SELECTED STATUTES ON TRUSTS AND ESTATES

2020 Edition

Selected and Edited by

MARK L. ASCHER
Hayden W. Head Regents Chair for Faculty Excellence
University of Texas

GRAYSON M.P. McCOUCH
Gerald Sohn Professor of Law
University of Florida

WEST
ACADEMIC
PUBLISHING

© West, a Thomson business, 2001–2005, 2007
© 2009, 2010, 2012 Thomson Reuters
© 2014–2019 LEG, Inc. d/b/a West Academic
© 2020 LEG, Inc. d/b/a West Academic
  444 Cedar Street, Suite 700
  St. Paul, MN 55101
  1-877-888-1330

Printed in the United States of America

ISBN: 978-1-64708-074-7

PREFACE

This volume contains nineteen uniform acts relevant to courses dealing with wills, trusts, decedents' estates and related topics:

1. the Uniform Probate Code;
2. the Uniform Trust Code;
3. the Uniform Custodial Trust Act;
4. the Uniform Directed Trust Act;
5. the Uniform Disclaimer of Property Interests Act (1999);
6. the Uniform Electronic Wills Act;
7. the Uniform Estate Tax Apportionment Act (2003);
8. the Revised Uniform Fiduciary Access to Digital Assets Act (2015);
9. the Uniform Fiduciary Income and Principal Act;
10. the Uniform Guardianship, Conservatorship, and Other Protective Arrangements Act;
11. the Uniform Power of Attorney Act (2006);
12. the Uniform Powers of Appointment Act;
13. the Uniform Principal and Income Act (1997);
14. the Uniform Prudent Investor Act;
15. the Uniform Real Property Transfer on Death Act;
16. the Uniform Simultaneous Death Act (1940);
17. the Uniform Statutory Rule Against Perpetuities;
18. the Uniform Transfers to Minors Act; and
19. the Uniform Trust Decanting Act.

These acts and the accompanying official comments are promulgated by the National Conference of Commissioners on Uniform State Laws (NCCUSL), and are reproduced here with permission. The official comments explain the purpose and intent of the statutory provisions and the changes they make in prior law. From time to time, the NCCUSL continues to update both the acts themselves and the official comments. We have attempted to reproduce each in its most current version. We have included most, but not all, of the statutory provisions, indicating all omissions. As to the official comments, we have been more selective. Within any particular comment, we have indicated all omissions, but, when omitting an entire comment, we have done so without additional indication.

We welcome comments and suggestions.

MARK L. ASCHER

GRAYSON M.P. McCOUCH

January 2020

TABLE OF CONTENTS

SELECTED STATUTES ON TRUSTS AND ESTATES

2020 Edition

UNIFORM PROBATE CODE*

ARTICLE I
GENERAL PROVISIONS, DEFINITIONS AND PROBATE JURISDICTION OF COURT

PART 1
SHORT TITLE, CONSTRUCTION, GENERAL PROVISIONS

PART 2
DEFINITIONS

PART 3
SCOPE, JURISDICTION AND COURTS

PART 4
NOTICE, PARTIES AND REPRESENTATION IN ESTATE LITIGATION AND OTHER MATTERS

PART 1

SHORT TITLE, CONSTRUCTION, GENERAL PROVISIONS

Section 1–101. Short Title.

This [act] shall be known and may be cited as the Uniform Probate Code.

Section 1–102. Purposes; Rule of Construction.

(a) This [code] shall be liberally construed and applied to promote its underlying purposes and policies.

(b) The underlying purposes and policies of this [code] are:

(1) to simplify and clarify the law concerning the affairs of decedents, missing persons, protected persons, minors and incapacitated persons;

(2) to discover and make effective the intent of a decedent in distribution of his property;

(3) to promote a speedy and efficient system for liquidating the estate of the decedent and making distribution to his successors;

(4) to facilitate use and enforcement of certain trusts;

(5) to make uniform the law among the various jurisdictions.

Section 1–103. Supplementary General Principles of Law Applicable.

Unless displaced by the particular provisions of this [code], the principles of law and equity supplement its provisions.

Section 1–104. Severability.

If any provision of this [code] or the application thereof to any person or circumstances is held invalid, the invalidity shall not affect other provisions or applications of the [code] which can be given effect without the invalid provision or application, and to this end the provisions of this [code] are declared to be severable.

Section 1–105. Construction Against Implied Repeal.

This [code] is a general act intended as a unified coverage of its subject matter and no part of it shall be deemed impliedly repealed by subsequent legislation if it can reasonably be avoided.

Section 1–106. Effect of Fraud and Evasion.

Whenever fraud has been perpetrated in connection with any proceeding or in any statement filed under this [code] or if fraud is used to avoid or circumvent the provisions or purposes of this [code], any person injured thereby may obtain appropriate relief against the perpetrator of the fraud or restitution from any person (other than a bona fide purchaser) benefitting from the fraud, whether innocent or not. Any proceeding must be commenced within two years after the discovery of the fraud, but no proceeding may be brought against one not a perpetrator of the fraud later than five years after the time of commission of the fraud. This section has no bearing on remedies relating to fraud practiced on a decedent during his lifetime which affects the succession of his estate.

Section 1–107. Evidence of Death or Status.

In addition to the rules of evidence in courts of general jurisdiction, the following rules relating to a determination of death and status apply:

(1) Death occurs when an individual [is determined to be dead under the Uniform Determination of Death Act (1978/1980)] [has sustained either (i) irreversible cessation of circulatory

2

and respiratory functions or (ii) irreversible cessation of all functions of the entire brain, including the brain stem. A determination of death must be made in accordance with accepted medical standards].

(2)   A certified or authenticated copy of a death certificate purporting to be issued by an official or agency of the place where the death purportedly occurred is prima facie evidence of the fact, place, date, and time of death and the identity of the decedent.

(3)   A certified or authenticated copy of any record or report of a governmental agency, domestic or foreign, that an individual is missing, detained, dead, or alive is prima facie evidence of the status and of the dates, circumstances, and places disclosed by the record or report.

(4)   In the absence of prima facie evidence of death under paragraph (2) or (3), the fact of death may be established by clear and convincing evidence, including circumstantial evidence.

(5)   An individual whose death is not established under the preceding paragraphs who is absent for a continuous period of five years, during which he [or she] has not been heard from, and whose absence is not satisfactorily explained after diligent search or inquiry, is presumed to be dead. His [or her] death is presumed to have occurred at the end of the period unless there is sufficient evidence for determining that death occurred earlier.

(6)   In the absence of evidence disputing the time of death stated on a document described in paragraph (2) or (3), a document described in paragraph (2) or (3) that states a time of death 120 hours or more after the time of death of another individual, however the time of death of the other individual is determined, establishes by clear and convincing evidence that the individual survived the other individual by 120 hours.

Section 1–108. Acts by Holder of General Power.

For the purpose of granting consent or approval with regard to the acts or accounts of a personal representative or trustee, including relief from liability or penalty for failure to post bond, to register a trust, or to perform other duties, and for purposes of consenting to modification or termination of a trust or to deviation from its terms, the sole holder or all co-holders of a presently exercisable general power of appointment, including one in the form of a power of amendment or revocation, are deemed to act for beneficiaries to the extent their interests (as objects, takers in default, or otherwise) are subject to the power.

Section 1–109. Cost of Living Adjustment of Certain Dollar Amounts.

(a)   In this section:

(1)   "CPI" means the Consumer Price Index (Annual Average) for All Urban Consumers (CPI-U): U.S. City Average—All items, reported by the Bureau of Labor Statistics, United States Department of Labor or its successor or, if the index is discontinued, an equivalent index reported by a federal authority. If no such index is reported, the term means the substitute index chosen by [insert appropriate state agency]; and

(2)   "Reference base index" means the CPI for calendar year [insert year immediately preceding the year in which this section takes effect].

(b)   The dollar amounts stated in Sections 2–102, [2–102A,] 2–202(b), 2–402, 2–403, 2–405, and 3–1201 apply to the estate of a decedent who died in or after [insert year in which this section takes effect], but for the estate of a decedent who died after [insert year after the year in which this section takes effect], these dollar amounts must be increased or decreased if the CPI for the calendar year immediately preceding the year of death exceeds or is less than the reference base index. The amount of any increase or decrease is computed by multiplying each dollar amount by the percentage by which the CPI for the calendar year immediately preceding the year of death exceeds or is less than the reference base index. If any increase or decrease produced by the computation is not a multiple of $100, the increase or decrease is rounded down, if an increase, or up, if a decrease, to the next multiple of $100, but for the purpose of Section 2–405, the periodic installment amount is the lump-sum amount divided by 12. If the CPI for [insert year immediately before the effective date of this section] is changed by the Bureau of Labor Statistics, the reference base index must be revised using the rebasing factor reported by the Bureau of Labor Statistics, or other comparable data if a rebasing factor is not reported.

[(c) Before February 1, [insert year after the year in which this section takes effect], and before February 1 of each succeeding year, the [insert appropriate state agency] shall publish a cumulative list, beginning with the dollar amounts effective for the estate of a decedent who died in [insert year after the year in which this section takes effect], of each dollar amount as increased or decreased under this section.]

PART 2

DEFINITIONS

Section 1–201. General Definitions.

Subject to additional definitions contained in the subsequent [articles] that are applicable to specific [articles], [parts], or sections, and unless the context otherwise requires, in this [code]:

(1) "Agent" includes an attorney-in-fact under a durable or nondurable power of attorney, an individual authorized to make decisions concerning another's health care, and an individual authorized to make decisions for another under a natural death act.

(2) "Application" means a written request to the Registrar for an order of informal probate or appointment under [Part] 3 of [Article] III.

(3) "Beneficiary," as it relates to a trust beneficiary, includes a person who has any present or future interest, vested or contingent, and also includes the owner of an interest by assignment or other transfer; as it relates to a charitable trust, includes any person entitled to enforce the trust; as it relates to a "beneficiary of a beneficiary designation," refers to a beneficiary of an insurance or annuity policy, of an account with POD designation, of a security registered in beneficiary form (TOD), or of a pension, profit-sharing, retirement, or similar benefit plan, or other nonprobate transfer at death; and, as it relates to a "beneficiary designated in a governing instrument," includes a grantee of a deed, a devisee, a trust beneficiary, a beneficiary of a beneficiary designation, a donee, appointee, or taker in default of a power of appointment, or a person in whose favor a power of attorney or a power held in any individual, fiduciary, or representative capacity is exercised.

(4) "Beneficiary designation" refers to a governing instrument naming a beneficiary of an insurance or annuity policy, of an account with POD designation, of a security registered in beneficiary form (TOD), or of a pension, profit-sharing, retirement, or similar benefit plan, or other nonprobate transfer at death.

(5) "Child" means an individual of any age whose parentage is established under [cite to Uniform Parentage Act (2017)][cite to state's parentage act][applicable state law].

(6) "Claims," in respect to estates of decedents and protected persons, includes liabilities of the decedent or protected person, whether arising in contract, in tort, or otherwise, and liabilities of the estate which arise at or after the death of the decedent or after the appointment of a conservator, including funeral expenses and expenses of administration. The term does not include estate or inheritance taxes, or demands or disputes regarding title of a decedent or protected person to specific assets alleged to be included in the estate.

(7) "Conservator" is as defined in Section 5–102.

(8) "Court" means the [. . . . . Court or branch] in this state having jurisdiction in matters relating to the affairs of decedents.

(9) "Descendant" of an individual means all of his [or her] descendants of all generations, with the relationship of parent and child at each generation being determined by the definition of child and parent contained in this [code].

(10) "Devise," when used as a noun, means a testamentary disposition of real or personal property and, when used as a verb, means to dispose of real or personal property by will.

(11) "Devisee" means a person designated in a will to receive a devise. For the purposes of [Article] III, in the case of a devise to an existing trust or trustee, or to a trustee or trust described by will, the trust or trustee is the devisee and the beneficiaries are not devisees.

(12) "Distributee" means any person who has received property of a decedent from his [or her] personal representative other than as a creditor or purchaser. A testamentary trustee is a distributee only to the extent of distributed assets or increment thereto remaining in his [or her] hands. A beneficiary of a testamentary trust to whom the trustee has distributed property received from a personal representative is a distributee of the personal representative. For the purposes of this provision, "testamentary trustee" includes a trustee to whom assets are transferred by will, to the extent of the devised assets.

(13) "Estate" includes the property of the decedent, trust, or other person whose affairs are subject to this [code] as originally constituted and as it exists from time to time during administration.

(14) "Exempt property" means that property of a decedent's estate which is described in Section 2–403.

(15) "Fiduciary" includes a personal representative, guardian, conservator, and trustee.

(16) "Foreign personal representative" means a personal representative appointed by another jurisdiction.

(17) "Formal proceedings" means proceedings conducted before a judge with notice to interested persons.

(18) "Governing instrument" means a deed, will, trust, insurance or annuity policy, account with POD designation, security registered in beneficiary form (TOD), transfer on death (TOD) deed, pension, profit-sharing, retirement, or similar benefit plan, instrument creating or exercising a power of appointment or a power of attorney, or a dispositive, appointive, or nominative instrument of any similar type.

(19) "Guardian" is as defined in Section 5–102.

(20) "Heirs," except as controlled by Section 2–711, means persons, including the surviving spouse and the state, who are entitled under the statutes of intestate succession to the property of a decedent.

(21) "Incapacitated person" means an individual described in Section 5–102.

(22) "Informal proceedings" means those conducted without notice to interested persons by an officer of the court acting as a registrar for probate of a will or appointment of a personal representative.

(23) "Interested person" includes heirs, devisees, children, spouses, creditors, beneficiaries, and any others having a property right in or claim against a trust estate or the estate of a decedent, ward, or protected person. It also includes persons having priority for appointment as personal representative, and other fiduciaries representing interested persons. The meaning as it relates to particular persons may vary from time to time and must be determined according to the particular purposes of, and matter involved in, any proceeding.

(24) "Issue" of an individual means descendant.

(25) "Joint tenants with the right of survivorship" and "community property with the right of survivorship" includes co-owners of property held under circumstances that entitle one or more to the whole of the property on the death of the other or others, but excludes forms of co-ownership registration in which the underlying ownership of each party is in proportion to that party's contribution.

(26) "Lease" includes an oil, gas, or other mineral lease.

(27) "Letters" includes letters testamentary, letters of guardianship, letters of administration, and letters of conservatorship.

(28) "Minor" has the meaning described in Section 5–102.

(29) "Mortgage" means any conveyance, agreement, or arrangement in which property is encumbered or used as security.

(30) "Nonresident decedent" means a decedent who was domiciled in another jurisdiction at the time of his [or her] death.

(31) "Organization" means a corporation, business trust, estate, trust, partnership, joint venture, association, government or governmental subdivision or agency, or any other legal or commercial entity.

(32) "Parent" means an individual who has established a parent-child relationship under [cite to Uniform Parentage Act (2017)][cite to state's parentage act][applicable state law].

(33) "Payor" means a trustee, insurer, business entity, employer, government, governmental agency or subdivision, or any other person authorized or obligated by law or a governing instrument to make payments.

(34) "Person" means an individual or an organization.

(35) "Personal representative" includes executor, administrator, successor personal representative, special administrator, and persons who perform substantially the same function under the law governing their status. "General personal representative" excludes special administrator.

(36) "Petition" means a written request to the court for an order after notice.

(37) "Proceeding" includes action at law and suit in equity.

(38) "Property" includes both real and personal property or any interest therein and means anything that may be the subject of ownership.

(39) "Protected person" is as defined in Section 5–102.

(40) "Protective proceeding" means a proceeding under [Part] 4 of [Article] V.

(41) "Record" means information that is inscribed on a tangible medium or that is stored in an electronic or other medium and is retrievable in perceivable form.

(42) "Registrar" refers to the official of the court designated to perform the functions of Registrar as provided in Section 1–307.

(43) "Security" includes any note, stock, treasury stock, bond, debenture, evidence of indebtedness, certificate of interest or participation in an oil, gas, or mining title or lease or in payments out of production under such a title or lease, collateral trust certificate, transferable share, voting trust certificate or, in general, any interest or instrument commonly known as a security, or any certificate of interest or participation, any temporary or interim certificate, receipt, or certificate of deposit for, or any warrant or right to subscribe to or purchase, any of the foregoing.

(44) "Settlement," in reference to a decedent's estate, includes the full process of administration, distribution, and closing.

(45) "Sign" means, with present intent to authenticate or adopt a record other than a will:

    (A)   to execute or adopt a tangible symbol; or

    (B)   to attach to or logically associate with the record an electronic symbol, sound, or process.

(46) "Special administrator" means a personal representative as described by Sections 3–614 through 3–618.

(47) "State" means a state of the United States, the District of Columbia, the Commonwealth of Puerto Rico, or any territory or insular possession subject to the jurisdiction of the United States.

(48) "Successor personal representative" means a personal representative, other than a special administrator, who is appointed to succeed a previously appointed personal representative.

(49) "Successors" means persons, other than creditors, who are entitled to property of a decedent under his [or her] will or this [code].

(50) "Supervised administration" refers to the proceedings described in [Article] III, [Part] 5.

(51) "Survive" means that an individual has neither predeceased an event, including the death of another individual, nor is deemed to have predeceased an event under this [code]. The term includes its derivatives, such as "survives", "survived", "survivor", or "surviving".

(52) "Testacy proceeding" means a proceeding to establish a will or determine intestacy.

(53) "Testator" includes an individual of either sex.

(54) "Trust" includes an express trust, private or charitable, with additions thereto, wherever and however created. The term also includes a trust created or determined by judgment or decree under which the trust is to be administered in the manner of an express trust. The term excludes other constructive trusts and excludes resulting trusts, conservatorships, personal representatives, trust accounts as defined in [Article] VI, custodial arrangements pursuant to [each state should list its legislation, including that relating to [gifts] [transfers] to minors, dealing with special custodial situations], business trusts providing for certificates to be issued to beneficiaries, common trust funds, voting trusts, security arrangements, liquidation trusts, and trusts for the primary purpose of paying debts, dividends, interest, salaries, wages, profits, pensions, or employee benefits of any kind, and any arrangement under which a person is nominee or escrowee for another.

(55) "Trustee" includes an original, additional, or successor trustee, whether or not appointed or confirmed by court.

(56) "Ward" means an individual described in Section 5–102.

(57) "Will" includes codicil and any testamentary instrument that merely appoints an executor, revokes or revises another will, nominates a guardian, or expressly excludes or limits the right of an individual or class to succeed to property of the decedent passing by intestate succession.

[FOR ADOPTION IN COMMUNITY PROPERTY STATES]

[(58) "Separate property" (if necessary, to be defined locally in accordance with existing concept in adopting state).

(59) "Community property" (if necessary, to be defined locally in accordance with existing concept in adopting state).]

PART 3

SCOPE, JURISDICTION AND COURTS

Section 1–301. Territorial Application.

Except as otherwise provided in this code, this code applies to:

(1) the affairs and estates of decedents, missing persons, and persons to be protected, domiciled in this state,

(2) the property of nonresidents located in this state or property coming into the control of a fiduciary who is subject to the laws of this state,

(3) incapacitated persons and minors in this state,

(4) survivorship and related accounts in this state, and

(5) trusts subject to administration in this state.

Section 1–302. Subject Matter Jurisdiction.

(a) To the full extent permitted by the constitution, the court has jurisdiction over all subject matter relating to

(1) estates of decedents, including construction of wills and determination of heirs and successors of decedents, and estates of protected persons;

(2) protection of minors and incapacitated persons; and

(3) trusts.

(b) The court has full power to make orders, judgments and decrees and take all other action necessary and proper to administer justice in the matters which come before it.

(c) The court has jurisdiction over protective proceedings and guardianship proceedings.

(d) If both guardianship and protective proceedings as to the same person are commenced or pending in the same court, the proceedings may be consolidated.

Section 1–303. Venue; Multiple Proceedings; Transfer.

(a) Where a proceeding under this [code] could be maintained in more than one place in this state, the court in which the proceeding is first commenced has the exclusive right to proceed.

(b) If proceedings concerning the same estate, protected person, ward, or trust are commenced in more than one court of this state, the court in which the proceeding was first commenced shall continue to hear the matter, and the other courts shall hold the matter in abeyance until the question of venue is decided, and if the ruling court determines that venue is properly in another court, it shall transfer the proceeding to the other court.

(c) If a court finds that in the interest of justice a proceeding or a file should be located in another court of this state, the court making the finding may transfer the proceeding or file to the other court.

Section 1–304. Practice in Court.

Unless specifically provided to the contrary in this [code] or unless inconsistent with its provisions, the rules of civil procedure including the rules concerning vacation of orders and appellate review govern formal proceedings under this [code].

Section 1–305. Records and Certified Copies.

The [Clerk of Court] shall keep a record for each decedent, ward, protected person or trust involved in any document which may be filed with the court under this [code], including petitions and applications, demands for notices or bonds, trust registrations, and of any orders or responses relating thereto by the Registrar or court, and establish and maintain a system for indexing, filing or recording which is sufficient to enable users of the records to obtain adequate information. Upon payment of the fees required by law the clerk must issue certified copies of any probated wills, letters issued to personal representatives, or any other record or paper filed or recorded. Certificates relating to probated wills must indicate whether the decedent was domiciled in this state and whether the probate was formal or informal. Certificates relating to letters must show the date of appointment.

Section 1–306. Jury Trial.

(a) If duly demanded, a party is entitled to trial by jury in [a formal testacy proceeding and] any proceeding in which any controverted question of fact arises as to which any party has a constitutional right to trial by jury.

(b) If there is no right to trial by jury under subsection (a) or the right is waived, the court in its discretion may call a jury to decide any issue of fact, in which case the verdict is advisory only.

Section 1–307. Registrar; Powers.

The acts and orders which this [code] specifies as performable by the Registrar may be performed either by a judge of the court or by a person, including the clerk, designated by the court by a written order filed and recorded in the office of the court.

Section 1–308. Appeals.

Appellate review, including the right to appellate review, interlocutory appeal, provisions as to time, manner, notice, appeal bond, stays, scope of review, record on appeal, briefs, arguments and power of the appellate court, is governed by the rules applicable to the appeals to the [Supreme Court] in equity cases from the [court of general jurisdiction], except that in proceedings where jury trial has been had as a matter of right, the rules applicable to the scope of review in jury cases apply.

Section 1–309. Qualifications of Judge.

A judge of the court must have the same qualifications as a judge of the [court of general jurisdiction.]

Section 1–310. Oath or Affirmation on Filed Documents.

Except as otherwise specifically provided in this [code] or by rule, every document filed with the court under this [code] including applications, petitions, and demands for notice, shall be deemed to include an oath, affirmation, or statement to the effect that its representations are true as far as the person executing or filing it knows or is informed, and penalties for perjury may follow deliberate falsification therein.

PART 4

NOTICE, PARTIES AND REPRESENTATION IN ESTATE LITIGATION AND OTHER MATTERS

Section 1–401. Notice; Method and Time of Giving.

(a) If notice of a hearing on any petition is required and except for specific notice requirements as otherwise provided, the petitioner shall cause notice of the time and place of hearing of any petition to be given to any interested person or his attorney if he has appeared by attorney or requested that notice be sent to his attorney. Notice shall be given:

(1) by mailing a copy thereof at least 14 days before the time set for the hearing by certified, registered or ordinary first class mail addressed to the person being notified at the post office address given in his demand for notice, if any, or at his office or place of residence, if known;

(2) by delivering a copy thereof to the person being notified personally at least 14 days before the time set for the hearing; or

(3) if the address, or identity of any person is not known and cannot be ascertained with reasonable diligence, by publishing at least once a week for 3 consecutive weeks, a copy thereof in a newspaper having general circulation in the county where the hearing is to be held, the last publication of which is to be at least 10 days before the time set for the hearing.

(b) The court for good cause shown may provide for a different method or time of giving notice for any hearing.

(c) Proof of the giving of notice shall be made on or before the hearing and filed in the proceeding.

Section 1–402. Notice; Waiver.

A person, including a guardian ad litem, conservator, or other fiduciary, may waive notice by a writing signed by him or his attorney and filed in the proceeding. A person for whom a guardianship or other protective order is sought, a ward, or a protected person may not waive notice.

Section 1–403. Pleadings; When Parties Bound by Others; Notice.

In formal proceedings involving trusts or estates of decedents, minors, protected persons, or incapacitated persons, and in judicially supervised settlements, the following rules apply:

(1) Interests to be affected must be described in pleadings that give reasonable information to owners by name or class, by reference to the instrument creating the interests or in another appropriate manner.

(2) A person is bound by an order binding another in the following cases:

(A) An order binding the sole holder or all co-holders of a power of revocation or a presently exercisable general power of appointment, including one in the form of a power of amendment, binds other persons to the extent their interests as objects, takers in default, or otherwise are subject to the power.

(B) To the extent there is no conflict of interest between them or among persons represented:

(i) an order binding a conservator binds the person whose estate the conservator controls;

(ii) an order binding a guardian binds the ward if no conservator of the ward's estate has been appointed;

(iii) an order binding a trustee binds beneficiaries of the trust in proceedings to probate a will establishing or adding to a trust, to review the acts or accounts of a former fiduciary, and in proceedings involving creditors or other third parties;

(iv) an order binding a personal representative binds persons interested in the undistributed assets of a decedent's estate in actions or proceedings by or against the estate; and

(v) an order binding a sole holder or all co-holders of a general testamentary power of appointment binds other persons to the extent their interests as objects, takers in default, or otherwise are subject to the power.

(C) Unless otherwise represented, a minor or an incapacitated, unborn, or unascertained person is bound by an order to the extent the person's interest is adequately represented by another party having a substantially identical interest in the proceeding.

(3) If no conservator or guardian has been appointed, a parent may represent a minor child.

(4) Notice is required as follows:

(A) The notice prescribed by Section 1–401 must be given to every interested person or to one who can bind an interested person as described in paragraph (2)(A) or (B). Notice may be given both to a person and to another who may bind the person.

(B) Notice is given to unborn or unascertained persons who are not represented under paragraph (2)(A) or (B) by giving notice to all known persons whose interests in the proceedings are substantially identical to those of the unborn or unascertained persons.

(5) At any point in a proceeding, a court may appoint a guardian ad litem to represent the interest of a minor, an incapacitated, unborn, or unascertained person, or a person whose identity or address is unknown, if the court determines that representation of the interest otherwise would be inadequate. If not precluded by conflict of interests, a guardian ad litem may be appointed to represent

several persons or interests. The court shall state its reasons for appointing a guardian ad litem as a part of the record of the proceeding.

ARTICLE II

INTESTACY, WILLS, AND DONATIVE TRANSFERS

PART 1
INTESTATE SUCCESSION

SUBPART 1. GENERAL RULES

SUBPART 2. PARENT-CHILD RELATIONSHIP

PART 2
ELECTIVE SHARE OF SURVIVING SPOUSE

PART 7
RULES OF CONSTRUCTION APPLICABLE TO WILLS
AND OTHER GOVERNING INSTRUMENTS

PART 8
GENERAL PROVISIONS CONCERNING PROBATE
AND NONPROBATE TRANSFERS

PART 9
STATUTORY RULE AGAINST PERPETUITIES; HONORARY TRUSTS

SUBPART 1. UNIFORM STATUTORY RULE AGAINST PERPETUITIES (1986/1990)

[The Uniform Statutory Rule Against Perpetuities (1986/1990)
is reproduced elsewhere in this volume.]

SUBPART 2. HONORARY TRUSTS

PART 10
UNIFORM INTERNATIONAL WILLS ACT (1977)

[omitted]

PART 11
UNIFORM DISCLAIMER OF PROPERTY INTERESTS ACT (1999/2006)

[The Uniform Disclaimer of Property Interests Act (1999/2006)
is reproduced elsewhere in this volume.]

PART 1

INTESTATE SUCCESSION

SUBPART 1. GENERAL RULES

Section 2–101. Intestate Estate.

(a) Any part of a decedent's estate not effectively disposed of by will passes by intestate succession to the decedent's heirs as prescribed in this [code], except as modified by the decedent's will.

(b) A decedent by will may expressly exclude or limit the right of an individual or class to succeed to property of the decedent passing by intestate succession. If that individual or a member of that class survives the decedent, the share of the decedent's intestate estate to which that individual or class would have succeeded passes as if that individual or each member of that class had disclaimed the intestate share.

Comment

* * * [S]ubsection (b) authorizes the decedent, by will, to exclude or limit the right of an individual or class to share in the decedent's intestate estate, in effect disinheriting that individual or class. By specifically authorizing so-called negative wills, subsection (b) reverses the usually accepted common-law rule, which defeats a testator's intent for no sufficient reason. * * *

Whether or not in an individual case the decedent's will has excluded or limited the right of an individual or class to take a share of the decedent's intestate estate is a question of construction. A clear case would be one in which the decedent's will expressly states that an individual is to receive none of the decedent's estate. Examples would be testamentary language such as "my brother, Hector, is not to receive any of my property" or "Brother Hector is disinherited."

Another rather clear case would be one in which the will states that an individual is to receive only a nominal devise, such as "I devise $50.00 to my brother, Hector, and no more."

An individual need not be identified by name to be excluded. Thus, if brother Hector is the decedent's only brother, Hector could be identified by a term such as "my brother." A group or class of relatives (such as "my brothers and sisters") can also be excluded under this provision.

Subsection (b) establishes the consequence of a disinheritance—the share of the decedent's intestate estate to which the disinherited individual or class would have succeeded passes as if that individual or class had disclaimed the intestate share. Thus, if the decedent's will provides that brother Hector is to receive $50.00 and no more, Hector is entitled to the $50.00 devise (because Hector is *not* treated as having predeceased the decedent for purposes of *testate* succession), but the portion of the decedent's *intestate* estate to which Hector would have succeeded passes as if Hector had disclaimed his intestate share. * * *

Section 2–102. Share of Spouse.

The intestate share of a decedent's surviving spouse is:

(1) the entire intestate estate if:

    (A) no descendant or parent of the decedent survives the decedent; or

    (B) all of the decedent's surviving descendants are also descendants of the surviving spouse and there is no other descendant of the surviving spouse who survives the decedent;

(2) the first [$300,000], plus three-fourths of any balance of the intestate estate, if no descendant of the decedent survives the decedent, but a parent of the decedent survives the decedent;

(3) the first [$225,000], plus one-half of any balance of the intestate estate, if all of the decedent's surviving descendants are also descendants of the surviving spouse and the surviving spouse has one or more surviving descendants who are not descendants of the decedent;

(4)   the first [$150,000], plus one-half of any balance of the intestate estate, if one or more of the decedent's surviving descendants are not descendants of the surviving spouse.

[ALTERNATIVE PROVISION FOR COMMUNITY PROPERTY STATES]

[Section 2–102A. Share of Spouse.

(a)   The intestate share of a decedent's surviving spouse in separate property is:

    (1)   the entire intestate estate if:

        (A)   no descendant or parent of the decedent survives the decedent; or

        (B)   all of the decedent's surviving descendants are also descendants of the surviving spouse and there is no other descendant of the surviving spouse who survives the decedent;

    (2)   the first [$300,000], plus three-fourths of any balance of the intestate estate, if no descendant of the decedent survives the decedent, but a parent of the decedent survives the decedent;

    (3)   the first [$225,000], plus one-half of any balance of the intestate estate, if all of the decedent's surviving descendants are also descendants of the surviving spouse and the surviving spouse has one or more surviving descendants who are not descendants of the decedent;

    (4)   the first [$150,000], plus one-half of any balance of the intestate estate, if one or more of the decedent's surviving descendants are not descendants of the surviving spouse.

(b)   The one-half of community property belonging to the decedent passes to the [surviving spouse] as the intestate share.]

Section 2–103. Share of Heirs Other Than Surviving Spouse.

(a)   [Definitions.] In this section:

    (1)   "Deceased parent", "deceased grandparent", or "deceased spouse" means a parent, grandparent, or spouse who either predeceased the decedent or is deemed under this [article] to have predeceased the decedent.

    (2)   "Surviving spouse", "surviving descendant", "surviving parent", or "surviving grandparent" means a spouse, descendant, parent, or grandparent who neither predeceased the decedent nor is deemed under this [article] to have predeceased the decedent.

(b)   [Heirs Other Than Surviving Spouse.] Any part of the intestate estate not passing under Section 2–102 to the decedent's surviving spouse passes to the decedent's descendants or parents as provided in subsections (c) and (d). If there is no surviving spouse, the entire intestate estate passes to the decedent's descendants, parents, or other heirs as provided in subsections (c) through (j).

(c)   [Surviving Descendant.] If a decedent is survived by one or more descendants, any part of the intestate estate not passing to the surviving spouse passes by representation to the decedent's surviving descendants.

(d)   [Surviving Parent.] If a decedent is not survived by a descendant but is survived by one or more parents, any part of the intestate estate not passing to the surviving spouse is distributed as follows:

    (1)   The intestate estate or part is divided into as many equal shares as there are:

        (A)   surviving parents; and

        (B)   deceased parents with one or more surviving descendants, if any, as determined under subsection (e).

    (2)   One share passes to each surviving parent.

(3) The balance of the intestate estate or part, if any, passes by representation to the surviving descendants of the decedent's deceased parents, as determined under subsection (e).

(e) [When Parent Survives: Computation of Shares of Surviving Descendants of Deceased Parent.] The following rules apply under subsection (d) to determine whether a deceased parent of the decedent is treated as having a surviving descendant:

(1) If all the surviving descendants of one or more deceased parents also are descendants of one or more surviving parents and none of those surviving parents has any other surviving descendant, those descendants are deemed to have predeceased the decedent.

(2) If two or more deceased parents have the same surviving descendants and none of those deceased parents has any other surviving descendant, those deceased parents are deemed to be one deceased parent with surviving descendants.

(f) [Surviving Descendant of Deceased Parent.] If a decedent is not survived by a descendant or parent but is survived by one or more descendants of a parent, the intestate estate passes by representation to the surviving descendants of the decedent's deceased parents.

(g) [Surviving Grandparent.] If a decedent is not survived by a descendant, parent, or descendant of a parent but is survived by one or more grandparents, the intestate estate is distributed as follows:

(1) The intestate estate is divided into as many equal shares as there are:

(A) surviving grandparents; and

(B) deceased grandparents with one or more surviving descendants, if any, as determined under subsection (h).

(2) One share passes to each surviving grandparent.

(3) The balance of the intestate estate, if any, passes by representation to the surviving descendants of the decedent's deceased grandparents, as determined under subsection (h).

(h) [When Grandparent Survives: Computation of Shares of Surviving Descendants of Deceased Grandparent.] The following rules apply under subsection (g) to determine whether a deceased grandparent of the decedent is treated as having a surviving descendant:

(1) If all the surviving descendants of one or more deceased grandparents also are descendants of one or more surviving grandparents and none of those surviving grandparents has any other surviving descendant, those descendants are deemed to have predeceased the decedent.

(2) If two or more deceased grandparents have the same surviving descendants and none of those deceased grandparents has any other surviving descendant, those deceased grandparents are deemed to be one deceased grandparent with surviving descendants.

(i) [Surviving Descendant of Deceased Grandparent.] If a decedent is not survived by a descendant, parent, descendant of a parent, or grandparent but is survived by one or more descendants of a grandparent, the intestate estate passes by representation to the surviving descendants of the decedent's deceased grandparents.

(j) [Surviving Descendant of Deceased Spouse.] If a decedent is not survived by a descendant, parent, descendant of a parent, grandparent, or descendant of a grandparent but is survived by one or more descendants of one or more deceased spouses, the intestate estate passes by representation to the surviving descendants of the decedent's deceased spouse or spouses.

Comment

This section provides for inheritance by descendants of the decedent, parents and their descendants, grandparents and collateral relatives descended from grandparents, and descendants of a deceased spouse or deceased spouses who are not also descendants of the decedent; in line with modern policy, it eliminates more remote relatives tracing through great-grandparents. * * *

Subsection (b). Subsection (b) states the well-established rule that this section governs the part of the decedent's intestate estate not passing to the decedent's surviving spouse under Section 2–102—or the entire intestate estate if the decedent has no surviving spouse.

Subsection (c). Subsection (c) states the well-established rule that if the decedent is survived by one or more descendants, the intestate estate or part thereof not passing to the surviving spouse passes by representation to the decedent's surviving descendants.

Example 1. G, the intestate, has a surviving spouse, S, and three surviving children, A, B, and C, who are also children of S. S has no other children. Section 2–102 provides that the entire intestate estate passes to S. Nothing passes under this section.

Example 2. Same facts as Example 1, except that S predeceased G. The intestate estate passes by representation to G's surviving children—A, B, and C—under subsection (c). "By representation" in subsection (c) is defined in Section 2–106(b). The result is that A, B, and C each inherit 1/3 of G's intestate estate.

Subsection (d). If the decedent is not survived by any descendants but is survived by one or more parents, subsection (d) provides that any part of the intestate estate not passing to the surviving spouse is distributed according to a three-step procedure:

(1)   The intestate estate or part is divided into as many equal shares as there are (A) surviving parents and (B) deceased parents with one or more surviving descendants, if any.

(2)   One share passes to each surviving parent.

(3)   The balance of the intestate estate or part, if any, passes by representation to the surviving descendants of the decedent's deceased parents.

Example 3. G, the intestate, had two parents, P1 and P2. P1 also had one other child, A. P2 also had two other children, B and C. G was predeceased by P2 and was survived by P1, A, B, and C. The intestate estate is divided into two equal shares, because there is one surviving parent (P1) and one deceased parent with surviving descendants (P2). One share passes to P1, who inherits 1/2 of G's intestate estate. The balance passes by representation to the surviving descendants of P2: B and C. "By representation" in subsection (d) is defined in Section 2–106(c). The result is that B and C each inherit 1/4 of G's intestate estate. * * * Note that B and C inherit in Example 3 as G's siblings without regard to the fact that they are half-siblings. See Section 2–107. * * *

Subsection (f). If the decedent is not survived by a descendant or parent but is survived by one or more descendants of a parent, subsection (f) provides that the intestate estate passes by representation to the surviving descendants of the decedent's deceased parents.

Example 4. Same facts as Example 3, except that P1 and P2 predeceased G and that A, B, and C survived G. The intestate estate passes by representation to the surviving descendants (A, B, and C) of G's deceased parents (P1 and P2). "By representation" in subsection (f) is defined in Section 2–106(d). The result is that A, B, and C each inherit 1/3 of G's intestate estate.

Subsection (g). If the decedent is not survived by a descendant, parent, or descendant of a parent but is survived by one or more grandparents, subsection (g) provides that the intestate estate is distributed according to a three-step procedure:

(1)   The intestate estate is divided into as many equal shares as there are (A) surviving grandparents and (B) deceased grandparents with one or more surviving descendants, if any.

(2)   One share passes to each surviving grandparent.

(3)   The balance of the intestate estate, if any, passes by representation to the surviving descendants of the decedent's deceased grandparents.

Example 5. G, the intestate, was survived by one grandparent, GP1, who had a daughter (G's aunt), A. G was predeceased by a second grandparent, GP2, who had two sons (G's uncles), B and C. G was survived by GP1, A, B, and C. The intestate estate is divided into two equal shares, because there is one surviving grandparent (GP1) and one deceased grandparent with surviving descendants (GP2). One share passes to GP1, who inherits 1/2 of G's intestate estate. The balance passes by representation to the surviving descendants of GP2: B and C. "By representation" in subsection (g) is defined in Section 2–106(e). The result is that B and C each inherit 1/4 of G's intestate estate. * * *

Subsection (i). If the decedent is not survived by a descendant, parent, descendant of a parent, or grandparent, subsection (i) provides that the intestate estate passes by representation to the surviving descendants of the decedent's deceased grandparents.

Example 6. Same facts as Example 5, except that G was survived only by A, B, and C. The intestate estate passes by representation to the surviving descendants (A, B, and C) of G's deceased grandparents (GP1 and GP2). "By representation" in subsection (i) is defined in Section 2–106(f). The result is that A, B, and C each inherit 1/3 of G's intestate estate.

Subsection (j). This subsection * * * grants inheritance rights to descendants of the intestate's deceased spouse(s) who are not also descendants of the intestate. The term deceased spouse refers to an individual to whom the intestate was married at the individual's death.

Example 7. G, the intestate, was survived only by A and B (the children of G's predeceased spouse S1) and by C (the child of G's predeceased spouse S2). A, B, and C are not descendants of G. The intestate estate passes by representation to the surviving descendants (A, B, and C) of G's deceased spouses (S1 and S2). "By representation" in subsection (j) is defined in Section 2–106(g). The result is that A, B, and C each inherit 1/3 of G's intestate estate.

Subsections (e) and (h). Subsections (e) and (h) deal with two special cases. The first arises when a surviving parent and a predeceased parent (or a surviving grandparent and a predeceased grandparent) have exactly the same descendants who survive the decedent. To achieve the correct results when calculating the intestate shares, these subsections provide that those descendants of the predeceased parent (or grandparent) are deemed to have predeceased the decedent.

Example 8. G, the intestate, had two parents, P1 and P2. P1 survived G; P2 predeceased G. P1 and P2 had two other children, A and B, both of whom survived G. Under subsection (d), G's intestate estate is divided into only one share, for P1. The reason is subsection (e)(1): because the surviving descendants of P2 (A and B) are the same as the surviving descendants of P1, those descendants are ignored ("deemed to have predeceased").

Example 9. G, the intestate, was survived by a grandparent, GP1, and by two descendants (A and B) of GP1 who are also descendants of a predeceased grandparent, GP2. Under subsection (g), G's intestate estate is divided into only one share, for GP1. The reason is subsection (h)(1): because the surviving descendants of GP2 (A and B) are the same as the surviving descendants of GP1, those descendants are ignored ("deemed to have predeceased").

The second special case addressed by subsections (e) and (h) arises when two or more deceased parents (or two or more deceased grandparents) have exactly the same descendants who survive the decedent. To achieve the correct results when calculating the intestate shares, these subsections provide that those deceased parents are deemed to be one deceased parent (or those deceased grandparents are deemed to be one deceased grandparent).

Example 10. G, the intestate, had three parents, P1, P2, and P3. P1 survived G; P2 and P3 predeceased G. P2 and P3 had two children, A and B, who survived G. Under subsection (d), the intestate estate is divided into two shares: one for P1 and one for the descendants (A and B) of P2 and P3, who are deemed to be one deceased parent rather than two, under subsection (e)(2). The share passing to A and B passes to them by representation. "By representation" in subsection (d) is defined in Section 2–106(c). The result is that A and B each inherit 1/4 of G's intestate estate.

Example 11. G, the intestate, was survived by a grandparent, GP1, and by the descendants (A and B) of G's predeceased grandparents GP2 and GP3. Under subsection (g), the intestate estate is divided into two shares: one for GP1 and one for the descendants (A and B) of GP2 and GP3, who are deemed to be one deceased grandparent rather than two, under subsection (h)(2). The share passing to A and B passes to them by representation. "By representation" in subsection (g) is defined in Section 2–106(e). The result is that A and B each inherit 1/4 of G's intestate estate.

More Than Two Parents; More Than Two Sets of Grandparents. The Uniform Parentage Act (2017) recognizes the possibility that a child may have more than two parents, hence more than two sets of grandparents. As revised in 2019, the rules of this section apply equally well irrespective of the number of parents or grandparents. * * *

Section 2–104. Requirement of Survival by 120 Hours; Gestational Period; Pregnancy After Decedent's Death.

(a) [Definitions.] In this section:

(1) "Assisted reproduction" means a method of causing pregnancy other than sexual intercourse.

(2) "Gestational period" means the time between the start of a pregnancy and birth.

(b) [Requirement of Survival by 120 Hours; Gestational Period; Pregnancy After Decedent's Death.] For purposes of intestate succession, homestead allowance, and exempt property, and except as otherwise provided in subsection (c), the following rules apply:

(1) An individual born before a decedent's death who fails to survive the decedent by 120 hours is deemed to have predeceased the decedent. If it is not established by clear and convincing evidence that an individual born before a decedent's death survived the decedent by 120 hours, it is deemed that the individual failed to survive for the required period.

(2) If the decedent dies during a gestational period that results in the birth of an individual who lives at least 120 hours after birth, that individual is deemed to be living at the decedent's death. If it is not established by clear and convincing evidence that the individual lived 120 hours after birth, it is deemed that the individual failed to survive for the required period.

(3) If the decedent dies before the start of a pregnancy by assisted reproduction resulting in the birth of an individual who lives at least 120 hours after birth, that individual is deemed to be living at the decedent's death if [the decedent's personal representative, not later than [6] months after the decedent's death, received notice or had actual knowledge of an intent to use genetic material in the assisted reproduction and]:

(A) the embryo was in utero not later than [36] months after the decedent's death; or

(B) the individual was born not later than [45] months after the decedent's death.

(c) [Section Inapplicable if Estate Would Pass to State.] This section does not apply if its application would cause the estate to pass to the state under Section 2–105.

Section 2–105. No Taker.

If there is no taker under the provisions of this [article], the intestate estate passes to the state.

Section 2–106. Representation.

(a) [Definitions.] In this section:

(1) "Deceased descendant", "deceased parent", "deceased grandparent", or "deceased spouse" means a descendant, parent, grandparent, or spouse who either predeceased the decedent or is deemed under this [article] to have predeceased the decedent.

(2) "Surviving descendant" means a descendant who neither predeceased the decedent nor is deemed under this [article] to have predeceased the decedent.

(b) [Decedent's Descendants.] If, under Section 2–103(c), all or part of a decedent's intestate estate passes by representation to the decedent's surviving descendants, the estate or part is divided into as many equal shares as there are (i) surviving descendants in the generation nearest to the decedent which contains one or more surviving descendants and (ii) deceased descendants in the same generation who left surviving descendants, if any. Each surviving descendant in the nearest generation is allocated one share. The remaining shares, if any, are combined and then divided in the same manner among the surviving descendants of the deceased descendants as if the surviving descendants who were allocated a share and their surviving descendants had predeceased the decedent.

(c) [Descendants of Parent When Parent Survives.] If a decedent is survived by one or more parents and, under Section 2–103(d) and (e), the balance of the decedent's intestate estate or part passes by representation to the surviving descendants of one or more of the decedent's deceased parents, the balance passes to those descendants as if they were the decedent's surviving descendants under subsection (b).

(d) [Descendants of Parent When No Parent Survives.] If a decedent is not survived by a parent and, under Section 2–103(f), the decedent's intestate estate passes by representation to the surviving descendants of one or more of the decedent's deceased parents, the intestate estate passes to those descendants as if they were the decedent's surviving descendants under subsection (b).

(e) [Descendants of Grandparent When Grandparent Survives.] If a decedent is survived by one or more grandparents and, under Section 2–103(g) and (h), the balance of the decedent's intestate estate passes by representation to the surviving descendants of one or more of the decedent's deceased grandparents, the balance passes to those descendants as if they were the decedent's surviving descendants under subsection (b).

(f) [Descendants of Grandparent When No Grandparent Survives.] If a decedent is not survived by a grandparent and, under Section 2–103(i), the decedent's intestate estate passes by representation to the surviving descendants of one or more of the decedent's deceased grandparents, the intestate estate passes to those descendants as if they were the decedent's surviving descendants under subsection (b).

(g) [Descendants of Deceased Spouse.] If a decedent is survived by descendants of one or more deceased spouses and, under Section 2–103(j), the decedent's intestate estate passes by representation to the surviving descendants of one or more of the decedent's deceased spouses, the intestate estate passes to those descendants as if they were the decedent's surviving descendants under subsection (b).

Comment

This section adopts the system of representation called per capita at each generation. The per-capita-at-each-generation system provides equal shares to those equally related. * * *

To illustrate the differences among the three systems [i.e., per capita at each generation, per stirpes, and pre-1990 UPC], consider a family, in which G is the intestate. G has 3 children, A, B, and C. Child A has 3 children, U, V, and W. Child B has 1 child, X. Child C has 2 children, Y and Z. Consider four variations.

Variation 1: All three children survive G.

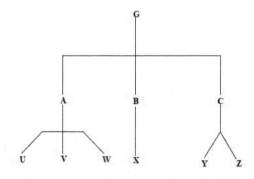

Solution: All three systems reach the same result: A, B, and C take 1/3 each.

Variation 2: One child, A, predeceases G; the other two survive G.

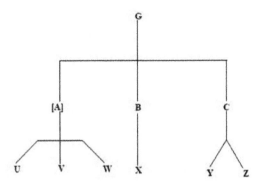

Solution: Again, all three systems reach the same result: B and C take 1/3 each; U, V, and W take 1/9 each.

Variation 3: All three children predecease G.

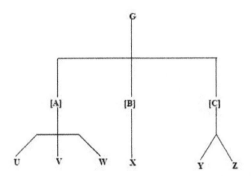

Solution: The pre-1990 UPC and the 1990 UPC systems reach the same result: U, V, W, X, Y, and Z take 1/6 each.

The per-stirpes system gives a different result: U, V, and W take 1/9 each; X takes 1/3; and Y and Z take 1/6 each.

Variation 4: Two of the three children, A and B predecease G; C survives G.

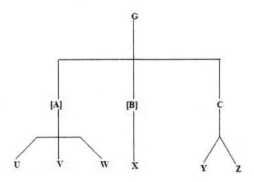

Solution: In this instance, the current UPC system (per capita at each generation) departs from the pre-1990 UPC system. Under the current UPC system, C takes 1/3 and the other two 1/3 shares are combined into a single share (amounting to 2/3 of the estate) and distributed as if C, Y and Z had predeceased G; the result is that U, V, W, and X take 1/6 each.

Although the pre-1990 UPC rejected the per-stirpes system, the result reached under the pre-1990 UPC was aligned with the per-stirpes system in this instance: C would have taken 1/3, X would have taken 1/3, and U, V, and W would have taken 1/9 each. * * *

Effect of Disclaimer. By virtue of Section 2–1106(b)(3)(A), an heir cannot use a disclaimer to effect a change in the division of an intestate's estate. To illustrate this point, consider the following example:

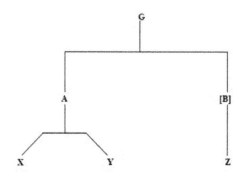

As it stands, G's intestate estate is divided into two equal parts: A takes half and B's child, Z, takes the other half. Suppose, however, that A files a disclaimer under Section 2–1105. A cannot affect the basic division of G's intestate estate by this maneuver. Section 2–1106(b)(3)(A) provides that "the disclaimed interest passes as if the disclaimant had died immediately before the time of distribution [except that] if, by law . . . , the descendants of the disclaimant would share in the disclaimed interest by any method of representation had the disclaimant died before the time of distribution, the disclaimed interest passes only to the descendants of the disclaimant who survive the time of distribution." In this example, the "disclaimed interest" is A's share (1/2) of G's estate; thus the 1/2 interest renounced by A devolves to A's children, X and Y, who take 1/4 each.

If Section 2–1106(b)(3)(A) had provided that G's "estate" is to be divided as if A predeceased G, A could have used his disclaimer to increase the share going to his children from 1/2 of 2/3 (1/3 for each child) and to decrease Z's share to 1/3. The careful wording of Section 2–1106(b)(3)(A), however, prevents A from manipulating the result by this method. * * *

Section 2–107. Inheritance Without Regard to Number of Common Ancestors in Same Generation.

An heir inherits without regard to how many common ancestors in the same generation the heir shares with the decedent.

Section 2–108. [Reserved].

Section 2–109. Advancements.

(a) If an individual dies intestate as to all or a portion of the estate, property the decedent gave during the decedent's lifetime to an individual who, at the decedent's death, is an heir is treated as an advancement against the heir's intestate share only if (i) the decedent declared in a contemporaneous writing or the heir acknowledged in writing that the gift is an advancement or (ii) the decedent's contemporaneous writing or the heir's written acknowledgment otherwise indicates that the gift is to be taken into account in computing the division and distribution of the decedent's intestate estate.

(b) For purposes of subsection (a), property advanced is valued as of the time the heir came into possession or enjoyment of the property or as of the time of the decedent's death, whichever first occurs.

(c) If the recipient of the property fails to survive the decedent, the property is not taken into account in computing the division and distribution of the decedent's intestate estate, unless the decedent's contemporaneous writing provides otherwise.

Comment

Purpose of the 1990 Revisions. This section was revised so that an advancement can be taken into account with respect to the intestate portion of a partially intestate estate.

Other than these revisions, and a few stylistic and clarifying amendments, the original content of the section is maintained, under which the common law relating to advancements is altered by requiring written evidence of the intent that an inter-vivos gift be an advancement.

The statute is phrased in terms of the donee being an heir "at the decedent's death." The donee need not be a prospective heir at the time of the gift. For example, if the intestate, G, made an inter-vivos gift intended to be an advancement to a grandchild at a time when the intestate's child who is the grandchild's parent is alive, the grandchild would not then be a prospective heir. Nevertheless, if G's intent that the gift be an advancement is contained in a written declaration or acknowledgment as provided in subsection (a), the gift is regarded as an advancement if G's child (who is the grandchild's parent) predeceases G, making the grandchild an heir.

To be an advancement, the gift need not be an outright gift; it can be in the form of a will substitute, such as designating the donee as the beneficiary of the intestate's life-insurance policy or the beneficiary of the remainder interest in a revocable inter-vivos trust. * * *

Computation of Shares—Hotchpot Method. This section does not specify the method of taking an advancement into account in distributing the decedent's intestate estate. That process, called the hotchpot method, is provided by the common law. The hotchpot method is illustrated by the following example.

Example: G died intestate, survived by his wife (W) and his three children (A, B, and C) by a prior marriage. G's probate estate is valued at $190,000. During his lifetime, G had advanced A $50,000 and B $10,000. G memorialized both gifts in a writing declaring his intent that they be advancements.

Solution. The first step in the hotchpot method is to add the value of the advancements to the value of G's probate estate. This combined figure is called the hotchpot estate.

In this case, G's hotchpot estate preliminarily comes to $250,000 ($190,000 + $50,000 + $10,000). W's intestate share of a $250,000 estate under section 2–102(4) is $200,000 ($150,000 + 1/2 of $100,000). The remaining $50,000 is divided equally among A, B, and C, or $16,667 each. This calculation reveals that A has received an advancement greater than the share to which he is entitled; A can retain the $50,000 advancement, but is not entitled to any additional amount. A and A's $50,000 advancement are therefore disregarded and the process is begun over.

Once A and A's $50,000 advancement are disregarded, G's revised hotchpot estate is $200,000 ($190,000 + $10,000). W's intestate share is $175,000 ($150,000 + 1/2 of $50,000). The remaining $25,000 is divided equally between B and C, or $12,500 each. From G's intestate estate, B receives $2,500 (B already having received $10,000 of his ultimate $12,500 share as an advancement); and C receives $12,500. The final division of G's probate estate is $175,000 to W, zero to A, $2,500 to B, and $12,500 to C.

Effect if Advancee Predeceases the Decedent; Disclaimer. If a decedent had made an advancement to a person who predeceased the decedent, the last sentence of Section 2–109 provides that the advancement is not taken into account in computing the intestate share of the recipient's descendants (unless the decedent's declaration provides otherwise). The rationale is that there is no guarantee that the recipient's descendants received the advanced property or its value from the recipient's estate.

To illustrate the application of the last sentence of Section 2–109, consider this case: During her lifetime, G had advanced $10,000 to her son, A. G died intestate, leaving a probate estate of $50,000. G was survived by her daughter, B, and by A's child, X. A predeceased G.

G's advancement to A is *disregarded*. G's $50,000 intestate estate is divided into two equal shares, half ($25,000) going to B and the other half ($25,000) going to A's child, X.

Now, suppose that A survived G. In this situation, of course, the advancement to A is taken into account in the division of G's intestate estate. Under the hotchpot method, illustrated above, G's hotchpot estate is $60,000 (probate estate of $50,000 plus advancement to A of $10,000). A takes half of this $60,000 amount, or $30,000, but is charged with already having received $10,000 of it. Consequently, A takes only a 2/5 share ($20,000) of G's intestate estate, and B takes the remaining 3/5 share ($30,000).

Note that A cannot use a disclaimer under Section 2–1105 in effect to give his child, X, a larger share than A was entitled to. Under Section 2–1106(b)(3)(A), the effect of a disclaimer by A is that the disclaimant's "interest" devolves to A's descendants as if the disclaimant had predeceased the decedent. The "interest" that A renounced was a right to a 2/5 share of G's estate, not a 1/2 share. Consequently, A's 2/5 share ($20,000) passes to A's child, X. * * *

Section 2–110. Debts to Decedent.

A debt owed to a decedent is not charged against the intestate share of any individual except the debtor. If the debtor fails to survive the decedent, the debt is not taken into account in computing the intestate share of the debtor's descendants.

Section 2–111. Alienage.

No individual is disqualified to take as an heir because the individual or an individual through whom he [or she] claims is or has been an alien.

[Section 2–112. Dower and Curtesy Abolished.

The estates of dower and curtesy are abolished.]

Section 2–113. Individual Related to Decedent Through More Than One Line.

An individual who is related to a decedent through more than one line of relationship is entitled to only a single share based on the relationship that would entitle the individual to the largest share. The individual and the individual's descendants are deemed to have predeceased the decedent with respect to a line of relationship resulting in a smaller share.

Section 2–114. Parent Barred from Inheriting in Certain Circumstances.

(a)   A parent is barred from inheriting from or through a child of the parent if:

(1)   the parent's parental rights were terminated and the parent-child relationship was not judicially reestablished; or

(2)   the child died before reaching [18] years of age and there is clear and convincing evidence that immediately before the child's death the parental rights of the parent could have been terminated under law of this state other than this [code] on the basis of nonsupport, abandonment, abuse, neglect, or other actions or inactions of the parent toward the child.

(b)   For the purpose of intestate succession from or through the deceased child, a parent who is barred from inheriting under this section is deemed to have predeceased the child.

(c)   Except as otherwise provided in Section 2–119(b), the termination of a parent's parental rights to a child has no effect on the right of the child or a descendant of the child to inherit from or through the parent.

SUBPART 2. PARENT-CHILD RELATIONSHIP

Section 2–115. Definitions.

In this [subpart]:

(1)   "Adoptee" means an individual who is adopted.

(2)   "Assisted reproduction" means a method of causing pregnancy other than sexual intercourse.

(3) "De facto parent" means an individual who is adjudicated on the basis of de facto parentage under [cite to Uniform Parentage Act (2017)][cite to state's parentage act][applicable state law] to be a parent of a child.

(4) "Relative" means a grandparent or a descendant of a grandparent.

Section 2–116. Scope.

The rules in this [subpart] concerning a parent-child relationship apply for the purpose of intestate succession.

Section 2–117. No Distinction Based on Marital Status of Parent.

A parent-child relationship extends equally to every child and parent, regardless of the marital status of the parent.

Section 2–118. Parent-Child Relationship Established Through Adoption or De Facto Parentage.

(a) [Parent-Child Relationship Established Through Adoption.] A parent-child relationship exists between an adoptee and the adoptee's adoptive parent.

(b) [Parent-Child Relationship Established Through De Facto Parentage.] A parent-child relationship exists between an individual and the individual's de facto parent.

Section 2–119. Effect of Adoption; Effect of De Facto Parentage.

(a) [Definitions.] In this section:

(1) "Parent before the adjudication" means an individual who is a parent of a child:

(A) immediately before another individual is adjudicated a de facto parent of the child; or

(B) immediately before dying, or being deemed under this [article] to have died, and before another individual is adjudicated a de facto parent of the child.

(2) "Parent before the adoption" means an individual who is a parent of a child:

(A) immediately before another individual adopts the child; or

(B) immediately before dying, or being deemed under this [article] to have died, and before another individual adopts the child.

(b) [Effect of Adoption on Parent Before the Adoption.] A parent-child relationship does not exist between an adoptee and an individual who was the adoptee's parent before the adoption unless:

(1) otherwise provided by [court order or] law other than this [code]; or

(2) the adoption:

(A) was by the spouse of a parent before the adoption;

(B) was by a relative or the spouse or surviving spouse of a relative of a parent before the adoption; or

(C) occurred after the death of a parent before the adoption.

(c) [Effect of De Facto Parentage on Parent Before the Adjudication.] Except as otherwise provided by a court order [under Uniform Parentage Act (2017) Section 613], an adjudication that an individual is a child of a de facto parent does not affect a parent-child relationship between the child and an individual who was the child's parent before the adjudication.

Comment

* * * Effect of Termination of Parental Rights. If parental rights are terminated for a parent before the adoption, that parent is barred from inheriting from the child under Section 2–114(a)(1). Under Section 2–114(b), that parent is treated as having predeceased the child for purposes of intestate succession from or through the child. Notwithstanding that an individual's parental rights have been terminated before or at the time of an adoption, that individual qualifies as a "parent before the adoption" under this section because that individual "is a parent of a child immediately before ... being deemed to have died" under Section 2–114(b) "and before another individual adopts that child." In accordance with Section 2–114(c) and subsection (b)(2) of this section, the child of such a parent continues to have the right to inherit from or through that parent. See the following examples.

Subsection (b): Adoption and Parents Before the Adoption. The opening clause of subsection (b) states the general rule that a parent-child relationship does not exist between an adopted child and the child's parents before the adoption. This rule recognizes that an adoption severs the parent-child relationship between the adopted child and the child's parents before the adoption. The adoption gives the adopted child a replacement family, sometimes referred to in the case law as "a fresh start". * * * Subsection (b) also states, however, that there are exceptions to this general rule to the extent provided by court order or law other than this Code, or as provided in subsections (b)(1) and (2).

Subsection (b)(1): Otherwise Provided by Court Order or Law. The parent-child relationship between an adoptee and the parents before the adoption remains intact if a court order or law other than this Code so provides.

Subsection (b)(2)(A): Stepchild Adopted by Stepparent. When a stepparent adopts a stepchild, subsection (b)(2)(A) provides that a parent-child relationship continues to exist between the child and the child's parent or parents before the adoption, subject to Section 2–114(a) and (b) if applicable. See Section 2–114 and the following examples.

Example 1. A and B were married and had two children, X and Y. A and B got divorced, and B married C. C adopted X and Y. The court did not terminate the parental rights of A or B. Under subsection (b)(2)(A), X and Y remain A's and B's children and under Section 2–118(a) are C's children for all purposes of intestate succession.

Example 2. Same facts as Example 1 except that A's parental rights were terminated before or when C adopted X and Y. Under Section 2–114(a)(1) and (b), for the purpose of intestate succession from or through X, A is deemed to have predeceased X, and for the purpose of intestate succession from or through Y, A is deemed to have predeceased Y. Under Sections 2–114(c) and subsection (b)(2)(A) of this section, X and Y remain the children of A and have the right to inherit from and through A.

Subsection (b)(2)(B): Individual Adopted by Relative of a Parent Before the Adoption. Under subsection (b)(2)(B), a child who is adopted by a relative of a parent, or by the spouse or surviving spouse of such a relative, remains a child of the parent or parents before the adoption, subject to Section 2–114(a) and (b) if applicable. See Section 2–114 and the following examples.

Example 3. A and B, a married couple with a four-year old child, X, were badly injured in an automobile accident and were no longer able to care for X. Thereafter, B's sister, S adopted X. The court did not terminate the parental rights of A or B. A and A's parent, P, then died intestate in that order. Under subsection (b)(2)(B), X remains A's child and P's grandchild for all purposes of intestate succession.

Example 4. Same facts as Example 3 except that X died intestate survived only by A, B, and S. Under subsections (b) and (b)(2)(B), A, B, and S have the right to inherit from X because X was a child of A, B, and S.

Example 5. Same facts as Example 3 except that the parental rights of A and B were terminated when S adopted X. Under Section 2–114(c) and subsection (b)(2)(B) of this section, X remains A's child and P's grandchild and has the right to inherit from and through A and P.

Example 6. Same facts as Example 5 except that X died intestate, survived by A, B, and P, but not by S. Under Section 2–114(a)(1) and (b), for the purpose of intestate succession from or through X, A and B are deemed to have predeceased X. Under Section 2–114(c) and subsection (b)(2)(B) of this section, P remains X's grandfather and has the right to inherit from X.

Subsection (b)(2)(C): Individual Adopted After Death of a Parent Before the Adoption. Usually, a post-death adoption does not remove a child from contact with the parent or parents before the adoption. Once a child has taken root in a family, an adoption after the death of a parent before the adoption is likely to be by someone chosen or approved of by the family. In such a case, the child does not become estranged from the family. Such an adoption does not "remove" the child from the families of the parent or parents before the adoption. Such a child continues to be a child of parents before the adoption, as well as a child of the adoptive parents, subject to Section 2–114(a) and (b) if applicable.

Example 7. A and B, a married couple with a four-year old child, X, were badly injured in an automobile accident. A subsequently died. B, who remained seriously injured, was no longer able to care for X. Thereafter, B's close friend, F, adopted X. A's parent, P, then died intestate. Under subsection (b)(2)(C), X remains P's grandchild (A's child) for all purposes of intestate succession.

Example 8. Same facts as Example 7 except that after F adopted X and before P died, B, F, and X died intestate in that order. Under subsections (b) and (b)(2)(C), X had the right to inherit from B and F because X was a child of B and a child of F. Under subsection (b)(2)(C), at X's death, P remains X's grandparent and has the right to inherit from X.

Subsection (c): Child of De Facto Parent. Unless provided otherwise by court order, an adjudication that an individual is a child of a de facto parent does not affect a parent-child relationship between the individual and the individual's parent or parents before the adjudication.

Example 9. A and B were unmarried cohabitants. With A's consent, B commenced a proceeding on the basis of de facto parentage to be adjudicated a parent of A's four-year-old child, X. The court adjudicated B on that basis to be a parent of X. After the adjudication, A died. Later, A's parent, P, died intestate. Under subsection (c), X is P's grandchild (A's child) and has the right to inherit from P.

Example 10. Same facts as Example 9 except that, after B was adjudicated X's parent, A, B, and X died intestate in that order, and P survived X. Under subsection (c), X had the right to inherit from A and B because X was a child of A and a child of B. Under subsection (c), at X's death, P remains X's grandparent and has the right to inherit from X.

Example 11. A and B were married and had a child, X. When X was four years old, A and B divorced, and B married C. When X was twelve years old, C commenced, with the consent of A and B, a proceeding on the basis of de facto parentage to be adjudicated a parent of X. The court did not terminate the parental rights of A or B when it adjudicated C to be a parent of X. Later, X died intestate, survived only by A, B, and C. Under Section 2–118(b) and subsection (c) of this section, A, B, and C are parents of X and have the right to inherit from X.

Section 2–120. Individual Conceived by Assisted Reproduction But Not Born to Gestational or Genetic Surrogate.

Except as otherwise provided under Section 2–121, parentage of an individual conceived by assisted reproduction is determined under [cite to Uniform Parentage Act (2017) Article 7 other than Section 708(b)(2)][cite to equivalent provisions of state's parentage act][applicable state law].

Comment

The promulgation of the Uniform Parentage Act (2017) [UPA (2017)] enables this section to incorporate by reference almost all of the provisions of Article 7 of the UPA (2017). The one provision inappropriate to incorporate here is Section 708(b)(2), which denies the existence of a parent-child relationship if an individual born as a result of a posthumous pregnancy fails to satisfy certain time limits. For illustrations of why these time limits on the existence of a parent-child relationship are inappropriate in the context of intestate succession, consider the following examples.

Example 1. S, facing impending death, deposited genetic material in a medical facility. Five years later, S's surviving spouse used the genetic material to give birth to a child, C. Assume that all of the requirements in the UPA (2017) for S's parentage of C are satisfied except the time limits in Section 708(b)(2). After C's birth, S's parent P died intestate, survived only by P's grandchild X and by C. Under this Code, C, who is in being at P's death, is, considered a grandchild of P (i.e., a child of S) for the purpose of determining P's heirs. P's intestate estate is divided equally between X and C.

Example 2. S, facing impending death, deposited genetic material in a medical facility. Five years later, S's parent P died intestate, survived only by P's grandchild, X. Two months after P's death, S's surviving spouse notified P's personal representative of an intent to use S's genetic material to have a child. Fifteen months after P's death, the embryo was in utero, and twenty-four months after P's death, S's surviving spouse gave birth to a child, C, who then satisfied the 120-hour requirement of survival in Section 2–104(b)(3). Assume that all of the requirements in the UPA (2017) for S's parentage of C are satisfied except the time limits in Section 708(b)(2). Under this Code, C is considered a grandchild of P (i.e., a child of S) for the purpose of determining P's heirs. P's intestate estate is divided equally between X and C. * * *

Section 2–121. Individual Born to Gestational or Genetic Surrogate.

Parentage of an individual conceived by assisted reproduction and born to a gestational or genetic surrogate is determined under [cite to Uniform Parentage Act (2017) Article 8 other than Sections 810(b)(2) and 817(b)(2)][cite to equivalent provisions of state's parentage act][applicable state law].

Comment

The promulgation of the Uniform Parentage Act (2017) [UPA (2017)] enables this section to incorporate by reference almost all of the provisions of Article 8 of the UPA (2017). The two provisions inappropriate to incorporate here are Sections 810(b)(2) and 817(b)(2), which deny the existence of a parent-child relationship if an individual born as a result of a posthumous pregnancy fails to satisfy certain time limits. For illustrations of why these time limits on the existence of a parent-child relationship are inappropriate in the context of intestate succession, consider the following examples.

Example 1. S, facing impending death, deposited genetic material in a medical facility. S and S's spouse entered into an agreement with a surrogate. Five years later, S's surviving spouse arranged for the transfer of the genetic material to the surrogate. The surrogate gave birth to C. Assume that all of the requirements in the UPA (2017) for S's parentage of C are satisfied except the time limits in Sections 810(b)(2) and 817(b)(2). After C's birth, S's parent P died intestate, survived only by P's grandchild X and by C. Under this Code, C, who is in being at P's death, is considered a grandchild of P (i.e., a child of S) for the purpose of determining P's heirs. P's intestate estate is divided equally between X and C.

Example 2. S, facing impending death, deposited genetic material in a medical facility. S and S's spouse entered into an agreement with a surrogate. Five years later, S's parent P died intestate, survived only by P's grandchild, X. Two months after P's death, S's surviving spouse notified P's personal representative of an intent to use S's genetic material to have a child by surrogacy. Fifteen months after P's death, the embryo was in utero, and twenty-four months after P's death, the surrogate gave birth to C, who then satisfied the 120-hour requirement of survival in Section 2–104(b)(3). Assume that all of the requirements in the UPA (2017) for S's parentage of C are satisfied except the time limits in Sections 810(b)(2) and 817(b)(2). Under this Code, C is considered a grandchild of P (i.e., a child of S) for the purpose of determining P's heirs. P's intestate estate is divided equally between X and C. * * *

Section 2–122. Equitable Adoption.

This [subpart] does not affect the doctrine of equitable adoption.

PART 2

ELECTIVE SHARE OF SURVIVING SPOUSE

General Comment

The elective share of the surviving spouse was fundamentally revised in 1990 and was reorganized and clarified in 1993 and 2008. The main purpose of the revisions is to bring elective-share law into line with the contemporary view of marriage as an economic partnership. The economic partnership theory of marriage is already implemented under the equitable-distribution system applied in both the common-law and community-property states when a marriage ends in divorce. When a marriage ends in death, that theory is also already implemented under the community-property system and under the system promulgated in the Model Marital Property Act. In the common-law states, however, elective-share law has not caught up to the partnership theory of marriage.

The general effect of implementing the partnership theory in elective-share law is to increase the entitlement of a surviving spouse in a long-term marriage in cases in which the marital assets were disproportionately titled in the decedent's name; and to decrease or even eliminate the entitlement of a surviving spouse in a long-term marriage in cases in which the marital assets were more or less equally titled or disproportionately titled in the surviving spouse's name. A further general effect is to decrease or even eliminate the entitlement of a surviving spouse in a short-term, later-in-life marriage (typically a post-widowhood remarriage) in which neither spouse contributed much, if anything, to the acquisition of the other's wealth, except that a special supplemental elective-share amount is provided in cases in which the surviving spouse would otherwise be left without sufficient funds for support.

The Partnership Theory of Marriage

The partnership theory of marriage, sometimes also called the marital-sharing theory, is stated in various ways. Sometimes it is thought of "as an expression of the presumed intent of husbands and wives to pool their fortunes on an equal basis, share and share alike." M. Glendon, The Transformation of Family Law 131 (1989). Under this approach, the economic rights of each spouse are seen as deriving from an unspoken marital bargain under which the partners agree that each is to enjoy a half interest in the fruits of the marriage, i.e., in the property nominally acquired by and titled in the sole name of either partner during the marriage (other than in property acquired by gift or inheritance). A decedent who disinherits his or her surviving spouse is seen as having reneged on the bargain. Sometimes the theory is expressed in restitutionary terms, a return-of-contribution notion. Under this approach, the law grants each spouse an entitlement to compensation for non-monetary contributions to the marital enterprise, as "a recognition of the activity of one spouse in the home and to compensate not only for this activity but for opportunities lost." Id. * * *

No matter how the rationale is expressed, the community-property system, including that version of community law promulgated in the Model Marital Property Act, recognizes the partnership theory, but it is sometimes thought that the common-law system denies it. In the ongoing marriage, it is true that the basic principle in the common-law (title-based) states is that marital status does not affect the ownership of property. The regime is one of separate property. Each spouse owns all that he or she earns. By contrast, in the community-property states, each spouse acquires an ownership interest in half the property the other earns during the marriage. By granting each spouse *upon acquisition* an immediate half interest in the earnings of the other, the community-property regimes directly recognize that the couple's enterprise is in essence collaborative.

The common-law states, however, also give effect or purport to give effect to the partnership theory when a marriage is dissolved by divorce. If the marriage ends in divorce, a spouse who sacrificed his or her financial-earning opportunities to contribute so-called domestic services to the marital enterprise (such as child-rearing and homemaking) stands to be recompensed. All states now follow the equitable-distribution system upon divorce, under which "broad discretion [is given to] trial courts to assign to either spouse property acquired during the marriage, irrespective of title, taking into account the circumstances of the particular case and recognizing the value of the contributions of a nonworking spouse or homemaker to the acquisition of that property. Simply stated, the system of equitable distribution views marriage as essentially a shared enterprise or joint undertaking in the nature of a partnership to which both spouses contribute—directly and indirectly, financially and nonfinancially—the fruits of which are distributable at divorce." J. Gregory, The Law of Equitable Distribution ¶ 1.03, at p. 1–6 (1989).

The other situation in which spousal property rights figure prominently is disinheritance at death. The original (pre-1990) Uniform Probate Code, along with almost all other non-UPC common-law states, treats this as one of the few instances in American law where the decedent's testamentary freedom with respect to his or her title-based ownership interests must be curtailed. No matter what the decedent's intent, the original Uniform Probate Code and almost all of the non-UPC common-law states recognize that the surviving spouse does have some claim to a portion of the decedent's estate. These statutes provide the spouse a so-called forced share. The forced share is expressed as an option that the survivor can elect or let lapse during the administration of the decedent's estate, hence in the UPC the forced share is termed the "elective" share.

Elective-share law in the common-law states, however, has not caught up to the partnership theory of marriage. Under typical American elective-share law, including the elective share provided by the original

Uniform Probate Code, a surviving spouse may claim a one-third share of the decedent's estate—not the 50 percent share of the couple's combined assets that the partnership theory would imply.

Long-term Marriages. To illustrate the discrepancy between the partnership theory and conventional elective-share law, consider first a long-term marriage, in which the couple's combined assets were accumulated mostly during the course of the marriage. The original elective-share fraction of one-third of the decedent's estate plainly does not implement a partnership principle. The actual result depends on which spouse happens to die first and on how the property accumulated during the marriage was nominally titled.

Example 1—Long-term Marriage under Conventional Forced-share Law. Consider A and B, who were married in their twenties or early thirties; they never divorced, and A died at age, say, 70, survived by B. For whatever reason, A left a will entirely disinheriting B.

Throughout their long life together, the couple managed to accumulate assets worth $600,000, marking them as a somewhat affluent but hardly wealthy couple.

Under conventional elective-share law, B's ultimate entitlement depends on the manner in which these $600,000 in assets were nominally titled as between them. B could end up much poorer or much richer than a 50/50 partnership principle would suggest. The reason is that under conventional elective-share law, B has a claim to one-third of A's "estate."

Marital Assets Disproportionately Titled in Decedent's Name; Conventional Elective-share Law Frequently Entitles Survivor to Less Than Equal Share of Marital Assets. If all the marital assets were titled in A's name, B's claim against A's estate would only be for $200,000—well below B's $300,000 entitlement produced by the partnership/marital-sharing principle.

If $500,000 of the marital assets were titled in A's name, B's claim against A's estate would still only be for $166,667 (1/3 of $500,000), which when combined with B's "own" $100,000 yields a $266,667 cut for B—still below the $300,000 figure produced by the partnership/marital-sharing principle.

Marital Assets Equally Titled; Conventional Elective-share Law Entitles Survivor to Disproportionately Large Share. If $300,000 of the marital assets were titled in A's name, B would still have a claim against A's estate for $100,000, which when combined with B's "own" $300,000 yields a $400,000 cut for B—well above the $300,000 amount to which the partnership/marital-sharing principle would lead.

Marital Assets Disproportionately Titled in Survivor's Name; Conventional Elective-share Law Entitles Survivor to Magnify the Disproportion. If only $200,000 were titled in A's name, B would still have a claim against A's estate for $66,667 (1/3 of $200,000), even though B was *already* overcompensated as judged by the partnership/marital-sharing theory.

Short-term, Later-in-Life Marriages. Short-term marriages, particularly the post-widowhood remarriage occurring later in life, present different considerations. Because each spouse in this type of marriage typically comes into the marriage owning assets derived from a former marriage, the one-third fraction of the decedent's estate far exceeds a 50/50 division of assets acquired during the marriage.

Example 2—Short-term, Later-in-Life Marriage under Conventional Elective-share Law. Consider B and C. A year or so after A's death, B married C. Both B and C are in their seventies, and after five years of marriage, B dies survived by C. Both B and C have adult children and a few grandchildren by their prior marriages, and each naturally would prefer to leave most or all of his or her property to those children.

The value of the couple's combined assets is $600,000, $300,000 of which is titled in B's name (the decedent) and $300,000 of which is titled in C's name (the survivor).

For reasons that are not immediately apparent, conventional elective-share law gives the survivor, C, a right to claim one-third of B's estate, thereby shrinking B's estate (and hence the share of B's children by B's prior marriage to A) by $100,000 (reducing it to $200,000) while supplementing C's assets (which will likely go to C's children by C's prior marriage) by $100,000 (increasing their value to $400,000).

Conventional elective-share law, in other words, basically rewards the children of the remarried spouse who manages to outlive the other, arranging for those children a windfall share of one third of the "loser's" estate. The "winning" spouse who chanced to survive gains a windfall, for this "winner" is unlikely to have made a contribution, monetary or otherwise, to the "loser's" wealth remotely worth one-third.

The Redesigned Elective Share

The redesigned elective share is intended to bring elective-share law into line with the partnership theory of marriage.

In the long-term marriage illustrated in *Example 1*, the effect of implementing a partnership theory is to increase the entitlement of the surviving spouse when the marital assets were disproportionately titled in the decedent's name; and to decrease or even eliminate the entitlement of the surviving spouse when the marital assets were more or less equally titled or disproportionately titled in the surviving spouse's name. Put differently, the effect is both to reward the surviving spouse who sacrificed his or her financial-earning opportunities in order to contribute so-called domestic services to the marital enterprise and to deny an additional windfall to the surviving spouse in whose name the fruits of a long-term marriage were mostly titled.

In the short-term, later-in-life marriage illustrated in *Example 2*, the effect of implementing a partnership theory is to decrease or even eliminate the entitlement of the surviving spouse because in such a marriage neither spouse is likely to have contributed much, if anything, to the acquisition of the other's wealth. Put differently, the effect is to deny a windfall to the survivor who contributed little to decedent's wealth, and ultimately to deny a windfall to the survivor's children by a prior marriage at the expense of the decedent's children by a prior marriage. Bear in mind that in such a marriage, which produces no children, a decedent who disinherits or largely disinherits the surviving spouse may not be acting so much from malice or spite toward the surviving spouse, but from a natural instinct to want to leave most or all of his or her property to the children of his or her former, long-term marriage. In hardship cases, however, as explained later, a special supplemental elective-share amount is provided when the surviving spouse would otherwise be left without sufficient funds for support. * * *

Specific Features of the Redesigned Elective Share

Because ease of administration and predictability of result are prized features of the probate system, the redesigned elective share implements the marital-partnership theory by means of a mechanically determined approximation system. Under the redesigned elective share, there is no need to identify which of the couple's property was earned during the marriage and which was acquired prior to the marriage or acquired during the marriage by gift or inheritance. For further discussion of the reasons for choosing this method, see Waggoner, "Spousal Rights in Our Multiple-Marriage Society: The Revised Uniform Probate Code," 26 Real Prop. Prob. & Tr. J. 683 (1992).

Section 2–202(a)—The "Elective-share Amount." Under Section 2–202(a), the elective-share amount is equal to 50 percent of the value of the "marital-property portion of the augmented estate." The marital-property portion of the augmented estate, which is determined under Section 2–203(b), increases with the length of the marriage. The longer the marriage, the larger the "marital-property portion of the augmented estate." The sliding scale adjusts for the correspondingly greater contribution to the acquisition of the couple's marital property in a marriage of 15 years than in a marriage of 15 days. Specifically, the "marital-property portion of the augmented estate" starts low and increases annually according to a graduated schedule until it reaches 100 percent. After one year of marriage, the marital-property portion of the augmented estate is six percent of the augmented estate and it increases with each additional year of marriage until it reaches the maximum 100 percent level after 15 years of marriage.

Section 2–203—The "Augmented Estate." The elective-share percentage of 50 percent is applied to the value of the "marital-property portion of the augmented estate." As defined in Section 2–203, the "augmented estate" equals the value of the couple's *combined* assets, not merely the value of the assets nominally titled in the decedent's name.

More specifically, the "augmented estate" is composed of the sum of four elements:

Section 2–204—the value of the decedent's net probate estate;

Section 2–205—the value of the decedent's nonprobate transfers to others, consisting of will-substitute-type inter-vivos transfers made by the decedent to others than the surviving spouse;

Section 2–206—the value of the decedent's nonprobate transfers to the surviving spouse, consisting of will-substitute-type inter-vivos transfers made by the decedent to the surviving spouse; and

Section 2–207—the value of the surviving spouse's net assets at the decedent's death, plus any property that would have been in the surviving spouse's nonprobate transfers to others under Section 2–205 had the surviving spouse been the decedent.

Section 2–203(b)—The "Marital-property portion" of the Augmented Estate. Section 2–203(b) defines the marital-property portion of the augmented estate.

Section 2–202(a)—The "Elective-share Amount." Section 2–202(a) requires the elective-share percentage of 50 percent to be applied to the value of the marital-property portion of the augmented estate. This calculation yields the "elective-share amount"—the amount to which the surviving spouse is entitled. If the elective-share percentage were to be applied only to the marital-property portion of the decedent's assets, a surviving spouse who has already been overcompensated in terms of the way the marital-property portion of the couple's assets have been nominally titled would receive a further windfall under the elective-share system. The marital-property portion of the couple's assets, in other words, would not be equalized. By applying the elective-share percentage of 50 percent to the marital-property portion of the augmented estate (the couple's combined assets), the redesigned system denies any significance to how the spouses took title to particular assets.

Section 2–209—Satisfying the Elective-share Amount. Section 2–209 determines how the elective-share amount is to be satisfied. Under Section 2–209, the decedent's net probate estate and nonprobate transfers to others are liable to contribute to the satisfaction of the elective-share amount only to the extent the elective-share amount is not fully satisfied by the sum of the following amounts:

Subsection (a)(1)—amounts that pass or have passed from the decedent to the surviving spouse by testate or intestate succession and amounts included in the augmented estate under Section 2–206, i.e., the value of the decedent's nonprobate transfers to the surviving spouse; and

Subsection (a)(2)—the marital-property portion of amounts included in the augmented estate under Section 2–207.

If the combined value of these amounts equals or exceeds the elective-share amount, the surviving spouse is not entitled to any further amount from recipients of the decedent's net probate estate or nonprobate transfers to others, unless the surviving spouse is entitled to a supplemental elective-share amount under Section 2–202(b).

Example 3—15-Year or Longer Marriage under Redesigned Elective Share; Marital Assets Disproportionately Titled in Decedent's Name. A and B were married to each other more than 15 years. A died, survived by B. A's will left nothing to B, and A made no nonprobate transfers to B. A made nonprobate transfers to others in the amount of $100,000 as defined in Section 2–205.

	Augmented Estate	Marital-Property Portion (100%)
A's net probate estate	$300,000	$300,000
A's nonprobate transfers to others	$100,000	$100,000
A's nonprobate transfers to B	$0	$0
B's assets and nonprobate transfers to others	$200,000	$200,000
Augmented Estate	$600,000	$600,000
Elective-Share Amount (50% of Marital-property portion) $300,000		
Less Amount Already Satisfied.. $200,000		
Unsatisfied Balance.. $100,000		

Under Section 2–209(a)(2), the full value of B's assets ($200,000) counts first toward satisfying B's entitlement. B, therefore, is treated as already having received $200,000 of B's ultimate entitlement of $300,000. Section 2–209(c) makes A's net probate estate and nonprobate transfers to others liable for the unsatisfied balance of the elective-share amount, $100,000, which is the amount needed to bring B's own $200,000 up to $300,000.

Example 4—15-Year or Longer Marriage under Redesigned Elective Share; Marital Assets Disproportionately Titled in Survivor's Name. As in *Example 3*, A and B were married to each other more than 15 years. A died, survived by B. A's will left nothing to B, and A made no nonprobate transfers to B. A made nonprobate transfers to others in the amount of $50,000 as defined in Section 2–205.

	Augmented Estate	Marital-Property Portion (100%)
A's net probate estate	$150,000	$150,000
A's nonprobate transfers to others	$50,000	$50,000
A's nonprobate transfers to B	$0	$0
B's assets and nonprobate transfers to others	$400,000	$400,000
Augmented Estate	$600,000	$600,000
Elective-Share Amount (50% of Marital-property portion) $300,000		
Less Amount Already Satisfied.. $400,000		
Unsatisfied Balance...$0		

Under Section 2–209(a)(2), the full value of B's assets ($400,000) counts first toward satisfying B's entitlement. B, therefore, is treated as already having received more than B's ultimate entitlement of $300,000. B has no claim on A's net probate estate or nonprobate transfers to others.

In a marriage that has lasted less than 15 years, only a portion of the survivor's assets—not all—count toward making up the elective-share amount. This is because, in these shorter-term marriages, the marital-property portion of the survivor's assets under Section 2–203(b) is less than 100% and, under Section 2–209(a)(2), the portion of the survivor's assets that count toward making up the elective-share amount is limited to the marital-property portion of those assets.

To explain why this is appropriate requires further elaboration of the underlying theory of the redesigned system. The system avoids the classification and tracing-to-source problems in determining the marital-property portion of the couple's assets. This is accomplished under Section 2–203(b) by applying an ever-increasing percentage, as the length of the marriage increases, to the couple's combined assets without regard to when or how those assets were acquired. By approximation, the redesigned system equates the marital-property portion of the couple's combined assets with the couple's marital assets—assets subject to equalization under the partnership/marital-sharing theory. Thus, in a marriage that has endured long enough for the marital-property portion of their assets to be 60% under Section 2–203(b), 60% of each spouse's assets are treated as marital assets. Section 2–209(a)(2) therefore counts only 60% of the survivor's assets toward making up the elective-share amount.

Example 5—Under 15-Year Marriage under the Redesigned Elective Share; Marital Assets Disproportionately Titled in Decedent's Name. A and B were married to each other more than 5 but less than 6 years. A died, survived by B. A's will left nothing to B, and A made no nonprobate transfers to B. A made nonprobate transfers to others in the amount of $100,000 as defined in Section 2–205.

	Augmented Estate	Marital-Property Portion (30%)
A's net probate estate	$300,000	$90,000
A's nonprobate transfers to others	$100,000	$30,000
A's nonprobate transfers to B	$0	$0
B's assets and nonprobate transfers to others	$200,000	$60,000
Augmented Estate	$600,000	$180,000
Elective-Share Amount (50% of Marital-property portion) $90,000		
Less Amount Already Satisfied... $60,000		
Unsatisfied Balance.. $30,000		

Under Section 2–209(a)(2), the marital-property portion of B's assets (30% of $200,000, or $60,000) counts first toward satisfying B's entitlement. B, therefore, is treated as already having received $60,000 of B's ultimate entitlement of $90,000. Under Section 2–209(c), B has a claim on A's net probate estate and nonprobate transfers to others of $30,000. * * *

The Support Theory

The partnership/marital-sharing theory is not the only driving force behind elective-share law. Another theoretical basis for elective-share law is that the spouses' mutual duties of support during their joint lifetimes should be continued in some form after death in favor of the survivor, as a claim on the decedent's estate. Current elective-share law implements this theory poorly. The fixed fraction, whether it is the typical one-third or some other fraction, disregards the survivor's actual need. A one-third share may be inadequate to the surviving spouse's needs, especially in a modest estate. On the other hand, in a very large estate, it may go far beyond the survivor's needs. In either a modest or a large estate, the survivor may or may not have ample independent means, and this factor, too, is disregarded in conventional elective-share law. The redesigned elective share system implements the support theory by granting the survivor a supplemental elective-share amount related to the survivor's actual needs. In implementing a support rationale, the length of the marriage is quite irrelevant. Because the duty of support is founded upon status, it arises at the time of the marriage.

Section 2–202(b)—The "Supplemental Elective-share Amount." Section 2–202(b) is the provision that implements the support theory by providing a supplemental elective-share amount of $75,000. The $75,000 figure is bracketed to indicate that individual states may wish to select a higher or lower amount.

In satisfying this $75,000 amount, the surviving spouse's own titled-based ownership interests count first toward making up this supplemental amount; included in the survivor's assets for this purpose are amounts shifting to the survivor at the decedent's death and amounts owing to the survivor from the decedent's estate under the accrual-type elective-share apparatus discussed above, but excluded are (1) amounts going to the survivor under the Code's probate exemptions and allowances and (2) the survivor's Social Security benefits (and other governmental benefits, such as Medicare insurance coverage). If the survivor's assets are less than the $75,000 minimum, then the survivor is entitled to whatever additional portion of the decedent's estate is necessary, up to 100 percent of it, to bring the survivor's assets up to that minimum level. In the case of a late marriage, in which the survivor is perhaps aged in the mid-seventies, the minimum figure plus the probate exemptions and allowances (which under the Code amount to a minimum of another $64,500) is pretty much on target—in conjunction with Social Security payments and other governmental benefits—to provide the survivor with a fairly adequate means of support.

Example 6—Supplemental Elective-share Amount. After A's death in *Example 1*, B married C. Five years later, B died, survived by C. B's will left nothing to C, and B made no nonprobate transfers to C. B made no nonprobate transfers to others as defined in Section 2–205.

	Augmented Estate	Marital-Property Portion (30%)
B's net probate estate	$90,000	$27,000
B's nonprobate transfers to others	$0	$0
B's nonprobate transfers to C	$0	$0
C's assets and nonprobate transfers to others	$10,000	$3,000
Augmented Estate	$100,000	$30,000
Elective-Share Amount (50% of Marital-property portion) $15,000		
Less Amount Already Satisfied... $3,000		
Unsatisfied Balance.. $12,000		

Solution under Redesigned Elective Share. Under Section 2–209(a)(2), $3,000 (30%) of C's assets count first toward making up C's elective-share amount; under Section 2–209(c), the remaining $12,000 elective-share amount would come from B's net probate estate.

Application of Section 2–202(b) shows that C is entitled to a supplemental elective-share amount. The calculation of C's supplemental elective-share amount begins by determining the sum of the amounts described in sections:

2–207...$10,000

2–209(a)(1).. 0

Elective-share amount payable from decedent's probate estate under

    Section 2–209(c) $12,000

Total...$22,000

The above calculation shows that C is entitled to a supplemental elective-share amount under Section 2–202(b) of $53,000 ($75,000 minus $22,000). The supplemental elective-share amount is payable entirely from B's net probate estate, as prescribed in Section 2–209(c).

The end result is that C is entitled to $65,000 ($12,000 + $53,000) by way of elective share from B's net probate estate (and nonprobate transfers to others, had there been any). Sixty-five thousand dollars is the amount necessary to bring C's $10,000 in assets up to $75,000.

Decedent's Nonprobate Transfers to Others

The pre-1990 Code made great strides toward preventing "fraud on the spouse's share." The problem of "fraud on the spouse's share" arises when the decedent seeks to evade the spouse's elective share by engaging in various kinds of nominal inter-vivos transfers. To render that type of behavior ineffective, the original Code adopted the augmented-estate concept, which extended the elective-share entitlement to property that was the subject of specified types of inter-vivos transfer, such as revocable inter-vivos trusts.

In the redesign of the elective share, the augmented-estate concept has been strengthened. The pre-1990 Code left several loopholes ajar in the augmented estate—a notable one being life insurance the decedent buys, naming someone other than his or her surviving spouse as the beneficiary. With appropriate protection for the insurance company that pays off before receiving notice of an elective-share claim, the redesigned elective-share system includes these types of insurance policies in the augmented estate as part of the decedent's nonprobate transfers to others under Section 2–205. * * *

Section 2–201. Definitions.

In this [part]:

(1)   As used in sections other than Section 2–205, "decedent's nonprobate transfers to others" means the amounts that are included in the augmented estate under Section 2–205.

(2)   "Fractional interest in property held in joint tenancy with the right of survivorship," whether the fractional interest is unilaterally severable or not, means the fraction, the numerator of which is one and the denominator of which, if the decedent was a joint tenant, is one plus the number of joint tenants who survive the decedent and which, if the decedent was not a joint tenant, is the number of joint tenants.

(3)   "Marriage," as it relates to a transfer by the decedent during marriage, means any marriage of the decedent to the decedent's surviving spouse.

(4)   "Nonadverse party" means a person who does not have a substantial beneficial interest in the trust or other property arrangement that would be adversely affected by the exercise or nonexercise of the power that he [or she] possesses respecting the trust or other property arrangement. A person having a general power of appointment over property is deemed to have a beneficial interest in the property.

(5)   "Power" or "power of appointment" includes a power to designate the beneficiary of a beneficiary designation.

(6)   "Presently exercisable general power of appointment" means a power of appointment under which, at the time in question, the decedent held a power to create a present or future interest in the

decedent, the decedent's creditors, the decedent's estate, or creditors of the decedent's estate, whether or not the decedent then had the capacity to exercise the power. The term includes a power to revoke or invade the principal of a trust or other property arrangement.

(7) "Property" includes values subject to a beneficiary designation.

(8) "Right to income" includes a right to payments under a commercial or private annuity, an annuity trust, a unitrust, or a similar arrangement.

(9) "Transfer", as it relates to a transfer by or of the decedent, includes:

(A) an exercise or release of a presently exercisable general power of appointment held by the decedent,

(B) a lapse at death of a presently exercisable general power of appointment held by the decedent, and

(C) an exercise, release, or lapse of a general power of appointment that the decedent reserved or of a power described in Section 2–205(2)(B) that the decedent conferred on a nonadverse party.

Section 2–202. Elective Share.

(a) **[Elective-Share Amount.]** The surviving spouse of a decedent who dies domiciled in this state has a right of election, under the limitations and conditions stated in this [part], to take an elective-share amount equal to 50 percent of the value of the marital-property portion of the augmented estate.

(b) **[Supplemental Elective-Share Amount.]** If the sum of the amounts described in Sections 2–207, 2–209(a)(1), and that part of the elective-share amount payable from the decedent's net probate estate and nonprobate transfers to others under Section 2–209(c) and (d) is less than [$75,000], the surviving spouse is entitled to a supplemental elective-share amount equal to [$75,000], minus the sum of the amounts described in those sections. The supplemental elective-share amount is payable from the decedent's net probate estate and from recipients of the decedent's nonprobate transfers to others in the order of priority set forth in Section 2–209(c) and (d).

(c) **[Effect of Election on Statutory Benefits.]** If the right of election is exercised by or on behalf of the surviving spouse, the surviving spouse's homestead allowance, exempt property, and family allowance, if any, are not charged against but are in addition to the elective-share and supplemental elective-share amounts.

(d) **[Non-Domiciliary.]** The right, if any, of the surviving spouse of a decedent who dies domiciled outside this state to take an elective share in property in this state is governed by the law of the decedent's domicile at death.

Section 2–203. Composition of the Augmented Estate; Marital-Property Portion.

(a) Subject to Section 2–208, the value of the augmented estate, to the extent provided in Sections 2–204, 2–205, 2–206, and 2–207, consists of the sum of the values of all property, whether real or personal, movable or immovable, tangible or intangible, wherever situated, that constitute:

(1) the decedent's net probate estate;

(2) the decedent's nonprobate transfers to others;

(3) the decedent's nonprobate transfers to the surviving spouse; and

(4) the surviving spouse's property and nonprobate transfers to others.

Alternative A

(b)　The value of the marital-property portion of the augmented estate consists of the sum of the values of the four components of the augmented estate as determined under subsection (a) multiplied by the following percentage:

If the decedent and the spouse were married to each other:	The percentage is:
Less than 1 year	3%
1 year but less than 2 years	6%
2 years but less than 3 years	12%
3 years but less than 4 years	18%
4 years but less than 5 years	24%
5 years but less than 6 years	30%
6 years but less than 7 years	36%
7 years but less than 8 years	42%
8 years but less than 9 years	48%
9 years but less than 10 years	54%
10 years but less than 11 years	60%
11 years but less than 12 years	68%
12 years but less than 13 years	76%
13 years but less than 14 years	84%
14 years but less than 15 years	92%
15 years or more	100%

Alternative B

(b)　The value of the marital-property portion of the augmented estate equals the value of that portion of the augmented estate that would be marital property at the decedent's death under [the Model Marital Property Act] [copy in definition from Model Marital Property Act, including the presumption that all property is marital property] [copy in other definition chosen by the enacting state].

End of Alternatives

Section 2–204. Decedent's Net Probate Estate.

The value of the augmented estate includes the value of the decedent's probate estate, reduced by funeral and administration expenses, homestead allowance, family allowances, exempt property, and enforceable claims.

Comment

This section * * * establishes as the first component of the augmented estate the value of the decedent's probate estate, reduced by funeral and administration expenses, homestead allowance (Section 2–402), family allowances (Section 2–404), exempt property (Section 2–403), and enforceable claims. * * *

Various aspects of Section 2–204 are illustrated by Examples 10, 11, and 12 in the Comment to Section 2–205, below.

Section 2-205. Decedent's Nonprobate Transfers to Others.

The value of the augmented estate includes the value of the decedent's nonprobate transfers to others, not included under Section 2-204, of any of the following types, in the amount provided respectively for each type of transfer:

(1) Property owned or owned in substance by the decedent immediately before death that passed outside probate at the decedent's death. Property included under this category consists of:

(A) Property over which the decedent alone, immediately before death, held a presently exercisable general power of appointment. The amount included is the value of the property subject to the power, to the extent the property passed at the decedent's death, by exercise, release, lapse, in default, or otherwise, to or for the benefit of any person other than the decedent's estate or surviving spouse.

(B) The decedent's fractional interest in property held by the decedent in joint tenancy with the right of survivorship. The amount included is the value of the decedent's fractional interest, to the extent the fractional interest passed by right of survivorship at the decedent's death to a surviving joint tenant other than the decedent's surviving spouse.

(C) The decedent's ownership interest in property or accounts held in POD, TOD, or co-ownership registration with the right of survivorship. The amount included is the value of the decedent's ownership interest, to the extent the decedent's ownership interest passed at the decedent's death to or for the benefit of any person other than the decedent's estate or surviving spouse.

(D) Proceeds of insurance, including accidental death benefits, on the life of the decedent, if the decedent owned the insurance policy immediately before death or if and to the extent the decedent alone and immediately before death held a presently exercisable general power of appointment over the policy or its proceeds. The amount included is the value of the proceeds, to the extent they were payable at the decedent's death to or for the benefit of any person other than the decedent's estate or surviving spouse.

(2) Property transferred in any of the following forms by the decedent during marriage:

(A) Any irrevocable transfer in which the decedent retained the right to the possession or enjoyment of, or to the income from, the property if and to the extent the decedent's right terminated at or continued beyond the decedent's death. The amount included is the value of the fraction of the property to which the decedent's right related, to the extent the fraction of the property passed outside probate to or for the benefit of any person other than the decedent's estate or surviving spouse.

(B) Any transfer in which the decedent created a power over income or property, exercisable by the decedent alone or in conjunction with any other person, or exercisable by a nonadverse party, to or for the benefit of the decedent, creditors of the decedent, the decedent's estate, or creditors of the decedent's estate. The amount included with respect to a power over property is the value of the property subject to the power, and the amount included with respect to a power over income is the value of the property that produces or produced the income, to the extent the power in either case was exercisable at the decedent's death to or for the benefit of any person other than the decedent's surviving spouse or to the extent the property passed at the decedent's death, by exercise, release, lapse, in default, or otherwise, to or for the benefit of any person other than the decedent's estate or surviving spouse. If the power is a power over both income and property and the preceding sentence produces different amounts, the amount included is the greater amount.

(3) Property that passed during marriage and during the two-year period next preceding the decedent's death as a result of a transfer by the decedent if the transfer was of any of the following types:

(A) Any property that passed as a result of the termination of a right or interest in, or power over, property that would have been included in the augmented estate under paragraph (1)(A), (B), or (C), or under paragraph (2), if the right, interest, or power had not terminated until the decedent's death. The amount included is the value of the property that would have been included under those paragraphs if the property were valued at the time the right, interest, or power terminated, and is included only to the extent the property passed upon termination to or for the benefit of any person other than the decedent or the decedent's estate, spouse, or surviving spouse. As used in this subparagraph, "termination," with respect to a right or interest in property, occurs when the right or interest terminated by the terms of the governing instrument or the decedent transferred or relinquished the right or interest, and, with respect to a power over property, occurs when the power terminated by exercise, release, lapse, default, or otherwise, but, with respect to a power described in paragraph (1)(A), "termination" occurs when the power terminated by exercise or release, but not otherwise.

(B) Any transfer of or relating to an insurance policy on the life of the decedent if the proceeds would have been included in the augmented estate under paragraph (1)(D) had the transfer not occurred. The amount included is the value of the insurance proceeds to the extent the proceeds were payable at the decedent's death to or for the benefit of any person other than the decedent's estate or surviving spouse.

(C) Any transfer of property, to the extent not otherwise included in the augmented estate, made to or for the benefit of a person other than the decedent's surviving spouse. The amount included is the value of the transferred property to the extent the transfers to any one donee in either of the two years exceeded [$12,000] [the amount excludable from taxable gifts under 26 U.S.C. Section 2503(b) [or its successor] on the date next preceding the date of the decedent's death].

Comment

This section * * * establishes as the second component of the augmented estate the value of the decedent's nonprobate transfers to others. * * *

This component is divided into three basic categories: (1) property owned or owned in substance by the decedent immediately before death that passed outside probate to persons other than the surviving spouse; (2) property transferred by the decedent during marriage that passed outside probate to persons other than the surviving spouse; and (3) property transferred by the decedent during marriage and during the two-year period next preceding the decedent's death. Various aspects of each category and each subdivision within each category are discussed and illustrated below.

Paragraph (1)—Property Owned or Owned in Substance by the Decedent. This category covers property that the decedent owned or owned in substance immediately before death and that passed outside probate at the decedent's death to a person or persons other than the surviving spouse. * * *

Various aspects of paragraph (1) are illustrated by the following examples. Other examples illustrating various aspects of this paragraph are *Example 19* in this Comment, below, and *Examples 20* and *21* in the Comment to Section 2–206, below. In each of the following examples, G is the decedent and S is the decedent's surviving spouse.

Example 1—General Testamentary Power. G's mother, M, created a testamentary trust, providing for the income to go to G for life, remainder in corpus to such persons, including G, G's creditors, G's estate, or the creditors of G's estate, as G by will appoints; in default of appointment, to X. G died, survived by S and X. G's will did not exercise his power in favor of S.

The value of the corpus of the trust at G's death is not included in the augmented estate under paragraph (1)(A), regardless of whether G exercised the power in favor of someone other than S or let the power lapse, so that the trust corpus passed in default of appointment to X. Section 2–205(1)(A) only applies to *presently exercisable* general powers; G's power was a general *testamentary* power. (Note that paragraph (2)(B) does cover property subject to a general *testamentary* power, but only if the power was created by G during marriage. G's general testamentary power was created by M and hence not covered by paragraph (2)(B).)

Example 2—Nongeneral Power and "5-and-5" Power. G's father, F, created a testamentary trust, providing for the income to go to G for life, remainder in corpus to such persons, except G, G's creditors, G's estate, or the creditors of G's estate, as G by will appoints; in default of appointment, to X. G was also given a noncumulative annual power to withdraw an amount equal to the greater of $5,000 or five percent of the trust corpus. G died, survived by S and X. G did not exercise her power in favor of S.

G's power over the remainder interest does not cause inclusion of the value of the full corpus in the augmented estate under paragraph (1)(A) because that power was a *nongeneral* power.

The value of the greater of $5,000 or five percent of the corpus of the trust *at G's death* is included in the augmented estate under paragraph (1)(A), to the extent that that property passed at G's death, by exercise, release, lapse, in default, or otherwise, to or for the benefit of any person other than the decedent's estate or surviving spouse, because that portion of the trust corpus was subject to a *presently exercisable general* power of appointment held by G immediately before G's death. No additional amount is included, however, whether G exercised the withdrawal power or allowed it to lapse in the years prior to G's death. (Note that paragraph (3)(A) is inapplicable to this case. That paragraph only applies to property subject to powers *created by the decedent during marriage* that lapse within the two-year period next preceding the decedent's death.)

Example 3—Revocable Inter-Vivos Trust. G created a revocable inter-vivos trust, providing for the income to go to G for life, remainder in corpus to such persons, except G, G's creditors, G's estate, or the creditors of G's estate, as G by will appoints; in default of appointment, to X. G died, survived by S and X. G never exercised his power to revoke, and the corpus of the trust passed at G's death to X.

Regardless of whether G created the trust before or after marrying S, the value of the corpus of the trust at G's death is included in the augmented estate under paragraph (1)(A) because, immediately before G's death, the trust corpus was subject to a presently exercisable general power of appointment (the power to revoke: see Section 2–201(6)) held by G.

(Note that if G created the trust during marriage, paragraph (2)(B) also requires inclusion of the value of the trust corpus. Because these two subparagraphs overlap, and because both subparagraphs include the same value, Section 2–208(c) provides that the value of the trust corpus is included under one but not both subparagraphs.)

Example 4—Joint Tenancy. G, X, and Y owned property in joint tenancy. G died, survived by S, X, and Y.

Because G's fractional interest in the property immediately before death was one-third, and because that one-third fractional interest passed by right of survivorship to X and Y at G's death, one-third of the value of the property at G's death is included in the augmented estate under paragraph (1)(B). This is the result whether or not under local law G had the unilateral right to sever her fractional interest. See Section 2–201(2).

Example 5—TOD Registered Securities and POD Account. G registered securities that G owned in TOD form. G also contributed all the funds in a savings account that G registered in POD Form. X was designated to take the securities and Y was designated to take the savings account on G's death. G died, survived by S, X, and Y.

Because G was the sole owner of the securities immediately before death (see Sections 6–302 and 6–306), and because ownership of the securities passed to X upon G's death (see Section 6–307), the full value of the securities at G's death is included in the augmented estate under paragraph (1)(C). Because G contributed all the funds in the savings account, G's ownership interest in the savings account immediately before death was 100 percent (see Section 6–211). Because that 100 percentage ownership interest passed by right of survivorship to Y at G's death, the full value of the account at G's death is included in the augmented estate under paragraph (1)(C).

Example 6—Joint Checking Account. G, X, and Y were registered as co-owners of a joint checking account. G contributed 75 percent of the funds in the account. G died, survived by S, X, and Y.

G's ownership interest in the account immediately before death, determined under Section 6–211, was 75 percent of the account. Because that percentage ownership interest passed by right of survivorship to X and Y at G's death, 75 percent of the value of the account at G's death is included in the augmented estate under paragraph (1)(C).

Example 7—Joint Checking Account. G's mother, M, added G's name to her checking account so that G could pay her bills for her. M contributed all the funds in the account. The account was registered in co-ownership form with right of survivorship. G died, survived by S and M.

Because G had contributed none of his own funds to the account, G's ownership interest in the account immediately before death, determined under Section 6–211, was zero. Consequently, no part of the value of the account at G's death is included in the augmented estate under paragraph (1)(C).

Example 8—Life Insurance. G, as owner of a life-insurance policy insuring her life, designated X and Y as the beneficiaries of that policy. G died owning the policy, survived by S, X, and Y.

The full value of the proceeds of that policy is included in the augmented estate under paragraph (1)(D).

Paragraph (2)—Property Transferred by the Decedent During Marriage. This category covers property that the decedent transferred in specified forms during "marriage" (defined in Section 2–201(3) as "any marriage of the decedent to the decedent's surviving spouse"). If the decedent and the surviving spouse were married to each other more than once, transfers that took place during any of their marriages to each other count as transfers during marriage.

The word "transfer," as it relates to a transfer by or of the decedent, is defined in Section 2–201(10), as including "(A) an exercise or release of a presently exercisable general power of appointment held by the decedent, (B) a lapse at death of a presently exercisable general power of appointment held by the decedent, and (C) an exercise, release, or lapse of a general power of appointment that the decedent created in himself [or herself] and of a power described in Section 2–205(2)(B) that the decedent conferred on a nonadverse party." * * *

Various aspects of paragraph (2) are illustrated by the following examples. Other examples illustrating various aspects of this paragraph are *Examples 1* and *3*, above, and *Example 22* in the Comment to Section 2–206, below. In the following examples, as in the examples above, G is the decedent and S is the decedent's surviving spouse.

Example 9—Retained Income Interest for Life. Before death, and during marriage, G created an irrevocable inter-vivos trust, providing for the income to be paid annually to G for life, then for the corpus of the trust to go to X. G died, survived by S and X.

The value of the corpus of the trust at G's death is included in the augmented estate under paragraph (2)(A). This paragraph applies to a retained income interest that terminates at the decedent's death, as here. The amount included is the value of the property that passes outside probate to any person other than the decedent's estate or surviving spouse, which in this case is the full value of the corpus that passes outside probate to X.

Had G retained the right to only one-half of the income, with the other half payable to Y for G's lifetime, only one half of the value of the corpus at G's death would have been included under paragraph (2)(A) because that paragraph specifies that "the amount included is the value of the fraction of the property to which the decedent's right related." Note, however, that if G had created the trust within two years before death, paragraph (3)(C) would require the inclusion of the value at the date the trust was established of the other half of the income interest for G's life and of the remainder interest in the other half of the corpus, each value to be reduced by as much as $10,000 as appropriate under the facts, taking into account other gifts made to Y and to X in the same year, if any.

Example 10—Retained Unitrust Interest for a Term. Before death, and during marriage, G created an irrevocable inter-vivos trust, providing for a fixed percentage of the value of the corpus of the trust (determined annually) to be paid annually to G for 10 years, then for the corpus of the trust (and any accumulated income) to go to X. G died six years after the trust was created, survived by S and X.

The full value of the corpus at G's death is included in the augmented estate under a combination of Sections 2–204 and 2–205(2)(A).

Section 2–205(2)(A) requires the inclusion of the commuted value of X's remainder interest at G's death. This paragraph applies to a retained income interest, which under Section 2–201(8) includes a unitrust interest. Moreover, Section 2–205(2)(A) not only applies to a retained income interest that terminates at the decedent's death, but also applies to a retained income interest that continues beyond the decedent's death, as here. The amount included is the value of the interest that passes outside probate to a person other than the decedent's estate or surviving spouse, which in this case is the commuted value of X's remainder interest at G's death.

Section 2–204 requires the inclusion of the commuted value of the remaining four years of G's unitrust interest because that interest passes through G's probate estate to G's devisees or heirs.

Because both the four-year unitrust interest and the remainder interest that directly succeeds it are included in the augmented estate, there is no need to derive separate values for X's remainder interest and for G's remaining unitrust interest. The sum of the two values will equal the full value of the corpus, and that is the value that is included in the augmented estate. (Note, however, that *for purposes of Section 2–209 (Sources from Which Elective Share Payable)*, it might become necessary to derive separate values for these two interests.)

Had the trust been revocable, the end-result would have been the same. The only difference would be that the revocability of the trust would cause paragraph (2)(A) to be inapplicable, but would also cause overlapping application of paragraphs (1)(A) and (2)(B) to X's remainder interest. Because each of these paragraphs yields the same value, Section 2–208(c) would require the commuted value of X's remainder interest to be included in the augmented estate under any one, but only one, of them. Note that neither paragraphs (1)(A) nor (2)(B) would apply to G's remaining four-year term because that four-year term would have passed to G's estate by lapse of G's power to revoke. As above, the commuted value of G's remaining four-year term would be included in the augmented estate under Section 2–204, obviating the need to derive separate valuations of G's four-year term and X's remainder interest.

Example 11—Personal Residence Trust. Before death, and during marriage, G created an irrevocable inter-vivos trust of G's personal residence, retaining the right to occupy the residence for 10 years, then for the residence to go to X. G died six years after the trust was created, survived by S and X.

The full value of the residence at G's death is included in the augmented estate under a combination of Sections 2–204 and 2–205(2)(A).

Section 2–205(2)(A) requires the inclusion of the commuted value of X's remainder interest at G's death. This paragraph applies to a retained right to possession that continues beyond the decedent's death, as here. The amount included is the value of the interest that passes outside probate to a person other than the decedent's estate or surviving spouse, which in this case is the commuted value of X's remainder interest at G's death.

Section 2–204 requires the inclusion of the commuted value of G's remaining four-year term because that interest passes through G's probate estate to G's devisees or heirs.

As in *Example 10*, there is no need to derive separate valuations of the remaining four-year term and the remainder interest that directly succeeds it. The sum of the two values will equal the full value of the residence at G's death, and that is the amount included in the augmented estate. (Note, however, that *for purposes of Section 2–209 (Sources from Which Elective Share Payable)*, it might become necessary to derive separate values for these two interests.)

Example 12—Retained Annuity Interest for a Term. Before death, and during marriage, G created an irrevocable inter-vivos trust, providing for a fixed dollar amount to be paid annually to G for 10 years, then for half of the corpus of the trust to go to X; the other half was to remain in trust for an additional five years, after which time the remaining corpus was to go to X. G died 14 years after the trust was created, survived by S and X.

The value of the one-half of the corpus of the trust remaining at G's death is included in the augmented estate under a combination of Sections 2–204 and 2–205(2)(A). The other one-half of the corpus of the trust that was distributed to X four years before G's death is not included in the augmented estate.

Section 2–205(2)(A) requires the inclusion of the commuted value of X's remainder interest in half of the corpus of the trust. This section applies to a retained income interest, which under Section 2–201(8), includes an annuity interest that continues beyond the decedent's death, as here. The amount included is the value of the interest that passes outside probate to a person other than the decedent's estate or surviving spouse, which in this case is the commuted value of X's remainder interest at G's death.

Section 2–204 requires the inclusion of the commuted value of the remaining one year of G's annuity interest in half of the corpus of the trust, which passed through G's probate estate to G's devisees or heirs.

There is no need to derive separate valuations of G's remaining annuity interest and X's remainder interest that directly succeeds it. The sum of the two values will equal the full value of the remaining one-half of the corpus of the trust at G's death, and that is the amount included in the augmented estate. (Note, however, that *for purposes of Section 2–209 (Sources from Which Elective Share Payable)*, it might become necessary to derive separate values for these two interests.)

Had G died eleven years after the trust was created, so that the termination of half of the trust would have occurred within the two-year period next preceding G's death, the value of the half of the corpus of the trust that was distributed to X 10 years after the trust was created would also have been included in the augmented estate under Section 2–205(3)(A).

Example 13—Commercial Annuity. Before G's death, and during marriage, G purchased three commercial annuities from an insurance company. Annuity One was a single-life annuity that paid a fixed sum to G annually and that contained a refund feature payable to X if G died within 10 years. Annuity Two was a single-life annuity that paid a fixed sum to G annually, but contained no refund feature. Annuity Three was a self and survivor annuity that paid a fixed sum to G annually for life, and then paid a fixed sum annually to X for life. G died six years after purchasing the annuities, survived by S and X.

Annuity One: The value of the refund payable to X at G's death under Annuity One is included in the augmented estate under paragraph (2)(A). G retained an income interest, as defined in Section 2–201(8), that terminated at G's death. The amount included is the value of the interest that passes outside probate to a person other than the decedent's estate or surviving spouse, which in this case is the refund amount to which X is entitled.

Annuity Two: Annuity Two does not cause any value to be included in the augmented estate because it expired at G's death; although G retained an income interest, as defined in Section 2–201(8), that terminated at G's death, nothing passed outside probate to any person other than G's estate or surviving spouse.

Annuity Three: The commuted value at G's death of the annuity payable to X under Annuity Three is included in the augmented estate under paragraph (2)(A). G retained an income interest, as defined in Section 2–201(8), that terminated at G's death. The amount included is the value of the interest that passes outside probate to a person other than the decedent's estate or surviving spouse, which in this case is the commuted value of X's right to the annuity payments for X's lifetime.

Example 14—Joint Power. Before death, and during marriage, G created an inter-vivos trust, providing for the income to go to X for life, remainder in corpus at X's death to X's then-living descendants, by representation; if none, to a specified charity. G retained a power, exercisable only with the consent of X, allowing G to withdraw all or any portion of the corpus at any time during G's lifetime. G died without exercising the power, survived by S and X.

The value of the corpus of the trust at G's death is included in the augmented estate under paragraph (2)(B). This paragraph applies to a power created by the decedent over the corpus of the trust that is exercisable by the decedent "in conjunction with any other person," who in this case is X. Note that the fact that X has an interest in the trust that would be adversely affected by the exercise of the power in favor of G is irrelevant. The amount included is the full value of the corpus of the trust at G's death because the power related to the full corpus of the trust and the full corpus passed at the decedent's death, by lapse or default of the power, to a person other than the decedent's estate or surviving spouse—X, X's descendants, and the specified charity.

Example 15—Power in Nonadverse Party. Before death, and during marriage, G created an inter-vivos trust, providing for the income to go to X for life, remainder in corpus to X's then-living descendants, by representation; if none, to a specified charity. G conferred a power on the trustee, a bank, to distribute, in the trustee's complete and uncontrolled discretion, all or any portion of the trust corpus to G or to X. One year before G's death, the trustee distributed $50,000 of trust corpus to G and $40,000 of trust corpus to X. G died, survived by S and X.

The full value of the portion of the corpus of the trust remaining at G's death is included in the augmented estate under paragraph (2)(B). This paragraph applies to a power created by the decedent over the corpus of the trust that is exercisable by a "nonadverse party." As defined in Section 2–201(4), the term "nonadverse party" is "a person who does not have a substantial beneficial interest in the trust or other property arrangement that would be adversely affected by the exercise or nonexercise of the power that he [or she] possesses respecting the trust or other property arrangement." The trustee in this case is a nonadverse party. The amount included is the full value of the corpus of the trust at G's death because the trustee's power related to the full corpus of the trust and the full corpus passed at the decedent's death, by lapse or default of the power, to a person other than the decedent's estate or surviving spouse—X, X's descendants, and the specified charity.

In addition to the full value of the remaining corpus at G's death, an additional amount is included in the augmented estate because of the $40,000 distribution of corpus to X within two years before G's death. As defined in Section 2–201(9), a transfer of the decedent includes the exercise "of a power described in Section 2–205(2)(B) that the decedent conferred on a nonadverse party." Consequently, the $40,000 distribution to X is considered to be a transfer of the decedent within two years before death, and is included in the augmented estate under paragraph (3)(C) to the extent it exceeded $12,000 of the aggregate gifts to X that year. If no other gifts were made to X in that year, the amount included would be $28,000 ($40,000 – $12,000).

Paragraph (3)—Property Transferred by the Decedent During Marriage and During the Two-Year Period Next Preceding the Decedent's Death. This paragraph—called the two-year rule— requires inclusion in the augmented estate of the value of property that the decedent transferred in specified forms during marriage and within two years of death. The word "transfer," as it relates to a transfer by or of the decedent, is defined in Section 2–201(9), as including "(A) an exercise or release of a presently exercisable general power of appointment held by the decedent, (B) a lapse at death of a presently exercisable general power of appointment held by the decedent, and (C) an exercise, release, or lapse of a general power of appointment that the decedent created in himself [or herself] and of a power described in Section 2–205(2)(B) that the decedent conferred on a nonadverse party." * * *

Various aspects of paragraph (3) are illustrated by the following examples. Other examples illustrating various aspects of this paragraph are *Examples 2, 9, 12, 14*, and *15*, above, and *Examples 33* and *34* in the Comment to Section 2–207, below. In the following examples, as in the examples above, G is the decedent and S is the decedent's surviving spouse.

Example 16—Retained Income Interest Terminating Within Two Years Before Death. Before death, and during marriage, G created an irrevocable inter-vivos trust, providing for the income to go to G for 10 years, then for the corpus of the trust to go to X. G died 11 years after the trust was created, survived by S and X. G was married to S when the trust terminated.

The full value of the corpus of the trust at the date of its termination is included in the augmented estate under paragraph (3)(A). The full value of the corpus at death would have been included in the augmented estate under paragraph (2)(A) had G's income interest not terminated until death; G's income interest terminated within the two-year period next preceding G's death; G was married to S when the trust was created and when the income interest terminated; and the trust corpus upon termination passed to a person other than S, G, or G's estate.

Example 17—Personal Residence Trust Terminating Within Two Years Before Death. Before death, and during marriage, G created an irrevocable inter-vivos trust of G's personal residence, retaining the right to occupy the residence for 10 years, then for the residence to go to X. G died eleven years after the trust was created, survived by S and X. G was married to S when the right to possession terminated.

The full value of the residence at the date the trust terminated is included in the augmented estate under paragraph (3)(A). The full value of the residence would have been included in the augmented estate under paragraph (2)(A) had G's right to possession not terminated until death; G's right to possession terminated within the two-year period next preceding G's death; G was married to S when the trust was created and when the right to possession terminated; and the residence passed upon termination to a person other than S, G, or G's estate.

Example 18—Irrevocable Assignment of Life-Insurance Policy Within Two Years Before Death. In *Example 8*, G irrevocably assigned the life-insurance policy to X and Y within two years preceding G's death. G was married to S when the policy was assigned. G died, survived by S, X, and Y.

The full value of the proceeds are included in the augmented estate under paragraph (3)(B). The full value of the proceeds would have been included in the augmented estate under paragraph (1)(D) had G owned the policy at death; G assigned the policy within the two-year period next preceding G's death; G was married to S when the policy was assigned; and the proceeds were payable to a person other than S or G's estate.

Example 19—Property Purchased in Joint Tenancy Within Two Years Before Death. Within two years before death, and during marriage, G and X purchased property in joint tenancy; G contributed $75,000 of the $100,000 purchase price and X contributed $25,000. G died, survived by S and X.

Regardless of when or by whom the property was purchased, the value at G's death of G's fractional interest of one-half is included in the augmented estate under paragraph (1)(B) because G's half passed to X as surviving joint tenant. Because the property was purchased within two years before death, and during marriage, and because G's contribution exceeded the value of G's fractional interest in the property, the excess contribution of $25,000 constitutes a gift to X within the two-year period next preceding G's death. Consequently, an additional $13,000 ($25,000 minus $12,000) is included in the augmented estate under paragraph (3)(C) as a gift to X.

Had G provided all of the $100,000 purchase price, then paragraph (3)(C) would require $38,000 ($50,000 minus $12,000) to be included in the augmented estate (in addition to the inclusion of one-half the value of the property at G's death under paragraph (1)(B)).

Had G provided one-half or less of the $100,000 purchase price, then G would not have made a gift to X within the two-year period next preceding G's death. Half the value of the property at G's death would still be included in the augmented estate under paragraph (1)(B), however. * * *

Section 2–206. Decedent's Nonprobate Transfers to the Surviving Spouse.

Excluding property passing to the surviving spouse under the federal Social Security system, the value of the augmented estate includes the value of the decedent's nonprobate transfers to the decedent's surviving spouse, which consist of all property that passed outside probate at the decedent's death from the decedent to the surviving spouse by reason of the decedent's death, including:

(1)   the decedent's fractional interest in property held as a joint tenant with the right of survivorship, to the extent that the decedent's fractional interest passed to the surviving spouse as surviving joint tenant,

(2)   the decedent's ownership interest in property or accounts held in co-ownership registration with the right of survivorship, to the extent the decedent's ownership interest passed to the surviving spouse as surviving co-owner, and

(3)   all other property that would have been included in the augmented estate under Section 2–205(1) or (2) had it passed to or for the benefit of a person other than the decedent's spouse, surviving spouse, the decedent, or the decedent's creditors, estate, or estate creditors.

Comment

This section * * * establishes as the third component of the augmented estate the value of the decedent's nonprobate transfers to the decedent's surviving spouse. * * *

Various aspects of Section 2–206 are illustrated by the following examples. In these examples, as in the examples in the Comment to Section 2–205, above, G is the decedent and S is the decedent's surviving spouse.

Example 20—Tenancy by the Entirety. G and S own property in tenancy by the entirety. G died, survived by S.

Because the definition in Section 1–201 of "joint tenants with the right of survivorship" includes tenants by the entirety, the provisions of Section 2–206 relating to joint tenancies with right of survivorship apply to tenancies by the entirety.

In total, therefore, the full value of the property is included in the augmented estate—G's one-half under Section 2–206(1) and S's one-half under Section 2–207(a)(1)(A).

Section 2–206(1) requires the inclusion of the value of G's one-half fractional interest because it passed to S as surviving joint tenant.

Section 2–207(a)(1)(A) requires the inclusion of S's one-half fractional interest. Because G was a joint tenant immediately before G's death, S's fractional interest, for purposes of Section 2–207, is determined immediately before G's death, disregarding the fact that G predeceased S. Immediately before G's death, S's fractional interest was then a one-half fractional interest. Despite Section 2–205(1)(B), none of S's fractional interest is included under Section 2–207(a)(2) because that provision does not apply to fractional interests that are included under Section 2–207(a)(1)(A). Consequently, the value of S's one-half interest is included under Section 2–207(a)(1)(A) but not under Section 2–207(a)(2).

Example 21—Joint Tenancy. G, S, and X own property in joint tenancy. G died more than two years after the property was titled in that form, survived by S and X.

In total, two-thirds of the value of the property at G's death is included in the augmented estate—one-sixth under Section 2–205, one-sixth under Section 2–206, and one-third under Section 2–207.

Section 2–205(1)(B) requires the inclusion of half of the value of G's one-third fractional interest because that half passed by right of survivorship to X.

Section 2–206(1) requires the inclusion of the value of the other half of G's one-third fractional interest because that half passed to S as surviving joint tenant.

Section 2–207(a)(1)(A) requires the inclusion of the value of S's one-third interest. Because G was a joint tenant immediately before G's death, S's fractional interest, for purposes of Section 2–207, is determined immediately before G's death, disregarding the fact that G predeceased S. Immediately before G's death, S's fractional interest was then a one-third fractional interest. Despite Section 2–205(1)(B), none of S's fractional interest is included under Section 2–207(a)(2) because that provision does not apply to fractional interests that are included under Section 2–207(a)(1)(A). Consequently, the value of S's one-third fractional interest is included in the augmented estate under Section 2–207(a)(1)(A) but not under Section 2–207(a)(2).

Example 22—Income Interest Passing to Surviving Spouse. Before death, and during marriage, G created an irrevocable inter-vivos trust, providing for the income to go to G for life, then for the income to go to S for life, then for the corpus of the trust to go to X. G died, survived by S and X.

The full value of the corpus of the trust at G's death is included in the augmented estate under a combination of Sections 2–205 and 2–206.

Section 2–206(3) requires the inclusion of the commuted value of S's income interest. Note that, although S owns the income interest as of G's death, the value of S's income interest is not included under Section 2–207 because Section 2–207 only includes property interests that are not included under Section 2–206.

Section 2–205(2)(A) requires the inclusion of the commuted value of X's remainder interest.

Example 23—Corpus Passing to Surviving Spouse. Before death, and during marriage, G created an irrevocable inter-vivos trust, providing for the income to go to G for life, then for the corpus of the trust to go to S. G died, survived by S.

The value of the corpus of the trust at G's death is included in the augmented estate under Section 2–206(3). Note that, although S owns the corpus as of G's death, the value of S's ownership interest in the corpus is not included under Section 2–207 because Section 2–207 only includes property interests that are not included under Section 2–206.

Example 24—TOD Registered Securities, POD Account, and Life Insurance Payable to Surviving Spouse. In *Examples 5* and *8* in the Comment to Section 2–205, G designated S to take the securities on death, registered S as the beneficiary of the POD savings account, and named S as the beneficiary of the life-insurance policy.

The same values that were included in the augmented estate under Section 2–205(1) in those examples are included in the augmented estate under Section 2–206.

Example 25—Joint Checking Account. G and S were registered as co-owners of a joint checking account. G contributed 75 percent of the funds in the account and S contributed 25 percent of the funds. G died, survived by S.

G's ownership interest in the account immediately before death, determined under Section 6–211, was 75 percent of the account. Because that percentage ownership interest passed by right of survivorship to S at G's death, 75 percent of the value of the account at G's death is included in the augmented estate under Section 2–206. The remaining 25 percent of the account is included in the augmented estate under Section 2–207. * * *

Section 2–207. Surviving Spouse's Property and Nonprobate Transfers to Others.

(a) **[Included Property.]** Except to the extent included in the augmented estate under Section 2–204 or 2–206, the value of the augmented estate includes the value of:

    (1)   property that was owned by the decedent's surviving spouse at the decedent's death, including:

        (A)   the surviving spouse's fractional interest in property held in joint tenancy with the right of survivorship,

        (B)   the surviving spouse's ownership interest in property or accounts held in co-ownership registration with the right of survivorship, and

        (C)   property that passed to the surviving spouse by reason of the decedent's death, but not including the spouse's right to homestead allowance, family allowance, exempt property, or payments under the federal Social Security system; and

    (2)   property that would have been included in the surviving spouse's nonprobate transfers to others, other than the spouse's fractional and ownership interests included under subsection (a)(1)(A) or (B), had the spouse been the decedent.

(b) **[Time of Valuation.]** Property included under this section is valued at the decedent's death, taking the fact that the decedent predeceased the spouse into account, but, for purposes of subsection (a)(1)(A) and (B), the values of the spouse's fractional and ownership interests are determined immediately before the decedent's death if the decedent was then a joint tenant or a co-owner of the property or accounts. For purposes of subsection (a)(2), proceeds of insurance that would have been included in the spouse's nonprobate transfers to others under Section 2–205(1)(D) are not valued as if he [or she] were deceased.

(c) **[Reduction for Enforceable Claims.]** The value of property included under this section is reduced by enforceable claims against the surviving spouse.

Comment

This section * * * establishes as the fourth component of the augmented estate the value of property owned by the surviving spouse at the decedent's death plus the value of amounts that would have been includible in the surviving spouse's nonprobate transfers to others had the spouse been the decedent, reduced by enforceable claims against that property or that spouse, as provided in Sections 2–207(c) and 2–208(b)(1). Property owned by the decedent's surviving spouse does not include the value of enhancements to the surviving spouse's earning capacity (e.g., the value of a law, medical, or business degree).

Note that amounts that would have been includible in the surviving spouse's nonprobate transfers to others under Section 2–205(1)(D) are not valued as if he or she were deceased. Thus, if, at the decedent's death, the surviving spouse owns a $1 million life-insurance policy on his or her life, payable to his or her sister, that policy would not be valued at its face value of $1 million, but rather could be valued under the method used in the federal estate tax under Treas. Reg. § 20.2031–8. * * *

Various aspects of Section 2–207 are illustrated by the following examples. Other examples illustrating various aspects of this section are *Examples 20, 21, 22, 23,* and *25* in the Comment to Section 2–206. In the following examples, as in the examples in the Comments to Sections 2–205 and 2–206, above, G is the decedent and S is the decedent's surviving spouse.

Example 26—Inter-Vivos Trust Created by Surviving Spouse; Corpus Payable to Spouse at Decedent's Death. Before G's death, and during marriage, S created an irrevocable inter-vivos trust, providing for the income to go to G for life, then for the corpus of the trust to go to S. G died, survived by S.

The value of the corpus of the trust at G's death is included in the augmented estate under Section 2–207(a)(1) as either an interest owned by S at G's death or as an interest that passed to the spouse by reason of G's death.

Example 27—Inter-Vivos Trust Created by Another; Income Payable to Spouse for Life. Before G's death, X created an irrevocable inter-vivos trust, providing for the income to go to S for life, then for the income to go to G for life, then for the corpus of the trust to go to Y. G died, survived by S and Y.

The commuted value of S's income interest as of G's death is included in the augmented estate under Section 2–207(a), as a property interest owned by the surviving spouse at the decedent's death.

Example 28—Inter-Vivos Trust Created by Another; Income Payable to Spouse for Life. Before G's death, X created an irrevocable inter-vivos trust, providing for the income to go to G for life, then for the income to go to S for life, then for the corpus of the trust to go to Y. G died, survived by S and Y.

The commuted value of S's income interest at the decedent's death is included in the augmented estate under Section 2–207(a)(1), as either a property interest owned by the surviving spouse at the decedent's death or a property interest that passed to the surviving spouse by reason of the decedent's death.

Example 29—Life Insurance on Decedent's Life Owned by Surviving Spouse; Proceeds Payable to Spouse. Before G's death, S bought a life-insurance policy on G's life, naming S as the beneficiary. G died, survived by S.

The value of the proceeds of the life-insurance policy is included in the augmented estate under Section 2–207(a)(1), as property owned by the surviving spouse at the decedent's death.

Example 30—Life Insurance on Decedent's Life Owned by Another; Proceeds Payable to Spouse. Before G's death, X brought a life-insurance policy on G's life, naming S as the beneficiary. G died, survived by S.

The value of the proceeds of the life-insurance policy is included in the augmented estate under Section 2–207(a)(1)(C), as property that passed to the surviving spouse by reason of the decedent's death.

Example 31—Joint Tenancy Between Spouse and Another. S and Y own property in joint tenancy. G died, survived by S and Y.

The value of S's one-half fractional interest at G's death is included in the augmented estate under Section 2–207(a)(1)(A). Despite Section 2–205(1)(B), none of S's fractional interest is included under Section 2–207(a)(2) because that provision does not apply to fractional interests required to be included under Section 2–207(a)(1)(A). Consequently, the value of S's one-half is included under Section 2–207(a)(1)(A) but not under Section 2–207(a)(2).

Example 32—Inter-Vivos Trust with Retained Income Interest Created by Surviving Spouse. Before G's death, and during marriage, S created an irrevocable inter-vivos trust, providing for the income to go to S for life, then for the income to go to G for life, then for the corpus of the trust to go to X. G died, survived by S and X.

The value of the trust corpus at G's death is included in the augmented estate under Section 2–207(a)(2) because, if S were the decedent, that value would be included in the spouse's nonprobate transfers to others under Section 2–205(2)(A). Note that property included under Section 2–207 is valued at the decedent's death, taking the fact that the decedent predeceased the spouse into account. Thus, G's remainder in income for life is extinguished, and the full value of the corpus is included in the augmented estate under Section 2–207(a)(2). The commuted value of S's income interest would also be included under Section 2–207(a)(1) but for the fact that Section 2–208(c) provides that when two provisions apply to the same property interest, the interest is not included under both provisions, but is included under the provision yielding the highest value. Consequently, since Section 2–207(a)(2) yields a higher value (the full corpus) than Section 2–207(a)(1) (the income interest), and since the income interest is part of the value of the corpus, and hence both provisions apply to the same property interest, the full corpus is included under Section 2–207(a)(2) and nothing is included under Section 2–207(a)(1).

Example 33—Inter-Vivos Trust Created by Decedent; Income to Surviving Spouse. More than two years before G's death, and during marriage, G created an irrevocable inter-vivos trust, providing for the income to go to S for life, then for the corpus of the trust to go to X. G died, survived by S and X.

The commuted value of S's income interest as of G's death is included in the augmented estate under Section 2–207. If G had created the trust within the two-year period next preceding G's death, the commuted value of X's remainder interest as of the date of the creation of the trust (less $12,000, assuming G made no other gifts to X in that year) would also have been included in the augmented estate under Section 2–205(3)(C).

Example 34—Inter-Vivos Trust Created by Surviving Spouse; No Retained Interest or Power. More than two years before G's death, and during marriage, S created an irrevocable inter-vivos trust, providing for the income to go to G for life, then for the corpus of the trust to go to Y. G died, survived by S and Y.

The value of the trust is not included in the augmented estate. If S had created the trust within the two-year period next preceding G's death, the commuted value of Y's remainder interest as of the date of the creation of the trust (less $10,000, assuming no other gifts to Y in that year) would have been included in the augmented estate under Section 2–207(a)(2) because if S were the decedent, the value of the remainder interest would have been included in S's nonprobate transfers to others under Section 2–205(3)(C). * * *

Section 2–208. Exclusions, Valuation, and Overlapping Application.

(a) [Exclusions.] The value of any property is excluded from the decedent's nonprobate transfers to others:

    (1) to the extent the decedent received adequate and full consideration in money or money's worth for a transfer of the property; or

    (2) if the property was transferred with the written joinder of, or if the transfer was consented to in writing before or after the transfer by, the surviving spouse.

(b) [Valuation.] The value of property:

    (1) included in the augmented estate under Section 2–205, 2–206, or 2–207 is reduced in each category by enforceable claims against the included property; and

    (2) includes the commuted value of any present or future interest and the commuted value of amounts payable under any trust, life insurance settlement option, annuity contract, public or private pension, disability compensation, death benefit or retirement plan, or any similar arrangement, exclusive of the federal Social Security system.

(c) [Overlapping Application; No Double Inclusion.] In case of overlapping application to the same property of the paragraphs or subparagraphs of Section 2–205, 2–206, or 2–207, the property is included in the augmented estate under the provision yielding the greatest value, and under only one overlapping provision if they all yield the same value.

Section 2–209. Sources from Which Elective Share Payable.

(a) [Elective-Share Amount Only.] In a proceeding for an elective share, the following are applied first to satisfy the elective-share amount and to reduce or eliminate any contributions due from the decedent's net probate estate and recipients of the decedent's nonprobate transfers to others:

    (1) amounts included in the augmented estate under Section 2–204 which pass or have passed to the surviving spouse by testate or intestate succession and amounts included in the augmented estate under Section 2–206; and

(2) the marital-property portion of amounts included in the augmented estate under Section 2–207.

(b) [Marital-Property Portion.] The marital-property portion under subsection (a)(2) is computed by multiplying the value of the amounts included in the augmented estate under Section 2–207 by the percentage of the augmented estate set forth in the schedule in Section 2–203(b) appropriate to the length of time the spouse and the decedent were married to each other.

(c) [Unsatisfied Balance of Elective-Share Amount; Supplemental Elective-Share Amount.] If, after the application of subsection (a), the elective-share amount is not fully satisfied or the surviving spouse is entitled to a supplemental elective-share amount, amounts included in the decedent's net probate estate, other than assets passing to the surviving spouse by testate or intestate succession, and in the decedent's nonprobate transfers to others under Section 2–205(1), (2), and (3)(B) are applied first to satisfy the unsatisfied balance of the elective-share amount or the supplemental elective-share amount. The decedent's net probate estate and that portion of the decedent's nonprobate transfers to others are so applied that liability for the unsatisfied balance of the elective-share amount or for the supplemental elective-share amount is apportioned among the recipients of the decedent's net probate estate and of that portion of the decedent's nonprobate transfers to others in proportion to the value of their interests therein.

(d) [Unsatisfied Balance of Elective-Share and Supplemental Elective-Share Amounts.] If, after the application of subsections (a) and (c), the elective-share or supplemental elective-share amount is not fully satisfied, the remaining portion of the decedent's nonprobate transfers to others is so applied that liability for the unsatisfied balance of the elective-share or supplemental elective-share amount is apportioned among the recipients of the remaining portion of the decedent's nonprobate transfers to others in proportion to the value of their interests therein.

(e) [Unsatisfied Balance Treated as General Pecuniary Devise.] The unsatisfied balance of the elective-share or supplemental elective-share amount as determined under subsection (c) or (d) is treated as a general pecuniary devise for purposes of Section 3–904.

Section 2–210. Personal Liability of Recipients.

(a) Only original recipients of the decedent's nonprobate transfers to others, and the donees of the recipients of the decedent's nonprobate transfers to others, to the extent the donees have the property or its proceeds, are liable to make a proportional contribution toward satisfaction of the surviving spouse's elective-share or supplemental elective-share amount. A person liable to make contribution may choose to give up the proportional part of the decedent's nonprobate transfers to him [or her] or to pay the value of the amount for which he [or she] is liable.

(b) If any section or part of any section of this [part] is preempted by federal law with respect to a payment, an item of property, or any other benefit included in the decedent's nonprobate transfers to others, a person who, not for value, receives the payment, item of property, or any other benefit is obligated to return the payment, item of property, or benefit, or is personally liable for the amount of the payment or the value of that item of property or benefit, as provided in Section 2–209, to the person who would have been entitled to it were that section or part of that section not preempted.

Comment

Federal Preemption of State Law. See the comment to Section 2–804 for a discussion of federal preemption. * * *

Section 2–211. Proceeding for Elective Share; Time Limit.

(a) Except as provided in subsection (b), the election must be made by filing in the court and mailing or delivering to the personal representative, if any, a petition for the elective share within nine months after the date of the decedent's death, or within six months after the probate of the decedent's will, whichever limitation later expires. The surviving spouse must give notice of the time and place set for hearing to persons interested in the estate and to the distributees and recipients of portions of the augmented estate whose interests will be adversely affected by the taking of the elective share. Except as provided in subsection (b), the decedent's nonprobate transfers to others are not included within the augmented estate for the purpose of computing the elective share, if the petition is filed more than nine months after the decedent's death.

(b) Within nine months after the decedent's death, the surviving spouse may petition the court for an extension of time for making an election. If, within nine months after the decedent's death, the spouse gives notice of the petition to all persons interested in the decedent's nonprobate transfers to others, the court for cause shown by the surviving spouse may extend the time for election. If the court grants the spouse's petition for an extension, the decedent's nonprobate transfers to others are not excluded from the augmented estate for the purpose of computing the elective-share and supplemental elective-share amounts, if the spouse makes an election by filing in the court and mailing or delivering to the personal representative, if any, a petition for the elective share within the time allowed by the extension.

(c) The surviving spouse may withdraw his [or her] demand for an elective share at any time before entry of a final determination by the court.

(d) After notice and hearing, the court shall determine the elective-share and supplemental elective-share amounts, and shall order its payment from the assets of the augmented estate or by contribution as appears appropriate under Sections 2–209 and 2–210. If it appears that a fund or property included in the augmented estate has not come into the possession of the personal representative, or has been distributed by the personal representative, the court nevertheless shall fix the liability of any person who has any interest in the fund or property or who has possession thereof, whether as trustee or otherwise. The proceeding may be maintained against fewer than all persons against whom relief could be sought, but no person is subject to contribution in any greater amount than he [or she] would have been under Sections 2–209 and 2–210 had relief been secured against all persons subject to contribution.

(e) An order or judgment of the court may be enforced as necessary in suit for contribution or payment in other courts of this state or other jurisdictions.

Section 2–212. Right of Election Personal to Surviving Spouse; Incapacitated Surviving Spouse.

(a) **[Surviving Spouse Must Be Living at Time of Election.]** The right of election may be exercised only by a surviving spouse who is living when the petition for the elective share is filed in the court under Section 2–211(a). If the election is not exercised by the surviving spouse personally, it may be exercised on the surviving spouse's behalf by his [or her] conservator, guardian, or agent under the authority of a power of attorney.

Alternative A

(b) **[Incapacitated Surviving Spouse.]** If the election is exercised on behalf of a surviving spouse who is an incapacitated person, that portion of the elective-share and supplemental elective-share amounts due from the decedent's probate estate and recipients of the decedent's nonprobate transfers to others under Section 2–209(c) and (d) must be placed in a custodial trust for the benefit of the surviving spouse under the provisions of the [Enacting state] Uniform Custodial Trust Act, except as modified below. For the purposes of this subsection, an election on behalf of a surviving spouse by an agent under a durable power of attorney is presumed to be on behalf of a surviving spouse who is an incapacitated person. For purposes of the custodial trust established by this subsection, (i) the electing guardian, conservator, or agent is the custodial trustee, (ii) the surviving spouse is the beneficiary, and (iii) the custodial trust is deemed to have been created by the decedent spouse by written transfer that takes effect at the decedent spouse's death and that directs the custodial trustee to administer the custodial trust as for an incapacitated beneficiary.

(c) [Custodial Trust.] For the purposes of subsection (b), the [Enacting state] Uniform Custodial Trust Act must be applied as if Section 6(b) thereof were repealed and Sections 2(e), 9(b), and 17(a) were amended to read as follows:

(1) Neither an incapacitated beneficiary nor anyone acting on behalf of an incapacitated beneficiary has a power to terminate the custodial trust; but if the beneficiary regains capacity, the beneficiary then acquires the power to terminate the custodial trust by delivering to the custodial trustee a writing signed by the beneficiary declaring the termination. If not previously terminated, the custodial trust terminates on the death of the beneficiary.

(2) If the beneficiary is incapacitated, the custodial trustee shall expend so much or all of the custodial trust property as the custodial trustee considers advisable for the use and benefit of the beneficiary and individuals who were supported by the beneficiary when the beneficiary became incapacitated, or who are legally entitled to support by the beneficiary. Expenditures may be made in the manner, when, and to the extent that the custodial trustee determines suitable and proper, without court order but with regard to other support, income, and property of the beneficiary [exclusive of] [and] benefits of medical or other forms of assistance from any state or federal government or governmental agency for which the beneficiary must qualify on the basis of need.

(3) Upon the beneficiary's death, the custodial trustee shall transfer the unexpended custodial trust property in the following order: (i) under the residuary clause, if any, of the will of the beneficiary's predeceased spouse against whom the elective share was taken, as if that predeceased spouse died immediately after the beneficiary; or (ii) to that predeceased spouse's heirs under Section 2–711 of [this state's] Uniform Probate Code.

Alternative B

(b) [Incapacitated Surviving Spouse.] If the election is exercised on behalf of a surviving spouse who is an incapacitated person, the court must set aside that portion of the elective-share and supplemental elective-share amounts due from the decedent's probate estate and recipients of the decedent's nonprobate transfers to others under Section 2–209(c) and (d) and must appoint a trustee to administer that property for the support of the surviving spouse. For the purposes of this subsection, an election on behalf of a surviving spouse by an agent under a durable power of attorney is presumed to be on behalf of a surviving spouse who is an incapacitated person. The trustee must administer the trust in accordance with the following terms and such additional terms as the court determines appropriate:

(1) Expenditures of income and principal may be made in the manner, when, and to the extent that the trustee determines suitable and proper for the surviving spouse's support, without court order but with regard to other support, income, and property of the surviving spouse [exclusive of] [and] benefits of medical or other forms of assistance from any state or federal government or governmental agency for which the surviving spouse must qualify on the basis of need.

(2) During the surviving spouse's incapacity, neither the surviving spouse nor anyone acting on behalf of the surviving spouse has a power to terminate the trust; but if the surviving spouse regains capacity, the surviving spouse then acquires the power to terminate the trust and acquire full ownership of the trust property free of trust, by delivering to the trustee a writing signed by the surviving spouse declaring the termination.

(3) Upon the surviving spouse's death, the trustee shall transfer the unexpended trust property in the following order: (i) under the residuary clause, if any, of the will of the predeceased spouse against whom the elective share was taken, as if that predeceased spouse died immediately after the surviving spouse; or (ii) to the predeceased spouse's heirs under Section 2–711.

End of Alternatives

Section 2–213. Effect of Premarital or Marital Agreement on Right to Elect and Other Rights.

(a)   In this section, "agreement" includes a subsequent agreement that affirms, modifies, or waives an earlier agreement.

(b)   The right of election of a surviving spouse and the rights of the surviving spouse to homestead allowance, exempt property, and family allowance, or any of them, may be affirmed, modified, or waived, only by a written agreement signed by the surviving spouse, before or after marriage. The agreement is enforceable without consideration.

(c)   An agreement under subsection (b) is not enforceable if the surviving spouse proves that:

(1)   the agreement was involuntary or the result of duress;

(2)   the surviving spouse did not have access to independent legal representation under subsection (d);

(3)   unless the surviving spouse had independent legal representation when the agreement was executed, the agreement did not include an explanation in plain language of the rights under subsection (b) being affirmed, modified, or waived; or

(4)   before signing the agreement, the surviving spouse did not receive adequate financial disclosure under subsection (e).

(d)   A surviving spouse had access to independent legal representation if:

(1)   before signing an agreement, the surviving spouse had a reasonable time to:

(A)   decide whether to retain a lawyer to provide independent legal representation; and

(B)   locate a lawyer to provide independent legal representation, obtain the lawyer's advice, and consider the advice provided; and

(2)   the other spouse was represented by a lawyer and the surviving spouse had the financial ability to retain a lawyer or the other spouse agreed to pay the reasonable fees and expenses of independent legal representation.

(e)   A surviving spouse had adequate financial disclosure under this section if the surviving spouse:

(1)   received a reasonably accurate description and good-faith estimate of the value of the property, liabilities, and income of the other spouse;

(2)   expressly waived, in a separate signed record, the right to financial disclosure beyond the disclosure provided; or

(3)   had adequate knowledge or a reasonable basis for having adequate knowledge of the information described in paragraph (1).

(f)   A court may refuse to enforce a term of an agreement under subsection (b) if, in the context of the agreement taken as a whole[:]

[(1)] the term was unconscionable at the time of signing[; or

(2)   enforcement of the term would result in substantial hardship for the surviving spouse because of a material change in circumstances arising after the agreement was signed].

(g)   An issue of unconscionability [or substantial hardship] of an agreement is for decision by the court as a matter of law.

(h)   Unless an agreement under subsection (b) provides to the contrary, a waiver of "all rights," or equivalent language, in the property or estate of a present or prospective spouse or a complete property settlement entered into after or in anticipation of separation or divorce is a waiver of all rights of elective share, homestead allowance, exempt property, and family allowance by the spouse in the property of the other spouse and a renunciation of all benefits that would otherwise pass to the renouncing spouse by intestate succession or by virtue of any will executed before the waiver or property settlement.

Section 2–214. Protection of Payors and Other Third Parties.

(a) Although under Section 2–205 a payment, item of property, or other benefit is included in the decedent's nonprobate transfers to others, a payor or other third party is not liable for having made a payment or transferred an item of property or other benefit to a beneficiary designated in a governing instrument, or for having taken any other action in good faith reliance on the validity of a governing instrument, upon request and satisfactory proof of the decedent's death, before the payor or other third party received written notice from the surviving spouse or spouse's representative of an intention to file a petition for the elective share or that a petition for the elective share has been filed. A payor or other third party is liable for payments made or other actions taken after the payor or other third party received written notice of an intention to file a petition for the elective share or that a petition for the elective share has been filed.

(b) A written notice of intention to file a petition for the elective share or that a petition for the elective share has been filed must be mailed to the payor's or other third party's main office or home by registered or certified mail, return receipt requested, or served upon the payor or other third party in the same manner as a summons in a civil action. Upon receipt of written notice of intention to file a petition for the elective share or that a petition for the elective share has been filed, a payor or other third party may pay any amount owed or transfer or deposit any item of property held by it to or with the court having jurisdiction of the probate proceedings relating to the decedent's estate, or if no proceedings have been commenced, to or with the court having jurisdiction of probate proceedings relating to decedents' estates located in the county of the decedent's residence. The court shall hold the funds or item of property, and, upon its determination under Section 2–211(d), shall order disbursement in accordance with the determination. If no petition is filed in the court within the specified time under Section 2–211(a) or, if filed, the demand for an elective share is withdrawn under Section 2–211(c), the court shall order disbursement to the designated beneficiary. Payments or transfers to the court or deposits made into court discharge the payor or other third party from all claims for amounts so paid or the value of property so transferred or deposited.

(c) Upon petition to the probate court by the beneficiary designated in a governing instrument, the court may order that all or part of the property be paid to the beneficiary in an amount and subject to conditions consistent with this [part].

PART 3

SPOUSE AND CHILDREN UNPROVIDED FOR IN WILLS

Section 2–301. Entitlement of Spouse; Premarital Will.

(a) If a testator's surviving spouse married the testator after the testator executed his [or her] will, the surviving spouse is entitled to receive, as an intestate share, no less than the value of the share of the estate he [or she] would have received if the testator had died intestate as to that portion of the testator's estate, if any, that neither is devised to a child of the testator who was born before the testator married the surviving spouse and who is not a child of the surviving spouse nor is devised to a descendant of such a child or passes under Sections 2–603 or 2–604 to such a child or to a descendant of such a child, unless:

(1) it appears from the will or other evidence that the will was made in contemplation of the testator's marriage to the surviving spouse;

(2) the will expresses the intention that it is to be effective notwithstanding any subsequent marriage; or

(3)   the testator provided for the spouse by transfer outside the will and the intent that the transfer be in lieu of a testamentary provision is shown by the testator's statements or is reasonably inferred from the amount of the transfer or other evidence.

(b)   In satisfying the share provided by this section, devises made by the will to the testator's surviving spouse, if any, are applied first, and other devises, other than a devise to a child of the testator who was born before the testator married the surviving spouse and who is not a child of the surviving spouse or a devise or substitute gift under Sections 2–603 or 2–604 to a descendant of such a child, abate as provided in Section 3–902.

Comment

Purpose and Scope of the Revisions. This section applies only to a premarital will, a will executed prior to the testator's marriage to his or her surviving spouse. If the decedent and the surviving spouse were married to each other more than once, a premarital will is a will executed by the decedent at any time when they were not married to each other but not a will executed during a prior marriage. This section reflects the view that the intestate share of the spouse in that portion of the testator's estate not devised to certain of the testator's children, under trust or not, (or that is not devised to their descendants, under trust or not, or does not pass to their descendants under the antilapse statute) is what the testator would want the spouse to have if he or she had thought about the relationship of his or her old will to the new situation.

Under this section, a surviving spouse who married the testator after the testator executed his or her will may be entitled to a certain minimum amount of the testator's estate. The surviving spouse's entitlement under this section, if any, is granted automatically; it need not be elected. If the surviving spouse exercises his or her right to take an elective share, amounts provided under this section count toward making up the elective-share amount by virtue of the language in subsection (a) stating that the amount provided by this section is treated as "an intestate share." Under Section 2–209(a)(1), amounts passing to the surviving spouse by intestate succession count first toward making up the spouse's elective-share amount.

Subsection (a). Subsection (a) is revised to make it clear that a surviving spouse who, by a premarital will, is devised, under trust or not, less than the share of the testator's estate he or she would have received had the testator died intestate as to that part of the estate, if any, not devised to certain of the testator's children, under trust or not, (or that is not devised to their descendants, under trust or not, or does not pass to their descendants under the antilapse statute) is entitled to be brought up to that share. Subsection (a) was amended in 1993 to make it clear that any lapsed devise that passes under Section 2–604 to a child of the testator by a prior marriage, rather than only to a descendant of such a child, is covered.

Example. G's will devised the residue of his estate "to my two children, A and B, in equal shares." A and B are children of G's prior marriage. G is survived by A and by G's new spouse, X. B predeceases G, without leaving any descendants who survived G by 120 hours. Under Section 2–604, B's half of the residue passes to G's child, A. A is a child of the testator's prior marriage but not a descendant of B. X's rights under Section 2–301 are to take an intestate share in that portion of G's estate not covered by the residuary clause. * * *

Subsection (b). Subsection (b) is also revised to provide that the value of any premarital devise to the surviving spouse, equitable or legal, is used first to satisfy the spouse's entitlement under this section, before any other devises suffer abatement. This revision is made necessary by the revision of subsection (a): If the existence or amount of a premarital devise to the surviving spouse is irrelevant, any such devise must be counted toward and not be in addition to the ultimate share to which the spouse is entitled. Normally, a devise in favor of the person whom the testator *later* marries will be a specific or general devise, not a residuary devise. The effect under the pre-1990 version of subsection (b) was that the surviving spouse could take the intestate share under Section 2–301, which in the pre-1990 version was satisfied out of the residue (under the rules of abatement in Section 3–902), *plus* the devise in his or her favor. The revision of subsection (b) prevents this "double dipping," so to speak. * * *

Section 2–302. Omitted Child.

(a)   [Parent-Child Relationship Established After Execution of Will.] Except as provided in subsection (b), if a testator becomes a parent of a child after the execution of the testator's will and fails to provide in the will for the child, the omitted child receives a share in the estate as follows:

(1)   If the testator had no child living when the testator executed the will, the omitted child receives a share in the estate equal in value to that which the child would have received had the testator died intestate, unless the will devised all or substantially all of the estate to another parent of the omitted child and that parent survives the testator and is entitled to take under the will.

(2)   If the testator had one or more children living when the testator executed the will, and the will devised property or an interest in property to one or more of the then-living children, the omitted child is entitled to share in the testator's estate as follows:

(A)   The portion of the testator's estate in which the omitted child is entitled to share is limited to devises made to the testator's then-living children under the will.

(B)   The omitted child is entitled to receive the share of the testator's estate, as limited in subparagraph (A), that the child would have received had the testator included all omitted children with the children to whom devises were made under the will and had given an equal share of the estate to each child.

(C)   To the extent feasible, the interest granted the omitted child under this section must be of the same character, whether equitable or legal, present or future, as that devised to the testator's then-living children under the will.

(D)   In the satisfaction of a share provided by this paragraph, devises to the testator's children who were living when the will was executed abate ratably. In abating the devises of the then-living children, the court shall preserve to the maximum extent possible the character of the testamentary plan adopted by the testator.

(b)   [Intentional Omission of Child; Provision for Child Outside Will.] Neither subsection (a)(1) nor subsection (a)(2) applies if:

(1)   it appears from the will that the omission was intentional; or

(2)   the testator provided for the omitted child by transfer outside the will and the intent that the transfer be in lieu of a testamentary provision is shown by the testator's statements or is reasonably inferred from the amount of the transfer or other evidence.

(c)   [Omission of Child Believed Dead.] If at the time of execution of the will the testator fails to provide in the will for a living child solely because the testator believes the child to be dead, the child is entitled to share in the estate as if the child were an omitted child.

(d)   [Abatement.] In the satisfaction of a share provided by subsection (a)(1), devises made by the will abate under Section 3–902.

Comment

This section provides for both the case where a child was born or adopted after the execution of the will and not foreseen at the time and thus not provided for in the will, and the rare case where a testator omits a child because of the mistaken belief that the child is dead. * * *

Basic Purposes and Scope of 1990 Revisions. This section was substantially revised in 1990. The revisions had two basic objectives. The first was to provide that a will that devised, under trust or not, all or substantially all of the testator's estate to the other parent of the omitted child prevents an after-born or after-adopted child from taking an intestate share if none of the testator's children was living when the testator executed the will. (Under this rule, the other parent must survive the testator and be entitled to take under the will.)

Under the pre-1990 Code, such a will prevented the omitted child's entitlement only if the testator had one or more children living when the testator executed the will. The rationale for the revised rule is found in the empirical evidence * * * that suggests that even testators with children tend to devise their entire estates to their surviving spouses, especially in smaller estates. The testator's purpose is not to disinherit the children; rather, such a will evidences a purpose to trust the surviving parent to use the property for the benefit of the children, as appropriate. This attitude of trust of the surviving parent carries over to the case where none of the children have been born when the will is executed.

The second basic objective of the 1990 revisions was to provide that if the testator had children when the testator executed the will, and if the will made provision for one or more of the then-living children, an omitted after-born or after-adopted child does not take a full intestate share (which might be substantially larger or substantially smaller than given to the living children). Rather, the omitted after-born or after-adopted child participates on a pro rata basis in the property devised, under trust or not, to the then-living children.

A more detailed description of the rules as revised in 1990 follows.

No Child Living When Will Executed. If the testator had no child living when the testator executed the will, subsection (a)(1) provided that an omitted after-born or after-adopted child receives the share the child would have received had the testator died intestate, unless the will devised, under trust or not, all or substantially all of the estate to the other parent of the omitted child. If the will did devise, under trust or not, all or substantially all of the estate to the other parent of the omitted child, and if that other parent survives the testator and is entitled to take under the will, the omitted after-born or after-adopted child receives no share of the estate. In the case of an after-adopted child, the term "other parent" refers to the other adopting parent. (The other parent of the omitted child might survive the testator, but not be entitled to take under the will because, for example, that devise, under trust or not, to the other parent was revoked under Section 2–803 or 2–804.)

One or More Children Living When Will Executed. If the testator had one or more children living when the will was executed, subsection (a)(2), which implements the second basic objective stated above, provided that an omitted after-born or after-adopted child only receives a share of the testator's estate if the testator's will devised property or an equitable or legal interest in property to one or more of the children living at the time the will was executed; if not, the omitted after-born or after-adopted child receives nothing.

* * * Subsection (a)(2) is illustrated by the following example.

Example. When G executed her will, she had two living children, A and B. Her will devised $7,500 to each child. After G executed her will, she had another child, C.

C is entitled to $5,000. $2,500 (1/3 of $7,500) of C's entitlement comes from A's $7,500 devise (reducing it to $5,000); and $2,500 (1/3 of $7,500) comes from B's $7,500 devise (reducing it to $5,000).

Variation. If G's will had devised $10,000 to A and $5,000 to B, C would be entitled to $5,000. $3,333 (1/3 of $10,000) of C's entitlement comes from A's $10,000 devise (reducing it to $6,667); and $1,667 (1/3 of $5,000) comes from B's $5,000 devise (reducing it to $3,333).

Subsection (b) Exceptions. To preclude operation of subsection (a)(1) or (2), the testator's will need not make any provision, even nominal in amount, for a testator's present or future children; under subsection (b)(1), a simple recital in the will that the testator intends to make no provision for then living children or any the testator thereafter may have would be sufficient. * * *

The moving party has the burden of proof on the elements of subsections (b)(1) and (2).

Subsection (c). Subsection (c) addresses the problem that arises if at the time of execution of the will the testator fails to provide for a living child solely because the testator believes the child to be dead. Extrinsic evidence is admissible to determine whether the testator omitted the living child solely because the testator believed the child to be dead. * * * If the child was omitted solely because of that belief, the child is entitled to share in the estate as if the child were an omitted after-born or after-adopted child.

Abatement Under Subsection (d). Under subsection (d) and Section 3–902, any intestate estate would first be applied to satisfy the intestate share of an omitted after-born or after-adopted child under subsection (a)(1). * * *

PART 4

EXEMPT PROPERTY AND ALLOWANCES

Section 2–401. Applicable Law.

This [part] applies to the estate of a decedent who dies domiciled in this state. Rights to homestead allowance, exempt property, and family allowance for a decedent who dies not domiciled in this state are governed by the law of the decedent's domicile at death.

Section 2–402. Homestead Allowance.

A decedent's surviving spouse is entitled to a homestead allowance of [$22,500]. If there is no surviving spouse, each minor child and each dependent child of the decedent is entitled to a homestead allowance amounting to [$22,500] divided by the number of minor and dependent children of the decedent. The homestead allowance is exempt from and has priority over all claims against the estate. Homestead allowance is in addition to any share passing to the surviving spouse or minor or dependent child by the will of the decedent, unless otherwise provided, by intestate succession, or by way of elective share.

[Section 2–402A. Constitutional Homestead.

The value of any constitutional right of homestead in the family home received by a surviving spouse or child must be charged against the spouse or child's homestead allowance to the extent the family home is part of the decedent's estate or would have been but for the homestead provision of the constitution.]

Section 2–403. Exempt Property.

In addition to the homestead allowance, the decedent's surviving spouse is entitled from the estate to a value, not exceeding $15,000 in excess of any security interests therein, in household furniture, automobiles, furnishings, appliances, and personal effects. If there is no surviving spouse, the decedent's children are entitled jointly to the same value. If encumbered chattels are selected and the value in excess of security interests, plus that of other exempt property, is less than $15,000, or if there is not $15,000 worth of exempt property in the estate, the spouse or children are entitled to other assets of the estate, if any, to the extent necessary to make up the $15,000 value. Rights to exempt property and assets needed to make up a deficiency of exempt property have priority over all claims against the estate, but the right to any assets to make up a deficiency of exempt property abates as necessary to permit earlier payment of homestead allowance and family allowance. These rights are in addition to any benefit or share passing to the surviving spouse or children by the decedent's will, unless otherwise provided, by intestate succession, or by way of elective share.

Section 2–404. Family Allowance.

(a) In addition to the right to homestead allowance and exempt property, the decedent's surviving spouse and minor children whom the decedent was obligated to support and children who were in fact being supported by the decedent are entitled to a reasonable allowance in money out of the estate for their maintenance during the period of administration, which allowance may not continue for longer than one year if the estate is inadequate to discharge allowed claims. The allowance may be paid as a lump sum or in periodic installments. It is payable to the surviving spouse, if living, for the use of the surviving spouse and minor and dependent children; otherwise to the children, or persons having their care and custody. If a minor child or dependent child is not living with the surviving spouse, the allowance may be made partially to the child or his [or her] guardian or other person having the child's care and custody, and partially to the spouse, as their needs may appear. The family allowance is exempt from and has priority over all claims except the homestead allowance.

(b) The family allowance is not chargeable against any benefit or share passing to the surviving spouse or children by the will of the decedent, unless otherwise provided, by intestate succession or by way of elective share. The death of any person entitled to family allowance terminates the right to allowances not yet paid.

Section 2–405. Source, Determination, and Documentation.

(a)   If the estate is otherwise sufficient, property specifically devised may not be used to satisfy rights to homestead allowance or exempt property. Subject to this restriction, the surviving spouse, guardians of minor children, or children who are adults may select property of the estate as homestead allowance and exempt property. The personal representative may make those selections if the surviving spouse, the children, or the guardians of the minor children are unable or fail to do so within a reasonable time or there is no guardian of a minor child. The personal representative may execute an instrument or deed of distribution to establish the ownership of property taken as homestead allowance or exempt property. The personal representative may determine the family allowance in a lump sum not exceeding $27,000 or periodic installments not exceeding $2,250 per month for one year, and may disburse funds of the estate in payment of the family allowance and any part of the homestead allowance payable in cash. The personal representative or an interested person aggrieved by any selection, determination, payment, proposed payment, or failure to act under this section may petition the court for appropriate relief, which may include a family allowance other than that which the personal representative determined or could have determined.

(b)   If the right to an elective share is exercised on behalf of a surviving spouse who is an incapacitated person, the personal representative may add any unexpended portions payable under the homestead allowance, exempt property, and family allowance to the trust established under Section 2–212(b).

PART 5

WILLS, WILL CONTRACTS, AND CUSTODY AND DEPOSIT OF WILLS

Section 2–501. Who May Make Will.

An individual 18 or more years of age who is of sound mind may make a will.

Section 2–502. Execution; Witnessed or Notarized Wills; Holographic Wills.

(a)   **[Witnessed or Notarized Wills.]** Except as otherwise provided in subsection (b) and in Sections 2–503, 2–506, and 2–513, a will must be:

(1)   in writing;

(2)   signed by the testator or in the testator's name by some other individual in the testator's conscious presence and by the testator's direction; and

(3)   either:

(A)   signed by at least two individuals, each of whom signed within a reasonable time after the individual witnessed either the signing of the will as described in paragraph (2) or the testator's acknowledgment of that signature or acknowledgment of the will; or

(B)   acknowledged by the testator before a notary public or other individual authorized by law to take acknowledgments.

(b)   **[Holographic Wills.]** A will that does not comply with subsection (a) is valid as a holographic will, whether or not witnessed, if the signature and material portions of the document are in the testator's handwriting.

(c)   **[Extrinsic Evidence.]** Intent that a document constitute the testator's will can be established by extrinsic evidence, including, for holographic wills, portions of the document that are not in the testator's handwriting.

Comment

Subsection (a): Witnessed or Notarized Wills. Three formalities for execution of a witnessed or notarized will are imposed. Subsection (a)(1) requires the will to be in writing. Any reasonably permanent record is sufficient. * * *

Under subsection (a)(2), the testator must sign the will or some other individual must sign the testator's name in the testator's presence and by the testator's direction. If the latter procedure is followed, and someone else signs the testator's name, the so-called "conscious presence" test is codified, under which a signing is sufficient if it was done in the testator's conscious presence, i.e., within the range of the testator's senses such as hearing; the signing need not have occurred within the testator's line of sight. * * *

Signing may be by mark, nickname, or initials, subject to the general rules relating to that which constitutes a "signature." * * * There is no requirement that the testator "publish" the document as his or her will, or that he or she request the witnesses to sign, or that the witnesses sign in the presence of the testator or of each other. The testator may sign the will outside the presence of the witnesses, if he or she later acknowledges to the witnesses that the signature is his or hers (or that his or her name was signed by another) or that the document is his or her will. An acknowledgment need not be expressly stated, but can be inferred from the testator's conduct. * * *

There is no requirement that the testator's signature be at the end of the will; thus, if the testator writes his or her name in the body of the will and intends it to be his or her signature, the statute is satisfied. * * *

Under subsection (a)(3)(A), the witnesses must sign as witnesses * * *, and must sign within a reasonable time after having witnessed the testator's act of signing or acknowledgment. There is, however, no requirement that the witnesses sign before the testator's death. In a particular case, the reasonable-time requirement could be satisfied even if the witnesses sign after the testator's death.

Under subsection (a)(3)(B), a will, whether or not it is properly witnessed under subsection (a)(3)(A), can be acknowledged by the testator before a notary public or other individual authorized by law to take acknowledgments. * * *

Allowing notarized wills as an optional method of execution addresses cases that have begun to emerge in which the supervising attorney, with the client and all witnesses present, circulates one or more estate-planning documents for signature, and fails to notice that the client or one of the witnesses has unintentionally neglected to sign one of the documents. * * * This often, but not always, arises when the attorney prepares multiple estate-planning documents—a will, a durable power of attorney, a health-care power of attorney, and perhaps a revocable trust. It is common practice, and sometimes required by state law, that the documents other than the will be notarized. It would reduce confusion and chance for error if all of these documents could be executed with the same formality. * * *

A will that does not meet the requirements of subsection (a) may be valid under subsection (b) as a holograph or under the harmless-error rule of Section 2–503.

Subsection (b): Holographic Wills. This subsection authorizes holographic wills. * * * Subsection (b) enables a testator to write his or her own will in handwriting. There need be no witnesses. The only requirement is that the signature and the material portions of the document be in the testator's handwriting.

By requiring only the "material portions of the document" to be in the testator's handwriting (rather than requiring, as some existing statutes do, that the will be "entirely" in the decedent's handwriting), a holograph may be valid even though immaterial parts such as date or introductory wording are printed, typed, or stamped.

A valid holograph can also be executed on a printed will form if the material portions of the document are handwritten. The fact, for example, that the will form contains printed language such as "I give, devise, and bequeath to _____" does not disqualify the document as a holographic will, as long as the testator fills out the remaining portion of the dispositive provision in his or her own hand.

Subsection (c): Extrinsic Evidence. Under subsection (c), testamentary intent can be shown by extrinsic evidence, including for holographic wills the printed, typed, or stamped portions of the form or document. Handwritten alterations, if signed, of a validly executed nonhandwritten will can operate as a holographic codicil to the will. If necessary, the handwritten codicil can derive meaning, and hence validity as a holographic codicil, from nonhandwritten portions of the document. * * *

Section 2–503. Harmless Error.

Although a document or writing added upon a document was not executed in compliance with Section 2–502, the document or writing is treated as if it had been executed in compliance with that section if the proponent of the document or writing establishes by clear and convincing evidence that the decedent intended the document or writing to constitute:

(1)   the decedent's will,

(2)   a partial or complete revocation of the will,

(3)   an addition to or an alteration of the will, or

(4)   a partial or complete revival of his [or her] formerly revoked will or of a formerly revoked portion of the will.

Comment

Purpose of New Section. By way of dispensing power, this new section allows the probate court to excuse a harmless error in complying with the formal requirements for executing or revoking a will. * * *

Evidence from South Australia suggests that the dispensing power will be applied mainly in two sorts of cases. See Langbein, [Excusing Harmless Errors in the Execution of Wills: A Report on Australia's Tranquil Revolution in Probate Law, 87 Colum. L. Rev. 1, 15–33 (1987)]. When the testator misunderstands the attestation requirements of Section 2–502(a) and neglects to obtain one or both witnesses, new Section 2–503 permits the proponents of the will to prove that the defective execution did not result from irresolution or from circumstances suggesting duress or trickery—in other words, that the defect was harmless to the purpose of the formality. The measure reduces the tension between holographic wills and the two-witness requirement for attested wills under Section 2–502(a). Ordinarily, the testator who attempts to make an attested will but blunders will still have achieved a level of formality that compares favorably with that permitted for holographic wills under the Code.

The other recurrent class of case in which the dispensing power has been invoked in South Australia entails alterations to a previously executed will. Sometimes the testator adds a clause, that is, the testator attempts to interpolate a defectively executed codicil. More frequently, the amendment has the character of a revision—the testator crosses out former text and inserts replacement terms. Lay persons do not always understand that the execution and revocation requirements of Section 2–502 call for fresh execution in order to modify a will; rather, lay persons often think that the original execution has continuing effect.

By placing the burden of proof upon the proponent of a defective instrument, and by requiring the proponent to discharge that burden by clear and convincing evidence (which courts at the trial and appellate levels are urged to police with rigor), Section 2–503 imposes procedural standards appropriate to the seriousness of the issue. * * *

The larger the departure from Section 2–502 formality, the harder it will be to satisfy the court that the instrument reflects the testator's intent. Whereas the South Australian and Israeli courts lightly excuse breaches of the attestation requirements, they have never excused noncompliance with the requirement that a will be in writing, and they have been extremely reluctant to excuse noncompliance with the signature requirement. See Langbein, supra, at 23–29, 49–50. The main circumstance in which the South Australian courts have excused signature errors has been in the recurrent class of cases in which two wills are prepared for simultaneous execution by two testators, typically husband and wife, and each mistakenly signs the will prepared for the other. * * *

Section 2–504. Self-Proved Will.

(a)   A will that is executed with attesting witnesses may be simultaneously executed, attested, and made self-proved, by acknowledgment thereof by the testator and affidavits of the witnesses, each made before an officer authorized to administer oaths under the laws of the state in which execution occurs and evidenced by the officer's certificate, under official seal, in substantially the following form:

I, _____, the testator, sign my name to this instrument this ___ day of _____,
    (name)

and being first duly sworn, do hereby declare to the undersigned authority that I sign and execute this instrument as my will and that I sign it willingly (or willingly direct another to sign for me), that I execute it as my free and voluntary act for the purposes therein expressed, and that I am [18] years of age or older, of sound mind, and under no constraint or undue influence.

                                                                 _____
                                                                 Testator

We, _____, _____, the witnesses, sign our names to this instrument,
    (name)   (name)

being first duly sworn, and do hereby declare to the undersigned authority that the testator signs and executes this instrument as (his) (her) will and that (he) (she) signs and executes this instrument as (his) (her) will and that (he) (she) signs it willingly (or willingly directs another to sign for (him) (her)), and that each of us, in the presence and hearing of the testator, hereby signs this will as witness and the testator's signing, and that to the best of our knowledge the testator is [18] years or age or older, of sound mind, and under no constraint or undue influence.

                                                                  _____
                                                                 Witness

                                                                    _____
                                                                 Witness

State of   _____
County of _____

Subscribed, sworn to and acknowledged before me by _____, the testator, and subscribed and sworn to before me by _____, and _____, witnesses, this ___ day of _____.

(Seal)

                                          (Signed) _____
                                                (Official capacity of officer)

(b)   A will that is executed with attesting witnesses may be made self-proved at any time after its execution by the acknowledgment thereof by the testator and the affidavits of the witnesses, each made before an officer authorized to administer oaths under the laws of the state in which the acknowledgment occurs and evidenced by the officer's certificate, under official seal, attached or annexed to the will in substantially the following form:

State of   _____
County of _____

We, _____, _____, and _____, the testator and the witnesses,
    (name)   (name)   (name)

respectively, whose names are signed to the attached or foregoing instrument, being first duly sworn, do hereby declare to the undersigned authority that the testator signed and executed the instrument as the testator's will and that (he) (she) had signed willingly (or willingly directed another to sign for (him) (her)), and that (he) (she) executed it as (his) (her) free and voluntary act for the purposes therein expressed, and that each of the witnesses, in the presence and hearing of the testator, signed the will as witness and that to the best of (his) (her) knowledge the testator was at that time [18] years or age or older, of sound mind, and under no constraint or undue influence.

_____
Testator

_____
Witness

_____
Witness

Subscribed, sworn to and acknowledged before me by _____, the testator, and subscribed and sworn to before me by _____, and _____, witnesses, this ____ day of _____.

(Seal)

(Signed) _____
(Official capacity of officer)

(c)   A signature affixed to a self-proving affidavit attached to a will is considered a signature affixed to the will, if necessary to prove the will's due execution.

Comment

A self-proved will may be admitted to probate as provided in Sections 3–303, 3–405, and 3–406 without the testimony of any attesting witness, but otherwise it is treated no differently from a will not self proved. Thus, a self-proved will may be contested (except in regard to questions of proper execution), revoked, or amended by a codicil in exactly the same fashion as a will not self proved. The procedural advantage of a self-proved will is limited to formal testacy proceedings because Section 3–303, which deals with informal probate, dispenses with the necessity of testimony of witnesses even though the instrument is not self proved under this section. * * *

Section 2–505. Who May Witness.

(a)   An individual generally competent to be a witness may act as a witness to a will.

(b)   The signing of a will by an interested witness does not invalidate the will or any provision of it.

Comment

This section carries forward the position of the pre-1990 Code. The position adopted simplifies the law relating to interested witnesses. Interest no longer disqualifies a person as a witness, nor does it invalidate or forfeit a gift under the will. Of course, the purpose of this change is not to foster use of interested witnesses, and attorneys will continue to use disinterested witnesses in execution of wills. But the rare and innocent use of a member of the testator's family on a home-drawn will is not penalized.

This approach does not increase appreciably the opportunity for fraud or undue influence. A substantial devise by will to a person who is one of the witnesses to the execution of the will is itself a suspicious circumstance, and the devise might be challenged on grounds of undue influence. The requirement of disinterested witnesses has not succeeded in preventing fraud and undue influence; and in most cases of undue influence, the influencer is careful not to sign as a witness, but to procure disinterested witnesses. * * *

Section 2–506. Choice of Law as to Execution.

A written will is valid if executed in compliance with Section 2–502 or 2–503 or if its execution complies with the law at the time of execution of the place where the will is executed, or of the law of the place where at the time of execution or at the time of death the testator is domiciled, has a place of abode, or is a national.

Section 2–507. Revocation by Writing or by Act.

(a)   A will or any part thereof is revoked:

(1)   by executing a subsequent will that revokes the previous will or part expressly or by inconsistency; or

(2)   by performing a revocatory act on the will, if the testator performed the act with the intent and for the purpose of revoking the will or part or if another individual performed the act in the testator's conscious presence and by the testator's direction. For purposes of this paragraph, "revocatory act on the will" includes burning, tearing, canceling, obliterating, or destroying the will or any part of it. A burning, tearing, or canceling is a "revocatory act on the will," whether or not the burn, tear, or cancellation touched any of the words on the will.

(b)   If a subsequent will does not expressly revoke a previous will, the execution of the subsequent will wholly revokes the previous will by inconsistency if the testator intended the subsequent will to replace rather than supplement the previous will.

(c)   The testator is presumed to have intended a subsequent will to replace rather than supplement a previous will if the subsequent will makes a complete disposition of the testator's estate. If this presumption arises and is not rebutted by clear and convincing evidence, the previous will is revoked; only the subsequent will is operative on the testator's death.

(d)   The testator is presumed to have intended a subsequent will to supplement rather than replace a previous will if the subsequent will does not make a complete disposition of the testator's estate. If this presumption arises and is not rebutted by clear and convincing evidence, the subsequent will revokes the previous will only to the extent the subsequent will is inconsistent with the previous will; each will is fully operative on the testator's death to the extent they are not inconsistent.

Comment

Purpose and Scope of Revisions. Revocation of a will may be by either a subsequent will or an authorized act done to the document. Revocation by subsequent will cannot be effective unless the subsequent will is valid.

Revocation by Inconsistency. As originally promulgated, this section provided no standard by which the courts were to determine whether in a given case a subsequent will with no revocation clause revokes a prior will, wholly or partly, by inconsistency. * * * Under [subsections (b), (c), and (d)], the question whether the subsequent will was intended to replace rather than supplement the previous will depends upon whether the second will makes a complete disposition of the testator's estate. If the second will does make a complete disposition of the testator's estate, a presumption arises that the second will was intended to replace the previous will. If the second will does not make a complete disposition of the testator's estate, a presumption arises that the second will was intended to supplement rather than replace the previous will. The rationale is that, when the second will does not make a complete disposition of the testator's estate, the second will is more in the nature of a codicil to the first will. * * *

Example. Five years before her death, G executed a will (Will #1), devising her antique desk to A; $20,000 to B; and the residue of her estate to C. Two years later, A died, and G executed another will (Will #2), devising her antique desk to A's spouse, X; $10,000 to B; and the residue of her estate to C. Will #2 neither expressly revoked Will #1 nor made any other reference to it. G's net probate estate consisted of her antique desk (worth $10,000) and other property (worth $90,000). X, B, and C survived G by 120 hours.

Solution. Will #2 was presumptively intended by G to replace Will #1 because Will #2 made a complete disposition of G's estate. Unless this presumption is rebutted by clear and convincing evidence, Will #1 is wholly revoked; only Will #2 is operative on G's death.

If, however, Will #2 had not contained a residuary clause, and hence had not made a complete disposition of G's estate, "Will #2" is more in the nature of a codicil to Will #1, and the solution would be different. Now, Will #2 would presumptively be treated as having been intended to supplement rather than replace Will #1. In the absence of evidence clearly and convincingly rebutting this presumption, Will #1 would be revoked only to the extent Will #2 is inconsistent with it; both wills would be operative on G's death, to the extent they are not inconsistent. As to the devise of the antique desk, Will #2 is inconsistent with Will #1, and the antique desk would go to X. There being no residuary clause in Will #2, there is nothing in Will #2 that is inconsistent with the residuary clause in Will #1, and so the residue would go to C. The more difficult question relates to the cash devises in the two wills. The question whether they are inconsistent with one another is a question of interpretation in the individual case. Section 2–507 does not establish a presumption one way or the other on that question. If the court finds that the cash devises are inconsistent with one another, i.e., if the court finds that the cash devise in Will #2 was intended to replace rather than supplement the cash devise in Will #1, then B takes $10,000. But if the court finds that the cash devises are not inconsistent with one another, B would take $30,000.

Revocatory Act. In the case of an act of revocation done to the document, subsection (a)(2) is revised to provide that a burning, tearing, or canceling is a sufficient revocatory act even though the act does not touch any of the words on the will. This is consistent with cases on burning or tearing * * *, but inconsistent with most, but not all, cases on cancellation * * * . By substantial authority, it is held that removal of the testator's signature—by, for example, lining it through, erasing or obliterating it, tearing or cutting it out of the document, or removing the entire signature page—constitutes a sufficient revocatory act to revoke the entire will. * * *

Subsection (a)(2) is also revised to codify the "conscious-presence" test. As revised, subsection (a)(2) provides that, if the testator does not perform the revocatory act, but directs another to perform the act, the act is a sufficient revocatory act if the other individual performs it in the testator's conscious presence. The act need not be performed in the testator's line of sight. * * *

Revocatory Intent. To effect a revocation, a revocatory act must be accompanied by revocatory intent. Determining whether a revocatory act was accompanied by revocatory intent may involve exploration of extrinsic evidence, including the testator's statements as to intent.

Partial Revocation. This section specifically permits partial revocation.

Dependent Relative Revocation. Each court is free to apply its own doctrine of dependent relative revocation. See generally Palmer, "Dependent Relative Revocation and Its Relation to Relief for Mistake," 69 Mich.L.Rev. 989 (1971). Note, however, that dependent relative revocation should less often be necessary under the revised provisions of the Code. Dependent relative revocation is the law of second best, i.e., its application does not produce the result the testator actually intended, but is designed to come as close as possible to that intent. A precondition to the application of dependent relative revocation is, or should be, good evidence of the testator's actual intention; without that, the court has no basis for determining which of several outcomes comes the closest to that actual intention.

When there is good evidence of the testator's actual intention, however, the revised provisions of the Code would usually facilitate the effectuation of the result the testator actually intended. If, for example, the testator by revocatory act revokes a second will for the purpose of reviving a former will, the evidence necessary to establish the testator's intent to revive the former will should be sufficient under Section 2–509 to effect a revival of the former will, making the application of dependent relative revocation as to the second will unnecessary. If, by revocatory act, the testator revokes a will in conjunction with an effort to execute a new will, the evidence necessary to establish the testator's intention that the new will be valid should, in most cases, be sufficient under Section 2–503 to give effect to the new will, making the application of dependent relative revocation as to the old will unnecessary. If the testator lines out parts of a will or dispositive provision in conjunction with an effort to alter the will's terms, the evidence necessary to establish the testator's intention that the altered terms be valid should be sufficient under Section 2–503 to give effect to the will as altered, making dependent relative revocation as to the lined-out parts unnecessary.

Section 2–508. Revocation by Change of Circumstances.

Except as provided in Sections 2–803 and 2–804, a change of circumstances does not revoke a will or any part of it.

Section 2–509. Revival of Revoked Will.

(a)   If a subsequent will that wholly revoked a previous will is thereafter revoked by a revocatory act under Section 2–507(a)(2), the previous will remains revoked unless it is revived. The previous will is revived if it is evident from the circumstances of the revocation of the subsequent will or from the testator's contemporary or subsequent declarations that the testator intended the previous will to take effect as executed.

(b)   If a subsequent will that partly revoked a previous will is thereafter revoked by a revocatory act under Section 2–507(a)(2), a revoked part of the previous will is revived unless it is evident from the circumstances of the revocation of the subsequent will or from the testator's contemporary or subsequent declarations that the testator did not intend the revoked part to take effect as executed.

(c)   If a subsequent will that revoked a previous will in whole or in part is thereafter revoked by another, later, will, the previous will remains revoked in whole or in part, unless it or its revoked part is revived. The previous will or its revoked part is revived to the extent it appears from the terms of the later will that the testator intended the previous will to take effect.

Comment

Purpose and Scope of Revisions. Although a will takes effect as a revoking instrument when it is executed, it takes effect as a dispositive instrument at death. Once revoked, therefore, a will is ineffective as a dispositive instrument unless it has been revived. This section covers the standards to be applied in determining whether a will (Will #1) that was revoked by a subsequent will (Will #2), either expressly or by inconsistency, has been revived by the revocation of the subsequent will, i.e., whether the revocation of Will #2 (the revoking will) revives Will #1 (the will that Will #2 revoked).

As revised, this section is divided into three subsections. Subsections (a) and (b) cover the effect of revoking Will #2 (the revoking will) by a revocatory act under Section 2–507(a)(2). Under subsection (a), if Will #2 (the revoking will) wholly revoked Will #1, the revocation of Will #2 does not revive Will #1 unless "it is evident from the circumstances of the revocation of [Will #2] or from the testator's contemporary or subsequent declarations that the testator intended [Will #1] to take effect as executed." This standard places the burden of persuasion on the proponent of Will #1 to establish that the decedent's intention was that Will #1 is to be his or her valid will. Testimony regarding the decedent's statements at the time he or she revokes Will #2 or at a later date can be admitted. Indeed, all relevant evidence of intention is to be considered by the court on this question * * * .

The pre-1990 version of this section did not distinguish between complete and partial revocation. Regardless of whether Will #2 wholly or partly revoked Will #1, the pre-1990 version presumed against revival of Will #1 when Will #2 was revoked by act.

As revised, this section properly treats the two situations as distinguishable. The presumption against revival imposed by subsection (a) is justified because where Will #2 wholly revoked Will #1, the testator understood or should have understood that Will #1 had no continuing effect. Consequently, subsection (a) properly presumes that the testator's act of revoking Will #2 was not accompanied by an intent to revive Will #1.

Subsection (b) establishes the opposite presumption where Will #2 (the revoking will) revoked Will #1 only in part. In this case, the revocation of Will #2 revives the revoked part or parts of Will #1 unless "it is evident from the circumstances of the revocation of [Will #2] or from the testator's contemporary or subsequent declarations that the testator did not intend the revoked part to take effect as executed." This standard places the burden of persuasion on the party arguing that the revoked part or parts of Will #1 were not revived. The justification is that where Will #2 only partly revoked Will #1, Will #2 is only a codicil to Will #1, and the testator knows (or should know) that Will #1 does have continuing effect. Consequently, subsection (b) properly presumes that the testator's act of revoking Will #2 (the codicil) was accompanied by an intent to revive or reinstate the revoked parts of Will #1.

Subsection (c) covers the effect on Will #1 of revoking Will #2 (the revoking will) by another, later, will (Will #3). Will #1 remains revoked except to the extent that Will #3 shows an intent to have Will #1 effective. * * *

Section 2–510. Incorporation by Reference.

A writing in existence when a will is executed may be incorporated by reference if the language of the will manifests this intent and describes the writing sufficiently to permit its identification.

Section 2-511. Uniform Testamentary Additions to Trusts Act (1991).

(a) A will may validly devise property to the trustee of a trust established or to be established (i) during the testator's lifetime by the testator, by the testator and some other person, or by some other person, including a funded or unfunded life insurance trust, although the settlor has reserved any or all rights of ownership of the insurance contracts, or (ii) at the testator's death by the testator's devise to the trustee, if the trust is identified in the testator's will and its terms are set forth in a written instrument, other than a will, executed before, concurrently with, or after the execution of the testator's will or in another individual's will if that other individual has predeceased the testator, regardless of the existence, size, or character of the corpus of the trust. The devise is not invalid because the trust is amendable or revocable, or because the trust was amended after the execution of the will or the testator's death.

(b) Unless the testator's will provides otherwise, property devised to a trust described in subsection (a) is not held under a testamentary trust of the testator, but it becomes a part of the trust to which it is devised, and must be administered and disposed of in accordance with the provisions of the governing instrument setting forth the terms of the trust, including any amendments thereto made before or after the testator's death.

(c) Unless the testator's will provides otherwise, a revocation or termination of the trust before the testator's death causes the devise to lapse.

Section 2-512. Events of Independent Significance.

A will may dispose of property by reference to acts and events that have significance apart from their effect upon the dispositions made by the will, whether they occur before or after the execution of the will or before or after the testator's death. The execution or revocation of another individual's will is such an event.

Section 2-513. Separate Writing Identifying Devise of Certain Types of Tangible Personal Property.

Whether or not the provisions relating to holographic wills apply, a will may refer to a written statement or list to dispose of items of tangible personal property not otherwise specifically disposed of by the will, other than money. To be admissible under this section as evidence of the intended disposition, the writing must be signed by the testator and must describe the items and the devisees with reasonable certainty. The writing may be referred to as one to be in existence at the time of the testator's death; it may be prepared before or after the execution of the will; it may be altered by the testator after its preparation; and it may be a writing that has no significance apart from its effect on the dispositions made by the will.

Comment

Purpose and Scope of Revision. As part of the broader policy of effectuating a testator's intent and of relaxing formalities of execution, this section permits a testator to refer in his or her will to a separate document disposing of tangible personalty other than money. * * *

The language "items of tangible personal property" does not require that the separate document specifically itemize each item of tangible personal property covered. The only requirement is that the document describe the items covered "with reasonable certainty." Consequently, a document referring to "all my tangible personal property other than money" or to "all my tangible personal property located in my office" or using similar catch-all type of language would normally be sufficient.

The separate document disposing of an item or items of tangible personal property may be prepared after execution of the will, so would not come within Section 2-510 on incorporation by reference. It may even be altered from time to time. The only requirement is that the document be signed by the testator. The pre-1990 version of this section gave effect to an unsigned document if it was in the testator's handwriting. The revisions remove the language giving effect to such an unsigned document. The purpose is to prevent a mere handwritten draft from becoming effective without sufficient indication that the testator intended it to be effective. The signature requirement is designed to prevent mere drafts from becoming effective against the testator's wishes. An unsigned document could still be given effect under Section 2–503, however, if the proponent could carry the burden of proving by clear and convincing evidence that the testator intended the document to be effective.

The typical case covered by this section would be a list of personal effects and the persons whom the decedent desired to take specified items.

Sample Clause. Section 2–513 might be utilized by a clause in the decedent's will such as the following:

I might leave a written statement or list disposing of items of tangible personal property. If I do and if my written statement or list is found and is identified as such by my Personal Representative no later than 30 days after the probate of this will, then my written statement or list is to be given effect to the extent authorized by law and is to take precedence over any contrary devise or devises of the same item or items of property in this will.

Section 2–513 only authorizes disposition of tangible personal property "not otherwise specifically disposed of by the will." The sample clause above is consistent with this restriction. By providing that the written statement or list takes precedence over any contrary devise in the will, a contrary devise is made conditional upon the written statement or list not contradicting it; if the written statement or list does contradict a devise in the will, the will does not otherwise specifically dispose of the property.

If, however, the clause in the testator's will does not provide that the written statement or list is to take precedence over any contrary devise in the will (or contain a provision having similar effect), then the written statement or list is ineffective to the extent it purports to dispose of items of property that were otherwise specifically disposed of by the will.

Section 2–514. Contracts Concerning Succession.

A contract to make a will or devise, or not to revoke a will or devise, or to die intestate, if executed after the effective date of this [article], may be established only by (i) provisions of a will stating material provisions of the contract, (ii) an express reference in a will to a contract and extrinsic evidence proving the terms of the contract, or (iii) a writing signed by the decedent evidencing the contract. The execution of a joint will or mutual wills does not create a presumption of a contract not to revoke the will or wills.

Section 2–515. Deposit of Will With Court in Testator's Lifetime.

A will may be deposited by the testator or the testator's agent with any court for safekeeping, under rules of the court. The will must be sealed and kept confidential. During the testator's lifetime, a deposited will must be delivered only to the testator or to a person authorized in writing signed by the testator to receive the will. A conservator may be allowed to examine a deposited will of a protected testator under procedures designed to maintain the confidential character of the document to the extent possible, and to ensure that it will be resealed and kept on deposit after the examination. Upon being informed of the testator's death, the court shall notify any person designated to receive the will and deliver it to that person on request; or the court may deliver the will to the appropriate court.

Section 2–516. Duty of Custodian of Will; Liability.

After the death of a testator and on request of an interested person, a person having custody of a will of the testator shall deliver it with reasonable promptness to a person able to secure its probate and if none is known, to an appropriate court. A person who wilfully fails to deliver a will is liable to any person aggrieved for any damages that may be sustained by the failure. A person who wilfully refuses or fails to deliver a will after being ordered by the court in a proceeding brought for the purpose of compelling delivery is subject to penalty for contempt of court.

Section 2–517. Penalty Clause for Contest.

A provision in a will purporting to penalize an interested person for contesting the will or instituting other proceedings relating to the estate is unenforceable if probable cause exists for instituting proceedings.

PART 6

RULES OF CONSTRUCTION APPLICABLE ONLY TO WILLS

Section 2–601. Scope.

In the absence of a finding of a contrary intention, the rules of construction in this [part] control the construction of a will.

Comment

Purpose and Scope of 1990 Revisions. Common-law rules of construction yield to a finding of a contrary intention. The pre-1990 version of this section provided that the rules of construction in Part 6 yielded only to a "contrary intention indicated by the will." To align the statutory rules of construction in Part 6 with those established at common law, this section was revised in 1990 so that the rules of construction yield to a "finding of a contrary intention." As revised, evidence extrinsic to the will as well as the content of the will itself is admissible for the purpose of rebutting the rules of construction in Part 6.

As originally promulgated, this section began with the sentence: "The intention of a testator as expressed in his will controls the legal effect of his dispositions." This sentence was removed primarily because it was inappropriate and unnecessary in a part of the Code containing rules of construction. Deleting this sentence did not signify a retreat from the widely accepted proposition that a testator's intention controls the legal effect of his or her dispositions.

A further reason for deleting this sentence is that a possible, though unintended, reading of the sentence might have been that it prevented the judicial adoption of a general reformation doctrine for wills * * * .

Section 2–602. Will May Pass All Property and After-Acquired Property.

A will may provide for the passage of all property the testator owns at death and all property acquired by the estate after the testator's death.

Section 2–603. Antilapse; Deceased Devisee; Class Gifts.

(a) **[Definitions.]** In this section:

(1) "Alternative devise" means a devise that is expressly created by the will and, under the terms of the will, can take effect instead of another devise on the happening of one or more events, including survival of the testator or failure to survive the testator, whether an event is expressed in condition-precedent, condition-subsequent, or any other form. A residuary clause constitutes an alternative devise with respect to a nonresiduary devise only if the will specifically provides that, upon lapse or failure, the nonresiduary devise, or nonresiduary devises in general, pass under the residuary clause.

(2) "Class member" includes an individual who fails to survive the testator but who would have taken under a devise in the form of a class gift had he [or she] survived the testator.

(3) "Descendant of a grandparent", as used in subsection (b), means an individual who qualifies as a descendant of a grandparent of the testator or of the donor of a power of appointment under the (i) rules of construction applicable to a class gift created in the testator's will if the devise or exercise of the power is in the form of a class gift or (ii) rules for intestate succession if the devise or exercise of the power is not in the form of a class gift.

(4) "Descendants", as used in the phrase "surviving descendants" of a deceased devisee or class member in subsections (b)(1) and (2), mean the descendants of a deceased devisee or class member who would take under a class gift created in the testator's will.

(5) "Devise" includes an alternative devise, a devise in the form of a class gift, and an exercise of a power of appointment.

(6) "Devisee" includes (i) a class member if the devise is in the form of a class gift, (ii) an individual or class member who was deceased at the time the testator executed his [or her] will as well as an individual or class member who was then living but who failed to survive the testator, and (iii) an appointee under a power of appointment exercised by the testator's will.

(7) "Stepchild" means a child of the surviving, deceased, or former spouse of the testator or of the donor of a power of appointment, and not of the testator or donor.

(8) "Surviving", in the phrase "surviving devisees" or "surviving descendants", means devisees or descendants who neither predeceased the testator nor are deemed to have predeceased the testator under Section 2–702.

(9) "Testator" includes the donee of a power of appointment if the power is exercised in the testator's will.

(b) [Substitute Gift.] If a devisee fails to survive the testator and is a grandparent, a descendant of a grandparent, or a stepchild of either the testator or the donor of a power of appointment exercised by the testator's will, the following apply:

(1) Except as provided in paragraph (4), if the devise is not in the form of a class gift and the deceased devisee leaves surviving descendants, a substitute gift is created in the devisee's surviving descendants. They take by representation the property to which the devisee would have been entitled had the devisee survived the testator.

(2) Except as provided in paragraph (4), if the devise is in the form of a class gift, other than a devise to "issue," "descendants," "heirs of the body," "heirs," "next of kin," "relatives," or "family," or a class described by language of similar import, a substitute gift is created in the surviving descendants of any deceased devisee. The property to which the devisees would have been entitled had all of them survived the testator passes to the surviving devisees and the surviving descendants of the deceased devisees. Each surviving devisee takes the share to which he [or she] would have been entitled had the deceased devisees survived the testator. Each deceased devisee's surviving descendants who are substituted for the deceased devisee take by representation the share to which the deceased devisee would have been entitled had the deceased devisee survived the testator. For the purposes of this paragraph, "deceased devisee" means a class member who failed to survive the testator and left one or more surviving descendants.

(3) For the purposes of Section 2–601, words of survivorship, such as in a devise to an individual "if he survives me," or in a devise to "my surviving children," are not, in the absence of additional evidence, a sufficient indication of an intent contrary to the application of this section.

(4) If the will creates an alternative devise with respect to a devise for which a substitute gift is created by paragraph (1) or (2), the substitute gift is superseded by the alternative devise if:

(A) the alternative devise is in the form of a class gift and one or more members of the class is entitled to take under the will; or

(B) the alternative devise is not in the form of a class gift and the expressly designated devisee of the alternative devise is entitled to take under the will.

(5) Unless the language creating a power of appointment expressly excludes the substitution of the descendants of an appointee for the appointee, a surviving descendant of a deceased appointee of a power of appointment can be substituted for the appointee under this section, whether or not the descendant is an object of the power.

(c) [More Than One Substitute Gift; Which One Takes.] If, under subsection (b), substitute gifts are created and not superseded with respect to more than one devise and the devises are alternative devises, one to the other, the determination of which of the substitute gifts takes effect is resolved as follows:

(1) Except as provided in paragraph (2), the devised property passes under the primary substitute gift.

(2) If there is a younger-generation devise, the devised property passes under the younger-generation substitute gift and not under the primary substitute gift.

(3) In this subsection:

(A) "Primary devise" means the devise that would have taken effect had all the deceased devisees of the alternative devises who left surviving descendants survived the testator.

(B) "Primary substitute gift" means the substitute gift created with respect to the primary devise.

(C) "Younger-generation devise" means a devise that (i) is to a descendant of a devisee of the primary devise, (ii) is an alternative devise with respect to the primary devise, (iii) is a devise for which a substitute gift is created, and (iv) would have taken effect had all the deceased devisees who left surviving descendants survived the testator except the deceased devisee or devisees of the primary devise.

(D) "Younger-generation substitute gift" means the substitute gift created with respect to the younger-generation devise.

Comment

Purpose and Scope. Section 2–603 is a comprehensive antilapse statute that resolves a variety of interpretive questions that have arisen under standard antilapse statutes, including the antilapse statute of the pre-1990 Code.

Theory of Lapse. [T]he common-law rule of lapse is predicated on the principle that a will transfers property at the testator's death, not when the will is executed, and on the principle that property cannot be transferred to a deceased individual. Under the rule of lapse, all devises are automatically and by law conditioned on survivorship of the testator. A devise to a devisee who predeceases the testator fails (lapses); the devised property does not pass to the devisee's estate, to be distributed according to the devisee's will or pass by intestate succession from the devisee. (Section 2–702 modifies the rule of lapse by presumptively conditioning devises on a 120-hour period of survival.)

"Antilapse" Statutes—Rationale of Section 2–603. Statutes such as Section 2–603 are commonly called "antilapse" statutes. An antilapse statute is remedial in nature, tending to preserve equality of treatment among different lines of succession. Although Section 2–603 is a rule of construction, and hence under Section 2–601 yields to a finding of a contrary intention, the remedial character of the statute means that it should be given the widest possible latitude to operate in considering whether the testator had formed a contrary intent. * * *

The 120-hour Survivorship Period. In effect, the requirement of survival of the testator's death means survival of the 120-hour period following the testator's death. This is because, under Section 2–702(a), "an individual who is not established to have survived an event . . . by 120 hours is deemed to have predeceased the event." As made clear by subsection (a)(8), for the purposes of Section 2–603, the "event" to which Section 2–702(a) relates is the testator's death.

General Rule of Section 2–603—Subsection (b). Subsection (b) states the general rule of Section 2–603. Subsection (b)(1) applies to individual devises; subsection (b)(2) applies to devises in class gift form. * * * Together, subsections (b)(1) and (2) show that the "antilapse" label is somewhat misleading. Strictly speaking, these subsections do not reverse the common-law rule of lapse. They do not abrogate the law-imposed condition of survivorship, so that devised property passes to the estates of predeceasing devisees. Subsections (b)(1) and (2) leave the law-imposed condition of survivorship intact, but modify the devolution of lapsed devises by providing a statutory substitute gift in the case of specified relatives. The statutory substitute gift is to the devisee's descendants who survive the testator by 120 hours; they take the property to which the devisee would have been entitled had the devisee survived the testator by 120 hours.

Class Gifts. In line with modern policy, subsection (b)(2) continues the pre-1990 Code's approach of expressly extending the antilapse protection to class gifts. Subsection (b)(2) applies to single-generation class gifts * * * in which one or more class members fail to survive the testator (by 120 hours) leaving descendants who survive the testator (by 120 hours); in order for the subsection to apply, it is not necessary that any of the class members survive the testator (by 120 hours). Multiple-generation class gifts, i.e., class gifts to "issue," "descendants," "heirs of the body," "heirs," "next of kin," "relatives," "family," or a class described by language of similar import are excluded, however, because antilapse protection is unnecessary in class gifts of these types. They already contain within themselves the idea of representation, under which a deceased class member's descendants are substituted for him or her. See Sections 2–708, 2–709, 2–711 * * * .

"Void" Gifts. By virtue of subsection (a)(6), subsection (b) applies to the so-called "void" gift, where the devisee is dead at the time of execution of the will. Though contrary to some decisions, it seems likely that the testator would want the descendants of a person included, for example, in a class term but dead when the will is made to be treated like the descendants of another member of the class who was alive at the time the will was executed but who dies before the testator.

Protected Relatives. The specified relatives whose devises are protected by this section are the testator's grandparents and their descendants and the testator's stepchildren or, in the case of a testamentary exercise of a power of appointment, the testator's (donee's) or donor's grandparents and their descendants and the testator's or donor's stepchildren. * * *

Section 2–603 extends the "antilapse" protection to devises to the testator's own stepchildren. The term "stepchild" is defined in subsection (a)(5). Antilapse protection is not extended to devises to descendants of the testator's stepchildren or to stepchildren of any of the testator's relatives. As to the testator's own stepchildren, note that under Section 2–804 a devise to a stepchild might be revoked if the testator and the stepchild's adoptive or genetic parent become divorced; the antilapse statute does not, of course, apply to a deceased stepchild's devise if it was revoked by Section 2–804. Subsections (b)(1) and (2) give this result by providing that the substituted descendants take the property to which the deceased devisee or deceased class member would have been entitled if he or she had survived the testator. If a deceased stepchild whose devise was revoked by Section 2–804 had survived the testator, that stepchild would not have been entitled to his or her devise, and so his or her descendants take nothing, either.

Other than stepchildren, devisees related to the testator by affinity are not protected by this section.

Section 2–603 Applicable to Testamentary Exercise of a Power of Appointment Where Appointee Fails to Survive the Testator. Subsections (a)(5), (6), (7), (9), and (b)(5) extend the protection of this section to appointees under a power of appointment exercised by the testator's will. The extension of the antilapse statute to powers of appointment is a step long overdue. * * *

Substitute Gifts. The substitute gifts provided for by subsections (b)(1) and (2) are to the deceased devisee's descendants. * * *

The 120-hour survival requirement stated in Section 2–702 does not require descendants who would be substituted for their parent by this section to survive their parent by any set period. Thus, if a devisee who is a protected relative survives the testator by less than 120 hours, the substitute gift is to the devisee's descendants who survive the testator by 120 hours; survival of the devisee by 120 hours is not required.

The statutory substitute gift is divided among the devisee's descendants "by representation," a phrase defined in Section 2–709(b).

Section 2–603 Restricted to Wills. Section 2–603 is applicable only when a devisee of a will predeceases the testator. It does not apply to beneficiary designations in life-insurance policies, retirement plans, or transfer-on-death accounts, nor does it apply to inter-vivos trusts, whether revocable or irrevocable. See, however, Sections 2–706 and 2–707 for rules of construction applicable when the beneficiary of a life-insurance policy, a retirement plan, or a transfer-on-death account predeceases the decedent or when the beneficiary of a future interest is not living when the interest is to take effect in possession or enjoyment.

Contrary Intention—the Rationale of Subsection (b)(3). An antilapse statute is a rule of construction, designed to carry out presumed intention. In effect, Section 2–603 declares that when a testator devises property "to A (a specified relative)," the testator (if he or she had thought further about it) is presumed to have wanted to add: "but if A is not alive (120 hours after my death), I devise the property in A's stead to A's descendants (who survive me by 120 hours)."

Under Section 2–601, the rule of Section 2–603 yields to a finding of a contrary intention. A foolproof means of expressing a contrary intention is to add to a devise the phrase "and not to [the devisee's] descendants." * * * In the case of a power of appointment, the phrase "and not to an appointee's descendants" can be added by the donor of the power in the document creating the power of appointment, if the donor does not want the antilapse statute to apply to an appointment under a power. * * * In addition, adding to the residuary clause a phrase such as "including all lapsed or failed devises," adding to a nonresiduary devise a phrase such as "if the devisee does not survive me, the devise is to pass under the residuary clause," or adding a separate clause providing generally that "if the devisee of any nonresiduary devise does not survive me, the devise is to pass under the residuary clause" makes the residuary clause an "alternative devise." Under subsection (b)(4), * * * an alternative devise supersedes a substitute gift created by subsection (b)(1) or (2) if: (A) the alternative devise is in the form of a class gift and one or more members of the class is entitled to take under the will; or (B) the alternative devise is not in the form of a class gift and the expressly designated devisee of the alternative devise is entitled to take under the will. See infra *Example 3.*

A much-litigated question is whether mere words of survivorship—such as in a devise "to my daughter, A, if A survives me" or "to my surviving children"—*automatically* defeat the antilapse statute. Lawyers who believe that the attachment of words of survivorship to a devise is a foolproof method of defeating an antilapse statute are mistaken. The very fact that the question is litigated so frequently is itself proof that the use of mere words of survivorship is far from foolproof. In addition, the results of the litigated cases are divided on the question. * * *

Subsection (b)(3) adopts the position that mere words of survivorship do not—by themselves, *in the absence of additional evidence*—lead to *automatic* defeat of the antilapse statute. As noted in French, "Antilapse Statutes Are Blunt Instruments: A Blueprint for Reform," 37 Hastings L.J. 335, 369 (1985), "courts have tended to accord too much significance to survival requirements when deciding whether to apply antilapse statutes."

A formalistic argument sometimes employed by courts adopting the view that words of survivorship automatically defeat the antilapse statute is that, when words of survivorship are used, there is nothing upon which the antilapse statute can operate; the devise itself, it is said, is eliminated by the devisee's having predeceased the testator. The language of subsections (b)(1) and (2), however, nullify this formalistic argument by providing that the predeceased devisee's descendants take the property to which the devisee would have been entitled had the devisee survived the testator.

Another objection to applying the antilapse statute is that mere words of survivorship somehow establish a contrary intention. The argument is that attaching words of survivorship indicates that the testator thought about the matter and intentionally did not provide a substitute gift to the devisee's descendants. At best, this is an inference only, which may or may not accurately reflect the testator's actual intention. An equally plausible inference is that the words of survivorship are in the testator's will merely because the testator's lawyer used a will form with words of survivorship. The testator who went to lawyer X and ended up with a will containing devises with a survivorship requirement could by chance have gone to lawyer Y and ended up with a will containing devises with no survivorship requirement—with no different intent on the testator's part from one case to the other.

Even a lawyer's deliberate use of mere words of survivorship to defeat the antilapse statute does not guarantee that the lawyer's intention represents the client's intention. Any linkage between the lawyer's intention and the client's intention is speculative unless the lawyer discussed the matter with the client. Especially in the case of younger-generation devisees, such as the client's children or nieces and nephews, it cannot be assumed that all clients, on their own, have anticipated the possibility that the devisee will predecease the client and will have thought through who should take the devised property in case the never-anticipated event happens.

If, however, evidence establishes that the lawyer did discuss the question with the client, and that the client decided that, for example, if the client's child predeceases the client, the deceased child's children (the client's grandchildren) should not take the devise in place of the deceased child, then the combination of the words of survivorship and the extrinsic evidence of the client's intention would support a finding of a contrary intention under Section 2–601. See *Example 1*, below. For this reason, Sections 2–601 and 2–603 will not expose lawyers to malpractice liability for the amount that, in the absence of the finding of the contrary intention, would have passed under the antilapse statute to a deceased devisee's descendants. The success of a malpractice claim depends upon sufficient evidence of a client's intention and the lawyer's failure to carry out that intention. In a case in which there is evidence that the client did not want the antilapse statute to apply, that evidence would support a finding of a contrary intention under Section 2–601, thus preventing the client's intention from being defeated by Section 2–603 and protecting the lawyer from liability for the amount that, in the absence of the finding of a contrary intention, would have passed under the antilapse statute to a deceased devisee's descendants.

Any inference about actual intention to be drawn from mere words of survivorship is especially problematic in the case of will substitutes such as life insurance, where it is less likely that the insured had the assistance of a lawyer in drafting the beneficiary designation. Although Section 2–603 only applies to wills, a companion provision is Section 2–706, which applies to will substitutes, including life insurance. Section 2–706 also contains language similar to that in subsection (b)(3), directing that words of survivorship do not, in the absence of additional evidence, indicate an intent contrary to the application of this section. It would be anomalous to provide one rule for wills and a different rule for will substitutes.

The basic operation of Section 2–603 is illustrated in the following example:

Example 1. G's will devised "$10,000 to my surviving children." G had two children, A and B. A predeceased G, leaving a child, X, who survived G by 120 hours. B also survived G by 120 hours.

Solution: Under subsection (b)(2), X takes $5,000 and B takes $5,000. The substitute gift to A's descendant, X, is not defeated by the fact that the devise is a class gift nor, under subsection (b)(3), is it automatically defeated by the fact that the word "surviving" is used.

Note that subsection (b)(3) provides that words of survivorship are not by themselves to be taken as expressing a contrary intention for purposes of Section 2–601. Under Section 2–601, a finding of a contrary intention could appropriately be based on affirmative evidence that G deliberately used the words of survivorship to defeat the antilapse statute. In the case of such a finding, B would take the full $10,000 devise. Relevant evidence tending to support such a finding might be a pre-execution letter or memorandum to G from G's attorney stating that G's attorney used the word "surviving" for the purpose of assuring that if one of G's children were to predecease G, that child's descendants would not take the predeceased child's share under any statute or rule of law.

In the absence of persuasive evidence of a contrary intent, however, the antilapse statute, being remedial in nature, and tending to preserve equality among different lines of succession, should be given the widest possible chance to operate and should be defeated only by a finding of intention that *directly contradicts* the substitute gift created by the statute. Mere words of survivorship—by themselves—do not directly contradict the statutory substitute gift to the descendants of a deceased devisee. The common law of lapse already conditions all devises on survivorship (and Section 2–702 presumptively conditions all devises on survivorship by 120 hours). As noted above, the antilapse statute does not reverse the law-imposed requirement of survivorship in any strict sense; it merely alters the devolution of lapsed devises by substituting the deceased devisee's descendants in place of those who would otherwise take. Thus, mere words of survivorship merely *duplicate* the law-imposed survivorship requirement deriving from the rule of lapse, and do not contradict the statutory substitute gift created by subsection (b)(1) or (2).

Subsection (b)(4). Under subsection (b)(4), * * * a statutory substitute gift is superseded if the testator's will expressly provides for its own alternative devisee and if: (A) the alternative devise is in the form of a class gift and one or more members of the class is entitled to take under the will; or (B) the alternative devise is not in the form of a class gift and the expressly designated devisee of the alternative devise is entitled to take under the will. For example, the statute's substitute gift would be superseded in the case of a devise "to A if A survives me; if not, to B," where B survived the testator but A predeceased the testator leaving descendants who survived the testator. Under subsection (b)(4), B, not A's descendants, would take. In the same example, however, it should be noted that A's descendants *would* take under the statute if B as well as A predeceased the testator, for in that case B (the "expressly designated devisee of the alternative devise") would not be entitled to take under the will. This would be true even if B left descendants who survived the testator; B's descendants are not "expressly designated devisees of the alternative devise."

It should also be noted that, for purposes of Section 2–601, an alternative devise might indicate a contrary intention even if subsection (b)(4) is inapplicable. To illustrate this point, consider a variation of *Example 1*. Suppose that in *Example 1*, G's will devised "$10,000 to my surviving children, *but if none of my children survives me, to the descendants of deceased children.*" The alternative devise to the descendants of deceased children would not cause the substitute gift to X to be superseded under subsection (b)(4) because the condition precedent to the alternative devise—"if none of my children survives me"—was not satisfied; one of G's children, B, survived G. Hence the alternative devisees would not be entitled to take under the will. Nevertheless, the italicized language would indicate that G did not intend to substitute descendants of deceased children unless all of G's children failed to survive G. Thus, although A predeceased G leaving a child, X, who survived G by 120 hours, X would not be substituted for A. B, G's surviving child, would take the whole $10,000 devise.

The above variation of *Example 1* is to be distinguished from other variations, such as one in which G's will devised "$10,000 to my surviving children, *but if none of my children survives me, to my brothers and sisters.*" The italicized language in this variation would not indicate that G did not intend to substitute descendants of deceased children unless all of G's children failed to survive G. In addition, even if one or more of G's brothers and sisters survived G, the alternative devise would not cause the substitute gift to X to be superseded under subsection (b)(4); the alternative devisees would not be entitled to take under the will because the alternative devise is expressly conditioned on none of G's children surviving G. Thus, X would be substituted for A, allowing X and B to divide the $10,000 equally (as in the original version of *Example 1*.)

Subsection (b)(4) is further illustrated by the following examples:

Example 2. G's will devised "$10,000 to my sister, S" and devised "the rest, residue, and remainder of my estate to X-Charity." S predeceased G, leaving a child, N, who survived G by 120 hours.

Solution: S's $10,000 devise goes to N, not to X-Charity. The residuary clause does not create an "alternative devise," as defined in subsection (a)(1), because neither it nor any other language in the will specifically provides that S's $10,000 devise or lapsed or failed devises in general pass under the residuary clause.

Example 3. Same facts as *Example 2*, except that G's residuary clause devised "the rest, residue, and remainder of my estate, including all failed and lapsed devises, to X-Charity."

Solution: S's $10,000 devise goes to X-Charity, not to N. Under subsection (b)(4), the substitute gift to N created by subsection (b)(1) is superseded. The residuary clause expressly creates an "alternative devise," as defined in subsection (a)(1), in favor of X-Charity and that alternative devisee, X-Charity, is entitled to take under the will.

Example 4. G's will devised "$10,000 to my two children, A and B, or to the survivor of them." A predeceased G, leaving a child, X, who survived G by 120 hours. B also survived G by 120 hours.

Solution: B takes the full $10,000. Because the takers of the $10,000 devise are both named and numbered ("my *two* children, *A and B*"), the devise is not in the form of a class gift. * * * The substance of the devise is as if it read "half of $10,000 to A, but if A predeceases me, that half to B if B survives me and the other half of $10,000 to B, but if B predeceases me, that other half to A if A survives me." With respect to each half, A and B have alternative devises, one to the other. Subsection (b)(1) creates a substitute gift to A's descendant, X, with respect to A's alternative devise in each half. Under subsection (b)(4), however, that substitute gift to X with respect to each half is superseded by the alternative devise to B because the alternative devisee, B, survived G by 120 hours and is entitled to take under G's will.

Example 5. G's will devised "$10,000 to my two children, A and B, or to the survivor of them." A and B predeceased G. A left a child, X, who survived G by 120 hours; B died childless.

Solution: X takes the full $10,000. Because the devise itself is in the same form as the one in *Example 4*, the substance of the devise is as if it read "half of $10,000 to A, but if A predeceases me, that half to B if B survives me and the other half of $10,000 to B, but if B predeceases me, that other half to A if A survives me." With respect to each half, A and B have alternative devises, one to the other. As in *Example 4*, subsection (b)(1) creates a substitute gift to A's descendant, X, with respect to A's alternative devise in each half. Unlike the situation in *Example 4*, however, neither substitute gift to X is superseded under subsection (b)(4) by the alternative devise to B because, in this case, the alternative devisee, B, failed to survive G by 120 hours and is therefore not entitled to take either half under G's will.

Note that the order of deaths as between A and B is irrelevant. The phrase "or to the survivor" does not mean the survivor as between them if they both predecease G; it refers to the one who survives G if one but not the other survives G.

Example 6. G's will devised "$10,000 to my son, A, if he is living at my death; if not, to A's children." A predeceased G. A's child, X, also predeceased G. A's other child, Y, and X's children, M and N, survived G by 120 hours.

Solution: Half of the devise ($5,000) goes to Y. The other half ($5,000) goes to M and N.

Because A failed to survive G by 120 hours and left descendants who survived G by 120 hours, subsection (b)(1) substitutes A's descendants who survived G by 120 hours for A. But that substitute gift is superseded under subsection (b)(4) by the alternative devise to A's children. Under subsection (b)(4), * * * an alternative devise supersedes a substitute gift if the alternative devise is in the form of a class gift and one or more members of the class is entitled to take under the will. Because the alternative devise is in the form of a class gift * * * , and because one member of the class, Y, survived the testator and is entitled to take, the substitute gift under subsection (b)(1) is superseded.

Because the alternative devise to A's children is in the form of a class gift, however, and because one of the class members, X, failed to survive G by 120 hours and left descendants who survived G by 120 hours, subsection (b)(2) applies and substitutes M and N for X.

Subsection (c). Subsection (c) is necessary because there can be cases in which subsections (b)(1) or (2) create substitute gifts with respect to two or more alternative devises of the same property, and those substitute gifts are not superseded under the terms of subsection (b)(4). Subsection (c) provides the tie-breaking mechanism for such situations.

The initial step is to determine which of the alternative devises would take effect had all the devisees themselves survived the testator (by 120 hours). In subsection (c), this devise is called the "primary devise." Unless subsection (c)(2) applies, subsection (c)(1) provides that the devised property passes under substitute gift created with respect to the primary devise. This substitute gift is called the "primary substitute gift." Thus, the devised property goes to the descendants of the devisee or devisees of the primary devise.

Subsection (c)(2) provides an exception to this rule. Under subsection (c)(2), the devised property does not pass under the primary substitute gift if there is a "younger-generation devise"—defined as a devise that (i) is to a descendant of a devisee of the primary devise, (ii) is an alternative devise with respect to the primary devise, (iii) is a devise for which a substitute gift is created, and (iv) would have taken effect had all the deceased devisees who left surviving descendants survived the testator except the deceased devisee or devisees of the primary devise. If there is a younger-generation devise, the devised property passes under the "younger-generation substitute gift"—defined as the substitute gift created with respect to the younger-generation devise.

Subsection (c) is illustrated by the following examples:

Example 7. G's will devised "$5,000 to my son, A, if he is living at my death; if not, to my daughter, B" and devised "$7,500 to my daughter, B, if she is living at my death; if not, to my son, A." A and B predeceased G, both leaving descendants who survived G by 120 hours.

Solution: A's descendants take the $5,000 devise as substitute takers for A, and B's descendants take the $7,500 devise as substitute takers for B. In the absence of a finding based on affirmative evidence such as described in the solution to *Example 1*, the mere words of survivorship do not by themselves indicate a contrary intent.

Both devises require application of subsection (c). In the case of both devises, the statute produces a substitute gift for the devise to A and for the devise to B, each devise being an alternative devise, one to the other. The question of which of the substitute gifts takes effect is resolved by determining which of the devisees themselves would take the devised property if both A and B had survived G by 120 hours.

With respect to the devise of $5,000, the primary devise is to A because A would have taken the devised property had both A and B survived G by 120 hours. Consequently, the primary substitute gift is to A's descendants and that substitute gift prevails over the substitute gift to B's descendants.

With respect to the devise of $7,500, the primary devise is to B because B would have taken the devised property had both A and B survived G by 120 hours, and so the substitute gift to B's descendants is the primary substitute gift and it prevails over the substitute gift to A's descendants.

Subsection (c)(2) is inapplicable because there is no younger-generation devise. Neither A nor B is a descendant of the other.

Example 8. G's will devised "$10,000 to my son, A, if he is living at my death; if not, to A's children, X and Y." A and X predeceased G. A's child, Y, and X's children, M and N, survived G by 120 hours.

Solution: Half of the devise ($5,000) goes to Y. The other half ($5,000) goes to M and N. The disposition of the latter half requires application of subsection (c).

Subsection (b)(1) produces substitute gifts as to that half for the devise of that half to A and for the devise of that half to X, each of these devises being alternative devises, one to the other. The primary devise is to A. But there is also a younger-generation devise, the alternative devise to X. X is a descendant of A, X would take if X but not A survived G by 120 hours, and the devise is one for which a substitute gift is created by subsection (b)(1). So, the younger-generation substitute gift, which is to X's descendants (M and N), prevails over the primary substitute gift, which is to A's descendants (Y, M, and N).

Note that the outcome of this example is the same as in *Example 6.*

Example 9. Same facts as *Example 5*, except that both A and B predeceased the testator and both left descendants who survived the testator by 120 hours.

Solution: A's descendants take half ($5,000) and B's descendants take half ($5,000).

As to the half devised to A, subsection (b)(1) produces a substitute gift to A's descendants and a substitute gift to B's descendants (because the language "or to the survivor of them" created an alternative devise in B of A's half). As to the half devised to B, subsection (b)(1) produces a substitute gift to B's descendants and a substitute gift to A's descendants (because the language "or to the survivor of them" created an alternative devise in A of B's half). Thus, with respect to each half, resort must be had to subsection (c) to determine which substitute gift prevails.

Under subsection (c)(1), each half passes under the primary substitute gift. The primary devise as to A's half is to A and the primary devise as to B's half is to B because, if both A and B had survived G by 120 hours, A would have taken half ($5,000) and B would have taken half ($5,000). Neither A nor B is a descendant of the other, so subsection (c)(2) does not apply. Only if one were a descendant of the other would the other's descendants take it all, under the rule of subsection (c)(2). * * *

Section 2–604. Failure of Testamentary Provision.

(a) Except as provided in Section 2–603, a devise, other than a residuary devise, that fails for any reason becomes a part of the residue.

(b) Except as provided in Section 2–603, if the residue is devised to two or more persons, the share of a residuary devisee that fails for any reason passes to the other residuary devisee, or to other residuary devisees in proportion to the interest of each in the remaining part of the residue.

Section 2–605. Increase in Securities; Accessions.

(a) If a testator executes a will that devises securities and the testator then owned securities that meet the description in the will, the devise includes additional securities owned by the testator at death to the extent the additional securities were acquired by the testator after the will was executed as a result of the testator's ownership of the described securities and are securities of any of the following types:

(1) securities of the same organization acquired by reason of action initiated by the organization or any successor, related, or acquiring organization, excluding any acquired by exercise of purchase options;

(2) securities of another organization acquired as a result of a merger, consolidation, reorganization, or other distribution by the organization or any successor, related, or acquiring organization; or

(3) securities of the same organization acquired as a result of a plan of reinvestment.

(b) Distributions in cash before death with respect to a described security are not part of the devise.

Comment

Purpose and Scope of Revisions. The rule of subsection (a), as revised, relates to a devise of securities (such as a devise of 100 shares of XYZ Company), regardless of whether that devise is characterized as a general or specific devise. If the testator executes a will that makes a devise of securities and if the testator then owned securities that meet the description in the will, then the devisee is entitled not only to the described securities to the extent they are owned by the testator at death; the devisee is also entitled to any additional securities owned by the testator at death that were acquired by the testator during his or her lifetime after the will was executed and were acquired as a result of the testator's ownership of the described securities by reason of an action specified in subsection (a)(1), (2), or (3), such as the declaration of stock splits or stock dividends or spinoffs of a subsidiary. * * *

Subsection (a) Not Exclusive. Subsection (a) is not exclusive, i.e., it is not to be understood as setting forth the only conditions under which additional securities of the types described in subsections (a)(1) through (3) are included in the devise. For example, the express terms of subsection (a) do not apply to a case in which the testator owned the described securities when he or she executed the will, but later sold (or otherwise disposed of) those securities, and then later purchased (or otherwise acquired) securities that meet the description in the will, following which additional securities of the type or types described in subsection (a)(1), (2), or (3) are acquired as a result of the testator's ownership of the later-acquired securities. Nor do the express terms of subsection (a) apply to a similar (but less likely) case in which the testator did not own the described securities when he or she executed the will, but later purchased (or otherwise acquired) such securities. Subsection (a) does not preclude a court, in an appropriate case, from deciding that additional securities of the type described in subsection (a)(1), (2), or (3) acquired as a result of the testator's ownership of the later-acquired securities pass under the devise in either of these two cases, or in other cases if appropriate. * * *

Section 2–606. Nonademption of Specific Devises; Unpaid Proceeds of Sale, Condemnation, or Insurance; Sale by Conservator or Agent.

(a) A specific devisee has a right to specifically devised property in the testator's estate at the testator's death and to:

(1) any balance of the purchase price, together with any security agreement, owed by a purchaser at the testator's death by reason of sale of the property;

(2) any amount of a condemnation award for the taking of the property unpaid at death;

(3) any proceeds unpaid at death on fire or casualty insurance on or other recovery for injury to the property;

(4) any property owned by the testator at death and acquired as a result of foreclosure, or obtained in lieu of foreclosure, of the security interest for a specifically devised obligation;

(5) any real property or tangible personal property owned by the testator at death which the testator acquired as a replacement for specifically devised real property or tangible personal property; and

(6) if not covered by paragraphs (1) through (5), a pecuniary devise equal to the value as of its date of disposition of other specifically devised property disposed of during the testator's

lifetime but only to the extent it is established that ademption would be inconsistent with the testator's manifested plan of distribution or that at the time the will was made, the date of disposition or otherwise, the testator did not intend ademption of the devise.

(b)   If specifically devised property is sold or mortgaged by a conservator or by an agent acting within the authority of a durable power of attorney for an incapacitated principal, or a condemnation award, insurance proceeds, or recovery for injury to the property is paid to a conservator or to an agent acting within the authority of a durable power of attorney for an incapacitated principal, the specific devisee has the right to a general pecuniary devise equal to the net sale price, the amount of the unpaid loan, the condemnation award, the insurance proceeds, or the recovery.

(c)   The right of a specific devisee under subsection (b) is reduced by any right the devisee has under subsection (a).

(d)   For the purposes of the references in subsection (b) to a conservator, subsection (b) does not apply if after the sale, mortgage, condemnation, casualty, or recovery, it was adjudicated that the testator's incapacity ceased and the testator survived the adjudication for at least one year.

(e)   For the purposes of the references in subsection (b) to an agent acting within the authority of a durable power of attorney for an incapacitated principal, (i) "incapacitated principal" means a principal who is an incapacitated person, (ii) no adjudication of incapacity before death is necessary, and (iii) the acts of an agent within the authority of a durable power of attorney are presumed to be for an incapacitated principal.

Comment

Purpose and Scope of Revisions. Under the "identity" theory followed by most courts, the common-law doctrine of ademption by extinction is that a specific devise is adeemed—rendered ineffective—if the specifically devised property is not owned by the testator at death. In applying the "identity" theory, courts do not inquire into the testator's intent to determine whether the testator's objective in disposing of the specifically devised property was to revoke the devise. The only thing that matters is that the property is no longer owned at death. The application of the "identity" theory of ademption has resulted in harsh results in a number of cases, where it was reasonably clear that the testator did not intend to revoke the devise. * * *

Recently, some courts have begun to break away from the "identity" theory and adopt instead the so-called "intent" theory. * * * The major import of the revisions of this section is to adopt the "intent" theory in subsections (a)(5) and (6).

Subsection (a)(5) does not import a tracing principle into the question of ademption, but rather should be seen as a sensible "mere change in form" principle.

Example 1. G's will devised to X "my 1984 Ford." After she executed her will, she sold her 1984 Ford and bought a 1988 Buick; later, she sold the 1988 Buick and bought a 1993 Chrysler. She still owned the 1993 Chrysler when she died. Under subsection (a)(5), X takes the 1993 Chrysler.

Variation. If G had sold her 1984 Ford (or any of the replacement cars) and used the proceeds to buy shares in a mutual fund, which she owned at death, subsection (a)(5) does not give X the shares in the mutual fund. If G owned an automobile at death as a replacement for her 1984 Ford, however, X would be entitled to that automobile, even though it was bought with funds other than the proceeds of the sale of the 1984 Ford.

Subsection (a)(6) applies only to the extent the specifically devised property is not in the testator's estate at death and its value or its replacement is not covered by the provisions of subsections (a)(1) through (5). In that event, subsection (a)(6) allows the devisee claiming that an ademption has not occurred to establish that the facts and circumstances indicate that ademption of the devise was not intended by the testator or that ademption of the devise is inconsistent with the testator's manifested plan of distribution.

Example 2. G's will devised to his son, A, "that diamond ring I inherited from grandfather" and devised to his daughter, B, "that diamond brooch I inherited from grandmother." After G executed his will, a burglar entered his home and stole the diamond ring (but not the diamond brooch, as it was in G's safety deposit box at his bank).

Under subsection (a)(6), A could likely establish that G intended A's devise to not adeem or that ademption would be inconsistent with G's manifested plan of distribution. In fact, G's equalizing devise to B affirmatively indicates that ademption is inconsistent with G's manifested plan of distribution. The likely result is that, under subsection (a)(6), A would be entitled to the value of the diamond ring.

Example 3. G's will devised her painting titled *The Bar* by Edouard Manet to X. After executing her will, G donated the painting to a museum. G's deliberate act of giving away the specifically devised property is a fact and circumstance indicating that ademption of the devise was intended. In the absence of persuasive evidence to the contrary, therefore, X would not be entitled to the value of the painting. * * *

Section 2–607. Nonexoneration.

A specific devise passes subject to any mortgage interest existing at the date of death, without right of exoneration, regardless of a general directive in the will to pay debts.

Section 2–608. Exercise of Power of Appointment.

In the absence of a requirement that a power of appointment be exercised by a reference, or by an express or specific reference, to the power, a general residuary clause in a will, or a will making general disposition of all of the testator's property, expresses an intention to exercise a power of appointment held by the testator only if (i) the power is a general power exercisable in favor of the powerholder's estate and the creating instrument does not contain an effective gift if the power is not exercised or (ii) the testator's will manifests an intention to include the property subject to the power.

Comment

General Residuary Clause. This section, in conjunction with Section 2–601, provides that a general residuary clause (such as "All the residue of my estate, I devise to. . . .") in the testator's will or a will making general disposition of all of the testator's property (such as "All of my estate, I devise to. . . .") is presumed to express an intent to exercise a power of appointment only if one or the other of two circumstances or sets of circumstances are satisfied. One such circumstance (whether the power is general or nongeneral) is if the testator's will manifests an intention to include the property subject to the power. A simple example of a residuary clause that manifests such an intention is a so-called "blending" clause, such as "All the residue of my estate, including any property over which I have a power of appointment, I devise to. . . ."

The other circumstance under which a general residuary clause or a will making general disposition of all of the testator's property is presumed to express an intent to exercise a power is if the power is a *general* power exercisable in favor of the powerholder's estate *and* the instrument that created the power does not contain an effective gift over in the event the power is not exercised (a "gift in default"). In well planned estates, a general power of appointment will be accompanied by a gift in default. The gift-in-default clause is ordinarily expected to take effect; it is not merely an after-thought just in case the power is not exercised. The power is not expected to be exercised, and in fact is often conferred mainly to gain a tax benefit * * * . A general power should not be exercised in such a case without clear evidence of an intent to appoint.

In poorly planned estates, on the other hand, there may be no gift-in-default clause. In the absence of a gift-in-default clause, it seems better to let the property pass under the powerholder's will than force it to return to the donor's estate, for the reason that the donor died before the powerholder died and it seems better to avoid forcing a reopening of the donor's estate. * * *

Section 2–609. Ademption by Satisfaction.

(a)   Property a testator gave in his [or her] lifetime to a person is treated as a satisfaction of a devise in whole or in part, only if (i) the will provides for deduction of the gift, (ii) the testator declared in a contemporaneous writing that the gift is in satisfaction of the devise or that its value is to be deducted from the value of the devise, or (iii) the devisee acknowledged in writing that the gift is in satisfaction of the devise or that its value is to be deducted from the value of the devise.

(b) For purposes of partial satisfaction, property given during lifetime is valued as of the time the devisee came into possession or enjoyment of the property or at the testator's death, whichever occurs first.

(c) If the devisee fails to survive the testator, the gift is treated as a full or partial satisfaction of the devise, as appropriate, in applying Sections 2–603 and 2–604, unless the testator's contemporaneous writing provides otherwise.

Comment

Scope and Purpose of Revisions. In addition to minor stylistic changes, this section is revised to delete the requirement that the gift in satisfaction of a devise be made to the devisee. The purpose is to allow the testator to satisfy a devise to A by making a gift to B. Consider why this might be desirable. G's will made a $20,000 devise to his child, A. G was a widower. Shortly before his death, G in consultation with his lawyer decided to take advantage of the $10,000 annual gift tax exclusion and sent a check for $10,000 to A and another check for $10,000 to A's spouse, B. The checks were accompanied by a letter from G explaining that the gifts were made for tax purposes and were in lieu of the $20,000 devise to A. The removal of the phrase "to that person" from the statute allows the $20,000 devise to be fully satisfied by the gifts to A and B.

This section parallels Section 2–109 on advancements and follows the same policy of requiring written evidence that lifetime gifts are to be taken into account in the distribution of an estate, whether testate or intestate. * * *

To be a gift in satisfaction, the gift need not be an outright gift; it can be in the form of a will substitute, such as designating the devisee as the beneficiary of the testator's life-insurance policy or the beneficiary of the remainder interest in a revocable inter-vivos trust.

Subsection (b) on value accords with Section 2–109 and applies if, for example, property such as stock is given. If the devise is specific, a gift of the specific property to the devisee during lifetime adeems the devise by extinction rather than by satisfaction, and this section would be inapplicable. Unlike the common law of satisfaction, however, specific devises are not excluded from the rule of this section. If, for example, the testator makes a devise of a specific item of property, and subsequently makes a gift of cash or other property to the devisee, accompanied by the requisite written intent that the gift satisfies the devise, the devise is satisfied under this section even if the subject of the specific devise is still in the testator's estate at death (and hence would not be adeemed under the doctrine of ademption by extinction).

Under subsection (c), if a devisee to whom a gift in satisfaction is made predeceases the testator and his or her descendants take under Section 2–603 or 2–604, they take the same devise as their ancestor would have taken had the ancestor survived the testator; if the devise is reduced by reason of this section as to the ancestor, it is automatically reduced as to the devisee's descendants. In this respect, the rule in testacy differs from that in intestacy; see Section 2–109(c).

PART 7

RULES OF CONSTRUCTION APPLICABLE TO WILLS AND OTHER GOVERNING INSTRUMENTS

Section 2–701. Scope.

In the absence of a finding of a contrary intention, the rules of construction in this [part] control the construction of a governing instrument. The rules of construction in this [part] apply to a governing instrument of any type, except as the application of a particular section is limited by its terms to a specific type or types of provision or governing instrument.

Section 2–702. Requirement of Survival by 120 Hours.

(a) [Requirement of Survival by 120 Hours Under Probate Code.] For the purposes of this [code], except as provided in subsection (d), an individual who is not established by clear and convincing evidence to have survived an event, including the death of another individual, by 120 hours is deemed to have predeceased the event.

(b) [Requirement of Survival by 120 Hours under Governing Instrument.] Except as provided in subsection (d), for purposes of a provision of a governing instrument that relates to an individual surviving an event, including the death of another individual, an individual who is not established by clear and convincing evidence to have survived the event by 120 hours is deemed to have predeceased the event.

(c) [Co-owners With Right of Survivorship; Requirement of Survival by 120 Hours.] Except as provided in subsection (d), if (i) it is not established by clear and convincing evidence that one of two co-owners with right of survivorship survived the other co-owner by 120 hours, one-half of the property passes as if one had survived by 120 hours and one-half as if the other had survived by 120 hours and (ii) there are more than two co-owners and it is not established by clear and convincing evidence that at least one of them survived the others by 120 hours, the property passes in the proportion that one bears to the whole number of co-owners. For the purposes of this subsection, "co-owners with right of survivorship" includes joint tenants, tenants by the entireties, and other co-owners of property or accounts held under circumstances that entitles one or more to the whole of the property or account on the death of the other or others.

(d) [Exceptions.] Survival by 120 hours is not required if:

(1) the governing instrument contains language dealing explicitly with simultaneous deaths or deaths in a common disaster and that language is operable under the facts of the case;

(2) the governing instrument expressly indicates that an individual is not required to survive an event, including the death of another individual, by any specified period or expressly requires the individual to survive the event by a specified period; but survival of the event or the specified period must be established by clear and convincing evidence;

(3) the imposition of a 120-hour requirement of survival would cause a nonvested property interest or a power of appointment to fail to qualify for validity under Section 2–901(a)(1), (b)(1), or (c)(1) or to become invalid under Section 2–901(a)(2), (b)(2), or (c)(2); but survival must be established by clear and convincing evidence; or

(4) the application of a 120-hour requirement of survival to multiple governing instruments would result in an unintended failure or duplication of a disposition; but survival must be established by clear and convincing evidence.

(e) [Protection of Payors and Other Third Parties.]

(1) A payor or other third party is not liable for having made a payment or transferred an item of property or any other benefit to a beneficiary designated in a governing instrument who, under this section, is not entitled to the payment or item of property, or for having taken any other action in good faith reliance on the beneficiary's apparent entitlement under the terms of the governing instrument, before the payor or other third party received written notice of a claimed lack of entitlement under this section. A payor or other third party is liable for a payment made or other action taken after the payor or other third party received written notice of a claimed lack of entitlement under this section.

(2) Written notice of a claimed lack of entitlement under paragraph (1) must be mailed to the payor's or other third party's main office or home by registered or certified mail, return receipt requested, or served upon the payor or other third party in the same manner as a summons in a civil action. Upon receipt of written notice of a claimed lack of entitlement under this section, a payor or other third party may pay any amount owed or transfer or deposit any item of property held by it to or with the court having jurisdiction of the probate proceedings relating to the decedent's estate, or if no proceedings have been commenced, to or with the court having jurisdiction of probate proceedings relating to decedents' estates located in the county of the decedent's residence. The court shall hold the funds or item of property and, upon its

determination under this section, shall order disbursement in accordance with the determination. Payments, transfers, or deposits made to or with the court discharge the payor or other third party from all claims for the value of amounts paid to or items of property transferred to or deposited with the court.

(f) [Protection of Bona Fide Purchasers; Personal Liability of Recipient.]

(1) A person who purchases property for value and without notice, or who receives a payment or other item of property in partial or full satisfaction of a legally enforceable obligation, is neither obligated under this section to return the payment, item of property, or benefit nor is liable under this section for the amount of the payment or the value of the item of property or benefit. But a person who, not for value, receives a payment, item of property, or any other benefit to which the person is not entitled under this section is obligated to return the payment, item of property, or benefit, or is personally liable for the amount of the payment or the value of the item of property or benefit, to the person who is entitled to it under this section.

(2) If this section or any part of this section is preempted by federal law with respect to a payment, an item of property, or any other benefit covered by this section, a person who, not for value, receives the payment, item of property, or any other benefit to which the person is not entitled under this section is obligated to return the payment, item of property, or benefit, or is personally liable for the amount of the payment or the value of the item of property or benefit, to the person who would have been entitled to it were this section or part of this section not preempted.

Comment

Scope and Purpose of Revision. This section parallels Section 2–104, which requires an heir to survive the intestate by 120 hours in order to inherit.

The scope of this section is expanded to cover all provisions of a governing instrument and this Code that relate to an individual surviving an event (including the death of another individual). * * *

Note that subsection (d)(1) provides that the 120-hour requirement of survival is inapplicable if the governing instrument "contains language dealing explicitly with simultaneous deaths or deaths in a common disaster and that language is operable under the facts of the case." The application of this provision is illustrated by the following example.

Example. G died leaving a will devising her entire estate to her husband, H, adding that "in the event he dies before I do, at the same time that I do, or under circumstances as to make it doubtful who died first," my estate is to go to my brother Melvin. H died about 38 hours after G's death, both having died as a result of injuries sustained in an automobile accident.

Under subsection (b), G's estate passes under the alternative devise to Melvin because H's failure to survive G by 120 hours means that H is deemed to have predeceased G. The language in the governing instrument does not, under subsection (d)(1), nullify the provision that causes H, because of his failure to survive G by 120 hours, to be deemed to have predeceased G. Although the governing instrument does contain language dealing with simultaneous deaths, that language is not operable under the facts of the case because H did not die before G, at the same time as G, or under circumstances as to make it doubtful who died first.

Note that subsection (d)(4) provides that the 120-hour requirement of survival is inapplicable if "the application of this section to multiple governing instruments would result in an unintended failure or duplication of a disposition." The application of this provision is illustrated by the following example.

Example. Pursuant to a common plan, H and W executed mutual wills with reciprocal provisions. Their intention was that a $50,000 charitable devise would be made on the death of the survivor. To that end, H's will devised $50,000 to the charity if W predeceased him. W's will devised $50,000 to the charity if H predeceased her. Subsequently, H and W were involved in a common accident. W survived H by 48 hours.

Were it not for subsection (d)(4), not only would the charitable devise in W's will be effective, because H in fact predeceased W, but the charitable devise in H's will would also be effective, because W's failure to survive H by 120 hours would result in her being deemed to have predeceased H. Because this would result in an unintended duplication of the $50,000 devise, subsection (d)(4) provides that the 120-hour requirement of survival is inapplicable. Thus, only the $50,000 charitable devise in W's will is effective.

Subsection (d)(4) also renders the 120-hour requirement of survival inapplicable had H and W died in circumstances in which it could not be established by clear and convincing evidence that either survived the other. In such a case, an appropriate result might be to give effect to the common plan by paying half of the intended $50,000 devise from H's estate and half from W's estate.

Federal Preemption of State Law. See the Comment to Section 2–804 for a discussion of federal preemption. * * *

Section 2–703. Choice of Law as to Meaning and Effect of Governing Instrument.

The meaning and legal effect of a governing instrument is determined by the local law of the state selected in the governing instrument, unless the application of that law is contrary to the provisions relating to the elective share described in [Part] 2, the provisions relating to exempt property and allowances described in [Part] 4, or any other public policy of this state otherwise applicable to the disposition.

Section 2–704. Power of Appointment; Compliance With Specific Reference Requirement.

A powerholder's substantial compliance with a formal requirement of appointment imposed in a governing instrument by the donor, including a requirement that the instrument exercising the power of appointment make reference or specific reference to the power, is sufficient, if:

(1) the powerholder knows of and intends to exercise the power; and

(2) the powerholder's manner of attempted exercise does not impair a material purpose of the donor in imposing the requirement.

Comment

Rationale of Section. In the creation of powers of appointment, it has become common estate-planning practice to require that the powerholder can exercise the power only by making reference (or express or specific reference) to it. The question of whether the powerholder has made a sufficiently specific reference is much litigated. The precise question often is whether a so-called blanket-exercise clause—a clause referring to "any property over which I have a power of appointment"—constitutes a sufficient reference to a particular power to exercise that power. * * *

Section 2–704 adopts a substantial-compliance rule. If it could be shown that the powerholder had knowledge of and intended to exercise the power, the blanket-exercise clause would be sufficient to exercise the power, unless it could be shown that the donor had a material purpose in insisting on the specific-reference requirement. * * *

Section 2–705. Class Gifts Construed to Accord With Intestate Succession; Exceptions.

(a) **[Definitions.]** In this section:

(1) "Assisted reproduction" has the meaning set forth in Section 2–115.

(2) "De facto parent" has the meaning set forth in Section 2–115.

(3) "Distribution date" means the time when an immediate or a postponed class gift is to take effect in possession or enjoyment.

(4) "Gestational period" has the meaning set forth in Section 2–104.

(5) "In-law" includes a stepchild.

(6) "Relative" has the meaning set forth in Section 2–115.

(b) **[Terms of Relationship.]** Except as otherwise provided in subsections (c) and (d), a class gift in a governing instrument which uses a term of relationship to identify the class members is construed in accordance with the rules for intestate succession.

(c) **[In-Laws.]** A class gift in a governing instrument excludes in-laws unless:

(1) when the governing instrument was executed, the class was then and foreseeably would be empty; or

(2) the language or circumstances otherwise establish that in-laws were intended to be included.

(d) **[Transferor Not Parent.]** In construing a governing instrument of a transferor who is not a parent of an individual, the individual is not considered the child of the parent unless:

(1) the parent, a relative of the parent, or the spouse or surviving spouse of the parent or of a relative of the parent performed functions customarily performed by a parent before the individual reached [18] years of age; or

(2) the parent intended to perform functions under paragraph (1) but was prevented from doing so by death or another reason, if the intent is proved by clear and convincing evidence.

(e) **[Class-Closing Rules.]** The following rules apply for purposes of the class-closing rules:

(1) If a particular time is during a gestational period that results in the birth of an individual who lives at least 120 hours after birth, the individual is deemed to be living at that time.

(2) If the start of a pregnancy resulting in the birth of an individual occurs after the death of the individual's parent and the distribution date is the death of the parent, the individual is deemed to be living on the distribution date if [the person with the power to appoint or distribute among the class members received notice or had actual knowledge, not later than [6] months after the parent's death, of an intent to use genetic material in assisted reproduction and] the individual lives at least 120 hours after birth and:

(A) the embryo was in utero not later than [36] months after the deceased parent's death; or

(B) the individual was born not later than [45] months after the deceased parent's death.

(3) An individual who is in the process of being adopted when the class closes is treated as adopted when the class closes if the adoption is subsequently granted.

(4) An individual who is in the process of being adjudicated a child of a de facto parent when the class closes is treated as a child of the de facto parent when the class closes, if the parentage is subsequently established.

Comment

This section facilitates a modern construction of gifts that identify the recipient by reference to a relationship to someone; usually these gifts will be class gifts.

The rules set forth in this section are rules of construction, which under Section 2–701 are controlling in the absence of a finding of a contrary intention.

Subsection (a): Definitions. With two exceptions, the definitions in subsection (a) rely on definitions contained in the Code's intestacy sections. The exceptions are the definition of "in-law," which is defined to include a stepchild, and the definition of "distribution date," which is relevant to the class-closing rules contained in subsection (e). Distribution date is defined as the date when an immediate or postponed class gift takes effect in possession or enjoyment.

Subsection (b): Terms of Relationship. Subsection (b) provides that—subject to the exceptions contained in subsections (d) and (d), which are discussed below—a class gift that uses a term of relationship—such as "spouses", "children", "grandchildren", "descendants", "issue", "parents", "grandparents", brothers", "sisters", "nephews", or "nieces"—to identify the takers is construed in accordance with the rules for intestate succession. Thus, for example, a class gift to "spouses" is construed in accordance with Section 2–102, which makes no distinction between same-sex and opposite-sex spouses. Similarly, a class gift to an individual's "siblings" is construed in accordance with Section 2–107, which treats siblings equally without regard to how many common ancestors in the same generation they share.

Default rules. The rules in this section are default rules. Under Section 2–701, the rules in this section yield if there is a finding of a contrary intention. One circumstance in which a court should not find a contrary intention is when the governing instrument contains a provision excluding a child born to parents who are not married to each other, but the provision does not say anything about a child conceived by assisted reproduction. The question presented is whether such a provision excluding a nonmarital child also applies to a child resulting from a posthumous pregnancy after death has ended a marriage. In a strictly literal sense, a child resulting from a posthumous pregnancy is a nonmarital child. * * * This interpretation should be rejected. A child resulting from a posthumous pregnancy after death has ended a marriage should be considered a marital child, not a nonmarital child. A provision in a will, trust, or other governing instrument that relates to the exclusion of a nonmarital child, without more, likely was not inserted with a child resulting from a posthumous pregnancy in mind. Unless the provision of the governing instrument excluding a nonmarital child manifests an intent also to exclude a child resulting from a posthumous pregnancy after death has ended a marriage, the provision should not be interpreted to exclude such a child. For similar reasons, a provision in a governing instrument excluding a nonmarital child which does not say anything about a child conceived by assisted reproduction should not be construed to exclude a child born to a gestational or genetic surrogate if the intended parents are married, whether the child is born while the intended parents are alive or after the death of an intended parent.

Posthumous Pregnancy: Time Limits on Parentage in the Uniform Parentage Act (2017) Inapplicable. Sections 708(b)(2), 810(b)(2), and 817(b)(2) of the Uniform Parentage Act (2017) [UPA (2017)] impose time limits on the posthumous creation of parent-child relationships. These time limits do not apply here. Subsection (b) provides that class gifts are construed in accordance with the rules for intestate succession. The rules for intestate succession include Sections 2–120 and 2–121, which incorporate most of the provisions of the UPA (2017) but not these time limits. These time limits are unnecessary and inappropriate in construing a term of relationship in a class gift because the class membership already is governed by the class-closing rules. * * *

Class Closing. As provided in subsection (e), inclusion in a class is subject to the class-closing rules.

Subsection (c): In-Laws. Subsection (c) provides that class gifts are construed to exclude in-laws (relatives by marriage, including stepchildren), unless (1) when the governing instrument was executed, the class was then and foreseeably would be empty or (2) the language or circumstances otherwise establish that in-laws (relatives by marriage, including stepchildren) were intended to be included. * * * As recognized in * * * subsection (c) * * *, there are situations in which the circumstances would tend to include a relative by marriage. As provided in subsection (e), inclusion in a class is subject to the class-closing rules.

One situation in which the circumstances would tend to establish an intent to include a relative by marriage is the situation in which, looking at the facts existing when the governing instrument was executed, the class was then and foreseeably would be empty unless the transferor intended to include relatives by marriage.

Example 1. G's will devised property in trust, directing the trustee to pay the income in equal shares "to G's children who are living on each income payment date and on the death of G's last surviving child, to distribute the trust property to G's issue then living, such issue to take per stirpes, and if no issue of G is then living, to distribute the trust property to the X Charity." When G executed her will, she was past the usual childbearing age, had no children of her own, and was married to a man who had four children by a previous marriage. These children had lived with G and her husband for many years, but G had never adopted them. Under these circumstances, it is reasonable to conclude that when G referred to her "children" in her will she was referring to her stepchildren. Thus her stepchildren should be included in the presumptive meaning of the gift "to G's children" and the issue of her stepchildren should be included in the presumptive meaning of the gift "to G's issue." If G, at the time she executed her will, had children of her own, in the absence of additional facts, G's stepchildren should not be included in the presumptive meaning of the gift to "G's children" or in the gift to "G's issue."

Example 2. G's will devised property in trust, directing the trustee to pay the income to G's wife W for life, and on her death, to distribute the trust property to "my grandchildren." W had children by a prior marriage who were G's stepchildren. G never had any children of his own and he never adopted his stepchildren. It is reasonable to conclude that under these circumstances G meant the children of his stepchildren when his will gave the future interest under the trust to G's "grandchildren."

Example 3. G's will devised property in trust, directing the trustee to pay the income "to my daughter for life and on her death, to distribute the trust property to her children." When G executed his will, his son had died, leaving surviving the son's wife, G's daughter-in-law, and two children. G had no daughter of his own. Under these circumstances, the conclusion is justified that G's daughter-in-law is the "daughter" referred to in G's will.

Another situation in which the circumstances would tend to establish an intent to include a relative by marriage is the case of reciprocal wills, as illustrated in Example 4 * * * .

Example 4. G's will devised her entire estate "to my husband if he survives me, but if not, to my nieces and nephews." G's husband H predeceased her. H's will devised his entire estate "to my wife if she survives me, but if not, to my nieces and nephews." Both G and H had nieces and nephews. In these circumstances, "my nieces and nephews" is construed to include G's nieces and nephews by marriage. Were it otherwise, the combined estates of G and H would pass only to the nieces and nephews of the spouse who happened to survive.

Still another situation in which the circumstances would tend to establish an intent to include a relative by marriage is a case in which an ancestor participated in raising a relative by marriage.

Example 5. G's will devised property in trust, directing the trustee to pay the income in equal shares "to my nieces and nephews living on each income payment date until the death of the last survivor of my nieces and nephews, at which time the trust shall terminate and the trust property shall be distributed to the X Charity." G's wife W was deceased when G executed his will. W had one brother who predeceased her. G and W took the brother's children, the wife's nieces and nephews, into their home and raised them. G had one sister who predeceased him, and G and W were close to her children, G's nieces and nephews. Under these circumstances, the conclusion is justified that the disposition "to my nieces and nephews" includes the children of W's brother as well as the children of G's sister.

The language of the disposition may also establish an intent to include relatives by marriage, as illustrated in Examples 6, 7, and 8.

Example 6. G's will devised half of his estate to his wife W and half to "my children." G had one child by a prior marriage, and W had two children by a prior marriage. G did not adopt his stepchildren. G's relationship with his stepchildren was close, and he participated in raising them. The use of the plural "children" is a factor indicating that G intended to include his stepchildren in the class gift to his children.

Example 7. G's will devised the residue of his estate to "my nieces and nephews named herein before." G's niece by marriage was referred to in two earlier provisions as "my niece." The previous reference to her as "my niece" indicates that G intended to include her in the residuary devise.

Example 8. G's will devised the residue of her estate "in twenty-five (25) separate equal shares, so that there shall be one (1) such share for each of my nieces and nephews who shall survive me, and one (1) such share for each of my nieces and nephews who shall not survive me but who shall have left a child or children surviving me." G had 22 nieces and nephews by blood or adoption and three nieces and nephews by marriage. The reference to twenty-five nieces and nephews indicates that G intended to include her three nieces and nephews by marriage in the residuary devise.

Subsection (d): Transferor Not Parent. The general theory of subsection (d) is that a transferor who is not the parent of an individual would want the individual to be included in a class gift as a child of the individual's parent only if (1) the parent, a relative of the parent, or the spouse or surviving spouse of the parent or of a relative of the parent performed functions customarily performed by a parent before the individual reached the age of majority, or (2) the parent intended to perform such functions but was prevented from doing so by death or some other reason, if such intent is proved by clear and convincing evidence. * * *

As provided in subsection (e) of this section, inclusion of an individual in a class is subject to the class-closing rules.

Example 9. G's will created a trust, providing for income to G's daughter, A, for life, remainder in corpus to A's descendants who survive A, by representation. A and A's husband adopted a 47-year old man, X. Because A did not function as a parent of X before X reached the age of [18], X would not be included as a member of the class of A's descendants who take the corpus of G's trust on A's death.

If, however, A executed a will containing a devise to her "children" or designated her "children" as beneficiary of her life insurance policy, X would be included in the class. Under Section 2–118, X is A's child for purposes of intestate succession. Subsection (d) is inapplicable because the transferor, A, is the parent.

Subsection (e): Class-Closing Rules. In order for an individual to be a taker under a class gift that uses a term of relationship to identify the class members, the individual must (1) qualify as a class member under subsections (b), (c), and (d) and (2) not be excluded by the class-closing rules. For an exposition of the class-closing rules, see Restatement (Third) of Property: Wills and Other Donative Transfers § 15.1. Section 15.1 provides that, "unless the language or circumstances establish that the transferor had a different intention, a class gift that has not yet closed physiologically closes to future entrants on the distribution date if a beneficiary of the class gift is then entitled to distribution."

Subsection (e)(1): Class Closing During a Gestational Period. Subsection (e)(1) codifies the well-accepted rule that if a particular time is during a gestational period that results in the birth of an individual who lives at least 120 hours after birth, that individual is deemed to be living at that particular time.

Subsection (e)(2): Children of Assisted Reproduction; Class Gift in Which Distribution Date is Deceased Parent's Death. Subsection (e)(2) changes the class-closing rules in one respect. If the start of a pregnancy resulting in the birth of an individual occurs after the death of the individual's parent, and if the distribution date is the deceased parent's death, then the individual is treated as living on the distribution date if the individual lives 120 hours after birth and either (1) the embryo was in utero no later than 36 months after the deceased parent's death or (2) the individual was born no later than 45 months after the deceased parent's death. Bracketed language imposes an additional requirement: that the person with the power to appoint or distribute the property receive notice or have actual knowledge within [6] months of the parent's death of intent to use genetic material in assisted reproduction and thereby affect the class membership.

The 36-month period in subsection (e)(2) is designed to allow a surviving spouse or partner a period of grieving, time to decide whether to go forward with assisted reproduction, and a reasonable allowance for unsuccessful attempts to achieve a pregnancy. The 36-month period also coincides with Section 3–1006, under which an heir is allowed to recover property improperly distributed or its value from any distributee during the later of three years after the decedent's death or one year after distribution. If the assisted-reproduction procedure is performed in a medical facility, the date when the child is in utero will ordinarily be made evident by medical records. In some cases, however, the procedure is not performed in a medical facility, and so such evidence may be lacking. Providing an alternative of birth within 45 months is designed to provide certainty in such cases. The 45-month period is based on the 36-month period with an additional nine months tacked on to allow for a normal period of pregnancy.

Example 10. G, a member of the armed forces, executed a military will under 10 U.S.C. § 1044d shortly before being deployed to a war zone. G's will devised "90 percent of my estate to my wife W and 10 percent of my estate to my children." G also left frozen sperm at a sperm bank in case he should be killed in action. G was killed in action. After G's death, W decided to become inseminated with his frozen sperm so that she could have his child. If either (1) the embryo was in utero within 36 months after G's death or (2) the child was born within 45 months after G's death, and if the child lived 120 hours after birth (see Section 2–702), the child is treated as living at G's death and is included in the class.

Example 11. G, a member of the armed forces, executed a military will under 10 U.S.C. § 1044d shortly before being deployed to a war zone. G's will devised "90 percent of my estate to my husband H and 10 percent of my estate to my issue by representation." G also left frozen embryos in case she should be killed in action. G was killed in action. After G's death, H arranged for the embryos to be implanted in the uterus of a surrogate. If either (1) the embryo was in utero within 36 months after G's death or (2) the child was born within 45 months after G's death, and if the child lived 120 hours after birth (see Section 2–702), the child is treated as living at G's death and is included in the class.

Example 12. The will of G's mother created a testamentary trust, directing the trustee to pay the income to G for life, then to distribute the trust principal to G's children. When G's mother died, G was married but had no children. Shortly after being diagnosed with leukemia, G feared that he would be rendered infertile by the disease or by the treatment for the disease, so he left frozen sperm at a sperm bank. After G's death, G's widow decided to become inseminated with his frozen sperm so that she could have his child. If either (1) the embryo was in utero within 36 months after G's death or (2) the child was born within 45 months after G's death, and if the child lived 120 hours after birth (see Section 2–702), the child is treated as living at G's death and is included in the class.

Subsection (e)(2) Inapplicable Unless Pregnancy Is Posthumous and Distribution Date Arises at Deceased Parent's Death. Subsection (e)(2) only applies if there is a posthumous pregnancy and if the distribution date arises at the deceased parent's death. Subsection (e)(2) does not apply if the pregnancy is not posthumous. It also does not apply if the distribution date arises before or after the deceased parent's death. The reason is that in all of these cases the special rule in (e)(2) is not needed. Instead, the ordinary class-closing rules—including subsections (e)(1), (e)(3), and (e)(4)—suffice. * * *

A case that reached the same result that would be reached under this section is In re Martin B., 841 N.Y.S.2d 207 (Sur. Ct. 2007). In that case, two children (who were conceived posthumously and were born to a deceased father's widow approximately three and five years after his death) were included in class gifts of principal to the deceased father's "issue" or "descendants". The children would be included under this section because (1) the requirements in the UPA (2017) for a parent-child relationship between the children and the deceased father were satisfied other than the time limits rendered inapplicable by subsection (b), which references the rules for intestate succession, including Section 2–120, (2) the distribution dates arose after the deceased father's death, and (3) the children were living on the distribution dates, thus satisfying subsection (e)(1).

Martin B. illustrates why the time limits in Sections 708(b)(2), 810(b)(2), and 817(b)(2) of the UPA (2017) are not needed or appropriate in the construction of class gifts. The rules for class closing govern. Consider also the following examples.

Example 13. G created a revocable inter vivos trust shortly before his death. The trustee was directed to pay the income to G for life, then "to pay the income to my wife, W, for life, then to distribute the trust principal by representation to my descendants who survive W." When G died, G and W had no children. Shortly before G's death and after being diagnosed with leukemia, G feared that he would be rendered infertile by the disease or by the treatment for the disease, so he left frozen sperm at a sperm bank. Assume that the parentage requirements of the UPA (2017) were satisfied except for the time limits in Section 708(b)(2) of that Act. After G's death, W decided to become inseminated with G's frozen sperm so that she could have his child. The child, X, was born five years after G's death. W raised X. Upon W's death many years later, X was a grown adult. X is entitled to receive the trust principal, because (1) X was living on the distribution date, and (2) the requirements for a parent-child relationship between G and X were satisfied except for the time limits in Section 708(b)(2) of the UPA (2017). These time limits are rendered inapplicable by subsection (b), which references the rules for intestate succession, including Section 2–120.

Example 14. The will of G's mother created a testamentary trust, directing the trustee to pay the income to G for life, then "to pay the income by representation to G's issue from time to time living, and at the death of G's last surviving child, to distribute the trust principal by representation to G descendants who survive G's last surviving child." When G's mother died, G was married but had no children. Shortly after being diagnosed with leukemia, G feared that he would be rendered infertile by the disease or by the treatment for the disease, so he left frozen sperm at a sperm bank. Assume that the parentage requirements of the UPA (2017) were satisfied except for the time limits in Section 708(b)(2) of that Act. After G's death, G's widow decided to become inseminated with his frozen sperm so that she could have his child. If either (1) the embryo was in utero within 36 months after G's death or (2) the child was born within 45 months after G's death, and if the child lived 120 hours after birth, the child is treated as living at G's death and is included in the class-gift of income for which the distribution date is G's death. Whether or not G's widow later decides to use his frozen sperm to have another child or children, G's child or children would be included in or excluded from the class-gift of income of subsequent income distributions (assuming they live 120 hours after birth) based on the ordinary class-closing rules. The reason is that an income interest in class-gift form is treated as creating separate class gifts in which the distribution date is the time of each successive income payment. * * * Regarding the remainder interest in principal that takes effect in possession on the death of G's last living child, the then-living descendants of G's children would take the trust principal.

Subsections (e)(3) and (e)(4). For purposes of the class-closing rules, an individual who is in the process of being adopted when the class closes is treated as adopted when the class closes if the adoption is subsequently granted. An individual is "in the process of being adopted" if a legal proceeding to adopt the individual had been filed before the class closed. However, the phrase "in the process of being adopted" is not intended to be limited to the filing of a legal proceeding, but is intended to grant flexibility to find on a case by case basis that the process commenced earlier.

Similarly, under subsection (e)(4), an individual who is in the process of being adjudicated a child of a de facto parent when the class closes is treated as a child of that de facto parent when the class closes if the de facto parentage is subsequently established. * * *

Section 2–706. Life Insurance; Retirement Plan; Account With POD Designation; Transfer-on-Death Registration; Deceased Beneficiary.

(a) **[Definitions.]** In this section:

(1) "Alternative beneficiary designation" means a beneficiary designation that is expressly created by the governing instrument and, under the terms of the governing instrument, can take effect instead of another beneficiary designation on the happening of one or more events, including survival of the decedent or failure to survive the decedent, whether an event is expressed in condition-precedent, condition-subsequent, or any other form.

(2) "Beneficiary" means the beneficiary of a beneficiary designation under which the beneficiary must survive the decedent and includes (i) a class member if the beneficiary designation is in the form of a class gift and (ii) an individual or class member who was deceased at the time the beneficiary designation was executed as well as an individual or class member who was then living but who failed to survive the decedent, but excludes a joint tenant of a joint tenancy with the right of survivorship and a party to a joint and survivorship account.

(3) "Beneficiary designation" includes an alternative beneficiary designation and a beneficiary designation in the form of a class gift.

(4) "Class member" includes an individual who fails to survive the decedent but who would have taken under a beneficiary designation in the form of a class gift had he [or she] survived the decedent.

(5) "Descendant of a grandparent", as used in subsection (b), means an individual who qualifies as a descendant of a grandparent of the decedent under the (i) rules of construction applicable to a class gift created in the decedent's beneficiary designation if the beneficiary designation is in the form of a class gift or (ii) rules for intestate succession if the beneficiary designation is not in the form of a class gift.

(6) "Descendants", as used in the phrase "surviving descendants" of a deceased beneficiary or class member in subsections (b)(1) and (2), mean the descendants of a deceased beneficiary or class member who would take under a class gift created in the beneficiary designation.

(7) "Stepchild" means a child of the decedent's surviving, deceased, or former spouse, and not of the decedent.

(8) "Surviving", in the phrase "surviving beneficiaries" or "surviving descendants", means beneficiaries or descendants who neither predeceased the decedent nor are deemed to have predeceased the decedent under Section 2–702.

(b) [Substitute Gift.] If a beneficiary fails to survive the decedent and is a grandparent, a descendant of a grandparent, or a stepchild of the decedent, the following apply:

(1) Except as provided in paragraph (4), if the beneficiary designation is not in the form of a class gift and the deceased beneficiary leaves surviving descendants, a substitute gift is created in the beneficiary's surviving descendants. They take by representation the property to which the beneficiary would have been entitled had the beneficiary survived the decedent.

(2) Except as provided in paragraph (4), if the beneficiary designation is in the form of a class gift, other than a beneficiary designation to "issue," "descendants," "heirs of the body," "heirs," "next of kin," "relatives," or "family," or a class described by language of similar import, a substitute gift is created in the surviving descendants of any deceased beneficiary. The property to which the beneficiaries would have been entitled had all of them survived the decedent passes to the surviving beneficiaries and the surviving descendants of the deceased beneficiaries. Each surviving beneficiary takes the share to which he [or she] would have been entitled had the deceased beneficiaries survived the decedent. Each deceased beneficiary's surviving descendants who are substituted for the deceased beneficiary take by representation the share to which the deceased beneficiary would have been entitled had the deceased beneficiary survived the decedent. For the purposes of this paragraph, "deceased beneficiary" means a class member who failed to survive the decedent and left one or more surviving descendants.

(3) For the purposes of Section 2–701, words of survivorship, such as in a beneficiary designation to an individual "if he survives me," or in a beneficiary designation to "my surviving children," are not, in the absence of additional evidence, a sufficient indication of an intent contrary to the application of this section.

(4) If a governing instrument creates an alternative beneficiary designation with respect to a beneficiary designation for which a substitute gift is created by paragraph (1) or (2), the substitute gift is superseded by the alternative beneficiary designation if:

(A) the alternative beneficiary designation is in the form of a class gift and one or more members of the class is entitled to take; or

(B) the alternative beneficiary designation is not in the form of a class gift and the expressly designated beneficiary of the alternative beneficiary designation is entitled to take.

(c) [More Than One Substitute Gift; Which One Takes.] If, under subsection (b), substitute gifts are created and not superseded with respect to more than one beneficiary designation and the beneficiary designations are alternative beneficiary designations, one to the other, the determination of which of the substitute gifts takes effect is resolved as follows:

(1) Except as provided in paragraph (2), the property passes under the primary substitute gift.

(2) If there is a younger-generation beneficiary designation, the property passes under the younger-generation substitute gift and not under the primary substitute gift.

(3) In this subsection:

(A) "Primary beneficiary designation" means the beneficiary designation that would have taken effect had all the deceased beneficiaries of the alternative beneficiary designations who left surviving descendants survived the decedent.

(B) "Primary substitute gift" means the substitute gift created with respect to the primary beneficiary designation.

(C) "Younger-generation beneficiary designation" means a beneficiary designation that (i) is to a descendant of a beneficiary of the primary beneficiary designation, (ii) is an alternative beneficiary designation with respect to the primary beneficiary designation, (iii) is a beneficiary designation for which a substitute gift is created, and (iv) would have taken effect had all the deceased beneficiaries who left surviving descendants survived the decedent except the deceased beneficiary or beneficiaries of the primary beneficiary designation.

(D) "Younger-generation substitute gift" means the substitute gift created with respect to the younger-generation beneficiary designation.

(d) [Protection of Payors.]

(1) A payor is protected from liability in making payments under the terms of the beneficiary designation until the payor has received written notice of a claim to a substitute gift under this section. Payment made before the receipt of written notice of a claim to a substitute gift under this section discharges the payor, but not the recipient, from all claims for the amounts paid. A payor is liable for a payment made after the payor has received written notice of the claim. A recipient is liable for a payment received, whether or not written notice of the claim is given.

(2) The written notice of the claim must be mailed to the payor's main office or home by registered or certified mail, return receipt requested, or served upon the payor in the same manner as a summons in a civil action. Upon receipt of written notice of the claim, a payor may pay any amount owed by it to the court having jurisdiction of the probate proceedings relating to the decedent's estate or, if no proceedings have been commenced, to the court having jurisdiction of probate proceedings relating to decedents' estates located in the county of the decedent's residence. The court shall hold the funds and, upon its determination under this section, shall order disbursement in accordance with the determination. Payment made to the court discharges the payor from all claims for the amounts paid.

(e) [Protection of Bona Fide Purchasers; Personal Liability of Recipient.]

(1) A person who purchases property for value and without notice, or who receives a payment or other item of property in partial or full satisfaction of a legally enforceable obligation, is neither obligated under this section to return the payment, item of property, or benefit nor is liable under this section for the amount of the payment or the value of the item of property or benefit. But a person who, not for value, receives a payment, item of property, or any other benefit to which the person is not entitled under this section is obligated to return the payment, item of property, or benefit, or is personally liable for the amount of the payment or the value of the item of property or benefit, to the person who is entitled to it under this section.

(2) If this section or any part of this section is preempted by federal law with respect to a payment, an item of property, or any other benefit covered by this section, a person who, not for value, receives the payment, item of property, or any other benefit to which the person is not entitled under this section is obligated to return the payment, item of property, or benefit, or is personally liable for the amount of the payment or the value of the item of property or benefit, to the person who would have been entitled to it were this section or part of this section not preempted.

Comment

Purpose. This section provides an antilapse statute for "beneficiary designations," under which the beneficiary must survive the decedent. The term "beneficiary designation" is defined in Section 1–201 as "a governing instrument naming a beneficiary of an insurance or annuity policy, of an account with POD designation, of a security registered in beneficiary form (TOD), or of a pension, profit-sharing, retirement, or similar benefit plan, or other nonprobate transfer at death."

The terms of this section parallel those of Section 2–603, except that the provisions relating to payor protection and personal liability of recipients have been added. The Comment to Section 2–603 contains an elaborate exposition of Section 2–603, together with examples illustrating its application. That Comment, in addition to the examples given below, should aid understanding of Section 2–706. For a discussion of the reasons why Section 2–706 should not be preempted by federal law, see the Comment to Section 2–804. * * *

Example 1. G is the owner of a life-insurance policy. When the policy was taken out, G was married to S; G and S had two young children, A and B. G died 45 years after the policy was taken out. S predeceased G. A survived G by 120 hours and B predeceased G leaving three children (X, Y, and Z) who survived G by 120 hours. G's policy names S as the primary beneficiary of the policy, but because S predeceased G, the secondary (contingent) beneficiary designation became operative. The secondary (contingent) beneficiary designation of G's policy states: "equally to the then living children born of the marriage of G and S."

The printed terms of G's policy provide:

If two or more persons are designated as beneficiary, the beneficiary will be the designated person or persons who survive the Insured, and if more than one survive, they will share equally.

Solution: The printed clause constitutes an "alternative beneficiary designation" for purposes of subsection (b)(4), which supersedes the substitute gift to B's descendants created by subsection (b)(2). A is entitled to all of the proceeds of the policy.

Example 2. The facts are the same as in *Example 1*, except that G's policy names "A and B" as secondary (contingent) beneficiaries. The printed terms of the policy provide:

If any designated Beneficiary predeceases the Insured, the interest of such Beneficiary will terminate and shall be shared equally by such of the Beneficiaries as survive the Insured.

Solution: The printed clause constitutes an "alternative beneficiary designation" for purposes of subsection (b)(4), which supersedes the substitute gift to B's descendants created by subsection (b)(1). A is entitled to all of the proceeds of the policy.

Example 3. The facts are the same as *Examples 1* or *2*, except that the printed terms of the policy do not contain either quoted clause or a similar one.

Solution: Under Section 2–706, A would be entitled to half of the policy proceeds and X, Y, and Z would divide the other half equally.

Example 4. The facts are the same as *Example 3*, except that the policy has a beneficiary designation that provides that, if the adjacent box is checked, the share of any deceased beneficiary shall be paid "in one sum and in equal shares to the children of that beneficiary who survive." G did *not* check the box adjacent to this option.

Solution: G's deliberate decision not to check the box providing for the share of any deceased beneficiary to go to that beneficiary's children constitutes a clear indication of a contrary intention for purposes of Section 2–701. A would be entitled to all of the proceeds of the policy.

Example 5. G's life-insurance policy names her niece, A, as primary beneficiary, and provides that if A does not survive her, the proceeds are to go to her niece B, as contingent beneficiary. A predeceased G, leaving children who survived G by 120 hours. B survived G by 120 hours.

Solution: The contingent beneficiary designation constitutes an "alternative beneficiary designation" for purposes of subsection (b)(4), which supersedes the substitute gift to A's descendants created by subsection (b)(1). The proceeds go to B, not to A's children.

Example 6. G's life-insurance policy names her niece, A, as primary beneficiary and provides that if A does not survive her, the proceeds are to go to her niece B, as contingent beneficiary. The printed terms of the policy specifically state that if neither the primary nor secondary beneficiaries survive the policyholder, the proceeds are payable to the policyholder's estate. A predeceased G, leaving children who survived G by 120 hours. B also predeceased G, leaving children who survived G by 120 hours.

Solution: The second contingent beneficiary designation to G's estate constitutes an "alternative beneficiary designation" for purposes of subsection (b)(4), which supersedes the substitute gifts to A's and B's descendants created by subsection (b)(1). The proceeds go to G's estate, not to A's children or to B's children. * * *

Section 2–707. Survivorship With Respect to Future Interests Under Terms of Trust; Substitute Takers.

(a) **[Definitions.]** In this section:

(1) "Alternative future interest" means an expressly created future interest that can take effect in possession or enjoyment instead of another future interest on the happening of one or more events, including survival of an event or failure to survive an event, whether an event is expressed in condition-precedent, condition-subsequent, or any other form. A residuary clause in a will does not create an alternative future interest with respect to a future interest created in a nonresiduary devise in the will, whether or not the will specifically provides that lapsed or failed devises are to pass under the residuary clause.

(2) "Beneficiary" means the beneficiary of a future interest and includes a class member if the future interest is in the form of a class gift.

(3) "Class member" includes an individual who fails to survive the distribution date but who would have taken under a future interest in the form of a class gift had he [or she] survived the distribution date.

(4) "Descendants", in the phrase "surviving descendants" of a deceased beneficiary or class member in subsections (b)(1) and (2), mean the descendants of a deceased beneficiary or class member who would take under a class gift created in the trust.

(5) "Distribution date," with respect to a future interest, means the time when the future interest is to take effect in possession or enjoyment. The distribution date need not occur at the beginning or end of a calendar day, but can occur at a time during the course of a day.

(6) "Future interest" includes an alternative future interest and a future interest in the form of a class gift.

(7) "Future interest under the terms of a trust" means a future interest that was created by a transfer creating a trust or to an existing trust or by an exercise of a power of appointment to an existing trust, directing the continuance of an existing trust, designating a beneficiary of an existing trust, or creating a trust.

(8) "Surviving", in the phrase "surviving beneficiaries" or "surviving descendants", means beneficiaries or descendants who neither predeceased the distribution date nor are deemed to have predeceased the distribution date under Section 2–702.

(b) **[Survivorship Required; Substitute Gift.]** A future interest under the terms of a trust is contingent on the beneficiary's surviving the distribution date. If a beneficiary of a future interest under the terms of a trust fails to survive the distribution date, the following apply:

(1) Except as provided in paragraph (4), if the future interest is not in the form of a class gift and the deceased beneficiary leaves surviving descendants, a substitute gift is created in the beneficiary's surviving descendants. They take by representation the property to which the beneficiary would have been entitled had the beneficiary survived the distribution date.

(2) Except as provided in paragraph (4), if the future interest is in the form of a class gift, other than a future interest to "issue," "descendants," "heirs of the body," "heirs," "next of kin," "relatives," or "family," or a class described by language of similar import, a substitute gift is created in the surviving descendants of any deceased beneficiary. The property to which the beneficiaries would have been entitled had all of them survived the distribution date passes to the surviving beneficiaries and the surviving descendants of the deceased beneficiaries. Each surviving beneficiary takes the share to which he [or she] would have been entitled had the deceased beneficiaries survived the distribution date. Each deceased beneficiary's surviving descendants who are substituted for the deceased beneficiary take by representation the share to which the deceased beneficiary would have been entitled had the deceased beneficiary survived

the distribution date. For the purposes of this paragraph, "deceased beneficiary" means a class member who failed to survive the distribution date and left one or more surviving descendants.

(3) For the purposes of Section 2–701, words of survivorship attached to a future interest are not, in the absence of additional evidence, a sufficient indication of an intent contrary to the application of this section. Words of survivorship include words of survivorship that relate to the distribution date or to an earlier or an unspecified time, whether those words of survivorship are expressed in condition-precedent, condition-subsequent, or any other form.

(4) If the governing instrument creates an alternative future interest with respect to a future interest for which a substitute gift is created by paragraph (1) or (2), the substitute gift is superseded by the alternative future interest if:

(A) the alternative future interest is in the form of a class gift and one or more members of the class is entitled to take in possession or enjoyment; or

(B) the alternative future interest is not in the form of a class gift and the expressly designated beneficiary of the alternative future interest is entitled to take in possession or enjoyment.

(c) **[More Than One Substitute Gift; Which One Takes.]** If, under subsection (b), substitute gifts are created and not superseded with respect to more than one future interest and the future interests are alternative future interests, one to the other, the determination of which of the substitute gifts takes effect is resolved as follows:

(1) Except as provided in paragraph (2), the property passes under the primary substitute gift.

(2) If there is a younger-generation future interest, the property passes under the younger-generation substitute gift and not under the primary substitute gift.

(3) In this subsection:

(A) "Primary future interest" means the future interest that would have taken effect had all the deceased beneficiaries of the alternative future interests who left surviving descendants survived the distribution date.

(B) "Primary substitute gift" means the substitute gift created with respect to the primary future interest.

(C) "Younger-generation future interest" means a future interest that (i) is to a descendant of a beneficiary of the primary future interest, (ii) is an alternative future interest with respect to the primary future interest, (iii) is a future interest for which a substitute gift is created, and (iv) would have taken effect had all the deceased beneficiaries who left surviving descendants survived the distribution date except the deceased beneficiary or beneficiaries of the primary future interest.

(D) "Younger-generation substitute gift" means the substitute gift created with respect to the younger-generation future interest.

(d) **[If No Other Takers, Property Passes Under Residuary Clause or to Transferor's Heirs.]** Except as provided in subsection (e), if, after the application of subsections (b) and (c), there is no surviving taker, the property passes in the following order:

(1) if the trust was created in a nonresiduary devise in the transferor's will or in a codicil to the transferor's will, the property passes under the residuary clause in the transferor's will; for purposes of this section, the residuary clause is treated as creating a future interest under the terms of a trust.

(2) if no taker is produced by the application of paragraph (1), the property passes to the transferor's heirs under Section 2–711.

(e) [If No Other Takers and If Future Interest Created by Exercise of Power of Appointment.] If, after the application of subsections (b) and (c), there is no surviving taker and if the future interest was created by the exercise of a power of appointment:

    (1)   the property passes under the donor's gift-in-default clause, if any, which clause is treated as creating a future interest under the terms of a trust; and

    (2)   if no taker is produced by the application of paragraph (1), the property passes as provided in subsection (d). For purposes of subsection (d), "transferor" means the donor if the power was a nongeneral power and means the donee if the power was a general power.

Comment

Rationale. The objective of this section is to project the antilapse idea into the area of future interests, thus preventing disinheritance of a descending line that has one or more members living on the distribution date and preventing a share from passing down a descending line that has died out by the distribution date.

Scope. This section applies only to future interests under the terms of a trust. For shorthand purposes, references in this Comment to the term "future interest" refer to a future interest under the terms of a trust. The rationale for restricting this section to future interests under the terms of a trust is that legal life estates in land, followed by indefeasibly vested remainder interests, are still created in some localities, often with respect to farmland. In such cases, the legal life tenant and the person holding the remainder interest can, together, give good title in the sale of the land. If the antilapse idea were injected into this type of situation, the ability of the parties to sell the land would be impaired if not destroyed because the antilapse idea would, in effect, create a contingent substitute remainder interest in the present and future descendants of the person holding the remainder interest.

Structure. The structure of this section substantially parallels the structure of the regular antilapse statute, Section 2–603, and the antilapse-type statute relating to beneficiary designations, Section 2–706.

Common-law Background. At common law, conditions of survivorship are not implied with respect to future interests. The rule against implying a condition of survivorship applies whether the future interest is created in trust or otherwise and whether the future interest is or is not in the form of a class gift. The only exception, where a condition of survivorship is implied at common law, is in the case of a multiple-generation class gift. * * * For example, in the simple case of a trust, "income to husband, A, for life, remainder to daughter, B," B's interest is not defeated at common law if she predeceases A; B's interest would pass through her estate to her successors in interest (probably either her residuary legatees or heirs * * *), who would become entitled to possession when A died. If any of B's successors in interest died before A, the interest held by that deceased successor in interest would likewise pass through his or her estate to his or her successors in interest; and so on. Thus, a benefit of a statutory provision reversing the common-law rule and providing substitute takers is that it prevents cumbersome and costly distributions to and through the estates of deceased beneficiaries of future interests, who may have died long before the distribution date.

Subsection (b). Subsection (b) imposes a condition of survivorship on future interests to the distribution date—defined as the time when the future interest is to take effect in possession or enjoyment. The requirement of survivorship imposed by subsection (b) applies whether or not the deceased beneficiary leaves descendants who survive the distribution date and are takers of a substitute gift provided by subsection (b)(1) or (2). Imposing a condition of survivorship on a future interest when the deceased beneficiary did not leave descendants who survive the distribution date prevents a share from passing down a descending line that has died out by the distribution date. Imposing a condition of survivorship on a future interest when the deceased beneficiary did leave descendants who survive the distribution date, and providing a substitute gift to those descendants, prevents disinheritance of a descending line that has one or more living members on the distribution date.

The 120-hour Survivorship Period. In effect, the requirement of survival of the distribution date means survival of the 120-hour period following the distribution date. This is because, under Section 2–702(a), "an individual who is not established to have survived an event . . . by 120 hours is deemed to have predeceased the event." As made clear by subsection (a)(7), for the purposes of Section 2–707, the "event" to which Section 2–702(a) relates is the distribution date.

Note that the "distribution date" need not occur at the beginning or end of a calendar day, but can occur at a time during the course of a day, such as the time of death of an income beneficiary.

References in Section 2–707 and in this Comment to survival of the distribution date should be understood as referring to survival of the distribution date by 120 hours.

Ambiguous Survivorship Language. Subsection (b) serves another purpose. It resolves a frequently litigated question arising from ambiguous language of survivorship, such as in a trust, "income to A for life, remainder in corpus to my surviving children." * * *

The first sentence of subsection (b), in combination with paragraph (3), imposes a condition of survivorship to the distribution date (the time of possession or enjoyment) even when an express condition of survivorship to an earlier time has been imposed. Thus, in a trust like "income to A for life, remainder in corpus to B, but if B predeceases A, to B's children who survive B," the first sentence of subsection (b) combined with paragraph (3) requires B's children to survive (by 120 hours) the death of the income beneficiary, A.

Rule of Construction. Note that Section 2–707 is a rule of construction. It is qualified by the rule set forth in Section 2–701, and thus it yields to a finding of a contrary intention. Consequently, in trusts like "income to A for life, remainder in corpus to B whether or not B survives A," or "income to A for life, remainder in corpus to B or B's estate," this section would not apply and, should B predecease A, B's future interest would pass through B's estate to B's successors in interest, who would become entitled to possession or enjoyment at A's death.

Classification. Subsection (b) renders a future interest "contingent" on the beneficiary's survival of the distribution date. As a result, future interests are "nonvested" and subject to the Rule Against Perpetuities. To prevent an injustice from resulting because of this, the Uniform Statutory Rule Against Perpetuities, which has a wait-and-see element, is incorporated into the Code as Article II, Part 9.

Substitute Gifts. Section 2–707 not only imposes a condition of survivorship to the distribution date; like its antilapse counterparts, Sections 2–603 and 2–706, it provides substitute takers in cases of a beneficiary's failure to survive the distribution date.

The statutory substitute gift is divided among the devisee's descendants "by representation," a phrase defined in Section 2–709(b). * * *

Subsection (b)(1)—Future Interests Not in the Form of a Class Gift. Subsection (b)(1) applies to non-class gifts, such as the "income to A for life, remainder in corpus to B" trust discussed above. If B predeceases A, subsection (b)(1) creates a substitute gift with respect to B's future interest; the substitute gift is to B's descendants who survive A (by 120 hours).

Subsection (b)(2)—Class Gift Future Interests. Subsection (b)(2) applies to single-generation class gifts, such as in a trust "income to A for life, remainder in corpus to A's children." * * * Suppose that A had two children, X and Y. X predeceases A; Y survives A. Subsection (b)(2) creates a substitute gift with respect to any of A's children who fail to survive A (by 120 hours) leaving descendants who survive A (by 120 hours). Thus, if X left descendants who survived A (by 120 hours), those descendants would take X's share; if X left no descendants who survived A (by 120 hours), Y would take it all.

Subsection (b)(2) does not apply to future interests to multiple-generation classes such as "issue," "descendants," "heirs of the body," "heirs," "next of kin," "distributees," "relatives," "family," or the like. The reason is that these types of class gifts have their own internal systems of representation, and so the substitute gift provided by subsection (b)(1) would be out of place with respect to these types of future interests. * * * The first sentence of subsection (b) and subsection (d) do apply, however. For example, suppose a nonresiduary devise "to A for life, remainder to A's issue, by representation." If A leaves issue surviving him (by 120 hours), they take. But if A leaves no issue surviving him (by 120 hours), the testator's residuary devisees are the takers.

Subsection (b)(4). Subsection (b)(4) * * * provides that, if a governing instrument creates an alternative future interest with respect to a future interest for which a substitute gift is created by paragraph (1) or (2), the substitute gift is superseded by the alternative future interest if: (A) the alternative future interest is in the form of a class gift and one or more members of the class is entitled to take in possession or enjoyment; or (B) the alternative future interest is not in the form of a class gift and the expressly designated beneficiary of the alternative future interest is entitled to take in possession or enjoyment. Consider, for example, a trust under which the income is to be paid to A for life, remainder in corpus to B if B survives A, but if not to C if C survives A. If B predeceases A, leaving descendants who survive A (by 120 hours), subsection (b)(1) creates a substitute gift to those descendants. But, if C survives A (by 120 hours), the alternative future interest in C supersedes the substitute gift to B's descendants. Upon A's death, the trust corpus passes to C.

Subsection (c). Subsection (c) is necessary because there can be cases in which subsections (b)(1) or (2) create substitute gifts with respect to two or more alternative future interests, and those substitute gifts are not superseded under the terms of subsection (b)(4). Subsection (c) provides the tie-breaking mechanism for such situations.

The initial step is to determine which of the alternative future interests would take effect had all the beneficiaries themselves survived the distribution date (by 120 hours). In subsection (c), this future interest is called the "primary future interest." Unless subsection (c)(2) applies, subsection (c)(1) provides that the property passes under the substitute gift created with respect to the primary future interest. This substitute gift is called the "primary substitute gift." Thus, the property goes to the descendants of the beneficiary or beneficiaries of the primary future interest.

Subsection (c)(2) provides an exception to this rule. Under subsection (c)(2), the property does not pass under the primary substitute gift if there is a "younger-generation future interest"—defined as a future interest that (i) is to a descendant of a beneficiary of the primary future interest, (ii) is an alternative future interest with respect to the primary future interest, (iii) is a future interest for which a substitute gift is created, and (iv) would have taken effect had all the deceased beneficiaries who left surviving descendants survived the distribution date except the deceased beneficiary or beneficiaries of the primary future interest. If there is a younger-generation future interest, the property passes under the "younger-generation substitute gift"—defined as the substitute gift created with respect to the younger-generation future interest.

Subsection (d). Since it is possible that, after the application of subsections (b) and (c), there are no substitute gifts, a back-stop set of substitute takers is provided in subsection (d)—the transferor's residuary devisees or heirs. Note that the transferor's residuary clause is treated as creating a future interest and, as such, is subject to this section. Note also that the meaning of the back-stop gift to the transferor's heirs is governed by Section 2–711, under which the gift is to the transferor's heirs determined as if the transferor died when A died. Thus there will always be a set of substitute takers, even if it turns out to be the State. If the transferor's surviving spouse has remarried after the transferor's death but before A's death, he or she would not be a taker under this provision.

Examples. The application of Section 2–707 is illustrated by the following examples. Note that, in each example, the "distribution date" is the time of the income beneficiary's death. Assume, in each example, that an individual who is described as having "survived" the income beneficiary's death survived the income beneficiary's death by 120 hours or more.

Example 1. A nonresiduary devise in G's will created a trust, income to A for life, remainder in corpus to B if B survives A. G devised the residue of her estate to a charity. B predeceased A. At A's death, B's child, X, is living.

Solution: On A's death, the trust property goes to X, not to the charity. Because B's future interest is not in the form of a class gift, subsection (b)(1) applies, not subsection (b)(2). Subsection (b)(1) creates a substitute gift with respect to B's future interest; the substitute gift is to B's child, X. Under subsection (b)(3), the words of survivorship attached to B's future interest ("to B if B survives A") do not indicate an intent contrary to the creation of that substitute gift. Nor, under subsection (b)(4), is that substitute gift superseded by an alternative future interest because, as defined in subsection (a)(1), G's residuary clause does not create an alternative future interest. In the normal lapse situation, a residuary clause does not supersede the substitute gift created by the antilapse statute, and the same analysis applies to this situation as well.

Example 2. Same as *Example 1*, except that B left no descendants who survived A.

Solution: Subsection (b)(1) does not create a substitute gift with respect to B's future interest because B left no descendants who survived A. This brings subsection (d) into operation, under which the trust property passes to the charity under G's residuary clause.

Example 3. G created an irrevocable inter-vivos trust, income to A for life, remainder in corpus to B if B survives A. B predeceased A. At A's death, G and X, B's child, are living.

Solution: X takes the trust property. Because B's future interest is not in the form of a class gift, subsection (b)(1) applies, not subsection (b)(2). Subsection (b)(1) creates a substitute gift with respect to B's future interest; the substitute gift is to B's child, X. Under subsection (b)(3), the words of survivorship ("to B if B survives A") do not indicate an intent contrary to the creation of that substitute gift. Nor, under subsection (b)(4), is the substitute gift superseded by an alternative future interest; G's reversion is not an alternative future interest as defined in subsection (a)(1) because it was not *expressly* created.

Example 4. G created an irrevocable inter-vivos trust, income to A for life, remainder in corpus to B if B survives A; if not, to C. B predeceased A. At A's death, C and B's child are living.

Solution: C takes the trust property. Because B's future interest is not in the form of a class gift, subsection (b)(1) applies, not subsection (b)(2). Subsection (b)(1) creates a substitute gift with respect to B's future interest; the substitute gift is to B's child, X. Under subsection (b)(3), the words of survivorship ("to B if B survives A") do not indicate an intent contrary to the creation of that substitute gift. But, under subsection (b)(4), the substitute gift to B's child is superseded by the alternative future interest held by C because C, having survived A (by 120 hours), is entitled to take in possession or enjoyment.

Example 5. G created an irrevocable inter-vivos trust, income to A for life, remainder in corpus to B, but if B predeceases A, to the person B appoints by will. B predeceased A. B's will exercised his power of appointment in favor of C. C survives A. B's child, X, also survives A.

Solution: B's appointee, C, takes the trust property, not B's child, X. Because B's future interest is not in the form of a class gift, subsection (b)(1) applies, not subsection (b)(2). Subsection (b)(1) creates a substitute gift with respect to B's future interest; the substitute gift is to B's child, X. Under subsection (b)(3), the words of survivorship ("to B if B survives A") do not indicate an intent contrary to the creation of that substitute gift. But, under subsection (b)(4), the substitute gift to B's child is superseded by the alternative future interest held by C because C, having survived A (by 120 hours), is entitled to take in possession or enjoyment. Because C's future interest was created in "a" governing instrument (B's will), it counts as an "alternative future interest."

Example 6. G creates an irrevocable inter-vivos trust, income to A for life, remainder in corpus to A's children who survive A; if none, to B. A's children predecease A, leaving descendants, X and Y, who survive A. B also survives A.

Solution: On A's death, the trust property goes to B, not to X and Y. Because the future interest in A's children is in the form of a class gift * * *, subsection (b)(2) applies, not subsection (b)(1). Subsection (b)(2) creates a substitute gift with respect to the future interest in A's children; the substitute gift is to the descendants of A's children, X and Y. Under subsection (b)(3), the words of survivorship ("to A's children who survive A") do not indicate an intent contrary to the creation of that substitute gift. But, under subsection (b)(4), the alternative future interest to B supersedes the substitute gift to the descendants of A's children because B survived A.

Alternative Facts: One of A's children, J, survives A; A's other child, K, predeceases A, leaving descendants, X and Y, who survive A. B also survives A.

Solution: J takes half the trust property and X and Y split the other half. Although there is an alternative future interest (in B) and although B did survive A, the alternative future interest was conditioned on none of A's children surviving A. Because that condition was not satisfied, the expressly designated beneficiary of that alternative future interest, B, is not entitled to take in possession or enjoyment. Thus, the alternative future interest in B does not supersede the substitute gift to K's descendants, X and Y.

Example 7. G created an irrevocable inter-vivos trust, income to A for life, remainder in corpus to B if B survives A; if not, to C. B and C predecease A. At A's death, B's child and C's child are living.

Solution: Subsection (b)(1) produces substitute gifts with respect to B's future interest and with respect to C's future interest. B's future interest and C's future interest are alternative future interests, one to the other. B's future interest is expressly conditioned on B's surviving A. C's future interest is conditioned on B's predeceasing A and C's surviving A. The condition that C survive A does not arise from express language in G's trust but from the first sentence of subsection (b); that sentence makes C's future interest contingent on C's surviving A. Thus, because neither B nor C survived A, neither B nor C is entitled to take in possession or enjoyment. So, under subsection (b)(4), neither substitute gift, created with respect to the future interests in B and C, is superseded by an alternative future interest. Consequently, resort must be had to subsection (c) to break the tie to determine which substitute gift takes effect.

Under subsection (c), B is the beneficiary of the "primary future interest" because B would have been entitled to the trust property had both B and C survived A. Unless subsection (c)(2) applies, the trust property passes to B's child as the taker under the "primary substitute gift."

Subsection (c)(2) would only apply if C's future interest qualifies as a "younger-generation future interest." This depends upon whether C is a descendant of B, for C's future interest satisfies the other requirements necessary to make it a younger-generation future interest. If C was a descendant of B, the substitute gift to C's child would be a "younger-generation substitute gift" and would become effective instead of the "primary substitute gift" to B's descendants. But if C was not a descendant of B, the property would pass under the "primary substitute gift" to B's descendants.

Example 8. G created an irrevocable inter-vivos trust, income to A for life, remainder in corpus to A's children who survive A; if none, to B. All of A's children predecease A. X and Y, who are descendants of one or more of A's children, survive A. B predeceases A, leaving descendants, M and N, who survive A.

Solution: On A's death, the trust property passes to X and Y under the "primary substitute gift," unless B was a descendant of any of A's children.

Subsection (b)(2) produces substitute gifts with respect to A's children who predeceased A leaving descendants who survived A. Subsection (b)(1) creates a substitute gift with respect to B's future interest. A's children's future interest and B's future interest are alternative future interests, one to the other. A's children's future interest is expressly conditioned on surviving A. B's future interest is conditioned on none of A's children surviving A and on B's surviving A. The condition of survivorship as to B's future interest does not arise because of express language in G's trust but because of the first sentence of subsection (b); that sentence makes B's future interest contingent on B's surviving A. Thus, because none of A's children survived A, and because B did not survive A, none of A's children nor B is entitled to take in possession or enjoyment. So, under subsection (b)(4), neither substitute gift—i.e., neither the one created with respect to the future interest in A's children nor the one created with respect to the future interest in B—is superseded by an alternative future interest. Consequently, resort must be had to subsection (c) to break the tie to determine which substitute gift takes effect.

Under subsection (c), A's children are the beneficiaries of the "primary future interest" because they would have been entitled to the trust property had all of them and B survived A. Unless subsection (c)(2) applies, the trust property passes to X and Y as the takers under the "primary substitute gift." Subsection (c)(2) would only apply if B's future interest qualifies as a "younger-generation future interest." This depends upon whether B is a descendant of any of A's children, for B's future interest satisfies the other requirements necessary to make it a "younger-generation future interest." If B was a descendant of one of A's children, the substitute gift to B's children, M and N, would be a "younger-generation substitute gift" and would become effective instead of the "primary substitute gift" to X and Y. But if B was not a descendant of any of A's children, the property would pass under the "primary substitute gift" to X and Y.

Example 9. G's will devised property in trust, income to niece Lilly for life, corpus on Lilly's death to her children; should Lilly die without leaving children, the corpus shall be equally divided among my nephews and nieces then living, the child or children of nieces who may be deceased to take the share their mother would have been entitled to if living.

Lilly never had any children. G had 3 nephews and 2 nieces in addition to Lilly. All 3 nephews and both nieces predeceased Lilly. A child of one of the nephews survived Lilly. One of the nieces had 8 children, 7 of whom survived Lilly. The other niece had one child, who did not survive Lilly. (This example is based on the facts of Bomberger's Estate, 32 A.2d 729 (Pa.1943).)

Solution: The trust property goes to the 7 children of the nieces who survived Lilly. The substitute gifts created by subsection (b)(2) to the nephew's son or to the nieces' children are superseded under subsection (b)(4) because there is an alternative future interest (the "child or children of nieces who may be deceased") and expressly designated beneficiaries of that alternative future interest (the 7 children of the nieces) are living at Lilly's death and are entitled to take in possession or enjoyment.

Example 10. G devised the residue of his estate in trust, income to his wife, W, for life, remainder in corpus to their children, John and Florence; if either John or Florence should predecease W, leaving descendants, such descendants shall take the share their parent would have taken if living.

G's son, John, survived W. G's daughter, Florence, predeceased W. Florence never had any children. Florence's husband survived W. (This example is based on the facts of Matter of Kroos, 99 N.E.2d 222 (N.Y.1951).)

Solution: John, of course, takes his half of the trust property. Because Florence left no descendants who survived W, subsection (b)(1) does not create a substitute gift with respect to Florence's future interest in her half. Subsection (d)(1) is inapplicable because G's trust was not created in a nonresiduary devise or in a codicil to G's will. Subsection (d)(2) therefore becomes applicable, under which Florence's half goes to G's heirs determined as if G died when W died, i.e., John. See Section 2–711. * * *

Section 2–708. Class Gifts to "Descendants," "Issue," or "Heirs of the Body"; Form of Distribution if None Specified.

If a class gift in favor of "descendants," "issue," or "heirs of the body" does not specify the manner in which the property is to be distributed among the class members, the property is distributed among the class members who are living when the interest is to take effect in possession or enjoyment, in such shares as they would receive, under the applicable law of intestate succession, if the designated ancestor had then died intestate owning the subject matter of the class gift.

Section 2–709. Representation; Per Capita at Each Generation; Per Stirpes.

(a) **[Definitions.]** In this section:

(1) "Deceased child" or "deceased descendant" means a child or a descendant who either predeceased the distribution date or is deemed to have predeceased the distribution date under Section 2–702.

(2) "Distribution date," with respect to an interest, means the time when the interest is to take effect in possession or enjoyment. The distribution date need not occur at the beginning or end of a calendar day, but can occur at a time during the course of a day.

(3) "Surviving ancestor," "surviving child," or "surviving descendant" means an ancestor, a child, or a descendant who neither predeceased the distribution date nor is deemed to have predeceased the distribution date under Section 2–702.

(b) **[Representation; Per Capita at Each Generation.]** If an applicable statute or a governing instrument calls for property to be distributed "by representation" or "per capita at each generation," the property is divided into as many equal shares as there are (i) surviving descendants in the generation nearest to the designated ancestor which contains one or more surviving descendants and (ii) deceased descendants in the same generation who left surviving descendants, if any. Each surviving descendant in the nearest generation is allocated one share. The remaining shares, if any, are combined and then divided in the same manner among the surviving descendants of the deceased descendants as if the surviving descendants who were allocated a share and their surviving descendants had predeceased the distribution date.

(c) **[Per Stirpes.]** If a governing instrument calls for property to be distributed "per stirpes," the property is divided into as many equal shares as there are (i) surviving children of the designated ancestor and (ii) deceased children who left surviving descendants. Each surviving child, if any, is allocated one share. The share of each deceased child with surviving descendants is divided in the same manner, with subdivision repeating at each succeeding generation until the property is fully allocated among surviving descendants.

(d) [Deceased Descendant With No Surviving Descendant Disregarded.] For the purposes of subsections (b) and (c), an individual who is deceased and left no surviving descendant is disregarded, and an individual who leaves a surviving ancestor who is a descendant of the designated ancestor is not entitled to a share.

Section 2–710. Worthier-Title Doctrine Abolished.

The doctrine of worthier title is abolished as a rule of law and as a rule of construction. Language in a governing instrument describing the beneficiaries of a disposition as the transferor's "heirs," "heirs at law," "next of kin," "distributees," "relatives," or "family," or language of similar import, does not create or presumptively create a reversionary interest in the transferor.

Section 2–711. Interests in "Heirs" and Like.

If an applicable statute or a governing instrument calls for a present or future distribution to or creates a present or future interest in a designated individual's "heirs," "heirs at law," "next of kin," "relatives," or "family," or language of similar import, the property passes to those persons, including the state, and in such shares as would succeed to the designated individual's intestate estate under the intestate succession law of the designated individual's domicile if the designated individual died when the disposition is to take effect in possession or enjoyment. If the designated individual's surviving spouse is living but is remarried at the time the disposition is to take effect in possession or enjoyment, the surviving spouse is not an heir of the designated individual.

PART 8

GENERAL PROVISIONS CONCERNING PROBATE AND NONPROBATE TRANSFERS

Section 2–801. [Reserved].

Section 2–802. Effect of Divorce, Annulment, and Decree of Separation.

(a) An individual who is divorced from the decedent or whose marriage to the decedent has been annulled is not a surviving spouse unless, by virtue of a subsequent marriage, the individual is married to the decedent at the time of death. A decree of separation that does not terminate the marriage is not a divorce for purposes of this section.

(b) For purposes of [Parts] 1, 2, 3, and 4 of this [article], and of Section 3–203, a surviving spouse does not include:

(1) an individual who obtains or consents to a final decree or judgment of divorce from the decedent or an annulment of their marriage, which decree or judgment is not recognized as valid in this state, unless subsequently they participate in a marriage ceremony purporting to marry each to the other or live together as spouses;

(2) an individual who, following an invalid decree or judgment of divorce or annulment obtained by the decedent, participates in a marriage ceremony with a third individual; or

(3) an individual who was a party to a valid proceeding concluded by an order purporting to terminate all marital property rights.

Section 2–803. Effect of Homicide on Intestate Succession, Wills, Trusts, Joint Assets, Life Insurance, and Beneficiary Designations.

(a) **[Definitions.]** In this section:

(1) "Disposition or appointment of property" includes a transfer of an item of property or any other benefit to a beneficiary designated in a governing instrument.

(2) "Governing instrument" means a governing instrument executed by the decedent.

(3) "Revocable", with respect to a disposition, appointment, provision, or nomination, means one under which the decedent, at the time of or immediately before death, was alone empowered, by law or under the governing instrument, to cancel the designation in favor of the killer, whether or not the decedent was then empowered to designate the decedent in place of the killer and whether or not the decedent then had capacity to exercise the power.

(b) **[Forfeiture of Statutory Benefits.]** An individual who feloniously and intentionally kills the decedent forfeits all benefits under this [article] with respect to the decedent's estate, including an intestate share, an elective share, an omitted spouse's or child's share, a homestead allowance, exempt property, and a family allowance. If the decedent died intestate, the decedent's intestate estate passes as if the killer disclaimed the intestate share.

(c) **[Revocation of Benefits Under Governing Instruments.]** The felonious and intentional killing of the decedent:

(1) revokes any revocable (i) disposition or appointment of property made by the decedent to the killer in a governing instrument, (ii) provision in a governing instrument conferring a general or nongeneral power of appointment on the killer, and (iii) nomination of the killer in a governing instrument, nominating or appointing the killer to serve in any fiduciary or representative capacity, including a personal representative, executor, trustee, or agent; and

(2) severs the interests of the decedent and killer in property held by them at the time of the killing as joint tenants with the right of survivorship [or as community property with the right of survivorship], transforming the interests of the decedent and killer into equal tenancies in common.

(d) **[Effect of Severance.]** A severance under subsection (c)(2) does not affect any third-party interest in property acquired for value and in good faith reliance on an apparent title by survivorship in the killer unless a writing declaring the severance has been noted, registered, filed, or recorded in records appropriate to the kind and location of the property which are relied upon, in the ordinary course of transactions involving such property, as evidence of ownership.

(e) **[Effect of Revocation.]** Provisions of a governing instrument are given effect as if the killer disclaimed all provisions revoked by this section or, in the case of a revoked nomination in a fiduciary or representative capacity, as if the killer predeceased the decedent.

(f) **[Wrongful Acquisition of Property.]** A wrongful acquisition of property or interest by a killer not covered by this section must be treated in accordance with the principle that a killer cannot profit from the killer's wrong.

(g) **[Felonious and Intentional Killing; How Determined.]** After all right to appeal has been exhausted, a judgment of conviction establishing criminal accountability for the felonious and intentional killing of the decedent conclusively establishes the convicted individual as the decedent's killer for purposes of this section. In the absence of a conviction, the court, upon the petition of an interested person, must determine whether, under the preponderance of evidence standard, the individual would be found criminally accountable for the felonious and intentional killing of the decedent. If the court determines that, under that standard, the individual would be found criminally accountable for the felonious and intentional killing of the decedent, the determination conclusively establishes that individual as the decedent's killer for purposes of this section.

(h) [Protection of Payors and Other Third Parties.]

(1) A payor or other third party is not liable for having made a payment or transferred an item of property or any other benefit to a beneficiary designated in a governing instrument affected by an intentional and felonious killing, or for having taken any other action in good faith reliance on the validity of the governing instrument, upon request and satisfactory proof of the decedent's death, before the payor or other third party received written notice of a claimed forfeiture or revocation under this section. A payor or other third party is liable for a payment made or other action taken after the payor or other third party received written notice of a claimed forfeiture or revocation under this section.

(2) Written notice of a claimed forfeiture or revocation under paragraph (1) must be mailed to the payor's or other third party's main office or home by registered or certified mail, return receipt requested, or served upon the payor or other third party in the same manner as a summons in a civil action. Upon receipt of written notice of a claimed forfeiture or revocation under this section, a payor or other third party may pay any amount owed or transfer or deposit any item of property held by it to or with the court having jurisdiction of the probate proceedings relating to the decedent's estate, or if no proceedings have been commenced, to or with the court having jurisdiction of probate proceedings relating to decedents' estates located in the county of the decedent's residence. The court shall hold the funds or item of property and, upon its determination under this section, shall order disbursement in accordance with the determination. Payments, transfers, or deposits made to or with the court discharge the payor or other third party from all claims for the value of amounts paid to or items of property transferred to or deposited with the court.

(i) [Protection of Bona Fide Purchasers; Personal Liability of Recipient.]

(1) A person who purchases property for value and without notice, or who receives a payment or other item of property in partial or full satisfaction of a legally enforceable obligation, is neither obligated under this section to return the payment, item of property, or benefit nor is liable under this section for the amount of the payment or the value of the item of property or benefit. But a person who, not for value, receives a payment, item of property, or any other benefit to which the person is not entitled under this section is obligated to return the payment, item of property, or benefit, or is personally liable for the amount of the payment or the value of the item of property or benefit, to the person who is entitled to it under this section.

(2) If this section or any part of this section is preempted by federal law with respect to a payment, an item of property, or any other benefit covered by this section, a person who, not for value, receives the payment, item of property, or any other benefit to which the person is not entitled under this section is obligated to return the payment, item of property, or benefit, or is personally liable for the amount of the payment or the value of the item of property or benefit, to the person who would have been entitled to it were this section or part of this section not preempted.

Comment

* * * [T]his section is confined to felonious and intentional killing and excludes the accidental manslaughter killing. Subsection (g) leaves no doubt that, for purposes of this section, a killing can be "felonious and intentional," whether or not the killer has actually been convicted in a criminal prosecution. Under subsection (g), after all right to appeal has been exhausted, a judgment of conviction establishing criminal accountability for the felonious and intentional killing of the decedent conclusively establishes the convicted individual as the decedent's killer for purposes of this section. Acquittal, however, does not preclude the acquitted individual from being regarded as the decedent's killer for purposes of this section.

This is because different considerations as well as a different burden of proof enter into the finding of criminal accountability in the criminal prosecution. Hence it is possible that the defendant on a murder charge may be found not guilty and acquitted, but if the same person claims as an heir, devisee, or beneficiary of a revocable beneficiary designation, etc. of the decedent, the probate court, upon the petition of an interested person, may find that, under a preponderance of the evidence standard, he or she would be found criminally accountable for the felonious and intentional killing of the decedent and thus be barred under this section from sharing in the affected property. In fact, in many of the cases arising under this section there may be no criminal prosecution because the killer has committed suicide.

It is now well accepted that the matter dealt with is not exclusively criminal in nature but is also a proper matter for probate courts. The concept that a wrongdoer may not profit by his or her own wrong is a civil concept, and the probate court is the proper forum to determine the effect of killing on succession to the decedent's property covered by this section. * * *

The phrases "criminal accountability" and "criminally accountable" for the felonious and intentional killing of the decedent not only include criminal accountability as an actor or direct perpetrator, but also as an accomplice or co-conspirator. * * *

Federal Preemption of State Law. See the Comment to Section 2–804 for a discussion of federal preemption. * * *

Section 2–804. Revocation of Probate and Nonprobate Transfers by Divorce; No Revocation by Other Changes of Circumstances.

(a) [Definitions.] In this section:

(1) "Disposition or appointment of property" includes a transfer of an item of property or any other benefit to a beneficiary designated in a governing instrument.

(2) "Divorce or annulment" means any divorce or annulment, or any dissolution or declaration of invalidity of a marriage, that would exclude the spouse as a surviving spouse within the meaning of Section 2–802. A decree of separation that does not terminate the marriage is not a divorce for purposes of this section.

(3) "Divorced individual" includes an individual whose marriage has been annulled.

(4) "Governing instrument" means a governing instrument executed by the divorced individual before the divorce or annulment of the marriage to the divorced individual's former spouse.

(5) "Relative of the divorced individual's former spouse" means an individual who is related to the divorced individual's former spouse by application of the rules establishing parent-child relationships under [[Subpart] 2 of [Part] 1] or affinity and who, after the divorce or annulment, is not related to the divorced individual by application of the rules establishing parent-child relationships under [[Subpart] 2 of [Part] 1] or affinity.

(6) "Revocable," with respect to a disposition, appointment, provision, or nomination, means one under which the divorced individual, at the time of the divorce or annulment, was alone empowered, by law or under the governing instrument, to cancel the designation in favor of the divorced individual's former spouse or relative of the former spouse, whether or not the divorced individual was then empowered to designate the divorced individual in place of the former spouse or relative of the former spouse and whether or not the divorced individual then had the capacity to exercise the power.

(b) [Revocation Upon Divorce.] Except as provided by the express terms of a governing instrument, a court order, or a contract relating to the division of the marital estate made between the divorced individuals before or after the marriage, divorce, or annulment, the divorce or annulment of a marriage:

(1) revokes any revocable:

(A) disposition or appointment of property made by a divorced individual to the divorced individual's former spouse in a governing instrument and any disposition or appointment created by law or in a governing instrument to a relative of the divorced individual's former spouse,

(B)   provision in a governing instrument conferring a general or nongeneral power of appointment on the divorced individual's former spouse or on a relative of the divorced individual's former spouse, and

(C)   nomination in a governing instrument, nominating a divorced individual's former spouse or a relative of the divorced individual's former spouse to serve in any fiduciary or representative capacity, including a personal representative, executor, trustee, conservator, agent, or guardian; and

(2)   severs the interests of the former spouses in property held by them at the time of the divorce or annulment as joint tenants with the right of survivorship [or as community property with the right of survivorship], transforming the interests of the former spouses into equal tenancies in common.

(c)   [Effect of Severance.] A severance under subsection (b)(2) does not affect any third-party interest in property acquired for value and in good faith reliance on an apparent title by survivorship in the survivor of the former spouses unless a writing declaring the severance has been noted, registered, filed, or recorded in records appropriate to the kind and location of the property which are relied upon, in the ordinary course of transactions involving such property, as evidence of ownership.

(d)   [Effect of Revocation.] Provisions of a governing instrument are given effect as if the former spouse and relatives of the former spouse disclaimed all provisions revoked by this section or, in the case of a revoked nomination in a fiduciary or representative capacity, as if the former spouse and relatives of the former spouse died immediately before the divorce or annulment.

(e)   [Revival if Divorce Nullified.] Provisions revoked solely by this section are revived by the divorced individual's remarriage to the former spouse or by a nullification of the divorce or annulment.

(f)   [No Revocation for Other Change of Circumstances.] No change of circumstances other than as described in this section and in Section 2–803 effects a revocation.

(g)   [Protection of Payors and Other Third Parties.]

(1)   A payor or other third party is not liable for having made a payment or transferred an item of property or any other benefit to a beneficiary designated in a governing instrument affected by a divorce, annulment, or remarriage, or for having taken any other action in good faith reliance on the validity of the governing instrument, before the payor or other third party received written notice of the divorce, annulment, or remarriage. A payor or other third party is liable for a payment made or other action taken after the payor or other third party received written notice of a claimed forfeiture or revocation under this section.

(2)   Written notice of the divorce, annulment, or remarriage under subsection (g)(1) must be mailed to the payor's or other third party's main office or home by registered or certified mail, return receipt requested, or served upon the payor or other third party in the same manner as a summons in a civil action. Upon receipt of written notice of the divorce, annulment, or remarriage, a payor or other third party may pay any amount owed or transfer or deposit any item of property held by it to or with the court having jurisdiction of the probate proceedings relating to the decedent's estate or, if no proceedings have been commenced, to or with the court having jurisdiction of probate proceedings relating to decedents' estates located in the county of the decedent's residence. The court shall hold the funds or item of property and, upon its determination under this section, shall order disbursement or transfer in accordance with the determination. Payments, transfers, or deposits made to or with the court discharge the payor or other third party from all claims for the value of amounts paid to or items of property transferred to or deposited with the court.

(h)   [Protection of Bona Fide Purchasers; Personal Liability of Recipient.]

(1)   A person who purchases property from a former spouse, relative of a former spouse, or any other person for value and without notice, or who receives from a former spouse, relative of a former spouse, or any other person a payment or other item of property in partial or full

satisfaction of a legally enforceable obligation, is neither obligated under this section to return the payment, item of property, or benefit nor is liable under this section for the amount of the payment or the value of the item of property or benefit. But a former spouse, relative of a former spouse, or other person who, not for value, received a payment, item of property, or any other benefit to which that person is not entitled under this section is obligated to return the payment, item of property, or benefit, or is personally liable for the amount of the payment or the value of the item of property or benefit, to the person who is entitled to it under this section.

(2) If this section or any part of this section is preempted by federal law with respect to a payment, an item of property, or any other benefit covered by this section, a former spouse, relative of the former spouse, or any other person who, not for value, received a payment, item of property, or any other benefit to which that person is not entitled under this section is obligated to return that payment, item of property, or benefit, or is personally liable for the amount of the payment or the value of the item of property or benefit, to the person who would have been entitled to it were this section or part of this section not preempted.

Comment

Purpose and Scope of Revision. * * * The revisions expand the section to cover "will substitutes" such as revocable inter-vivos trusts, life-insurance and retirement-plan beneficiary designations, transfer-on-death accounts, and other revocable dispositions to the former spouse that the divorced individual established before the divorce (or annulment). As revised, this section also effects a severance of the interests of the former spouses in property that they held at the time of the divorce (or annulment) as joint tenants with the right of survivorship; their co-ownership interests become tenancies in common. * * *

Revoking Benefits of the Former Spouse's Relatives. In several cases, including Clymer v. Mayo, 473 N.E.2d 1084 (Mass. 1985), and Estate of Coffed, 387 N.E.2d 1209 (N.Y. 1979), the result of treating the former spouse as predeceasing the testator was that a gift in the governing instrument was triggered in favor of relatives of the former spouse who, after the divorce, were no longer relatives of the testator. In the Massachusetts case, the former spouse's nieces and nephews ended up with an interest in the property. In the New York case, the winners included the former spouse's child by a prior marriage. * * * Given that, during divorce process or in the aftermath of the divorce, the former spouse's relatives are likely to side with the former spouse, breaking down or weakening any former ties that may previously have developed between the transferor and the former spouse's relatives, seldom would the transferor have favored such a result. This section, therefore, also revokes these gifts. * * *

Federal Preemption of State Law. The Employee Retirement Income Security Act of 1974 (ERISA) federalizes pension and employee benefit law. Section 514(a) of ERISA, 29 U.S.C. § 1144(a), provides that the provisions of Titles I and IV of ERISA "shall supersede any and all State laws insofar as they may now or hereafter relate to any employee benefit plan" governed by ERISA.

ERISA's preemption clause is extraordinarily broad. ERISA Section 514(a) does not merely preempt state laws that conflict with specific provisions in ERISA. Rather, it preempts "any and all State laws" insofar as they "relate to" any ERISA-governed employee benefit plan.

A complex body of case law has arisen concerning the question of whether to apply ERISA Section 514(a) to preempt state law in circumstances in which ERISA supplies no substantive regulation. For example, until 1984, ERISA contained no authorization for the enforcement of state domestic relations decrees against pension accounts, but the federal courts were virtually unanimous in refusing to apply ERISA preemption against such state decrees. See, e.g., American Telephone & Telegraph Co. v. Merry, 592 F.2d 118 (2d Cir. 1979). The Retirement Equity Act of 1984 amended ERISA to add Sections 206(d)(3) and 514(b)(7), confirming the judicially created exception for state domestic relations decrees.

The federal courts have been less certain about whether to defer to state probate law. In Board of Trustees of Western Conference of Teamsters Pension Trust Fund v. H.F. Johnson, Inc., 830 F.2d 1009 (9th Cir. 1987), the court held that ERISA preempted the Montana nonclaim statute (which is Section 3–803 of the Uniform Probate Code). On the other hand, in Mendez-Bellido v. Board of Trustees, 709 F. Supp. 329 (E.D.N.Y. 1989), the court applied the New York "slayer-rule" against an ERISA preemption claim, reasoning that "state laws prohibiting murderers from receiving death benefits are relatively uniform [and therefore] there is little threat of creating a 'patchwork scheme of regulations' " that ERISA sought to avoid. * * *

It is to be hoped that the federal courts will show sensitivity to the primary role of state law in the field of probate and nonprobate transfers. To the extent that the federal courts think themselves unable to craft exceptions to ERISA's preemption language, it is open to them to apply state law concepts as federal common law. Because the Uniform Probate Code contemplates multistate applicability, it is well suited to be the model for federal common law absorption. * * *

Another avenue of reconciliation between ERISA preemption and the primacy of state law in this field is envisioned in subsection (h)(2) of this section. It imposes a personal liability for pension payments that pass to a former spouse or relative of a former spouse. This provision respects ERISA's concern that federal law govern the administration of the plan, while still preventing unjust enrichment that would result if an unintended beneficiary were to receive the pension benefits. Federal law has no interest in working a broader disruption of state probate and nonprobate transfer law than is required in the interest of smooth administration of pension and employee benefit plans.

Regrettably, the U.S. Supreme Court decided in Hillman v. Maretta, 133 S.Ct. 1943 (2013), that a Virginia statute essentially equivalent to subsection (h)(2) of this section was pre-empted by the federal law known as FEGLIA (the Federal Employees' Group Life Insurance Act of 1954) * * * . The Court's decision in *Hillman* has many unfortunate consequences. First, the decision frustrates the dominant purpose of wealth transfer law, which is to implement the transferor's intention. The result in *Hillman*, that the decedent's ex-spouse remained entitled to the proceeds of the decedent's life insurance policy purchased through a program established by FEGLIA, frustrates the decedent's intention. Second, the *Hillman* decision ignores the decades-long trend of unifying the law governing probate and nonprobate transfers. The revocation-on-divorce rule has long been a part of probate law (see, e.g., pre-1990 Section 2–508). In 1990, this section extended the rule of revocation on divorce to nonprobate transfers. Third, the decision in *Hillman* fosters a division between state- and federally-regulated nonprobate mechanisms. If the decedent in *Hillman* had purchased a life insurance policy individually, rather than through the FEGLIA program, the policy would have been governed by the Virginia counterpart of this section. * * *

Section 2–805. Reformation to Correct Mistakes.

The court may reform the terms of a governing instrument, even if unambiguous, to conform the terms to the transferor's intention if it is proved by clear and convincing evidence what the transferor's intention was and that the terms of the governing instrument were affected by a mistake of fact or law, whether in expression or inducement.

Section 2–806. Modification to Achieve Transferor's Tax Objectives.

To achieve the transferor's tax objectives, the court may modify the terms of a governing instrument in a manner that is not contrary to the transferor's probable intention. The court may provide that the modification has retroactive effect.

PART 9

STATUTORY RULE AGAINST PERPETUITIES; HONORARY TRUSTS

SUBPART 1. UNIFORM STATUTORY RULE AGAINST PERPETUITIES (1986/1990)

[The Uniform Statutory Rule Against Perpetuities (1986/1990)
is reproduced elsewhere in this volume.]

SUBPART 2. HONORARY TRUSTS

[Section 2-907. Honorary Trusts; Trusts for Pets.

(a) [Honorary Trust.] Subject to subsection (c), if (i) a trust is for a specific lawful noncharitable purpose or for lawful noncharitable purposes to be selected by the trustee and (ii) there is no definite or definitely ascertainable beneficiary designated, the trust may be performed by the trustee for [21] years but no longer, whether or not the terms of the trust contemplate a longer duration.

(b) [Trust for Pets.] Subject to this subsection and subsection (c), a trust for the care of a designated domestic or pet animal is valid. The trust terminates when no living animal is covered by the trust. A governing instrument must be liberally construed to bring the transfer within this subsection, to presume against the merely precatory or honorary nature of the disposition, and to carry out the general intent of the transferor. Extrinsic evidence is admissible in determining the transferor's intent.

(c) [Additional Provisions Applicable to Honorary Trusts and Trusts for Pets.] In addition to the provisions of subsection (a) or (b), a trust covered by either of those subsections is subject to the following provisions:

(1) Except as expressly provided otherwise in the trust instrument, no portion of the principal or income may be converted to the use of the trustee or to any use other than for the trust's purposes or for the benefit of a covered animal.

(2) Upon termination, the trustee shall transfer the unexpended trust property in the following order:

(A) as directed in the trust instrument;

(B) if the trust was created in a nonresiduary clause in the transferor's will or in a codicil to the transferor's will, under the residuary clause in the transferor's will; and

(C) if no taker is produced by the application of subparagraph (A) or (B), to the transferor's heirs under Section 2-711.

(3) For the purposes of Section 2-707, the residuary clause is treated as creating a future interest under the terms of a trust.

(4) The intended use of the principal or income can be enforced by an individual designated for that purpose in the trust instrument or, if none, by an individual appointed by a court upon application to it by an individual.

(5) Except as ordered by the court or required by the trust instrument, no filing, report, registration, periodic accounting, separate maintenance of funds, appointment, or fee is required by reason of the existence of the fiduciary relationship of the trustee.

(6) A court may reduce the amount of the property transferred, if it determines that that amount substantially exceeds the amount required for the intended use. The amount of the reduction, if any, passes as unexpended trust property under subsection (c)(2).

(7) If no trustee is designated or no designated trustee is willing or able to serve, a court shall name a trustee. A court may order the transfer of the property to another trustee, if required to assure that the intended use is carried out and if no successor trustee is designated in the trust instrument or if no designated successor trustee agrees to serve or is able to serve. A court may also make such other orders and determinations as shall be advisable to carry out the intent of the transferor and the purpose of this section.]

PART 10

UNIFORM INTERNATIONAL WILLS ACT (1977)

[omitted]

PART 11

UNIFORM DISCLAIMER OF PROPERTY INTERESTS ACT (1999/2006)

[The Uniform Disclaimer of Property Interests Act (1999/2006)
is reproduced elsewhere in this volume.]

ARTICLE III
PROBATE OF WILLS AND ADMINISTRATION

PART 1
GENERAL PROVISIONS

PART 2
VENUE FOR PROBATE AND ADMINISTRATION; PRIORITY TO ADMINISTER; DEMAND FOR NOTICE

PART 3
INFORMAL PROBATE AND APPOINTMENT PROCEEDINGS; SUCCESSION WITHOUT ADMINISTRATION

SUBPART 1. INFORMAL PROBATE AND APPOINTMENT PROCEEDINGS

SUBPART 2. SUCCESSION WITHOUT ADMINISTRATION

PART 4
FORMAL TESTACY AND APPOINTMENT PROCEEDINGS

PART 5
SUPERVISED ADMINISTRATION

PART 6
PERSONAL REPRESENTATIVE; APPOINTMENT, CONTROL
AND TERMINATION OF AUTHORITY

PART 7
DUTIES AND POWERS OF PERSONAL REPRESENTATIVES

PART 8
CREDITORS' CLAIMS

PART 9
SPECIAL PROVISIONS RELATING TO DISTRIBUTION

PART 9A
UNIFORM ESTATE TAX APPORTIONMENT ACT (2003)

[The Uniform Estate Tax Apportionment Act (2003)
is reproduced elsewhere in this volume.]

PART 10
CLOSING ESTATES

PART 11
COMPROMISE OF CONTROVERSIES

PART 12
COLLECTION OF PERSONAL PROPERTY BY AFFIDAVIT AND SUMMARY ADMINISTRATION PROCEDURE FOR SMALL ESTATES

PART 1

GENERAL PROVISIONS

Section 3–101. Devolution of Estate at Death; Restrictions.

The power of a person to leave property by will, and the rights of creditors, devisees, and heirs to his property are subject to the restrictions and limitations contained in this [code] to facilitate the prompt settlement of estates. Upon the death of a person, his real and personal property devolves to the persons to whom it is devised by his last will or to those indicated as substitutes for them in cases involving lapse, renunciation, or other circumstances affecting the devolution of testate estate, or in the absence of testamentary disposition, to his heirs, or to those indicated as substitutes for them in cases involving renunciation or other circumstances affecting devolution of intestate estates, subject to homestead allowance, exempt property and family allowance, to rights of creditors, elective share of the surviving spouse, and to administration.

ALTERNATIVE SECTION FOR COMMUNITY PROPERTY STATES

[Section 3–101A. Devolution of Estate at Death; Restrictions.

The power of a person to leave property by will, and the rights of creditors, devisees, and heirs to the decedent's property are subject to the restrictions and limitations contained in this [code] to facilitate the prompt settlement of estates. Upon death, the decedent's separate property devolves to the persons to whom it is devised by the decedent's will, or to those indicated as substitutes for them in cases involving lapse, renunciation or other circumstances affecting the devolution of testate estates, or in the absence of testamentary disposition to the decedent's heirs, or to those indicated as substitutes for them in cases involving renunciation or other circumstances affecting the devolution of intestate estates. The decedent's share of community property devolves to the persons to whom it is devised by the decedent's will, or in the absence of testamentary disposition, to the decedent's heirs, but the community property which is under the management and control of the decedent is subject to the decedent's debts and administration, and that portion of the community property which is not under the management and control of the decedent but which is necessary to carry out the provisions of the decedent's will is subject to administration; but the devolution of all the above described property is subject to rights to homestead allowance, exempt property and family allowances, to renunciation, to rights of creditors, [elective share of the surviving spouse] and to administration.]

Section 3–102. Necessity of Order of Probate for Will.

Except as provided in Section 3–1201, to be effective to prove the transfer of any property or to nominate an executor, a will must be declared to be valid by an order of informal probate by the Registrar, or an adjudication of probate by the court.

Section 3–103. Necessity of Appointment for Administration.

Except as otherwise provided in [Article] IV, to acquire the powers and undertake the duties and liabilities of a personal representative of a decedent, a person must be appointed by order of the court or Registrar, qualify and be issued letters. Administration of an estate is commenced by the issuance of letters.

Section 3–104. Claims Against Decedent; Necessity of Administration.

No proceeding to enforce a claim against the estate of a decedent or his successors may be revived or commenced before the appointment of a personal representative. After the appointment and until distribution, all proceedings and actions to enforce a claim against the estate are governed by the procedure prescribed by this [article]. After distribution a creditor whose claim has not been barred may recover from the distributees as provided in Section 3–1004 or from a former personal representative individually liable as provided in Section 3–1005. This section has no application to a proceeding by a secured creditor of the decedent to enforce his right to his security except as to any deficiency judgment which might be sought therein.

Section 3–105. Proceedings Affecting Devolution and Administration; Jurisdiction of Subject Matter.

Persons interested in decedents' estates may apply to the Registrar for determination in the informal proceedings provided in this [article], and may petition the court for orders in formal proceedings within the court's jurisdiction including but not limited to those described in this [article]. The court has exclusive jurisdiction of formal proceedings to determine how decedents' estates subject to the laws of this state are to be administered, expended and distributed. The court has concurrent jurisdiction of any other action or proceeding concerning a succession or to which an estate, through a personal representative, may be a party, including actions to determine title to property alleged to belong to the estate, and of any action or proceeding in which property distributed by a personal representative or its value is sought to be subjected to rights of creditors or successors of the decedent.

Section 3–106. Proceedings Within the Exclusive Jurisdiction of Court; Service; Jurisdiction Over Persons.

In proceedings within the exclusive jurisdiction of the court where notice is required by this [code] or by rule, and in proceedings to construe probated wills or determine heirs which concern estates that have not been and cannot now be open for administration, interested persons may be bound by the orders of the court in respect to property in or subject to the laws of this state by notice in conformity with Section 1–401. An order is binding as to all who are given notice of the proceeding though less than all interested persons are notified.

Section 3–107. Scope of Proceedings; Proceedings Independent; Exception.

Unless supervised administration as described in [Part 5] is involved,

(1) each proceeding before the court or Registrar is independent of any other proceeding involving the same estate;

(2) petitions for formal orders of the court may combine various requests for relief in a single proceeding if the orders sought may be finally granted without delay. Except as required for proceedings which are particularly described by other sections of this [article], no petition is defective because it fails to embrace all matters which might then be the subject of a final order;

(3) proceedings for probate of wills or adjudications of no will may be combined with proceedings for appointment of personal representatives; and

(4) a proceeding for appointment of a personal representative is concluded by an order making or declining the appointment.

Section 3–108. Probate, Testacy and Appointment Proceedings; Ultimate Time Limit.

(a) No informal probate or appointment proceeding or formal testacy or appointment proceeding, other than a proceeding to probate a will previously probated at the testator's domicile and appointment proceedings relating to an estate in which there has been a prior appointment, may be commenced more than three years after the decedent's death, except:

(1) if a previous proceeding was dismissed because of doubt about the fact of the decedent's death, appropriate probate, appointment, or testacy proceedings may be maintained at any time thereafter upon a finding that the decedent's death occurred before the initiation of the previous proceeding and the applicant or petitioner has not delayed unduly in initiating the subsequent proceeding;

(2) appropriate probate, appointment, or testacy proceedings may be maintained in relation to the estate of an absent, disappeared or missing person for whose estate a conservator

has been appointed, at any time within three years after the conservator becomes able to establish the death of the protected person;

(3) a proceeding to contest an informally probated will and to secure appointment of the person with legal priority for appointment in the event the contest is successful, may be commenced within the later of twelve months from the informal probate or three years from the decedent's death;

(4) an informal appointment or a formal testacy or appointment proceeding may be commenced thereafter if no proceedings concerning the succession or estate administration has occurred within the three year period after the decedent's death, but the personal representative has no right to possess estate assets as provided in Section 3–709 beyond that necessary to confirm title thereto in the successors to the estate and claims other than expenses of administration may not be presented against the estate; and

(5) a formal testacy proceeding may be commenced at any time after three years from the decedent's death for the purpose of establishing an instrument to direct or control the ownership of property passing or distributable after the decedent's death from one other than the decedent when the property is to be appointed by the terms of the decedent's will or is to pass or be distributed as a part of the decedent's estate or its transfer is otherwise to be controlled by the terms of the decedent's will.

(b) These limitations do not apply to proceedings to construe probated wills or determine heirs of an intestate.

(c) In cases under subsection (a)(1) or (2), the date on which a testacy or appointment proceeding is properly commenced shall be deemed to be the date of the decedent's death for purposes of other limitations provisions of this [code] which relate to the date of death.

Section 3–109. Statutes of Limitation on Decedent's Cause of Action.

No statute of limitation running on a cause of action belonging to a decedent which had not been barred as of the date of his death, shall apply to bar a cause of action surviving the decedent's death sooner than four months after death. A cause of action which, but for this section, would have been barred less than four months after death, is barred after four months unless tolled.

PART 2

VENUE FOR PROBATE AND ADMINISTRATION; PRIORITY TO ADMINISTER; DEMAND FOR NOTICE

Section 3–201. Venue for First and Subsequent Estate Proceedings; Location of Property.

(a) Venue for the first informal or formal testacy or appointment proceedings after a decedent's death is:

(1) in the [county] where the decedent had his domicile at the time of his death; or

(2) if the decedent was not domiciled in this state, in any [county] where property of the decedent was located at the time of his death.

(b) Venue for all subsequent proceedings within the exclusive jurisdiction of the court is in the place where the initial proceeding occurred, unless the initial proceeding has been transferred as provided in Section 1–303 or subsection (c).

(c) If the first proceeding was informal, on application of an interested person and after notice to the proponent in the first proceeding, the court, upon finding that venue is elsewhere, may transfer the proceeding and the file to the other court.

(d) For the purpose of aiding determinations concerning location of assets which may be relevant in cases involving non-domiciliaries, a debt, other than one evidenced by investment or commercial paper or other instrument in favor of a non-domiciliary is located where the debtor resides or, if the debtor is a person other than an individual, at the place where it has its principal office. Commercial paper, investment paper and other instruments are located where the instrument is. An interest in property held in trust is located where the trustee may be sued.

Section 3-202. Appointment or Testacy Proceedings; Conflicting Claim of Domicile in Another State.

If conflicting claims as to the domicile of a decedent are made in a formal testacy or appointment proceeding commenced in this state, and in a testacy or appointment proceeding after notice pending at the same time in another state, the court of this state must stay, dismiss, or permit suitable amendment in, the proceeding here unless it is determined that the local proceeding was commenced before the proceeding elsewhere. The determination of domicile in the proceeding first commenced must be accepted as determinative in the proceeding in this state.

Section 3-203. Priority Among Persons Seeking Appointment as Personal Representative.

(a) Whether the proceedings are formal or informal, persons who are not disqualified have priority for appointment in the following order:

(1) the person with priority as determined by a probated will including a person nominated by a power conferred in a will;

(2) the surviving spouse of the decedent who is a devisee of the decedent;

(3) other devisees of the decedent;

(4) the surviving spouse of the decedent;

(5) other heirs of the decedent;

(6) 45 days after the death of the decedent, any creditor.

(b) An objection to an appointment can be made only in formal proceedings. In case of objection the priorities stated in subsection (a) apply except that

(1) if the estate appears to be more than adequate to meet exemptions and costs of administration but inadequate to discharge anticipated unsecured claims, the court, on petition of creditors, may appoint any qualified person;

(2) in case of objection to appointment of a person other than one whose priority is determined by will by an heir or devisee appearing to have a substantial interest in the estate, the court may appoint a person who is acceptable to heirs and devisees whose interests in the estate appear to be worth in total more than half of the probable distributable value, or, in default of this accord any suitable person.

(c) A person entitled to letters under paragraphs (2) through (5) of subsection (a) above, and a person aged [18] and over who would be entitled to letters but for his age, may nominate a qualified person to act as personal representative. Any person aged [18] and over may renounce his right to nominate or to an appointment by appropriate writing filed with the court. When two or more persons share a priority, those of them who do not renounce must concur in nominating another to act for them, or in applying for appointment.

(d) Conservators of the estates of protected persons, or if there is no conservator, any guardian except a guardian ad litem of a minor or incapacitated person, may exercise the same right to nominate, to object to another's appointment, or to participate in determining the preference of a majority in interest of the heirs and devisees that the protected person or ward would have if qualified for appointment.

(e) Appointment of one who does not have priority, including priority resulting from renunciation or nomination determined pursuant to this section, may be made only in formal proceedings. Before appointing one without priority, the court must determine that those having priority, although given notice of the proceedings, have failed to request appointment or to nominate another for appointment, and that administration is necessary.

(f) No person is qualified to serve as a personal representative who is:

(1) under the age of [21];

(2) a person whom the court finds unsuitable in formal proceedings.

(g) A personal representative appointed by a court of the decedent's domicile has priority over all other persons except where the decedent's will nominates different persons to be personal representative in this state and in the state of domicile. The domiciliary personal representative may nominate another, who shall have the same priority as the domiciliary personal representative.

(h) This section governs priority for appointment of a successor personal representative but does not apply to the selection of a special administrator.

Section 3–204. Demand for Notice of Order or Filing Concerning Decedent's Estate.

Any person desiring notice of any order or filing pertaining to a decedent's estate in which he has a financial or property interest, may file a demand for notice with the court at any time after the death of the decedent stating the name of the decedent, the nature of his interest in the estate, and the demandant's address or that of his attorney. The clerk shall mail a copy of the demand to the personal representative if one has been appointed. After filing of a demand, no order or filing to which the demand relates shall be made or accepted without notice as prescribed in Section 1–401 to the demandant or his attorney. The validity of an order which is issued or filing which is accepted without compliance with this requirement shall not be affected by the error, but the petitioner receiving the order or the person making the filing may be liable for any damage caused by the absence of notice. The requirement of notice arising from a demand under this provision may be waived in writing by the demandant and shall cease upon the termination of his interest in the estate.

PART 3

INFORMAL PROBATE AND APPOINTMENT PROCEEDINGS; SUCCESSION WITHOUT ADMINISTRATION

SUBPART 1. INFORMAL PROBATE AND APPOINTMENT PROCEEDINGS

Section 3–301. Informal Probate or Appointment Proceedings; Application; Contents.

(a) Applications for informal probate or informal appointment shall be directed to the Registrar, and verified by the applicant to be accurate and complete to the best of his knowledge and belief as to the following information:

(1) Every application for informal probate of a will or for informal appointment of a personal representative, other than a special or successor representative, shall contain the following:

(A) a statement of the interest of the applicant;

(B) the name, and date of death of the decedent, his age, and the county and state of his domicile at the time of death, and the names and addresses of the spouse, children, heirs and devisees and the ages of any who are minors so far as known or ascertainable with reasonable diligence by the applicant;

(C) if the decedent was not domiciled in the state at the time of his death, a statement showing venue;

(D) a statement identifying and indicating the address of any personal representative of the decedent appointed in this state or elsewhere whose appointment has not been terminated;

(E) a statement indicating whether the applicant has received a demand for notice, or is aware of any demand for notice of any probate or appointment proceeding concerning the decedent that may have been filed in this state or elsewhere; and

(F) that the time limit for informal probate or appointment as provided in this [article] has not expired either because three years or less have passed since the decedent's death, or, if more than three years from death have passed, circumstances as described by Section 3–108 authorizing tardy probate or appointment have occurred.

(2) An application for informal probate of a will shall state the following in addition to the statements required by paragraph (1):

(A) that the original of the decedent's last will is in the possession of the court, or accompanies the application, or that an authenticated copy of a will probated in another jurisdiction accompanies the application;

(B) that the applicant, to the best of his knowledge, believes the will to have been validly executed;

(C) that after the exercise of reasonable diligence, the applicant is unaware of any instrument revoking the will, and that the applicant believes that the instrument which is the subject of the application is the decedent's last will.

(3) An application for informal appointment of a personal representative to administer an estate under a will shall describe the will by date of execution and state the time and place of probate or the pending application or petition for probate. The application for appointment shall adopt the statements in the application or petition for probate and state the name, address and priority for appointment of the person whose appointment is sought.

(4) An application for informal appointment of an administrator in intestacy shall state in addition to the statements required by paragraph (1):

(A) that after the exercise of reasonable diligence, the applicant is unaware of any unrevoked testamentary instrument relating to property having a situs in this state under Section 1–301, or, a statement why any such instrument of which he may be aware is not being probated;

(B) the priority of the person whose appointment is sought and the names of any other persons having a prior or equal right to the appointment under Section 3–203.

(5) An application for appointment of a personal representative to succeed a personal representative appointed under a different testacy status shall refer to the order in the most recent testacy proceeding, state the name and address of the person whose appointment is sought and of the person whose appointment will be terminated if the application is granted, and describe the priority of the applicant.

(6) An application for appointment of a personal representative to succeed a personal representative who has tendered a resignation as provided in 3–610(c), or whose appointment has been terminated by death or removal, shall adopt the statements in the application or petition which led to the appointment of the person being succeeded except as specifically changed or corrected, state the name and address of the person who seeks appointment as successor, and describe the priority of the applicant.

(b) By verifying an application for informal probate, or informal appointment, the applicant submits personally to the jurisdiction of the court in any proceeding for relief from fraud relating to the application, or for perjury, that may be instituted against him.

Section 3–302. Informal Probate; Duty of Registrar; Effect of Informal Probate.

Upon receipt of an application requesting informal probate of a will, the Registrar, upon making the findings required by Section 3–303 shall issue a written statement of informal probate if at least 120 hours have elapsed since the decedent's death. Informal probate is conclusive as to all persons until superseded by an order in a formal testacy proceeding. No defect in the application or procedure relating thereto which leads to informal probate of a will renders the probate void.

Section 3–303. Informal Probate; Proof and Findings Required.

(a)   In an informal proceeding for original probate of a will, the Registrar shall determine whether:

(1)   the application is complete;

(2)   the applicant has made oath or affirmation that the statements contained in the application are true to the best of his knowledge and belief;

(3)   the applicant appears from the application to be an interested person as defined in Section 1–201(23);

(4)   on the basis of the statements in the application, venue is proper;

(5)   an original, duly executed and apparently unrevoked will is in the Registrar's possession;

(6)   any notice required by Section 3–204 has been given and that the application is not within Section 3–304; and

(7)   it appears from the application that the time limit for original probate has not expired.

(b)   The application shall be denied if it indicates that a personal representative has been appointed in another [county] of this state or except as provided in subsection (d) below, if it appears that this or another will of the decedent has been the subject of a previous probate order.

(c)   A will which appears to have the required signatures and which contains an attestation clause showing that requirements of execution under Section 2–502, 2–503 or 2–506 have been met shall be probated without further proof. In other cases, the Registrar may assume execution if the will appears to have been properly executed, or he may accept a sworn statement or affidavit of any person having knowledge of the circumstances of execution, whether or not the person was a witness to the will.

(d)   Informal probate of a will which has been previously probated elsewhere may be granted at any time upon written application by any interested person, together with deposit of an authenticated copy of the will and of the statement probating it from the office or court where it was first probated.

(e)   A will from a place which does not provide for probate of a will after death and which is not eligible for probate under subsection (a) above, may be probated in this state upon receipt by the Registrar of a duly authenticated copy of the will and a duly authenticated certificate of its legal custodian that the copy filed is a true copy and that the will has become operative under the law of the other place.

Section 3–304. Informal Probate; Unavailable in Certain Cases.

Applications for informal probate which relate to one or more of a known series of testamentary instruments (other than a will and one or more codicils thereto), the latest of which does not expressly revoke the earlier, shall be declined.

Section 3–305. Informal Probate; Registrar Not Satisfied.

If the Registrar is not satisfied that a will is entitled to be probated in informal proceedings because of failure to meet the requirements of Sections 3–303 and 3–304 or any other reason, he may decline the application. A declination of informal probate is not an adjudication and does not preclude formal probate proceedings.

Section 3–306. Informal Probate; Notice Requirements.

[*]   The moving party must give notice as described by Section 1–401 of his application for informal probate to any person demanding it pursuant to Section 3–204, and to any personal representative of the decedent whose appointment has not been terminated. No other notice of informal probate is required.

[(b)   If an informal probate is granted, within 30 days thereafter the applicant shall give written information of the probate to the heirs and devisees. The information shall include the name and address of the applicant, the name and location of the court granting the informal probate, and the date of the probate. The information shall be delivered or sent by ordinary mail to each of the heirs and devisees whose address is reasonably available to the applicant. No duty to give information is incurred if a personal representative is appointed who is required to give the written information required by Section 3–705. An applicant's failure to give information as required by this section is a breach of his duty to the heirs and devisees but does not affect the validity of the probate.]

Section 3–307. Informal Appointment Proceedings; Delay in Order; Duty of Registrar; Effect of Appointment.

(a)   Upon receipt of an application for informal appointment of a personal representative other than a special administrator as provided in Section 3–614, if at least 120 hours have elapsed since the decedent's death, the Registrar, after making the findings required by Section 3–308, shall appoint the applicant subject to qualification and acceptance; provided, that if the decedent was a non-resident, the Registrar shall delay the order of appointment until 30 days have elapsed since death unless the personal representative appointed at the decedent's domicile is the applicant, or unless the decedent's will directs that his estate be subject to the laws of this state.

(b)   The status of personal representative and the powers and duties pertaining to the office are fully established by informal appointment. An appointment, and the office of personal representative created thereby, is subject to termination as provided in Sections 3–608 through 3–612, but is not subject to retroactive vacation.

Section 3–308. Informal Appointment Proceedings; Proof and Findings Required.

(a)   In informal appointment proceedings, the Registrar must determine whether:

(1)   the application for informal appointment of a personal representative is complete;

(2)   the applicant has made oath or affirmation that the statements contained in the application are true to the best of his knowledge and belief;

(3)   the applicant appears from the application to be an interested person as defined in Section 1–201(23);

(4)   on the basis of the statements in the application, venue is proper;

(5)   any will to which the requested appointment relates has been formally or informally probated; but this requirement does not apply to the appointment of a special administrator;

(6)   any notice required by Section 3–204 has been given;

(7)   from the statements in the application, the person whose appointment is sought has priority entitling him to the appointment.

(b)   Unless Section 3–612 controls, the application must be denied if it indicates that a personal representative who has not filed a written statement of resignation as provided in Section 3–610(c) has been appointed in this or another [county] of this state, that (unless the applicant is the domiciliary

---

[*] This paragraph becomes subsection (a) if optional subsection (b) is accepted.

personal representative or his nominee) the decedent was not domiciled in this state and that a personal representative whose appointment has not been terminated has been appointed by a court in the state of domicile, or that other requirements of this section have not been met.

Section 3–309. Informal Appointment Proceedings; Registrar Not Satisfied.

If the Registrar is not satisfied that a requested informal appointment of a personal representative should be made because of failure to meet the requirements of Sections 3–307 and 3–308, or for any other reason, he may decline the application. A declination of informal appointment is not an adjudication and does not preclude appointment in formal proceedings.

Section 3–310. Informal Appointment Proceedings; Notice Requirements.

The moving party must give notice as described by Section 1–401 of his intention to seek an appointment informally:

(1) to any person demanding it pursuant to Section 3–204; and

(2) to any person having a prior or equal right to appointment not waived in writing and filed with the court. No other notice of an informal appointment proceeding is required.

Section 3–311. Informal Appointment Unavailable in Certain Cases.

If an application for informal appointment indicates the existence of a possible unrevoked testamentary instrument which may relate to property subject to the laws of this state, and which is not filed for probate in this court, the Registrar shall decline the application.

SUBPART 2. SUCCESSION WITHOUT ADMINISTRATION

Section 3–312. Universal Succession; In General.

The heirs of an intestate or the residuary devisees under a will, excluding minors and incapacitated, protected, or unascertained persons, may become universal successors to the decedent's estate by assuming personal liability for (i) taxes, (ii) debts of the decedent, (iii) claims against the decedent or the estate, and (iv) distributions due other heirs, devisees, and persons entitled to property of the decedent as provided in Sections 3–313 through 3–322.

Section 3–313. Universal Succession; Application; Contents.

(a) An application to become universal successors by the heirs of an intestate or the residuary devisees under a will must be directed to the Registrar, signed by each applicant, and verified to be accurate and complete to the best of the applicant's knowledge and belief as follows:

(1) An application by heirs of an intestate must contain the statements required by Section 3–301(a)(1) and (4)(A) and state that the applicants constitute all the heirs other than minors and incapacitated, protected, or unascertained persons.

(2) An application by residuary devisees under a will must be combined with a petition for informal probate if the will has not been admitted to probate in this state and must contain the statements required by Section 3–301(a)(1) and (2). If the will has been probated in this state, an application by residuary devisees must contain the statements required by Section 3–301(a)(2)(C). An application by residuary devisees must state that the applicants constitute the residuary devisees of the decedent other than any minors and incapacitated, protected, or unascertained persons. If the estate is partially intestate, all of the heirs other than minors and incapacitated, protected, or unascertained persons must join as applicants.

(b) The application must state whether letters of administration are outstanding, whether a petition for appointment of a personal representative of the decedent is pending in any court of this state, and that the applicants waive their right to seek appointment of a personal representative.

(c) The application may describe in general terms the assets of the estate and must state that the applicants accept responsibility for the estate and assume personal liability for (i) taxes, (ii) debts of the decedent, (iii) claims against the decedent or the estate and (iv) distributions due other heirs, devisees, and persons entitled to property of the decedent as provided in Sections 3–316 through 3–322.

Section 3–314. Universal Succession; Proof and Findings Required.

(a) The Registrar shall grant the application if:

(1) the application is complete in accordance with Section 3–313;

(2) all necessary persons have joined and have verified that the statements contained therein are true, to the best knowledge and belief of each;

(3) venue is proper;

(4) any notice required by Section 3–204 has been given or waived;

(5) the time limit for original probate or appointment proceedings has not expired and the applicants claim under a will;

(6) the application requests informal probate of a will, the application and findings conform with Sections 3–301(a)(2) and 3–303(a), (c), (d), and (e) so the will is admitted to probate; and

(7) none of the applicants is a minor or an incapacitated or protected person.

(b) The Registrar shall deny the application if letters of administration are outstanding.

(c) Except as provided in Section 3–322, the Registrar shall deny the application if any creditor, heir, or devisee who is qualified by Section 3–605 to demand bond files an objection.

Section 3–315. Universal Succession; Duty of Registrar; Effect of Statement of Universal Succession.

Upon receipt of an application under Section 3–313, if at least 120 hours have elapsed since the decedent's death, the Registrar, upon granting the application, shall issue a written statement of universal succession describing the estate as set forth in the application and stating that the applicants (i) are the universal successors to the assets of the estate as provided in Section 3–312, (ii) have assumed liability for the obligations of the decedent, and (iii) have acquired the powers and liabilities of universal successors. The statement of universal succession is evidence of the universal successors' title to the assets of the estate. Upon its issuance, the powers and liabilities of universal successors provided in Sections 3–316 through 3–322 attach and are assumed by the applicants.

Section 3–316. Universal Succession; Universal Successors' Powers.

Upon the Registrar's issuance of a statement of universal succession:

(1) Universal successors have full power of ownership to deal with the assets of the estate subject to the limitations and liabilities in this [subpart]. The universal successors shall proceed expeditiously to settle and distribute the estate without adjudication but if necessary may invoke the jurisdiction of the court to resolve questions concerning the estate.

(2) Universal successors have the same powers as distributees from a personal representative under Sections 3–908 and 3–909 and third persons with whom they deal are protected as provided in Section 3–910.

(3) For purposes of collecting assets in another state whose law does not provide for universal succession, universal successors have the same standing and power as personal representatives or distributees in this state.

Section 3–317. Universal Succession; Universal Successors' Liability to Creditors, Other Heirs, Devisees and Persons Entitled to Decedent's Property; Liability of Other Persons Entitled to Property.

(a) In the proportions and subject to the limits expressed in Section 3–321, universal successors assume all liabilities of the decedent that were not discharged by reason of death and liability for all taxes, claims against the decedent or the estate, and charges properly incurred after death for the preservation of the estate, to the extent those items, if duly presented, would be valid claims against the decedent's estate.

(b) In the proportions and subject to the limits expressed in Section 3–321, universal successors are personally liable to other heirs, devisees, and persons entitled to property of the decedent for the assets or amounts that would be due those heirs, were the estate administered, but no allowance having priority over devisees may be claimed for attorney's fees or charges for preservation of the estate in excess of reasonable amounts properly incurred.

(c) Universal successors are entitled to their interests in the estate as heirs or devisees subject to priority and abatement pursuant to Section 3–902 and to agreement pursuant to Section 3–912.

(d) Other heirs, devisees, and persons to whom assets have been distributed have the same powers and liabilities as distributees under Sections 3–908, 3–909, and 3–910.

(e) Absent breach of fiduciary obligations or express undertaking, a fiduciary's liability is limited to the assets received by the fiduciary.

Section 3–318. Universal Succession; Universal Successors' Submission to Jurisdiction; When Heirs or Devisees May Not Seek Administration.

(a) Upon issuance of the statement of universal succession, the universal successors become subject to the personal jurisdiction of the courts of this state in any proceeding that may be instituted relating to the estate or to any liability assumed by them.

(b) Any heir or devisee who voluntarily joins in an application under Section 3–313 may not subsequently seek appointment of a personal representative.

Section 3–319. Universal Succession; Duty of Universal Successors; Information to Heirs and Devisees.

Not later than 30 days after issuance of the statement of universal succession, each universal successor shall inform the heirs and devisees who did not join in the application of the succession without administration. The information must be delivered or be sent by ordinary mail to each of the heirs and devisees whose address is reasonably available to the universal successors. The information must include the names and addresses of the universal successors, indicate that it is being sent to persons who have or may have some interest in the estate, and describe the court where the application and statement of universal succession has been filed. The failure of a universal successor to give this information is a breach of duty to the persons concerned but does not affect the validity of the approval of succession without administration or the powers or liabilities of the universal successors. A universal successor may inform other persons of the succession without administration by delivery or by ordinary first class mail.

Section 3–320. Universal Succession; Universal Successors' Liability for Restitution to Estate.

If a personal representative is subsequently appointed, universal successors are personally liable for restitution of any property of the estate to which they are not entitled as heirs or devisees of the decedent and their liability is the same as a distributee under Section 3–909, subject to the provisions of Sections 3–317 and 3–321 and the limitations of Section 3–1006.

Section 3-321. Universal Succession; Liability of Universal Successors for Claims, Expenses, Intestate Shares and Devises.

The liability of universal successors is subject to any defenses that would have been available to the decedent. Other than liability arising from fraud, conversion, or other wrongful conduct of a universal successor, the personal liability of each universal successor to any creditor, claimant, other heir, devisee, or person entitled to decedent's property may not exceed the proportion of the claim that the universal successor's share bears to the share of all heirs and residuary devisees.

Section 3-322. Universal Succession; Remedies of Creditors, Other Heirs, Devisees or Persons Entitled to Decedent's Property.

In addition to remedies otherwise provided by law, any creditor, heir, devisee, or person entitled to decedent's property qualified under Section 3–605, may demand bond of universal successors. If the demand for bond precedes the granting of an application for universal succession, it must be treated as an objection under Section 3–314(c) unless it is withdrawn, the claim satisfied, or the applicants post bond in an amount sufficient to protect the demandant. If the demand for bond follows the granting of an application for universal succession, the universal successors, within 10 days after notice of the demand, upon satisfying the claim or posting bond sufficient to protect the demandant, may disqualify the demandant from seeking administration of the estate.

PART 4

FORMAL TESTACY AND APPOINTMENT PROCEEDINGS

Section 3-401. Formal Testacy Proceedings; Nature; When Commenced.

A formal testacy proceeding is litigation to determine whether a decedent left a valid will. A formal testacy proceeding may be commenced by an interested person filing a petition as described in Section 3–402(a) in which he requests that the court, after notice and hearing, enter an order probating a will, or a petition to set aside an informal probate of a will or to prevent informal probate of a will which is the subject of a pending application, or a petition in accordance with Section 3–402(b) for an order that the decedent died intestate.

A petition may seek formal probate of a will without regard to whether the same or a conflicting will has been informally probated. A formal testacy proceeding may, but need not, involve a request for appointment of a personal representative.

During the pendency of a formal testacy proceeding, the Registrar shall not act upon any application for informal probate of any will of the decedent or any application for informal appointment of a personal representative of the decedent.

Unless a petition in a formal testacy proceeding also requests confirmation of the previous informal appointment, a previously appointed personal representative, after receipt of notice of the commencement of a formal probate proceeding, must refrain from exercising his power to make any further distribution of the estate during the pendency of the formal proceeding. A petitioner who seeks the appointment of a different personal representative in a formal proceeding also may request an order restraining the acting personal representative from exercising any of the powers of his office and requesting the appointment of a special administrator. In the absence of a request, or if the request is denied, the commencement of a formal proceeding has no effect on the powers and duties of a previously appointed personal representative other than those relating to distribution.

Section 3-402. Formal Testacy or Appointment Proceedings; Petition; Contents.

(a) Petitions for formal probate of a will, or for adjudication of intestacy with or without request for appointment of a personal representative, must be directed to the court, request a judicial order after notice and hearing and contain further statements as indicated in this section. A petition for formal probate of a will

(1)   requests an order as to the testacy of the decedent in relation to a particular instrument which may or may not have been informally probated and determining the heirs,

(2)   contains the statements required for informal applications as stated in the six subparagraphs under Section 3–301(a)(1), the statements required by subparagraphs (B) and (C) of Section 3–301(a)(2), and

(3)   states whether the original of the last will of the decedent is in the possession of the court or accompanies the petition.

If the original will is neither in the possession of the court nor accompanies the petition and no authenticated copy of a will probated in another jurisdiction accompanies the petition, the petition also must state the contents of the will, and indicate that it is lost, destroyed, or otherwise unavailable.

(b)   A petition for adjudication of intestacy and appointment of an administrator in intestacy must request a judicial finding and order that the decedent left no will and determining the heirs, contain the statements required by paragraphs (1) and (4) of Section 3–301(a) and indicate whether supervised administration is sought. A petition may request an order determining intestacy and heirs without requesting the appointment of an administrator, in which case, the statements required by subparagraph (B) of Section 3–301(a)(4) above may be omitted.

Section 3–403. Formal Testacy Proceedings; Notice of Hearing on Petition.

(a)   Upon commencement of a formal testacy proceeding, the court shall fix a time and place of hearing. Notice shall be given in the manner prescribed by Section 1–401 by the petitioner to the persons herein enumerated and to any additional person who has filed a demand for notice under Section 3–204 of this [code].

Notice shall be given to the following persons: the surviving spouse, children, and other heirs of the decedent, the devisees and executors named in any will that is being, or has been, probated, or offered for informal or formal probate in the [county], or that is known by the petitioner to have been probated, or offered for informal or formal probate elsewhere, and any personal representative of the decedent whose appointment has not been terminated. Notice may be given to other persons. In addition, the petitioner shall give notice by publication to all unknown persons and to all known persons whose addresses are unknown who have any interest in the matters being litigated.

(b)   If it appears by the petition or otherwise that the fact of the death of the alleged decedent may be in doubt, or on the written demand of any interested person, a copy of the notice of the hearing on said petition shall be sent by registered mail to the alleged decedent at his last known address. The court shall direct the petitioner to report the results of, or make and report back concerning, a reasonably diligent search for the alleged decedent in any manner that may seem advisable, including any or all of the following methods:

(1)   by inserting in one or more suitable periodicals a notice requesting information from any person having knowledge of the whereabouts of the alleged decedent;

(2)   by notifying law enforcement officials and public welfare agencies in appropriate locations of the disappearance of the alleged decedent;

(3)   by engaging the services of an investigator.

The costs of any search so directed shall be paid by the petitioner if there is no administration or by the estate of the decedent in case there is administration.

Section 3–404. Formal Testacy Proceedings; Written Objections to Probate.

Any party to a formal proceeding who opposes the probate of a will for any reason shall state in his pleadings his objections to probate of the will.

Section 3-405. Formal Testacy Proceedings; Uncontested Cases; Hearings and Proof.

If a petition in a testacy proceeding is unopposed, the court may order probate or intestacy on the strength of the pleadings if satisfied that the conditions of Section 3-409 have been met, or conduct a hearing in open court and require proof of the matters necessary to support the order sought. If evidence concerning execution of the will is necessary, the affidavit or testimony of one of any attesting witnesses to the instrument is sufficient. If the affidavit or testimony of an attesting witness is not available, execution of the will may be proved by other evidence or affidavit.

Section 3-406. Formal Testacy Proceedings; Contested Cases.

In a contested case in which the proper execution of a will is at issue, the following rules apply:

(1)   If the will is self-proved pursuant to Section 2-504, the will satisfies the requirements for execution without the testimony of any attesting witness, upon filing the will and the acknowledgment and affidavits annexed or attached to it, unless there is evidence of fraud or forgery affecting the acknowledgment or affidavit.

(2)   If the will is notarized pursuant to Section 2-502(a)(3)(B), but not self-proved, there is a rebuttable presumption that the will satisfies the requirements for execution upon filing the will.

(3)   If the will is witnessed pursuant to Section 2-502(a)(3)(A), but not notarized or self-proved, the testimony of at least one of the attesting witnesses is required to establish proper execution if the witness is within this state, competent, and able to testify. Proper execution may be established by other evidence, including an affidavit of an attesting witness. An attestation clause that is signed by the attesting witnesses raises a rebuttable presumption that the events recited in the clause occurred.

Section 3-407. Formal Testacy Proceedings; Burdens in Contested Cases.

In contested cases, petitioners who seek to establish intestacy have the burden of establishing prima facie proof of death, venue, and heirship. Proponents of a will have the burden of establishing prima facie proof of due execution in all cases, and, if they are also petitioners, prima facie proof of death and venue. Contestants of a will have the burden of establishing lack of testamentary intent or capacity, undue influence, fraud, duress, mistake or revocation. Parties have the ultimate burden of persuasion as to matters with respect to which they have the initial burden of proof. If a will is opposed by the petition for probate of a later will revoking the former, it shall be determined first whether the later will is entitled to probate, and if a will is opposed by a petition for a declaration of intestacy, it shall be determined first whether the will is entitled to probate.

Section 3-408. Formal Testacy Proceedings; Will Construction; Effect of Final Order in Another Jurisdiction.

A final order of a court of another state determining testacy, the validity or construction of a will, made in a proceeding involving notice to and an opportunity for contest by all interested persons must be accepted as determinative by the courts of this state if it includes, or is based upon, a finding that the decedent was domiciled at his death in the state where the order was made.

Section 3-409. Formal Testacy Proceedings; Order; Foreign Will.

After the time required for any notice has expired, upon proof of notice, and after any hearing that may be necessary, if the court finds that the testator is dead, venue is proper and that the proceeding was commenced within the limitation prescribed by Section 3-108, it shall determine the decedent's domicile at death, his heirs and his state of testacy. Any will found to be valid and unrevoked shall be formally probated. Termination of any previous informal appointment of a personal representative, which may be appropriate in view of the relief requested and findings, is governed by Section 3-612. The petition shall be dismissed or appropriate amendment allowed if the court is not satisfied that the alleged decedent is dead. A will from a place which does not provide for probate of a will after death, may be proved for probate in this state by a duly authenticated certificate of its legal custodian that the copy introduced is a true copy and that the will has become effective under the law of the other place.

Section 3–410. Formal Testacy Proceedings; Probate of More Than One Instrument.

If two or more instruments are offered for probate before a final order is entered in a formal testacy proceeding, more than one instrument may be probated if neither expressly revokes the other or contains provisions which work a total revocation by implication. If more than one instrument is probated, the order shall indicate what provisions control in respect to the nomination of an executor, if any. The order may, but need not, indicate how any provisions of a particular instrument are affected by the other instrument. After a final order in a testacy proceeding has been entered, no petition for probate of any other instrument of the decedent may be entertained, except incident to a petition to vacate or modify a previous probate order and subject to the time limits of Section 3–412.

Section 3–411. Formal Testacy Proceedings; Partial Intestacy.

If it becomes evident in the course of a formal testacy proceeding that, though one or more instruments are entitled to be probated, the decedent's estate is or may be partially intestate, the court shall enter an order to that effect.

Section 3–412. Formal Testacy Proceedings; Effect of Order; Vacation.

Subject to appeal and subject to vacation as provided in this section and in Section 3–413, a formal testacy order under Sections 3–409 to 3–411, including an order that the decedent left no valid will and determining heirs, is final as to all persons with respect to all issues concerning the decedent's estate that the court considered or might have considered incident to its rendition relevant to the question of whether the decedent left a valid will, and to the determination of heirs, except that:

(1) The court shall entertain a petition for modification or vacation of its order and probate of another will of the decedent if it is shown that the proponents of the later-offered will: (i) were unaware of its existence at the time of the earlier proceeding: or (ii) were unaware of the earlier proceeding and were given no notice thereof, except by publication.

(2) If intestacy of all or part of the estate has been ordered, the determination of heirs of the decedent may be reconsidered if it is shown that one or more persons were omitted from the determination and it is also shown that the persons were unaware of their relationship to the decedent, were unaware of his death or were given no notice of any proceeding concerning his estate, except by publication.

(3) A petition for vacation under paragraph (1) or (2) must be filed prior to the earlier of the following time limits:

(A) if a personal representative has been appointed for the estate, the time of entry of any order approving final distribution of the estate, or, if the estate is closed by statement, six months after the filing of the closing statement;

(B) whether or not a personal representative has been appointed for the estate of the decedent, the time prescribed by Section 3–108 when it is no longer possible to initiate an original proceeding to probate a will of the decedent; or

(C) twelve months after the entry of the order sought to be vacated.

(4) The order originally rendered in the testacy proceeding may be modified or vacated, if appropriate under the circumstances, by the order of probate of the later-offered will or the order redetermining heirs.

(5) The finding of the fact of death is conclusive as to the alleged decedent only if notice of the hearing on the petition in the formal testacy proceeding was sent by registered or certified mail addressed to the alleged decedent at his last known address and the court finds that a search under Section 3–403(b) was made.

If the alleged decedent is not dead, even if notice was sent and search was made, he may recover estate assets in the hands of the personal representative. In addition to any remedies available to the alleged decedent by reason of any fraud or intentional wrongdoing, the alleged decedent may recover any estate or its proceeds from distributees that is in their hands, or the value of distributions received by them, to the extent that any recovery from distributees is equitable in view of all of the circumstances.

Section 3–413. Formal Testacy Proceedings; Vacation of Order for Other Cause.

For good cause shown, an order in a formal testacy proceeding may be modified or vacated within the time allowed for appeal.

Section 3–414. Formal Proceedings Concerning Appointment of Personal Representative.

(a) A formal proceeding for adjudication regarding the priority or qualification of one who is an applicant for appointment as personal representative, or of one who previously has been appointed personal representative in informal proceedings, if an issue concerning the testacy of the decedent is or may be involved, is governed by Section 3–402, as well as by this section. In other cases, the petition shall contain or adopt the statements required by Section 3–301(1) and describe the question relating to priority or qualification of the personal representative which is to be resolved. If the proceeding precedes any appointment of a personal representative, it shall stay any pending informal appointment proceedings as well as any commenced thereafter. If the proceeding is commenced after appointment, the previously appointed personal representative, after receipt of notice thereof, shall refrain from exercising any power of administration except as necessary to preserve the estate or unless the court orders otherwise.

(b) After notice to interested persons, including all persons interested in the administration of the estate as successors under the applicable assumption concerning testacy, any previously appointed personal representative and any person having or claiming priority for appointment as personal representative, the court shall determine who is entitled to appointment under Section 3–203, make a proper appointment and, if appropriate, terminate any prior appointment found to have been improper as provided in cases of removal under Section 3–611.

PART 5

SUPERVISED ADMINISTRATION

Section 3–501. Supervised Administration; Nature of Proceeding.

Supervised administration is a single in rem proceeding to secure complete administration and settlement of a decedent's estate under the continuing authority of the court which extends until entry of an order approving distribution of the estate and discharging the personal representative or other order terminating the proceeding. A supervised personal representative is responsible to the court, as well as to the interested parties, and is subject to directions concerning the estate made by the court on its own motion or on the motion of any interested party. Except as otherwise provided in this [part], or as otherwise ordered by the court, a supervised personal representative has the same duties and powers as a personal representative who is not supervised.

Section 3–502. Supervised Administration; Petition; Order.

A petition for supervised administration may be filed by any interested person or by a personal representative at any time or the prayer for supervised administration may be joined with a petition in a testacy or appointment proceeding. If the testacy of the decedent and the priority and qualification of any personal representative have not been adjudicated previously, the petition for supervised administration shall include the matters required of a petition in a formal testacy proceeding and the notice requirements and procedures applicable to a formal testacy proceeding apply. If not previously adjudicated, the court shall adjudicate the testacy of the decedent and questions relating to the priority and qualifications of the personal representative in any case involving a request for supervised administration, even though the request for supervised administration may be denied. After notice to interested persons, the court shall order supervised administration of a decedent's estate:

(1) if the decedent's will directs supervised administration, it shall be ordered unless the court finds that circumstances bearing on the need for supervised administration have changed since the execution of the will and that there is no necessity for supervised administration;

(2) if the decedent's will directs unsupervised administration, supervised administration shall be ordered only upon a finding that it is necessary for protection of persons interested in the estate; or

(3) in other cases if the court finds that supervised administration is necessary under the circumstances.

Section 3–503. Supervised Administration; Effect on Other Proceedings.

(a) The pendency of a proceeding for supervised administration of a decedent's estate stays action on any informal application then pending or thereafter filed.

(b) If a will has been previously probated in informal proceedings, the effect of the filing of a petition for supervised administration is as provided for formal testacy proceedings by Section 3–401.

(c) After he has received notice of the filing of a petition for supervised administration, a personal representative who has been appointed previously shall not exercise his power to distribute any estate. The filing of the petition does not affect his other powers and duties unless the court restricts the exercise of any of them pending full hearing on the petition.

Section 3–504. Supervised Administration; Powers of Personal Representative.

Unless restricted by the court, a supervised personal representative has, without interim orders approving exercise of a power, all powers of personal representatives under this [code], but he shall not exercise his power to make any distribution of the estate without prior order of the court. Any other restriction on the power of a personal representative which may be ordered by the court must be endorsed on his letters of appointment and, unless so endorsed, is ineffective as to persons dealing in good faith with the personal representative.

Section 3–505. Supervised Administration; Interim Orders; Distribution and Closing Orders.

Unless otherwise ordered by the court, supervised administration is terminated by order in accordance with time restrictions, notices and contents of orders prescribed for proceedings under Section 3–1001. Interim orders approving or directing partial distributions or granting other relief may be issued by the court at any time during the pendency of a supervised administration on the application of the personal representative or any interested person.

PART 6

PERSONAL REPRESENTATIVE; APPOINTMENT, CONTROL AND TERMINATION OF AUTHORITY

Section 3–601. Qualification.

Prior to receiving letters, a personal representative shall qualify by filing with the appointing court any required bond and a statement of acceptance of the duties of the office.

Section 3–602. Acceptance of Appointment; Consent to Jurisdiction.

By accepting appointment, a personal representative submits personally to the jurisdiction of the court in any proceeding relating to the estate that may be instituted by any interested person. Notice of any proceeding shall be delivered to the personal representative, or mailed to him by ordinary first class mail at his address as listed in the application or petition for appointment or as thereafter reported to the court and to his address as then known to the petitioner.

Section 3–603. Bond Not Required Without Court Order; Exceptions.

No bond is required of a personal representative appointed in informal proceedings, except (i) upon the appointment of a special administrator; (ii) when an executor or other personal representative is appointed to administer an estate under a will containing an express requirement of bond or (iii) when bond is required under Section 3–605. Bond may be required by court order at the time of appointment of a personal representative appointed in any formal proceeding except that bond is not required of a personal representative appointed in formal proceedings if the will relieves the personal representative of bond, unless bond has been requested by an interested party and the court is satisfied that it is desirable. Bond required by any will may be dispensed with in formal proceedings upon determination by the court that it is not necessary. No bond is required of any personal representative who, pursuant to statute, has deposited cash or collateral with an agency of this state to secure performance of his duties.

Section 3–604. Bond Amount; Security; Procedure; Reduction.

If bond is required and the provisions of the will or order do not specify the amount, unless stated in his application or petition, the person qualifying shall file a statement under oath with the Registrar indicating his best estimate of the value of the personal estate of the decedent and of the income expected from the personal and real estate during the next year, and he shall execute and file a bond with the Registrar, or give other suitable security, in an amount not less than the estimate. The Registrar shall determine that the bond is duly executed by a corporate surety, or one or more individual sureties whose performance is secured by pledge of personal property, mortgage on real property or other adequate security. The Registrar may permit the amount of the bond to be reduced by the value of assets of the estate deposited with a domestic financial institution (as defined in Section 6–101) in a manner that prevents their unauthorized disposition. On petition of the personal representative or another interested person the court may excuse a requirement of bond, increase or reduce the amount of the bond, release sureties, or permit the substitution of another bond with the same or different sureties.

Section 3–605. Demand for Bond by Interested Person.

Any person apparently having an interest in the estate worth in excess of [$5,000], or any creditor having a claim in excess of [$5,000], may make a written demand that a personal representative give bond. The demand must be filed with the Registrar and a copy mailed to the personal representative, if appointment and qualification have occurred. Thereupon, bond is required, but the requirement ceases if the person demanding bond ceases to be interested in the estate, or if bond is excused as provided in Section 3–603 or 3–604. After he has received notice and until the filing of the bond or cessation of the requirement of bond, the personal representative shall refrain from exercising any powers of his office except as necessary to preserve the estate. Failure of the personal representative to meet a requirement of bond by giving suitable bond within 30 days after receipt of notice is cause for his removal and appointment of a successor personal representative.

Section 3–606. Terms and Conditions of Bonds.

(a)　The following requirements and provisions apply to any bond required by this [part]:

(1)　Bonds shall name the [state] as obligee for the benefit of the persons interested in the estate and shall be conditioned upon the faithful discharge by the fiduciary of all duties according to law.

(2)　Unless otherwise provided by the terms of the approved bond, sureties are jointly and severally liable with the personal representative and with each other. The address of sureties shall be stated in the bond.

(3)   By executing an approved bond of a personal representative, the surety consents to the jurisdiction of the probate court which issued letters to the primary obligor in any proceedings pertaining to the fiduciary duties of the personal representative and naming the surety as a party. Notice of any proceeding shall be delivered to the surety or mailed to him by registered or certified mail at his address as listed with the court where the bond is filed and to his address as then known to the petitioner.

(4)   On petition of a successor personal representative, any other personal representative of the same decedent, or any interested person, a proceeding in the court may be initiated against a surety for breach of the obligation of the bond of the personal representative.

(5)   The bond of the personal representative is not void after the first recovery but may be proceeded against from time to time until the whole penalty is exhausted.

(b)   No action or proceeding may be commenced against the surety on any matter as to which an action or proceeding against the primary obligor is barred by adjudication or limitation.

Section 3–607. Order Restraining Personal Representative.

(a)   On petition of any person who appears to have an interest in the estate, the court by temporary order may restrain a personal representative from performing specified acts of administration, disbursement, or distribution, or exercise of any powers or discharge of any duties of his office, or make any other order to secure proper performance of his duty, if it appears to the court that the personal representative otherwise may take some action which would jeopardize unreasonably the interest of the applicant or of some other interested person. Persons with whom the personal representative may transact business may be made parties.

(b)   The matter shall be set for hearing within 10 days unless the parties otherwise agree. Notice as the court directs shall be given to the personal representative and his attorney of record, if any, and to any other parties named defendant in the petition.

Section 3–608. Termination of Appointment; General.

Termination of appointment of a personal representative occurs as indicated in Sections 3–609 to 3–612, inclusive. Termination ends the right and power pertaining to the office of personal representative as conferred by this [code] or any will, except that a personal representative, at any time prior to distribution or until restrained or enjoined by court order, may perform acts necessary to protect the estate and may deliver the assets to a successor representative. Termination does not discharge a personal representative from liability for transactions or omissions occurring before termination, or relieve him of the duty to preserve assets subject to his control, to account therefor and to deliver the assets. Termination does not affect the jurisdiction of the court over the personal representative, but terminates his authority to represent the estate in any pending or future proceeding.

Section 3–609. Termination of Appointment; Death or Disability.

The death of a personal representative or the appointment of a conservator for the estate of a personal representative, terminates his appointment. Until appointment and qualification of a successor or special representative to replace the deceased or protected representative, the representative of the estate of the deceased or protected personal representative, if any, has the duty to protect the estate possessed and being administered by his decedent or ward at the time his appointment terminates, has the power to perform acts necessary for protection and shall account for and deliver the estate assets to a successor or special personal representative upon his appointment and qualification.

Section 3–610. Termination of Appointment; Voluntary.

(a)   An appointment of a personal representative terminates as provided in Section 3–1003, one year after the filing of a closing statement.

(b) An order closing an estate as provided in Section 3–1001 or 3–1002 terminates an appointment of a personal representative.

(c) A personal representative may resign his position by filing a written statement of resignation with the Registrar after he has given at least 15 days written notice to the persons known to be interested in the estate. If no one applies or petitions for appointment of a successor representative within the time indicated in the notice, the filed statement of resignation is ineffective as a termination of appointment and in any event is effective only upon the appointment and qualification of a successor representative and delivery of the assets to him.

Section 3–611. Termination of Appointment by Removal; Cause; Procedure.

(a) A person interested in the estate may petition for removal of a personal representative for cause at any time. Upon filing of the petition, the court shall fix a time and place for hearing. Notice shall be given by the petitioner to the personal representative, and to other persons as the court may order. Except as otherwise ordered as provided in Section 3–607, after receipt of notice of removal proceedings, the personal representative shall not act except to account, to correct maladministration or preserve the estate. If removal is ordered, the court also shall direct by order the disposition of the assets remaining in the name of, or under the control of, the personal representative being removed.

(b) Cause for removal exists when removal would be in the best interests of the estate, or if it is shown that a personal representative or the person seeking his appointment intentionally misrepresented material facts in the proceedings leading to his appointment, or that the personal representative has disregarded an order of the court, has become incapable of discharging the duties of his office, or has mismanaged the estate or failed to perform any duty pertaining to the office. Unless the decedent's will directs otherwise, a personal representative appointed at the decedent's domicile, incident to securing appointment of himself or his nominee as ancillary personal representative, may obtain removal of another who was appointed personal representative in this state to administer local assets.

Section 3–612. Termination of Appointment; Change of Testacy Status.

Except as otherwise ordered in formal proceedings, the probate of a will subsequent to the appointment of a personal representative in intestacy or under a will which is superseded by formal probate of another will, or the vacation of an informal probate of a will subsequent to the appointment of the personal representative thereunder, does not terminate the appointment of the personal representative although his powers may be reduced as provided in Section 3–401. Termination occurs upon appointment in informal or formal appointment proceedings of a person entitled to appointment under the later assumption concerning testacy. If no request for new appointment is made within 30 days after expiration of time for appeal from the order in formal testacy proceedings, or from the informal probate, changing the assumption concerning testacy, the previously appointed personal representative upon request may be appointed personal representative under the subsequently probated will, or as in intestacy as the case may be.

Section 3–613. Successor Personal Representative.

[Parts] 3 and 4 of this [article] govern proceedings for appointment of a personal representative to succeed one whose appointment has been terminated. After appointment and qualification, a successor personal representative may be substituted in all actions and proceedings to which the former personal representative was a party, and no notice, process or claim which was given or served upon the former personal representative need be given to or served upon the successor in order to preserve any position or right the person giving the notice or filing the claim may thereby have obtained or preserved with reference to the former personal representative. Except as otherwise ordered by the court, the successor personal representative has the powers and duties in respect to the continued administration which the former personal representative would have had if his appointment had not been terminated.

Section 3–614. Special Administrator; Appointment.

A special administrator may be appointed:

(1) informally by the Registrar on the application of any interested person when necessary to protect the estate of a decedent prior to the appointment of a general personal representative or if a prior appointment has been terminated as provided in Section 3–609;

(2) in a formal proceeding by order of the court on the petition of any interested person and finding, after notice and hearing, that appointment is necessary to preserve the estate or to secure its proper administration including its administration in circumstances where a general personal representative cannot or should not act. If it appears to the court that an emergency exists, appointment may be ordered without notice.

Section 3–615. Special Administrator; Who May Be Appointed.

(a) If a special administrator is to be appointed pending the probate of a will which is the subject of a pending application or petition for probate, the person named executor in the will shall be appointed if available, and qualified.

(b) In other cases, any proper person may be appointed special administrator.

Section 3–616. Special Administrator; Appointed Informally; Powers and Duties.

A special administrator appointed by the Registrar in informal proceedings pursuant to Section 3–614(1) has the duty to collect and manage the assets of the estate, to preserve them, to account therefor and to deliver them to the general personal representative upon his qualification. The special administrator has the power of a personal representative under the [code] necessary to perform his duties.

Section 3–617. Special Administrator; Formal Proceedings; Power and Duties.

A special administrator appointed by order of the court in any formal proceeding has the power of a general personal representative except as limited in the appointment and duties as prescribed in the order. The appointment may be for a specified time, to perform particular acts or on other terms as the court may direct.

Section 3–618. Termination of Appointment; Special Administrator.

The appointment of a special administrator terminates in accordance with the provisions of the order of appointment or on the appointment of a general personal representative. In other cases, the appointment of a special administrator is subject to termination as provided in Sections 3–608 through 3–611.

PART 7

DUTIES AND POWERS OF PERSONAL REPRESENTATIVES

Section 3–701. Time of Accrual of Duties and Powers.

The duties and powers of a personal representative commence upon his appointment. The powers of a personal representative relate back in time to give acts by the person appointed which are beneficial to the estate occurring prior to appointment the same effect as those occurring thereafter. Prior to appointment, a person named executor in a will may carry out written instructions of the decedent relating to his body, funeral and burial arrangements. A personal representative may ratify and accept acts on behalf of the estate done by others where the acts would have been proper for a personal representative.

Section 3–702. Priority Among Different Letters.

A person to whom general letters are issued first has exclusive authority under the letters until his appointment is terminated or modified. If, through error, general letters are afterwards issued to another, the first appointed representative may recover any property of the estate in the hands of the representative subsequently appointed, but the acts of the latter done in good faith before notice of the first letters are not void for want of validity of appointment.

Section 3–703. General Duties; Relation and Liability to Persons Interested in Estate; Standing to Sue.

(a)   A personal representative is a fiduciary who shall observe the standards of care applicable to trustees. A personal representative is under a duty to settle and distribute the estate of the decedent in accordance with the terms of any probated and effective will and this [code], and as expeditiously and efficiently as is consistent with the best interests of the estate. He shall use the authority conferred upon him by this [code], the terms of the will, if any, and any order in proceedings to which he is party for the best interests of successors to the estate.

(b)   A personal representative may not be surcharged for acts of administration or distribution if the conduct in question was authorized at the time. Subject to other obligations of administration, an informally probated will is authority to administer and distribute the estate according to its terms. An order of appointment of a personal representative, whether issued in informal or formal proceedings, is authority to distribute apparently intestate assets to the heirs of the decedent if, at the time of distribution, the personal representative is not aware of a pending testacy proceeding, a proceeding to vacate an order entered in an earlier testacy proceeding, a formal proceeding questioning his appointment or fitness to continue, or a supervised administration proceeding. This section does not affect the duty of the personal representative to administer and distribute the estate in accordance with the rights of claimants whose claims have been allowed, the surviving spouse, any minor and dependent children and any pretermitted child of the decedent as described elsewhere in this [code].

(c)   Except as to proceedings which do not survive the death of the decedent, a personal representative of a decedent domiciled in this state at his death has the same standing to sue and be sued in the courts of this state and the courts of any other jurisdiction as his decedent had immediately prior to death.

(d)   A personal representative may not be surcharged for a distribution that does not take into consideration the possibility of posthumous pregnancy unless the personal representative[, not later than [6] months after the decedent's death,] received notice or had actual knowledge of an intent to use genetic material in assisted reproduction.

Section 3–704. Personal Representative to Proceed Without Court Order; Exception.

A personal representative shall proceed expeditiously with the settlement and distribution of a decedent's estate and, except as otherwise specified or ordered in regard to a supervised personal representative, do so without adjudication, order, or direction of the court, but he may invoke the jurisdiction of the court, in proceedings authorized by this [code], to resolve questions concerning the estate or its administration.

Section 3–705. Duty of Personal Representative; Information to Heirs and Devisees.

Not later than 30 days after his appointment every personal representative, except any special administrator, shall give information of his appointment to the heirs and devisees, including, if there has been no formal testacy proceeding and if the personal representative was appointed on the assumption that the decedent died intestate, the devisees in any will mentioned in the application for appointment of a personal representative. The information shall be delivered or sent by ordinary mail to each of the heirs and devisees whose address is reasonably available to the personal representative. The duty does not extend to require information to persons who have been adjudicated in a prior formal testacy proceeding to have no interest in the estate. The information shall include the name and address of the personal representative, indicate that it is being sent to persons who have or may have some interest in the estate being administered, indicate whether bond has been filed, and describe the court where papers relating to the estate are on file. The information shall state that the estate is being administered by the personal representative under the [State] Probate Code without supervision by the court but that recipients are entitled to information regarding the administration from the personal representative and can petition the court in any matter relating to the estate, including distribution of assets and expenses of administration. The personal representative's failure to give this information is a breach of his duty to the persons concerned but does not affect the validity of his appointment, his powers or other duties. A personal representative may inform other persons of his appointment by delivery or ordinary first class mail.

Section 3–706. Duty of Personal Representative; Inventory and Appraisement.

Within three months after his appointment, a personal representative, who is not a special administrator or a successor to another representative who has previously discharged this duty, shall prepare and file or mail an inventory of property owned by the decedent at the time of his death, listing it with reasonable detail, and indicating as to each listed item, its fair market value as of the date of the decedent's death, and the type and amount of any encumbrance that may exist with reference to any item.

The personal representative shall send a copy of the inventory to interested persons who request it. He may also file the original of the inventory with the court.

Section 3–707. Employment of Appraisers.

The personal representative may employ a qualified and disinterested appraiser to assist him in ascertaining the fair market value as of the date of the decedent's death of any asset the value of which may be subject to reasonable doubt. Different persons may be employed to appraise different kinds of assets included in the estate. The names and addresses of any appraiser shall be indicated on the inventory with the item or items he appraised.

Section 3–708. Duty of Personal Representative; Supplementary Inventory.

If any property not included in the original inventory comes to the knowledge of a personal representative or if the personal representative learns that the value or description indicated in the original inventory for any item is erroneous or misleading, he shall make a supplementary inventory or appraisement showing the market value as of the date of the decedent's death of the new item or the revised market value or descriptions, and the appraisers or other data relied upon, if any, and file it with the court if the original inventory was filed, or furnish copies thereof or information thereof to persons interested in the new information.

Section 3–709. Duty of Personal Representative; Possession of Estate.

Except as otherwise provided by a decedent's will, every personal representative has a right to, and shall take possession or control of, the decedent's property, except that any real property or tangible personal property may be left with or surrendered to the person presumptively entitled thereto unless or until, in the judgment of the personal representative, possession of the property by him will be necessary for purposes of administration. The request by a personal representative for delivery of any property possessed by an heir or devisee is conclusive evidence, in any action against the heir or devisee for possession thereof, that the possession of the property by the personal representative is necessary for purposes of administration. The personal representative shall pay taxes on, and take all steps reasonably necessary for the management, protection and preservation of, the estate in his possession. He may maintain an action to recover possession of property or to determine the title thereto.

Section 3–710. Power to Avoid Transfers.

The property liable for the payment of unsecured debts of a decedent includes all property transferred by him by any means which is in law void or voidable as against his creditors, and subject to prior liens, the right to recover this property, so far as necessary for the payment of unsecured debts of the decedent, is exclusively in the personal representative.

Section 3–711. Powers of Personal Representatives; In General.

[(a)] Until termination of his appointment a personal representative has the same power over the title to property of the estate that an absolute owner would have, in trust however, for the benefit of the creditors and others interested in the estate. This power may be exercised without notice, hearing, or order of court.

[(b) A personal representative has access to and authority over a digital asset of the decedent to the extent provided by [the Revised Uniform Fiduciary Access to Digital Assets Act] or by order of court.]

Section 3–712. Improper Exercise of Power; Breach of Fiduciary Duty.

If the exercise of power concerning the estate is improper, the personal representative is liable to interested persons for damage or loss resulting from breach of his fiduciary duty to the same extent as a trustee of an express trust. The rights of purchasers and others dealing with a personal representative shall be determined as provided in Sections 3–713 and 3–714.

Section 3–713. Sale, Encumbrance or Transaction Involving Conflict of Interest; Voidable; Exceptions.

Any sale or encumbrance to the personal representative, his spouse, agent or attorney, or any corporation or trust in which he has a substantial beneficial interest, or any transaction which is affected by a substantial conflict of interest on the part of the personal representative, is voidable by any person interested in the estate except one who has consented after fair disclosure, unless

(1)   the will or a contract entered into by the decedent expressly authorized the transaction; or

(2)   the transaction is approved by the court after notice to interested persons.

Section 3–714. Persons Dealing With Personal Representative; Protection.

A person who in good faith either assists a personal representative or deals with him for value is protected as if the personal representative properly exercised his power. The fact that a person knowingly deals with a personal representative does not alone require the person to inquire into the existence of a power or the propriety of its exercise. Except for restrictions on powers of supervised personal representatives which are endorsed on letters as provided in Section 3–504, no provision in any will or order of court purporting to limit the power of a personal representative is effective except as to persons with actual knowledge thereof. A person is not bound to see to the proper application of estate assets paid or delivered to a personal representative. The protection here expressed extends to instances in which some procedural irregularity or jurisdictional defect occurred in proceedings leading to the issuance of letters, including a case in which the alleged decedent is found to be alive. The protection here expressed is not by substitution for that provided by comparable provisions of the laws relating to commercial transactions and laws simplifying transfers of securities by fiduciaries.

Section 3–715. Transactions Authorized for Personal Representatives; Exceptions.

Except as restricted or otherwise provided by the will or by an order in a formal proceeding and subject to the priorities stated in Section 3–902, a personal representative, acting reasonably for the benefit of the interested persons, may properly:

(1) retain assets owned by the decedent pending distribution or liquidation including those in which the representative is personally interested or which are otherwise improper for trust investment;

(2) receive assets from fiduciaries, or other sources;

(3) perform, compromise or refuse performance of the decedent's contracts that continue as obligations of the estate, as he may determine under the circumstances. In performing enforceable contracts by the decedent to convey or lease land, the personal representative, among other possible courses of action, may:

(A) execute and deliver a deed of conveyance for cash payment of all sums remaining due or the purchaser's note for the sum remaining due secured by a mortgage or deed of trust on the land; or

(B) deliver a deed in escrow with directions that the proceeds, when paid in accordance with the escrow agreement, be paid to the successors of the decedent, as designated in the escrow agreement;

(4) satisfy written charitable pledges of the decedent irrespective of whether the pledges constituted binding obligations of the decedent or were properly presented as claims, if in the judgment of the personal representative the decedent would have wanted the pledges completed under the circumstances;

(5) if funds are not needed to meet debts and expenses currently payable and are not immediately distributable, deposit or invest liquid assets of the estate, including moneys received from the sale of other assets, in federally insured interest-bearing accounts, readily marketable secured loan arrangements or other prudent investments which would be reasonable for use by trustees generally;

(6) acquire or dispose of an asset, including land in this or another state, for cash or on credit, at public or private sale; and manage, develop, improve, exchange, partition, change the character of, or abandon an estate asset;

(7) make ordinary or extraordinary repairs or alterations in buildings or other structures, demolish any improvements, raze existing or erect new party walls or buildings;

(8) subdivide, develop or dedicate land to public use; make or obtain the vacation of plats and adjust boundaries; or adjust differences in valuation on exchange or partition by giving or receiving considerations; or dedicate easements to public use without consideration;

(9) enter for any purpose into a lease as lessor or lessee, with or without option to purchase or renew, for a term within or extending beyond the period of administration;

(10) enter into a lease or arrangement for exploration and removal of minerals or other natural resources or enter into a pooling or unitization agreement;

(11) abandon property when, in the opinion of the personal representative, it is valueless, or is so encumbered, or is in condition that it is of no benefit to the estate;

(12) vote stocks or other securities in person or by general or limited proxy;

(13) pay calls, assessments, and other sums chargeable or accruing against or on account of securities, unless barred by the provisions relating to claims;

(14) hold a security in the name of a nominee or in other form without disclosure of the interest of the estate but the personal representative is liable for any act of the nominee in connection with the security so held;

(15) insure the assets of the estate against damage, loss and liability and himself against liability as to third persons;

(16) borrow money with or without security to be repaid from the estate assets or otherwise; and advance money for the protection of the estate;

(17) effect a fair and reasonable compromise with any debtor or obligor, or extend, renew or in any manner modify the terms of any obligation owing to the estate. If the personal representative holds a mortgage, pledge or other lien upon property of another person, he may, in lieu of foreclosure, accept a conveyance or transfer of encumbered assets from the owner thereof in satisfaction of the indebtedness secured by lien;

(18) pay taxes, assessments, compensation of the personal representative, and other expenses incident to the administration of the estate;

(19) sell or exercise stock subscription or conversion rights; consent, directly or through a committee or other agent, to the reorganization, consolidation, merger, dissolution, or liquidation of a corporation or other business enterprise;

(20) allocate items of income or expense to either estate income or principal, as permitted or provided by law;

(21) employ persons, including attorneys, auditors, investment advisors, or agents, even if they are associated with the personal representative, to advise or assist the personal representative in the performance of his administrative duties; act without independent investigation upon their recommendations; and instead of acting personally, employ one or more agents to perform any act of administration, whether or not discretionary;

(22) prosecute or defend claims, or proceedings in any jurisdiction for the protection of the estate and of the personal representative in the performance of his duties;

(23) sell, mortgage, or lease any real or personal property of the estate or any interest therein for cash, credit, or for part cash and part credit, and with or without security for unpaid balances;

(24) continue any unincorporated business or venture in which the decedent was engaged at the time of his death (i) in the same business form for a period of not more than 4 months from the date of appointment of a general personal representative if continuation is a reasonable means of preserving the value of the business including good will, (ii) in the same business form for any additional period of time that may be approved by order of the court in a formal proceeding to which the persons interested in the estate are parties; or (iii) throughout the period of administration if the business is incorporated by the personal representative and if none of the probable distributees of the business who are competent adults object to its incorporation and retention in the estate;

(25) incorporate any business or venture in which the decedent was engaged at the time of his death;

(26) provide for exoneration of the personal representative from personal liability in any contract entered into on behalf of the estate;

(27) satisfy and settle claims and distribute the estate as provided in this [code].

Section 3–716. Powers and Duties of Successor Personal Representative.

A successor personal representative has the same power and duty as the original personal representative to complete the administration and distribution of the estate, as expeditiously as possible, but he shall not exercise any power expressly made personal to the executor named in the will.

Section 3–717. Co-representatives; When Joint Action Required.

If two or more persons are appointed co-representatives and unless the will provides otherwise, the concurrence of all is required on all acts connected with the administration and distribution of the estate. This restriction does not apply when any co-representative receives and receipts for property due the estate, when the concurrence of all cannot readily be obtained in the time reasonably available for emergency action necessary to preserve the estate, or when a co-representative has been delegated to act for the others. Persons dealing with a co-representative if actually unaware that another has been appointed to serve with him or if advised by the personal representative with whom they deal that he has authority to act alone for any of the reasons mentioned herein, are as fully protected as if the person with whom they dealt had been the sole personal representative.

Section 3–718. Powers of Surviving Personal Representative.

Unless the terms of the will otherwise provide, every power exercisable by personal co-representatives may be exercised by the one or more remaining after the appointment of one or more is terminated, and if one of two or more nominated as co-executors is not appointed, those appointed may exercise all the powers incident to the office.

Section 3–719. Compensation of Personal Representative.

A personal representative is entitled to reasonable compensation for his services. If a will provides for compensation of the personal representative and there is no contract with the decedent regarding compensation, he may renounce the provision before qualifying and be entitled to reasonable compensation. A personal representative also may renounce his right to all or any part of the compensation. A written renunciation of fee may be filed with the court.

Section 3–720. Expenses in Estate Litigation.

If any personal representative or person nominated as personal representative defends or prosecutes any proceeding in good faith, whether successful or not he is entitled to receive from the estate his necessary expenses and disbursements including reasonable attorneys' fees incurred.

Section 3–721. Proceedings for Review of Employment of Agents and Compensation of Personal Representatives and Employees of Estate.

After notice to all interested persons or on petition of an interested person or on appropriate motion if administration is supervised, the propriety of employment of any person by a personal representative including any attorney, auditor, investment advisor or other specialized agent or assistant, the reasonableness of the compensation of any person so employed, or the reasonableness of the compensation determined by the personal representative for his own services, may be reviewed by the court. Any person who has received excessive compensation from an estate for services rendered may be ordered to make appropriate refunds.

PART 8

CREDITORS' CLAIMS

Section 3–801. Notice to Creditors.

(a) Unless notice has already been given under this section, a personal representative upon appointment [may] [shall] publish a notice to creditors once a week for three successive weeks in a newspaper of general circulation in the [county] announcing the appointment and the personal representative's address and notifying creditors of the estate to present their claims within four months after the date of the first publication of the notice or be forever barred.

(b) A personal representative may give written notice by mail or other delivery to a creditor, notifying the creditor to present his [or her] claim within four months after the published notice, if given as provided in subsection (a), or within 60 days after the mailing or other delivery of the notice, whichever is later, or be forever barred. Written notice must be the notice described in subsection (a) above or a similar notice.

(c) The personal representative is not liable to a creditor or to a successor of the decedent for giving or failing to give notice under this section.

Section 3–802. Statutes of Limitations.

(a)   Unless an estate is insolvent, the personal representative, with the consent of all successors whose interests would be affected, may waive any defense of limitations available to the estate. If the defense is not waived, no claim barred by a statute of limitations at the time of the decedent's death may be allowed or paid.

(b)   The running of a statute of limitations measured from an event other than death or the giving of notice to creditors is suspended for four months after the decedent's death, but resumes thereafter as to claims not barred by other sections.

(c)   For purposes of a statute of limitations, the presentation of a claim pursuant to Section 3–804 is equivalent to commencement of a proceeding on the claim.

Section 3–803. Limitations on Presentation of Claims.

(a)   All claims against a decedent's estate which arose before the death of the decedent, including claims of the state and any subdivision thereof, whether due or to become due, absolute or contingent, liquidated or unliquidated, founded on contract, tort, or other legal basis, if not barred earlier by another statute of limitations or non-claim statute, are barred against the estate, the personal representative, the heirs and devisees, and nonprobate transferees of the decedent, unless presented within the earlier of the following:

(1)   one year after the decedent's death; or

(2)   the time provided by Section 3–801(b) for creditors who are given actual notice, and within the time provided in 3–801(a) for all creditors barred by publication.

(b)   A claim described in subsection (a) which is barred by the non-claim statute of the decedent's domicile before the giving of notice to creditors in this state is barred in this state.

(c)   All claims against a decedent's estate which arise at or after the death of the decedent, including claims of the state and any subdivision thereof, whether due or to become due, absolute or contingent, liquidated or unliquidated, founded on contract, tort, or other legal basis, are barred against the estate, the personal representative, and the heirs and devisees of the decedent, unless presented as follows:

(1)   a claim based on a contract with the personal representative, within four months after performance by the personal representative is due; or

(2)   any other claim, within the later of four months after it arises, or the time specified in subsection (a)(1).

(d)   Nothing in this section affects or prevents:

(1)   any proceeding to enforce any mortgage, pledge, or other lien upon property of the estate;

(2)   to the limits of the insurance protection only, any proceeding to establish liability of the decedent or the personal representative for which he is protected by liability insurance; or

(3)   collection of compensation for services rendered and reimbursement for expenses advanced by the personal representative or by the attorney or accountant for the personal representative of the estate.

Section 3–804. Manner of Presentation of Claims.

Claims against a decedent's estate may be presented as follows:

(1)   The claimant may deliver or mail to the personal representative a written statement of the claim indicating its basis, the name and address of the claimant, and the amount claimed, or may file a written statement of the claim, in the form prescribed by rule, with the clerk of the court. The claim is deemed presented on the first to occur of receipt of the written statement of claim by the personal

representative, or the filing of the claim with the court. If a claim is not yet due, the date when it will become due shall be stated. If the claim is contingent or unliquidated, the nature of the uncertainty shall be stated. If the claim is secured, the security shall be described. Failure to describe correctly the security, the nature of any uncertainty, and the due date of a claim not yet due does not invalidate the presentation made.

(2) The claimant may commence a proceeding against the personal representative in any court where the personal representative may be subjected to jurisdiction, to obtain payment of his claim against the estate, but the commencement of the proceeding must occur within the time limited for presenting the claim. No presentation of claim is required in regard to matters claimed in proceedings against the decedent which were pending at the time of his death.

(3) If a claim is presented under paragraph (1), no proceeding thereon may be commenced more than 60 days after the personal representative has mailed a notice of disallowance; but, in the case of a claim which is not presently due or which is contingent or unliquidated, the personal representative may consent to an extension of the 60-day period, or to avoid injustice the court, on petition, may order an extension of the 60-day period, but in no event shall the extension run beyond the applicable statute of limitations.

Section 3–805. Classification of Claims.

(a) If the applicable assets of the estate are insufficient to pay all claims in full, the personal representative shall make payment in the following order:

(1) costs and expenses of administration;

(2) reasonable funeral expenses;

(3) debts and taxes with preference under federal law;

(4) reasonable and necessary medical and hospital expenses of the last illness of the decedent, including compensation of persons attending him;

(5) debts and taxes with preference under other laws of this state;

(6) all other claims.

(b) No preference shall be given in the payment of any claim over any other claim of the same class, and a claim due and payable shall not be entitled to a preference over claims not due.

Section 3–806. Allowance of Claims.

(a) As to claims presented in the manner described in Section 3–804 within the time limit prescribed in 3–803, the personal representative may mail a notice to any claimant stating that the claim has been disallowed. If, after allowing or disallowing a claim, the personal representative changes his decision concerning the claim, he shall notify the claimant. The personal representative may not change a disallowance of a claim after the time for the claimant to file a petition for allowance or to commence a proceeding on the claim has run and the claim has been barred. Every claim which is disallowed in whole or in part by the personal representative is barred so far as not allowed unless the claimant files a petition for allowance in the court or commences a proceeding against the personal representative not later than 60 days after the mailing of the notice of disallowance or partial allowance if the notice warns the claimant of the impending bar. Failure of the personal representative to mail notice to a claimant of action on his claim for 60 days after the time for original presentation of the claim has expired has the effect of a notice of allowance.

(b) After allowing or disallowing a claim the personal representative may change the allowance or disallowance as hereafter provided. The personal representative may prior to payment change the allowance to a disallowance in whole or in part, but not after allowance by a court order or judgment or an order directing payment of the claim. He shall notify the claimant of the change to disallowance, and the disallowed claim is then subject to bar as provided in subsection (a). The personal representative may change a disallowance to an allowance, in whole or in part, until it is barred under subsection (a); after it is barred, it may be allowed and paid only if the estate is solvent and all successors whose interests would be affected consent.

(c) Upon the petition of the personal representative or of a claimant in a proceeding for the purpose, the court may allow in whole or in part any claim or claims presented to the personal representative or filed with the clerk of the court in due time and not barred by subsection (a). Notice in this proceeding shall be given to the claimant, the personal representative and those other persons interested in the estate as the court may direct by order entered at the time the proceeding is commenced.

(d) A judgment in a proceeding in another court against a personal representative to enforce a claim against a decedent's estate is an allowance of the claim.

(e) Unless otherwise provided in any judgment in another court entered against the personal representative, allowed claims bear interest at the legal rate for the period commencing 60 days after the time for original presentation of the claim has expired unless based on a contract making a provision for interest, in which case they bear interest in accordance with that provision.

Section 3–807. Payment of Claims.

(a) Upon the expiration of the earlier of the time limitations provided in Section 3–803 for the presentation of claims, the personal representative shall proceed to pay the claims allowed against the estate in the order of priority prescribed, after making provision for homestead, family and support allowances, for claims already presented that have not yet been allowed or whose allowance has been appealed, and for unbarred claims that may yet be presented, including costs and expenses of administration. By petition to the court in a proceeding for the purpose, or by appropriate motion if the administration is supervised, a claimant whose claim has been allowed but not paid may secure an order directing the personal representative to pay the claim to the extent funds of the estate are available to pay it.

(b) The personal representative at any time may pay any just claim that has not been barred, with or without formal presentation, but is personally liable to any other claimant whose claim is allowed and who is injured by its payment if:

(1) payment was made before the expiration of the time limit stated in subsection (a) and the personal representative failed to require the payee to give adequate security for the refund of any of the payment necessary to pay other claimants; or

(2) payment was made, due to negligence or willful fault of the personal representative, in such manner as to deprive the injured claimant of priority.

Section 3–808. Individual Liability of Personal Representative.

(a) Unless otherwise provided in the contract, a personal representative is not individually liable on a contract properly entered into in his fiduciary capacity in the course of administration of the estate unless he fails to reveal his representative capacity and identify the estate in the contract.

(b) A personal representative is individually liable for obligations arising from ownership or control of the estate or for torts committed in the course of administration of the estate only if he is personally at fault.

(c) Claims based on contracts entered into by a personal representative in his fiduciary capacity, on obligations arising from ownership or control of the estate or on torts committed in the course of estate administration may be asserted against the estate by proceeding against the personal representative in his fiduciary capacity, whether or not the personal representative is individually liable therefor.

(d) Issues of liability as between the estate and the personal representative individually may be determined in a proceeding for accounting, surcharge or indemnification or other appropriate proceeding.

Section 3–809. Secured Claims.

Payment of a secured claim is upon the basis of the amount allowed if the creditor surrenders his security; otherwise payment is upon the basis of one of the following:

(1)   if the creditor exhausts his security before receiving payment, [unless precluded by other law] upon the amount of the claim allowed less the fair value of the security; or

(2)   if the creditor does not have the right to exhaust his security or has not done so, upon the amount of the claim allowed less the value of the security determined by converting it into money according to the terms of the agreement pursuant to which the security was delivered to the creditor, or by the creditor and personal representative by agreement, arbitration, compromise or litigation.

Section 3–810. Claims Not Due and Contingent or Unliquidated Claims.

(a)   If a claim which will become due at a future time or a contingent or unliquidated claim becomes due or certain before the distribution of the estate, and if the claim has been allowed or established by a proceeding, it is paid in the same manner as presently due and absolute claims of the same class.

(b)   In other cases the personal representative or, on petition of the personal representative or the claimant in a special proceeding for the purpose, the court may provide for payment as follows:

(1)   if the claimant consents, he may be paid the present or agreed value of the claim, taking any uncertainty into account;

(2)   arrangement for future payment, or possible payment, on the happening of the contingency or on liquidation may be made by creating a trust, giving a mortgage, obtaining a bond or security from a distributee, or otherwise.

Section 3–811. Counterclaims.

In allowing a claim the personal representative may deduct any counterclaim which the estate has against the claimant. In determining a claim against an estate a court shall reduce the amount allowed by the amount of any counterclaims and, if the counterclaims exceed the claim, render a judgment against the claimant in the amount of the excess. A counterclaim, liquidated or unliquidated, may arise from a transaction other than that upon which the claim is based. A counterclaim may give rise to relief exceeding in amount or different in kind from that sought in the claim.

Section 3–812. Execution and Levies Prohibited.

No execution may issue upon nor may any levy be made against any property of the estate under any judgment against a decedent or a personal representative, but this section shall not be construed to prevent the enforcement of mortgages, pledges or liens upon real or personal property in an appropriate proceeding.

Section 3–813. Compromise of Claims.

When a claim against the estate has been presented in any manner, the personal representative may, if it appears for the best interest of the estate, compromise the claim, whether due or not due, absolute or contingent, liquidated or unliquidated.

Section 3–814. Encumbered Assets.

If any assets of the estate are encumbered by mortgage, pledge, lien, or other security interest, the personal representative may pay the encumbrance or any part thereof, renew or extend any obligation secured by the encumbrance or convey or transfer the assets to the creditor in satisfaction of his lien, in whole or in part, whether or not the holder of the encumbrance has presented a claim, if it appears to be for the best interest of the estate. Payment of an encumbrance does not increase the share of the distributee entitled to the encumbered assets unless the distributee is entitled to exoneration.

Section 3-815. Administration in More Than One State; Duty of Personal Representative.

(a) All assets of estates being administered in this state are subject to all claims, allowances and charges existing or established against the personal representative wherever appointed.

(b) If the estate either in this state or as a whole is insufficient to cover all family exemptions and allowances determined by the law of the decedent's domicile, prior charges and claims, after satisfaction of the exemptions, allowances and charges, each claimant whose claim has been allowed either in this state or elsewhere in administrations of which the personal representative is aware, is entitled to receive payment of an equal proportion of his claim. If a preference or security in regard to a claim is allowed in another jurisdiction but not in this state, the creditor so benefited is to receive dividends from local assets only upon the balance of his claim after deducting the amount of the benefit.

(c) In case the family exemptions and allowances, prior charges and claims of the entire estate exceed the total value of the portions of the estate being administered separately and this state is not the state of the decedent's last domicile, the claims allowed in this state shall be paid their proportion if local assets are adequate for the purpose, and the balance of local assets shall be transferred to the domiciliary personal representative. If local assets are not sufficient to pay all claims allowed in this state the amount to which they are entitled, local assets shall be marshalled so that each claim allowed in this state is paid its proportion as far as possible, after taking into account all dividends on claims allowed in this state from assets in other jurisdictions.

Section 3-816. Final Distribution to Domiciliary Representative.

The estate of a non-resident decedent being administered by a personal representative appointed in this state shall, if there is a personal representative of the decedent's domicile willing to receive it, be distributed to the domiciliary personal representative for the benefit of the successors of the decedent unless (i) by virtue of the decedent's will, if any, and applicable choice of law rules, the successors are identified pursuant to the local law of this state without reference to the local law of the decedent's domicile; (ii) the personal representative of this state, after reasonable inquiry, is unaware of the existence or identity of a domiciliary personal representative; or (iii) the court orders otherwise in a proceeding for a closing order under Section 3-1001 or incident to the closing of a supervised administration. In other cases, distribution of the estate of a decedent shall be made in accordance with the other [parts] of this [article].

PART 9

SPECIAL PROVISIONS RELATING TO DISTRIBUTION

Section 3-901. Successors' Rights if No Administration.

In the absence of administration, the heirs and devisees are entitled to the estate in accordance with the terms of a probated will or the laws of intestate succession. Devisees may establish title by the probated will to devised property. Persons entitled to property by homestead allowance, exemption or intestacy may establish title thereto by proof of the decedent's ownership, his death, and their relationship to the decedent. Successors take subject to all charges incident to administration, including the claims of creditors and allowances of surviving spouse and dependent children, and subject to the rights of others resulting from abatement, retainer, advancement, and ademption.

Section 3-902. Distribution; Order in Which Assets Appropriated; Abatement.

(a) Except as provided in subsection (b) and except as provided in connection with the share of the surviving spouse who elects to take an elective share, shares of distributees abate, without any preference or priority as between real and personal property, in the following order: (i) property not disposed of by the will; (ii) residuary devises; (iii) general devises; (iv) specific devises. For purposes of abatement, a general devise charged on any specific property or fund is a specific devise to the extent of the value of the property on which it is charged, and upon the failure or insufficiency of the property on which it is charged, a general devise to the extent of the failure or insufficiency. Abatement within each classification is in proportion to the amounts of property each of the beneficiaries would have received if full distribution of the property had been made in accordance with the terms of the will.

(b) If the will expresses an order of abatement, or if the testamentary plan or the express or implied purpose of the devise would be defeated by the order of abatement stated in subsection (a), the shares of the distributees abate as may be found necessary to give effect to the intention of the testator.

Alternative A

(c) If the subject of a preferred devise is sold or used incident to administration, abatement shall be achieved by appropriate adjustments in, or contribution from, other interests in the remaining assets.

Alternative B

(c) If an estate of a decedent consists partly of separate property and partly of community property, the debts and expenses of administration shall be apportioned and charged against the different kinds of property in proportion to the relative value thereof.

(d) If the subject of a preferred devise is sold or used incident to administration, abatement shall be achieved by appropriate adjustments in, or contribution from, other interests in the remaining assets.

End of Alternatives

Section 3–903. Right of Retainer.

The amount of a non-contingent indebtedness of a successor to the estate if due, or its present value if not due, shall be offset against the successor's interest; but the successor has the benefit of any defense which would be available to him in a direct proceeding for recovery of the debt.

Section 3–904. Interest on General Pecuniary Devise.

General pecuniary devises bear interest at the legal rate beginning one year after the first appointment of a personal representative until payment, unless a contrary intent is indicated by the will.

Section 3–905. Penalty Clause for Contest.

A provision in a will purporting to penalize any interested person for contesting the will or instituting other proceedings relating to the estate is unenforceable if probable cause exists for instituting proceedings.

Section 3–906. Distribution in Kind; Valuation; Method.

(a) Unless a contrary intention is indicated by the will, the distributable assets of a decedent's estate shall be distributed in kind to the extent possible through application of the following provisions:

(1) A specific devisee is entitled to distribution of the thing devised to him, and a spouse or child who has selected particular assets of an estate as provided in Section 2–403 shall receive the items selected.

(2) Any homestead or family allowance or devise of a stated sum of money may be satisfied in kind provided

(A) the person entitled to the payment has not demanded payment in cash;

(B) the property distributed in kind is valued at fair market value as of the date of its distribution, and

(C) no residuary devisee has requested that the asset in question remain a part of the residue of the estate.

(3) For the purpose of valuation under paragraph (2) securities regularly traded on recognized exchanges, if distributed in kind, are valued at the price for the last sale of like securities traded on the business day prior to distribution, or if there was no sale on that day, at the median between amounts bid and offered at the close of that day. Assets consisting of sums owed the decedent or the estate by solvent debtors as to which there is no known dispute or defense are valued at the sum due with accrued interest or discounted to the date of distribution. For assets which do not have readily ascertainable values, a valuation as of a date not more than 30 days prior to the date of distribution, if otherwise reasonable, controls. For purposes of facilitating distribution, the personal representative may ascertain the value of the assets as of the time of the proposed distribution in any reasonable way, including the employment of qualified appraisers, even if the assets may have been previously appraised.

(4) The residuary estate shall be distributed in any equitable manner.

(b) After the probable charges against the estate are known, the personal representative may mail or deliver a proposal for distribution to all persons who have a right to object to the proposed distribution. The right of any distributee to object to the proposed distribution on the basis of the kind or value of asset he is to receive, if not waived earlier in writing, terminates if he fails to object in writing received by the personal representative within 30 days after mailing or delivery of the proposal.

Section 3–907. Distribution in Kind; Evidence.

If distribution in kind is made, the personal representative shall execute an instrument or deed of distribution assigning, transferring or releasing the assets to the distributee as evidence of the distributee's title to the property.

Section 3–908. Distribution; Right or Title of Distributee.

Proof that a distributee has received an instrument or deed of distribution of assets in kind, or payment in distribution, from a personal representative, is conclusive evidence that the distributee has succeeded to the interest of the estate in the distributed assets, as against all persons interested in the estate, except that the personal representative may recover the assets or their value if the distribution was improper.

Section 3–909. Improper Distribution; Liability of Distributee.

Unless the distribution or payment no longer can be questioned because of adjudication, estoppel, or limitation, a distributee of property improperly distributed or paid, or a claimant who was improperly paid, is liable to return the property improperly received and its income since distribution if he has the property. If he does not have the property, then he is liable to return the value as of the date of disposition of the property improperly received and its income and gain received by him.

Section 3–910. Purchasers From Distributees Protected.

If property distributed in kind or a security interest therein is acquired for value by a purchaser from or lender to a distributee who has received an instrument or deed of distribution from the personal representative, or is so acquired by a purchaser from or lender to a transferee from such distributee, the purchaser or lender takes title free of rights of any interested person in the estate and incurs no personal liability to the estate, or to any interested person, whether or not the distribution was proper or supported by court order or the authority of the personal representative was terminated before execution of the instrument or deed. This section protects a purchaser from or lender to a distributee who, as personal representative, has executed a deed of distribution to himself, as well as a purchaser from or lender to any other distributee or his transferee. To be protected under this provision, a purchaser or lender need not inquire whether a personal representative acted properly in making the distribution in kind, even if the personal representative and the distributee are the same

150

person, or whether the authority of the personal representative had terminated before the distribution. Any recorded instrument described in this section on which a state documentary fee is noted pursuant to [insert appropriate reference] shall be prima facie evidence that such transfer was made for value.

Section 3–911. Partition for Purpose of Distribution.

When two or more heirs or devisees are entitled to distribution of undivided interests in any real or personal property of the estate, the personal representative or one or more of the heirs or devisees may petition the court prior to the formal or informal closing of the estate, to make partition. After notice to the interested heirs or devisees, the court shall partition the property in the same manner as provided by the law for civil actions of partition. The court may direct the personal representative to sell any property which cannot be partitioned without prejudice to the owners and which cannot conveniently be allotted to any one party.

Section 3–912. Private Agreements Among Successors to Decedent Binding on Personal Representative.

Subject to the rights of creditors and taxing authorities, competent successors may agree among themselves to alter the interests, shares, or amounts to which they are entitled under the will of the decedent, or under the laws of intestacy, in any way that they provide in a written contract executed by all who are affected by its provisions. The personal representative shall abide by the terms of the agreement subject to his obligation to administer the estate for the benefit of creditors, to pay all taxes and costs of administration, and to carry out the responsibilities of his office for the benefit of any successors of the decedent who are not parties. Personal representatives of decedents' estates are not required to see to the performance of trusts if the trustee thereof is another person who is willing to accept the trust. Accordingly, trustees of a testamentary trust are successors for the purposes of this section. Nothing herein relieves trustees of any duties owed to beneficiaries of trusts.

Section 3–913. Distributions to Trustee.

(a) Before distributing to a trustee, the personal representative may require that the trust be registered if the state in which it is to be administered provides for registration and that the trustee inform the beneficiaries as provided in [Section 813 of the Uniform Trust Code].

(b) If the trust instrument does not excuse the trustee from giving bond, the personal representative may petition the appropriate court to require that the trustee post bond if he apprehends that distribution might jeopardize the interests of persons who are not able to protect themselves, and he may withhold distribution until the court has acted.

(c) No inference of negligence on the part of the personal representative shall be drawn from his failure to exercise the authority conferred by subsections (a) and (b).

[Section 3–914. Disposition of Unclaimed Assets.

(a) If an heir, devisee or claimant cannot be found, the personal representative shall distribute the share of the missing person to his conservator, if any, otherwise to the [state treasurer] to become a part of the [state escheat fund].

(b) The money received by [state treasurer] shall be paid to the person entitled on proof of his right thereto or, if the [state treasurer] refuses or fails to pay, the person may petition the court which appointed the personal representative, whereupon the court upon notice to the [state treasurer] may determine the person entitled to the money and order the [treasurer] to pay it to him. No interest is allowed thereon and the heir, devisee or claimant shall pay all costs and expenses incident to the proceeding. If no petition is made to the [court] within 8 years after payment to the [state treasurer], the right of recovery is barred.]

Section 3–915. Distribution to Person Under Disability.

(a) A personal representative may discharge his obligation to distribute to any person under legal disability by distributing in a manner expressly provided in the will.

(b) Unless contrary to an express provision in the will, the personal representative may discharge his obligation to distribute to a minor or person under other disability as authorized by Section 5–104 or any other statute. If the personal representative knows that a conservator has been appointed or that a proceeding for appointment of a conservator is pending, the personal representative is authorized to distribute only to the conservator.

(c) If the heir or devisee is under disability other than minority, the personal representative is authorized to distribute to:

(1) an attorney in fact who has authority under a power of attorney to receive property for that person; or

(2) the spouse, parent or other close relative with whom the person under disability resides if the distribution is of amounts not exceeding [$10,000] a year, or property not exceeding [$50,000] in value, unless the court authorizes a larger amount or greater value.

Persons receiving money or property for the disabled person are obligated to apply the money or property to the support of that person, but may not pay themselves except by way of reimbursement for out-of-pocket expenses for goods and services necessary for the support of the disabled person. Excess sums must be preserved for future support of the disabled person. The personal representative is not responsible for the proper application of money or property distributed pursuant to this subsection.

Section 3–916. [Reserved].

PART 9A

UNIFORM ESTATE TAX APPORTIONMENT ACT (2003)

[The Uniform Estate Tax Apportionment Act (2003)
is reproduced elsewhere in this volume.]

PART 10

CLOSING ESTATES

Section 3–1001. Formal Proceedings Terminating Administration; Testate or Intestate; Order of General Protection.

(a) A personal representative or any interested person may petition for an order of complete settlement of the estate. The personal representative may petition at any time, and any other interested person may petition after one year from the appointment of the original personal representative except that no petition under this section may be entertained until the time for presenting claims which arose prior to the death of the decedent has expired. The petition may request the court to determine testacy, if not previously determined, to consider the final account or compel or approve an accounting and distribution, to construe any will or determine heirs and adjudicate the final settlement and distribution of the estate. After notice to all interested persons and hearing the court may enter an order or orders, on appropriate conditions, determining the persons entitled to distribution of the estate, and, as circumstances require, approving settlement and directing or approving distribution of the estate and discharging the personal representative from further claim or demand of any interested person.

(b) If one or more heirs or devisees were omitted as parties in, or were not given notice of, a previous formal testacy proceeding, the court, on proper petition for an order of complete settlement of the estate under this section, and after notice to the omitted or unnotified persons and other interested parties determined to be interested on the assumption that the previous order concerning testacy is conclusive as to those given notice of the earlier proceeding, may determine testacy as it affects the omitted persons and confirm or alter the previous order of testacy as it affects all interested persons as appropriate in the light of the new proofs. In the absence of objection by an omitted or unnotified person, evidence received in the original testacy proceeding shall constitute prima facie proof of due execution of any will previously admitted to probate, or of the fact that the decedent left no valid will if the prior proceedings determined this fact.

Section 3–1002. Formal Proceedings Terminating Testate Administration; Order Construing Will Without Adjudicating Testacy.

A personal representative administering an estate under an informally probated will or any devisee under an informally probated will may petition for an order of settlement of the estate which will not adjudicate the testacy status of the decedent. The personal representative may petition at any time, and a devisee may petition after one year, from the appointment of the original personal representative, except that no petition under this section may be entertained until the time for presenting claims which arose prior to the death of the decedent has expired. The petition may request the court to consider the final account or compel or approve an accounting and distribution, to construe the will and adjudicate final settlement and distribution of the estate. After notice to all devisees and the personal representative and hearing, the court may enter an order or orders, on appropriate conditions, determining the persons entitled to distribution of the estate under the will, and, as circumstances require, approving settlement and directing or approving distribution of the estate and discharging the personal representative from further claim or demand of any devisee who is a party to the proceeding and those he represents. If it appears that a part of the estate is intestate, the proceedings shall be dismissed or amendments made to meet the provisions of Section 3–1001.

Section 3–1003. Closing Estates; By Sworn Statement of Personal Representative.

(a) Unless prohibited by order of the court and except for estates being administered in supervised administration proceedings, a personal representative may close an estate by filing with the court no earlier than six months after the date of original appointment of a general personal representative for the estate, a verified statement stating that the personal representative, or a previous personal representative, has:

(1) determined that the time limited for presentation of creditors' claims has expired.

(2) fully administered the estate of the decedent by making payment, settlement, or other disposition of all claims that were presented, expenses of administration and estate, inheritance and other death taxes, except as specified in the statement, and that the assets of the estate have been distributed to the persons entitled. If any claims remain undischarged, the statement must state whether the personal representative has distributed the estate subject to possible liability with the agreement of the distributees or state in detail other arrangements that have been made to accommodate outstanding liabilities; and

(3) sent a copy of the statement to all distributees of the estate and to all creditors or other claimants of whom the personal representative is aware whose claims are neither paid nor barred and has furnished a full account in writing of the personal representative's administration to the distributees whose interests are affected thereby.

(b) If no proceedings involving the personal representative are pending in the court one year after the closing statement is filed, the appointment of the personal representative terminates.

Section 3-1004. Liability of Distributees to Claimants.

After assets of an estate have been distributed and subject to Section 3–1006, an undischarged claim not barred may be prosecuted in a proceeding against one or more distributees. No distributee shall be liable to claimants for amounts received as exempt property, homestead or family allowances, or for amounts in excess of the value of his distribution as of the time of distribution. As between distributees, each shall bear the cost of satisfaction of unbarred claims as if the claim had been satisfied in the course of administration. Any distributee who shall have failed to notify other distributees of the demand made upon him by the claimant in sufficient time to permit them to join in any proceeding in which the claim was asserted against him loses his right of contribution against other distributees.

Section 3-1005. Limitations on Proceedings Against Personal Representative.

Unless previously barred by adjudication and except as provided in the closing statement, the rights of successors and of creditors whose claims have not otherwise been barred against the personal representative for breach of fiduciary duty are barred unless a proceeding to assert the same is commenced within six months after the filing of the closing statement. The rights thus barred do not include rights to recover from a personal representative for fraud, misrepresentation, or inadequate disclosure related to the settlement of the decedent's estate.

Section 3-1006. Limitations on Actions and Proceedings Against Distributees.

Unless previously adjudicated in a formal testacy proceeding or in a proceeding settling the accounts of a personal representative or otherwise barred, the claim of a claimant to recover from a distributee who is liable to pay the claim, and the right of an heir or devisee, or of a successor personal representative acting in their behalf, to recover property improperly distributed or its value from any distributee is forever barred at the later of three years after the decedent's death or one year after the time of its distribution, but all claims of creditors of the decedent are barred one year after the decedent's death. This section does not bar an action to recover property or value received as a result of fraud.

Section 3-1007. Certificate Discharging Liens Securing Fiduciary Performance.

After his appointment has terminated, the personal representative, his sureties, or any successor of either, upon the filing of a verified application showing, so far as is known by the applicant, that no action concerning the estate is pending in any court, is entitled to receive a certificate from the Registrar that the personal representative appears to have fully administered the estate in question. The certificate evidences discharge of any lien on any property given to secure the obligation of the personal representative in lieu of bond or any surety, but does not preclude action against the personal representative or the surety.

Section 3-1008. Subsequent Administration.

If other property of the estate is discovered after an estate has been settled and the personal representative discharged or after one year after a closing statement has been filed, the court upon petition of any interested person and upon notice as it directs may appoint the same or a successor personal representative to administer the subsequently discovered estate. If a new appointment is made, unless the court orders otherwise, the provisions of this [code] apply as appropriate; but no claim previously barred may be asserted in the subsequent administration.

PART 11

COMPROMISE OF CONTROVERSIES

Section 3-1101. Effect of Approval of Agreements Involving Trusts, Inalienable Interests, or Interests of Third Persons.

A compromise of any controversy as to admission to probate of any instrument offered for formal probate as the will of a decedent, the construction, validity, or effect of any governing instrument, the rights or interests in the estate of the decedent, of any successor, or the administration of the estate, if approved in a formal proceeding in the court for that purpose, is binding on all the parties thereto including those unborn, unascertained or who could not be located. An approved compromise is binding even though it may affect a trust or an inalienable interest. A compromise does not impair the rights of creditors or of taxing authorities who are not parties to it.

Section 3-1102. Procedure for Securing Court Approval of Compromise.

The procedure for securing court approval of a compromise is as follows:

(1)   The terms of the compromise shall be set forth in an agreement in writing which shall be executed by all competent persons and parents acting for any minor child having beneficial interests or having claims which will or may be affected by the compromise. Execution is not required by any person whose identity cannot be ascertained or whose whereabouts is unknown and cannot reasonably be ascertained.

(2)   Any interested person, including the personal representative, if any, or a trustee, then may submit the agreement to the court for its approval and for execution by the personal representative, the trustee of every affected testamentary trust, and other fiduciaries and representatives.

(3)   After notice to all interested persons or their representatives, including the personal representative of any estate and all affected trustees of trusts, the court, if it finds that the contest or controversy is in good faith and that the effect of the agreement upon the interests of persons represented by fiduciaries or other representatives is just and reasonable, shall make an order approving the agreement and directing all fiduciaries subject to its jurisdiction to execute the agreement. Minor children represented only by their parents may be bound only if their parents join with other competent persons in execution of the compromise. Upon the making of the order and the execution of the agreement, all further disposition of the estate is in accordance with the terms of the agreement.

PART 12

COLLECTION OF PERSONAL PROPERTY BY AFFIDAVIT AND SUMMARY ADMINISTRATION PROCEDURE FOR SMALL ESTATES

Section 3-1201. Collection of Personal Property by Affidavit.

(a)   Thirty days after the death of a decedent, any person indebted to the decedent or having possession of tangible personal property or an instrument evidencing a debt, obligation, stock or chose in action belonging to the decedent shall make payment of the indebtedness or deliver the tangible personal property or an instrument evidencing a debt, obligation, stock or chose in action to a person claiming to be the successor of the decedent upon being presented an affidavit made by or on behalf of the successor stating that:

(1)   the value of the entire estate, wherever located, less liens and encumbrances, does not exceed $25,000;

(2)   30 days have elapsed since the death of the decedent;

(3)   no application or petition for the appointment of a personal representative is pending or has been granted in any jurisdiction; and

(4)   the claiming successor is entitled to payment or delivery of the property.

(b)   A transfer agent of any security shall change the registered ownership on the books of a corporation from the decedent to the successor or successors upon the presentation of an affidavit as provided in subsection (a).

Section 3-1202. Effect of Affidavit.

The person paying, delivering, transferring, or issuing personal property or the evidence thereof pursuant to affidavit is discharged and released to the same extent as if he dealt with a personal representative of the decedent. He is not required to see to the application of the personal property or evidence thereof or to inquire into the truth of any statement in the affidavit. If any person to whom an affidavit is delivered refuses to pay, deliver, transfer, or issue any personal property or evidence thereof, it may be recovered or its payment, delivery, transfer, or issuance compelled upon proof of their right in a proceeding brought for the purpose by or on behalf of the persons entitled thereto. Any person to whom payment, delivery, transfer or issuance is made is answerable and accountable therefor to any personal representative of the estate or to any other person having a superior right.

Section 3-1203. Small Estates; Summary Administration Procedure.

If it appears from the inventory and appraisal that the value of the entire estate, less liens and encumbrances, does not exceed homestead allowance, exempt property, family allowance, costs and expenses of administration, reasonable funeral expenses, and reasonable and necessary medical and hospital expenses of the last illness of the decedent, the personal representative, without giving notice to creditors, may immediately disburse and distribute the estate to the persons entitled thereto and file a closing statement as provided in Section 3-1204.

Section 3-1204. Small Estates; Closing by Sworn Statement of Personal Representative.

(a)   Unless prohibited by order of the court and except for estates being administered by supervised personal representatives, a personal representative may close an estate administered under the summary procedures of Section 3-1203 by filing with the court, at any time after disbursement and distribution of the estate, a verified statement stating that:

(1)   to the best knowledge of the personal representative, the value of the entire estate, less liens and encumbrances, did not exceed homestead allowance, exempt property, family allowance, costs and expenses of administration, reasonable funeral expenses, and reasonable, necessary medical and hospital expenses of the last illness of the decedent;

(2)   the personal representative has fully administered the estate by disbursing and distributing it to the persons entitled thereto; and

(3)   the personal representative has sent a copy of the closing statement to all distributees of the estate and to all creditors or other claimants of whom he is aware whose claims are neither paid nor barred and has furnished a full account in writing of his administration to the distributees whose interests are affected.

(b)   If no actions or proceedings involving the personal representative are pending in the court one year after the closing statement is filed, the appointment of the personal representative terminates.

(c)   A closing statement filed under this section has the same effect as one filed under Section 3-1003.

ARTICLE IV

FOREIGN PERSONAL REPRESENTATIVES; ANCILLARY ADMINISTRATION

PART 1
DEFINITIONS

PART 2
POWERS OF FOREIGN PERSONAL REPRESENTATIVES

PART 3
JURISDICTION OVER FOREIGN REPRESENTATIVES

PART 4
JUDGMENTS AND PERSONAL REPRESENTATIVE

PART 1

DEFINITIONS

Section 4–101. Definitions.

In this [article]

(1)   "local administration" means administration by a personal representative appointed in this state pursuant to appointment proceedings described in [Article] III.

(2)   "local personal representative" includes any personal representative appointed in this state pursuant to appointment proceedings described in [Article] III and excludes foreign personal representatives who acquire the power of a local personal representative pursuant to Section 4–205.

(3)   "resident creditor" means a person domiciled in, or doing business in this state, who is, or could be, a claimant against an estate of a non-resident decedent.

PART 2

POWERS OF FOREIGN PERSONAL REPRESENTATIVES

Section 4–201. Payment of Debt and Delivery of Property to Domiciliary Foreign Personal Representative Without Local Administration.

At any time after the expiration of 60 days from the death of a nonresident decedent, any person indebted to the estate of the nonresident decedent or having possession or control of personal property, or of an instrument evidencing a debt, obligation, stock or chose in action belonging to the estate of the nonresident decedent may pay the debt, deliver the personal property, or the instrument evidencing the debt, obligation, stock or chose in action, to the domiciliary foreign personal representative of the nonresident decedent upon being presented with proof of his appointment and an affidavit made by or on behalf of the representative stating:

(1)   the date of the death of the nonresident decedent,

(2)   that no local administration, or application or petition therefor, is pending in this state,

(3)   that the domiciliary foreign personal representative is entitled to payment or delivery.

Section 4–202. Payment or Delivery Discharges.

Payment or delivery made in good faith on the basis of the proof of authority and affidavit releases the debtor or person having possession of the personal property to the same extent as if payment or delivery had been made to a local personal representative.

Section 4–203. Resident Creditor Notice.

Payment or delivery under Section 4–201 may not be made if a resident creditor of the nonresident decedent has notified the debtor of the nonresident decedent or the person having possession of the personal property belonging to the nonresident decedent that the debt should not be paid nor the property delivered to the domiciliary foreign personal representative.

Section 4–204. Proof of Authority—Bond.

If no local administration or application or petition therefor is pending in this state, a domiciliary foreign personal representative may file with a court in this state in a [county] in which property belonging to the decedent is located, authenticated copies of his appointment and of any official bond he has given.

Section 4–205. Powers.

A domiciliary foreign personal representative who has complied with Section 4–204 may exercise as to assets in this state all powers of a local personal representative and may maintain actions and proceedings in this state subject to any conditions imposed upon nonresident parties generally.

Section 4–206. Power of Representatives in Transition.

The power of a domiciliary foreign personal representative under Section 4–201 or 4–205 shall be exercised only if there is no administration or application therefor pending in this state. An application or petition for local administration of the estate terminates the power of the foreign personal representative to act under Section 4–205, but the local court may allow the foreign personal representative to exercise limited powers to preserve the estate. No person who, before receiving actual notice of a pending local administration, has changed his position in reliance upon the powers of a foreign personal representative shall be prejudiced by reason of the application or petition for, or grant of, local administration. The local personal representative is subject to all duties and obligations which have accrued by virtue of the exercise of the powers by the foreign personal representative and may be substituted for him in any action or proceedings in this state.

Section 4–207. Ancillary and Other Local Administrations; Provisions Governing.

In respect to a nonresident decedent, the provisions of [Article] III of this [code] govern:

(1) proceedings, if any, in a court of this state for probate of the will, appointment, removal, supervision, and discharge of the local personal representative, and any other order concerning the estate; and

(2) the status, powers, duties and liabilities of any local personal representative and the rights of claimants, purchasers, distributees and others in regard to a local administration.

PART 3

JURISDICTION OVER FOREIGN REPRESENTATIVES

Section 4–301. Jurisdiction by Act of Foreign Personal Representative.

A foreign personal representative submits personally to the jurisdiction of the courts of this state in any proceeding relating to the estate by (i) filing authenticated copies of his appointment as provided in Section 4–204, (ii) receiving payment of money or taking delivery of personal property under Section 4–201, or (iii) doing any act as a personal representative in this state which would have given the state jurisdiction over him as an individual. Jurisdiction under (ii) is limited to the money or value of personal property collected.

Section 4–302. Jurisdiction by Act of Decedent.

In addition to jurisdiction conferred by Section 4–301, a foreign personal representative is subject to the jurisdiction of the courts of this state to the same extent that his decedent was subject to jurisdiction immediately prior to death.

Section 4–303. Service on Foreign Personal Representative.

(a) Service of process may be made upon the foreign personal representative by registered or certified mail, addressed to his last reasonably ascertainable address, requesting a return receipt signed by addressee only. Notice by ordinary first class mail is sufficient if registered or certified mail service to the addressee is unavailable. Service may be made upon a foreign personal representative in the manner in which service could have been made under other laws of this state on either the foreign personal representative or his decedent immediately prior to death.

(b) If service is made upon a foreign personal representative as provided in subsection (a), he shall be allowed at least [30] days within which to appear or respond.

PART 4

JUDGMENTS AND PERSONAL REPRESENTATIVE

Section 4–401. Effect of Adjudication for or Against Personal Representative.

An adjudication rendered in any jurisdiction in favor of or against any personal representative of the estate is as binding on the local personal representative as if he were a party to the adjudication.

ARTICLE V

UNIFORM GUARDIANSHIP AND PROTECTIVE PROCEEDINGS ACT (1997/1998)

PART 1
GENERAL PROVISIONS

PART 4
PROTECTION OF PROPERTY OF PROTECTED PERSON

PART 1

GENERAL PROVISIONS

Section 5–101. Short Title.

This [article] may be cited as the Uniform Guardianship and Protective Proceedings Act.

Section 5–102. Definitions.

In this [article]:

(1) "Conservator" means a person who is appointed by a court to manage the estate of a protected person. The term includes a limited conservator.

(2) "Court" means the [designate appropriate court].

(3) "Guardian" means a person who has qualified as a guardian of a minor or incapacitated person pursuant to appointment by a parent or spouse, or by the court. The term includes a limited, emergency, and temporary substitute guardian but not a guardian ad litem.

(4) "Incapacitated person" means an individual who, for reasons other than being a minor, is unable to receive and evaluate information or make or communicate decisions to such an extent that the individual lacks the ability to meet essential requirements for physical health, safety, or self-care, even with appropriate technological assistance.

(5) "Legal representative" includes the lawyer for the respondent, a representative payee, a guardian or conservator acting for a respondent in this state or elsewhere, a trustee or custodian of a trust or custodianship of which the respondent is a beneficiary, and an agent designated under a power of attorney, whether for health care or property, in which the respondent is identified as the principal.

(6) "Minor" means an unemancipated individual who has not attained [18] years of age.

(7) "Parent" means a parent whose parental rights have not been terminated.

(8) "Protected person" means a minor or other individual for whom a conservator has been appointed or other protective order has been made.

(9) "Respondent" means an individual for whom the appointment of a guardian or conservator or other protective order is sought.

(10) "Ward" means an individual for whom a guardian has been appointed.

Section 5–103. [Reserved].

Section 5–104. Facility of Transfer.

(a) Unless a person required to transfer money or personal property to a minor knows that a conservator has been appointed or that a proceeding for appointment of a conservator of the estate of the minor is pending, the person may do so, as to an amount or value not exceeding [$10,000] a year, by transferring it to:

(1) a person who has the care and custody of the minor and with whom the minor resides;

(2) a guardian of the minor;

(3) a custodian under the Uniform Transfers To Minors Act or custodial trustee under the Uniform Custodial Trust Act; or

(4) a financial institution as a deposit in an interest-bearing account or certificate in the sole name of the minor and giving notice of the deposit to the minor.

(b) A person who transfers money or property in compliance with this section is not responsible for its proper application.

(c) A guardian or other person who receives money or property for a minor under subsection (a)(1) or (2) may only apply it to the support, care, education, health, and welfare of the minor, and may not derive a personal financial benefit except for reimbursement for necessary expenses. Any excess must be preserved for the future support, care, education, health, and welfare of the minor, and any balance must be transferred to the minor upon emancipation or attaining majority.

Section 5–105. Delegation of Power by Parent or Guardian.

A parent or guardian of a minor or incapacitated person, by a power of attorney, may delegate to another person, for a period not exceeding six months, any power regarding care, custody, or property of the minor or ward, except the power to consent to marriage or adoption.

Section 5–106. Subject-Matter Jurisdiction.

(a) Except to the extent the guardianship is subject to the [insert citation to Uniform Child Custody Jurisdiction and Enforcement Act], the court of this state has jurisdiction over guardianship for minors domiciled or present in this state. The court of this state has jurisdiction over protective proceedings for minors domiciled in or having property located in this state.

(b) The court of this state has jurisdiction over guardianship and protective proceedings for an adult individual as provided in the [insert citation to Uniform Adult Guardianship and Protective Proceedings Jurisdiction Act].

Section 5–107. Transfer of Jurisdiction.

(a) Except as otherwise provided in subsection (b), the following rules apply:

(1) After the appointment of a guardian or conservator or entry of another protective order, the court making the appointment or entering the order may transfer the proceeding to a court in another [county] in this state or to another state if the court is satisfied that a transfer will serve the best interest of the ward or protected person.

(2) If a guardianship or protective proceeding is pending in another state or a foreign country and a petition for guardianship or protective proceeding is filed in a court in this state, the court in this state shall notify the original court and, after consultation with the original court, assume or decline jurisdiction, whichever is in the best interest of the ward or protected person.

(3) A guardian, conservator, or like fiduciary appointed in another state may petition the court for appointment as a guardian or conservator in this state if venue in this state is or will be established. The appointment may be made upon proof of appointment in the other state and presentation of a certified copy of the portion of the court record in the other state specified by the court in this state. Notice of hearing on the petition, together with a copy of the petition, must be given to the ward or protected person, if the ward or protected person has attained 14 years of age, and to the persons who would be entitled to notice if the regular procedures for appointment of a guardian or conservator under this [article] were applicable. The court shall make the appointment in this state unless it concludes that the appointment would not be in the best interest of the ward or protected person. On the filing of an acceptance of office and any required bond, the court shall issue appropriate letters of guardianship or conservatorship. Not later than 14 days after an appointment, the guardian or conservator shall send or deliver a copy of the order of appointment to the ward or protected person, if the ward or protected person has attained 14 years of age, and to all persons given notice of the hearing on the petition.

(b) This section does not apply to a guardianship or protective proceeding for an adult individual that is subject to the transfer provisions of [insert citation to Article 3 of the Uniform Adult Guardianship and Protective Proceedings Jurisdiction Act (2007)].

Section 5–108. Venue.

(a)   Venue for a guardianship proceeding for a minor is in the [county] of this state in which the minor resides or is present at the time the proceeding is commenced.

(b)   Venue for a guardianship proceeding for an incapacitated person is in the [county] of this state in which the respondent resides and, if the respondent has been admitted to an institution by order of a court of competent jurisdiction, in the [county] in which the court is located. Venue for the appointment of an emergency or a temporary substitute guardian of an incapacitated person is also in the [county] in which the respondent is present.

(c)   Venue for a protective proceeding is in the [county] of this state in which the respondent resides, whether or not a guardian has been appointed in another place or, if the respondent does not reside in this state, in any [county] of this state in which property of the respondent is located.

(d)   If a proceeding under this [article] is brought in more than one [county] in this state, the court of the [county] in which the proceeding is first brought has the exclusive right to proceed unless that court determines that venue is properly in another court or that the interests of justice otherwise require that the proceeding be transferred.

Section 5–109. [Reserved].

Section 5–110. Letters of Office.

Upon the guardian's filing of an acceptance of office, the court shall issue appropriate letters of guardianship. Upon the conservator's filing of an acceptance of office and any required bond, the court shall issue appropriate letters of conservatorship. Letters of guardianship must indicate whether the guardian was appointed by the court, a parent, or the spouse. Any limitation on the powers of a guardian or conservator or of the assets subject to a conservatorship must be endorsed on the guardian's or conservator's letters.

Section 5–111. Effect of Acceptance of Appointment.

By accepting appointment, a guardian or conservator submits personally to the jurisdiction of the court in any proceeding relating to the guardianship or conservatorship. The petitioner shall send or deliver notice of any proceeding to the guardian or conservator at the guardian's or conservator's address shown in the court records and at any other address then known to the petitioner.

Section 5–112. Termination of or Change in Guardian's or Conservator's Appointment.

(a)   The appointment of a guardian or conservator terminates upon the death, resignation, or removal of the guardian or conservator or upon termination of the guardianship or conservatorship. A resignation of a guardian or conservator is effective when approved by the court. [A parental or spousal appointment as guardian under an informally probated will terminates if the will is later denied probate in a formal proceeding.] Termination of the appointment of a guardian or conservator does not affect the liability of either for previous acts or the obligation to account for money and other assets of the ward or protected person.

(b)   A ward, protected person, or person interested in the welfare of a ward or protected person may petition for removal of a guardian or conservator on the ground that removal would be in the best interest of the ward or protected person or for other good cause. A guardian or conservator may petition for permission to resign. A petition for removal or permission to resign may include a request for appointment of a successor guardian or conservator.

(c)   The court may appoint an additional guardian or conservator at any time, to serve immediately or upon some other designated event, and may appoint a successor guardian or conservator in the event of a vacancy or make the appointment in contemplation of a vacancy, to serve if a vacancy occurs. An additional or successor guardian or conservator may file an acceptance of appointment at any time after the appointment, but not later than 30 days after the occurrence of the vacancy or other designated event. The additional or successor guardian or conservator becomes eligible to act on the occurrence of the vacancy or designated event, or the filing of the acceptance of appointment, whichever last occurs. A successor guardian or conservator succeeds to the predecessor's powers, and a successor conservator succeeds to the predecessor's title to the protected person's assets.

Section 5–113. Notice.

(a)   Except as otherwise ordered by the court for good cause, if notice of a hearing on a petition is required, other than a notice for which specific requirements are otherwise provided, the petitioner shall give notice of the time and place of the hearing to the person to be notified. Notice must be given in compliance with [insert the applicable rule of civil procedure], at least 14 days before the hearing.

(b)   Proof of notice must be made before or at the hearing and filed in the proceeding.

(c)   A notice under this [article] must be given in plain language.

Section 5–114. Waiver of Notice.

A person may waive notice by a writing signed by the person or the person's attorney and filed in the proceeding. However, a respondent, ward, or protected person may not waive notice.

Section 5–115. Guardian Ad Litem.

At any stage of a proceeding, a court may appoint a guardian ad litem if the court determines that representation of the interest otherwise would be inadequate. If not precluded by a conflict of interest, a guardian ad litem may be appointed to represent several individuals or interests. The court shall state on the record the duties of the guardian ad litem and its reasons for the appointment.

Section 5–116. Request for Notice; Interested Persons.

An interested person not otherwise entitled to notice who desires to be notified before any order is made in a guardianship proceeding, including a proceeding after the appointment of a guardian, or in a protective proceeding, may file a request for notice with the clerk of the court in which the proceeding is pending. The clerk shall send or deliver a copy of the request to the guardian and to the conservator if one has been appointed. A request is not effective unless it contains a statement showing the interest of the person making it and the address of that person or a lawyer to whom notice is to be given. The request is effective only as to proceedings conducted after its filing. A governmental agency paying or planning to pay benefits to the respondent or protected person is an interested person in a protective proceeding.

Section 5–117. Multiple Appointments or Nominations.

If a respondent or other person makes more than one written appointment or nomination of a guardian or a conservator, the most recent controls.

PART 2

GUARDIANSHIP OF MINOR

Section 5–201. Appointment and Status of Guardian.

A person becomes a guardian of a minor by parental appointment or upon appointment by the court. The guardianship continues until terminated, without regard to the location of the guardian or minor ward.

Section 5–202. Parental Appointment of Guardian.

(a)   A guardian may be appointed by will or other signed writing by a parent for any minor child the parent has or may have in the future. The appointment may specify the desired limitations on the powers to be given to the guardian. The appointing parent may revoke or amend the appointment before confirmation by the court.

(b)   Upon petition of an appointing parent and a finding that the appointing parent will likely become unable to care for the child within [two] years, and after notice as provided in Section 5–205(a), the court, before the appointment becomes effective, may confirm the parent's selection of a guardian and terminate the rights of others to object.

(c)   Subject to Section 5–203, the appointment of a guardian becomes effective upon the appointing parent's death, an adjudication that the parent is an incapacitated person, or a written determination by a physician who has examined the parent that the parent is no longer able to care for the child, whichever first occurs.

(d)   The guardian becomes eligible to act upon the filing of an acceptance of appointment, which must be filed within 30 days after the guardian's appointment becomes effective. The guardian shall:

(1)   file the acceptance of appointment and a copy of the will with the court of the [county] in which the will was or could be probated or, in the case of another appointing instrument, file the acceptance of appointment and the appointing instrument with the court of the [county] in which the minor resides or is present; and

(2)   give written notice of the acceptance of appointment to the appointing parent, if living, the minor, if the minor has attained 14 years of age, and a person other than the parent having care and custody of the minor.

(e)   Unless the appointment was previously confirmed by the court, the notice given under subsection (d)(2) must include a statement of the right of those notified to terminate the appointment by filing a written objection in the court as provided in Section 5–203.

(f)   Unless the appointment was previously confirmed by the court, within 30 days after filing the notice and the appointing instrument, a guardian shall petition the court for confirmation of the appointment, giving notice in the manner provided in Section 5–205(a).

(g)   The appointment of a guardian by a parent does not supersede the parental rights of either parent. If both parents are dead or have been adjudged incapacitated persons, an appointment by the last parent who died or was adjudged incapacitated has priority. An appointment by a parent which is effected by filing the guardian's acceptance under a will probated in the state of the testator's domicile is effective in this state.

(h)   The powers of a guardian who timely complies with the requirements of subsections (d) and (f) relate back to give acts by the guardian which are of benefit to the minor and occurred on or after the date the appointment became effective the same effect as those that occurred after the filing of the acceptance of the appointment.

(i)   The authority of a guardian appointed under this section terminates upon the first to occur of the appointment of a guardian by the court or the giving of written notice to the guardian of the filing of an objection pursuant to Section 5–203.

Section 5–203. Objection by Minor or Others to Parental Appointment.

Until the court has confirmed an appointee under Section 5–202, a minor who is the subject of an appointment by a parent and who has attained 14 years of age, the other parent, or a person other than a parent or guardian having care or custody of the minor may prevent or terminate the appointment at any time by filing a written objection in the court in which the appointing instrument is filed and giving notice of the objection to the guardian and any other persons entitled to notice of the acceptance of the appointment. An objection may be withdrawn, and if withdrawn is of no effect. The objection does not preclude judicial appointment of the person selected by the parent. The court may treat the filing of an objection as a petition for the appointment of an emergency or a temporary guardian under Section 5–204, and proceed accordingly.

Section 5–204. Judicial Appointment of Guardian: Conditions for Appointment.

(a)   A minor or a person interested in the welfare of a minor may petition for appointment of a guardian.

(b)   The court may appoint a guardian for a minor if the court finds the appointment is in the minor's best interest, and:

(1)   the parents consent;

(2)   all parental rights have been terminated; or

(3)   the parents are unwilling or unable to exercise their parental rights.

(c)   If a guardian is appointed by a parent pursuant to Section 5–202 and the appointment has not been prevented or terminated under Section 5–203, that appointee has priority for appointment. However, the court may proceed with another appointment upon a finding that the appointee under Section 5–202 has failed to accept the appointment within 30 days after notice of the guardianship proceeding.

(d)   If necessary and on petition or motion and whether or not the conditions of subsection (b) have been established, the court may appoint a temporary guardian for a minor upon a showing that an immediate need exists and that the appointment would be in the best interest of the minor. Notice in the manner provided in Section 5–113 must be given to the parents and to a minor who has attained 14 years of age. Except as otherwise ordered by the court, the temporary guardian has the authority of an unlimited guardian, but the duration of the temporary guardianship may not exceed six months. Within five days after the appointment, the temporary guardian shall send or deliver a copy of the order to all individuals who would be entitled to notice of hearing under Section 5–205.

(e)   If the court finds that following the procedures of this [part] will likely result in substantial harm to a minor's health or safety and that no other person appears to have authority to act in the circumstances, the court, on appropriate petition, may appoint an emergency guardian for the minor. The duration of the guardian's authority may not exceed [30] days and the guardian may exercise only the powers specified in the order. Reasonable notice of the time and place of a hearing on the petition for appointment of an emergency guardian must be given to the minor, if the minor has attained 14 years of age, to each living parent of the minor, and a person having care or custody of the minor, if other than a parent. The court may dispense with the notice if it finds from affidavit or testimony that the minor will be substantially harmed before a hearing can be held on the petition. If the guardian is appointed without notice, notice of the appointment must be given within 48 hours after the appointment and a hearing on the appropriateness of the appointment held within [five] days after the appointment.

Section 5–205. Judicial Appointment of Guardian: Procedure.

(a)   After a petition for appointment of a guardian is filed, the court shall schedule a hearing, and the petitioner shall give notice of the time and place of the hearing, together with a copy of the petition, to:

(1)   the minor, if the minor has attained 14 years of age and is not the petitioner;

(2)   any person alleged to have had the primary care and custody of the minor during the 60 days before the filing of the petition;

(3)   each living parent of the minor or, if there is none, the adult nearest in kinship that can be found;

(4)   any person nominated as guardian by the minor if the minor has attained 14 years of age;

(5)   any appointee of a parent whose appointment has not been prevented or terminated under Section 5–203; and

(6)   any guardian or conservator currently acting for the minor in this state or elsewhere.

(b)   The court, upon hearing, shall make the appointment if it finds that a qualified person seeks appointment, venue is proper, the required notices have been given, the conditions of Section 5–204(b) have been met, and the best interest of the minor will be served by the appointment. In other cases, the court may dismiss the proceeding or make any other disposition of the matter that will serve the best interest of the minor.

(c)   If the court determines at any stage of the proceeding, before or after appointment, that the interests of the minor are or may be inadequately represented, it may appoint a lawyer to represent the minor, giving consideration to the choice of the minor if the minor has attained 14 years of age.

Section 5–206. Judicial Appointment of Guardian: Priority of Minor's Nominee; Limited Guardianship.

(a)   The court shall appoint as guardian a person whose appointment will be in the best interest of the minor. The court shall appoint a person nominated by the minor, if the minor has attained 14 years of age, unless the court finds the appointment will be contrary to the best interest of the minor.

(b)   In the interest of developing self-reliance of a ward or for other good cause, the court, at the time of appointment or later, on its own motion or on motion of the minor ward or other interested person, may limit the powers of a guardian otherwise granted by this [part] and thereby create a limited guardianship. Following the same procedure, the court may grant additional powers or withdraw powers previously granted.

Section 5–207. Duties of Guardian.

(a)   Except as otherwise limited by the court, a guardian of a minor ward has the duties and responsibilities of a parent regarding the ward's support, care, education, health, and welfare. A guardian shall act at all times in the ward's best interest and exercise reasonable care, diligence, and prudence.

(b)   A guardian shall:

(1)   become or remain personally acquainted with the ward and maintain sufficient contact with the ward to know of the ward's capacities, limitations, needs, opportunities, and physical and mental health;

(2)   take reasonable care of the ward's personal effects and bring a protective proceeding if necessary to protect other property of the ward;

(3)   expend money of the ward which has been received by the guardian for the ward's current needs for support, care, education, health, and welfare;

(4)   conserve any excess money of the ward for the ward's future needs, but if a conservator has been appointed for the estate of the ward, the guardian shall pay the money at least quarterly to the conservator to be conserved for the ward's future needs;

(5)   report the condition of the ward and account for money and other assets in the guardian's possession or subject to the guardian's control, as ordered by the court on application of any person interested in the ward's welfare or as required by court rule; and

(6)   inform the court of any change in the ward's custodial dwelling or address.

Section 5–208. Powers of Guardian.

(a)   Except as otherwise limited by the court, a guardian of a minor ward has the powers of a parent regarding the ward's support, care, education, health, and welfare.

(b)   A guardian may:

    (1)   apply for and receive money for the support of the ward otherwise payable to the ward's parent, guardian, or custodian under the terms of any statutory system of benefits or insurance or any private contract, devise, trust, conservatorship, or custodianship;

    (2)   if otherwise consistent with the terms of any order by a court of competent jurisdiction relating to custody of the ward, take custody of the ward and establish the ward's place of custodial dwelling, but may only establish or move the ward's custodial dwelling outside the state upon express authorization of the court;

    (3)   if a conservator for the estate of a ward has not been appointed with existing authority, commence a proceeding, including an administrative proceeding, or take other appropriate action to compel a person to support the ward or to pay money for the benefit of the ward;

    (4)   consent to medical or other care, treatment, or service for the ward;

    (5)   consent to the marriage of the ward; and

    (6)   if reasonable under all of the circumstances, delegate to the ward certain responsibilities for decisions affecting the ward's well-being.

    (c)   The court may specifically authorize the guardian to consent to the adoption of the ward.

Section 5-209. Rights and Immunities of Guardian.

    (a)   A guardian is entitled to reasonable compensation for services as guardian and to reimbursement for room, board, and clothing provided by the guardian to the ward, but only as approved by the court. If a conservator, other than the guardian or a person who is affiliated with the guardian, has been appointed for the estate of the ward, reasonable compensation and reimbursement to the guardian may be approved and paid by the conservator without order of the court.

    (b)   A guardian need not use the guardian's personal funds for the ward's expenses. A guardian is not liable to a third person for acts of the ward solely by reason of the guardianship. A guardian is not liable for injury to the ward resulting from the negligence or act of a third person providing medical or other care, treatment, or service for the ward except to the extent that a parent would be liable under the circumstances.

Section 5-210. Termination of Guardianship; Other Proceedings After Appointment.

    (a)   A guardianship of a minor terminates upon the minor's death, adoption, emancipation or attainment of majority or as ordered by the court.

    (b)   A ward or a person interested in the welfare of a ward may petition for any order that is in the best interest of the ward. The petitioner shall give notice of the hearing on the petition to the ward, if the ward has attained 14 years of age and is not the petitioner, the guardian, and any other person as ordered by the court.

PART 3

GUARDIANSHIP OF INCAPACITATED PERSON

Section 5-301. Appointment and Status of Guardian.

    A person becomes a guardian of an incapacitated person by a parental or spousal appointment or upon appointment by the court. The guardianship continues until terminated, without regard to the location of the guardian or ward.

Section 5-302. Appointment of Guardian by Will or Other Writing.

    (a)   A parent, by will or other signed writing, may appoint a guardian for an unmarried child who the parent believes is an incapacitated person, specify desired limitations on the powers to be given to the guardian, and revoke or amend the appointment before confirmation by the court.

(b)   An individual, by will or other signed writing, may appoint a guardian for the individual's spouse who the appointing spouse believes is an incapacitated person, specify desired limitations on the powers to be given to the guardian, and revoke or amend the appointment before confirmation by the court.

(c)   The incapacitated person, the person having care or custody of the incapacitated person if other than the appointing parent or spouse, or the adult nearest in kinship to the incapacitated person may file a written objection to an appointment, unless the court has confirmed the appointment under subsection (d). The filing of the written objection terminates the appointment. An objection may be withdrawn and, if withdrawn, is of no effect. The objection does not preclude judicial appointment of the person selected by the parent or spouse. Notice of the objection must be given to the guardian and any other person entitled to notice of the acceptance of the appointment. The court may treat the filing of an objection as a petition for the appointment of an emergency guardian under Section 5–312 or for the appointment of a limited or unlimited guardian under Section 5–304 and proceed accordingly.

(d)   Upon petition of the appointing parent or spouse, and a finding that the appointing parent or spouse will likely become unable to care for the incapacitated person within [two] years, and after notice as provided in this section, the court, before the appointment becomes effective, may confirm the appointing parent's or spouse's selection of a guardian and terminate the rights of others to object.

Section 5–303. Appointment of Guardian by Will or Other Writing: Effectiveness; Acceptance; Confirmation.

(a)   The appointment of a guardian under Section 5–302 becomes effective upon the death of the appointing parent or spouse, the adjudication of incapacity of the appointing parent or spouse, or a written determination by a physician who has examined the appointing parent or spouse that the appointing parent or spouse is no longer able to care for the incapacitated person, whichever first occurs.

(b)   A guardian appointed under Section 5–302 becomes eligible to act upon the filing of an acceptance of appointment, which must be filed within 30 days after the guardian's appointment becomes effective. The guardian shall:

(1)   file the notice of acceptance of appointment and a copy of the will with the court of the [county] in which the will was or could be probated or, in the case of another appointing instrument, file the acceptance of appointment and the appointing instrument with the court in the [county] in which the incapacitated person resides or is present; and

(2)   give written notice of the acceptance of appointment to the appointing parent or spouse if living, the incapacitated person, a person having care or custody of the incapacitated person other than the appointing parent or spouse, and the adult nearest in kinship.

(c)   Unless the appointment was previously confirmed by the court, the notice given under subsection (b)(2) must include a statement of the right of those notified to terminate the appointment by filing a written objection as provided in Section 5–302.

(d)   An appointment effected by filing the guardian's acceptance under a will probated in the state of the testator's domicile is effective in this state.

(e)   Unless the appointment was previously confirmed by the court, within 30 days after filing the notice and the appointing instrument, a guardian appointed under Section 5–302 shall file a petition in the court for confirmation of the appointment. Notice of the filing must be given in the manner provided in Section 5–309.

(f)   The authority of a guardian appointed under Section 5–302 terminates upon the appointment of a guardian by the court or the giving of written notice to the guardian of the filing of an objection pursuant to Section 5–302, whichever first occurs.

(g)   The appointment of a guardian under this section is not a determination of incapacity.

(h) The powers of a guardian who timely complies with the requirements of subsections (b) and (e) relate back to give acts by the guardian which are of benefit to the incapacitated person and occurred on or after the date the appointment became effective the same effect as those that occurred after the filing of the acceptance of appointment.

Section 5–304. Judicial Appointment of Guardian: Petition.

(a) An individual or a person interested in the individual's welfare may petition for a determination of incapacity, in whole or in part, and for the appointment of a limited or unlimited guardian for the individual.

(b) The petition must set forth the petitioner's name, residence, current address if different, relationship to the respondent, and interest in the appointment and, to the extent known, state or contain the following with respect to the respondent and the relief requested:

(1) the respondent's name, age, principal residence, current street address, and, if different, the address of the dwelling in which it is proposed that the respondent will reside if the appointment is made;

(2) the name and address of the respondent's:

(A) spouse, or if the respondent has none, an adult with whom the respondent has resided for more than six months before the filing of the petition; and

(B) adult children or, if the respondent has none, the respondent's parents and adult brothers and sisters, or if the respondent has none, at least one of the adults nearest in kinship to the respondent who can be found;

(3) the name and address of any person responsible for care or custody of the respondent;

(4) the name and address of any legal representative of the respondent;

(5) the name and address of any person nominated as guardian by the respondent;

(6) the name and address of any proposed guardian and the reason why the proposed guardian should be selected;

(7) the reason why guardianship is necessary, including a brief description of the nature and extent of the respondent's alleged incapacity;

(8) if an unlimited guardianship is requested, the reason why limited guardianship is inappropriate and, if a limited guardianship is requested, the powers to be granted to the limited guardian; and

(9) a general statement of the respondent's property with an estimate of its value, including any insurance or pension, and the source and amount of any other anticipated income or receipts.

Section 5–305. Judicial Appointment of Guardian: Preliminaries to Hearing.

(a) Upon receipt of a petition to establish a guardianship, the court shall set a date and time for hearing the petition and appoint a [visitor]. The duties and reporting requirements of the [visitor] are limited to the relief requested in the petition. The [visitor] must be an individual having training or experience in the type of incapacity alleged.

Alternative A

(b) The court shall appoint a lawyer to represent the respondent in the proceeding if:

(1) requested by the respondent;

(2) recommended by the [visitor]; or

(3) the court determines that the respondent needs representation.

Alternative B

(b) Unless the respondent is represented by a lawyer, the court shall appoint a lawyer to represent the respondent in the proceeding, regardless of the respondent's ability to pay.

End of Alternatives

(c) The [visitor] shall interview the respondent in person and, to the extent that the respondent is able to understand:

(1) explain to the respondent the substance of the petition, the nature, purpose, and effect of the proceeding, the respondent's rights at the hearing, and the general powers and duties of a guardian;

(2) determine the respondent's views about the proposed guardian, the proposed guardian's powers and duties, and the scope and duration of the proposed guardianship;

(3) inform the respondent of the right to employ and consult with a lawyer at the respondent's own expense and the right to request a court-appointed lawyer; and

(4) inform the respondent that all costs and expenses of the proceeding, including respondent's attorney's fees, will be paid from the respondent's estate.

(d) In addition to the duties imposed by subsection (c), the [visitor] shall:

(1) interview the petitioner and the proposed guardian;

(2) visit the respondent's present dwelling and any dwelling in which the respondent will live if the appointment is made;

(3) obtain information from any physician or other person who is known to have treated, advised, or assessed the respondent's relevant physical or mental condition; and

(4) make any other investigation the court directs.

(e) The [visitor] shall promptly file a report in writing with the court, which must include:

(1) a recommendation as to whether a lawyer should be appointed to represent the respondent;

(2) a summary of daily functions the respondent can manage without assistance, could manage with the assistance of supportive services or benefits, including use of appropriate technological assistance, and cannot manage;

(3) recommendations regarding the appropriateness of guardianship, including as to whether less restrictive means of intervention are available, the type of guardianship, and, if a limited guardianship, the powers to be granted to the limited guardian;

(4) a statement of the qualifications of the proposed guardian, together with a statement as to whether the respondent approves or disapproves of the proposed guardian, and the powers and duties proposed or the scope of the guardianship;

(5) a statement as to whether the proposed dwelling meets the respondent's individual needs;

(6) a recommendation as to whether a professional evaluation or further evaluation is necessary; and

(7) any other matters the court directs.

Section 5–306. Judicial Appointment of Guardian: Professional Evaluation.

At or before a hearing under this [part], the court may order a professional evaluation of the respondent and shall order the evaluation if the respondent so demands. If the court orders the evaluation, the respondent must be examined by a physician, psychologist, or other individual appointed by the court who is qualified to evaluate the respondent's alleged impairment. The examiner shall promptly file a written report with the court. Unless otherwise directed by the court, the report must contain:

(1) a description of the nature, type, and extent of the respondent's specific cognitive and functional limitations;

(2) an evaluation of the respondent's mental and physical condition and, if appropriate, educational potential, adaptive behavior, and social skills;

(3) a prognosis for improvement and a recommendation as to the appropriate treatment or habilitation plan; and

(4) the date of any assessment or examination upon which the report is based.

Section 5–307. Confidentiality of Records.

The written report of a [visitor] and any professional evaluation are confidential and must be sealed upon filing, but are available to:

(1) the court;

(2) the respondent without limitation as to use;

(3) the petitioner, the [visitor], and the petitioner's and respondent's lawyers, for purposes of the proceeding; and

(4) other persons for such purposes as the court may order for good cause.

Section 5–308. Judicial Appointment of Guardian: Presence and Rights at Hearing.

(a) Unless excused by the court for good cause, the proposed guardian shall attend the hearing. The respondent shall attend and participate in the hearing, unless excused by the court for good cause. The respondent may present evidence and subpoena witnesses and documents; examine witnesses, including any court-appointed physician, psychologist, or other individual qualified to evaluate the alleged impairment, and the [visitor]; and otherwise participate in the hearing. The hearing may be held in a location convenient to the respondent and may be closed upon the request of the respondent and a showing of good cause.

(b) Any person may request permission to participate in the proceeding. The court may grant the request, with or without hearing, upon determining that the best interest of the respondent will be served. The court may attach appropriate conditions to the participation.

Section 5–309. Notice.

(a) A copy of a petition for guardianship and notice of the hearing on the petition must be served personally on the respondent. The notice must include a statement that the respondent must be physically present unless excused by the court, inform the respondent of the respondent's rights at the hearing, and include a description of the nature, purpose, and consequences of an appointment. A failure to serve the respondent with a notice substantially complying with this subsection precludes the court from granting the petition.

(b) In a proceeding to establish a guardianship, notice of the hearing must be given to the persons listed in the petition. Failure to give notice under this subsection does not preclude the appointment of a guardian or the making of a protective order.

(c) Notice of the hearing on a petition for an order after appointment of a guardian, together with a copy of the petition, must be given to the ward, the guardian, and any other person the court directs.

(d)   A guardian shall give notice of the filing of the guardian's report, together with a copy of the report, to the ward and any other person the court directs. The notice must be delivered or sent within 14 days after the filing of the report.

Section 5–310. Who May Be Guardian: Priorities.

(a)   Subject to subsection (c), the court in appointing a guardian shall consider persons otherwise qualified in the following order of priority:

(1)   a guardian, other than a temporary or emergency guardian, currently acting for the respondent in this state or elsewhere;

(2)   a person nominated as guardian by the respondent, including the respondent's most recent nomination made in a durable power of attorney, if at the time of the nomination the respondent had sufficient capacity to express a preference;

(3)   an agent appointed by the respondent under [a durable power of attorney for health care] [the Uniform Health-Care Decisions Act (1993)];

(4)   the spouse of the respondent or a person nominated by will or other signed writing of a deceased spouse;

(5)   an adult child of the respondent;

(6)   a parent of the respondent, or an individual nominated by will or other signed writing of a deceased parent; and

(7)   an adult with whom the respondent has resided for more than six months before the filing of the petition.

(b)   With respect to persons having equal priority, the court shall select the one it considers best qualified. The court, acting in the best interest of the respondent, may decline to appoint a person having priority and appoint a person having a lower priority or no priority.

(c)   An owner, operator, or employee of [a long-term-care institution] at which the respondent is receiving care may not be appointed as guardian unless related to the respondent by blood, marriage, or adoption.

Section 5–311. Findings; Order of Appointment.

(a)   The court may:

(1)   appoint a limited or unlimited guardian for a respondent only if it finds by clear and convincing evidence that:

(A)   the respondent is an incapacitated person; and

(B)   the respondent's identified needs cannot be met by less restrictive means, including use of appropriate technological assistance; or

(2)   with appropriate findings, treat the petition as one for a protective order under Section 5–401, enter any other appropriate order, or dismiss the proceeding.

(b)   The court, whenever feasible, shall grant to a guardian only those powers necessitated by the ward's limitations and demonstrated needs and make appointive and other orders that will encourage the development of the ward's maximum self-reliance and independence.

(c)   Within 14 days after an appointment, a guardian shall send or deliver to the ward and to all other persons given notice of the hearing on the petition a copy of the order of appointment, together with a notice of the right to request termination or modification.

Section 5–312. Emergency Guardian.

(a) If the court finds that compliance with the procedures of this [part] will likely result in substantial harm to the respondent's health, safety, or welfare, and that no other person appears to have authority and willingness to act in the circumstances, the court, on petition by a person interested in the respondent's welfare, may appoint an emergency guardian whose authority may not exceed [60] days and who may exercise only the powers specified in the order. Immediately upon receipt of the petition for an emergency guardianship, the court shall appoint a lawyer to represent the respondent in the proceeding. Except as otherwise provided in subsection (b), reasonable notice of the time and place of a hearing on the petition must be given to the respondent and any other persons as the court directs.

(b) An emergency guardian may be appointed without notice to the respondent and the respondent's lawyer only if the court finds from affidavit or testimony that the respondent will be substantially harmed before a hearing on the appointment can be held. If the court appoints an emergency guardian without notice to the respondent, the respondent must be given notice of the appointment within 48 hours after the appointment. The court shall hold a hearing on the appropriateness of the appointment within [five] days after the appointment.

(c) Appointment of an emergency guardian, with or without notice, is not a determination of the respondent's incapacity.

(d) The court may remove an emergency guardian at any time. An emergency guardian shall make any report the court requires. In other respects, the provisions of this [article] concerning guardians apply to an emergency guardian.

Section 5–313. Temporary Substitute Guardian.

(a) If the court finds that a guardian is not effectively performing the guardian's duties and that the welfare of the ward requires immediate action, it may appoint a temporary substitute guardian for the ward for a specified period not exceeding six months. Except as otherwise ordered by the court, a temporary substitute guardian so appointed has the powers set forth in the previous order of appointment. The authority of any unlimited or limited guardian previously appointed by the court is suspended as long as a temporary substitute guardian has authority. If an appointment is made without previous notice to the ward or the affected guardian, the court, within five days after the appointment, shall inform the ward or guardian of the appointment.

(b) The court may remove a temporary substitute guardian at any time. A temporary substitute guardian shall make any report the court requires. In other respects, the provisions of this [article] concerning guardians apply to a temporary substitute guardian.

Section 5–314. Duties of Guardian.

(a) Except as otherwise limited by the court, a guardian shall make decisions regarding the ward's support, care, education, health, and welfare. A guardian shall exercise authority only as necessitated by the ward's limitations and, to the extent possible, shall encourage the ward to participate in decisions, act on the ward's own behalf, and develop or regain the capacity to manage the ward's personal affairs. A guardian, in making decisions, shall consider the expressed desires and personal values of the ward to the extent known to the guardian. A guardian at all times shall act in the ward's best interest and exercise reasonable care, diligence, and prudence.

(b) A guardian shall:

(1) become or remain personally acquainted with the ward and maintain sufficient contact with the ward to know of the ward's capacities, limitations, needs, opportunities, and physical and mental health;

(2) take reasonable care of the ward's personal effects and bring protective proceedings if necessary to protect the property of the ward;

(3) expend money of the ward that has been received by the guardian for the ward's current needs for support, care, education, health, and welfare;

(4) conserve any excess money of the ward for the ward's future needs, but if a conservator has been appointed for the estate of the ward, the guardian shall pay the money to the conservator, at least quarterly, to be conserved for the ward's future needs;

(5) immediately notify the court if the ward's condition has changed so that the ward is capable of exercising rights previously removed; and

(6) inform the court of any change in the ward's custodial dwelling or address.

Section 5–315. Powers of Guardian.

(a) Except as otherwise limited by the court, a guardian may:

(1) apply for and receive money payable to the ward or the ward's guardian or custodian for the support of the ward under the terms of any statutory system of benefits or insurance or any private contract, devise, trust, conservatorship, or custodianship;

(2) if otherwise consistent with the terms of any order by a court of competent jurisdiction relating to custody of the ward, take custody of the ward and establish the ward's place of custodial dwelling, but may only establish or move the ward's place of dwelling outside this state upon express authorization of the court;

(3) if a conservator for the estate of the ward has not been appointed with existing authority, commence a proceeding, including an administrative proceeding, or take other appropriate action to compel a person to support the ward or to pay money for the benefit of the ward;

(4) consent to medical or other care, treatment, or service for the ward;

(5) consent to the marriage [or divorce] of the ward; and

(6) if reasonable under all of the circumstances, delegate to the ward certain responsibilities for decisions affecting the ward's well-being.

(b) The court may specifically authorize the guardian to consent to the adoption of the ward.

Section 5–316. Rights and Immunities of Guardian; Limitations.

(a) A guardian is entitled to reasonable compensation for services as guardian and to reimbursement for room, board, and clothing provided to the ward, but only as approved by order of the court. If a conservator, other than the guardian or one who is affiliated with the guardian, has been appointed for the estate of the ward, reasonable compensation and reimbursement to the guardian may be approved and paid by the conservator without order of the court.

(b) A guardian need not use the guardian's personal funds for the ward's expenses. A guardian is not liable to a third person for acts of the ward solely by reason of the relationship. A guardian who exercises reasonable care in choosing a third person providing medical or other care, treatment, or service for the ward is not liable for injury to the ward resulting from the wrongful conduct of the third party.

(c) A guardian, without authorization of the court, may not revoke a power of attorney for health care [made pursuant to the Uniform Health-Care Decisions Act (1993)] of which the ward is the principal. If a power of attorney for health care [made pursuant to the Uniform Health-Care Decisions Act (1993)] is in effect, absent an order of the court to the contrary, a health-care decision of the agent takes precedence over that of a guardian.

(d) A guardian may not initiate the commitment of a ward to a [mental health-care] institution except in accordance with the state's procedure for involuntary civil commitment.

Section 5–317. Reports; Monitoring of Guardianship.

(a)　Within 30 days after appointment, a guardian shall report to the court in writing on the condition of the ward and account for money and other assets in the guardian's possession or subject to the guardian's control. A guardian shall report at least annually thereafter and whenever ordered by the court. A report must state or contain:

(1)　the current mental, physical, and social condition of the ward;

(2)　the living arrangements for all addresses of the ward during the reporting period;

(3)　the medical, educational, vocational, and other services provided to the ward and the guardian's opinion as to the adequacy of the ward's care;

(4)　a summary of the guardian's visits with the ward and activities on the ward's behalf and the extent to which the ward has participated in decision-making;

(5)　if the ward is institutionalized, whether the guardian considers the current plan for care, treatment, or habilitation to be in the ward's best interest;

(6)　plans for future care; and

(7)　a recommendation as to the need for continued guardianship and any recommended changes in the scope of the guardianship.

(b)　The court may appoint a [visitor] to review a report, interview the ward or guardian, and make any other investigation the court directs.

(c)　The court shall establish a system for monitoring guardianships, including the filing and review of annual reports.

Section 5–318. Termination or Modification of Guardianship.

(a)　A guardianship terminates upon the death of the ward or upon order of the court.

(b)　On petition of a ward, a guardian, or another person interested in the ward's welfare, the court may terminate a guardianship if the ward no longer needs the assistance or protection of a guardian. The court may modify the type of appointment or powers granted to the guardian if the extent of protection or assistance previously granted is currently excessive or insufficient or the ward's capacity to provide for support, care, education, health, and welfare has so changed as to warrant that action.

(c)　Except as otherwise ordered by the court for good cause, the court, before terminating a guardianship, shall follow the same procedures to safeguard the rights of the ward as apply to a petition for guardianship. Upon presentation by the petitioner of evidence establishing a prima facie case for termination, the court shall order the termination unless it is proven that continuation of the guardianship is in the best interest of the ward.

PART 4

PROTECTION OF PROPERTY OF PROTECTED PERSON

Section 5–401. Protective Proceeding.

Upon petition and after notice and hearing, the court may appoint a limited or unlimited conservator or make any other protective order provided in this [part] in relation to the estate and affairs of:

(1)　a minor, if the court determines that the minor owns money or property requiring management or protection that cannot otherwise be provided or has or may have business affairs that may be put at risk or prevented because of the minor's age, or that money is needed for support and education and that protection is necessary or desirable to obtain or provide money; or

(2) any individual, including a minor, if the court determines that, for reasons other than age:

(A) by clear and convincing evidence, the individual is unable to manage property and business affairs because of an impairment in the ability to receive and evaluate information or make decisions, even with the use of appropriate technological assistance, or because the individual is missing, detained, or unable to return to the United States; and

(B) by a preponderance of evidence, the individual has property that will be wasted or dissipated unless management is provided or money is needed for the support, care, education, health, and welfare of the individual or of individuals who are entitled to the individual's support and that protection is necessary or desirable to obtain or provide money.

Section 5-402. Jurisdiction Over Business Affairs of Protected Person.

After the service of notice in a proceeding seeking a conservatorship or other protective order and until termination of the proceeding, the court in which the petition is filed has:

(1) exclusive jurisdiction to determine the need for a conservatorship or other protective order;

(2) exclusive jurisdiction to determine how the estate of the protected person which is subject to the laws of this state must be managed, expended, or distributed to or for the use of the protected person, individuals who are in fact dependent upon the protected person, or other claimants; and

(3) concurrent jurisdiction to determine the validity of claims against the person or estate of the protected person and questions of title concerning assets of the estate.

Section 5-403. Original Petition for Appointment or Protective Order.

(a) The following may petition for the appointment of a conservator or for any other appropriate protective order:

(1) the person to be protected;

(2) an individual interested in the estate, affairs, or welfare of the person to be protected, including a parent, guardian, or custodian; or

(3) a person who would be adversely affected by lack of effective management of the property and business affairs of the person to be protected.

(b) A petition under subsection (a) must set forth the petitioner's name, residence, current address if different, relationship to the respondent, and interest in the appointment or other protective order, and, to the extent known, state or contain the following with respect to the respondent and the relief requested:

(1) the respondent's name, age, principal residence, current street address, and, if different, the address of the dwelling where it is proposed that the respondent will reside if the appointment is made;

(2) if the petition alleges impairment in the respondent's ability to receive and evaluate information, a brief description of the nature and extent of the respondent's alleged impairment;

(3) if the petition alleges that the respondent is missing, detained, or unable to return to the United States, a statement of the relevant circumstances, including the time and nature of the disappearance or detention and a description of any search or inquiry concerning the respondent's whereabouts;

(4) the name and address of the respondent's:

(A) spouse or, if the respondent has none, an adult with whom the respondent has resided for more than six months before the filing of the petition; and

(B) adult children or, if the respondent has none, the respondent's parents and adult brothers and sisters or, if the respondent has none, at least one of the adults nearest in kinship to the respondent who can be found;

(5) the name and address of the person responsible for care or custody of the respondent;

(6) the name and address of any legal representative of the respondent;

(7) a general statement of the respondent's property with an estimate of its value, including any insurance or pension, and the source and amount of other anticipated income or receipts; and

(8) the reason why a conservatorship or other protective order is in the best interest of the respondent.

(c) If a conservatorship is requested, the petition must also set forth to the extent known:

(1) the name and address of any proposed conservator and the reason why the proposed conservator should be selected;

(2) the name and address of any person nominated as conservator by the respondent if the respondent has attained 14 years of age; and

(3) the type of conservatorship requested and, if an unlimited conservatorship, the reason why limited conservatorship is inappropriate or, if a limited conservatorship, the property to be placed under the conservator's control and any limitation on the conservator's powers and duties.

Section 5–404. Notice.

(a) A copy of the petition and the notice of hearing on a petition for conservatorship or other protective order must be served personally on the respondent, but if the respondent's whereabouts is unknown or personal service cannot be made, service on the respondent must be made by [substituted service] [or] [publication]. The notice must include a statement that the respondent must be physically present unless excused by the court, inform the respondent of the respondent's rights at the hearing, and, if the appointment of a conservator is requested, include a description of the nature, purpose, and consequences of an appointment. A failure to serve the respondent with a notice substantially complying with this subsection precludes the court from granting the petition.

(b) In a proceeding to establish a conservatorship or for another protective order, notice of the hearing must be given to the persons listed in the petition. Failure to give notice under this subsection does not preclude the appointment of a conservator or the making of another protective order.

(c) Notice of the hearing on a petition for an order after appointment of a conservator or making of another protective order, together with a copy of the petition, must be given to the protected person, if the protected person has attained 14 years of age and is not missing, detained, or unable to return to the United States, any conservator of the protected person's estate, and any other person as ordered by the court.

(d) A conservator shall give notice of the filing of the conservator's inventory, report, or plan of conservatorship, together with a copy of the inventory, report, or plan of conservatorship to the protected person and any other person the court directs. The notice must be delivered or sent within 14 days after the filing of the inventory, report, or plan of conservatorship.

Section 5–405. Original Petition: Minors; Preliminaries to Hearing.

(a) Upon the filing of a petition to establish a conservatorship or for another protective order for the reason that the respondent is a minor, the court shall set a date for hearing. If the court determines at any stage of the proceeding that the interests of the minor are or may be inadequately represented, it may appoint a lawyer to represent the minor, giving consideration to the choice of the minor if the minor has attained 14 years of age.

(b) While a petition to establish a conservatorship or for another protective order is pending, after preliminary hearing and without notice to others, the court may make orders to preserve and apply the property of the minor as may be required for the support of the minor or individuals who are in fact dependent upon the minor. The court may appoint a [master] to assist in that task.

Section 5–406. Original Petition: Preliminaries to Hearing.

(a) Upon the filing of a petition for a conservatorship or other protective order for a respondent for reasons other than being a minor, the court shall set a date for hearing. The court shall appoint a [visitor] unless the petition does not request the appointment of a conservator and the respondent is represented by a lawyer. The duties and reporting requirements of the [visitor] are limited to the relief requested in the petition. The [visitor] must be an individual having training or experience in the type of incapacity alleged.

Alternative A

(b) The court shall appoint a lawyer to represent the respondent in the proceeding if:

(1) requested by the respondent;

(2) recommended by the [visitor]; or

(3) the court determines that the respondent needs representation.

Alternative B

(b) Unless the respondent is represented by a lawyer, the court shall appoint a lawyer to represent the respondent in the proceeding, regardless of the respondent's ability to pay.

End of Alternatives

(c) The [visitor] shall interview the respondent in person and, to the extent that the respondent is able to understand:

(1) explain to the respondent the substance of the petition and the nature, purpose, and effect of the proceeding;

(2) if the appointment of a conservator is requested, inform the respondent of the general powers and duties of a conservator and determine the respondent's views regarding the proposed conservator, the proposed conservator's powers and duties, and the scope and duration of the proposed conservatorship;

(3) inform the respondent of the respondent's rights, including the right to employ and consult with a lawyer at the respondent's own expense, and the right to request a court-appointed lawyer; and

(4) inform the respondent that all costs and expenses of the proceeding, including respondent's attorney's fees, will be paid from the respondent's estate.

(d) In addition to the duties imposed by subsection (c), the [visitor] shall:

(1) interview the petitioner and the proposed conservator, if any; and

(2) make any other investigation the court directs.

(e) The [visitor] shall promptly file a report with the court, which must include:

(1) a recommendation as to whether a lawyer should be appointed to represent the respondent;

(2) recommendations regarding the appropriateness of a conservatorship, including whether less restrictive means of intervention are available, the type of conservatorship, and, if a limited conservatorship, the powers and duties to be granted the limited conservator, and the assets over which the conservator should be granted authority;

(3)   a statement of the qualifications of the proposed conservator, together with a statement as to whether the respondent approves or disapproves of the proposed conservator, and a statement of the powers and duties proposed or the scope of the conservatorship;

(4)   a recommendation as to whether a professional evaluation or further evaluation is necessary; and

(5)   any other matters the court directs.

(f)   The court may also appoint a physician, psychologist, or other individual qualified to evaluate the alleged impairment to conduct an examination of the respondent.

(g)   While a petition to establish a conservatorship or for another protective order is pending, after preliminary hearing and without notice to others, the court may issue orders to preserve and apply the property of the respondent as may be required for the support of the respondent or individuals who are in fact dependent upon the respondent. The court may appoint a [master] to assist in that task.

Section 5–407. Confidentiality of Records.

The written report of a [visitor] and any professional evaluation are confidential and must be sealed upon filing, but are available to:

(1)   the court;

(2)   the respondent without limitation as to use;

(3)   the petitioner, the [visitor], and the petitioner's and respondent's lawyers, for purposes of the proceeding; and

(4)   other persons for such purposes as the court may order for good cause.

Section 5–408. Original Petition: Procedure at Hearing.

(a)   Unless excused by the court for good cause, a proposed conservator shall attend the hearing. The respondent shall attend and participate in the hearing, unless excused by the court for good cause. The respondent may present evidence and subpoena witnesses and documents, examine witnesses, including any court-appointed physician, psychologist, or other individual qualified to evaluate the alleged impairment, and the [visitor], and otherwise participate in the hearing. The hearing may be held in a location convenient to the respondent and may be closed upon request of the respondent and a showing of good cause.

(b)   Any person may request permission to participate in the proceeding. The court may grant the request, with or without hearing, upon determining that the best interest of the respondent will be served. The court may attach appropriate conditions to the participation.

Section 5–409. Original Petition: Orders.

(a)   If a proceeding is brought for the reason that the respondent is a minor, after a hearing on the petition, upon finding that the appointment of a conservator or other protective order is in the best interest of the minor, the court shall make an appointment or other appropriate protective order.

(b)   If a proceeding is brought for reasons other than that the respondent is a minor, after a hearing on the petition, upon finding that a basis exists for a conservatorship or other protective order, the court shall make the least restrictive order consistent with its findings. The court shall make orders necessitated by the protected person's limitations and demonstrated needs, including appointive and other orders that will encourage the development of maximum self-reliance and independence of the protected person.

(c)   Within 14 days after an appointment, the conservator shall deliver or send a copy of the order of appointment, together with a statement of the right to seek termination or modification, to the protected person, if the protected person has attained 14 years of age and is not missing, detained, or unable to return to the United States, and to all other persons given notice of the petition.

(d) The appointment of a conservator or the entry of another protective order is not a determination of incapacity of the protected person.

Section 5–410. Powers of Court.

(a) After hearing and upon determining that a basis for a conservatorship or other protective order exists, the court has the following powers, which may be exercised directly or through a conservator:

(1) with respect to a minor for reasons of age, all the powers over the estate and business affairs of the minor which may be necessary for the best interest of the minor and members of the minor's immediate family; and

(2) with respect to an adult, or to a minor for reasons other than age, for the benefit of the protected person and individuals who are in fact dependent on the protected person for support, all the powers over the estate and business affairs of the protected person which the person could exercise if the person were an adult, present, and not under conservatorship or other protective order.

(b) Subject to Section 5–110 requiring endorsement of limitations on the letters of office, the court may limit at any time the powers of a conservator otherwise conferred and may remove or modify any limitation.

Section 5–411. Required Court Approval.

(a) After notice to interested persons and upon express authorization of the court, a conservator may:

(1) make gifts, except as otherwise provided in Section 5–427(b);

(2) convey, release, or disclaim contingent and expectant interests in property, including marital property rights and any right of survivorship incident to joint tenancy or tenancy by the entireties;

(3) exercise or release a power of appointment;

(4) create a revocable or irrevocable trust of property of the estate, whether or not the trust extends beyond the duration of the conservatorship, or revoke or amend a trust revocable by the protected person;

(5) exercise rights to elect options and change beneficiaries under insurance policies and annuities or surrender the policies and annuities for their cash value;

(6) exercise any right to an elective share in the estate of the protected person's deceased spouse and to renounce or disclaim any interest by testate or intestate succession or by transfer inter vivos; and

(7) make, amend, or revoke the protected person's will.

(b) A conservator, in making, amending, or revoking the protected person's will, shall comply with [the state's statute for executing wills].

(c) The court, in exercising or in approving a conservator's exercise of the powers listed in subsection (a), shall consider primarily the decision that the protected person would have made, to the extent that the decision can be ascertained. The court shall also consider:

(1) the financial needs of the protected person and the needs of individuals who are in fact dependent on the protected person for support and the interest of creditors;

(2) possible reduction of income, estate, inheritance, or other tax liabilities;

(3)   eligibility for governmental assistance;

(4)   the protected person's previous pattern of giving or level of support;

(5)   the existing estate plan;

(6)   the protected person's life expectancy and the probability that the conservatorship will terminate before the protected person's death; and

(7)   any other factors the court considers relevant.

(d)   Without authorization of the court, a conservator may not revoke or amend a durable power of attorney of which the protected person is the principal. If a durable power of attorney is in effect, absent a court order to the contrary, a decision of the agent takes precedence over that of a conservator.

Section 5–412. Protective Arrangements and Single Transactions.

(a)   If a basis is established for a protective order with respect to an individual, the court, without appointing a conservator, may:

(1)   authorize, direct, or ratify any transaction necessary or desirable to achieve any arrangement for security, service, or care meeting the foreseeable needs of the protected person, including:

(A)   payment, delivery, deposit, or retention of funds or property;

(B)   sale, mortgage, lease, or other transfer of property;

(C)   purchase of an annuity;

(D)   making a contract for life care, deposit contract, or contract for training and education; or

(E)   addition to or establishment of a suitable trust[, including a trust created under the Uniform Custodial Trust Act (1987)]; and

(2)   authorize, direct, or ratify any other contract, trust, will, or transaction relating to the protected person's property and business affairs, including a settlement of a claim, upon determining that it is in the best interest of the protected person.

(b)   In deciding whether to approve a protective arrangement or other transaction under this section, the court shall consider the factors described in Section 5–411(c).

(c)   The court may appoint a [master] to assist in the accomplishment of any protective arrangement or other transaction authorized under this section. The [master] has the authority conferred by the order and shall serve until discharged by order after report to the court.

Section 5–413. Who May Be Conservator: Priorities.

(a)   Except as otherwise provided in subsection (d), the court, in appointing a conservator, shall consider persons otherwise qualified in the following order of priority:

(1)   a conservator, guardian of the estate, or other like fiduciary appointed or recognized by an appropriate court of any other jurisdiction in which the protected person resides;

(2)   a person nominated as conservator by the respondent, including the respondent's most recent nomination made in a durable power of attorney, if the respondent has attained 14 years of age and at the time of the nomination had sufficient capacity to express a preference;

(3)   an agent appointed by the respondent to manage the respondent's property under a durable power of attorney;

(4)   the spouse of the respondent;

(5)   an adult child of the respondent;

(6)   a parent of the respondent; and

(7)   an adult with whom the respondent has resided for more than six months before the filing of the petition.

(b)   A person having priority under subsection (a)(1), (4), (5), or (6) may designate in writing a substitute to serve instead and thereby transfer the priority to the substitute.

(c)   With respect to persons having equal priority, the court shall select the one it considers best qualified. The court, acting in the best interest of the protected person, may decline to appoint a person having priority and appoint a person having a lower priority or no priority.

(d)   An owner, operator, or employee of [a long-term care institution] at which the respondent is receiving care may not be appointed as conservator unless related to the respondent by blood, marriage, or adoption.

Section 5–414. Petition for Order Subsequent to Appointment.

(a)   A protected person or a person interested in the welfare of a protected person may file a petition in the appointing court for an order:

(1)   requiring bond or collateral or additional bond or collateral, or reducing bond;

(2)   requiring an accounting for the administration of the protected person's estate;

(3)   directing distribution;

(4)   removing the conservator and appointing a temporary or successor conservator;

(5)   modifying the type of appointment or powers granted to the conservator if the extent of protection or management previously granted is currently excessive or insufficient or the protected person's ability to manage the estate and business affairs has so changed as to warrant the action; or

(6)   granting other appropriate relief.

(b)   A conservator may petition the appointing court for instructions concerning fiduciary responsibility.

(c)   Upon notice and hearing the petition, the court may give appropriate instructions and make any appropriate order.

Section 5–415. Bond.

The court may require a conservator to furnish a bond conditioned upon faithful discharge of all duties of the conservatorship according to law, with sureties as it may specify. Unless otherwise directed by the court, the bond must be in the amount of the aggregate capital value of the property of the estate in the conservator's control, plus one year's estimated income, and minus the value of assets deposited under arrangements requiring an order of the court for their removal and the value of any real property that the fiduciary, by express limitation, lacks power to sell or convey without court authorization. The court, in place of sureties on a bond, may accept collateral for the performance of the bond, including a pledge of securities or a mortgage of real property.

Section 5–416. Terms and Requirements of Bond.

(a)   The following rules apply to any bond required:

(1)   Except as otherwise provided by the terms of the bond, sureties and the conservator are jointly and severally liable.

(2)   By executing the bond of a conservator, a surety submits to the jurisdiction of the court that issued letters to the primary obligor in any proceeding pertaining to the fiduciary duties of the conservator in which the surety is named as a party. Notice of any proceeding must be sent

or delivered to the surety at the address shown in the court records at the place where the bond is filed and to any other address then known to the petitioner.

(3) On petition of a successor conservator or any interested person, a proceeding may be brought against a surety for breach of the obligation of the bond of the conservator.

(4) The bond of the conservator may be proceeded against until liability under the bond is exhausted.

(b) A proceeding may not be brought against a surety on any matter as to which an action or proceeding against the primary obligor is barred.

Section 5–417. Compensation and Expenses.

If not otherwise compensated for services rendered, a guardian, conservator, lawyer for the respondent, lawyer whose services resulted in a protective order or in an order beneficial to a protected person's estate, or any other person appointed by the court is entitled to reasonable compensation from the estate. Compensation may be paid and expenses reimbursed without court order. If the court determines that the compensation is excessive or the expenses are inappropriate, the excessive or inappropriate amount must be repaid to the estate.

Section 5–418. General Duties of Conservator; Plan.

(a) A conservator, in relation to powers conferred by this [part] or implicit in the title acquired by virtue of the proceeding, is a fiduciary and shall observe the standards of care applicable to a trustee.

(b) A conservator may exercise authority only as necessitated by the limitations of the protected person, and to the extent possible, shall encourage the person to participate in decisions, act in the person's own behalf, and develop or regain the ability to manage the person's estate and business affairs.

(c) Within 60 days after appointment, a conservator shall file with the appointing court a plan for protecting, managing, expending, and distributing the assets of the protected person's estate. The plan must be based on the actual needs of the person and take into consideration the best interest of the person. The conservator shall include in the plan steps to develop or restore the person's ability to manage the person's property, an estimate of the duration of the conservatorship, and projections of expenses and resources.

(d) In investing an estate, selecting assets of the estate for distribution, and invoking powers of revocation or withdrawal available for the use and benefit of the protected person and exercisable by the conservator, a conservator shall take into account any estate plan of the person known to the conservator and may examine the will and any other donative, nominative, or other appointive instrument of the person.

Section 5–419. Inventory; Records.

(a) Within 60 days after appointment, a conservator shall prepare and file with the appointing court a detailed inventory of the estate subject to the conservatorship, together with an oath or affirmation that the inventory is believed to be complete and accurate as far as information permits.

(b) A conservator shall keep records of the administration of the estate and make them available for examination on reasonable request of an interested person.

Section 5–420. Reports; Appointment of [Visitor]; Monitoring.

(a) A conservator shall report to the court for administration of the estate annually unless the court otherwise directs, upon resignation or removal, upon termination of the conservatorship, and at other times as the court directs. An order, after notice and hearing, allowing an intermediate report of a conservator adjudicates liabilities concerning the matters adequately disclosed in the accounting.

An order, after notice and hearing, allowing a final report adjudicates all previously unsettled liabilities relating to the conservatorship.

(b) A report must state or contain:

(1) a list of the assets of the estate under the conservator's control and a list of the receipts, disbursements, and distributions during the period for which the report is made;

(2) a list of the services provided to the protected person; and

(3) any recommended changes in the plan for the conservatorship as well as a recommendation as to the continued need for conservatorship and any recommended changes in the scope of the conservatorship.

(c) The court may appoint a [visitor] to review a report or plan, interview the protected person or conservator, and make any other investigation the court directs. In connection with a report, the court may order a conservator to submit the assets of the estate to an appropriate examination to be made in a manner the court directs.

(d) The court shall establish a system for monitoring conservatorships, including the filing and review of conservators' reports and plans.

Section 5–421. Title by Appointment.

(a) The appointment of a conservator vests title in the conservator as trustee to all property of the protected person, or to the part thereof specified in the order, held at the time of appointment or thereafter acquired. An order vesting title in the conservator to only a part of the property of the protected person creates a conservatorship limited to assets specified in the order.

(b) Letters of conservatorship are evidence of vesting title of the protected person's assets in the conservator. An order terminating a conservatorship transfers title to assets remaining subject to the conservatorship, including any described in the order, to the formerly protected person or the person's successors.

(c) Subject to the requirements of other statutes governing the filing or recordation of documents of title to land or other property, letters of conservatorship and orders terminating conservatorships may be filed or recorded to give notice of title as between the conservator and the protected person.

Section 5–422. Protected Person's Interest Inalienable.

(a) Except as otherwise provided in subsections (c) and (d), the interest of a protected person in property vested in a conservator is not transferable or assignable by the protected person. An attempted transfer or assignment by the protected person, although ineffective to affect property rights, may give rise to a claim against the protected person for restitution or damages which, subject to presentation and allowance, may be satisfied as provided in Section 5–429.

(b) Property vested in a conservator by appointment and the interest of the protected person in that property are not subject to levy, garnishment, or similar process for claims against the protected person unless allowed under Section 5–429.

(c) A person without knowledge of the conservatorship who in good faith and for security or substantially equivalent value receives delivery from a protected person of tangible personal property of a type normally transferred by delivery of possession, is protected as if the protected person or transferee had valid title.

(d) A third party who deals with the protected person with respect to property vested in a conservator is entitled to any protection provided in other law.

Section 5-423. Sale, Encumbrance, or Other Transaction Involving Conflict of Interest.

Any transaction involving the conservatorship estate which is affected by a substantial conflict between the conservator's fiduciary and personal interests is voidable unless the transaction is expressly authorized by the court after notice to interested persons. A transaction affected by a substantial conflict between personal and fiduciary interests includes any sale, encumbrance, or other transaction involving the conservatorship estate entered into by the conservator, the spouse, descendant, agent, or lawyer of a conservator, or a corporation or other enterprise in which the conservator has a substantial beneficial interest.

Section 5-424. Protection of Person Dealing With Conservator.

(a) A person who assists or deals with a conservator in good faith and for value in any transaction other than one requiring a court order under Section 5-410 or 5-411 is protected as though the conservator properly exercised the power. That a person knowingly deals with a conservator does not alone require the person to inquire into the existence of a power or the propriety of its exercise, but restrictions on powers of conservators which are endorsed on letters as provided in Section 5-110 are effective as to third persons. A person who pays or delivers assets to a conservator is not responsible for their proper application.

(b) Protection provided by this section extends to any procedural irregularity or jurisdictional defect that occurred in proceedings leading to the issuance of letters and is not a substitute for protection provided to persons assisting or dealing with a conservator by comparable provisions in other law relating to commercial transactions or to simplifying transfers of securities by fiduciaries.

Section 5-425. Powers of Conservator in Administration.

(a) Except as otherwise qualified or limited by the court in its order of appointment and endorsed on the letters, a conservator has all of the powers granted in this section and any additional powers granted by law to a trustee in this state.

(b) A conservator, acting reasonably and in an effort to accomplish the purpose of the appointment, and without further court authorization or confirmation, may:

(1) collect, hold, and retain assets of the estate, including assets in which the conservator has a personal interest and real property in another state, until the conservator considers that disposition of an asset should be made;

(2) receive additions to the estate;

(3) continue or participate in the operation of any business or other enterprise;

(4) acquire an undivided interest in an asset of the estate in which the conservator, in any fiduciary capacity, holds an undivided interest;

(5) invest assets of the estate as though the conservator were a trustee;

(6) deposit money of the estate in a financial institution, including one operated by the conservator;

(7) acquire or dispose of an asset of the estate, including real property in another state, for cash or on credit, at public or private sale, and manage, develop, improve, exchange, partition, change the character of, or abandon an asset of the estate;

(8) make ordinary or extraordinary repairs or alterations in buildings or other structures, demolish any improvements, and raze existing or erect new party walls or buildings;

(9) subdivide, develop, or dedicate land to public use, make or obtain the vacation of plats and adjust boundaries, adjust differences in valuation or exchange or partition by giving or receiving considerations, and dedicate easements to public use without consideration;

(10) enter for any purpose into a lease as lessor or lessee, with or without option to purchase or renew, for a term within or extending beyond the term of the conservatorship;

(11) enter into a lease or arrangement for exploration and removal of minerals or other natural resources or enter into a pooling or unitization agreement;

(12) grant an option involving disposition of an asset of the estate and take an option for the acquisition of any asset;

(13) vote a security, in person or by general or limited proxy;

(14) pay calls, assessments, and any other sums chargeable or accruing against or on account of securities;

(15) sell or exercise stock subscription or conversion rights;

(16) consent, directly or through a committee or other agent, to the reorganization, consolidation, merger, dissolution, or liquidation of a corporation or other business enterprise;

(17) hold a security in the name of a nominee or in other form without disclosure of the conservatorship so that title to the security may pass by delivery;

(18) insure the assets of the estate against damage or loss and the conservator against liability with respect to a third person;

(19) borrow money, with or without security, to be repaid from the estate or otherwise and advance money for the protection of the estate or the protected person and for all expenses, losses, and liability sustained in the administration of the estate or because of the holding or ownership of any assets, for which the conservator has a lien on the estate as against the protected person for advances so made;

(20) pay or contest any claim, settle a claim by or against the estate or the protected person by compromise, arbitration, or otherwise, and release, in whole or in part, any claim belonging to the estate to the extent the claim is uncollectible;

(21) pay taxes, assessments, compensation of the conservator and any guardian, and other expenses incurred in the collection, care, administration, and protection of the estate;

(22) allocate items of income or expense to income or principal of the estate, as provided by other law, including creation of reserves out of income for depreciation, obsolescence, or amortization or for depletion of minerals or other natural resources;

(23) pay any sum distributable to a protected person or individual who is in fact dependent on the protected person by paying the sum to the distributee or by paying the sum for the use of the distributee:

(A) to the guardian of the distributee;

(B) to a distributee's custodian under [the Uniform Transfers to Minors Act (1983/1986)] or custodial trustee under [the Uniform Custodial Trust Act (1987)]; or

(C) if there is no guardian, custodian, or custodial trustee, to a relative or other person having physical custody of the distributee;

(24) prosecute or defend actions, claims, or proceedings in any jurisdiction for the protection of assets of the estate and of the conservator in the performance of fiduciary duties; and

(25) execute and deliver all instruments that will accomplish or facilitate the exercise of the powers vested in the conservator.

Section 5–426. Delegation.

(a) A conservator may not delegate to an agent or another conservator the entire administration of the estate, but a conservator may otherwise delegate the performance of functions that a prudent trustee of comparable skills may delegate under similar circumstances.

(b) The conservator shall exercise reasonable care, skill, and caution in:

(1) selecting an agent;

(2) establishing the scope and terms of a delegation, consistent with the purposes and terms of the conservatorship;

(3) periodically reviewing an agent's overall performance and compliance with the terms of the delegation; and

(4) redressing an action or decision of an agent which would constitute a breach of trust if performed by the conservator.

(c) A conservator who complies with subsections (a) and (b) is not liable to the protected person or to the estate for the decisions or actions of the agent to whom a function was delegated.

(d) In performing a delegated function, an agent shall exercise reasonable care to comply with the terms of the delegation.

(e) By accepting a delegation from a conservator subject to the law of this state, an agent submits to the jurisdiction of the courts of this state.

Section 5–427. Principles of Distribution by Conservator.

(a) Unless otherwise specified in the order of appointment and endorsed on the letters of appointment or contrary to the plan filed pursuant to Section 5–418, a conservator may expend or distribute income or principal of the estate of the protected person without further court authorization or confirmation for the support, care, education, health, and welfare of the protected person and individuals who are in fact dependent on the protected person, including the payment of child or spousal support, in accordance with the following rules:

(1) A conservator shall consider recommendations relating to the appropriate standard of support, care, education, health, and welfare for the protected person or an individual who is in fact dependent on the protected person made by a guardian, if any, and, if the protected person is a minor, the conservator shall consider recommendations made by a parent.

(2) A conservator may not be surcharged for money paid to persons furnishing support, care, education, or benefit to a protected person, or an individual who is in fact dependent on the protected person, in accordance with the recommendations of a parent or guardian of the protected person unless the conservator knows that the parent or guardian derives personal financial benefit therefrom, including relief from any personal duty of support, or the recommendations are not in the best interest of the protected person.

(3) In making distributions under this subsection, the conservator shall consider:

(A) the size of the estate, the estimated duration of the conservatorship, and the likelihood that the protected person, at some future time, may be fully self-sufficient and able to manage business affairs and the estate;

(B) the accustomed standard of living of the protected person and individuals who are in fact dependent on the protected person; and

(C) other money or sources used for the support of the protected person.

(4) Money expended under this subsection may be paid by the conservator to any person, including the protected person, as reimbursement for expenditures that the conservator might have made, or in advance for services to be rendered to the protected person if it is reasonable to

expect the services will be performed and advance payments are customary or reasonably necessary under the circumstances.

(b) If an estate is ample to provide for the distributions authorized by subsection (a), a conservator for a protected person other than a minor may make gifts that the protected person might have been expected to make, in amounts that do not exceed in the aggregate for any calendar year 20 percent of the income of the estate in that year.

Section 5–428. Death of Protected Person.

[(a)] If a protected person dies, the conservator shall deliver to the court for safekeeping any will of the protected person which may have come into the conservator's possession, inform the personal representative or beneficiary named in the will of the delivery, and retain the estate for delivery to the personal representative of the decedent or to another person entitled to it.

[(b) If a personal representative has not been appointed within 40 days after the death of a protected person and an application or petition for appointment is not before the court, the conservator may apply to exercise the powers and duties of a personal representative in order to administer and distribute the decedent's estate. Upon application for an order conferring upon the conservator the powers of a personal representative, after notice given by the conservator to any person nominated as personal representative by any will of which the applicant is aware, the court may grant the application upon determining that there is no objection and endorse the letters of conservatorship to note that the formerly protected person is deceased and that the conservator has acquired all of the powers and duties of a personal representative.

(c) The issuance of an order under this section has the effect of an order of appointment of a personal representative [as provided in Section 3–308 and [Parts] 6 through 10 of [Article] III]. However, the estate in the name of the conservator, after administration, may be distributed to the decedent's successors without retransfer to the conservator as personal representative.]

Section 5–429. Presentation and Allowance of Claims.

(a) A conservator may pay, or secure by encumbering assets of the estate, claims against the estate or against the protected person arising before or during the conservatorship upon their presentation and allowance in accordance with the priorities stated in subsection (d). A claimant may present a claim by:

    (1) sending or delivering to the conservator a written statement of the claim, indicating its basis, the name and address of the claimant, and the amount claimed; or

    (2) filing a written statement of the claim, in a form acceptable to the court, with the clerk of court and sending or delivering a copy of the statement to the conservator.

(b) A claim is deemed presented on receipt of the written statement of claim by the conservator or the filing of the claim with the court, whichever first occurs. A presented claim is allowed if it is not disallowed by written statement sent or delivered by the conservator to the claimant within 60 days after its presentation. The conservator before payment may change an allowance to a disallowance in whole or in part, but not after allowance under a court order or judgment or an order directing payment of the claim. The presentation of a claim tolls the running of any statute of limitations relating to the claim until 30 days after its disallowance.

(c) A claimant whose claim has not been paid may petition the court for determination of the claim at any time before it is barred by a statute of limitations and, upon due proof, procure an order for its allowance, payment, or security by encumbering assets of the estate. If a proceeding is pending against a protected person at the time of appointment of a conservator or is initiated against the protected person thereafter, the moving party shall give to the conservator notice of any proceeding that could result in creating a claim against the estate.

(d) If it appears that the estate is likely to be exhausted before all existing claims are paid, the conservator shall distribute the estate in money or in kind in payment of claims in the following order:

(1)   costs and expenses of administration;

(2)   claims of the federal or state government having priority under other law;

(3)   claims incurred by the conservator for support, care, education, health, and welfare previously provided to the protected person or individuals who are in fact dependent on the protected person;

(4)   claims arising before the conservatorship; and

(5)   all other claims.

(e)   Preference may not be given in the payment of a claim over any other claim of the same class, and a claim due and payable may not be preferred over a claim not due.

(f)   If assets of the conservatorship are adequate to meet all existing claims, the court, acting in the best interest of the protected person, may order the conservator to grant a security interest in the conservatorship estate for the payment of any or all claims at a future date.

Section 5–430. Personal Liability of Conservator.

(a)   Except as otherwise agreed, a conservator is not personally liable on a contract properly entered into in a fiduciary capacity in the course of administration of the estate unless the conservator fails to reveal in the contract the representative capacity and identify the estate.

(b)   A conservator is personally liable for obligations arising from ownership or control of property of the estate or for other acts or omissions occurring in the course of administration of the estate only if personally at fault.

(c)   Claims based on contracts entered into by a conservator in a fiduciary capacity, obligations arising from ownership or control of the estate, and claims based on torts committed in the course of administration of the estate may be asserted against the estate by proceeding against the conservator in a fiduciary capacity, whether or not the conservator is personally liable therefor.

(d)   A question of liability between the estate and the conservator personally may be determined in a proceeding for accounting, surcharge, or indemnification, or in another appropriate proceeding or action.

[(e)   A conservator is not personally liable for any environmental condition on or injury resulting from any environmental condition on land solely by reason of an acquisition of title under Section 5–421.]

Section 5–431. Termination of Proceedings.

(a)   A conservatorship terminates upon the death of the protected person or upon order of the court. Unless created for reasons other than that the protected person is a minor, a conservatorship created for a minor also terminates when the protected person attains majority or is emancipated.

(b)   Upon the death of a protected person, the conservator shall conclude the administration of the estate by distribution to the person's successors. The conservator shall file a final report and petition for discharge within [30] days after distribution.

(c)   On petition of a protected person, a conservator, or another person interested in a protected person's welfare, the court may terminate the conservatorship if the protected person no longer needs the assistance or protection of a conservator. Termination of the conservatorship does not affect a conservator's liability for previous acts or the obligation to account for funds and assets of the protected person.

(d)   Except as otherwise ordered by the court for good cause, before terminating a conservatorship, the court shall follow the same procedures to safeguard the rights of the protected person that apply to a petition for conservatorship. Upon the establishment of a prima facie case for termination, the court shall order termination unless it is proved that continuation of the conservatorship is in the best interest of the protected person.

(e)   Upon termination of a conservatorship and whether or not formally distributed by the conservator, title to assets of the estate passes to the formerly protected person or the person's successors. The order of termination must provide for expenses of administration and direct the conservator to execute appropriate instruments to evidence the transfer of title or confirm a distribution previously made and to file a final report and a petition for discharge upon approval of the final report.

(f)   The court shall enter a final order of discharge upon the approval of the final report and satisfaction by the conservator of any other conditions placed by the court on the conservator's discharge.

Section 5–432. Registration of Guardianship Orders.

If a guardian has been appointed in another state and a petition for the appointment of a guardian is not pending in this state, the guardian appointed in the other state, after giving notice to the appointing court of an intent to register, may register the guardianship order in this state by filing as a foreign judgment in a court, in any appropriate [county] of this state, certified copies of the order and letters of office.

Section 5–433. Registration of Protective Orders.

If a conservator has been appointed in another state and a petition for a protective order is not pending in this state, the conservator appointed in the other state, after giving notice to the appointing court of an intent to register, may register the protective order in this state by filing as a foreign judgment in a court of this state, in any [county] in which property belonging to the protected person is located, certified copies of the order and letters of office and of any bond.

Section 5–434. Effect of Registration.

(a)   Upon registration of a guardianship or protective order from another state, the guardian or conservator may exercise in this state all powers authorized in the order of appointment except as prohibited under the laws of this state, including maintaining actions and proceedings in this state and, if the guardian or conservator is not a resident of this state, subject to any conditions imposed upon nonresident parties.

(b)   A court of this state may grant any relief available under this [article] and other law of this state to enforce a registered order.

ARTICLE 5A

UNIFORM ADULT GUARDIANSHIP AND PROTECTIVE PROCEEDINGS JURISDICTION ACT (2007)

PART 1
GENERAL PROVISIONS

PART 1

GENERAL PROVISIONS

Section 5A–101. Short Title.

This [article] may be cited as the Uniform Adult Guardianship and Protective Proceedings Jurisdiction Act (2007).

Section 5A–102. Definitions.

In this [article]:

(1) "Adult" means an individual who has attained [18] years of age.

(2) "Conservator" means a person appointed by the court to administer the property of an adult as provided in [Article] V.

(3) "Guardian" means a person appointed by the court to make decisions regarding the person of an adult as provided in [Article] V.

(4) "Guardianship order" means an order appointing a guardian.

(5) "Guardianship proceeding" means a judicial proceeding in which an order for the appointment of a guardian is sought or has been issued.

(6) "Incapacitated person" means an adult for whom a guardian has been appointed.

(7) "Party" means the respondent, petitioner, guardian, conservator, or any other person allowed by the court to participate in a guardianship or protective proceeding.

(8) "Protected person" means an adult for whom a protective order has been issued.

(9) "Protective order" means an order appointing a conservator or other order related to management of an adult's property.

(10) "Protective proceeding" means a judicial proceeding in which a protective order is sought or has been issued.

(11) "Respondent" means an adult for whom a protective order or the appointment of a guardian is sought.

Section 5A–103. International Application of [Article].

A court of this state may treat a foreign country as if it were a state for the purpose of applying this [part] and [parts] 2 and 3.

Section 5A–104. Communication Between Courts.

[(a)] A court of this state may communicate with a court in another state concerning a proceeding arising under this [article]. The court may allow the parties to participate in the communication. [Except as otherwise provided in subsection (b), the court shall make a record of the communication. The record may be limited to the fact that the communication occurred.

(b) Courts may communicate concerning schedules, calendars, court records, and other administrative matters without making a record.]

Section 5A–105. Cooperation Between Courts.

(a) In a guardianship or protective proceeding in this state, a court of this state may request the appropriate court of another state to do any of the following:

(1) hold an evidentiary hearing;

(2) order a person in that state to produce evidence or give testimony pursuant to procedures of that state;

(3) order that an evaluation or assessment be made of the respondent;

(4) order any appropriate investigation of a person involved in a proceeding;

(5) forward to the court of this state a certified copy of the transcript or other record of a hearing under paragraph (1) or any other proceeding, any evidence otherwise produced under paragraph (2), and any evaluation or assessment prepared in compliance with an order under paragraph (3) or (4);

(6)   issue any order necessary to assure the appearance in the proceeding of a person whose presence is necessary for the court to make a determination, including the respondent or the incapacitated or protected person;

(7)   issue an order authorizing the release of medical, financial, criminal, or other relevant information in that state, including protected health information as defined in 45 C.F.R 160.103[, as amended].

(b)   If a court of another state in which a guardianship or protective proceeding is pending requests assistance of the kind provided in subsection (a), a court of this state has jurisdiction for the limited purpose of granting the request or making reasonable efforts to comply with the request.

Section 5A–106. Taking Testimony in Another State.

(a)   In a guardianship or protective proceeding, in addition to other procedures that may be available, testimony of a witness who is located in another state may be offered by deposition or other means allowable in this state for testimony taken in another state. The court on its own motion may order that the testimony of a witness be taken in another state and may prescribe the manner in which and the terms upon which the testimony is to be taken.

(b)   In a guardianship or protective proceeding, a court in this state may permit a witness located in another state to be deposed or to testify by telephone or audiovisual or other electronic means. A court of this state shall cooperate with the court of the other state in designating an appropriate location for the deposition or testimony.

[(c)   Documentary evidence transmitted from another state to a court of this state by technological means that do not produce an original writing may not be excluded from evidence on an objection based on the best evidence rule.]

PART 2

JURISDICTION

Section 5A–201. Definitions; Significant Connection Factors.

(a)   In this [part]:

(1)   "Emergency" means a circumstance that likely will result in substantial harm to a respondent's health, safety, or welfare, and for which the appointment of a guardian is necessary because no other person has authority and is willing to act on the respondent's behalf;

(2)   "Home state" means the state in which the respondent was physically present, including any period of temporary absence, for at least six consecutive months immediately before the filing of a petition for a protective order or the appointment of a guardian; or if none, the state in which the respondent was physically present, including any period of temporary absence, for at least six consecutive months ending within the six months prior to the filing of the petition.

(3)   "Significant-connection state" means a state, other than the home state, with which a respondent has a significant connection other than mere physical presence and in which substantial evidence concerning the respondent is available.

(b)   In determining under Section 5A–203 and Section 5A–301(e) whether a respondent has a significant connection with a particular state, the court shall consider:

(1)   the location of the respondent's family and other persons required to be notified of the guardianship or protective proceeding;

(2)   the length of time the respondent at any time was physically present in the state and the duration of any absence;

(3)   the location of the respondent's property; and

(4)   the extent to which the respondent has ties to the state such as voting registration, state or local tax return filing, vehicle registration, driver's license, social relationship, and receipt of services.

Section 5A–202. Exclusive Basis.

This [part] provides the exclusive jurisdictional basis for a court of this state to appoint a guardian or issue a protective order for an adult.

Section 5A–203. Jurisdiction.

A court of this state has jurisdiction to appoint a guardian or issue a protective order for a respondent if:

(1)   this state is the respondent's home state;

(2)   on the date the petition is filed, this state is a significant-connection state and:

(A)   the respondent does not have a home state or a court of the respondent's home state has declined to exercise jurisdiction because this state is a more appropriate forum; or

(B)   the respondent has a home state, a petition for an appointment or order is not pending in a court of that state or another significant-connection state, and, before the court makes the appointment or issues the order:

(i)   a petition for an appointment or order is not filed in the respondent's home state;

(ii)   an objection to the court's jurisdiction is not filed by a person required to be notified of the proceeding; and

(iii)   the court in this state concludes that it is an appropriate forum under the factors set forth in Section 5A–206;

(3)   this state does not have jurisdiction under either paragraph (1) or (2), the respondent's home state and all significant-connection states have declined to exercise jurisdiction because this state is the more appropriate forum, and jurisdiction in this state is consistent with the constitutions of this state and the United States; or

(4)   the requirements for special jurisdiction under Section 5A–204 are met.

Section 5A–204. Special Jurisdiction.

(a)   A court of this state lacking jurisdiction under Section 5A–203 has special jurisdiction to do any of the following:

(1)   appoint a guardian in an emergency for a term not exceeding [90] days for a respondent who is physically present in this state;

(2)   issue a protective order with respect to real or tangible personal property located in this state;

(3)   appoint a guardian or conservator for an incapacitated or protected person for whom a provisional order to transfer the proceeding from another state has been issued under procedures similar to Section 5A–301.

(b)   If a petition for the appointment of a guardian in an emergency is brought in this state and this state was not the respondent's home state on the date the petition was filed, the court shall dismiss the proceeding at the request of the court of the home state, if any, whether dismissal is requested before or after the emergency appointment.

Section 5A–205. Exclusive and Continuing Jurisdiction.

Except as otherwise provided in Section 5A–204, a court that has appointed a guardian or issued a protective order consistent with this [article] has exclusive and continuing jurisdiction over the proceeding until it is terminated by the court or the appointment or order expires by its own terms.

Section 5A–206. Appropriate Forum.

(a)   A court of this state having jurisdiction under Section 5A–203 to appoint a guardian or issue a protective order may decline to exercise its jurisdiction if it determines at any time that a court of another state is a more appropriate forum.

(b)   If a court of this state declines to exercise its jurisdiction under subsection (a), it shall either dismiss or stay the proceeding. The court may impose any condition the court considers just and proper, including the condition that a petition for the appointment of a guardian or issuance of a protective order be filed promptly in another state.

(c)   In determining whether it is an appropriate forum, the court shall consider all relevant factors, including:

(1)   any expressed preference of the respondent;

(2)   whether abuse, neglect, or exploitation of the respondent has occurred or is likely to occur and which state could best protect the respondent from the abuse, neglect, or exploitation;

(3)   the length of time the respondent was physically present in or was a legal resident of this or another state;

(4)   the distance of the respondent from the court in each state;

(5)   the financial circumstances of the respondent's estate;

(6)   the nature and location of the evidence;

(7)   the ability of the court in each state to decide the issue expeditiously and the procedures necessary to present evidence;

(8)   the familiarity of the court of each state with the facts and issues in the proceeding; and

(9)   if an appointment were made, the court's ability to monitor the conduct of the guardian or conservator.

Section 5A–207. Jurisdiction Declined By Reason of Conduct.

(a)   If at any time a court of this state determines that it acquired jurisdiction to appoint a guardian or issue a protective order because of unjustifiable conduct, the court may:

(1)   decline to exercise jurisdiction;

(2)   exercise jurisdiction for the limited purpose of fashioning an appropriate remedy to ensure the health, safety, and welfare of the respondent or the protection of the respondent's property or prevent a repetition of the unjustifiable conduct, including staying the proceeding until a petition for the appointment of a guardian or issuance of a protective order is filed in a court of another state having jurisdiction; or

(3)   continue to exercise jurisdiction after considering:

(A)   the extent to which the respondent and all persons required to be notified of the proceedings have acquiesced in the exercise of the court's jurisdiction;

(B)   whether it is a more appropriate forum than the court of any other state under the factors set forth in Section 5A–206(c); and

(C) whether the court of any other state would have jurisdiction under factual circumstances in substantial conformity with the jurisdictional standards of Section 5A–203.

(b)   If a court of this state determines that it acquired jurisdiction to appoint a guardian or issue a protective order because a party seeking to invoke its jurisdiction engaged in unjustifiable conduct, it may assess against that party necessary and reasonable expenses, including attorney's fees, investigative fees, court costs, communication expenses, witness fees and expenses, and travel expenses. The court may not assess fees, costs, or expenses of any kind against this state or a governmental subdivision, agency, or instrumentality of this state unless authorized by law other than this [article].

Section 5A–208. Notice of Proceeding.

If a petition for the appointment of a guardian or issuance of a protective order is brought in this state and this state was not the respondent's home state on the date the petition was filed, in addition to complying with the notice requirements of this state, notice of the petition must be given to those persons who would be entitled to notice of the petition if a proceeding were brought in the respondent's home state. The notice must be given in the same manner as notice is required to be given in this state.

Section 5A–209. Proceedings in More Than One State.

Except for a petition for the appointment of a guardian in an emergency or issuance of a protective order limited to property located in this state under Section 5A–204(a)(1) or (2), if a petition for the appointment of a guardian or issuance of a protective order is filed in this state and in another state and neither petition has been dismissed or withdrawn, the following rules apply:

(1)   If the court in this state has jurisdiction under Section 5A–203, it may proceed with the case unless a court in another state acquires jurisdiction under provisions similar to Section 5A–203 before the appointment or issuance of the order.

(2)   If the court in this state does not have jurisdiction under Section 5A–203, whether at the time the petition is filed or at any time before the appointment or issuance of the order, the court shall stay the proceeding and communicate with the court in the other state. If the court in the other state has jurisdiction, the court in this state shall dismiss the petition unless the court in the other state determines that the court in this state is a more appropriate forum.

PART 3

TRANSFER OF GUARDIANSHIP OR CONSERVATORSHIP

Section 5A–301. Transfer of Guardianship or Conservatorship to Another State.

(a)   A guardian or conservator appointed in this state may petition the court to transfer the guardianship or conservatorship to another state.

(b)   Notice of a petition under subsection (a) must be given to the persons that would be entitled to notice of a petition in this state for the appointment of a guardian or conservator.

(c)   On the court's own motion or on request of the guardian or conservator, the incapacitated or protected person, or other person required to be notified of the petition, the court shall hold a hearing on a petition filed pursuant to subsection (a).

(d)   The court shall issue an order provisionally granting a petition to transfer a guardianship and shall direct the guardian to petition for guardianship in the other state if the court is satisfied that the guardianship will be accepted by the court in the other state and the court finds that:

(1)   the incapacitated person is physically present in or is reasonably expected to move permanently to the other state;

(2)   an objection to the transfer has not been made or, if an objection has been made, the objector has not established that the transfer would be contrary to the interests of the incapacitated person; and

(3)   plans for care and services for the incapacitated person in the other state are reasonable and sufficient.

(e)   The court shall issue a provisional order granting a petition to transfer a conservatorship and shall direct the conservator to petition for conservatorship in the other state if the court is satisfied that the conservatorship will be accepted by the court of the other state and the court finds that:

(1)   the protected person is physically present in or is reasonably expected to move permanently to the other state, or the protected person has a significant connection to the other state considering the factors in Section 5A-201(b);

(2)   an objection to the transfer has not been made or, if an objection has been made, the objector has not established that the transfer would be contrary to the interests of the protected person; and

(3)   adequate arrangements will be made for management of the protected person's property.

(f)   The court shall issue a final order confirming the transfer and terminating the guardianship or conservatorship upon its receipt of:

(1)   a provisional order accepting the proceeding from the court to which the proceeding is to be transferred which is issued under provisions similar to Section 5A-302; and

(2)   the documents required to terminate a guardianship or conservatorship in this state.

Section 5A-302. Accepting Guardianship or Conservatorship Transferred From Another State.

(a)   To confirm transfer of a guardianship or conservatorship transferred to this state under provisions similar to Section 5A-301, the guardian or conservator must petition the court in this state to accept the guardianship or conservatorship. The petition must include a certified copy of the other state's provisional order of transfer.

(b)   Notice of a petition under subsection (a) must be given to those persons that would be entitled to notice if the petition were a petition for the appointment of a guardian or issuance of a protective order in both the transferring state and this state. The notice must be given in the same manner as notice is required to be given in this state.

(c)   On the court's own motion or on request of the guardian or conservator, the incapacitated or protected person, or other person required to be notified of the proceeding, the court shall hold a hearing on a petition filed pursuant to subsection (a).

(d)   The court shall issue an order provisionally granting a petition filed under subsection (a) unless:

(1)   an objection is made and the objector establishes that transfer of the proceeding would be contrary to the interests of the incapacitated or protected person; or

(2)   the guardian or conservator is ineligible for appointment in this state.

(e)   The court shall issue a final order accepting the proceeding and appointing the guardian or conservator as guardian or conservator in this state upon its receipt from the court from which the proceeding is being transferred of a final order issued under provisions similar to Section 5A-301 transferring the proceeding to this state.

(f) Not later than [90] days after issuance of a final order accepting transfer of a guardianship or conservatorship, the court shall determine whether the guardianship or conservatorship needs to be modified to conform to the law of this state.

(g) In granting a petition under this section, the court shall recognize a guardianship or conservatorship order from the other state, including the determination of the incapacitated or protected person's incapacity and the appointment of the guardian or conservator.

(h) The denial by a court of this state of a petition to accept a guardianship or conservatorship transferred from another state does not affect the ability of the guardian or conservator to seek appointment as guardian or conservator in this state under [insert statutory references to this state's ordinary procedures law for the appointment of guardian or conservator] if the court has jurisdiction to make an appointment other than by reason of the provisional order of transfer.

PART 4

REGISTRATION AND RECOGNITION OF ORDERS FROM OTHER STATES

Section 5A–401. Registration of Guardianship Orders.

If a guardian has been appointed in another state and a petition for the appointment of a guardian is not pending in this state, the guardian appointed in the other state, after giving notice to the appointing court of an intent to register, may register the guardianship order in this state by filing as a foreign judgment in a court, in any appropriate [county] of this state, certified copies of the order and letters of office.

Section 5A–402. Registration of Protective Orders.

If a conservator has been appointed in another state and a petition for a protective order is not pending in this state, the conservator appointed in the other state, after giving notice to the appointing court of an intent to register, may register the protective order in this state by filing as a foreign judgment in a court of this state, in any [county] in which property belonging to the protected person is located, certified copies of the order and letters of office and of any bond.

Section 5A–403. Effect of Registration.

(a) Upon registration of a guardianship or protective order from another state, the guardian or conservator may exercise in this state all powers authorized in the order of appointment except as prohibited under the laws of this state, including maintaining actions and proceedings in this state and, if the guardian or conservator is not a resident of this state, subject to any conditions imposed upon nonresident parties.

(b) A court of this state may grant any relief available under this [article] and other law of this state to enforce a registered order.

ARTICLE 5B

UNIFORM POWER OF ATTORNEY ACT (2006)

[The Uniform Power of Attorney Act (2006)
is reproduced elsewhere in this volume.]

ARTICLE VI

NONPROBATE TRANSFERS ON DEATH

PART 1
PROVISIONS RELATING TO EFFECT OF DEATH

PART 2
UNIFORM MULTIPLE-PERSON ACCOUNTS ACT (1989/1998)

SUBPART 1
DEFINITIONS AND GENERAL PROVISIONS

SUBPART 2
OWNERSHIP AS BETWEEN PARTIES AND OTHERS

SUBPART 3
PROTECTION OF FINANCIAL INSTITUTIONS

PART 3
UNIFORM TOD SECURITY REGISTRATION ACT (1989/1998)

PART 4
UNIFORM REAL PROPERTY TRANSFER ON DEATH ACT (2009)

[The Uniform Real Property Transfer on Death Act
(2009) is reproduced elsewhere in this volume.]

PART 1

PROVISIONS RELATING TO EFFECT OF DEATH

Section 6–101. Nonprobate Transfers on Death.

A provision for a nonprobate transfer on death in an insurance policy, contract of employment, bond, mortgage, promissory note, certificated or uncertificated security, account agreement, custodial agreement, deposit agreement, compensation plan, pension plan, individual retirement plan, employee benefit plan, trust, conveyance, deed of gift, marital property agreement, or other written instrument of a similar nature is nontestamentary. This subsection includes a written provision that:

(1)   money or other benefits due to, controlled by, or owned by a decedent before death must be paid after the decedent's death to a person whom the decedent designates either in the instrument or in a separate writing, including a will, executed either before or at the same time as the instrument, or later;

(2)   money due or to become due under the instrument ceases to be payable in the event of death of the promisee or the promisor before payment or demand; or

(3)   any property controlled by or owned by the decedent before death which is the subject of the instrument passes to a person the decedent designates either in the instrument or in a separate writing, including a will, executed either before or at the same time as the instrument, or later.

Comment

This section is a revised version of former Section 6–201 of the original Uniform Probate Code, which authorized a variety of contractual arrangements that had sometimes been treated as testamentary in prior law. * * *

Because the modes of transfer authorized by an instrument under this section are declared to be nontestamentary, the instrument does not have to be executed in compliance with the formalities for wills prescribed under Section 2–502; nor does the instrument have to be probated, nor does the personal representative have any power or duty with respect to the assets.

The sole purpose of this section is to prevent the transfers authorized here from being treated as testamentary. This section does not invalidate other arrangements by negative implication. Thus, this section does not speak to the phenomenon of the oral trust to hold property at death for named persons, an arrangement already generally enforceable under trust law. * * *

Section 6–102. Liability of Nonprobate Transferees for Creditor Claims and Statutory Allowances.

(a)   In this section, "nonprobate transfer" means a valid transfer effective at death, other than a transfer of a survivorship interest in a joint tenancy of real estate, by a transferor whose last domicile was in this state to the extent that the transferor immediately before death had power, acting alone, to prevent the transfer by revocation or withdrawal and instead to use the property for the benefit of the transferor or apply it to discharge claims against the transferor's probate estate.

(b) Except as otherwise provided by statute, a transferee of a nonprobate transfer is subject to liability to any probate estate of the decedent for allowed claims against decedent's probate estate and statutory allowances to the decedent's spouse and children to the extent the estate is insufficient to satisfy those claims and allowances. The liability of a nonprobate transferee may not exceed the value of nonprobate transfers received or controlled by that transferee.

(c) Nonprobate transferees are liable for the insufficiency described in subsection (b) in the following order of priority:

(1) a transferee designated in the decedent's will or any other governing instrument, as provided in the instrument;

(2) the trustee of a trust serving as the principal nonprobate instrument in the decedent's estate plan as shown by its designation as devisee of the decedent's residuary estate or by other facts or circumstances, to the extent of the value of the nonprobate transfer received or controlled;

(3) other nonprobate transferees, in proportion to the values received.

(d) Unless otherwise provided by the trust instrument, interests of beneficiaries in all trusts incurring liabilities under this section abate as necessary to satisfy the liability, as if all of the trust instruments were a single will and the interests were devises under it.

(e) A provision made in one instrument may direct the apportionment of the liability among the nonprobate transferees taking under that or any other governing instrument. If a provision in one instrument conflicts with a provision in another, the later one prevails.

(f) Upon due notice to a nonprobate transferee, the liability imposed by this section is enforceable in proceedings in this state, whether or not the transferee is located in this state.

(g) A proceeding under this section may not be commenced unless the personal representative of the decedent's estate has received a written demand for the proceeding from the surviving spouse or a child, to the extent that statutory allowances are affected, or a creditor. If the personal representative declines or fails to commence a proceeding after demand, a person making demand may commence the proceeding in the name of the decedent's estate, at the expense of the person making the demand and not of the estate. A personal representative who declines in good faith to commence a requested proceeding incurs no personal liability for declining.

(h) A proceeding under this section must be commenced within one year after the decedent's death, but a proceeding on behalf of a creditor whose claim was allowed after proceedings challenging disallowance of the claim may be commenced within 60 days after final allowance of the claim.

(i) Unless a written notice asserting that a decedent's probate estate is nonexistent or insufficient to pay allowed claims and statutory allowances has been received from the decedent's personal representative, the following rules apply:

(1) Payment or delivery of assets by a financial institution, registrar, or other obligor, to a nonprobate transferee in accordance with the terms of the governing instrument controlling the transfer releases the obligor from all claims for amounts paid or assets delivered.

(2) A trustee receiving or controlling a nonprobate transfer is released from liability under this section with respect to any assets distributed to the trust's beneficiaries. Each beneficiary to the extent of the distribution received becomes liable for the amount of the trustee's liability attributable to assets received by the beneficiary.

Comment

* * * [T]his section clarifies that the recipients of nonprobate transfers can be required to contribute to pay allowed claims and statutory allowances to the extent the probate estate is inadequate. The maximum liability for a single nonprobate transferee is the value of the transfer. Values are determined under

subsection (b) as of the time when the benefits are "received or controlled by that transferee." This would be the date of the decedent's death for nonprobate transfers made by means of a revocable trust, and date of receipt for other nonprobate transfers. Two or more transferees are severally liable for the portion of the liability based on the value of the transfers received by each. * * *

If there are no probate assets, a creditor or other person seeking to use this Section 6–102 would first need to secure appointment of a personal representative to invoke Code procedures for establishing a creditor's claim as "allowed." * * *

If a state's insurance laws do not exempt or protect a particular insurance death benefit, the insured's creditors would not be able to establish a "nonprobate transfer" under subsection (a) except to the extent of any cash surrender value generated by premiums paid by the insured that the insured could have obtained immediately before death. * * *

The definition of "nonprobate transfer" in subsection (a) includes revocable transfers by a decedent; it does not include a transfer at death incident to a decedent's exercise or non-exercise of a presently exercisable general power of appointment created by another person. The drafters decided against including such powers even though presently exercisable general powers of appointment are subject to the Code's augmented estate provisions dealing with protection of a surviving spouse from disinheritance. Spousal protection against disinheritance by the other spouse supports the institution of marriage; creditors are better able to fend for themselves than financially disadvantaged surviving spouses. In addition, a presently exercisable general power of appointment created by another person is commonly viewed as a provision in the trust creator's instrument designed to provide flexibility in the estate plan rather than as a gift to the donee. * * *

* * * By excluding real estate joint tenancies, stability of title and ease of title examination is preserved. Moreover, real estate joint tenancies have served for generations to keep the share of a couple's real estate owned by the first to die out of probate and away from estate creditors. This familiar arrangement need not be disturbed incident to expanding the ability of decedents' creditors to reach newly recognized nonprobate transfers at death.

No view is expressed as to whether a survivorship interest in personal or intangible property registered in two or more names as joint tenants with right of survivorship would come within Section 6–102(a). The outcome might depend on who originated the registration and whether severance by any co-owner acting alone was possible immediately preceding a co-owner's death.

* * * Section 6–211 and related sections of the Code make it clear that parties to a joint and survivor account separately own values in the account in proportion to net contributions. Hence, a surviving joint account depositor who had contributed to the balance on deposit prior to the death of the other party is subject to the remedies described in this section only to the extent of new account values gained through survival of the decedent. * * *

PART 2

UNIFORM MULTIPLE-PERSON ACCOUNTS ACT (1989/1998)

SUBPART 1

DEFINITIONS AND GENERAL PROVISIONS

Section 6–201. Definitions.

In this [part]:

(1) "Account" means a contract of deposit between a depositor and a financial institution, and includes a checking account, savings account, certificate of deposit, and share account.

(2) "Agent" means a person authorized to make account transactions for a party.

(3) "Beneficiary" means a person named as one to whom sums on deposit in an account are payable on request after death of all parties or for whom a party is named as trustee.

(4) "Financial institution" means an organization authorized to do business under state or federal laws relating to financial institutions, and includes a bank, trust company, savings bank, building and loan association, savings and loan company or association, and credit union.

(5) "Multiple-party account" means an account payable on request to one or more of two or more parties, whether or not a right of survivorship is mentioned.

(6) "Party" means a person who, by the terms of an account, has a present right, subject to request, to payment from the account other than as a beneficiary or agent.

(7) "Payment" of sums on deposit includes withdrawal, payment to a party or third person pursuant to check or other request, and a pledge of sums on deposit by a party, or a set-off, reduction, or other disposition of all or part of an account pursuant to a pledge.

(8) "POD designation" means the designation of (i) a beneficiary in an account payable on request to one party during the party's lifetime and on the party's death to one or more beneficiaries, or to one or more parties during their lifetimes and on death of all of them to one or more beneficiaries, or (ii) a beneficiary in an account in the name of one or more parties as trustee for one or more beneficiaries if the relationship is established by the terms of the account and there is no subject of the trust other than the sums on deposit in the account, whether or not payment to the beneficiary is mentioned.

(9) "Receive," as it relates to notice to a financial institution, means receipt in the office or branch office of the financial institution in which the account is established, but if the terms of the account require notice at a particular place, in the place required.

(10) "Request" means a request for payment complying with all terms of the account, including special requirements concerning necessary signatures and regulations of the financial institution; but, for purposes of this [part], if terms of the account condition payment on advance notice, a request for payment is treated as immediately effective and a notice of intent to withdraw is treated as a request for payment.

(11) "Sums on deposit" means the balance payable on an account, including interest and dividends earned, whether or not included in the current balance, and any deposit life insurance proceeds added to the account by reason of death of a party.

(12) "Terms of the account" includes the deposit agreement and other terms and conditions, including the form, of the contract of deposit.

Section 6–202. Limitation on Scope of Part.

This [part] does not apply to:

(1) an account established for a partnership, joint venture, or other organization for a business purpose,

(2) an account controlled by one or more persons as an agent or trustee for a corporation, unincorporated association, or charitable or civic organization, or

(3) a fiduciary or trust account in which the relationship is established other than by the terms of the account.

Section 6–203. Types of Account; Existing Accounts.

(a) An account may be for a single party or multiple parties. A multiple-party account may be with or without a right of survivorship between the parties. Subject to Section 6–212(c), either a single-party account or a multiple-party account may have a POD designation, an agency designation, or both.

(b) An account established before, on, or after the effective date of this [part], whether in the form prescribed in Section 6–204 or in any other form, is either a single-party account or a multiple-party account, with or without right of survivorship, and with or without a POD designation or an agency designation, within the meaning of this [part], and is governed by this [part].

Section 6–204. Forms.

(a) A contract of deposit that contains provisions in substantially the following form establishes the type of account provided, and the account is governed by the provisions of this [part] applicable to an account of that type:

UNIFORM SINGLE- OR MULTIPLE-PARTY ACCOUNT FORM

PARTIES [Name One or More Parties]:

_____   _____

OWNERSHIP [Select One And Initial]:

_____ SINGLE-PARTY ACCOUNT

_____ MULTIPLE-PARTY ACCOUNT

Parties own account in proportion to net contributions unless there is clear and convincing evidence of a different intent.

RIGHTS AT DEATH [Select One And Initial]:

_____ SINGLE-PARTY ACCOUNT

At death of party, ownership passes as part of party's estate.

_____ SINGLE-PARTY ACCOUNT WITH POD (PAY ON DEATH) DESIGNATION

[Name One Or More Beneficiaries]:

_____   _____

At death of party, ownership passes to POD beneficiaries and is not part of party's estate.

_____ MULTIPLE-PARTY ACCOUNT WITH RIGHT OF SURVIVORSHIP

At death of party, ownership passes to surviving parties.

_____ MULTIPLE-PARTY ACCOUNT WITH RIGHT OF SURVIVORSHIP AND POD (PAY ON DEATH) DESIGNATION

[Name One Or More Beneficiaries]:

_____   _____

At death of last surviving party, ownership passes to POD beneficiaries and is not part of last surviving party's estate.

_____ MULTIPLE-PARTY ACCOUNT WITHOUT RIGHT OF SURVIVORSHIP

At death of party, deceased party's ownership passes as part of deceased party's estate.

AGENCY (POWER OF ATTORNEY) DESIGNATION [Optional]

Agents may make account transactions for parties but have no ownership or rights at death unless named as POD beneficiaries.

[To Add Agency Designation To Account, Name One Or More Agents]:

_____   _____

[Select One And Initial]:

_____ AGENCY DESIGNATION SURVIVES DISABILITY OR INCAPACITY OF PARTIES

_____ AGENCY DESIGNATION TERMINATES ON DISABILITY OR INCAPACITY OF PARTIES

(b)   A contract of deposit that does not contain provisions in substantially the form provided in subsection (a) is governed by the provisions of this [part] applicable to the type of account that most nearly conforms to the depositor's intent.

Section 6–205. Designation of Agent.

(a)   By a writing signed by all parties, the parties may designate as agent of all parties on an account a person other than a party.

(b)   Unless the terms of an agency designation provide that the authority of the agent terminates on disability or incapacity of a party, the agent's authority survives disability and incapacity. The agent may act for a disabled or incapacitated party until the authority of the agent is terminated.

(c)   Death of the sole party or last surviving party terminates the authority of an agent.

Section 6–206. Applicability of Part.

The provisions of [Subpart] 2 concerning beneficial ownership as between parties or as between parties and beneficiaries apply only to controversies between those persons and their creditors and other successors, and do not apply to the right of those persons to payment as determined by the terms of the account. [Subpart] 3 governs the liability and set-off rights of financial institutions that make payments pursuant to it.

SUBPART 2

OWNERSHIP AS BETWEEN PARTIES AND OTHERS

Section 6–211. Ownership During Lifetime.

(a)   In this section, "net contribution" of a party means the sum of all deposits to an account made by or for the party, less all payments from the account made to or for the party which have not been paid to or applied to the use of another party and a proportionate share of any charges deducted from the account, plus a proportionate share of any interest or dividends earned, whether or not included in the current balance. The term includes deposit life insurance proceeds added to the account by reason of death of the party whose net contribution is in question.

(b)   During the lifetime of all parties, an account belongs to the parties in proportion to the net contribution of each to the sums on deposit, unless there is clear and convincing evidence of a different intent. As between parties married to each other, in the absence of proof otherwise, the net contribution of each is presumed to be an equal amount.

(c)   A beneficiary in an account having a POD designation has no right to sums on deposit during the lifetime of any party.

(d)   An agent in an account with an agency designation has no beneficial right to sums on deposit.

Section 6–212. Rights at Death.

(a)   Except as otherwise provided in this [part], on death of a party sums on deposit in a multiple-party account belong to the surviving party or parties. If two or more parties survive and one is the surviving spouse of the decedent, the amount to which the decedent, immediately before death, was beneficially entitled under Section 6–211 belongs to the surviving spouse. If two or more parties survive and none is the surviving spouse of the decedent, the amount to which the decedent, immediately before death, was beneficially entitled under Section 6–211 belongs to the surviving parties in equal shares, and augments the proportion to which each survivor, immediately before the decedent's death, was beneficially entitled under Section 6–211, and the right of survivorship continues between the surviving parties.

(b)   In an account with a POD designation:

(1)   On death of one of two or more parties, the rights in sums on deposit are governed by subsection (a).

(2)   On death of the sole party or the last survivor of two or more parties, sums on deposit belong to the surviving beneficiary or beneficiaries. If two or more beneficiaries survive, sums on deposit belong to them in equal and undivided shares, and there is no right of survivorship in the event of death of a beneficiary thereafter. If no beneficiary survives, sums on deposit belong to the estate of the last surviving party.

(c)   Sums on deposit in a single-party account without a POD designation, or in a multiple-party account that, by the terms of the account, is without right of survivorship, are not affected by death of a party, but the amount to which the decedent, immediately before death, was beneficially entitled under Section 6–211 is transferred as part of the decedent's estate. A POD designation in a multiple-party account without right of survivorship is ineffective. For purposes of this section, designation of an account as a tenancy in common establishes that the account is without right of survivorship.

(d)   The ownership right of a surviving party or beneficiary, or of the decedent's estate, in sums on deposit is subject to requests for payment made by a party before the party's death, whether paid by the financial institution before or after death, or unpaid. The surviving party or beneficiary, or the decedent's estate, is liable to the payee of an unpaid request for payment. The liability is limited to a proportionate share of the amount transferred under this section, to the extent necessary to discharge the request for payment.

Section 6–213. Alteration of Rights.

(a)   Rights at death of a party under Section 6–212 are determined by the terms of the account at the death of the party. A party may alter the terms of the account by a notice signed by the party and given to the financial institution to change the terms of the account or to stop or vary payment under the terms of the account. To be effective, the notice must be received by the financial institution during the party's lifetime.

(b)   A right of survivorship arising from the express terms of the account, Section 6–212, or a POD designation, may not be altered by will.

Section 6–214. Accounts and Transfers Nontestamentary.

Except as provided in [Part] 2 of [Article] II (elective share of surviving spouse) or as a consequence of, and to the extent directed by, Section 6–215, a transfer resulting from the application of Section 6–212 is effective by reason of the terms of the account involved and this [part] and is not testamentary or subject to [Articles] I through IV (estate administration).

Section 6–215. [Reserved].

Section 6–216. Community Property and Tenancy by the Entireties.

(a)   A deposit of community property in an account does not alter the community character of the property or community rights in the property, but a right of survivorship between parties married to each other arising from the express terms of the account or Section 6–212 may not be altered by will.

(b)   This [part] does not affect the law governing tenancy by the entireties.

SUBPART 3

PROTECTION OF FINANCIAL INSTITUTIONS

Section 6–221. Authority of Financial Institution.

A financial institution may enter into a contract of deposit for a multiple-party account to the same extent it may enter into a contract of deposit for a single-party account, and may provide for a

POD designation and an agency designation in either a single-party account or a multiple-party account. A financial institution need not inquire as to the source of a deposit to an account or as to the proposed application of a payment from an account.

Section 6–222. Payment on Multiple-Party Account.

A financial institution, on request, may pay sums on deposit in a multiple-party account to:

(1) one or more of the parties, whether or not another party is disabled, incapacitated, or deceased when payment is requested and whether or not the party making the request survives another party; or

(2) the personal representative, if any, or, if there is none, the heirs or devisees of a deceased party if proof of death is presented to the financial institution showing that the deceased party was the survivor of all other persons named on the account either as a party or beneficiary, unless the account is without right of survivorship under Section 6–212.

Section 6–223. Payment on POD Designation.

A financial institution, on request, may pay sums on deposit in an account with a POD designation to:

(1) one or more of the parties, whether or not another party is disabled, incapacitated, or deceased when the payment is requested and whether or not a party survives another party;

(2) the beneficiary or beneficiaries, if proof of death is presented to the financial institution showing that the beneficiary or beneficiaries survived all persons named as parties; or

(3) the personal representative, if any, or, if there is none, the heirs or devisees of a deceased party, if proof of death is presented to the financial institution showing that the deceased party was the survivor of all other persons named on the account either as a party or beneficiary.

Section 6–224. Payment to Designated Agent.

A financial institution, on request of an agent under an agency designation for an account, may pay to the agent sums on deposit in the account, whether or not a party is disabled, incapacitated, or deceased when the request is made or received, and whether or not the authority of the agent terminates on the disability or incapacity of a party.

Section 6–225. Payment to Minor.

If a financial institution is required or permitted to make payment pursuant to this [part] to a minor designated as a beneficiary, payment may be made pursuant to the Uniform Transfers to Minors Act (1983/1986).

Section 6–226. Discharge.

(a) Payment made pursuant to this [part] in accordance with the terms of the account discharges the financial institution from all claims for amounts so paid, whether or not the payment is consistent with the beneficial ownership of the account as between parties, beneficiaries, or their successors. Payment may be made whether or not a party, beneficiary, or agent is disabled, incapacitated, or deceased when payment is requested, received, or made.

(b) Protection under this section does not extend to payments made after a financial institution has received written notice from a party, or from the personal representative, surviving spouse, or heir or devisee of a deceased party, to the effect that payments in accordance with the terms of the account, including one having an agency designation, should not be permitted, and the financial institution has had a reasonable opportunity to act on it when the payment is made. Unless the notice is withdrawn by the person giving it, the successor of any deceased party must concur in a request for payment if the financial institution is to be protected under this section. Unless a financial institution has been served with process in an action or proceeding, no other notice or other information shown to have been available to the financial institution affects its right to protection under this section.

(c) A financial institution that receives written notice pursuant to this section or otherwise has reason to believe that a dispute exists as to the rights of the parties may refuse, without liability, to make payments in accordance with the terms of the account.

(d) Protection of a financial institution under this section does not affect the rights of parties in disputes between themselves or their successors concerning the beneficial ownership of sums on deposit in accounts or payments made from accounts.

Section 6–227. Set-Off.

Without qualifying any other statutory right to set-off or lien and subject to any contractual provision, if a party is indebted to a financial institution, the financial institution has a right to set-off against the account. The amount of the account subject to set-off is the proportion to which the party is, or immediately before death was, beneficially entitled under Section 6–211 or, in the absence of proof of that proportion, an equal share with all parties.

PART 3

UNIFORM TOD SECURITY REGISTRATION ACT (1989/1998)

Section 6–301. Definitions.

In this [part]:

(1) "Beneficiary form" means a registration of a security which indicates the present owner of the security and the intention of the owner regarding the person who will become the owner of the security upon the death of the owner.

(2) "Register," including its derivatives, means to issue a certificate showing the ownership of a certificated security or, in the case of an uncertificated security, to initiate or transfer an account showing ownership of securities.

(3) "Registering entity" means a person who originates or transfers a security title by registration, and includes a broker maintaining security accounts for customers and a transfer agent or other person acting for or as an issuer of securities.

(4) "Security" means a share, participation, or other interest in property, in a business, or in an obligation of an enterprise or other issuer, and includes a certificated security, an uncertificated security, and a security account.

(5) "Security account" means (i) a reinvestment account associated with a security, a securities account with a broker, a cash balance in a brokerage account, cash, interest, earnings, or dividends earned or declared on a security in an account, a reinvestment account, or a brokerage account, whether or not credited to the account before the owner's death, or (ii) a cash balance or other property held for or due to the owner of a security as a replacement for or product of an account security, whether or not credited to the account before the owner's death.

Section 6–302. Registration in Beneficiary Form; Sole or Joint Tenancy Ownership.

Only individuals whose registration of a security shows sole ownership by one individual or multiple ownership by two or more with right of survivorship, rather than as tenants in common, may obtain registration in beneficiary form. Multiple owners of a security registered in beneficiary form hold as joint tenants with right of survivorship, as tenants by the entireties, or as owners of community property held in survivorship form, and not as tenants in common.

Section 6–303. Registration in Beneficiary Form; Applicable Law.

A security may be registered in beneficiary form if the form is authorized by this or a similar statute of the state of organization of the issuer or registering entity, the location of the registering entity's principal office, the office of its transfer agent or its office making the registration, or by this or a similar statute of the law of the state listed as the owner's address at the time of registration. A registration governed by the law of a jurisdiction in which this or similar legislation is not in force or was not in force when a registration in beneficiary form was made is nevertheless presumed to be valid and authorized as a matter of contract law.

Section 6–304. Origination of Registration in Beneficiary Form.

A security, whether evidenced by certificate or account, is registered in beneficiary form when the registration includes a designation of a beneficiary to take the ownership at the death of the owner or the deaths of all multiple owners.

Section 6–305. Form of Registration in Beneficiary Form.

Registration in beneficiary form may be shown by the words "transfer on death" or the abbreviation "TOD," or by the words "pay on death" or the abbreviation "POD," after the name of the registered owner and before the name of a beneficiary.

Section 6–306. Effect of Registration in Beneficiary Form.

The designation of a TOD beneficiary on a registration in beneficiary form has no effect on ownership until the owner's death. A registration of a security in beneficiary form may be canceled or changed at any time by the sole owner or all then surviving owners without the consent of the beneficiary.

Section 6–307. Ownership on Death of Owner.

On death of a sole owner or the last to die of all multiple owners, ownership of securities registered in beneficiary form passes to the beneficiary or beneficiaries who survive all owners. On proof of death of all owners and compliance with any applicable requirements of the registering entity, a security registered in beneficiary form may be reregistered in the name of the beneficiary or beneficiaries who survive the death of all owners. Until division of the security after the death of all owners, multiple beneficiaries surviving the death of all owners hold their interests as tenants in common. If no beneficiary survives the death of all owners, the security belongs to the estate of the deceased sole owner or the estate of the last to die of all multiple owners.

Section 6–308. Protection of Registering Entity.

(a) A registering entity is not required to offer or to accept a request for security registration in beneficiary form. If a registration in beneficiary form is offered by a registering entity, the owner requesting registration in beneficiary form assents to the protections given to the registering entity by this [part].

(b) By accepting a request for registration of a security in beneficiary form, the registering entity agrees that the registration will be implemented on death of the deceased owner as provided in this [part].

(c) A registering entity is discharged from all claims to a security by the estate, creditors, heirs, or devisees of a deceased owner if it registers a transfer of the security in accordance with Section 6–307 and does so in good faith reliance (i) on the registration, (ii) on this [part], and (iii) on information provided to it by affidavit of the personal representative of the deceased owner, or by the surviving beneficiary or by the surviving beneficiary's representatives, or other information available to the registering entity. The protections of this [part] do not extend to a reregistration or payment made after a registering entity has received written notice from any claimant to any interest in the security objecting to implementation of a registration in beneficiary form. No other notice or other information available to the registering entity affects its right to protection under this [part].

(d)   The protection provided by this [part] to the registering entity of a security does not affect the rights of beneficiaries in disputes between themselves and other claimants to ownership of the security transferred or its value or proceeds.

Section 6–309. Nontestamentary Transfer on Death.

A transfer on death resulting from a registration in beneficiary form is effective by reason of the contract regarding the registration between the owner and the registering entity and this [part] and is not testamentary.

Section 6–310. Terms, Conditions, and Forms for Registration.

(a)   A registering entity offering to accept registrations in beneficiary form may establish the terms and conditions under which it will receive requests (i) for registrations in beneficiary form, and (ii) for implementation of registrations in beneficiary form, including requests for cancellation of previously registered TOD beneficiary designations and requests for reregistration to effect a change of beneficiary. The terms and conditions so established may provide for proving death, avoiding or resolving any problems concerning fractional shares, designating primary and contingent beneficiaries, and substituting a named beneficiary's descendants to take in the place of the named beneficiary in the event of the beneficiary's death. Substitution may be indicated by appending to the name of the primary beneficiary the letters LDPS, standing for "lineal descendants per stirpes." This designation substitutes a deceased beneficiary's descendants who survive the owner for a beneficiary who fails to so survive, the descendants to be identified and to share in accordance with the law of the beneficiary's domicile at the owner's death governing inheritance by descendants of an intestate. Other forms of identifying beneficiaries who are to take on one or more contingencies, and rules for providing proofs and assurances needed to satisfy reasonable concerns by registering entities regarding conditions and identities relevant to accurate implementation of registrations in beneficiary form, may be contained in a registering entity's terms and conditions.

(b)   The following are illustrations of registrations in beneficiary form which a registering entity may authorize:

(1)   Sole owner-sole beneficiary: John S Brown TOD (or POD) John S Brown Jr.

(2)   Multiple owners-sole beneficiary: John S Brown Mary B Brown JT TEN TOD John S Brown Jr.

(3)   Multiple owners-primary and secondary (substituted) beneficiaries: John S Brown Mary B Brown JT TEN TOD John S Brown Jr SUB BENE Peter Q Brown *or* John S Brown Mary B Brown JT TEN TOD John S Brown Jr LDPS.

[Section 6–311. Application of Part.

This [part] applies to registrations of securities in beneficiary form made before or after [effective date], by decedents dying on or after [effective date].]

PART 4

UNIFORM REAL PROPERTY TRANSFER ON DEATH ACT (2009)

[The Uniform Real Property Transfer on Death Act (2009) is reproduced elsewhere in this volume.]

ARTICLE VII
TRUST ADMINISTRATION

[withdrawn]

ARTICLE VIII
EFFECTIVE DATE AND REPEALER

[omitted]

APPENDIX

PRE-1990 ARTICLE II
INTESTATE SUCCESSION AND WILLS

PART 1
INTESTATE SUCCESSION

PART 2
ELECTIVE SHARE OF SURVIVING SPOUSE

PART 3
SPOUSE AND CHILDREN UNPROVIDED FOR IN WILLS

PART 4
EXEMPT PROPERTY AND ALLOWANCES

APPENDIX

PART 5
WILLS

PART 6
RULES OF CONSTRUCTION

PART 7
CONTRACTUAL ARRANGEMENTS RELATING TO DEATH

PART 8
GENERAL PROVISIONS

PART 9
CUSTODY AND DEPOSIT OF WILLS

PART 10
UNIFORM INTERNATIONAL WILLS ACT [INTERNATIONAL WILL; INFORMATION REGISTRATION]

[omitted]

PART 1

INTESTATE SUCCESSION

Section 2–101. [Intestate Estate.]

Any part of the estate of a decedent not effectively disposed of by his will passes to his heirs as prescribed in the following sections of this Code.

Section 2–102. [Share of the Spouse.]

The intestate share of the surviving spouse is:

(1)   if there is no surviving issue or parent of the decedent, the entire intestate estate;

(2)   if there is no surviving issue but the decedent is survived by a parent or parents, the first [$50,000], plus one-half of the balance of the intestate estate;

(3)   if there are surviving issue all of whom are issue of the surviving spouse also, the first [$50,000], plus one-half of the balance of the intestate estate;

(4)   if there are surviving issue one or more of whom are not issue of the surviving spouse, one-half of the intestate estate.

ALTERNATIVE PROVISION FOR COMMUNITY PROPERTY STATES

[Section 2–102A. [Share of the Spouse.]

The intestate share of the surviving spouse is as follows:

(1)   as to separate property

(i)   if there is no surviving issue or parent of the decedent, the entire intestate estate;

(ii)   if there is no surviving issue but the decedent is survived by a parent or parents, the first [$50,000], plus one-half of the balance of the intestate estate;

(iii)   if there are surviving issue all of whom are issue of the surviving spouse also, the first [$50,000], plus one-half of the balance of the intestate estate;

(iv)   if there are surviving issue one or more of whom are not issue of the surviving spouse, one-half of the intestate estate.

(2)   as to community property

(i)   the one-half of community property which belongs to the decedent passes to the [surviving spouse].]

Section 2–103. [Shares of Heirs Other Than Surviving Spouse.]

The part of the intestate estate not passing to the surviving spouse under Section 2–102, or the entire intestate estate if there is no surviving spouse, passes as follows:

(1)   to the issue of the decedent; if they are all of the same degree of kinship to the decedent they take equally, but if of unequal degree, then those of more remote degree take by representation;

(2)   if there is no surviving issue, to his parent or parents equally;

(3)   if there is no surviving issue or parent, to the issue of the parents or either of them by representation;

(4)   if there is no surviving issue, parent or issue of a parent, but the decedent is survived by one or more grandparents or issue of grandparents, half of the estate passes to the paternal grandparents if both survive, or to the surviving paternal grandparent, or to the issue of the paternal grandparents if both are deceased, the issue taking equally if they are all of the same degree of kinship to the decedent, but if of unequal degree those of more remote degree take by representation; and the other half passes to the maternal relatives in the same manner; but if there be no surviving grandparent or issue of grandparent on either the paternal or the maternal side, the entire estate passes to the relatives on the other side in the same manner as the half.

Section 2–104. [Requirement That Heir Survive Decedent for 120 Hours.]

Any person who fails to survive the decedent by 120 hours is deemed to have predeceased the decedent for purposes of homestead allowance, exempt property and intestate succession, and the decedent's heirs are determined accordingly. If the time of death of the decedent or of the person who would otherwise be an heir, or the times of death of both, cannot be determined, and it cannot be established that the person who would otherwise be an heir has survived the decedent by 120 hours, it is deemed that the person failed to survive for the required period. This section is not to be applied where its application would result in a taking of intestate estate by the state under Section 2–105.

Section 2–105. [No Taker.]

If there is no taker under the provisions of this Article, the intestate estate passes to the [state].

Section 2–106. [Representation.]

If representation is called for by this Code, the estate is divided into as many shares as there are surviving heirs in the nearest degree of kinship and deceased persons in the same degree who left issue who survive the decedent, each surviving heir in the nearest degree receiving one share and the share of each deceased person in the same degree being divided among his issue in the same manner.

Comment

Under the system of intestate succession in effect in some states, property is directed to be divided "per stirpes" among issue or descendants of identified ancestors. Applying a meaning commonly associated with the quoted words, the estate is first divided into the number indicated by the number of children of the ancestor who survive, *or* who leave issue who survive. If, for example, the property is directed to issue "per stirpes" of the intestate's parents, the first division would be by the number of children of parents (other than the intestate) who left issue surviving even though no person of this generation survives. Thus, if the survivors are a child and a grandchild of a deceased brother of the intestate and five children of his deceased sister, the brother's descendants would divide one-half and the five children of the sister would divide the other half. Yet, if the parent of the brother's grandchild also had survived, most statutes would give the seven nephews and nieces equal shares because it is commonly provided that if all surviving kin are in equal degree, they take per capita.

The draft rejects this pattern and keys to a system which assures that the first and principal division of the estate will be with reference to a generation which includes one or more living members.

Section 2–107. [Kindred of Half Blood.]

Relatives of the half blood inherit the same share they would inherit if they were of the whole blood.

Section 2–108. [Afterborn Heirs.]

Relatives of the decedent conceived before his death but born thereafter inherit as if they had been born in the lifetime of the decedent.

Section 2–109. [Meaning of Child and Related Terms.]

If, for purposes of intestate succession, a relationship of parent and child must be established to determine succession by, through, or from a person,

(1)   an adopted person is the child of an adopting parent and not of the natural parents except that adoption of a child by the spouse of a natural parent has no effect on the relationship between the child and either natural parent.

(2)   In cases not covered by Paragraph (1), a person is the child of its parents regardless of the marital status of its parents and the parent and child relationship may be established under the [Uniform Parentage Act].

Alternative subsection (2) for states that have
not adopted the Uniform Parentage Act.

[(2)   In cases not covered by Paragraph (1), a person born out of wedlock is a child of the mother. That person is also a child of the father, if:

(i)   the natural parents participated in a marriage ceremony before or after the birth of the child, even though the attempted marriage is void; or

(ii)   the paternity is established by an adjudication before the death of the father or is established thereafter by clear and convincing proof, but the paternity established under this subparagraph is ineffective to qualify the father or his kindred to inherit from or through the child unless the father has openly treated the child as his, and has not refused to support the child.]

Section 2–110. [Advancements.]

If a person dies intestate as to all his estate, property which he gave in his lifetime to an heir is treated as an advancement against the latter's share of the estate only if declared in a contemporaneous writing by the decedent or acknowledged in writing by the heir to be an advancement. For this purpose the property advanced is valued as of the time the heir came into possession or enjoyment of the property or as of the time of death of the decedent, whichever first occurs. If the recipient of the property fails to survive the decedent, the property is not taken into account in computing the intestate share to be received by the recipient's issue, unless the declaration or acknowledgment provides otherwise.

Comment

This section alters the common law relating to advancements by requiring written evidence of the intent that an inter vivos gift be an advancement. The statute is phrased in terms of the donee being an "heir" because the transaction is regarded as of decedent's death; of course, the donee is only a prospective heir at the time of the transfer during lifetime. Most inter vivos transfers today are intended to be absolute gifts or are carefully integrated into a total estate plan. If the donor intends that any transfer during lifetime be deducted from the donee's share of his estate, the donor may either execute a will so providing or, if he intends to die intestate, charge the gift as an advance by a writing within the present section. The present section applies only when the decedent died intestate and not when he leaves a will.

This section applies to advances to collaterals (such as nephews and nieces) as well as to lineal descendants. The statute does not spell out the method of taking account in the advance, since this process is well settled by the common law and is not a source of litigation.

Section 2–111. [Debts to Decedent.]

A debt owed to the decedent is not charged against the intestate share of any person except the debtor. If the debtor fails to survive the decedent, the debt is not taken into account in computing the intestate share of the debtor's issue.

Section 2–112. [Alienage.]

No person is disqualified to take as an heir because he or a person through whom he claims is or has been an alien.

[Section 2–113. [Dower and Curtesy Abolished.]

The estates of dower and curtesy are abolished.]

Section 2–114. [Persons Related to Decedent Through Two Lines.]

A person who is related to the decedent through 2 lines of relationship is entitled to only a single share based on the relationship which would entitle him to the larger share.

PART 2

ELECTIVE SHARE OF SURVIVING SPOUSE

Section 2–201. [Right to Elective Share.]

(a) If a married person domiciled in this state dies, the surviving spouse has a right of election to take an elective share of one-third of the augmented estate under the limitations and conditions hereinafter stated.

(b) If a married person not domiciled in this state dies, the right, if any, of the surviving spouse to take an elective share in property in this state is governed by the law of the decedent's domicile at death.

Section 2–202. [Augmented Estate.]

The augmented estate means the estate reduced by funeral and administration expenses, homestead allowance, family allowances and exemptions, and enforceable claims, to which is added the sum of the following amounts:

(1) The value of property transferred to anyone other than a bona fide purchaser by the decedent at any time during marriage, to or for the benefit of any person other than the surviving spouse, to the extent that the decedent did not receive adequate and full consideration in money or money's worth for the transfer, if the transfer is of any of the following types:

(i) any transfer under which the decedent retained at the time of his death the possession or enjoyment of, or right to income from, the property;

(ii) any transfer to the extent that the decedent retained at the time of his death a power, either alone or in conjunction with any other person, to revoke or to consume, invade or dispose of the principal for his own benefit;

(iii) any transfer whereby property is held at the time of decedent's death by decedent and another with right of survivorship;

(iv) any transfer made to a donee within two years of death of the decedent to the extent that the aggregate transfers to any one donee in either of the years exceed $3,000.00.

Any transfer is excluded if made with the written consent or joinder of the surviving spouse. Property is valued as of the decedent's death except that property given irrevocably to a donee during lifetime of the decedent is valued as of the date the donee came into possession or enjoyment if that occurs first. Nothing herein shall cause to be included in the augmented estate any life insurance, accident insurance, joint annuity, or pension payable to a person other than the surviving spouse.

(2) The value of property owned by the surviving spouse at the decedent's death, plus the value of property transferred by the spouse at any time during marriage to any person other than the decedent which would have been includible in the spouse's augmented estate if the surviving spouse

had predeceased the decedent to the extent the owned or transferred property is derived from the decedent by any means other than testate or intestate succession without a full consideration in money or money's worth. For purposes of this paragraph:

(i)   Property derived from the decedent includes, but is not limited to, any beneficial interest of the surviving spouse in a trust created by the decedent during his lifetime, any property appointed to the spouse by the decedent's exercise of a general or special power of appointment also exercisable in favor of others than the spouse, any proceeds of insurance (including accidental death benefits) on the life of the decedent attributable to premiums paid by him, any lump sum immediately payable and the commuted value of the proceeds of annuity contracts under which the decedent was the primary annuitant attributable to premiums paid by him, the commuted value of amounts payable after the decedent's death under any public or private pension, disability compensation, death benefit or retirement plan, exclusive of the Federal Social Security system, by reason of service performed or disabilities incurred by the decedent, any property held at the time of decedent's death by decedent and the surviving spouse with right of survivorship, any property held by decedent and transferred by contract to the surviving spouse by reason of the decedent's death and the value of the share of the surviving spouse resulting from rights in community property in this or any other state formerly owned with the decedent. Premiums paid by the decedent's employer, his partner, a partnership of which he was a member, or his creditors, are deemed to have been paid by the decedent.

(ii)   Property owned by the spouse at the decedent's death is valued as of the date of death. Property transferred by the spouse is valued at the time the transfer became irrevocable, or at the decedent's death, whichever occurred first. Income earned by included property prior to the decedent's death is not treated as property derived from the decedent.

(iii) Property owned by the surviving spouse as of the decedent's death, or previously transferred by the surviving spouse, is presumed to have been derived from the decedent except to the extent that the surviving spouse establishes that it was derived from another source.

(3)   For purposes of this section a bona fide purchaser is a purchaser for value in good faith and without notice of any adverse claim. Any recorded instrument on which a state documentary fee is noted pursuant to [insert appropriate reference] is prima facie evidence that the transfer described therein was made to a bona fide purchaser.

Comment

The purpose of the concept of augmenting the probate estate in computing the elective share is twofold: (1) to prevent the owner of wealth from making arrangements which transmit his property to others by means other than probate deliberately to defeat the right of the surviving spouse to a share, and (2) to prevent the surviving spouse from electing a share of the probate estate when the spouse has received a fair share of the total wealth of the decedent either during the lifetime of the decedent or at death by life insurance, joint tenancy assets and other nonprobate arrangements. Thus essentially two separate groups of property are added to the net probate estate to arrive at the augmented net estate which is the basis for computing the one-third share of the surviving spouse. In the first category are transfers by the decedent during his lifetime which are essentially will substitutes, arrangements which give him continued benefits or controls over the property. However, only transfers during the marriage are included in this category. This makes it possible for a person to provide for children by a prior marriage, as by a revocable living trust, without concern that such provisions will be upset by later marriage. The limitation to transfers during marriage reflects some of the policy underlying community property. What kinds of transfers should be included here is a matter of reasonable difference of opinion. The finespun tests of the Federal Estate Tax Law might be utilized, of course. However, the objectives of a tax law are different from those involved here in the Probate Code, and the present section is therefore more limited. It is intended to reach the kinds of transfers readily usable to defeat an elective share in only the probate estate.

In the second category of assets, property of the surviving spouse derived from the decedent and property derived from the decedent which the spouse has, in turn, given away in a transaction that is will-like in effect or purpose, the scope is much broader. Thus a person can during his lifetime make outright gifts to relatives and they are not included in this first category unless they are made within two years of death (the exception being designed to prevent a person from depleting his estate in contemplation of death). But the time when the surviving spouse derives her wealth from the decedent is immaterial; thus if a husband has purchased a home in the wife's name and made systematic gifts to the wife over many years, the home and accumulated wealth she owns at his death as a result of such gifts ought to, and under this section do, reduce her share of the augmented estate. Likewise, for policy reasons life insurance is not included in the first category of transfers to other persons, because it is not ordinarily purchased as a way of depleting the probate estate and avoiding the elective share of the spouse; but life insurance proceeds payable to the surviving spouse are included in the second category, because it seems unfair to allow a surviving spouse to disturb the decedent's estate plan if the spouse has received ample provision from life insurance. In this category no distinction is drawn as to whether the transfers are made before or after marriage.

Depending on the circumstances it is obvious that this section will operate in the long run to decrease substantially the number of elections. This is because the statute will encourage and provide a legal base for counseling of testators against schemes to disinherit the spouse, and because the spouse can no longer elect in cases where substantial provision is made by joint tenancy, life insurance, lifetime gifts, living trusts set up by the decedent, and the other numerous nonprobate arrangements by which wealth is today transferred. On the other hand the section should provide realistic protection against disinheritance of the spouse in the rare case where decedent tries to achieve that purpose by depleting his probate estate.

The augmented net estate approach embodied in this section is relatively complex and assumes that litigation may be required in cases in which the right to an elective share is asserted. The proposed scheme should not complicate administration in well-planned or routine cases, however, because the spouse's rights are freely releasable under Section 2–204 and because of the time limits in Section 2–205. * * *

Section 2–203. [Right of Election Personal to Surviving Spouse.]

The right of election of the surviving spouse may be exercised only during his lifetime by him. In the case of a protected person, the right of election may be exercised only by order of the court in which protective proceedings as to his property are pending, after finding that exercise is necessary to provide adequate support for the protected person during his probable life expectancy.

Section 2–204. [Waiver of Right to Elect and of Other Rights.]

The right of election of a surviving spouse and the rights of the surviving spouse to homestead allowance, exempt property and family allowance, or any of them, may be waived, wholly or partially, before or after marriage, by a written contract, agreement or waiver signed by the party waiving after fair disclosure. Unless it provides to the contrary, a waiver of "all rights" (or equivalent language) in the property or estate of a present or prospective spouse or a complete property settlement entered into after or in anticipation of separation or divorce is a waiver of all rights to elective share, homestead allowance, exempt property and family allowance by each spouse in the property of the other and a renunciation by each of all benefits which would otherwise pass to him from the other by intestate succession or by virtue of the provisions of any will executed before the waiver or property settlement.

Section 2–205. [Proceeding for Elective Share; Time Limit.]

(a) The surviving spouse may elect to take his elective share in the augmented estate by filing in the Court and mailing or delivering to the personal representative, if any, a petition for the elective share within 9 months after the date of death, or within 6 months after the probate of the decedent's will, whichever limitation last expires. However, non-probate transfers, described in Section 2–202(1), shall not be included within the augmented estate for the purpose of computing the elective share, if the petition is filed later than 9 months after death.

The Court may extend the time for election as it sees fit for cause shown by the surviving spouse before the time for election has expired.

(b)   The surviving spouse shall give notice of the time and place set for hearing to persons interested in the estate and to the distributees and recipients of portions of the augmented net estate whose interests will be adversely affected by the taking of the elective share.

(c)   The surviving spouse may withdraw his demand for an elective share at any time before entry of a final determination by the Court.

(d)   After notice and hearing, the Court shall determine the amount of the elective share and shall order its payment from the assets of the augmented net estate or by contribution as appears appropriate under Section 2–207. If it appears that a fund or property included in the augmented net estate has not come into the possession of the personal representative, or has been distributed by the personal representative, the Court nevertheless shall fix the liability of any person who has any interest in the fund or property or who has possession thereof, whether as trustee or otherwise. The proceeding may be maintained against fewer than all persons against whom relief could be sought, but no person is subject to contribution in any greater amount than he would have been if relief had been secured against all persons subject to contribution.

(e)   The order or judgment of the Court may be enforced as necessary in suit for contribution or payment in other courts of this state or other jurisdictions.

Section 2–206. [Effect of Election on Benefits by Will or Statute.]

A surviving spouse is entitled to homestead allowance, exempt property, and family allowance, whether or not he elects to take an elective share.

Section 2–207. [Charging Spouse With Gifts Received; Liability of Others for Balance of Elective Share.]

(a)   In the proceeding for an elective share, values included in the augmented estate which pass or have passed to the surviving spouse, or which would have passed to the spouse but were renounced, are applied first to satisfy the elective share and to reduce any contributions due from other recipients of transfers included in the augmented estate. For purposes of this subsection, the electing spouse's beneficial interest in any life estate or in any trust shall be computed as if worth one half of the total value of the property subject to the life estate, or of the trust estate, unless higher or lower values for these interests are established by proof.

(b)   Remaining property of the augmented estate is so applied that liability for the balance of the elective share of the surviving spouse is equitably apportioned among the recipients of the augmented estate in proportion to the value of their interests therein.

(c)   Only original transferees from, or appointees of, the decedent and their donees, to the extent the donees have the property or its proceeds, are subject to the contribution to make up the elective share of the surviving spouse. A person liable to contribution may choose to give up the property transferred to him or to pay its value as of the time it is considered in computing the augmented estate.

PART 3

SPOUSE AND CHILDREN UNPROVIDED FOR IN WILLS

Section 2–301. [Omitted Spouse.]

(a)   If a testator fails to provide by will for his surviving spouse who married the testator after the execution of the will, the omitted spouse shall receive the same share of the estate he would have received if the decedent left no will unless it appears from the will that the omission was intentional or the testator provided for the spouse by transfer outside the will and the intent that the transfer be in lieu of a testamentary provision is shown by statements of the testator or from the amount of the transfer or other evidence.

(b)　In satisfying a share provided by this section, the devises made by the will abate as provided in Section 3–902.

Section 2–302. [Pretermitted Children.]

(a)　If a testator fails to provide in his will for any of his children born or adopted after the execution of his will, the omitted child receives a share in the estate equal in value to that which he would have received if the testator had died intestate unless:

(1)　it appears from the will that the omission was intentional;

(2)　when the will was executed the testator had one or more children and devised substantially all his estate to the other parent of the omitted child; or

(3)　the testator provided for the child by transfer outside the will and the intent that the transfer be in lieu of a testamentary provision is shown by statements of the testator or from the amount of the transfer or other evidence.

(b)　If at the time of execution of the will the testator fails to provide in his will for a living child solely because he believes the child to be dead, the child receives a share in the estate equal in value to that which he would have received if the testator had died intestate.

(c)　In satisfying a share provided by this section, the devises made by the will abate as provided in Section 3–902.

PART 4

EXEMPT PROPERTY AND ALLOWANCES

Section 2–401. [Homestead Allowance.]

A surviving spouse of a decedent who was domiciled in this state is entitled to a homestead allowance of [$5,000]. If there is no surviving spouse, each minor child and each dependent child of the decedent is entitled to a homestead allowance amounting to [$5,000] divided by the number of minor and dependent children of the decedent. The homestead allowance is exempt from and has priority over all claims against the estate. Homestead allowance is in addition to any share passing to the surviving spouse or minor or dependent child by the will of the decedent unless otherwise provided, by intestate succession or by way of elective share.

[Section 2–401A. [Constitutional Homestead.]

The value of any constitutional right of homestead in the family home received by a surviving spouse or child shall be charged against that spouse or child's homestead allowance to the extent that the family home is part of the decedent's estate or would have been but for the homestead provision of the constitution.]

Section 2–402. [Exempt Property.]

In addition to the homestead allowance, the surviving spouse of a decedent who was domiciled in this state is entitled from the estate to value not exceeding $3,500 in excess of any security interests therein in household furniture, automobiles, furnishings, appliances and personal effects. If there is no surviving spouse, children of the decedent are entitled jointly to the same value. If encumbered chattels are selected and if the value in excess of security interests, plus that of other exempt property, is less than $3,500, or if there is not $3,500 worth of exempt property in the estate, the spouse or children are entitled to other assets of the estate, if any, to the extent necessary to make up the $3,500 value. Rights to exempt property and assets needed to make up a deficiency of exempt property have priority over all claims against the estate, except that the right to any assets to make up a deficiency of exempt property shall abate as necessary to permit prior payment of homestead allowance and family allowance. These rights are in addition to any benefit or share passing to the surviving spouse or children by the will of the decedent unless otherwise provided, by intestate succession, or by way of elective share.

Section 2-403. [Family Allowance.]

In addition to the right to homestead allowance and exempt property, if the decedent was domiciled in this state, the surviving spouse and minor children whom the decedent was obligated to support and children who were in fact being supported by him are entitled to a reasonable allowance in money out of the estate for their maintenance during the period of administration, which allowance may not continue for longer than one year if the estate is inadequate to discharge allowed claims. The allowance may be paid as a lump sum or in periodic installments. It is payable to the surviving spouse, if living, for the use of the surviving spouse and minor and dependent children; otherwise to the children, or persons having their care and custody; but in case any minor child or dependent child is not living with the surviving spouse, the allowance may be made partially to the child or his guardian or other person having his care and custody, and partially to the spouse, as their needs may appear. The family allowance is exempt from and has priority over all claims but not over the homestead allowance.

The family allowance is not chargeable against any benefit or share passing to the surviving spouse or children by the will of the decedent unless otherwise provided, by intestate succession, or by way of elective share. The death of any person entitled to family allowance terminates his right to allowances not yet paid.

Section 2-404. [Source, Determination and Documentation.]

If the estate is otherwise sufficient, property specifically devised is not used to satisfy rights to homestead and exempt property. Subject to this restriction, the surviving spouse, the guardians of the minor children, or children who are adults may select property of the estate as homestead allowance and exempt property. The personal representative may make these selections if the surviving spouse, the children or the guardians of the minor children are unable or fail to do so within a reasonable time or if there are no guardians of the minor children. The personal representative may execute an instrument or deed of distribution to establish the ownership of property taken as homestead allowance or exempt property. He may determine the family allowance in a lump sum not exceeding $6,000 or periodic installments not exceeding $500 per month for one year, and may disburse funds of the estate in payment of the family allowance and any part of the homestead allowance payable in cash. The personal representative or any interested person aggrieved by any selection, determination, payment, proposed payment, or failure to act under this section may petition the Court for appropriate relief, which relief may provide a family allowance larger or smaller than that which the personal representative determined or could have determined.

PART 5

WILLS

Section 2-501. [Who May Make a Will.]

Any person 18 or more years of age who is of sound mind may make a will.

Section 2-502. [Execution.]

Except as provided for holographic wills, writings within Section 2-513, and wills within Section 2-506, every will shall be in writing signed by the testator or in the testator's name by some other person in the testator's presence and by his direction, and shall be signed by at least 2 persons each of whom witnessed either the signing or the testator's acknowledgment of the signature or of the will.

Comment

The formalities for execution of a witnessed will have been reduced to a minimum. Execution under this section normally would be accomplished by signature of the testator and of two witnesses; each of the persons signing as witnesses must "witness" any of the following: the signing of the will by the testator, an acknowledgment by the testator that the signature is his, or an acknowledgment by the testator that the document is his will. Signing by the testator may be by mark under general rules relating to what constitutes a signature; or the will may be signed on behalf of the testator by another person signing the testator's name at his direction and in his presence. There is no requirement that the testator publish the document as his will, or that he request the witnesses to sign, or that the witnesses sign in the presence of the testator or of each other. The testator may sign the will outside the presence of the witnesses if he later acknowledges to the witnesses that the signature is his or that the document is his will, and they sign as witnesses. There is no requirement that the testator's signature be at the end of the will; thus, if he writes his name in the body of the will and intends it to be his signature, this would satisfy the statute. The intent is to validate wills which meet the minimal formalities of the statute.

A will which does not meet these requirements may be valid under Section 2–503 as a holograph.

Section 2–503. [Holographic Will.]

A will which does not comply with Section 2–502 is valid as a holographic will, whether or not witnessed, if the signature and the material provisions are in the handwriting of the testator.

Comment

This section enables a testator to write his own will in his handwriting. There need be no witnesses. The only requirement is that the signature and the material provisions of the will be in the testator's handwriting. By requiring only the "material provisions" to be in the testator's handwriting (rather than requiring, as some existing statutes do, that the will be "entirely" in the testator's handwriting) a holograph may be valid even though immaterial parts such as date or introductory wording be printed or stamped. A valid holograph might even be executed on some printed will forms if the printed portion could be eliminated and the handwritten portion could evidence the testator's will. For persons unable to obtain legal assistance, the holographic will may be adequate.

Section 2–504. [Self-proved Will.]

(a) Any will may be simultaneously executed, attested, and made self-proved, by acknowledgment thereof by the testator and affidavits of the witnesses, each made before an officer authorized to administer oaths under the laws of the state where execution occurs and evidenced by the officer's certificate, under official seal, in substantially the following form:

I, _____, the testator, sign my name to this instrument this _____ day of _____, 19__, and being first duly sworn, do hereby declare to the undersigned authority that I sign and execute this instrument as my last will and that I sign it willingly (or willingly direct another to sign for me), that I execute it as my free and voluntary act for the purposes therein expressed, and that I am eighteen years of age or older, of sound mind, and under no constraint or undue influence.

_____
                                                                                    Testator

We, _____, _____, the witnesses, sign our names to this instrument, being first duly sworn, and do hereby declare to the undersigned authority that the testator signs and executes this instrument as his last will and that he signs it willingly (or willingly directs another to sign for him), and that each of us, in the presence and hearing of the testator, hereby signs this will as witness to the testator's signing, and that to the best of our knowledge the testator is eighteen years of age or older, of sound mind, and under no constraint or undue influence.

_____
Witness

_____
Witness

The State of _____
County of _____

    Subscribed, sworn to and acknowledged before me by _____, the testator, and subscribed and sworn to before me by _____, and _____, witnesses, this _____ day of _____.

    (Seal)

                    (Signed) _____

                    (Official capacity of officer)

    (b)   An attested will may at any time subsequent to its execution be made self-proved by the acknowledgment thereof by the testator and the affidavits of the witnesses, each made before an officer authorized to administer oaths under the laws of the state where the acknowledgment occurs and evidenced by the officer's certificate, under the official seal, attached or annexed to the will in substantially the following form:

The State of _____
County of _____

    We, _____, _____, and _____, the testator and the witnesses, respectively, whose names are signed to the attached or foregoing instrument, being first duly sworn, do hereby declare to the undersigned authority that the testator signed and executed the instrument as his last will and that he had signed willingly (or willingly directed another to sign for him), and that he executed it as his free and voluntary act for the purposes therein expressed, and that each of the witnesses, in the presence and hearing of the testator, signed the will as witness and that to the best of his knowledge the testator was at that time eighteen years of age or older, of sound mind and under no constraint or undue influence

_____
Testator

_____
Witness

_____
Witness

    Subscribed, sworn to and acknowledged before me by _____, the testator, and subscribed and sworn to before me by _____, and _____, witnesses, this _____ day of _____.

    (Seal)

                    (Signed) _____
                    (Official capacity of officer)

Comment

    A self-proved will may be admitted to probate as provided in Sections 3–303, 3–405 and 3–406 without the testimony of any subscribing witness, but otherwise it is treated no differently than a will not self-proved. Thus, a self-proved will may be contested (except in regard to signature requirements), revoked, or amended by a codicil in exactly the same fashion as a will not self-proved. * * *

Section 2–505. [Who May Witness.]

    (a)   Any person generally competent to be a witness may act as a witness to a will.

(b) A will or any provision thereof is not invalid because the will is signed by an interested witness.

Comment

This section simplifies the law relating to interested witnesses. Interest no longer disqualifies a person as a witness, nor does it invalidate or forfeit a gift under the will. Of course, the purpose of this change is not to foster use of interested witnesses, and attorneys will continue to use disinterested witnesses in execution of wills. But the rare and innocent use of a member of the testator's family on a home-drawn will would no longer be penalized. This change does not increase appreciably the opportunity for fraud or undue influence. A substantial gift by will to a person who is one of the witnesses to the execution of the will would itself be a suspicious circumstance, and the gift could be challenged on grounds of undue influence. The requirement of disinterested witnesses has not succeeded in preventing fraud and undue influence; and in most cases of undue influence, the influencer is careful not to sign as witness but to use disinterested witnesses. * * *

Section 2–506. [Choice of Law as to Execution.]

A written will is valid if executed in compliance with Section 2–502 or 2–503 or if its execution complies with the law at the time of execution of the place where the will is executed, or of the law of the place where at the time of execution or at the time of death the testator is domiciled, has a place of abode or is a national.

Section 2–507. [Revocation by Writing or by Act.]

A will or any part thereof is revoked

(1)   by a subsequent will which revokes the prior will or part expressly or by inconsistency; or

(2)   by being burned, torn, canceled, obliterated, or destroyed, with the intent and for the purpose of revoking it by the testator or by another person in his presence and by his direction.

Comment

Revocation of a will may be by either a subsequent will or an act done to the document. If revocation is by a subsequent will, it must be properly executed. This section employs the traditional language which has been interpreted by the courts in many cases. It leaves to the Court the determination of whether a subsequent will which has no express revocation clause is inconsistent with the prior will so as to revoke it wholly or partially, and in the case of an act done to the document the determination of whether the act is a sufficient burning, tearing, canceling, obliteration or destruction and was done with the intent and for the purpose of revoking. The latter necessarily involves exploration of extrinsic evidence, including statements of testator as to intent.

The section specifically permits partial revocation. Each Court is free to apply its own doctrine of dependent relative revocation. * * *

Section 2–508. [Revocation by Divorce; No Revocation by Other Changes of Circumstances.]

If after executing a will the testator is divorced or his marriage annulled, the divorce or annulment revokes any disposition or appointment of property made by the will to the former spouse, any provision conferring a general or special power of appointment on the former spouse, and any nomination of the former spouse as executor, trustee, conservator, or guardian, unless the will expressly provides otherwise. Property prevented from passing to a former spouse because of revocation by divorce or annulment passes as if the former spouse failed to survive the decedent, and other provisions conferring some power or office on the former spouse are interpreted as if the spouse failed to survive the decedent. If provisions are revoked solely by this section, they are revived by testator's remarriage to the former spouse. For purposes of this section, divorce or annulment means any divorce or annulment which would exclude the spouse as a surviving spouse within the meaning of Section 2–802(b). A decree of separation which does not terminate the status of husband and wife is not a divorce for purposes of this section. No change of circumstances other than as described in this section revokes a will.

Section 2-509. [Revival of Revoked Will.]

(a)   If a second will which, had it remained effective at death, would have revoked the first will in whole or in part, is thereafter revoked by acts under Section 2-507, the first will is revoked in whole or in part unless it is evident from the circumstances of the revocation of the second will or from testator's contemporary or subsequent declarations that he intended the first will to take effect as executed.

(b)   If a second will which, had it remained effective at death, would have revoked the first will in whole or in part, is thereafter revoked by a third will, the first will is revoked in whole or in part, except to the extent it appears from the terms of the third will that the testator intended the first will to take effect.

Comment

This section adopts a limited revival doctrine. If testator executes will no. 1 and later executes will no. 2, revoking will no. 1 and still later revokes will no. 2 by act such as destruction, there is a question as to whether testator intended to die intestate or have will no. 1 revived as his last will. Under this section will no. 1 can be probated as testator's last will if his intent to that effect can be established. For this purpose testimony as to his statements at the time he revokes will no. 2 or at a later date can be admitted. If will no. 2 is revoked by a third will, will no. 1 would remain revoked except to the extent that will no. 3 showed an intent to have will no. 1 effective.

Section 2-510. [Incorporation by Reference.]

Any writing in existence when a will is executed may be incorporated by reference if the language of the will manifests this intent and describes the writing sufficiently to permit its identification.

Section 2-511. [Testamentary Additions to Trusts.]

A devise or bequest, the validity of which is determinable by the law of this state, may be made by a will to the trustee of a trust established or to be established by the testator or by the testator and some other person or by some other person (including a funded or unfunded life insurance trust, although the trustor has reserved any or all rights of ownership of the insurance contracts) if the trust is identified in the testator's will and its terms are set forth in a written instrument (other than a will) executed before or concurrently with the execution of the testator's will or in the valid last will of a person who has predeceased the testator (regardless of the existence, size, or character of the corpus of the trust). The devise is not invalid because the trust is amendable or revocable, or because the trust was amended after the execution of the will or after the death of the testator. Unless the testator's will provides otherwise, the property so devised (1) is not deemed to be held under a testamentary trust of the testator but becomes a part of the trust to which it is given and (2) shall be administered and disposed of in accordance with the provisions of the instrument or will setting forth the terms of the trust, including any amendments thereto made before the death of the testator (regardless of whether made before or after the execution of the testator's will), and, if the testator's will so provides, including any amendments to the trust made after the death of the testator. A revocation or termination of the trust before the death of the testator causes the devise to lapse.

Section 2-512. [Events of Independent Significance.]

A will may dispose of property by reference to acts and events which have significance apart from their effect upon the dispositions made by the will, whether they occur before or after the execution of the will or before or after the testator's death. The execution or revocation of a will of another person is such an event.

Section 2-513. [Separate Writing Identifying Bequest of Tangible Property.]

Whether or not the provisions relating to holographic wills apply, a will may refer to a written statement or list to dispose of items of tangible personal property not otherwise specifically disposed of by the will, other than money, evidences of indebtedness, documents of title, and securities, and property used in trade or business. To be admissible under this section as evidence of the intended disposition, the writing must either be in the handwriting of the testator or be signed by him and must describe the items and the devisees with reasonable certainty. The writing may be referred to as one to be in existence at the time of the testator's death; it may be prepared before or after the execution of the will; it may be altered by the testator after its preparation; and it may be a writing which has no significance apart from its effect upon the dispositions made by the will.

Comment

As part of the broader policy of effectuating a testator's intent and of relaxing formalities of execution, this section permits a testator to refer in his will to a separate document disposing of certain tangible personalty. The separate document may be prepared after execution of the will, so would not come within Section 2–510 on incorporation by reference. It may even be altered from time to time. It need only be either in the testator's handwriting or signed by him. The typical case would be a list of personal effects and the persons whom the testator desired to take specified items.

PART 6

RULES OF CONSTRUCTION

Section 2–601. [Requirement That Devisee Survive Testator by 120 Hours.]

A devisee who does not survive the testator by 120 hours is treated as if he predeceased the testator, unless the will of decedent contains some language dealing explicitly with simultaneous deaths or deaths in a common disaster, or requiring that the devisee survive the testator or survive the testator for a stated period in order to take under the will.

Section 2–602. [Choice of Law as to Meaning and Effect of Wills.]

The meaning and legal effect of a disposition in a will shall be determined by the local law of a particular state selected by the testator in his instrument unless the application of that law is contrary to the provisions relating to the elective share described in Part 2 of this Article, the provisions relating to exempt property and allowances described in Part 4 of this Article, or any other public policy of this State otherwise applicable to the disposition.

Section 2–603. [Rules of Construction and Intention.]

The intention of a testator as expressed in his will controls the legal effect of his dispositions. The rules of construction expressed in the succeeding sections of this Part apply unless a contrary intention is indicated by the will.

Section 2–604. [Construction That Will Passes All Property; After-Acquired Property.]

A will is construed to pass all property which the testator owns at his death including property acquired after the execution of the will.

Section 2–605. [Anti-lapse; Deceased Devisee; Class Gifts.]

If a devisee who is a grandparent or a lineal descendant of a grandparent of the testator is dead at the time of execution of the will, fails to survive the testator, or is treated as if he predeceased the testator, the issue of the deceased devisee who survive the testator by 120 hours take in place of the deceased devisee and if they are all of the same degree of kinship to the devisee they take equally, but if of unequal degree then those of more remote degree take by representation. One who would have been a devisee under a class gift if he had survived the testator is treated as a devisee for purposes of this section whether his death occurred before or after the execution of the will.

Section 2–606. [Failure of Testamentary Provision.]

(a)   Except as provided in Section 2–605 if a devise other than a residuary devise fails for any reason, it becomes a part of the residue.

(b)   Except as provided in Section 2–605 if the residue is devised to two or more persons and the share of one of the residuary devisees fails for any reason, his share passes to the other residuary devisee, or to other residuary devisees in proportion to their interests in the residue.

Section 2–607. [Change in Securities; Accessions; Nonademption.]

(a)   If the testator intended a specific devise of certain securities rather than the equivalent value thereof, the specific devisee is entitled only to:

(1)   as much of the devised securities as is a part of the estate at time of the testator's death;

(2)   any additional or other securities of the same entity owned by the testator by reason of action initiated by the entity excluding any acquired by exercise of purchase options;

(3)   securities of another entity owned by the testator as a result of a merger, consolidation, reorganization or other similar action initiated by the entity; and

(4)   any additional securities of the entity owned by the testator as a result of a plan of reinvestment.

(b)   Distributions prior to death with respect to a specifically devised security not provided for in subsection (a) are not part of the specific devise.

Section 2–608. [Nonademption of Specific Devises in Certain Cases; Unpaid Proceeds of Sale, Condemnation or Insurance; Sale by Conservator.]

(a)   A specific devisee has the right to the remaining specifically devised property and:

(1)   any balance of the purchase price (together with any security interest) owing from a purchaser to the testator at death by reason of sale of the property;

(2)   any amount of a condemnation award for the taking of the property unpaid at death;

(3)   any proceeds unpaid at death on fire or casualty insurance on the property; and

(4)   property owned by testator at his death as a result of foreclosure, or obtained in lieu of foreclosure, of the security for a specifically devised obligation.

(b)   If specifically devised property is sold by a conservator or an agent acting within the authority of a durable power of attorney for a principal who is under a disability, or if a condemnation award or insurance proceeds are paid to a conservator or an agent acting within the authority of a durable power of attorney for a principal who is under a disability as a result of condemnation, fire, or casualty, the specific devisee has the right to a general pecuniary devise equal to the net sale price, the condemnation award, or the insurance proceeds. This subsection does not apply if after the sale, condemnation or casualty, it is adjudicated that the disability of the testator has ceased and the testator survives the adjudication by one year. The right of the specific devisee under this subsection is reduced by any right he has under subsection (a).

Section 2–609. [Non-Exoneration.]

A specific devise passes subject to any mortgage interest existing at the date of death, without right of exoneration, regardless of a general directive in the will to pay debts.

Section 2–610. [Exercise of Power of Appointment.]

A general residuary clause in a will, or a will making general disposition of all of the testator's property, does not exercise a power of appointment held by the testator unless specific reference is made to the power or there is some other indication of intention to include the property subject to the power.

Section 2–611. [Construction of Generic Terms to Accord With Relationships as Defined for Intestate Succession.]

Halfbloods, adopted persons, and persons born out of wedlock are included in class gift terminology and terms of relationship in accordance with rules for determining relationships for purposes of intestate succession. [However, a person born out of wedlock is not treated as the child of the father unless the person is openly and notoriously so treated by the father.]

Section 2–612. [Ademption by Satisfaction.]

Property which a testator gave in his lifetime to a person is treated as a satisfaction of a devise to that person in whole or in part, only if the will provides for deduction of the lifetime gift, or the testator declares in a contemporaneous writing that the gift is to be deducted from the devise or is in satisfaction of the devise, or the devisee acknowledges in writing that the gift is in satisfaction. For purpose of partial satisfaction, property given during lifetime is valued as of the time the devisee came into possession or enjoyment of the property or as of the time of death of the testator, whichever occurs first.

Comment

This section parallels Section 2–110 on advancements and follows the same policy of requiring written evidence that lifetime gifts are to be taken into account in distribution of an estate, whether testate or intestate. * * * Some wills expressly provide for lifetime advances by a hotchpot clause. Where the will is silent, the above section would require either the testator to declare in writing that the gift is an advance or satisfaction or the devisee to acknowledge the same in writing. * * * If a devisee to whom an advancement is made predeceases the testator and his issue take under 2–605, they take the same devise as their ancestor; if the devise is reduced by reason of this section as to the ancestor, it is automatically reduced as to his issue. In this respect the rule in testacy differs from that in intestacy; see Section 2–110.

PART 7

CONTRACTUAL ARRANGEMENTS RELATING TO DEATH

Section 2–701. [Contracts Concerning Succession.]

A contract to make a will or devise, or not to revoke a will or devise, or to die intestate, if executed after the effective date of this Act, can be established only by (1) provisions of a will stating material provisions of the contract; (2) an express reference in a will to a contract and extrinsic evidence proving the terms of the contract; or (3) a writing signed by the decedent evidencing the contract. The execution of a joint will or mutual wills does not create a presumption of a contract not to revoke the will or wills.

PART 8

GENERAL PROVISIONS

Section 2–801. [Renunciation of Succession.]

(a) A person or the representative of an incapacitated or protected person, who is an heir, devisee, person succeeding to a renounced interest, beneficiary under a testamentary instrument, or appointee under a power of appointment exercised by a testamentary instrument, may renounce in whole or in part the right of succession to any property or interest therein, including a future interest, by filing a written renunciation under this Section. The right to renounce does not survive the death of the person having it. The instrument shall (1) describe the property or interest renounced, (2) declare the renunciation and extent thereof, and (3) be signed by the person renouncing.

(b)(1) An instrument renouncing a present interest shall be filed not later than [9] months after the death of the decedent or the donee of the power.

(2)   An instrument renouncing a future interest may be filed not later than [9] months after the event determining that the taker of the property or interest is finally ascertained and his interest is indefeasibly vested.

(3)   The renunciation shall be filed in the [probate] court of the county in which proceedings have been commenced for the administration of the estate of the deceased owner or deceased donee of the power or, if they have not been commenced, in which they could be commenced. A copy of the renunciation shall be delivered in person or mailed by registered or certified mail to any personal representative, or other fiduciary of the decedent or donee of the power. If real property or an interest therein is renounced, a copy of the renunciation may be recorded in the office of the [Recorder of Deeds] of the county in which the real estate is situated.*

(c)   Unless the decedent or donee of the power has otherwise provided, the property or interest renounced devolves as though the person renouncing had predeceased the decedent or, if the person renouncing is designated to take under a power of appointment exercised by a testamentary instrument, as though the person renouncing had predeceased the donee of the power. A future interest that takes effect in possession or enjoyment after the termination of the estate or interest renounced takes effect as though the person renouncing had predeceased the decedent or the donee of the power. A renunciation relates back for all purposes to the date of the death of the decedent or the donee of the power.

(d)(1) The right to renounce property or an interest therein is barred by (i) an assignment, conveyance, encumbrance, pledge, or transfer of the property or interest, or a contract therefor, (ii) a written waiver of the right to renounce, (iii) an acceptance of the property or interest or benefit thereunder, or (iv) a sale of the property or interest under judicial sale made before the renunciation is effected.

(2)   The right to renounce exists notwithstanding any limitation on the interest of the person renouncing in the nature of a spendthrift provision or similar restriction.

(3)   A renunciation or a written waiver of the right to renounce is binding upon the person renouncing or person waiving and all persons claiming through or under him.

(e)   This Section does not abridge the right of a person to waive, release, disclaim, or renounce property or an interest therein under any other statute.

(f)   An interest in property existing on the effective date of this Section as to which the time for filing a renunciation under this Section would have begun to run were this Section in effect when the interest was created, may be renounced within [9] months after the effective date of this Section.

Section 2–802. [Effect of Divorce, Annulment, and Decree of Separation.]

(a)   A person who is divorced from the decedent or whose marriage to the decedent has been annulled is not a surviving spouse unless, by virtue of a subsequent marriage, he is married to the decedent at the time of death. A decree of separation which does not terminate the status of husband and wife is not a divorce for purposes of this section.

(b)   For purposes of Parts 1, 2, 3 & 4 of this Article, and of Section 3–203, a surviving spouse does not include:

(1)   a person who obtains or consents to a final decree or judgment of divorce from the decedent or an annulment of their marriage, which decree or judgment is not recognized as valid in this state, unless they subsequently participate in a marriage ceremony purporting to marry each to the other, or subsequently live together as man and wife;

---

*   If Torrens system is in effect, add provisions to comply with local law.

(2)   a person who, following a decree or judgment of divorce or annulment obtained by the decedent, participates in a marriage ceremony with a third person; or

(3)   a person who was a party to a valid proceeding concluded by an order purporting to terminate all marital property rights.

[Section 2–803. [Effect of Homicide on Intestate Succession, Wills, Joint Assets, Life Insurance and Beneficiary Designations.]

(a)   A surviving spouse, heir or devisee who feloniously and intentionally kills the decedent is not entitled to any benefits under the will or under this Article, and the estate of decedent passes as if the killer had predeceased the decedent. Property appointed by the will of the decedent to or for the benefit of the killer passes as if the killer had predeceased the decedent.

(b)   Any joint tenant who feloniously and intentionally kills another joint tenant thereby effects a severance of the interest of the decedent so that the share of the decedent passes as his property and the killer has no rights by survivorship. This provision applies to joint tenancies [and tenancies by the entirety] in real and personal property, joint and multiple-party accounts in banks, savings and loan associations, credit unions and other institutions, and any other form of co-ownership with survivorship incidents.

(c)   A named beneficiary of a bond, life insurance policy, or other contractual arrangement who feloniously and intentionally kills the principal obligee or the person upon whose life the policy is issued is not entitled to any benefit under the bond, policy or other contractual arrangement, and it becomes payable as though the killer had predeceased the decedent.

(d)   Any other acquisition of property or interest by the killer shall be treated in accordance with the principles of this section.

(e)   A final judgment of conviction of felonious and intentional killing is conclusive for purposes of this section. In the absence of a conviction of felonious and intentional killing the Court may determine by a preponderance of evidence whether the killing was felonious and intentional for purposes of this section.

(f)   This section does not affect the rights of any person who, before rights under this section have been adjudicated, purchases from the killer for value and without notice property which the killer would have acquired except for this section, but the killer is liable for the amount of the proceeds or the value of the property. Any insurance company, bank, or other obligor making payment according to the terms of its policy or obligation is not liable by reason of this section unless prior to payment it has received at its home office or principal address written notice of a claim under this section.]

PART 9

CUSTODY AND DEPOSIT OF WILLS

Section 2–901. [Deposit of Will With Court in Testator's Lifetime.]

A will may be deposited by the testator or his agent with any Court for safekeeping, under rules of the Court. The will shall be kept confidential. During the testator's lifetime a deposited will shall be delivered only to him or to a person authorized in writing signed by him to receive the will. A conservator may be allowed to examine a deposited will of a protected testator under procedures designed to maintain the confidential character of the document to the extent possible, and to assure that it will be resealed and left on deposit after the examination. Upon being informed of the testator's death, the Court shall notify any person designated to receive the will and deliver it to him on request; or the Court may deliver the will to the appropriate Court.

Section 2–902. [Duty of Custodian of Will; Liability.]

After the death of a testator and on request of an interested person, any person having custody of a will of the testator shall deliver it with reasonable promptness to a person able to secure its probate and if none is known, to an appropriate Court. Any person who wilfully fails to deliver a will is liable to any person aggrieved for the damages which may be sustained by the failure. Any person who wilfully refuses or fails to deliver a will after being ordered by the Court in a proceeding brought for the purpose of compelling delivery is subject to penalty for contempt of Court.

PART 10

UNIFORM INTERNATIONAL WILLS ACT [INTERNATIONAL WILL; INFORMATION REGISTRATION]

[omitted]

APPENDIX
PRE-1989 ARTICLE VI
NON-PROBATE TRANSFERS

PART 1
MULTIPLE-PARTY ACCOUNTS

PART 1

MULTIPLE-PARTY ACCOUNTS

Section 6–101. [Definitions.]

In this part, unless the context otherwise requires:

(1) "account" means a contract of deposit of funds between a depositor and a financial institution, and includes a checking account, savings account, certificate of deposit, share account and other like arrangement;

(2) "beneficiary" means a person named in a trust account as one for whom a party to the account is named as trustee;

(3) "financial institution" means any organization authorized to do business under state or federal laws relating to financial institutions, including, without limitation, banks and trust companies, savings banks, building and loan associations, savings and loan companies or associations, and credit unions;

(4) "joint account" means an account payable on request to one or more of two or more parties whether or not mention is made of any right of survivorship;

(5) a "multiple-party account" is any of the following types of account: (i) a joint account, (ii) a P.O.D. account, or (iii) a trust account. It does not include accounts established for deposit of funds of a partnership, joint venture, or other association for business purposes, or accounts controlled by one

or more persons as the duly authorized agent or trustee for a corporation, unincorporated association, charitable or civic organization or a regular fiduciary or trust account where the relationship is established other than by deposit agreement;

(6) "net contribution" of a party to a joint account as of any given time is the sum of all deposits thereto made by or for him, less all withdrawals made by or for him which have not been paid to or applied to the use of any other party, plus a pro rata share of any interest or dividends included in the current balance. The term includes, in addition, any proceeds of deposit life insurance added to the account by reason of the death of the party whose net contribution is in question;

(7) "party" means a person who, by the terms of the account, has a present right, subject to request, to payment from a multiple-party account. A P.O.D. payee or beneficiary of a trust account is a party only after the account becomes payable to him by reason of his surviving the original payee or trustee. Unless the context otherwise requires, it includes a guardian, conservator, personal representative, or assignee, including an attaching creditor, of a party. It also includes a person identified as a trustee of an account for another whether or not a beneficiary is named, but it does not include any named beneficiary unless he has a present right of withdrawal;

(8) "payment" of sums on deposit includes withdrawal, payment on check or other directive of a party, and any pledge of sums on deposit by a party and any set-off, or reduction or other disposition of all or part of an account pursuant to a pledge;

(9) "proof of death" includes a death certificate or record or report which is prima facie proof of death under Section 1–107;

(10) "P.O.D. account" means an account payable on request to one person during his lifetime and on his death to one or more P.O.D. payees, or to one or more persons during their lifetimes and on the death of all of them to one or more P.O.D. payees;

(11) "P.O.D. payee" means a person designated on a P.O.D. account as one to whom the account is payable on request after the death of one or more persons;

(12) "request" means a proper request for withdrawal, or a check or order for payment, which complies with all conditions of the account, including special requirements concerning necessary signatures and regulations of the financial institution; but if the financial institution conditions withdrawal or payment on advance notice, for purposes of this part the request for withdrawal or payment is treated as immediately effective and a notice of intent to withdraw is treated as a request for withdrawal;

(13) "sums on deposit" means the balance payable on a multiple-party account including interest, dividends, and in addition any deposit life insurance proceeds added to the account by reason of the death of a party;

(14) "trust account" means an account in the name of one or more parties as trustee for one or more beneficiaries where the relationship is established by the form of the account and the deposit agreement with the financial institution and there is no subject of the trust other than the sums on deposit in the account; it is not essential that payment to the beneficiary be mentioned in the deposit agreement. A trust account does not include a regular trust account under a testamentary trust or a trust agreement which has significance apart from the account, or a fiduciary account arising from a fiduciary relation such as attorney-client;

(15) "withdrawal" includes payment to a third person pursuant to check or other directive of a party.

Section 6–102. [Ownership As Between Parties, and Others; Protection of Financial Institutions.]

The provisions of Sections 6–103 to 6–105 concerning beneficial ownership as between parties, or as between parties and P.O.D. payees or beneficiaries of multiple-party accounts, are relevant only to controversies between these persons and their creditors and other successors, and have no bearing on the power of withdrawal of these persons as determined by the terms of account contracts. The provisions of Sections 6–108 to 6–113 govern the liability of financial institutions who make payments pursuant thereto, and their set-off rights.

Section 6–103. [Ownership During Lifetime.]

(a)   A joint account belongs, during the lifetime of all parties, to the parties in proportion to the net contributions by each to the sums on deposit, unless there is clear and convincing evidence of a different intent.

(b)   A P.O.D. account belongs to the original payee during his lifetime and not to the P.O.D. payee or payees; if two or more parties are named as original payees, during their lifetimes rights as between them are governed by subsection (a) of this section.

(c)   Unless a contrary intent is manifested by the terms of the account or the deposit agreement or there is other clear and convincing evidence of an irrevocable trust, a trust account belongs beneficially to the trustee during his lifetime, and if two or more parties are named as trustee on the account, during their lifetimes beneficial rights as between them are governed by subsection (a) of this section. If there is an irrevocable trust, the account belongs beneficially to the beneficiary.

Section 6–104. [Right of Survivorship.]

(a)   Sums remaining on deposit at the death of a party to a joint account belong to the surviving party or parties as against the estate of the decedent unless there is clear and convincing evidence of a different intention at the time the account is created. If there are 2 or more surviving parties, their respective ownerships during lifetime shall be in proportion to their previous ownership interests under Section 6–103 augmented by an equal share for each survivor of any interest the decedent may have owned in the account immediately before his death; and the right of survivorship continues between the surviving parties.

(b)   if the account is a P.O.D. account;

(1)   on death of one of 2 or more original payees the rights to any sums remaining on deposit are governed by subsection (a);

(2)   on death of the sole original payee or of the survivor of two or more original payees, any sums remaining on deposit belong to the P.O.D. payee or payees if surviving, or to the survivor of them if one or more die before the original payee; if 2 or more P.O.D. payees survive, there is no right of survivorship in the event of death of a P.O.D. payee thereafter unless the terms of the account or deposit agreement expressly provide for survivorship between them.

(c)   if the account is a trust account;

(1)   on death of one of 2 or more trustees, the rights to any sums remaining on deposit are governed by subsection (a);

(2)   on death of the sole trustee or the survivor of 2 or more trustees, any sums remaining on deposit belong to the person or persons named as beneficiaries, if surviving, or to the survivor of them if one or more die before the trustee, unless there is clear evidence of a contrary intent; if 2 or more beneficiaries survive, there is no right of survivorship in event of death of any beneficiary thereafter unless the terms of the account or deposit agreement expressly provide for survivorship between them.

(d)   In other cases, the death of any party to a multiple-party account has no effect on beneficial ownership of the account other than to transfer the rights of the decedent as part of his estate.

(e)   A right of survivorship arising from the express terms of the account or under this section, a beneficiary designation in a trust account, or a P.O.D. payee designation, cannot be changed by will.

Section 6–105. [Effect of Written Notice to Financial Institution.]

The provisions of Section 6–104 as to rights of survivorship are determined by the form of the account at the death of a party. This form may be altered by written order given by a party to the financial institution to change the form of the account or to stop or vary payment under the terms of the account. The order or request must be signed by a party, received by the financial institution during the party's lifetime, and not countermanded by other written order of the same party during his lifetime.

Section 6–106. [Accounts and Transfers Nontestamentary.]

Any transfers resulting from the application of Section 6–104 are effective by reason of the account contracts involved and this statute and are not to be considered as testamentary or subject to Articles I through IV, except as provided in Sections 2–201 through 2–207, and except as a consequence of, and to the extent directed by, Section 6–107.

Section 6–107. [Rights of Creditors.]

No multiple-party account will be effective against an estate of a deceased party to transfer to a survivor sums needed to pay debts, taxes, and expenses of administration, including statutory allowances to the surviving spouse, minor children and dependent children, if other assets of the estate are insufficient. A surviving party, P.O.D. payee, or beneficiary who receives payment from a multiple-party account after the death of a deceased party shall be liable to account to his personal representative for amounts the decedent owned beneficially immediately before his death to the extent necessary to discharge the claims and charges mentioned above remaining unpaid after application of the decedent's estate. No proceeding to assert this liability shall be commenced unless the personal representative has received a written demand by a surviving spouse, a creditor or one acting for a minor or dependent child of the decedent, and no proceeding shall be commenced later than two years following the death of the decedent. Sums recovered by the personal representative shall be administered as part of the decedent's estate. This section shall not affect the right of a financial institution to make payment on multiple-party accounts according to the terms thereof, or make it liable to the estate of a deceased party unless before payment the institution has been served with process in a proceeding by the personal representative.

Section 6–108. [Financial Institution Protection; Payment on Signature of One Party.]

Financial institutions may enter into multiple-party accounts to the same extent that they may enter into single-party accounts. Any multiple-party account may be paid, on request, to any one or more of the parties. A financial institution shall not be required to inquire as to the source of funds received for deposit to a multiple-party account, or to inquire as to the proposed application of any sum withdrawn from an account, for purposes of establishing net contributions.

Section 6–109. [Financial Institution Protection; Payment After Death or Disability; Joint Account.]

Any sums in a joint account may be paid, on request, to any party without regard to whether any other party is incapacitated or deceased at the time the payment is demanded; but payment may not be made to the personal representative or heirs of a deceased party unless proofs of death are presented to the financial institution showing that the decedent was the last surviving party or unless there is no right of survivorship under Section 6–104.

Section 6–110. [Financial Institution Protection; Payment of P.O.D. Account.]

Any P.O.D. account may be paid, on request, to any original party to the account. Payment may be made, on request, to the P.O.D. payee or to the personal representative or heirs of a deceased P.O.D. payee upon presentation to the financial institution of proof of death showing that the P.O.D. payee survived all persons named as original payees. Payment may be made to the personal representative or heirs of a deceased original payee if proof of death is presented to the financial institution showing that his decedent was the survivor of all other persons named on the account either as an original payee or as P.O.D. payee.

Section 6–111. [Financial Institution Protection; Payment of Trust Account.]

Any trust account may be paid, on request, to any trustee. Unless the financial institution has received written notice that the beneficiary has a vested interest not dependent upon his surviving the trustee, payment may be made to the personal representative or heirs of a deceased trustee if proof of death is presented to the financial institution showing that his decedent was the survivor of all other persons named on the account either as trustee or beneficiary. Payment may be made, on request, to the beneficiary upon presentation to the financial institution of proof of death showing that the beneficiary or beneficiaries survived all persons named as trustees.

Section 6–112. [Financial Institution Protection; Discharge.]

Payment made pursuant to Sections 6–108, 6–109, 6–110 or 6–111 discharges the financial institution from all claims for amounts so paid whether or not the payment is consistent with the beneficial ownership of the account as between parties, P.O.D. payees, or beneficiaries, or their successors. The protection here given does not extend to payments made after a financial institution has received written notice from any party able to request present payment to the effect that withdrawals in accordance with the terms of the account should not be permitted. Unless the notice is withdrawn by the person giving it, the successor of any deceased party must concur in any demand for withdrawal if the financial institution is to be protected under this section. No other notice or any other information shown to have been available to a financial institution shall affect its right to the protection provided here. The protection here provided shall have no bearing on the rights of parties in disputes between themselves or their successors concerning the beneficial ownership of funds in, or withdrawn from, multiple-party accounts.

Section 6–113. [Financial Institution Protection; Set-off.]

Without qualifying any other statutory right to set-off or lien and subject to any contractual provision, if a party to a multiple-party account is indebted to a financial institution, the financial institution has a right to set-off against the account in which the party has or had immediately before his death a present right of withdrawal. The amount of the account subject to set-off is that proportion to which the debtor is, or was immediately before his death, beneficially entitled, and in the absence of proof of net contributions, to an equal share with all parties having present rights of withdrawal.

PART 2

PROVISIONS RELATING TO EFFECT OF DEATH

Section 6–201. [Provisions for Payment or Transfer at Death.]

(a) Any of the following provisions in an insurance policy, contract of employment, bond, mortgage, promissory note, deposit agreement, pension plan, trust agreement, conveyance or any other written instrument effective as a contract, gift, conveyance, or trust is deemed to be nontestamentary, and this Code does not invalidate the instrument or any provision:

   (1) that money or other benefits theretofore due to, controlled or owned by a decedent shall be paid after his death to a person designated by the decedent in either the instrument or a separate writing, including a will, executed at the same time as the instrument or subsequently;

   (2) that any money due or to become due under the instrument shall cease to be payable in event of the death of the promisee or the promissor before payment or demand; or

(3) that any property which is the subject of the instrument shall pass to a person designated by the decedent in either the instrument or a separate writing, including a will, executed at the same time as the instrument or subsequently.

(b)   Nothing in this section limits the rights of creditors under other laws of this state.

Comment

This section authorizes a variety of contractual arrangements which have in the past been treated as testamentary. For example most courts treat as testamentary a provision in a promissory note that if the payee dies before payment is made the note shall be paid to another named person, or a provision in a land contract that if the seller dies before payment is completed the balance shall be cancelled and the property shall belong to the vendee. These provisions often occur in family arrangements. The result of holding the provisions testamentary is usually to invalidate them because not executed in accordance with the statute of wills. On the other hand the same courts have for years upheld beneficiary designations in life insurance contracts. Similar kinds of problems are arising in regard to beneficiary designations in pension funds and under annuity contracts. The analogy of the power of appointment provides some historical base for solving some of these problems aside from a validating statute. However, there appear to be no policy reasons for continuing to treat these varied arrangements as testamentary. The revocable living trust and the multiple-party bank accounts, as well as the experience with United States government bonds payable on death to named beneficiaries, have demonstrated that the evils envisioned if the statute of wills is not rigidly enforced simply do not materialize. The fact that these provisions often are part of a business transaction and in any event are evidenced by a writing eliminate the danger of "fraud."

Because the types of provisions described in the statute are characterized as nontestamentary, the instrument does not have to be executed in compliance with Section 2–502; nor does it have to be probated, nor does the personal representative have any power or duty with respect to the assets involved.

The sole purpose of this section is to eliminate the testamentary characterization from the arrangements falling within the terms of the section. It does not invalidate other arrangements by negative implication. Thus it is not intended by this section to embrace oral trusts to hold property at death for named persons; such arrangements are already generally enforceable under trust law.

UNIFORM TRUST CODE*

ARTICLE 1. GENERAL PROVISIONS AND DEFINITIONS

ARTICLE 2. JUDICIAL PROCEEDINGS

ARTICLE 3. REPRESENTATION

ARTICLE 4. CREATION, VALIDITY, MODIFICATION, AND TERMINATION OF TRUST

UNIFORM TRUST CODE

UNIFORM TRUST CODE

ARTICLE 9. UNIFORM PRUDENT INVESTOR ACT

[The Uniform Prudent Investor Act is reproduced elsewhere in this volume.]

ARTICLE 10. LIABILITY OF TRUSTEES AND RIGHTS OF PERSONS DEALING WITH TRUSTEE

ARTICLE 11. MISCELLANEOUS PROVISIONS

―――――――

ARTICLE 1

GENERAL PROVISIONS AND DEFINITIONS

Section 101. Short Title.

This [Act] may be cited as the Uniform Trust Code.

Section 102. Scope.

This [Code] applies to express trusts, charitable or noncharitable, and trusts created pursuant to a statute, judgment, or decree that requires the trust to be administered in the manner of an express trust.

Comment

The Uniform Trust Code, while comprehensive, applies only to express trusts. Excluded from the Code's coverage are resulting and constructive trusts, which are not express trusts but remedial devices imposed by law. * * *

The Uniform Trust Code is directed primarily at trusts that arise in an estate planning or other donative context, but express trusts can arise in other contexts. For example, a trust created pursuant to a divorce action would be included, even though such a trust is not donative but is created pursuant to a bargained-for exchange. Commercial trusts come in numerous forms, including trusts created pursuant to a state business trust act and trusts created to administer specified funds, such as to pay a pension or to manage pooled investments. Commercial trusts are often subject to special-purpose legislation and case law, which in some respects displace the usual rules stated in this Code. * * *

Express trusts also may be created by means of court judgment or decree. Examples include trusts created to hold the proceeds of personal injury recoveries and trusts created to hold the assets of a protected person in a conservatorship proceeding. * * *

Section 103. Definitions.

In this [Code]:

(1) "Action," with respect to an act of a trustee, includes a failure to act.

(2) "Ascertainable standard" means a standard relating to an individual's health, education, support, or maintenance within the meaning of Section 2041(b)(1)(A) or 2514(c)(1) of the Internal Revenue Code of 1986, as in effect on [the effective date of this [Code] [amendment] [, or as later amended]].

(3) "Beneficiary" means a person that:

(A) has a present or future beneficial interest in a trust, vested or contingent; or

(B) in a capacity other than that of trustee, holds a power of appointment over trust property.

(4) "Charitable trust" means a trust, or portion of a trust, created for a charitable purpose described in Section 405(a).

(5) "[Conservator]" means a person appointed by the court to administer the estate of a minor or adult individual.

(6) "Environmental law" means a federal, state, or local law, rule, regulation, or ordinance relating to protection of the environment.

(7) "[Guardian]" means a person appointed by the court [, a parent, or a spouse] to make decisions regarding the support, care, education, health, and welfare of a minor or adult individual. The term does not include a guardian ad litem.

(8) "Interests of the beneficiaries" means the beneficial interests provided in the terms of the trust.

(9) "Jurisdiction," with respect to a geographic area, includes a State or country.

(10) "Person" means an individual, corporation, business trust, estate, trust, partnership, limited liability company, association, joint venture, government; governmental subdivision, agency, or instrumentality; public corporation, or any other legal or commercial entity.

(11) "Power of withdrawal" means a presently exercisable general power of appointment other than a power: (A) exercisable by a trustee and limited by an ascertainable standard; or (B) exercisable by another person only upon consent of the trustee or a person holding an adverse interest.

(12) "Property" means anything that may be the subject of ownership, whether real or personal, legal or equitable, or any interest therein.

(13) "Qualified beneficiary" means a beneficiary who, on the date the beneficiary's qualification is determined:

    (A)   is a distributee or permissible distributee of trust income or principal;

    (B)   would be a distributee or permissible distributee of trust income or principal if the interests of the distributees described in subparagraph (A) terminated on that date without causing the trust to terminate; or

    (C)   would be a distributee or permissible distributee of trust income or principal if the trust terminated on that date.

(14) "Revocable," as applied to a trust, means revocable by the settlor without the consent of the trustee or a person holding an adverse interest.

(15) "Settlor" means a person, including a testator, who creates, or contributes property to, a trust. If more than one person creates or contributes property to a trust, each person is a settlor of the portion of the trust property attributable to that person's contribution except to the extent another person has the power to revoke or withdraw that portion.

(16) "Spendthrift provision" means a term of a trust which restrains both voluntary and involuntary transfer of a beneficiary's interest.

(17) "State" means a State of the United States, the District of Columbia, Puerto Rico, the United States Virgin Islands, or any territory or insular possession subject to the jurisdiction of the United States. The term includes an Indian tribe or band recognized by federal law or formally acknowledged by a State.

(18) "Terms of a trust" means:

    (A)   Except as otherwise provided in subparagraph (B), the manifestation of the settlor's intent regarding a trust's provisions as:

        (i)   expressed in the trust instrument; or

        (ii)   established by other evidence that would be admissible in a judicial proceeding; or

    (B)   the trust's provisions, as established, determined, or amended by:

        (i)   a trustee or other person in accordance with applicable law; [or]

        (ii)   a court order; [[or]

        (iii)   a nonjudicial settlement agreement under [Section 111]].

(19) "Trust instrument" means an instrument executed by the settlor that contains terms of the trust, including any amendments thereto.

(20) "Trustee" includes an original, additional, and successor trustee, and a cotrustee.

Comment

* * * "Beneficiary" (paragraph (3)) refers only to a beneficiary of a trust as defined in the Uniform Trust Code. In addition to living and ascertained individuals, beneficiaries may be unborn or unascertained. * * * The term "beneficiary" includes not only beneficiaries who received their interests under the terms of the trust but also beneficiaries who received their interests by other means, including by assignment, exercise of a power of appointment, resulting trust upon the failure of an interest, gap in a disposition, operation of an antilapse statute upon the predecease of a named beneficiary, or upon termination of the trust. The fact that a person incidentally benefits from the trust does not mean that the person is a beneficiary. For example, neither a trustee nor persons hired by the trustee become beneficiaries merely because they receive compensation from the trust. * * *

The definition of "beneficiary" includes only those who hold beneficial interests in the trust. Because a charitable trust is not created to benefit ascertainable beneficiaries but to benefit the community at large * * *, persons receiving distributions from a charitable trust are not beneficiaries as that term is defined in this Code. However, pursuant to Section 110(b), also granted rights of a qualified beneficiary under the Code are charitable organizations expressly designated to receive distributions under the terms of a charitable trust but only if [their] beneficial interests [are] sufficient to satisfy the definition of qualified beneficiary for a noncharitable trust.

The phrase "interests of the beneficiaries" (paragraph (8)) is used with some frequency in the Uniform Trust Code. The definition clarifies that the interests are as provided in the terms of the trust and not as determined by the beneficiaries. * * *

The definition of "property" (paragraph (12)) is intended to be as expansive as possible and to encompass anything that may be the subject of ownership. Included are choses in action, claims, and interests created by beneficiary designations under policies of insurance, financial instruments, and deferred compensation and other retirement arrangements, whether revocable or irrevocable. Any such property interest is sufficient to support creation of a trust. * * *

Due to the difficulty of identifying beneficiaries whose interests are remote and contingent, and because such beneficiaries are not likely to have much interest in the day-to-day affairs of the trust, the Uniform Trust Code uses the concept of "qualified beneficiary" (paragraph (13)) to limit the class of beneficiaries to whom certain notices must be given or consents received. * * *

The qualified beneficiaries consist of the beneficiaries currently eligible to receive a distribution from the trust together with those who might be termed the first-line remaindermen. These are the beneficiaries who would become eligible to receive distributions were the event triggering the termination of a beneficiary's interest or of the trust itself to occur on the date in question. Such a terminating event will typically be the death or deaths of the beneficiaries currently eligible to receive the income. * * *

The qualified beneficiaries who take upon termination of the beneficiary's interest or of the trust can include takers in default of the exercise of a power of appointment. The term can also include the persons entitled to receive the trust property pursuant to the exercise of a power of appointment. Because the exercise of a testamentary power of appointment is not effective until the testator's death and probate of the will, the qualified beneficiaries do not include appointees under the will of a living person. * * *

The definition of "revocable" (paragraph (14)) clarifies that revocable trusts include only trusts whose revocation is substantially within the settlor's control. The fact that the settlor becomes incapacitated does not convert a revocable trust into an irrevocable trust. The trust remains revocable until the settlor's death or the power of revocation is released. * * *

The definition of "settlor" (paragraph (15)) refers to the person who creates, or contributes property to, a trust, whether by will, self-declaration, transfer of property to another person as trustee, or exercise of a power of appointment. * * * Determining the identity of the "settlor" is usually not an issue. The same person will both sign the trust instrument and fund the trust. Ascertaining the identity of the settlor becomes more difficult when more than one person signs the trust instrument or funds the trust. The fact that a person is designated as the "settlor" by the terms of the trust is not necessarily determinative. For example, the person who executes the trust instrument may be acting as the agent for the person who will be funding the trust. In that case, the person funding the trust, and not the person signing the trust instrument, will be the settlor. Should more than one person contribute to a trust, all of the contributors will ordinarily be treated as settlors in proportion to their respective contributions, regardless of which one signed the trust instrument. * * *

In the case of a revocable trust employed as a will substitute, gifts to the trust's creator are sometimes made by placing the gifted property directly into the trust. To recognize that such a donor is not intended to be treated as a settlor, the definition of "settlor" excludes a contributor to a trust that is revocable by another person or over which another person has a power of withdrawal. Thus, a parent who contributes to a child's revocable trust would not be treated as one of the trust's settlors. The definition of settlor would treat the child as the sole settlor of the trust to the extent of the child's proportionate contribution. Pursuant to Section 603(d), the child's power of withdrawal over the trust would also result in the child being treated as the settlor with respect to the portion of the trust attributable to the parent's contribution. * * *

"Terms of a trust" (paragraph (18)) is a defined term used frequently in the Uniform Trust Code. While the wording of a written trust instrument is almost always the most important determinant of a trust's terms, the definition is not so limited. Oral statements, the situation of the beneficiaries, the purposes of the trust, the circumstances under which the trust is to be administered, and, to the extent the settlor was otherwise silent, rules of construction, all may have a bearing on determining a trust's meaning. * * *

A manifestation of a settlor's intention does not constitute evidence of a trust's terms if it would be inadmissible in a judicial proceeding in which the trust's terms are in question. * * * For example, in many States a trust of real property is unenforceable unless evidenced by a writing, although Section 407 of this Code does not so require, leaving this issue to be covered by separate statute if the enacting jurisdiction so elects. Evidence otherwise relevant to determining the terms of a trust may also be excluded under other principles of law, such as the parol evidence rule. * * *

Section 104. Knowledge.

(a) Subject to subsection (b), a person has knowledge of a fact if the person:

　　(1) has actual knowledge of it;

　　(2) has received a notice or notification of it; or

　　(3) from all the facts and circumstances known to the person at the time in question, has reason to know it.

(b) An organization that conducts activities through employees has notice or knowledge of a fact involving a trust only from the time the information was received by an employee having responsibility to act for the trust, or would have been brought to the employee's attention if the organization had exercised reasonable diligence. An organization exercises reasonable diligence if it maintains reasonable routines for communicating significant information to the employee having responsibility to act for the trust and there is reasonable compliance with the routines. Reasonable diligence does not require an employee of the organization to communicate information unless the communication is part of the individual's regular duties or the individual knows a matter involving the trust would be materially affected by the information.

Section 105. Default and Mandatory Rules.

(a) Except as otherwise provided in the terms of the trust, this [Code] governs the duties and powers of a trustee, relations among trustees, and the rights and interests of a beneficiary.

(b) The terms of a trust prevail over any provision of this [Code] except:

　　(1) the requirements for creating a trust;

　　(2) [subject to [Uniform Directed Trust Act Sections 9, 11, and 12],] the duty of a trustee to act in good faith and in accordance with the terms and purposes of the trust and the interests of the beneficiaries;

　　(3) the requirement that a trust and its terms be for the benefit of its beneficiaries, and that the trust have a purpose that is lawful, not contrary to public policy, and possible to achieve;

　　(4) the power of the court to modify or terminate a trust under Sections 410 through 416;

(5)   the effect of a spendthrift provision and the rights of certain creditors and assignees to reach a trust as provided in [Article] 5;

(6)   the power of the court under Section 702 to require, dispense with, or modify or terminate a bond;

(7)   the power of the court under Section 708(b) to adjust a trustee's compensation specified in the terms of the trust which is unreasonably low or high;

[(8) the duty under Section 813(b)(2) and (3) to notify qualified beneficiaries of an irrevocable trust who have attained 25 years of age of the existence of the trust, of the identity of the trustee, and of their right to request trustee's reports;]

[(9) the duty under Section 813(a) to respond to the request of a [qualified] beneficiary of an irrevocable trust for trustee's reports and other information reasonably related to the administration of a trust;]

(10) the effect of an exculpatory term under Section 1008;

(11) the rights under Sections 1010 through 1013 of a person other than a trustee or beneficiary;

(12) periods of limitation for commencing a judicial proceeding; [and]

(13) the power of the court to take such action and exercise such jurisdiction as may be necessary in the interests of justice [; and

(14) the subject-matter jurisdiction of the court and venue for commencing a proceeding as provided in Sections 203 and 204].

Comment

Subsection (a) emphasizes that the Uniform Trust Code is primarily a default statute. While this Code provides numerous procedural rules on which a settlor may wish to rely, the settlor is generally free to override these rules and to prescribe the conditions under which the trust is to be administered. With only limited exceptions, the duties and powers of a trustee, relations among trustees, and the rights and interests of a beneficiary are as specified in the terms of the trust.

Subsection (b) lists the items not subject to override in the terms of the trust. * * *

Subsection (b)(1) confirms that the requirements for a trust's creation, such as the necessary level of capacity and the requirement that a trust have a legal purpose, are controlled by statute and common law, not by the settlor. * * * Subsection (b)(12) makes clear that the settlor may not reduce any otherwise applicable period of limitations for commencing a judicial proceeding. * * * Subsection (b)(2) provides that the terms may not eliminate a trustee's duty to act in good faith and in accordance with the purposes of the trust and the interests of the beneficiaries. * * * Subsection (b)(3) provides that the terms may not eliminate the requirement that a trust and its terms must be for the benefit of the beneficiaries. * * *

The terms of a trust may not deny a court authority to take such action as necessary in the interests of justice, including requiring that a trustee furnish bond. Subsection (b)(6), (13). * * * The power of the court to modify or terminate a trust under Sections 410 through 416 is not subject to variation in the terms of the trust. Subsection (b)(4). However, all of these Code sections involve situations which the settlor could have addressed had the settlor had sufficient foresight. These include situations where the purpose of the trust has been achieved, a mistake was made in the trust's creation, or circumstances have arisen that were not anticipated by the settlor.

Section 813 imposes a general obligation to keep the beneficiaries informed as well as several specific notice requirements. Subsections (b)(8) and (b)(9), which were placed in brackets and made optional by a 2004 amendment, specify limits on the settlor's ability to waive these information requirements. With respect to beneficiaries age 25 or older, a settlor may dispense with all of the requirements of Section 813 except for the duties to inform the beneficiaries of the existence of the trust, of the identity of the trustee, and to provide a beneficiary upon request with such reports as the trustee may have prepared. Among the specific requirements that a settlor may waive include the duty to provide a beneficiary upon request with a copy of the trust instrument * * * and the requirement that the trustee provide annual reports to the qualified beneficiaries * * * . The furnishing of a copy of the entire trust instrument and preparation of annual reports may be required in a particular case, however, if such information is requested by a beneficiary and is reasonably related to the trust's administration.

Responding to the desire of some settlors that younger beneficiaries not know of the trust's bounty until they have reached an age of maturity and self-sufficiency, subsection (b)(8) allows a settlor to provide that the trustee need not even inform beneficiaries under age 25 of the existence of the trust. However, pursuant to subsection (b)(9), if the younger beneficiary learns of the trust and requests information, the trustee must respond. * * *

Waiver by a settlor of the trustee's duty to keep the beneficiaries informed of the trust's administration does not otherwise affect the trustee's duties. The trustee remains accountable to the beneficiaries for the trustee's actions.

Neither subsection (b)(8) nor (b)(9) apply to revocable trusts. The settlor of a revocable trust may waive all reporting to the beneficiaries, even in the event the settlor loses capacity. * * *

* * * [Sections 105(b)(8) and 105(b)(9)] were placed in brackets out of a recognition that there is a lack of consensus on the extent to which a settlor ought to be able to waive reporting to beneficiaries, and that there is little chance that the states will enact Sections 105(b)(8) and (b)(9) with any uniformity.

The policy debate is succinctly stated in Joseph Kartiganer & Raymond H. Young, *The UTC: Help for Beneficiaries and Their Attorneys*, Prob. & Prop., Mar./April 2003, at 18, 20:

> The beneficiaries' rights to information and reports are among the most important provisions in the UTC. They also are among the provisions that have attracted the most attention. The UTC provisions reflect a compromise position between opposing viewpoints.

> Objections raised to beneficiaries' rights to information include the wishes of some settlors who believe that knowledge of trust benefits would not be good for younger beneficiaries, encouraging them to take up a life of ease rather than work and be productive citizens. Sometimes trustees themselves desire secrecy and freedom from interference by beneficiaries.

> The policy arguments on the other side are: that the essence of the trust relationship is accounting to the beneficiaries; that it is wise administration to account and inform beneficiaries, to avoid the greater danger of the beneficiary learning of a breach or possible breach long after the event; and that there are practical difficulties with secrecy (for example, the trustee must tell a child that he or she is not eligible for financial aid at college because the trust will pay, and must determine whether to accumulate income at high income tax rates or pay it out for inclusion in the beneficiary's own return). Furthermore, there is the practical advantage of a one-year statute of limitations when the beneficiary is informed of the trust transactions and advised of the bar if no claim is made within the year. * * * In the absence of notice, the trustee is exposed to liability until five years after the trustee ceases to serve, the interests of beneficiaries end, or the trust terminates. * * *

Section 106. Common Law of Trusts; Principles of Equity.

The common law of trusts and principles of equity supplement this [Code], except to the extent modified by this [Code] or another statute of this State.

Section 107. Governing Law.

The meaning and effect of the terms of a trust are determined by:

(1) the law of the jurisdiction designated in the terms unless the designation of that jurisdiction's law is contrary to a strong public policy of the jurisdiction having the most significant relationship to the matter at issue; or

(2) in the absence of a controlling designation in the terms of the trust, the law of the jurisdiction having the most significant relationship to the matter at issue.

Comment

This section provides rules for determining the law that will govern the meaning and effect of particular trust terms. The law to apply to determine whether a trust has been validly created is determined under Section 403.

Paragraph (1) allows a settlor to select the law that will govern the meaning and effect of the terms of the trust. The jurisdiction selected need not have any other connection to the trust. The settlor is free to select the governing law regardless of where the trust property may be physically located, whether it consists of real or personal property, and whether the trust was created by will or during the settlor's lifetime. This section does not attempt to specify the strong public policies sufficient to invalidate a settlor's choice of governing law. These public policies will vary depending upon the locale and may change over time.

Paragraph (2) provides a rule for trusts without governing law provisions—the meaning and effect of the trust's terms are to be determined by the law of the jurisdiction having the most significant relationship to the matter at issue. Factors to consider in determining the governing law include the place of the trust's creation, the location of the trust property, and the domicile of the settlor, the trustee, and the beneficiaries. * * * Other more general factors that may be pertinent in particular cases include the relevant policies of the forum, the relevant policies of other interested jurisdictions and degree of their interest, the protection of justified expectations and certainty, and predictability and uniformity of result. * * * Usually, the law of the trust's principal place of administration will govern administrative matters and the law of the place having the most significant relationship to the trust's creation will govern the dispositive provisions. * * *

Section 108. Principal Place of Administration.

(a) Without precluding other means for establishing a sufficient connection with the designated jurisdiction, terms of a trust designating the principal place of administration are valid and controlling if:

    (1) a trustee's principal place of business is located in or a trustee is a resident of the designated jurisdiction; or

    (2) all or part of the administration occurs in the designated jurisdiction.

(b) A trustee is under a continuing duty to administer the trust at a place appropriate to its purposes, its administration, and the interests of the beneficiaries.

(c) Without precluding the right of the court to order, approve, or disapprove a transfer, the trustee, in furtherance of the duty prescribed by subsection (b), may transfer the trust's principal place of administration to another State or to a jurisdiction outside of the United States.

(d) The trustee shall notify the qualified beneficiaries of a proposed transfer of a trust's principal place of administration not less than 60 days before initiating the transfer. The notice of proposed transfer must include:

    (1) the name of the jurisdiction to which the principal place of administration is to be transferred;

    (2) the address and telephone number at the new location at which the trustee can be contacted;

    (3) an explanation of the reasons for the proposed transfer;

    (4) the date on which the proposed transfer is anticipated to occur; and

    (5) the date, not less than 60 days after the giving of the notice, by which the qualified beneficiary must notify the trustee of an objection to the proposed transfer.

(e) The authority of a trustee under this section to transfer a trust's principal place of administration terminates if a qualified beneficiary notifies the trustee of an objection to the proposed transfer on or before the date specified in the notice.

(f)   In connection with a transfer of the trust's principal place of administration, the trustee may transfer some or all of the trust property to a successor trustee designated in the terms of the trust or appointed pursuant to Section 704.

Comment

This section prescribes rules relating to a trust's principal place of administration. Locating a trust's principal place of administration will ordinarily determine which court has primary if not exclusive jurisdiction over the trust. * * *

Because of the difficult and variable situations sometimes involved, the Uniform Trust Code does not attempt to further define principal place of administration. A trust's principal place of administration ordinarily will be the place where the trustee is located. Determining the principal place of administration becomes more difficult, however, when cotrustees are located in different States or when a single institutional trustee has trust operations in more than one State. In such cases, other factors may become relevant, including the place where the trust records are kept or trust assets held, or in the case of an institutional trustee, the place where the trust officer responsible for supervising the account is located. * * *

A settlor expecting to name a trustee or cotrustees with significant contacts in more than one State may eliminate possible uncertainty about the location of the trust's principal place of administration by specifying the jurisdiction in the terms of the trust. Under subsection (a), a designation in the terms of the trust is controlling if (1) a trustee is a resident of or has its principal place of business in the designated jurisdiction, or (2) all or part of the administration occurs in the designated jurisdiction. Designating the principal place of administration should be distinguished from designating the law to determine the meaning and effect of the trust's terms, as authorized by Section 107. A settlor is free to designate one jurisdiction as the principal place of administration and another to govern the meaning and effect of the trust's provisions.

Subsection (b) provides that a trustee is under a continuing duty to administer the trust at a place appropriate to its purposes, its administration, and the interests of the beneficiaries. * * * Ordinarily, absent a substantial change of circumstances, the trustee may assume that the original place of administration is also the appropriate place of administration. The duty to administer the trust at an appropriate place may also dictate that the trustee not move the trust.

Subsections (c)–(f) provide a procedure for changing the principal place of administration to another State or country. Such changes are often beneficial. A change may be desirable to secure a lower state income tax rate, or because of relocation of the trustee or beneficiaries, the appointment of a new trustee, or a change in the location of the trust investments. The procedure for transfer specified in this section applies only in the absence of a contrary provision in the terms of the trust. * * * To facilitate transfer in the typical case, where all concur that a transfer is either desirable or is at least not harmful, a transfer can be accomplished without court approval unless a qualified beneficiary objects. To allow the qualified beneficiaries sufficient time to review a proposed transfer, the trustee must give the qualified beneficiaries at least 60 days prior notice of the transfer. Notice must be given not only to qualified beneficiaries as defined in Section 103(13) but also to those granted the rights of qualified beneficiaries under Section 110. To assure that those receiving notice have sufficient information upon which to make a decision, minimum contents of the notice are specified. If a qualified beneficiary objects, a trustee wishing to proceed with the transfer must seek court approval. * * *

While transfer of the principal place of administration will normally change the governing law with respect to administrative matters, a transfer does not normally alter the controlling law with respect to the validity of the trust and the construction of its dispositive provisions. * * *

Section 109. Methods and Waiver of Notice.

(a)   Notice to a person under this [Code] or the sending of a document to a person under this [Code] must be accomplished in a manner reasonably suitable under the circumstances and likely to result in receipt of the notice or document. Permissible methods of notice or for sending a document include first-class mail, personal delivery, delivery to the person's last known place of residence or place of business, or a properly directed electronic message.

(b)   Notice otherwise required under this [Code] or a document otherwise required to be sent under this [Code] need not be provided to a person whose identity or location is unknown to and not reasonably ascertainable by the trustee.

(c)   Notice under this [Code] or the sending of a document under this [Code] may be waived by the person to be notified or sent the document.

(d)   Notice of a judicial proceeding must be given as provided in the applicable rules of civil procedure.

Section 110. Others Treated as Qualified Beneficiaries.

(a)   Whenever notice to qualified beneficiaries of a trust is required under this [Code], the trustee must also give notice to any other beneficiary who has sent the trustee a request for notice.

(b)   A charitable organization expressly designated to receive distributions under the terms of a charitable trust has the rights of a qualified beneficiary under this [Code] if the charitable organization, on the date the charitable organization's qualification is being determined:

(A)   is a distributee or permissible distributee of trust income or principal;

(B)   would be a distributee or permissible distributee of trust income or principal upon the termination of the interests of other distributees or permissible distributees then receiving or eligible to receive distributions; or

(C)   would be a distributee or permissible distributee of trust income or principal if the trust terminated on that date.

(c)   A person appointed to enforce a trust created for the care of an animal or another noncharitable purpose as provided in Section 408 or 409 has the rights of a qualified beneficiary under this [Code].

[(d)   The [attorney general of this State] has the rights of a qualified beneficiary with respect to a charitable trust having its principal place of administration in this State.]

Comment

Under the Uniform Trust Code, certain notices need be given only to the "qualified" beneficiaries. * * * Subsection (a) of this section authorizes other beneficiaries to receive one or more of these notices by filing a request for notice with the trustee.

Under the Code, certain actions, such as the appointment of a successor trustee, can be accomplished by the consent of the qualified beneficiaries. * * * Subsection (a) only addresses notice, not required consent. A person who requests notice under subsection (a) does not thereby acquire a right to participate in actions that can be taken only upon consent of the qualified beneficiaries.

Charitable trusts do not have beneficiaries in the usual sense. However, certain persons, while not technically beneficiaries, do have an interest in seeing that the trust is enforced. In the case of a charitable trust, this includes the state's attorney general and charitable organizations expressly designated to receive distributions under the terms of the trust. Under subsection (b), charitable organizations expressly designated in the terms of the trust to receive distributions and who would qualify as a qualified beneficiary were the trust noncharitable, are granted the rights of qualified beneficiaries under the Code. Because the charitable organization must be expressly named in the terms of the trust and must be designated to receive distributions, excluded are organizations that might receive distributions in the trustee's discretion but that are not named in the trust's terms. Requiring that the organization have an interest similar to that of a beneficiary of a private trust also denies the rights of a qualified beneficiary to organizations holding remote remainder interests. * * *

Subsection (c) similarly grants the rights of qualified beneficiaries to persons appointed by the terms of the trust or by the court to enforce a trust created for an animal or other trust with a valid purpose but no ascertainable beneficiary. * * *

Section 111. Nonjudicial Settlement Agreements.

(a) For purposes of this section, "interested persons" means persons whose consent would be required in order to achieve a binding settlement were the settlement to be approved by the court.

(b) Except as otherwise provided in subsection (c), interested persons may enter into a binding nonjudicial settlement agreement with respect to any matter involving a trust.

(c) A nonjudicial settlement agreement is valid only to the extent it does not violate a material purpose of the trust and includes terms and conditions that could be properly approved by the court under this [Code] or other applicable law.

(d) Matters that may be resolved by a nonjudicial settlement agreement include:

(1) the interpretation or construction of the terms of the trust;

(2) the approval of a trustee's report or accounting;

(3) direction to a trustee to refrain from performing a particular act or the grant to a trustee of any necessary or desirable power;

(4) the resignation or appointment of a trustee and the determination of a trustee's compensation;

(5) transfer of a trust's principal place of administration; and

(6) liability of a trustee for an action relating to the trust.

(e) Any interested person may request the court to approve a nonjudicial settlement agreement, to determine whether the representation as provided in [Article] 3 was adequate, and to determine whether the agreement contains terms and conditions the court could have properly approved.

Comment

While the Uniform Trust Code recognizes that a court may intervene in the administration of a trust to the extent its jurisdiction is invoked by interested persons or otherwise provided by law * * * , resolution of disputes by nonjudicial means is encouraged. This section facilitates the making of such agreements by giving them the same effect as if approved by the court. To achieve such certainty, however, subsection (c) requires that the nonjudicial settlement must contain terms and conditions that a court could properly approve. Under this section, a nonjudicial settlement cannot be used to produce a result not authorized by law, such as to terminate a trust in an impermissible manner.

Trusts ordinarily have beneficiaries who are minors, incapacitated, unborn or unascertained. Because such beneficiaries cannot signify their consent to an agreement, binding settlements can ordinarily be achieved only through the application of doctrines such as virtual representation or appointment of a guardian ad litem, doctrines traditionally available only in the case of judicial settlements. The effect of this section and the Uniform Trust Code more generally is to allow for such binding representation even if the agreement is not submitted for approval to a court. For the rules on representation, including appointments of representatives by the court to approve particular settlements, see Article 3.

Subsection (d) is a nonexclusive list of matters to which a nonjudicial settlement may pertain. * * * The fact that the trustee and beneficiaries may resolve a matter nonjudicially does not mean that beneficiary approval is required. For example, a trustee may resign pursuant to Section 705 solely by giving notice to the qualified beneficiaries and any cotrustees. But a nonjudicial settlement between the trustee and beneficiaries will frequently prove helpful in working out the terms of the resignation.

Because of the great variety of matters to which a nonjudicial settlement may be applied, this section does not attempt to precisely define the "interested persons" whose consent is required to obtain a binding settlement as provided in subsection (a). However, the consent of the trustee would ordinarily be required to obtain a binding settlement with respect to matters involving a trustee's administration, such as approval of a trustee's report or resignation.

[Section 112. Rules of Construction.

The rules of construction that apply in this State to the interpretation of and disposition of property by will also apply as appropriate to the interpretation of the terms of a trust and the disposition of the trust property.]

Comment

* * * The revocable trust is used primarily as a will substitute, with its key provision being the determination of the persons to receive the trust property upon the settlor's death. Given this functional equivalence between the revocable trust and a will, the rules for interpreting the disposition of property at death should be the same whether the individual has chosen a will or revocable trust as the individual's primary estate planning instrument. Over the years, the legislatures of the States and the courts have developed a series of rules of construction reflecting the legislative or judicial understanding of how the average testator would wish to dispose of property in cases where the will is silent or insufficiently clear. Few legislatures have yet to extend these rules of construction to revocable trusts, and even fewer to irrevocable trusts, although a number of courts have done so as a matter of judicial construction. * * *

Because of the wide variation among the States on the rules of construction applicable to wills, this Code does not attempt to prescribe the exact rules to be applied to trusts but instead adopts the philosophy * * * that the rules applicable to trusts ought to be the same, whatever those rules might be. * * *

[Section 113. Insurable Interest of Trustee.

(a) In this section, "settlor" means a person that executes a trust instrument. The term includes a person for which a fiduciary or agent is acting.

(b) A trustee of a trust has an insurable interest in the life of an individual insured under a life insurance policy that is owned by the trustee of the trust acting in a fiduciary capacity or that designates the trust itself as the owner if, on the date the policy is issued:

    (1) the insured is:

        (A) a settlor of the trust; or

        (B) an individual in whom a settlor of the trust has, or would have had if living at the time the policy was issued, an insurable interest; and

    (2) the life insurance proceeds are primarily for the benefit of one or more trust beneficiaries that have[:

        (A)] an insurable interest in the life of the insured [; or

        (B) a substantial interest engendered by love and affection in the continuation of the life of the insured and, if not already included under subparagraph (A), who are:

            (i) related within the third degree or closer, as measured by the civil law system of determining degrees of relation, either by blood or law, to the insured; or

            (ii) stepchildren of the insured].]

Comment

* * * [T]he purpose of [Section 113] is to clarify when, for purposes of the Code, a trustee has an insurable interest in an individual whose life is to be the subject of an insurance policy to fund the trust. Clarification of this area of law * * * will provide a reliable basis upon which trust and estate planning practitioners may draft trust instruments that involve the eventual payment of expected death benefits. * * *

Subsection (b) carries forward the widely approved rule that the time at which insurable interest in a life insurance policy is determined is the date the policy is issued, otherwise understood as the inception of the policy. Thus, if on the date the policy is issued the trustee has an insurable interest in the individual whose life is insured, the policy is not subject to being declared void for lack of such an interest. Under the reasoning that an individual has an unlimited insurable interest in his or her own life, subsection (b) provides that a trustee has an insurable interest in the settlor's own life. If an individual, as settlor, has created a trust to hold a life insurance policy on his or her own life, has funded that trust with the policy or with money to pay its premiums, and has selected the trustee of the trust, it follows that the trustee should have the same insurable interest that the settlor has in his or her own life. Similarly, recognizing that an individual may purchase insurance on the life of anyone in whom that individual has an insurable interest up to, generally speaking, the amount of that interest, subsection (b) provides that the trustee has an insurable interest in an individual in whom the settlor has, or would have had if living at the time the policy was issued, an insurable interest.

* * *

ARTICLE 2

JUDICIAL PROCEEDINGS

Section 201. Role of Court in Administration of Trust.

(a)   The court may intervene in the administration of a trust to the extent its jurisdiction is invoked by an interested person or as provided by law.

(b)   A trust is not subject to continuing judicial supervision unless ordered by the court.

(c)   A judicial proceeding involving a trust may relate to any matter involving the trust's administration, including a request for instructions and an action to declare rights.

Comment

While the Uniform Trust Code encourages the resolution of disputes without resort to the courts by providing such options as the nonjudicial settlement authorized by Section 111, the court is always available to the extent its jurisdiction is invoked by interested persons. The jurisdiction of the court with respect to trust matters is inherent and historical and also includes the ability to act on its own initiative, to appoint a special master to investigate the facts of a case, and to provide a trustee with instructions even in the absence of an actual dispute.

Contrary to the trust statutes in some States, the Uniform Trust Code does not create a system of routine or mandatory court supervision. While subsection (b) authorizes a court to direct that a particular trust be subject to continuing court supervision, the court's intervention will normally be confined to the particular matter brought before it.

Subsection (c) makes clear that the court's jurisdiction may be invoked even absent an actual dispute. Traditionally, courts in equity have heard petitions for instructions and have issued declaratory judgments if there is a reasonable doubt as to the extent of the trustee's powers or duties. The court will not ordinarily instruct trustees on how to exercise discretion, however. * * * This section does not limit the court's equity jurisdiction. Beyond mentioning petitions for instructions and actions to declare rights, subsection (c) does not attempt to list the types of judicial proceedings involving trust administration that might be brought by a trustee or beneficiary. * * *

Section 202. Jurisdiction Over Trustee and Beneficiary.

(a)   By accepting the trusteeship of a trust having its principal place of administration in this State or by moving the principal place of administration to this State, the trustee submits personally to the jurisdiction of the courts of this State regarding any matter involving the trust.

(b)   With respect to their interests in the trust, the beneficiaries of a trust having its principal place of administration in this State are subject to the jurisdiction of the courts of this State regarding any matter involving the trust. By accepting a distribution from such a trust, the recipient submits personally to the jurisdiction of the courts of this State regarding any matter involving the trust.

(c)   This section does not preclude other methods of obtaining jurisdiction over a trustee, beneficiary, or other person receiving property from the trust.

Comment

This section clarifies that the courts of the principal place of administration have jurisdiction to enter orders relating to the trust that will be binding on both the trustee and beneficiaries. Consent to jurisdiction does not dispense with any required notice, however. * * *

The jurisdiction conferred over the trustee and beneficiaries by this section does not preclude jurisdiction by courts elsewhere on some other basis. Furthermore, the fact that the courts in a new State acquire jurisdiction under this section following a change in a trust's principal place of administration does not necessarily mean that the courts of the former principal place of administration lose jurisdiction, particularly as to matters involving events occurring prior to the transfer.

The jurisdiction conferred by this section is limited. Pursuant to subsection (b), until a distribution is made, jurisdiction over a beneficiary is limited to the beneficiary's interests in the trust. Personal jurisdiction over a beneficiary is conferred only upon the making of a distribution. Subsection (b) also gives the court jurisdiction over other recipients of distributions. This would include individuals who receive distributions in the mistaken belief they are beneficiaries. * * *

[Section 203. Subject-Matter Jurisdiction.

(a) The [designate] court has exclusive jurisdiction of proceedings in this State brought by a trustee or beneficiary concerning the administration of a trust.

(b) The [designate] court has concurrent jurisdiction with other courts of this State of other proceedings involving a trust.]

[Section 204. Venue.

(a) Except as otherwise provided in subsection (b), venue for a judicial proceeding involving a trust is in the [county] of this State in which the trust's principal place of administration is or will be located and, if the trust is created by will and the estate is not yet closed, in the [county] in which the decedent's estate is being administered.

(b) If a trust has no trustee, venue for a judicial proceeding for the appointment of a trustee is in a [county] of this State in which a beneficiary resides, in a [county] in which any trust property is located, and if the trust is created by will, in the [county] in which the decedent's estate was or is being administered.]

ARTICLE 3

REPRESENTATION

Section 301. Representation: Basic Effect.

(a)   Notice to a person who may represent and bind another person under this [article] has the same effect as if notice were given directly to the other person.

(b)   The consent of a person who may represent and bind another person under this [article] is binding on the person represented unless the person represented objects to the representation before the consent would otherwise have become effective.

(c)   Except as otherwise provided in Sections [411 and] 602, a person who under this [article] may represent a settlor who lacks capacity may receive notice and give a binding consent on the settlor's behalf.

[(d) A settlor may not represent and bind a beneficiary under this [article] with respect to the termination or modification of a trust under Section 411(a).]

Comment

* * * Subsection (a) validates substitute notice to a person who may represent and bind another person as provided in the succeeding sections of this article. Notice to the substitute has the same effect as if given directly to the other person. Subsection (a) does not apply to notice of a judicial proceeding. Pursuant to Section 109(d), notice of a judicial proceeding must be given as provided in the applicable rules of civil procedure, which may require that notice not only be given to the representative but also to the person represented. * * *

Subsection (b) deals with the effect of a consent, whether by actual or virtual representation. * * *

A consent by a representative bars a later objection by the person represented, but a consent is not binding if the person represented raises an objection prior to the date the consent would otherwise become effective. The possibility that a beneficiary might object to a consent given on the beneficiary's behalf will not be germane in many cases because the person represented will be unborn or unascertained. However, the representation principles of this article will sometimes apply to adult and competent beneficiaries. * * *

Section 302. Representation by Holder of General Testamentary Power of Appointment.

To the extent there is no conflict of interest between the holder of a general testamentary power of appointment and the persons represented with respect to the particular question or dispute, the holder may represent and bind persons whose interests, as permissible appointees, takers in default, or otherwise, are subject to the power.

Comment

This section specifies the circumstances under which a holder of a general testamentary power of appointment may receive notices on behalf of and otherwise represent and bind persons whose interests are subject to the power, whether as permissible appointees, takers in default, or otherwise. Such representation is allowed except to the extent there is a conflict of interest with respect to the particular matter or dispute. Typically, the holder of a general testamentary power of appointment is also a life income beneficiary of the trust * * * . Without the exception for conflict of interest, the holder of the power could act in a way that could enhance the holder's income interests to the detriment of the appointees or takers in default, whoever they may be.

Section 303. Representation by Fiduciaries and Parents.

To the extent there is no conflict of interest between the representative and the person represented or among those being represented with respect to a particular question or dispute:

(1) a [conservator] may represent and bind the estate that the [conservator] controls;

(2) a [guardian] may represent and bind the ward if a [conservator] of the ward's estate has not been appointed;

(3) an agent having authority to act with respect to the particular question or dispute may represent and bind the principal;

(4) a trustee may represent and bind the beneficiaries of the trust;

(5) a personal representative of a decedent's estate may represent and bind persons interested in the estate; and

(6) a parent may represent and bind the parent's minor or unborn child if a [conservator] or [guardian] for the child has not been appointed.

Comment

This section allows for representation of persons by their fiduciaries (conservators, guardians, agents, trustees, and personal representatives), a principle that has long been part of the law. Paragraph (6), which allows parents to represent their children, is more recent * * * . This section is not limited to representation of beneficiaries. It also applies to representation of the settlor. Representation is not available if the fiduciary or parent is in a conflict position with respect to the particular matter or dispute, however. A typical conflict would be where the fiduciary or parent seeking to represent the beneficiary is either the trustee or holds an adverse beneficial interest.

Paragraph (2) authorizes a guardian to bind and represent a ward if a conservator of the ward's estate has not been appointed. Granting a guardian authority to represent the ward with respect to interests in the trust can avoid the need to seek appointment of a conservator. * * *

Paragraph (3) authorizes an agent to represent a principal only to the extent the agent has authority to act with respect to the particular question or dispute. Pursuant to Sections 411 and 602, an agent may represent a settlor with respect to the amendment, revocation or termination of the trust only to the extent this authority is expressly granted either in the trust or the power. Otherwise, depending on the particular question or dispute, a general grant of authority in the power may be sufficient to confer the necessary authority.

Section 304. Representation by Person Having Substantially Identical Interest.

Unless otherwise represented, a minor, incapacitated, or unborn individual, or a person whose identity or location is unknown and not reasonably ascertainable, may be represented by and bound by another having a substantially identical interest with respect to the particular question or dispute, but only to the extent there is no conflict of interest between the representative and the person represented.

Comment

This section authorizes a person with a substantially identical interest with respect to a particular question or dispute to represent and bind an otherwise unrepresented minor, incapacitated or unborn individual, or person whose location is unknown and not reasonably ascertainable. * * *

Typically, the interests of the representative and the person represented will be identical. A common example would be a trust providing for distribution to the settlor's children as a class, with an adult child being able to represent the interests of children who are either minors or unborn. Exact identity of interests is not required, only substantial identity with respect to the particular question or dispute. Whether such identity is present may depend on the nature of the interest. For example, a presumptive remainderman may be able to represent alternative remaindermen with respect to approval of a trustee's report but not with respect to interpretation of the remainder provision or termination of the trust. Even if the beneficial interests of the representative and person represented are identical, representation is not allowed in the event of conflict of interest. The representative may have interests outside of the trust that are adverse to the interest of the person represented, such as a prior relationship with the trustee or other beneficiaries. * * *

Section 305. Appointment of Representative.

(a) If the court determines that an interest is not represented under this [article], or that the otherwise available representation might be inadequate, the court may appoint a [representative] to receive notice, give consent, and otherwise represent, bind, and act on behalf of a minor, incapacitated, or unborn individual, or a person whose identity or location is unknown. A [representative] may be appointed to represent several persons or interests.

(b) A [representative] may act on behalf of the individual represented with respect to any matter arising under this [Code], whether or not a judicial proceeding concerning the trust is pending.

(c) In making decisions, a [representative] may consider general benefit accruing to the living members of the individual's family.

Comment

* * * Unlike a guardian ad litem, under this section a representative can be appointed to act with respect to a nonjudicial settlement or to receive a notice on a beneficiary's behalf. Furthermore, in making decisions, a representative may consider general benefit accruing to living members of the family. * * * The court may appoint a representative to act for a person even if the person could be represented under another section of this article.

ARTICLE 4

CREATION, VALIDITY, MODIFICATION, AND TERMINATION OF TRUST

Section 401. Methods of Creating Trust.

A trust may be created by:

(1)   transfer of property to another person as trustee during the settlor's lifetime or by will or other disposition taking effect upon the settlor's death;

(2)   declaration by the owner of property that the owner holds identifiable property as trustee; or

(3)   exercise of a power of appointment in favor of a trustee.

Comment

* * * Under the methods specified for creating a trust in this section, a trust is not created until it receives property. * * * The property interest necessary to fund and create a trust need not be substantial. A revocable designation of the trustee as beneficiary of a life insurance policy or employee benefit plan has long been understood to be a property interest sufficient to create a trust. * * * Furthermore, the property interest need not be transferred contemporaneously with the signing of the trust instrument. A trust instrument signed during the settlor's lifetime is not rendered invalid simply because the trust was not created until property was transferred to the trustee at a much later date, including by contract after the settlor's death. * * *

A trust can also be created by a promise that creates enforceable rights in a person who immediately or later holds these rights as trustee. * * *

A trust created by self-declaration is best created by reregistering each of the assets that comprise the trust into the settlor's name as trustee. However, such reregistration is not necessary to create the trust. * * * A declaration of trust can be funded merely by attaching a schedule listing the assets that are to be subject to the trust without executing separate instruments of transfer. But such practice can make it difficult to later confirm title with third party transferees and for this reason is not recommended. * * *

Section 402. Requirements for Creation.

(a)   A trust is created only if:

(1)   the settlor has capacity to create a trust;

(2)   the settlor indicates an intention to create the trust;

(3)   the trust has a definite beneficiary or is:

(A)   a charitable trust;

(B)   a trust for the care of an animal, as provided in Section 408; or

(C)   a trust for a noncharitable purpose, as provided in Section 409;

(4)   the trustee has duties to perform; and

(5)   the same person is not the sole trustee and sole beneficiary.

(b)   A beneficiary is definite if the beneficiary can be ascertained now or in the future, subject to any applicable rule against perpetuities.

(c)   A power in a trustee to select a beneficiary from an indefinite class is valid. If the power is not exercised within a reasonable time, the power fails and the property subject to the power passes to the persons who would have taken the property had the power not been conferred.

Comment

Subsection (a) codifies the basic requirements for the creation of a trust. To create a valid trust, the settlor must indicate an intention to create a trust. * * * But only such manifestations of intent as are admissible as proof in a judicial proceeding may be considered. * * *

To create a trust, a settlor must have the requisite mental capacity. To create a revocable or testamentary trust, the settlor must have the capacity to make a will. To create an irrevocable trust, the settlor must have capacity during lifetime to transfer the property free of trust. * * *

Subsection (a)(3) requires that a trust, other than a charitable trust, a trust for the care of an animal, or a trust for another valid noncharitable purpose, have a definite beneficiary. While some beneficiaries will be definitely ascertained as of the trust's creation, subsection (b) recognizes that others may be ascertained in the future as long as this occurs within the applicable perpetuities period. The definite beneficiary requirement does not prevent a settlor from making a disposition in favor of a class of persons. Class designations are valid as long as the membership of the class will be finally determined within the applicable perpetuities period. * * *

Subsection (a)(4) recites standard doctrine that a trust is created only if the trustee has duties to perform. * * * Trustee duties are usually active, but a validating duty may also be passive, implying only that the trustee has an obligation not to interfere with the beneficiary's enjoyment of the trust property. Such passive trusts, while valid under this Code, may be terminable under the enacting jurisdiction's Statute of Uses. * * *

Subsection (a)(5) addresses the doctrine of merger, which, as traditionally stated, provides that a trust is not created if the settlor is the sole trustee and sole beneficiary of *all* beneficial interests. * * * The doctrine of merger is properly applicable only if all beneficial interests, both life interests and remainders, are vested in the same person, whether in the settlor or someone else. An example of a trust to which the doctrine of merger would apply is a trust of which the settlor is sole trustee, sole beneficiary for life, and with the remainder payable to the settlor's probate estate. * * *

Subsection (c) allows a settlor to empower the trustee to select the beneficiaries even if the class from whom the selection may be made cannot be ascertained. Such a provision would fail under traditional doctrine; it is an imperative power with no designated beneficiary capable of enforcement. Such a provision is valid, however, under * * * this Code * * * if there is at least one person who can meet the description. If the trustee does not exercise the power within a reasonable time, the power fails and the property will pass by resulting trust. * * *

Section 403. Trusts Created in Other Jurisdictions.

A trust not created by will is validly created if its creation complies with the law of the jurisdiction in which the trust instrument was executed, or the law of the jurisdiction in which, at the time of creation:

(1)   the settlor was domiciled, had a place of abode, or was a national;

(2)   a trustee was domiciled or had a place of business; or

(3)   any trust property was located.

Section 404. Trust Purposes.

A trust may be created only to the extent its purposes are lawful, not contrary to public policy, and possible to achieve. A trust and its terms must be for the benefit of its beneficiaries.

Comment

* * * A trust with a purpose that is unlawful or against public policy is invalid. Depending on when the violation occurred, the trust may be invalid at its inception or it may become invalid at a later date. The invalidity may also affect only particular provisions. Generally, a trust has a purpose which is illegal if (1) its performance involves the commission of a criminal or tortious act by the trustee; (2) the settlor's purpose in creating the trust was to defraud creditors or others; or (3) the consideration for the creation of the trust was illegal. * * * Purposes violative of public policy include those that tend to encourage criminal or tortious

conduct, that interfere with freedom to marry or encourage divorce, that limit religious freedom, or which are frivolous or capricious. * * *

* * * The general purpose of trusts having identifiable beneficiaries is to benefit those beneficiaries in accordance with their interests as defined in the trust's terms. The requirement of this section that a trust and its terms be for the benefit of its beneficiaries * * * implements this general purpose. While a settlor has considerable latitude in specifying how a particular trust purpose is to be pursued, the administrative and other nondispositive trust terms must reasonably relate to this purpose and not divert the trust property to achieve a trust purpose that is invalid, such as one which is frivolous or capricious. * * *

Section 405. Charitable Purposes; Enforcement.

(a)   A charitable trust may be created for the relief of poverty, the advancement of education or religion, the promotion of health, governmental or municipal purposes, or other purposes the achievement of which is beneficial to the community.

(b)   If the terms of a charitable trust do not indicate a particular charitable purpose or beneficiary, the court may select one or more charitable purposes or beneficiaries. The selection must be consistent with the settlor's intention to the extent it can be ascertained.

(c)   The settlor of a charitable trust, among others, may maintain a proceeding to enforce the trust.

Comment

The required purposes of a charitable trust specified in subsection (a) restate * * * well-established categories of charitable purposes * * * which ultimately derive from the Statute of Charitable Uses, 43 Eliz. I, c.4 (1601). The directive to the courts to validate purposes the achievement of which are beneficial to the community has proved to be remarkably adaptable over the centuries. * * *

Charitable trusts are subject to the restriction in Section 404 that a trust purpose must be legal and not contrary to public policy. This would include trusts that involve invidious discrimination. * * *

Under subsection (b), a trust that states a general charitable purpose does not fail if the settlor neglected to specify a particular charitable purpose or organization to receive distributions. The court may instead validate the trust by specifying particular charitable purposes or recipients, or delegate to the trustee the framing of an appropriate scheme. * * *

Subsection (b) does not apply to the long-established estate planning technique of delegating to the trustee the selection of the charitable purposes or recipients. In that case, judicial intervention to supply particular terms is not necessary to validate the creation of the trust. The necessary terms instead will be supplied by the trustee. * * * Judicial intervention under subsection (b) will become necessary only if the trustee fails to make a selection. * * *

* * * [S]ubsection (c) grants a settlor standing to maintain an action to enforce a charitable trust. The grant of standing to the settlor does not negate the right of the state attorney general or persons with special interests to enforce either the trust or their interests. * * *

Section 406. Creation of Trust Induced by Fraud, Duress, or Undue Influence.

A trust is void to the extent its creation was induced by fraud, duress, or undue influence.

Section 407. Evidence of Oral Trust.

Except as required by a statute other than this [Code], a trust need not be evidenced by a trust instrument, but the creation of an oral trust and its terms may be established only by clear and convincing evidence.

Comment

While it is always advisable for a settlor to reduce a trust to writing, the Uniform Trust Code follows established law in recognizing oral trusts. Such trusts are viewed with caution, however. The requirement of this section that an oral trust can be established only by clear and convincing evidence is a higher standard than is in effect in many States. * * *

Absent some specific statutory provision, such as a provision requiring that transfers of real property be in writing, a trust need not be evidenced by a writing. * * *

Section 408. Trust for Care of Animal.

(a)   A trust may be created to provide for the care of an animal alive during the settlor's lifetime. The trust terminates upon the death of the animal or, if the trust was created to provide for the care of more than one animal alive during the settlor's lifetime, upon the death of the last surviving animal.

(b)   A trust authorized by this section may be enforced by a person appointed in the terms of the trust or, if no person is so appointed, by a person appointed by the court. A person having an interest in the welfare of the animal may request the court to appoint a person to enforce the trust or to remove a person appointed.

(c)   Property of a trust authorized by this section may be applied only to its intended use, except to the extent the court determines that the value of the trust property exceeds the amount required for the intended use. Except as otherwise provided in the terms of the trust, property not required for the intended use must be distributed to the settlor, if then living, otherwise to the settlor's successors in interest.

Comment

This section and the next section of the Code validate so called honorary trusts. Unlike honorary trusts created pursuant to the common law of trusts, which are arguably no more than powers of appointment, the trusts created by this and the next section are valid and enforceable. * * *

This section addresses a particular type of honorary trust, the trust for the care of an animal. * * * A trust for the care of an animal may last for the life of the animal. While the animal will ordinarily be alive on the date the trust is created, an animal may be added as a beneficiary after that date as long as the addition is made prior to the settlor's death. Animals in gestation but not yet born at the time of the trust's creation may also be covered by its terms. A trust authorized by this section may be created to benefit one designated animal or several designated animals.

Subsection (b) addresses enforcement. * * *

* * * If the trust is created for the care of an animal, a person with an interest in the welfare of the animal has standing to petition for an appointment. The person appointed by the court to enforce the trust should also be a person who has exhibited an interest in the animal's welfare. * * *

Subsection (c) addresses the problem of excess funds. If the court determines that the trust property exceeds the amount needed for the intended purpose and that the terms of the trust do not direct the disposition, a resulting trust is ordinarily created in the settlor or settlor's successors in interest. * * *

Section 409. Noncharitable Trust Without Ascertainable Beneficiary.

Except as otherwise provided in Section 408 or by another statute, the following rules apply:

(1)   A trust may be created for a noncharitable purpose without a definite or definitely ascertainable beneficiary or for a noncharitable but otherwise valid purpose to be selected by the trustee. The trust may not be enforced for more than [21] years.

(2)   A trust authorized by this section may be enforced by a person appointed in the terms of the trust or, if no person is so appointed, by a person appointed by the court.

(3)   Property of a trust authorized by this section may be applied only to its intended use, except to the extent the court determines that the value of the trust property exceeds the amount required for the intended use. Except as otherwise provided in the terms of the trust, property not required for the intended use must be distributed to the settlor, if then living, otherwise to the settlor's successors in interest.

Comment

This section authorizes two types of trusts without ascertainable beneficiaries; trusts for general but noncharitable purposes, and trusts for a specific noncharitable purpose other than the care of an animal, on which see Section 408. Examples of trusts for general noncharitable purposes include a bequest of money to be distributed to such objects of benevolence as the trustee might select. Unless such attempted disposition was interpreted as charitable, at common law the disposition was honorary only and did not create a trust. Under this section, however, the disposition is enforceable as a trust for a period of up to 21 years * * * .

The most common example of a trust for a specific noncharitable purpose is a trust for the care of a cemetery plot. The lead-in language to the section recognizes that some special purpose trusts, particularly those for care of cemetery plots, are subject to other statutes. Such legislation will typically endeavor to facilitate perpetual care as opposed to care limited to 21 years as under this section. * * *

Section 410. Modification or Termination of Trust; Proceedings for Approval or Disapproval.

(a) In addition to the methods of termination prescribed by Sections 411 through 414, a trust terminates to the extent the trust is revoked or expires pursuant to its terms, no purpose of the trust remains to be achieved, or the purposes of the trust have become unlawful, contrary to public policy, or impossible to achieve.

(b) A proceeding to approve or disapprove a proposed modification or termination under Sections 411 through 416, or trust combination or division under Section 417, may be commenced by a trustee or beneficiary, [and a proceeding to approve or disapprove a proposed modification or termination under Section 411 may be commenced by the settlor]. The settlor of a charitable trust may maintain a proceeding to modify the trust under Section 413.

Comment

Subsection (a) lists the grounds on which trusts typically terminate. * * *

Withdrawal of the trust property is not an event terminating a trust. The trust remains in existence although the trustee has no duties to perform unless and until property is later contributed to the trust. * * *

Section 411. Modification or Termination of Noncharitable Irrevocable Trust by Consent.

[(a) [A noncharitable irrevocable trust may be modified or terminated upon consent of the settlor and all beneficiaries, even if the modification or termination is inconsistent with a material purpose of the trust.] [If, upon petition, the court finds that the settlor and all beneficiaries consent to the modification or termination of a noncharitable irrevocable trust, the court shall approve the modification or termination even if the modification or termination is inconsistent with a material purpose of the trust.] A settlor's power to consent to a trust's modification or termination may be exercised by an agent under a power of attorney only to the extent expressly authorized by the power of attorney or the terms of the trust; by the settlor's [conservator] with the approval of the court supervising the [conservatorship] if an agent is not so authorized; or by the settlor's [guardian] with the approval of the court supervising the [guardianship] if an agent is not so authorized and a conservator has not been appointed. [This subsection does not apply to irrevocable trusts created before or to revocable trusts that become irrevocable before [the effective date of this [Code] [amendment].]]

(b) A noncharitable irrevocable trust may be terminated upon consent of all of the beneficiaries if the court concludes that continuance of the trust is not necessary to achieve any material purpose of the trust. A noncharitable irrevocable trust may be modified upon consent of all of the beneficiaries if the court concludes that modification is not inconsistent with a material purpose of the trust.

[(c) A spendthrift provision in the terms of the trust is not presumed to constitute a material purpose of the trust.]

(d)   Upon termination of a trust under subsection (a) or (b), the trustee shall distribute the trust property as agreed by the beneficiaries.

(e)   If not all of the beneficiaries consent to a proposed modification or termination of the trust under subsection (a) or (b), the modification or termination may be approved by the court if the court is satisfied that:

> (1)   if all of the beneficiaries had consented, the trust could have been modified or terminated under this section; and

> (2)   the interests of a beneficiary who does not consent will be adequately protected.

Comment

This section describes the circumstances in which termination or modification of a noncharitable irrevocable trust may be compelled by the beneficiaries, with or without the concurrence of the settlor. * * *

Subsection (a) * * * states the test for termination or modification by the beneficiaries with the concurrence of the settlor. * * *

Subsection (b) states the test for termination or modification by unanimous consent of the beneficiaries without the concurrence of the settlor. The rules on trust termination in Subsections (a)–(b) carries forward the *Claflin* rule, first stated in the famous case of Claflin v. Claflin, 20 N.E. 454 (Mass. 1889). * * *

The provisions of Article 3 on representation, virtual representation and the appointment and approval of representatives appointed by the court apply to the determination of whether all beneficiaries have signified consent under this section. The authority to consent on behalf of another person, however, does not include authority to consent over the other person's objection. * * * A consent given by a representative is invalid to the extent there is a conflict of interest between the representative and the person represented. Given this limitation, virtual representation of a beneficiary's interest by another beneficiary pursuant to Section 304 will rarely be available in a trust termination case, although it should be routinely available in cases involving trust modification, such as a grant to the trustee of additional powers. If virtual or other form of representation is unavailable, Section 305 of the Code permits the court to appoint a representative who may give the necessary consent to the proposed modification or termination on behalf of the minor, incapacitated, unborn, or unascertained beneficiary. The ability to use virtual and other forms of representation to consent on a beneficiary's behalf to a trust termination or modification has not traditionally been part of the law, although there are some notable exceptions. * * *

Subsection (a) also addresses the authority of an agent, conservator, or guardian to act on a settlor's behalf. Consistent with Section 602 on revocation or modification of a revocable trust, the section assumes that a settlor, in granting an agent general authority, did not intend for the agent to have authority to consent to the termination or modification of a trust, authority that could be exercised to radically alter the settlor's estate plan. In order for an agent to validly consent to a termination or modification of the settlor's revocable trust, such authority must be expressly conveyed either in the power or in the terms of the trust.

Subsection (a), however, does not impose restrictions on consent by a conservator or guardian, other than prohibiting such action if the settlor is represented by an agent. The section instead leaves the issue of a conservator's or guardian's authority to local law. * * *

* * * Unlike termination by the beneficiaries alone under subsection (b), termination with the concurrence of the settlor does not require a finding that the trust no longer serves a material purpose. No finding of failure of material purpose is required because all parties with a possible interest in the trust's continuation, both the settlor and beneficiaries, agree there is no further need for the trust. * * *

Subsection (b) * * * allows modification by beneficiary action. The beneficiaries may modify any term of the trust if the modification is not inconsistent with a material purpose of the trust. * * * Under the Code, however, Section 706 is the exclusive provision on removal of trustees. Section 706(b)(4) recognizes that a request for removal upon unanimous agreement of the qualified beneficiaries is a factor for the court to consider, but before removing the trustee the court must also find that such action best serves the interests of all the beneficiaries, that removal is not inconsistent with a material purpose of the trust, and that a suitable cotrustee or successor trustee is available. * * *

The requirement that the trust no longer serve a material purpose before it can be terminated by the beneficiaries does not mean that the trust has no remaining function. In order to be material, the purpose remaining to be performed must be of some significance * * * .

Subsection (c) of this section deals with the effect of a spendthrift provision on the right of a beneficiary to concur in a trust termination or modification. * * * Spendthrift terms have sometimes been construed to constitute a material purpose without inquiry into the intention of the particular settlor. * * * This result is troublesome because spendthrift provisions are often added to instruments with little thought. Subsection (c) * * * does not negate the possibility that continuation of a trust to assure spendthrift protection might have been a material purpose of the particular settlor. The question of whether that was the intent of a particular settlor is instead a matter of fact to be determined on the totality of the circumstances.

Subsection (d) recognizes that the beneficiaries' power to compel termination of the trust includes the right to direct how the trust property is to be distributed. While subsection (a) requires the settlor's consent to terminate an irrevocable trust, the settlor does not control the subsequent distribution of the trust property. Once termination has been approved, how the trust property is to be distributed is solely for the beneficiaries to decide.

Subsection (e) * * * addresses situations in which a termination or modification is requested by less than all the beneficiaries, either because a beneficiary objects, the consent of a beneficiary cannot be obtained, or representation is either unavailable or its application uncertain. Subsection (e) allows the court to fashion an appropriate order protecting the interests of the nonconsenting beneficiaries while at the same time permitting the remainder of the trust property to be distributed without restriction. The order of protection for the nonconsenting beneficiaries might include partial continuation of the trust, the purchase of an annuity, or the valuation and cashout of the interest. * * *

Section 412. Modification or Termination Because of Unanticipated Circumstances or Inability to Administer Trust Effectively.

(a) The court may modify the administrative or dispositive terms of a trust or terminate the trust if, because of circumstances not anticipated by the settlor, modification or termination will further the purposes of the trust. To the extent practicable, the modification must be made in accordance with the settlor's probable intention.

(b) The court may modify the administrative terms of a trust if continuation of the trust on its existing terms would be impracticable or wasteful or impair the trust's administration.

(c) Upon termination of a trust under this section, the trustee shall distribute the trust property in a manner consistent with the purposes of the trust.

Comment

This section broadens the court's ability to apply equitable deviation to terminate or modify a trust. Subsection (a) allows a court to modify the dispositive provisions of the trust as well as its administrative terms. For example, modification of the dispositive provisions to increase support of a beneficiary might be appropriate if the beneficiary has become unable to provide for support due to poor health or serious injury. * * * The purpose of the "equitable deviation" authorized by subsection (a) is not to disregard the settlor's intent but to modify inopportune details to effectuate better the settlor's broader purposes. Among other things, equitable deviation may be used to modify administrative or dispositive terms due to the failure to anticipate economic change or the incapacity of a beneficiary. * * * While it is necessary that there be circumstances not anticipated by the settlor before the court may grant relief under subsection (a), the circumstances may have been in existence when the trust was created. * * *

Subsection (b) broadens the court's ability to modify the administrative terms of a trust. The standard under subsection (b) is similar to the standard for applying cy pres to a charitable trust. * * * Subsections (a) and (b) are not mutually exclusive. Many situations justifying modification of administrative terms under subsection (a) will also justify modification under subsection (b). Subsection (b) is also an application of the requirement in Section 404 that a trust and its terms must be for the benefit of its beneficiaries. * * * Although the settlor is granted considerable latitude in defining the purposes of the trust, the principle that a trust have a purpose which is for the benefit of its beneficiaries precludes unreasonable restrictions on the use of trust property. * * *

Upon termination of a trust under this section, subsection (c) requires that the trust be distributed in a manner consistent with the purposes of the trust. As under the doctrine of cy pres, effectuating a distribution consistent with the purposes of the trust requires an examination of what the settlor would have intended had the settlor been aware of the unanticipated circumstances. Typically, such terminating distributions will be made to the qualified beneficiaries, often in proportion to the actuarial value of their interests, although the section does not so prescribe. * * *

Modification under this section, because it does not require beneficiary action, is not precluded by a spendthrift provision.

Section 413. Cy Pres.

(a) Except as otherwise provided in subsection (b), if a particular charitable purpose becomes unlawful, impracticable, impossible to achieve, or wasteful:

(1) the trust does not fail, in whole or in part;

(2) the trust property does not revert to the settlor or the settlor's successors in interest; and

(3) the court may apply cy pres to modify or terminate the trust by directing that the trust property be applied or distributed, in whole or in part, in a manner consistent with the settlor's charitable purposes.

(b) A provision in the terms of a charitable trust that would result in distribution of the trust property to a noncharitable beneficiary prevails over the power of the court under subsection (a) to apply cy pres to modify or terminate the trust only if, when the provision takes effect:

(1) the trust property is to revert to the settlor and the settlor is still living; or

(2) fewer than 21 years have elapsed since the date of the trust's creation.

Comment

Subsection (a) codifies the court's inherent authority to apply cy pres. The power may be applied to modify an administrative or dispositive term. The court may order the trust terminated and distributed to other charitable entities. Partial termination may also be ordered if the trust property is more than sufficient to satisfy the trust's current purposes. Subsection (a) * * * modifies the doctrine of cy pres by presuming that the settlor had a general charitable intent when a particular charitable purpose becomes impossible or impracticable to achieve. Traditional doctrine did not supply that presumption, leaving it to the courts to determine whether the settlor had a general charitable intent. If such an intent is found, the trust property is applied to other charitable purposes. If not, the charitable trust fails. * * * In the great majority of cases the settlor would prefer that the property be used for other charitable purposes. Courts are usually able to find a general charitable purpose to which to apply the property, no matter how vaguely such purpose may have been expressed by the settlor. Under subsection (a), if the particular purpose for which the trust was created becomes impracticable, unlawful, impossible to achieve, or wasteful, the trust does not fail. The court instead must either modify the terms of the trust or distribute the property of the trust in a manner consistent with the settlor's charitable purposes.

The settlor, with one exception, may mandate that the trust property pass to a noncharitable beneficiary upon failure of a particular charitable purpose. Responding to concerns about the clogging of title and other administrative problems caused by remote default provisions upon failure of a charitable purpose, subsection (b) invalidates a gift over to a noncharitable beneficiary upon failure of a particular charitable purpose unless the trust property is to revert to a living settlor or fewer than 21 years have elapsed since the trust's creation. * * *

* * * Pursuant to Sections 405(c) and 410(b), a petition requesting a court to enforce a charitable trust or to apply cy pres may be maintained by a settlor. Such actions can also be maintained by a cotrustee, the state attorney general, or by a person having a special interest in the charitable disposition. * * *

Section 414. Modification or Termination of Uneconomic Trust.

(a)   After notice to the qualified beneficiaries, the trustee of a trust consisting of trust property having a total value less than [$50,000] may terminate the trust if the trustee concludes that the value of the trust property is insufficient to justify the cost of administration.

(b)   The court may modify or terminate a trust or remove the trustee and appoint a different trustee if it determines that the value of the trust property is insufficient to justify the cost of administration.

(c)   Upon termination of a trust under this section, the trustee shall distribute the trust property in a manner consistent with the purposes of the trust.

(d)   This section does not apply to an easement for conservation or preservation.

Comment

Subsection (a) assumes that a trust with a value of $50,000 or less is sufficiently likely to be inefficient to administer that a trustee should be able to terminate it without the expense of a judicial termination proceeding. * * * Because subsection (a) is a default rule, a settlor is free to set a higher or lower figure or to specify different procedures or to prohibit termination without a court order. * * *

Subsection (b) allows the court to modify or terminate a trust if the costs of administration would otherwise be excessive in relation to the size of the trust. The court may terminate a trust under this section even if the settlor has forbidden it. See Section 105(b)(4). Judicial termination under this subsection may be used whether or not the trust is larger or smaller than $50,000.

When considering whether to terminate a trust under either subsection (a) or (b), the trustee or court should consider the purposes of the trust. Termination under this section is not always wise. Even if administrative costs may seem excessive in relation to the size of the trust, protection of the assets from beneficiary mismanagement may indicate that the trust be continued. The court may be able to reduce the costs of administering the trust by appointing a new trustee.

Upon termination of a trust under this section, subsection (c) requires that the trust property be distributed in a manner consistent with the purposes of the trust. * * * Distribution under this section will typically be made to the qualified beneficiaries in proportion to the actuarial value of their interests. * * *

Because termination of a trust under this section is initiated by the trustee or ordered by the court, termination is not precluded by a spendthrift provision.

Section 415. Reformation to Correct Mistakes.

The court may reform the terms of a trust, even if unambiguous, to conform the terms to the settlor's intention if it is proved by clear and convincing evidence that both the settlor's intent and the terms of the trust were affected by a mistake of fact or law, whether in expression or inducement.

Comment

* * * This section applies whether the mistake is one of expression or one of inducement. A mistake of expression occurs when the terms of the trust misstate the settlor's intention, fail to include a term that was intended to be included, or include a term that was not intended to be included. A mistake in the inducement occurs when the terms of the trust accurately reflect what the settlor intended to be included or excluded but this intention was based on a mistake of fact or law. * * * Mistakes of expression are frequently caused by scriveners' errors while mistakes of inducement often trace to errors of the settlor.

Reformation is different from resolving an ambiguity. Resolving an ambiguity involves the interpretation of language already in the instrument. Reformation, on the other hand, may involve the addition of language not originally in the instrument, or the deletion of language originally included by mistake, if necessary to conform the instrument to the settlor's intent. Because reformation may involve the addition of language to the instrument, or the deletion of language that may appear clear on its face, reliance on extrinsic evidence is essential. To guard against the possibility of unreliable or contrived evidence in such circumstance, the higher standard of clear and convincing proof is required. * * *

In determining the settlor's original intent, the court may consider evidence relevant to the settlor's intention even though it contradicts an apparent plain meaning of the text. The objective of the plain meaning rule, to protect against fraudulent testimony, is satisfied by the requirement of clear and convincing proof. * * *

Section 416. Modification to Achieve Settlor's Tax Objectives.

To achieve the settlor's tax objectives, the court may modify the terms of a trust in a manner that is not contrary to the settlor's probable intention. The court may provide that the modification has retroactive effect.

Comment

* * * The modification authorized here allows the terms of the trust to be changed to meet the settlor's tax-saving objective as long as the resulting terms, particularly the dispositive provisions, are not inconsistent with the settlor's probable intent. * * *

Whether a modification made by the court under this section will be recognized under federal tax law is a matter of federal law. Absent specific statutory or regulatory authority, binding recognition is normally given only to modifications made prior to the taxing event, for example, the death of the testator or settlor in the case of the federal estate tax. * * *

Section 417. Combination and Division of Trusts.

After notice to the qualified beneficiaries, a trustee may combine two or more trusts into a single trust or divide a trust into two or more separate trusts, if the result does not impair rights of any beneficiary or adversely affect achievement of the purposes of the trust.

Comment

* * * This section allows a trustee to combine two or more trusts even though their terms are not identical. Typically the trusts to be combined will have been created by different members of the same family and will vary on only insignificant details, such as the presence of different perpetuities savings periods. The more the dispositive provisions of the trusts to be combined differ from each other the more likely it is that a combination would impair some beneficiary's interest, hence the less likely that the combination can be approved. Combining trusts may prompt more efficient trust administration and is sometimes an alternative to terminating an uneconomic trust as authorized by Section 414. Administrative economies promoted by combining trusts include a potential reduction in trustees' fees, particularly if the trustee charges a minimum fee per trust, the ability to file one trust income tax return instead of multiple returns, and the ability to invest a larger pool of capital more effectively. Particularly if the terms of the trust are identical, available administrative economies may suggest that the trustee has a responsibility to pursue a combination. * * *

Division of trusts is often beneficial and, in certain circumstances, almost routine. Division of trusts is frequently undertaken due to a desire to obtain maximum advantage of exemptions available under the federal generation-skipping tax. While the terms of the trusts which result from such a division are identical, the division will permit differing investment objectives to be pursued and allow for discretionary distributions to be made from one trust and not the other. Given the substantial tax benefits often involved, a failure by the trustee to pursue a division might in certain cases be a breach of fiduciary duty. The opposite could also be true if the division is undertaken to increase fees or to fit within the small trust termination provision. * * *

This section authorizes a trustee to divide a trust even if the trusts that result are dissimilar. Conflicts among beneficiaries, including differing investment objectives, often invite such a division, although as in the case with a proposed combination of trusts, the more the terms of the divided trusts diverge from the original plan, the less likely it is that the settlor's purposes would be achieved and that the division could be approved.

This section does not require that a combination or division be approved either by the court or by the beneficiaries. Prudence may dictate, however, that court approval under Section 410 be sought and beneficiary consent obtained whenever the terms of the trusts to be combined or the trusts that will result from a division differ substantially one from the other. * * *

While the consent of the beneficiaries is not necessary before a trustee may combine or divide trusts under this section, advance notice to the qualified beneficiaries of the proposed combination or division is required. * * *

ARTICLE 5

CREDITOR'S CLAIMS; SPENDTHRIFT AND DISCRETIONARY TRUSTS

Section 501. Rights of Beneficiary's Creditor or Assignee.

To the extent a beneficiary's interest is not subject to a spendthrift provision, the court may authorize a creditor or assignee of the beneficiary to reach the beneficiary's interest by attachment of present or future distributions to or for the benefit of the beneficiary or other means. The court may limit the award to such relief as is appropriate under the circumstances.

Comment

This section applies only if the trust does not contain a spendthrift provision or the spendthrift provision does not apply to a particular beneficiary's interest. A settlor may subject to spendthrift protection the interests of certain beneficiaries but not others. A settlor may also subject only a portion of the trust to spendthrift protection such as an interest in the income but not principal. * * *

Absent a valid spendthrift provision, a creditor may ordinarily reach the interest of a beneficiary the same as any other of the beneficiary's assets. * * * This section does not prescribe the procedures ("other means") for reaching a beneficiary's interest or of priority among claimants, leaving those issues to the enacting State's laws on creditor rights. The section does clarify, however, that an order obtained against the trustee, whatever state procedure may have been used, may extend to future distributions whether made directly to the beneficiary or to others for the beneficiary's benefit. By allowing an order to extend to future payments, the need for the creditor periodically to return to court will be reduced.

Because proceedings to satisfy a claim are equitable in nature, the second sentence of this section ratifies the court's discretion to limit the award as appropriate under the circumstances. In exercising its discretion to limit relief, the court may appropriately consider the circumstances of a beneficiary and the beneficiary's family. * * *

Section 502. Spendthrift Provision.

(a)   A spendthrift provision is valid only if it restrains both voluntary and involuntary transfer of a beneficiary's interest.

(b)   A term of a trust providing that the interest of a beneficiary is held subject to a "spendthrift trust," or words of similar import, is sufficient to restrain both voluntary and involuntary transfer of the beneficiary's interest.

(c)   A beneficiary may not transfer an interest in a trust in violation of a valid spendthrift provision and, except as otherwise provided in this [article], a creditor or assignee of the beneficiary may not reach the interest or a distribution by the trustee before its receipt by the beneficiary.

Comment

Under this section, a settlor has the power to restrain the transfer of a beneficiary's interest, regardless of whether the beneficiary has an interest in income, in principal, or in both. Unless one of the exceptions under this article applies, a creditor of the beneficiary is prohibited from attaching a protected interest and may only attempt to collect directly from the beneficiary after payment is made. * * *

For a spendthrift provision to be effective under this Code, it must prohibit both the voluntary and involuntary transfer of the beneficiary's interest, that is, a settlor may not allow a beneficiary to assign while prohibiting a beneficiary's creditor from collecting, and vice versa. * * * A spendthrift provision valid under this Code will also be recognized as valid in a federal bankruptcy proceeding. * * *

Subsection (b) * * * allows a settlor to provide maximum spendthrift protection simply by stating in the instrument that all interests are held subject to a "spendthrift trust" or words of similar effect.

A disclaimer, because it is a refusal to accept ownership of an interest and not a transfer of an interest already owned, is not affected by the presence or absence of a spendthrift provision. * * * Releases and exercises of powers of appointment are also not affected because they are not transfers of property. * * *

A spendthrift provision is ineffective against a beneficial interest retained by the settlor. * * *

A valid spendthrift provision makes it impossible for a beneficiary to make a legally binding transfer, but the trustee may choose to honor the beneficiary's purported assignment. The trustee may recommence distributions to the beneficiary at anytime. The beneficiary, not having made a binding transfer, can withdraw the beneficiary's direction but only as to future payments. * * *

Section 503. Exceptions to Spendthrift Provision.

(a)   In this section, "child" includes any person for whom an order or judgment for child support has been entered in this or another State.

(b)   A spendthrift provision is unenforceable against:

(1)   a beneficiary's child, spouse, or former spouse who has a judgment or court order against the beneficiary for support or maintenance;

(2)   a judgment creditor who has provided services for the protection of a beneficiary's interest in the trust; and

(3)   a claim of this State or the United States to the extent a statute of this State or federal law so provides.

(c)   A claimant against which a spendthrift provision cannot be enforced may obtain from a court an order attaching present or future distributions to or for the benefit of the beneficiary. The court may limit the award to such relief as is appropriate under the circumstances.

Comment

This section exempts the claims of certain categories of creditors from the effects of a spendthrift restriction and specifies the remedies such exemption creditors may take to satisfy their claims.

* * * [S]ubsection (b)(1) [provides an exception] for judgments or orders to support a beneficiary's child or current or former spouse * * * . The effect of this exception is to permit the claimant for unpaid support to attach present or future distributions that would otherwise be made to the beneficiary. Distributions subject to attachment include distributions required by the express terms of the trust, such as mandatory payments of income, and distributions the trustee has otherwise decided to make, such as through the exercise of discretion. Subsection (b)(1), unlike Section 504, does not authorize the spousal or child claimant to compel a distribution from the trust. * * *

The exception in subsection (b)(2) for a judgment creditor who has provided services for the protection of a beneficiary's interest in the trust * * * allows a beneficiary of modest means to overcome an obstacle preventing the beneficiary's obtaining services essential to the protection or enforcement of the beneficiary's rights under the trust. * * *

Subsection (b)(3) * * * exempts certain governmental claims from a spendthrift restriction. Federal preemption guarantees that certain federal claims, such as claims by the Internal Revenue Service, may bypass a spendthrift provision no matter what this Code might say. * * * Regarding claims by state governments, this subsection recognizes that States take a variety of approaches with respect to collection, depending on whether the claim is for unpaid taxes, for care provided at an institution, or for other charges. Acknowledging this diversity, subsection (c) does not prescribe a rule, but refers to other statutes of the State on whether particular claims are subject to or exempted from spendthrift provisions.

* * * [T]his Code does not create an exception to the spendthrift restriction for creditors who have furnished necessary services or supplies to the beneficiary. Most of these cases involve claims by governmental entities, which the drafters concluded are better handled by the enactment of special legislation as authorized by subsection (b)(3). The drafters also declined to create an exception for tort claimants. * * *

Subsection (c) provides that the only remedy available to an exception creditor is attachment of present or future distributions [to or for the benefit of the beneficiary]. Depending on other creditor law of the state, additional remedies may be available should a beneficiary's interest not be subject to a spendthrift provision. Section 501, which applies in such situations, provides that the creditor may reach the beneficiary's interest under that section by attachment or "other means." * * *

Section 504. Discretionary Trusts; Effect of Standard.

(a) In this section, "child" includes any person for whom an order or judgment for child support has been entered in this or another State.

(b) Except as otherwise provided in subsection (c), whether or not a trust contains a spendthrift provision, a creditor of a beneficiary may not compel a distribution that is subject to the trustee's discretion, even if:

(1) the discretion is expressed in the form of a standard of distribution; or

(2) the trustee has abused the discretion.

(c) To the extent a trustee has not complied with a standard of distribution or has abused a discretion:

(1) a distribution may be ordered by the court to satisfy a judgment or court order against the beneficiary for support or maintenance of the beneficiary's child, spouse, or former spouse; and

(2) the court shall direct the trustee to pay to the child, spouse, or former spouse such amount as is equitable under the circumstances but not more than the amount the trustee would have been required to distribute to or for the benefit of the beneficiary had the trustee complied with the standard or not abused the discretion.

(d) This section does not limit the right of a beneficiary to maintain a judicial proceeding against a trustee for an abuse of discretion or failure to comply with a standard for distribution.

(e) If the trustee's or cotrustee's discretion to make distributions for the trustee's or cotrustee's own benefit is limited by an ascertainable standard, a creditor may not reach or compel distribution of the beneficial interest except to the extent the interest would be subject to the creditor's claim were the beneficiary not acting as trustee or cotrustee.

Comment

This section addresses the ability of a beneficiary's creditor to reach the beneficiary's discretionary trust interest, whether or not the exercise of the trustee's discretion is subject to a standard. This section * * * eliminates the distinction between discretionary and support trusts, unifying the rules for all trusts fitting within either of the former categories. * * * By eliminating this distinction, the rights of a creditor are the same whether the distribution standard is discretionary, subject to a standard, or both. Other than for a claim by a child, spouse or former spouse, a beneficiary's creditor may not reach the beneficiary's interest. Eliminating this distinction affects only the rights of creditors. The [effect] of this change is limited to the rights of creditors. It does not affect the rights of a beneficiary to compel a distribution. Whether the trustee has a duty in a given situation to make a distribution depends on factors such as the breadth of the discretion granted and whether the terms of the trust include a support or other standard. * * *

Subsection (b), which establishes the general rule, forbids a creditor from compelling a distribution from the trust, even if the trustee has failed to comply with the standard of distribution or has abused a discretion. Under subsection (d), the power to force a distribution due to an abuse of discretion or failure to comply with a standard belongs solely to the beneficiary. * * *

Subsection (c) creates an exception for support claims of a child, spouse, or former spouse who has a judgment or order against a beneficiary for support or maintenance. While a creditor of a beneficiary generally may not assert that a trustee has abused a discretion or failed to comply with a standard of distribution, such a claim may be asserted by the beneficiary's child, spouse, or former spouse enforcing a judgment or court order against the beneficiary for unpaid support or maintenance. The court must direct the trustee to pay the child, spouse or former spouse such amount as is equitable under the circumstances but not in excess of the amount the trustee was otherwise required to distribute to or for the benefit of the beneficiary. Before fixing this amount, the court having jurisdiction over the trust should consider that in setting the respective support award, the family court has already considered the respective needs and assets of the family. The Uniform Trust Code does not prescribe a particular procedural method for enforcing a judgment or order against the trust, leaving that matter to local collection law.

Section 505. Creditor's Claim Against Settlor.

(a)   Whether or not the terms of a trust contain a spendthrift provision, the following rules apply:

    (1)   During the lifetime of the settlor, the property of a revocable trust is subject to claims of the settlor's creditors.

    (2)   With respect to an irrevocable trust, a creditor or assignee of the settlor may reach the maximum amount that can be distributed to or for the settlor's benefit. If a trust has more than one settlor, the amount the creditor or assignee of a particular settlor may reach may not exceed the settlor's interest in the portion of the trust attributable to that settlor's contribution.

    (3)   After the death of a settlor, and subject to the settlor's right to direct the source from which liabilities will be paid, the property of a trust that was revocable at the settlor's death is subject to claims of the settlor's creditors, costs of administration of the settlor's estate, the expenses of the settlor's funeral and disposal of remains, and [statutory allowances] to a surviving spouse and children to the extent the settlor's probate estate is inadequate to satisfy those claims, costs, expenses, and [allowances].

(b)   For purposes of this section:

    (1)   during the period the power may be exercised, the holder of a power of withdrawal is treated in the same manner as the settlor of a revocable trust to the extent of the property subject to the power; and

    (2)   upon the lapse, release, or waiver of the power, the holder is treated as the settlor of the trust only to the extent the value of the property affected by the lapse, release, or waiver exceeds the greater of the amount specified in Section 2041(b)(2) or 2514(e) of the Internal Revenue Code of 1986, or Section 2503(b) of the Internal Revenue Code of 1986, in each case as in effect on [the effective date of this [Code]] [, or as later amended].

Comment

Subsection (a)(1) states what is now a well accepted conclusion, that a revocable trust is subject to the claims of the settlor's creditors while the settlor is living. * * * Such claims were not allowed at common law, however. * * * Because a settlor usually also retains a beneficial interest that a creditor may reach under subsection (a)(2), the common law rule, were it retained in this Code, would be of little significance. * * *

Subsection (a)(2) * * * follows traditional doctrine in providing that a settlor who is also a beneficiary may not use the trust as a shield against the settlor's creditors. * * * Under the Code, whether the trust contains a spendthrift provision or not, a creditor of the settlor may reach the maximum amount that the trustee could have paid to the settlor-beneficiary. If the trustee has discretion to distribute the entire income and principal to the settlor, the effect of this subsection is to place the settlor's creditors in the same position as if the trust had not been created. * * *

This section does not address possible rights against a settlor who was insolvent at the time of the trust's creation or was rendered insolvent by the transfer of property to the trust. This subject is instead left to the State's law on fraudulent transfers. A transfer to the trust by an insolvent settlor might also constitute a voidable preference under federal bankruptcy law.

Subsection (a)(3) recognizes that a revocable trust is usually employed as a will substitute. As such, the trust assets, following the death of the settlor, should be subject to the settlor's debts and other charges. However, in accordance with traditional doctrine, the assets of the settlor's probate estate must normally first be exhausted before the assets of the revocable trust can be reached. This section does not attempt to address the procedural issues raised by the need first to exhaust the decedent's probate estate before reaching the assets of the revocable trust. Nor does this section address the priority of creditor claims or liability of the decedent's other nonprobate assets for the decedent's debts and other charges. * * *

Subsection (b)(1) treats a power of withdrawal as the equivalent of a power of revocation because the two powers are functionally identical. * * * If the power is unlimited, the property subject to the power will be fully subject to the claims of the power holder's creditors, the same as the power holder's other assets. If the power holder retains the power until death, the property subject to the power may be liable for claims and statutory allowances to the extent the power holder's probate estate is insufficient to satisfy those claims and allowances. For powers limited either in time or amount, such as a right to withdraw a $10,000 annual exclusion contribution within 30 days, this subsection would limit the creditor to the $10,000 contribution and require the creditor to take action prior to the expiration of the 30-day period.

Upon the lapse, release, or waiver of a power of withdrawal, the property formerly subject to the power will normally be subject to the claims of the power holder's creditors and assignees the same as if the power holder were the settlor of a now irrevocable trust. Pursuant to subsection (a)(2), a creditor or assignee of the power holder generally may reach the power holder's entire beneficial interest in the trust, whether or not distribution is subject to the trustee's discretion. However, * * * subsection (b)(2) creates an exception for trust property which was subject to a *Crummey* or five and five power. Upon the lapse, release, or waiver of a power of withdrawal, the holder is treated as the settlor of the trust only to the extent the value of the property subject to the power at the time of the lapse, release, or waiver exceeded the greater of the amounts specified in IRC §§ 2041(b)(2) or 2514(e) [greater of 5% or $5,000], or IRC § 2503(b) [$10,000 in 2001]. * * *

Section 506. Overdue Distribution.

(a) In this section, "mandatory distribution" means a distribution of income or principal which the trustee is required to make to a beneficiary under the terms of the trust, including a distribution upon termination of the trust. The term does not include a distribution subject to the exercise of the trustee's discretion even if (1) the discretion is expressed in the form of a standard of distribution, or (2) the terms of the trust authorizing a distribution couple language of discretion with language of direction.

(b) Whether or not a trust contains a spendthrift provision, a creditor or assignee of a beneficiary may reach a mandatory distribution of income or principal, including a distribution upon termination of the trust, if the trustee has not made the distribution to the beneficiary within a reasonable time after the mandated distribution date.

Comment

The effect of a spendthrift provision is generally to insulate totally a beneficiary's interest until a distribution is made and received by the beneficiary. * * * But this section, along with several other sections in this article, recognizes exceptions to this general rule. Whether a trust contains a spendthrift provision or not, a trustee should not be able to avoid creditor claims against a beneficiary by refusing to make a distribution required to be made by the express terms of the trust. On the other hand, a spendthrift provision would become largely a nullity were a beneficiary's creditors able to attach all required payments as soon as they became due. This section reflects a compromise between these two competing principles. A creditor can reach a mandatory distribution, including a distribution upon termination, if the trustee has failed to make the payment within a reasonable time after the required distribution date. Following this reasonable period, payments mandated by the express terms of the trust are in effect being held by the trustee as agent for the beneficiary and should be treated as part of the beneficiary's personal assets. * * *

Section 507. Personal Obligations of Trustee.

Trust property is not subject to personal obligations of the trustee, even if the trustee becomes insolvent or bankrupt.

Comment

Because the beneficiaries of the trust hold the beneficial interest in the trust property and the trustee holds only legal title without the benefits of ownership, the creditors of the trustee have only a personal claim against the trustee. * * * Similarly, a personal creditor of the trustee who attaches trust property to satisfy the debt does not acquire title as a bona fide purchaser even if the creditor is unaware of the trust.

* * * The protection afforded by this section is consistent with that provided by the Bankruptcy Code. Property in which the trustee holds legal title as trustee is not part of the trustee's bankruptcy estate. * * *

ARTICLE 6

REVOCABLE TRUSTS

Section 601. Capacity of Settlor of Revocable Trust.

The capacity required to create, amend, revoke, or add property to a revocable trust, or to direct the actions of the trustee of a revocable trust, is the same as that required to make a will.

Comment

* * * The revocable trust is used primarily as a will substitute, with its key provision being the determination of the persons to receive the trust property upon the settlor's death. To solidify the use of the revocable trust as a device for transferring property at death, the settlor usually also executes a pourover will. The use of a pourover will assures that property not transferred to the trust during life will be combined with the property the settlor did manage to convey. Given this primary use of the revocable trust as a device for disposing of property at death, the capacity standard for wills rather than that for lifetime gifts should apply. The application of the capacity standard for wills does not mean that the revocable trust must be executed with the formalities of a will. * * *

Section 602. Revocation or Amendment of Revocable Trust.

(a)   Unless the terms of a trust expressly provide that the trust is irrevocable, the settlor may revoke or amend the trust. This subsection does not apply to a trust created under an instrument executed before [the effective date of this [Code]].

(b)   If a revocable trust is created or funded by more than one settlor:

(1)   to the extent the trust consists of community property, the trust may be revoked by either spouse acting alone but may be amended only by joint action of both spouses;

(2)   to the extent the trust consists of property other than community property, each settlor may revoke or amend the trust with regard [to] the portion of the trust property attributable to that settlor's contribution; and

(3)   upon the revocation or amendment of the trust by fewer than all of the settlors, the trustee shall promptly notify the other settlors of the revocation or amendment.

(c)   The settlor may revoke or amend a revocable trust:

(1)   by substantial compliance with a method provided in the terms of the trust; or

(2)   if the terms of the trust do not provide a method or the method provided in the terms is not expressly made exclusive, by:

(A)   a later will or codicil that expressly refers to the trust or specifically devises property that would otherwise have passed according to the terms of the trust; or

(B)   any other method manifesting clear and convincing evidence of the settlor's intent.

(d)   Upon revocation of a revocable trust, the trustee shall deliver the trust property as the settlor directs.

(e)   A settlor's powers with respect to revocation, amendment, or distribution of trust property may be exercised by an agent under a power of attorney only to the extent expressly authorized by the terms of the trust or the power.

(f)   A [conservator] of the settlor or, if no [conservator] has been appointed, a [guardian] of the settlor may exercise a settlor's powers with respect to revocation, amendment, or distribution of trust property only with the approval of the court supervising the [conservatorship] or [guardianship].

(g)   A trustee who does not know that a trust has been revoked or amended is not liable to the settlor or settlor's successors in interest for distributions made and other actions taken on the assumption that the trust had not been amended or revoked.

Comment

Subsection (a), which provides that a settlor may revoke or modify a trust unless the terms of the trust expressly state that the trust is irrevocable, changes the common law. * * * This Code presumes revocability when the instrument is silent because the instrument was likely drafted by a nonprofessional, who intended the trust as a will substitute. * * * Because professional drafters habitually spell out whether or not a trust is revocable, subsection (a) will have limited application.

A power of revocation includes the power to amend. An unrestricted power to amend may also include the power to revoke a trust. * * *

Subsection (b) * * * provides default rules for revocation or amendment of a trust having several settlors. The settlor's authority to revoke or modify the trust depends on whether the trust contains community property. To the extent the trust contains community property, the trust may be revoked by either spouse acting alone but may be amended only by joint action of both spouses. The purpose of this provision, and the reason for the use of joint trusts in community property states, is to preserve the community character of property transferred to the trust. While community property does not prevail in a majority of states, contributions of community property to trusts created in noncommunity property states does occur. This is due to the mobility of settlors, and the fact that community property retains its community character when a couple move from a community to a noncommunity state. * * *

With respect to separate property contributed to the trust, or all property of the trust if none of the trust property consists of community property, subsection (b) provides that each settlor may revoke or amend the trust as to the portion of the trust contributed by that settlor. The inclusion of a rule for contributions of separate property does not mean that the drafters of this Code concluded that the use of joint trusts should be encouraged. The rule is included because of the widespread use of joint trusts in noncommunity property states in recent years. Due to the desire to preserve the community character of trust property, joint trusts are a necessity in community property states. Unless community property will be contributed to the trust, no similarly important reason exists for the creation of a joint trust in a noncommunity property state. Joint trusts are often poorly drafted, confusing the dispositive provisions of the respective settlors. Their use can also lead to unintended tax consequences. * * *

Subsection (b) does not address the many technical issues that can arise in determining the settlors' proportionate contribution to a joint trust. Most problematic are contributions of jointly-owned property. In the case of joint tenancies in real estate, each spouse would presumably be treated as having made an equal contribution because of the right to sever the interest and convert it into a tenancy in common. This is in contrast to joint accounts in financial institutions, ownership of which in most States is based not on fractional interest but on actual dollar contribution. * * * Most difficult may be determining a contribution rule for entireties property. * * *

Subsection (c) * * * specifies the method of revocation and amendment. Revocation of a trust differs fundamentally from revocation of a will. Revocation of a will, because a will is not effective until death, cannot affect an existing fiduciary relationship. With a trust, however, because a revocation will terminate an already existing fiduciary relationship, there is a need to protect a trustee who might act without knowledge that the trust has been revoked. There is also a need to protect trustees against the risk that they will misperceive the settlor's intent and mistakenly assume that an informal document or communication constitutes a revocation when that was not in fact the settlor's intent. To protect trustees against these risks, drafters habitually insert provisions providing that a revocable trust may be revoked only by delivery to the trustee of a formal revoking document. Some courts require strict compliance with the stated formalities. Other courts, recognizing that the formalities were inserted primarily for the trustee's and not the settlor's benefit, will accept other methods of revocation as long as the settlor's intent is clear. * * *

This Code tries to effectuate the settlor's intent to the maximum extent possible while at the same time protecting a trustee against inadvertent liability. While notice to the trustee of a revocation is good practice, this section does not make the giving of such notice a prerequisite to a trust's revocation. To protect a trustee who has not been notified of a revocation or amendment, subsection (g) provides that a trustee who does not know that a trust has been revoked or amended is not liable to the settlor or settlor's successors in interest for distributions made and other actions taken on the assumption that the trust, as unamended, was still in effect. However, to honor the settlor's intent, subsection (c) generally honors a settlor's clear expression of intent even if inconsistent with stated formalities in the terms of the trust.

Under subsection (c), the settlor may revoke or amend a revocable trust by substantial compliance with the method specified in the terms of the trust or by a later will or codicil or any other method manifesting clear and convincing evidence of the settlor's intent. Only if the method specified in the terms of the trust is made exclusive is use of the other methods prohibited. Even then, a failure to comply with a technical requirement, such as required notarization, may be excused as long as compliance with the method specified in the terms of the trust is otherwise substantial.

While revocation of a trust will ordinarily continue to be accomplished by signing and delivering a written document to the trustee, other methods, such as a physical act or an oral statement coupled with a withdrawal of the property, might also demonstrate the necessary intent. These less formal methods, because they provide less reliable indicia of intent, will often be insufficient, however. The method specified in the terms of the trust is a reliable safe harbor and should be followed whenever possible.

Revocation or amendment by will is mentioned in subsection (c) not to encourage the practice but to make clear that it is not precluded by omission. * * * Situations do arise, particularly in death-bed cases, where revocation by will may be the only practicable method. In such cases, a will, a solemn document executed with a high level of formality, may be the most reliable method for expressing intent. A revocation in a will ordinarily becomes effective only upon probate of the will following the testator's death. * * *

A residuary clause in a will disposing of the estate differently than the trust is alone insufficient to revoke or amend a trust. The provision in the will must either be express or the will must dispose of specific assets contrary to the terms of the trust. The substantial body of law on revocation of Totten trusts by will offers helpful guidance. * * *

Subsection (e) * * * authorizes an agent under a power of attorney to revoke or modify a revocable trust only to the extent the terms of the trust or power of attorney expressly so permit. An express provision is required because most settlors usually intend that the revocable trust, and not the power of attorney, function as the settlor's principal property management device. The power of attorney is usually intended as a backup for assets not transferred to the revocable trust or to address specific topics, such as the power to sign tax returns or apply for government benefits, which may be beyond the authority of a trustee or are not customarily granted to a trustee. * * *

Many state conservatorship statutes authorize a conservator to exercise the settlor's power of revocation with the prior approval of the court supervising the conservatorship. * * * Subsection (f) ratifies this practice. Under the Code, a conservator may exercise a settlor's power of revocation, amendment, or right to withdraw trust property upon approval of the court supervising the conservatorship. Because a settlor often creates a revocable trust for the very purpose of avoiding conservatorship, this power should be exercised by the court reluctantly. Settlors concerned about revocation by a conservator may wish to deny a conservator a power to revoke. However, while such a provision in the terms of the trust is entitled to considerable weight, the court may override the restriction if it concludes that the action is necessary in the interests of justice. * * *

Section 603. Settlor's Powers; Powers of Withdrawal.

(a)   To the extent a trust is revocable by a settlor, a trustee may follow a direction of the settlor that is contrary to the terms of the trust. To the extent a trust is revocable by a settlor in conjunction with a person other than a trustee or person holding an adverse interest, the trustee may follow a direction from the settlor and the other person holding the power to revoke even if the direction is contrary to the terms of the trust.

(b)   To the extent a trust is revocable [and the settlor has capacity to revoke the trust], rights of the beneficiaries are subject to the control of, and the duties of the trustee are owed exclusively to, the settlor.

(c)   During the period the power may be exercised, the holder of a power of withdrawal has the rights of a settlor of a revocable trust under this section to the extent of the property subject to the power.

Comment

This section recognizes that the settlor of a revocable trust is in control of the trust and should have the right to enforce the trust. Pursuant to this section, the duty under Section 813 to inform and report to beneficiaries is owed to the settlor of a revocable trust as long as the settlor has capacity.

If the settlor loses capacity, subsection (b) no longer applies, with the consequence that the rights of the beneficiaries are no longer subject to the settlor's control. The beneficiaries are then entitled to request information concerning the trust and the trustee must provide the beneficiaries with annual trustee reports and whatever other information may be required under Section 813. However, because this section may be freely overridden in the terms of the trust, a settlor is free to deny the beneficiaries these rights, even to the point of directing the trustee not to inform them of the existence of the trust. Also, should an incapacitated settlor later regain capacity, the beneficiaries' rights will again be subject to the settlor's control.

Typically, the settlor of a revocable trust will also be the sole or primary beneficiary of the trust, and the settlor has control over whether to take action against a trustee for breach of trust. Upon the settlor's incapacity, any right of action the settlor-trustee may have against the trustee for breach of trust occurring while the settlor had capacity will pass to the settlor's agent or conservator, who would succeed to the settlor's right to have property restored to the trust. Following the death or incapacity of the settlor, the beneficiaries would have a right to maintain an action against a trustee for breach of trust. However, with respect to actions occurring prior to the settlor's death or incapacity, an action by the beneficiaries could be barred by the settlor's consent or by other events such as approval of the action by a successor trustee. * * *

Subsection (c) makes clear that a holder of a power of withdrawal has the same powers over the trust as the settlor of a revocable trust. Equal treatment is warranted due to the holder's equivalent power to control the trust. * * *

Section 604. Limitation on Action Contesting Validity of Revocable Trust; Distribution of Trust Property.

(a)   A person may commence a judicial proceeding to contest the validity of a trust that was revocable at the settlor's death within the earlier of:

(1)   [three] years after the settlor's death; or

(2)   [120] days after the trustee sent the person a copy of the trust instrument and a notice informing the person of the trust's existence, of the trustee's name and address, and of the time allowed for commencing a proceeding.

(b)   Upon the death of the settlor of a trust that was revocable at the settlor's death, the trustee may proceed to distribute the trust property in accordance with the terms of the trust. The trustee is not subject to liability for doing so unless:

(1)   the trustee knows of a pending judicial proceeding contesting the validity of the trust; or

(2)   a potential contestant has notified the trustee of a possible judicial proceeding to contest the trust and a judicial proceeding is commenced within 60 days after the contestant sent the notification.

(c)   A beneficiary of a trust that is determined to have been invalid is liable to return any distribution received.

Comment

This section provides finality to the question of when a contest of a revocable trust may be brought. The section is designed to allow an adequate time in which to bring a contest while at the same time permitting the expeditious distribution of the trust property following the settlor's death.

A trust can be contested on a variety of grounds. For example, the contestant may allege that no trust was created due to lack of intent to create a trust or lack of capacity (see Section 402), that undue influence, duress, or fraud was involved in the trust's creation (see Section 406), or that the trust had been revoked or modified (see Section 602). A "contest" is an action to invalidate all or part of the terms of the trust or of property transfers to the trustee. An action against a beneficiary or other person for intentional interference with an inheritance or gift, not being a contest, is not subject to this section. * * * Nor does this section preclude an action to determine the validity of a trust that is brought during the settlor's lifetime, such as a petition for a declaratory judgment, if such action is authorized by other law. * * *

This section applies only to a revocable trust that becomes irrevocable by reason of the settlor's death. A trust that became irrevocable by reason of the settlor's lifetime release of the power to revoke is outside its scope. A revocable trust does not become irrevocable upon a settlor's loss of capacity. Pursuant to Section 602, the power to revoke may be exercised by the settlor's agent, conservator, or guardian, or personally by the settlor if the settlor regains capacity.

Subsection (a) specifies a time limit on when a contest can be brought. A contest is barred upon the first to occur of two possible events. The maximum possible time for bringing a contest is three years from the settlor's death. This should provide potential contestants with ample time in which to determine whether they have an interest that will be affected by the trust, even if formal notice of the trust is lacking. * * *

A trustee who wishes to shorten the contest period may do so by giving notice. * * * [S]ubsection (a)(2) bars a contest by a potential contestant 120 days after the date the trustee sent that person a copy of the trust instrument and informed the person of the trust's existence, of the trustee's name and address, and of the time allowed for commencing a contest. * * *

Because only a small minority of trusts are actually contested, trustees should not be restrained from making distributions because of concern about possible liability should a contest later be filed. Absent a protective statute, a trustee is ordinarily absolutely liable for misdelivery of the trust assets, even if the trustee reasonably believed that the distribution was proper. * * * Subsection (b) addresses liability concerns by allowing the trustee, upon the settlor's death, to proceed expeditiously to distribute the trust property. The trustee may distribute the trust property in accordance with the terms of the trust until and unless the trustee receives notice of a pending judicial proceeding contesting the validity of the trust, or until notified by a potential contestant of a possible contest, followed by its filing within 60 days.

Even though a distribution in compliance with subsection (b) discharges the trustee from potential liability, subsection (c) makes the beneficiaries of what later turns out to have been an invalid trust liable to return any distribution received. Issues as to whether the distribution must be returned with interest, or with income earned or profit made are not addressed in this section but are left to the law of restitution.

For purposes of notices under this section, the substitute representation principles of Article 3 are applicable. * * *

ARTICLE 7

OFFICE OF TRUSTEE

Section 701. Accepting or Declining Trusteeship.

(a)   Except as otherwise provided in subsection (c), a person designated as trustee accepts the trusteeship:

(1)   by substantially complying with a method of acceptance provided in the terms of the trust; or

(2)   if the terms of the trust do not provide a method or the method provided in the terms is not expressly made exclusive, by accepting delivery of the trust property, exercising powers or performing duties as trustee, or otherwise indicating acceptance of the trusteeship.

(b)   A person designated as trustee who has not yet accepted the trusteeship may reject the trusteeship. A designated trustee who does not accept the trusteeship within a reasonable time after knowing of the designation is deemed to have rejected the trusteeship.

(c)   A person designated as trustee, without accepting the trusteeship, may:

(1)   act to preserve the trust property if, within a reasonable time after acting, the person sends a rejection of the trusteeship to the settlor or, if the settlor is dead or lacks capacity, to a qualified beneficiary; and

(2)   inspect or investigate trust property to determine potential liability under environmental or other law or for any other purpose.

Comment

This section, which specifies the requirements for a valid acceptance of the trusteeship, implicates many of the same issues that arise in determining whether a trust has been revoked. Consequently, the two provisions track each other closely. * * * Procedures specified in the terms of the trust are recognized, but only substantial, not literal compliance is required. A failure to meet technical requirements, such as notarization of the trustee's signature, does not result in a failure to accept. Ordinarily, the trustee will indicate acceptance by signing the trust instrument or signing a separate written instrument. However, this section validates any other method demonstrating the necessary intent, such as by knowingly exercising trustee powers, unless the terms of the trust make the specified method exclusive. This section also does not preclude an acceptance by estoppel. * * *

To avoid the inaction that can result if the person designated as trustee fails to communicate a decision either to accept or to reject the trusteeship, subsection (b) provides that a failure to accept within a reasonable time constitutes a rejection of the trusteeship. What will constitute a reasonable time depends on the facts and circumstances of the particular case. A major consideration is possible harm that might occur if a vacancy in a trusteeship is not filled in a timely manner. A trustee's rejection normally precludes a later acceptance but does not cause the trust to fail. * * *

A person designated as trustee who decides not to accept the trusteeship need not provide a formal rejection, but a clear and early communication is recommended. The appropriate recipient of the rejection depends upon the circumstances. Ordinarily, it would be appropriate to communicate the rejection to the person who informed the designee of the proposed trusteeship. If judicial proceedings involving the trust are pending, the rejection could be filed with the court. In the case of a person named as trustee of a revocable trust, it would be appropriate to communicate the rejection to the settlor. In any event, it would be best to inform a beneficiary with a significant interest in the trust because that beneficiary might be more motivated than others to seek appointment of a new trustee.

Subsection (c)(1) makes clear that a nominated trustee may act expeditiously to protect the trust property without being considered to have accepted the trusteeship. However, upon conclusion of the intervention, the nominated trustee must send a rejection of office to the settlor, if living and competent, otherwise to a qualified beneficiary.

Because of the potential liability that can inhere in trusteeship, subsection (c)(2) allows a person designated as trustee to inspect the trust property without accepting the trusteeship. The condition of real property is a particular concern, including possible tort liability for the condition of the premises or liability for violation of state or federal environmental laws * * * .

Section 702. Trustee's Bond.

(a) A trustee shall give bond to secure performance of the trustee's duties only if the court finds that a bond is needed to protect the interests of the beneficiaries or is required by the terms of the trust and the court has not dispensed with the requirement.

(b) The court may specify the amount of a bond, its liabilities, and whether sureties are necessary. The court may modify or terminate a bond at any time.

[(c) A regulated financial-service institution qualified to do trust business in this State need not give bond, even if required by the terms of the trust.]

Comment

* * * Because a bond is required only if the terms of the trust require bond or a bond is found by the court to be necessary to protect the interests of beneficiaries, bond should rarely be required under this Code.

Despite the ability of the court pursuant to Section 105(b)(6) to override a term of the trust waiving bond, the court should order bond in such cases only for good reasons. Similarly, the court should rarely dispense with bond if the settlor directed that the trustee give bond. * * *

Section 703. Cotrustees.

(a) Cotrustees who are unable to reach a unanimous decision may act by majority decision.

(b) If a vacancy occurs in a cotrusteeship, the remaining cotrustees may act for the trust.

(c) [Subject to [Uniform Directed Trust Act Section 12], a][A] cotrustee must participate in the performance of a trustee's function unless the cotrustee is unavailable to perform the function because of absence, illness, disqualification under other law, or other temporary incapacity or the cotrustee has properly delegated the performance of the function to another trustee.

(d) If a cotrustee is unavailable to perform duties because of absence, illness, disqualification under other law, or other temporary incapacity, and prompt action is necessary to achieve the purposes of the trust or to avoid injury to the trust property, the remaining cotrustee or a majority of the remaining cotrustees may act for the trust.

(e) A trustee may not delegate to a cotrustee the performance of a function the settlor reasonably expected the trustees to perform jointly. Unless a delegation was irrevocable, a trustee may revoke a delegation previously made.

(f) Except as otherwise provided in subsection (g), a trustee who does not join in an action of another trustee is not liable for the action.

(g) [Subject to [Uniform Directed Trust Act Section 12], each][Each] trustee shall exercise reasonable care to:

(1) prevent a cotrustee from committing a serious breach of trust; and

(2) compel a cotrustee to redress a serious breach of trust.

(h) A dissenting trustee who joins in an action at the direction of the majority of the trustees and who notified any cotrustee of the dissent at or before the time of the action is not liable for the action unless the action is a serious breach of trust.

Comment

* * * Cotrustees are appointed for a variety of reasons. Having multiple decision-makers serves as a safeguard against eccentricity or misconduct. Cotrustees are often appointed to gain the advantage of differing skills, perhaps a financial institution for its permanence and professional skills, and a family member to maintain a personal connection with the beneficiaries. On other occasions, cotrustees are appointed to make certain that all family lines are represented in the trust's management.

Cotrusteeship should not be called for without careful reflection. Division of responsibility among cotrustees is often confused, the accountability of any individual trustee is uncertain, obtaining consent of all trustees can be burdensome, and unless an odd number of trustees is named deadlocks requiring court resolution can occur. Potential problems can be reduced by addressing division of responsibilities in the terms of the trust. Like the other sections of this article, this section is freely subject to modification in the terms of the trust. * * *

Subsection (a) * * * rejects the common law rule * * * requiring unanimity among the trustees of a private trust. * * *

Under subsection (b), a majority of the remaining trustees may act for the trust when a vacancy occurs in a cotrusteeship. * * *

Pursuant to subsection (c), a cotrustee must participate in the performance of a trustee function unless the cotrustee has properly delegated performance to another cotrustee, or the cotrustee is unable to participate due to temporary incapacity or disqualification under other law. Other laws under which a cotrustee might be disqualified include federal securities law and the ERISA prohibited transactions rules. Subsection (d) authorizes a cotrustee to assume some or all of the functions of another trustee who is unavailable to perform duties as provided in subsection (c).

Subsection (e) addresses the extent to which a trustee may delegate the performance of functions to a cotrustee. The standard differs from the standard for delegation to an agent as provided in Section 807 because the two situations are different. * * * Subsection (e) is premised on the assumption that the settlor selected cotrustees for a specific reason and that this reason ought to control the scope of a permitted delegation to a cotrustee. Subsection (e) prohibits a trustee from delegating to another trustee functions the settlor reasonably expected the trustees to perform jointly. The exact extent to which a trustee may delegate functions to another trustee in a particular case will vary depending on the reasons the settlor decided to appoint cotrustees. The better practice is to address the division of functions in the terms of the trust * * * .

By permitting the trustees to act by a majority, this section contemplates that there may be a trustee or trustees who might dissent. Trustees who dissent from the acts of a cotrustee are in general protected from liability. Subsection (f) protects trustees who refused to join in the action. Subsection (h) protects a dissenting trustee who joined the action at the direction of the majority, such as to satisfy a demand of the other side to a transaction, if the trustee expressed the dissent to a cotrustee at or before the time of the action in question. However, the protections provided by subsections (f) and (h) no longer apply if the action constitutes a serious breach of trust. In that event, subsection (g) may impose liability against a dissenting trustee for failing to take reasonable steps to rectify the improper conduct. * * *

Section 704. Vacancy in Trusteeship; Appointment of Successor.

(a) A vacancy in a trusteeship occurs if:

    (1)   a person designated as trustee rejects the trusteeship;

    (2)   a person designated as trustee cannot be identified or does not exist;

    (3)   a trustee resigns;

    (4)   a trustee is disqualified or removed;

    (5)   a trustee dies; or

    (6)   a [guardian] or [conservator] is appointed for an individual serving as trustee.

(b) If one or more cotrustees remain in office, a vacancy in a trusteeship need not be filled. A vacancy in a trusteeship must be filled if the trust has no remaining trustee.

(c)　A vacancy in a trusteeship of a noncharitable trust that is required to be filled must be filled in the following order of priority:

> (1)　by a person designated in the terms of the trust to act as successor trustee;
>
> (2)　by a person appointed by unanimous agreement of the qualified beneficiaries; or
>
> (3)　by a person appointed by the court.

(d)　A vacancy in a trusteeship of a charitable trust that is required to be filled must be filled in the following order of priority:

> (1)　by a person designated in the terms of the trust to act as successor trustee;
>
> (2)　by a person selected by the charitable organizations expressly designated to receive distributions under the terms of the trust [if the [attorney general] concurs in the selection]; or
>
> (3)　by a person appointed by the court.

(e)　Whether or not a vacancy in a trusteeship exists or is required to be filled, the court may appoint an additional trustee or special fiduciary whenever the court considers the appointment necessary for the administration of the trust.

Comment

* * * Good drafting practice suggests that the terms of the trust deal expressly with the problem of vacancies, naming successors and specifying the procedure for filling vacancies. This section applies only if the terms of the trust fail to specify a procedure. * * *

Subsection (b) provides that a vacancy in the cotrusteeship must be filled only if the trust has no remaining trustee. * * * However, as provided in subsection [(e)], the court, exercising its inherent equity authority, may always appoint additional trustees if the appointment would promote better administration of the trust. * * *

Absent an effective provision in the terms of the trust, subsection (c)(2) permits a vacancy in the trusteeship to be filled, without the need for court approval, by a person selected by unanimous agreement of the qualified beneficiaries. * * *

If the qualified beneficiaries fail to make an appointment, subsection (c)(3) authorizes the court to fill the vacancy. In making the appointment, the court should consider the objectives and probable intention of the settlor, the promotion of the proper administration of the trust, and the interests and wishes of the beneficiaries. * * *

Section 705. Resignation of Trustee.

(a)　A trustee may resign:

> (1)　upon at least 30 days' notice to the qualified beneficiaries, the settlor, if living, and all cotrustees; or
>
> (2)　with the approval of the court.

(b)　In approving a resignation, the court may issue orders and impose conditions reasonably necessary for the protection of the trust property.

(c)　Any liability of a resigning trustee or of any sureties on the trustee's bond for acts or omissions of the trustee is not discharged or affected by the trustee's resignation.

Comment

This section rejects the common law rule that a trustee may resign only with permission of the court * * *. Concluding that the default rule ought to approximate standard drafting practice, the Drafting Committee provided in subsection (a) that a trustee may resign by giving notice to the qualified beneficiaries and any cotrustee. A resigning trustee may also follow the traditional method and resign with approval of the court. * * *

Section 706. Removal of Trustee.

(a)   The settlor, a cotrustee, or a beneficiary may request the court to remove a trustee, or a trustee may be removed by the court on its own initiative.

(b)   The court may remove a trustee if:

(1)   the trustee has committed a serious breach of trust;

(2)   lack of cooperation among cotrustees substantially impairs the administration of the trust;

(3)   because of unfitness, unwillingness, or persistent failure of the trustee to administer the trust effectively, the court determines that removal of the trustee best serves the interests of the beneficiaries; or

(4)   there has been a substantial change of circumstances or removal is requested by all of the qualified beneficiaries, the court finds that removal of the trustee best serves the interests of all of the beneficiaries and is not inconsistent with a material purpose of the trust, and a suitable cotrustee or successor trustee is available.

(c)   Pending a final decision on a request to remove a trustee, or in lieu of or in addition to removing a trustee, the court may order such appropriate relief under Section 1001(b) as may be necessary to protect the trust property or the interests of the beneficiaries.

Comment

Subsection (a), contrary to the common law, grants the settlor of an irrevocable trust the right to petition for removal of a trustee. The right to petition for removal does not give the settlor of an irrevocable trust any other rights, such as the right to an annual report or to receive other information concerning administration of the trust. * * *

Subsection (b) lists the grounds for removal of the trustee. * * * A trustee may be removed for untoward action, such as for a serious breach of trust, but the section is not so limited. A trustee may also be removed under a variety of circumstances in which the court concludes that the trustee is not best serving the interests of the beneficiaries. * * * Removal for conduct detrimental to the interests of the beneficiaries is a well-established standard for removal of a trustee. * * *

Subsection (b)(1) * * * makes clear that not every breach of trust justifies removal of the trustee. The breach must be "serious." A serious breach of trust may consist of a single act that causes significant harm or involves flagrant misconduct. A serious breach of trust may also consist of a series of smaller breaches, none of which individually justify removal when considered alone, but which do so when considered together. A particularly appropriate circumstance justifying removal of the trustee is a serious breach of the trustee's duty to keep the beneficiaries reasonably informed of the administration of the trust or to comply with a beneficiary's request for information as required by Section 813. Failure to comply with this duty may make it impossible for the beneficiaries to protect their interests. It may also mask more serious violations by the trustee.

The lack of cooperation among trustees justifying removal under subsection (b)(2) need not involve a breach of trust. The key factor is whether the administration of the trust is significantly impaired by the trustees' failure to agree. Removal is particularly appropriate if the naming of an even number of trustees, combined with their failure to agree, has resulted in deadlock requiring court resolution. The court may remove one or more or all of the trustees. * * *

Subsection (b)(2) deals only with lack of cooperation among cotrustees, not with friction between the trustee and beneficiaries. Friction between the trustee and beneficiaries is ordinarily not a basis for removal. However, removal might be justified if a communications breakdown is caused by the trustee or appears to be incurable. * * *

Subsection (b)(3) authorizes removal for a variety of grounds, including unfitness, unwillingness, or persistent failure to administer the trust effectively. Removal in any of these cases is allowed only if it best serves the interests of the beneficiaries. * * * "Unfitness" may include not only mental incapacity but also lack of basic ability to administer the trust. Before removing a trustee for unfitness the court should consider the extent to which the problem might be cured by a delegation of functions the trustee is personally incapable of performing. "Unwillingness" includes not only cases where the trustee refuses to act but also a pattern of indifference to some or all of the beneficiaries. * * * A "persistent failure to administer the trust effectively" might include a long-term pattern of mediocre performance, such as consistently poor investment results when compared to comparable trusts.

It has traditionally been more difficult to remove a trustee named by the settlor than a trustee named by the court, particularly if the settlor at the time of the appointment was aware of the trustee's failings. * * * Because of the discretion normally granted to a trustee, the settlor's confidence in the judgment of the particular person whom the settlor selected to act as trustee is entitled to considerable weight. This deference to the settlor's choice can weaken or dissolve if a substantial change in the trustee's circumstances occurs. To honor a settlor's reasonable expectations, subsection (b)(4) lists a substantial change of circumstances as a possible basis for removal of the trustee. Changed circumstances justifying removal of a trustee might include a substantial change in the character of the service or location of the trustee. A corporate reorganization of an institutional trustee is not itself a change of circumstances if it does not affect the service provided the individual trust account. Before removing a trustee on account of changed circumstances, the court must also conclude that removal is not inconsistent with a material purpose of the trust, that it will best serve the interests of the beneficiaries, and that a suitable cotrustee or successor trustee is available.

Subsection (b)(4) * * * allows the qualified beneficiaries to request removal of the trustee if the designation of the trustee was not a material purpose of the trust. Before removing the trustee the court must also find that removal will best serve the interests of the beneficiaries and that a suitable cotrustee or successor trustee is available. * * *

Section 707. Delivery of Property by Former Trustee.

(a)   Unless a cotrustee remains in office or the court otherwise orders, and until the trust property is delivered to a successor trustee or other person entitled to it, a trustee who has resigned or been removed has the duties of a trustee and the powers necessary to protect the trust property.

(b)   A trustee who has resigned or been removed shall proceed expeditiously to deliver the trust property within the trustee's possession to the cotrustee, successor trustee, or other person entitled to it.

Comment

This section addresses the continuing authority and duty of a resigning or removed trustee. Subject to the power of the court to make other arrangements or unless a cotrustee remains in office, a resigning or removed trustee has continuing authority until the trust property is delivered to a successor. If a cotrustee remains in office, there is no reason to grant a resigning or removed trustee any continuing authority, and none is granted under this section. * * *

There is ample authority in the Uniform Trust Code for the appointment of a special fiduciary, an appointment which can avoid the need for a resigning or removed trustee to exercise residual powers until a successor can take office. * * *

If the former trustee has died, the Uniform Trust Code does not require that the trustee's personal representative windup the deceased trustee's administration. Nor is a trustee's conservator or guardian required to complete the former trustee's administration if the trustee's authority terminated due to an adjudication of incapacity. * * *

Section 708. Compensation of Trustee.

(a)   If the terms of a trust do not specify the trustee's compensation, a trustee is entitled to compensation that is reasonable under the circumstances.

(b)   If the terms of a trust specify the trustee's compensation, the trustee is entitled to be compensated as specified, but the court may allow more or less compensation if:

(1)   the duties of the trustee are substantially different from those contemplated when the trust was created; or

(2)   the compensation specified by the terms of the trust would be unreasonably low or high.

Comment

Subsection (a) establishes a standard of reasonable compensation. Relevant factors in determining this compensation * * * include the custom of the community; the trustee's skill, experience, and facilities; the time devoted to trust duties; the amount and character of the trust property; the degree of difficulty, responsibility and risk assumed in administering the trust, including in making discretionary distributions; the nature and costs of services rendered by others; and the quality of the trustee's performance. * * *

In setting compensation, the services actually performed and responsibilities assumed by the trustee should be closely examined. A downward adjustment of fees may be appropriate if a trustee has delegated significant duties to agents, such as the delegation of investment authority to outside managers. * * * On the other hand, a trustee with special skills, such as those of a real estate agent, may be entitled to extra compensation for performing services that would ordinarily be delegated. * * *

* * * [E]ach trustee, including a cotrustee, is entitled to reasonable compensation under the circumstances. The fact that a trust has more than one trustee does not mean that the trustees together are entitled to more compensation than had either acted alone. Nor does the appointment of more than one trustee mean that the trustees are eligible to receive the compensation in equal shares. The total amount of the compensation to be paid and how it will be divided depend on the totality of the circumstances. Factors to be considered include the settlor's reasons for naming more than one trustee and the level of responsibility assumed and exact services performed by each trustee. Often the fees of cotrustees will be in the aggregate higher than the fees for a single trustee because of the duty of each trustee to participate in administration and not delegate to a cotrustee duties the settlor expected the trustees to perform jointly. * * * The trust may benefit in such cases from the enhanced quality of decision-making resulting from the collective deliberations of the trustees.

Financial institution trustees normally base their fees on published fee schedules. Published fee schedules are subject to the same standard of reasonableness under the Uniform Trust Code as are other methods for computing fees. The courts have generally upheld published fee schedules but this is not automatic. Among the more litigated topics is the issue of termination fees. Termination fees are charged upon termination of the trust and sometimes upon transfer of the trust to a successor trustee. Factors relevant to whether the fee is appropriate include the actual work performed; whether a termination fee was authorized in the terms of the trust; whether the fee schedule specified the circumstances in which a termination fee would be charged; whether the trustee's overall fees for administering the trust from the date of the trust's creation, including the termination fee, were reasonable; and the general practice in the community regarding termination fees. Because significantly less work is normally involved, termination fees are less appropriate upon transfer to a successor trustee than upon termination of the trust. * * *

This Code does not take a specific position on whether dual fees may be charged when a trustee hires its own law firm to represent the trust. The trend is to authorize dual compensation as long as the overall fees are reasonable. * * *

Subsection (b) permits the terms of the trust to override the reasonable compensation standard, subject to the court's inherent equity power to make adjustments downward or upward in appropriate circumstances. Compensation provisions should be drafted with care. Common questions include whether a provision in the terms of the trust setting the amount of the trustee's compensation is binding on a successor trustee, whether a dispositive provision for the trustee in the terms of the trust is in addition to or in lieu of the trustee's regular compensation, and whether a dispositive provision for the trustee is conditional on the person performing services as trustee. * * *

Compensation may be set by agreement. A trustee may enter into an agreement with the beneficiaries for lesser or increased compensation, although an agreement increasing compensation is not binding on a nonconsenting beneficiary. * * *

Section 709. Reimbursement of Expenses.

(a)   A trustee is entitled to be reimbursed out of the trust property, with interest as appropriate, for:

     (1)   expenses that were properly incurred in the administration of the trust; and

     (2)   to the extent necessary to prevent unjust enrichment of the trust, expenses that were not properly incurred in the administration of the trust.

(b)   An advance by the trustee of money for the protection of the trust gives rise to a lien against trust property to secure reimbursement with reasonable interest.

Comment

A trustee has the authority to expend trust funds as necessary in the administration of the trust, including expenses incurred in the hiring of agents. * * *

Subsection (a)(1) clarifies that a trustee is entitled to reimbursement from the trust for incurring expenses within the trustee's authority. The trustee may also withhold appropriate reimbursement for expenses before making distributions to the beneficiaries. * * * A trustee is ordinarily not entitled to reimbursement for incurring unauthorized expenses. Such expenses are normally the personal responsibility of the trustee.

As provided in subsection (a)(2), a trustee is entitled to reimbursement for unauthorized expenses only if the unauthorized expenditures benefitted the trust. The purpose of this provision * * * is not to ratify the unauthorized conduct of the trustee, but to prevent unjust enrichment of the trust. Given this purpose, a court, on appropriate grounds, may delay or even deny reimbursement for expenses which benefitted the trust. Appropriate grounds include: (1) whether the trustee acted in bad faith in incurring the expense; (2) whether the trustee knew that the expense was inappropriate; (3) whether the trustee reasonably believed the expense was necessary for the preservation of the trust estate; (4) whether the expense has resulted in a benefit; and (5) whether indemnity can be allowed without defeating or impairing the purposes of the trust. * * *

ARTICLE 8

DUTIES AND POWERS OF TRUSTEE

Section 801. Duty to Administer Trust.

Upon acceptance of a trusteeship, the trustee shall administer the trust in good faith, in accordance with its terms and purposes and the interests of the beneficiaries, and in accordance with this [Code].

Comment

This section confirms that a primary duty of a trustee is to follow the terms and purposes of the trust and to do so in good faith. Only if the terms of a trust are silent or for some reason invalid on a particular issue does this Code govern the trustee's duties. This section also confirms that a trustee does not have a duty to act until the trustee has accepted the trusteeship. * * *

Section 802. Duty of Loyalty.

(a)   A trustee shall administer the trust solely in the interests of the beneficiaries.

(b)   Subject to the rights of persons dealing with or assisting the trustee as provided in Section 1012, a sale, encumbrance, or other transaction involving the investment or management of trust property entered into by the trustee for the trustee's own personal account or which is otherwise affected by a conflict between the trustee's fiduciary and personal interests is voidable by a beneficiary affected by the transaction unless:

(1)   the transaction was authorized by the terms of the trust;

(2)   the transaction was approved by the court;

(3)   the beneficiary did not commence a judicial proceeding within the time allowed by Section 1005;

(4)   the beneficiary consented to the trustee's conduct, ratified the transaction, or released the trustee in compliance with Section 1009; or

(5)   the transaction involves a contract entered into or claim acquired by the trustee before the person became or contemplated becoming trustee.

(c)   A sale, encumbrance, or other transaction involving the investment or management of trust property is presumed to be affected by a conflict between personal and fiduciary interests if it is entered into by the trustee with:

(1)   the trustee's spouse;

(2)   the trustee's descendants, siblings, parents, or their spouses;

(3)   an agent or attorney of the trustee; or

(4)   a corporation or other person or enterprise in which the trustee, or a person that owns a significant interest in the trustee, has an interest that might affect the trustee's best judgment.

(d)   A transaction between a trustee and a beneficiary that does not concern trust property but that occurs during the existence of the trust or while the trustee retains significant influence over the beneficiary and from which the trustee obtains an advantage is voidable by the beneficiary unless the trustee establishes that the transaction was fair to the beneficiary.

(e)   A transaction not concerning trust property in which the trustee engages in the trustee's individual capacity involves a conflict between personal and fiduciary interests if the transaction concerns an opportunity properly belonging to the trust.

(f) An investment by a trustee in securities of an investment company or investment trust to which the trustee, or its affiliate, provides services in a capacity other than as trustee is not presumed to be affected by a conflict between personal and fiduciary interests if the investment otherwise complies with the prudent investor rule of [Article] 9. In addition to its compensation for acting as trustee, the trustee may be compensated by the investment company or investment trust for providing those services out of fees charged to the trust. If the trustee receives compensation from the investment company or investment trust for providing investment advisory or investment management services, the trustee must at least annually notify the persons entitled under Section 813 to receive a copy of the trustee's annual report of the rate and method by which that compensation was determined.

(g) In voting shares of stock or in exercising powers of control over similar interests in other forms of enterprise, the trustee shall act in the best interests of the beneficiaries. If the trust is the sole owner of a corporation or other form of enterprise, the trustee shall elect or appoint directors or other managers who will manage the corporation or enterprise in the best interests of the beneficiaries.

(h) This section does not preclude the following transactions, if fair to the beneficiaries:

(1) an agreement between a trustee and a beneficiary relating to the appointment or compensation of the trustee;

(2) payment of reasonable compensation to the trustee;

(3) a transaction between a trust and another trust, decedent's estate, or [conservatorship] of which the trustee is a fiduciary or in which a beneficiary has an interest;

(4) a deposit of trust money in a regulated financial-service institution operated by the trustee; or

(5) an advance by the trustee of money for the protection of the trust.

(i) The court may appoint a special fiduciary to make a decision with respect to any proposed transaction that might violate this section if entered into by the trustee.

Comment

This section addresses the duty of loyalty, perhaps the most fundamental duty of the trustee. Subsection (a) states the general principle * * *. A trustee owes a duty of loyalty to the beneficiaries, a principle which is sometimes expressed as the obligation of the trustee not to place the trustee's own interests over those of the beneficiaries. Most but not all violations of the duty of loyalty concern transactions involving the trust property, but breaches of the duty can take other forms. * * *

The duty of loyalty applies to both charitable and noncharitable trusts, even though the beneficiaries of charitable trusts are indefinite. In the case of a charitable trust, the trustee must administer the trust solely in the interests of effectuating the trust's charitable purposes. * * *

Duty of loyalty issues often arise in connection with the settlor's designation of the trustee. For example, it is not uncommon that the trustee will also be a beneficiary. Or the settlor will name a friend or family member who is an officer of a company in which the settlor owns stock. In such cases, settlors should be advised to consider addressing in the terms of the trust how such conflicts are to be handled. Section 105 authorizes a settlor to override an otherwise applicable duty of loyalty in the terms of the trust. Sometimes the override is implied. The grant to a trustee of authority to make a discretionary distribution to a class of beneficiaries that includes the trustee implicitly authorizes the trustee to make distributions for the trustee's own benefit.

Subsection (b) states the general rule with respect to transactions involving trust property that are affected by a conflict of interest. A transaction affected by a conflict between the trustee's fiduciary and personal interests is voidable by a beneficiary who is affected by the transaction. Subsection (b) carries out the "no further inquiry" rule by making transactions involving trust property entered into by a trustee for the trustee's own personal account voidable without further proof. Such transactions are irrebuttably presumed to be affected by a conflict between personal and fiduciary interests. It is immaterial whether the trustee acts in good faith or pays a fair consideration. * * *

The rule is less severe with respect to transactions involving trust property entered into with persons who have close business or personal ties with the trustee. Under subsection (c), a transaction between a trustee and certain relatives and business associates is presumptively voidable, not void. Also presumptively voidable are transactions with corporations or other enterprises in which the trustee, or a person who owns a significant interest in the trustee, has an interest that might affect the trustee's best judgment. The presumption is rebutted if the trustee establishes that the transaction was not affected by a conflict between personal and fiduciary interests. Among the factors tending to rebut the presumption are whether the consideration was fair and whether the other terms of the transaction are similar to those that would be transacted with an independent party.

Even where the presumption under subsection (c) does not apply, a transaction may still be voided by a beneficiary if the beneficiary proves that a conflict between personal and fiduciary interests existed and that the transaction was affected by the conflict. The right of a beneficiary to void a transaction affected by a conflict of interest is optional. If the transaction proves profitable to the trust and unprofitable to the trustee, the beneficiary will likely allow the transaction to stand. * * *

As provided in subsection (b), no breach of the duty of loyalty occurs if the transaction was authorized by the terms of the trust or approved by the court, or if the beneficiary failed to commence a judicial proceeding within the time allowed or chose to ratify the transaction, either prior to or subsequent to its occurrence. In determining whether a beneficiary has consented to a transaction, the principles of representation from Article 3 may be applied.

Subsection (b)(5) * * * allows a trustee to implement a contract or pursue a claim that the trustee entered into or acquired before the person became or contemplated becoming trustee. While this subsection allows the transaction to proceed without automatically being voidable by a beneficiary, the transaction is not necessarily free from scrutiny. In implementing the contract or pursuing the claim, the trustee must still complete the transaction in a way that avoids a conflict between the trustee's fiduciary and personal interests. Because avoiding such a conflict will frequently be difficult, the trustee should consider petitioning the court to appoint a special fiduciary, as authorized by subsection (i), to work out the details and complete the transaction.

Subsection (d) creates a presumption that a transaction between a trustee and a beneficiary not involving trust property is an abuse by the trustee of a confidential relationship with the beneficiary. This subsection has limited scope. If the trust has terminated, there must be proof that the trustee's influence with the beneficiary remained. Furthermore, whether or not the trust has terminated, there must be proof that the trustee obtained an advantage from the relationship. The fact the trustee profited is insufficient to show an abuse if a third party would have similarly profited in an arm's length transaction. * * *

Subsection (e) * * * allows a beneficiary to void a transaction entered into by the trustee that involved an opportunity belonging to the trust * * *. While normally associated with corporations and with their directors and officers, what is usually referred to as the corporate opportunity doctrine also applies to other types of fiduciary. The doctrine prohibits the trustee's pursuit of certain business activities, such as entering into a business in direct competition with a business owned by the trust, or the purchasing of an investment that the facts suggest the trustee was expected to purchase for the trust. * * *

Subsection (f) creates an exception to the no further inquiry rule for trustee investment in mutual funds. This exception applies even though the mutual fund company pays the financial-service institution trustee a fee for providing investment advice and other services, such as custody, transfer agent, and distribution, that would otherwise be provided by agents of the fund. Mutual funds offer several advantages for fiduciary investing. By comparison with common trust funds, mutual fund shares may be distributed in-kind when trust interests terminate, avoiding liquidation and the associated recognition of gain for tax purposes. Mutual funds commonly offer daily pricing, which gives trustees and beneficiaries better information about performance. Because mutual funds can combine fiduciary and nonfiduciary accounts, they can achieve larger size, which can enhance diversification and produce economies of scale that can lower investment costs.

Mutual fund investment also has a number of potential disadvantages. It adds another layer of expense to the trust, and it causes the trustee to lose control over the nature and timing of transactions in the fund. Trustee investment in mutual funds sponsored by the trustee, its affiliate, or from which the trustee receives extra fees has given rise to litigation implicating the trustee's duty of loyalty, the duty to invest with prudence, and the right to receive only reasonable compensation. Because financial institution trustees ordinarily provide advisory services to and receive compensation from the very funds in which they invest trust assets, the contention is made that investing the assets of individual trusts in these funds is imprudent and motivated by the effort to generate additional fee income. Because the financial institution trustee often will also charge its regular fee for administering the trust, the contention is made that the financial institution trustee's total compensation, both direct and indirect, is excessive.

Subsection (f) attempts to retain the advantages of mutual funds while at the same time making clear that such investments are subject to traditional fiduciary responsibilities. Nearly all of the States have enacted statutes authorizing trustees to invest in funds from which the trustee might derive additional compensation. * * * Subsection (f) makes clear that such dual investment-fee arrangements are not automatically presumed to involve a conflict between the trustee's personal and fiduciary interests, but subsection (f) does not otherwise waive or lessen a trustee's fiduciary obligations. The trustee, in deciding whether to invest in a mutual fund, must not place its own interests ahead of those of the beneficiaries. The investment decision must also comply with the enacting jurisdiction's prudent investor rule. To obtain the protection afforded by subsection (f), the trustee must disclose at least annually to the beneficiaries entitled to receive a copy of the trustee's annual report the rate and method by which the additional compensation was determined. Furthermore, the selection of a mutual fund, and the resulting delegation of certain of the trustee's functions, may be taken into account under Section 708 in setting the trustee's regular compensation. * * *

Section 803. Impartiality.

If a trust has two or more beneficiaries, the trustee shall act impartially in investing, managing, and distributing the trust property, giving due regard to the beneficiaries' respective interests.

Comment

The duty of impartiality is an important aspect of the duty of loyalty. * * * The differing beneficial interests for which the trustee must act impartially include those of the current beneficiaries versus those of beneficiaries holding interests in the remainder; and among those currently eligible to receive distributions. In fulfilling the duty to act impartially, the trustee should be particularly sensitive to allocation of receipts and disbursements between income and principal and should consider, in an appropriate case, a reallocation of income to the principal account and vice versa, if allowable under local law. * * *

The duty to act impartially does not mean that the trustee must treat the beneficiaries equally. Rather, the trustee must treat the beneficiaries equitably in light of the purposes and terms of the trust. A settlor who prefers that the trustee, when making decisions, generally favor the interests of one beneficiary over those of others should provide appropriate guidance in the terms of the trust. * * *

Section 804. Prudent Administration.

A trustee shall administer the trust as a prudent person would, by considering the purposes, terms, distributional requirements, and other circumstances of the trust. In satisfying this standard, the trustee shall exercise reasonable care, skill, and caution.

Comment

The duty to administer a trust with prudence is a fundamental duty of the trustee. This duty does not depend on whether the trustee receives compensation. * * *

* * * This section appropriately bases the standard on the purposes and other circumstances of the particular trust.

A settlor who wishes to modify the standard of care specified in this section is free to do so, but there is a limit. Section 1008 prohibits a settlor from exculpating a trustee from liability for breach of trust committed in bad faith or with reckless indifference to the purposes of the trust or to the interests of the beneficiaries.

Section 805. Costs of Administration.

In administering a trust, the trustee may incur only costs that are reasonable in relation to the trust property, the purposes of the trust, and the skills of the trustee.

Comment

* * * The duty not to incur unreasonable costs applies when a trustee decides whether and how to delegate to agents, as well as to other aspects of trust administration. In deciding whether and how to delegate, the trustee must be alert to balancing projected benefits against the likely costs. To protect the beneficiary against excessive costs, the trustee should also be alert to adjusting compensation for functions which the trustee has delegated to others. * * *

Section 806. Trustee's Skills.

A trustee who has special skills or expertise, or is named trustee in reliance upon the trustee's representation that the trustee has special skills or expertise, shall use those special skills or expertise.

Section 807. Delegation by Trustee.

(a)   A trustee may delegate duties and powers that a prudent trustee of comparable skills could properly delegate under the circumstances. The trustee shall exercise reasonable care, skill, and caution in:

(1)   selecting an agent;

(2)   establishing the scope and terms of the delegation, consistent with the purposes and terms of the trust; and

(3)   periodically reviewing the agent's actions in order to monitor the agent's performance and compliance with the terms of the delegation.

(b)   In performing a delegated function, an agent owes a duty to the trust to exercise reasonable care to comply with the terms of the delegation.

(c)   A trustee who complies with subsection (a) is not liable to the beneficiaries or to the trust for an action of the agent to whom the function was delegated.

(d)   By accepting a delegation of powers or duties from the trustee of a trust that is subject to the law of this State, an agent submits to the jurisdiction of the courts of this State.

Comment

* * * This section encourages and protects the trustee in making delegations appropriate to the facts and circumstances of the particular trust. Whether a particular function is delegable is based on whether it is a function that a prudent trustee might delegate under similar circumstances. For example, delegating some administrative and reporting duties might be prudent for a family trustee but unnecessary for a corporate trustee.

This section applies only to delegation to agents, not to delegation to a cotrustee. * * *

Section 808. [Reserved].

Section 809. Control and Protection of Trust Property.

A trustee shall take reasonable steps to take control of and protect the trust property.

Comment

* * * The duty to take control of and safeguard trust property is an aspect of the trustee's duty of prudent administration as provided in Section 804. * * * The duty to take control normally means that the trustee must take physical possession of tangible personal property and securities belonging to the trust, and must secure payment of any choses in action. * * * This section, like the other sections in this part, is subject to alteration by the terms of the trust. * * * For example, the settlor may provide that the spouse

may occupy the settlor's former residence rent free, in which event the spouse's occupancy would prevent the trustee from taking possession.

Section 810. Recordkeeping and Identification of Trust Property.

(a)　A trustee shall keep adequate records of the administration of the trust.

(b)　A trustee shall keep trust property separate from the trustee's own property.

(c)　Except as otherwise provided in subsection (d), a trustee shall cause the trust property to be designated so that the interest of the trust, to the extent feasible, appears in records maintained by a party other than a trustee or beneficiary.

(d)　If the trustee maintains records clearly indicating the respective interests, a trustee may invest as a whole the property of two or more separate trusts.

Comment

The duty to keep adequate records stated in subsection (a) is implicit in the duty to act with prudence (Section 804) and the duty to report to beneficiaries (Section 813). * * *

The duty to earmark trust assets and the duty of a trustee not to mingle the assets of the trust with the trustee's own are closely related. * * * Subsection (c) makes the requirement that assets be earmarked more precise * * * by requiring that the interest of the trust must appear in the records of a third party, such as a bank, brokerage firm, or transfer agent. Because of the serious risk of mistake or misappropriation even if disclosure is made to the beneficiaries, showing the interest of the trust solely in the trustee's own internal records is insufficient. Section 816(7)(B), which allows a trustee to hold securities in nominee form, is not inconsistent with this requirement. While securities held in nominee form are not specifically registered in the name of the trustee, they are properly earmarked because the trustee's holdings are indicated in the records maintained by an independent party, such as in an account at a brokerage firm.

Earmarking is not practical for all types of assets. With respect to assets not subject to registration, such as tangible personal property and bearer bonds, arranging for the trust's ownership interest to be reflected on the records of a third-party custodian would not be feasible. For this reason, subsection (c) waives separate recordkeeping for these types of assets. Under subsection (b), however, the duty of the trustee not to mingle these or any other trust assets with the trustee's own remains absolute.

Subsection (d) * * * allows a trustee to use the property of two or more trusts to make joint investments, even though under traditional principles a joint investment would violate the duty to earmark. A joint investment frequently is more economical than attempting to invest the funds of each trust separately. Also, the risk of misappropriation or mistake is less when the trust property is invested jointly with the property of another trust than when pooled with the property of the trustee or other person.

Section 811. Enforcement and Defense of Claims.

A trustee shall take reasonable steps to enforce claims of the trust and to defend claims against the trust.

Section 812. Collecting Trust Property.

A trustee shall take reasonable steps to compel a former trustee or other person to deliver trust property to the trustee, and to redress a breach of trust known to the trustee to have been committed by a former trustee.

Comment

This section is a specific application of Section 811 on the duty to enforce claims, which includes a claim for trust property held by a former trustee or others, and a claim against a predecessor trustee for breach of trust. The duty imposed by this section is not absolute. Pursuit of a claim is not required if the amount of the claim, costs of suit and enforcement, and likelihood of recovery, make such action uneconomic. * * * [T]his section only requires a successor trustee to redress breaches of trust "known" to have been committed by the predecessor. * * *

Section 813. Duty to Inform and Report.

(a)   A trustee shall keep the qualified beneficiaries of the trust reasonably informed about the administration of the trust and of the material facts necessary for them to protect their interests. Unless unreasonable under the circumstances, a trustee shall promptly respond to a beneficiary's request for information related to the administration of the trust.

(b)   A trustee:

(1)   upon request of a beneficiary, shall promptly furnish to the beneficiary a copy of the trust instrument;

(2)   within 60 days after accepting a trusteeship, shall notify the qualified beneficiaries of the acceptance and of the trustee's name, address, and telephone number;

(3)   within 60 days after the date the trustee acquires knowledge of the creation of an irrevocable trust, or the date the trustee acquires knowledge that a formerly revocable trust has become irrevocable, whether by the death of the settlor or otherwise, shall notify the qualified beneficiaries of the trust's existence, of the identity of the settlor or settlors, of the right to request a copy of the trust instrument, and of the right to a trustee's report as provided in subsection (c); and

(4)   shall notify the qualified beneficiaries in advance of any change in the method or rate of the trustee's compensation.

(c)   A trustee shall send to the distributees or permissible distributees of trust income or principal, and to other qualified or nonqualified beneficiaries who request it, at least annually and at the termination of the trust, a report of the trust property, liabilities, receipts, and disbursements, including the source and amount of the trustee's compensation, a listing of the trust assets and, if feasible, their respective market values. Upon a vacancy in a trusteeship, unless a cotrustee remains in office, a report must be sent to the qualified beneficiaries by the former trustee. A personal representative, [conservator], or [guardian] may send the qualified beneficiaries a report on behalf of a deceased or incapacitated trustee.

(d)   A beneficiary may waive the right to a trustee's report or other information otherwise required to be furnished under this section. A beneficiary, with respect to future reports and other information, may withdraw a waiver previously given.

(e)   Subsections (b)(2) and (3) do not apply to a trustee who accepts a trusteeship before [the effective date of this [Code]], to an irrevocable trust created before [the effective date of this [Code]], or to a revocable trust that becomes irrevocable before [the effective date of this [Code]].

Comment

The duty to keep the beneficiaries reasonably informed of the administration of the trust is a fundamental duty of a trustee. * * * [S]ubsection (a) of this section limits the duty to keep the beneficiaries informed to the qualified beneficiaries. * * * The result of this limitation is that the information need not be furnished to beneficiaries with remote remainder interests unless they have made a request to the trustee. * * *

Subsection (a) requires that the trustee keep the qualified beneficiaries of the trust reasonably informed about the administration of the trust and of the material facts necessary for them to protect their interests. This may include a duty to communicate to a qualified beneficiary information about the administration of the trust that is reasonably necessary to enable the beneficiary to enforce the beneficiary's rights and to prevent or redress a breach of trust. * * * With respect to the permissible distributees, the duty articulated in subsection (a) would ordinarily be satisfied by providing the beneficiary with a copy of the annual report mandated by subsection (c). Otherwise, the trustee is not ordinarily under a duty to furnish information to a beneficiary in the absence of a specific request for the information. * * * However, special circumstances may require that the trustee take affirmative steps to provide additional information. For example, if the trustee is dealing with the beneficiary on the trustee's own account, the trustee must communicate material facts relating to the transaction that the trustee knows or should know. * * *

Furthermore, to enable the beneficiaries to take action to protect their interests, the trustee may be required to provide advance notice of transactions involving real estate, closely-held business interests, and other assets that are difficult to value or to replace. * * * The trustee is justified in not providing such advance disclosure if disclosure is forbidden by other law, as under federal securities laws, or if disclosure would be seriously detrimental to the interests of the beneficiaries, for example, when disclosure would cause the loss of the only serious buyer.

Subsection (a) also requires that the trustee promptly respond to the request of any beneficiary, whether qualified or not, for information related to the administration of the trust. Performance is excused only if compliance is unreasonable under the circumstances. Within the bounds of the reasonableness limit, this provision allows the beneficiary to determine what information is relevant to protect the beneficiary's interest. Should a beneficiary so request, subsection (b)(1) also requires the trustee to furnish the beneficiary with a complete copy of the trust instrument and not merely with those portions the trustee deems relevant to the beneficiary's interest. * * *

The drafters of this Code decided to leave open for further consideration by the courts the extent to which a trustee may claim attorney-client privilege against a beneficiary seeking discovery of attorney-client communications between the trustee and the trustee's attorney. The courts are split because of the important values that are in tension on this question. * * *

To enable beneficiaries to protect their interests effectively, it is essential that they know the identity of the trustee. Subsection (b)(2) requires that a trustee inform the qualified beneficiaries within 60 days of the trustee's acceptance of office and of the trustee's name, address and telephone number. Similar to the obligation imposed on a personal representative following admission of the will to probate, subsection (b)(3) requires the trustee of a revocable trust to inform the qualified beneficiaries of the trust's existence within 60 days after the settlor's death. These two duties can overlap. If the death of the settlor happens also to be the occasion for the appointment of a successor trustee, the new trustee of the formerly revocable trust would need to inform the qualified beneficiaries both of the trustee's acceptance and of the trust's existence. * * *

Subsection (c) requires the trustee to furnish the current beneficiaries and other beneficiaries who request it with a copy of a trustee's report at least annually and upon termination of the trust. Unless a cotrustee remains in office, the former trustee also must provide a report to all of the qualified beneficiaries upon the trustee's resignation or removal. If the vacancy occurred because of the former trustee's death or adjudication of incapacity, a report may, but need not be provided by the former trustee's personal representative, conservator, or guardian.

The Uniform Trust Code employs the term "report" instead of "accounting" in order to negate any inference that the report must be prepared in any particular format or with a high degree of formality. The reporting requirement might even be satisfied by providing the beneficiaries with copies of the trust's income tax returns and monthly brokerage account statements if the information on those returns and statements is complete and sufficiently clear. The key factor is not the format chosen but whether the report provides the beneficiaries with the information necessary to protect their interests. * * *

Subsection (d) allows trustee reports and other required information to be waived by a beneficiary. A beneficiary may also withdraw a consent. However, a waiver of a trustee's report or other information does not relieve the trustee from accountability and potential liability for matters that the report or other information would have disclosed. * * *

Section 814. Discretionary Powers; Tax Savings.

(a)   Notwithstanding the breadth of discretion granted to a trustee in the terms of the trust, including the use of such terms as "absolute", "sole", or "uncontrolled", the trustee shall exercise a discretionary power in good faith and in accordance with the terms and purposes of the trust and the interests of the beneficiaries.

(b)   Subject to subsection (d), and unless the terms of the trust expressly indicate that a rule in this subsection does not apply:

(1) a person other than a settlor who is a beneficiary and trustee of a trust that confers on the trustee a power to make discretionary distributions to or for the trustee's personal benefit may exercise the power only in accordance with an ascertainable standard; and

(2) a trustee may not exercise a power to make discretionary distributions to satisfy a legal obligation of support that the trustee personally owes another person.

(c) A power whose exercise is limited or prohibited by subsection (b) may be exercised by a majority of the remaining trustees whose exercise of the power is not so limited or prohibited. If the power of all trustees is so limited or prohibited, the court may appoint a special fiduciary with authority to exercise the power.

(d) Subsection (b) does not apply to:

(1) a power held by the settlor's spouse who is the trustee of a trust for which a marital deduction, as defined in Section 2056(b)(5) or 2523(e) of the Internal Revenue Code of 1986, as in effect on [the effective date of this [Code]] [, or as later amended], was previously allowed;

(2) any trust during any period that the trust may be revoked or amended by its settlor; or

(3) a trust if contributions to the trust qualify for the annual exclusion under Section 2503(c) of the Internal Revenue Code of 1986, as in effect on [the effective date of this [Code]] [, or as later amended].

Comment

Despite the breadth of discretion purportedly granted by the wording of a trust, no grant of discretion to a trustee, whether with respect to management or distribution, is ever absolute. A grant of discretion establishes a range within which the trustee may act. The greater the grant of discretion, the broader the range. Pursuant to subsection (a), a trustee's exercise of discretion must be in good faith. Consistent with the trustee's duty to administer the trust * * *, the trustee's exercise must also be in accordance with the terms and purposes of the trust and the interests of the beneficiaries. * * *

Subsection (a) requires a trustee exercise a discretionary power in good faith and in accordance with the terms and purposes of the trust and the interests of the beneficiaries. * * * [S]ubsection (a) does not impose an obligation that a trustee's decision be within the bounds of a reasonable judgment, although such an interpretive standard may be imposed by the courts if the document adds a standard whereby the reasonableness of the trustee's judgment can be tested. * * *

An abuse by the trustee of the discretion granted in the terms of the trust is a breach of trust that can result in surcharge. * * * The standard stated in subsection (a) applies only to powers which are to be exercised in a fiduciary as opposed to a nonfiduciary capacity.

Subsections (b) through (d) rewrite the terms of a trust that might otherwise result in adverse estate and gift tax consequences to a beneficiary-trustee. This Code does not generally address the subject of tax curative provisions. * * *

Section 815. General Powers of Trustee.

(a) A trustee, without authorization by the court, may exercise:

(1) powers conferred by the terms of the trust; and

(2) except as limited by the terms of the trust:

(A) all powers over the trust property which an unmarried competent owner has over individually owned property;

(B) any other powers appropriate to achieve the proper investment, management, and distribution of the trust property; and

(C) any other powers conferred by this [Code].

(b) The exercise of a power is subject to the fiduciary duties prescribed by this [article].

Comment

This section is intended to grant trustees the broadest possible powers, but to be exercised always in accordance with the duties of the trustee and any limitations stated in the terms of the trust. This broad authority is denoted by granting the trustee the powers of an unmarried competent owner of individually owned property, unlimited by restrictions that might be placed on it by marriage, disability, or cotenancy. * * *

A power differs from a duty. A duty imposes an obligation or a mandatory prohibition. A power, on the other hand, is a discretion, the exercise of which is not obligatory. The existence of a power, however created or granted, does not speak to the question of whether it is prudent under the circumstances to exercise the power. * * *

Section 816. Specific Powers of Trustee.

Without limiting the authority conferred by Section 815, a trustee may:

(1) collect trust property and accept or reject additions to the trust property from a settlor or any other person;

(2) acquire or sell property, for cash or on credit, at public or private sale;

(3) exchange, partition, or otherwise change the character of trust property;

(4) deposit trust money in an account in a regulated financial-service institution;

(5) borrow money, with or without security, and mortgage or pledge trust property for a period within or extending beyond the duration of the trust;

(6) with respect to an interest in a proprietorship, partnership, limited liability company, business trust, corporation, or other form of business or enterprise, continue the business or other enterprise and take any action that may be taken by shareholders, members, or property owners, including merging, dissolving, or otherwise changing the form of business organization or contributing additional capital;

(7) with respect to stocks or other securities, exercise the rights of an absolute owner, including the right to:

    (A) vote, or give proxies to vote, with or without power of substitution, or enter into or continue a voting trust agreement;

    (B) hold a security in the name of a nominee or in other form without disclosure of the trust so that title may pass by delivery;

    (C) pay calls, assessments, and other sums chargeable or accruing against the securities, and sell or exercise stock subscription or conversion rights; and

    (D) deposit the securities with a depositary or other regulated financial-service institution;

(8) with respect to an interest in real property, construct, or make ordinary or extraordinary repairs to, alterations to, or improvements in, buildings or other structures, demolish improvements, raze existing or erect new party walls or buildings, subdivide or develop land, dedicate land to public use or grant public or private easements, and make or vacate plats and adjust boundaries;

(9) enter into a lease for any purpose as lessor or lessee, including a lease or other arrangement for exploration and removal of natural resources, with or without the option to purchase or renew, for a period within or extending beyond the duration of the trust;

(10) grant an option involving a sale, lease, or other disposition of trust property or acquire an option for the acquisition of property, including an option exercisable beyond the duration of the trust, and exercise an option so acquired;

(11) insure the property of the trust against damage or loss and insure the trustee, the trustee's agents, and beneficiaries against liability arising from the administration of the trust;

(12) abandon or decline to administer property of no value or of insufficient value to justify its collection or continued administration;

(13) with respect to possible liability for violation of environmental law:

(A) inspect or investigate property the trustee holds or has been asked to hold, or property owned or operated by an organization in which the trustee holds or has been asked to hold an interest, for the purpose of determining the application of environmental law with respect to the property;

(B) take action to prevent, abate, or otherwise remedy any actual or potential violation of any environmental law affecting property held directly or indirectly by the trustee, whether taken before or after the assertion of a claim or the initiation of governmental enforcement;

(C) decline to accept property into trust or disclaim any power with respect to property that is or may be burdened with liability for violation of environmental law;

(D) compromise claims against the trust which may be asserted for an alleged violation of environmental law; and

(E) pay the expense of any inspection, review, abatement, or remedial action to comply with environmental law;

(14) pay or contest any claim, settle a claim by or against the trust, and release, in whole or in part, a claim belonging to the trust;

(15) pay taxes, assessments, compensation of the trustee and of employees and agents of the trust, and other expenses incurred in the administration of the trust;

(16) exercise elections with respect to federal, state, and local taxes;

(17) select a mode of payment under any employee benefit or retirement plan, annuity, or life insurance payable to the trustee, exercise rights thereunder, including exercise of the right to indemnification for expenses and against liabilities, and take appropriate action to collect the proceeds;

(18) make loans out of trust property, including loans to a beneficiary on terms and conditions the trustee considers to be fair and reasonable under the circumstances, and the trustee has a lien on future distributions for repayment of those loans;

(19) pledge trust property to guarantee loans made by others to the beneficiary;

(20) appoint a trustee to act in another jurisdiction with respect to trust property located in the other jurisdiction, confer upon the appointed trustee all of the powers and duties of the appointing trustee, require that the appointed trustee furnish security, and remove any trustee so appointed;

(21) pay an amount distributable to a beneficiary who is under a legal disability or who the trustee reasonably believes is incapacitated, by paying it directly to the beneficiary or applying it for the beneficiary's benefit, or by:

(A) paying it to the beneficiary's [conservator] or, if the beneficiary does not have a [conservator], the beneficiary's [guardian];

(B) paying it to the beneficiary's custodian under [the Uniform Transfers to Minors Act] or custodial trustee under [the Uniform Custodial Trust Act], and, for that purpose, creating a custodianship or custodial trust;

(C) if the trustee does not know of a [conservator], [guardian], custodian, or custodial trustee, paying it to an adult relative or other person having legal or physical care or custody of the beneficiary, to be expended on the beneficiary's behalf; or

(D) managing it as a separate fund on the beneficiary's behalf, subject to the beneficiary's continuing right to withdraw the distribution;

(22) on distribution of trust property or the division or termination of a trust, make distributions in divided or undivided interests, allocate particular assets in proportionate or disproportionate shares, value the trust property for those purposes, and adjust for resulting differences in valuation;

(23) resolve a dispute concerning the interpretation of the trust or its administration by mediation, arbitration, or other procedure for alternative dispute resolution;

(24) prosecute or defend an action, claim, or judicial proceeding in any jurisdiction to protect trust property and the trustee in the performance of the trustee's duties;

(25) sign and deliver contracts and other instruments that are useful to achieve or facilitate the exercise of the trustee's powers; and

(26) on termination of the trust, exercise the powers appropriate to wind up the administration of the trust and distribute the trust property to the persons entitled to it.

Comment

This section enumerates specific powers commonly included in trust instruments and in trustee powers legislation. All the powers listed are subject to alteration in the terms of the trust. * * * The powers listed add little of substance not already granted by Section 815 and powers conferred elsewhere in the Code * * * . While the Committee drafting this Code discussed dropping the list of specific powers, it concluded that the demand of third parties to see language expressly authorizing specific transactions justified retention of a detailed list. * * *

Section 817. Distribution Upon Termination.

(a) Upon termination or partial termination of a trust, the trustee may send to the beneficiaries a proposal for distribution. The right of any beneficiary to object to the proposed distribution terminates if the beneficiary does not notify the trustee of an objection within 30 days after the proposal was sent but only if the proposal informed the beneficiary of the right to object and of the time allowed for objection.

(b) Upon the occurrence of an event terminating or partially terminating a trust, the trustee shall proceed expeditiously to distribute the trust property to the persons entitled to it, subject to the right of the trustee to retain a reasonable reserve for the payment of debts, expenses, and taxes.

(c) A release by a beneficiary of a trustee from liability for breach of trust is invalid to the extent:

(1) it was induced by improper conduct of the trustee; or

(2) the beneficiary, at the time of the release, did not know of the beneficiary's rights or of the material facts relating to the breach.

Comment

* * * Subsection (a) * * * addresses the dilemma that sometimes arises when the trustee is reluctant to make distribution until the beneficiary approves but the beneficiary is reluctant to approve until the assets are in hand. The procedure made available under subsection (a) facilitates the making of non-pro-rata distributions. However, whenever practicable it is normally better practice to obtain the advance written consent of the beneficiaries to a proposed plan of distribution. * * *

The failure of a beneficiary to object to a plan of distribution pursuant to subsection (a) is not a release as provided in subsection (c) or Section 1009. A release requires an affirmative act by a beneficiary and is not accomplished upon a mere failure to object. * * *

Subsection (b) recognizes that upon an event terminating or partially terminating a trust, expeditious distribution should be encouraged to the extent reasonable under the circumstances. However, a trustee is entitled to retain a reasonable reserve for payment of debts, expenses, and taxes. * * *

Subsection (c) is an application of Section 1009. Section 1009 addresses the validity of any type of release that a beneficiary might give. Subsection (c) is more limited, dealing only with releases given upon termination of the trust. Factors affecting the validity of a release include adequacy of disclosure, whether the beneficiary had a legal incapacity and was not represented under Article 3, and whether the trustee engaged in any improper conduct. * * *

ARTICLE 9

UNIFORM PRUDENT INVESTOR ACT

[The Uniform Prudent Investor Act is reproduced elsewhere in this volume.]

ARTICLE 10

LIABILITY OF TRUSTEES AND RIGHTS OF PERSONS DEALING WITH TRUSTEE

Section 1001. Remedies for Breach of Trust.

(a)   A violation by a trustee of a duty the trustee owes to a beneficiary is a breach of trust.

(b)   To remedy a breach of trust that has occurred or may occur, the court may:

(1)   compel the trustee to perform the trustee's duties;

(2)   enjoin the trustee from committing a breach of trust;

(3)   compel the trustee to redress a breach of trust by paying money, restoring property, or other means;

(4)   order a trustee to account;

(5)   appoint a special fiduciary to take possession of the trust property and administer the trust;

(6)   suspend the trustee;

(7)   remove the trustee as provided in Section 706;

(8)   reduce or deny compensation to the trustee;

(9)   subject to Section 1012, void an act of the trustee, impose a lien or a constructive trust on trust property, or trace trust property wrongfully disposed of and recover the property or its proceeds; or

(10)   order any other appropriate relief.

Comment

This section codifies the remedies available to rectify or to prevent a breach of trust for violation of a duty owed to a beneficiary. * * *

This section identifies the available remedies but does not attempt to cover the refinements and exceptions developed in case law. The availability of a remedy in a particular circumstance will be determined not only by this Code but also by the common law of trusts and principles of equity. * * *

Beneficiaries and cotrustees have standing to bring a petition to remedy a breach of trust. Following a successor trustee's acceptance of office, a successor trustee has standing to sue a predecessor for breach of trust. * * * A person who may represent a beneficiary's interest under Article 3 would have standing to bring a petition on behalf of the person represented. In the case of a charitable trust, those with standing include the state attorney general, a charitable organization expressly entitled to receive benefits under the terms of the trust, and other persons with a special interest. * * * A person appointed to enforce a trust for an animal or a trust for a noncharitable purpose would have standing to sue for a breach of trust. * * *

Section 1002. Damages for Breach of Trust.

(a)   A trustee who commits a breach of trust is liable to the beneficiaries affected for the greater of:

(1)   the amount required to restore the value of the trust property and trust distributions to what they would have been had the breach not occurred; or

(2)   the profit the trustee made by reason of the breach.

(b)   Except as otherwise provided in this subsection, if more than one trustee is liable to the beneficiaries for a breach of trust, a trustee is entitled to contribution from the other trustee or trustees. A trustee is not entitled to contribution if the trustee was substantially more at fault than another trustee or if the trustee committed the breach of trust in bad faith or with reckless indifference to the purposes of the trust or the interests of the beneficiaries. A trustee who received a benefit from the breach of trust is not entitled to contribution from another trustee to the extent of the benefit received.

Comment

* * * If a trustee commits a breach of trust, the beneficiaries may either affirm the transaction or, if a loss has occurred, hold the trustee liable for the amount necessary to compensate fully for the consequences of the breach. This may include recovery of lost income, capital gain, or appreciation that would have resulted from proper administration. Even if a loss has not occurred, the trustee may not benefit from the improper action and is accountable for any profit the trustee made by reason of the breach. * * *

For purposes of this section and Section 1003, "profit" does not include the trustee's compensation. A trustee who has committed a breach of trust is entitled to reasonable compensation for administering the trust unless the court reduces or denies the trustee compensation pursuant to Section 1001(b)(8).

* * * Cotrustees are jointly and severally liable for a breach of trust if there was joint participation in the breach. Joint and several liability also is imposed on a nonparticipating cotrustee who, as provided in Section 703(g), failed to exercise reasonable care (1) to prevent a cotrustee from committing a serious breach of trust, or (2) to compel a cotrustee to redress a serious breach of trust. Joint and several liability normally carries with it a right in any trustee to seek contribution from a cotrustee to the extent the trustee has paid more than the trustee's proportionate share of the liability. Subsection (b) * * * creates an exception. A trustee who was substantially more at fault or committed the breach of trust in bad faith or with reckless indifference to the purposes of the trust or the interests of the beneficiaries is not entitled to contribution from the other trustees.

Determining degrees of comparative fault is a question of fact. The fact that one trustee was more culpable or more active than another does not necessarily establish that this trustee was substantially more at fault. Nor is a trustee substantially less at fault because the trustee did not actively participate in the breach. * * * Among the factors to consider: (1) Did the trustee fraudulently induce the other trustee to join in the breach? (2) Did the trustee commit the breach intentionally while the other trustee was at most negligent? (3) Did the trustee, because of greater experience or expertise, control the actions of the other trustee? (4) Did the trustee alone commit the breach with liability imposed on the other trustee only because of an improper delegation or failure to properly monitor the actions of the cotrustee? * * *

Section 1003. Damages in Absence of Breach.

(a)   A trustee is accountable to an affected beneficiary for any profit made by the trustee arising from the administration of the trust, even absent a breach of trust.

(b)   Absent a breach of trust, a trustee is not liable to a beneficiary for a loss or depreciation in the value of trust property or for not having made a profit.

Comment

The principle on which a trustee's duty of loyalty is premised is that a trustee should not be allowed to use the trust as a means for personal profit other than for routine compensation earned. While most instances of personal profit involve situations where the trustee has breached the duty of loyalty, not all cases of personal profit involve a breach of trust. Subsection (a) * * * holds a trustee accountable for any profit made, even absent a breach of trust * * * . A typical example of a profit is receipt by the trustee of a commission or bonus from a third party for actions relating to the trust's administration. * * *

A trustee is not an insurer. * * * [S]ubsection (b) provides that absent a breach of trust a trustee is not liable for a loss or depreciation in the value of the trust property or for failure to make a profit.

Section 1004. Attorney's Fees and Costs.

In a judicial proceeding involving the administration of a trust, the court, as justice and equity may require, may award costs and expenses, including reasonable attorney's fees, to any party, to be paid by another party or from the trust that is the subject of the controversy.

Section 1005. Limitation of Action Against Trustee.

(a) A beneficiary may not commence a proceeding against a trustee for breach of trust more than one year after the date the beneficiary or a representative of the beneficiary was sent a report that adequately disclosed the existence of a potential claim for breach of trust and informed the beneficiary of the time allowed for commencing a proceeding.

(b) A report adequately discloses the existence of a potential claim for breach of trust if it provides sufficient information so that the beneficiary or representative knows of the potential claim or should have inquired into its existence.

(c) If subsection (a) does not apply, a judicial proceeding by a beneficiary against a trustee for breach of trust must be commenced within five years after the first to occur of:

(1)   the removal, resignation, or death of the trustee;

(2)   the termination of the beneficiary's interest in the trust; or

(3)   the termination of the trust.

Comment

The one-year and five-year limitations periods under this section are not the only means for barring an action by a beneficiary. A beneficiary may be foreclosed by consent, release, or ratification as provided in Section 1009. Claims may also be barred by principles such as estoppel and laches arising in equity under the common law of trusts. * * *

The representative referred to in subsection (a) is the person who may represent and bind a beneficiary as provided in Article 3. During the time that a trust is revocable and the settlor has capacity, the person holding the power to revoke is the one who must receive the report. * * *

This section addresses only the issue of when the clock will start to run for purposes of the statute of limitations. If the trustee wishes to foreclose possible claims immediately, a consent to the report or other information may be obtained pursuant to Section 1009. * * *

Subsection (a) applies only if the trustee has furnished a report. The one-year statute of limitations does not begin to run against a beneficiary who has waived the furnishing of a report as provided in Section 813(d).

Subsection (c) is intended to provide some ultimate repose for actions against a trustee. It applies to cases in which the trustee has failed to report to the beneficiaries or the report did not meet the disclosure requirements of subsection (b). It also applies to beneficiaries who did not receive notice of the report, whether personally or through representation. While the five-year limitations period will normally begin to run on termination of the trust, it can also begin earlier. If a trustee leaves office prior to the termination of the trust, the limitations period for actions against that particular trustee begins to run on the date the trustee leaves office. If a beneficiary receives a final distribution prior to the date the trust terminates, the limitations period for actions by that particular beneficiary begins to run on the date of final distribution.

If a trusteeship terminates by reason of death, a claim against the trustee's estate for breach of fiduciary duty would, like other claims against the trustee's estate, be barred by a probate creditor's claim statute even though the statutory period prescribed by this section has not yet expired.

This section does not specifically provide that the statutes of limitations under this section are tolled for fraud or other misdeeds, the drafters preferring to leave the resolution of this question to other law of the State.

Section 1006. Reliance on Trust Instrument.

A trustee who acts in reasonable reliance on the terms of the trust as expressed in the trust instrument is not liable to a beneficiary for a breach of trust to the extent the breach resulted from the reliance.

Comment

It sometimes happens that the intended terms of the trust differ from the apparent meaning of the trust instrument. This can occur because the court, in determining the terms of the trust, is allowed to consider evidence extrinsic to the trust instrument. * * * Furthermore, if a trust is reformed on account of mistake of fact or law, as authorized by Section 415, provisions of a trust instrument can be deleted or contradicted and provisions not in the trust instrument may be added. The concept of the "terms of a trust," both as defined in this Code and as used in the doctrine of reformation, is intended to effectuate the principle that a trust should be administered and distributed in accordance with the settlor's intent. However, a trustee should also be able to administer a trust with some dispatch and without concern that a reasonable reliance on the terms of the trust instrument is misplaced. This section protects a trustee who so relies on a trust instrument but only to the extent the breach of trust resulted from such reliance. * * *

This section protects a trustee only if the trustee's reliance is reasonable. For example, a trustee's reliance on the trust instrument would not be justified if the trustee is aware of a prior court decree or binding nonjudicial settlement agreement clarifying or changing the terms of the trust.

Section 1007. Event Affecting Administration or Distribution.

If the happening of an event, including marriage, divorce, performance of educational requirements, or death, affects the administration or distribution of a trust, a trustee who has exercised reasonable care to ascertain the happening of the event is not liable for a loss resulting from the trustee's lack of knowledge.

Comment

This section * * * is designed to encourage trustees to administer trusts expeditiously and without undue concern about liability for failure to ascertain external facts, often of a personal nature, that might affect administration or distribution of the trust. The common law, contrary to this section, imposed absolute liability against a trustee for misdelivery regardless of the trustee's level of care. * * * The events listed in this section are not exclusive. A trustee who has exercised reasonable care to ascertain the occurrence of other events, such as the attainment by a beneficiary of a certain age, is also protected from liability.

Section 1008. Exculpation of Trustee.

(a) A term of a trust relieving a trustee of liability for breach of trust is unenforceable to the extent that it:

(1) relieves the trustee of liability for breach of trust committed in bad faith or with reckless indifference to the purposes of the trust or the interests of the beneficiaries; or

(2) was inserted as the result of an abuse by the trustee of a fiduciary or confidential relationship to the settlor.

(b) An exculpatory term drafted or caused to be drafted by the trustee is invalid as an abuse of a fiduciary or confidential relationship unless the trustee proves that the exculpatory term is fair under the circumstances and that its existence and contents were adequately communicated to the settlor.

Comment

Even if the terms of the trust attempt to completely exculpate a trustee for the trustee's acts, the trustee must always comply with a certain minimum standard. As provided in subsection (a), a trustee must always act in good faith with regard to the purposes of the trust and the interests of the beneficiaries. * * *

Subsection (b) disapproves of cases * * * which held that an exculpatory clause in a trust instrument drafted by the trustee was valid because the beneficiary could not prove that the clause was inserted as a result of an abuse of a fiduciary relationship. * * * Subsection (b) responds to the danger that the insertion of such a clause by the fiduciary or its agent may have been undisclosed or inadequately understood by the settlor. To overcome the presumption of abuse in subsection (b), the trustee must establish that the clause was fair and that its existence and contents were adequately communicated to the settlor. In determining whether the clause was fair, the court may wish to examine: (1) the extent of the prior relationship between the settlor and trustee; (2) whether the settlor received independent advice; (3) the sophistication of the settlor with respect to business and fiduciary matters; (4) the trustee's reasons for inserting the clause; and (5) the scope of the particular provision inserted. * * *

The requirements of subsection (b) are satisfied if the settlor was represented by independent counsel. If the settlor was represented by independent counsel, the settlor's attorney is considered the drafter of the instrument even if the attorney used the trustee's form. Because the settlor's attorney is an agent of the settlor, disclosure of an exculpatory term to the settlor's attorney is disclosure to the settlor.

Section 1009. Beneficiary's Consent, Release, or Ratification.

A trustee is not liable to a beneficiary for breach of trust if the beneficiary consented to the conduct constituting the breach, released the trustee from liability for the breach, or ratified the transaction constituting the breach, unless:

(1)   the consent, release, or ratification of the beneficiary was induced by improper conduct of the trustee; or

(2)   at the time of the consent, release, or ratification, the beneficiary did not know of the beneficiary's rights or of the material facts relating to the breach.

Comment

* * * A consent, release, or affirmance under this section may occur either before or after the approved conduct. This section requires an affirmative act by the beneficiary. A failure to object is not sufficient. * * * A consent is binding on a consenting beneficiary although other beneficiaries have not consented. * * * To constitute a valid consent, the beneficiary must know of the beneficiary's rights and of the material facts relating to the breach. * * * If the beneficiary's approval involves a self-dealing transaction, the approval is binding only if the transaction was fair and reasonable. * * *

An approval by the settlor of a revocable trust or by the holder of a presently exercisable power of withdrawal binds all the beneficiaries. * * * A beneficiary is also bound to the extent an approval is given by a person authorized to represent the beneficiary as provided in Article 3.

Section 1010. Limitation on Personal Liability of Trustee.

(a)   Except as otherwise provided in the contract, a trustee is not personally liable on a contract properly entered into in the trustee's fiduciary capacity in the course of administering the trust if the trustee in the contract disclosed the fiduciary capacity.

(b)   A trustee is personally liable for torts committed in the course of administering a trust, or for obligations arising from ownership or control of trust property, including liability for violation of environmental law, only if the trustee is personally at fault.

(c)   A claim based on a contract entered into by a trustee in the trustee's fiduciary capacity, on an obligation arising from ownership or control of trust property, or on a tort committed in the course of administering a trust, may be asserted in a judicial proceeding against the trustee in the trustee's fiduciary capacity, whether or not the trustee is personally liable for the claim.

Comment

* * * [S]ubsection (a) protects a trustee who reveals the fiduciary relationship either by indicating a signature as trustee or by simply referring to the trust. The protection afforded the trustee by this section applies only to contracts that are properly entered into in the trustee's fiduciary capacity, meaning that the trustee is exercising an available power and is not violating a duty. This section does not excuse any liability the trustee may have for breach of trust.

Subsection (b) addresses trustee liability arising from ownership or control of trust property and for torts occurring incident to the administration of the trust. Liability in such situations is imposed on the trustee personally only if the trustee was personally at fault, either intentionally or negligently. * * *

Subsection (c) alters the common law rule that a trustee could not be sued in a representative capacity if the trust estate was not liable.

[Section 1011. Interest as General Partner.

(a)   Except as otherwise provided in subsection (c) or unless personal liability is imposed in the contract, a trustee who holds an interest as a general partner in a general or limited partnership is not personally liable on a contract entered into by the partnership after the trust's acquisition of the interest if the fiduciary capacity was disclosed in the contract or in a statement previously filed pursuant to the [Uniform Partnership Act or Uniform Limited Partnership Act].

(b)   Except as otherwise provided in subsection (c), a trustee who holds an interest as a general partner is not personally liable for torts committed by the partnership or for obligations arising from ownership or control of the interest unless the trustee is personally at fault.

(c)   The immunity provided by this section does not apply if an interest in the partnership is held by the trustee in a capacity other than that of trustee or is held by the trustee's spouse or one or more of the trustee's descendants, siblings, or parents, or the spouse of any of them.

(d)   If the trustee of a revocable trust holds an interest as a general partner, the settlor is personally liable for contracts and other obligations of the partnership as if the settlor were a general partner.]

Comment

Section 1010 protects a trustee from personal liability on contracts that the trustee enters into on behalf of the trust. Section 1010 also absolves a trustee from liability for torts committed in administering the trust unless the trustee was personally at fault. It does not protect a trustee from personal liability for contracts entered into or torts committed by a general or limited partnership of which the trustee was a general partner. That is the purpose of this section * * * .

Special protection is not needed for other business interests that the trustee may own, such as an interest as a limited partner, a membership interest in an LLC, or an interest as a corporate shareholder. In these cases the nature of the entity or the interest owned by the trustee carries with it its own limitation on liability. * * *

Section 1012. Protection of Person Dealing With Trustee.

(a)   A person other than a beneficiary who in good faith assists a trustee, or who in good faith and for value deals with a trustee, without knowledge that the trustee is exceeding or improperly exercising the trustee's powers is protected from liability as if the trustee properly exercised the power.

(b)   A person other than a beneficiary who in good faith deals with a trustee is not required to inquire into the extent of the trustee's powers or the propriety of their exercise.

(c)   A person who in good faith delivers assets to a trustee need not ensure their proper application.

(d)   A person other than a beneficiary who in good faith assists a former trustee, or who in good faith and for value deals with a former trustee, without knowledge that the trusteeship has terminated is protected from liability as if the former trustee were still a trustee.

(e)   Comparable protective provisions of other laws relating to commercial transactions or transfer of securities by fiduciaries prevail over the protection provided by this section.

Comment

* * * Subsection (a) protects two different classes; persons other than beneficiaries who assist a trustee with a transaction, and persons other than beneficiaries who deal with the trustee for value. As long as the assistance was provided or the transaction was entered into in good faith and without knowledge, third persons in either category are protected in the transaction even if the trustee was exceeding or improperly exercising the power. * * *

Subsection (b) confirms that a third party who is acting in good faith is not charged with a duty to inquire into the extent of a trustee's powers or the propriety of their exercise. The third party may assume that the trustee has the necessary power. Consequently, there is no need to request or examine a copy of the trust instrument. A third party who wishes assurance that the trustee has the necessary authority instead should request a certification of trust as provided in Section 1013. Subsection (b) * * * [is] intended to negate the rule, followed by some courts, that a third party is charged with constructive notice of the trust instrument and its contents. * * *

Section 1013. Certification of Trust.

(a)   Instead of furnishing a copy of the trust instrument to a person other than a beneficiary, the trustee may furnish to the person a certification of trust containing the following information:

(1)   that the trust exists and the date the trust instrument was executed;

(2)   the identity of the settlor;

(3)   the identity and address of the currently acting trustee;

(4)   the powers of the trustee;

(5)   the revocability or irrevocability of the trust and the identity of any person holding a power to revoke the trust;

(6)   the authority of cotrustees to sign or otherwise authenticate and whether all or less than all are required in order to exercise powers of the trustee;

(7)   the trust's taxpayer identification number; and

(8)   the manner of taking title to trust property.

(b)   A certification of trust may be signed or otherwise authenticated by any trustee.

(c)   A certification of trust must state that the trust has not been revoked, modified, or amended in any manner that would cause the representations contained in the certification of trust to be incorrect.

(d)   A certification of trust need not contain the dispositive terms of a trust.

(e)   A recipient of a certification of trust may require the trustee to furnish copies of those excerpts from the original trust instrument and later amendments which designate the trustee and confer upon the trustee the power to act in the pending transaction.

(f)   A person who acts in reliance upon a certification of trust without knowledge that the representations contained therein are incorrect is not liable to any person for so acting and may assume without inquiry the existence of the facts contained in the certification. Knowledge of the terms of the trust may not be inferred solely from the fact that a copy of all or part of the trust instrument is held by the person relying upon the certification.

(g)   A person who in good faith enters into a transaction in reliance upon a certification of trust may enforce the transaction against the trust property as if the representations contained in the certification were correct.

(h)   A person making a demand for the trust instrument in addition to a certification of trust or excerpts is liable for damages if the court determines that the person did not act in good faith in demanding the trust instrument.

(i)   This section does not limit the right of a person to obtain a copy of the trust instrument in a judicial proceeding concerning the trust.

Comment

This section * * * is designed to protect the privacy of a trust instrument by discouraging requests from persons other than beneficiaries for complete copies of the instrument in order to verify a trustee's authority. Even absent this section, such requests are usually unnecessary. Pursuant to Section 1012(b), a third person proceeding in good faith is not required to inquire into the extent of the trustee's powers or the propriety of their exercise. This section adds another layer of protection.

Third persons frequently insist on receiving a copy of the complete trust instrument solely to verify a specific and narrow authority of the trustee to engage in a particular transaction. * * * A certification of trust is a document signed by a currently acting trustee that may include excerpts from the trust instrument necessary to facilitate the particular transaction. A certification provides the third party with an assurance of authority without having to disclose the trust's dispositive provisions. Nor is there a need for third persons who may already have a copy of the instrument to pry into its provisions. Persons acting in reliance on a certification may assume the truth of the certification even if they have a complete copy of the trust instrument in their possession.

Subsections (a) through (c) specify the required contents of a certification. Subsection (d) clarifies that the certification need not include the trust's dispositive terms. A certification, however, normally will contain the administrative terms of the trust relevant to the transaction. Subsection (e) provides that the third party may make this a condition of acceptance. Subsections (f) and (g) protect a third party who relies on the certification. The third party may assume that the certification is true, and is not charged with constructive knowledge of the terms of the trust instrument even if the third party has a copy.

To encourage compliance with this section, a person demanding a trust instrument after already being offered a certification may be liable under subsection (h) for damages if the refusal to accept the certification is determined not to have been in good faith. A person acting in good faith would include a person required to examine a complete copy of the trust instrument pursuant to due diligence standards or as required by other law. Examples of such due diligence and legal requirements include (1) in connection with transactions to be executed in the capital markets where documentary standards have been established in connection with underwriting concerns; (2) to satisfy documentary requirements established by state or local government or regulatory agency; (3) to satisfy documentary requirements established by a state or local government or regulatory agency; and (4) where the insurance rates or premiums or other expenses of the party would be higher absent the availability of the documentation. * * *

ARTICLE 11

MISCELLANEOUS PROVISIONS

UNIFORM CUSTODIAL TRUST ACT*

PREFATORY NOTE

This Uniform Act provides for the creation of a statutory custodial trust for adults to be governed by the provisions of the Act whenever property is delivered to another "as custodial trustee under the (Enacting state) Uniform Custodial Trust Act." The provisions of this Act are based on trust analogies to concepts developed and used in establishing custodianships for minors under the Uniform Transfers to Minors Act (UTMA). The Custodial Trust Act is designed to provide a statutory standby inter vivos trust for individuals who typically are not very affluent or sophisticated, and possibly represented by attorneys engaged in general rather than specialized estate practice. The most frequent use of this trust would be in response to the commonly occurring need of elderly individuals to provide for the future management of assets in the event of incapacity. The statute will also be available for accomplishing distribution of funds by judgment debtors and others to incapacitated persons for whom a conservator has not been appointed. Since this Act allows any person, competent to transfer property, to create custodial trusts for the benefit of themselves or others, with the beneficial interest in custodial trust property in the beneficiary and not in the custodial trustee, its potential for use is extensive. Although the most frequent use probably will be by elderly persons, it is also available for a parent to establish a custodial trust for an adult child who may be incapacitated; for adult persons in the military, or those leaving the country temporarily, to place their property with another for management without relinquishing beneficial ownership of their property; or for young people who have received property under the Uniform Transfers to Minors Act to continue a custodial trust as adults in order to obtain the benefit and convenience of management services performed by the custodial trustee.

This Act follows the approach taken by the Uniform Transfers to Minors Act and allows any kind of property, real or personal, tangible or intangible, to be made the subject of a transfer to a custodial trustee for the benefit of a beneficiary. However, the most typical transaction envisioned would involve a person who would transfer intangible property, such as securities or bank accounts, to a custodial trustee but with retention by the transferor of direction over the property. Later, this direction could be relinquished, or it could be lost upon incapacity. The objective of the statute is to provide a simple trust that is uncomplicated in its creation, administration, and termination. The potential for tax problems is minimized by permitting the beneficiary in most instances to retain control while the beneficiary has capacity to manage the assets effectively. The statute contains an asset specific transfer provision that it is believed will be simple to use and will gain the acceptance of the securities and financial industry. A simple transfer document, examples of which are set forth in the Act, and a receipt from the custodian, also in the Act, would provide for identification of beneficiaries or distributees upon death of the beneficiary. Protection is extended to third parties dealing with the custodian. Although the Act is patterned on the Uniform Transfers to Minors Act and meshes into the Uniform Probate Code, it is appropriate for enactment as well in states which have not adopted either UTMA or the UPC.

An adult beneficiary, who is not incapacitated, may: (1) terminate the custodial trust on demand (Section 2(e)); (2) receive so much of the income or custodial property as he or she may request from time to time (Section 9(a)); and (3) give the custodial trustee binding instructions for investment or management (Section 7(b)). In the absence of direction by the beneficiary, who is not incapacitated, the custodial trustee manages the property subject to the standard of care that would be observed by a prudent person dealing with the property of another and is not limited by other statutory restrictions on investments by fiduciaries. (Section 7).

A principal feature of the Custodial Trust under this Act is designed to protect the beneficiary and his or her dependents against the perils of the beneficiary's possible future incapacity without the necessity of a conservatorship. Under Section 10, the incapacity of the beneficiary does not terminate (1) the custodial trust, (2) the designation of a successor custodial trustee, (3) any power or authority of the custodial trustee, or (4) the immunities of third persons relying on actions of the custodial trustee. The custodial trustee continues to manage the property as a discretionary trust under the prudent person standard for the benefit of the incapacitated beneficiary. * * *

Section 1. Definitions.

As used in this [Act]:

(1)   "Adult" means an individual who is at least 18 years of age.

(2)   "Beneficiary" means an individual for whom property has been transferred to or held under a declaration of trust by a custodial trustee for the individual's use and benefit under this [Act].

(3)   "Conservator" means a person appointed or qualified by a court to manage the estate of an individual or a person legally authorized to perform substantially the same functions.

(4)   "Court" means the [_____] court of this State.

(5)   "Custodial trust property" means an interest in property transferred to or held under a declaration of trust by a custodial trustee under this [Act] and the income from and proceeds of that interest.

(6)   "Custodial trustee" means a person designated as trustee of a custodial trust under this [Act] or a substitute or successor to the person designated.

(7)   "Guardian" means a person appointed or qualified by a court as a guardian of an individual, including a limited guardian, but not a person who is only a guardian ad litem.

(8)   "Incapacitated" means lacking the ability to manage property and business affairs effectively by reason of mental illness, mental deficiency, physical illness or disability, chronic use of drugs, chronic intoxication, confinement, detention by a foreign power, disappearance, minority, or other disabling cause.

(9)   "Legal representative" means a personal representative or conservator.

(10) "Member of the beneficiary's family" means a beneficiary's spouse, descendant, stepchild, parent, stepparent, grandparent, brother, sister, uncle, or aunt, whether of the whole or half blood or by adoption.

(11) "Person" means an individual, corporation, business trust, estate, trust, partnership, joint venture, association, or any other legal or commercial entity.

(12) "Personal representative" means an executor, administrator, or special administrator of a decedent's estate, a person legally authorized to perform substantially the same functions, or a successor to any of them.

(13) "State" means a state, territory, or possession of the United States, the District of Columbia, or the Commonwealth of Puerto Rico.

(14) "Transferor" means a person who creates a custodial trust by transfer or declaration.

(15) "Trust company" means a financial institution, corporation, or other legal entity, authorized to exercise general trust powers.

Section 2. Custodial Trust; General.

(a)   A person may create a custodial trust of property by a written transfer of the property to another person, evidenced by registration or by other instrument of transfer, executed in any lawful manner, naming as beneficiary, an individual who may be the transferor, in which the transferee is designated, in substance, as custodial trustee under the [Enacting state] Uniform Custodial Trust Act.

(b)   A person may create a custodial trust of property by a written declaration, evidenced by registration of the property or by other instrument of declaration executed in any lawful manner, describing the property and naming as beneficiary an individual other than the declarant, in which the declarant as titleholder is designated, in substance, as custodial trustee under the [Enacting state] Uniform Custodial Trust Act. A registration or other declaration of trust for the sole benefit of the declarant is not a custodial trust under this [Act].

(c)   Title to custodial trust property is in the custodial trustee and the beneficial interest is in the beneficiary.

(d)   Except as provided in subsection (e), a transferor may not terminate a custodial trust.

(e)   The beneficiary, if not incapacitated, or the conservator of an incapacitated beneficiary, may terminate a custodial trust by delivering to the custodial trustee a writing signed by the beneficiary or conservator declaring the termination. If not previously terminated, the custodial trust terminates on the death of the beneficiary.

(f)   Any person may augment existing custodial trust property by the addition of other property pursuant to this [Act].

(g)   The transferor may designate, or authorize the designation of, a successor custodial trustee in the trust instrument.

(h)   This [Act] does not displace or restrict other means of creating trusts. A trust whose terms do not conform to this [Act] may be enforceable according to its terms under other law.

Section 3. Custodial Trustee for Future Payment or Transfer.

(a)   A person having the right to designate the recipient of property payable or transferable upon a future event may create a custodial trust upon the occurrence of the future event by designating in writing the recipient, followed in substance by: "as custodial trustee for _____ (name of beneficiary) under the [Enacting state] Uniform Custodial Trust Act."

(b)   Persons may be designated as substitute or successor custodial trustees to whom the property must be paid or transferred in the order named if the first designated custodial trustee is unable or unwilling to serve.

(c)   A designation under this section may be made in a will, a trust, a deed, a multiple-party account, an insurance policy, an instrument exercising a power of appointment, or a writing designating a beneficiary of contractual rights. Otherwise, to be effective, the designation must be registered with or delivered to the fiduciary, payor, issuer, or obligor of the future right.

Section 4. Form and Effect of Receipt and Acceptance by Custodial Trustee, Jurisdiction.

(a)   Obligations of a custodial trustee, including the obligation to follow directions of the beneficiary, arise under this [Act] upon the custodial trustee's acceptance, express or implied, of the custodial trust property.

(b)   The custodial trustee's acceptance may be evidenced by a writing stating in substance:

CUSTODIAL TRUSTEE'S RECEIPT AND ACCEPTANCE

I, _____ (name of custodial trustee) acknowledge receipt of the custodial trust property described below or in the attached instrument and accept the custodial trust as custodial trustee for _____ (name of beneficiary) under the [Enacting state] Uniform Custodial Trust Act. I undertake to administer and distribute the custodial trust property pursuant to the [Enacting state] Uniform Custodial Trust Act. My obligations as custodial trustee are subject to the directions of the beneficiary unless the beneficiary is designated as, is, or becomes incapacitated. The custodial trust property consists of _____.

Dated: _____

_____
(Signature of Custodial
Trustee)

(c)   Upon accepting custodial trust property, a person designated as custodial trustee under this [Act] is subject to personal jurisdiction of the court with respect to any matter relating to the custodial trust.

Section 5. Transfer to Custodial Trustee by Fiduciary or Obligor; Facility of Payment.

(a)   Unless otherwise directed by an instrument designating a custodial trustee pursuant to Section 3, a person, including a fiduciary other than a custodial trustee, who holds property of or owes a debt to an incapacitated individual not having a conservator may make a transfer to an adult member of the beneficiary's family or to a trust company as custodial trustee for the use and benefit of the incapacitated individual. If the value of the property or the debt exceeds [$20,000], the transfer is not effective unless authorized by the court.

(b)   A written acknowledgment of delivery, signed by a custodial trustee, is a sufficient receipt and discharge for property transferred to the custodial trustee pursuant to this section.

Section 6. Multiple Beneficiaries; Separate Custodial Trusts; Survivorship.

(a)   Beneficial interests in a custodial trust created for multiple beneficiaries are deemed to be separate custodial trusts of equal undivided interests for each beneficiary. Except in a transfer or declaration for use and benefit of spouses, for whom survivorship is presumed, a right of survivorship does not exist unless the instrument creating the custodial trust specifically provides for survivorship [or survivorship is required as to community or marital property].

(b)   Custodial trust property held under this [Act] by the same custodial trustee for the use and benefit of the same beneficiary may be administered as a single custodial trust.

(c)   A custodial trustee of custodial trust property held for more than one beneficiary shall separately account to each beneficiary pursuant to Sections 7 and 15 for the administration of the custodial trust.

Section 7. General Duties of Custodial Trustee.

(a)   If appropriate, a custodial trustee shall register or record the instrument vesting title to custodial trust property.

(b)   If the beneficiary is not incapacitated, a custodial trustee shall follow the directions of the beneficiary in the management, control, investment, or retention of the custodial trust property. In the absence of effective contrary direction by the beneficiary while not incapacitated, the custodial trustee shall observe the standard of care that would be observed by a prudent person dealing with property of another and is not limited by any other law restricting investments by fiduciaries. However, a custodial trustee, in the custodial trustee's discretion, may retain any custodial trust property received from the transferor. If a custodial trustee has a special skill or expertise or is named custodial trustee on the basis of representation of a special skill or expertise, the custodial trustee shall use that skill or expertise.

(c)   Subject to subsection (b), a custodial trustee shall take control of and collect, hold, manage, invest, and reinvest custodial trust property.

(d)   A custodial trustee at all times shall keep custodial trust property of which the custodial trustee has control, separate from all other property in a manner sufficient to identify it clearly as custodial trust property of the beneficiary. Custodial trust property, the title to which is subject to recordation, is so identified if an appropriate instrument so identifying the property is recorded, and custodial trust property subject to registration is so identified if it is registered, or held in an account in the name of the custodial trustee, designated in substance: "as custodial trustee for _____ (name of beneficiary) under the [Enacting state] Uniform Custodial Trust Act."

(e)   A custodial trustee shall keep records of all transactions with respect to custodial trust property, including information necessary for the preparation of tax returns, and shall make the records and information available at reasonable times to the beneficiary or legal representative of the beneficiary.

(f)   The exercise of a durable power of attorney for an incapacitated beneficiary is not effective to terminate or direct the administration or distribution of a custodial trust.

Section 8. General Powers of Custodial Trustee.

(a)   A custodial trustee, acting in a fiduciary capacity, has all the rights and powers over custodial trust property which an unmarried adult owner has over individually owned property, but a custodial trustee may exercise those rights and powers in a fiduciary capacity only.

(b)   This section does not relieve a custodial trustee from liability for a violation of Section 7.

Section 9. Use of Custodial Trust Property.

(a)   A custodial trustee shall pay to the beneficiary or expend for the beneficiary's use and benefit so much or all of the custodial trust property as the beneficiary while not incapacitated may direct from time to time.

(b)   If the beneficiary is incapacitated, the custodial trustee shall expend so much or all of the custodial trust property as the custodial trustee considers advisable for the use and benefit of the beneficiary and individuals who were supported by the beneficiary when the beneficiary became incapacitated, or who are legally entitled to support by the beneficiary. Expenditures may be made in the manner, when, and to the extent that the custodial trustee determines suitable and proper, without court order and without regard to other support, income, or property of the beneficiary.

(c) A custodial trustee may establish checking, savings, or other similar accounts of reasonable amounts under which either the custodial trustee or the beneficiary may withdraw funds from, or draw checks against, the accounts. Funds withdrawn from, or checks written against, the account by the beneficiary are distributions of custodial trust property by the custodial trustee to the beneficiary.

Section 10. Determination of Incapacity; Effect.

(a) The custodial trustee shall administer the custodial trust as for an incapacitated beneficiary if (i) the custodial trust was created under Section 5, (ii) the transferor has so directed in the instrument creating the custodial trust, or (iii) the custodial trustee has determined that the beneficiary is incapacitated.

(b) A custodial trustee may determine that the beneficiary is incapacitated in reliance upon (i) previous direction or authority given by the beneficiary while not incapacitated, including direction or authority pursuant to a durable power of attorney, (ii) the certificate of the beneficiary's physician, or (iii) other persuasive evidence.

(c) If a custodial trustee for an incapacitated beneficiary reasonably concludes that the beneficiary's incapacity has ceased, or that circumstances concerning the beneficiary's ability to manage property and business affairs have changed since the creation of a custodial trust directing administration as for an incapacitated beneficiary, the custodial trustee may administer the trust as for a beneficiary who is not incapacitated.

(d) On petition of the beneficiary, the custodial trustee, or other person interested in the custodial trust property or the welfare of the beneficiary, the court shall determine whether the beneficiary is incapacitated.

(e) Absent determination of incapacity of the beneficiary under subsection (b) or (d), a custodial trustee who has reason to believe that the beneficiary is incapacitated shall administer the custodial trust in accordance with the provisions of this [Act] applicable to an incapacitated beneficiary.

(f) Incapacity of a beneficiary does not terminate (i) the custodial trust, (ii) any designation of a successor custodial trustee, (iii) rights or powers of the custodial trustee, or (iv) any immunities of third persons acting on instructions of the custodial trustee.

Section 11. Exemption of Third Person From Liability.

A third person in good faith and without a court order may act on instructions of, or otherwise deal with, a person purporting to make a transfer as, or purporting to act in the capacity of, a custodial trustee. In the absence of knowledge to the contrary, the third person is not responsible for determining:

(1) the validity of the purported custodial trustee's designation;

(2) the propriety of, or the authority under this [Act] for, any action of the purported custodial trustee;

(3) the validity or propriety of an instrument executed or instruction given pursuant to this [Act] either by the person purporting to make a transfer or declaration or by the purported custodial trustee; or

(4) the propriety of the application of property vested in the purported custodial trustee.

Section 12. Liability to Third Person.

(a) A claim based on a contract entered into by a custodial trustee acting in a fiduciary capacity, an obligation arising from the ownership or control of custodial trust property, or a tort committed in the course of administering the custodial trust, may be asserted by a third person against the custodial trust property by proceeding against the custodial trustee in a fiduciary capacity, whether or not the custodial trustee or the beneficiary is personally liable.

(b)   A custodial trustee is not personally liable to a third person:

(1)   on a contract properly entered into in a fiduciary capacity unless the custodial trustee fails to reveal that capacity or to identify the custodial trust in the contract; or

(2)   for an obligation arising from control of custodial trust property or for a tort committed in the course of the administration of the custodial trust unless the custodial trustee is personally at fault.

(c)   A beneficiary is not personally liable to a third person for an obligation arising from beneficial ownership of custodial trust property or for a tort committed in the course of administration of the custodial trust unless the beneficiary is personally in possession of the custodial trust property giving rise to the liability or is personally at fault.

(d)   Subsections (b) and (c) do not preclude actions or proceedings to establish liability of the custodial trustee or beneficiary to the extent the person sued is protected as the insured by liability insurance.

Section 13. Declination, Resignation, Incapacity, Death, or Removal of Custodial Trustee, Designation of Successor Custodial Trustee.

(a)   Before accepting the custodial trust property, a person designated as custodial trustee may decline to serve by notifying the person who made the designation, the transferor, or the transferor's legal representative. If an event giving rise to a transfer has not occurred, the substitute custodial trustee designated under Section 3 becomes the custodial trustee, or, if a substitute custodial trustee has not been designated, the person who made the designation may designate a substitute custodial trustee pursuant to Section 3. In other cases, the transferor or the transferor's legal representative may designate a substitute custodial trustee.

(b)   A custodial trustee who has accepted the custodial trust property may resign by (i) delivering written notice to a successor custodial trustee, if any, the beneficiary and, if the beneficiary is incapacitated, to the beneficiary's conservator, if any, and (ii) transferring or registering, or recording an appropriate instrument relating to, the custodial trust property, in the name of, and delivering the records to, the successor custodial trustee identified under subsection (c).

(c)   If a custodial trustee or successor custodial trustee is ineligible, resigns, dies, or becomes incapacitated, the successor designated under Section 2(g) or 3 becomes custodial trustee. If there is no effective provision for a successor, the beneficiary, if not incapacitated, may designate a successor custodial trustee. If the beneficiary is incapacitated, or fails to act within 90 days after the ineligibility, resignation, death, or incapacity of the custodial trustee, the beneficiary's conservator becomes successor custodial trustee. If the beneficiary does not have a conservator or the conservator fails to act, the resigning custodial trustee may designate a successor custodial trustee.

(d)   If a successor custodial trustee is not designated pursuant to subsection (c), the transferor, the legal representative of the transferor or of the custodial trustee, an adult member of the beneficiary's family, the guardian of the beneficiary, a person interested in the custodial trust property, or a person interested in the welfare of the beneficiary, may petition the court to designate a successor custodial trustee.

(e)   A custodial trustee who declines to serve or resigns, or the legal representative of a deceased or incapacitated custodial trustee, as soon as practicable, shall put the custodial trust property and records in the possession and control of the successor custodial trustee. The successor custodial trustee may enforce the obligation to deliver custodial trust property and records and becomes responsible for each item as received.

(f)   A beneficiary, the beneficiary's conservator, an adult member of the beneficiary's family, a guardian of the person of the beneficiary, a person interested in the custodial trust property, or a person interested in the welfare of the beneficiary, may petition the court to remove the custodial trustee for cause and designate a successor custodial trustee, to require the custodial trustee to furnish a bond or other security for the faithful performance of fiduciary duties, or for other appropriate relief.

Section 14. Expenses, Compensation, and Bond of Custodial Trustee.

Except as otherwise provided in the instrument creating the custodial trust, in an agreement with the beneficiary, or by court order, a custodial trustee:

(1) is entitled to reimbursement from custodial trust property for reasonable expenses incurred in the performance of fiduciary services;

(2) has a noncumulative election, to be made no later than six months after the end of each calendar year, to charge a reasonable compensation for fiduciary services performed during that year; and

(3) need not furnish a bond or other security for the faithful performance of fiduciary duties.

Section 15. Reporting and Accounting by Custodial Trustee; Determination of Liability of Custodial Trustee.

(a) Upon the acceptance of custodial trust property, the custodial trustee shall provide a written statement describing the custodial trust property and shall thereafter provide a written statement of the administration of the custodial trust property (i) once each year, (ii) upon request at reasonable times by the beneficiary or the beneficiary's legal representative, (iii) upon resignation or removal of the custodial trustee, and (iv) upon termination of the custodial trust. The statements must be provided to the beneficiary or to the beneficiary's legal representative, if any. Upon termination of the beneficiary's interest, the custodial trustee shall furnish a current statement to the person to whom the custodial trust property is to be delivered.

(b) A beneficiary, the beneficiary's legal representative, an adult member of the beneficiary's family, a person interested in the custodial trust property, or a person interested in the welfare of the beneficiary may petition the court for an accounting by the custodial trustee or the custodial trustee's legal representative.

(c) A successor custodial trustee may petition the court for an accounting by a predecessor custodial trustee.

(d) In an action or proceeding under this [Act] or in any other proceeding, the court may require or permit the custodial trustee or the custodial trustee's legal representative to account. The custodial trustee or the custodial trustee's legal representative may petition the court for approval of final accounts.

(e) If a custodial trustee is removed, the court shall require an accounting and order delivery of the custodial trust property and records to the successor custodial trustee and the execution of all instruments required for transfer of the custodial trust property.

(f) On petition of the custodial trustee or any person who could petition for an accounting, the court, after notice to interested persons, may issue instructions to the custodial trustee or review the propriety of the acts of a custodial trustee or the reasonableness of compensation determined by the custodial trustee for the services of the custodial trustee or others.

Section 16. Limitations of Action Against Custodial Trustee.

(a) Except as provided in subsection (c), unless previously barred by adjudication, consent, or limitation, a claim for relief against a custodial trustee for accounting or breach of duty is barred as to a beneficiary, a person to whom custodial trust property is to be paid or delivered, or the legal representative of an incapacitated or deceased beneficiary or payee:

(1) who has received a final account or statement fully disclosing the matter unless an action or proceeding to assert the claim is commenced within two years after receipt of the final account or statement; or

(2) who has not received a final account or statement fully disclosing the matter unless an action or proceeding to assert the claim is commenced within three years after the termination of the custodial trust.

(b) Except as provided in subsection (c), a claim for relief to recover from a custodial trustee for fraud, misrepresentation, or concealment related to the final settlement of the custodial trust or concealment of the existence of the custodial trust, is barred unless an action or proceeding to assert the claim is commenced within five years after the termination of the custodial trust.

(c) A claim for relief is not barred by this section if the claimant:

(1) is a minor, until the earlier of two years after the claimant becomes an adult or dies;

(2) is an incapacitated adult, until the earliest of two years after (i) the appointment of a conservator, (ii) the removal of the incapacity, or (iii) the death of the claimant; or

(3) was an adult, now deceased, who was not incapacitated, until two years after the claimant's death.

Section 17. Distribution on Termination.

(a) Upon termination of a custodial trust, the custodial trustee shall transfer the unexpended custodial trust property:

(1) to the beneficiary, if not incapacitated or deceased;

(2) to the conservator or other recipient designated by the court for an incapacitated beneficiary; or

(3) upon the beneficiary's death, in the following order:

(i) as last directed in a writing signed by the deceased beneficiary while not incapacitated and received by the custodial trustee during the life of the deceased beneficiary;

(ii) to the survivor of multiple beneficiaries if survivorship is provided for pursuant to Section 6;

(iii) as designated in the instrument creating the custodial trust; or

(iv) to the estate of the deceased beneficiary.

(b) If, when the custodial trust would otherwise terminate, the distributee is incapacitated, the custodial trust continues for the use and benefit of the distributee as beneficiary until the incapacity is removed or the custodial trust is otherwise terminated.

(c) Death of a beneficiary does not terminate the power of the custodial trustee to discharge obligations of the custodial trustee or beneficiary incurred before the termination of the custodial trust.

Comment

* * * The direction to the custodial trustee by the beneficiary, who is not incapacitated, for distribution on termination of the custodial trust may be in any written form clearly identifying the distributee. For example, the following direction would be adequate under the statute:

I, _____ (name of beneficiary) hereby direct _____ (name of trustee) as custodial trustee, to transfer and pay the unexpended balance of the custodial trust property of which I am beneficiary to _____ as distributee on the termination of the trust at my death. In the event of the prior death of _____ above named as distributee, I designate _____ as distributee of the custodial trust property.

Signed

(signature)
Beneficiary

Date _____

Receipt Acknowledged

(signature)
Custodial Trustee

Date _____

Section 18. Methods and Forms for Creating Custodial Trusts.

(a) If a transaction, including a declaration with respect to or a transfer of specific property, otherwise satisfies applicable law, the criteria of Section 2 are satisfied by:

(1)   the execution and either delivery to the custodial trustee or recording of an instrument in substantially the following form:

TRANSFER UNDER THE [ENACTING STATE]
UNIFORM CUSTODIAL TRUST ACT

I, _____ (name of transferor or name and representative capacity if a fiduciary), transfer to _____ (name of trustee other than transferor), as custodial trustee for _____ (name of beneficiary) as beneficiary and _____ as distributee on termination of the trust in absence of direction by the beneficiary under the [Enacting state] Uniform Custodial Trust Act, the following: (insert a description of the custodial trust property legally sufficient to identify and transfer each item of property).

Dated: _____

_____
(Signature); or

(2)   the execution and the recording or giving notice of its execution to the beneficiary of an instrument in substantially the following form:

DECLARATION OF TRUST UNDER THE [ENACTING STATE]
UNIFORM CUSTODIAL TRUST ACT

I, _____ (name of owner of property), declare that henceforth I hold as custodial trustee for _____ (name of beneficiary other than transferor) as beneficiary and _____ as distributee on termination of the trust in absence of direction by the beneficiary under the [Enacting state] Uniform Custodial Trust Act, the following: (Insert a description of the custodial trust property legally sufficient to identify and transfer each item of property).

Dated: _____

_____
(Signature)

(b) Customary methods of transferring or evidencing ownership of property may be used to create a custodial trust, including any of the following:

(1)   registration of a security in the name of a trust company, an adult other than the transferor, or the transferor if the beneficiary is other than the transferor, designated in substance "as custodial trustee for _____ (name of beneficiary) under the [Enacting state] Uniform Custodial Trust Act";

(2)   delivery of a certificated security, or a document necessary for the transfer of an uncertificated security, together with any necessary endorsement, to an adult other than the

transferor or to a trust company as custodial trustee, accompanied by an instrument in substantially the form prescribed in subsection (a)(1);

(3) payment of money or transfer of a security held in the name of a broker or a financial institution or its nominee to a broker or financial institution for credit to an account in the name of a trust company, an adult other than the transferor, or the transferor if the beneficiary is other than the transferor, designated in substance: "as custodial trustee for _____ (name of beneficiary) under the [Enacting state] Uniform Custodial Trust Act";

(4) registration of ownership of a life or endowment insurance policy or annuity contract with the issuer in the name of a trust company, an adult other than the transferor, or the transferor if the beneficiary is other than the transferor, designated in substance: "as custodial trustee for _____ (name of beneficiary) under the [Enacting state] Uniform Custodial Trust Act";

(5) delivery of a written assignment to an adult other than the transferor or to a trust company whose name in the assignment is designated in substance by the words: "as custodial trustee for _____ (name of beneficiary) under the [Enacting state] Uniform Custodial Trust Act";

(6) irrevocable exercise of a power of appointment, pursuant to its terms, in favor of a trust company, an adult other than the donee of the power, or the donee who holds the power if the beneficiary is other than the donee, whose name in the appointment is designated in substance: "as custodial trustee for _____ (name of beneficiary) under the [Enacting state] Uniform Custodial Trust Act";

(7) delivery of a written notification or assignment of a right to future payment under a contract to an obligor which transfers the right under the contract to a trust company, an adult other than the transferor, or the transferor if the beneficiary is other than the transferor, whose name in the notification or assignment is designated in substance: "as custodial trustee for _____ (name of beneficiary) under the [Enacting state] Uniform Custodial Trust Act";

(8) execution, delivery, and recordation of a conveyance of an interest in real property in the name of a trust company, an adult other than the transferor, or the transferor if the beneficiary is other than the transferor, designated in substance: "as custodial trustee for _____ (name of beneficiary) under the [Enacting state] Uniform Custodial Trust Act";

(9) issuance of a certificate of title by an agency of a state or of the United States which evidences title to tangible personal property:

(i) issued in the name of a trust company, an adult other than the transferor, or the transferor if the beneficiary is other than the transferor, designated in substance: "as custodial trustee for _____ (name of beneficiary) under the [Enacting state] Uniform Custodial Trust Act"; or

(ii) delivered to a trust company or an adult other than the transferor or endorsed by the transferor to that person, designated in substance: "as custodial trustee for _____ (name of beneficiary) under the [Enacting state] Uniform Custodial Trust Act"; or

(10) execution and delivery of an instrument of gift to a trust company or an adult other than the transferor, designated in substance: "as custodial trustee for _____ (name of beneficiary) under the [Enacting state] Uniform Custodial Trust Act."

Section 19. Applicable Law. [omitted]

Section 20. Uniformity of Application and Construction. [omitted]

Section 21. Short Title.

This [Act] may be cited as the "[Name of Enacting State] Uniform Custodial Trust Act."

Section 22. Severability. [omitted]

Section 23. Effective Date. [omitted]

UNIFORM DIRECTED TRUST ACT*

PREFATORY NOTE

Background. The Uniform Directed Trust Act addresses an increasingly common arrangement in contemporary estate planning and asset management known as a "directed trust." In a directed trust, the terms of the trust grant a person other than a trustee a power over some aspect of the trust's administration. There is no consistent vocabulary to describe the person other than a trustee that holds a power in a directed trust. Several terms are common in practice, including "trust protector," "trust adviser," and "trust director." There is much uncertainty in existing law about the fiduciary status of a nontrustee that has a power over a trust and about the fiduciary duty of a trustee, sometimes called an "administrative trustee" or "directed trustee," with regard to actions taken or directed by the nontrustee. * * *

Under the Uniform Directed Trust Act, a power over a trust held by a nontrustee is called a "power of direction." The holder of a power of direction is called a "trust director." A trustee that is subject to a power of direction is called a "directed trustee." The main contribution of the act is to address the many complications created by giving a power of direction to a trust director, including the fiduciary duty of a trust director and the fiduciary duty of a directed trustee.

Enabling Settlor Autonomy Consistent with Fiduciary Minimums. By validating terms of a trust that grant a trust director a power of direction, the Uniform Directed Trust Act promotes settlor autonomy in accordance with the principle of freedom of disposition. At the same time, the act imposes a mandatory minimum of fiduciary duty on both a directed trustee and a trust director in accordance with the traditional principle that a trust is a fiduciary relationship. * * *

Structure of the Act. The heart of the Uniform Directed Trust Act appears in Sections 6 through 11, which address the powers and duties of a trust director and a directed trustee. Sections 6 through 8 address the kinds of powers that the terms of a trust can grant to a trust director and the default

---

and mandatory fiduciary duties of the director. Section 9 addresses the fiduciary duty of a directed trustee. Sections 10 and 11 further elaborate the duties of a trust director and directed trustee, prescribing specific rules for information sharing and monitoring among trust directors and trustees. * * *

Fiduciary Duty in a Directed Trust. Under the Uniform Directed Trust Act, a trust director has the same default and mandatory fiduciary duties as a trustee in a like position and under similar circumstances (Section 8). In complying with a trust director's exercise of a power of direction, a directed trustee is liable only for the trustee's own "willful misconduct" (Section 9). The logic behind these rules is that in a directed trust the trust director functions much like a trustee in an undirected trust. Accordingly, the trust director should have the same duties as a trustee in the exercise or nonexercise of the director's power of direction, and the fiduciary duty of the directed trustee is reduced with respect to the director's power of direction. * * *

In summary, under the Uniform Directed Trust Act a beneficiary's main recourse for misconduct by a trust director is an action against the director for breach of the director's fiduciary duty to the beneficiary. The beneficiary also has recourse against a directed trustee, but only to the extent of the trustee's own willful misconduct. Compared with a non-directed trust in which a trustee holds all power over the trust, a directed trust subject to this act provides for more aggregate fiduciary duties owed to a beneficiary. All of the usual duties of trusteeship are preserved in the trust director, and in addition the directed trustee has a duty to avoid willful misconduct.

Section 1. Short Title.

This [act] may be cited as the Uniform Directed Trust Act.

Section 2. Definitions.

In this [act]:

(1) "Breach of trust" includes a violation by a trust director or trustee of a duty imposed on that director or trustee by the terms of the trust, this [act], or law of this state other than this [act] pertaining to trusts.

(2) "Directed trust" means a trust for which the terms of the trust grant a power of direction.

(3) "Directed trustee" means a trustee that is subject to a trust director's power of direction.

(4) "Person" means an individual, estate, business or nonprofit entity, public corporation, government or governmental subdivision, agency, or instrumentality, or other legal entity.

(5) "Power of direction" means a power over a trust granted to a person by the terms of the trust to the extent the power is exercisable while the person is not serving as a trustee. The term includes a power over the investment, management, or distribution of trust property or other matters of trust administration. The term excludes the powers described in Section 5(b).

(6) "Settlor" means a person, including a testator, that creates, or contributes property to, a trust. If more than one person creates or contributes property to a trust, each person is a settlor of the portion of the trust property attributable to that person's contribution except to the extent another person has the power to revoke or withdraw that portion.

(7) "State" means a state of the United States, the District of Columbia, Puerto Rico, the United States Virgin Islands, or any other territory or possession subject to the jurisdiction of the United States.

(8) "Terms of a trust" means:

(A) except as otherwise provided in subparagraph (B), the manifestation of the settlor's intent regarding a trust's provisions as:

(i) expressed in the trust instrument; or

      (ii)   established by other evidence that would be admissible in a judicial proceeding; or

   (B)   the trust's provisions as established, determined, or amended by:

      (i)   a trustee or trust director in accordance with applicable law; [or]

      (ii)   court order[; or

      (iii)   a nonjudicial settlement agreement under [Uniform Trust Code Section 111]].

   (9)   "Trust director" means a person that is granted a power of direction by the terms of a trust to the extent the power is exercisable while the person is not serving as a trustee. The person is a trust director whether or not the terms of the trust refer to the person as a trust director and whether or not the person is a beneficiary or settlor of the trust.

   (10)   "Trustee" includes an original, additional, and successor trustee, and a cotrustee.

Comment

(1) Breach of trust. The definition of "breach of trust" in paragraph (1) makes clear that the term includes a breach by a trust director or a trustee of a duty imposed on that director or trustee by the terms of the trust, this act, or other law pertaining to trusts. * * *

In defining a breach of trust to include a breach of a duty imposed by this act, it is important to recognize that some of the duties imposed by this act are default rules that may be varied by the terms of the trust. The drafting committee contemplated that a trust director or a trustee would not be in breach of trust for conduct that was authorized by the terms of a trust to the extent that those terms are permissible under this act or other applicable law. * * *

(3) Directed trustee. The definition of "directed trustee" in paragraph (3) refers only to a trustee that is subject to direction by a trust director. A trustee that is subject to direction by a cotrustee is not for that reason a directed trustee, as paragraphs (5) and (9) exclude a person from being a trust director while that person is serving as trustee. The term "directed trustee" thus includes many but not all trustees that in practice are sometimes called "administrative trustees." Relations between multiple trustees are governed by the law of cotrusteeship as modified by Section 12. * * *

(5) Power of direction. The definition of "power of direction" in paragraph (5) is expansive. It includes any "power over a trust" to the extent the power is exercisable at a time the power holder is not serving as a trustee. A power of direction may be structured as a power to direct the trustee in the exercise of the trustee's powers—for example, a power to direct the trustee in the investment or management of the trust property. A power of direction may also be structured as a power to act independently—for example, by amending the terms of a trust or releasing a trustee from liability.

The definition includes a power only to the extent the power is exercisable at a time the power holder is not serving as a trustee. The purpose of this limitation is to exclude a person serving as trustee from the definition of a trust director, even though as trustee the person will inevitably have a "power over a trust." A trust director, in other words, is someone other than a trustee. The contribution of this act is to address the complications created by giving a person other than a trustee—that is, a trust director—a power over a trust. A power over a trust held by a trustee is governed by existing trust fiduciary law. * * *

(9) Trust director. The definition of a "trust director" in paragraph (9) refers to a person other than a serving trustee that is granted a power of direction by the terms of a trust. Such a person is a trust director even if the terms of the trust or the parties call the person a "trust adviser" or "trust protector" or otherwise purport to disclaim trust director status. A person may be a trust director even if the person is a beneficiary or settlor of the trust, though certain powers of a beneficiary and a settlor are excluded from the application of this act by Section 5.

A serving trustee cannot be a "trust director" for the same reasons that under paragraph (5) a power over a trust cannot be a "power of direction" while the person that holds the power is serving as a trustee. Relations between multiple trustees are governed by the law of cotrusteeship as modified by Section 12. * * *

Section 3. Application; Principal Place of Administration.

(a)   This [act] applies to a trust, whenever created, that has its principal place of administration in this state, subject to the following rules:

(1)   If the trust was created before [the effective date of this [act]], this [act] applies only to a decision or action occurring on or after [the effective date of this [act]].

(2)   If the principal place of administration of the trust is changed to this state on or after [the effective date of this [act]], this [act] applies only to a decision or action occurring on or after the date of the change.

(b)   Without precluding other means to establish a sufficient connection with the designated jurisdiction in a directed trust, terms of the trust which designate the principal place of administration of the trust are valid and controlling if:

(1)   a trustee's principal place of business is located in or a trustee is a resident of the designated jurisdiction;

(2)   a trust director's principal place of business is located in or a trust director is a resident of the designated jurisdiction; or

(3)   all or part of the administration occurs in the designated jurisdiction.

Comment

Subsection (a). Subsection (a) addresses two matters. First, because powers and duties in a directed trust are matters of trust administration, * * * this subsection follows the prevailing conflict of laws rule by linking application of this act to the trust's principal place of administration. As with other matters of administration, the parties are protected against inconsistent court orders by the common law principle of "primary supervision." * * *

Second, this subsection applies this act to all trusts administered in an enacting state regardless of whether the trust was in existence on the effective date of this act. However, under subsections (a)(1) and (2), this act applies only with respect to a decision or action occurring on or after the effective date or, if the trust's principal place of administration was changed to the enacting state after the effective date, only with respect to a decision or action occurring on or after that change. * * *

Subsection (b). Subsection (b) * * * establishes a safe harbor for a settlor's designation of the principal place of administration for a directed trust. Such a designation is valid if (1) a trustee is located in the designated jurisdiction, (2) a trust director is located in the designated jurisdiction, or (3) at least some of the trust administration occurs in the designated jurisdiction. * * *

Section 4. Common Law and Principles of Equity.

The common law and principles of equity supplement this [act], except to the extent modified by this [act] or law of this state other than this [act].

Section 5. Exclusions.

(a)   In this section, "power of appointment" means a power that enables a person acting in a nonfiduciary capacity to designate a recipient of an ownership interest in or another power of appointment over trust property.

(b)   This [act] does not apply to a:

(1)   power of appointment;

(2)   power to appoint or remove a trustee or trust director;

(3)   power of a settlor over a trust to the extent the settlor has a power to revoke the trust;

(4)   power of a beneficiary over a trust to the extent the exercise or nonexercise of the power affects the beneficial interest of:

(A) the beneficiary; or

(B) another beneficiary represented by the beneficiary[under Uniform Trust Code Sections 301 through 305] with respect to the exercise or nonexercise of the power; or

(5) power over a trust if:

(A) the terms of the trust provide that the power is held in a nonfiduciary capacity; and

(B) the power must be held in a nonfiduciary capacity to achieve the settlor's tax objectives under the United States Internal Revenue Code of 1986[, as amended][, and regulations issued thereunder][, as amended].

(c) Unless the terms of a trust provide otherwise, a power granted to a person to designate a recipient of an ownership interest in or power of appointment over trust property which is exercisable while the person is not serving as a trustee is a power of appointment and not a power of direction.

Comment

This section excludes five categories of powers that the drafting committee concluded should not be covered by this act for reasons of policy, coverage by other law, or both. Questions regarding a power that falls within one of these exclusions, such as the duty of the holder of the power and the duty of a trustee or other person subject to the power, are governed by law other than this act.

(1) Power of appointment. Subsection (b)(1) excludes a "power of appointment," which is defined by subsection (a) to mean "a power that enables a person acting in a nonfiduciary capacity to designate a recipient of an ownership interest in or another power of appointment over trust property." * * *

The exclusion prescribed by subsection (b)(1) applies only to a nonfiduciary power of appointment. It does not apply to a fiduciary power of distribution. Thus, if the terms of a trust grant a person a fiduciary power to direct a distribution of trust property, and the power is exercisable while the person is not serving as trustee, then the power is a power of direction subject to this act.

To resolve doubt about whether a power over distribution is a power of appointment or a power of direction, subsection (c) prescribes a rule of construction under which a power over distribution is a power of appointment, and so is not held in a fiduciary capacity, unless the terms of the trust provide that the power is held in a fiduciary capacity.

A power in a serving trustee to designate a recipient of an ownership interest in or a power of appointment over trust property can never be a power of direction, because a serving trustee can never be a trust director (see Sections 2(5) and (9)). Whether a power over distribution granted to a serving trustee is held in a fiduciary capacity (making it a fiduciary distributive power) or is instead a nonfiduciary power of appointment is governed by law other than this act * * * .

(2) Power to appoint or remove. Subsection (b)(2) excludes "a power to appoint or remove a trustee or trust director." This exclusion addresses the compelling suggestion to the drafting committee that granting a person a power to appoint or remove a trustee is a common drafting practice that arose separately from the phenomenon of directed trusts. * * *

(3) Revocable trust. Subsection (b)(3) excludes a power of a settlor over a trust to the extent the settlor has a power to revoke the trust. The drafting committee intended that this exception would apply only to that portion of a trust over which the settlor has a power to revoke, that is, "to the extent" of the settlor's power to revoke. * * *

Without the exclusion of this subsection, the definitions contained in paragraphs (3), (5), and (9) of Section 2 could have been read to transform a settlor's power over a revocable trust into fiduciary powers of a trust director, thus subjecting the settlor to the fiduciary duties of a trust director under Section 8 and the trustee to the modified fiduciary duties of a directed trustee under Sections 9 through 11.

To the extent that a conservator or agent of the settlor may exercise the settlor's power to revoke, * * * subsection (b)(3) of this section would apply to the conservator or agent. A nonfiduciary power in a person other than the settlor to withdraw the trust property is a power of appointment that would fall within subsection (b)(1).

(4) Power of a beneficiary. Paragraph (4) excludes a power of a beneficiary to the extent that the exercise or nonexercise of the power affects (A) the beneficial interest of the beneficiary, or (B) the beneficial interest of another beneficiary who is represented by the beneficiary under virtual representation law.

Subparagraph (A) follows from traditional law, under which "[a] power that is for the sole benefit of the person holding the power is not a fiduciary power." * * * Thus, for example, a power in a beneficiary to release a trustee from a claim by the beneficiary is excluded from this act. To the extent the power affects another person, however, then it is not for the sole benefit of the person holding the power. Hence, a power over a trust held by a beneficiary may be a power of direction subject to this act if it affects the beneficial interest of another beneficiary. For example, a power in a beneficiary to release the trustee from a claim by another beneficiary is not excluded by this paragraph unless the power to bind the other beneficiary arises by reason of virtual representation.

The same rules apply if the beneficiary's power is jointly held. Thus, for example, if the terms of a trust provide that a trustee may be released from liability by a majority of the beneficiaries, and a majority of the beneficiaries grants such a release, then those beneficiaries would be acting as trust directors to the extent the release bound other beneficiaries by reason of the power other than by virtual representation. * * *

The carve-out for virtual representation in subparagraph (B) reflects the drafting committee's intent not to impose the fiduciary rules of this act on top of the law of virtual representation, which contains its own limits and safeguards. Without the exclusion of this subsection, the definitions contained in paragraphs (5) and (9) of Section 2 could have been read to transform a beneficiary who represented another beneficiary by virtual representation into a trust director. * * *

(5) The settlor's tax objectives. Subsection (b)(5) excludes a power if (A) the terms of the trust provide that the power is held in a nonfiduciary capacity, and (B) the power must be held in a nonfiduciary capacity to achieve the settlor's tax objectives under federal tax law. This exclusion is responsive to multiple suggestions to the drafting committee that certain powers held by a person other than a trustee must be nonfiduciary to achieve the settlor's federal tax objectives.

For example, to ensure that a trust is a grantor trust for federal income tax purposes, a common practice is to include in the trust instrument a provision that allows the settlor or another person to substitute assets of the trust for assets of an equivalent value, exercisable in a nonfiduciary capacity. * * *

Section 6. Powers of Trust Director.

(a)   Subject to Section 7, the terms of a trust may grant a power of direction to a trust director.

(b)   Unless the terms of a trust provide otherwise:

(1)   a trust director may exercise any further power appropriate to the exercise or nonexercise of a power of direction granted to the director under subsection (a); and

(2)   trust directors with joint powers must act by majority decision.

Comment

Validating a trust director. Subsection (a) validates a provision for a trust director in the terms of a trust. This subsection does not provide any powers to a trust director by default. Nor does it specify the scope of a power of direction. The existence and scope of a power of direction must instead be specified by the terms of a trust. A trust director may be named by the terms of the trust, by a procedure prescribed by the terms of the trust, or in accordance with Section 16(6).

Breadth of subsection (a). Without limiting the definition of a "power of direction" in Section 2(5), the drafting committee specifically contemplated that subsection (a) would validate terms of a trust that grant a power to a trust director to:

- direct investments, including a power to:

    o   acquire, dispose of, exchange, or retain an investment;

- o   make or take loans;

- o   vote proxies for securities held in trust;

- o   adopt a particular valuation of trust property or determine the frequency or methodology of valuation;

- o   adjust between principal and income or convert to a unitrust;

- o   manage a business held in the trust; or

- o   select a custodian for trust assets;

- modify, reform, terminate, or decant a trust;

- direct a trustee's or another director's delegation of the trustee's or other director's powers;

- change the principal place of administration, situs, or governing law of the trust;

- ascertain the happening of an event that affects the administration of the trust;

- determine the capacity of a trustee, settlor, director, or beneficiary of the trust;

- determine the compensation to be paid to a trustee or trust director;

- prosecute, defend, or join an action, claim, or judicial proceeding relating to the trust;

- grant permission before a trustee or another director may exercise a power of the trustee or other director; or

- release a trustee or another trust director from liability for an action proposed or previously taken by the trustee or other director. * * *

Pet and other noncharitable purpose trust enforcers. Statutes in every state validate a trust for a pet animal and certain other noncharitable purposes. Following Uniform Probate Code § 2–907(c)(4) (1993) and Uniform Trust Code §§ 408(b) and 409(2) (2000), most of these statutes authorize enforcement of the trust by a person named in the terms of the trust. In a state that enacts this act, such a person would be a trust director.

Exclusions. Like the other provisions of this act, this section does not apply to matters that are excluded by Section 5. Thus, because Sections 5(b)(1)–(2) exclude a "power of appointment," and a "power to appoint or remove a trustee or trust director," subsection 6(a) does not authorize the granting of such powers. Instead, such a power is governed by law other than this act.

Subsection (b). Subsection (b) prescribes two rules of construction that apply unless the terms of a trust provide otherwise.

(1) Further appropriate powers. Subsection (b)(1) prescribes a default rule under which a trust director may exercise any "further" power that is "appropriate" to the director's exercise of the director's express powers granted by the terms of the trust under subsection (a). * * * Appropriateness should be judged in relation to the purpose for which the power was granted and the function being carried out by the director. Examples of further powers that might be appropriate include a power to: (1) incur reasonable costs and direct indemnification for those costs; (2) make a report or accounting to a beneficiary or other interested party; (3) direct a trustee to issue a certification of trust under Uniform Trust Code § 1013 (2000); (4) prosecute, defend, or join an action, claim, or judicial proceeding relating to a trust; or (5) employ a professional to assist or advise the director in the exercise or nonexercise of the director's powers.

Delegation by trust director. In some circumstances, it may be appropriate under subsection (b)(1) for a trust director to exercise a further power to delegate the director's powers, much as it may sometimes be appropriate for a trustee to delegate its powers. Under Section 8, a trust director is subject to the same fiduciary duty regarding delegation as a trustee in a like position and under similar circumstances. In most states, therefore, a trust director would be required to exercise reasonable care, skill, and caution in selecting, instructing, and monitoring an agent, and a director that did so would not be liable for the action of the agent. * * *

(2) Majority decision. Subsection (b)(2) provides a default rule of majority action for multiple trust directors with "joint powers," such as a three-person committee with a power of direction over investment or distribution. Majority action is the prevailing default for cotrustees. * * *

The duty and liability of a trust director is governed by Section 8, which applies the fiduciary duty of trusteeship to a trust director. Thus, under Section 8(a)(1)(B), a trust director that holds a power of direction jointly with a trustee or another trust director would be subject to the fiduciary duty of a cotrustee.

Section 7. Limitations on Trust Director.

A trust director is subject to the same rules as a trustee in a like position and under similar circumstances in the exercise or nonexercise of a power of direction or further power under Section 6(b)(1) regarding:

(1) a payback provision in the terms of a trust necessary to comply with the reimbursement requirements of Medicaid law in Section 1917 of the Social Security Act, 42 U.S.C. Section 1396p(d)(4)(A)[, as amended][, and regulations issued thereunder][, as amended]; and

(2) a charitable interest in the trust, including notice regarding the interest to [the Attorney General].

Comment

This section applies to a trust director the same rules that apply to a trustee in two specific situations in which many states have particular regulatory interests. The first, in paragraph (1), concerns a payback provision necessary to comply with the reimbursement requirements of Medicaid law in a trust for a beneficiary with a disability. The second, in paragraph (2), concerns a charitable interest in a trust.

In both circumstances, this section imposes all the same rules that would apply to a trustee in a like position and under similar circumstances. For example, many states require a trustee to give notice to the Attorney General before taking certain actions with respect to a charitable interest in a trust. Some states also disempower a trustee from taking certain actions with respect to a payback provision in a trust meant to comply with the reimbursement requirements of Medicaid law. * * *

Section 8. Duty and Liability of Trust Director.

(a) Subject to subsection (b), with respect to a power of direction or further power under Section 6(b)(1):

(1) a trust director has the same fiduciary duty and liability in the exercise or nonexercise of the power:

(A) if the power is held individually, as a sole trustee in a like position and under similar circumstances; or

(B) if the power is held jointly with a trustee or another trust director, as a cotrustee in a like position and under similar circumstances; and

(2) the terms of the trust may vary the director's duty or liability to the same extent the terms of the trust could vary the duty or liability of a trustee in a like position and under similar circumstances.

(b) Unless the terms of a trust provide otherwise, if a trust director is licensed, certified, or otherwise authorized or permitted by law other than this [act] to provide health care in the ordinary course of the director's business or practice of a profession, to the extent the director acts in that capacity, the director has no duty or liability under this [act].

(c) The terms of a trust may impose a duty or liability on a trust director in addition to the duties and liabilities under this section.

Comment

Duty and liability of a trust director. This section addresses the duty and liability of a trust director. It should be read in conjunction with Section 10, which governs information sharing among directed trustees and trust directors, and Section 11, which eliminates certain duties to monitor, inform, or give advice. The drafting committee contemplated that this section, along with Sections 10 and 11, would prescribe the mandatory minimum fiduciary duties of a trust director, displacing any contrary mandatory minimum such as under Uniform Trust Code § 105 (2005).

Subsection (a). Subsection (a) imposes the same fiduciary duties on a trust director that would apply to a trustee in a like position and under similar circumstances. A trust director with a power to make or direct investments, for example, has the same duties that would apply to a trustee with the same power, including a duty to act prudently, in the sole interest of the beneficiaries, and impartially with due regard for the respective interests of the beneficiaries. * * * The theory behind subsection (a) is that if a trust director has a power of direction, the director is the most appropriate person to bear the duty associated with the exercise or nonexercise of that power. Put differently, in a directed trust, a trust director functions much like a trustee in a non-directed trust, and thus should have the same duties as a trustee.

Accordingly, subsection (a)(1) sets the default duties of a trust director by absorbing the default duties that would ordinarily apply to a trustee in a like position and under similar circumstances. Subsection (a)(2) sets the mandatory minimum duties of a trust director by absorbing the mandatory minimum duties that the terms of a trust cannot vary for a trustee in a like position and under similar circumstances. The default and mandatory rules applicable to a trustee include those prescribed by the other provisions of this act. * * *

Absorption of existing trust fiduciary law. Subsection (a) operates by absorbing existing state law rather than by inventing a new body of law. Absorbing existing state law in this manner offers several advantages. First, it avoids the need to spell out the entirety of trust fiduciary law. * * * Second, absorbing the trust fiduciary law of each enacting state accommodates diversity across the states in the particulars of a trustee's default and mandatory fiduciary duties, such as the duties to diversify and to give information to the beneficiaries, both of which have become increasingly differentiated across the states. Third, absorption allows for changes to the law of a trustee's fiduciary duties to be absorbed automatically into the duties of a trust director without need for periodic conforming revisions to this act.

Varied circumstances of trust directors. In applying the law of trustee fiduciary duties to a trust director, a court must make use of the flexibility built into fiduciary law. Courts have long applied the duties of loyalty and prudence across a wide array of circumstances, including many different kinds of trusts as well as other fiduciary relationships, such as corporations and agencies. Fiduciary principles are thus amenable to application in a context-specific manner that is sensitive to the particular circumstances and structure of each directed trust. In assessing the actions of a director that holds a power to modify a trust, for example, a court should apply the standards of loyalty and prudence in a manner that is appropriate to the particular context, including the trust's terms and purposes and the director's particular powers.

The trust director's duty of disclosure. Under subsection (a), a trust director is subject to the same duties of disclosure as a trustee in a like position and under similar circumstances. For example, if a trust director intends to direct a nonroutine transaction, to change "investment ... strategies," or to take "significant actions ... involving hard-to-value assets or special sensitivity to beneficiaries," the director is under a duty of affirmative advance disclosure, just like a trustee. * * * A trust director's disclosure duties are limited, however, by Section 11, which eliminates certain duties to monitor, inform, or give advice.

Sole versus joint powers. Under subsection (a), a trust director has the same fiduciary duties as a sole trustee when a power of direction is held individually and the same fiduciary duties as a cotrustee when a power of direction is held jointly. A trust director that individually holds a power to amend the trust, for example, does not have the duties of a cotrustee to monitor the actions of the trustee concerning investments or the actions of another trust director concerning the determination of a beneficiary's capacity.

Subject to Section 11, a trust director that holds a power of direction jointly with a trustee or another trust director, by contrast, has the duties of a cotrustee regarding the actions of that trustee or other trust director that are within the scope of the jointly held power. Thus, a trust director that jointly exercises a power to direct investments with other trust directors has the same fiduciary duties as a cotrustee regarding its own actions and the actions of the other directors with respect to the power. Under subsection (a)(2), a settlor may vary the duty and liability of a trust director that holds a power of direction jointly to the same extent the settlor could vary the duty and liability of a cotrustee under Section 12 or otherwise.

Springing powers without a duty to monitor. The drafting committee contemplated that a settlor could construct a trust director's power to be springing such that the director would not be under a continuous obligation to monitor the administration of the trust. For example, a settlor could grant a trust director a power to direct a distribution, but only if the director was requested to do so by a beneficiary. A director holding such a power would not be under a duty to act unless requested to do so by a beneficiary. Moreover, because under subsection (a)(2) a settlor can vary the fiduciary duties of a trust director to the same extent that the settlor could vary the fiduciary duties of a trustee, under Uniform Trust Code § 105(b)(2) (2004) the terms of a trust could waive all of the director's otherwise applicable duties other than the duty "to act in good faith and in accordance with the terms and purposes of the trust and the interests of the beneficiaries." A director with a power to direct a distribution upon a beneficiary's request, for example, would be subject to this mandatory duty when it responds to a beneficiary's request.

Extended discretion. Under subsection (a), if the terms of a trust give a trust director extended discretion, such as "sole," "absolute," or "uncontrolled" discretion, those terms would have the same effect on the duty and liability of the director as they would have for a trustee. Under prevailing law, a trustee with extended discretion may not "act in bad faith or for some purpose or motive other than to accomplish the purposes of the discretionary power." * * *

Exculpation or exoneration. A trust director is likewise subject to the same rules as a trustee with regard to an exculpation or exoneration clause. Under prevailing law, * * * an exculpation or exoneration clause cannot protect a trustee against liability for acting in bad faith or with reckless indifference. Under subsection (a)(2) of this section, the same rules would apply to an exculpation or exoneration clause for a trust director. Thus, if the terms of a trust provide that a director can never be liable to a beneficiary, then the trust director would have the same liability as a trustee would have under a similar exculpatory clause.

Directed director. The terms of a trust may provide that a trust director has a power over a trust that requires another director to comply with the director's exercise or nonexercise of the power. In other words, a director may have the power to direct another director. In such a trust, subsection (a)(1) would absorb for the directed director the same fiduciary duties that would apply to a directed trustee. A directed director would thus be subject to the willful misconduct standard that Section 9 applies to a directed trustee. Under subsection (a)(2), the terms of a trust may vary the duty of a directed director to the same extent they could vary the duty of a directed trustee.

Subsection (b)—health-care professionals. Subsection (b) refers to a trust director who is "licensed, certified, or otherwise authorized or permitted by law . . . to provide health care in the ordinary course of the director's business or practice of a profession." This phrasing is based on the definition of "health-care provider" in Uniform Health-Care Decisions Act § 1(8) (1993). To the extent that a trust director acts in the director's business or practice of a profession to provide health care, the director is relieved from duty and liability under this act unless the terms of the trust provide otherwise.

This subsection addresses the concern that a health-care professional might refuse appointment as a trust director if such service would expose the professional to fiduciary duty under this act. For example, the terms of a trust might call for a health-care professional to determine the capacity or sobriety of a beneficiary or the capacity of a settlor. In making such a determination, under subsection (b) the health-care professional would not be subject to duty or liability under this act.

Although the professional would not be subject to duty or liability under this act, the professional would remain subject to any rules and regulations otherwise applicable to the professional, such as the rules of medical ethics. The professional would also be subject to the other provisions of this act that do not create a duty or liability, such as the rules of construction prescribed by Sections 6(b) and 16. Moreover, a trustee subject to a direction by a health-care professional under subsection (b) of this section is still subject to the duties under Section 9 to take reasonable action to comply with the professional's direction and to avoid willful misconduct in doing so.

Subsection (c)—no ceiling on duties. Subsection (c) confirms that the duties under this section are defaults and minimums, not ceilings. The terms of a trust may impose further duties in addition to those prescribed by this section.

Section 9. Duty and Liability of Directed Trustee.

(a)   Subject to subsection (b), a directed trustee shall take reasonable action to comply with a trust director's exercise or nonexercise of a power of direction or further power under Section 6(b)(1), and the trustee is not liable for the action.

(b)   A directed trustee must not comply with a trust director's exercise or nonexercise of a power of direction or further power under Section 6(b)(1) to the extent that by complying the trustee would engage in willful misconduct.

(c)   An exercise of a power of direction under which a trust director may release a trustee or another trust director from liability for breach of trust is not effective if:

(1)   the breach involved the trustee's or other director's willful misconduct;

(2)   the release was induced by improper conduct of the trustee or other director in procuring the release; or

(3)   at the time of the release, the director did not know the material facts relating to the breach.

(d)   A directed trustee that has reasonable doubt about its duty under this section may petition the [court] for instructions.

(e)   The terms of a trust may impose a duty or liability on a directed trustee in addition to the duties and liabilities under this section.

Comment

Duties of a directed trustee. This section addresses the duty and liability of a directed trustee. It should be read in conjunction with Section 10, which governs information sharing among directed trustees and trust directors, and Section 11, which eliminates certain duties to monitor, inform, or advise. The drafting committee contemplated that this section, along with Sections 10 and 11, would prescribe the mandatory minimum fiduciary duties of a directed trustee, displacing any contrary mandatory minimum such as under Uniform Trust Code § 105 (2005).

Subsection (a)—duty to take reasonable action; nonliability other than under subsection (b). Subject to subsection (b), subsection (a) requires a directed trustee to take reasonable action to comply with a trust director's exercise or nonexercise of the director's power of direction or further power under Section 6(b)(1) and provides that the trustee is not liable for so acting.

The duty of a trustee in subsection (a) to take reasonable action depends on context. A power of direction under which a trust director may give a trustee an express direction will require the trustee to comply by following the direction. A power that requires a trustee to obtain permission from a trust director before acting imposes a duty on the trustee to obtain the required permission. A power that allows a director to amend the trust imposes a duty on the trustee to take reasonable action to facilitate the amendment and then comply with its terms. The duty prescribed by subsection (a) is to take reasonable action to comply with whatever the terms of the trust require of a trustee in connection with a trust director's exercise or nonexercise of the director's power of direction or further power under Section 6(b)(1).

A trustee's duty to take reasonable action is limited by the scope of the trust director's power of direction. A directed trustee should not comply with a direction that is outside of the director's power of direction and beyond the director's further powers under Section 6(b)(1). To do so would violate the trustee's duty under subsection (a) and the trustee's background duty to act in accordance with the terms of the trust. * * * For example, an attempt by a director to exercise a power of direction in a form contrary to that required by the terms of the trust, such as an oral direction if the terms of the trust require a writing, is not within the trust director's power.

Subsection (a) requires a trustee to act reasonably as it carries out the acts necessary to comply with a trust director's exercise or nonexercise of the director's powers. If a trust director with a power to direct investments directs the trustee to purchase a particular security, for example, the trustee must take care to ensure that the security is purchased within a reasonable time and at reasonable cost and must refrain from self-dealing and conflicts of interest in doing so.

The duty to take reasonable action under subsection (a) does not, however, impose a duty to ensure that the substance of the direction is reasonable. To the contrary, subject to subsection (b), a trustee that takes reasonable action to comply with a power of direction is not liable for so acting even if the substance of the direction is unreasonable. In other words, subject to the willful misconduct rule of subsection (b), a trustee is liable only for its own breach of trust in executing a direction, and not for the director's breach of trust in giving the direction. Returning to the example of a direction to purchase a security, the trustee is not required to assess whether the purchase of the security would be prudent in relation to the trust's investment portfolio; the trustee is only required to execute the purchase reasonably.

Powers jointly held with a trust director. A trustee may hold a power of direction jointly with a trust director. For example, the terms of a trust may confer a power to determine the capacity of a beneficiary upon a committee of people, and the committee may include both the trustee and the beneficiary's son, who is a trust director. When a trustee holds a power jointly with a trust director, the trustee continues to have the normal duties of a trustee regarding its own exercise or nonexercise of the joint power. Subsection (a), in other words, does not relieve the trustee from the trustee's normal duties as to powers that belong directly to the trustee, including powers held jointly with a trust director. In deciding how to vote as a member of the committee to determine the beneficiary's capacity, for example, the trustee would be subject to the same duties as if it held its power jointly with another trustee instead of with another trust director.

A trustee's participation in joint decisionmaking with a trust director, however, must be distinguished from the trustee's execution of those joint decisions. Although the trustee is subject to the normal fiduciary duties of trusteeship in making a decision jointly with a trust director, the trustee is subject to the reduced duty of subsections (a) and (b) in executing the decision. Returning to the example of a committee including a trustee with power to determine a beneficiary's capacity, the trustee has its normal fiduciary duties in deciding how to cast its vote about whether the beneficiary lacks capacity. But the trustee has only the duties prescribed by subsections (a) and (b) when the trustee takes action to comply with the decision of the committee.

Powers to veto or approve. The terms of a trust may give a trust director a power to veto or approve the actions of a trustee. A trustee, for example, may have the power to invest trust property, subject to the power of a trust director to review and override the trustee's decision. A trustee that operates under this kind of veto or approval power has the normal duties of a trustee regarding the trustee's exercise of its own powers, but has only the duties of a directed trustee regarding the trust director's exercise of its power to veto or approve. Thus, the trustee would be subject to the normal duty of prudence in deciding which investments to propose to a director, but then would be subject only to the willful misconduct rule of subsection (b) in choosing whether to comply with the director's veto or disapproval of the proposed investments.

Subsection (b)—willful misconduct. Subsection (b) provides an exception to the duty of compliance prescribed by subsection (a). Under subsection (b), a trustee must not comply with a trust director's exercise or nonexercise of a power of direction or a further power under Section 6(b)(1) to the extent that by complying the trustee would engage in "willful misconduct."

The willful misconduct standard in subsection (b) is to be distinguished from the duty to take reasonable action in subsection (a). The reasonable action rule of subsection (a) applies to the manner by which a trustee complies with a power of direction. The willful misconduct standard of subsection (b) applies to the decision of whether to comply with a power of direction.

The willful misconduct standard in subsection (b) is a mandatory minimum. The terms of a trust may not reduce a trustee's duty below the standard of willful misconduct. Terms of a trust that attempt to give a trustee no duty or to indicate that a trustee is not a fiduciary or is an "excluded fiduciary" or other such language are not enforceable under subsection (b). Instead, such provisions should be construed to provide for the willful misconduct standard of subsection (b).

The drafting committee settled upon the "willful misconduct" standard after a review of the existing directed trust statutes. Roughly speaking, the existing statutes fall into two groups. In one group, which constitutes a majority, are the statutes that provide that a directed trustee has no duty or liability for complying with an exercise of a power of direction. * * *

The policy rationale for these no duty statutes is that duty should follow power. If a director has the exclusive authority to exercise a power of direction, then the director should be the exclusive bearer of fiduciary duty in the exercise or nonexercise of the power. Placing the exclusive duty on a director does not diminish the total duty owed to a beneficiary, because a settlor of a directed trust could have chosen to make the trust director the sole trustee instead. Thus, on greater-includes-the-lesser reasoning, a settlor who could have named a trust director to serve instead as a trustee should also be able to give the trust director the duties of the trustee. Under the no duty statutes, a beneficiary's only recourse for misconduct by the trust director is an action against the director for breach of the director's fiduciary duty to the beneficiary.

In the other group of statutes, * * * a directed trustee is not liable for complying with a direction of a trust director unless by so doing the directed trustee would personally engage in "willful" or "intentional" misconduct. The policy rationale for these statutes is that, because a trustee stands at the center of a trust, the trustee must bear at least some duty even if the trustee is acting under the direction of a director. Although the settlor could have made the trust director the sole trustee, the settlor did not actually do so— and under traditional understandings of trust law, a trustee must always be accountable to a beneficiary in some way. * * *

The states in the second group also recognize, however, that to facilitate the settlor's intent that the trust director rather than the directed trustee be the primary or even sole decisionmaker, it is appropriate to reduce the trustee's duty below the usual level with respect to a matter subject to a power of direction. Accordingly, under these statutes a beneficiary's main recourse for misconduct by the trust director is an action against the director for breach of the director's fiduciary duty to the beneficiary. The beneficiary also has recourse against the trustee, but only if the trustee's compliance with the director's exercise or nonexercise of the director's powers amounted to "willful misconduct" by the trustee. Relative to a non-directed trust, this second approach has the effect of increasing the total fiduciary duties owed to a beneficiary. All of the usual duties of trusteeship are preserved in the trust director, but in addition the directed trustee has a duty to avoid willful misconduct.

After extensive deliberation and debate, the drafting committee opted to follow the second group of statutes on the grounds that this model is more consistent with traditional fiduciary policy. * * *

Subsection (c)—release by trust director. The terms of a trust may empower a trust director to release a trustee or another trust director from liability for breach of trust. If the director grants such a release, the trustee or other director is not liable to the extent of the release. The terms of a trust may authorize such a release to be given at any time, whether before or after the trustee or other director acts. The precise scope of a power of release and the manner of its exercise depend on the terms of the trust.

Although a settlor has wide latitude in designing a power of direction, subsection (c) prescribes three mandatory safeguards that limit a director's power to release a trustee or other director from liability. First, consistent with the policy of subsection (b), a trustee or other director cannot be released for a breach that involves the trustee's or the other director's own willful misconduct. Second, consistent with prevailing law governing a release of a trustee by a beneficiary, a release by a trust director is not enforceable if it was procured by the improper conduct of the trustee or other director. Third, again consistent with prevailing law governing a release of a trustee by a beneficiary, a release by a trust director is not enforceable if at the time of the release the director did not know the material facts relating to the breach. * * *

Subsection (d)—petition for instructions. Subsection (d) confirms that, in accordance with existing law, a directed trustee that has reasonable doubt about its duty under this section may petition the court for instructions. * * * The safe harbor of this subsection is permissive rather than mandatory. Though a trustee may satisfy its duties by petitioning for instructions, this subsection does not require a trustee to petition.

Subsection (e)—no ceiling on duties. Subsection (e) confirms that the duties prescribed by this section are defaults and minimums, not ceilings. The terms of a trust may impose further duties in addition to those prescribed by this section.

Section 10. Duty to Provide Information to Trust Director or Trustee.

(a) Subject to Section 11, a trustee shall provide information to a trust director to the extent the information is reasonably related both to:

(1) the powers or duties of the trustee; and

(2)   the powers or duties of the director.

(b)   Subject to Section 11, a trust director shall provide information to a trustee or another trust director to the extent the information is reasonably related both to:

(1)   the powers or duties of the director; and

(2)   the powers or duties of the trustee or other director.

(c)   A trustee that acts in reliance on information provided by a trust director is not liable for a breach of trust to the extent the breach resulted from the reliance, unless by so acting the trustee engages in willful misconduct.

(d)   A trust director that acts in reliance on information provided by a trustee or another trust director is not liable for a breach of trust to the extent the breach resulted from the reliance, unless by so acting the trust director engages in willful misconduct.

Comment

Subsections (a) and (b)—Duty to provide information. This section imposes duties on trustees and trust directors to provide information to each other. Subsection (a) imposes this duty on a directed trustee, and subsection (b) imposes this duty on a trust director. The drafting committee contemplated that the duties created by this section would provide trustees and trust directors with sufficient information to fulfill their obligations under trust law as well as other law, including banking, securities, and tax law.

Disclosure to beneficiaries. This section governs disclosure of information to trustees and trust directors. The duty of a trust director to disclose information to a beneficiary is governed by Section 8, which prescribes the fiduciary duties of a trust director, subject to Section 11. The duty of a trustee to disclose information to a beneficiary is governed by the background law of an enacting state under Section 4 as modified by Section 11, which limits a directed trustee's duty to inform a beneficiary about the actions of a trust director.

Reasonableness. This section relies heavily on the concept of reasonableness. Information must be disclosed only if it is reasonably related both to the powers or duties of the person making the disclosure and to the powers or duties of the person receiving the disclosure. The information must be reasonably related to the powers or duties of the person making the disclosure, because otherwise that person cannot be expected to possess the information. The information must also be reasonably related to the powers or duties of the person receiving the disclosure, because otherwise that person would not need the information. Examples of matters that might require disclosure under this section include asset valuations, modifications to the terms of a trust, changes to investment policy or strategy, distributions, changes in accounting procedure or valuations, and removal or appointment of trustees and trust directors.

Both an affirmative and a responsive duty to inform. This section imposes an affirmative duty to provide information (even in the absence of a request for that information) as well as a responsive duty to reply to requests for information. For example, if a trust director exercises a power to modify the terms of a trust, the director would have an affirmative duty to inform the trustees and other trust directors whose powers or duties are reasonably related to the amendment whether or not the trustees or other trust directors inquired about it. Similarly, the director would have a responsive duty to provide information about the amendment upon a request by a trustee or another trust director whose powers or duties were reasonably related to the amendment.

Interaction with Section 11. The duties of a trustee (in subsection (a)) and of a trust director (in subsection (b)) to disclose information are subject to the limitations of Section 11. Thus, although a trustee has a duty under this section to disclose information that is related to both the powers or duties of the trustee and the powers or duties of the director, a trustee does not have a duty to inform or give advice to the trust director concerning instances in which the trustee would have exercised the director's powers differently. The same is true for a trust director. * * *

*Subsections (c) and (d)—*Subsection (c) provides a safe harbor for a trustee that acts in reliance on information provided by a trust director. Subsection (d) provides a similar safe harbor for a trust director for information provided by a trustee or other trust director. Under both subsections, the safe harbor only applies if the trustee or trust director that acts in reliance on the information is not engaged in willful misconduct. For example, subsection (c) protects a trustee if the trustee acts in reliance on a trust director's valuation of an asset, unless by accepting the valuation the trustee would engage in willful misconduct. As in Section 9, the rationale for the safe harbor and willful misconduct limit is to implement the settlor's division of labor subject to a mandatory fiduciary minimum.

No ceiling on duties to share information. This section imposes a mandatory floor, rather than a ceiling, on a directed trustee's and a trust director's duty to share information. The terms of a trust may specify more extensive duties of information sharing among directed trustees and trust directors.

Section 11. No Duty to Monitor, Inform, or Advise.

(a) Unless the terms of a trust provide otherwise:

  (1) a trustee does not have a duty to:

    (A) monitor a trust director; or

    (B) inform or give advice to a settlor, beneficiary, trustee, or trust director concerning an instance in which the trustee might have acted differently than the director; and

  (2) by taking an action described in paragraph (1), a trustee does not assume the duty excluded by paragraph (1).

(b) Unless the terms of a trust provide otherwise:

  (1) a trust director does not have a duty to:

    (A) monitor a trustee or another trust director; or

    (B) inform or give advice to a settlor, beneficiary, trustee, or another trust director concerning an instance in which the director might have acted differently than a trustee or another trust director; and

  (2) by taking an action described in paragraph (1), a trust director does not assume the duty excluded by paragraph (1).

Comment

Following existing statutes. Subsection (a) provides that a trustee does not have a duty to monitor a trust director or inform or give advice to a settlor, beneficiary, trustee, or trust director concerning instances in which the trustee might have acted differently than the director. Many existing state statutes are to similar effect, though the language in this section is simpler and more direct. Subsection (b) applies the same rule to a trust director regarding the actions of a trustee or another trust director. * * *

Survival of trustee's and trust director's general duty of disclosure. Although this section confirms that a directed trustee has no duty to monitor a trust director or inform or give advice to others concerning instances in which the trustee might have acted differently than the director, this section does not relieve a trustee of its ordinary duties to disclose, report, or account under otherwise applicable law * * * . The same is true for a trust director, on whom Section 8(a) imposes the fiduciary duties of a trustee.

For example, if a trust director has a power to direct investments, this section would relieve a directed trustee of any duty to advise a beneficiary about the risks of the director's decision to concentrate the investment portfolio. The trustee would remain under a duty, however, to make periodic reports or accountings to the beneficiary and to answer reasonable inquiries by the beneficiary about the administration of the trust to the extent required by otherwise applicable law. The trustee would also remain under the duty imposed by Section 10 to provide a trust director with information reasonably related to its powers and duties.

No assumption of duty. In addition to waiving a directed trustee's duty to monitor, inform, or give advice as under subsection (a)(1), many state statutes go further and also provide that if a trustee for some reason chooses to monitor, inform, or give advice, these activities will be deemed to be "administrative actions." * * * The purpose of these provisions is to ensure that if a directed trustee chooses for some reason to monitor, inform, or give advice, the trustee does not assume a continuing obligation to do so or concede a prior duty to have done so. This section dispenses with the opacity of an administrative classification and achieves the intended result more directly. Subsection (a)(2) provides that if a trustee monitors, informs, or gives advice about the actions of a trust director, the trustee does not thereby assume a duty to do so. Subsection (b)(2) applies the same rule for a trust director.

Section 12. Application to Cotrustee.

The terms of a trust may relieve a cotrustee from duty and liability with respect to another cotrustee's exercise or nonexercise of a power of the other cotrustee to the same extent that in a directed trust a directed trustee is relieved from duty and liability with respect to a trust director's power of direction under Sections 9 through 11.

Comment

Traditional law. Under traditional law, each cotrustee "has a duty to use reasonable care to prevent a cotrustee from committing a breach of trust and, if a breach of trust occurs, to obtain redress." * * * This rule applies even if the settlor limits the role or function of one of the cotrustees. "Even in matters for which a trustee is relieved of responsibility, . . . if the trustee knows that a co-trustee is committing or attempting to commit a breach of trust, the trustee has a duty to take reasonable steps to prevent the fiduciary misconduct." * * * Moreover, "even in the absence of any duty to intervene or grounds for suspicion, a trustee is entitled to request and receive reasonable information regarding an aspect of trust administration in which the trustee is not required to participate." * * * These rules for cotrusteeship contrast with the less demanding fiduciary standards for a directed trusteeship under Sections 9, 10, and 11 of this act.

Settlor autonomy. This section allows a settlor to choose either fiduciary regime for a cotrusteeship—the traditional rules of cotrusteeship or the more permissive rules of a directed trusteeship. There seems little reason to prohibit a settlor from applying the fiduciary rules of this act to a cotrusteeship given that the settlor could choose the more permissive rules of a directed trusteeship by labeling one of the cotrustees as a trust director and another as a directed trustee. The rationale for permitting the terms of a trust to reduce the duty of a cotrustee that is subject to direction by another trustee is the same as the rationale for permitting the terms of a trust to reduce the duty of a directed trustee. In both instances, a trustee must act according to directions from another person and therefore the other person, not the trustee, should bear the full fiduciary responsibility for the action.

Accordingly, if the terms of a trust so provide, a cotrustee may have only the duty required by the reasonable action and willful misconduct standards specified in Section 9, and be subject to the narrower rules governing information sharing and monitoring specified in Sections 10 and 11, with respect to another cotrustee's exercise or nonexercise of a power of that other cotrustee. If the terms of a trust indicate that a directed cotrustee is to have no duty or is not a fiduciary, then the effect will be to reduce the cotrustee's duties to those prescribed by Sections 9 through 11, just as would be the effect of similar language for a directed trustee.

Mechanics of choosing directed trustee duties. Under this section the default rule is that, if a settlor names cotrustees, the traditional law of cotrusteeship applies. The fiduciary duties of directed trusteeship will only apply to a cotrustee if the terms of the trust manifest such an intent. Whether this section applies to a given trust is thus a question of construction. * * *

For example, a familiar drafting strategy is to name cotrustees but also to provide that in the event of disagreement about a particular matter the decision of a specified trustee controls and the other cotrustee has no liability in that event. Under traditional law, notwithstanding this provision, the other cotrustee would be liable if it did not take reasonable steps to prevent a breach by the controlling cotrustee. Under this section, on a prospective basis the other cotrustee would be liable only for its own willful misconduct akin to a directed trustee.

Cotrustees as directed trustees and trust directors. The terms of a trust can place a cotrustee in a position of either giving direction, like a trust director, or taking direction, like a directed trustee. This section only applies to a cotrustee that takes direction. This section does not address the duties of a cotrustee that is not directed. Nor does this section address the duties of a cotrustee that gives direction. Under Section 8, the background law of an enacting state that applies to a directing cotrustee also applies to a similarly situated trustee. The drafting committee intended that the language "with respect to another cotrustee's exercise or nonexercise of a power of the other cotrustee" would refer only to a power of another cotrustee and not a power held jointly with the directed cotrustee, because a cotrustee cannot be thought of as taking direction from another cotrustee if the two cotrustees exercise a power jointly.

No third-party effects. Although this section changes the degree to which the terms of a trust may reduce a cotrustee's duty and liability, it does not alter the rules that affect the rights of third parties who contract with or otherwise interact with a cotrustee. The principal difference between cotrusteeship and directed trusteeship is that in a cotrusteeship every cotrustee has title to the trust property, whereas in a directed trusteeship, title to trust property belongs only to the trustee, and not to the trust director. The placement of title can have important consequences for dealings with third parties and for tax, property, and other bodies of law outside of trust law. This section does not change the rights of third parties who deal with a cotrustee in the cotrustee's capacity as such.

Section 13. Limitation of Action Against Trust Director.

(a)   An action against a trust director for breach of trust must be commenced within the same limitation period as[under Uniform Trust Code Section 1005] for an action for breach of trust against a trustee in a like position and under similar circumstances.

(b)   A report or accounting has the same effect on the limitation period for an action against a trust director for breach of trust that the report or accounting would have[under Uniform Trust Code Section 1005] in an action for breach of trust against a trustee in a like position and under similar circumstances.

Comment

This section absorbs for a trust director the law of an enacting state governing limitations on an action against a trustee. A limitation applies to a trust director as it would to a trustee in a like position and under similar circumstances. Whether the law is default or mandatory as applied to a trust director, for example, is determined by whether it is default or mandatory as applied to a trustee.

Subsection (a) extends to a trust director the same limits on liability that a trustee enjoys under the law of an enacting state by way of a statutory limitations period, such as under Uniform Trust Code § 1005(c) (2000). The limitations period absorbed by subsection (a) applies to all claims against a trust director for breach of trust, whether by a beneficiary, a trustee, another trust director, or some other party.

Subsection (b) extends to a trust director the same limitation period that a trustee enjoys under the law of an enacting state arising from the making of a report or accounting, such as under Uniform Trust Code § 1005(a)–(b) (2000). The rule of subsection (b) applies regardless of whether the report or accounting was made by the trust director. A trust director may therefore be protected by a report or accounting made by a trustee or another trust director even though the director did not make the report or accounting, so long as the report or accounting fairly discloses the relevant facts of the director's conduct.

Laches, which strictly speaking is an equitable defense rather than a limitations period, would apply to an action against a trust director under Section 14.

Section 14. Defenses in Action Against Trust Director.

In an action against a trust director for breach of trust, the director may assert the same defenses a trustee in a like position and under similar circumstances could assert in an action for breach of trust against the trustee.

Comment

Absorption. This section makes available to a trust director the same defenses that are available to a trustee in a like position and under similar circumstances in an action for breach of trust. A trust director can assert any defense that would be available to a trustee in a comparable action for breach of trust under existing state law, including:

- laches or estoppel * * * ;
- consent, release, or ratification by a beneficiary * * * ;
- reasonable reliance on the terms of a trust * * * ; and

- reasonable care in ascertaining the happening of an event affecting administration or distribution * * * .

Section 15. Jurisdiction Over Trust Director.

(a) By accepting appointment as a trust director of a trust subject to this [act], the director submits to personal jurisdiction of the courts of this state regarding any matter related to a power or duty of the director.

(b) This section does not preclude other methods of obtaining jurisdiction over a trust director.

Comment

Under subsection (a), by accepting appointment as a trust director of a trust subject to this act, the director submits to personal jurisdiction of the courts of this state with respect to "any matter related to a power or duty of the director." This subsection does not apply to a person that has not accepted appointment as a trust director (the question of whether a person has accepted appointment is governed by Section 16(1)). * * *

Jurisdiction over a person that has accepted appointment as trust director is mandatory. The terms of a trust or an agreement among the trust director and other parties cannot negate personal jurisdiction over a trust director under this section. However, this section does not preclude a court from declining to exercise jurisdiction under the doctrine of forum non conveniens. * * *

Section 16. Office of Trust Director.

Unless the terms of a trust provide otherwise, the rules applicable to a trustee apply to a trust director regarding the following matters:

(1) acceptance[under Uniform Trust Code Section 701];

(2) giving of bond to secure performance[under Uniform Trust Code Section 702];

(3) reasonable compensation[under Uniform Trust Code Section 708];

(4) resignation[under Uniform Trust Code Section 705];

(5) removal[under Uniform Trust Code Section 706]; and

(6) vacancy and appointment of successor[under Uniform Trust Code Section 704].

Comment

This section applies the law of trusteeship to a trust directorship with regard to seven subjects. Whether the law is default or mandatory as applied to a trust director depends on whether it is default or mandatory as applied to a trustee.

Paragraph (1)—acceptance. This paragraph absorbs an enacting state's law governing acceptance of a trusteeship, * * * for application to acceptance of a trust directorship. However, whereas a trustee is expected to participate actively in the administration of the trust, and is therefore usually capable of signaling acceptance by conduct, some trust directors, such as a director with a power to determine the settlor's competence, may not take any action for long stretches of time, if ever. This delay in action may complicate acceptance by conduct.

Paragraph (2)—bond. This paragraph absorbs an enacting state's law governing bond to secure performance by a trustee, * * * for application to bond by a trust director. The drafting committee assumed that bond would seldom be required for a trust director, as in the usual case the director would not have custody of the trust property.

Paragraph (3)—reasonable compensation. This paragraph absorbs an enacting state's law governing reasonable compensation of a trustee, * * * for application to compensation of a trust director. The drafting committee contemplated that, just as in total "the reasonable fees for multiple trustees may be higher than for a single trustee," * * * so too the total reasonable fees for a trust with a directed trustee and a trust director may be higher than for a single trustee.

Reasonable compensation for a trust director will vary based on the nature of the director's powers, and in some circumstances may well be zero. A state that provides a statutory commission for a trustee should therefore refrain from using the commission for a trust director and should instead use a rule of reasonable compensation. Statutory trustee commissions will often overcompensate a trust director, especially a director that does not participate actively on an ongoing basis in the administration of the trust. The problem will be especially serious in a trust with multiple such directors.

Moreover, the reasonable compensation of a directed trustee is likely to be less than that for a trustee that is not directed. An apt analogy is to a trustee that hires others to "render services expected or normally to be performed by the trustee." * * *

Paragraph (4)—resignation. This paragraph absorbs an enacting state's law governing resignation by a trustee, * * * for application to resignation by a trust director.

Paragraph (5)—removal. This subsection absorbs an enacting state's law governing removal of a trustee * * * for application to removal of a trust director.

Paragraph (6)—vacancy. This section absorbs an enacting state's law applicable to a vacancy in a trusteeship for application to a vacancy in a trust directorship. For example, under Uniform Trust Code § 704 (2004), "a vacancy in a trusteeship need not be filled" if "one or more cotrustees remain in office." So too, if three of five trust directors with a joint power to determine the settlor's capacity remain in office, the court "need not" fill the vacancies, though the vacancies should be filled if doing so would be more consistent with the settlor's plan. Likewise, if the sole trust director with power over investment of the trust property ceases to serve, in most circumstances the vacancy should be filled, and this is true even if other directors with unrelated powers remain in office. An apt analogy is to a trust with several cotrustees, each of whom has controlling authority over different aspects of the trust's administration. If any of those trustees ceases to serve, in many circumstances a court should appoint a successor even though other cotrustees remain in office.

Costs and indemnification. The power of a trust director to incur reasonable costs and to direct indemnification for expenses would in most cases be covered by Section 6(b)(1).

Section 17. Uniformity of Application and Construction. [omitted]

Section 18. Relation to Electronic Signatures in Global and National Commerce Act. [omitted]

Section 19. Repeals; Conforming Amendments. [omitted]

Section 20. Effective Date. [omitted]

UNIFORM DISCLAIMER OF PROPERTY INTERESTS ACT (1999)*

PREFATORY NOTE

The Uniform Disclaimer of Property Interests Act (UDPIA) replaces three Uniform Acts promulgated in 1978 (Uniform Disclaimer of Property Interests Act, Uniform Disclaimer of Transfers by Will, Intestacy or Appointment Act, and Uniform Disclaimer of Transfers under Nontestamentary Instruments Act) * * * . The new Act is the most comprehensive disclaimer statute ever written. It is designed to allow every sort of disclaimer, including those that are useful for tax planning purposes. It does not, however, include a specific time limit on the making of any disclaimer. Because a disclaimer is a refusal to accept, the only bar to a disclaimer should be acceptance of the offer. In addition, in almost all jurisdictions disclaimers can be used for more than tax planning. A proper disclaimer will often keep the disclaimed property from the disclaimant's creditors. In short, the new Act is an enabling statute which prescribes all the rules for refusing a proffered interest in or power over property and the effect of that refusal on the power or interest while leaving the effect of the refusal itself to other law. Section 13(e) explicitly states that a disclaimer may be barred or limited by law other than the Act.

The decision not to include a specific time limit—to "decouple" the disclaimer statute from the time requirement applicable to a "qualified disclaimer" under IRC § 2518—is also designed to reduce confusion. The older Uniform Acts and almost all the current state statutes (many of which are based on those Acts) were drafted in the wake of the passage of IRC § 2518 in 1976. That provision replaced the "reasonable time" requirement of prior law with a requirement that a disclaimer must be made within nine months of the creation of the interest disclaimed if the disclaimer is to be a "qualified disclaimer" which is not regarded as transfer by the disclaimant. The statutes that were written in

---

response to this new provision of tax law reflected the nine month time limit. Under most of these statutes (including the older Uniform Acts and former Section 2–801) a disclaimer must be made within nine months of the creation of a present interest (for example, as disclaimer of an outright gift under a will must be made within nine months of the decedent's death), which corresponds to the requirement of IRC § 2518. A future interest, however, may be disclaimed within nine months of the time the interest vests in possession or enjoyment (for example, a remainder whether or not contingent on surviving the holder of the life income interest must be disclaimed within nine months of the death of the life income beneficiary). The time limit for future interests does not correspond to IRC § 2518 which generally requires that a qualified disclaimer of a future interest be made within nine months of the interest's creation, no matter how contingent it may then be. The nine-month time limit of the existing statutes really is a trap. While it superficially conforms to IRC § 2518, its application to the disclaimer of future interests does not. The removal of all mention of time limits will clearly signal the practitioner that the requirements for a tax qualified disclaimer are set by different law.

The elimination of the time limit is not the only change from current statutes. The Act abandons the concept of "relates back" as a proxy for when a disclaimer becomes effective. Instead, by stating specifically when a disclaimer becomes effective and explicitly stating in Section 5(f) that a disclaimer "is not a transfer, assignment, or release," the Act makes clear the results of refusing property or powers through a disclaimer. Second, UDPIA creates rules for several types of disclaimers that have not been explicitly addressed in previous statutes. The Act provides detailed rules for the disclaimer of interests in jointly held property (Section 7). Such disclaimers have important uses especially in tax planning, but their status under current law is not clear. Furthermore, although current statutes mention the disclaimer of jointly held property, they provide no details. Recent developments in the law of qualified disclaimers of jointly held property make fuller treatment of such disclaimers necessary. Section 8 addresses the disclaimer by trustees of property that would otherwise become part of the trust. The disclaimer of powers of appointment and other powers not held in a fiduciary capacity is treated in Section 9 and disclaimers by appointees, objects, and takers in default of exercise of a power of appointment is the subject of Section 10. Finally, Section 11 provides rules for the disclaimer of powers held in a fiduciary capacity.

Section 1. Short Title.

This [Act] may be cited as the "Uniform Disclaimer of Property Interests Act (1999)."

Section 2. Definitions.

In this [Act]:

(1) "Disclaimant" means the person to whom a disclaimed interest or power would have passed had the disclaimer not been made.

(2) "Disclaimed interest" means the interest that would have passed to the disclaimant had the disclaimer not been made.

(3) "Disclaimer" means the refusal to accept an interest in or power over property.

(4) "Fiduciary" means a personal representative, trustee, agent acting under a power of attorney, or other person authorized to act as a fiduciary with respect to the property of another person.

(5) "Jointly held property" means property held in the name of two or more persons under an arrangement in which all holders have concurrent interests and under which the last surviving holder is entitled to the whole of the property.

(6) "Person" means an individual, corporation, business trust, estate, trust, partnership, limited liability company, association, joint venture, government; governmental subdivision, agency, or instrumentality; public corporation, or any other legal or commercial entity.

(7) "State" means a State of the United States, the District of Columbia, Puerto Rico, the United States Virgin Islands, or any territory or insular possession subject to the jurisdiction of the United

States. The term includes an Indian tribe or band, or Alaskan native village, recognized by federal law or formally acknowledged by a State.

(8)   "Trust" means:

(A)   an express trust, charitable or noncharitable, with additions thereto, whenever and however created; and

(B)   a trust created pursuant to a statute, judgment, or decree which requires the trust to be administered in the manner of an express trust.

Comment

The definition of "disclaimant" (subsection (1)) limits the term to the person who would have received the disclaimed property or power if the disclaimer had not been made. The disclaimant is not necessarily the person making the disclaimer, who may be a guardian, custodian, or other fiduciary acting for the disclaimant or the personal representative of the disclaimant's estate.

The term "disclaimed interest" (subsection (2)) refers to the subject matter of a disclaimer of an interest in property and provides a compact term the use of which simplifies the drafting of Section 6.

The definition of "disclaimer" (subsection (3)) expands previous definitions. Prior Uniform Acts provided for a disclaimer of "the right of succession to any property or interest therein" and former UPC Section 2–801 referred to "an interest in or with respect to property or an interest therein." These previously authorized types of disclaimers are continued by the present language referring to "an interest in . . . property." The language referring to "power over property" broadens the permissible scope of disclaimers to include any power over property that gives the power-holder a right to control property, whether it be cast in the form of a power of appointment or a fiduciary's management power over property or discretionary power of distribution over income or corpus.

Under the Act, a "fiduciary" (defined in subsection (4)) is given the power to disclaim except where specifically prohibited by state law or by the document creating the fiduciary relationship. *See* Section 5(b).

The term "jointly held property" (subsection (5)) includes not only a traditional joint tenancy but also other property that is "held," but may not be "owned," by two or more persons with a right of survivorship. One form of such property is a joint bank account between parties who are not married to each other which, under the laws of many States, is owned by the parties in proportion to their deposits. (*See* UPC § 6–211(b).) This "holding" concept, as opposed to "owning," may also be true with joint brokerage accounts under the law of some States. *See* Treas. Regs. § 25.2518–2(c)(4). * * *

Section 3. Scope.

This [Act] applies to disclaimers of any interest in or power over property, whenever created.

Section 4. [Act] Supplemented by Other Law.

(a)   Unless displaced by a provision of this [Act], the principles of law and equity supplement this [Act].

(b)   This [Act] does not limit any right of a person to waive, release, disclaim, or renounce an interest in or power over property under a law other than this [Act].

Comment

The supplementation of the provisions of the Act by the principles of law and equity in Section 2–1104(a) is important because the Act is not a complete statement of the law relating to disclaimers. For example, Section 2–1105(b) permits a trustee to disclaim, yet the disclaiming trustee must still adhere to all applicable fiduciary duties. * * * Similarly, the provisions of Section 2–1113 on bars to disclaiming are subject to supplementation by equitable principles. * * *

Not only are the provisions of the Act supplemented by the principles of law and equity, but under Section 2–1104(b) the provisions of the Act do not preempt other law that creates the right to reject an interest in or power over property. The growth of the law would be unduly restricted were the provisions of the Act completely to displace other law.

Section 5. Power to Disclaim; General Requirements; When Irrevocable.

(a)   A person may disclaim, in whole or part, any interest in or power over property, including a power of appointment. A person may disclaim the interest or power even if its creator imposed a spendthrift provision or similar restriction on transfer or a restriction or limitation on the right to disclaim.

(b)   Except to the extent a fiduciary's right to disclaim is expressly restricted or limited by another statute of this State or by the instrument creating the fiduciary relationship, a fiduciary may disclaim, in whole or part, any interest in or power over property, including a power of appointment, whether acting in a personal or representative capacity. A fiduciary may disclaim the interest or power even if its creator imposed a spendthrift provision or similar restriction on transfer or a restriction or limitation on the right to disclaim, or an instrument other than the instrument that created the fiduciary relationship imposed a restriction or limitation on the right to disclaim.

(c)   To be effective, a disclaimer must be in a writing or other record, declare the disclaimer, describe the interest or power disclaimed, be signed by the person making the disclaimer, and be delivered or filed in the manner provided in Section 12. In this subsection:

(1)   "record" means information that is inscribed on a tangible medium or that is stored in an electronic or other medium and is retrievable in perceivable form; and

(2)   "signed" means, with present intent to authenticate or adopt a record, to:

(A)   execute or adopt a tangible symbol; or

(B)   attach to or logically associate with the record an electronic sound, symbol, or process.

(d)   A partial disclaimer may be expressed as a fraction, percentage, monetary amount, term of years, limitation of a power, or any other interest or estate in the property.

(e)   A disclaimer becomes irrevocable when it is delivered or filed pursuant to Section 12 or when it becomes effective as provided in Sections 6 through 11, whichever occurs later.

(f)   A disclaimer made under this [Act] is not a transfer, assignment, or release.

Comment

Subsections (a) and (b) give both persons (as defined in Section 2(6)) and fiduciaries (as defined in Section 2(4)) a broad power to disclaim both interests in and powers over property. In both instances, the ability to disclaim interests is comprehensive; it does not matter whether the disclaimed interest is vested, either in interest or in possession. For example, Father's will creates a testamentary trust which is to pay income to his descendants and after the running of the traditional perpetuities period is to terminate and be distributed to his descendants then living by representation. If at any time there are no descendants, the trust is to terminate and be distributed to collateral relatives. At the time of Father's death he has many descendants and the possibility of his line dying out and the collateral relatives taking under the trust is remote in the extreme. Nevertheless, under the Act the collateral relatives may disclaim their contingent remainders. (In order to make a qualified disclaimer for tax purposes, however, they must disclaim them within 9 months of Father's death.) Every sort of power may also be disclaimed.

Subsection (a) continues the provisions of current law by making ineffective any attempt to limit the right to disclaim which the creator of an interest or non-fiduciary power seeks to impose on a person. This provision follows from the principle behind all disclaimers—no one can be forced to accept property—and extends that principle to powers over property.

This Act also gives fiduciaries broad powers to disclaim both interests and powers. A fiduciary who may also be a beneficiary of the fiduciary arrangement may disclaim in either capacity. For example, a trustee who is also one of several beneficiaries of a trust may have the power to invade trust principal for the beneficiaries. The trustee may disclaim the power as trustee under Section 11 or may disclaim as a holder of a power of appointment under Section 9. Subsection (b) also gives fiduciaries the right to disclaim in spite of spendthrift or similar restrictions given, but subjects that right to a restriction applicable only to fiduciaries. As a policy matter, the creator of a trust or other arrangement creating a fiduciary relationship should be able to prevent a fiduciary accepting office under the arrangement from altering the parameters of the relationship. This reasoning also applies to fiduciary relationships created by statute such as those governing conservatorships and guardianships. Subsection (b) therefore does not override express restrictions on disclaimers contained in the instrument creating the fiduciary relationship or in other statutes of the State. * * *

Subsection (d) specifically allows a partial disclaimer of an interest in property or of a power over property, and gives the disclaimant wide latitude in describing the portion disclaimed. For example, a residuary beneficiary of an estate may disclaim a fraction or percentage of the residue or may disclaim specific property included in the residue (all the shares of X corporation or a specific number of shares). A devisee or donee may disclaim specific acreage or an undivided fraction or carve out a life estate or remainder from a larger interest in real or personal property. (It must be noted, however, that a disclaimer by a devisee or donee which seeks to "carve out" a remainder or life estate is not a "qualified disclaimer" for tax purposes, Treas. Reg. § 25.2518–3(b).)

Subsection (e) makes the disclaimer irrevocable on the later to occur of (i) delivery or filing or (ii) its becoming effective under the section governing the disclaimer of the particular power or interest. A disclaimer must be "irrevocable" in order to be a qualified disclaimer for tax purposes. Since a disclaimer under this Act becomes effective at the time significant for tax purposes, a disclaimer under this Act will always meet the irrevocability requirement for tax qualification. The interaction of the Act and the requirements for a tax qualified disclaimer can be illustrated by analyzing a disclaimer of an interest in a revocable lifetime trust.

Example 1. G creates a revocable lifetime trust which will terminate on G's death and distribute the trust property to G's surviving descendants by representation. G's son, S, determines that he would prefer his share of G's estate to pass to his descendants and executes a disclaimer of his interest in the revocable trust. The disclaimer is then delivered to G (*see* Section 12(e)(3)). The disclaimer is not irrevocable at that time, however, because it will not become effective until G's death when the trust becomes irrevocable (*see* Section 6(b)(1)). Because the disclaimer will not become irrevocable until it becomes effective at G's death, S may recall the disclaimer before G's death and, if he does so, the disclaimer will have no effect.

Subsection (f) restates the long standing rule that a disclaimer is a true refusal to accept and not an act by which the disclaimant transfers, assigns, or releases the disclaimed interest. This subsection states the effect and meaning of the traditional "relation back" doctrine of prior Acts. * * *

Section 6. Disclaimer of Interest in Property.

(a)   In this section:

(1)   "Future interest" means an interest that takes effect in possession or enjoyment, if at all, later than the time of its creation.

(2)   "Time of distribution" means the time when a disclaimed interest would have taken effect in possession or enjoyment.

(b)   Except for a disclaimer governed by Section 7 or 8, the following rules apply to a disclaimer of an interest in property:

(1)   The disclaimer takes effect as of the time the instrument creating the interest becomes irrevocable, or, if the interest arose under the law of intestate succession, as of the time of the intestate's death.

(2)   The disclaimed interest passes according to any provision in the instrument creating the interest providing for the disposition of the interest, should it be disclaimed, or of disclaimed interests in general.

(3)   If the instrument does not contain a provision described in paragraph (2), the following rules apply:

(A)   If the disclaimant is not an individual, the disclaimed interest passes as if the disclaimant did not exist.

(B) If the disclaimant is an individual, except as otherwise provided in subparagraphs (C) and (D), the disclaimed interest passes as if the disclaimant had died immediately before the time of distribution.

(C) If by law or under the instrument, the descendants of the disclaimant would share in the disclaimed interest by any method of representation had the disclaimant died before the time of distribution, the disclaimed interest passes only to the descendants of the disclaimant who survive the time of distribution.

(D) If the disclaimed interest would pass to the disclaimant's estate had the disclaimant died before the time of distribution, the disclaimed interest instead passes by representation to the descendants of the disclaimant who survive the time of distribution. If no descendant of the disclaimant survives the time of distribution, the disclaimed interest passes to those persons, including the state but excluding the disclaimant, and in such shares as would succeed to the transferor's intestate estate under the intestate succession law of the transferor's domicile had the transferor died at the time of distribution. However, if the transferor's surviving spouse is living but is remarried at the time of distribution, the transferor is deemed to have died unmarried at the time of distribution.

(4) Upon the disclaimer of a preceding interest, a future interest held by a person other than the disclaimant takes effect as if the disclaimant had died or ceased to exist immediately before the time of distribution, but a future interest held by the disclaimant is not accelerated in possession or enjoyment.

Comment

* * * Section 6(b)(1) makes a disclaimer of an interest in property effective as of the time the instrument creating the interest becomes irrevocable or at the decedent's death if the interest is created by intestate succession. A will and a revocable trust are irrevocable at the testator's or settlor's death. Inter vivos trusts may also be irrevocable at their creation or may become irrevocable before the settlor's death. A beneficiary designation is also irrevocable at death, unless it is made irrevocable at an earlier time. This provision continues the provision of Uniform Acts on this subject, but with different wording. Previous Acts have stated that the disclaimer "relates back" to some time before the disclaimed interest was created. The relation back doctrine gives effect to the special nature of the disclaimer as a refusal to accept. Because the disclaimer "relates back," the disclaimant is regarded as never having had an interest in the disclaimed property. A disclaimer by a devisee against whom there is an outstanding judgment will prevent the creditor from reaching the property the debtor would otherwise inherit. This Act continues the effect of the relation back doctrine, not by using the specific words, but by directly stating what the relation back doctrine has been interpreted to mean. Sections 2(3) and 5(f) taken together define a disclaimer as a refusal to accept which is not a transfer or release, and subsection (b)(1) of this section makes the disclaimer effective as of the time the creator cannot revoke the interest. Nothing in the statute, however, prevents the legislatures or the courts from limiting the effect of the disclaimer as refusal doctrine in specific situations or generally. *See* the Comments to Section 13 below.

Section 6(b)(2) allows the creator of the instrument to control the disposition of the disclaimed interest by express provision in the instrument. The provision may apply to a particular interest. "I give to my cousin A the sum of ten thousand dollars ($10,000) and should he disclaim any part of this gift, I give the part disclaimed to my cousin B." The provision may also apply to all disclaimed interests. A residuary clause beginning "I give my residuary estate, including all disclaimed interests to. . . ." is such a provision.

Sections 6(b)(3)(B), (C), and (D) apply if Section 6(b)(2) does not and if the disclaimant is an individual. Because "disclaimant" is defined as the person to whom the disclaimed interest would have passed had the disclaimer not been made (Section 2(1)), these paragraphs would apply to disclaimers by fiduciaries on behalf of individuals. The general rule is that the disclaimed interest passes as if the disclaimant had died immediately before the time of distribution defined in Section 6(a)(2). The application of this general rule to present interests given to named individuals is illustrated by the following examples:

Example 1(a). T's will devised "ten thousand dollars ($10,000) to my brother, B." B disclaims the entire devise. B is deemed to have predeceased T, and, therefore B's gift has lapsed. If the State's antilapse statute applies, it will direct the passing of the disclaimed interest. Under UPC § 2–603(b)(1), for example, B's descendants who survive T by 120 hours will take the devise by representation.

Example 1(b). T's will devised "ten thousand dollars ($10,000) to my friend, F." F disclaims the entire devise. F is deemed to predecease T and the gift has lapsed. Few antilapse statutes apply to devises to non-family members. Under UPC § 2–603(b), which saves from lapse only gifts made to certain relatives, the devise would lapse and pass through the residuary clause of the will.

Example 1(c). T's will devised "ten thousand dollars ($10,000) to my brother, B, but if B does not survive me, to my children." If B disclaims the devise, he will be deemed to have predeceased T and the alternative gift to T's children will dispose of the devise.

Present interests are also given to the surviving members of a class or group of persons. Perhaps the most common example of this gift is a devise of the testator's residuary estate "to my descendants who survive me by representation." Under the system of distribution among multi-generational classes used in the Uniform Probate Code § 2–709 and similar statutes, division of the property to be distributed begins in the eldest generation in which there are living people. The following example illustrates a problem that can arise.

Example 2(a). T's will devised "the residue of my estate to my descendants who survive me by representation." T is survived by son S and daughter D. Son has two living children and D has one. S disclaims his interest. The disclaimed interest is one-half of the residuary estate, the interest S would have received had he not disclaimed. Section 6(b)(3)(B) provides that the disclaimed interest passes as if S had predeceased T. If Section 6(b)(3) stopped there, S's children would take one-half of the disclaimed interest and D would take the other half under every system of "representation" that commonly exists. S's disclaimer should not have that effect, however, but should pass what he would have taken to his children. Section 6(b)(3)(C) solves the problem. It provides that the entire disclaimed interest passes only to S's descendants because they would share in the interest had S truly predeceased T.

The provision also solves a problem that exists when the disclaimant is the only representative of an older generation.

Example 2(b). Assume the same facts as *Example 2(a)*, but D has predeceased T. T is survived, therefore, by S, S's two children, and D's child. S disclaims. Again, the disclaimed interest is one-half of the residuary estate and it passes as if S had predeceased T. Had S actually predeceased T, the three grandchildren of S would have shared equally in T's residuary estate because they are all in the same generation. Were the three grandchildren to share equally in the disclaimed interest, S's two children would each receive one-third of the one-half while D's child would receive one-third of the one-half in addition to the one-half of the residuary estate received as the representative of his or her late parent. Section 6(b)(3)(C) again applies to insure that S's children receive one-half of the residue, exactly the interest S would have received but for the disclaimer.

The disclaimer of future interests created by will leads to a different problem. The effective date of the disclaimer of the future interest, the testator's death, is earlier in time than the distribution date. This in turn leads to a possible anomaly illustrated by the following example.

Example 3. Father's will creates a testamentary trust for Mother who is to receive all the income for life. At her death, the trust is to be distributed to Father and Mother's surviving descendants by representation. Mother is survived by son S and daughter D. Son has two living children and D has one. Son decides that he would prefer his share of the trust to pass to his children and disclaims. The disclaimer must be made within nine months of Father's death if it is to be a qualified disclaimer for tax purposes. Under prior Acts and former UPC § 2–801, the interest would have passed as if Son had predeceased Father. A problem could arise if, at Mother's death, one or more of S's children living at that time were born after Father's death. It would be possible to argue that had S predeceased Father the afterborn children would not exist and that D and S's two children living at the time of Father's death are entitled to all of the trust property.

The problem illustrated in *Example 3* is solved by Section 6(b)(3)(B). The disclaimed interest would have taken effect in possession or enjoyment, that is, Son would be entitled to receive one-half of the trust property, at Mother's death. Under paragraph (3)(B) Son is deemed to have died immediately before Mother's death even though under Section 6(b)(1) the disclaimer is effective as of Father's death. There is no doubt, therefore, that S's children living at the distribution date, whenever born, are entitled to the share of the trust property S would have received and, as *Examples 2(a)* and *2(b)* show, they will take exactly what S would have received but for the disclaimer. Had S actually died before Mother, he would have received nothing at Mother's death whether or not the disclaimer had been made. There is nothing to pass to S's children and they take as representatives of S under the representational scheme in effect.

Future interests may or may not be conditioned on survivorship. The following examples illustrate disclaimers of future interests not expressly conditioned on survival.

Example 4(a). G's revocable trust directs the trustee to pay "ten thousand dollars ($10,000) to the grantor's brother, B" at the termination of the trust on G's death. B disclaims the entire gift immediately after G's death. B is deemed to have predeceased G because it is at G's death that the interest given B will come into possession and enjoyment. Had B not disclaimed he would have received $10,000 at that time. The recipient of the disclaimed interest will be determined by the law that applies to gifts of future interests to persons who die before the interest comes into possession and enjoyment. Traditional analysis would regard the gift to B as a vested interest subject to divestment by G's power to revoke the trust. So long as G has not revoked the gift, the interest would pass through B's estate to B's successors in interest. Yet If B's successors in interest are selected by B's will, the disclaimer cannot be a qualified disclaimer for tax purposes. This problem does not arise in a jurisdiction with UPC § 2–707(b), because the interest passes not through B's estate but rather to B's descendants who survive G by 120 hours by representation. Because the antilapse mechanism of UPC § 2–707 is not limited to gifts to relatives, a disclaimer by a friend rather than a brother would have the same result. For jurisdictions without UPC § 2–707, however, Section 6(b)(3)(D) provides an equivalent solution: a disclaimed interest that would otherwise pass through B's estate instead passes to B's descendants who survive G by representation.

Example 4(b). G's revocable trust directed that on his death the trust property is to be distributed to his three children, A, B, and C. A disclaims immediately after G's death and is deemed to predecease the distribution date, which is G's death. The traditional analysis applies exactly as it does in *Example 4(a)*. The only condition on A's gift would be G's not revoking the trust. A is not explicitly required to survive G. * * * The interest would pass to A's successors in interest. If those successors are selected by A's will, the disclaimer cannot be a qualified disclaimer for tax purposes. UPC § 2–707(b) provides that A's interest passes by representation to A's descendants who survive G by 120 hours. For jurisdictions without UPC § 2–707, Section 6(b)(3)(D) reaches the same result.

Example 4(c). G conveys land "to A for life, remainder to B." B disclaims immediately after the conveyance. Traditional analysis regards B's remainder as vested; it is not contingent on surviving A. This classification is unaffected by whether or not the jurisdiction has adopted UPC § 2–707, because that section only applies to future interests in trust; it does not apply to future interests not in trust, such as the one in this example created directly in land. To the extent that B's remainder is transmissible through B's estate, B's disclaimer cannot be a qualified disclaimer for tax purposes. Section 6(b)(3)(D) resolves the problem: a disclaimed interest that would otherwise pass through B's estate instead passes as if it were controlled by UPC §§ 2–707 and 2–711. Because UPC § 2–707 only applies to future interests in trust, jurisdictions enacting Section 6 should enact Section 6(b)(3)(D) whether or not they have enacted UPC § 2–707.

Section 6(b)(3)(A) provides a rule for the passing of property interests disclaimed by persons other than individuals. Because Section 8 applies to disclaimers by trustees of property that would otherwise pass to the trust, Section 6(b)(3)(A) principally applies to disclaimers by corporations, partnerships, and the other entities listed in the definition of "person" in Section 2(6). A charity, for example, might wish to disclaim property the acceptance of which would be incompatible with its purposes.

Section 6(b)(4) continues the provision of prior Uniform Acts and UPC § 2–801 on this subject providing for the acceleration of future interests on the making of the disclaimer, except that future interests in the disclaimant do not accelerate. The workings of Section 6(b)(4) are illustrated by the following examples.

Example 5(a). Father's will creates a testamentary trust to pay income to his son S for his life, and on his death to pay the remainder to S's descendants then living, by representation. If S disclaims his life income interest in the trust, he will be deemed to have died immediately before Father's death. The disclaimed interest, S's income interest, came into possession and enjoyment at Father's death as would any present interest created by will (*see Examples 1(a), (b),* and *(c)*), and, therefore, the time of distribution is Father's death. If the income beneficiary of a testamentary trust does not survive the testator, the income interest is not created and the next interest in the trust takes effect. Since the next interest in Father's trust is the remainder in S's descendants, the trust property will pass to S's descendants who survive Father by representation. It is immaterial under the statute that the actual situation at the S's death might be different with different descendants entitled to the remainder.

Example 5(b). Mother's will creates a testamentary trust to pay the income to her daughter D until she reaches age 35 at which time the trust is to terminate and the trust property distributed in equal shares to D and her three siblings. D disclaims her income interest. The remainder interests in her three siblings accelerate and they each receive one-fourth of the trust property. D's remainder interest does not accelerate, however, and she must wait until she is 35 to receive her fourth of the trust property. * * *

Section 7. Disclaimer of Rights of Survivorship in Jointly Held Property.

(a)   Upon the death of a holder of jointly held property, a surviving holder may disclaim, in whole or part, the greater of:

(1)   a fractional share of the property determined by dividing the number one by the number of joint holders alive immediately before the death of the holder to whose death the disclaimer relates; or

(2)   all of the property except that part of the value of the entire interest attributable to the contribution furnished by the disclaimant.

(b)   A disclaimer under subsection (a) takes effect as of the death of the holder of jointly held property to whose death the disclaimer relates.

(c)   An interest in jointly held property disclaimed by a surviving holder of the property passes as if the disclaimant predeceased the holder to whose death the disclaimer relates.

Comment

The various forms of ownership in which "joint property," as defined in Section 1(5), can be held include common law joint tenancies and any statutory variation that preserves the right of survivorship. The common law was unsettled whether a surviving joint tenant had any right to renounce his interest in jointly-owned property and if so to what extent. * * * Specifically, if A and B owned real estate or securities as joint tenants with right of survivorship and A died, the problem was whether B might disclaim what was given to him originally upon creation of the estate, or, if not, whether he could nevertheless reject the incremental portion derived through the right of survivorship. There was also a question of whether a joint bank account should be treated differently from jointly-owned securities or real estate for the purpose of disclaimer.

This common law of disclaimers of jointly held property must be set against the rapid developments in the law of tax qualified disclaimers of jointly held property. Since the previous Uniform Acts were drafted, the law regarding tax qualified disclaimers of joint property interests has been clarified. * * *

The amended final Regulations, § 25.2518–2(c)(4)(i) allow a surviving joint tenant or tenant by the entireties to disclaim that portion of the tenancy to which he or she succeeds upon the death of the first joint tenant (1/2 where there are two joint tenants) whether or not the tenancy could have been unilaterally severed under local law and regardless of the proportion of consideration furnished by the disclaimant. The Regulations also create a special rule for joint tenancies between spouses created after July 14, 1988 where the spouse of the donor is not a United States citizen. In that case, the donee spouse may disclaim any portion of the joint tenancy includible in the donor spouse's gross estate under IRC § 2040, which creates a contribution rule. Thus the surviving non-citizen spouse may disclaim all of the joint tenancy property if the deceased spouse provided all the consideration for the tenancy's creation.

The amended final Regulations, § 25.2518–2(c)(4)(iii) also recognize the unique features of joint bank accounts, and allow the disclaimer by a survivor of that part of the account contributed by the decedent, so long as the decedent could have regained that portion during life by unilateral action, bar the disclaimer of that part of the account attributable to the survivor's contributions, and explicitly extend the rule governing joint bank accounts to brokerage and other investment accounts, such as mutual fund accounts, held in joint name.

These developments in the tax law of disclaimers are reflected in subsection (a). The subsection allows a surviving holder of jointly held property to disclaim the greater of the accretive share, the part of the jointly held property which augments the survivor's interest in the property, and all of the property that is not attributable to the disclaimant's contribution to the jointly held property. In the usual joint tenancy or tenancy by the entireties between husband and wife, the survivor will always be able to disclaim one-half of the property. If the disclaimer conforms to the requirements of IRC § 2518, it will be a qualified disclaimer. In addition the surviving spouse can disclaim all of the property attributable to the decedent's contribution, a provision which will allow the non-citizen spouse to take advantage of the contribution rule of the final Regulations. The contribution rule of subsection (a)(2) will also allow surviving holders of joint property arrangements other than joint tenancies to make a tax qualified disclaimer under the rules applicable to those joint arrangements. For example, if A contributes 60% and B contributes 40% to a joint bank account and they allow the interest on the funds to accumulate, on B's death A can disclaim 40% of the account; on A's death B can disclaim 60% of the account. (Note that under subsection (a)(1) A can disclaim up to 50% of the account on B's death because there are two joint account holders, but the disclaimer would not be fully tax qualified. As previously noted, a tax qualified disclaimer is limited to 40% of the account.) If the account belonged to the parties during their joint lives in proportion to their contributions, the disclaimers in this example can be tax qualified disclaimers if all the requirements of IRC § 2518 are met.

Subsection (b) provides that the disclaimer is effective as of the death of the joint holder which triggers the survivorship feature of the joint property arrangement. The disclaimant, therefore, has no interest in and has not transferred the disclaimed interest.

Subsection (c) provides that the disclaimed interest passes as if the disclaimant had predeceased the holder to whose death the disclaimer relates. Where there are two joint holders, a disclaimer by the survivor results in the disclaimed property passing as part of the deceased joint holder's estate because under this subsection, the deceased joint holder is the survivor as to the portion disclaimed. If a married couple owns the family home in joint tenancy, therefore, a disclaimer by the survivor under subsection (a)(1) results in one-half of the home passing through the decedent's estate. The surviving spouse and whoever receives the interest through the decedent's estate are tenants in common in the house. In the proper circumstances, the disclaimed one-half could help to use up the decedent's unified credit. Without the disclaimer, the interest would automatically qualify for the marital deduction, perhaps wasting part of the decedent's applicable exclusion amount.

In a multiple holder joint property arrangement, the disclaimed interest will belong to the other joint holder or holders.

Example 1. A, B, and C make equal contributions to the purchase of Blackacre, to which they take title as joint tenants with right of survivorship. On partition each would receive 1/3 of Blackacre and any of them could convert his or her interest to a 1/3 tenancy in common interest by unilateral severance (which, of course, would have to be accomplished in accordance with state law). On A's death, B and C may each, if they wish, disclaim up to 1/3 of the property under 2–1107(a)(1). Should one of them disclaim the full 1/3, the disclaimant will be deemed to predecease A.

Assume that B so disclaims. With respect to the 1/3 undivided interest that now no longer belongs to A the only surviving joint holder is C. C therefore owns that 1/3 interest as tenant in common with the joint tenancy. Should C predecease B, the 1/3 tenancy in common interest will pass through C's estate and B will be the sole owner of an undivided 2/3 interest in Blackacre as the survivor of the joint tenancy. Should B predecease C, C will be the sole owner of Blackacre in fee simple absolute.

Alternatively, assume that both B and C make valid disclaimers after A's death. They are both deemed to have predeceased A, A is the sole survivor of the joint tenancy and Blackacre passes through A's estate.

Finally, assume that A provided all the consideration for the purchase of Blackacre. On A's death, B and C can each disclaim the entire property under 2–1107(a)(2). If they both do so, Blackacre will pass through A's estate. If only one of B or C disclaims the entire property, the one who does not will be the sole owner of Blackacre as the only surviving joint tenant. Such a disclaimer would not be completely tax qualified, however. The Regulations limit a tax qualified disclaimer to no more than 1/3 of the property. If, however, B or C were the first to die, A could still disclaim the 1/3 interest that no longer belongs to the decedent under 7(a)(1) [UPC 2–1107(a)(1)], the disclaimer would be a qualified disclaimer for tax purposes under the Regulations, and the result is that the other surviving joint tenant owns 1/3 of Blackacre as tenant in common with the joint tenancy. * * *

Section 8. Disclaimer of Interest by Trustee.

If a trustee disclaims an interest in property that otherwise would have become trust property, the interest does not become trust property.

Comment

Section 8 deals with disclaimer of a right to receive property into a trust, and thus applies only to trustees. (A disclaimer of a right to receive property by a fiduciary acting on behalf of an individual, such as a personal representative, conservator, guardian, or agent is governed by the section of the statute applicable to the type of interest being disclaimed.) The instrument under which the right to receive the property was created may govern the disposition of the property in the event of a disclaimer by providing for a disposition when the trust does not exist. When the instrument does not make such a provision, the doctrine of resulting trust will carry the property back to the donor. The effect of the actions of co-trustees will depend on the state law governing the action of multiple trustees. Every disclaimer by a trustee must be compatible with the trustee's fiduciary obligations.

Section 9. Disclaimer of Power of Appointment or Other Power Not Held in Fiduciary Capacity.

If a holder disclaims a power of appointment or other power not held in a fiduciary capacity, the following rules apply:

(1) If the holder has not exercised the power, the disclaimer takes effect as of the time the instrument creating the power becomes irrevocable.

(2) If the holder has exercised the power and the disclaimer is of a power other than a presently exercisable general power of appointment, the disclaimer takes effect immediately after the last exercise of the power.

(3) The instrument creating the power is construed as if the power expired when the disclaimer became effective.

Section 10. Disclaimer by Appointee, Object, or Taker in Default of Exercise of Power of Appointment.

(a) A disclaimer of an interest in property by an appointee of a power of appointment takes effect as of the time the instrument by which the holder exercises the power becomes irrevocable.

(b) A disclaimer of an interest in property by an object or taker in default of an exercise of a power of appointment takes effect as of the time the instrument creating the power becomes irrevocable.

Comment

Section 10 governs disclaimers by those who may or do receive an interest in property through the exercise of a power of appointment. At the time of the creation of a power of appointment, the creator of the power, besides giving the power to the holder of the power, can also limit the objects of the power (the permissible appointees of the property subject to the power) and also name those who are to take if the power is not exercised, persons referred to as takers in default.

Section 10 provides rules for disclaimers by all of these persons: subsection (a) is concerned with a disclaimer by a person who actually receives an interest in property through the exercise of a power of appointment, and subsection (b) recognizes a disclaimer by a taker in default or permissible appointee before the power is exercised. These two situations are quite different. An appointee is in the same position as any devisee or beneficiary of a trust. He or she may receive a present or future interest depending on how the holder of the power exercises it. Subsection (a), therefore, makes the disclaimer effective as of the time the instrument exercising the power—giving the interest to the disclaimant—becomes irrevocable. If the holder of the power created an interest in the appointee, the effect of the disclaimer is governed by Section 6. If the holder created another power in the appointee, the effect of the disclaimer is governed by Section 9.

Example 1. Mother's will creates a testamentary trust for daughter D. The trustees are to pay all income to D for her life and have discretion to invade principal for D's maintenance. On D's death she may appoint the trust property by will among her then living descendants. In default of appointment the property is to be distributed by representation to D's descendants who survive her. D is the donee, her descendants are the permissible appointees and the takers in default. D exercises her power by appointing the trust property in three equal shares to her children A, B, and C. The three children are the appointees. A disclaims. Under subsection (a) A's disclaimer is effective as of D's death (the time at which the will exercising the power became irrevocable). Because A disclaimed an interest in property, the effect of the disclaimer is governed by Section 6(b). If D's will makes no provisions for the disposition of the interest should it be disclaimed or of disclaimed interests in general (Section 6(b)(2)), the interest passes as if A predeceased the time of distribution which is D's death. An appointment to a person who is dead at the time of the appointment is ineffective except as provided by an antilapse statute. * * * Since antilapse statutes usually apply to devises to children and grandchildren, the disclaimed interest would pass to A's descendants by representation.

A taker in default or a permissible object of appointment is traditionally regarded as having a type of future interest. * * * The future interest will come into possession and enjoyment when the question of whether or not the power is to be exercised is resolved. For testamentary powers that time is the death of the holder.

Subsection (b) provides that a disclaimer by an object or taker in default takes effect as of the time the instrument creating the power becomes effective. Because the disclaimant is disclaiming an interest in property, albeit a future interest, the effect of the disclaimer is governed by Section 6. The effect of these rules is illustrated by the following examples.

Example 2(a). The facts are the same as *Example 1*, except A disclaims before D's death and D's will does not exercise the power. Under subsection (b) A's disclaimer is effective as of Mother's death which is the time when the instrument creating the power, Mother's will, became irrevocable. Because A disclaimed an interest in property, the effect of the disclaimer is governed by Section 6(b). If Mother's will makes no provision for the disposition of the interest should it be disclaimed or of disclaimed interests in general (Section 6(b)(2)), the interest passes under Section 6(b)(3) as if the disclaimant had died immediately before the time of distribution. Thus, A is deemed to have died immediately before D's death, which is the time of distribution. If A actually survives D, the disclaimed interest is one-third of the trust property; it will pass as if A predeceased D, and the result is the same as in *Example 1*. If A does predecease D he would have received nothing and there is no disclaimed interest. The disclaimer has no effect on the passing of the trust property.

Example 2(b). The facts are the same as in *Example 2(a)* except D does exercise her power of appointment to give one-third of the trust property to each of her three children, A, B, and C. A's disclaimer means the disclaimed interest will pass as if he predeceased D and the result is the same as in *Example 1*.

In addition, if all the objects and takers in default disclaim before the power is exercised the power of appointment is destroyed. * * *

Section 11. Disclaimer of Power Held in Fiduciary Capacity.

(a)   If a fiduciary disclaims a power held in a fiduciary capacity which has not been exercised, the disclaimer takes effect as of the time the instrument creating the power becomes irrevocable.

(b)   If a fiduciary disclaims a power held in a fiduciary capacity which has been exercised, the disclaimer takes effect immediately after the last exercise of the power.

(c)   A disclaimer under this section is effective as to another fiduciary if the disclaimer so provides and the fiduciary disclaiming has the authority to bind the estate, trust, or other person for whom the fiduciary is acting.

Comment

Section 11 governs disclaimers by fiduciaries of powers held in their fiduciary capacity. Examples include a right to remove and replace a trustee or a trustee's power to make distributions of income or principal. Such disclaimers have not been specifically dealt with in prior Uniform Acts although they could prove useful in several situations. A trustee who is also a beneficiary may want to disclaim a power to invade principal for himself for tax purposes. A trustee of a trust for the benefit for a surviving spouse who also has the power to invade principal for the decedent's descendants may wish to disclaim the power in order to qualify the trust for the marital deduction. * * *

The section refers to fiduciary in the singular. It is possible, of course, for a trust to have two or more co-trustees and an estate to have two or more co-personal representatives. This Act leaves the effect of actions of multiple fiduciaries to the general rules in effect in each State relating to multiple fiduciaries. For example, if the general rule is that a majority of trustees can make binding decisions, a disclaimer by two of three co-trustees of a power is effective. A dissenting co-trustee could follow whatever procedure state law prescribes for disassociating him or herself from the action of the majority. A sole trustee burdened with a power to invade principal for a group of beneficiaries including him or herself who wishes to disclaim the power but yet preserve the possibility of another trustee exercising the power would seek the appointment of a disinterested co-trustee to exercise the power and then disclaim the power for him or herself. The subsection thus makes the disclaimer effective only as to the disclaiming fiduciary unless the disclaimer states otherwise. If the disclaimer does attempt to bind other fiduciaries, be they co-fiduciaries or successor fiduciaries, the effect of the disclaimer will depend on local law.

As with any action by a fiduciary, a disclaimer of fiduciary powers must be compatible with the fiduciary's duties.

Section 12. Delivery or Filing.

(a)   In this section, "beneficiary designation" means an instrument, other than an instrument creating a trust, naming the beneficiary of:

(1)   an annuity or insurance policy;

(2)   an account with a designation for payment on death;

(3)   a security registered in beneficiary form;

(4)   a pension, profit-sharing, retirement, or other employment-related benefit plan; or

(5)   any other nonprobate transfer at death.

(b)   Subject to subsections (c) through (*l*), delivery of a disclaimer may be effected by personal delivery, first-class mail, or any other method likely to result in its receipt.

(c)   In the case of an interest created under the law of intestate succession or an interest created by will, other than an interest in a testamentary trust:

(1)   a disclaimer must be delivered to the personal representative of the decedent's estate; or

(2)   if no personal representative is then serving, it must be filed with a court having jurisdiction to appoint the personal representative.

(d)   In the case of an interest in a testamentary trust:

(1)   a disclaimer must be delivered to the trustee then serving, or if no trustee is then serving, to the personal representative of the decedent's estate; or

(2)   if no personal representative is then serving, it must be filed with a court having jurisdiction to enforce the trust.

(e)   In the case of an interest in an inter vivos trust:

(1)   a disclaimer must be delivered to the trustee then serving;

(2)   if no trustee is then serving, it must be filed with a court having jurisdiction to enforce the trust; or

(3)   if the disclaimer is made before the time the instrument creating the trust becomes irrevocable, it must be delivered to the settlor of a revocable trust or the transferor of the interest.

(f)   In the case of an interest created by a beneficiary designation which is disclaimed before the designation becomes irrevocable, the disclaimer must be delivered to the person making the beneficiary designation.

(g)   In the case of an interest created by a beneficiary designation which is disclaimed after the designation becomes irrevocable:

(1)   the disclaimer of an interest in personal property must be delivered to the person obligated to distribute the interest; and

(2)   the disclaimer of an interest in real property must be recorded in [the office of the county recorder of deeds] of the [county] where the real property that is the subject of the disclaimer is located.

(h)   In the case of a disclaimer by a surviving holder of jointly held property, the disclaimer must be delivered to the person to whom the disclaimed interest passes.

(i)   In the case of a disclaimer by an object or taker in default of exercise of a power of appointment at any time after the power was created:

(1)   the disclaimer must be delivered to the holder of the power or to the fiduciary acting under the instrument that created the power; or

(2)   if no fiduciary is then serving, it must be filed with a court having authority to appoint the fiduciary.

(j)   In the case of a disclaimer by an appointee of a nonfiduciary power of appointment:

(1)   the disclaimer must be delivered to the holder, the personal representative of the holder's estate or to the fiduciary under the instrument that created the power; or

(2)   if no fiduciary is then serving, it must be filed with a court having authority to appoint the fiduciary.

(k)   In the case of a disclaimer by a fiduciary of a power over a trust or estate, the disclaimer must be delivered as provided in subsection (c), (d), or (e), as if the power disclaimed were an interest in property.

(l)   In the case of a disclaimer of a power by an agent, the disclaimer must be delivered to the principal or the principal's representative.

Section 13. When Disclaimer Barred or Limited.

(a)   A disclaimer is barred by a written waiver of the right to disclaim.

(b)   A disclaimer of an interest in property is barred if any of the following events occur before the disclaimer becomes effective:

(1)   the disclaimant accepts the interest sought to be disclaimed;

(2)   the disclaimant voluntarily assigns, conveys, encumbers, pledges, or transfers the interest sought to be disclaimed or contracts to do so; or

(3)   a judicial sale of the interest sought to be disclaimed occurs.

(c)   A disclaimer, in whole or part, of the future exercise of a power held in a fiduciary capacity is not barred by its previous exercise.

(d) A disclaimer, in whole or part, of the future exercise of a power not held in a fiduciary capacity is not barred by its previous exercise unless the power is exercisable in favor of the disclaimant.

(e) A disclaimer is barred or limited if so provided by law other than this [Act].

(f) A disclaimer of a power over property which is barred by this section is ineffective. A disclaimer of an interest in property which is barred by this section takes effect as a transfer of the interest disclaimed to the persons who would have taken the interest under this [Act] had the disclaimer not been barred.

Comment

The 1978 Act required that an effective disclaimer be made within nine months of the event giving rise to the right to disclaim (e.g., nine months from the death of the decedent or donee of a power or the vesting of a future interest). The nine month period corresponded in some situations with the Internal Revenue Code provisions governing qualified tax disclaimers. Under the common law an effective disclaimer had to be made only within a "reasonable" time.

This Act specifically rejects a time requirement for making a disclaimer. Recognizing that disclaimers are used for purposes other than tax planning, a disclaimer can be made effectively under the Act so long as the disclaimant is not barred from disclaiming the property or interest or has not waived the right to disclaim. Persons seeking to make tax qualified disclaimers will continue to have to conform to the requirements of the Internal Revenue Code. * * *

Subsection (e), unlike the 1978 Act, specifies that "other law" may bar the right to disclaim. Some States * * * bar a disclaimer by an insolvent disclaimant. In others a disclaimer by an insolvent debtor is treated as a fraudulent "transfer". * * * A number of States refuse to recognize a disclaimer used to qualify the disclaimant for Medicaid or other public assistance. These decisions often rely on the definition of "transfer" in the federal Medical Assistance Handbook which includes a "waiver" of the right to receive an inheritance (see 42 U.S.C.A. § 1396p(e)(1)). * * * It is also likely that state policies will begin to address the question of disclaimers of real property on which an environmental hazard is located in order to avoid saddling the State, as title holder of last resort, with the resulting liability, although the need for fiduciaries to disclaim property subject to environmental liability has probably been diminished by the 1996 amendments to CERCLA by the Asset Conservation Act of 1996 (PL 104–208). These larger policy issues are not addressed in this Act and must, therefore, continue to be addressed by the States. * * *

Section 14. Tax Qualified Disclaimer.

Notwithstanding any other provision of this [Act], if as a result of a disclaimer or transfer the disclaimed or transferred interest is treated pursuant to the provisions of Title 26 of the United States Code, as now or hereafter amended, or any successor statute thereto, and the regulations promulgated thereunder, as never having been transferred to the disclaimant, then the disclaimer or transfer is effective as a disclaimer under this [Act].

Section 15. Recording of Disclaimer.

If an instrument transferring an interest in or power over property subject to a disclaimer is required or permitted by law to be filed, recorded, or registered, the disclaimer may be so filed, recorded, or registered. Except as otherwise provided in Section 12(g)(2), failure to file, record, or register the disclaimer does not affect its validity as between the disclaimant and persons to whom the property interest or power passes by reason of the disclaimer.

Section 16. Application to Existing Relationships. [omitted]

Section 17. Relation to Electronic Signatures in Global and National Commerce Act. [omitted]

Section 18. Uniformity of Application and Construction. [omitted]

Section 19. Severability Clause. [omitted]

Section 20. Effective Date. [omitted]

Section 21. Repeals. [omitted]

UNIFORM ELECTRONIC WILLS ACT*

PREFATORY NOTE

Electronic Wills Under Existing Statutes. People increasingly turn to electronic tools to accomplish life's tasks, including legal tasks. They use computers, tablets, or smartphones to execute electronically a variety of estate planning documents, including pay-on-death and transfer-on-death beneficiary designations and powers of attorney. Some people assume that they will be able to execute all their estate planning documents electronically, and they prefer to do so for efficiency, cost savings, or other reasons. Indeed, a few cases involving wills executed on electronic devices have already arisen. * * *

Goals of the E-Wills Act. Estate planning lawyers, notaries, and software providers are among those interested in electronic wills. * * *

* * * The E-Wills Act seeks:

- To allow a testator to execute a will electronically, while maintaining the safeguards wills law provides for wills executed on something tangible (usually paper);

- To create execution requirements that, if followed, will result in a valid will without a court hearing to determine validity, if no one contests the will; and

- To develop a process that would not enshrine a particular business model in the statutes.

The E-Wills Act seeks to preserve the four functions served by will formalities * * * . Those four functions are:

- Evidentiary—the will provides permanent and reliable evidence of the testator's intent.

- Channeling—the testator's intent is expressed in a way that is understood by those who will interpret it so that the courts and personal representatives can process the will efficiently and without litigation.

- Ritual (cautionary)—the testator has a serious intent to dispose of property in the way indicated and the instrument is in final form and not a draft.

- Protective—the testator has capacity and is protected from undue influence, fraud, delusion and coercion. The instrument is not the product of forgery or perjury. * * *

Electronic Execution of Estate Planning Documents. * * * Many documents authorizing nonprobate transfers of property are already executed electronically, and property owners have become accustomed to being able to use electronic beneficiary designations in connection with various will substitutes. The idea of permitting an electronic designation to control the transfer of property at death is already well accepted.

Section 1. Short Title.

This [act] may be cited as the Uniform Electronic Wills Act.

Section 2. Definitions.

In this [act]:

(1) "Electronic" means relating to technology having electrical, digital, magnetic, wireless, optical, electromagnetic, or similar capabilities.

[(2) "Electronic presence" means the relationship of two or more individuals in different locations communicating in real time to the same extent as if the individuals were physically present in the same location.]

(3) "Electronic will" means a will executed electronically in compliance with Section 5(a).

(4) "Record" means information that is inscribed on a tangible medium or that is stored in an electronic or other medium and is retrievable in perceivable form.

(5) "Sign" means, with present intent to authenticate or adopt a record:

   (A) to execute or adopt a tangible symbol; or

   (B) to affix to or logically associate with the record an electronic symbol or process.

(6) "State" means a state of the United States, the District of Columbia, Puerto Rico, the United States Virgin Islands, or any territory or insular possession subject to the jurisdiction of the United States. The term includes a federally recognized Indian tribe.

(7) "Will" includes a codicil and any testamentary instrument that merely appoints an executor, revokes or revises another will, nominates a guardian, or expressly excludes or limits the right of an individual or class to succeed to property of the decedent passing by intestate succession.

Comment

Paragraph 2. Electronic Presence. An electronic will may be executed with the testator and all of the necessary witnesses present in one physical location. In that case the state's rules concerning presence for non-electronic wills, which may require line-of-sight presence or conscious presence, will apply. *See* Section 3. Because the E-Wills Act does not provide a separate definition of physical presence, a state's existing rules for presence will apply to determine physical presence.

An electronic will is also valid if the witnesses are in the electronic presence of the testator, *see* Section 5. This definition provides for the meaning of electronic presence. Permitting electronic presence will make it easier for testators in remote locations and testators with limited mobility to execute their wills. The witnesses and testator must be able to communicate in "real time," a term that means "the actual time during which something takes place." * * * The term is used in connection with electronic communication to mean that the people communicating do so without a delay in the exchange of information. * * *

In the definition of electronic presence, "to the same extent" includes accommodations for people who are differently-abled. The definition does not provide specific accommodations due to the concern that any attempt at specificity would be too restrictive and to allow the standards to keep current with future advances in technology.

Paragraph 5. Sign. The term "logically associated" is used in the definition of sign, without further definition. * * * Although often used in connection with a signature, the term is used * * * in the E-Wills Act to refer both to a document that may be logically associated with another document as well as to a signature logically associated with a document. * * *

Section 3. Law Applicable to Electronic Will; Principles of Equity.

An electronic will is a will for all purposes of the law of this state. The law of this state applicable to wills and principles of equity apply to an electronic will, except as modified by this [act].

Comment

The first sentence of this Section is didactic, and emphatically ensures that an electronic will is treated as a traditional one for all purposes.

In this Section "law" means both common law and statutory law. Law other than the E-Wills Act continues to supply rules related to wills, unless the E-Wills Act modifies a state's other law related to wills.

The common law requires that a testator intend that the writing be the testator's will. * * *

A number of protective doctrines attempt to ensure that a document being probated as a will reflects the intent of the testator. Wills statutes typically include capacity requirements related to mental capacity and age. A minor cannot execute a valid will. * * * Other requirements for validity may be left to the common law. A writing that appears to be a will may be challenged based on allegations of undue influence, duress, or fraud. * * * The statutory and common law requirements that apply to wills in general also apply to electronic wills.

Laws related to qualifications to serve as a witness also apply to electronic wills. * * *

Section 4. Choice of Law Regarding Execution.

A will executed electronically but not in compliance with Section 5(a) is an electronic will under this [act] if executed in compliance with the law of the jurisdiction where the testator is:

(1)   physically located when the will is signed; or

(2)   domiciled or resides when the will is signed or when the testator dies.

Comment

Under the common law, the execution requirements for a will depended on the situs of real property, as to the real property, and the domicile of the testator, for personal property. * * * The statutes of many states now treat as valid a will that was validly executed under the law of the state where the will was executed or where the testator was domiciled. * * * For a non-electronic will, the testator will necessarily be in the state where the will is executed. Many state statutes also permit the law of the testator's domicile when the testator dies to apply. * * *

Some of the state statutes permitting electronic wills treat an electronic will as executed in the state and valid under the state law even if the testator is not physically in the state at the time of execution. * * * The Uniform Law Commission concluded that a state should not be required to accept an electronic will as valid if the state's domiciliary executed the will without being physically present in the state authorizing electronic wills.

Section 4 reflects the policy that a will valid where the testator was physically located should be given effect using the law of the state where executed. The E-Wills Act does not require a state to give effect to a will executed by a testator using the law of another state unless the testator resides, is domiciled, or is physically present in the other state when the testator executes the will.

Example: Gina lived in Connecticut and was domiciled there. During a trip to Nevada Gina executes an electronic will, following the requirements of Nevada law. The will is valid in Nevada and also in Connecticut, because Gina was physically present in a state that authorizes electronic wills when she executed her will. Now assume that Gina never leaves the state of Connecticut. While at home she goes online, prepares a will, and executes it electronically using Nevada law. The will is valid in Nevada but not in Connecticut, unless Connecticut adopts the E-Wills Act.

This rule is consistent with current law for non-electronic wills. The rule is necessary, because otherwise someone living in a state that authorizes electronic wills might execute a will there and then move to a state that does not authorize electronic wills and be forced to make a new will or die intestate if unable or unwilling to execute another will. An electronic will executed in compliance with the law of the state where the testator was physically located should be given effect, even if the testator later moves to another state, just as a non-electronic will would be given effect. A rule that would invalidate a will properly executed under the law of the state where the testator was physically present at the time of execution, especially if the testator was domiciled there, could trap an unwary testator and result in intestacy.

Example: Dennis lived in Nevada for 20 years. He met with a lawyer to have a will prepared, and when the will was ready for execution his lawyer suggested executing the will from his house, using the lawyer's electronic platform. Dennis executed the will in compliance with Nevada law in force at the time of execution, using the lawyer's electronic platform and providing the required identification. The lawyer had no concerns about Dennis's capacity and no worries that someone was unduly influencing him. Two years later Dennis moved to Connecticut where his daughter lived. Dennis died in Connecticut, with the Nevada will as his last valid will. Connecticut should give effect to Dennis's will, regardless of whether its execution would have otherwise been valid under Connecticut law.

Section 5. Execution of Electronic Will.

(a)   Subject to Section 8(d)[and except as provided in Section 6], an electronic will must be:

   (1)   a record that is readable as text at the time of signing under paragraph (2);

   (2)   signed by:

      (A)   the testator; or

      (B)   another individual in the testator's name, in the testator's physical presence and by the testator's direction; and

   (3)   [either:

      (A)] signed in the physical [or electronic] presence of the testator by at least two individuals[, each of whom is a resident of a state and physically located in a state at the time of signing and] within a reasonable time after witnessing:

      [(A)] [(i)] the signing of the will under paragraph (2); or

      [(B)] [(ii)] the testator's acknowledgment of the signing of the will under paragraph (2) or acknowledgement of the will [; or

      (B)   acknowledged by the testator before and in the physical [or electronic] presence of a notary public or other individual authorized by law to notarize records electronically].

(b)   Intent of a testator that the record under subsection (a)(1) be the testator's electronic will may be established by extrinsic evidence.

Comment

The E-Wills Act does not duplicate all rules related to valid wills, and except as otherwise provided in the E-Wills Act, a state's existing requirements for valid wills will apply to electronic wills. Section 5 follows the formalities required in UPC § 2–502. A state with different formalities should modify this Section to conform to its requirements. Under Section 5 an electronic will can be valid if executed electronically, even if the testator and witnesses are in different locations.

Some states allow a will to be self-proved if the testator and witnesses sign an affidavit detailing the procedures followed in executing the will. The UPC treats the self-proving affidavit as creating a conclusive presumption that the signature requirements were met and a rebuttable presumption that other requirements for a valid will were met. * * * Rather than create extra requirements to validate an electronic will, the E-Wills Act creates extra requirements to make an electronic will self-proving when the testator and witnesses are in different locations. *See* Section 8.

Requirement of a Writing. Statutes that apply to non-electronic wills require that a will be "in writing." * * *

UPC § 2–502 requires that a will be "in writing" and the comment to that section says, "Any reasonably permanent record is sufficient." The E-Wills Act requires that the provisions of an electronic will be readable as text (and not as computer code, for example) at the time the testator executed the will. The E-Wills Act incorporates the requirement of writing by requiring that an electronic will be readable as text.

One example of an electronic record readable as text is a will inscribed with a stylus on a tablet. *See In re Estate of Javier Castro*, Case No. 2013ES00140, Court of Common Pleas Probate Division, Lorain County, Ohio (June 19, 2013). An electronic will may also be a word processing document that exists on a computer or a cell phone but has not been printed. Under the E-Wills Act, the issue for these wills is not whether a writing exists but whether the testator signed the will and the witnesses attested it.

The Uniform Law Commission decided to retain the requirement that a will be in writing. Thus, the E-Wills Act does not permit an audio or audio-visual recording of an individual describing the individual's testamentary wishes to constitute a will. However, an audio-visual recording of the execution of a will may provide valuable evidence concerning the validity of the will.

The use of a voice activated computer program can create text that can meet the requirements of a will. For example, a testator could dictate the will to a computer using voice recognition software. If the computer converts the spoken words to text *before* the testator executes the will, the will meets that requirement that it be a record readable as text at the time of execution.

Electronic Signature. In *Castro*, the testator signed his name as an electronic image using a stylus. A signature in this form is a signature for purposes of the E-Wills Act. The definition of "sign" includes a "tangible symbol" or an "electronic symbol or process" made with the intent to authenticate the record being signed. Thus, a typed signature would be sufficient if typed with the intent that it be a signature. A signature typed in a cursive font or a pasted electronic copy of a signature would also be sufficient, if made with the intent that it be a signature. As e-signing develops, other types of symbols or processes may be used, with the important element being that the testator intended the action taken to be a signature validating the electronic will.

Requirement of Witnesses. Wills law includes a witness requirement for several reasons: (1) evidentiary—to identify persons who can answer questions about the voluntariness and coherence of the testator and whether undue influence played a role in the creation and execution of the will, (2) cautionary—to signal to the testator that signing the document has serious consequences, and (3) protective—to deter coercion, fraud, duress, and undue influence. Section 5 requires witnesses for a validly executed will.

Will substitutes—tools authorizing nonprobate transfers—typically do not require witnesses, and a testator acting without legal assistance may not realize that witnesses are necessary for an electronic will. The harmless error doctrine has been used to give effect to an electronic will executed without witnesses when the testator's intent was clear. * * * A state concerned that electronic wills will be invalidated due to lack of witnesses should consider adopting the harmless error provision in Section 6 of the E-Wills Act, even if the state has not adopted a similar provision for judicially correcting harmless error in execution.

Remote Witnesses. Because electronic wills may be executed via the internet, the question arises whether the witnesses to the testator's signature must be in the physical presence of the testator or whether electronic presence such as via a webcam and microphone will suffice. Some online providers of wills offer remote witnessing as a service. The E-Wills Act does not include additional requirements for electronic wills executed with remote witnesses, but Section 8 imposes additional requirements before a will executed with remote witnesses can be considered self-proving.

The usefulness of witnesses who can testify about the testator's apparent state of mind if a will is challenged for lack of capacity or undue influence may be limited, because a witness who observes the testator sign the will may not have sufficient contact with the testator to have knowledge of capacity or undue influence. This is true whether the witnesses are in the physical or electronic presence of the testator. Nonetheless, the current legal standards and procedures address the situation adequately and remote attestation should not create significant new evidentiary burdens. The E-Wills Act errs on the side of not creating hurdles that result in denying probate to wills that represent the intent of their testators.

Reasonable Time. The witnesses must sign within a reasonable time after witnessing the testator sign or acknowledge the signing or the will. The Comment to UPC § 2–502 notes that the statute does not require that the witness sign before the testator dies, but some cases have held that signing after the testator's death is not "within a reasonable time." * * * Other cases have held a will valid even though a witness signed after the testator's death. * * * For electronic wills, a state's rules applicable to non-electronic wills apply.

Notarized Wills. A small number of states permit a notary public to validate the execution of a will in lieu of witnesses. Paragraph (3)(b) follows UPC § 2–502(a)(3)(B) and provides that a will can be validated if the testator acknowledges the will before a notary, even if the will is not attested by two witnesses. Because remote online notarization includes protection against tampering, other states may want to include the option for the benefit of additional security.

[Section 6. Harmless Error.

Alternative A

A record readable as text not executed in compliance with Section 5(a) is deemed to comply with Section 5(a) if the proponent of the record establishes by clear-and-convincing evidence that the decedent intended the record to be:

(1)   the decedent's will;

(2)   a partial or complete revocation of the decedent's will;

(3)   an addition to or modification of the decedent's will; or

(4)   a partial or complete revival of the decedent's formerly revoked will or part of the will.

Alternative B

[Cite to Section 2–503 of the Uniform Probate Code or comparable provision of the law of this state] applies to a will executed electronically.

End of Alternatives]

Comment

The harmless error doctrine was added to the UPC in 1990. Since then 11 states have adopted the rule. The Comments to UPC § 2–503 describe the development of the doctrine in Australia, Canada, and Israel, and cite to a number of studies and articles. * * *

The focus of the harmless error doctrine is the testator's intent. A court can excuse a defect in the execution formalities if the proponent of the defective will can establish by clear and convincing evidence that the testator intended the writing to be the testator's will. The will formalities serve as proxies for testamentary intent, and harmless error doctrine replaces strict compliance with the formalities with direct evidence of that intent.

The harmless error doctrine may be particularly important in connection with electronic wills because a testator executing an electronic will without legal assistance may assume that an electronic will is valid even if not witnessed. The high standard of proof that the testator intended the writing to serve as will should protect against abuse.

A number of cases both in the United States and in Australia have involved electronic wills written shortly before the testator committed suicide. The circumstances surrounding the writing have led the courts in those cases to use harmless error to validate the wills, despite the lack of witnesses. * * *

Although in these cases the wills have been given effect, a will drafted in contemplation of suicide may be subject to challenge based on concerns about capacity. Even if a state adopts the harmless error doctrine, the other requirements for a valid will, including testamentary capacity and a lack of undue influence, will apply.

Section 7. Revocation.

(a)   An electronic will may revoke all or part of a previous will.

(b)   All or part of an electronic will is revoked by:

(1)   a subsequent will that revokes all or part of the electronic will expressly or by inconsistency; or

    (2)   a physical act, if it is established by a preponderance of the evidence that the testator, with the intent of revoking all or part of the will, performed the act or directed another individual who performed the act in the testator's physical presence.

Comment

Revocation by physical act is permitted for non-electronic wills. The difficulty with physical revocation of an electronic will is that multiple copies of an electronic will may exist. Although a subsequent will may revoke an electronic will, a testator may assume that a will may be deleted by using a delete or trash function on a computer, as well as by other physical means. Guided by the goal of giving effect to the intent of most testators, the E-Wills Act permits revocation by physical act.

Although a will may be revoked by physical act, revocation by subsequent will under subsection (a)(1) is the preferred, and more reliable, method of revocation. The lack of a certain outcome when revocation by physical act is used makes this form of revocation problematic.

Physical Act Revocation. The E-Wills Act does not define physical act, which could include deleting a file with the click of a mouse or smashing a flash drive with a hammer. If an electronic will is stored with a third party that provides a designated mechanism for revocation, such as a delete button, and the testator intentionally pushes the button, the testator has used a physical act. If a testator prints a copy of an electronic will, writing "revoked" on the copy would be a physical act. Typing "revoked" on an electronic copy would also constitute a physical act, if the electronic will had not been notarized in a manner that locked the document.

Sending an email that says, "I revoke my will," is not a physical act performed on the will itself because the email is separate from the will. The email could revoke the will under subsection (a)(1) as a subsequent will, if the email met the formalities required under Section 5(a) or met the burden of proof under Section 6. Of course, if there were a separate physical act, such as deleting an electronic will on an electronic device, such an email could be useful evidence in interpreting the testator's intent.

If a testator uses a physical act to revoke an electronic will, the party arguing that the testator intended to revoke the will must prove the testator's intent.

Multiple Originals. Although multiple copies of an electronic will may exist, a physical act performed on one of them by the testator with the intent to revoke will be sufficient to revoke the will. Traditional law applicable to duplicate originals supports this rule. * * *

Intent to Revoke. Revocation by physical act requires that the testator intend to revoke the will. The E-Wills Act uses a preponderance of the evidence standard, which may be more likely to give effect to the intent of testators with electronic wills than would a clear and convincing evidence standard. A testator might assume that by deleting a document the testator has revoked it, and a higher evidentiary standard could give effect to wills that testators intended to revoke. The standard may increase the risk of a false positive but should decrease the risk of a false negative. The preponderance of the evidence standard is consistent with the law for non-electronic wills. * * *

Example: Alejandro executes a will electronically, using a service that provides witnesses and a notary. A year later Alejandro decides to revoke the will, but he is not ready to make a new will. He goes to the website of the company that is storing his will, enters his login information, and gets to a page that gives him the option to revoke the will by pressing a button labeled revoke. He affirms the decision when a pop-up screen asks if he is certain he wants to revoke his will. When Alejandro dies, his sister (the beneficiary of the electronic will) produces a copy he had sent her. The company provides information indicating that he had revoked the will, following the company's protocol to revoke a will. The evidence is sufficient to establish that Alejandro intended to revoke his will, and under the E-Wills Act Alejandro's compliance with the company's protocol would qualify as a physical act revocation. His sister will be unsuccessful in her attempt to probate the copy she has.

Example: Yvette writes a will on her electronic tablet and executes it electronically, with two neighbors serving as witnesses. She saves a copy on her home computer. The will gives her estate to her nephew. Some years later Yvette decides she would prefer for her estate to be divided by her two intestate heirs, the nephew and a niece. Yvette deletes the will file on her computer, forgetting that she had given her tablet, which still has the will on it, to her nephew. She deleted the file with the intent to revoke her will, and she tells one of the witnesses as well as her niece that she has done so. When she dies her nephew produces the tablet and asserts that the will is her valid will. Her niece and the witness can testify that Yvette intended to revoke her will by the physical act of deleting the duplicate original on her computer. Under the E-Wills Act, a court could reasonably conclude that a preponderance of the evidence supports a finding of a physical act revocation. If the will on the computer had been deleted but the only person who could testify about Yvette's intent was the niece, the court might conclude that the niece's self-interest made her testimony less persuasive. The evidence in that case might not meet the preponderance of the evidence standard, especially if the niece had access to Yvette's computer.

Lost Wills. A testator's accidental deletion of an electronic will should not be considered revocation of the will. However, the common law "lost will" presumption may apply. Under the common law, if a will last known to be in the possession of the testator cannot be found at the testator's death, a presumption of revocation may apply. The soft presumption is that the testator destroyed the will with the intent to revoke it. * * * The presumption can be overcome with extrinsic evidence that provides another explanation for the will's disappearance. A house fire might have destroyed the testator's files. A testator may have misplaced or inadvertently discarded files; age or poor health may make such inadvertence more likely. A person with motive to revoke and access to the testator's files might have destroyed the will. The presumption does not apply if the will was in the possession of someone other than the testator.

If the document cannot be found and the presumption of revocation is overcome or does not apply, the contents of the will can be proved through a copy or testimony of the person who drafted the will.

Physical Act by Someone Other than Testator. A testator may direct someone else to perform a physical act on a will for the purpose of revoking it. The testator must be in the physical presence of the person performing the act, not merely in the person's electronic presence. The use of "physical presence" is intended to mean that the state's rules on presence in connection with wills apply—either line of sight or conscious presence. UPC § 2–507(a)(2) relies on conscious presence.

Section 8. Electronic Will Attested and Made Self-Proving at Time of Execution.

(a)   An electronic will may be simultaneously executed, attested, and made self-proving by acknowledgment of the testator and affidavits of the witnesses.

(b)   The acknowledgment and affidavits under subsection (a) must be:

(1)   made before an officer authorized to administer oaths under law of the state in which execution occurs [or, if fewer than two attesting witnesses are physically present in the same location as the testator at the time of signing under Section 5(a)(2), before an officer authorized under [cite to Revised Uniform Law on Notarial Acts Section 14A (2018) or comparable provision of the law of this state]]; and

(2)   evidenced by the officer's certificate under official seal affixed to or logically associated with the electronic will.

(c)   The acknowledgment and affidavits under subsection (a) must be in substantially the following form:

I, _____, the testator, and being sworn, declare to the undersigned officer that I sign

(name)

this instrument as my electronic will, I willingly sign it or willingly direct another individual to sign it for me, I execute it as my voluntary act for the purposes expressed in this instrument, and I am [18] years of age or older, of sound mind, and under no constraint or undue influence.

_____
Testator

We, _____, and _____, witnesses, being sworn, declare to the undersigned

(name)   (name)

officer that the testator signed this instrument as the testator's electronic will, that the testator willingly signed it or willingly directed another individual to sign for the testator, and that each of us, in the physical [or electronic] presence of the testator, signs this instrument as witness to the testator's signing, and to the best of our knowledge the testator is [18] years of age or older, of sound mind, and under no constraint or undue influence.

_____
Witness

_____
Witness

Certificate of officer:

State of _____

[County] of _____

    Subscribed, sworn to, and acknowledged before me by _____, the testator, and
                                 (name)

subscribed and sworn to before me by _____ and _____, witnesses, this ___ day of
                      (name)   (name)

_____, ___.

(Seal)

_____
(Signed)

_____
(Capacity of officer)

    (d) A signature physically or electronically affixed to an affidavit that is affixed to or logically associated with an electronic will under this [act] is deemed a signature of the electronic will under Section 5(a).

Comment

    If an officer authorized to administer oaths (a notary) is in a state that has adopted Section 14A of RULONA or a comparable statute, the notary need not be physically present. However, if the state has not adopted a statute allowing remote online notarization, the notary must be physically present in order to administer the oath under the law of that state.

    Remote Online Notarization. Section 14A of RULONA provides additional protection through a notarization process referred to as "remote online notarization." In remote online notarization, the person signing a document appears before a notary using audio-video technology. Depending on state law, the document can be paper or digital, but the signer and the notary are in two different places. Extra security measures are taken to establish the signer's identity.

    The E-Wills Act requires additional steps to make an electronic will with remote attestation self-proving. If the testator and necessary witnesses are in the same physical location, the will can be made self-proving using a notary who can notarize an electronic document but who is not authorized to use remote online notarization. However, if anyone necessary to the execution of the will is not in the same physical location as the testator, the will can be made self-proving only if remote online notarization is used.

    Signatures on Affidavit Used to Execute Will. Subsection (d) addresses the problem that arises when a testator and witnesses sign an affidavit, mistakenly thinking they are signing the will itself. UPC § 2–504(c) incorporated this provision into the UPC in 1990 to counteract judicial interpretations in some states that had invalidated wills where this mistake had occurred.

Time of Affidavit. Under the UPC a will may be made self-proving at a time later than execution. The E-Wills Act does not permit the execution of a self-proving affidavit for an electronic will other than at the time of execution of the electronic will. An electronic will has metadata that will show the date of execution, and if an affidavit is logically associated with an electronic will at a later date, the date of the electronic will and the protection provided by the self-proving affidavit may be uncertain. If a testator fails to make an electronic will self-proving simultaneously with the will's execution, the testator can later re-execute the electronic will. The additional burden on the testator is justified given the possible confusion and loss of protection that could result from a later completion of an affidavit.

Section 9. Certification of Paper Copy.

An individual may create a certified paper copy of an electronic will by affirming under penalty of perjury that a paper copy of the electronic will is a complete, true, and accurate copy of the electronic will. If the electronic will is made self-proving, the certified paper copy of the will must include the self-proving affidavits.

Section 10. Uniformity of Application and Construction. [omitted]

Section 11. Transitional Provision. [omitted]

Section 12. Effective Date. [omitted]

UNIFORM ESTATE TAX APPORTIONMENT ACT (2003)*

PREFATORY NOTE

The Internal Revenue Code places the primary responsibility for paying federal estate taxes on the decedent's executor and empowers, but does not direct, the executor to collect from recipients of certain non-probate transfers included in the taxable estate a prorated portion of the estate tax attributable to those types of property. In the absence of specific contrary directions of the decedent, the Code generally provides as to other transfers that taxes are to be borne by the persons who would bear that cost if the taxes were paid by the executor prior to distributing the estate. The determination of who should bear the ultimate burden of the estate taxes is left to state law.

If a state does not have a statutory apportionment law, the burden of the estate taxes generally will fall on residuary beneficiaries of the probate estate. This means that recipients of many types of nonprobate assets (such as beneficiaries of revocable trusts and surviving joint tenants) may be exonerated from paying a portion of the tax. Also, it generates a risk that residual gifts to the spouse or a charity may result in a smaller deduction and a larger tax. A number of states have adopted legislation apportioning the burden of estates taxes among the beneficiaries. * * *

The Act [advances the principle] that the decedent's expressed intentions govern apportionment of an estate tax. Statutory apportionment applies only to the extent there is no clear and effective decedent's tax burden direction to the contrary. Under the statutory scheme, marital and charitable beneficiaries generally are insulated from bearing any of the estate tax, and a decedent's direction that estate tax be paid from a gift to be shared by a spouse or charity with another is construed to locate the tax burden only on the taxable portion of the gift. The Act provides relief for persons forced to pay estate tax on values passing to others whose interests, though contributing to the tax, are unreachable by the fiduciary. * * *

Section 1. Short Title.

This [act] may be cited as the Uniform Estate Tax Apportionment Act.

Section 2. Definitions.

In this [act]:

(1)   "Apportionable estate" means the value of the gross estate as finally determined for purposes of the estate tax to be apportioned reduced by:

(A)   any claim or expense allowable as a deduction for purposes of the tax;

(B)   the value of any interest in property that, for purposes of the tax, qualifies for a marital or charitable deduction or otherwise is deductible or is exempt; and

(C)   any amount added to the decedent's gross estate because of a gift tax on transfers made before death.

(2)   "Estate tax" means a federal, state, or foreign tax imposed because of the death of an individual and interest and penalties associated with the tax. The term does not include an inheritance tax, income tax, or generation-skipping transfer tax other than a generation-skipping transfer tax incurred on a direct skip taking effect at death.

(3)   "Gross estate" means, with respect to an estate tax, all interests in property subject to the tax.

(4)   "Person" means an individual, corporation, business trust, estate, trust, partnership, limited liability company, association, joint venture, public corporation, government, governmental subdivision, agency, or instrumentality, or any other legal or commercial entity.

(5)   "Ratable" means apportioned or allocated pro rata according to the relative values of interests to which the term is to be applied. "Ratably" has a corresponding meaning.

(6)   "Time-limited interest" means an interest in property which terminates on a lapse of time or on the occurrence or nonoccurrence of an event or which is subject to the exercise of discretion that could transfer a beneficial interest to another person. The term does not include a cotenancy unless the cotenancy itself is a time-limited interest.

(7)   "Value" means, with respect to an interest in property, fair market value as finally determined for purposes of the estate tax that is to be apportioned, reduced by any outstanding debt secured by the interest without reduction for taxes paid or required to be paid or for any special valuation adjustment.

Section 3. Apportionment by Will or Other Dispositive Instrument.

(a)   Except as otherwise provided in subsection (c), the following rules apply:

(1)   To the extent that a provision of a decedent's will expressly and unambiguously directs the apportionment of an estate tax, the tax must be apportioned accordingly.

(2)   Any portion of an estate tax not apportioned pursuant to paragraph (1) must be apportioned in accordance with any provision of a revocable trust of which the decedent was the settlor which expressly and unambiguously directs the apportionment of an estate tax. If conflicting apportionment provisions appear in two or more revocable trust instruments, the provision in the most recently dated instrument prevails. For purposes of this paragraph:

(A)   a trust is revocable if it was revocable immediately after the trust instrument was executed, even if the trust subsequently becomes irrevocable; and

(B)   the date of an amendment to a revocable trust instrument is the date of the amended instrument only if the amendment contains an apportionment provision.

(3)   If any portion of an estate tax is not apportioned pursuant to paragraph (1) or (2), and a provision in any other dispositive instrument expressly and unambiguously directs that any interest in the property disposed of by the instrument is or is not to be applied to the payment of the estate tax attributable to the interest disposed of by the instrument, the provision controls the apportionment of the tax to that interest.

(b)   Subject to subsection (c), and unless the decedent expressly and unambiguously directs the contrary, the following rules apply:

(1)   If an apportionment provision directs that a person receiving an interest in property under an instrument is to be exonerated from the responsibility to pay an estate tax that would otherwise be apportioned to the interest,

(A)   the tax attributable to the exonerated interest must be apportioned among the other persons receiving interests passing under the instrument, or

(B)   if the values of the other interests are less than the tax attributable to the exonerated interest, the deficiency must be apportioned ratably among the other persons receiving interests in the apportionable estate that are not exonerated from apportionment of the tax.

(2)   If an apportionment provision directs that an estate tax is to be apportioned to an interest in property a portion of which qualifies for a marital or charitable deduction, the estate tax must first be apportioned ratably among the holders of the portion that does not qualify for a marital or charitable deduction and then apportioned ratably among the holders of the deductible portion to the extent that the value of the nondeductible portion is insufficient.

(3)   Except as otherwise provided in paragraph (4), if an apportionment provision directs that an estate tax be apportioned to property in which one or more time-limited interests exist, other than interests in specified property under Section 7, the tax must be apportioned to the principal of that property, regardless of the deductibility of some of the interests in that property.

(4)   If an apportionment provision directs that an estate tax is to be apportioned to the holders of interests in property in which one or more time-limited interests exist and a charity has an interest that otherwise qualifies for an estate tax charitable deduction, the tax must first be apportioned, to the extent feasible, to interests in property that have not been distributed to the persons entitled to receive the interests.

(c)   A provision that apportions an estate tax is ineffective to the extent that it increases the tax apportioned to a person having an interest in the gross estate over which the decedent had no power to transfer immediately before the decedent executed the instrument in which the apportionment direction was made. For purposes of this subsection, a testamentary power of appointment is a power to transfer the property that is subject to the power.

Comment

A decedent's direction will not control the apportionment of taxes unless it explicitly refers to the payment of an estate tax and is specific and unambiguous as to the direction it makes for that payment. For example, a testamentary direction that "all debts and expenses of and claims against me or my estate are to be paid out of the residuary of my probate estate" is not an express direction for the payment of estate taxes and will not control apportionment. While an estate tax is a claim against the estate, a will's direction for payment of claims that does not explicitly mention estate taxes is likely to be a boiler plate that was written with no intention of controlling tax apportionment. To protect against an inadvertent inclusion of estate tax payment in a general provision of that nature, the Act requires that the direction explicitly mention estate taxes.

On the other hand, a direction in a will that "all taxes arising as a result of my death, whether attributable to assets passing under this will or otherwise, be paid out of the residue of my probate estate" satisfies the Act's requirement for an explicit mention of estate taxes and is specific and unambiguous as to what properties are to bear the payment of those taxes.

Whether other directions of a decedent that explicitly mention estate taxes comply with the Act's requirement that they be specific and unambiguous is a matter for judicial construction. For example, there is a split among judicial decisions as to whether a direction such as "all estate taxes be paid out of the residue of my estate" is ambiguous because it is unclear whether it is intended to apply to taxes attributable to nonprobate assets. To the extent that it is determined that a decedent failed to apportion an estate tax, then the Act will apply to apportion that amount of the tax. * * *

[T]he Act provides an order of priority for a decedent's provisions for estate tax allocations. To the extent that a decedent makes an express and unambiguous provision by will, that provision will trump any competing provision in another instrument. To the extent that the will does not expressly and unambiguously provide for the allocation of some estate taxes, an express and unambiguous provision in a revocable trust instrument will control. If the decedent executed more than one revocable trust instrument, the express provisions in the instrument that was executed most recently will control. In determining which revocable trust instrument was executed most recently, the date of any amendment containing an express and unambiguous apportionment provision will be taken into account. In the event that the allocation of estate taxes is not fully provided for by the decedent's will or revocable trust instrument, an express and unambiguous provision in other instruments executed by the decedent controls to the extent that the provision applies to the property disposed of in that instrument. An example of a provision in an instrument disposing of property, other than a will or revocable trust instrument, is a provision in a designation of a beneficiary of life insurance proceeds either that the proceeds will or will not be used to pay a portion of estate taxes. A designation of that form will be honored if there is no conflicting valid provision in a will or revocable trust instrument. * * *

The federal estate tax laws enable a decedent's personal representative to collect a portion of the decedent's federal estate tax from the recipients of certain nonprobate property that is included in the decedent's gross estate. See e.g., §§ 2206 to 2207B of the Internal Revenue Code. There is a conflict among the courts as to whether those federal provisions preempt a State law apportionment provision. Choosing the position that there is no federal preemption, the Act apportions taxes without regard to the federal provisions. The federal provisions are not apportionment statutes; rather, they simply empower the personal representative to collect a portion of the estate tax that is attributable to the property included in the decedent's gross estate and do not direct use of the collected amounts by the personal representative. The rights granted to the personal representative by federal law for the collection of assets from nonprobate beneficiaries do not conflict either with the apportionment of taxes by State law or with other rights of collection granted by State law. Since there is no conflict, this Act does not include a direction as to whether federal or State law takes priority. * * *

If a decedent directs that estate taxes be paid from properties, some of which qualify for a marital or charitable deduction, the provision making that direction may designate the extent to which the charitable or marital interests will or will not bear a portion of the tax. If the decedent makes no provision as to whether the marital or charitable interests bear a portion of the tax, the Act provides a default rule that exempts the marital or charitable interests from payment of the tax to the extent that it is feasible to do so. * * *

If a decedent had made an irrevocable transfer during his life, over which the decedent did not retain a power to make a subsequent transfer, and if that transfer is included in the decedent's gross estate for estate tax purposes, a portion of the estate tax will be apportioned to the transferee unless the decedent effectively provides otherwise in a will, revocable trust or other instrument. While, by an express provision in the appropriate instrument, a decedent can reduce the amount of tax apportioned to such inter vivos transfers, the decedent is not permitted to increase the amount of tax apportioned to such a transferee. If a decedent attempts to do so, whether directly by apportioning more estate tax to the inter vivos transfer or indirectly by insulating some person interested in the gross estate from all or part of that person's share of the estate tax, the amount of estate tax that is apportioned to the transferee of an irrevocable inter vivos transfer will not be greater than the amount that would have been apportioned to that transferee if the decedent had made no provision for apportionment in another instrument. * * *

Section 4. Statutory Apportionment of Estate Taxes.

To the extent that apportionment of an estate tax is not controlled by an instrument described in Section 3 and except as otherwise provided in Sections 6 and 7, the following rules apply:

(1)   Subject to paragraphs (2), (3), and (4), the estate tax is apportioned ratably to each person that has an interest in the apportionable estate.

(2)   A generation-skipping transfer tax incurred on a direct skip taking effect at death is charged to the person to which the interest in property is transferred.

(3)   If property is included in the decedent's gross estate because of Section 2044 of the Internal Revenue Code of 1986 or any similar estate tax provision, the difference between the total estate tax for which the decedent's estate is liable and the amount of estate tax for which the decedent's estate would have been liable if the property had not been included in the decedent's gross estate is apportioned ratably among the holders of interests in the property. The balance of the tax, if any, is apportioned ratably to each other person having an interest in the apportionable estate.

(4)   Except as otherwise provided in Section 3(b)(4) and except as to property to which Section 7 applies, an estate tax apportioned to persons holding interests in property subject to a time-limited interest must be apportioned, without further apportionment, to the principal of that property.

Section 5. Credits and Deferrals.

Except as otherwise provided in Sections 6 and 7, the following rules apply to credits and deferrals of estate taxes:

(1)   A credit resulting from the payment of gift taxes or from estate taxes paid on property previously taxed inures ratably to the benefit of all persons to which the estate tax is apportioned.

(2)   A credit for state or foreign estate taxes inures ratably to the benefit of all persons to which the estate tax is apportioned, except that the amount of a credit for a state or foreign tax paid by a beneficiary of the property on which the state or foreign tax was imposed, directly or by a charge against the property, inures to the benefit of the beneficiary.

(3)   If payment of a portion of an estate tax is deferred because of the inclusion in the gross estate of a particular interest in property, the benefit of the deferral inures ratably to the persons to which the estate tax attributable to the interest is apportioned. The burden of any interest charges incurred on a deferral of taxes and the benefit of any tax deduction associated with the accrual or payment of the interest charge is allocated ratably among the persons receiving an interest in the property.

Section 6. Insulated Property: Advancement of Tax.

(a)   In this section:

(1)   "Advanced fraction" means a fraction that has as its numerator the amount of the advanced tax and as its denominator the value of the interests in insulated property to which that tax is attributable.

(2)   "Advanced tax" means the aggregate amount of estate tax attributable to interests in insulated property which is required to be advanced by uninsulated holders under subsection (c).

(3)   "Insulated property" means property subject to a time-limited interest which is included in the apportionable estate but is unavailable for payment of an estate tax because of impossibility or impracticability.

(4)   "Uninsulated holder" means a person who has an interest in uninsulated property.

(5)   "Uninsulated property" means property included in the apportionable estate other than insulated property.

(b)   If an estate tax is to be advanced pursuant to subsection (c) by persons holding interests in uninsulated property subject to a time-limited interest other than property to which Section 7 applies, the tax must be advanced, without further apportionment, from the principal of the uninsulated property.

(c)   Subject to Section 9(b) and (d), an estate tax attributable to interests in insulated property must be advanced ratably by uninsulated holders. If the value of an interest in uninsulated property is less than the amount of estate taxes otherwise required to be advanced by the holder of that interest, the deficiency must be advanced ratably by the persons holding interests in properties that are excluded from the apportionable estate under Section 2(1)(B) as if those interests were in uninsulated property.

(d)   A court having jurisdiction to determine the apportionment of an estate tax may require a beneficiary of an interest in insulated property to pay all or part of the estate tax otherwise apportioned to the interest if the court finds that it would be substantially more equitable for that beneficiary to bear the tax liability personally than for that part of the tax to be advanced by uninsulated holders.

(e)   When a distribution of insulated property is made, each uninsulated holder may recover from the distributee a ratable portion of the advanced fraction of the property distributed. To the extent that undistributed insulated property ceases to be insulated, each uninsulated holder may recover from the property a ratable portion of the advanced fraction of the total undistributed property.

(f)   Upon a distribution of insulated property for which, pursuant to subsection (d), the distributee becomes obligated to make a payment to uninsulated holders, a court may award an uninsulated holder a recordable lien on the distributee's property to secure the distributee's obligation to that uninsulated holder.

Comment

* * * Since the estate tax apportioned to the owners of insulated property cannot be collected from the property, the tax is to be paid (as an advancement) by persons having interests in other assets of the estate (uninsulated holders), provided however that the total tax attributed to and advanced by an uninsulated holder cannot exceed the value of that person's interest in the uninsulated property. * * * If the amount of the aggregate tax apportioned to and to be advanced by an uninsulated holder exceeds the value of that holder's interest in the uninsulated property, then the deficiency shall be apportioned to the holders of interests in properties that otherwise qualify for charitable or marital deductions. In such cases, those charitable and marital properties are reclassified as uninsulated properties, and so the beneficiaries of those properties will be uninsulated holders who will have a right of recovery from the distributees of insulated properties for which they paid a portion of the estate tax. * * *

The tax attributable to the insulated property that is required to be paid by the uninsulated holders is referred to as an "advanced tax." To permit the uninsulated holders who bear the advanced tax to be reimbursed, the Act effectively provides the uninsulated holders with a phantom percentage interest in the property whose transfer is the source of the advanced tax. While the phantom percentage interest of the uninsulated holder remains constant, its value will increase or decrease as the value of the property changes. The phantom percentage interest is determined by dividing the advanced tax by the aggregate value of insulated properties as determined for purposes of the estate tax. When a distribution of insulated property is made, a percentage of that distribution must be paid over to the uninsulated holders; and this is a personal obligation of the distributee. If it were not for this Section, the uninsulated holders would have had a right of reimbursement under Section 10 for the amount of their outlay from the distributees; but instead, subsection (e) gives them a right to a fraction of the distributed amount rather than to a fixed dollar amount. The amount collected from a distributee is divided among the uninsulated holders according to the percentage of the advanced tax that they paid.

It is important to note that the uninsulated holders do not have an actual interest in the insulated property and have no lien or security interest in that property while it is in the possession of the trust or fund. The uninsulated holders only have a claim against the persons who receive distributions from the trust or fund which holds the insulated property. The only exception is where previously insulated property loses its insulation so that it can be reached by the uninsulated holders without violating any prohibition against alienation of interests. Once insulated property is in the hands of a distributee, subsection (f) permits the uninsulated holders to seek a lien on the distributee's property for the amount owed to them; but there is no lien or other encumbrance on the insulated property while it is in the possession of the trust or fund. * * *

In certain circumstances, it would be more equitable to require the beneficiary of an interest in insulated property to bear the tax on that interest than to reapportion it to others. For example, if the beneficiary's interest is one that will become possessory in a short period of time, so that the beneficiary will soon have possession of assets from the fund or trust, it would be more equitable to place personal liability on that beneficiary; and the court has discretion to do so. In determining whether a beneficiary is likely to obtain possession of all or a significant part of the beneficiary's interest in the insulated property, the court can consider not only distributions that are required to be made to the beneficiary, but also distributions that, based on an examination of the history of the administration of the fund or trust, are likely to be made in the near future. Subsection (d) provides the court with the discretion to make that determination. While a beneficiary's receipt of a distribution from the trust or fund would make that beneficiary liable to uninsulated holders who paid the advanced tax, that places a burden of collection on the uninsulated holders; and so, when the distribution is likely to be made to a beneficiary within a short period of time, it would be more equitable to have that beneficiary bear the tax.

Section 7. Apportionment and Recapture of Special Elective Benefits.

(a) In this section:

(1) "Special elective benefit" means a reduction in an estate tax obtained by an election for:

(A) a reduced valuation of specified property that is included in the gross estate;

(B) a deduction from the gross estate, other than a marital or charitable deduction, allowed for specified property; or

(C) an exclusion from the gross estate of specified property.

(2) "Specified property" means property for which an election has been made for a special elective benefit.

(b) If an election is made for one or more special elective benefits, an initial apportionment of a hypothetical estate tax must be computed as if no election for any of those benefits had been made. The aggregate reduction in estate tax resulting from all elections made must be allocated among holders of interests in the specified property in the proportion that the amount of deduction, reduced valuation, or exclusion attributable to each holder's interest bears to the aggregate amount of deductions, reduced valuations, and exclusions obtained by the decedent's estate from the elections. If the estate tax initially apportioned to the holder of an interest in specified property is reduced to zero, any excess amount of reduction reduces ratably the estate tax apportioned to other persons that receive interests in the apportionable estate.

(c) An additional estate tax imposed to recapture all or part of a special elective benefit must be charged to the persons that are liable for the additional tax under the law providing for the recapture.

Comment

The types of special elective benefits at which this provision is aimed are currently set forth in §§ 2031(c), 2032A, and 2057 of the Internal Revenue Code of 1986. * * * The purpose of this Section is to define how the benefit of an estate tax reduction of this or a similar type will be allocated and how any additional estate tax imposed to recapture some of that tax benefit will be allocated. * * *

The allocation of the aggregate tax reduction obtained from all special elective benefits is made among the holders of interests in the specified properties in accordance with the reduction of the decedent's taxable estate that is attributable to each holder's interest. Since the determination of the amount of estate tax benefit is made by applying the marginal rate of estate tax to the reduced value of the gross estate, it is necessary to aggregate the tax reduction obtained from all of the special election benefits so that the greater tax reduction obtained from using a marginal rate is not duplicated by applying that rate to several distinct reductions.

Once the amount of estate tax that is apportioned to the holder of an interest in specified property is determined, it will have to be paid. The holders of interests in a specified property may have difficulty paying that tax. To pay the tax, the holders will have to sell the property, borrow against it, use other funds to pay the tax, or defer the payment of the tax under tax deferral provisions and pay the tax in installments with income produced by the property. If they were to sell the property, the special elective benefit would be lost; so a sale is not a viable option. Accordingly, the requirement of Sections 3(b)(3), 4(4), and 6(b) that the estate tax or an advanced tax be paid from the principal of property subject to a time-limited interest does not apply to properties for which an election for a special elective benefit is made. The solution chosen in Section 6(c) and (e) of having other persons interested in the apportionable estate pay the tax and then collect reimbursement from distributees of the property is not practical here because there would be difficulty in determining what income was derived from the property itself, and there would be no trustee or other fiduciary to see that the amounts were turned over to the persons who paid the tax. So, that approach was not adopted. Instead, Sections 4(1) and this section apportion the estate tax to the holders of the interests in the properties who, facing the obligation to pay, can determine the best method for obtaining the funds to make that payment.

If additional estate taxes are imposed to recapture some or all of a special elective benefit, Section 7 follows the allocation of liability imposed by the estate tax law that generated the additional tax. The burden of the additional estate tax will be borne by the persons who hold interests in the specified property at the time that the additional tax payment is made, and those persons may not be the same ones who held the specified property when the special elective benefit was allowed and so derived the benefit of that election.

Section 8. Securing Payment of Estate Tax From Property in Possession of Fiduciary.

(a)   A fiduciary may defer a distribution of property until the fiduciary is satisfied that adequate provision for payment of the estate tax has been made.

(b)   A fiduciary may withhold from a distributee an amount equal to the amount of estate tax apportioned to an interest of the distributee.

(c)   As a condition to a distribution, a fiduciary may require the distributee to provide a bond or other security for the portion of the estate tax apportioned to the distributee.

Section 9. Collection of Estate Tax by Fiduciary.

(a)   A fiduciary responsible for payment of an estate tax may collect from any person the tax apportioned to and the tax required to be advanced by the person.

(b)   Except as otherwise provided in Section 6, any estate tax due from a person that cannot be collected from the person may be collected by the fiduciary from other persons in the following order of priority:

(1)   any person having an interest in the apportionable estate which is not exonerated from the tax;

(2)   any other person having an interest in the apportionable estate;

(3)   any person having an interest in the gross estate.

(c)   A domiciliary fiduciary may recover from an ancillary personal representative the estate tax apportioned to the property controlled by the ancillary personal representative.

(d)   The total tax collected from a person pursuant to this [act] may not exceed the value of the person's interest.

Comment

If a fiduciary is unable to collect from a person the estate tax apportioned to that person or to be advanced by that person, the fiduciary is authorized to collect the deficiency from any person interested in the apportionable estate whose interest is not exonerated from tax apportionment. The fiduciary is not obliged to collect the deficiency ratably from such persons. At the fiduciary's discretion, the fiduciary is authorized to collect all of the deficiency from one person or from several persons in any proportion that the fiduciary chooses. The reason that the fiduciary is not required to collect a deficiency ratably is that the payment of the estate tax should not be delayed because of difficulties in collecting from a number of persons.

If the amount collected from persons whose interests in the apportionable estate is not exonerated from tax apportionment is insufficient to make up the deficiency, the fiduciary can then collect any remaining deficiency from persons interested in the apportionable estate whose interests are exonerated from tax apportionment. This class excludes persons holding interests in property that qualified for a marital or charitable deduction since those interests are excluded from the apportionable estate. Again, the fiduciary is not required to collect the remaining deficiency ratably from the persons holding exonerated interests.

Finally, if the amount collected from persons holding exonerated interests is insufficient, the fiduciary can collect the balance from persons holding interests that qualify for a marital or charitable deduction. The fiduciary is not required to make that collection ratably.

Anyone who pays more than his share of an estate tax or an advanced tax has a ratable right of reimbursement from those who did not pay their share. If requested, the fiduciary may assist in collecting that reimbursement.

Section 10. Right of Reimbursement.

(a)   A person required under Section 9 to pay an estate tax greater than the amount due from the person under Section 3 or 4 has a right to reimbursement from another person to the extent that the other person has not paid the tax required by Section 3 or 4 and a right to reimbursement ratably from other persons to the extent that each has not contributed a portion of the amount collected under Section 9(b).

(b)   A fiduciary may enforce the right of reimbursement under subsection (a) on behalf of the person that is entitled to the reimbursement and shall take reasonable steps to do so if requested by the person.

Section 11. Action to Determine or Enforce Act.

A fiduciary, transferee, or beneficiary of the gross estate may maintain an action for declaratory judgment to have a court determine and enforce this [act].

Section 12. Uniformity of Application and Construction. [omitted]

[Section 13. Severability.] [omitted]

Section 14. Delayed Application. [omitted]

Section 15. Effective Date. [omitted]

[Section 16. Repeals.] [omitted]

REVISED UNIFORM FIDUCIARY ACCESS TO DIGITAL ASSETS ACT (2015)*

Section 1. Short Title.

This [act] may be cited as the Revised Uniform Fiduciary Access to Digital Assets Act (2015).

Section 2. Definitions.

In this [act]:

(1)   "Account" means an arrangement under a terms-of-service agreement in which a custodian carries, maintains, processes, receives, or stores a digital asset of the user or provides goods or services to the user.

(2)   "Agent" means an attorney-in-fact granted authority under a durable or nondurable power of attorney.

(3)   "Carries" means engages in the transmission of an electronic communication.

(4)   "Catalogue of electronic communications" means information that identifies each person with which a user has had an electronic communication, the time and date of the communication, and the electronic address of the person.

(5)   "[Conservator]" means a person appointed by a court to manage the estate of a living individual. The term includes a limited [conservator].

---

(6) "Content of an electronic communication" means information concerning the substance or meaning of the communication which:

(A) has been sent or received by a user;

(B) is in electronic storage by a custodian providing an electronic-communication service to the public or is carried or maintained by a custodian providing a remote-computing service to the public; and

(C) is not readily accessible to the public.

(7) "Court" means the [insert name of court in this state having jurisdiction in matters relating to the content of this act].

(8) "Custodian" means a person that carries, maintains, processes, receives, or stores a digital asset of a user.

(9) "Designated recipient" means a person chosen by a user using an online tool to administer digital assets of the user.

(10) "Digital asset" means an electronic record in which an individual has a right or interest. The term does not include an underlying asset or liability unless the asset or liability is itself an electronic record.

(11) "Electronic" means relating to technology having electrical, digital, magnetic, wireless, optical, electromagnetic, or similar capabilities.

(12) "Electronic communication" has the meaning set forth in 18 U.S.C. Section 2510(12)[, as amended].

(13) "Electronic-communication service" means a custodian that provides to a user the ability to send or receive an electronic communication.

(14) "Fiduciary" means an original, additional, or successor personal representative, [conservator], agent, or trustee.

(15) "Information" means data, text, images, videos, sounds, codes, computer programs, software, databases, or the like.

(16) "Online tool" means an electronic service provided by a custodian that allows the user, in an agreement distinct from the terms-of-service agreement between the custodian and user, to provide directions for disclosure or nondisclosure of digital assets to a third person.

(17) "Person" means an individual, estate, business or nonprofit entity, public corporation, government or governmental subdivision, agency, or instrumentality, or other legal entity.

(18) "Personal representative" means an executor, administrator, special administrator, or person that performs substantially the same function under law of this state other than this [act].

(19) "Power of attorney" means a record that grants an agent authority to act in the place of a principal.

(20) "Principal" means an individual who grants authority to an agent in a power of attorney.

(21) "[Protected person]" means an individual for whom a [conservator] has been appointed. The term includes an individual for whom an application for the appointment of a [conservator] is pending.

(22) "Record" means information that is inscribed on a tangible medium or that is stored in an electronic or other medium and is retrievable in perceivable form.

(23) "Remote-computing service" means a custodian that provides to a user computer-processing services or the storage of digital assets by means of an electronic communications system, as defined in 18 U.S.C. Section 2510(14)[, as amended].

(24) "Terms-of-service agreement" means an agreement that controls the relationship between a user and a custodian.

(25) "Trustee" means a fiduciary with legal title to property under an agreement or declaration that creates a beneficial interest in another. The term includes a successor trustee.

(26) "User" means a person that has an account with a custodian.

(27) "Will" includes a codicil, testamentary instrument that only appoints an executor, and instrument that revokes or revises a testamentary instrument.

Comment

* * * The definition of "account" is broadly worded to encompass any contractual arrangement subject to a terms-of-service agreement, but limited for the purpose of this act by the requirement that the custodian carry, maintain, process, receive, or store a digital asset of the user.

The definition of "digital asset" expressly excludes underlying assets such as funds held in an online bank account. Because records may exist in both electronic and non-electronic formats, this definition clarifies the scope of the act and the limitation on the type of records to which it applies. The term includes types of electronic records currently in existence and yet to be invented. It includes any type of electronically-stored information, such as: 1) information stored on a user's computer and other digital devices; 2) content uploaded onto websites; and 3) rights in digital property. It also includes records that are either the catalogue or the content of an electronic communication. * * *

The term "catalogue of electronic communications" is designed to cover log-type information about an electronic communication such as the email addresses of the sender and the recipient, and the date and time the communication was sent.

The term "content of an electronic communication" is adapted from 18 U.S.C. Section 2510(8), which provides that content: "when used with respect to any wire, oral, or electronic communication, includes any information concerning the substance, purport, or meaning of that communication." The definition is designed to cover only content subject to the coverage of Section 2702 of the Electronic Communications Privacy Act (ECPA), 18 U.S.C. Section 2510 et seq.; it does not include content not subject to ECPA. Consequently, the "content of an electronic communication", as used later throughout Revised UFADAA, refers *only* to information in the body of an electronic message that is not readily accessible to the public; if the information were readily accessible to the public, it would not be subject to the privacy protections of federal law under ECPA. * * * Example: X uses a Twitter account to send a message. If the tweet is sent only to other people who have been granted access to X's tweets, then it meets Revised UFADAA's definition of "content of an electronic communication." But, if the tweet is completely public with no access restrictions, then it does not meet the act's definition of "content of an electronic communication." ECPA does not apply to private e-mail service providers, such as employers and educational institutions. * * *

A "user" is a person that has an account with a custodian, and includes a deceased individual that entered into the agreement while alive. A fiduciary can be a user when the fiduciary opens the account. * * *

A "custodian" includes any entity that provides or stores electronic data for an account holder.

The fiduciary's access to a record defined as a "digital asset" does not mean the fiduciary *owns* the asset or may engage in transactions with the asset. Consider, for example, a fiduciary's legal rights with respect to funds in a bank account or securities held with a broker or other custodian, regardless of whether the bank, broker, or custodian has a brick-and-mortar presence. This act affects electronic records concerning the bank account or securities, but does not affect the authority to engage in transfers of title or other commercial transactions in the funds or securities, even though such transfers or other transactions might occur electronically. Revised UFADAA only deals with the right of the fiduciary to access all relevant electronic communications and digital assets accessible through the online account. An entity may not refuse to provide access to online records any more than the entity can refuse to provide the fiduciary with access to hard copy records.

An "electronic communication" is a particular type of digital asset subject to the privacy protections of the Electronic Communications Privacy Act. It includes email, text messages, instant messages, and any other electronic communication between private parties. The definition of "electronic communication" is that set out in 18 U.S.C. Section 2510(12):

> "electronic communication" means any transfer of signs, signals, writing, images, sounds, data, or intelligence of any nature transmitted in whole or in part by a wire, radio, electromagnetic, photoelectronic or photooptical system that affects interstate or foreign commerce, but does not include—
>
> (A)   any wire or oral communication;
>
> (B)   any communication made through a tone-only paging device;
>
> (C)   any communication from a tracking device (as defined in section 3117 of this title); or
>
> (D)   electronic funds transfer information stored by a financial institution in a communications system used for the electronic storage and transfer of funds.

* * * The definition of "remote-computing service" * * * refers to 18 U.S.C. Section 2510(14), which defines an electronic communications system as: "any wire, radio, electromagnetic, photooptical or photoelectronic facilities for the transmission of wire or electronic communications, and any computer facilities or related electronic equipment for the electronic storage of such communications." * * *

An "online tool" is a mechanism by which a user names an individual to manage the user's digital assets after the occurrence of a future event, such as the user's death or incapacity. The named individual is referred to as the "designated recipient" in the act to differentiate the person from a fiduciary. A designated recipient may perform many of the same tasks as a fiduciary, but is not held to the same legal standard of conduct. * * *

Section 3. Applicability.

(a)   This [act] applies to:

(1)   a fiduciary acting under a will or power of attorney executed before, on, or after [the effective date of this [act]];

(2)   a personal representative acting for a decedent who died before, on, or after [the effective date of this [act]];

(3)   a [conservatorship] proceeding commenced before, on, or after [the effective date of this [act]]; and

(4)   a trustee acting under a trust created before, on, or after [the effective date of this [act]].

(b)   This [act] applies to a custodian if the user resides in this state or resided in this state at the time of the user's death.

(c)   This [act] does not apply to a digital asset of an employer used by an employee in the ordinary course of the employer's business.

Comment

This act does not change the substantive rules of other laws, such as agency, banking, conservatorship, contract, copyright, criminal, fiduciary, privacy, probate, property, security, trust, or other applicable law except to vest fiduciaries with authority, according to the provisions of this act, to access or copy digital assets of a decedent, protected person, principal, settlor, or trustee. * * *

Subsection (b) clarifies that the act does not apply to a fiduciary's access to an employer's internal email system.

Example 1—Fiduciary access to an employee e-mail account. D dies, employed by Company Y. Company Y has an internal e-mail communication system, available only to Y's employees, and used by them in the ordinary course of Y's business. D's personal representative, R, believes that D used Company Y's e-mail system to effectuate some financial transactions that R cannot find through other means. R requests access from Company Y to the e-mails.

Company Y is not a custodian subject to the act. Under Section 2(8), a custodian must carry, maintain or store a user's digital assets. A user, under Section 2(26) must have an account, and an account, in turn, is defined under Section 2(1) as a contractual arrangement subject to a terms-of-service agreement. Company Y, like most employers, did not enter into a terms-of-service agreement with D, so Y is not a custodian.

Example 2—Employee of electronic-communication service provider. D dies, employed by Company Y. Company Y is an electronic-communication service provider. Company Y has an internal e-mail communication system, available only to Y's employees and used by them in the ordinary course of Y's business. D used the internal Company Y system. When not at work, D also used an electronic-communication service system that Company Y provides to the public. D's personal representative, R, believes that D used Company Y's internal e-mail system as well as Company Y's electronic-communication system available to the public to effectuate some financial transactions. R seeks access to both communication systems.

As is true in Example 1, Company Y is not a custodian subject to the act for purposes of the internal email system. The situation is different with respect to R's access to Company Y's system that is available to the public. Assuming that Company Y can disclose the communications under federal law and R meets the other requirements of this act, Company Y must disclose them to R.

Section 4. User Direction for Disclosure of Digital Assets.

(a)   A user may use an online tool to direct the custodian to disclose or not to disclose some or all of the user's digital assets, including the content of electronic communications. If the online tool allows the user to modify or delete a direction at all times, a direction regarding disclosure using an online tool overrides a contrary direction by the user in a will, trust, power of attorney, or other record.

(b)   If a user has not used an online tool to give direction under subsection (a) or if the custodian has not provided an online tool, the user may allow or prohibit in a will, trust, power of attorney, or other record, disclosure to a fiduciary of some or all of the user's digital assets, including the content of electronic communications sent or received by the user.

(c)   A user's direction under subsection (a) or (b) overrides a contrary provision in a terms-of-service agreement that does not require the user to act affirmatively and distinctly from the user's assent to the terms of service.

Comment

This section addresses the relationship of online tools, other records documenting the user's intent, and terms-of-service agreements. In some instances, there may be a conflict between the directions provided by a user in an online tool that limits access by other parties to the user's digital assets, and the user's estate planning or other personal documents that purport to authorize access for specified persons in identified situations. The act attempts to balance these interests by establishing a three-tier priority system for determining the user's intent with respect to any digital asset.

Subsection (a) gives top priority to a user's wishes as expressed using an online tool. If a custodian of digital assets allows the user to provide directions for handling those digital assets in case of the user's death or incapacity, and the user does so, that provides the clearest possible indication of the user's intent and is specifically limited to those particular digital assets.

If the user does not give direction using an online tool, but makes provisions in an estate plan for the disposition of digital assets, subsection (b) gives legal effect to the user's directions. The fiduciary charged with managing the user's digital assets must provide a copy of the relevant document to the custodian when requesting access. See Sections 7 through 14.

If the user provides no other direction, the terms-of-service governing the account will apply. If the terms-of-service do not address fiduciary access to digital assets, the default rules provided in this act will apply.

Section 5. Terms-of-Service Agreement.

(a)   This [act] does not change or impair a right of a custodian or a user under a terms-of-service agreement to access and use digital assets of the user.

(b)   This [act] does not give a fiduciary any new or expanded rights other than those held by the user for whom, or for whose estate, the fiduciary acts or represents.

(c)   A fiduciary's access to digital assets may be modified or eliminated by a user, by federal law, or by a terms-of-service agreement if the user has not provided direction under Section 4.

Comment

This section clarifies that, to the extent that a custodian gives a fiduciary access to an account pursuant to Section 6, the account's terms-of-service agreement applies equally to the original user and to a fiduciary acting for the original user. A fiduciary is subject to the same terms and conditions of the user's agreement with the custodian. This section does not require a custodian to permit a fiduciary to assume a user's terms-of-service agreement if the custodian can otherwise comply with Section 6.

Section 6. Procedure for Disclosing Digital Assets.

(a)   When disclosing digital assets of a user under this [act], the custodian may at its sole discretion:

(1)   grant a fiduciary or designated recipient full access to the user's account;

(2)   grant a fiduciary or designated recipient partial access to the user's account sufficient to perform the tasks with which the fiduciary or designated recipient is charged; or

(3)   provide a fiduciary or designated recipient a copy in a record of any digital asset that, on the date the custodian received the request for disclosure, the user could have accessed if the user were alive and had full capacity and access to the account.

(b)   A custodian may assess a reasonable administrative charge for the cost of disclosing digital assets under this [act].

(c)   A custodian need not disclose under this [act] a digital asset deleted by a user.

(d)   If a user directs or a fiduciary requests a custodian to disclose under this [act] some, but not all, of the user's digital assets, the custodian need not disclose the assets if segregation of the assets would impose an undue burden on the custodian. If the custodian believes the direction or request imposes an undue burden, the custodian or fiduciary may seek an order from the court to disclose:

(1)   a subset limited by date of the user's digital assets;

(2)   all of the user's digital assets to the fiduciary or designated recipient;

(3)   none of the user's digital assets; or

(4)   all of the user's digital assets to the court for review in camera.

Comment

This section governs a custodian's response to a request for disclosure of a user's digital assets.

Subsection (a) gives the custodian of digital assets a choice of methods for disclosing digital assets to an authorized fiduciary. Each custodian has a different business model and may prefer one method over another.

Subsection (b) allows a custodian to assess a reasonable administrative charge for the cost of disclosure. This is intended to be analogous to the charge any business may assess for administrative tasks outside the ordinary course of its business to comply with a court order.

Subsection (c) states that any digital asset deleted by the user need not be disclosed, even if recoverable by the custodian. Deletion is assumed to be a good indication that the user did not intend for a fiduciary to have access.

Subsection (d) addresses requests that are unduly burdensome because they require segregation of digital assets. For example, a fiduciary's request for disclosure of "any email pertaining to financial matters" would require a custodian to sort through the full list of emails and cull any irrelevant messages before disclosure. If a custodian receives an unduly burdensome request of this sort, it may decline to disclose the digital assets, and either the fiduciary or custodian may seek guidance from a court.

Section 7. Disclosure of Content of Electronic Communications of Deceased User.

If a deceased user consented or a court directs disclosure of the contents of electronic communications of the user, the custodian shall disclose to the personal representative of the estate of the user the content of an electronic communication sent or received by the user if the representative gives the custodian:

(1)   a written request for disclosure in physical or electronic form;

(2)   a [certified] copy of the death certificate of the user;

(3)   a [certified] copy of [the letter of appointment of the representative or a small-estate affidavit or court order];

(4)   unless the user provided direction using an online tool, a copy of the user's will, trust, power of attorney, or other record evidencing the user's consent to disclosure of the content of electronic communications; and

(5)   if requested by the custodian:

(A)   a number, username, address, or other unique subscriber or account identifier assigned by the custodian to identify the user's account;

(B)   evidence linking the account to the user; or

(C)   a finding by the court that:

(i)   the user had a specific account with the custodian, identifiable by the information specified in subparagraph (A);

(ii)   disclosure of the content of electronic communications of the user would not violate 18 U.S.C. Section 2701 et seq.[, as amended], 47 U.S.C. Section 222[, as amended], or other applicable law;

(iii)   unless the user provided direction using an online tool, the user consented to disclosure of the content of electronic communications; or

(iv)   disclosure of the content of electronic communications of the user is reasonably necessary for administration of the estate.

Comment

The Electronic Communications Privacy Act (ECPA) distinguishes between the permissible disclosure of the "content" of an electronic communication, covered in 18 U.S.C. Section 2702(b), and of "a record or other information pertaining to a" subscriber or customer, covered in 18 U.S.C. Section 2702(c) * * * . Section 7 concerns disclosure of content; Section 8 covers disclosure of non-content and other digital assets of the user.

Content-based material can, in turn, be divided into two types of communications: those received by the user and those sent. Federal law, 18 U.S.C. Section 2702(b) permits a custodian to divulge the contents of a communication "(1) to an addressee or intended recipient of such communication or an agent of such addressee or intended recipient" or "(3) with the lawful consent of the originator or an addressee or intended recipient of such communication, or the subscriber in the case of remote computing service."

Consequently, when the user is the "addressee or intended recipient," material can be disclosed either to that individual or to an agent for that person, 18 U.S.C. Section 2702(b)(1), and it can also be disclosed to third parties with the "lawful consent" of the addressee or intended recipient. 18 U.S.C. Section 2702(b)(3). Material for which the user is the "originator" (or the "subscriber" to a remote computing service) can be disclosed to third parties only with the account holder's "lawful consent." 18 U.S.C. Section 2702(b)(3). * * * By contrast to content-based material, non-content material can be disclosed either with the lawful consent of the user or to any person (other than a governmental entity) even without lawful consent. This information includes material about any communication sent, such as the addressee, sender, date/time, and other subscriber data, which this act defines as the "catalogue of electronic communications." * * *

Therefore, Section 7 gives the personal representative access to digital assets if the user consented to disclosure or if a court orders disclosure. To obtain access, the personal representative must provide the documentation specified by Section 7. First, the personal representative must give the custodian a written request for disclosure, a copy of the death certificate, a document establishing the authority of the personal representative, and, in the absence of an online tool, a record evidencing the user's consent to disclosure. When requesting disclosure, the fiduciary must write or email the custodian. The form of the request is limited, and does not, for example, include video, Tweet, instant message or other forms of communication.

Second, if the custodian requests, then the personal representative can be required to establish that the requested information is necessary for estate administration and the account is attributable to the decedent. Different custodians may have different procedures. Thus a custodian may request that the personal representative obtain a court order, and such an order must include findings that: 1) the user had a specific account with the custodian, 2) that disclosure of the content of electronic communications of the user would not violate the SCA or other law, 3) unless the user provided direction using an online tool, that the user consented to disclosure of the content of electronic communications, or 4) that disclosure of the content of electronic communications of a user is reasonably necessary for administration of the estate.

Section 8. Disclosure of Other Digital Assets of Deceased User.

Unless the user prohibited disclosure of digital assets or the court directs otherwise, a custodian shall disclose to the personal representative of the estate of a deceased user a catalogue of electronic communications sent or received by the user and digital assets, other than the content of electronic communications, of the user, if the representative gives the custodian:

(1)   a written request for disclosure in physical or electronic form;

(2)   a [certified] copy of the death certificate of the user;

(3)   a [certified] copy of [the letter of appointment of the representative or a small-estate affidavit or court order]; and

(4)   if requested by the custodian:

(A)   a number, username, address, or other unique subscriber or account identifier assigned by the custodian to identify the user's account;

(B)   evidence linking the account to the user;

(C)   an affidavit stating that disclosure of the user's digital assets is reasonably necessary for administration of the estate; or

(D)   a finding by the court that:

(i)   the user had a specific account with the custodian, identifiable by the information specified in subparagraph (A); or

(ii)   disclosure of the user's digital assets is reasonably necessary for administration of the estate.

Comment

* * * Section 8 requires disclosure of all other digital assets, unless prohibited by the decedent or directed by the court, once the personal representative provides a written request, a death certificate and a certified copy of the letter of appointment. In addition, the custodian may request a court order, and such an order must include findings that the decedent had a specific account with the custodian and that disclosure of the decedent's digital assets is reasonably necessary for administration of the estate. Thus,

Section 8 was intended to give personal representatives default access to the "catalogue" of electronic communications and other digital assets not protected by federal privacy law.

Section 9. Disclosure of Content of Electronic Communications of Principal.

To the extent a power of attorney expressly grants an agent authority over the content of electronic communications sent or received by the principal and unless directed otherwise by the principal or the court, a custodian shall disclose to the agent the content if the agent gives the custodian:

(1)   a written request for disclosure in physical or electronic form;

(2)   an original or copy of the power of attorney expressly granting the agent authority over the content of electronic communications of the principal;

(3)   a certification by the agent, under penalty of perjury, that the power of attorney is in effect; and

(4)   if requested by the custodian:

(A)   a number, username, address, or other unique subscriber or account identifier assigned by the custodian to identify the principal's account; or

(B)   evidence linking the account to the principal.

Comment

An agent has access to the content of electronic communications only when the power of attorney explicitly grants access. Section 10 concerns disclosure of other digital assets of the principal.

When a power of attorney contains the consent of the principal, ECPA does not prevent the agent from exercising authority over the content of an electronic communication. * * * There should be no question that an explicit delegation of authority in a power of attorney constitutes authorization from the user to access digital assets and provides "lawful consent" to allow disclosure of the content of an electronic communication from an electronic-communication service or a remote-computing service pursuant to applicable law. Both authorization and lawful consent are important because 18 U.S.C. Section 2701 deals with intentional access without authorization and 18 U.S.C. Section 2702 allows a service provider to disclose with lawful consent. * * *

When requesting access, the agent must write or email the custodian (see the comments in Section 7). The agent must also give the custodian an original or copy of the power of attorney expressly granting the agent authority over the contents of electronic communications of the principal to the agent and a certification by the agent, under penalty of perjury, that the power of attorney is in effect. In addition, if requested by the custodian, the agent must provide a unique subscriber or account identifier assigned by the custodian to identify the principal's account or other evidence linking the account to the principal.

Section 10. Disclosure of Other Digital Assets of Principal.

Unless otherwise ordered by the court, directed by the principal, or provided by a power of attorney, a custodian shall disclose to an agent with specific authority over digital assets or general authority to act on behalf of a principal a catalogue of electronic communications sent or received by the principal and digital assets, other than the content of electronic communications, of the principal if the agent gives the custodian:

(1)   a written request for disclosure in physical or electronic form;

(2)   an original or a copy of the power of attorney that gives the agent specific authority over digital assets or general authority to act on behalf of the principal;

(3)   a certification by the agent, under penalty of perjury, that the power of attorney is in effect; and

(4)   if requested by the custodian:

(A)   a number, username, address, or other unique subscriber or account identifier assigned by the custodian to identify the principal's account; or

(B)   evidence linking the account to the principal.

Comment

This section establishes that the agent has default authority over all of the principal's digital assets, other than the content of the principal's electronic communications. When requesting access, the agent must write or email the custodian (see the comments in Section 7).

The agent must also give the custodian an original or copy of the power of attorney and a certification by the agent, under penalty of perjury, that the power of attorney is in effect. Also, if requested by the custodian, the agent must provide a unique subscriber or account identifier assigned by the custodian to identify the principal's account, or some evidence linking the account to the principal.

Section 11. Disclosure of Digital Assets Held in Trust When Trustee Is Original User.

Unless otherwise ordered by the court or provided in a trust, a custodian shall disclose to a trustee that is an original user of an account any digital asset of the account held in trust, including a catalogue of electronic communications of the trustee and the content of electronic communications.

Comment

Section 11 provides that trustees who are original account holders can access all digital assets held in the trust. There should be no question that a trustee who is the original account holder will have full access to all digital assets. This includes the content of electronic communications, as access to content is presumed with respect to assets for which the trustee is the initial account holder. A trustee may have title to digital assets when the trustee opens an account as trustee; under those circumstances, the trustee can access the content of each digital asset that is in an account for which the trustee is the original account holder, not necessarily each digital asset held in the trust.

Section 12. Disclosure of Contents of Electronic Communications Held in Trust When Trustee Not Original User.

Unless otherwise ordered by the court, directed by the user, or provided in a trust, a custodian shall disclose to a trustee that is not an original user of an account the content of an electronic communication sent or received by an original or successor user and carried, maintained, processed, received, or stored by the custodian in the account of the trust if the trustee gives the custodian:

(1)   a written request for disclosure in physical or electronic form;

(2)   a certified copy of the trust instrument[or a certification of the trust under [cite trust-certification statute, such as Uniform Trust Code Section 1013]] that includes consent to disclosure of the content of electronic communications to the trustee;

(3)   a certification by the trustee, under penalty of perjury, that the trust exists and the trustee is a currently acting trustee of the trust; and

(4)   if requested by the custodian:

(A)   a number, username, address, or other unique subscriber or account identifier assigned by the custodian to identify the trust's account; or

(B)   evidence linking the account to the trust.

Comment

For accounts that are transferred into a trust by the settlor or in another manner, a trustee is not the original user of the account, and the trustee's authority is qualified. Thus, Section 12, governing disclosure of content of electronic communications from those accounts, requires consent.

Section 12 addresses situations involving an inter vivos transfer of a digital asset into a trust, a transfer into a testamentary trust, or a transfer via a pourover will or other governing instrument of a digital asset into a trust. In those situations, a trustee becomes a successor user when the settlor transfers a digital asset into the trust. There should be no question that the trustee with legal title to the digital asset was authorized by the settlor to access the digital assets so transferred, including both the catalogue and content of an electronic communication, and this provides "lawful consent" to allow disclosure of the content of an electronic communication from an electronic-communication service or a remote-computing service pursuant to applicable law. * * * Nonetheless, Sections 12 and 13 distinguish between the catalogue and content of an electronic communication in case there are any questions about whether the form in which property transferred into a trust is held constitutes lawful consent. Both authorization and lawful consent are important because 18 U.S.C. Section 2701 deals with intentional access without authorization and because 18 U.S.C. Section 2702 allows a service provider to disclose with lawful consent.

The underlying trust documents and default trust law will supply the allocation of responsibilities between and among trustees. When requesting access, the trustee must write or email the custodian (see comments to Section 7). The trustee must also give the custodian an original or copy of the trust that includes consent to disclosure of the content of electronic communications to the trustee and a certification by the trustee, under penalty of perjury, that the trust exists and that the trustee is a currently acting trustee of the trust. Also, if requested by the custodian, the trustee must provide a unique subscriber or account identifier assigned by the custodian to identify the trust's account, or some evidence linking the account to the trust.

Section 13. Disclosure of Other Digital Assets Held in Trust When Trustee Not Original User.

Unless otherwise ordered by the court, directed by the user, or provided in a trust, a custodian shall disclose, to a trustee that is not an original user of an account, a catalogue of electronic communications sent or received by an original or successor user and stored, carried, or maintained by the custodian in an account of the trust and any digital assets, other than the content of electronic communications, in which the trust has a right or interest if the trustee gives the custodian:

(1)   a written request for disclosure in physical or electronic form;

(2)   a certified copy of the trust instrument [or a certification of the trust under [cite trust-certification statute, such as Uniform Trust Code Section 1013]];

(3)   a certification by the trustee, under penalty of perjury, that the trust exists and the trustee is a currently acting trustee of the trust; and

(4)   if requested by the custodian:

(A)   a number, username, address, or other unique subscriber or account identifier assigned by the custodian to identify the trust's account; or

(B)   evidence linking the account to the trust.

Comment

Section 13 governs digital assets other than the contents of electronic communications, so it does not require the settlor's consent.

When requesting access, the trustee must write or email the custodian (see Comments to Section 7).

The trustee must also give the custodian an original or copy of the trust, and a certification by the trustee, under penalty of perjury, that the trust exists and that the trustee is a currently acting trustee of the trust. Also, if requested by the custodian, the trustee must provide a unique subscriber or account identifier assigned by the custodian to identify the trust's account, or some evidence linking the account to the trust.

Section 14. Disclosure of Digital Assets to [Conservator] of [Protected Person].

(a)   After an opportunity for a hearing under [state conservatorship law], the court may grant a [conservator] access to the digital assets of a [protected person].

(b)   Unless otherwise ordered by the court or directed by the user, a custodian shall disclose to a [conservator] the catalogue of electronic communications sent or received by a [protected person] and any digital assets, other than the content of electronic communications, in which the [protected person] has a right or interest if the [conservator] gives the custodian:

(1)   a written request for disclosure in physical or electronic form;

(2)   a [certified] copy of the court order that gives the [conservator] authority over the digital assets of the [protected person]; and

(3)   if requested by the custodian:

(A)   a number, username, address, or other unique subscriber or account identifier assigned by the custodian to identify the account of the [protected person]; or

(B)   evidence linking the account to the [protected person].

(c)   A [conservator] with general authority to manage the assets of a [protected person] may request a custodian of the digital assets of the [protected person] to suspend or terminate an account of the [protected person] for good cause. A request made under this section must be accompanied by a [certified] copy of the court order giving the [conservator] authority over the protected person's property.

Comment

When a conservator is appointed to represent a protected person's interests, the protected person may still retain some right to privacy in their personal communications. Therefore, Section 14 does not permit conservators to request disclosure of a protected person's electronic communications on the basis of the conservatorship order alone. To access a protected person's digital assets and a catalogue of electronic communications, a conservator must be specifically authorized by the court to do so. This requirement for express judicial authority over digital assets does not limit the fiduciary's authority over the underlying assets, such as funds held in a bank account. * * *

State law will establish the criteria for when a court will grant power to the conservator.

For example, UPC Section 5–411(c) requires the court to consider the decision the protected person would have made as well as a list of other factors. Existing state law may also set out the requisite standards for a conservator's actions. The conservator must exercise authority in the interests of the protected person. When requesting access to digital assets in which the protected person has a right or interest, the conservator must write or email the custodian (see comments to Section 7).

The conservator must also give the custodian a certified copy of the court order that gives the conservator authority over the protected person's digital assets. Also, if requested by the custodian, the conservator must provide a unique subscriber or account identifier assigned by the custodian to identify the protected person's account, or some evidence linking the account to the protected person. The custodian is required to disclose the digital assets so requested. * * *

Section 15. Fiduciary Duty and Authority.

(a)   The legal duties imposed on a fiduciary charged with managing tangible property apply to the management of digital assets, including:

(1)   the duty of care;

(2)   the duty of loyalty; and

(3)   the duty of confidentiality.

(b)   A fiduciary's authority with respect to a digital asset of a user:

(1)   except as otherwise provided in Section 4, is subject to the applicable terms of service;

(2)   is subject to other applicable law, including copyright law;

(3)   is limited by the scope of the fiduciary's duties; and

(4)   may not be used to impersonate the user.

(c)   A fiduciary with authority over the property of a decedent, [protected person], principal, or settlor has the right to access any digital asset in which the decedent, [protected person], principal, or settlor had a right or interest and that is not held by a custodian or subject to a terms-of-service agreement.

(d)   A fiduciary acting within the scope of the fiduciary's duties is an authorized user of the property of the decedent, [protected person], principal, or settlor for the purpose of applicable computer-fraud and unauthorized-computer-access laws, including [this state's law on unauthorized computer access].

(e)   A fiduciary with authority over the tangible, personal property of a decedent, [protected person], principal, or settlor:

(1)   has the right to access the property and any digital asset stored in it; and

(2)   is an authorized user for the purpose of computer-fraud and unauthorized-computer-access laws, including [this state's law on unauthorized computer access].

(f)   A custodian may disclose information in an account to a fiduciary of the user when the information is required to terminate an account used to access digital assets licensed to the user.

(g)   A fiduciary of a user may request a custodian to terminate the user's account. A request for termination must be in writing, in either physical or electronic form, and accompanied by:

(1)   if the user is deceased, a [certified] copy of the death certificate of the user;

(2)   a [certified] copy of the [letter of appointment of the representative or a small-estate affidavit or court order,] court order, power of attorney, or trust giving the fiduciary authority over the account; and

(3)   if requested by the custodian:

(A)   a number, username, address, or other unique subscriber or account identifier assigned by the custodian to identify the user's account;

(B)   evidence linking the account to the user; or

(C)   a finding by the court that the user had a specific account with the custodian, identifiable by the information specified in subparagraph (A).

Comment

The original version of UFADAA incorporated fiduciary duties by reference to "other law." This proved to be confusing and led to enactment difficulty. Section 15 specifies the nature, extent and limitation of the fiduciary's authority over digital assets. Subsection (a) expressly imposes all fiduciary duties to the management of digital assets, including the duties of care, loyalty and confidentiality. Subsection (b) specifies that a fiduciary's authority over digital assets is subject to the terms-of-service agreement, except to the extent the terms-of-service agreement provision is overridden by an action taken pursuant to Section 4, and it reinforces the applicability of copyright and fiduciary duties. Finally, subsection 15(b) prohibits a fiduciary's authority being used to impersonate a user. Subsection 15(c) permits the fiduciary to access all digital assets not in an account or subject to a terms-of-service agreement. Subsection 15(d) further specifies that the fiduciary is an authorized user under any applicable law on unauthorized computer access.

Subsection 15(g) gives the fiduciary the option of requesting that an account be terminated, if termination would not violate a fiduciary duty.

This issue concerning the parameters of the fiduciary's authority potentially arises in two situations: 1) the fiduciary obtains access to a password or the like directly from the account holder, as would be true in various circumstances such as for the trustee of an inter vivos trust or someone who has stored passwords in a written or electronic list and those passwords are then transmitted to the fiduciary; and 2) the fiduciary obtains access pursuant to this act.

This section clarifies that the fiduciary has the same authority as the user if the user were the one exercising the authority (note that, where the user has died, this means that the fiduciary has the same access as the user had immediately before death). This means that the fiduciary's authority to access the digital asset is the same as the user except where, pursuant to Section 4, the user has explicitly opted out of fiduciary access. In exercising its responsibilities, the fiduciary is subject to the duties and obligations established pursuant to state fiduciary law, and is liable for breach of those duties. Note that even if the digital asset were illegally obtained by the account holder, the fiduciary would still need access in order to handle that asset appropriately. There may, for example, be tax consequences that the fiduciary would be obligated to report.

However, this section does not require a custodian to permit a fiduciary to assume a user's terms-of-service agreement if the custodian can otherwise comply with Section 6.

In exercising its responsibilities, the fiduciary is subject to the same limitations as the user more generally. For example, a fiduciary cannot delete an account if this would be fraudulent. Similarly, if the user could challenge provisions in a terms-of-service agreement, then the fiduciary is also able to do so. * * *

Subsection (b) is designed to establish that the fiduciary is authorized to obtain or access digital assets in accordance with other applicable laws. The language mirrors that used in Title II of the Electronic Communications Privacy Act of 1986 (ECPA), also known as the Stored Communications Act, 18 U.S.C. Section 2701 *et seq.* (2006) * * * . The subsection clarifies that state law treats the fiduciary as "authorized" under state laws criminalizing unauthorized access.

State laws vary in their coverage but typically prohibit unauthorized computer access. By defining the fiduciary as an authorized user in subsection (d), the fiduciary has authorization under applicable law to access the digital assets under state computer trespass laws.

Federal courts may look to these provisions to guide their interpretations of ECPA and the federal Computer Fraud and Abuse Act (CFAA), but fiduciaries should understand that federal courts may not view such provisions as dispositive in determining whether access to a user's account violated federal criminal law.

Subsection (e) clarifies that the fiduciary is authorized to access digital assets stored on tangible personal property of the decedent, protected person, principal, or settlor, such as laptops, computers, smartphones or storage media, exempting fiduciaries from application for purposes of state or federal laws on unauthorized computer access. For criminal law purposes, this clarifies that the fiduciary is authorized to access all of the account holder's digital assets, whether held locally or remotely.

Example 1—Access to digital assets by personal representative. D dies with a will that is silent with respect to digital assets. D has a bank account for which D received only electronic statements, D has stored photos in a cloud-based Internet account, and D has an e-mail account with a company that provides electronic-communication services to the public. The personal representative of D's estate needs access to the electronic bank account statements, the photo account, and e-mails.

The personal representative of D's estate has the authority to access D's electronic banking statements and D's photo account, which both fall under the act's definition of a "digital asset." This means that, if these accounts are password-protected or otherwise unavailable to the personal representative, then the bank and the photo account service must give access to the personal representative when the request is made in accordance with Section 9. If the terms-of-service agreement permits D to transfer the accounts electronically, then the personal representative of D's estate can use that procedure for transfer as well.

The personal representative of D's estate is also able to request that the e-mail account service provider grant access to e-mails sent or received by D; ECPA permits the service provider to release the catalogue to the personal representative. The service provider also must provide the personal representative access to the content of an electronic communication sent or received by D if the service provider is permitted under

18 U.S.C. Section 2702(b) to disclose the content. The bank may release the catalogue of electronic communications or content of an electronic communication for which it is the originator or the addressee because the bank is not subject to the ECPA.

Example 2—Access to digital assets by agent. X creates a power of attorney designating A as X's agent. The power of attorney expressly grants A authority over X's digital assets, including the content of an electronic communication. X has a bank account for which X receives only electronic statements, X has stored photos in a cloud-based Internet account, and X has a game character and in-game property associated with an online game. X also has an e-mail account with a company that provides electronic-communication services to the public.

A has the authority to access X's electronic bank statements, the photo account, the game character and in-game property associated with the online game, all of which fall under the act's definition of a "digital asset." This means that, if these accounts are password-protected or otherwise unavailable to A as X's agent, then the bank, the photo account service provider, and the online game service provider must give access to A when the request is made in accordance with Section 9. If the terms-of-service agreement permits X to transfer the accounts electronically, then A as X's agent can use that procedure for transfer as well.

As X's agent, A is also able to request that the e-mail account service provider grant access to e-mails sent or received by X; ECPA permits the service provider to release the catalogue. The service provider also must provide A access to the content of an electronic communication sent or received by X if the service provider is permitted under 18 U.S.C. Section 2702(b) to disclose the content. The bank may release the catalogue of electronic communications or content of an electronic communication for which it is the originator or the addressee because the bank is not subject to the ECPA.

Example 3—Access to digital assets by trustee. T is the trustee of a trust established by S. As trustee of the trust, T opens a bank account for which T receives only electronic statements. S transfers into the trust to T as trustee (in compliance with a terms-of-service agreement) a game character and in-game property associated with an online game and a cloud-based Internet account in which S has stored photos. S also transfers to T as trustee (in compliance with the terms-of-service agreement) an e-mail account with a company that provides electronic-communication services to the public.

T is an original user with respect to the bank account that T opened, and T has the ability to access the electronic banking statements. T, as successor user to S, may access the game character and in-game property associated with the online game and the photo account, which both fall under the act's definition of a "digital asset." This means that, if these accounts are password-protected or otherwise unavailable to T as trustee, then the bank, the photo account service provider, and the online game service provider must give access to T when the request is made in accordance with the act. If the terms-of-service agreement permits the user to transfer the accounts electronically, then T as trustee can use that procedure for transfer as well.

T as successor user of the e-mail account for which S was previously the user is also able to request that the e-mail account service provider grant access to e-mails sent or received by S; the ECPA permits the service provider to release the catalogue. The service provider also must provide T access to the content of an electronic communication sent or received by S if the service provider is permitted under 18 U.S.C. Section 2702(b) to disclose the content. The bank may release the catalogue of electronic communications or content of an electronic communication for which it is the originator or the addressee because the bank is not subject to the ECPA.

Section 16. Custodian Compliance and Immunity.

(a) Not later than [60] days after receipt of the information required under Sections 7 through 14, a custodian shall comply with a request under this [act] from a fiduciary or designated recipient to disclose digital assets or terminate an account. If the custodian fails to comply, the fiduciary or designated recipient may apply to the court for an order directing compliance.

(b) An order under subsection (a) directing compliance must contain a finding that compliance is not in violation of 18 U.S.C. Section 2702[, as amended].

(c) A custodian may notify the user that a request for disclosure or to terminate an account was made under this [act].

(d)   A custodian may deny a request under this [act] from a fiduciary or designated recipient for disclosure of digital assets or to terminate an account if the custodian is aware of any lawful access to the account following the receipt of the fiduciary's request.

(e)   This [act] does not limit a custodian's ability to obtain or require a fiduciary or designated recipient requesting disclosure or termination under this [act] to obtain a court order which:

(1)   specifies that an account belongs to the [protected person] or principal;

(2)   specifies that there is sufficient consent from the [protected person] or principal to support the requested disclosure; and

(3)   contains a finding required by law other than this [act].

(f)   A custodian and its officers, employees, and agents are immune from liability for an act or omission done in good faith in compliance with this [act].

Comment

This section establishes that custodians are protected from liability when they act in accordance with the procedures of this act and in good faith. The types of actions covered include disclosure as well as transfer of copies. The critical issue in conferring immunity is the source of the liability. Direct liability is not subject to immunity; indirect liability is subject to immunity.

Direct liability could only arise from noncompliance with a judicial order issued under sections 7 to 15. Upon determination of a right of access under those sections, a court may issue an order to grant access under section 16. Section 16(b) requires that an order directing compliance contain a finding that compliance is not in violation of 18 U.S.C. Section 2702. Noncompliance with that order would give rise to liability for contempt. There is no immunity from this liability.

Indirect liability could arise from granting a right of access under this act. Access to a digital asset might invade the privacy or the harm the reputation of the decedent, protected person, principal, or settlor, it might harm the family or business of the decedent, protected person, principal, or settlor, and it might harm other persons. The grantor of access to the digital asset is immune from liability arising out of any of these circumstances if the grantor acted in good faith to comply with this act. If there is a judicial order under section 16, compliance with the order establishes good faith. Absent a judicial order under section 16, good faith must be established by the grantor's assessment of the requirements of this act. Further, Section 16(e) allows the custodian to verify that the account belongs to the person represented by the fiduciary.

Section 17. Uniformity of Application and Construction. [omitted]

Section 18. Relation to Electronic Signatures in Global and National Commerce Act. [omitted]

[Section 19. Severability.] [omitted]

Section 20. Repeals; Conforming Amendments. [omitted]

Section 21. Effective Date. [omitted]

UNIFORM FIDUCIARY INCOME AND PRINCIPAL ACT*

[Article] 1
GENERAL PROVISIONS

[Article] 2
FIDUCIARY DUTIES AND JUDICIAL REVIEW

[Article] 3
UNITRUST

[Article] 4
ALLOCATION OF RECEIPTS

[PART] 1
RECEIPTS FROM ENTITY

[PART] 2
RECEIPTS NOT NORMALLY APPORTIONED

---

*   Copyright © 2018 by the National Conference of Commissioners on Uniform State Laws.

UNIFORM FIDUCIARY INCOME AND PRINCIPAL ACT

[PART] 3
RECEIPTS NORMALLY APPORTIONED

[Article] 5
ALLOCATION OF DISBURSEMENTS

[Article] 6
DEATH OF INDIVIDUAL OR TERMINATION OF INCOME INTEREST

[Article] 7
APPORTIONMENT AT BEGINNING AND END OF INCOME INTEREST

[Article] 8
MISCELLANEOUS PROVISIONS

[ARTICLE] 1

GENERAL PROVISIONS

Section 101. Short Title.

This [act] may be cited as the Uniform Fiduciary Income and Principal Act.

Section 102. Definitions.

In this [act]:

(1) "Accounting period" means a calendar year, unless a fiduciary selects another period of 12 calendar months or approximately 12 calendar months. The term includes a part of a calendar year or another period of 12 calendar months or approximately 12 calendar months which begins when an income interest begins or ends when an income interest ends.

(2) "Asset-backed security" means a security that is serviced primarily by the cash flows of a discrete pool of fixed or revolving receivables or other financial assets that by their terms convert into cash within a finite time. The term includes rights or other assets that ensure the servicing or timely distribution of proceeds to the holder of the asset-backed security. The term does not include an asset to which Section 401, 409, or 414 applies.

(3) "Beneficiary" includes:

(A) for a trust:

(i) a current beneficiary, including a current income beneficiary and a beneficiary that may receive only principal;

(ii) a remainder beneficiary; and

(iii) any other successor beneficiary;

(B) for an estate, an heir[, legatee,] and devisee; and

(C) for a life estate or term interest, a person that holds a life estate, term interest, or remainder or other interest following a life estate or term interest.

(4) "Court" means [the court in this state having jurisdiction relating to a trust, estate, or life estate or other term interest described in Section 103(2)].

(5) "Current income beneficiary" means a beneficiary to which a fiduciary may distribute net income, whether or not the fiduciary also may distribute principal to the beneficiary.

(6) "Distribution" means a payment or transfer by a fiduciary to a beneficiary in the beneficiary's capacity as a beneficiary, made under the terms of the trust, without consideration other than the beneficiary's right to receive the payment or transfer under the terms of the trust. "Distribute", "distributed", and "distributee" have corresponding meanings.

(7) "Estate" means a decedent's estate. The term includes the property of the decedent as the estate is originally constituted and the property of the estate as it exists at any time during administration.

(8) "Fiduciary" includes a trustee,[trust director determined under [Section 2(9) of the Uniform Directed Trust Act,]] personal representative, life tenant, holder of a term interest, and person acting under a delegation from a fiduciary. The term includes a person that holds property for a successor beneficiary whose interest may be affected by an allocation of receipts and expenditures between income and principal. If there are two or more co-fiduciaries, the term includes all co-fiduciaries acting under the terms of the trust and applicable law.

(9) "Income" means money or other property a fiduciary receives as current return from principal. The term includes a part of receipts from a sale, exchange, or liquidation of a principal asset, to the extent provided in [Article] 4.

(10) "Income interest" means the right of a current income beneficiary to receive all or part of net income, whether the terms of the trust require the net income to be distributed or authorize the net income to be distributed in the fiduciary's discretion. The term includes the right of a current beneficiary to use property held by a fiduciary.

(11) "Independent person" means a person that is not:

(A) for a trust:

(i) [a qualified beneficiary determined under [Uniform Trust Code Section 103(13)]][a beneficiary that is a distributee or permissible distributee of trust income or principal or would be a distributee or permissible distributee of trust income or principal if either the trust or the interests of the distributees or permissible distributees of trust income or principal were terminated, assuming no power of appointment is exercised];

(ii) a settlor of the trust; or

(iii) an individual whose legal obligation to support a beneficiary may be satisfied by a distribution from the trust;

(B) for an estate, a beneficiary;

(C) a spouse, parent, brother, sister, or issue of an individual described in subparagraph (A) or (B);

(D) a corporation, partnership, limited liability company, or other entity in which persons described in subparagraphs (A) through (C), in the aggregate, have voting control; or

(E) an employee of a person described in subparagraph (A), (B), (C), or (D).

(12) "Mandatory income interest" means the right of a current income beneficiary to receive net income that the terms of the trust require the fiduciary to distribute.

(13) "Net income" means the total allocations during an accounting period to income under the terms of a trust and this [act] minus the disbursements during the period, other than distributions, allocated to income under the terms of the trust and this [act]. To the extent the trust is a unitrust under [Article] 3, the term means the unitrust amount determined under [Article] 3. The term includes an adjustment from principal to income under Section 203. The term does not include an adjustment from income to principal under Section 203.

(14) "Person" means an individual, estate, trust, business or nonprofit entity, public corporation, government or governmental subdivision, agency, or instrumentality, or other legal entity.

(15) "Personal representative" means an executor, administrator, successor personal representative, special administrator, or person that performs substantially the same function with respect to an estate under the law governing the person's status.

(16) "Principal" means property held in trust for distribution to, production of income for, or use by a current or successor beneficiary.

(17) "Record" means information that is inscribed on a tangible medium or that is stored in an electronic or other medium and is retrievable in perceivable form.

(18) "Settlor" means a person, including a testator, that creates or contributes property to a trust. If more than one person creates or contributes property to a trust, the term includes each person, to the extent of the trust property attributable to that person's contribution, except to the extent another person has the power to revoke or withdraw that portion.

(19) "Special tax benefit" means:

(A) exclusion of a transfer to a trust from gifts described in Section 2503(b) of the Internal Revenue Code of 1986[, as amended,] 26 U.S.C. Section 2503(b)[, as amended,] because of the qualification of an income interest in the trust as a present interest in property;

(B) status as a qualified subchapter S trust described in Section 1361(d)(3) of the Internal Revenue Code of 1986[, as amended,] 26 U.S.C. Section 1361(d)(3)[, as amended,] at a time the trust holds stock of an S corporation described in Section 1361(a)(1) of the Internal Revenue Code of 1986[, as amended,] 26 U.S.C. Section 1361(a)(1)[, as amended];

(C) an estate or gift tax marital deduction for a transfer to a trust under Section 2056 or 2523 of the Internal Revenue Code of 1986[, as amended,] 26 U.S.C. Section 2056 or 2523[, as amended,] which depends or depended in whole or in part on the right of the settlor's spouse to receive the net income of the trust;

(D) exemption in whole or in part of a trust from the federal generation-skipping transfer tax imposed by Section 2601 of the Internal Revenue Code of 1986[, as amended,] 26 U.S.C. Section 2601[, as amended,] because the trust was irrevocable on September 25, 1985, if there is any possibility that:

    (i) a taxable distribution, as defined in Section 2612(b) of the Internal Revenue Code of 1986[, as amended,] 26 U.S.C. Section 2612(b)[, as amended], could be made from the trust; or

    (ii) a taxable termination, as defined in Section 2612(a) of the Internal Revenue Code of 1986[, as amended,] 26 U.S.C. Section 2612(a)[, as amended], could occur with respect to the trust; or

(E) an inclusion ratio, as defined in Section 2642(a) of the Internal Revenue Code of 1986[, as amended,] 26 U.S.C. Section 2642(a)[, as amended], of the trust which is less than one, if there is any possibility that:

    (i) a taxable distribution, as defined in Section 2612(b) of the Internal Revenue Code of 1986[, as amended,] 26 U.S.C. Section 2612(b)[, as amended], could be made from the trust; or

    (ii) a taxable termination, as defined in Section 2612(a) of the Internal Revenue Code of 1986[, as amended,] 26 U.S.C. Section 2612(a)[, as amended], could occur with respect to the trust.

(20) "Successive interest" means the interest of a successor beneficiary.

(21) "Successor beneficiary" means a person entitled to receive income or principal or to use property when an income interest or other current interest ends.

(22) "Terms of a trust" means:

(A) except as otherwise provided in subparagraph (B), the manifestation of the settlor's intent regarding a trust's provisions as

    (i) expressed in the trust instrument; or

    (ii) established by other evidence that would be admissible in a judicial proceeding;

(B) the trust's provisions as established, determined, or amended by:

    (i) a trustee or trust director in accordance with applicable law; [or]

    (ii) court order[; or

    (iii) a nonjudicial settlement agreement under [Uniform Trust Code Section 111]];

(C) for an estate, a will; or

(D)　for a life estate or term interest, the corresponding manifestation of the rights of the beneficiaries.

(23)　"Trust":

(A)　includes:

(i)　an express trust, private or charitable, with additions to the trust, wherever and however created; and

(ii)　a trust created or determined by judgment or decree under which the trust is to be administered in the manner of an express trust; and

(B)　does not include:

(i)　a constructive trust;

(ii)　a resulting trust, conservatorship, guardianship, multi-party account, custodial arrangement for a minor, business trust, voting trust, security arrangement, liquidation trust, or trust for the primary purpose of paying debts, dividends, interest, salaries, wages, profits, pensions, retirement benefits, or employee benefits of any kind; or

(iii)　an arrangement under which a person is a nominee, escrowee, or agent for another.

(24)　"Trustee" means a person, other than a personal representative, that owns or holds property for the benefit of a beneficiary. The term includes an original, additional, or successor trustee, whether or not appointed or confirmed by a court.

(25)　"Will" means any testamentary instrument recognized by applicable law which makes a legally effective disposition of an individual's property, effective at the individual's death. The term includes a codicil or other amendment to a testamentary instrument.

Section 103. Scope.

Except as otherwise provided in the terms of a trust or this [act], this [act] applies to:

(1)　a trust or estate; and

(2)　a life estate or other term interest in which the interest of one or more persons will be succeeded by the interest of one or more other persons.

Section 104. Governing Law.

Except as otherwise provided in the terms of a trust or this [act], this [act] applies when this state is the principal place of administration of a trust or estate or the situs of property that is not held in a trust or estate and is subject to a life estate or other term interest described in Section 103(2). By accepting the trusteeship of a trust having its principal place of administration in this state or by moving the principal place of administration of a trust to this state, the trustee submits to the application of this [act] to any matter within the scope of this [act] involving the trust.

[ARTICLE] 2

FIDUCIARY DUTIES AND JUDICIAL REVIEW

Section 201. Fiduciary Duties; General Principles.

(a)   In making an allocation or determination or exercising discretion under this [act], a fiduciary shall:

(1)   act in good faith, based on what is fair and reasonable to all beneficiaries;

(2)   administer a trust or estate impartially, except to the extent the terms of the trust manifest an intent that the fiduciary shall or may favor one or more beneficiaries;

(3)   administer the trust or estate in accordance with the terms of the trust, even if there is a different provision in this [act]; and

(4)   administer the trust or estate in accordance with this [act], except to the extent the terms of the trust provide otherwise or authorize the fiduciary to determine otherwise.

(b)   A fiduciary's allocation, determination, or exercise of discretion under this [act] is presumed to be fair and reasonable to all beneficiaries. A fiduciary may exercise a discretionary power of administration given to the fiduciary by the terms of the trust, and an exercise of the power which produces a result different from a result required or permitted by this [act] does not create an inference that the fiduciary abused the fiduciary's discretion.

(c)   A fiduciary shall:

(1)   add a receipt to principal, to the extent neither the terms of the trust nor this [act] allocates the receipt between income and principal; and

(2)   charge a disbursement to principal, to the extent neither the terms of the trust nor this [act] allocates the disbursement between income and principal.

(d)   A fiduciary may exercise the power to adjust under Section 203, convert an income trust to a unitrust under Section 303(a)(1), change the percentage or method used to calculate a unitrust amount under Section 303(a)(2), or convert a unitrust to an income trust under Section 303(a)(3), if the fiduciary determines the exercise of the power will assist the fiduciary to administer the trust or estate impartially.

(e)   Factors the fiduciary must consider in making the determination under subsection (d) include:

(1)   the terms of the trust;

(2)   the nature, distribution standards, and expected duration of the trust;

(3)   the effect of the allocation rules, including specific adjustments between income and principal, under [Articles] 4 through 7;

(4)   the desirability of liquidity and regularity of income;

(5)   the desirability of the preservation and appreciation of principal;

(6)   the extent to which an asset is used or may be used by a beneficiary;

(7)   the increase or decrease in the value of principal assets, reasonably determined by the fiduciary;

(8)   whether and to what extent the terms of the trust give the fiduciary power to accumulate income or invade principal or prohibit the fiduciary from accumulating income or invading principal;

(9)   the extent to which the fiduciary has accumulated income or invaded principal in preceding accounting periods;

(10) the effect of current and reasonably expected economic conditions; and

(11) the reasonably expected tax consequences of the exercise of the power.

Section 202. Judicial Review of Exercise of Discretionary Power[; Request for Instruction].

(a)   In this section, "fiduciary decision" means:

(1)   a fiduciary's allocation between income and principal or other determination regarding income and principal required or authorized by the terms of the trust or this [act];

(2)   the fiduciary's exercise or nonexercise of a discretionary power regarding income and principal granted by the terms of the trust or this [act], including the power to adjust under Section 203, convert an income trust to a unitrust under Section 303(a)(1), change the percentage or method used to calculate a unitrust amount under Section 303(a)(2), or convert a unitrust to an income trust under Section 303(a)(3); or

(3)   the fiduciary's implementation of a decision described in paragraph (1) or (2).

(b)   The court may not order a fiduciary to change a fiduciary decision unless the court determines that the fiduciary decision was an abuse of the fiduciary's discretion.

(c)   If the court determines that a fiduciary decision was an abuse of the fiduciary's discretion, the court may order a remedy authorized by law[, including Uniform Trust Code Section 1001]. To place the beneficiaries in the positions the beneficiaries would have occupied if there had not been an abuse of the fiduciary's discretion, the court may order:

(1)   the fiduciary to exercise or refrain from exercising the power to adjust under Section 203;

(2)   the fiduciary to exercise or refrain from exercising the power to convert an income trust to a unitrust under Section 303(a)(1), change the percentage or method used to calculate a unitrust amount under Section 303(a)(2), or convert a unitrust to an income trust under Section 303(a)(3);

(3)   the fiduciary to distribute an amount to a beneficiary;

(4)   a beneficiary to return some or all of a distribution; or

(5)   the fiduciary to withhold an amount from one or more future distributions to a beneficiary.

[(d) On [petition] by a fiduciary for instruction, the court may determine whether a proposed fiduciary decision will result in an abuse of the fiduciary's discretion. If the [petition] describes the proposed decision, contains sufficient information to inform the beneficiary of the reasons for making the proposed decision and the facts on which the fiduciary relies, and explains how the beneficiary will be affected by the proposed decision, a beneficiary that opposes the proposed decision has the burden to establish that it will result in an abuse of the fiduciary's discretion.]

Section 203. Fiduciary's Power to Adjust.

(a)   Except as otherwise provided in the terms of a trust or this section, a fiduciary, in a record, without court approval, may adjust between income and principal if the fiduciary determines the exercise of the power to adjust will assist the fiduciary to administer the trust or estate impartially.

(b)   This section does not create a duty to exercise or consider the power to adjust under subsection (a) or to inform a beneficiary about the applicability of this section.

(c)   A fiduciary that in good faith exercises or fails to exercise the power to adjust under subsection (a) is not liable to a person affected by the exercise or failure to exercise.

(d)   In deciding whether and to what extent to exercise the power to adjust under subsection (a), a fiduciary shall consider all factors the fiduciary considers relevant, including relevant factors in Section 201(e) and the application of Sections 401(i), 408, and 413.

(e)   A fiduciary may not exercise the power under subsection (a) to make an adjustment or under Section 408 to make a determination that an allocation is insubstantial if:

(1)   the adjustment or determination would reduce the amount payable to a current income beneficiary from a trust that qualifies for a special tax benefit, except to the extent the adjustment is made to provide for a reasonable apportionment of the total return of the trust between the current income beneficiary and successor beneficiaries;

(2)   the adjustment or determination would change the amount payable to a beneficiary, as a fixed annuity or a fixed fraction of the value of the trust assets, under the terms of the trust;

(3)   the adjustment or determination would reduce an amount that is permanently set aside for a charitable purpose under the terms of the trust, unless both income and principal are set aside for the charitable purpose;

(4)   possessing or exercising the power would cause a person to be treated as the owner of all or part of the trust for federal income tax purposes;

(5)   possessing or exercising the power would cause all or part of the value of the trust assets to be included in the gross estate of an individual for federal estate tax purposes;

(6)   possessing or exercising the power would cause an individual to be treated as making a gift for federal gift tax purposes;

(7)   the fiduciary is not an independent person;

(8)   the trust is irrevocable and provides for income to be paid to the settlor and possessing or exercising the power would cause the adjusted principal or income to be considered an available resource or available income under a public-benefit program; or

(9)   the trust is a unitrust under [Article] 3.

(f)   If subsection (e)(4), (5), (6), or (7) applies to a fiduciary:

(1)   a co-fiduciary to which subsection (e)(4) through (7) does not apply may exercise the power to adjust, unless the exercise of the power by the remaining co-fiduciary or co-fiduciaries is not permitted by the terms of the trust or law other than this [act]; or

(2)   if there is no co-fiduciary to which subsection (e)(4) through (7) does not apply, the fiduciary may appoint a co-fiduciary to which subsection (e)(4) through (7) does not apply, which may be a special fiduciary with limited powers, and the appointed co-fiduciary may exercise the power to adjust under subsection (a), unless the appointment of a co-fiduciary or the exercise of the power by a co-fiduciary is not permitted by the terms of the trust or law other than this [act].

(g)   A fiduciary may release or delegate to a co-fiduciary the power to adjust under subsection (a) if the fiduciary determines that the fiduciary's possession or exercise of the power will or may:

(1)   cause a result described in subsection (e)(1) through (6) or (8); or

(2)   deprive the trust of a tax benefit or impose a tax burden not described in subsection (e)(1) through (6).

(h)   A fiduciary's release or delegation to a co-fiduciary under subsection (g) of the power to adjust under subsection (a):

(1)   must be in a record;

(2)   applies to the entire power, unless the release or delegation provides a limitation, which may be a limitation to the power to adjust:

    (A)   from income to principal;

    (B)   from principal to income;

    (C)   for specified property; or

    (D)   in specified circumstances;

(3)   for a delegation, may be modified by a re-delegation under this subsection by the co-fiduciary to which the delegation is made; and

(4)   subject to paragraph (3), is permanent, unless the release or delegation provides a specified period, including a period measured by the life of an individual or the lives of more than one individual.

(i)   Terms of a trust which deny or limit the power to adjust between income and principal do not affect the application of this section, unless the terms of the trust expressly deny or limit the power to adjust under subsection (a).

(j)   The exercise of the power to adjust under subsection (a) in any accounting period may apply to the current period, the immediately preceding period, and one or more subsequent periods.

(k)   A description of the exercise of the power to adjust under subsection (a) must be:

(1)   included in a report, if any, sent to beneficiaries under [Uniform Trust Code Section 813(c)]; or

(2)   communicated at least annually to [the qualified beneficiaries determined under [Uniform Trust Code Section 103(13)], other than [the Attorney General]][all beneficiaries that receive or are entitled to receive income from the trust or would be entitled to receive a distribution of principal if the trust were terminated at the time the notice is sent, assuming no power of appointment is exercised].

[ARTICLE] 3

UNITRUST

Section 301. Definitions.

In this [article]:

(1) "Applicable value" means the amount of the net fair market value of a trust taken into account under Section 307.

(2) "Express unitrust" means a trust for which, under the terms of the trust without regard to this [article], income or net income must or may be calculated as a unitrust amount.

(3) "Income trust" means a trust that is not a unitrust.

(4) "Net fair market value of a trust" means the fair market value of the assets of the trust, less the noncontingent liabilities of the trust.

(5) "Unitrust" means a trust for which net income is a unitrust amount. The term includes an express unitrust.

(6) "Unitrust amount" means an amount computed by multiplying a determined value of a trust by a determined percentage. For a unitrust administered under a unitrust policy, the term means the applicable value, multiplied by the unitrust rate.

(7) "Unitrust policy" means a policy described in Sections 305 through 309 and adopted under Section 303.

(8) "Unitrust rate" means the rate used to compute the unitrust amount under paragraph (6) for a unitrust administered under a unitrust policy.

Section 302. Application; Duties and Remedies.

(a) Except as otherwise provided in subsection (b), this [article] applies to:

(1) an income trust, unless the terms of the trust expressly prohibit use of this [article] by a specific reference to this [article] or an explicit expression of intent that net income not be calculated as a unitrust amount; and

(2) an express unitrust, except to the extent the terms of the trust explicitly:

(A) prohibit use of this [article] by a specific reference to this [article];

(B) prohibit conversion to an income trust; or

(C) limit changes to the method of calculating the unitrust amount.

(b) This [article] does not apply to a trust described in Section 170(f)(2)(B), 642(c)(5), 664(d), 2702(a)(3)(A)(ii) or (iii), or 2702(b) of the Internal Revenue Code of 1986[, as amended,] 26 U.S.C. Section 170(f)(2)(B), 642(c)(5), 664(d), 2702(a)(3)(A)(ii) or (iii), or 2702(b)[, as amended].

(c) An income trust to which this [article] applies under subsection (a)(1) may be converted to a unitrust under this [article] regardless of the terms of the trust concerning distributions. Conversion to a unitrust under this [article] does not affect other terms of the trust concerning distributions of income or principal.

(d) This [article] applies to an estate only to the extent a trust is a beneficiary of the estate. To the extent of the trust's interest in the estate, the estate may be administered as a unitrust, the administration of the estate as a unitrust may be discontinued, or the percentage or method used to calculate the unitrust amount may be changed, in the same manner as for a trust under this [article].

(e)   This [article] does not create a duty to take or consider action under this [article] or to inform a beneficiary about the applicability of this [article].

(f)   A fiduciary that in good faith takes or fails to take an action under this [article] is not liable to a person affected by the action or inaction.

Section 303. Authority of Fiduciary.

(a)   A fiduciary, without court approval, by complying with subsections (b) and (f), may:

(1)   convert an income trust to a unitrust if the fiduciary adopts in a record a unitrust policy for the trust providing:

(A)   that in administering the trust the net income of the trust will be a unitrust amount rather than net income determined without regard to this [article]; and

(B)   the percentage and method used to calculate the unitrust amount;

(2)   change the percentage or method used to calculate a unitrust amount for a unitrust if the fiduciary adopts in a record a unitrust policy or an amendment or replacement of a unitrust policy providing changes in the percentage or method used to calculate the unitrust amount; or

(3)   convert a unitrust to an income trust if the fiduciary adopts in a record a determination that, in administering the trust, the net income of the trust will be net income determined without regard to this [article] rather than a unitrust amount.

(b)   A fiduciary may take an action under subsection (a) if:

(1)   the fiduciary determines that the action will assist the fiduciary to administer a trust impartially;

(2)   the fiduciary sends a notice in a record, in the manner required by Section 304, describing and proposing to take the action;

(3)   the fiduciary sends a copy of the notice under paragraph (2) to each settlor of the trust which is:

(A)   if an individual, living; or

(B)   if not an individual, in existence;

(4)   at least one member of each class[of the qualified beneficiaries determined under [Uniform Trust Code Section 103(13)], other than [the Attorney General],] receiving the notice under paragraph (2) is:

(A)   if an individual, legally competent; [or]

(B)   if not an individual, in existence; [or

(C)   represented in the manner provided in Section 304(b);] and

(5)   the fiduciary does not receive, by the date specified in the notice under Section 304[(d)(5)][(c)(5)], an objection in a record to the action proposed under paragraph (2) from a person to which the notice under paragraph (2) is sent.

(c)   If a fiduciary receives, not later than the date stated in the notice under Section 304[(d)(5)][(c)(5)], an objection in a record described in Section 304[(d)(4)][(c)(4)] to a proposed action, the fiduciary or a beneficiary may request the court to have the proposed action taken as proposed, taken with modifications, or prevented. A person described in Section 304(a) may oppose the proposed action in the proceeding under this subsection, whether or not the person:

(1)   consented under Section 304[(c)][(b)]; or

(2)   objected under Section 304[(d)(4)][(c)(4)].

(d)   If, after sending a notice under subsection (b)(2), a fiduciary decides not to take the action proposed in the notice, the fiduciary shall notify in a record each person described in Section 304(a) of the decision not to take the action and the reasons for the decision.

(e)   If a beneficiary requests in a record that a fiduciary take an action described in subsection (a) and the fiduciary declines to act or does not act within 90 days after receiving the request, the beneficiary may request the court to direct the fiduciary to take the action requested.

(f)   In deciding whether and how to take an action authorized by subsection (a), or whether and how to respond to a request by a beneficiary under subsection (e), a fiduciary shall consider all factors relevant to the trust and the beneficiaries, including relevant factors in Section 201(e).

(g)   A fiduciary may release or delegate the power to convert an income trust to a unitrust under subsection (a)(1), change the percentage or method used to calculate a unitrust amount under subsection (a)(2), or convert a unitrust to an income trust under subsection (a)(3), for a reason described in Section 203(g) and in the manner described in Section 203(h).

Section 304. Notice.

Alternative A

(a)   A notice required by Section 303(b)(2) must be sent in a manner authorized under [Uniform Trust Code Section 109] to:

(1)   the qualified beneficiaries determined under [Uniform Trust Code Section 103(13)], other than [the Attorney General]; [and]

(2)   [each person acting as trust director of the trust under the Uniform Directed Trust Act][each person that is granted a power over the trust by the terms of the trust, to the extent the power is exercisable when the person is not then serving as a trustee:

(A)   including a:

(i)   power over the investment, management, or distribution of trust property or other matters of trust administration; and

(ii)   power to appoint or remove a trustee or person described in this paragraph; and

(B)   excluding a:

(i)   power of appointment;

(ii)   power of a beneficiary over the trust, to the extent the exercise or nonexercise of the power affects the beneficial interest of the beneficiary or another beneficiary represented by the beneficiary under [Uniform Trust Code Sections 301 through 305] with respect to the exercise or nonexercise of the power; and

(iii)   power over the trust if the terms of the trust provide that the power is held in a nonfiduciary capacity and the power must be held in a nonfiduciary capacity to achieve a tax objective under the Internal Revenue Code of 1986[, as amended,] 26 U.S.C.[, as amended]][; and

(3)   each person that is granted a power by the terms of the trust to appoint or remove a trustee or person described in paragraph (2), to the extent the power is exercisable when the person that exercises the power is not then serving as a trustee or person described in paragraph (2)].

(b)   The representation provisions of [Uniform Trust Code Sections 301 through 305] apply to notice under this section.

Alternative B

(a)   A notice required by Section 303(b)(2) must be sent to:

(1)   all beneficiaries that receive or are entitled to receive income from the trust or would be entitled to receive a distribution of principal if the trust were terminated at the time the notice is sent, assuming no power of appointment is exercised; [and]

(2)   [each person acting as trust director of the trust under the Uniform Directed Trust Act][each person that is granted a power over the trust by the terms of the trust, to the extent the power is exercisable when the person is not then serving as a trustee:

(A)   including a:

(i)   power over the investment, management, or distribution of trust property or other matters of trust administration; and

(ii)   power to appoint or remove a trustee or person described in this paragraph; and

(B)   excluding a:

(i)   power of appointment;

(ii)   power of a beneficiary over the trust, to the extent the exercise or nonexercise of the power affects the beneficial interest of the beneficiary; and

(iii)   power over the trust if the terms of the trust provide that the power is held in a nonfiduciary capacity and the power must be held in a nonfiduciary capacity to achieve a tax objective under the Internal Revenue Code of 1986[, as amended,] 26 U.S.C.[, as amended]][; and

(3)   each person that is granted a power by the terms of the trust to appoint or remove a trustee or person described in paragraph (2), to the extent the power is exercisable when the person that exercises the power is not then serving as a trustee or person described in paragraph (2)].

End of Alternatives

[(c)][(b)]   A person may consent in a record at any time to action proposed under Section 303(b)(2). A notice required by Section 303(b)(2) need not be sent to a person that consents under this subsection.

[(d)][(c)]   A notice required by Section 303(b)(2) must include:

(1)   the action proposed under Section 303(b)(2);

(2)   for a conversion of an income trust to a unitrust, a copy of the unitrust policy adopted under Section 303(a)(1);

(3)   for a change in the percentage or method used to calculate the unitrust amount, a copy of the unitrust policy or amendment or replacement of the unitrust policy adopted under Section 303(a)(2);

(4)   a statement that the person to which the notice is sent may object to the proposed action by stating in a record the basis for the objection and sending or delivering the record to the fiduciary;

(5)   the date by which an objection under paragraph (4) must be received by the fiduciary, which must be at least 30 days after the date the notice is sent;

(6)   the date on which the action is proposed to be taken and the date on which the action is proposed to take effect;

(7)   the name and contact information of the fiduciary; and

(8)   the name and contact information of a person that may be contacted for additional information.

Section 305. Unitrust Policy.

(a)   In administering a unitrust under this [article], a fiduciary shall follow a unitrust policy adopted under Section 303(a)(1) or (2) or amended or replaced under Section 303(a)(2).

(b)   A unitrust policy must provide:

(1)   the unitrust rate or the method for determining the unitrust rate under Section 306;

(2)   the method for determining the applicable value under Section 307; and

(3)   the rules described in Sections 306 through 309 which apply in the administration of the unitrust, whether the rules are:

(A)   mandatory, as provided in Sections 307(a) and 308(a); or

(B)   optional, as provided in Sections 306, 307(b), 308(b), and 309(a), to the extent the fiduciary elects to adopt those rules.

Section 306. Unitrust Rate.

(a)   Except as otherwise provided in Section 309(b)(1), a unitrust rate may be:

(1)   a fixed unitrust rate; or

(2)   a unitrust rate that is determined for each period using:

(A)   a market index or other published data; or

(B)   a mathematical blend of market indices or other published data over a stated number of preceding periods.

(b)   Except as otherwise provided in Section 309(b)(1), a unitrust policy may provide:

(1)   a limit on how high the unitrust rate determined under subsection (a)(2) may rise;

(2)   a limit on how low the unitrust rate determined under subsection (a)(2) may fall;

(3)   a limit on how much the unitrust rate determined under subsection (a)(2) may increase over the unitrust rate for the preceding period or a mathematical blend of unitrust rates over a stated number of preceding periods;

(4)   a limit on how much the unitrust rate determined under subsection (a)(2) may decrease below the unitrust rate for the preceding period or a mathematical blend of unitrust rates over a stated number of preceding periods; or

(5)   a mathematical blend of any of the unitrust rates determined under subsection (a)(2) and paragraphs (1) through (4).

Section 307. Applicable Value.

(a)   A unitrust policy must provide the method for determining the fair market value of an asset for the purpose of determining the unitrust amount, including:

(1)   the frequency of valuing the asset, which need not require a valuation in every period; and

(2)   the date for valuing the asset in each period in which the asset is valued.

(b)   Except as otherwise provided in Section 309(b)(2), a unitrust policy may provide methods for determining the amount of the net fair market value of the trust to take into account in determining the applicable value, including:

(1)   obtaining an appraisal of an asset for which fair market value is not readily available;

(2)   exclusion of specific assets or groups or types of assets;

(3)   other exceptions or modifications of the treatment of specific assets or groups or types of assets;

(4)   identification and treatment of cash or property held for distribution;

(5)   use of:

(A)   an average of fair market values over a stated number of preceding periods; or

(B)   another mathematical blend of fair market values over a stated number of preceding periods;

(6)   a limit on how much the applicable value of all assets, groups of assets, or individual assets may increase over:

(A)   the corresponding applicable value for the preceding period; or

(B)   a mathematical blend of applicable values over a stated number of preceding periods;

(7)   a limit on how much the applicable value of all assets, groups of assets, or individual assets may decrease below:

(A)   the corresponding applicable value for the preceding period; or

(B)   a mathematical blend of applicable values over a stated number of preceding periods;

(8)   the treatment of accrued income and other features of an asset which affect value; and

(9)   determining the liabilities of the trust, including treatment of liabilities to conform with the treatment of assets under paragraphs (1) through (8).

Section 308. Period.

(a)   A unitrust policy must provide the period used under Sections 306 and 307. Except as otherwise provided in Section 309(b)(3), the period may be:

(1)   a calendar year;

(2)   a 12-month period other than a calendar year;

(3)   a calendar quarter;

(4)   a three-month period other than a calendar quarter; or

(5)   another period.

(b)   Except as otherwise provided in Section 309(b), a unitrust policy may provide standards for:

(1)   using fewer preceding periods under Section 306(a)(2)(B) or (b)(3) or (4) if:

(A)   the trust was not in existence in a preceding period; or

(B)   market indices or other published data are not available for a preceding period;

(2)   using fewer preceding periods under Section 307(b)(5)(A) or (B), (6)(B), or (7)(B) if:

(A)   the trust was not in existence in a preceding period; or

(B)   fair market values are not available for a preceding period; and

(3)   prorating the unitrust amount on a daily basis for a part of a period in which the trust or the administration of the trust as a unitrust or the interest of any beneficiary commences or terminates.

Section 309. Special Tax Benefits; Other Rules.

(a) A unitrust policy may:

    (1) provide methods and standards for:

        (A) determining the timing of distributions;

        (B) making distributions in cash or in kind or partly in cash and partly in kind; or

        (C) correcting an underpayment or overpayment to a beneficiary based on the unitrust amount if there is an error in calculating the unitrust amount;

    (2) specify sources and the order of sources, including categories of income for federal income tax purposes, from which distributions of a unitrust amount are paid; or

    (3) provide other standards and rules the fiduciary determines serve the interests of the beneficiaries.

(b) If a trust qualifies for a special tax benefit or a fiduciary is not an independent person:

    (1) the unitrust rate established under Section 306 may not be less than three percent or more than five percent;

    (2) the only provisions of Section 307 which apply are Section 307(a) and (b)(1), (4), (5)(A), and (9);

    (3) the only period that may be used under Section 308 is a calendar year under Section 308(a)(1); and

    (4) the only other provisions of Section 308 which apply are Section 308(b)(2)(A) and (3).

[ARTICLE] 4

ALLOCATION OF RECEIPTS

[PART] 1

RECEIPTS FROM ENTITY

Section 401. Character of Receipts From Entity.

(a) In this section:

(1) "Capital distribution" means an entity distribution of money which is a:

(A) return of capital; or

(B) distribution in total or partial liquidation of the entity.

(2) "Entity":

(A) means a corporation, partnership, limited liability company, regulated investment company, real estate investment trust, common trust fund, or any other organization or arrangement in which a fiduciary owns or holds an interest, whether or not the entity is a taxpayer for federal income tax purposes; and

(B) does not include:

(i) a trust or estate to which Section 402 applies;

(ii) a business or other activity to which Section 403 applies which is not conducted by an entity described in subparagraph (A);

(iii) an asset-backed security; or

(iv) an instrument or arrangement to which Section 416 applies.

(3) "Entity distribution" means a payment or transfer by an entity made to a person in the person's capacity as an owner or holder of an interest in the entity.

(b) In this section, an attribute or action of an entity includes an attribute or action of any other entity in which the entity owns or holds an interest, including an interest owned or held indirectly through another entity.

(c) Except as otherwise provided in subsection (d)(2) through (4), a fiduciary shall allocate to income:

(1) money received in an entity distribution; and

(2) tangible personal property of nominal value received from the entity.

(d) A fiduciary shall allocate to principal:

(1) property received in an entity distribution which is not:

(A) money; or

(B) tangible personal property of nominal value;

(2) money received in an entity distribution in an exchange for part or all of the fiduciary's interest in the entity, to the extent the entity distribution reduces the fiduciary's interest in the entity relative to the interests of other persons that own or hold interests in the entity;

(3) money received in an entity distribution that the fiduciary determines or estimates is a capital distribution; and

(4)   money received in an entity distribution from an entity that is:

(A)   a regulated investment company or real estate investment trust if the money received is a capital gain dividend for federal income tax purposes; or

(B)   treated for federal income tax purposes comparably to the treatment described in subparagraph (A).

(e)   A fiduciary may determine or estimate that money received in an entity distribution is a capital distribution:

(1)   by relying without inquiry or investigation on a characterization of the entity distribution provided by or on behalf of the entity, unless the fiduciary:

(A)   determines, on the basis of information known to the fiduciary, that the characterization is or may be incorrect; or

(B)   owns or holds more than 50 percent of the voting interest in the entity;

(2)   by determining or estimating, on the basis of information known to the fiduciary or provided to the fiduciary by or on behalf of the entity, that the total amount of money and property received by the fiduciary in the entity distribution or a series of related entity distributions is or will be greater than 20 percent of the fair market value of the fiduciary's interest in the entity; or

(3)   if neither paragraph (1) nor (2) applies, by considering the factors in subsection (f) and the information known to the fiduciary or provided to the fiduciary by or on behalf of the entity.

(f)   In making a determination or estimate under subsection (e)(3), a fiduciary may consider:

(1)   a characterization of an entity distribution provided by or on behalf of the entity;

(2)   the amount of money or property received in:

(A)   the entity distribution; or

(B)   what the fiduciary determines is or will be a series of related entity distributions;

(3)   the amount described in paragraph (2) compared to the amount the fiduciary determines or estimates is, during the current or preceding accounting periods:

(A)   the entity's operating income;

(B)   the proceeds of the entity's sale or other disposition of:

(i)   all or part of the business or other activity conducted by the entity;

(ii)   one or more business assets that are not sold to customers in the ordinary course of the business or other activity conducted by the entity; or

(iii)   one or more assets other than business assets, unless the entity's primary activity is to invest in assets to realize gain on the disposition of all or some of the assets;

(C)   if the entity's primary activity is to invest in assets to realize gain on the disposition of all or some of the assets, the gain realized on the disposition;

(D)   the entity's regular, periodic entity distributions;

(E)   the amount of money the entity has accumulated;

(F)   the amount of money the entity has borrowed;

(G)   the amount of money the entity has received from the sources described in Sections 407, 410, 411, and 412; and

(H)   the amount of money the entity has received from a source not otherwise described in this paragraph; and

(4)   any other factor the fiduciary determines is relevant.

(g)   If, after applying subsections (c) through (f), a fiduciary determines that a part of an entity distribution is a capital distribution but is in doubt about the amount of the entity distribution which is a capital distribution, the fiduciary shall allocate to principal the amount of the entity distribution which is in doubt.

(h)   If a fiduciary receives additional information about the application of this section to an entity distribution before the fiduciary has paid part of the entity distribution to a beneficiary, the fiduciary may consider the additional information before making the payment to the beneficiary and may change a decision to make the payment to the beneficiary.

(i)   If a fiduciary receives additional information about the application of this section to an entity distribution after the fiduciary has paid part of the entity distribution to a beneficiary, the fiduciary is not required to change or recover the payment to the beneficiary but may consider that information in determining whether to exercise the power to adjust under Section 203.

Section 402. Distribution From Trust or Estate.

A fiduciary shall allocate to income an amount received as a distribution of income, including a unitrust distribution under [Article] 3, from a trust or estate in which the fiduciary has an interest, other than an interest the fiduciary purchased in a trust that is an investment entity, and shall allocate to principal an amount received as a distribution of principal from the trust or estate. If a fiduciary purchases, or receives from a settlor, an interest in a trust that is an investment entity, Section 401, 415, or 416 applies to a receipt from the trust.

Section 403. Business or Other Activity Conducted by Fiduciary.

(a)   This section applies to a business or other activity conducted by a fiduciary if the fiduciary determines that it is in the interests of the beneficiaries to account separately for the business or other activity instead of:

(1)   accounting for the business or other activity as part of the fiduciary's general accounting records; or

(2)   conducting the business or other activity through an entity described in Section 401(a)(2)(A).

(b)   A fiduciary may account separately under this section for the transactions of a business or other activity, whether or not assets of the business or other activity are segregated from other assets held by the fiduciary.

(c)   A fiduciary that accounts separately under this section for a business or other activity:

(1)   may determine:

(A)   the extent to which the net cash receipts of the business or other activity must be retained for:

(i)   working capital;

(ii)   the acquisition or replacement of fixed assets; and

(iii)   other reasonably foreseeable needs of the business or other activity; and

(B)   the extent to which the remaining net cash receipts are accounted for as principal or income in the fiduciary's general accounting records for the trust;

(2)   may make a determination under paragraph (1) separately and differently from the fiduciary's decisions concerning distributions of income or principal; and

(3)   shall account for the net amount received from the sale of an asset of the business or other activity, other than a sale in the ordinary course of the business or other activity, as

principal in the fiduciary's general accounting records for the trust, to the extent the fiduciary determines that the net amount received is no longer required in the conduct of the business or other activity.

(d)   Activities for which a fiduciary may account separately under this section include:

(1)   retail, manufacturing, service, and other traditional business activities;

(2)   farming;

(3)   raising and selling livestock and other animals;

(4)   managing rental properties;

(5)   extracting minerals, water, and other natural resources;

(6)   growing and cutting timber;

(7)   an activity to which Section 414, 415, or 416 applies; and

(8)   any other business conducted by the fiduciary.

[PART] 2

RECEIPTS NOT NORMALLY APPORTIONED

Section 404. Principal Receipts.

A fiduciary shall allocate to principal:

(1)   to the extent not allocated to income under this [act], an asset received from:

(A)   an individual during the individual's lifetime;

(B)   an estate;

(C)   a trust on termination of an income interest; or

(D)   a payor under a contract naming the fiduciary as beneficiary;

(2)   except as otherwise provided in this [article], money or other property received from the sale, exchange, liquidation, or change in form of a principal asset;

(3)   an amount recovered from a third party to reimburse the fiduciary because of a disbursement described in Section 502(a) or for another reason to the extent not based on loss of income;

(4)   proceeds of property taken by eminent domain, except that proceeds awarded for loss of income in an accounting period are income if a current income beneficiary had a mandatory income interest during the period;

(5)   net income received in an accounting period during which there is no beneficiary to which a fiduciary may or must distribute income; and

(6)   other receipts as provided in [Part] 3.

Section 405. Rental Property.

To the extent a fiduciary does not account for the management of rental property as a business under Section 403, the fiduciary shall allocate to income an amount received as rent of real or personal property, including an amount received for cancellation or renewal of a lease. An amount received as a refundable deposit, including a security deposit or a deposit that is to be applied as rent for future periods:

(1)   must be added to principal and held subject to the terms of the lease, except as otherwise provided by law other than this [act]; and

(2) is not allocated to income or available for distribution to a beneficiary until the fiduciary's contractual obligations have been satisfied with respect to that amount.

Section 406. Receipt on Obligation to Be Paid in Money.

(a) This section does not apply to an obligation to which Section 409, 410, 411, 412, 414, 415, or 416 applies.

(b) A fiduciary shall allocate to income, without provision for amortization of premium, an amount received as interest on an obligation to pay money to the fiduciary, including an amount received as consideration for prepaying principal.

(c) A fiduciary shall allocate to principal an amount received from the sale, redemption, or other disposition of an obligation to pay money to the fiduciary. A fiduciary shall allocate to income the increment in value of a bond or other obligation for the payment of money bearing no stated interest but payable or redeemable, at maturity or another future time, in an amount that exceeds the amount in consideration of which it was issued.

Section 407. Insurance Policy or Contract.

(a) This section does not apply to a contract to which Section 409 applies.

(b) Except as otherwise provided in subsection (c), a fiduciary shall allocate to principal the proceeds of a life insurance policy or other contract received by the fiduciary as beneficiary, including a contract that insures against damage to, destruction of, or loss of title to an asset. The fiduciary shall allocate dividends on an insurance policy to income to the extent premiums on the policy are paid from income and to principal to the extent premiums on the policy are paid from principal.

(c) A fiduciary shall allocate to income proceeds of a contract that insures the fiduciary against loss of:

(1) occupancy or other use by a current income beneficiary;

(2) income; or

(3) subject to Section 403, profits from a business.

[PART] 3

RECEIPTS NORMALLY APPORTIONED

Section 408. Insubstantial Allocation Not Required.

(a) If a fiduciary determines that an allocation between income and principal required by Section 409, 410, 411, 412, or 415 is insubstantial, the fiduciary may allocate the entire amount to principal, unless Section 203(e) applies to the allocation.

(b) A fiduciary may presume an allocation is insubstantial under subsection (a) if:

(1) the amount of the allocation would increase or decrease net income in an accounting period, as determined before the allocation, by less than 10 percent; and

(2) the asset producing the receipt to be allocated has a fair market value less than 10 percent of the total fair market value of the assets owned or held by the fiduciary at the beginning of the accounting period.

(c) The power to make a determination under subsection (a) may be:

(1) exercised by a co-fiduciary in the manner described in Section 203(f); or

(2) released or delegated for a reason described in Section 203(g) and in the manner described in Section 203(h).

Section 409. Deferred Compensation, Annuity, or Similar Payment.

(a)   In this section:

(1)   "Internal income of a separate fund" means the amount determined under subsection (b).

(2)   "Marital trust" means a trust:

(A)   of which the settlor's surviving spouse is the only current income beneficiary and is entitled to a distribution of all the current net income of the trust; and

(B)   that qualifies for a marital deduction with respect to the settlor's estate under Section 2056 of the Internal Revenue Code of 1986[, as amended,] 26 U.S.C. Section 2056[, as amended,] because:

(i)   an election to qualify for a marital deduction under Section 2056(b)(7) of the Internal Revenue Code of 1986[, as amended,] 26 U.S.C. Section 2056(b)(7)[, as amended,] has been made; or

(ii)   the trust qualifies for a marital deduction under Section 2056(b)(5) of the Internal Revenue Code of 1986[, as amended,] 26 U.S.C. Section 2056(b)(5)[, as amended].

(3)   "Payment" means an amount a fiduciary may receive over a fixed number of years or during the life of one or more individuals because of services rendered or property transferred to the payor in exchange for future amounts the fiduciary may receive. The term includes an amount received in money or property from the payor's general assets or from a separate fund created by the payor.

(4)   "Separate fund" includes a private or commercial annuity, an individual retirement account, and a pension, profit-sharing, stock-bonus, or stock-ownership plan.

(b)   For each accounting period, the following rules apply to a separate fund:

(1)   The fiduciary shall determine the internal income of the separate fund as if the separate fund were a trust subject to this [act].

(2)   If the fiduciary cannot determine the internal income of the separate fund under paragraph (1), the internal income of the separate fund is deemed to equal [insert a number at least three and not more than five] percent of the value of the separate fund, according to the most recent statement of value preceding the beginning of the accounting period.

(3)   If the fiduciary cannot determine the value of the separate fund under paragraph (2), the value of the separate fund is deemed to equal the present value of the expected future payments, as determined under Section 7520 of the Internal Revenue Code of 1986[, as amended,] 26 U.S.C. Section 7520[, as amended], for the month preceding the beginning of the accounting period for which the computation is made.

(c)   A fiduciary shall allocate a payment received from a separate fund during an accounting period to income, to the extent of the internal income of the separate fund during the period, and the balance to principal.

(d)   The fiduciary of a marital trust shall:

(1)   withdraw from a separate fund the amount the current income beneficiary of the trust requests the fiduciary to withdraw, not greater than the amount by which the internal income of the separate fund during the accounting period exceeds the amount the fiduciary otherwise receives from the separate fund during the period;

(2)   transfer from principal to income the amount the current income beneficiary requests the fiduciary to transfer, not greater than the amount by which the internal income of the

separate fund during the period exceeds the amount the fiduciary receives from the separate fund during the period after the application of paragraph (1); and

    (3)   distribute to the current income beneficiary as income:

        (A)   the amount of the internal income of the separate fund received or withdrawn during the period; and

        (B)   the amount transferred from principal to income under paragraph (2).

    (e)   For a trust, other than a marital trust, of which one or more current income beneficiaries are entitled to a distribution of all the current net income, the fiduciary shall transfer from principal to income the amount by which the internal income of a separate fund during the accounting period exceeds the amount the fiduciary receives from the separate fund during the period.

Section 410. Liquidating Asset.

    (a)   In this section, "liquidating asset" means an asset whose value will diminish or terminate because the asset is expected to produce receipts for a limited time. The term includes a leasehold, patent, copyright, royalty right, and right to receive payments during a period of more than one year under an arrangement that does not provide for the payment of interest on the unpaid balance.

    (b)   This section does not apply to a receipt subject to Section 401, 409, 411, 412, 414, 415, 416, or 503.

    (c)   A fiduciary shall allocate:

    (1)   to income:

        (A)   a receipt produced by a liquidating asset, to the extent the receipt does not exceed [insert a number at least three and not more than five] percent of the value of the asset; or

        (B)   if the fiduciary cannot determine the value of the asset, 10 percent of the receipt; and

    (2)   to principal, the balance of the receipt.

Section 411. Minerals, Water, and Other Natural Resources.

    (a)   To the extent a fiduciary does not account for a receipt from an interest in minerals, water, or other natural resources as a business under Section 403, the fiduciary shall allocate the receipt:

    (1)   to income, to the extent received:

        (A)   as delay rental or annual rent on a lease;

        (B)   as a factor for interest or the equivalent of interest under an agreement creating a production payment; or

        (C)   on account of an interest in renewable water;

    (2)   to principal, if received from a production payment, to the extent paragraph (1)(B) does not apply; or

    (3)   between income and principal equitably, to the extent received:

        (A)   on account of an interest in non-renewable water;

        (B)   as a royalty, shut-in-well payment, take-or-pay payment, or bonus; or

        (C)   from a working interest or any other interest not provided for in paragraph (1) or (2) or subparagraph (A) or (B).

    (b)   This section applies to an interest owned or held by a fiduciary whether or not a settlor was extracting minerals, water, or other natural resources before the fiduciary owned or held the interest.

(c) An allocation of a receipt under subsection (a)(3) is presumed to be equitable if the amount allocated to principal is equal to the amount allowed by the Internal Revenue Code of 1986[, as amended,] 26 U.S.C.[, as amended,] as a deduction for depletion of the interest.

(d) If a fiduciary owns or holds an interest in minerals, water, or other natural resources before [the effective date of this [act]], the fiduciary may allocate receipts from the interest as provided in this section or in the manner used by the fiduciary before [the effective date of this [act]]. If the fiduciary acquires an interest in minerals, water, or other natural resources on or after [the effective date of this [act]], the fiduciary shall allocate receipts from the interest as provided in this section.

Section 412. Timber.

(a) To the extent a fiduciary does not account for receipts from the sale of timber and related products as a business under Section 403, the fiduciary shall allocate the net receipts:

(1) to income, to the extent the amount of timber cut from the land does not exceed the rate of growth of the timber;

(2) to principal, to the extent the amount of timber cut from the land exceeds the rate of growth of the timber or the net receipts are from the sale of standing timber;

(3) between income and principal if the net receipts are from the lease of land used for growing and cutting timber or from a contract to cut timber from land, by determining the amount of timber cut from the land under the lease or contract and applying the rules in paragraphs (1) and (2); or

(4) to principal, to the extent advance payments, bonuses, and other payments are not allocated under paragraph (1), (2), or (3).

(b) In determining net receipts to be allocated under subsection (a), a fiduciary shall deduct and transfer to principal a reasonable amount for depletion.

(c) This section applies to land owned or held by a fiduciary whether or not a settlor was cutting timber from the land before the fiduciary owned or held the property.

(d) If a fiduciary owns or holds an interest in land used for growing and cutting timber before [the effective date of this [act]], the fiduciary may allocate net receipts from the sale of timber and related products as provided in this section or in the manner used by the fiduciary before [the effective date of this [act]]. If the fiduciary acquires an interest in land used for growing and cutting timber on or after [the effective date of this [act]], the fiduciary shall allocate net receipts from the sale of timber and related products as provided in this section.

Section 413. Marital Deduction Property Not Productive of Income.

(a) If a trust received property for which a gift or estate tax marital deduction was allowed and the settlor's spouse holds a mandatory income interest in the trust, the spouse may require the trustee, to the extent the trust assets otherwise do not provide the spouse with sufficient income from or use of the trust assets to qualify for the deduction, to:

(1) make property productive of income;

(2) convert property to property productive of income within a reasonable time; or

(3) exercise the power to adjust under Section 203.

(b) The trustee may decide which action or combination of actions in subsection (a) to take.

Section 414. Derivative or Option.

(a) In this section, "derivative" means a contract, instrument, other arrangement, or combination of contracts, instruments, or other arrangements, the value, rights, and obligations of which are, in whole or in part, dependent on or derived from an underlying tangible or intangible asset, group of tangible or intangible assets, index, or occurrence of an event. The term includes stocks, fixed income securities, and financial instruments and arrangements based on indices, commodities, interest rates, weather-related events, and credit-default events.

(b)   To the extent a fiduciary does not account for a transaction in derivatives as a business under Section 403, the fiduciary shall allocate 10 percent of receipts from the transaction and 10 percent of disbursements made in connection with the transaction to income and the balance to principal.

(c)   Subsection (d) applies if:

(1)   a fiduciary:

(A)   grants an option to buy property from a trust, whether or not the trust owns the property when the option is granted;

(B)   grants an option that permits another person to sell property to the trust; or

(C)   acquires an option to buy property for the trust or an option to sell an asset owned by the trust; and

(2)   the fiduciary or other owner of the asset is required to deliver the asset if the option is exercised.

(d)   If this subsection applies, the fiduciary shall allocate 10 percent to income and the balance to principal of the following amounts:

(1)   an amount received for granting the option;

(2)   an amount paid to acquire the option; and

(3)   gain or loss realized on the exercise, exchange, settlement, offset, closing, or expiration of the option.

Section 415. Asset-Backed Security.

(a)   Except as otherwise provided in subsection (b), a fiduciary shall allocate to income a receipt from or related to an asset-backed security, to the extent the payor identifies the payment as being from interest or other current return, and to principal the balance of the receipt.

(b)   If a fiduciary receives one or more payments in exchange for part or all of the fiduciary's interest in an asset-backed security, including a liquidation or redemption of the fiduciary's interest in the security, the fiduciary shall allocate to income 10 percent of receipts from the transaction and 10 percent of disbursements made in connection with the transaction, and to principal the balance of the receipts and disbursements.

Section 416. Other Financial Instrument or Arrangement.

A fiduciary shall allocate receipts from or related to a financial instrument or arrangement not otherwise addressed by this [act]. The allocation must be consistent with Sections 414 and 415.

[ARTICLE] 5

ALLOCATION OF DISBURSEMENTS

Section 501. Disbursement From Income.

Subject to Section 504, and except as otherwise provided in Section 601(c)(2) or (3), a fiduciary shall disburse from income:

(1)   one-half of:

(A)   the regular compensation of the fiduciary and any person providing investment advisory, custodial, or other services to the fiduciary, to the extent income is sufficient; and

(B)   an expense for an accounting, judicial or nonjudicial proceeding, or other matter that involves both income and successive interests, to the extent income is sufficient;

(2)   the balance of the disbursements described in paragraph (1), to the extent a fiduciary that is an independent person determines that making those disbursements from income would be in the interests of the beneficiaries;

(3)   another ordinary expense incurred in connection with administration, management, or preservation of property and distribution of income, including interest, an ordinary repair, regularly recurring tax assessed against principal, and an expense of an accounting, judicial or nonjudicial proceeding, or other matter that involves primarily an income interest, to the extent income is sufficient; and

(4)   a premium on insurance covering loss of a principal asset or income from or use of the asset.

Section 502. Disbursement From Principal.

(a)   Subject to Section 505, and except as otherwise provided in Section 601(c)(2), a fiduciary shall disburse from principal:

(1)   the balance of the disbursements described in Section 501(1) and (3), after application of Section 501(2);

(2)   the fiduciary's compensation calculated on principal as a fee for acceptance, distribution, or termination;

(3)   a payment of an expense to prepare for or execute a sale or other disposition of property;

(4)   a payment on the principal of a trust debt;

(5)   a payment of an expense of an accounting, judicial or nonjudicial proceeding, or other matter that involves primarily principal, including a proceeding to construe the terms of the trust or protect property;

(6)   a payment of a premium for insurance, including title insurance, not described in Section 501(4), of which the fiduciary is the owner and beneficiary;

(7)   a payment of an estate or inheritance tax or other tax imposed because of the death of a decedent, including penalties, apportioned to the trust; and

(8)   a payment:

(A)   related to environmental matters, including:

(i)   reclamation;

(ii)   assessing environmental conditions;

(iii)   remedying and removing environmental contamination;

(iv) monitoring remedial activities and the release of substances;

(v) preventing future releases of substances;

(vi) collecting amounts from persons liable or potentially liable for the costs of activities described in clauses (i) through (v);

(vii) penalties imposed under environmental laws or regulations;

(viii) other actions to comply with environmental laws or regulations;

(ix) statutory or common law claims by third parties; and

(x) defending claims based on environmental matters; and

(B) for a premium for insurance for matters described in subparagraph (A).

(b) If a principal asset is encumbered with an obligation that requires income from the asset to be paid directly to a creditor, the fiduciary shall transfer from principal to income an amount equal to the income paid to the creditor in reduction of the principal balance of the obligation.

Section 503. Transfer From Income to Principal for Depreciation.

(a) In this section, "depreciation" means a reduction in value due to wear, tear, decay, corrosion, or gradual obsolescence of a tangible asset having a useful life of more than one year.

(b) A fiduciary may transfer to principal a reasonable amount of the net cash receipts from a principal asset that is subject to depreciation, but may not transfer any amount for depreciation:

(1) of the part of real property used or available for use by a beneficiary as a residence;

(2) of tangible personal property held or made available for the personal use or enjoyment of a beneficiary; or

(3) under this section, to the extent the fiduciary accounts:

(A) under Section 410 for the asset; or

(B) under Section 403 for the business or other activity in which the asset is used.

(c) An amount transferred to principal under this section need not be separately held.

Section 504. Reimbursement of Income From Principal.

(a) If a fiduciary makes or expects to make an income disbursement described in subsection (b), the fiduciary may transfer an appropriate amount from principal to income in one or more accounting periods to reimburse income.

(b) To the extent the fiduciary has not been and does not expect to be reimbursed by a third party, income disbursements to which subsection (a) applies include:

(1) an amount chargeable to principal but paid from income because principal is illiquid;

(2) a disbursement made to prepare property for sale, including improvements and commissions; and

(3) a disbursement described in Section 502(a).

(c) If an asset whose ownership gives rise to an income disbursement becomes subject to a successive interest after an income interest ends, the fiduciary may continue to make transfers under subsection (a).

Section 505. Reimbursement of Principal From Income.

(a) If a fiduciary makes or expects to make a principal disbursement described in subsection (b), the fiduciary may transfer an appropriate amount from income to principal in one or more accounting periods to reimburse principal or provide a reserve for future principal disbursements.

(b)   To the extent a fiduciary has not been and does not expect to be reimbursed by a third party, principal disbursements to which subsection (a) applies include:

(1)   an amount chargeable to income but paid from principal because income is not sufficient;

(2)   the cost of an improvement to principal, whether a change to an existing asset or the construction of a new asset, including a special assessment;

(3)   a disbursement made to prepare property for rental, including tenant allowances, leasehold improvements, and commissions;

(4)   a periodic payment on an obligation secured by a principal asset, to the extent the amount transferred from income to principal for depreciation is less than the periodic payment; and

(5)   a disbursement described in Section 502(a).

(c)   If an asset whose ownership gives rise to a principal disbursement becomes subject to a successive interest after an income interest ends, the fiduciary may continue to make transfers under subsection (a).

Section 506. Income Taxes.

(a)   A tax required to be paid by a fiduciary which is based on receipts allocated to income must be paid from income.

(b)   A tax required to be paid by a fiduciary which is based on receipts allocated to principal must be paid from principal, even if the tax is called an income tax by the taxing authority.

(c)   Subject to subsection (d) and Sections 504, 505, and 507, a tax required to be paid by a fiduciary on a share of an entity's taxable income in an accounting period must be paid from:

(1)   income and principal proportionately to the allocation between income and principal of receipts from the entity in the period; and

(2)   principal to the extent the tax exceeds the receipts from the entity in the period.

(d)   After applying subsections (a) through (c), a fiduciary shall adjust income or principal receipts, to the extent the taxes the fiduciary pays are reduced because of a deduction for a payment made to a beneficiary.

Section 507. Adjustment Between Income and Principal Because of Taxes.

(a)   A fiduciary may make an adjustment between income and principal to offset the shifting of economic interests or tax benefits between current income beneficiaries and successor beneficiaries which arises from:

(1)   an election or decision the fiduciary makes regarding a tax matter, other than a decision to claim an income tax deduction to which subsection (b) applies;

(2)   an income tax or other tax imposed on the fiduciary or a beneficiary as a result of a transaction involving the fiduciary or a distribution by the fiduciary; or

(3)   ownership by the fiduciary of an interest in an entity a part of whose taxable income, whether or not distributed, is includable in the taxable income of the fiduciary or a beneficiary.

(b)   If the amount of an estate tax marital or charitable deduction is reduced because a fiduciary deducts an amount paid from principal for income tax purposes instead of deducting it for estate tax purposes and, as a result, estate taxes paid from principal are increased and income taxes paid by the fiduciary or a beneficiary are decreased, the fiduciary shall charge each beneficiary that benefits from the decrease in income tax to reimburse the principal from which the increase in estate tax is paid. The total reimbursement must equal the increase in the estate tax, to the extent the principal used to pay the increase would have qualified for a marital or charitable deduction but for the payment. The share of the reimbursement for each fiduciary or beneficiary whose income taxes are reduced must be the same as its share of the total decrease in income tax.

(c)   A fiduciary that charges a beneficiary under subsection (b) may offset the charge by obtaining payment from the beneficiary, withholding an amount from future distributions to the beneficiary, or adopting another method or combination of methods.

[ARTICLE] 6

DEATH OF INDIVIDUAL OR TERMINATION OF INCOME INTEREST

Section 601. Determination and Distribution of Net Income.

(a)   This section applies when:

(1)   the death of an individual results in the creation of an estate or trust; or

(2)   an income interest in a trust terminates, whether the trust continues or is distributed.

(b)   A fiduciary of an estate or trust with an income interest that terminates shall determine, under subsection [(g)][(e)] and [Articles] 4, 5, and 7, the amount of net income and net principal receipts received from property specifically given to a beneficiary. The fiduciary shall distribute the net income and net principal receipts to the beneficiary that is to receive the specific property.

(c)   A fiduciary shall determine the income and net income of an estate or income interest in a trust which terminates, other than the amount of net income determined under subsection (b), under [Articles] 4, 5, and 7 and by:

(1)   including in net income all income from property used or sold to discharge liabilities;

(2)   paying from income or principal, in the fiduciary's discretion, fees of attorneys, accountants, and fiduciaries, court costs and other expenses of administration, and interest on estate and inheritance taxes and other taxes imposed because of the decedent's death, but the fiduciary may pay the expenses from income of property passing to a trust for which the fiduciary claims a federal estate tax marital or charitable deduction only to the extent:

(A)   the payment of the expenses from income will not cause the reduction or loss of the deduction; or

(B)   the fiduciary makes an adjustment under Section 507(b); and

(3)   paying from principal other disbursements made or incurred in connection with the settlement of the estate or the winding up of an income interest that terminates, including:

(A)   to the extent authorized by the decedent's will, the terms of the trust, or applicable law, debts, funeral expenses, disposition of remains, family allowances, estate and inheritance taxes, and other taxes imposed because of the decedent's death; and

(B)   related penalties that are apportioned, by the decedent's will, the terms of the trust, or applicable law, to the estate or income interest that terminates.

[(d) If a decedent's will, the terms of a trust, or applicable law provides for the payment of interest or the equivalent of interest to a beneficiary that receives a pecuniary amount outright, the fiduciary shall make the payment from net income determined under subsection (c) or from principal to the extent net income is insufficient.

(e)   If a beneficiary is to receive a pecuniary amount outright from a trust after an income interest ends because of an income beneficiary's death, and no payment of interest or the equivalent of interest is provided for by the terms of the trust or applicable law, the fiduciary shall pay the interest or the equivalent of interest to which the beneficiary would be entitled under applicable law if the pecuniary amount were required to be paid under a will.]

[(f)][(d)]   A fiduciary shall distribute net income[remaining after payments required by subsections (d) and (e)] in the manner described in Section 602 to all other beneficiaries, including a beneficiary that receives a pecuniary amount in trust, even if the beneficiary holds an unqualified power to withdraw assets from the trust or other presently exercisable general power of appointment over the trust.

[(g)][(e)] A fiduciary may not reduce principal or income receipts from property described in subsection (b) because of a payment described in Section 501 or 502, to the extent the decedent's will, the terms of the trust, or applicable law requires the fiduciary to make the payment from assets other than the property or to the extent the fiduciary recovers or expects to recover the payment from a third party. The net income and principal receipts from the property must be determined by including the amount the fiduciary receives or pays regarding the property, whether the amount accrued or became due before, on, or after the date of the decedent's death or an income interest's terminating event, and making a reasonable provision for an amount the estate or income interest may become obligated to pay after the property is distributed.

Section 602. Distribution to Successor Beneficiary.

(a) Except to the extent [Article] 3 applies for a beneficiary that is a trust, each beneficiary described in Section [601(f)][601(d)] is entitled to receive a share of the net income equal to the beneficiary's fractional interest in undistributed principal assets, using values as of the distribution date. If a fiduciary makes more than one distribution of assets to beneficiaries to which this section applies, each beneficiary, including a beneficiary that does not receive part of the distribution, is entitled, as of each distribution date, to a share of the net income the fiduciary received after the decedent's death, an income interest's other terminating event, or the preceding distribution by the fiduciary.

(b) In determining a beneficiary's share of net income under subsection (a), the following rules apply:

(1) The beneficiary is entitled to receive a share of the net income equal to the beneficiary's fractional interest in the undistributed principal assets immediately before the distribution date.

(2) The beneficiary's fractional interest under paragraph (1) must be calculated:

(A) on the aggregate value of the assets as of the distribution date without reducing the value by any unpaid principal obligation; and

(B) without regard to:

(i) property specifically given to a beneficiary under the decedent's will or the terms of the trust; and

(ii) property required to pay pecuniary amounts not in trust.

(3) The distribution date under paragraph (1) may be the date as of which the fiduciary calculates the value of the assets if that date is reasonably near the date on which the assets are distributed.

(c) To the extent a fiduciary does not distribute under this section all the collected but undistributed net income to each beneficiary as of a distribution date, the fiduciary shall maintain records showing the interest of each beneficiary in the net income.

(d) If this section applies to income from an asset, a fiduciary may apply the rules in this section to net gain or loss realized from the disposition of the asset after the decedent's death, an income interest's terminating event, or the preceding distribution by the fiduciary.

[ARTICLE] 7

APPORTIONMENT AT BEGINNING AND END OF INCOME INTEREST

Section 701. When Right to Income Begins and Ends.

(a)   An income beneficiary is entitled to net income in accordance with the terms of the trust from the date an income interest begins. The income interest begins on the date specified in the terms of the trust or, if no date is specified, on the date an asset becomes subject to:

    (1)   the trust for the current income beneficiary; or

    (2)   a successive interest for a successor beneficiary.

(b)   An asset becomes subject to a trust under subsection (a)(1):

    (1)   for an asset that is transferred to the trust during the settlor's life, on the date the asset is transferred;

    (2)   for an asset that becomes subject to the trust because of a decedent's death, on the date of the decedent's death, even if there is an intervening period of administration of the decedent's estate; or

    (3)   for an asset that is transferred to a fiduciary by a third party because of a decedent's death, on the date of the decedent's death.

(c)   An asset becomes subject to a successive interest under subsection (a)(2) on the day after the preceding income interest ends, as determined under subsection (d), even if there is an intervening period of administration to wind up the preceding income interest.

(d)   An income interest ends on the day before an income beneficiary dies or another terminating event occurs or on the last day of a period during which there is no beneficiary to which a fiduciary may or must distribute income.

Section 702. Apportionment of Receipts and Disbursements When Decedent Dies or Income Interest Begins.

(a)   A fiduciary shall allocate an income receipt or disbursement, other than a receipt to which Section 601(b) applies, to principal if its due date occurs before the date on which:

    (1)   for an estate, the decedent died; or

    (2)   for a trust or successive interest, an income interest begins.

(b)   If the due date of a periodic income receipt or disbursement occurs on or after the date on which a decedent died or an income interest begins, a fiduciary shall allocate the receipt or disbursement to income.

(c)   If an income receipt or disbursement is not periodic or has no due date, a fiduciary shall treat the receipt or disbursement under this section as accruing from day to day. The fiduciary shall allocate to principal the portion of the receipt or disbursement accruing before the date on which a decedent died or an income interest begins, and to income the balance.

(d)   A receipt or disbursement is periodic under subsections (b) and (c) if:

    (1)   the receipt or disbursement must be paid at regular intervals under an obligation to make payments; or

    (2)   the payor customarily makes payments at regular intervals.

(e) An item of income or obligation is due under this section on the date the payor is required to make a payment. If a payment date is not stated, there is no due date.

(f) Distributions to shareholders or other owners from an entity to which Section 401 applies are due:

(1) on the date fixed by or on behalf of the entity for determining the persons entitled to receive the distribution;

(2) if no date is fixed, on the date of the decision by or on behalf of the entity to make the distribution; or

(3) if no date is fixed and the fiduciary does not know the date of the decision by or on behalf of the entity to make the distribution, on the date the fiduciary learns of the decision.

Section 703. Apportionment When Income Interest Ends.

(a) In this section, "undistributed income" means net income received on or before the date on which an income interest ends. The term does not include an item of income or expense which is due or accrued or net income that has been added or is required to be added to principal under the terms of the trust.

(b) Except as otherwise provided in subsection (c), when a mandatory income interest of a beneficiary ends, the fiduciary shall pay the beneficiary's share of the undistributed income that is not disposed of under the terms of the trust to the beneficiary or, if the beneficiary does not survive the date the interest ends, to the beneficiary's estate.

(c) If a beneficiary has an unqualified power to withdraw more than five percent of the value of a trust immediately before an income interest ends:

(1) the fiduciary shall allocate to principal the undistributed income from the portion of the trust which may be withdrawn; and

(2) subsection (b) applies only to the balance of the undistributed income.

(d) When a fiduciary's obligation to pay a fixed annuity or a fixed fraction of the value of assets ends, the fiduciary shall prorate the final payment as required to preserve an income tax, gift tax, estate tax, or other tax benefit.

[ARTICLE] 8

MISCELLANEOUS PROVISIONS

Section 801. Uniformity of Application and Construction. [omitted]

Section 802. Relationship to Electronic Signatures in Global and National Commerce Act. [omitted]

Section 803. Application to Trust or Estate. [omitted]

[Section 804. Severability.] [omitted]

Section 805. Repeals; Conforming Amendments. [omitted]

Section 806. Effective Date. [omitted]

UNIFORM GUARDIANSHIP, CONSERVATORSHIP, AND OTHER PROTECTIVE ARRANGEMENTS ACT*

[ARTICLE] 1
GENERAL PROVISIONS

Section

[ARTICLE] 2
GUARDIANSHIP OF MINOR

---

* Copyright © 2017 by the National Conference of Commissioners on Uniform State Laws.

UNIFORM GUARDIANSHIP, CONSERVATORSHIP, AND OTHER PROTECTIVE ARRANGEMENTS ACT

UNIFORM GUARDIANSHIP, CONSERVATORSHIP, AND OTHER PROTECTIVE ARRANGEMENTS ACT

[ARTICLE] 1

GENERAL PROVISIONS

Section 101. Short Title.

This [act] may be cited as the Uniform Guardianship, Conservatorship, and Other Protective Arrangements Act.

Section 102. Definitions.

In this [act]:

(1) "Adult" means an individual at least [18] years of age or an emancipated individual under [18] years of age.

(2) "Adult subject to conservatorship" means an adult for whom a conservator has been appointed under this [act].

(3) "Adult subject to guardianship" means an adult for whom a guardian has been appointed under this [act].

(4) "Claim" includes a claim against an individual or conservatorship estate, whether arising in contract, tort, or otherwise.

(5) "Conservator" means a person appointed by a court to make decisions with respect to the property or financial affairs of an individual subject to conservatorship. The term includes a co-conservator.

(6) "Conservatorship estate" means the property subject to conservatorship under this [act].

(7) "Full conservatorship" means a conservatorship that grants the conservator all powers available under this [act].

(8) "Full guardianship" means a guardianship that grants the guardian all powers available under this [act].

(9) "Guardian" means a person appointed by the court to make decisions with respect to the personal affairs of an individual. The term includes a co-guardian but does not include a guardian ad litem.

(10) "Guardian ad litem" means a person appointed to inform the court about, and to represent, the needs and best interest of an individual.

(11) "Individual subject to conservatorship" means an adult or minor for whom a conservator has been appointed under this [act].

(12) "Individual subject to guardianship" means an adult or minor for whom a guardian has been appointed under this [act].

(13) "Less restrictive alternative" means an approach to meeting an individual's needs which restricts fewer rights of the individual than would the appointment of a guardian or conservator. The term includes supported decision making, appropriate technological assistance, appointment of a representative payee, and appointment of an agent by the individual, including appointment under a [power of attorney for health care] or power of attorney for finances.

(14) "Letters of office" means a record issued by a court certifying a guardian's or conservator's authority to act.

(15) "Limited conservatorship" means a conservatorship that grants the conservator less than all powers available under this [act], grants powers over only certain property, or otherwise restricts the powers of the conservator.

(16) "Limited guardianship" means a guardianship that grants the guardian less than all powers available under this [act] or otherwise restricts the powers of the guardian.

(17) "Minor" means an unemancipated individual under [18] years of age.

(18) "Minor subject to conservatorship" means a minor for whom a conservator has been appointed under this [act].

(19) "Minor subject to guardianship" means a minor for whom a guardian has been appointed under this [act].

(20) "Parent" does not include an individual whose parental rights have been terminated.

(21) "Person" means an individual, estate, business or nonprofit entity, public corporation, government or governmental subdivision, agency, or instrumentality, or other legal entity.

(22) "Property" includes tangible and intangible property.

(23) "Protective arrangement instead of conservatorship" means a court order entered under Section 503.

(24) "Protective arrangement instead of guardianship" means a court order entered under Section 502.

(25) "Protective arrangement under [Article] 5" means a court order entered under Section 502 or 503.

(26) "Record", used as a noun, means information that is inscribed on a tangible medium or that is stored in an electronic or other medium and is retrievable in perceivable form.

(27) "Respondent" means an individual for whom appointment of a guardian or conservator or a protective arrangement instead of guardianship or conservatorship is sought.

(28) "Sign" means, with present intent to authenticate or adopt a record:

    (A)   to execute or adopt a tangible symbol; or

    (B)   to attach to or logically associate with the record an electronic symbol, sound, or process.

(29) "Standby guardian" means a person appointed by the court under Section 207.

(30) "State" means a state of the United States, the District of Columbia, Puerto Rico, the United States Virgin Islands, or any territory or insular possession subject to the jurisdiction of the United States. The term includes a federally recognized Indian tribe.

(31) "Supported decision making" means assistance from one or more persons of an individual's choosing in understanding the nature and consequences of potential personal and financial decisions, which enables the individual to make the decisions, and in communicating a decision once made if consistent with the individual's wishes.

Section 103. Supplemental Principles of Law and Equity Applicable.

Unless displaced by a particular provision of this [act], the principles of law and equity supplement its provisions.

Section 104. Subject-Matter Jurisdiction.

(a)   Except to the extent jurisdiction is precluded by [insert citation to Uniform Child Custody Jurisdiction and Enforcement Act], the [designate appropriate court] has jurisdiction over a guardianship for a minor domiciled or present in this state. The court has jurisdiction over a conservatorship or protective arrangement instead of conservatorship for a minor domiciled or having property in this state.

(b) The [designate appropriate court] has jurisdiction over a guardianship, conservatorship, or protective arrangement under [Article] 5 for an adult as provided in the [insert citation to Uniform Adult Guardianship and Protective Proceedings Jurisdiction Act].

(c) After notice is given in a proceeding for a guardianship, conservatorship, or protective arrangement under [Article] 5 and until termination of the proceeding, the court in which the petition is filed has:

(1) exclusive jurisdiction to determine the need for the guardianship, conservatorship, or protective arrangement;

(2) exclusive jurisdiction to determine how property of the respondent must be managed, expended, or distributed to or for the use of the respondent, an individual who is dependent in fact on the respondent, or other claimant;

(3) nonexclusive jurisdiction to determine the validity of a claim against the respondent or property of the respondent or a question of title concerning the property; and

(4) if a guardian or conservator is appointed, exclusive jurisdiction over issues related to administration of the guardianship or conservatorship.

(d) A court that appoints a guardian or conservator, or authorizes a protective arrangement under [Article] 5, has exclusive and continuing jurisdiction over the proceeding until the court terminates the proceeding or the appointment or protective arrangement expires by its terms.

Section 105. Transfer of Proceeding.

(a) This section does not apply to a guardianship or conservatorship for an adult which is subject to the transfer provisions of [insert citation to Article 3 of the Uniform Adult Guardianship and Protective Proceedings Jurisdiction Act].

(b) After appointment of a guardian or conservator, the court that made the appointment may transfer the proceeding to a court in another [county] in this state or another state if transfer is in the best interest of the individual subject to the guardianship or conservatorship.

(c) If a proceeding for a guardianship or conservatorship is pending in another state or a foreign country and a petition for guardianship or conservatorship for the same individual is filed in a court in this state, the court shall notify the court in the other state or foreign country and, after consultation with that court, assume or decline jurisdiction, whichever is in the best interest of the respondent.

(d) A guardian or conservator appointed in another state or country may petition the court for appointment as a guardian or conservator in this state for the same individual if jurisdiction in this state is or will be established. The appointment may be made on proof of appointment in the other state or foreign country and presentation of a certified copy of the part of the court record in the other state or country specified by the court in this state.

(e) Notice of hearing on a petition under subsection (d), together with a copy of the petition, must be given to the respondent, if the respondent is at least 12 years of age at the time of the hearing, and to the persons that would be entitled to notice if the procedures for appointment of a guardian or conservator under this [act] were applicable. The court shall make the appointment unless it determines the appointment would not be in the best interest of the respondent.

(f) Not later than 14 days after appointment under subsection (e), the guardian or conservator shall give a copy of the order of appointment to the individual subject to guardianship or conservatorship, if the individual is at least 12 years of age, and to all persons given notice of the hearing on the petition.

Section 106. Venue.

(a) Venue for a guardianship proceeding for a minor is in:

(1)   the [county] in which the minor resides or is present at the time the proceeding commences; or

(2)   the [county] in which another proceeding concerning the custody or parental rights of the minor is pending.

(b)   Venue for a guardianship proceeding or protective arrangement instead of guardianship for an adult is in:

(1)   the [county] in which the respondent resides;

(2)   if the respondent has been admitted to an institution by court order, the [county] in which the court is located; or

(3)   if the proceeding is for appointment of an emergency guardian for an adult, the [county] in which the respondent is present.

(c)   Venue for a conservatorship proceeding or protective arrangement instead of conservatorship is in:

(1)   the [county] in which the respondent resides, whether or not a guardian has been appointed in another [county] or other jurisdiction; or

(2)   if the respondent does not reside in this state, in any [county] in which property of the respondent is located.

(d)   If proceedings under this [act] are brought in more than one [county], the court of the [county] in which the first proceeding is brought has the exclusive right to proceed unless the court determines venue is properly in another court or the interest of justice otherwise requires transfer of the proceeding.

Section 107. Practice in Court.

(a)   Except as otherwise provided in this [act], the rules of evidence and civil procedure, including rules concerning appellate review, govern a proceeding under this [act].

(b)   If proceedings for a guardianship, conservatorship, or protective arrangement under [Article] 5 for the same individual are commenced or pending in the same court, the proceedings may be consolidated.

[(c)   A respondent may demand a jury trial in a proceeding under this [act] on the issue whether a basis exists for appointment of a guardian or conservator.]

Section 108. Letters of Office.

(a)   The court shall issue letters of office to a guardian on filing by the guardian of an acceptance of appointment.

(b)   The court shall issue letters of office to a conservator on filing by the conservator of an acceptance of appointment and filing of any required bond or compliance with any other asset-protection arrangement required by the court.

(c)   Limitations on the powers of a guardian or conservator or on the property subject to conservatorship must be stated on the letters of office.

(d)   The court at any time may limit the powers conferred on a guardian or conservator. The court shall issue new letters of office to reflect the limitation. The court shall give notice of the limitation to the guardian or conservator, individual subject to guardianship or conservatorship, each parent of a minor subject to guardianship or conservatorship, and any other person the court determines.

Section 109. Effect of Acceptance of Appointment.

On acceptance of appointment, a guardian or conservator submits to personal jurisdiction of the court in this state in any proceeding relating to the guardianship or conservatorship.

Section 110. Co-Guardian; Co-Conservator.

(a)   The court at any time may appoint a co-guardian or co-conservator to serve immediately or when a designated event occurs.

(b)   A co-guardian or co-conservator appointed to serve immediately may act when that co-guardian or co-conservator complies with Section 108.

(c)   A co-guardian or co-conservator appointed to serve when a designated event occurs may act when:

(1)   the event occurs; and

(2)   that co-guardian or co-conservator complies with Section 108.

(d)   Unless an order of appointment under subsection (a) or subsequent order states otherwise, co-guardians or co-conservators shall make decisions jointly.

Section 111. Judicial Appointment of Successor Guardian or Successor Conservator.

(a)   The court at any time may appoint a successor guardian or successor conservator to serve immediately or when a designated event occurs.

(b)   A person entitled under Section 202 or 302 to petition the court to appoint a guardian may petition the court to appoint a successor guardian. A person entitled under Section 402 to petition the court to appoint a conservator may petition the court to appoint a successor conservator.

(c)   A successor guardian or successor conservator appointed to serve when a designated event occurs may act as guardian or conservator when:

(1)   the event occurs; and

(2)   the successor complies with Section 108.

(d)   A successor guardian or successor conservator has the predecessor's powers unless otherwise provided by the court.

Section 112. Effect of Death, Removal, or Resignation of Guardian or Conservator.

(a)   Appointment of a guardian or conservator terminates on the death or removal of the guardian or conservator, or when the court under subsection (b) approves a resignation of the guardian or conservator.

(b)   A guardian or conservator must petition the court to resign. The petition may include a request that the court appoint a successor. Resignation of a guardian or conservator is effective on the date the resignation is approved by the court.

(c)   Death, removal, or resignation of a guardian or conservator does not affect liability for a previous act or the obligation to account for:

(1)   an action taken on behalf of the individual subject to guardianship or conservatorship; or

(2)   the individual's funds or other property.

Section 113. Notice of Hearing Generally.

(a)   Except as otherwise provided in Sections 203, 207, 303, 403, and 505, if notice of a hearing under this [act] is required, the movant shall give notice of the date, time, and place of the hearing to the person to be notified unless otherwise ordered by the court for good cause. Except as otherwise

459

provided in this [act], notice must be given in compliance with [insert citation to this state's rule of civil procedure] at least 14 days before the hearing.

(b)   Proof of notice of a hearing under this [act] must be made before or at the hearing and filed in the proceeding.

(c)   Notice of a hearing under this [act] must be in at least 16-point font, in plain language, and, to the extent feasible, in a language in which the person to be notified is proficient.

Section 114. Waiver of Notice.

(a)   Except as otherwise provided in subsection (b), a person may waive notice under this [act] in a record signed by the person or person's attorney and filed in the proceeding.

(b)   A respondent, individual subject to guardianship, individual subject to conservatorship, or individual subject to a protective arrangement under [Article] 5 may not waive notice under this [act].

Section 115. Guardian ad Litem.

The court at any time may appoint a guardian ad litem for an individual if the court determines the individual's interest otherwise would not be adequately represented. If no conflict of interest exists, a guardian ad litem may be appointed to represent multiple individuals or interests. The guardian ad litem may not be the same individual as the attorney representing the respondent. The court shall state the duties of the guardian ad litem and the reasons for the appointment.

Section 116. Request for Notice.

(a)   A person may file with the court a request for notice under this [act] if the person is:

(1)   not otherwise entitled to notice; and

(2)   interested in the welfare of a respondent, individual subject to guardianship or conservatorship, or individual subject to a protective arrangement under [Article] 5.

(b)   A request under subsection (a) must include a statement showing the interest of the person making the request and the address of the person or an attorney for the person to whom notice is to be given.

(c)   If the court approves a request under subsection (a), the court shall give notice of the approval to the guardian or conservator, if one has been appointed, or the respondent if no guardian or conservator has been appointed.

Section 117. Disclosure of Bankruptcy or Criminal History.

(a)   Before accepting appointment as a guardian or conservator, a person shall disclose to the court whether the person:

(1)   is or has been a debtor in a bankruptcy, insolvency, or receivership proceeding; or

(2)   been convicted of:

(A)   a felony;

(B)   a crime involving dishonesty, neglect, violence, or use of physical force; or

(C)   other crime relevant to the functions the individual would assume as guardian or conservator.

(b)   A guardian or conservator that engages or anticipates engaging an agent the guardian or conservator knows has been convicted of a felony, a crime involving dishonesty, neglect, violence, or use of physical force, or other crime relevant to the functions the agent is being engaged to perform promptly shall disclose that knowledge to the court.

(c)   If a conservator engages or anticipates engaging an agent to manage finances of the individual subject to conservatorship and knows the agent is or has been a debtor in a bankruptcy, insolvency, or receivership proceeding, the conservator promptly shall disclose that knowledge to the court.

Section 118. Multiple Nominations.

If a respondent or other person makes more than one nomination of a guardian or conservator, the latest in time governs.

Section 119. Compensation and Expenses; In General.

(a)   Unless otherwise compensated or reimbursed, an attorney for a respondent in a proceeding under this [act] is entitled to reasonable compensation for services and reimbursement of reasonable expenses from the property of the respondent.

(b)   Unless otherwise compensated or reimbursed, an attorney or other person whose services resulted in an order beneficial to an individual subject to guardianship or conservatorship or for whom a protective arrangement under [Article] 5 was ordered is entitled to reasonable compensation for services and reimbursement of reasonable expenses from the property of the individual.

(c)   The court must approve compensation and expenses payable under this section before payment. Approval is not required before a service is provided or an expense is incurred.

(d)   If the court dismisses a petition under this [act] and determines the petition was filed in bad faith, the court may assess the cost of any court-ordered professional evaluation or [visitor] against the petitioner.

Section 120. Compensation of Guardian or Conservator.

(a)   Subject to court approval, a guardian is entitled to reasonable compensation for services as guardian and to reimbursement for room, board, clothing, and other appropriate expenses advanced for the benefit of the individual subject to guardianship. If a conservator, other than the guardian or a person affiliated with the guardian, is appointed for the individual, reasonable compensation and reimbursement to the guardian may be approved and paid by the conservator without court approval.

(b)   Subject to court approval, a conservator is entitled to reasonable compensation for services and reimbursement for appropriate expenses from the property of the individual subject to conservatorship.

(c)   In determining reasonable compensation for a guardian or conservator, the court, or a conservator in determining reasonable compensation for a guardian as provided in subsection (a), shall consider:

(1)   the necessity and quality of the services provided;

(2)   the experience, training, professional standing, and skills of the guardian or conservator;

(3)   the difficulty of the services performed, including the degree of skill and care required;

(4)   the conditions and circumstances under which a service was performed, including whether the service was provided outside regular business hours or under dangerous or extraordinary conditions;

(5)   the effect of the services on the individual subject to guardianship or conservatorship;

(6)   the extent to which the services provided were or were not consistent with the guardian's plan under Section 316 or conservator's plan under Section 419; and

(7)   the fees customarily paid to a person that performs a like service in the community.

(d)   A guardian or conservator need not use personal funds of the guardian or conservator for the expenses of the individual subject to guardianship or conservatorship.

(e) If an individual subject to guardianship or conservatorship seeks to modify or terminate the guardianship or conservatorship or remove the guardian or conservator, the court may order compensation to the guardian or conservator for time spent opposing modification, termination, or removal only to the extent the court determines the opposition was reasonably necessary to protect the interest of the individual subject to guardianship or conservatorship.

Section 121. Liability of Guardian or Conservator for Act of Individual Subject to Guardianship or Conservatorship.

A guardian or conservator is not personally liable to another person solely because of the guardianship or conservatorship for an act or omission of the individual subject to guardianship or conservatorship.

Section 122. Petition After Appointment for Instruction or Ratification.

(a) A guardian or conservator may petition the court for instruction concerning fiduciary responsibility or ratification of a particular act related to the guardianship or conservatorship.

(b) On notice and hearing on a petition under subsection (a), the court may give an instruction and issue an appropriate order.

Section 123. Third-Party Acceptance of Authority of Guardian or Conservator.

(a) A person must not recognize the authority of a guardian or conservator to act on behalf of an individual subject to guardianship or conservatorship if:

(1) the person has actual knowledge or a reasonable belief that the letters of office of the guardian or conservator are invalid or the conservator or guardian is exceeding or improperly exercising authority granted by the court; or

(2) the person has actual knowledge that the individual subject to guardianship or conservatorship is subject to physical or financial abuse, neglect, exploitation, or abandonment by the guardian or conservator or a person acting for or with the guardian or conservator.

(b) A person may refuse to recognize the authority of a guardian or conservator to act on behalf of an individual subject to guardianship or conservatorship if:

(1) the guardian's or conservator's proposed action would be inconsistent with this [act]; or

(2) the person makes, or has actual knowledge that another person has made, a report to the [government agency providing protective services to adults or children] stating a good-faith belief that the individual subject to guardianship or conservatorship is subject to physical or financial abuse, neglect, exploitation, or abandonment by the guardian or conservator or a person acting for or with the guardian or conservator.

(c) A person that refuses to accept the authority of a guardian or conservator in accordance with subsection (b) may report the refusal and the reason for refusal to the court. The court on receiving the report shall consider whether removal of the guardian or conservator or other action is appropriate.

(d) A guardian or conservator may petition the court to require a third party to accept a decision made by the guardian or conservator on behalf of the individual subject to guardianship or conservatorship.

Section 124. Use of Agent by Guardian or Conservator.

(a) Except as otherwise provided in subsection (c), a guardian or conservator may delegate a power to an agent which a prudent guardian or conservator of comparable skills could delegate prudently under the circumstances if the delegation is consistent with the guardian's or conservator's fiduciary duties and the guardian's plan under Section 316 or conservator's plan under Section 419.

(b) In delegating a power under subsection (a), the guardian or conservator shall exercise reasonable care, skill, and caution in:

(1)   selecting the agent;

(2)   establishing the scope and terms of the agent's work in accordance with the guardian's plan under Section 316 or conservator's plan under Section 419;

(3)   monitoring the agent's performance and compliance with the delegation; and

(4)   redressing an act or omission of the agent which would constitute a breach of the guardian's or conservator's duties if done by the guardian or conservator.

(c)   A guardian or conservator may not delegate all powers to an agent.

(d)   In performing a power delegated under this section, an agent shall:

(1)   exercise reasonable care to comply with the terms of the delegation and use reasonable care in the performance of the power; and

(2)   if the guardian or conservator has delegated to the agent the power to make a decision on behalf of the individual subject to guardianship or conservatorship, use the same decision-making standard the guardian or conservator would be required to use.

(e)   By accepting a delegation of a power under subsection (a) from a guardian or conservator, an agent submits to the personal jurisdiction of the courts of this state in an action involving the agent's performance as agent.

(f)   A guardian or conservator that delegates and monitors a power in compliance with this section is not liable for the decision, act, or omission of the agent.

Section 125. Temporary Substitute Guardian or Conservator.

(a)   The court may appoint a temporary substitute guardian for an individual subject to guardianship for a period not exceeding six months if:

(1)   a proceeding to remove a guardian for the individual is pending; or

(2)   the court finds a guardian is not effectively performing the guardian's duties and the welfare of the individual requires immediate action.

(b)   The court may appoint a temporary substitute conservator for an individual subject to conservatorship for a period not exceeding six months if:

(1)   a proceeding to remove a conservator for the individual is pending; or

(2)   the court finds that a conservator for the individual is not effectively performing the conservator's duties and the welfare of the individual or the conservatorship estate requires immediate action.

(c)   Except as otherwise ordered by the court, a temporary substitute guardian or temporary substitute conservator appointed under this section has the powers stated in the order of appointment of the guardian or conservator. The authority of the existing guardian or conservator is suspended for as long as the temporary substitute guardian or conservator has authority.

(d)   The court shall give notice of appointment of a temporary substitute guardian or temporary substitute conservator, not later than [five] days after the appointment, to:

(1)   the individual subject to guardianship or conservatorship;

(2)   the affected guardian or conservator; and

(3)   in the case of a minor, each parent of the minor and any person currently having care or custody of the minor.

(e)   The court may remove a temporary substitute guardian or temporary substitute conservator at any time. The temporary substitute guardian or temporary substitute conservator shall make any report the court requires.

Section 126. Registration of Order; Effect.

(a) If a guardian has been appointed in another state for an individual, and a petition for guardianship for the individual is not pending in this state, the guardian appointed in the other state, after giving notice to the appointing court, may register the guardianship order in this state by filing as a foreign judgment, in a court of an appropriate [county] of this state, certified copies of the order and letters of office.

(b) If a conservator has been appointed in another state for an individual, and a petition for conservatorship for the individual is not pending in this state, the conservator appointed for the individual in the other state, after giving notice to the appointing court, may register the conservatorship in this state by filing as a foreign judgment, in a court of a [county] in which property belonging to the individual subject to conservatorship is located, certified copies of the order of conservatorship, letters of office, and any bond or other asset-protection arrangement required by the court.

(c) On registration under this section of a guardianship or conservatorship order from another state, the guardian or conservator may exercise in this state all powers authorized in the order except as prohibited by this [act] and law of this state other than this [act]. If the guardian or conservator is not a resident of this state, the guardian or conservator may maintain an action or proceeding in this state subject to any condition imposed by this state on an action or proceeding by a nonresident party.

(d) The court may grant any relief available under this [act] and law of this state other than this [act] to enforce an order registered under this section.

Section 127. Grievance Against Guardian or Conservator.

(a) An individual who is subject to guardianship or conservatorship, or person interested in the welfare of an individual subject to guardianship or conservatorship, that reasonably believes the guardian or conservator is breaching the guardian's or conservator's fiduciary duty or otherwise acting in a manner inconsistent with this [act] may file a grievance in a record with the court.

(b) Subject to subsection (c), after receiving a grievance under subsection (a), the court:

(1) shall review the grievance and, if necessary to determine the appropriate response, court records related to the guardianship or conservatorship;

(2) shall schedule a hearing if the individual subject to guardianship or conservatorship is an adult and the grievance supports a reasonable belief that:

(A) removal of the guardian and appointment of a successor may be appropriate under Section 318;

(B) termination or modification of the guardianship may be appropriate under Section 319;

(C) removal of the conservator and appointment of a successor may be appropriate under Section 430; or

(D) termination or modification of the conservatorship may be appropriate under Section 431; and

(3) may take any action supported by the evidence, including:

(A) ordering the guardian or conservator to provide the court a report, accounting, inventory, updated plan, or other information;

(B) appointing a guardian ad litem;

(C) appointing an attorney for the individual subject to guardianship or conservatorship; or

(D) holding a hearing.

(c) The court may decline to act under subsection (b) if a similar grievance was filed within the six months preceding the filing of the current grievance and the court followed the procedures of subsection (b) in considering the earlier grievance.

[Section 128. Delegation by Parent.

A parent of a minor, by a power of attorney, may delegate to another person for a period not exceeding [nine months] any of the parent's powers regarding care, custody, or property of the minor, other than power to consent to marriage or adoption.]

[ARTICLE] 2

GUARDIANSHIP OF MINOR

Section 201. Basis for Appointment of Guardian for Minor.

(a) A person becomes a guardian for a minor only on appointment by the court.

(b) The court may appoint a guardian for a minor who does not have a guardian if the court finds the appointment is in the minor's best interest and:

(1) each parent of the minor, after being fully informed of the nature and consequences of guardianship, consents;

(2) all parental rights have been terminated; or

(3) there is clear-and-convincing evidence that no parent of the minor is willing or able to exercise the powers the court is granting the guardian.

Section 202. Petition for Appointment of Guardian for Minor.

(a) A person interested in the welfare of a minor, including the minor, may petition for appointment of a guardian for the minor.

(b) A petition under subsection (a) must state the petitioner's name, principal residence, current street address, if different, relationship to the minor, interest in the appointment, the name and address of any attorney representing the petitioner, and, to the extent known, the following:

(1) the minor's name, age, principal residence, current street address, if different, and, if different, address of the dwelling in which it is proposed the minor will reside if the appointment is made;

(2) the name and current street address of the minor's parents;

(3) the name and address, if known, of each person that had primary care or custody of the minor for at least 60 days during the two years immediately before the filing of the petition or for at least 730 days during the five years immediately before the filing of the petition;

(4) the name and address of any attorney for the minor and any attorney for each parent of the minor;

(5) the reason guardianship is sought and would be in the best interest of the minor;

(6) the name and address of any proposed guardian and the reason the proposed guardian should be selected;

(7) if the minor has property other than personal effects, a general statement of the minor's property with an estimate of its value;

(8) whether the minor needs an interpreter, translator, or other form of support to communicate effectively with the court or understand court proceedings;

(9) whether any parent of the minor needs an interpreter, translator, or other form of support to communicate effectively with the court or understand court proceedings; and

(10) whether any other proceeding concerning the care or custody of the minor is pending in any court in this state or another jurisdiction.

Section 203. Notice of Hearing for Appointment of Guardian for Minor.

(a) If a petition is filed under Section 202, the court shall schedule a hearing and the petitioner shall:

(1)   serve notice of the date, time, and place of the hearing, together with a copy of the petition, personally on each of the following that is not the petitioner:

(A)   the minor, if the minor will be 12 years of age or older at the time of the hearing;

(B)   each parent of the minor or, if there is none, the adult nearest in kinship who can be found with reasonable diligence;

(C)   any adult with whom the minor resides;

(D)   each person that had primary care or custody of the minor for at least 60 days during the two years immediately before the filing of the petition or for at least 730 days during the five years immediately before the filing of the petition; and

(E)   any other person the court determines should receive personal service of notice; and

(2)   give notice under Section 113 of the date, time, and place of the hearing, together with a copy of the petition, to:

(A)   any person nominated as guardian by the minor, if the minor is 12 years of age or older;

(B)   any nominee of a parent;

(C)   each grandparent and adult sibling of the minor;

(D)   any guardian or conservator acting for the minor in any jurisdiction; and

(E)   any other person the court determines.

(b)   Notice required by subsection (a) must include a statement of the right to request appointment of an attorney for the minor or object to appointment of a guardian and a description of the nature, purpose, and consequences of appointment of a guardian.

(c)   The court may not grant a petition for guardianship of a minor if notice substantially complying with subsection (a)(1) is not served on:

(1)   the minor, if the minor is 12 years of age or older; and

(2)   each parent of the minor, unless the court finds by clear-and-convincing evidence that the parent cannot with due diligence be located and served or the parent waived, in a record, the right to notice.

(d)   If a petitioner is unable to serve notice under subsection (a)(1) on a parent of a minor or alleges that the parent waived, in a record, the right to notice under this section, the court shall appoint a [visitor] who shall:

(1)   interview the petitioner and the minor;

(2)   if the petitioner alleges the parent cannot be located, ascertain whether the parent cannot be located with due diligence; and

(3)   investigate any other matter relating to the petition the court directs.

Section 204. Attorney for Minor or Parent.

(a)   The court shall appoint an attorney to represent a minor who is the subject of a proceeding under Section 202 if:

(1)   requested by the minor and the minor is 12 years of age or older;

(2)   recommended by a guardian ad litem; or

(3)   the court determines the minor needs representation.

(b)   An attorney appointed under subsection (a) shall:

(1)   make a reasonable effort to ascertain the minor's wishes;

(2)   advocate for the minor's wishes to the extent reasonably ascertainable; and

(3)   if the minor's wishes are not reasonably ascertainable, advocate for the minor's best interest.

(c)   A minor who is the subject of a proceeding under Section 202 may retain an attorney to represent the minor in the proceeding.

(d)   A parent of a minor who is the subject of a proceeding under Section 202 may retain an attorney to represent the parent in the proceeding.

[(e)   The court shall appoint an attorney to represent a parent of a minor who is the subject of a proceeding under Section 202 if:

(1)   the parent objects to appointment of a guardian for the minor;

(2)   the court determines that counsel is needed to ensure that consent to appointment of a guardian is informed; or

(3)   the court otherwise determines the parent needs representation.]

Section 205. Attendance and Participation at Hearing for Appointment of Guardian for Minor.

(a)   The court shall require a minor who is the subject of a hearing under Section 203 to attend the hearing and allow the minor to participate in the hearing unless the court determines, by clear-and-convincing evidence presented at the hearing or a separate hearing, that:

(1)   the minor consistently and repeatedly refused to attend the hearing after being fully informed of the right to attend and, if the minor is 12 years of age or older, the potential consequences of failing to do so;

(2)   there is no practicable way for the minor to attend the hearing;

(3)   the minor lacks the ability or maturity to participate meaningfully in the hearing; or

(4)   attendance would be harmful to the minor.

(b)   Unless excused by the court for good cause, the person proposed to be appointed as guardian for a minor shall attend a hearing under Section 203.

(c)   Each parent of a minor who is the subject of a hearing under Section 203 has the right to attend the hearing.

(d)   A person may request permission to participate in a hearing under Section 203. The court may grant the request, with or without hearing, on determining that it is in the best interest of the minor who is the subject of the hearing. The court may impose appropriate conditions on the person's participation.

Section 206. Order of Appointment; Priority of Nominee; Limited Guardianship for Minor.

(a)   After a hearing under Section 203, the court may appoint a guardian for a minor, if appointment is proper under Section 201, dismiss the proceeding, or take other appropriate action consistent with this [act] or law of this state other than this [act].

(b)   In appointing a guardian under subsection (a), the following rules apply:

(1)   The court shall appoint a person nominated as guardian by a parent of the minor in a will or other record unless the court finds the appointment is contrary to the best interest of the minor.

(2)   If multiple parents have nominated different persons to serve as guardian, the court shall appoint the nominee whose appointment is in the best interest of the minor, unless the court finds that appointment of none of the nominees is in the best interest of the minor.

(3)   If a guardian is not appointed under paragraph (1) or (2), the court shall appoint the person nominated by the minor if the minor is 12 years of age or older unless the court finds that appointment is contrary to the best interest of the minor. In that case, the court shall appoint as guardian a person whose appointment is in the best interest of the minor.

(c)   In the interest of maintaining or encouraging involvement by a minor's parent in the minor's life, developing self-reliance of the minor, or for other good cause, the court, at the time of appointment of a guardian for the minor or later, on its own or on motion of the minor or other interested person, may create a limited guardianship by limiting the powers otherwise granted by this [article] to the guardian. Following the same procedure, the court may grant additional powers or withdraw powers previously granted.

(d)   The court, as part of an order appointing a guardian for a minor, shall state rights retained by any parent of the minor, which may include contact or visitation with the minor, decision making regarding the minor's health care, education, or other matter, or access to a record regarding the minor.

(e)   An order granting a guardianship for a minor must state that each parent of the minor is entitled to notice that:

(1)   the guardian has delegated custody of the minor subject to guardianship;

(2)   the court has modified or limited the powers of the guardian; or

(3)   the court has removed the guardian.

(f)   An order granting a guardianship for a minor must identify any person in addition to a parent of the minor which is entitled to notice of the events listed in subsection (e).

Section 207. Standby Guardian for Minor.

(a)   A standby guardian appointed under this section may act as guardian, with all duties and powers of a guardian under Sections 209 and 210, when no parent of the minor is willing or able to exercise the duties and powers granted to the guardian.

(b)   A parent of a minor, in a signed record, may nominate a person to be appointed by the court as standby guardian for the minor. The parent, in a signed record, may state desired limitations on the powers to be granted the standby guardian. The parent, in a signed record, may revoke or amend the nomination at any time before the court appoints a standby guardian.

(c)   The court may appoint a standby guardian for a minor on:

(1)   petition by a parent of the minor or a person nominated under subsection (b); and

(2)   finding that no parent of the minor likely will be able or willing to care for or make decisions with respect to the minor not later than [two years] after the appointment.

(d)   A petition under subsection (c)(1) must include the same information required under Section 202 for the appointment of a guardian for a minor.

(e)   On filing a petition under subsection (c)(1), the petitioner shall:

(1)   serve a copy of the petition personally on:

(A)   the minor, if the minor is 12 years of age or older, and the minor's attorney, if any;

(B)   each parent of the minor;

(C)   the person nominated as standby guardian; and

(D)   any other person the court determines; and

(2)   include with the copy of the petition served under paragraph (1) a statement of the right to request appointment of an attorney for the minor or to object to appointment of the standby guardian, and a description of the nature, purpose, and consequences of appointment of a standby guardian.

(f)   A person entitled to notice under subsection (e), not later than 60 days after service of the petition and statement, may object to appointment of the standby guardian by filing an objection with the court and giving notice of the objection to each other person entitled to notice under subsection (e).

(g)   If an objection is filed under subsection (f), the court shall hold a hearing to determine whether a standby guardian should be appointed and, if so, the person that should be appointed. If no objection is filed, the court may make the appointment.

(h)   The court may not grant a petition for a standby guardian of the minor if notice substantially complying with subsection (e) is not served on:

(1)   the minor, if the minor is 12 years of age or older; and

(2)   each parent of the minor, unless the court finds by clear-and-convincing evidence that the parent, in a record, waived the right to notice or cannot be located and served with due diligence.

(i)   If a petitioner is unable to serve notice under subsection (e) on a parent of the minor or alleges that a parent of the minor waived the right to notice under this section, the court shall appoint a [visitor] who shall:

(1)   interview the petitioner and the minor;

(2)   if the petitioner alleges the parent cannot be located and served, ascertain whether the parent cannot be located with due diligence; and

(3)   investigate any other matter relating to the petition the court directs.

(j)   If the court finds under subsection (c) that a standby guardian should be appointed, the following rules apply:

(1)   The court shall appoint the person nominated under subsection (b) unless the court finds the appointment is contrary to the best interest of the minor.

(2)   If the parents have nominated different persons to serve as standby guardian, the court shall appoint the nominee whose appointment is in the best interest of the minor, unless the court finds that appointment of none of the nominees is in the best interest of the minor.

(k)   An order appointing a standby guardian under this section must state that each parent of the minor is entitled to notice, and identify any other person entitled to notice, if:

(1)   the standby guardian assumes the duties and powers of the guardian;

(2)   the guardian delegates custody of the minor;

(3)   the court modifies or limits the powers of the guardian; or

(4)   the court removes the guardian.

(l)   Before assuming the duties and powers of a guardian, a standby guardian must file with the court an acceptance of appointment as guardian and give notice of the acceptance to:

(1)   each parent of the minor, unless the parent, in a record, waived the right to notice or cannot be located and served with due diligence;

(2)   the minor, if the minor is 12 years of age or older; and

(3)   any person, other than the parent, having care or custody of the minor.

(m) A person that receives notice under subsection (*l*) or any other person interested in the welfare of the minor may file with the court an objection to the standby guardian's assumption of duties and powers of a guardian. The court shall hold a hearing if the objection supports a reasonable belief that the conditions for assumption of duties and powers have not been satisfied.

Section 208. Emergency Guardian for Minor.

(a) On its own, or on petition by a person interested in a minor's welfare, the court may appoint an emergency guardian for the minor if the court finds:

(1) appointment of an emergency guardian is likely to prevent substantial harm to the minor's health, safety, or welfare; and

(2) no other person appears to have authority and willingness to act in the circumstances.

(b) The duration of authority of an emergency guardian for a minor may not exceed [60] days and the emergency guardian may exercise only the powers specified in the order of appointment. The emergency guardian's authority may be extended once for not more than [60] days if the court finds that the conditions for appointment of an emergency guardian in subsection (a) continue.

(c) Except as otherwise provided in subsection (d), reasonable notice of the date, time, and place of a hearing on a petition for appointment of an emergency guardian for a minor must be given to:

(1) the minor, if the minor is 12 years of age or older;

(2) any attorney appointed under Section 204;

(3) each parent of the minor;

(4) any person, other than a parent, having care or custody of the minor; and

(5) any other person the court determines.

(d) The court may appoint an emergency guardian for a minor without notice under subsection (c) and a hearing only if the court finds from an affidavit or testimony that the minor's health, safety, or welfare will be substantially harmed before a hearing with notice on the appointment can be held. If the court appoints an emergency guardian without notice to an unrepresented minor or the attorney for a represented minor, notice of the appointment must be given not later than 48 hours after the appointment to the individuals listed in subsection (c). Not later than [five] days after the appointment, the court shall hold a hearing on the appropriateness of the appointment.

(e) Appointment of an emergency guardian under this section, with or without notice, is not a determination that a basis exists for appointment of a guardian under Section 201.

(f) The court may remove an emergency guardian appointed under this section at any time. The emergency guardian shall make any report the court requires.

Section 209. Duties of Guardian for Minor.

(a) A guardian for a minor is a fiduciary. Except as otherwise limited by the court, a guardian for a minor has the duties and responsibilities of a parent regarding the minor's support, care, education, health, safety, and welfare. A guardian shall act in the minor's best interest and exercise reasonable care, diligence, and prudence.

(b) A guardian for a minor shall:

(1) be personally acquainted with the minor and maintain sufficient contact with the minor to know the minor's abilities, limitations, needs, opportunities, and physical and mental health;

(2) take reasonable care of the minor's personal effects and bring a proceeding for a conservatorship or protective arrangement instead of conservatorship if necessary to protect other property of the minor;

(3)   expend funds of the minor which have been received by the guardian for the minor's current needs for support, care, education, health, safety, and welfare;

(4)   conserve any funds of the minor not expended under paragraph (3) for the minor's future needs, but if a conservator is appointed for the minor, pay the funds at least quarterly to the conservator to be conserved for the minor's future needs;

(5)   report the condition of the minor and account for funds and other property of the minor in the guardian's possession or subject to the guardian's control, as required by court rule or ordered by the court on application of a person interested in the minor's welfare;

(6)   inform the court of any change in the minor's dwelling or address; and

(7)   in determining what is in the minor's best interest, take into account the minor's preferences to the extent actually known or reasonably ascertainable by the guardian.

Section 210. Powers of Guardian for Minor.

(a)   Except as otherwise limited by court order, a guardian of a minor has the powers a parent otherwise would have regarding the minor's support, care, education, health, safety, and welfare.

(b)   Except as otherwise limited by court order, a guardian for a minor may:

(1)   apply for and receive funds and benefits otherwise payable for the support of the minor to the minor's parent, guardian, or custodian under a statutory system of benefits or insurance or any private contract, devise, trust, conservatorship, or custodianship;

(2)   unless inconsistent with a court order entitled to recognition in this state, take custody of the minor and establish the minor's place of dwelling and, on authorization of the court, establish or move the minor's dwelling outside this state;

(3)   if the minor is not subject to conservatorship, commence a proceeding, including an administrative proceeding, or take other appropriate action to compel a person to support the minor or make a payment for the benefit of the minor;

(4)   consent to health or other care, treatment, or service for the minor; or

(5)   to the extent reasonable, delegate to the minor responsibility for a decision affecting the minor's well-being.

(c)   The court may authorize a guardian for a minor to consent to the adoption of the minor if the minor does not have a parent.

(d)   A guardian for a minor may consent to the marriage of the minor [if authorized by the court].

Section 211. Removal of Guardian for Minor; Termination of Guardianship; Appointment of Successor.

(a)   Guardianship under this [act] for a minor terminates:

(1)   on the minor's death, adoption, emancipation, or attainment of majority; or

(2)   when the court finds that the standard in Section 201 for appointment of a guardian is not satisfied, unless the court finds that:

(A)   termination of the guardianship would be harmful to the minor; and

(B)   the minor's interest in the continuation of the guardianship outweighs the interest of any parent of the minor in restoration of the parent's right to make decisions for the minor.

(b)   A minor subject to guardianship or a person interested in the welfare of the minor may petition the court to terminate the guardianship, modify the guardianship, remove the guardian and appoint a successor guardian, or remove a standby guardian and appoint a different standby guardian.

(c)   A petitioner under subsection (b) shall give notice of the hearing on the petition to the minor, if the minor is 12 years of age or older and is not the petitioner, the guardian, each parent of the minor, and any other person the court determines.

(d)   The court shall follow the priorities in Section 206(b) when selecting a successor guardian for a minor.

(e)   Not later than 30 days after appointment of a successor guardian for a minor, the court shall give notice of the appointment to the minor subject to guardianship, if the minor is 12 years of age or older, each parent of the minor, and any other person the court determines.

(f)   When terminating a guardianship for a minor under this section, the court may issue an order providing for transitional arrangements that will assist the minor with a transition of custody and is in the best interest of the minor.

(g)   A guardian for a minor that is removed shall cooperate with a successor guardian to facilitate transition of the guardian's responsibilities and protect the best interest of the minor.

[ARTICLE] 3

GUARDIANSHIP OF ADULT

Section 301. Basis for Appointment of Guardian for Adult.

(a)   On petition and after notice and hearing, the court may:

(1)   appoint a guardian for an adult if the court finds by clear-and-convincing evidence that:

(A)   the respondent lacks the ability to meet essential requirements for physical health, safety, or self-care because the respondent is unable to receive and evaluate information or make or communicate decisions, even with appropriate supportive services, technological assistance, or supported decision making; and

(B)   the respondent's identified needs cannot be met by a protective arrangement instead of guardianship or other less restrictive alternative; or

(2)   with appropriate findings, treat the petition as one for a conservatorship under [Article] 4 or protective arrangement under [Article] 5, issue any appropriate order, or dismiss the proceeding.

(b)   The court shall grant a guardian appointed under subsection (a) only those powers necessitated by the demonstrated needs and limitations of the respondent and issue orders that will encourage development of the respondent's maximum self-determination and independence. The court may not establish a full guardianship if a limited guardianship, protective arrangement instead of guardianship, or other less restrictive alternatives would meet the needs of the respondent.

Section 302. Petition for Appointment of Guardian for Adult.

(a)   A person interested in an adult's welfare, including the adult for whom the order is sought, may petition for appointment of a guardian for the adult.

(b)   A petition under subsection (a) must state the petitioner's name, principal residence, current street address, if different, relationship to the respondent, interest in the appointment, the name and address of any attorney representing the petitioner, and, to the extent known, the following:

(1)   the respondent's name, age, principal residence, current street address, if different, and, if different, address of the dwelling in which it is proposed the respondent will reside if the petition is granted;

(2)   the name and address of the respondent's:

(A)   spouse [or domestic partner] or, if the respondent has none, an adult with whom the respondent has shared household responsibilities for more than six months in the 12-month period immediately before the filing of the petition;

(B)   adult children or, if none, each parent and adult sibling of the respondent, or, if none, at least one adult nearest in kinship to the respondent who can be found with reasonable diligence; and

(C)   adult stepchildren whom the respondent actively parented during the stepchildren's minor years and with whom the respondent had an ongoing relationship in the two-year period immediately before the filing of the petition;

(3)   the name and current address of each of the following, if applicable:

(A)   a person responsible for care of the respondent;

(B)   any attorney currently representing the respondent;

(C)   any representative payee appointed by the Social Security Administration for the respondent;

(D)   a guardian or conservator acting for the respondent in this state or in another jurisdiction;

(E)   a trustee or custodian of a trust or custodianship of which the respondent is a beneficiary;

(F)   any fiduciary for the respondent appointed by the Department of Veterans Affairs;

(G)   an agent designated under a [power of attorney for health care] in which the respondent is identified as the principal;

(H)   an agent designated under a power of attorney for finances in which the respondent is identified as the principal;

(I)   a person nominated as guardian by the respondent;

(J)   a person nominated as guardian by the respondent's parent or spouse [or domestic partner] in a will or other signed record;

(K)   a proposed guardian and the reason the proposed guardian should be selected; and

(L)   a person known to have routinely assisted the respondent with decision making during the six months immediately before the filing of the petition;

(4)   the reason a guardianship is necessary, including a brief description of:

(A)   the nature and extent of the respondent's alleged need;

(B)   any protective arrangement instead of guardianship or other less restrictive alternatives for meeting the respondent's alleged need which have been considered or implemented;

(C)   if no protective arrangement instead of guardianship or other less restrictive alternatives have been considered or implemented, the reason they have not been considered or implemented; and

(D)   the reason a protective arrangement instead of guardianship or other less restrictive alternative is insufficient to meet the respondent's alleged need;

(5)   whether the petitioner seeks a limited guardianship or full guardianship;

(6)   if the petitioner seeks a full guardianship, the reason a limited guardianship or protective arrangement instead of guardianship is not appropriate;

(7)   if a limited guardianship is requested, the powers to be granted to the guardian;

(8)   the name and current address, if known, of any person with whom the petitioner seeks to limit the respondent's contact;

(9)   if the respondent has property other than personal effects, a general statement of the respondent's property, with an estimate of its value, including any insurance or pension, and the source and amount of other anticipated income or receipts; and

(10)   whether the respondent needs an interpreter, translator, or other form of support to communicate effectively with the court or understand court proceedings.

Section 303. Notice of Hearing for Appointment of Guardian for Adult.

(a)   On filing of a petition under Section 302 for appointment of a guardian for an adult, the court shall set a date, time, and place for hearing the petition.

(b)   A copy of a petition under Section 302 and notice of a hearing on the petition must be served personally on the respondent. The notice must inform the respondent of the respondent's rights at the hearing, including the right to an attorney and to attend the hearing. The notice must include a description of the nature, purpose, and consequences of granting the petition. The court may not grant the petition if notice substantially complying with this subsection is not served on the respondent.

(c)   In a proceeding on a petition under Section 302, the notice required under subsection (b) must be given to the persons required to be listed in the petition under Section 302(b)(1) through (3) and any other person interested in the respondent's welfare the court determines. Failure to give notice under this subsection does not preclude the court from appointing a guardian.

(d)   After the appointment of a guardian, notice of a hearing on a petition for an order under this [article], together with a copy of the petition, must be given to:

(1)   the adult subject to guardianship;

(2)   the guardian; and

(3)   any other person the court determines.

Section 304. Appointment and Role of [Visitor].

(a)   On receipt of a petition under Section 302 for appointment of a guardian for an adult, the court shall appoint a [visitor]. The [visitor] must be an individual with training or experience in the type of abilities, limitations, and needs alleged in the petition.

(b)   A [visitor] appointed under subsection (a) shall interview the respondent in person and, in a manner the respondent is best able to understand:

(1)   explain to the respondent the substance of the petition, the nature, purpose, and effect of the proceeding, the respondent's rights at the hearing on the petition, and the general powers and duties of a guardian;

(2)   determine the respondent's views about the appointment sought by the petitioner, including views about a proposed guardian, the guardian's proposed powers and duties, and the scope and duration of the proposed guardianship;

(3)   inform the respondent of the respondent's right to employ and consult with an attorney at the respondent's expense and the right to request a court-appointed attorney; and

(4)   inform the respondent that all costs and expenses of the proceeding, including respondent's attorney's fees, may be paid from the respondent's assets.

(c)   The [visitor] appointed under subsection (a) shall:

(1)   interview the petitioner and proposed guardian, if any;

(2)   visit the respondent's present dwelling and any dwelling in which it is reasonably believed the respondent will live if the appointment is made;

(3)   obtain information from any physician or other person known to have treated, advised, or assessed the respondent's relevant physical or mental condition; and

(4)   investigate the allegations in the petition and any other matter relating to the petition the court directs.

(d)   A [visitor] appointed under subsection (a) promptly shall file a report in a record with the court, which must include:

(1)   a recommendation whether an attorney should be appointed to represent the respondent;

(2)   a summary of self-care and independent-living tasks the respondent can manage without assistance or with existing supports, could manage with the assistance of appropriate supportive services, technological assistance, or supported decision making, and cannot manage;

(3) a recommendation regarding the appropriateness of guardianship, including whether a protective arrangement instead of guardianship or other less restrictive alternative for meeting the respondent's needs is available and:

(A) if a guardianship is recommended, whether it should be full or limited; and

(B) if a limited guardianship is recommended, the powers to be granted to the guardian;

(4) a statement of the qualifications of the proposed guardian and whether the respondent approves or disapproves of the proposed guardian;

(5) a statement whether the proposed dwelling meets the respondent's needs and whether the respondent has expressed a preference as to residence;

(6) a recommendation whether a professional evaluation under Section 306 is necessary;

(7) a statement whether the respondent is able to attend a hearing at the location court proceedings typically are held;

(8) a statement whether the respondent is able to participate in a hearing and which identifies any technology or other form of support that would enhance the respondent's ability to participate; and

(9) any other matter the court directs.

Section 305. Appointment and Role of Attorney for Adult.

Alternative A

(a) The court shall appoint an attorney to represent the respondent in a proceeding for appointment of a guardian for an adult if:

(1) the respondent requests an appointment;

(2) the [visitor] recommends an appointment; or

(3) the court determines the respondent needs representation.

Alternative B

(a) Unless the respondent in a proceeding for appointment of a guardian for an adult is represented by an attorney, the court shall appoint an attorney to represent the respondent, regardless of the respondent's ability to pay.

End of Alternatives

(b) An attorney representing the respondent in a proceeding for appointment of a guardian for an adult shall:

(1) make reasonable efforts to ascertain the respondent's wishes;

(2) advocate for the respondent's wishes to the extent reasonably ascertainable; and

(3) if the respondent's wishes are not reasonably ascertainable, advocate for the result that is the least restrictive in type, duration, and scope, consistent with the respondent's interests.

Section 306. Professional Evaluation.

(a) At or before a hearing on a petition for a guardianship for an adult, the court shall order a professional evaluation of the respondent:

(1) if the respondent requests the evaluation; or

(2) in other cases, unless the court finds that it has sufficient information to determine the respondent's needs and abilities without the evaluation.

(b)   If the court orders an evaluation under subsection (a), the respondent must be examined by a licensed physician, psychologist, social worker, or other individual appointed by the court who is qualified to evaluate the respondent's alleged cognitive and functional abilities and limitations and will not be advantaged or disadvantaged by a decision to grant the petition or otherwise have a conflict of interest. The individual conducting the evaluation promptly shall file report in a record with the court. Unless otherwise directed by the court, the report must contain:

(1)   a description of the nature, type, and extent of the respondent's cognitive and functional abilities and limitations;

(2)   an evaluation of the respondent's mental and physical condition and, if appropriate, educational potential, adaptive behavior, and social skills;

(3)   a prognosis for improvement and recommendation for the appropriate treatment, support, or habilitation plan; and

(4)   the date of the examination on which the report is based.

(c)   The respondent may decline to participate in an evaluation ordered under subsection (a).

Section 307. Attendance and Rights at Hearing.

(a)   Except as otherwise provided in subsection (b), a hearing under Section 303 may not proceed unless the respondent attends the hearing. If it is not reasonably feasible for the respondent to attend a hearing at the location court proceedings typically are held, the court shall make reasonable efforts to hold the hearing at an alternative location convenient to the respondent or allow the respondent to attend the hearing using real-time audio-visual technology.

(b)   A hearing under Section 303 may proceed without the respondent in attendance if the court finds by clear-and-convincing evidence that:

(1)   the respondent consistently and repeatedly has refused to attend the hearing after having been fully informed of the right to attend and the potential consequences of failing to do so; or

(2)   there is no practicable way for the respondent to attend and participate in the hearing even with appropriate supportive services and technological assistance.

(c)   The respondent may be assisted in a hearing under Section 303 by a person or persons of the respondent's choosing, assistive technology, or an interpreter or translator, or a combination of these supports. If assistance would facilitate the respondent's participation in the hearing, but is not otherwise available to the respondent, the court shall make reasonable efforts to provide it.

(d)   The respondent has a right to choose an attorney to represent the respondent at a hearing under Section 303.

(e)   At a hearing held under Section 303, the respondent may:

(1)   present evidence and subpoena witnesses and documents;

(2)   examine witnesses, including any court-appointed evaluator and the [visitor]; and

(3)   otherwise participate in the hearing.

(f)   Unless excused by the court for good cause, a proposed guardian shall attend a hearing under Section 303.

(g)   A hearing under Section 303 must be closed on request of the respondent and a showing of good cause.

(h)   Any person may request to participate in a hearing under Section 303. The court may grant the request, with or without a hearing, on determining that the best interest of the respondent will be served. The court may impose appropriate conditions on the person's participation.

Section 308. Confidentiality of Records.

(a)   The existence of a proceeding for or the existence of a guardianship for an adult is a matter of public record unless the court seals the record after:

(1)   the respondent or individual subject to guardianship requests the record be sealed; and

(2)   either:

(A)   the petition for guardianship is dismissed; or

(B)   the guardianship is terminated.

(b)   An adult subject to a proceeding for a guardianship, whether or not a guardian is appointed, an attorney designated by the adult, and a person entitled to notice under Section 310(e) or a subsequent order are entitled to access court records of the proceeding and resulting guardianship, including the guardian's plan under Section 316 and report under Section 317. A person not otherwise entitled to access court records under this subsection for good cause may petition the court for access to court records of the guardianship, including the guardian's report and plan. The court shall grant access if access is in the best interest of the respondent or adult subject to guardianship or furthers the public interest and does not endanger the welfare or financial interests of the adult.

[(c)   A report under Section 304 of a [visitor] or a professional evaluation under Section 306 is confidential and must be sealed on filing, but is available to:

(1)   the court;

(2)   the individual who is the subject of the report or evaluation, without limitation as to use;

(3)   the petitioner, [visitor], and petitioner's and respondent's attorneys, for purposes of the proceeding;

(4)   unless the court orders otherwise, an agent appointed under a [power of attorney for health care] or power of attorney for finances in which the respondent is the principal; and

(5)   any other person if it is in the public interest or for a purpose the court orders for good cause.]

Section 309. Who May Be Guardian for Adult; Order of Priority.

(a)   Except as otherwise provided in subsection (c), the court in appointing a guardian for an adult shall consider persons qualified to be guardian in the following order of priority:

(1)   a guardian, other than a temporary or emergency guardian, currently acting for the respondent in another jurisdiction;

(2)   a person nominated as guardian by the respondent, including the respondent's most recent nomination made in a power of attorney;

(3)   an agent appointed by the respondent under [a power of attorney for health care];

(4)   a spouse [or domestic partner] of the respondent; and

(5)   a family member or other individual who has shown special care and concern for the respondent.

(b)   If two or more persons have equal priority under subsection (a), the court shall select as guardian the person the court considers best qualified. In determining the best qualified person, the court shall consider the person's relationship with the respondent, the person's skills, the expressed wishes of the respondent, the extent to which the person and the respondent have similar values and preferences, and the likelihood the person will be able to perform the duties of a guardian successfully.

(c)   The court, acting in the best interest of the respondent, may decline to appoint as guardian a person having priority under subsection (a) and appoint a person having a lower priority or no priority.

(d)   A person that provides paid services to the respondent, or an individual who is employed by a person that provides paid services to the respondent or is the spouse, [domestic partner,] parent, or child of an individual who provides or is employed to provide paid services to the respondent, may not be appointed as guardian unless:

(1)   the individual is related to the respondent by blood, marriage, or adoption; or

(2)   the court finds by clear-and-convincing evidence that the person is the best qualified person available for appointment and the appointment is in the best interest of the respondent.

(e)   An owner, operator, or employee of [a long-term-care institution] at which the respondent is receiving care may not be appointed as guardian unless the owner, operator, or employee is related to the respondent by blood, marriage, or adoption.

Section 310. Order of Appointment for Guardian.

(a)   A court order appointing a guardian for an adult must:

(1)   include a specific finding that clear-and-convincing evidence established that the identified needs of the respondent cannot be met by a protective arrangement instead of guardianship or other less restrictive alternative, including use of appropriate supportive services, technological assistance, or supported decision making;

(2)   include a specific finding that clear-and-convincing evidence established the respondent was given proper notice of the hearing on the petition;

(3)   state whether the adult subject to guardianship retains the right to vote and, if the adult does not retain the right to vote, include findings that support removing that right [which must include a finding that the adult cannot communicate, with or without support, a specific desire to participate in the voting process]; and

(4)   state whether the adult subject to guardianship retains the right to marry and, if the adult does not retain the right to marry, include findings that support removing that right.

(b)   An adult subject to guardianship retains the right to vote unless the order under subsection (a) includes the statement required by subsection (a)(3). An adult subject to guardianship retains the right to marry unless the order under subsection (a) includes the findings required by subsection (a)(4).

(c)   A court order establishing a full guardianship for an adult must state the basis for granting a full guardianship and include specific findings that support the conclusion that a limited guardianship would not meet the functional needs of the adult subject to guardianship.

(d)   A court order establishing a limited guardianship for an adult must state the specific powers granted to the guardian.

(e)   The court, as part of an order establishing a guardianship for an adult, shall identify any person that subsequently is entitled to:

(1)   notice of the rights of the adult under Section 311(b);

(2)   notice of a change in the primary dwelling of the adult;

(3)   notice that the guardian has delegated:

(A)   the power to manage the care of the adult;

(B)   the power to make decisions about where the adult lives;

(C)   the power to make major medical decisions on behalf of the adult;

(D)   a power that requires court approval under Section 315; or

(E)   substantially all powers of the guardian;

(4)   notice that the guardian will be unavailable to visit the adult for more than two months or unavailable to perform the guardian's duties for more than one month;

(5)   a copy of the guardian's plan under Section 316 and the guardian's report under Section 317;

(6)   access to court records relating to the guardianship;

(7)   notice of the death or significant change in the condition of the adult;

(8)   notice that the court has limited or modified the powers of the guardian; and

(9)   notice of the removal of the guardian.

(f)   A spouse[, domestic partner,] and adult children of an adult subject to guardianship are entitled to notice under subsection (e) unless the court determines notice would be contrary to the preferences or prior directions of the adult subject to guardianship or not in the best interest of the adult.

Section 311. Notice of Appointment; Rights.

(a)   A guardian appointed under Section 309 shall give the adult subject to guardianship and all other persons given notice under Section 303 a copy of the order of appointment, together with notice of the right to request termination or modification. The order and notice must be given not later than 14 days after the appointment.

(b)   Not later than 30 days after appointment of a guardian under Section 309, the court shall give to the adult subject to guardianship, the guardian, and any other person entitled to notice under Section 310(e) or a subsequent order a statement of the rights of the adult subject to guardianship and procedures to seek relief if the adult is denied those rights. The statement must be in at least 16-point font, in plain language, and, to the extent feasible, in a language in which the adult subject to guardianship is proficient. The statement must notify the adult subject to guardianship of the right to:

(1)   seek termination or modification of the guardianship, or removal of the guardian, and choose an attorney to represent the adult in these matters;

(2)   be involved in decisions affecting the adult, including decisions about the adult's care, dwelling, activities, or social interactions, to the extent reasonably feasible;

(3)   be involved in health-care decision making to the extent reasonably feasible and supported in understanding the risks and benefits of health-care options to the extent reasonably feasible;

(4)   be notified at least 14 days before a change in the adult's primary dwelling or permanent move to a nursing home, mental-health facility, or other facility that places restrictions on the individual's ability to leave or have visitors unless the change or move is proposed in the guardian's plan under Section 316 or authorized by the court by specific order;

(5)   object to a change or move described in paragraph (4) and the process for objecting;

(6)   communicate, visit, or interact with others, including receiving visitors, and making or receiving telephone calls, personal mail, or electronic communications, including through social media, unless:

(A)   the guardian has been authorized by the court by specific order to restrict communications, visits, or interactions;

(B)   a protective order or protective arrangement instead of guardianship is in effect that limits contact between the adult and a person; or

(C) the guardian has good cause to believe restriction is necessary because interaction with a specified person poses a risk of significant physical, psychological, or financial harm to the adult, and the restriction is:

(i) for a period of not more than seven business days if the person has a family or pre-existing social relationship with the adult; or

(ii) for a period of not more than 60 days if the person does not have a family or pre-existing social relationship with the adult;

(7) receive a copy of the guardian's plan under Section 316 and the guardian's report under Section 317; and

(8) object to the guardian's plan or report.

Section 312. Emergency Guardian for Adult.

(a) On its own after a petition has been filed under Section 302, or on petition by a person interested in an adult's welfare, the court may appoint an emergency guardian for the adult if the court finds:

(1) appointment of an emergency guardian is likely to prevent substantial harm to the adult's physical health, safety, or welfare;

(2) no other person appears to have authority and willingness to act in the circumstances; and

(3) there is reason to believe that a basis for appointment of a guardian under Section 301 exists.

(b) The duration of authority of an emergency guardian for an adult may not exceed [60] days, and the emergency guardian may exercise only the powers specified in the order of appointment. The emergency guardian's authority may be extended once for not more than [60 days] if the court finds that the conditions for appointment of an emergency guardian in subsection (a) continue.

(c) Immediately on filing of a petition for appointment of an emergency guardian for an adult, the court shall appoint an attorney to represent the respondent in the proceeding. Except as otherwise provided in subsection (d), reasonable notice of the date, time, and place of a hearing on the petition must be given to the respondent, the respondent's attorney, and any other person the court determines.

(d) The court may appoint an emergency guardian for an adult without notice to the adult and any attorney for the adult only if the court finds from an affidavit or testimony that the respondent's physical health, safety, or welfare will be substantially harmed before a hearing with notice on the appointment can be held. If the court appoints an emergency guardian without giving notice under subsection (c), the court must:

(1) give notice of the appointment not later than 48 hours after the appointment to:

(A) the respondent;

(B) the respondent's attorney; and

(C) any other person the court determines; and

(2) hold a hearing on the appropriateness of the appointment not later than [five] days after the appointment.

(e) Appointment of an emergency guardian under this section is not a determination that a basis exists for appointment of a guardian under Section 301.

(f) The court may remove an emergency guardian appointed under this section at any time. The emergency guardian shall make any report the court requires.

Section 313. Duties of Guardian for Adult.

(a)   A guardian for an adult is a fiduciary. Except as otherwise limited by the court, a guardian for an adult shall make decisions regarding the support, care, education, health, and welfare of the adult subject to guardianship to the extent necessitated by the adult's limitations.

(b)   A guardian for an adult shall promote the self-determination of the adult and, to the extent reasonably feasible, encourage the adult to participate in decisions, act on the adult's own behalf, and develop or regain the capacity to manage the adult's personal affairs. In furtherance of this duty, the guardian shall:

(1)   become or remain personally acquainted with the adult and maintain sufficient contact with the adult, including through regular visitation, to know the adult's abilities, limitations, needs, opportunities, and physical and mental health;

(2)   to the extent reasonably feasible, identify the values and preferences of the adult and involve the adult in decisions affecting the adult, including decisions about the adult's care, dwelling, activities, or social interactions; and

(3)   make reasonable efforts to identify and facilitate supportive relationships and services for the adult.

(c)   A guardian for an adult at all times shall exercise reasonable care, diligence, and prudence when acting on behalf of or making decisions for the adult. In furtherance of this duty, the guardian shall:

(1)   take reasonable care of the personal effects, pets, and service or support animals of the adult and bring a proceeding for a conservatorship or protective arrangement instead of conservatorship if necessary to protect the adult's property;

(2)   expend funds and other property of the adult received by the guardian for the adult's current needs for support, care, education, health, and welfare;

(3)   conserve any funds and other property of the adult not expended under paragraph (2) for the adult's future needs, but if a conservator has been appointed for the adult, pay the funds and other property at least quarterly to the conservator to be conserved for the adult's future needs; and

(4)   monitor the quality of services, including long-term care services, provided to the adult.

(d)   In making a decision for an adult subject to guardianship, the guardian shall make the decision the guardian reasonably believes the adult would make if the adult were able unless doing so would unreasonably harm or endanger the welfare or personal or financial interests of the adult. To determine the decision the adult subject to guardianship would make if able, the guardian shall consider the adult's previous or current directions, preferences, opinions, values, and actions, to the extent actually known or reasonably ascertainable by the guardian.

(e)   If a guardian for an adult cannot make a decision under subsection (d) because the guardian does not know and cannot reasonably determine the decision the adult probably would make if able, or the guardian reasonably believes the decision the adult would make would unreasonably harm or endanger the welfare or personal or financial interests of the adult, the guardian shall act in accordance with the best interest of the adult. In determining the best interest of the adult, the guardian shall consider:

(1)   information received from professionals and persons that demonstrate sufficient interest in the welfare of the adult;

(2)   other information the guardian believes the adult would have considered if the adult were able to act; and

(3)   other factors a reasonable person in the circumstances of the adult would consider, including consequences for others.

(f)   A guardian for an adult immediately shall notify the court if the condition of the adult has changed so that the adult is capable of exercising rights previously removed.

Section 314. Powers of Guardian for Adult.

(a)   Except as limited by court order, a guardian for an adult may:

(1)   apply for and receive funds and benefits for the support of the adult, unless a conservator is appointed for the adult and the application or receipt is within the powers of the conservator;

(2)   unless inconsistent with a court order, establish the adult's place of dwelling;

(3)   consent to health or other care, treatment, or service for the adult;

(4)   if a conservator for the adult has not been appointed, commence a proceeding, including an administrative proceeding, or take other appropriate action to compel another person to support the adult or pay funds for the adult's benefit;

(5)   to the extent reasonable, delegate to the adult responsibility for a decision affecting the adult's well-being; and

(6)   receive personally identifiable health-care information regarding the adult.

(b)   The court by specific order may authorize a guardian for an adult to consent to the adoption of the adult.

[(c)   The court by specific order may authorize a guardian for an adult to:

(1)   consent or withhold consent to the marriage of the adult if the adult's right to marry has been removed under Section 310;

(2)   petition for divorce, dissolution, or annulment of marriage of the adult or a declaration of invalidity of the adult's marriage; or

(3)   support or oppose a petition for divorce, dissolution, or annulment of marriage of the adult or a declaration of invalidity of the adult's marriage.]

(d)   In determining whether to authorize a power under subsection (b) [or (c)], the court shall consider whether the underlying act would be in accordance with the adult's preferences, values, and prior directions and whether the underlying act would be in the adult's best interest.

(e)   In exercising a guardian's power under subsection (a)(2) to establish the adult's place of dwelling, the guardian shall:

(1)   select a residential setting the guardian believes the adult would select if the adult were able, in accordance with the decision-making standard in Section 313(d) and (e). If the guardian does not know and cannot reasonably determine what setting the adult subject to guardianship probably would choose if able, or the guardian reasonably believes the decision the adult would make would unreasonably harm or endanger the welfare or personal or financial interests of the adult, the guardian shall choose in accordance with Section 313(e) a residential setting that is consistent with the adult's best interest;

(2)   in selecting among residential settings, give priority to a residential setting in a location that will allow the adult to interact with persons important to the adult and meet the adult's needs in the least restrictive manner reasonably feasible unless to do so would be inconsistent with the decision-making standard in Section 313(d) and (e);

(3)   not later than 30 days after a change in the dwelling of the adult:

(A) give notice of the change to the court, the adult, and any person identified as entitled to the notice in the court order appointing the guardian or a subsequent order; and

(B) include in the notice the address and nature of the new dwelling and state whether the adult received advance notice of the change and whether the adult objected to the change;

(4) establish or move the permanent place of dwelling of the adult to a nursing home, mental-health facility, or other facility that places restrictions on the adult's ability to leave or have visitors only if:

(A) the establishment or move is in the guardian's plan under Section 316;

(B) the court authorizes the establishment or move; or

(C) the guardian gives notice of the establishment or move at least 14 days before the establishment or move to the adult and all persons entitled to notice under Section 310(e)(2) or a subsequent order, and no objection is filed;

(5) establish or move the place of dwelling of the adult outside this state only if consistent with the guardian's plan and authorized by the court by specific order; and

(6) take action that would result in the sale of or surrender of the lease to the primary dwelling of the adult only if:

(A) the action is specifically included in the guardian's plan under Section 316;

(B) the court authorizes the action by specific order; or

(C) notice of the action was given at least 14 days before the action to the adult and all persons entitled to the notice under Section 310(e)(2) or a subsequent order and no objection has been filed.

(f) In exercising a guardian's power under subsection (a)(3) to make health-care decisions, the guardian shall:

(1) involve the adult in decision making to the extent reasonably feasible, including, when practicable, by encouraging and supporting the adult in understanding the risks and benefits of health-care options;

(2) defer to a decision by an agent under a [power of attorney for health care] executed by the adult and cooperate to the extent feasible with the agent making the decision; and

(3) take into account:

(A) the risks and benefits of treatment options; and

(B) the current and previous wishes and values of the adult, if known or reasonably ascertainable by the guardian.

Section 315. Special Limitations on Guardian's Power.

(a) Unless authorized by the court by specific order, a guardian for an adult does not have the power to revoke or amend a [power of attorney for health care] or power of attorney for finances executed by the adult. If a [power of attorney for health care] is in effect, unless there is a court order to the contrary, a health-care decision of an agent takes precedence over that of the guardian and the guardian shall cooperate with the agent to the extent feasible. If a power of attorney for finances is in effect, unless there is a court order to the contrary, a decision by the agent which the agent is authorized to make under the power of attorney for finances takes precedence over that of the guardian and the guardian shall cooperate with the agent to the extent feasible.

(b) A guardian for an adult may not initiate the commitment of the adult to a [mental health] facility except in accordance with the state's procedure for involuntary civil commitment.

(c)   A guardian for an adult may not restrict the ability of the adult to communicate, visit, or interact with others, including receiving visitors and making or receiving telephone calls, personal mail, or electronic communications, including through social media, or participating in social activities, unless:

(1)   authorized by the court by specific order;

(2)   a protective order or a protective arrangement instead of guardianship is in effect that limits contact between the adult and a person; or

(3)   the guardian has good cause to believe restriction is necessary because interaction with a specified person poses a risk of significant physical, psychological, or financial harm to the adult and the restriction is:

(A)   for a period of not more than seven business days if the person has a family or pre-existing social relationship with the adult; or

(B)   for a period of not more than 60 days if the person does not have a family or pre-existing social relationship with the adult.

Section 316. Guardian's Plan.

(a)   A guardian for an adult, not later than 60 days after appointment and when there is a significant change in circumstances, or the guardian seeks to deviate significantly from the guardian's plan, shall file with the court a plan for the care of the adult. The plan must be based on the needs of the adult and take into account the best interest of the adult as well as the adult's preferences, values, and prior directions, to the extent known to or reasonably ascertainable by the guardian. The guardian shall include in the plan:

(1)   the living arrangement, services, and supports the guardian expects to arrange, facilitate, or continue for the adult;

(2)   social and educational activities the guardian expects to facilitate on behalf of the adult;

(3)   any person with whom the adult has a close personal relationship or relationship involving regular visitation and any plan the guardian has for facilitating visits with the person;

(4)   the anticipated nature and frequency of the guardian's visits and communication with the adult;

(5)   goals for the adult, including any goal related to the restoration of the adult's rights, and how the guardian anticipates achieving the goals;

(6)   whether the adult has an existing plan and, if so, whether the guardian's plan is consistent with the adult's plan; and

(7)   a statement or list of the amount the guardian proposes to charge for each service the guardian anticipates providing to the adult.

(b)   A guardian shall give notice of the filing of the guardian's plan under subsection (a), together with a copy of the plan, to the adult subject to guardianship, a person entitled to notice under Section 310(e) or a subsequent order, and any other person the court determines. The notice must include a statement of the right to object to the plan and be given not later than 14 days after the filing.

(c)   An adult subject to guardianship and any person entitled under subsection (b) to receive notice and a copy of the guardian's plan may object to the plan.

(d)   The court shall review the guardian's plan filed under subsection (a) and determine whether to approve the plan or require a new plan. In deciding whether to approve the plan, the court shall consider an objection under subsection (c) and whether the plan is consistent with the guardian's duties and powers under Sections 313 and 314. The court may not approve the plan until [30] days after its filing.

(e)   After the guardian's plan filed under this section is approved by the court, the guardian shall provide a copy of the plan to the adult subject to guardianship, a person entitled to notice under Section 310(e) or a subsequent order, and any other person the court determines.

Section 317. Guardian's Report; Monitoring of Guardianship.

(a)   A guardian for an adult, not later than 60 days after appointment and at least annually thereafter, shall file with the court a report in a record regarding the condition of the adult and accounting for funds and other property in the guardian's possession or subject to the guardian's control.

(b)   A report under subsection (a) must state or contain:

(1)   the mental, physical, and social condition of the adult;

(2)   the living arrangements of the adult during the reporting period;

(3)   a summary of the supported decision making, technological assistance, medical services, educational and vocational services, and other supports and services provided to the adult and the guardian's opinion as to the adequacy of the adult's care;

(4)   a summary of the guardian's visits with the adult, including the dates of the visits;

(5)   action taken on behalf of the adult;

(6)   the extent to which the adult has participated in decision making;

(7)   if the adult is living in a [mental health] facility or living in a facility that provides the adult with health-care or other personal services, whether the guardian considers the facility's current plan for support, care, treatment, or habilitation consistent with the adult's preferences, values, prior directions, and best interest;

(8)   anything of more than de minimis value which the guardian, any individual who resides with the guardian, or the spouse, [domestic partner,] parent, child, or sibling of the guardian has received from an individual providing goods or services to the adult;

(9)   if the guardian delegated a power to an agent, the power delegated and the reason for the delegation;

(10) any business relation the guardian has with a person the guardian has paid or that has benefited from the property of the adult;

(11) a copy of the guardian's most recently approved plan under Section 316 and a statement whether the guardian has deviated from the plan and, if so, how the guardian has deviated and why;

(12) plans for future care and support of the adult;

(13) a recommendation as to the need for continued guardianship and any recommended change in the scope of the guardianship; and

(14) whether any co-guardian or successor guardian appointed to serve when a designated event occurs is alive and able to serve.

(c)   The court may appoint a [visitor] to review a report submitted under this section or a guardian's plan submitted under Section 316, interview the guardian or adult subject to guardianship, or investigate any other matter involving the guardianship.

(d)   Notice of the filing under this section of a guardian's report, together with a copy of the report, must be given to the adult subject to guardianship, a person entitled to notice under Section 310(e) or a subsequent order, and any other person the court determines. The notice and report must be given not later than 14 days after the filing.

(e)   The court shall establish procedures for monitoring a report submitted under this section and review each report at least annually to determine whether:

(1)   the report provides sufficient information to establish the guardian has complied with the guardian's duties;

(2)   the guardianship should continue; and

(3)   the guardian's requested fees, if any, should be approved.

(f)   If the court determines there is reason to believe a guardian for an adult has not complied with the guardian's duties or the guardianship should be modified or terminated, the court:

(1)   shall notify the adult, the guardian, and any other person entitled to notice under Section 310(e) or a subsequent order;

(2)   may require additional information from the guardian;

(3)   may appoint a [visitor] to interview the adult or guardian or investigate any matter involving the guardianship; and

(4)   consistent with Sections 318 and 319, may hold a hearing to consider removal of the guardian, termination of the guardianship, or a change in the powers granted to the guardian or terms of the guardianship.

(g)   If the court has reason to believe fees requested by a guardian for an adult are not reasonable, the court shall hold a hearing to determine whether to adjust the requested fees.

(h)   A guardian for an adult may petition the court for approval of a report filed under this section. The court after review may approve the report. If the court approves the report, there is a rebuttable presumption the report is accurate as to a matter adequately disclosed in the report.

Section 318. Removal of Guardian for Adult; Appointment of Successor.

(a)   The court may remove a guardian for an adult for failure to perform the guardian's duties or for other good cause and appoint a successor guardian to assume the duties of guardian.

(b)   The court shall hold a hearing to determine whether to remove a guardian for an adult and appoint a successor guardian on:

(1)   petition of the adult, guardian, or person interested in the welfare of the adult, which contains allegations that, if true, would support a reasonable belief that removal of the guardian and appointment of a successor guardian may be appropriate, but the court may decline to hold a hearing if a petition based on the same or substantially similar facts was filed during the preceding six months;

(2)   communication from the adult, guardian, or person interested in the welfare of the adult which supports a reasonable belief that removal of the guardian and appointment of a successor guardian may be appropriate; or

(3)   determination by the court that a hearing would be in the best interest of the adult.

(c)   Notice of a petition under subsection (b)(1) must be given to the adult subject to guardianship, the guardian, and any other person the court determines.

(d)   An adult subject to guardianship who seeks to remove the guardian and have a successor guardian appointed has the right to choose an attorney to represent the adult in this matter. [If the adult is not represented by an attorney, the court shall appoint an attorney under the same conditions as in Section 305.] The court shall award reasonable attorney's fees to the attorney for the adult as provided in Section 119.

(e)   In selecting a successor guardian for an adult, the court shall follow the priorities under Section 309.

(f)   Not later than 30 days after appointing a successor guardian, the court shall give notice of the appointment to the adult subject to guardianship and any person entitled to notice under Section 310(e) or a subsequent order.

Section 319. Termination or Modification of Guardianship for Adult.

(a)   An adult subject to guardianship, the guardian for the adult, or a person interested in the welfare of the adult may petition for:

(1)   termination of the guardianship on the ground that a basis for appointment under Section 301 does not exist or termination would be in the best interest of the adult or for other good cause; or

(2)   modification of the guardianship on the ground that the extent of protection or assistance granted is not appropriate or for other good cause.

(b)   The court shall hold a hearing to determine whether termination or modification of a guardianship for an adult is appropriate on:

(1)   petition under subsection (a) which contains allegations that, if true, would support a reasonable belief that termination or modification of the guardianship may be appropriate, but the court may decline to hold a hearing if a petition based on the same or substantially similar facts was filed during the preceding six months;

(2)   communication from the adult, guardian, or person interested in the welfare of the adult which supports a reasonable belief that termination or modification of the guardianship may be appropriate, including because the functional needs of the adult or supports or services available to the adult have changed;

(3)   a report from a guardian or conservator which indicates that termination or modification may be appropriate because the functional needs of the adult or supports or services available to the adult have changed or a protective arrangement instead of guardianship or other less restrictive alternative for meeting the adult's needs is available; or

(4)   a determination by the court that a hearing would be in the best interest of the adult.

(c)   Notice of a petition under subsection (b)(1) must be given to the adult subject to guardianship, the guardian, and any other person the court determines.

(d)   On presentation of prima facie evidence for termination of a guardianship for an adult, the court shall order termination unless it is proven that a basis for appointment of a guardian under Section 301 exists.

(e)   The court shall modify the powers granted to a guardian for an adult if the powers are excessive or inadequate due to a change in the abilities or limitations of the adult, the adult's supports, or other circumstances.

(f)   Unless the court otherwise orders for good cause, before terminating or modifying a guardianship for an adult, the court shall follow the same procedures to safeguard the rights of the adult which apply to a petition for guardianship.

(g)   An adult subject to guardianship who seeks to terminate or modify the terms of the guardianship has the right to choose an attorney to represent the adult in the matter. [If the adult is not represented by an attorney, the court shall appoint an attorney under the same conditions as in Section 305.] The court shall award reasonable attorney's fees to the attorney for the adult as provided in Section 119.

[ARTICLE] 4

CONSERVATORSHIP

Section 401. Basis for Appointment of Conservator.

(a)   On petition and after notice and hearing, the court may appoint a conservator for the property or financial affairs of a minor if the court finds by a preponderance of evidence that appointment of a conservator is in the minor's best interest, and:

(1)   if the minor has a parent, the court gives weight to any recommendation of the parent whether an appointment is in the minor's best interest; and

(2)   either:

(A)   the minor owns funds or other property requiring management or protection that otherwise cannot be provided;

(B)   the minor has or may have financial affairs that may be put at unreasonable risk or hindered because of the minor's age; or

(C)   appointment is necessary or desirable to obtain or provide funds or other property needed for the support, care, education, health, or welfare of the minor.

(b)   On petition and after notice and hearing, the court may appoint a conservator for the property or financial affairs of an adult if the court finds by clear-and-convincing evidence that:

(1)   the adult is unable to manage property or financial affairs because:

(A)   of a limitation in the adult's ability to receive and evaluate information or make or communicate decisions, even with the use of appropriate supportive services, technological assistance, or supported decision making; or

(B)   the adult is missing, detained, or unable to return to the United States;

(2)   appointment is necessary to:

(A)   avoid harm to the adult or significant dissipation of the property of the adult; or

(B)   obtain or provide funds or other property needed for the support, care, education, health, or welfare of the adult or of an individual entitled to the adult's support; and

(3)   the respondent's identified needs cannot be met by a protective arrangement instead of conservatorship or other less restrictive alternative.

(c)   The court shall grant a conservator only those powers necessitated by demonstrated limitations and needs of the respondent and issue orders that will encourage development of the respondent's maximum self-determination and independence. The court may not establish a full conservatorship if a limited conservatorship, protective arrangement instead of conservatorship, or other less restrictive alternative would meet the needs of the respondent.

Section 402. Petition for Appointment of Conservator.

(a)   The following may petition for the appointment of a conservator:

(1)   the individual for whom the order is sought;

(2)   a person interested in the estate, financial affairs, or welfare of the individual, including a person that would be adversely affected by lack of effective management of property or financial affairs of the individual; or

(3)   the guardian for the individual.

(b)   A petition under subsection (a) must state the petitioner's name, principal residence, current street address, if different, relationship to the respondent, interest in the appointment, the name and address of any attorney representing the petitioner, and, to the extent known, the following:

(1)   the respondent's name, age, principal residence, current street address, if different, and, if different, address of the dwelling in which it is proposed the respondent will reside if the petition is granted;

(2)   the name and address of the respondent's:

(A)   spouse [or domestic partner] or, if the respondent has none, an adult with whom the respondent has shared household responsibilities for more than six months in the 12-month period before the filing of the petition;

(B)   adult children or, if none, each parent and adult sibling of the respondent, or, if none, at least one adult nearest in kinship to the respondent who can be found with reasonable diligence; and

(C)   adult stepchildren whom the respondent actively parented during the stepchildren's minor years and with whom the respondent had an ongoing relationship during the two years immediately before the filing of the petition;

(3)   the name and current address of each of the following, if applicable:

(A)   a person responsible for the care or custody of the respondent;

(B)   any attorney currently representing the respondent;

(C)   the representative payee appointed by the Social Security Administration for the respondent;

(D)   a guardian or conservator acting for the respondent in this state or another jurisdiction;

(E)   a trustee or custodian of a trust or custodianship of which the respondent is a beneficiary;

(F)   the fiduciary appointed for the respondent by the Department of Veterans Affairs;

(G)   an agent designated under a [power of attorney for health care] in which the respondent is identified as the principal;

(H)   an agent designated under a power of attorney for finances in which the respondent is identified as the principal;

(I)   a person known to have routinely assisted the respondent with decision making in the six-month period immediately before the filing of the petition;

(J)   any proposed conservator, including a person nominated by the respondent, if the respondent is 12 years of age or older; and

(K)   if the individual for whom a conservator is sought is a minor:

(i)   an adult not otherwise listed with whom the minor resides; and

(ii)   each person not otherwise listed that had primary care or custody of the minor for at least 60 days during the two years immediately before the filing of the petition or for at least 730 days during the five years immediately before the filing of the petition;

(4)   a general statement of the respondent's property with an estimate of its value, including any insurance or pension, and the source and amount of other anticipated income or receipts;

(5)   the reason conservatorship is necessary, including a brief description of:

(A)   the nature and extent of the respondent's alleged need;

(B)   if the petition alleges the respondent is missing, detained, or unable to return to the United States, the relevant circumstances, including the time and nature of the disappearance or detention and any search or inquiry concerning the respondent's whereabouts;

(C)   any protective arrangement instead of conservatorship or other less restrictive alternative for meeting the respondent's alleged need which has been considered or implemented;

(D)   if no protective arrangement or other less restrictive alternatives have been considered or implemented, the reason it has not been considered or implemented; and

(E)   the reason a protective arrangement or other less restrictive alternative is insufficient to meet the respondent's need;

(6)   whether the petitioner seeks a limited conservatorship or a full conservatorship;

(7)   if the petitioner seeks a full conservatorship, the reason a limited conservatorship or protective arrangement instead of conservatorship is not appropriate;

(8)   if the petition includes the name of a proposed conservator, the reason the proposed conservator should be appointed;

(9)   if the petition is for a limited conservatorship, a description of the property to be placed under the conservator's control and any requested limitation on the authority of the conservator;

(10) whether the respondent needs an interpreter, translator, or other form of support to communicate effectively with the court or understand court proceedings; and

(11) the name and address of an attorney representing the petitioner, if any.

Section 403. Notice and Hearing for Appointment of Conservator.

(a)   On filing of a petition under Section 402 for appointment of a conservator, the court shall set a date, time, and place for a hearing on the petition.

(b)   A copy of a petition under Section 402 and notice of a hearing on the petition must be served personally on the respondent. If the respondent's whereabouts are unknown or personal service cannot be made, service on the respondent must be made by [substituted service] [or] [publication]. The notice must inform the respondent of the respondent's rights at the hearing, including the right to an attorney and to attend the hearing. The notice must include a description of the nature, purpose, and consequences of granting the petition. The court may not grant a petition for appointment of a conservator if notice substantially complying with this subsection is not served on the respondent.

(c)   In a proceeding on a petition under Section 402, the notice required under subsection (b) must be given to the persons required to be listed in the petition under Section 402(b)(1) through (3) and any other person interested in the respondent's welfare the court determines. Failure to give notice under this subsection does not preclude the court from appointing a conservator.

(d)   After the appointment of a conservator, notice of a hearing on a petition for an order under this [article], together with a copy of the petition, must be given to:

(1)   the individual subject to conservatorship, if the individual is 12 years of age or older and not missing, detained, or unable to return to the United States;

(2)   the conservator; and

(3)   any other person the court determines.

Section 404. Order to Preserve or Apply Property While Proceeding Pending.

While a petition under Section 402 is pending, after preliminary hearing and without notice to others, the court may issue an order to preserve and apply property of the respondent as required for the support of the respondent or an individual who is in fact dependent on the respondent. The court may appoint a [master] to assist in implementing the order.

Section 405. Appointment and Role of [Visitor].

(a) If the respondent in a proceeding to appoint a conservator is a minor, the court may appoint a [visitor] to investigate a matter related to the petition or inform the minor or a parent of the minor about the petition or a related matter.

(b) If the respondent in a proceeding to appoint a conservator is an adult, the court shall appoint a [visitor] [unless the adult is represented by an attorney appointed by the court]. The duties and reporting requirements of the [visitor] are limited to the relief requested in the petition. The [visitor] must be an individual with training or experience in the type of abilities, limitations, and needs alleged in the petition.

(c) A [visitor] appointed under subsection (b) for an adult shall interview the respondent in person and in a manner the respondent is best able to understand:

(1) explain to the respondent the substance of the petition, the nature, purpose, and effect of the proceeding, the respondent's rights at the hearing on the petition, and the general powers and duties of a conservator;

(2) determine the respondent's views about the appointment sought by the petitioner, including views about a proposed conservator, the conservator's proposed powers and duties, and the scope and duration of the proposed conservatorship;

(3) inform the respondent of the respondent's right to employ and consult with an attorney at the respondent's expense and the right to request a court-appointed attorney; and

(4) inform the respondent that all costs and expenses of the proceeding, including respondent's attorney's fees, may be paid from the respondent's assets.

(d) A [visitor] appointed under subsection (b) for an adult shall:

(1) interview the petitioner and proposed conservator, if any;

(2) review financial records of the respondent, if relevant to the [visitor's] recommendation under subsection (e)(2);

(3) investigate whether the respondent's needs could be met by a protective arrangement instead of conservatorship or other less restrictive alternative and, if so, identify the arrangement or other less restrictive alternative; and

(4) investigate the allegations in the petition and any other matter relating to the petition the court directs.

(e) A [visitor] appointed under subsection (b) for an adult promptly shall file a report in a record with the court, which must include:

(1) a recommendation whether an attorney should be appointed to represent the respondent;

(2) a recommendation:

(A) regarding the appropriateness of conservatorship, or whether a protective arrangement instead of conservatorship or other less restrictive alternative for meeting the respondent's needs is available;

(B) if a conservatorship is recommended, whether it should be full or limited; and

(C) if a limited conservatorship is recommended, the powers to be granted to the conservator, and the property that should be placed under the conservator's control;

(3) a statement of the qualifications of the proposed conservator and whether the respondent approves or disapproves of the proposed conservator;

(4) a recommendation whether a professional evaluation under Section 407 is necessary;

(5) a statement whether the respondent is able to attend a hearing at the location court proceedings typically are held;

(6) a statement whether the respondent is able to participate in a hearing and which identifies any technology or other form of support that would enhance the respondent's ability to participate; and

(7) any other matter the court directs.

Section 406. Appointment and Role of Attorney.

Alternative A

(a) The court shall appoint an attorney to represent the respondent in a proceeding to appoint a conservator if:

(1) the respondent requests an appointment;

(2) the [visitor] recommends an appointment; or

(3) the court determines the respondent needs representation.

Alternative B

(a) Unless the respondent in a proceeding for appointment of a conservator is represented by an attorney, the court shall appoint an attorney to represent the respondent, regardless of the respondent's ability to pay.

End of Alternatives

(b) An attorney representing the respondent in a proceeding for appointment of a conservator shall:

(1) make reasonable efforts to ascertain the respondent's wishes;

(2) advocate for the respondent's wishes to the extent reasonably ascertainable; and

(3) if the respondent's wishes are not reasonably ascertainable, advocate for the result that is the least-restrictive in type, duration, and scope, consistent with the respondent's interests.

[(c) The court shall appoint an attorney to represent a parent of a minor who is the subject of a proceeding under Section 402 if:

(1) the parent objects to appointment of a conservator;

(2) the court determines that counsel is needed to ensure that consent to appointment of a conservator is informed; or

(3) the court otherwise determines the parent needs representation.]

Section 407. Professional Evaluation.

(a) At or before a hearing on a petition for conservatorship for an adult, the court shall order a professional evaluation of the respondent:

(1) if the respondent requests the evaluation; or

(2) in other cases, unless the court finds it has sufficient information to determine the respondent's needs and abilities without the evaluation.

(b)   If the court orders an evaluation under subsection (a), the respondent must be examined by a licensed physician, psychologist, social worker, or other individual appointed by the court who is qualified to evaluate the respondent's alleged cognitive and functional abilities and limitations and will not be advantaged or disadvantaged by a decision to grant the petition or otherwise have a conflict of interest. The individual conducting the evaluation promptly shall file a report in a record with the court. Unless otherwise directed by the court, the report must contain:

(1)   a description of the nature, type, and extent of the respondent's cognitive and functional abilities and limitations with regard to the management of the respondent's property and financial affairs;

(2)   an evaluation of the respondent's mental and physical condition and, if appropriate, educational potential, adaptive behavior, and social skills;

(3)   a prognosis for improvement with regard to the ability to manage the respondent's property and financial affairs; and

(4)   the date of the examination on which the report is based.

(c)   A respondent may decline to participate in an evaluation ordered under subsection (a).

Section 408. Attendance and Rights at Hearing.

(a)   Except as otherwise provided in subsection (b), a hearing under Section 403 may not proceed unless the respondent attends the hearing. If it is not reasonably feasible for the respondent to attend a hearing at the location court proceedings typically are held, the court shall make reasonable efforts to hold the hearing at an alternative location convenient to the respondent or allow the respondent to attend the hearing using real-time audio-visual technology.

(b)   A hearing under Section 403 may proceed without the respondent in attendance if the court finds by clear-and-convincing evidence that:

(1)   the respondent consistently and repeatedly has refused to attend the hearing after having been fully informed of the right to attend and the potential consequences of failing to do so;

(2)   there is no practicable way for the respondent to attend and participate in the hearing even with appropriate supportive services or technological assistance; or

(3)   the respondent is a minor who has received proper notice and attendance would be harmful to the minor.

(c)   The respondent may be assisted in a hearing under Section 403 by a person or persons of the respondent's choosing, assistive technology, or an interpreter or translator, or a combination of these supports. If assistance would facilitate the respondent's participation in the hearing, but is not otherwise available to the respondent, the court shall make reasonable efforts to provide it.

(d)   The respondent has a right to choose an attorney to represent the respondent at a hearing under Section 403.

(e)   At a hearing under Section 403, the respondent may:

(1)   present evidence and subpoena witnesses and documents;

(2)   examine witnesses, including any court-appointed evaluator and the [visitor]; and

(3)   otherwise participate in the hearing.

(f)   Unless excused by the court for good cause, a proposed conservator shall attend a hearing under Section 403.

(g)   A hearing under Section 403 must be closed on request of the respondent and a showing of good cause.

(h)   Any person may request to participate in a hearing under Section 403. The court may grant the request, with or without a hearing, on determining that the best interest of the respondent will be served. The court may impose appropriate conditions on the person's participation.

Section 409. Confidentiality of Records.

(a)   The existence of a proceeding for or the existence of conservatorship is a matter of public record unless the court seals the record after:

(1)   the respondent, the individual subject to conservatorship, or the parent of a minor subject to conservatorship requests the record be sealed; and

(2)   either:

(A)   the petition for conservatorship is dismissed; or

(B)   the conservatorship is terminated.

(b)   An individual subject to a proceeding for a conservatorship, whether or not a conservator is appointed, an attorney designated by the individual, and a person entitled to notice under Section 411(e) or a subsequent order may access court records of the proceeding and resulting conservatorship, including the conservator's plan under Section 419 and the conservator's report under Section 423. A person not otherwise entitled to access to court records under this section for good cause may petition the court for access to court records of the conservatorship, including the conservator's plan and report. The court shall grant access if access is in the best interest of the respondent or individual subject to conservatorship or furthers the public interest and does not endanger the welfare or financial interests of the respondent or individual.

[(c)   A report under Section 405 of a [visitor] or professional evaluation under Section 407 is confidential and must be sealed on filing, but is available to:

(1)   the court;

(2)   the individual who is the subject of the report or evaluation, without limitation as to use;

(3)   the petitioner, [visitor], and petitioner's and respondent's attorneys, for purposes of the proceeding;

(4)   unless the court directs otherwise, an agent appointed under a power of attorney for finances in which the respondent is identified as the principal; and

(5)   any other person if it is in the public interest or for a purpose the court orders for good cause.]

Section 410. Who May Be Conservator; Order of Priority.

(a)   Except as otherwise provided in subsection (c), the court in appointing a conservator shall consider persons qualified to be a conservator in the following order of priority:

(1)   a conservator, other than a temporary or emergency conservator, currently acting for the respondent in another jurisdiction;

(2)   a person nominated as conservator by the respondent, including the respondent's most recent nomination made in a power of attorney for finances;

(3)   an agent appointed by the respondent to manage the respondent's property under a power of attorney for finances;

(4)   a spouse [or domestic partner] of the respondent; and

(5)   a family member or other individual who has shown special care and concern for the respondent.

(b)   If two or more persons have equal priority under subsection (a), the court shall select as conservator the person the court considers best qualified. In determining the best qualified person, the court shall consider the person's relationship with the respondent, the person's skills, the expressed wishes of the respondent, the extent to which the person and the respondent have similar values and preferences, and the likelihood the person will be able to perform the duties of a conservator successfully.

(c)   The court, acting in the best interest of the respondent, may decline to appoint as conservator a person having priority under subsection (a) and appoint a person having a lower priority or no priority.

(d)   A person that provides paid services to the respondent, or an individual who is employed by a person that provides paid services to the respondent or is the spouse, [domestic partner,] parent, or child of an individual who provides or is employed to provide paid services to the respondent, may not be appointed as conservator unless:

(1)   the individual is related to the respondent by blood, marriage, or adoption; or

(2)   the court finds by clear-and-convincing evidence that the person is the best qualified person available for appointment and the appointment is in the best interest of the respondent.

(e)   An owner, operator, or employee of [a long-term-care institution] at which the respondent is receiving care may not be appointed as conservator unless the owner, operator, or employee is related to the respondent by blood, marriage, or adoption.

Section 411. Order of Appointment of Conservator.

(a)   A court order appointing a conservator for a minor must include findings to support appointment of a conservator and, if a full conservatorship is granted, the reason a limited conservatorship would not meet the identified needs of the minor.

(b)   A court order appointing a conservator for an adult must:

(1)   include a specific finding that clear-and-convincing evidence has established that the identified needs of the respondent cannot be met by a protective arrangement instead of conservatorship or other less restrictive alternative, including use of appropriate supportive services, technological assistance, or supported decision making; and

(2)   include a specific finding that clear-and-convincing evidence established the respondent was given proper notice of the hearing on the petition.

(c)   A court order establishing a full conservatorship for an adult must state the basis for granting a full conservatorship and include specific findings to support the conclusion that a limited conservatorship would not meet the functional needs of the adult.

(d)   A court order establishing a limited conservatorship must state the specific property placed under the control of the conservator and the powers granted to the conservator.

(e)   The court, as part of an order establishing a conservatorship, shall identify any person that subsequently is entitled to:

(1)   notice of the rights of the individual subject to conservatorship under Section 412(b);

(2)   notice of a sale of or surrender of a lease to the primary dwelling of the individual;

(3)   notice that the conservator has delegated a power that requires court approval under Section 414 or substantially all powers of the conservator;

(4)   notice that the conservator will be unavailable to perform the conservator's duties for more than one month;

(5)   a copy of the conservator's plan under Section 419 and the conservator's report under Section 423;

    (6)   access to court records relating to the conservatorship;

    (7)   notice of a transaction involving a substantial conflict between the conservator's fiduciary duties and personal interests;

    (8)   notice of the death or significant change in the condition of the individual;

    (9)   notice that the court has limited or modified the powers of the conservator; and

    (10) notice of the removal of the conservator.

    (f)   If an individual subject to conservatorship is an adult, the spouse[, domestic partner,] and adult children of the adult subject to conservatorship are entitled under subsection (e) to notice unless the court determines notice would be contrary to the preferences or prior directions of the adult subject to conservatorship or not in the best interest of the adult.

    (g)   If an individual subject to conservatorship is a minor, each parent and adult sibling of the minor is entitled under subsection (e) to notice unless the court determines notice would not be in the best interest of the minor.

Section 412. Notice of Order of Appointment; Rights.

    (a)   A conservator appointed under Section 411 shall give to the individual subject to conservatorship and to all other persons given notice under Section 403 a copy of the order of appointment, together with notice of the right to request termination or modification. The order and notice must be given not later than 14 days after the appointment.

    (b)   Not later than 30 days after appointment of a conservator under Section 411, the court shall give to the individual subject to conservatorship, the conservator, and any other person entitled to notice under Section 411(e) a statement of the rights of the individual subject to conservatorship and procedures to seek relief if the individual is denied those rights. The statement must be in plain language, in at least 16-point font, and to the extent feasible, in a language in which the individual subject to conservatorship is proficient. The statement must notify the individual subject to conservatorship of the right to:

    (1)   seek termination or modification of the conservatorship, or removal of the conservator, and choose an attorney to represent the individual in these matters;

    (2)   participate in decision making to the extent reasonably feasible;

    (3)   receive a copy of the conservator's plan under Section 419, the conservator's inventory under Section 420, and the conservator's report under Section 423; and

    (4)   object to the conservator's inventory, plan, or report.

    (c)   If a conservator is appointed for the reasons stated in Section 401(b)(1)(B) and the individual subject to conservatorship is missing, notice under this section to the individual is not required.

Section 413. Emergency Conservator.

    (a)   On its own or on petition by a person interested in an individual's welfare after a petition has been filed under Section 402, the court may appoint an emergency conservator for the individual if the court finds:

    (1)   appointment of an emergency conservator is likely to prevent substantial and irreparable harm to the individual's property or financial interests;

    (2)   no other person appears to have authority and willingness to act in the circumstances; and

    (3)   there is reason to believe that a basis for appointment of a conservator under Section 401 exists.

(b)   The duration of authority of an emergency conservator may not exceed [60] days and the emergency conservator may exercise only the powers specified in the order of appointment. The emergency conservator's authority may be extended once for not more than [60] days if the court finds that the conditions for appointment of an emergency conservator under subsection (a) continue.

(c)   Immediately on filing of a petition for an emergency conservator, the court shall appoint an attorney to represent the respondent in the proceeding. Except as otherwise provided in subsection (d), reasonable notice of the date, time, and place of a hearing on the petition must be given to the respondent, the respondent's attorney, and any other person the court determines.

(d)   The court may appoint an emergency conservator without notice to the respondent and any attorney for the respondent only if the court finds from an affidavit or testimony that the respondent's property or financial interests will be substantially and irreparably harmed before a hearing with notice on the appointment can be held. If the court appoints an emergency conservator without giving notice under subsection (c), the court must give notice of the appointment not later than 48 hours after the appointment to:

(1)   the respondent;

(2)   the respondent's attorney; and

(3)   any other person the court determines.

(e)   Not later than [five] days after the appointment, the court shall hold a hearing on the appropriateness of the appointment.

(f)   Appointment of an emergency conservator under this section is not a determination that a basis exists for appointment of a conservator under Section 401.

(g)   The court may remove an emergency conservator appointed under this section at any time. The emergency conservator shall make any report the court requires.

Section 414. Powers of Conservator Requiring Court Approval.

(a)   Except as otherwise ordered by the court, a conservator must give notice to persons entitled to notice under Section 403(d) and receive specific authorization by the court before the conservator may exercise with respect to the conservatorship the power to:

(1)   make a gift, except a gift of de minimis value;

(2)   sell, encumber an interest in, or surrender a lease to the primary dwelling of the individual subject to conservatorship;

(3)   convey, release, or disclaim a contingent or expectant interest in property, including marital property and any right of survivorship incident to joint tenancy or tenancy by the entireties;

(4)   exercise or release a power of appointment;

(5)   create a revocable or irrevocable trust of property of the conservatorship estate, whether or not the trust extends beyond the duration of the conservatorship, or revoke or amend a trust revocable by the individual subject to conservatorship;

(6)   exercise a right to elect an option or change a beneficiary under an insurance policy or annuity or surrender the policy or annuity for its cash value;

(7)   exercise a right to an elective share in the estate of a deceased spouse [or domestic partner] of the individual subject to conservatorship or renounce or disclaim a property interest; [and]

(8)   grant a creditor priority for payment over creditors of the same or higher class if the creditor is providing property or services used to meet the basic living and care needs of the

individual subject to conservatorship and preferential treatment otherwise would be impermissible under Section 428(e)[; and

(9)   make, modify, amend, or revoke the will of the individual subject to conservatorship in compliance with [the state's statute for executing a will]].

(b)   In approving a conservator's exercise of a power listed in subsection (a), the court shall consider primarily the decision the individual subject to conservatorship would make if able, to the extent the decision can be ascertained.

(c)   To determine under subsection (b) the decision the individual subject to conservatorship would make if able, the court shall consider the individual's prior or current directions, preferences, opinions, values, and actions, to the extent actually known or reasonably ascertainable by the conservator. The court also shall consider:

(1)   the financial needs of the individual subject to conservatorship and individuals who are in fact dependent on the individual subject to conservatorship for support, and the interests of creditors of the individual;

(2)   possible reduction of income, estate, inheritance, or other tax liabilities;

(3)   eligibility for governmental assistance;

(4)   the previous pattern of giving or level of support provided by the individual;

(5)   any existing estate plan or lack of estate plan of the individual;

(6)   the life expectancy of the individual and the probability the conservatorship will terminate before the individual's death; and

(7)   any other relevant factor.

(d)   A conservator may not revoke or amend a power of attorney for finances executed by the individual subject to conservatorship. If a power of attorney for finances is in effect, a decision of the agent takes precedence over that of the conservator, unless the court orders otherwise.

Section 415. Petition for Order After Appointment.

An individual subject to conservatorship or a person interested in the welfare of the individual may petition for an order:

(1)   requiring the conservator to furnish a bond or collateral or additional bond or collateral or allowing a reduction in a bond or collateral previously furnished;

(2)   requiring an accounting for the administration of the conservatorship estate;

(3)   directing distribution;

(4)   removing the conservator and appointing a temporary or successor conservator;

(5)   modifying the type of appointment or powers granted to the conservator, if the extent of protection or management previously granted is excessive or insufficient to meet the individual's needs, including because the individual's abilities or supports have changed;

(6)   rejecting or modifying the conservator's plan under Section 419, the conservator's inventory under Section 420, or the conservator's report under Section 423; or

(7)   granting other appropriate relief.

Section 416. Bond; Alternative Asset-Protection Arrangement.

(a)   Except as otherwise provided in subsection (c), the court shall require a conservator to furnish a bond with a surety the court specifies, or require an alternative asset-protection arrangement, conditioned on faithful discharge of all duties of the conservator. The court may waive the requirement only if the court finds that a bond or other asset-protection arrangement is not necessary to protect the interests of the individual subject to conservatorship. Except as otherwise provided in subsection (c), the court may not waive the requirement if the conservator is in the business of serving as a conservator and is being paid for the conservator's service.

(b)   Unless the court directs otherwise, the bond required under this section must be in the amount of the aggregate capital value of the conservatorship estate, plus one year's estimated income, less the value of property deposited under an arrangement requiring a court order for its removal and real property the conservator lacks power to sell or convey without specific court authorization. The court, in place of surety on a bond, may accept collateral for the performance of the bond, including a pledge of securities or a mortgage of real property.

(c)   [A regulated financial-service institution qualified to do trust business] in this state is not required to give a bond under this section.

Section 417. Terms and Requirements of Bond.

(a)   The following rules apply to the bond required under Section 416:

(1)   Except as otherwise provided by the bond, the surety and the conservator are jointly and severally liable.

(2)   By executing a bond provided by a conservator, the surety submits to the personal jurisdiction of the court that issued letters of office to the conservator in a proceeding relating to the duties of the conservator in which the surety is named as a party. Notice of the proceeding must be given to the surety at the address shown in the records of the court in which the bond is filed and any other address of the surety then known to the person required to provide the notice.

(3)   On petition of a successor conservator or person affected by a breach of the obligation of the bond, a proceeding may be brought against the surety for breach of the obligation of the bond.

(4)   A proceeding against the bond may be brought until liability under the bond is exhausted.

(b)   A proceeding may not be brought under this section against a surety of a bond on a matter as to which a proceeding against the conservator is barred.

(c)   If a bond under Section 416 is not renewed by the conservator, the surety or sureties immediately shall give notice to the court and the individual subject to conservatorship.

Section 418. Duties of Conservator.

(a)   A conservator is a fiduciary and has duties of prudence and loyalty to the individual subject to conservatorship.

(b)   A conservator shall promote the self-determination of the individual subject to conservatorship and, to the extent feasible, encourage the individual to participate in decisions, act on the individual's own behalf, and develop or regain the capacity to manage the individual's personal affairs.

(c)   In making a decision for an individual subject to conservatorship, the conservator shall make the decision the conservator reasonably believes the individual would make if able, unless doing so would fail to preserve the resources needed to maintain the individual's well-being and lifestyle or otherwise unreasonably harm or endanger the welfare or personal or financial interests of the individual. To determine the decision the individual would make if able, the conservator shall consider the individual's prior or current directions, preferences, opinions, values, and actions, to the extent actually known or reasonably ascertainable by the conservator.

(d)   If a conservator cannot make a decision under subsection (c) because the conservator does not know and cannot reasonably determine the decision the individual subject to conservatorship probably would make if able, or the conservator reasonably believes the decision the individual would

502

make would fail to preserve resources needed to maintain the individual's well-being and lifestyle or otherwise unreasonably harm or endanger the welfare or personal or financial interests of the individual, the conservator shall act in accordance with the best interest of the individual. In determining the best interest of the individual, the conservator shall consider:

(1) information received from professionals and persons that demonstrate sufficient interest in the welfare of the individual;

(2) other information the conservator believes the individual would have considered if the individual were able to act; and

(3) other factors a reasonable person in the circumstances of the individual would consider, including consequences for others.

(e) Except when inconsistent with the conservator's duties under subsections (a) through (d), a conservator shall invest and manage the conservatorship estate as a prudent investor would, by considering:

(1) the circumstances of the individual subject to conservatorship and the conservatorship estate;

(2) general economic conditions;

(3) the possible effect of inflation or deflation;

(4) the expected tax consequences of an investment decision or strategy;

(5) the role of each investment or course of action in relation to the conservatorship estate as a whole;

(6) the expected total return from income and appreciation of capital;

(7) the need for liquidity, regularity of income, and preservation or appreciation of capital; and

(8) the special relationship or value, if any, of specific property to the individual subject to conservatorship.

(f) The propriety of a conservator's investment and management of the conservatorship estate is determined in light of the facts and circumstances existing when the conservator decides or acts and not by hindsight.

(g) A conservator shall make a reasonable effort to verify facts relevant to the investment and management of the conservatorship estate.

(h) A conservator that has special skills or expertise, or is named conservator in reliance on the conservator's representation of special skills or expertise, has a duty to use the special skills or expertise in carrying out the conservator's duties.

(i) In investing, selecting specific property for distribution, and invoking a power of revocation or withdrawal for the use or benefit of the individual subject to conservatorship, a conservator shall consider any estate plan of the individual known or reasonably ascertainable to the conservator and may examine the will or other donative, nominative, or appointive instrument of the individual.

(j) A conservator shall maintain insurance on the insurable real and personal property of the individual subject to conservatorship, unless the conservatorship estate lacks sufficient funds to pay for insurance or the court finds:

(1) the property lacks sufficient equity; or

(2) insuring the property would unreasonably dissipate the conservatorship estate or otherwise not be in the best interest of the individual.

(k) If a power of attorney for finances is in effect, a conservator shall cooperate with the agent to the extent feasible.

(*l*) A conservator has access to and authority over a digital asset of the individual subject to conservatorship to the extent provided by [the Revised Uniform Fiduciary Access to Digital Assets Act] or court order.

(m) A conservator for an adult shall notify the court if the condition of the adult has changed so that the adult is capable of exercising rights previously removed. The notice must be given immediately on learning of the change.

Section 419. Conservator's Plan.

(a) A conservator, not later than 60 days after appointment and when there is a significant change in circumstances or the conservator seeks to deviate significantly from the conservator's plan, shall file with the court a plan for protecting, managing, expending, and distributing the assets of the conservatorship estate. The plan must be based on the needs of the individual subject to conservatorship and take into account the best interest of the individual as well as the individual's preferences, values, and prior directions, to the extent known to or reasonably ascertainable by the conservator. The conservator shall include in the plan:

    (1) a budget containing projected expenses and resources, including an estimate of the total amount of fees the conservator anticipates charging per year and a statement or list of the amount the conservator proposes to charge for each service the conservator anticipates providing to the individual;

    (2) how the conservator will involve the individual in decisions about management of the conservatorship estate;

    (3) any step the conservator plans to take to develop or restore the ability of the individual to manage the conservatorship estate; and

    (4) an estimate of the duration of the conservatorship.

(b) A conservator shall give notice of the filing of the conservator's plan under subsection (a), together with a copy of the plan, to the individual subject to conservatorship, a person entitled to notice under Section 411(e) or a subsequent order, and any other person the court determines. The notice must include a statement of the right to object to the plan and be given not later than 14 days after the filing.

(c) An individual subject to conservatorship and any person entitled under subsection (b) to receive notice and a copy of the conservator's plan may object to the plan.

(d) The court shall review the conservator's plan filed under subsection (a) and determine whether to approve the plan or require a new plan. In deciding whether to approve the plan, the court shall consider an objection under subsection (c) and whether the plan is consistent with the conservator's duties and powers. The court may not approve the plan until [30] days after its filing.

(e) After a conservator's plan under this section is approved by the court, the conservator shall provide a copy of the plan to the individual subject to conservatorship, a person entitled to notice under Section 411(e) or a subsequent order, and any other person the court determines.

Section 420. Inventory; Records.

(a) Not later than 60 days after appointment, a conservator shall prepare and file with the appointing court a detailed inventory of the conservatorship estate, together with an oath or affirmation that the inventory is believed to be complete and accurate as far as information permits.

(b) A conservator shall give notice of the filing of an inventory to the individual subject to conservatorship, a person entitled to notice under Section 411(e) or a subsequent order, and any other person the court determines. The notice must be given not later than 14 days after the filing.

(c)   A conservator shall keep records of the administration of the conservatorship estate and make them available for examination on reasonable request of the individual subject to conservatorship, a guardian for the individual, or any other person the conservator or the court determines.

Section 421. Administrative Powers of Conservator Not Requiring Court Approval.

(a)   Except as otherwise provided in Section 414 or qualified or limited in the court's order of appointment and stated in the letters of office, a conservator has all powers granted in this section and any additional power granted to a trustee by law of this state other than this [act].

(b)   A conservator, acting reasonably and consistent with the fiduciary duties of the conservator to accomplish the purpose of the conservatorship, without specific court authorization or confirmation, may with respect to the conservatorship estate:

(1)   collect, hold, and retain property, including property in which the conservator has a personal interest and real property in another state, until the conservator determines disposition of the property should be made;

(2)   receive additions to the conservatorship estate;

(3)   continue or participate in the operation of a business or other enterprise;

(4)   acquire an undivided interest in property in which the conservator, in a fiduciary capacity, holds an undivided interest;

(5)   invest assets;

(6)   deposit funds or other property in a financial institution, including one operated by the conservator;

(7)   acquire or dispose of property, including real property in another state, for cash or on credit, at public or private sale, and manage, develop, improve, exchange, partition, change the character of, or abandon property;

(8)   make ordinary or extraordinary repairs or alterations in a building or other structure, demolish any improvement, or raze an existing or erect a new party wall or building;

(9)   subdivide or develop land, dedicate land to public use, make or obtain the vacation of a plat and adjust a boundary, adjust a difference in valuation of land, exchange or partition land by giving or receiving consideration, and dedicate an easement to public use without consideration;

(10) enter for any purpose into a lease of property as lessor or lessee, with or without an option to purchase or renew, for a term within or extending beyond the term of the conservatorship;

(11) enter into a lease or arrangement for exploration and removal of minerals or other natural resources or a pooling or unitization agreement;

(12) grant an option involving disposition of property or accept or exercise an option for the acquisition of property;

(13) vote a security, in person or by general or limited proxy;

(14) pay a call, assessment, or other sum chargeable or accruing against or on account of a security;

(15) sell or exercise a stock subscription or conversion right;

(16) consent, directly or through a committee or agent, to the reorganization, consolidation, merger, dissolution, or liquidation of a corporation or other business enterprise;

(17) hold a security in the name of a nominee or in other form without disclosure of the conservatorship so that title to the security may pass by delivery;

(18) insure:

(A) the conservatorship estate, in whole or in part, against damage or loss in accordance with Section 418(j); and

(B) the conservator against liability with respect to a third person;

(19) borrow funds, with or without security, to be repaid from the conservatorship estate or otherwise;

(20) advance funds for the protection of the conservatorship estate or the individual subject to conservatorship and all expenses, losses, and liability sustained in the administration of the conservatorship estate or because of holding any property for which the conservator has a lien on the conservatorship estate;

(21) pay or contest a claim, settle a claim by or against the conservatorship estate or the individual subject to conservatorship by compromise, arbitration, or otherwise, or release, in whole or in part, a claim belonging to the conservatorship estate to the extent the claim is uncollectible;

(22) pay a tax, assessment, compensation of the conservator or any guardian, and other expense incurred in the collection, care, administration, and protection of the conservatorship estate;

(23) pay a sum distributable to the individual subject to conservatorship or an individual who is in fact dependent on the individual subject to conservatorship by paying the sum to the distributee or for the use of the distributee:

(A) to the guardian for the distributee;

(B) to the custodian of the distributee under [the Uniform Transfers to Minors Act] or custodial trustee under [the Uniform Custodial Trust Act]; or

(C) if there is no guardian, custodian, or custodial trustee, to a relative or other person having physical custody of the distributee;

(24) bring or defend an action, claim, or proceeding in any jurisdiction for the protection of the conservatorship estate or the conservator in the performance of the conservator's duties;

(25) structure the finances of the individual subject to conservatorship to establish eligibility for a public benefit, including by making gifts consistent with the individual's preferences, values, and prior directions, if the conservator's action does not jeopardize the individual's welfare and otherwise is consistent with the conservator's duties; and

(26) execute and deliver any instrument that will accomplish or facilitate the exercise of a power of the conservator.

Section 422. Distribution From Conservatorship Estate.

Except as otherwise provided in Section 414 or qualified or limited in the court's order of appointment and stated in the letters of office, and unless contrary to a conservator's plan under Section 419, the conservator may expend or distribute income or principal of the conservatorship estate without specific court authorization or confirmation for the support, care, education, health, or welfare of the individual subject to conservatorship or an individual who is in fact dependent on the individual subject to conservatorship, including the payment of child or spousal support, in accordance with the following rules:

(1) The conservator shall consider a recommendation relating to the appropriate standard of support, care, education, health, or welfare for the individual subject to conservatorship or individual who is dependent on the individual subject to conservatorship, made by a guardian for the individual

subject to conservatorship, if any, and, if the individual subject to conservatorship is a minor, a recommendation made by a parent of the minor.

(2) The conservator acting in compliance with the conservator's duties under Section 418 is not liable for an expenditure or distribution made based on a recommendation under paragraph (1) unless the conservator knows the expenditure or distribution is not in the best interest of the individual subject to conservatorship.

(3) In making an expenditure or distribution under this section, the conservator shall consider:

(A) the size of the conservatorship estate, the estimated duration of the conservatorship, and the likelihood the individual subject to conservatorship, at some future time, may be fully self-sufficient and able to manage the individual's financial affairs and the conservatorship estate;

(B) the accustomed standard of living of the individual subject to conservatorship and individual who is dependent on the individual subject to conservatorship;

(C) other funds or source used for the support of the individual subject to conservatorship; and

(D) the preferences, values, and prior directions of the individual subject to conservatorship.

(4) Funds expended or distributed under this section may be paid by the conservator to any person, including the individual subject to conservatorship, as reimbursement for expenditures the conservator might have made, or in advance for services to be provided to the individual subject to conservatorship or individual who is dependent on the individual subject to conservatorship if it is reasonable to expect the services will be performed and advance payment is customary or reasonably necessary under the circumstances.

Section 423. Conservator's Report and Accounting; Monitoring.

(a) A conservator shall file with the court a report in a record regarding the administration of the conservatorship estate annually unless the court otherwise directs, on resignation or removal, on termination of the conservatorship, and at any other time the court directs.

(b) A report under subsection (a) must state or contain:

(1) an accounting that lists property included in the conservatorship estate and the receipts, disbursements, liabilities, and distributions during the period for which the report is made;

(2) a list of the services provided to the individual subject to conservatorship;

(3) a copy of the conservator's most recently approved plan and a statement whether the conservator has deviated from the plan and, if so, how the conservator has deviated and why;

(4) a recommendation as to the need for continued conservatorship and any recommended change in the scope of the conservatorship;

(5) to the extent feasible, a copy of the most recent reasonably available financial statements evidencing the status of bank accounts, investment accounts, and mortgages or other debts of the individual subject to conservatorship with [all but the last four digits of the] account numbers and Social Security number redacted;

(6) anything of more than de minimis value which the conservator, any individual who resides with the conservator, or the spouse, [domestic partner,] parent, child, or sibling of the conservator has received from a person providing goods or services to the individual subject to conservatorship;

(7) any business relation the conservator has with a person the conservator has paid or that has benefited from the property of the individual subject to conservatorship; and

(8)   whether any co-conservator or successor conservator appointed to serve when a designated event occurs is alive and able to serve.

(c)   The court may appoint a [visitor] to review a report under this section or conservator's plan under Section 419, interview the individual subject to conservatorship or conservator, or investigate any other matter involving the conservatorship. In connection with the report, the court may order the conservator to submit the conservatorship estate to appropriate examination in a manner the court directs.

(d)   Notice of the filing under this section of a conservator's report, together with a copy of the report, must be provided to the individual subject to conservatorship, a person entitled to notice under Section 411(e) or a subsequent order, and other persons the court determines. The notice and report must be given not later than 14 days after filing.

(e)   The court shall establish procedures for monitoring a report submitted under this section and review each report at least annually to determine whether:

(1)   the reports provide sufficient information to establish the conservator has complied with the conservator's duties;

(2)   the conservatorship should continue; and

(3)   the conservator's requested fees, if any, should be approved.

(f)   If the court determines there is reason to believe a conservator has not complied with the conservator's duties or the conservatorship should not continue, the court:

(1)   shall notify the individual subject to conservatorship, the conservator, and any other person entitled to notice under Section 411(e) or a subsequent order;

(2)   may require additional information from the conservator;

(3)   may appoint a [visitor] to interview the individual subject to conservatorship or conservator or investigate any matter involving the conservatorship; and

(4)   consistent with Sections 430 and 431, may hold a hearing to consider removal of the conservator, termination of the conservatorship, or a change in the powers granted to the conservator or terms of the conservatorship.

(g)   If the court has reason to believe fees requested by a conservator are not reasonable, the court shall hold a hearing to determine whether to adjust the requested fees.

(h)   A conservator may petition the court for approval of a report filed under this section. The court after review may approve the report. If the court approves the report, there is a rebuttable presumption the report is accurate as to a matter adequately disclosed in the report.

(i)   An order, after notice and hearing, approving an interim report of a conservator filed under this Section adjudicates liabilities concerning a matter adequately disclosed in the report, as to a person given notice of the report or accounting.

(j)   An order, after notice and hearing, approving a final report filed under this Section discharges the conservator from all liabilities, claims, and causes of action by a person given notice of the report and the hearing as to a matter adequately disclosed in the report.

Section 424. Attempted Transfer of Property by Individual Subject to Conservatorship.

(a)   The interest of an individual subject to conservatorship in property included in the conservatorship estate is not transferrable or assignable by the individual and is not subject to levy, garnishment, or similar process for claims against the individual unless allowed under Section 428.

(b)   If an individual subject to conservatorship enters into a contract after having the right to enter the contract removed by the court, the contract is void against the individual and the individual's property but is enforceable against the person that contracted with the individual.

(c)   A person other than the conservator that deals with an individual subject to conservatorship with respect to property included in the conservatorship estate is entitled to protection provided by law of this state other than this [act].

Section 425. Transaction Involving Conflict of Interest.

A transaction involving a conservatorship estate which is affected by a substantial conflict between the conservator's fiduciary duties and personal interests is voidable unless the transaction is authorized by court order after notice to persons entitled to notice under Section 411(e) or a subsequent order. A transaction affected by a substantial conflict includes a sale, encumbrance, or other transaction involving the conservatorship estate entered into by the conservator, an individual with whom the conservator resides, the spouse, [domestic partner,] descendant, sibling, agent, or attorney of the conservator, or a corporation or other enterprise in which the conservator has a substantial beneficial interest.

Section 426. Protection of Person Dealing With Conservator.

(a)   A person that assists or deals with a conservator in good faith and for value in any transaction, other than a transaction requiring a court order under Section 414, is protected as though the conservator properly exercised any power in question. Knowledge by a person that the person is dealing with a conservator alone does not require the person to inquire into the existence of authority of the conservator or the propriety of the conservator's exercise of authority, but restrictions on authority stated in letters of office, or otherwise provided by law, are effective as to the person. A person that pays or delivers property to a conservator is not responsible for proper application of the property.

(b)   Protection under subsection (a) extends to a procedural irregularity or jurisdictional defect in the proceeding leading to the issuance of letters of office and does not substitute for protection for a person that assists or deals with a conservator provided by comparable provisions in law of this state other than this [act] relating to a commercial transaction or simplifying a transfer of securities by a fiduciary.

Section 427. Death of Individual Subject to Conservatorship.

(a)   If an individual subject to conservatorship dies, the conservator shall deliver to the court for safekeeping any will of the individual in the conservator's possession and inform the personal representative named in the will if feasible, or if not feasible, a beneficiary named in the will, of the delivery.

[(b) If 40 days after the death of an individual subject to conservatorship no personal representative has been appointed and no application or petition for appointment is before the court, the conservator may apply to exercise the powers and duties of a personal representative to administer and distribute the decedent's estate. The conservator shall give notice to a person nominated as personal representative by a will of the decedent of which the conservator is aware. The court may grant the application if there is no objection and endorse the letters of office to note that the individual formerly subject to conservatorship is deceased and the conservator has acquired the powers and duties of a personal representative.

(c)   Issuance of an order under this section has the effect of an order of appointment of a personal representative under [Section 3–308 and Parts 6 through 10 of Article III of the Uniform Probate Code]].

(d)   On the death of an individual subject to conservatorship, the conservator shall conclude the administration of the conservatorship estate as provided in Section 431.

Section 428. Presentation and Allowance of Claim.

(a)   A conservator may pay, or secure by encumbering property included in the conservatorship estate, a claim against the conservatorship estate or the individual subject to conservatorship arising before or during the conservatorship, on presentation and allowance in accordance with the priorities under subsection (d). A claimant may present a claim by:

(1) sending or delivering to the conservator a statement in a record of the claim, indicating its basis, the name and address of the claimant, and the amount claimed; or

(2) filing the claim with the court, in a form acceptable to the court, and sending or delivering a copy of the claim to the conservator.

(b) A claim under subsection (a) is presented on receipt by the conservator of the statement of the claim or the filing with the court of the claim, whichever first occurs. A presented claim is allowed if it is not disallowed in whole or in part by the conservator in a record sent or delivered to the claimant not later than 60 days after its presentation. Before payment, the conservator may change an allowance of the claim to a disallowance in whole or in part, but not after allowance under a court order or order directing payment of the claim. Presentation of a claim tolls until 30 days after disallowance of the claim the running of a statute of limitations that has not expired relating to the claim.

(c) A claimant whose claim under subsection (a) has not been paid may petition the court to determine the claim at any time before it is barred by a statute of limitations, and the court may order its allowance, payment, or security by encumbering property included in the conservatorship estate. If a proceeding is pending against the individual subject to conservatorship at the time of appointment of the conservator or is initiated thereafter, the moving party shall give the conservator notice of the proceeding if it could result in creating a claim against the conservatorship estate.

(d) If a conservatorship estate is likely to be exhausted before all existing claims are paid, the conservator shall distribute the estate in money or in kind in payment of claims in the following order:

(1) costs and expenses of administration;

(2) a claim of the federal or state government having priority under law other than this [act];

(3) a claim incurred by the conservator for support, care, education, health, or welfare previously provided to the individual subject to conservatorship or an individual who is in fact dependent on the individual subject to conservatorship;

(4) a claim arising before the conservatorship; and

(5) all other claims.

(e) Preference may not be given in the payment of a claim under subsection (d) over another claim of the same class. A claim due and payable may not be preferred over a claim not due unless:

(1) doing so would leave the conservatorship estate without sufficient funds to pay the basic living and health-care expenses of the individual subject to conservatorship; and

(2) the court authorizes the preference under Section 414(a)(8).

(f) If assets of a conservatorship estate are adequate to meet all existing claims, the court, acting in the best interest of the individual subject to conservatorship, may order the conservator to grant a security interest in the conservatorship estate for payment of a claim at a future date.

Section 429. Personal Liability of Conservator.

(a) Except as otherwise agreed by a conservator, the conservator is not personally liable on a contract properly entered into in a fiduciary capacity in the course of administration of the conservatorship estate unless the conservator fails to reveal the conservator's representative capacity in the contract or before entering into the contract.

(b) A conservator is personally liable for an obligation arising from control of property of the conservatorship estate or an act or omission occurring in the course of administration of the conservatorship estate only if the conservator is personally at fault.

(c)   A claim based on a contract entered into by a conservator in a fiduciary capacity, an obligation arising from control of property included in the conservatorship estate, or a tort committed in the course of administration of the conservatorship estate may be asserted against the conservatorship estate in a proceeding against the conservator in a fiduciary capacity, whether or not the conservator is personally liable for the claim.

(d)   A question of liability between a conservatorship estate and the conservator personally may be determined in a proceeding for accounting, surcharge, or indemnification or another appropriate proceeding or action.

Section 430. Removal of Conservator; Appointment of Successor.

(a)   The court may remove a conservator for failure to perform the conservator's duties or other good cause and appoint a successor conservator to assume the duties of the conservator.

(b)   The court shall hold a hearing to determine whether to remove a conservator and appoint a successor on:

(1)   petition of the individual subject to conservatorship, conservator, or person interested in the welfare of the individual which contains allegations that, if true, would support a reasonable belief that removal of the conservator and appointment of a successor may be appropriate, but the court may decline to hold a hearing if a petition based on the same or substantially similar facts was filed during the preceding six months;

(2)   communication from the individual subject to conservatorship, conservator, or person interested in the welfare of the individual which supports a reasonable belief that removal of the conservator and appointment of a successor may be appropriate; or

(3)   determination by the court that a hearing would be in the best interest of the individual subject to conservatorship.

(c)   Notice of a petition under subsection (b)(1) must be given to the individual subject to conservatorship, the conservator, and any other person the court determines.

(d)   An individual subject to conservatorship who seeks to remove the conservator and have a successor appointed has the right to choose an attorney to represent the individual in this matter. [If the individual is not represented by an attorney, the court shall appoint an attorney under the same conditions as in Section 406.] The court shall award reasonable attorney's fees to the attorney as provided in Section 119.

(e)   In selecting a successor conservator, the court shall follow the priorities under Section 410.

(f)   Not later than 30 days after appointing a successor conservator, the court shall give notice of the appointment to the individual subject to conservatorship and any person entitled to notice under Section 411(e) or a subsequent order.

Section 431. Termination or Modification of Conservatorship.

(a)   A conservatorship for a minor terminates on the earliest of:

(1)   a court order terminating the conservatorship;

(2)   the minor becoming an adult or, if the minor consents or the court finds by clear-and-convincing evidence that substantial harm to the minor's interests is otherwise likely, attaining 21 years of age;

(3)   emancipation of the minor; or

(4)   death of the minor.

(b)   A conservatorship for an adult terminates on order of the court or when the adult dies.

(c) An individual subject to conservatorship, the conservator, or a person interested in the welfare of the individual may petition for:

(1) termination of the conservatorship on the ground that a basis for appointment under Section 401 does not exist or termination would be in the best interest of the individual or for other good cause; or

(2) modification of the conservatorship on the ground that the extent of protection or assistance granted is not appropriate or for other good cause.

(d) The court shall hold a hearing to determine whether termination or modification of a conservatorship is appropriate on:

(1) petition under subsection (c) which contains allegations that, if true, would support a reasonable belief that termination or modification of the conservatorship may be appropriate, but the court may decline to hold a hearing if a petition based on the same or substantially similar facts was filed within the preceding six months;

(2) a communication from the individual subject to conservatorship, conservator, or person interested in the welfare of the individual which supports a reasonable belief that termination or modification of the conservatorship may be appropriate, including because the functional needs of the individual or supports or services available to the individual have changed;

(3) a report from a guardian or conservator which indicates that termination or modification may be appropriate because the functional needs or supports or services available to the individual have changed or a protective arrangement instead of conservatorship or other less restrictive alternative is available; or

(4) a determination by the court that a hearing would be in the best interest of the individual.

(e) Notice of a petition under subsection (c) must be given to the individual subject to conservatorship, the conservator, and any such other person the court determines.

(f) On presentation of prima facie evidence for termination of a conservatorship, the court shall order termination unless it is proven that a basis for appointment of a conservator under Section 401 exists.

(g) The court shall modify the powers granted to a conservator if the powers are excessive or inadequate due to a change in the abilities or limitations of the individual subject to conservatorship, the individual's supports, or other circumstances.

(h) Unless the court otherwise orders for good cause, before terminating a conservatorship, the court shall follow the same procedures to safeguard the rights of the individual subject to conservatorship which apply to a petition for conservatorship.

(i) An individual subject to conservatorship who seeks to terminate or modify the terms of the conservatorship has the right to choose an attorney to represent the individual in this matter. [If the individual is not represented by an attorney, the court shall appoint an attorney under the same conditions as in Section 406.] The court shall award reasonable attorney's fees to the attorney as provided in Section 119.

(j) On termination of a conservatorship other than by reason of the death of the individual subject to conservatorship, property of the conservatorship estate passes to the individual. The order of termination must direct the conservator to file a final report and petition for discharge on approval by the court of the final report.

(k) On termination of a conservatorship by reason of the death of the individual subject to conservatorship, the conservator promptly shall file a final report and petition for discharge on approval by the court of the final report. On approval of the final report, the conservator shall proceed expeditiously to distribute the conservatorship estate to the individual's estate or as otherwise ordered by the court. The conservator may take reasonable measures necessary to preserve the conservatorship estate until distribution can be made.

(*l*)   The court shall issue a final order of discharge on the approval by the court of the final report and satisfaction by the conservator of any other condition the court imposed on the conservator's discharge.

Section 432. Transfer for Benefit of Minor Without Appointment of Conservator.

(a)   Unless a person required to transfer funds or other property to a minor knows that a conservator for the minor has been appointed or a proceeding is pending for conservatorship, the person may transfer an amount or value not exceeding $[15,000] in a 12-month period to:

(1)   a person that has care or custody of the minor and with whom the minor resides;

(2)   a guardian for the minor;

(3)   a custodian under [the Uniform Transfers to Minors Act or Uniform Gifts to Minors Act]; or

(4)   a financial institution as a deposit in an interest-bearing account or certificate solely in the name of the minor and shall give notice to the minor of the deposit.

(b)   A person that transfers funds or other property under this section is not responsible for its proper application.

(c)   A person that receives funds or other property for a minor under subsection (a)(1) or (2) may apply it only to the support, care, education, health, or welfare of the minor, and may not derive a personal financial benefit from it, except for reimbursement for necessary expenses. Funds not applied for these purposes must be preserved for the future support, care, education, health, or welfare of the minor, and the balance, if any, transferred to the minor when the minor becomes an adult or otherwise is emancipated.

[ARTICLE] 5

OTHER PROTECTIVE AGREEMENTS

Section 501. Authority for Protective Arrangement.

(a)   Under this [article], a court:

(1)   on receiving a petition for a guardianship for an adult may order a protective arrangement instead of guardianship as a less restrictive alternative to guardianship; and

(2)   on receiving a petition for a conservatorship for an individual may order a protective arrangement instead of conservatorship as a less restrictive alternative to conservatorship.

(b)   A person interested in an adult's welfare, including the adult or a conservator for the adult, may petition under this [article] for a protective arrangement instead of guardianship.

(c)   The following persons may petition under this [article] for a protective arrangement instead of conservatorship:

(1)   the individual for whom the protective arrangement is sought;

(2)   a person interested in the property, financial affairs, or welfare of the individual, including a person that would be affected adversely by lack of effective management of property or financial affairs of the individual; and

(3)   the guardian for the individual.

Section 502. Basis for Protective Arrangement Instead of Guardianship for Adult.

(a)   After the hearing on a petition under Section 302 for a guardianship or under Section 501(b) for a protective arrangement instead of guardianship, the court may issue an order under subsection (b) for a protective arrangement instead of guardianship if the court finds by clear-and-convincing evidence that:

(1)   the respondent lacks the ability to meet essential requirements for physical health, safety, or self-care because the respondent is unable to receive and evaluate information or make or communicate decisions, even with appropriate supportive services, technological assistance, or supported decision making; and

(2)   the respondent's identified needs cannot be met by a less restrictive alternative.

(b)   If the court makes the findings under subsection (a), the court, instead of appointing a guardian, may:

(1)   authorize or direct a transaction necessary to meet the respondent's need for health, safety, or care, including:

(A)   a particular medical treatment or refusal of a particular medical treatment;

(B)   a move to a specified place of dwelling; or

(C)   visitation or supervised visitation between the respondent and another person;

(2)   restrict access to the respondent by a specified person whose access places the respondent at serious risk of physical, psychological, or financial harm; and

(3)   order other arrangements on a limited basis that are appropriate.

(c)   In deciding whether to issue an order under this section, the court shall consider the factors under Sections 313 and 314 which a guardian must consider when making a decision on behalf of an adult subject to guardianship.

Section 503. Basis for Protective Arrangement Instead of Conservatorship for Adult or Minor.

(a) After the hearing on a petition under Section 402 for conservatorship for an adult or under Section 501(c) for a protective arrangement instead of conservatorship for an adult, the court may issue an order under subsection (c) for a protective arrangement instead of conservatorship for the adult if the court finds by clear-and-convincing evidence that:

(1) the adult is unable to manage property or financial affairs because:

(A) of a limitation in the ability to receive and evaluate information or make or communicate decisions, even with appropriate supportive services, technological assistance, or supported decision making; or

(B) the adult is missing, detained, or unable to return to the United States;

(2) an order under subsection (c) is necessary to:

(A) avoid harm to the adult or significant dissipation of the property of the adult; or

(B) obtain or provide funds or other property needed for the support, care, education, health, or welfare of the adult or an individual entitled to the adult's support; and

(3) the respondent's identified needs cannot be met by a less restrictive alternative.

(b) After the hearing on a petition under Section 402 for conservatorship for a minor or under Section 501(c) for a protective arrangement instead of conservatorship for a minor, the court may issue an order under subsection (c) for a protective arrangement instead of conservatorship for the respondent if the court finds by a preponderance of the evidence that the arrangement is in the minor's best interest, and:

(1) if the minor has a parent, the court gives weight to any recommendation of the parent whether an arrangement is in the minor's best interest;

(2) either:

(A) the minor owns money or property requiring management or protection that otherwise cannot be provided;

(B) the minor has or may have financial affairs that may be put at unreasonable risk or hindered because of the minor's age; or

(C) the arrangement is necessary or desirable to obtain or provide funds or other property needed for the support, care, education, health, or welfare of the minor; and

(3) the order under subsection (c) is necessary or desirable to obtain or provide money needed for the support, care, education, health, or welfare of the minor.

(c) If the court makes the findings under subsection (a) or (b), the court, instead of appointing a conservator, may:

(1) authorize or direct a transaction necessary to protect the financial interest or property of the respondent, including:

(A) an action to establish eligibility for benefits;

(B) payment, delivery, deposit, or retention of funds or property;

(C) sale, mortgage, lease, or other transfer of property;

(D) purchase of an annuity;

(E) entry into a contractual relationship, including a contract to provide for personal care, supportive services, education, training, or employment;

(F) addition to or establishment of a trust;

(G)   ratification or invalidation of a contract, trust, will, or other transaction, including a transaction related to the property or business affairs of the respondent; or

(H)   settlement of a claim; or

(2)   restrict access to the respondent's property by a specified person whose access to the property places the respondent at serious risk of financial harm.

(d)   After the hearing on a petition under Section 501(a)(2) or (c), whether or not the court makes the findings under subsection (a) or (b), the court may issue an order to restrict access to the respondent or the respondent's property by a specified person that the court finds by clear-and-convincing evidence:

(1)   through fraud, coercion, duress, or the use of deception and control caused or attempted to cause an action that would have resulted in financial harm to the respondent or the respondent's property; and

(2)   poses a serious risk of substantial financial harm to the respondent or the respondent's property.

(e)   Before issuing an order under subsection (c) or (d), the court shall consider the factors under Section 418 a conservator must consider when making a decision on behalf of an individual subject to conservatorship.

(f)   Before issuing an order under subsection (c) or (d) for a respondent who is a minor, the court also shall consider the best interest of the minor, the preference of the parents of the minor, and the preference of the minor, if the minor is 12 years of age or older.

Section 504. Petition for Protective Arrangement.

A petition for a protective arrangement instead of guardianship or conservatorship must state the petitioner's name, principal residence, current street address, if different, relationship to the respondent, interest in the protective arrangement, the name and address of any attorney representing the petitioner, and, to the extent known, the following:

(1)   the respondent's name, age, principal residence, current street address, if different, and, if different, address of the dwelling in which it is proposed the respondent will reside if the petition is granted;

(2)   the name and address of the respondent's:

(A)   spouse [or domestic partner] or, if the respondent has none, an adult with whom the respondent has shared household responsibilities for more than six months in the 12-month period before the filing of the petition;

(B)   adult children or, if none, each parent and adult sibling of the respondent, or, if none, at least one adult nearest in kinship to the respondent who can be found with reasonable diligence; and

(C)   adult stepchildren whom the respondent actively parented during the stepchildren's minor years and with whom the respondent had an ongoing relationship in the two year period immediately before the filing of the petition;

(3)   the name and current address of each of the following, if applicable:

(A)   a person responsible for the care or custody of the respondent;

(B)   any attorney currently representing the respondent;

(C)   the representative payee appointed by the Social Security Administration for the respondent;

(D)   a guardian or conservator acting for the respondent in this state or another jurisdiction;

(E)   a trustee or custodian of a trust or custodianship of which the respondent is a beneficiary;

(F)   the fiduciary appointed for the respondent by the Department of Veterans Affairs;

(G)   an agent designated under a [power of attorney for health care] in which the respondent is identified as the principal;

(H)   an agent designated under a power of attorney for finances in which the respondent is identified as the principal;

(I)   a person nominated as guardian or conservator by the respondent if the respondent is 12 years of age or older;

(J)   a person nominated as guardian by the respondent's parent[,] [or] spouse [, or domestic partner]in a will or other signed record;

(K)   a person known to have routinely assisted the respondent with decision making in the six-month period immediately before the filing of the petition; and

(L)   if the respondent is a minor:

(i)   an adult not otherwise listed with whom the respondent resides; and

(ii)   each person not otherwise listed that had primary care or custody of the respondent for at least 60 days during the two years immediately before the filing of the petition or for at least 730 days during the five years immediately before the filing of the petition;

(4)   the nature of the protective arrangement sought;

(5)   the reason the protective arrangement sought is necessary, including a brief description of:

(A)   the nature and extent of the respondent's alleged need;

(B)   any less restrictive alternative for meeting the respondent's alleged need which has been considered or implemented;

(C)   if no less restrictive alternative has been considered or implemented, the reason less restrictive alternatives have not been considered or implemented; and

(D)   the reason other less restrictive alternatives are insufficient to meet the respondent's alleged need;

(6)   the name and current address, if known, of any person with whom the petitioner seeks to limit the respondent's contact;

(7)   whether the respondent needs an interpreter, translator, or other form of support to communicate effectively with the court or understand court proceedings;

(8)   if a protective arrangement instead of guardianship is sought and the respondent has property other than personal effects, a general statement of the respondent's property with an estimate of its value, including any insurance or pension, and the source and amount of any other anticipated income or receipts; and

(9)   if a protective arrangement instead of conservatorship is sought, a general statement of the respondent's property with an estimate of its value, including any insurance or pension, and the source and amount of other anticipated income or receipts.

Section 505. Notice and Hearing.

(a)   On filing of a petition under Section 501, the court shall set a date, time, and place for a hearing on the petition.

(b)   A copy of a petition under Section 501 and notice of a hearing on the petition must be served personally on the respondent. The notice must inform the respondent of the respondent's rights at the hearing, including the right to an attorney and to attend the hearing. The notice must include a description of the nature, purpose, and consequences of granting the petition. The court may not grant the petition if notice substantially complying with this subsection is not served on the respondent.

(c)   In a proceeding on a petition under Section 501, the notice required under subsection (b) must be given to the persons required to be listed in the petition under Section 504(1) through (3) and any other person interested in the respondent's welfare the court determines. Failure to give notice under this subsection does not preclude the court from granting the petition.

(d)   After the court has ordered a protective arrangement under this [article], notice of a hearing on a petition filed under this [act], together with a copy of the petition, must be given to the respondent and any other person the court determines.

Section 506. Appointment and Role of [Visitor].

(a)   On filing of a petition under Section 501 for a protective arrangement instead of guardianship, the court shall appoint a [visitor]. The [visitor] must be an individual with training or experience in the type of abilities, limitations, and needs alleged in the petition.

(b)   On filing of a petition under Section 501 for a protective arrangement instead of conservatorship for a minor, the court may appoint a [visitor] to investigate a matter related to the petition or inform the minor or a parent of the minor about the petition or a related matter.

(c)   On filing of a petition under Section 501 for a protective arrangement instead of conservatorship for an adult, the court shall appoint a [visitor][unless the respondent is represented by an attorney appointed by the court]. The [visitor] must be an individual with training or experience in the types of abilities, limitations, and needs alleged in the petition.

(d)   A [visitor] appointed under subsection (a) or (c) shall interview the respondent in person and in a manner the respondent is best able to understand:

(1)   explain to the respondent the substance of the petition, the nature, purpose, and effect of the proceeding, and the respondent's rights at the hearing on the petition;

(2)   determine the respondent's views with respect to the order sought;

(3)   inform the respondent of the respondent's right to employ and consult with an attorney at the respondent's expense and the right to request a court-appointed attorney;

(4)   inform the respondent that all costs and expenses of the proceeding, including respondent's attorney's fees, may be paid from the respondent's assets;

(5)   if the petitioner seeks an order related to the dwelling of the respondent, visit the respondent's present dwelling and any dwelling in which it is reasonably believed the respondent will live if the order is granted;

(6)   if a protective arrangement instead of guardianship is sought, obtain information from any physician or other person known to have treated, advised, or assessed the respondent's relevant physical or mental condition;

(7)   if a protective arrangement instead of conservatorship is sought, review financial records of the respondent, if relevant to the [visitor's] recommendation under subsection (e)(3); and

(8)   investigate the allegations in the petition and any other matter relating to the petition the court directs.

(e)   A [visitor] under this section promptly shall file a report in a record with the court, which must include:

(1)   a recommendation whether an attorney should be appointed to represent the respondent;

(2)   to the extent relevant to the order sought, a summary of self-care, independent-living tasks, and financial-management tasks the respondent:

(A)   can manage without assistance or with existing supports;

(B)   could manage with the assistance of appropriate supportive services, technological assistance, or supported decision making; and

(C)   cannot manage;

(3)   a recommendation regarding the appropriateness of the protective arrangement sought and whether a less restrictive alternative for meeting the respondent's needs is available;

(4)   if the petition seeks to change the physical location of the dwelling of the respondent, a statement whether the proposed dwelling meets the respondent's needs and whether the respondent has expressed a preference as to the respondent's dwelling;

(5)   a recommendation whether a professional evaluation under Section 508 is necessary;

(6)   a statement whether the respondent is able to attend a hearing at the location court proceedings typically are held;

(7)   a statement whether the respondent is able to participate in a hearing and which identifies any technology or other form of support that would enhance the respondent's ability to participate; and

(8)   any other matter the court directs.

Section 507. Appointment and Role of Attorney.

Alternative A

(a)   The court shall appoint an attorney to represent the respondent in a proceeding under this [article] if:

(1)   the respondent requests the appointment;

(2)   the [visitor] recommends the appointment; or

(3)   the court determines the respondent needs representation.

Alternative B

(a)   Unless the respondent in a proceeding under this [article] is represented by an attorney, the court shall appoint an attorney to represent the respondent, regardless of the respondent's ability to pay.

End of Alternatives

(b)   An attorney representing the respondent in a proceeding under this [article] shall:

(1)   make reasonable efforts to ascertain the respondent's wishes;

(2)   advocate for the respondent's wishes to the extent reasonably ascertainable; and

(3)   if the respondent's wishes are not reasonably ascertainable, advocate for the result that is the least restrictive alternative in type, duration, and scope, consistent with the respondent's interests.

[(c)   The court shall appoint an attorney to represent a parent of a minor who is the subject of a proceeding under this [article] if:

(1)   the parent objects to the entry of an order for a protective arrangement instead of guardianship or conservatorship;

(2)   the court determines that counsel is needed to ensure that consent to the entry of an order for a protective arrangement is informed; or

(3)   the court otherwise determines the parent needs representation.]

Section 508. Professional Evaluation.

(a)   At or before a hearing on a petition under this [article] for a protective arrangement, the court shall order a professional evaluation of the respondent:

(1)   if the respondent requests the evaluation; or

(2)   or in other cases, unless the court finds that it has sufficient information to determine the respondent's needs and abilities without the evaluation.

(b)   If the court orders an evaluation under subsection (a), the respondent must be examined by a licensed physician, psychologist, social worker, or other individual appointed by the court who is qualified to evaluate the respondent's alleged cognitive and functional abilities and limitations and will not be advantaged or disadvantaged by a decision to grant the petition or otherwise have a conflict of interest. The individual conducting the evaluation promptly shall file a report in a record with the court. Unless otherwise directed by the court, the report must contain:

(1)   a description of the nature, type, and extent of the respondent's cognitive and functional abilities and limitations;

(2)   an evaluation of the respondent's mental and physical condition and, if appropriate, educational potential, adaptive behavior, and social skills;

(3)   a prognosis for improvement, including with regard to the ability to manage the respondent's property and financial affairs if a limitation in that ability is alleged, and recommendation for the appropriate treatment, support, or habilitation plan; and

(4)   the date of the examination on which the report is based.

(c)   The respondent may decline to participate in an evaluation ordered under subsection (a).

Section 509. Attendance and Rights at Hearing.

(a)   Except as otherwise provided in subsection (b), a hearing under this [article] may not proceed unless the respondent attends the hearing. If it is not reasonably feasible for the respondent to attend a hearing at the location court proceedings typically are held, the court shall make reasonable efforts to hold the hearing at an alternative location convenient to the respondent or allow the respondent to attend the hearing using real-time audio-visual technology.

(b)   A hearing under this [article] may proceed without the respondent in attendance if the court finds by clear-and-convincing evidence that:

(1)   the respondent consistently and repeatedly has refused to attend the hearing after having been fully informed of the right to attend and the potential consequences of failing to do so;

(2)   there is no practicable way for the respondent to attend and participate in the hearing even with appropriate supportive services and technological assistance; or

(3)   the respondent is a minor who has received proper notice and attendance would be harmful to the minor.

(c)   The respondent may be assisted in a hearing under this [article] by a person or persons of the respondent's choosing, assistive technology, or an interpreter or translator, or a combination of these supports. If assistance would facilitate the respondent's participation in the hearing, but is not otherwise available to the respondent, the court shall make reasonable efforts to provide it.

(d)   The respondent has a right to choose an attorney to represent the respondent at a hearing under this [article].

(e)   At a hearing under this [article], the respondent may:

(1)   present evidence and subpoena witnesses and documents;

(2)   examine witnesses, including any court-appointed evaluator and the [visitor]; and

(3)   otherwise participate in the hearing.

(f)   A hearing under this [article] must be closed on request of the respondent and a showing of good cause.

(g)   Any person may request to participate in a hearing under this [article]. The court may grant the request, with or without a hearing, on determining that the best interest of the respondent will be served. The court may impose appropriate conditions on the person's participation.

Section 510. Notice of Order.

The court shall give notice of an order under this [article] to the individual who is subject to the protective arrangement instead of guardianship or conservatorship, a person whose access to the individual is restricted by the order, and any other person the court determines.

Section 511. Confidentiality of Records.

(a)   The existence of a proceeding for or the existence of a protective arrangement instead of guardianship or conservatorship is a matter of public record unless the court seals the record after:

(1)   the respondent, the individual subject to the protective arrangement, or the parent of a minor subject to the protective arrangement requests the record be sealed; and

(2)   either:

(A)   the proceeding is dismissed;

(B)   the protective arrangement is no longer in effect; or

(C)   an act authorized by the order granting the protective arrangement has been completed.

(b)   A respondent, an individual subject to a protective arrangement instead of guardianship or conservatorship, an attorney designated by the respondent or individual, a parent of a minor subject to a protective arrangement, and any other person the court determines are entitled to access court records of the proceeding and resulting protective arrangement. A person not otherwise entitled to access to court records under this subsection for good cause may petition the court for access. The court shall grant access if access is in the best interest of the respondent or individual subject to the protective arrangement or furthers the public interest and does not endanger the welfare or financial interests of the respondent or individual.

[(c)   A report of a [visitor] or professional evaluation generated in the course of a proceeding under this [article] must be sealed on filing but is available to:

(1)   the court;

(2)   the individual who is the subject of the report or evaluation, without limitation as to use;

(3)   the petitioner[, visitor,] and petitioner's and respondent's attorneys, for purposes of the proceeding;

(4)   unless the court orders otherwise, an agent appointed under a power of attorney for finances in which the respondent is the principal;

(5) if the order is for a protective arrangement instead of guardianship and unless the court orders otherwise, an agent appointed under a [power of attorney for health care] in which the respondent is identified as the principal; and

(6) any other person if it is in the public interest or for a purpose the court orders for good cause.]

Section 512. Appointment of [Master].

The court may appoint a [master] to assist in implementing a protective arrangement under this [article]. The [master] has the authority conferred by the order of appointment and serves until discharged by court order.

[[ARTICLE] 6

FORMS

Section 601. Use of Forms.

Use of the forms contained in this [article] is optional. Failure to use these forms does not prejudice any party.

Section 602. Petition for Guardianship for Minor.

This form may be used to petition for guardianship for a minor.

Petition for Guardianship for Minor

State of:

[County] of:

Name and address of attorney representing Petitioner, if applicable:

Note to Petitioner: This form can be used to petition for a guardian for a minor. A court may appoint a guardian for a minor who does not have a guardian if the court finds the appointment is in the minor's best interest, and: (1) the parents, after being fully informed of the nature and consequences of guardianship, consent; (2) all parental rights have been terminated; or (3) the court finds by clear-and-convincing evidence that the parents are unwilling or unable to exercise their parental rights.

1. **Information about the person filing this petition (the "Petitioner").**

   a. Name:

   b. Principal residence:

   c. Current street address (if different):

   d. Relationship to minor:

   e. Interest in this petition:

   f. Telephone number (optional):

   g. Email address (optional):

2. **Information about the minor alleged to need a guardian.**

   Provide the following information to the extent known.

   a. Name:

   b. Age:

   c. Principal residence:

   d. Current street address (if different):

   e. If Petitioner anticipates the minor moving, or seeks to move the minor, proposed new address:

   f. Does the minor need an interpreter, translator, or other form of support to communicate with the court or understand court proceedings? If so, please explain.

   g. Telephone number (optional):

   h. Email address (optional):

3. **Information about the minor's parent(s).**

    a.   Name(s) of living parent(s):

    b.   Current street address(es) of living parent(s):

    c.   Does any parent need an interpreter, translator, or other form of support to communicate with the court or understand court proceedings? If so, please explain.

4. **People who are required to be notified of this petition.** State the name and current address of the people listed in Appendix A.

5. **Appointment requested.** State the name and address of any proposed guardian and the reason the proposed guardian should be selected.

6. **State why Petitioner seeks the appointment.** Include a description of the nature and extent of the minor's alleged need.

7. **Property.** If the minor has property other than personal effects, state the minor's property with an estimate of its value.

8. **Other proceedings.** If there are any other proceedings concerning the care or custody of the minor currently pending in any court in this state or another jurisdiction, please describe them.

9. **Attorney(s).** If the minor or the minor's parent is represented by an attorney in this matter, state the name, [telephone number, email address,] and address of the attorney(s).

SIGNATURE

_____   _____

Signature of Petitioner   Date

_____   _____

Signature of Petitioner's Attorney if   Date
Petitioner is Represented by Counsel

Appendix A:

People whose name and address must be listed in Section 4
of this petition if they are not the Petitioner.

- The minor, if the minor is 12 years of age or older;
- Each parent of the minor or, if there are none, the adult nearest in kinship that can be found;
- An adult with whom the minor resides;
- Each person that had primary care or custody of the minor for at least 60 days during the two years immediately before the filing of the petition or for at least 730 days during the five years immediately before the filing of the petition;
- If the minor is 12 years of age or older, any person nominated as guardian by the minor;
- Any person nominated as guardian by a parent of the minor;
- The grandparents of the minor;
- Adult siblings of the minor; and
- Any current guardian or conservator for the minor appointed in this state or another jurisdiction.

Section 603. Petition for Guardianship, Conservatorship, or Protective Arrangement.

This form may be used to petition for:

(1)   guardianship for an adult;

(2)   conservatorship for an adult or minor;

(3)   a protective arrangement instead of guardianship for an adult; or

(4)   a protective arrangement instead of conservatorship for an adult or minor.

Petition for Guardianship, Conservatorship, or Protective Arrangement

State of:

[County] of:

Name and address of attorney representing Petitioner, if applicable:

Note to Petitioner: This form can be used to petition for a guardian, conservator, or both, or for a protective arrangement instead of either a guardianship or conservatorship. This form should not be used to petition for guardianship for a minor.

The court may appoint a guardian or order a protective arrangement instead of guardianship for an adult if the adult lacks the ability to meet essential requirements for physical health, safety, or self-care because (1) the adult is unable to receive and evaluate information or make or communicate decisions even with the use of supportive services, technological assistance, and supported decision-making, and (2) the adult's identified needs cannot be met by a less restrictive alternative.

The court may appoint a conservator or order a protective arrangement instead of conservatorship for an adult if (1) the adult is unable to manage property and financial affairs because of a limitation in the ability to receive and evaluate information or make or communicate decisions even with the use of supportive services, technological assistance, and supported decision making or the adult is missing, detained, or unable to return to the United States, and (2) appointment is necessary to avoid harm to the adult or significant dissipation of the property of the adult, or to obtain or provide funds or other property needed for the support, care, education, health, or welfare of the adult, or of an individual who is entitled to the adult's support, and protection is necessary or desirable to provide funds or other property for that purpose.

The court may appoint a conservator or order a protective arrangement instead of conservatorship for a minor if (1) the minor owns funds or other property requiring management or protection that cannot otherwise be provided; or (2) it would be in the minor's best interest, and the minor has or may have financial affairs that may be put at unreasonable risk or hindered because of the minor's age, or appointment is necessary or desirable to provide funds or other property needed for the support, care, education, health, or welfare of the minor.

The court may also order a protective arrangement instead of conservatorship that restricts access to an individual or an individual's property by a person that the court finds: (1) through fraud, coercion, duress, or the use of deception and control, caused, or attempted to cause, an action that would have resulted in financial harm to the individual or the individual's property; and (2) poses a serious risk of substantial financial harm to the individual or the individual's property.

1.   **Information about the person filing this petition (the "Petitioner").**

     a.   Name:

     b.   Principal residence:

     c.   Current street address (if different):

     d.   Relationship to Respondent:

     e.   Interest in this petition:

f.   Telephone number (optional):

g.   Email address (optional):

2.   **Information about the individual alleged to need protection (the "Respondent").** Provide the following information to the extent known.

a.   Name:

b.   Age:

c.   Principal residence:

d.   Current street address (if different):

e.   If Petitioner anticipates Respondent moving, or seeks to move Respondent, proposed new address:

f.   Does Respondent need an interpreter, translator, or other form of support to communicate with the court or understand court proceedings? If so, please explain.

g.   Telephone number (optional):

h.   Email address (optional):

3.   **People who are required to be notified of this petition.** State the name and address of the people listed in Appendix A.

4.   **Existing agents.** State the name and address of any person appointed as an agent under a power of attorney for finances or [power of attorney for health care], or who has been appointed as the individual's representative for payment of benefits.

5.   **Action requested.** State whether Petitioner is seeking appointment of a guardian, a conservator, or a protective arrangement instead of an appointment.

6.   **Order requested or appointment requested.** If seeking a protective arrangement instead of a guardianship or conservatorship, state the transaction or other action you want the court to order. If seeking appointment of a guardian or conservator, state the powers Petitioner requests the court grant to a guardian or conservator.

7.   **State why the appointment or protective arrangement sought is necessary.** Include a description of the nature and extent of Respondent's alleged need.

8.   **State all less restrictive alternatives to meeting Respondent's alleged need that have been considered or implemented.** Less restrictive alternatives could include supported decision making, technological assistance, or the appointment of an agent by Respondent including appointment under a [power of attorney for health care] or power of attorney for finances. If no alternative has been considered or implemented, state the reason why not.

9.   **Explain why less restrictive alternatives will not meet Respondent's alleged need.**

10. **Provide a general statement of Respondent's property and an estimate of its value.** Include any real property such as a house or land, insurance or pension, and the source and amount of any other anticipated income or receipts. As part of this statement, indicate, if known, how the property is titled (for example, is it jointly owned?).

11. **For a petition seeking appointment of a conservator. (skip this section if not asking for appointment of a conservator)**

a.   If seeking appointment of a conservator with all powers permissible under this state's law, explain why appointment of a conservator with fewer powers (i.e., a "limited conservatorship") or other protective arrangement instead of conservatorship will not meet the individual's alleged needs.

    b.   If seeking a limited conservatorship, state the property Petitioner requests be placed under the conservator's control and any proposed limitation on the conservator's powers and duties.

    c.   State the name and address of any proposed conservator and the reason the proposed conservator should be selected.

    d.   If Respondent is 12 years of age or older, state the name and address of any person Respondent nominates as conservator.

    e.   If alleging a limitation in Respondent's ability to receive and evaluate information, provide a brief description of the nature and extent of Respondent's alleged limitation.

    f.   If alleging that Respondent is missing, detained, or unable to return to the United States, state the relevant circumstances, including the time and nature of the disappearance or detention and a description of any search or inquiry concerning Respondent's whereabouts.

12. **For a petition seeking appointment of a guardian. (skip this section if not asking for appointment of a guardian)**

    a.   If seeking appointment of a guardian with all powers permissible under this state's law, explain why appointment of a guardian with fewer powers (i.e., a "limited guardianship") or other protective arrangement instead of guardianship will not meet the individual's alleged needs.

    b.   If seeking a limited guardianship, state the powers Petitioner requests be granted to the guardian.

    c.   State the name and address of any proposed guardian and the reason the proposed guardian should be selected.

    d.   State the name and address of any person nominated as guardian by Respondent, or, in a will or other signed writing or other record, by Respondent's parent or spouse [or domestic partner].

13. **Attorney.** If Petitioner, Respondent, or, if Respondent is a minor, Respondent's parent is represented by an attorney in this matter, state the name, [telephone number, email address, and] address of the attorney(s).

SIGNATURE

_____   _____

Signature of Petitioner   Date

_____   _____

Signature of Petitioner's Attorney if   Date
Petitioner is Represented by Counsel

Appendix A:

**People whose name and address must be listed in Section 3
of this petition, if they are not the Petitioner.**

•   Respondent's spouse [or domestic partner], or if Respondent has none, any adult with whom Respondent has shared household responsibilities in the past six months;

- Respondent's adult children, or, if Respondent has none, Respondent's parents and adult siblings, or if Respondent has none, one or more adults nearest in kinship to Respondent who can be found with reasonable diligence;

- Respondent's adult stepchildren whom Respondent actively parented during the stepchildren's minor years and with whom Respondent had an ongoing relationship within two years of this petition;

- Any person responsible for the care or custody of Respondent;

- Any attorney currently representing Respondent;

- Any representative payee for Respondent appointed by the Social Security Administration;

- Any current guardian or conservator for Respondent appointed in this state or another jurisdiction;

- Any trustee or custodian of a trust or custodianship of which Respondent is a beneficiary;

- Any Veterans Administration fiduciary for Respondent;

- Any person Respondent has designated as agent under a power of attorney for finances;

- Any person Respondent has designated as agent under a [power of attorney for health care];

- Any person known to have routinely assisted the individual with decision making in the previous six months;

- Any person Respondent nominates as guardian or conservator; and

- Any person nominated as guardian by Respondent's parent or spouse [or domestic partner] in a will or other signed writing or other record.

Section 604. Notification of Rights for Adult Subject to Guardianship or Conservatorship.

This form may be used to notify an adult subject to guardianship or conservatorship of the adult's rights under Sections 311 and 412.

Notification of Rights

You are getting this notice because a guardian, conservator, or both have been appointed for you. It tells you about some important rights you have. It does not tell you about all your rights. If you have questions about your rights, you can ask an attorney or another person, including your guardian or conservator, to help you understand your rights.

General rights:

You have the right to exercise any right the court has not given to your guardian or conservator.

You also have the right to ask the court to:

- end your guardianship, conservatorship, or both;

- increase or decrease the powers granted to your guardian, conservator, or both;

- make other changes that affect what your guardian or conservator can do or how they do it; and

- replace the person that was appointed with someone else.

You also have a right to hire an attorney to help you do any of these things.

Additional rights for persons for whom a guardian has been appointed:

As an adult subject to guardianship, you have a right to:

(1)   be involved in decisions affecting you, including decisions about your care, where you live, your activities, and your social interactions, to the extent reasonably feasible;

(2)   be involved in decisions about your health care to the extent reasonably feasible, and to have other people help you understand the risks and benefits of health-care options;

(3)   be notified at least 14 days in advance of a change in where you live or a permanent move to a nursing home, mental-health facility, or other facility that places restrictions on your ability to leave or have visitors, unless the guardian has proposed this change in the guardian's plan or the court has expressly authorized it;

(4)   ask the court to prevent your guardian from changing where you live or selling or surrendering your primary dwelling by [insert process for asking the court to prevent such a move];

(5)   vote and get married unless the court order appointing your guardian states that you cannot do so;

(6)   receive a copy of your guardian's report and your guardian's plan; and

(7)   communicate, visit, or interact with other people (this includes the right to have visitors, to make and receive telephone calls, personal mail, or electronic communications) unless:

- your guardian has been authorized by the court by specific order to restrict these communications, visits, or interactions;

- a protective order is in effect that limits contact between you and other people; or

- your guardian has good cause to believe the restriction is needed to protect you from significant physical, psychological, or financial harm and the restriction is for not more than seven business days if the person has a family or pre-existing social relationship with you or not more than 60 days if the person does not have that kind of relationship with you.

Additional rights for persons for whom a conservator has been appointed:

As an adult subject to conservatorship, you have a right to:

(1)   participate in decisions about how your property is managed to the extent feasible; and

(2)   receive a copy of your conservator's inventory, report, and plan.]

[ARTICLE] 7

MISCELLANEOUS PROVISIONS

UNIFORM POWER OF ATTORNEY ACT (2006)*

[ARTICLE] 1. GENERAL PROVISIONS

[ARTICLE] 2. AUTHORITY

[ARTICLE] 3. STATUTORY FORMS

[ARTICLE] 4. MISCELLANEOUS PROVISIONS

[ARTICLE] 1

GENERAL PROVISIONS

Section 101. Short Title.

This [act] may be cited as the Uniform Power of Attorney Act.

Section 102. Definitions.

In this [act]:

(1) "Agent" means a person granted authority to act for a principal under a power of attorney, whether denominated an agent, attorney-in-fact, or otherwise. The term includes an original agent, coagent, successor agent, and a person to which an agent's authority is delegated.

(2) "Durable," with respect to a power of attorney, means not terminated by the principal's incapacity.

(3) "Electronic" means relating to technology having electrical, digital, magnetic, wireless, optical, electromagnetic, or similar capabilities.

(4) "Good faith" means honesty in fact.

(5) "Incapacity" means inability of an individual to manage property or business affairs because the individual:

(A) has an impairment in the ability to receive and evaluate information or make or communicate decisions even with the use of technological assistance; or

(B) is:

(i) missing;

(ii) detained, including incarcerated in a penal system; or

(iii) outside the United States and unable to return.

(6) "Person" means an individual, corporation, business trust, estate, trust, partnership, limited liability company, association, joint venture, public corporation, government or governmental subdivision, agency, or instrumentality, or any other legal or commercial entity.

(7) "Power of attorney" means a writing or other record that grants authority to an agent to act in the place of the principal, whether or not the term power of attorney is used.

(8) "Presently exercisable general power of appointment," with respect to property or a property interest subject to a power of appointment, means power exercisable at the time in question to vest absolute ownership in the principal individually, the principal's estate, the principal's creditors, or the creditors of the principal's estate. The term includes a power of appointment not exercisable until the occurrence of a specified event, the satisfaction of an ascertainable standard, or the passage of a specified period only after the occurrence of the specified event, the satisfaction of the ascertainable standard, or the passage of the specified period. The term does not include a power exercisable in a fiduciary capacity or only by will.

(9) "Principal" means an individual who grants authority to an agent in a power of attorney.

(10) "Property" means anything that may be the subject of ownership, whether real or personal, or legal or equitable, or any interest or right therein.

(11) "Record" means information that is inscribed on a tangible medium or that is stored in an electronic or other medium and is retrievable in perceivable form.

(12) "Sign" means, with present intent to authenticate or adopt a record:

(A) to execute or adopt a tangible symbol; or

(B) to attach to or logically associate with the record an electronic sound, symbol, or process.

(13) "State" means a state of the United States, the District of Columbia, Puerto Rico, the United States Virgin Islands, or any territory or insular possession subject to the jurisdiction of the United States.

(14) "Stocks and bonds" means stocks, bonds, mutual funds, and all other types of securities and financial instruments, whether held directly, indirectly, or in any other manner. The term does not include commodity futures contracts and call or put options on stocks or stock indexes.

Section 103. Applicability.

This [act] applies to all powers of attorney except:

(1) a power to the extent it is coupled with an interest in the subject of the power, including a power given to or for the benefit of a creditor in connection with a credit transaction;

(2) a power to make health-care decisions;

(3) a proxy or other delegation to exercise voting rights or management rights with respect to an entity; and

(4) a power created on a form prescribed by a government or governmental subdivision, agency, or instrumentality for a governmental purpose.

Section 104. Power of Attorney Is Durable.

A power of attorney created under this [act] is durable unless it expressly provides that it is terminated by the incapacity of the principal.

Section 105. Execution of Power of Attorney.

A power of attorney must be signed by the principal or in the principal's conscious presence by another individual directed by the principal to sign the principal's name on the power of attorney. A signature on a power of attorney is presumed to be genuine if the principal acknowledges the signature before a notary public or other individual authorized by law to take acknowledgments.

Section 106. Validity of Power of Attorney.

(a) A power of attorney executed in this state on or after [the effective date of this [act]] is valid if its execution complies with Section 105.

(b) A power of attorney executed in this state before [the effective date of this [act]] is valid if its execution complied with the law of this state as it existed at the time of execution.

(c) A power of attorney executed other than in this state is valid in this state if, when the power of attorney was executed, the execution complied with:

(1) the law of the jurisdiction that determines the meaning and effect of the power of attorney pursuant to Section 107; or

(2) the requirements for a military power of attorney pursuant to 10 U.S.C. Section 1044b [, as amended].

(d) Except as otherwise provided by statute other than this [act], a photocopy or electronically transmitted copy of an original power of attorney has the same effect as the original.

Section 107. Meaning and Effect of Power of Attorney.

The meaning and effect of a power of attorney is determined by the law of the jurisdiction indicated in the power of attorney and, in the absence of an indication of jurisdiction, by the law of the jurisdiction in which the power of attorney was executed.

Section 108. Nomination of [Conservator or Guardian]; Relation of Agent to Court-Appointed Fiduciary.

(a) In a power of attorney, a principal may nominate a [conservator or guardian] of the principal's estate or [guardian] of the principal's person for consideration by the court if protective proceedings for the principal's estate or person are begun after the principal executes the power of attorney. [Except for good cause shown or disqualification, the court shall make its appointment in accordance with the principal's most recent nomination.]

(b) If, after a principal executes a power of attorney, a court appoints a [conservator or guardian] of the principal's estate or other fiduciary charged with the management of some or all of the principal's property, the agent is accountable to the fiduciary as well as to the principal. [The power of attorney is not terminated and the agent's authority continues unless limited, suspended, or terminated by the court.]

Section 109. When Power of Attorney Effective.

(a) A power of attorney is effective when executed unless the principal provides in the power of attorney that it becomes effective at a future date or upon the occurrence of a future event or contingency.

(b) If a power of attorney becomes effective upon the occurrence of a future event or contingency, the principal, in the power of attorney, may authorize one or more persons to determine in a writing or other record that the event or contingency has occurred.

(c) If a power of attorney becomes effective upon the principal's incapacity and the principal has not authorized a person to determine whether the principal is incapacitated, or the person authorized is unable or unwilling to make the determination, the power of attorney becomes effective upon a determination in a writing or other record by:

(1) a physician [or licensed psychologist] that the principal is incapacitated within the meaning of Section 102(5)(A); or

(2) an attorney at law, a judge, or an appropriate governmental official that the principal is incapacitated within the meaning of Section 102(5)(B).

(d) A person authorized by the principal in the power of attorney to determine that the principal is incapacitated may act as the principal's personal representative pursuant to the Health Insurance Portability and Accountability Act, Sections 1171 through 1179 of the Social Security Act, 42 U.S.C. Section 1320d, [as amended,] and applicable regulations, to obtain access to the principal's health-care information and communicate with the principal's health-care provider.

Section 110. Termination of Power of Attorney or Agent's Authority.

(a) A power of attorney terminates when:

(1) the principal dies;

(2) the principal becomes incapacitated, if the power of attorney is not durable;

(3) the principal revokes the power of attorney;

(4) the power of attorney provides that it terminates;

(5) the purpose of the power of attorney is accomplished; or

(6)   the principal revokes the agent's authority or the agent dies, becomes incapacitated, or resigns, and the power of attorney does not provide for another agent to act under the power of attorney.

(b)   An agent's authority terminates when:

(1)   the principal revokes the authority;

(2)   the agent dies, becomes incapacitated, or resigns;

(3)   an action is filed for the [dissolution] or annulment of the agent's marriage to the principal or their legal separation, unless the power of attorney otherwise provides; or

(4)   the power of attorney terminates.

(c)   Unless the power of attorney otherwise provides, an agent's authority is exercisable until the authority terminates under subsection (b), notwithstanding a lapse of time since the execution of the power of attorney.

(d)   Termination of an agent's authority or of a power of attorney is not effective as to the agent or another person that, without actual knowledge of the termination, acts in good faith under the power of attorney. An act so performed, unless otherwise invalid or unenforceable, binds the principal and the principal's successors in interest.

(e)   Incapacity of the principal of a power of attorney that is not durable does not revoke or terminate the power of attorney as to an agent or other person that, without actual knowledge of the incapacity, acts in good faith under the power of attorney. An act so performed, unless otherwise invalid or unenforceable, binds the principal and the principal's successors in interest.

(f)   The execution of a power of attorney does not revoke a power of attorney previously executed by the principal unless the subsequent power of attorney provides that the previous power of attorney is revoked or that all other powers of attorney are revoked.

Section 111. Coagents and Successor Agents.

(a)   A principal may designate two or more persons to act as coagents. Unless the power of attorney otherwise provides, each coagent may exercise its authority independently.

(b)   A principal may designate one or more successor agents to act if an agent resigns, dies, becomes incapacitated, is not qualified to serve, or declines to serve. A principal may grant authority to designate one or more successor agents to an agent or other person designated by name, office, or function. Unless the power of attorney otherwise provides, a successor agent:

(1)   has the same authority as that granted to the original agent; and

(2)   may not act until all predecessor agents have resigned, died, become incapacitated, are no longer qualified to serve, or have declined to serve.

(c)   Except as otherwise provided in the power of attorney and subsection (d), an agent that does not participate in or conceal a breach of fiduciary duty committed by another agent, including a predecessor agent, is not liable for the actions of the other agent.

(d)   An agent that has actual knowledge of a breach or imminent breach of fiduciary duty by another agent shall notify the principal and, if the principal is incapacitated, take any action reasonably appropriate in the circumstances to safeguard the principal's best interest. An agent that fails to notify the principal or take action as required by this subsection is liable for the reasonably foreseeable damages that could have been avoided if the agent had notified the principal or taken such action.

Section 112. Reimbursement and Compensation of Agent.

Unless the power of attorney otherwise provides, an agent is entitled to reimbursement of expenses reasonably incurred on behalf of the principal and to compensation that is reasonable under the circumstances.

Section 113. Agent's Acceptance.

Except as otherwise provided in the power of attorney, a person accepts appointment as an agent under a power of attorney by exercising authority or performing duties as an agent or by any other assertion or conduct indicating acceptance.

Section 114. Agent's Duties.

(a)   Notwithstanding provisions in the power of attorney, an agent that has accepted appointment shall:

(1)   act in accordance with the principal's reasonable expectations to the extent actually known by the agent and, otherwise, in the principal's best interest;

(2)   act in good faith; and

(3)   act only within the scope of authority granted in the power of attorney.

(b)   Except as otherwise provided in the power of attorney, an agent that has accepted appointment shall:

(1)   act loyally for the principal's benefit;

(2)   act so as not to create a conflict of interest that impairs the agent's ability to act impartially in the principal's best interest;

(3)   act with the care, competence, and diligence ordinarily exercised by agents in similar circumstances;

(4)   keep a record of all receipts, disbursements, and transactions made on behalf of the principal;

(5)   cooperate with a person that has authority to make health-care decisions for the principal to carry out the principal's reasonable expectations to the extent actually known by the agent and, otherwise, act in the principal's best interest; and

(6)   attempt to preserve the principal's estate plan, to the extent actually known by the agent, if preserving the plan is consistent with the principal's best interest based on all relevant factors, including:

(A)   the value and nature of the principal's property;

(B)   the principal's foreseeable obligations and need for maintenance;

(C)   minimization of taxes, including income, estate, inheritance, generation-skipping transfer, and gift taxes; and

(D)   eligibility for a benefit, a program, or assistance under a statute or regulation.

(c)   An agent that acts in good faith is not liable to any beneficiary of the principal's estate plan for failure to preserve the plan.

(d)   An agent that acts with care, competence, and diligence for the best interest of the principal is not liable solely because the agent also benefits from the act or has an individual or conflicting interest in relation to the property or affairs of the principal.

(e)   If an agent is selected by the principal because of special skills or expertise possessed by the agent or in reliance on the agent's representation that the agent has special skills or expertise, the special skills or expertise must be considered in determining whether the agent has acted with care, competence, and diligence under the circumstances.

(f)   Absent a breach of duty to the principal, an agent is not liable if the value of the principal's property declines.

(g)   An agent that exercises authority to delegate to another person the authority granted by the principal or that engages another person on behalf of the principal is not liable for an act, error of judgment, or default of that person if the agent exercises care, competence, and diligence in selecting and monitoring the person.

(h)   Except as otherwise provided in the power of attorney, an agent is not required to disclose receipts, disbursements, or transactions conducted on behalf of the principal unless ordered by a court or requested by the principal, a guardian, a conservator, another fiduciary acting for the principal, a governmental agency having authority to protect the welfare of the principal, or, upon the death of the principal, by the personal representative or successor in interest of the principal's estate. If so requested, within 30 days the agent shall comply with the request or provide a writing or other record substantiating why additional time is needed and shall comply with the request within an additional 30 days.

Section 115. Exoneration of Agent.

A provision in a power of attorney relieving an agent of liability for breach of duty is binding on the principal and the principal's successors in interest except to the extent the provision:

(1)   relieves the agent of liability for breach of duty committed dishonestly, with an improper motive, or with reckless indifference to the purposes of the power of attorney or the best interest of the principal; or

(2)   was inserted as a result of an abuse of a confidential or fiduciary relationship with the principal.

Section 116. Judicial Relief.

(a)   The following persons may petition a court to construe a power of attorney or review the agent's conduct, and grant appropriate relief:

(1)   the principal or the agent;

(2)   a guardian, conservator, or other fiduciary acting for the principal;

(3)   a person authorized to make health-care decisions for the principal;

(4)   the principal's spouse, parent, or descendant;

(5)   an individual who would qualify as a presumptive heir of the principal;

(6)   a person named as a beneficiary to receive any property, benefit, or contractual right on the principal's death or as a beneficiary of a trust created by or for the principal that has a financial interest in the principal's estate;

(7)   a governmental agency having regulatory authority to protect the welfare of the principal;

(8)   the principal's caregiver or another person that demonstrates sufficient interest in the principal's welfare; and

(9)   a person asked to accept the power of attorney.

(b)   Upon motion by the principal, the court shall dismiss a petition filed under this section, unless the court finds that the principal lacks capacity to revoke the agent's authority or the power of attorney.

Section 117. Agent's Liability.

An agent that violates this [act] is liable to the principal or the principal's successors in interest for the amount required to:

(1) restore the value of the principal's property to what it would have been had the violation not occurred; and

(2) reimburse the principal or the principal's successors in interest for the attorney's fees and costs paid on the agent's behalf.

Section 118. Agent's Resignation; Notice.

Unless the power of attorney provides a different method for an agent's resignation, an agent may resign by giving notice to the principal and, if the principal is incapacitated:

(1) to the [conservator or guardian], if one has been appointed for the principal, and a coagent or successor agent; or

(2) if there is no person described in paragraph (1), to:

(A) the principal's caregiver;

(B) another person reasonably believed by the agent to have sufficient interest in the principal's welfare; or

(C) a governmental agency having authority to protect the welfare of the principal.

Section 119. Acceptance of and Reliance Upon Acknowledged Power of Attorney.

(a) For purposes of this section and Section 120, "acknowledged" means purportedly verified before a notary public or other individual authorized to take acknowledgements.

(b) A person that in good faith accepts an acknowledged power of attorney without actual knowledge that the signature is not genuine may rely upon the presumption under Section 105 that the signature is genuine.

(c) A person that in good faith accepts an acknowledged power of attorney without actual knowledge that the power of attorney is void, invalid, or terminated, that the purported agent's authority is void, invalid, or terminated, or that the agent is exceeding or improperly exercising the agent's authority may rely upon the power of attorney as if the power of attorney were genuine, valid and still in effect, the agent's authority were genuine, valid and still in effect, and the agent had not exceeded and had properly exercised the authority.

(d) A person that is asked to accept an acknowledged power of attorney may request, and rely upon, without further investigation:

(1) an agent's certification under penalty of perjury of any factual matter concerning the principal, agent, or power of attorney;

(2) an English translation of the power of attorney if the power of attorney contains, in whole or in part, language other than English; and

(3) an opinion of counsel as to any matter of law concerning the power of attorney if the person making the request provides in a writing or other record the reason for the request.

(e) An English translation or an opinion of counsel requested under this section must be provided at the principal's expense unless the request is made more than seven business days after the power of attorney is presented for acceptance.

(f) For purposes of this section and Section 120, a person that conducts activities through employees is without actual knowledge of a fact relating to a power of attorney, a principal, or an agent if the employee conducting the transaction involving the power of attorney is without actual knowledge of the fact.

Alternative A

Section 120. Liability for Refusal to Accept Acknowledged Power of Attorney.

(a)   Except as otherwise provided in subsection (b):

(1)   a person shall either accept an acknowledged power of attorney or request a certification, a translation, or an opinion of counsel under Section 119(d) no later than seven business days after presentation of the power of attorney for acceptance;

(2)   if a person requests a certification, a translation, or an opinion of counsel under Section 119(d), the person shall accept the power of attorney no later than five business days after receipt of the certification, translation, or opinion of counsel; and

(3)   a person may not require an additional or different form of power of attorney for authority granted in the power of attorney presented.

(b)   A person is not required to accept an acknowledged power of attorney if:

(1)   the person is not otherwise required to engage in a transaction with the principal in the same circumstances;

(2)   engaging in a transaction with the agent or the principal in the same circumstances would be inconsistent with federal law;

(3)   the person has actual knowledge of the termination of the agent's authority or of the power of attorney before exercise of the power;

(4)   a request for a certification, a translation, or an opinion of counsel under Section 119(d) is refused;

(5)   the person in good faith believes that the power is not valid or that the agent does not have the authority to perform the act requested, whether or not a certification, a translation, or an opinion of counsel under Section 119(d) has been requested or provided; or

(6)   the person makes, or has actual knowledge that another person has made, a report to the [local adult protective services office] stating a good faith belief that the principal may be subject to physical or financial abuse, neglect, exploitation, or abandonment by the agent or a person acting for or with the agent.

(c)   A person that refuses in violation of this section to accept an acknowledged power of attorney is subject to:

(1)   a court order mandating acceptance of the power of attorney; and

(2)   liability for reasonable attorney's fees and costs incurred in any action or proceeding that confirms the validity of the power of attorney or mandates acceptance of the power of attorney.

Alternative B

Section 120. Liability for Refusal to Accept Acknowledged Statutory Form Power of Attorney.

(a)   In this section, "statutory form power of attorney" means a power of attorney substantially in the form provided in Section 301 or that meets the requirements for a military power of attorney pursuant to 10 U.S.C. Section 1044b [, as amended].

(b)   Except as otherwise provided in subsection (c):

(1)   a person shall either accept an acknowledged statutory form power of attorney or request a certification, a translation, or an opinion of counsel under Section 119(d) no later than seven business days after presentation of the power of attorney for acceptance;

(2) if a person requests a certification, a translation, or an opinion of counsel under Section 119(d), the person shall accept the statutory form power of attorney no later than five business days after receipt of the certification, translation, or opinion of counsel; and

(3) a person may not require an additional or different form of power of attorney for authority granted in the statutory form power of attorney presented.

(c) A person is not required to accept an acknowledged statutory form power of attorney if:

(1) the person is not otherwise required to engage in a transaction with the principal in the same circumstances;

(2) engaging in a transaction with the agent or the principal in the same circumstances would be inconsistent with federal law;

(3) the person has actual knowledge of the termination of the agent's authority or of the power of attorney before exercise of the power;

(4) a request for a certification, a translation, or an opinion of counsel under Section 119(d) is refused;

(5) the person in good faith believes that the power is not valid or that the agent does not have the authority to perform the act requested, whether or not a certification, a translation, or an opinion of counsel under Section 119(d) has been requested or provided; or

(6) the person makes, or has actual knowledge that another person has made, a report to the [local adult protective services office] stating a good faith belief that the principal may be subject to physical or financial abuse, neglect, exploitation, or abandonment by the agent or a person acting for or with the agent.

(d) A person that refuses in violation of this section to accept an acknowledged statutory form power of attorney is subject to:

(1) a court order mandating acceptance of the power of attorney; and

(2) liability for reasonable attorney's fees and costs incurred in any action or proceeding that confirms the validity of the power of attorney or mandates acceptance of the power of attorney.

End of Alternatives

Section 121. Principles of Law and Equity.

Unless displaced by a provision of this [act], the principles of law and equity supplement this [act].

Section 122. Laws Applicable to Financial Institutions and Entities.

This [act] does not supersede any other law applicable to financial institutions or other entities, and the other law controls if inconsistent with this [act].

Section 123. Remedies Under Other Law.

The remedies under this [act] are not exclusive and do not abrogate any right or remedy under the law of this state other than this [act].

[ARTICLE] 2

AUTHORITY

Section 201. Authority That Requires Specific Grant; Grant of General Authority.

(a)   An agent under a power of attorney may do the following on behalf of the principal or with the principal's property only if the power of attorney expressly grants the agent the authority and exercise of the authority is not otherwise prohibited by another agreement or instrument to which the authority or property is subject:

(1)   create, amend, revoke, or terminate an inter vivos trust;

(2)   make a gift;

(3)   create or change rights of survivorship;

(4)   create or change a beneficiary designation;

(5)   delegate authority granted under the power of attorney;

(6)   waive the principal's right to be a beneficiary of a joint and survivor annuity, including a survivor benefit under a retirement plan;

(7)   exercise fiduciary powers that the principal has authority to delegate; [or]

(8)   exercise authority over the content of electronic communications, as defined in 18 U.S.C. Section 2510(12)[, as amended,] sent or received by the principal[; or

(9)   disclaim property, including a power of appointment].

(b)   Notwithstanding a grant of authority to do an act described in subsection (a), unless the power of attorney otherwise provides, an agent that is not an ancestor, spouse, or descendant of the principal, may not exercise authority under a power of attorney to create in the agent, or in an individual to whom the agent owes a legal obligation of support, an interest in the principal's property, whether by gift, right of survivorship, beneficiary designation, disclaimer, or otherwise.

(c)   Subject to subsections (a), (b), (d), and (e), if a power of attorney grants to an agent authority to do all acts that a principal could do, the agent has the general authority described in Sections 204 through 216.

(d)   Unless the power of attorney otherwise provides, a grant of authority to make a gift is subject to Section 217.

(e)   Subject to subsections (a), (b), and (d), if the subjects over which authority is granted in a power of attorney are similar or overlap, the broadest authority controls.

(f)   Authority granted in a power of attorney is exercisable with respect to property that the principal has when the power of attorney is executed or acquires later, whether or not the property is located in this state and whether or not the authority is exercised or the power of attorney is executed in this state.

(g)   An act performed by an agent pursuant to a power of attorney has the same effect and inures to the benefit of and binds the principal and the principal's successors in interest as if the principal had performed the act.

Section 202. Incorporation of Authority.

(a)   An agent has authority described in this [article] if the power of attorney refers to general authority with respect to the descriptive term for the subjects stated in Sections 204 through 217 or cites the section in which the authority is described.

(b)   A reference in a power of attorney to general authority with respect to the descriptive term for a subject in Sections 204 through 217 or a citation to a section of Sections 204 through 217 incorporates the entire section as if it were set out in full in the power of attorney.

(c)   A principal may modify authority incorporated by reference.

Section 203. Construction of Authority Generally.

Except as otherwise provided in the power of attorney, by executing a power of attorney that incorporates by reference a subject described in Sections 204 through 217 or that grants to an agent authority to do all acts that a principal could do pursuant to Section 201(c), a principal authorizes the agent, with respect to that subject, to:

(1)   demand, receive, and obtain by litigation or otherwise, money or another thing of value to which the principal is, may become, or claims to be entitled, and conserve, invest, disburse, or use anything so received or obtained for the purposes intended;

(2)   contract in any manner with any person, on terms agreeable to the agent, to accomplish a purpose of a transaction and perform, rescind, cancel, terminate, reform, restate, release, or modify the contract or another contract made by or on behalf of the principal;

(3)   execute, acknowledge, seal, deliver, file, or record any instrument or communication the agent considers desirable to accomplish a purpose of a transaction, including creating at any time a schedule listing some or all of the principal's property and attaching it to the power of attorney;

(4)   initiate, participate in, submit to alternative dispute resolution, settle, oppose, or propose or accept a compromise with respect to a claim existing in favor of or against the principal or intervene in litigation relating to the claim;

(5)   seek on the principal's behalf the assistance of a court or other governmental agency to carry out an act authorized in the power of attorney;

(6)   engage, compensate, and discharge an attorney, accountant, discretionary investment manager, expert witness, or other advisor;

(7)   prepare, execute, and file a record, report, or other document to safeguard or promote the principal's interest under a statute or regulation;

(8)   communicate with any representative or employee of a government or governmental subdivision, agency, or instrumentality, on behalf of the principal;

(9)   access communications intended for, and communicate on behalf of the principal, whether by mail, electronic transmission, telephone, or other means; and

(10)   do any lawful act with respect to the subject and all property related to the subject.

Section 204. Real Property.

Unless the power of attorney otherwise provides, language in a power of attorney granting general authority with respect to real property authorizes the agent to:

(1)   demand, buy, lease, receive, accept as a gift or as security for an extension of credit, or otherwise acquire or reject an interest in real property or a right incident to real property;

(2)   sell; exchange; convey with or without covenants, representations, or warranties; quitclaim; release; surrender; retain title for security; encumber; partition; consent to partitioning; subject to an easement or covenant; subdivide; apply for zoning or other governmental permits; plat or consent to platting; develop; grant an option concerning; lease; sublease; contribute to an entity in exchange for an interest in that entity; or otherwise grant or dispose of an interest in real property or a right incident to real property;

(3)   pledge or mortgage an interest in real property or right incident to real property as security to borrow money or pay, renew, or extend the time of payment of a debt of the principal or a debt guaranteed by the principal;

(4)   release, assign, satisfy, or enforce by litigation or otherwise a mortgage, deed of trust, conditional sale contract, encumbrance, lien, or other claim to real property which exists or is asserted;

(5)   manage or conserve an interest in real property or a right incident to real property owned or claimed to be owned by the principal, including:

(A)   insuring against liability or casualty or other loss;

(B)   obtaining or regaining possession of or protecting the interest or right by litigation or otherwise;

(C)   paying, assessing, compromising, or contesting taxes or assessments or applying for and receiving refunds in connection with them; and

(D)   purchasing supplies, hiring assistance or labor, and making repairs or alterations to the real property;

(6)   use, develop, alter, replace, remove, erect, or install structures or other improvements upon real property in or incident to which the principal has, or claims to have, an interest or right;

(7)   participate in a reorganization with respect to real property or an entity that owns an interest in or right incident to real property and receive, and hold, and act with respect to stocks and bonds or other property received in a plan of reorganization, including:

(A)   selling or otherwise disposing of them;

(B)   exercising or selling an option, right of conversion, or similar right with respect to them; and

(C)   exercising any voting rights in person or by proxy;

(8)   change the form of title of an interest in or right incident to real property; and

(9)   dedicate to public use, with or without consideration, easements or other real property in which the principal has, or claims to have, an interest.

Section 205. Tangible Personal Property.

Unless the power of attorney otherwise provides, language in a power of attorney granting general authority with respect to tangible personal property authorizes the agent to:

(1)   demand, buy, receive, accept as a gift or as security for an extension of credit, or otherwise acquire or reject ownership or possession of tangible personal property or an interest in tangible personal property;

(2)   sell; exchange; convey with or without covenants, representations, or warranties; quitclaim; release; surrender; create a security interest in; grant options concerning; lease; sublease; or, otherwise dispose of tangible personal property or an interest in tangible personal property;

(3)   grant a security interest in tangible personal property or an interest in tangible personal property as security to borrow money or pay, renew, or extend the time of payment of a debt of the principal or a debt guaranteed by the principal;

(4)   release, assign, satisfy, or enforce by litigation or otherwise, a security interest, lien, or other claim on behalf of the principal, with respect to tangible personal property or an interest in tangible personal property;

(5)   manage or conserve tangible personal property or an interest in tangible personal property on behalf of the principal, including:

(A)   insuring against liability or casualty or other loss;

    (B)   obtaining or regaining possession of or protecting the property or interest, by litigation or otherwise;

    (C)   paying, assessing, compromising, or contesting taxes or assessments or applying for and receiving refunds in connection with taxes or assessments;

    (D)   moving the property from place to place;

    (E)   storing the property for hire or on a gratuitous bailment; and

    (F)   using and making repairs, alterations, or improvements to the property; and

    (6)   change the form of title of an interest in tangible personal property.

Section 206. Stocks and Bonds.

Unless the power of attorney otherwise provides, language in a power of attorney granting general authority with respect to stocks and bonds authorizes the agent to:

    (1)   buy, sell, and exchange stocks and bonds;

    (2)   establish, continue, modify, or terminate an account with respect to stocks and bonds;

    (3)   pledge stocks and bonds as security to borrow, pay, renew, or extend the time of payment of a debt of the principal;

    (4)   receive certificates and other evidences of ownership with respect to stocks and bonds; and

    (5)   exercise voting rights with respect to stocks and bonds in person or by proxy, enter into voting trusts, and consent to limitations on the right to vote.

Section 207. Commodities and Options.

Unless the power of attorney otherwise provides, language in a power of attorney granting general authority with respect to commodities and options authorizes the agent to:

    (1)   buy, sell, exchange, assign, settle, and exercise commodity futures contracts and call or put options on stocks or stock indexes traded on a regulated option exchange; and

    (2)   establish, continue, modify, and terminate option accounts.

Section 208. Banks and Other Financial Institutions.

Unless the power of attorney otherwise provides, language in a power of attorney granting general authority with respect to banks and other financial institutions authorizes the agent to:

    (1)   continue, modify, and terminate an account or other banking arrangement made by or on behalf of the principal;

    (2)   establish, modify, and terminate an account or other banking arrangement with a bank, trust company, savings and loan association, credit union, thrift company, brokerage firm, or other financial institution selected by the agent;

    (3)   contract for services available from a financial institution, including renting a safe deposit box or space in a vault;

    (4)   withdraw, by check, order, electronic funds transfer, or otherwise, money or property of the principal deposited with or left in the custody of a financial institution;

    (5)   receive statements of account, vouchers, notices, and similar documents from a financial institution and act with respect to them;

    (6)   enter a safe deposit box or vault and withdraw or add to the contents;

(7)   borrow money and pledge as security personal property of the principal necessary to borrow money or pay, renew, or extend the time of payment of a debt of the principal or a debt guaranteed by the principal;

(8)   make, assign, draw, endorse, discount, guarantee, and negotiate promissory notes, checks, drafts, and other negotiable or nonnegotiable paper of the principal or payable to the principal or the principal's order, transfer money, receive the cash or other proceeds of those transactions, and accept a draft drawn by a person upon the principal and pay it when due;

(9)   receive for the principal and act upon a sight draft, warehouse receipt, or other document of title whether tangible or electronic, or other negotiable or nonnegotiable instrument;

(10) apply for, receive, and use letters of credit, credit and debit cards, electronic transaction authorizations, and traveler's checks from a financial institution and give an indemnity or other agreement in connection with letters of credit; and

(11) consent to an extension of the time of payment with respect to commercial paper or a financial transaction with a financial institution.

Section 209. Operation of Entity or Business.

Subject to the terms of a document or an agreement governing an entity or an entity ownership interest, and unless the power of attorney otherwise provides, language in a power of attorney granting general authority with respect to operation of an entity or business authorizes the agent to:

(1)   operate, buy, sell, enlarge, reduce, or terminate an ownership interest;

(2)   perform a duty or discharge a liability and exercise in person or by proxy a right, power, privilege, or option that the principal has, may have, or claims to have;

(3)   enforce the terms of an ownership agreement;

(4)   initiate, participate in, submit to alternative dispute resolution, settle, oppose, or propose or accept a compromise with respect to litigation to which the principal is a party because of an ownership interest;

(5)   exercise in person or by proxy, or enforce by litigation or otherwise, a right, power, privilege, or option the principal has or claims to have as the holder of stocks and bonds;

(6)   initiate, participate in, submit to alternative dispute resolution, settle, oppose, or propose or accept a compromise with respect to litigation to which the principal is a party concerning stocks and bonds;

(7)   with respect to an entity or business owned solely by the principal:

(A)   continue, modify, renegotiate, extend, and terminate a contract made by or on behalf of the principal with respect to the entity or business before execution of the power of attorney;

(B)   determine:

(i)   the location of its operation;

(ii)   the nature and extent of its business;

(iii) the methods of manufacturing, selling, merchandising, financing, accounting, and advertising employed in its operation;

(iv)   the amount and types of insurance carried; and

(v)   the mode of engaging, compensating, and dealing with its employees and accountants, attorneys, or other advisors;

(C)   change the name or form of organization under which the entity or business is operated and enter into an ownership agreement with other persons to take over all or part of the operation of the entity or business; and

(D)   demand and receive money due or claimed by the principal or on the principal's behalf in the operation of the entity or business and control and disburse the money in the operation of the entity or business;

(8)   put additional capital into an entity or business in which the principal has an interest;

(9)   join in a plan of reorganization, consolidation, conversion, domestication, or merger of the entity or business;

(10) sell or liquidate all or part of an entity or business;

(11) establish the value of an entity or business under a buy-out agreement to which the principal is a party;

(12) prepare, sign, file, and deliver reports, compilations of information, returns, or other papers with respect to an entity or business and make related payments; and

(13) pay, compromise, or contest taxes, assessments, fines, or penalties and perform any other act to protect the principal from illegal or unnecessary taxation, assessments, fines, or penalties, with respect to an entity or business, including attempts to recover, in any manner permitted by law, money paid before or after the execution of the power of attorney.

Section 210. Insurance and Annuities.

Unless the power of attorney otherwise provides, language in a power of attorney granting general authority with respect to insurance and annuities authorizes the agent to:

(1)   continue, pay the premium or make a contribution on, modify, exchange, rescind, release, or terminate a contract procured by or on behalf of the principal which insures or provides an annuity to either the principal or another person, whether or not the principal is a beneficiary under the contract;

(2)   procure new, different, and additional contracts of insurance and annuities for the principal and the principal's spouse, children, and other dependents, and select the amount, type of insurance or annuity, and mode of payment;

(3)   pay the premium or make a contribution on, modify, exchange, rescind, release, or terminate a contract of insurance or annuity procured by the agent;

(4)   apply for and receive a loan secured by a contract of insurance or annuity;

(5)   surrender and receive the cash surrender value on a contract of insurance or annuity;

(6)   exercise an election;

(7)   exercise investment powers available under a contract of insurance or annuity;

(8)   change the manner of paying premiums on a contract of insurance or annuity;

(9)   change or convert the type of insurance or annuity with respect to which the principal has or claims to have authority described in this section;

(10) apply for and procure a benefit or assistance under a statute or regulation to guarantee or pay premiums of a contract of insurance on the life of the principal;

(11) collect, sell, assign, hypothecate, borrow against, or pledge the interest of the principal in a contract of insurance or annuity;

(12) select the form and timing of the payment of proceeds from a contract of insurance or annuity; and

(13) pay, from proceeds or otherwise, compromise or contest, and apply for refunds in connection with, a tax or assessment levied by a taxing authority with respect to a contract of insurance or annuity or its proceeds or liability accruing by reason of the tax or assessment.

Section 211. Estates, Trusts, and Other Beneficial Interests.

(a) In this section, "estate, trust, or other beneficial interest" means a trust, probate estate, guardianship, conservatorship, escrow, or custodianship or a fund from which the principal is, may become, or claims to be, entitled to a share or payment.

(b) Unless the power of attorney otherwise provides, language in a power of attorney granting general authority with respect to estates, trusts, and other beneficial interests authorizes the agent to:

(1) accept, receive, receipt for, sell, assign, pledge, or exchange a share in or payment from an estate, trust, or other beneficial interest;

(2) demand or obtain money or another thing of value to which the principal is, may become, or claims to be, entitled by reason of an estate, trust, or other beneficial interest, by litigation or otherwise;

(3) exercise for the benefit of the principal a presently exercisable general power of appointment held by the principal;

(4) initiate, participate in, submit to alternative dispute resolution, settle, oppose, or propose or accept a compromise with respect to litigation to ascertain the meaning, validity, or effect of a deed, will, declaration of trust, or other instrument or transaction affecting the interest of the principal;

(5) initiate, participate in, submit to alternative dispute resolution, settle, oppose, or propose or accept a compromise with respect to litigation to remove, substitute, or surcharge a fiduciary;

(6) conserve, invest, disburse, or use anything received for an authorized purpose; [and]

(7) transfer an interest of the principal in real property, stocks and bonds, accounts with financial institutions or securities intermediaries, insurance, annuities, and other property to the trustee of a revocable trust created by the principal as settlor [; and

(8) reject, renounce, disclaim, release, or consent to a reduction in or modification of a share in or payment from an estate, trust, or other beneficial interest].

Section 212. Claims and Litigation.

Unless the power of attorney otherwise provides, language in a power of attorney granting general authority with respect to claims and litigation authorizes the agent to:

(1) assert and maintain before a court or administrative agency a claim, claim for relief, cause of action, counterclaim, offset, recoupment, or defense, including an action to recover property or other thing of value, recover damages sustained by the principal, eliminate or modify tax liability, or seek an injunction, specific performance, or other relief;

(2) bring an action to determine adverse claims or intervene or otherwise participate in litigation;

(3) seek an attachment, garnishment, order of arrest, or other preliminary, provisional, or intermediate relief and use an available procedure to effect or satisfy a judgment, order, or decree;

(4) make or accept a tender, offer of judgment, or admission of facts, submit a controversy on an agreed statement of facts, consent to examination, and bind the principal in litigation;

(5) submit to alternative dispute resolution, settle, and propose or accept a compromise;

(6) waive the issuance and service of process upon the principal, accept service of process, appear for the principal, designate persons upon which process directed to the principal may be served, execute and file or deliver stipulations on the principal's behalf, verify pleadings, seek appellate review, procure and give surety and indemnity bonds, contract and pay for the preparation and

printing of records and briefs, receive, execute, and file or deliver a consent, waiver, release, confession of judgment, satisfaction of judgment, notice, agreement, or other instrument in connection with the prosecution, settlement, or defense of a claim or litigation;

(7)   act for the principal with respect to bankruptcy or insolvency, whether voluntary or involuntary, concerning the principal or some other person, or with respect to a reorganization, receivership, or application for the appointment of a receiver or trustee which affects an interest of the principal in property or other thing of value;

(8)   pay a judgment, award, or order against the principal or a settlement made in connection with a claim or litigation; and

(9)   receive money or other thing of value paid in settlement of or as proceeds of a claim or litigation.

Section 213. Personal and Family Maintenance.

(a)   Unless the power of attorney otherwise provides, language in a power of attorney granting general authority with respect to personal and family maintenance authorizes the agent to:

(1)   perform the acts necessary to maintain the customary standard of living of the principal, the principal's spouse, and the following individuals, whether living when the power of attorney is executed or later born:

(A)   the principal's children;

(B)   other individuals legally entitled to be supported by the principal; and

(C)   the individuals whom the principal has customarily supported or indicated the intent to support;

(2)   make periodic payments of child support and other family maintenance required by a court or governmental agency or an agreement to which the principal is a party;

(3)   provide living quarters for the individuals described in paragraph (1) by:

(A)   purchase, lease, or other contract; or

(B)   paying the operating costs, including interest, amortization payments, repairs, improvements, and taxes, for premises owned by the principal or occupied by those individuals;

(4)   provide normal domestic help, usual vacations and travel expenses, and funds for shelter, clothing, food, appropriate education, including postsecondary and vocational education, and other current living costs for the individuals described in paragraph (1);

(5)   pay expenses for necessary health care and custodial care on behalf of the individuals described in paragraph (1);

(6)   act as the principal's personal representative pursuant to the Health Insurance Portability and Accountability Act, Sections 1171 through 1179 of the Social Security Act, 42 U.S.C. Section 1320d, [as amended,] and applicable regulations, in making decisions related to the past, present, or future payment for the provision of health care consented to by the principal or anyone authorized under the law of this state to consent to health care on behalf of the principal;

(7)   continue any provision made by the principal for automobiles or other means of transportation, including registering, licensing, insuring, and replacing them, for the individuals described in paragraph (1);

(8)   maintain credit and debit accounts for the convenience of the individuals described in paragraph (1) and open new accounts; and

(9) continue payments incidental to the membership or affiliation of the principal in a religious institution, club, society, order, or other organization or to continue contributions to those organizations.

(b) Authority with respect to personal and family maintenance is neither dependent upon, nor limited by, authority that an agent may or may not have with respect to gifts under this [act].

Section 214. Benefits From Governmental Programs or Civil or Military Service.

(a) In this section, "benefits from governmental programs or civil or military service" means any benefit, program or assistance provided under a statute or regulation including Social Security, Medicare, and Medicaid.

(b) Unless the power of attorney otherwise provides, language in a power of attorney granting general authority with respect to benefits from governmental programs or civil or military service authorizes the agent to:

(1) execute vouchers in the name of the principal for allowances and reimbursements payable by the United States or a foreign government or by a state or subdivision of a state to the principal, including allowances and reimbursements for transportation of the individuals described in Section 213(a)(1), and for shipment of their household effects;

(2) take possession and order the removal and shipment of property of the principal from a post, warehouse, depot, dock, or other place of storage or safekeeping, either governmental or private, and execute and deliver a release, voucher, receipt, bill of lading, shipping ticket, certificate, or other instrument for that purpose;

(3) enroll in, apply for, select, reject, change, amend, or discontinue, on the principal's behalf, a benefit or program;

(4) prepare, file, and maintain a claim of the principal for a benefit or assistance, financial or otherwise, to which the principal may be entitled under a statute or regulation;

(5) initiate, participate in, submit to alternative dispute resolution, settle, oppose, or propose or accept a compromise with respect to litigation concerning any benefit or assistance the principal may be entitled to receive under a statute or regulation; and

(6) receive the financial proceeds of a claim described in paragraph (4) and conserve, invest, disburse, or use for a lawful purpose anything so received.

Section 215. Retirement Plans.

(a) In this section, "retirement plan" means a plan or account created by an employer, the principal, or another individual to provide retirement benefits or deferred compensation of which the principal is a participant, beneficiary, or owner, including a plan or account under the following sections of the Internal Revenue Code:

(1) an individual retirement account under Internal Revenue Code Section 408, 26 U.S.C. Section 408 [, as amended];

(2) a Roth individual retirement account under Internal Revenue Code Section 408A, 26 U.S.C. Section 408A [, as amended];

(3) a deemed individual retirement account under Internal Revenue Code Section 408(q), 26 U.S.C. Section 408(q) [, as amended];

(4) an annuity or mutual fund custodial account under Internal Revenue Code Section 403(b), 26 U.S.C. Section 403(b) [, as amended];

(5) a pension, profit-sharing, stock bonus, or other retirement plan qualified under Internal Revenue Code Section 401(a), 26 U.S.C. Section 401(a) [, as amended];

(6) a plan under Internal Revenue Code Section 457(b), 26 U.S.C. Section 457(b) [, as amended]; and

(7) a nonqualified deferred compensation plan under Internal Revenue Code Section 409A, 26 U.S.C. Section 409A [, as amended].

(b) Unless the power of attorney otherwise provides, language in a power of attorney granting general authority with respect to retirement plans authorizes the agent to:

(1) select the form and timing of payments under a retirement plan and withdraw benefits from a plan;

(2) make a rollover, including a direct trustee-to-trustee rollover, of benefits from one retirement plan to another;

(3) establish a retirement plan in the principal's name;

(4) make contributions to a retirement plan;

(5) exercise investment powers available under a retirement plan; and

(6) borrow from, sell assets to, or purchase assets from a retirement plan.

Section 216. Taxes.

Unless the power of attorney otherwise provides, language in a power of attorney granting general authority with respect to taxes authorizes the agent to:

(1) prepare, sign, and file federal, state, local, and foreign income, gift, payroll, property, Federal Insurance Contributions Act, and other tax returns, claims for refunds, requests for extension of time, petitions regarding tax matters, and any other tax-related documents, including receipts, offers, waivers, consents, including consents and agreements under Internal Revenue Code Section 2032A, 26 U.S.C. Section 2032A, [as amended,] closing agreements, and any power of attorney required by the Internal Revenue Service or other taxing authority with respect to a tax year upon which the statute of limitations has not run and the following 25 tax years;

(2) pay taxes due, collect refunds, post bonds, receive confidential information, and contest deficiencies determined by the Internal Revenue Service or other taxing authority;

(3) exercise any election available to the principal under federal, state, local, or foreign tax law; and

(4) act for the principal in all tax matters for all periods before the Internal Revenue Service, or other taxing authority.

Section 217. Gifts.

(a) In this section, a gift "for the benefit of" a person includes a gift to a trust, an account under the Uniform Transfers to Minors Act, and a tuition savings account or prepaid tuition plan as defined under Internal Revenue Code Section 529, 26 U.S.C. Section 529 [, as amended].

(b) Unless the power of attorney otherwise provides, language in a power of attorney granting general authority with respect to gifts authorizes the agent only to:

(1) make outright to, or for the benefit of, a person, a gift of any of the principal's property, including by the exercise of a presently exercisable general power of appointment held by the principal, in an amount per donee not to exceed the annual dollar limits of the federal gift tax exclusion under Internal Revenue Code Section 2503(b), 26 U.S.C. Section 2503(b), [as amended,] without regard to whether the federal gift tax exclusion applies to the gift, or if the principal's spouse agrees to consent to a split gift pursuant to Internal Revenue Code Section 2513, 26 U.S.C. 2513, [as amended,] in an amount per donee not to exceed twice the annual federal gift tax exclusion limit; and

(2)　consent, pursuant to Internal Revenue Code Section 2513, 26 U.S.C. Section 2513, [as amended,] to the splitting of a gift made by the principal's spouse in an amount per donee not to exceed the aggregate annual gift tax exclusions for both spouses.

(c)　An agent may make a gift of the principal's property only as the agent determines is consistent with the principal's objectives if actually known by the agent and, if unknown, as the agent determines is consistent with the principal's best interest based on all relevant factors, including:

(1)　the value and nature of the principal's property;

(2)　the principal's foreseeable obligations and need for maintenance;

(3)　minimization of taxes, including income, estate, inheritance, generation-skipping transfer, and gift taxes;

(4)　eligibility for a benefit, a program, or assistance under a statute or regulation; and

(5)　the principal's personal history of making or joining in making gifts.

[ARTICLE] 3

STATUTORY FORMS

Section 301. Statutory Form Power of Attorney.

A document substantially in the following form may be used to create a statutory form power of attorney that has the meaning and effect prescribed by this [act].

[INSERT NAME OF JURISDICTION]
STATUTORY FORM POWER OF ATTORNEY
IMPORTANT INFORMATION

This power of attorney authorizes another person (your agent) to make decisions concerning your property for you (the principal). Your agent will be able to make decisions and act with respect to your property (including your money) whether or not you are able to act for yourself. The meaning of authority over subjects listed on this form is explained in the Uniform Power of Attorney Act [insert citation].

This power of attorney does not authorize the agent to make health-care decisions for you.

You should select someone you trust to serve as your agent. Unless you specify otherwise, generally the agent's authority will continue until you die or revoke the power of attorney or the agent resigns or is unable to act for you.

Your agent is entitled to reasonable compensation unless you state otherwise in the Special Instructions.

This form provides for designation of one agent. If you wish to name more than one agent you may name a coagent in the Special Instructions. Coagents are not required to act together unless you include that requirement in the Special Instructions.

If your agent is unable or unwilling to act for you, your power of attorney will end unless you have named a successor agent. You may also name a second successor agent.

This power of attorney becomes effective immediately unless you state otherwise in the Special Instructions.

If you have questions about the power of attorney or the authority you are granting to your agent, you should seek legal advice before signing this form.

DESIGNATION OF AGENT

I _____ name the following person as my agent:
       (Name of Principal)

Name of Agent: _____

Agent's Address: _____

Agent's Telephone Number: _____

DESIGNATION OF SUCCESSOR AGENT(S) (OPTIONAL)

If my agent is unable or unwilling to act for me, I name as my successor agent:

Name of Successor Agent: _____

Successor Agent's Address: _____

Successor Agent's Telephone Number: _____

If my successor agent is unable or unwilling to act for me, I name as my second successor agent:

Name of Second Successor Agent: _____

Second Successor Agent's Address: _____

Second Successor Agent's Telephone Number: _____

GRANT OF GENERAL AUTHORITY

I grant my agent and any successor agent general authority to act for me with respect to the following subjects as defined in the Uniform Power of Attorney Act [insert citation]:

(INITIAL each subject you want to include in the agent's general authority. If you wish to grant general authority over all of the subjects you may initial "All Preceding Subjects" instead of initialing each subject.)

(___) Real Property

(___) Tangible Personal Property

(___) Stocks and Bonds

(___) Commodities and Options

(___) Banks and Other Financial Institutions

(___) Operation of Entity or Business

(___) Insurance and Annuities

(___) Estates, Trusts, and Other Beneficial Interests

(___) Claims and Litigation

(___) Personal and Family Maintenance

(___) Benefits from Governmental Programs or Civil or Military Service

(___) Retirement Plans

(___) Taxes

(___) All Preceding Subjects

GRANT OF SPECIFIC AUTHORITY (OPTIONAL)

My agent MAY NOT do any of the following specific acts for me UNLESS I have INITIALED the specific authority listed below:

(CAUTION: Granting any of the following will give your agent the authority to take actions that could significantly reduce your property or change how your property is distributed at your death. INITIAL ONLY the specific authority you WANT to give your agent.)

(___) Create, amend, revoke, or terminate an inter vivos trust

(___) Make a gift, subject to the limitations of the Uniform Power of Attorney Act [insert citation to Section 217 of the act] and any special instructions in this power of attorney

(___) Create or change rights of survivorship

(___) Create or change a beneficiary designation

(___) Authorize another person to exercise the authority granted under this power of attorney

(___) Waive the principal's right to be a beneficiary of a joint and survivor annuity, including a survivor benefit under a retirement plan

(___) Exercise fiduciary powers that the principal has authority to delegate

[(___) Disclaim or refuse an interest in property, including a power of appointment]

LIMITATION ON AGENT'S AUTHORITY

An agent that is not my ancestor, spouse, or descendant MAY NOT use my property to benefit the agent or a person to whom the agent owes an obligation of support unless I have included that authority in the Special Instructions.

SPECIAL INSTRUCTIONS (OPTIONAL)

You may give special instructions on the following lines:

_____

_____

_____

_____

_____

_____

EFFECTIVE DATE

This power of attorney is effective immediately unless I have stated otherwise in the Special Instructions.

NOMINATION OF [CONSERVATOR OR GUARDIAN] (OPTIONAL)

If it becomes necessary for a court to appoint a [conservator or guardian] of my estate or [guardian] of my person, I nominate the following person(s) for appointment:

Name of Nominee for [conservator or guardian] of my estate: _____

Nominee's Address: _____

Nominee's Telephone Number: _____

Name of Nominee for [guardian] of my person: _____

Nominee's Address: _____

Nominee's Telephone Number: _____

RELIANCE ON THIS POWER OF ATTORNEY

Any person, including my agent, may rely upon the validity of this power of attorney or a copy of it unless that person knows it has terminated or is invalid.

SIGNATURE AND ACKNOWLEDGMENT

_____   _____
Your Signature   Date

_____
Your Name Printed

_____
Your Address

_____
Your Telephone Number

State of _____
[County] of _____

This document was acknowledged before me on

_____ , by _____.
             (Date)   (Name of Principal)
                                                              (Seal, if any)

_____
Signature of Notary

My commission expires:

_____

[This document prepared by:

_____
_____]

IMPORTANT INFORMATION FOR AGENT

Agent's Duties

When you accept the authority granted under this power of attorney, a special legal relationship is created between you and the principal. This relationship imposes upon you legal duties that continue until you resign or the power of attorney is terminated or revoked. You must:

(1)   do what you know the principal reasonably expects you to do with the principal's property or, if you do not know the principal's expectations, act in the principal's best interest;

(2)   act in good faith;

(3)   do nothing beyond the authority granted in this power of attorney; and

(4)   disclose your identity as an agent whenever you act for the principal by writing or printing the name of the principal and signing your own name as "agent" in the following manner:

        (Principal's Name) by (Your Signature) as Agent

Unless the Special Instructions in this power of attorney state otherwise, you must also:

(1)   act loyally for the principal's benefit;

(2)   avoid conflicts that would impair your ability to act in the principal's best interest;

(3)   act with care, competence, and diligence;

(4)   keep a record of all receipts, disbursements, and transactions made on behalf of the principal;

(5)   cooperate with any person that has authority to make health-care decisions for the principal to do what you know the principal reasonably expects or, if you do not know the principal's expectations, to act in the principal's best interest; and

(6)   attempt to preserve the principal's estate plan if you know the plan and preserving the plan is consistent with the principal's best interest.

Termination of Agent's Authority

You must stop acting on behalf of the principal if you learn of any event that terminates this power of attorney or your authority under this power of attorney. Events that terminate a power of attorney or your authority to act under a power of attorney include:

(1)   death of the principal;

(2)   the principal's revocation of the power of attorney or your authority;

(3)   the occurrence of a termination event stated in the power of attorney;

(4)   the purpose of the power of attorney is fully accomplished; or

(5)   if you are married to the principal, a legal action is filed with a court to end your marriage, or for your legal separation, unless the Special Instructions in this power of attorney state that such an action will not terminate your authority.

Liability of Agent

The meaning of the authority granted to you is defined in the Uniform Power of Attorney Act [insert citation]. If you violate the Uniform Power of Attorney Act [insert citation] or act outside the authority granted, you may be liable for any damages caused by your violation.

If there is anything about this document or your duties that you do not understand, you should seek legal advice.

Section 302. Agent's Certification.

The following optional form may be used by an agent to certify facts concerning a power of attorney.

**AGENT'S CERTIFICATION AS TO THE VALIDITY OF
POWER OF ATTORNEY AND AGENT'S AUTHORITY**

State of _____

[County] of _____

I, _____ (Name of Agent), [certify] under penalty of perjury that _____ (Name of Principal) granted me authority as an agent or successor agent in a power of attorney dated _____.

I further [certify] that to my knowledge:

(1)   the Principal is alive and has not revoked the Power of Attorney or my authority to act under the Power of Attorney and the Power of Attorney and my authority to act under the Power of Attorney have not terminated;

(2)   if the Power of Attorney was drafted to become effective upon the happening of an event or contingency, the event or contingency has occurred;

(3)   if I was named as a successor agent, the prior agent is no longer able or willing to serve; and

(4)   _____

_____

_____

_____

(Insert other relevant statements)

SIGNATURE AND ACKNOWLEDGMENT

_____   _____
Agent's Signature   Date

_____
Agent's Name Printed

_____

_____
Agent's Address

_____
Agent's Telephone Number

This document was acknowledged before me on

_____, by   _____.

              (Date)   (Name of Agent)

                                                       (Seal, if any)

_____

Signature of Notary

My commission expires:

_____

[This document prepared by:

_____

_____]

[ARTICLE] 4

MISCELLANEOUS PROVISIONS

Section 401. Uniformity of Application and Construction. [omitted]

Section 402. Relation to Electronic Signatures in Global and National Commerce Act. [omitted]

Section 403. Effect on Existing Powers of Attorney. [omitted]

Section 404. Repeal. [omitted]

Section 405. Effective Date. [omitted]

UNIFORM POWERS OF APPOINTMENT ACT*

[ARTICLE] 1. GENERAL PROVISIONS

[ARTICLE] 2. CREATION, REVOCATION, AND AMENDMENT OF POWER OF APPOINTMENT

[ARTICLE] 3. EXERCISE OF POWER OF APPOINTMENT

[ARTICLE] 4. DISCLAIMER OR RELEASE; CONTRACT TO APPOINT OR NOT TO APPOINT

UNIFORM POWERS OF APPOINTMENT ACT

[ARTICLE] 5. RIGHTS OF POWERHOLDER'S CREDITORS IN APPOINTIVE PROPERTY

[ARTICLE] 6. MISCELLANEOUS PROVISIONS

[ARTICLE] 1

GENERAL PROVISIONS

Section 101. Short Title.

This [act] may be cited as the Uniform Powers of Appointment Act.

Section 102. Definitions.

In this [act]:

(1) "Appointee" means a person to which a powerholder makes an appointment of appointive property.

(2) "Appointive property" means the property or property interest subject to a power of appointment.

(3) "Blanket-exercise clause" means a clause in an instrument which exercises a power of appointment and is not a specific-exercise clause. The term includes a clause that:

(A) expressly uses the words "any power" in exercising any power of appointment the powerholder has;

(B) expressly uses the words "any property" in appointing any property over which the powerholder has a power of appointment; or

(C) disposes of all property subject to disposition by the powerholder.

(4) "Donor" means a person that creates a power of appointment.

(5) "Exclusionary power of appointment" means a power of appointment exercisable in favor of any one or more of the permissible appointees to the exclusion of the other permissible appointees.

(6) "General power of appointment" means a power of appointment exercisable in favor of the powerholder, the powerholder's estate, a creditor of the powerholder, or a creditor of the powerholder's estate.

(7) "Gift-in-default clause" means a clause identifying a taker in default of appointment.

(8) "Impermissible appointee" means a person that is not a permissible appointee.

(9) "Instrument" means a [writing][record].

(10) "Nongeneral power of appointment" means a power of appointment that is not a general power of appointment.

(11) "Permissible appointee" means a person in whose favor a powerholder may exercise a power of appointment.

(12) "Person" means an individual, estate, trust, business or nonprofit entity, public corporation, government or governmental subdivision, agency, or instrumentality, or other legal entity.

(13) "Power of appointment" means a power that enables a powerholder acting in a nonfiduciary capacity to designate a recipient of an ownership interest in or another power of appointment over the appointive property. The term does not include a power of attorney.

(14) "Powerholder" means a person in which a donor creates a power of appointment.

(15) "Presently exercisable power of appointment" means a power of appointment exercisable by the powerholder at the relevant time. The term:

(A) includes a power of appointment not exercisable until the occurrence of a specified event, the satisfaction of an ascertainable standard, or the passage of a specified time only after:

(i)   the occurrence of the specified event;

(ii)   the satisfaction of the ascertainable standard; or

(iii)   the passage of the specified time; and

(B)   does not include a power exercisable only at the powerholder's death.

(16) ["Record" means information that is inscribed on a tangible medium or that is stored in an electronic or other medium and is retrievable in perceivable form.]

(17) "Specific-exercise clause" means a clause in an instrument which specifically refers to and exercises a particular power of appointment.

(18) "Taker in default of appointment" means a person that takes all or part of the appointive property to the extent the powerholder does not effectively exercise the power of appointment.

(19) "Terms of the instrument" means the manifestation of the intent of the maker of the instrument regarding the instrument's provisions as expressed in the instrument or as may be established by other evidence that would be admissible in a legal proceeding.

Comment

Paragraph (1) defines an appointee as the person to which a powerholder makes an appointment of appointive property. For the definition of the related term, "permissible appointee," see paragraph (11).

Paragraph (2) defines appointive property as the property or property interest subject to a power of appointment. The effective creation of a power of appointment requires that there be appointive property. See Section 201.

Paragraphs (3) and (17) introduce the distinction between blanket-exercise and specific-exercise clauses. A specific-exercise clause exercises and specifically refers to the particular power of appointment in question, using language such as the following: "I exercise the power of appointment conferred upon me by my father's will as follows: I appoint [fill in details of appointment]." In contrast, a blanket-exercise clause exercises "any" power of appointment the powerholder may have, appoints "any" property over which the powerholder may have a power of appointment, or disposes of all property subject to disposition by the powerholder. The use of specific-exercise clauses is encouraged; the use of blanket-exercise clauses is discouraged. See Section 301 and the accompanying Comment.

Paragraphs (4) and (14) define the donor and the powerholder. The donor is the person who created the power of appointment. The powerholder is the person in whom the power of appointment was conferred or in whom the power was reserved. The traditional, but potentially confusing, term for powerholder is "donee." * * * In the case of a reserved power, the same person is both the donor and the powerholder.

Paragraph (5) introduces the distinction between exclusionary and nonexclusionary powers of appointment. An exclusionary power is one in which the donor has authorized the powerholder to appoint to any one or more of the permissible appointees to the exclusion of the other permissible appointees. For example, a power to appoint "to such of my descendants as the powerholder may select" is exclusionary, because the powerholder may appoint to any one or more of the donor's descendants to the exclusion of the other descendants. In contrast, a nonexclusionary power is one in which the powerholder cannot make an appointment that excludes any permissible appointee, or one or more designated permissible appointees, from a share of the appointive property. An example of a nonexclusionary power is a power "to appoint to all and every one of my children in such shares and proportions as the powerholder shall select." Here, the powerholder is not under a duty to exercise the power; but, if the powerholder does exercise the power, the appointment must abide by the power's nonexclusionary nature. See Sections 301 and 305. An instrument creating a power of appointment is construed as creating an exclusionary power unless the terms of the instrument manifest a contrary intent. See Section 203. The typical power of appointment is exclusionary. And in fact, only a power of appointment whose permissible appointees are "defined and limited" can be nonexclusionary. For elaboration of the well-accepted term of art "defined and limited," see Section 205 and the accompanying Comment.

Paragraphs (6) and (10) explain the distinction between general and nongeneral powers of appointment. A general power of appointment enables the powerholder to exercise the power in favor of one or more of the following: the powerholder, the powerholder's estate, the creditors of the powerholder, or the creditors of the powerholder's estate, regardless of whether the power is also exercisable in favor of others. A nongeneral power of appointment—sometimes called a "special" power of appointment—cannot be exercised in favor of the powerholder, the powerholder's estate, the creditors of the powerholder, or the creditors of the powerholder's estate. Estate planners often classify nongeneral powers as being either "broad" or "limited," depending on the range of permissible appointees. A power to appoint to anyone in the world except the powerholder, the powerholder's estate, and the creditors of either would be an example of a broad nongeneral power. In contrast, a power in the donor's spouse to appoint among the donor's descendants would be an example of a limited nongeneral power.

An instrument creating a power of appointment is construed as creating a general power unless the terms of the instrument manifest a contrary intent. See Section 203. A power to revoke, amend, or withdraw is a general power of appointment if it is exercisable in favor of the powerholder, the powerholder's estate, or the creditors of either. If the settlor of a trust empowers a trustee or another person to change a power of appointment from a general power into a nongeneral power, or vice versa, the power is either general or nongeneral depending on the scope of the power at any particular time.

Paragraph (7) defines the gift-in-default clause. In an instrument creating a power of appointment, the clause that identifies the taker in default is called the gift-in-default clause. A gift-in-default clause is not mandatory but is included in a well-drafted instrument.

Paragraphs (8) and (11) explain the distinction between impermissible and permissible appointees. The permissible appointees—known at common law as the "objects"—of a power of appointment may be narrowly defined (for example, "to such of the powerholder's descendants as the powerholder may select"), broadly defined (for example, "to such persons as the powerholder may select, except the powerholder, the powerholder's estate, the powerholder's creditors, or the creditors of the powerholder's estate"), or unlimited (for example, "to such persons as the powerholder may select"). A permissible appointee of a power of appointment does not, in that capacity, have a property interest that can be transferred to another. Otherwise, a permissible appointee could transform an impermissible appointee into a permissible appointee, exceeding the intended scope of the power and thereby violating the donor's intent. An appointment cannot benefit an impermissible appointee. See Section 307.

Paragraph (9) defines the term "instrument" as either a writing or a record, depending on the choice made by the enacting jurisdiction. The drafting committee had no clear preference between the two options. * * *

Paragraphs (12) and (16) contain the definitions of "person" and "record". With one exception, these are standard definitions approved by the Uniform Law Commission. The exception is that the word "trust" has been added to the definition of "person". Trust law in the United States is moving in the direction of viewing the trust as an entity, * * * but does not yet do so.

Paragraph (13) defines a power of appointment. A power of appointment is a power enabling the powerholder, acting in a nonfiduciary capacity, to designate recipients of ownership interests in or powers of appointment over the appointive property. (Powers held in a fiduciary capacity, such a trustee's power to "decant" property from one trust to another, are the subject of other uniform legislation.)

A power to revoke or amend a trust or a power to withdraw income or principal from a trust is a power of appointment, whether the power is reserved by the transferor or conferred on another. * * * A power to withdraw income or principal subject to an ascertainable standard is a postponed power, exercisable upon the satisfaction of the ascertainable standard. See the Comment to paragraph (15), below.

A power to direct a trustee to distribute income or principal to another is a power of appointment.

In this act, a fiduciary distributive power is not a power of appointment. Fiduciary distributive powers include a trustee's power to distribute principal to or for the benefit of an income beneficiary, or for some other individual, or to pay income or principal to a designated beneficiary, or to distribute income or principal among a defined group of beneficiaries. Unlike the exercise of a power of appointment, the exercise of a fiduciary distributive power is subject to fiduciary standards. Unlike a power of appointment, a fiduciary distributive power does not lapse upon the death of the fiduciary, but survives in a successor fiduciary. Nevertheless, a fiduciary distributive power, like a power of appointment, cannot be validly exercised in favor of or for the benefit of someone who is not a permissible appointee.

A power over the management of property, sometimes called an administrative power, is not a power of appointment. For example, a power of sale coupled with a power to invest the proceeds of the sale, as commonly held by a trustee of a trust, is not a power of appointment but is an administrative power. A power of sale merely authorizes the person to substitute money for the property sold but does not authorize the person to alter the beneficial interests in the substituted property.

A power to designate or replace a trustee or other fiduciary is not a power of appointment. A power to designate or replace a trustee or other fiduciary involves property management and is a power to designate only the nonbeneficial holder of property.

A power of attorney is not a power of appointment. See Restatement of Property § 318, Comment h: "A power of attorney, in the commonest sense of that term, creates the relationship of principal and agent . . . and is terminated by the death of the [principal]. In both of these characteristics such a power differs from a power of appointment. The latter does not create an agency relationship and, except in the case of a power reserved in the donor, it is usually expected that it will be exercised after the donor's death." * * * See also Uniform Power of Attorney Act §§ 102(7) (defining the holder of a power of attorney as an agent), 110(a)(1) (providing that the principal's death terminates a power of attorney).

A power to create or amend a beneficiary designation, for example with respect to the proceeds of a life insurance policy or of a pension plan, is not a power of appointment. An instrument creating a power of appointment must, among other things, transfer the appointive property. See Section 201 * * * .

On the authority of a powerholder to exercise the power of appointment by creating a new power of appointment, see Section 305. If a powerholder exercises a power by creating another power, the powerholder of the first power is the donor of the second power, and the powerholder of the second power is the appointee of the first power.

Paragraph (15) introduces the distinctions among powers of appointment based upon when the power can be exercised. (A power is exercised when the instrument of exercise is effective. Thus, a power exercised by deed is exercised when the deed is effective. The law of deeds typically requires, among other things, intent, delivery, and acceptance. A power exercised by will is exercised when the will is effective—at the testator's death, not when the will is executed.)

There are three categories here: a power of appointment is presently exercisable, postponed, or testamentary.

A power of appointment is presently exercisable if it is exercisable at the time in question. Typically, a presently exercisable power of appointment is exercisable at the time in question during the powerholder's life and also at the powerholder's death, e.g., by the powerholder's will. Thus, a power of appointment that is exercisable "by deed or will" is a presently exercisable power. To take another example, a power of appointment exercisable by the powerholder's last unrevoked instrument in writing is a presently exercisable power, because the powerholder can make a present exercise irrevocable by explicitly so providing in the instrument exercising the power. * * *

A power of appointment is presently exercisable even though, at the time in question, the powerholder can only appoint an *interest* that is revocable or subject to a condition. For example, suppose that a trust directs the trustee to pay the income to the powerholder for life, then to distribute the principal by representation to the powerholder's surviving descendants. The trust further provides that, if the powerholder leaves no surviving descendants, the principal is to be distributed "to such individuals as the powerholder shall appoint." The powerholder has a presently exercisable power of appointment, but the appointive property is a remainder interest that is conditioned on the powerholder leaving no surviving descendants.

A power is a postponed power—sometimes known as a deferred power—if it is not yet exercisable until the occurrence of a specified event, the satisfaction of an ascertainable standard, or the passage of a specified time. A postponed power becomes presently exercisable upon the occurrence of the specified event, the satisfaction of the ascertainable standard, or the passage of the specified time. * * *

A power is testamentary if it is not exercisable during the powerholder's life but only in the powerholder's will or in a nontestamentary instrument that is functionally similar to the powerholder's will, such as the powerholder's revocable trust that remains revocable until the powerholder's death. On the ability of a powerholder to exercise a testamentary power of appointment in such a revocable trust, see Section 304 and the accompanying Comment. * * *

Paragraph (18) defines a taker in default of appointment. A taker in default of appointment—often called the "taker in default"—has a property interest that can be transferred to another. If a taker in default transfers the interest to another, the transferee becomes a taker in default.

Paragraph (19) defines the "terms of the instrument" as the manifestation of the intent of the maker of the instrument regarding the instrument's provisions as expressed in the instrument or as may be established by other evidence that would be admissible in a legal proceeding. The maker of an instrument creating a power of appointment is the donor. The maker of an instrument exercising a power of appointment is the powerholder. * * *

Section 103. Governing Law.

Unless the terms of the instrument creating a power of appointment manifest a contrary intent:

(1) the creation, revocation, or amendment of the power is governed by the law of the donor's domicile at the relevant time; and

(2) the exercise, release, or disclaimer of the power, or the revocation or amendment of the exercise, release, or disclaimer of the power, is governed by the law of the powerholder's domicile at the relevant time.

Comment

This section provides default rules for determining the law governing the creation and exercise of, and related matters concerning, a power of appointment.

Unless the terms of the instrument creating the power provide otherwise, the actions of the donor—the creation, revocation, or amendment of the power—are governed by the law of the donor's domicile; and the actions of the powerholder—the exercise, release, or disclaimer, or the revocation or amendment thereof—are governed by the law of the powerholder's domicile.

In each case, the domicile is determined *at the relevant time*. For example, a donor's creation of a power is governed by the law of the donor's domicile at the time of the power's creation; and a donor's amendment of a power is governed by the law of the donor's domicile at the time of the amendment. Similarly, a powerholder's exercise of a power is governed by the law of the powerholder's domicile at the time of the exercise.

The standard "public policy" rules of choice of law naturally continue to apply. * * *

Paragraph (2) is a departure from older law. The older position was that the law of the donor's domicile governs acts both of the donor (such as the creation of the power) and of the powerholder (such as the exercise of the power). * * *

Paragraph (2) adopts the modern view that acts of the powerholder should be governed by the law of the powerholder's domicile, because that is the law the powerholder (or the powerholder's lawyer) is likely to know. * * *

Section 104. Common Law and Principles of Equity.

The common law and principles of equity supplement this [act], except to the extent modified by this [act] or law of this state other than this [act].

Comment

This act codifies those portions of the law of powers of appointment that are most amenable to codification. The act is supplemented by the common law and principles of equity. * * * The common law is not static but includes the contemporary and evolving rules of decision developed by the courts in exercise of their power to adapt the law to new situations and changing conditions. It also includes the traditional and broad equitable jurisdiction of the court, which the act in no way restricts.

The statutory text of the act is also supplemented by these Comments, which, like the Comments to any Uniform Act, may be relied on as a guide for interpretation. * * *

[ARTICLE] 2

CREATION, REVOCATION, AND AMENDMENT OF POWER OF APPOINTMENT

Section 201. Creation of Power of Appointment.

(a)   A power of appointment is created only if:

    (1)   the instrument creating the power:

        (A)   is valid under applicable law; and

        (B)   except as otherwise provided in subsection (b), transfers the appointive property; and

    (2)   the terms of the instrument creating the power manifest the donor's intent to create in a powerholder a power of appointment over the appointive property exercisable in favor of a permissible appointee.

(b)   Subsection (a)(1)(B) does not apply to the creation of a power of appointment by the exercise of a power of appointment.

(c)   A power of appointment may not be created in a deceased individual.

(d)   Subject to an applicable rule against perpetuities, a power of appointment may be created in an unborn or unascertained powerholder.

Comment

An instrument can only create a power of appointment if, under applicable law, the instrument itself is valid (or partially valid, see the next paragraph). Thus, for example, a *will* creating a power of appointment must be valid under the law—including choice of law (see Section 103)—applicable to wills. An *inter vivos trust* creating a power of appointment must be valid under the law—including choice of law (see Section 103)—applicable to inter vivos trusts. In part, this requirement of validity means that the instrument must be properly executed to the extent other law imposes requirements of execution. In addition, the creator of the instrument must have the capacity to execute the instrument and be free from undue influence and other wrongdoing. * * * The ability of an agent or guardian to create a power of appointment on behalf of a principal or ward is determined by other law, such as the Uniform Power of Attorney Act or the Uniform Guardianship and Protective Proceedings Act.

The instrument need not be entirely valid. A partially valid instrument creates a power of appointment if the provisions creating the power are valid.

In addition to being valid in the relevant provisions, an instrument creating a power of appointment must transfer the appointive property. The creation of a power of appointment—unlike the creation of a power of attorney—requires a transfer. * * * The term "transfer" includes a declaration by an owner of property that the owner holds the property as trustee. Such a declaration necessarily entails a transfer of legal title from the owner-as-owner to the owner-as-trustee; it also entails a transfer of all or some of the equitable interests in the property from the owner to the trust's beneficiaries. * * *

The requirement of a transfer presupposes that the donor has the right to transfer the property. An ordinary individual cannot create a power of appointment over the Brooklyn Bridge. Less fancifully, a donor cannot create a power of appointment if doing so would circumvent a valid restriction on the transfer of the property. For example, interests in unincorporated business organizations may have transfer restrictions arising from statute, contract, or both. A donor cannot use the creation of a power of appointment to circumvent a valid restriction on transfer.

The one exception to the requirement of a transfer is stated in subsection (b): by necessity, the requirement of a transfer does not apply to the creation of a power of appointment by the exercise of a power of appointment. On the ability of a powerholder to exercise the power by creating a new power of appointment, see Section 305.

In addition to the aforementioned requirements, an instrument creating a power of appointment must manifest the donor's intent to create in one or more powerholders a power of appointment over appointive property. This manifestation of intent does not require the use of particular words or phrases (such as "power of appointment"), but careful drafting should leave no doubt about the transferor's intent.

Sometimes the instrument is poorly drafted, raising the question whether the donor intended to create a power of appointment. In such a case, determining the donor's intent is a process of construction. * * *

The creation of a power of appointment requires that there be a donor, a powerholder (who may be the same as the donor), and appointive property. There must also be one or more permissible appointees, though these need not be restricted; a powerholder can be authorized to appoint to anyone. A donor is not required to designate a taker in default of appointment, although a well-drafted instrument will specify one or more takers in default.

Subsection (c) states the well-accepted rule that a power of appointment cannot be created in an individual who is deceased. If the powerholder dies before the effective date of an instrument purporting to confer a power of appointment, the power is not created, and an attempted exercise of the power is ineffective. (The effective date of a power of appointment created in a donor's will is the donor's death, not when the donor executes the will. The effective date of a power of appointment created in a donor's inter vivos trust is the date the trust is established, even if the trust is revocable. * * *

Nor is a power of appointment created if all the possible permissible appointees of the power are deceased when the transfer that is intended to create the power becomes legally operative. If all the possible permissible appointees of a power die after the power is created and before the powerholder exercises the power, the power terminates.

A power of appointment is not created if the permissible appointees are so indefinite that it is impossible to identify any person to whom the powerholder can appoint. If the description of the permissible appointees is such that one or more persons are identifiable, but it is not possible to determine whether other persons are within the description, the power is validly created, but an appointment can only be made to persons who can be identified as within the description of the permissible appointees.

Subsection (d) explains that a power of appointment can be conferred on an unborn or unascertained powerholder, subject to any applicable rule against perpetuities. This is a postponed power. The power arises on the powerholder's birth or ascertainment. The language creating the power as well as other factors such as the powerholder's capacity under applicable law determine whether the power is then presently exercisable, postponed, or testamentary. * * *

Section 202. Nontransferability.

A powerholder may not transfer a power of appointment. If a powerholder dies without exercising or releasing a power, the power lapses.

Comment

A power of appointment is nontransferable. The powerholder may not transfer the power to another person. (On the ability of the powerholder to exercise the power by conferring on a permissible appointee a new power of appointment over the appointive property, see Section 305.) If the powerholder dies without exercising or releasing the power, the power lapses. (If a power is held by multiple powerholders, which is rare, on the death of one powerholder that individual's power lapses but the power continues to be held by the surviving powerholders.) If the powerholder partially releases the power and dies without exercising the remaining part, the unexercised part of the power lapses. The power does not pass through the powerholder's estate to the powerholder's successors in interest.

The ability of an agent or guardian to create, revoke, exercise, or revoke the exercise of a power of appointment on behalf of a principal or ward is determined by other law, such as the Uniform Power of Attorney Act or the Uniform Guardianship and Protective Proceedings Act. * * *

Section 203. Presumption of Unlimited Authority.

Subject to Section 205, and unless the terms of the instrument creating a power of appointment manifest a contrary intent, the power is:

(1)   presently exercisable;

(2)   exclusionary; and

(3)   except as otherwise provided in Section 204, general.

Comment

In determining which type of power of appointment is created, the general principle of construction, articulated in this section, is that a power falls into the category giving the powerholder the maximum discretionary authority except to the extent the terms of the instrument creating the power restrict the powerholder's authority. Maximum discretion confers on the powerholder the flexibility to alter the donor's disposition in response to changing conditions.

In accordance with this presumption of unlimited authority, a power is general unless the terms of the creating instrument specify that the powerholder cannot exercise the power in favor of the powerholder, the powerholder's estate, or the creditors of either. A power is presently exercisable unless the terms of the creating instrument specify that the power can only be exercised at some later time or in some document such as a will that only takes effect at some later time. A power is exclusionary unless the terms of the creating instrument specify that a permissible appointee must receive a certain amount or portion of the appointive assets if the power is exercised.

This general principle of construction applies, unless the terms of the instrument creating the power of appointment provide otherwise. A well-drafted instrument intended to create a nongeneral or testamentary or nonexclusionary power will use clear language to achieve the desired objective. Not all instruments are well-drafted, however. A court may have to construe the terms of the instrument to discern the donor's intent. * * *

Section 204. Exception to Presumption of Unlimited Authority.

Unless the terms of the instrument creating a power of appointment manifest a contrary intent, the power is nongeneral if:

(1)   the power is exercisable only at the powerholder's death; and

(2)   the permissible appointees of the power are a defined and limited class that does not include the powerholder's estate, the powerholder's creditors, or the creditors of the powerholder's estate.

Comment

This section is designed to remedy a recurring drafting mistake. A testamentary power of appointment created in a defined and limited class that happens to include the powerholder is usually intended to be a nongeneral power. For example, a testamentary power created in one of the donor's descendants (such as the donor's child or grandchild) to appoint among the donor's "descendants" or "issue" is typically intended to be a nongeneral power. * * * Accordingly, the presumption of this Section is that such a power is nongeneral.

On the meaning of the well-accepted term of art "defined and limited," see the Comment to Section 205. * * *

Section 205. Rules of Classification.

(a)   In this section, "adverse party" means a person with a substantial beneficial interest in property which would be affected adversely by a powerholder's exercise or nonexercise of a power of appointment in favor of the powerholder, the powerholder's estate, a creditor of the powerholder, or a creditor of the powerholder's estate.

(b)   If a powerholder may exercise a power of appointment only with the consent or joinder of an adverse party, the power is nongeneral.

(c)   If the permissible appointees of a power of appointment are not defined and limited, the power is exclusionary.

Comment

Subsection (b) states a well-accepted and mandatory exception to the presumption of unlimited authority articulated in Section 203. If a power of appointment can be exercised only with the consent or joinder of an adverse party, the power is not a general power. An adverse party is an individual who has a substantial beneficial interest in the trust or other property arrangement that would be adversely affected by the exercise or nonexercise of the power in favor of the powerholder, the powerholder's estate, or the creditors of either. In this context, the word "substantial" is not subject to precise definition but must be determined in light of all the facts and circumstances. Consider the following examples.

Example 1. D transferred property in trust, directing the trustee "to pay the income to D's son S for life, remainder in corpus to such person or persons as S, with the joinder of X, shall appoint; in default of appointment, remainder to X." S's power is not a general power because X meets the definition of an adverse party.

Example 2. Same facts as Example 1, except that S's power is exercisable with the joinder of Y rather than with the joinder of X. Y has no property interest that could be adversely affected by the exercise of the power. Because Y is not an adverse party, S's power is general.

Whether the party whose consent or joinder is required is adverse or not is determined at the time in question. Consider the following example.

Example 3. Same facts as Example 2, except that, one month after D's creation of the trust, X transfers the remainder interest to Y. Before the transfer, Y is not an adverse party and S's power is general. After the transfer, Y is an adverse party and S's power is nongeneral.

Subsection (c) also states a longstanding mandatory rule. Only a power of appointment whose permissible appointees are defined and limited can be nonexclusionary. "Defined and limited" in this context is a well-accepted term of art. * * * In general, permissible appointees are "defined and limited" if they are defined and limited to a reasonable number. Typically, permissible appointees who are defined and limited are described in class-gift terms: a single-generation class such as "children," "grandchildren," "brothers and sisters," or "nieces and nephews," or a multiple-generation class such as "issue" or "descendants" or "heirs." Permissible appointees need not be described in class-gift terms to be defined and limited, however. The permissible appointees are also defined and limited if one or more permissible appointees are designated by name or otherwise individually identified.

If the permissible appointees are not defined and limited, the power is exclusionary irrespective of the donor's intent. A power exercisable, for example, in favor of "such person or persons other than the powerholder, the powerholder's estate, the creditors of the powerholder, and the creditors of the powerholder's estate" is an exclusionary power. An attempt by the donor to require the powerholder to appoint at least $X to each permissible appointee of the power is ineffective, because the permissible appointees of the power are so numerous that it would be administratively impossible to carry out the donor's expressed intent. The donor's expressed restriction is disregarded, and the powerholder may exclude any one or more of the permissible appointees in exercising the power.

In contrast, a power to appoint only to the powerholder's creditors or to the creditors of the powerholder's estate is a power in favor of a defined and limited class. Such a power could be nonexclusionary if, for example, the terms of the instrument creating the power provide that the power is a power to appoint "to such of the powerholder's estate creditors as the powerholder shall by will appoint, but if the powerholder exercises the power, the powerholder must appoint $X to a designated estate creditor or must appoint in full satisfaction of the powerholder's debt to a designated estate creditor."

If a power is determined to be nonexclusionary, it is to be inferred that the donor intends to require an appointment to confer a reasonable benefit upon each mandatory appointee. An appointment under which a mandatory appointee receives nothing, or only a nominal sum, violates this requirement and is forbidden. This doctrine is known as the doctrine forbidding illusory appointments. * * *

The terms of the instrument creating a power of appointment sometimes provide that no appointee shall receive any share in default of appointment unless the appointee consents to allow the amount of the appointment to be taken into account in calculating the fund to be distributed in default of appointment. This "hotchpot" language is used to minimize unintended inequalities of distribution among permissible appointees. Such a clause does not make the power nonexclusionary, because the terms do not prevent the powerholder from making an appointment that excludes a permissible appointee. * * *

Section 206. Power to Revoke or Amend.

A donor may revoke or amend a power of appointment only to the extent that:

(1)   the instrument creating the power is revocable by the donor; or

(2)   the donor reserves a power of revocation or amendment in the instrument creating the power of appointment.

Comment

The donor of a power of appointment has the authority to revoke or amend the power only to the extent the instrument creating the power is revocable by the donor or the donor reserves a power of revocation or amendment in the instrument creating the power.

For example, the donor's power to revoke or amend a revocable inter vivos trust carries with it the authority to revoke or amend any power of appointment created in the trust. However, to the extent an exercise of the power removes appointive property from the trust, the donor's authority to revoke or amend the power is eliminated, unless the donor expressly reserved authority to revoke or amend any transfer from the trust after the transfer is completed.

If an irrevocable inter vivos trust confers a presently exercisable power on someone who is not the settlor of the trust (the settlor being the donor of the power), the donor lacks authority to revoke or amend the power, except to the extent the donor reserved the authority to do so. If the donor did reserve the authority to revoke or amend the power, that authority is only effective until the powerholder irrevocably exercises the power.

If the same individual is both the donor and the powerholder, the donor in his or her capacity as powerholder can indirectly revoke or amend the power by a partial or total release of the power. See Section 402. After the power has been irrevocably exercised, however, the donor as donor is in no different position in regard to revoking or amending the exercise of the power than the donor would be if the donor and powerholder were different individuals.

The ability of an agent or guardian to revoke or amend a power of appointment on behalf of a principal or ward is determined by other law, such as the Uniform Power of Attorney Act or the Uniform Guardianship and Protective Proceedings Act.

Other law of the state may permit the reformation of an otherwise irrevocable instrument. See, for example, Uniform Probate Code § 2–805; Uniform Trust Code § 415. * * *

[ARTICLE] 3

EXERCISE OF POWER OF APPOINTMENT

Section 301. Requisites for Exercise of Power of Appointment.

A power of appointment is exercised only:

(1) if the instrument exercising the power is valid under applicable law;

(2) if the terms of the instrument exercising the power:

    (A) manifest the powerholder's intent to exercise the power; and

    (B) subject to Section 304, satisfy the requirements of exercise, if any, imposed by the donor; and

(3) to the extent the appointment is a permissible exercise of the power.

Comment

Paragraph (1) states the fundamental principle that an instrument can only exercise a power of appointment if the instrument, under applicable law, is valid (or partially valid, see the next paragraph). Thus, for example, a *will* exercising a power of appointment must be valid under the law—including choice of law (see Section 103)—applicable to wills. An *inter vivos trust* exercising a power of appointment must be valid under the law—including choice of law (see Section 103)—applicable to inter vivos trusts. In part, this means that the instrument must be properly executed to the extent other law imposes requirements of execution. In addition, the creator of the instrument must have the capacity to execute the instrument and be free from undue influence and other wrongdoing. * * * The ability of an agent or guardian to exercise a power of appointment on behalf of a principal or ward is determined by other law, such as the Uniform Power of Attorney Act or the Uniform Guardianship and Protective Proceedings Act.

The instrument need not be entirely valid. A partially valid instrument can exercise a power of appointment if the provisions exercising the power are valid.

Paragraph (2) requires the terms of the instrument exercising the power of appointment to manifest the powerholder's intent to exercise the power of appointment. Whether a powerholder has manifested an intent to exercise a power of appointment is a question of construction. * * * For example, a powerholder's disposition of appointive property may manifest an intent to exercise the power even though the powerholder does not refer to the power. * * * Paragraph (2) also requires that the terms of the instrument exercising the power must, subject to Section 304, satisfy the requirements of exercise, if any, imposed by the donor.

Language expressing an intent to exercise a power is clearest if it makes a specific reference to the creating instrument and exercises the power in unequivocal terms and with careful attention to the requirements of exercise, if any, imposed by the donor.

The recommended method for exercising a power of appointment is by a specific-exercise clause, using language such as the following: "I exercise the power of appointment conferred upon me by [my father's will] as follows: I appoint [fill in details of appointment]."

Not recommended is a blanket-exercise clause, which purports to exercise "any" power of appointment the powerholder may have, using language such as the following: "I exercise any power of appointment I may have as follows: I appoint [fill in details of appointment]." Although a blanket-exercise clause does manifest an intent to exercise any power of appointment the powerholder may have, such a clause raises the often-litigated question of whether it satisfies the requirement of specific reference imposed by the donor in the instrument creating the power.

A blending clause purports to blend the appointive property with the powerholder's own property in a common disposition. The exercise portion of a blending clause can take the form of a specific exercise or, more commonly, a blanket exercise. For example, a clause providing "All the residue of my estate, including the property over which I have a power of appointment under my mother's will, I devise as follows" is a blending clause with a specific exercise. A clause providing "All the residue of my estate, including any property over which I may have a power of appointment, I devise as follows" is a blending clause with a blanket exercise.

This act aims to eliminate any significance attached to the use of a blending clause. A blending clause has traditionally been regarded as significant in the application of the doctrines of "selective allocation" and "capture." This act eliminates the significance of such a clause under those doctrines. See Sections 308 (selective allocation) and 309 (capture). The use of a blending clause is more likely to be the product of the forms used by the powerholder's lawyer than a deliberate decision by the powerholder to facilitate the application of the doctrines of selective allocation or capture.

If the powerholder decides not to exercise a specific power or any power that the powerholder might have, it is important to consider whether to depend on mere silence to produce a nonexercise or to take definitive action to assure a nonexercise. Definitive action can take the form of a release during life (see Section 402) or a nonexercise clause in the powerholder's will or other relevant instrument. A nonexercise clause can take the form of a specific-nonexercise clause (for example, "I do not exercise the power of appointment conferred on me by my father's trust") or the form of a blanket-nonexercise clause (for example, "I do not exercise any power of appointment I may have").

In certain circumstances, different consequences depend on the powerholder's choice. Under Section 302, a residuary clause in the powerholder's will is treated as manifesting an intent to exercise a general power in certain limited circumstances if the powerholder silently failed to exercise the power, but not if the powerholder released the power or refrained in a record from exercising it. Under Section 310, unappointed property passes to the powerholder's estate in certain limited circumstances if the powerholder silently failed to exercise a general power, but passes to the donor or to the donor's successors in interest if the powerholder released the power.

Paragraph (3) provides that the exercise is valid only to the extent the exercise is permissible. On permissible and impermissible exercise, see Sections 305 to 307. * * *

Section 302. Intent to Exercise: Determining Intent From Residuary Clause.

(a)　In this section:

(1)　"Residuary clause" does not include a residuary clause containing a blanket-exercise clause or a specific-exercise clause.

(2)　"Will" includes a codicil and a testamentary instrument that revises another will.

(b)　A residuary clause in a powerholder's will, or a comparable clause in the powerholder's revocable trust, manifests the powerholder's intent to exercise a power of appointment only if:

(1)　the terms of the instrument containing the residuary clause do not manifest a contrary intent;

(2)　the power is a general power exercisable in favor of the powerholder's estate;

(3)　there is no gift-in-default clause or the clause is ineffective; and

(4)　the powerholder did not release the power.

Comment

This section addresses a question arising under Section 301(2)(A)—namely, whether the powerholder's intent to exercise a power of appointment is manifested by a garden-variety residuary clause such as "All the residue of my estate, I devise to . . . " or "All of my estate, I devise to. . . ." (The section also applies to a comparable provision in the powerholder's revocable trust, such as a provision providing for the distribution of the trust corpus.) This section does not address the effect of a residuary clause that contains a blanket exercise or a specific exercise of a power of appointment. On blanket-exercise and specific-exercise clauses, see the Comment to Section 301.

The rule of this section is that *in most circumstances* a garden-variety residuary clause does *not* manifest an intent to exercise a power of appointment.

Such a clause manifests an intent to exercise a power of appointment only in the rare circumstance when (1) the terms of the instrument containing the residuary clause do not manifest a contrary intent, (2) the power in question is a general power exercisable in favor of the powerholder's estate, (3) there is no gift-in-default clause or it is ineffective, and (4) the powerholder did not release the power.

In a well-planned estate, a power of appointment, whether general or nongeneral, is accompanied by a gift in default. In a less carefully planned estate, on the other hand, there may be no gift-in-default clause. Or, if there is such a clause, the clause may be wholly or partly ineffective. To the extent the donor did not provide for takers in default or the gift-in-default clause is ineffective, it is more efficient to attribute to the powerholder the intent to exercise a general power in favor of the powerholder's residuary devisees. The principal benefit of attributing to the powerholder the intent to exercise a general power is that it allows the property to pass under the powerholder's will instead of as part of the donor's estate. Because the donor's death would normally have occurred before the powerholder died, some of the donor's successors might themselves have predeceased the powerholder. It is more efficient to avoid tracing the interest through multiple estates to determine who are the present successors. Moreover, to the extent the donor did not provide for takers in default, it is also more in accord with the donor's probable intent for the powerholder's residuary clause to be treated as exercising the power.

A gift-in-default clause can be ineffective or partially ineffective for a variety of reasons. The clause might cover only part of the appointive property. The clause might be invalid because it violates a rule against perpetuities or some other rule, or it might be ineffective because it conditioned the interest of the takers in default on an uncertain event that did not happen, the most common of which is an unsatisfied condition of survival.

Under no circumstance does a residuary clause manifest an intent to exercise a nongeneral power. A residuary clause disposes of the powerholder's own property, and a nongeneral power is not an ownership-equivalent power. Similarly, a residuary clause does not manifest an intent to exercise a general power which is general only because it is exercisable in favor of the creditors of the powerholder or the creditors of the powerholder's estate. * * *

Section 303. Intent to Exercise: After-Acquired Power.

Unless the terms of the instrument exercising a power of appointment manifest a contrary intent:

(1) except as otherwise provided in paragraph (2), a blanket-exercise clause extends to a power acquired by the powerholder after executing the instrument containing the clause; and

(2) if the powerholder is also the donor of the power, the clause does not extend to the power unless there is no gift-in-default clause or the gift-in-default clause is ineffective.

Comment

Nothing in the law prevents a powerholder from exercising an after-acquired power—in other words, from exercising a power in an instrument executed before acquiring the power. The only question is one of construction: whether the powerholder *intended* by the earlier instrument to exercise the after-acquired power. (The term "after-acquired power" in this section refers only to an after-acquired power acquired before the powerholder's death. A power of appointment cannot be conferred on a deceased powerholder. See Section 201.)

If the instrument of exercise specifically identifies the power to be exercised, then the question of construction is readily answered: the specific-exercise clause expresses an intent to exercise the power, whether the power is after-acquired or not. However, if the instrument of exercise uses only a *blanket-exercise* clause, the question of whether the powerholder intended to exercise an after-acquired power is often harder to answer. The presumptions in this section provide default rules of construction on the powerholder's likely intent.

Paragraph (1) states the general rule of this section. Unless the terms of the instrument indicate that the powerholder had a different intent, a blanket-exercise clause extends to a power of appointment acquired after the powerholder executed the instrument containing the blanket-exercise clause. General references to then-present circumstances, such as "all the powers I have" or similar expressions, are not a sufficient indication of an intent to exclude an after-acquired power. In contrast, more precise language, such as "all powers I have at the date of execution of this will," does indicate an intent to exclude an after-acquired power.

It is important to remember that even if the terms of the instrument manifest an intent to exercise an after-acquired power, the intent may be ineffective, for example if the terms of the *donor's* instrument creating the power manifest an intent to preclude such an exercise. In the absence of an indication to the contrary, however, it is inferred that the time of the execution of the powerholder's exercising instrument is immaterial to the donor. Even if the donor declares that the property shall pass to such persons as the powerholder "shall" or "may" appoint, these terms do not suffice to indicate an intent to exclude exercise by an instrument previously executed, because these words may be construed to refer to the time when the exercising document becomes effective.

Paragraph (2) states an exception to the general rule of paragraph (1). If the powerholder is also the donor, a blanket-exercise clause in a preexisting instrument is rebuttably presumed *not* to manifest an intent to exercise a power later reserved in another donative transfer, unless the donor/powerholder did not provide for a taker in default of appointment or the gift-in-default clause is ineffective. * * *

Section 304. Substantial Compliance With Donor-Imposed Formal Requirement.

A powerholder's substantial compliance with a formal requirement of appointment imposed by the donor, including a requirement that the instrument exercising the power of appointment make reference or specific reference to the power, is sufficient if:

(1) the powerholder knows of and intends to exercise the power; and

(2) the powerholder's manner of attempted exercise of the power does not impair a material purpose of the donor in imposing the requirement.

Comment

This section adopts a substantial-compliance rule for donor-imposed formal requirements. This section only applies to formal requirements imposed *by the donor*. It does not apply to formal requirements imposed by law, such as the requirement that a will must be signed and attested. The section also does not apply to *substantive* requirements imposed by the donor, for example a requirement that the powerholder attain a certain age before the power is exercisable.

Whenever the donor imposes formal requirements with respect to the instrument of appointment that exceed the requirements imposed by law, the donor's purpose in imposing the additional requirements is relevant to whether the powerholder's attempted exercise satisfies the rule of this section. To the extent the powerholder's failure to comply with the additional requirements will not impair the accomplishment of a material purpose of the donor, the powerholder's attempted appointment in a manner that substantially complies with a donor-imposed requirement does not fail for lack of perfect compliance with that requirement.

For example, a donor's formal requirement that the power of appointment is exercisable "by will" may be satisfied by the powerholder's attempted exercise in a nontestamentary instrument that is functionally similar to a will, such as the powerholder's revocable trust that remains revocable until the powerholder's death. * * *

A formal requirement commonly imposed by the donor is that, in order to be effective, the powerholder's attempted exercise must make specific reference to the power. Specific-reference clauses were a pre-1942 invention designed to prevent an inadvertent exercise of a general power. The federal estate tax law then provided that the value of property subject to a general power was included in the powerholder's gross estate if the general power was exercised. The idea of requiring specific reference was designed to thwart unintended exercise and, hence, estate taxation.

The federal estate tax law has changed. For a general power created after October 21, 1942, estate tax consequences do not depend on whether the power is exercised.

Nevertheless, donors continue to impose specific-reference requirements. Because the original purpose of the specific-reference requirement was to prevent an inadvertent exercise of the power, it seems reasonable to presume that this is still the donor's purpose in doing so. Consequently, a specific-reference requirement still overrides any applicable state law that presumes that an ordinary residuary clause was intended to exercise a general power. Put differently: An ordinary residuary clause may manifest the powerholder's *intent to exercise* (under Section 301(2)(A)) but does not satisfy the *requirements of exercise* if the donor imposed a specific-reference requirement (this section and Section 301(2)(B)).

A more difficult question is whether a *blanket-exercise clause* satisfies a specific-reference requirement. If it could be shown that the powerholder had knowledge of and intended to exercise the power, the blanket-exercise clause would be sufficient to exercise the power, unless it could be shown that the donor's intent was not merely to prevent an inadvertent exercise of the power but instead that the donor had a material purpose in insisting on the specific-reference requirement. In such a case, the possibility of applying Uniform Probate Code § 2–805 * * * to reform the powerholder's attempted appointment to insert the required specific reference should be explored. * * *

Section 305. Permissible Appointment.

(a) A powerholder of a general power of appointment that permits appointment to the powerholder or the powerholder's estate may make any appointment, including an appointment in trust or creating a new power of appointment, that the powerholder could make in disposing of the powerholder's own property.

(b) A powerholder of a general power of appointment that permits appointment only to the creditors of the powerholder or of the powerholder's estate may appoint only to those creditors.

(c) Unless the terms of the instrument creating a power of appointment manifest a contrary intent, the powerholder of a nongeneral power may:

(1) make an appointment in any form, including an appointment in trust, in favor of a permissible appointee;

(2) create a general power in a permissible appointee;

(3) create a nongeneral power in any person to appoint to one or more of the permissible appointees of the original nongeneral power; or

(4) create a nongeneral power in a permissible appointee to appoint to one or more persons if the permissible appointees of the new nongeneral power include the permissible appointees of the original nongeneral power.

Comment

When a donor creates a general power under which an appointment can be made outright to the powerholder or the powerholder's estate, the necessary implication is that the powerholder may accomplish by an appointment to others whatever the powerholder could accomplish by first appointing to himself and then disposing of the property, including a disposition in trust or in the creation of a further power of appointment.

A general power to appoint only to the powerholder (even though it says "and to no one else") does not prevent the powerholder from exercising the power in favor of others. There is no reason to require the powerholder to transform the appointive assets into owned property and then, in a second step, to dispose of the owned property. Likewise, a general power to appoint only to the powerholder's estate (even though it says "and to no one else") does not prevent an exercise of the power by will in favor of others. There is no reason to require the powerholder to transform the appointive assets into estate property and then, in a second step, to dispose of the estate property by will.

Similarly, a general power to appoint to the powerholder may purport to allow only one exercise of the power, but such a restriction is ineffective and does not prevent multiple partial exercises of the power. To take another example, a general power to appoint to the powerholder or to the powerholder's estate may purport to restrict appointment to outright interests not in trust, but such a restriction is ineffective and does not prevent an appointment in trust.

An additional example will drive home the point. A general power to appoint to the powerholder or to the powerholder's estate may purport to forbid the powerholder from imposing conditions on the enjoyment of the property by the appointee. Such a restriction is ineffective and does not prevent an appointment subject to such conditions.

As stated in subsection (b), however, a general power to appoint only to the powerholder's creditors or the creditors of the powerholder's estate permits an appointment only to those creditors.

Except to the extent the terms of the instrument creating the power manifest a contrary intent, the powerholder of a nongeneral power has the same breadth of discretion in appointment to permissible appointees that the powerholder has in the disposition of the powerholder's owned property to permissible appointees of the power.

Thus, unless the terms of the instrument creating the power manifest a contrary intent, the powerholder of a nongeneral power has the authority to exercise the power by an appointment in trust. In order to manifest a contrary intent, the terms of the instrument creating the power must specifically prohibit an appointment in trust. So, for example, a power to appoint "to" the powerholder's descendants includes the authority to appoint in trust for the benefit of one or more of those descendants.

Similarly, unless the terms of the instrument creating the power manifest a contrary intent, the powerholder of a nongeneral power has the authority to exercise the power by creating a general power in a permissible appointee. The rationale for this rule is a straightforward application of the maxim that the greater includes the lesser. A powerholder of a nongeneral power may appoint outright to a permissible appointee, so the powerholder may instead create in a permissible appointee a general power.

Likewise, unless the terms of the instrument creating the power manifest a contrary intent, the powerholder of a nongeneral power may exercise the power by creating a new nongeneral power in *any* person, whether or not a permissible appointee, to appoint to some or all of the permissible appointees of the original nongeneral power. In order to manifest a contrary intent, the terms of the instrument creating the power must prohibit the creation of such powers. Language merely conferring the power of appointment on the powerholder does not suffice.

And finally, unless the terms of the instrument creating the power manifest a contrary intent, the powerholder of a nongeneral power may exercise the power by creating a new nongeneral power in a permissible appointee to appoint to one or more persons if the permissible appointees of the new nongeneral power include all of the permissible appointees of the original nongeneral power (other than the new powerholder, of course, given that the new power authorized by subsection (c)(4) is nongeneral). * * *

The rules of subsection (c) are default rules. The terms of the instrument creating the power may manifest a contrary intent. * * *

Section 306. Appointment to Deceased Appointee or Permissible Appointee's Descendant.

(a) [Subject to [refer to state law on antilapse], an] [An] appointment to a deceased appointee is ineffective.

(b) Unless the terms of the instrument creating a power of appointment manifest a contrary intent, a powerholder of a nongeneral power may exercise the power in favor of, or create a new power of appointment in, a descendant of a deceased permissible appointee whether or not the descendant is described by the donor as a permissible appointee.

Comment

Just as property cannot be transferred to an individual who is deceased * * *, a power of appointment cannot be effectively exercised in favor of a deceased appointee.

However, an antilapse statute may apply to trigger the substitution of the deceased appointee's descendants (or other substitute takers), unless the terms of the instrument creating or exercising the power of appointment manifest a contrary intent. Antilapse statutes typically provide, as a default rule of construction, that devises to certain relatives who predecease the testator pass instead to specified substitute takers, usually the descendants of the predeceased devisee who survive the testator. * * *

When an antilapse statute does not expressly address whether it applies to the exercise of a power of appointment, a court should construe it to apply to such an exercise. * * * The rationale underlying antilapse statutes, that of presumptively attributing to the testator the intent to substitute the descendants of a predeceased devisee, applies equally to the exercise of a power of appointment.

The substitute takers provided by an antilapse statute (typically the descendants of the deceased appointee) are treated as permissible appointees even if the description of permissible appointees provided by the donor does not expressly cover them. This rule corresponds to the rule applying antilapse statutes to class gifts. Antilapse statutes substitute the descendants of deceased class members, even if the class member's descendants are not members of the class. * * *

The donor of a power, general or nongeneral, can prohibit the application of an antilapse statute to the powerholder's appointment and, in the case of a nongeneral power, can prohibit an appointment to the descendants of a deceased permissible appointee, but must manifest an intent to do so in the terms of the instrument creating the power of appointment. A traditional gift-in-default clause does not manifest a contrary intent in either case, unless the clause provides that it is to take effect instead of the descendants of a deceased permissible appointee.

Subsection (b) provides that the descendants of a deceased permissible appointee are treated as permissible appointees of a nongeneral power of appointment. This rule is a logical extension of the application of antilapse statutes to appointments. If an antilapse statute can substitute the descendants of a deceased appointee, the powerholder should be allowed to appoint in favor of, or to create a new power of appointment in, a descendant (meaning, one or more descendants; the Uniform Law Commission uses the singular to include the plural) of a deceased permissible appointee.

Who qualifies as a "descendant" is defined by state law. * * *

Section 307. Impermissible Appointment.

(a) Except as otherwise provided in Section 306, an exercise of a power of appointment in favor of an impermissible appointee is ineffective.

(b) An exercise of a power of appointment in favor of a permissible appointee is ineffective to the extent the appointment is a fraud on the power.

Comment

The rules of this section apply to the extent the powerholder attempts to confer a beneficial interest in the appointive property on an impermissible appointee. For example, a nongeneral power may not be exercised in favor of the powerholder. And a nongeneral power in favor of the donor's descendants may not be exercised in favor of the donor's spouse (assuming the usual scenario wherein the spouse is not also a descendant).

To the extent an appointment is ineffective, it is invalid. But it bears emphasizing that an appointment that is partially valid remains partially valid. Partial invalidity does not doom the entire appointment.

The rules of this section do not apply to an appointment of a nonbeneficial interest—for example, the appointment of legal title to a trustee—if the beneficial interest is held by permissible appointees.

Nor do the rules of this section prohibit beneficial appointment to an impermissible appointee if the intent to benefit the impermissible appointee is not the powerholder's but rather is the intent of a permissible appointee in whose favor the powerholder has decided to exercise the power. In other words, if the powerholder makes a decision to exercise the power in favor of a permissible appointee, the permissible appointee may request the powerholder to transfer the appointive assets directly to an impermissible appointee. The appointment directly to the impermissible appointee in this situation is effective, being treated for all purposes as an appointment first to the permissible appointee followed by a transfer by the permissible appointee to the impermissible appointee.

The donor of a power of appointment sets the range of permissible appointees by designating the permissible appointees of the power. The rules of this section are concerned with attempts by the powerholder to exceed that authority. Such an attempt is called a fraud on the power and is ineffective. The term "fraud on the power" is a well-accepted term of art. * * *

Among the most common devices employed to commit a fraud on the power are: an appointment conditioned on the appointee conferring a benefit on an impermissible appointee; an appointment subject to a charge in favor of an impermissible appointee; an appointment upon a trust for the benefit of an impermissible appointee; an appointment in consideration of a benefit to an impermissible appointee; and an appointment primarily for the benefit of the permissible appointee's creditor if the creditor is an impermissible appointee. Each of these appointments is impermissible and ineffective. * * *

Section 308. Selective Allocation Doctrine.

If a powerholder exercises a power of appointment in a disposition that also disposes of property the powerholder owns, the owned property and the appointive property must be allocated in the permissible manner that best carries out the powerholder's intent.

Comment

The rule of this section is commonly known as the doctrine of selective allocation. This doctrine applies if the powerholder uses the same instrument to exercise a power of appointment and to dispose of property that the powerholder owns. For purposes of this section, the powerholder's will, any codicils to the powerholder's will, and any revocable trust created by the powerholder that did not become irrevocable before the powerholder's death are treated as the same instrument.

The doctrine of selective allocation provides that the owned property and the appointive property shall be allocated in the permissible manner that best carries out the powerholder's intent.

One situation that often calls for selective allocation is when the powerholder disposes of property to permissible and impermissible appointees. By allocating owned assets to the dispositions favoring impermissible appointees and allocating appointive assets to permissible appointees, the appointment is rendered effective. Consider the following example * * * .

Example. D died, leaving a will that devised property worth $100,000 to T in trust. T is directed to pay the net income to S (Donor's son) for life and then "to pay the principal to S's descendants as S shall by will appoint, and in default of appointment to pay the principal by representation to S's descendants then living, and if no descendant of S is then living, to pay the principal to X-Charity." S dies. The property over which S has the nongeneral power is worth $200,000 at his death. S's owned property at his death is worth $800,000. S's will provides as follows: "All property I own or over which I have any power of appointment shall be used first to pay my debts, expenses of administration, and death taxes, and the balance I give outright to my daughters." S's debts plus the death taxes payable on S's death plus the expenses of administering S's estate total $200,000. If S's owned property is allocated ratably to the payment of such $200,000, one-fifth of the $200,000 would be an ineffective appointment, because it would be to impermissible appointees. That one-fifth of $200,000 ($40,000 of the appointive assets) would pass in default of appointment, and the owned property would have to pick up the full payment of the debts, taxes, and expenses of administration. A selective allocation in the first instance of owned assets to the payment of debts, taxes, and expenses of administration leaves the appointive assets appointed only to permissible appointees of the nongeneral power and nothing passes in default of appointment.

The result of applying selective allocation is always one that the powerholder could have provided for in specific language, and one that the powerholder most probably would have provided for had he or she been aware of the difficulties inherent in the dispositive scheme. By the rule of selective allocation, courts undertake to prevent the dispositive plan from being frustrated by the ineptness of the powerholder or the powerholder's lawyer. * * *

Section 309. Capture Doctrine: Disposition of Ineffectively Appointed Property Under General Power.

To the extent a powerholder of a general power of appointment, other than a power to withdraw property from, revoke, or amend a trust, makes an ineffective appointment:

(1)   the gift-in-default clause controls the disposition of the ineffectively appointed property; or

(2)   if there is no gift-in-default clause or to the extent the clause is ineffective, the ineffectively appointed property:

(A)   passes to:

(i)   the powerholder if the powerholder is a permissible appointee and living; or

(ii)   if the powerholder is an impermissible appointee or deceased, the powerholder's estate if the estate is a permissible appointee; or

(B)   if there is no taker under subparagraph (A), passes under a reversionary interest to the donor or the donor's transferee or successor in interest.

Comment

This section applies when the powerholder of a general power makes an ineffective appointment. This section does not apply when the powerholder of a general power fails to exercise or releases the power. (On such fact-patterns, see instead Section 310.)

Nor does this section apply to an ineffective exercise of a power of revocation, amendment, or withdrawal—in each case, a power pertaining to a trust. To the extent a powerholder of one of these types of powers makes an ineffective appointment, the ineffectively appointed property remains in the trust.

The central rule of this section—in paragraph (1) and subparagraph (2)(A)—is a modern variation of the so-called "capture doctrine" adopted by a small body of case law * * * . Under that doctrine, the ineffectively appointed property passed to the powerholder or the powerholder's estate, but only if the ineffective appointment manifested an intent to assume control of the appointive property "for all purposes" and not merely for the limited purpose of giving effect to the attempted appointment. If the ineffective appointment manifested such an intent, the ineffective appointment was treated as an implied alternative appointment to the powerholder or the powerholder's estate, and thus took effect even if the donor provided for takers in default and one or more of the takers in default were otherwise entitled to take.

The capture doctrine was developed at a time when the donor's gift-in-default clause was considered an afterthought, inserted just in case the powerholder failed to exercise the power. Today, the donor's gift-in-default clause is typically carefully drafted and intended to take effect, unless circumstances change that would cause the powerholder to exercise the power. Consequently, if the powerholder exercises the power effectively, the exercise divests the interest of the takers in default. But if the powerholder makes an ineffective appointment, the powerholder's intent regarding the disposition of the ineffectively appointed property is problematic.

Whether or not the ineffective appointment manifested an intent to assume control of the appointive property "for all purposes" often depended on nothing more than whether the ineffective appointment was contained in a blending clause. The use of a blending clause rather than a direct-exercise clause, however, is typically the product of the drafting lawyer's forms rather than a deliberate choice of the powerholder.

This section alters the traditional capture doctrine in two ways: (1) the gift-in-default clause takes precedence over any implied alternative appointment to the powerholder or the powerholder's estate deduced from the use of a blending clause or otherwise; and (2) the ineffectively appointed property passes to the powerholder or the powerholder's estate only if there is no gift-in-default clause or to the extent the gift-in-default clause is ineffective. Nothing turns on whether the powerholder used a blending clause or somehow otherwise manifested an intent to assume control of the appointive property "for all purposes."

Subparagraph (2)(B) addresses the special case of a power of appointment that is general only because it is exercisable in favor of creditors, but not exercisable in favor of the powerholder or the powerholder's estate. This type of general power is sometimes used in generation-skipping transfer tax planning. However, this type of general power should not trigger the capture doctrine, because the powerholder and the powerholder's estate are impermissible appointees. Instead, ineffectively appointed property should pass under the gift-in-default clause (paragraph (1)) or, if there is no gift-in-default clause or it is ineffective, under a reversionary interest to the donor or the donor's transferee or successor in interest (subparagraph (2)(B)). * * *

Section 310. Disposition of Unappointed Property Under Released or Unexercised General Power.

To the extent a powerholder releases or fails to exercise a general power of appointment other than a power to withdraw property from, revoke, or amend a trust:

(1) the gift-in-default clause controls the disposition of the unappointed property; or

(2) if there is no gift-in-default clause or to the extent the clause is ineffective:

(A) except as otherwise provided in subparagraph (B), the unappointed property passes to:

(i) the powerholder if the powerholder is a permissible appointee and living; or

(ii) if the powerholder is an impermissible appointee or deceased, the powerholder's estate if the estate is a permissible appointee; or

(B) to the extent the powerholder released the power, or if there is no taker under subparagraph (A), the unappointed property passes under a reversionary interest to the donor or the donor's transferee or successor in interest.

Comment

The rules of this section apply to unappointed property under a general power of appointment. The rules do *not* apply to unappointed property under a power of revocation, amendment, or withdrawal—powers pertaining to a trust. If the powerholder releases or dies without exercising a power of revocation or amendment, the power to revoke expires and, unless someone else continues to have a power of revocation or amendment, the trust becomes irrevocable and unamendable. If the powerholder releases or dies without exercising a power to withdraw principal of a trust, the principal that the powerholder could have withdrawn, but did not, remains part of the trust.

The rationale for the rules of this section runs as follows. The gift-in-default clause controls the disposition of unappointed property to the extent the clause is effective. To the extent the gift-in-default clause is nonexistent or ineffective, the disposition of the unappointed property depends on whether the powerholder merely failed to exercise the power or whether the powerholder released the power. If the powerholder merely *failed to exercise* the power, the unappointed property passes to the powerholder or to the powerholder's estate (if these are permissible appointees). The rationale is the same as when the powerholder makes an ineffective appointment. If, however, the powerholder *released* the power, the powerholder has affirmatively chosen to reject the opportunity to gain ownership of the property, hence the unappointed property passes under a reversionary interest to the donor or to the donor's transferee or successor in interest.

These rules are illustrated by the following examples.

Example 1. D transfers property to T in trust, directing T to pay the income to S (D's son) for life, with a general testamentary power in S to appoint the principal of the trust, and in default of appointment the principal is to be distributed "to S's descendants who survive S, by representation, and if none, to X-Charity." S dies leaving a will that does not exercise the power. The principal passes under the gift-in-default clause to S's descendants who survive S, by representation.

Example 2. Same facts as Example 1, except that D's gift-in-default clause covered only half of the principal, and S died intestate. Half of the principal passes under the gift-in-default clause. The other half of the principal passes to S's estate for distribution to S's intestate heirs.

Example 3. Same facts as Example 2, except that S released the power before dying intestate. Half of the principal passes under the gift-in-default clause. The other half of the principal passes to D or to D's transferee or successor in interest.

In addition to governing a released general power, subparagraph (2)(B) also applies to the special case of an unexercised general power that is general only because it is exercisable in favor of creditors, but not exercisable in favor of the powerholder or the powerholder's estate. This type of general power is sometimes used in generation-skipping transfer tax planning. In such a case, unappointed property passes under the gift-in-default clause (paragraph (1)) or, if there is no gift-in-default clause or to the extent it is ineffective, under a reversionary interest to the donor or the donor's transferee or successor in interest (subparagraph (2)(B)). * * *

Section 311. Disposition of Unappointed Property Under Released or Unexercised Nongeneral Power.

To the extent a powerholder releases, ineffectively exercises, or fails to exercise a nongeneral power of appointment:

(1)   the gift-in-default clause controls the disposition of the unappointed property; or

(2)   if there is no gift-in-default clause or to the extent the clause is ineffective, the unappointed property:

     (A)   passes to the permissible appointees if:

         (i)   the permissible appointees are defined and limited; and

         (ii)   the terms of the instrument creating the power do not manifest a contrary intent; or

     (B)   if there is no taker under subparagraph (A), passes under a reversionary interest to the donor or the donor's transferee or successor in interest.

Comment

To the extent the powerholder of a nongeneral power releases, ineffectively exercises, or fails to exercise the power, thus causing the power to lapse, the gift-in-default clause controls the disposition of the unappointed property to the extent the gift-in-default clause is effective.

To the extent the gift-in-default clause is nonexistent or ineffective, the unappointed property passes to the permissible appointees of the power—including those who are substituted for permissible appointees under an antilapse statute (see Section 306)—if the permissible appointees are "defined and limited" (on the meaning of this term of art, see the Comment to Section 205) and the donor has not manifested an intent that the permissible appointees shall receive the appointive property only so far as the powerholder elects to appoint it to them. This rule of construction is based on the assumption that the donor intends the permissible appointees of the power to have the benefit of the property. The donor focused on transmitting the appointive property to the permissible appointees through an appointment, but if the powerholder fails to carry out this particular method of transfer, the donor's underlying intent to pass the appointive property to the defined and limited class of permissible appointees should be carried out. Subparagraph (2)(A) effectuates the donor's underlying intent by implying a gift in default of appointment to the defined and limited class of permissible appointees.

If the defined and limited class of permissible appointees is a multigenerational class, such as "descendants," "issue," "heirs," or "relatives," the default rule of construction is that they take by representation. * * * If the defined and limited class is a single-generation class, the default rule of construction is that the eligible class members take equally. * * *

No implied gift in default of appointment to the permissible appointees arises if the permissible appointees are identified in such broad and inclusive terms that they are not defined and limited. In such an event, the donor has no underlying intent to pass the appointive property to such permissible appointees. Similarly, if the donor manifests an intent that the defined and limited class of permissible appointees is to receive the appointive property only by appointment, the donor's manifestation of intent eliminates any implied gift in default to the permissible appointees. Subparagraph (2)(B) responds to these possibilities by providing for a reversionary interest to the donor or the donor's transferee or successor in interest.

The rules are illustrated by the following examples.

Example 1. D died, leaving a will devising property to T in trust. T is directed to pay the income to S (D's son) for life, and then to pay the principal "to such of S's descendants who survive S as S may appoint by will." D's will contains no gift-in-default clause. S dies without exercising the nongeneral power. The permissible appointees of the power constitute a defined and limited class. Accordingly, the principal of the trust passes at S's death to S's descendants who survive S, by representation.

Example 2. Same facts as Example 1, except that the permissible appointees of S's power of appointment are "such one or more persons, other than S, S's estate, S's creditors, or creditors of S's estate."

The permissible appointees do not constitute a defined and limited class. Accordingly, the principal of the trust passes, at S's death, under a reversionary interest to D or D's transferee or successor in interest. * * *

Section 312. Disposition of Unappointed Property if Partial Appointment to Taker in Default.

Unless the terms of the instrument creating or exercising a power of appointment manifest a contrary intent, if the powerholder makes a valid partial appointment to a taker in default of appointment, the taker in default of appointment may share fully in unappointed property.

Comment

If a powerholder makes a valid partial appointment to a taker in default, leaving some property unappointed, there is a question about whether that taker in default may also fully share in the unappointed property. In the first instance, the intent of the *donor* controls. In the absence of any indication of the donor's intent, it is assumed that the donor intends that the taker can take in both capacities. This rule presupposes that the donor contemplated that the taker in default who is an appointee could receive more of the appointive assets than a taker in default who is not an appointee. The donor can defeat this rule by manifesting a contrary intent in the instrument creating the power of appointment, thereby restricting the powerholder's freedom to benefit an appointee who is also a taker in default in both capacities. If the donor has not so manifested a contrary intent, the *powerholder* is free to exercise the power in favor of a taker in default who is a permissible appointee. Unless the powerholder manifests a contrary intent in the terms of the instrument exercising the power, it is assumed that the powerholder does not intend to affect in any way the disposition of any unappointed property. * * *

Section 313. Appointment to Taker in Default.

If a powerholder makes an appointment to a taker in default of appointment and the appointee would have taken the property under a gift-in-default clause had the property not been appointed, the power of appointment is deemed not to have been exercised and the appointee takes under the clause.

Comment

This section articulates the rule that, to the extent an appointee would have taken appointed property as a taker in default, the appointee takes under the gift-in-default clause rather than under the appointment.

Takers in default have future interests that may be defeated by an exercise of the power of appointment. To whatever extent the powerholder purports to appoint an interest already held in default of appointment, the powerholder does not exercise the power to alter the donor's disposition but merely declares an intent not to alter it. To the extent, however, that the appointed property *is different from* (e.g., is a lesser estate) or *exceeds the total of* the property the appointee would receive as a taker in default, the property passes under the appointment.

Usually it makes no difference whether the appointee takes as appointee or as taker in default. The principal difference arises in jurisdictions that follow the rule that the estate creditors of the powerholder of a general testamentary power that was conferred on the powerholder by another have no claim on the appointive property unless the powerholder has exercised the power. Although this act does not follow that rule regarding creditors' rights (see Section 502), some jurisdictions do. * * *

Section 314. Powerholder's Authority to Revoke or Amend Exercise.

A powerholder may revoke or amend an exercise of a power of appointment only to the extent that:

(1)   the powerholder reserves a power of revocation or amendment in the instrument exercising the power of appointment and, if the power is nongeneral, the terms of the instrument creating the power of appointment do not prohibit the reservation; or

(2)   the terms of the instrument creating the power of appointment provide that the exercise is revocable or amendable.

Comment

This section recognizes that a powerholder lacks the authority to revoke or amend an exercise of the power of appointment, except to the extent (1) the powerholder reserved a power of revocation or amendment in the instrument exercising the power of appointment and the terms of the instrument creating the power of appointment do not effectively prohibit the reservation, or (2) the donor provided that the exercise is revocable or amendable.

A powerholder who exercises a power of appointment is like any other transferor of property in regard to authority to revoke or amend the transfer. Hence, unless the powerholder (or the donor) in some appropriate manner manifests an intent that an appointment is revocable or amendable, the appointment is irrevocable.

The ability of an agent or guardian to revoke or amend the exercise of a power of appointment on behalf of a principal or ward is determined by other law, such as the Uniform Power of Attorney Act or the Uniform Guardianship and Protective Proceedings Act.

Other law of the state may permit the reformation of an otherwise irrevocable instrument. See, for example, Uniform Probate Code § 2–805; Uniform Trust Code § 415. * * *

[ARTICLE] 4

DISCLAIMER OR RELEASE; CONTRACT TO APPOINT OR NOT TO APPOINT

Section 401. Disclaimer.

As provided by [cite state law on disclaimer or the Uniform Disclaimer of Property Interests Act]:

(1)   A powerholder may disclaim all or part of a power of appointment.

(2)   A permissible appointee, appointee, or taker in default of appointment may disclaim all or part of an interest in appointive property.

Comment

A prospective powerholder cannot be compelled to accept the power of appointment, just as the prospective donee of a gift cannot be compelled to accept the gift.

A disclaimer is to be contrasted with a release. A release occurs after the powerholder accepts the power. A disclaimer prevents acquisition of the power, and consequently a powerholder who has accepted a power can no longer disclaim.

Disclaimer statutes frequently specify the time within which a disclaimer must be made. The Uniform Disclaimer of Property Interests Act (1999) (UDPIA) does not specify a time limit, but allows a disclaimer until a disclaimer is barred (see UDPIA § 13).

Disclaimer statutes customarily specify the methods for filing a disclaimer. UDPIA § 12 provides that the statutory methods must be followed. In the absence of such a requirement, statutory formalities for making a disclaimer of a power are not construed as exclusive, and any manifestation of the powerholder's intent not to accept the power may also suffice.

A partial disclaimer of a power of appointment leaves the powerholder possessed of the part of the power not disclaimed.

Just as an individual who would otherwise be a powerholder can avoid acquiring the power by disclaiming it, a person who otherwise would be a permissible appointee, appointee, or taker in default of appointment can avoid acquiring that status by disclaiming it.

The ability of an agent or guardian to disclaim on behalf of a principal or ward is determined by other law, such as the Uniform Power of Attorney Act or the Uniform Guardianship and Protective Proceedings Act. * * *

Section 402. Authority to Release.

A powerholder may release a power of appointment, in whole or in part, except to the extent the terms of the instrument creating the power prevent the release.

Comment

Whether a power of appointment is general or nongeneral, presently exercisable or testamentary, the powerholder has the authority to release the power in whole or in part, in the absence of an effective restriction on release imposed by the donor. A partial release is a release that narrows the freedom of choice otherwise available to the powerholder but does not eliminate the power. A partial release may relate either to the manner of exercising the power or to the persons in whose favor the power may be exercised.

If the powerholder did not create the power, so that the powerholder and donor are different individuals, the donor can effectively impose a restraint on release, but the donor must manifest an intent in the terms of the creating instrument to impose such a restraint.

If the powerholder created the power, so that the powerholder is also the donor, the donor/powerholder cannot effectively impose a restraint on release. A self-imposed restraint on release resembles a self-imposed restraint on alienation, which is ineffective. * * *

If the exercise of a power of appointment requires the action of two or more individuals, each powerholder has a power of appointment. If one but not the other joint powerholder releases the power, the power survives in the hands of the nonreleasing powerholder, unless the continuation of the power is inconsistent with the donor's purpose in creating the joint power. * * *

The ability of an agent or guardian to release a power of appointment on behalf of a principal or ward is determined by other law, such as the Uniform Power of Attorney Act or the Uniform Guardianship and Protective Proceedings Act. * * *

Section 403. Method of Release.

[(a) In this section, "record" means information that is inscribed on a tangible medium or that is stored in an electronic or other medium and is retrievable in perceivable form.

(b)] A powerholder of a releasable power of appointment may release the power in whole or in part:

(1) by substantial compliance with a method provided in the terms of the instrument creating the power; or

(2) if the terms of the instrument creating the power do not provide a method or the method provided in the terms of the instrument is not expressly made exclusive, by a record manifesting the powerholder's intent by clear and convincing evidence.

Comment

A powerholder may release the power of appointment by substantial compliance with the method specified in the terms of the instrument creating the power or any other method manifesting clear and convincing evidence of the powerholder's intent. Only if the method specified in the terms of the creating instrument is made exclusive is use of the other methods prohibited. Even then, a failure to comply with a technical requirement, such as required notarization, may be excused as long as compliance with the method specified in the terms of the creating instrument is otherwise substantial.

Examples of methods manifesting clear and convincing evidence of the powerholder's intent to release include: (1) delivering (by the same method of delivery that would make an instrument of transfer effective * * *) an instrument declaring the extent to which the power is released to an individual who could be adversely affected by an exercise of the power; (2) joining with some or all of the takers in default in making an otherwise effective transfer of an interest in the appointive property, in which case the power is released to the extent a subsequent exercise of the power would defeat the interest transferred; (3) contracting with an individual who could be adversely affected by an exercise of the power not to exercise the power, in which case the power is released to the extent a subsequent exercise of the power would violate the terms of the contract; and (4) communicating in a record an intent to release the power, in which case the power is released to the extent a subsequent exercise of the power would be contrary to manifested intent.

The black-letter of this section is based on Uniform Trust Code § 602(c). * * *

Section 404. Revocation or Amendment of Release.

A powerholder may revoke or amend a release of a power of appointment only to the extent that:

(1) the instrument of release is revocable by the powerholder; or

(2) the powerholder reserves a power of revocation or amendment in the instrument of release.

Comment

A release is typically irrevocable. If a powerholder wishes to retain the power to revoke or amend the release, the powerholder should so indicate in the instrument executing the release.

The ability of an agent or guardian to revoke or amend the release of a power of appointment on behalf of a principal or ward is determined by other law, such as the Uniform Power of Attorney Act or the Uniform Guardianship and Protective Proceedings Act.

Other law of the state may permit the reformation of an otherwise irrevocable instrument. See, for example, Uniform Probate Code § 2–805; Uniform Trust Code § 415. * * *

Section 405. Power to Contract: Presently Exercisable Power of Appointment.

A powerholder of a presently exercisable power of appointment may contract:

(1) not to exercise the power; or

(2) to exercise the power if the contract when made does not confer a benefit on an impermissible appointee.

Comment

A powerholder of a presently exercisable power may contract to make, or not to make, an appointment if the contract does not confer a benefit on an impermissible appointee. The rationale is that the power is presently exercisable, so the powerholder can presently enter into a contract concerning the appointment.

The contract may not confer a benefit on an impermissible appointee. Recall that a general power presently exercisable in favor of the powerholder or the powerholder's estate has no impermissible appointees. See Section 305(a). In contrast, a presently exercisable nongeneral power, or a general power presently exercisable only in favor of one or more of the creditors of the powerholder or the powerholder's estate, does have impermissible appointees. See Section 305(b)–(c).

A contract *not* to appoint assures that the appointive property will pass to the taker in default. A contract to appoint to a taker in default, if enforceable, has the same effect as a contract not to appoint.

The ability of an agent or guardian to contract on behalf of a principal or ward is determined by other law, such as the Uniform Power of Attorney Act or the Uniform Guardianship and Protective Proceedings Act. * * *

Section 406. Power to Contract: Power of Appointment Not Presently Exercisable.

A powerholder of a power of appointment that is not presently exercisable may contract to exercise or not to exercise the power only if the powerholder:

(1) is also the donor of the power; and

(2) has reserved the power in a revocable trust.

Comment

Except in the case of a power reserved by the donor in a revocable inter vivos trust, a contract to exercise, or not to exercise, a power of appointment that is not presently exercisable is unenforceable, because the powerholder does not have the authority to make a current appointment. If the powerholder was also the donor of the power and created the power in a revocable inter vivos trust, however, a contract to appoint is enforceable, because the donor-powerholder could have revoked the trust and recaptured ownership of the trust assets or could have amended the trust to change the power onto one that is presently exercisable.

In all other cases, the donor of a power not presently exercisable has manifested an intent that the selection of the appointees and the determination of the interests they are to receive are to be made in the light of the circumstances that exist on the date that the power becomes exercisable. Were a contract to be enforceable, the donor's intent would be defeated.

The ability of an agent or guardian to contract on behalf of a principal or ward is determined by other law, such as the Uniform Power of Attorney Act or the Uniform Guardianship and Protective Proceedings Act. * * *

Section 407. Remedy for Breach of Contract to Appoint or Not to Appoint.

The remedy for a powerholder's breach of a contract to appoint or not to appoint appointive property is limited to damages payable out of the appointive property or, if appropriate, specific performance of the contract.

Comment

This section sets forth a rule on remedy. The remedy for a powerholder's breach of an enforceable contract to appoint, or not to appoint, is limited to damages payable out of the appointive property or, if appropriate, specific performance. The powerholder's owned assets are not available to satisfy a judgment for damages. * * * This section does not address the *amount* of damages, which is determined by other law of the state, such as contract law.

[ARTICLE] 5

RIGHTS OF POWERHOLDER'S CREDITORS IN APPOINTIVE PROPERTY

Section 501. Creditor Claim: General Power Created by Powerholder.

(a) In this section, "power of appointment created by the powerholder" includes a power of appointment created in a transfer by another person to the extent the powerholder contributed value to the transfer.

(b) Appointive property subject to a general power of appointment created by the powerholder is subject to a claim of a creditor of the powerholder or of the powerholder's estate to the extent provided in [cite state law on fraudulent transfers or the Uniform Fraudulent Transfers Act].

(c) Subject to subsection (b), appointive property subject to a general power of appointment created by the powerholder is not subject to a claim of a creditor of the powerholder or the powerholder's estate to the extent the powerholder irrevocably appointed the property in favor of a person other than the powerholder or the powerholder's estate.

(d) Subject to subsections (b) and (c), and notwithstanding the presence of a spendthrift provision or whether the claim arose before or after the creation of the power of appointment, appointive property subject to a general power of appointment created by the powerholder is subject to a claim of a creditor of:

(1) the powerholder, to the same extent as if the powerholder owned the appointive property, if the power is presently exercisable; and

(2) the powerholder's estate, to the extent the estate is insufficient to satisfy the claim and subject to the right of a decedent to direct the source from which liabilities are paid, if the power is exercisable at the powerholder's death.

Comment

Subsection (b) states a well-settled rule: a donor of a power of appointment cannot use a fraudulent transfer to avoid creditors. If a donor fraudulently transfers appointive property, retaining a power of appointment, the donor/powerholder's creditors and the creditors of the donor/powerholder's estate may reach the appointive property as provided in the law of fraudulent transfers.

Subsection (c) also states a well-settled rule: if there is no fraudulent transfer, and the donor/powerholder has made an irrevocable appointment to a third party of the appointive property, the appointed property is beyond the reach of the donor/powerholder's creditors or the creditors of the donor/powerholder's estate. In other words, an irrevocable and nonfraudulent exercise of the general power by the donor/powerholder in favor of someone other than the powerholder or the powerholder's estate eliminates the ability of the powerholder's creditors or the creditors of the powerholder's estate to reach those assets.

Subsection (d) establishes rules governing the remaining fact-pattern: the donor has retained a general power of appointment but has made neither a fraudulent transfer nor an irrevocable appointment. In such a case, the following rules apply. If the donor retains a presently exercisable general power of appointment, the appointive property is subject to a claim of—and is reachable by—a creditor of the powerholder to the same extent as if the powerholder owned the appointive property. If the donor retains a general power of appointment exercisable at death, the appointive property is subject to a claim of—and is reachable by—a creditor of the donor/powerholder's estate (defined with reference to other law, but including costs of administration, expenses of the funeral and disposal of remains, and statutory allowances to the surviving spouse and children) to the extent the estate is insufficient, subject to the decedent's right to direct the source from which liabilities are paid. For the same rules in the context of a retained power to revoke a revocable trust, see Uniform Trust Code § 505(a). The application of these rules is not affected by the presence of a spendthrift provision or by whether the claim arose before or after the creation of the power of appointment. * * *

Subsection (a) enables all of these rules to apply even if the general power was not created in a transfer made by the powerholder. The rules will apply to the extent the powerholder contributed value to the transfer. * * * Consider the following examples * * * .

Example 1. D purchases Blackacre from A. Pursuant to D's request, A transfers Blackacre "to D for life, then to such person as D may by will appoint." The rule of subsection (d) applies to D's general testamentary power, though in form A created the power.

Example 2. A by will transfers Blackacre "to D for life, then to such persons as D may by will appoint." Blackacre is subject to mortgage indebtedness in favor of X in the amount of $10,000. The value of Blackacre is $20,000. D pays the mortgage indebtedness. The rule of subsection (d) applies to half of the value of Blackacre, though in form A's will creates the general power in D.

Example 3. D, an heir of A, contests A's will on the ground of undue influence on A by the principal beneficiary under A's will. The contest is settled by transferring part of A's estate to Trustee in trust. Under the trust, Trustee is directed "to pay the net income to D for life and, on D's death, the principal to such persons as D shall by will appoint." The rule of subsection (d) applies to the transfer in trust, though in form D did not create the general power.

The provisions of this section are designed to be consistent with Uniform Trust Code § 505(a). * * *

Section 502. Creditor Claim: General Power Not Created by Powerholder.

(a) Except as otherwise provided in subsection (b), appointive property subject to a general power of appointment created by a person other than the powerholder is subject to a claim of a creditor of:

    (1) the powerholder, to the extent the powerholder's property is insufficient, if the power is presently exercisable; and

    (2) the powerholder's estate, to the extent the estate is insufficient, subject to the right of a decedent to direct the source from which liabilities are paid.

(b) Subject to Section 504(c), a power of appointment created by a person other than the powerholder which is subject to an ascertainable standard relating to an individual's health, education, support, or maintenance within the meaning of 26 U.S.C. Section 2041(b)(1)(A) or 26 U.S.C. Section 2514(c)(1), [on the effective date of this [act]][as amended], is treated for purposes of this [article] as a nongeneral power.

Comment

Subsection (a) reaffirms the fundamental principle that a presently exercisable general power of appointment is an ownership-equivalent power. Consequently, subsection (b) provides that property subject to a presently exercisable general power of appointment is subject to the claims of the powerholder's creditors, to the extent the powerholder's property is insufficient. Furthermore, upon the powerholder's death, property subject to a general power of appointment is subject to creditors' claims against the powerholder's estate (defined with reference to other law, but including costs of administration, expenses of the funeral and disposal of remains, and statutory allowances to the surviving spouse and children) to the extent the estate is insufficient, subject to the decedent's right to direct the source from which liabilities are paid. In each case, whether the powerholder has or has not purported to exercise the power is immaterial.

Subsection (b) states an important exception. If the power is subject to an ascertainable standard within the meaning of 26 U.S.C. § 2041(b)(1)(A) or 26 U.S.C. § 2514(c)(1), the power is treated for purposes of this article as a nongeneral power, and the rights of the powerholder's creditors in the appointive property are governed by Sections 504(a) and (b).

Section 503. Power to Withdraw.

(a) For purposes of this [article], and except as otherwise provided in subsection (b), a power to withdraw property from a trust is treated, during the time the power may be exercised, as a presently exercisable general power of appointment to the extent of the property subject to the power to withdraw.

(b)   On the lapse, release, or waiver of a power to withdraw property from a trust, the power is treated as a presently exercisable general power of appointment only to the extent the value of the property affected by the lapse, release, or waiver exceeds the greater of the amount specified in 26 U.S.C. Section 2041(b)(2) and 26 U.S.C. Section 2514(e) or the amount specified in 26 U.S.C. Section 2503(b), [on the effective date of this [act]][as amended].

Comment

Subsection (a) treats a power of withdrawal as the equivalent of a presently exercisable general power of appointment, because the two are ownership-equivalent powers. Upon the lapse, release, or waiver of the power of withdrawal, subsection (b) follows the lead of Uniform Trust Code § 505(b)(2) in creating an exception for property subject to a Crummey or five and five power: the holder of the power of withdrawal is treated as a powerholder of a presently exercisable general power of appointment only to the extent the value of the property affected by the lapse, release, or waiver exceeds the greater of the amount specified in Internal Revenue Code §§ 2041(b)(2) and 2514(e) [greater of 5% or $5,000] or § 2503(b) [$13,000 in 2012].

Section 504. Creditor Claim: Nongeneral Power.

(a)   Except as otherwise provided in subsections (b) and (c), appointive property subject to a nongeneral power of appointment is exempt from a claim of a creditor of the powerholder or the powerholder's estate.

(b)   Appointive property subject to a nongeneral power of appointment is subject to a claim of a creditor of the powerholder or the powerholder's estate to the extent that the powerholder owned the property and, reserving the nongeneral power, transferred the property in violation of [cite state statute on fraudulent transfers or the Uniform Fraudulent Transfers Act].

(c)   If the initial gift in default of appointment is to the powerholder or the powerholder's estate, a nongeneral power of appointment is treated for purposes of this [article] as a general power.

Comment

Subsection (a) states the general rule of this section. Appointive property subject to a nongeneral power of appointment is exempt from a claim of a creditor of the powerholder or the powerholder's estate. The rationale for this general rule is that a nongeneral power of appointment is not an ownership-equivalent power, so the powerholder's creditors have no claim to the appointive assets.

Subsection (b) addresses an important exception: the fraudulent transfer. A fraudulent transfer arises if the powerholder formerly owned the appointive property covered by the nongeneral power and transferred the property in fraud of creditors, reserving the nongeneral power. In such a case, the creditors can reach the appointive property under the rules relating to fraudulent transfers.

Subsection (c) also addresses an important exception, arising when the initial gift in default of appointment is to the powerholder or the powerholder's estate. In such a case, the power of appointment, though in form a nongeneral power, is in substance a general power, and the rights of the powerholder's creditors in the appointive property are governed by Sections 501 and 502. * * *

[ARTICLE] 6

MISCELLANEOUS PROVISIONS

UNIFORM PRINCIPAL AND INCOME ACT (1997)*

[ARTICLE] 1. DEFINITIONS AND FIDUCIARY DUTIES

[ARTICLE] 2. DECEDENT'S ESTATE OR TERMINATING INCOME INTEREST

[ARTICLE] 3. APPORTIONMENT AT BEGINNING AND END OF INCOME INTEREST

[ARTICLE] 4. ALLOCATION OF RECEIPTS DURING ADMINISTRATION OF TRUST

[PART 1. RECEIPTS FROM ENTITIES]

[PART 2. RECEIPTS NOT NORMALLY APPORTIONED]

[PART 3. RECEIPTS NORMALLY APPORTIONED]

UNIFORM PRINCIPAL AND INCOME ACT

[ARTICLE] 5. ALLOCATION OF DISBURSEMENTS DURING ADMINISTRATION OF TRUST

[ARTICLE] 6. MISCELLANEOUS PROVISIONS

PREFATORY NOTE

This revision of the 1931 Uniform Principal and Income Act and the 1962 Revised Uniform Principal and Income Act has two purposes.

One purpose is to revise the 1931 and the 1962 Acts. Revision is needed to support the now widespread use of the revocable living trust as a will substitute, to change the rules in those Acts that experience has shown need to be changed, and to establish new rules to cover situations not provided for in the old Acts, including rules that apply to financial instruments invented since 1962.

The other purpose is to provide a means for implementing the transition to an investment regime based on principles embodied in the Uniform Prudent Investor Act, especially the principle of investing for total return rather than a certain level of "income" as traditionally perceived in terms of interest, dividends, and rents. * * *

[ARTICLE] 1

DEFINITIONS AND FIDUCIARY DUTIES

Section 101. Short Title.

This [Act] may be cited as the Uniform Principal and Income Act (1997).

Section 102. Definitions.

In this [Act]:

(1) "Accounting period" means a calendar year unless another 12-month period is selected by a fiduciary. The term includes a portion of a calendar year or other 12-month period that begins when an income interest begins or ends when an income interest ends.

(2) "Beneficiary" includes, in the case of a decedent's estate, an heir [, legatee,] and devisee and, in the case of a trust, an income beneficiary and a remainder beneficiary.

(3) "Fiduciary" means a personal representative or a trustee. The term includes an executor, administrator, successor personal representative, special administrator, and a person performing substantially the same function.

(4) "Income" means money or property that a fiduciary receives as current return from a principal asset. The term includes a portion of receipts from a sale, exchange, or liquidation of a principal asset, to the extent provided in [Article] 4.

(5) "Income beneficiary" means a person to whom net income of a trust is or may be payable.

(6) "Income interest" means the right of an income beneficiary to receive all or part of net income, whether the terms of the trust require it to be distributed or authorize it to be distributed in the trustee's discretion.

(7) "Mandatory income interest" means the right of an income beneficiary to receive net income that the terms of the trust require the fiduciary to distribute.

(8) "Net income" means the total receipts allocated to income during an accounting period minus the disbursements made from income during the period, plus or minus transfers under this [Act] to or from income during the period.

(9) "Person" means an individual, corporation, business trust, estate, trust, partnership, limited liability company, association, joint venture, government; governmental subdivision, agency, or instrumentality; public corporation, or any other legal or commercial entity.

(10) "Principal" means property held in trust for distribution to a remainder beneficiary when the trust terminates.

(11) "Remainder beneficiary" means a person entitled to receive principal when an income interest ends.

(12) "Terms of a trust" means the manifestation of the intent of a settlor or decedent with respect to the trust, expressed in a manner that admits of its proof in a judicial proceeding, whether by written or spoken words or by conduct.

(13) "Trustee" includes an original, additional, or successor trustee, whether or not appointed or confirmed by a court.

Section 103. Fiduciary Duties; General Principles.

(a) In allocating receipts and disbursements to or between principal and income, and with respect to any matter within the scope of [Articles] 2 and 3, a fiduciary:

(1)   shall administer a trust or estate in accordance with the terms of the trust or the will, even if there is a different provision in this [Act];

(2)   may administer a trust or estate by the exercise of a discretionary power of administration given to the fiduciary by the terms of the trust or the will, even if the exercise of the power produces a result different from a result required or permitted by this [Act];

(3)   shall administer a trust or estate in accordance with this [Act] if the terms of the trust or the will do not contain a different provision or do not give the fiduciary a discretionary power of administration; and

(4)   shall add a receipt or charge a disbursement to principal to the extent that the terms of the trust and this [Act] do not provide a rule for allocating the receipt or disbursement to or between principal and income.

(b) In exercising the power to adjust under Section 104(a) or a discretionary power of administration regarding a matter within the scope of this [Act], whether granted by the terms of a trust, a will, or this [Act], a fiduciary shall administer a trust or estate impartially, based on what is fair and reasonable to all of the beneficiaries, except to the extent that the terms of the trust or the will clearly manifest an intention that the fiduciary shall or may favor one or more of the beneficiaries. A determination in accordance with this [Act] is presumed to be fair and reasonable to all of the beneficiaries.

Comment

* * * **Fiduciary discretion.** The general rule is that if a discretionary power is conferred upon a trustee, the exercise of that power is not subject to control by a court except to prevent an abuse of discretion. Restatement (Second) of Trusts § 187. The situations in which a court will control the exercise of a trustee's discretion are discussed in the comments to § 187. See also id. § 233 Comment p.

Questions for which there is no provision. Section 103(a)(4) allocates receipts and disbursements to principal when there is no provision for a different allocation in the terms of the trust, the will, or the Act. This may occur because money is received from a financial instrument not available at the present time (inflation-indexed bonds might have fallen into this category had they been announced after this Act was approved by the Commissioners on Uniform State Laws) or because a transaction is of a type or occurs in a manner not anticipated by the Drafting Committee for this Act or the drafter of the trust instrument.

Allocating to principal a disbursement for which there is no provision in the Act or the terms of the trust preserves the income beneficiary's level of income in the year it is allocated to principal, but thereafter will reduce the amount of income produced by the principal. Allocating to principal a receipt for which there is no provision will increase the income received by the income beneficiary in subsequent years, and will eventually, upon termination of the trust, also favor the remainder beneficiary. Allocating these items to principal implements the rule that requires a trustee to administer the trust impartially, based on what is fair and reasonable to both income and remainder beneficiaries. However, if the trustee decides that an adjustment between principal and income is needed to enable the trustee to comply with Section 103(b), after considering the return from the portfolio as a whole, the trustee may make an appropriate adjustment under Section 104(a).

Duty of impartiality. Whenever there are two or more beneficiaries, a trustee is under a duty to deal impartially with them. Restatement of Trusts 3d: Prudent Investor Rule § 183 (1992). This rule applies whether the beneficiaries' interests in the trust are concurrent or successive. If the terms of the trust give the trustee discretion to favor one beneficiary over another, a court will not control the exercise of such discretion except to prevent the trustee from abusing it. Id. § 183, Comment a. "The precise meaning of the trustee's duty of impartiality and the balancing of competing interests and objectives inevitably are matters of judgment and interpretation. Thus, the duty and balancing are affected by the purposes, terms, distribution requirements, and other circumstances of the trust, not only at the outset but as they may change from time to time." Id. § 232, Comment c.

The terms of a trust may provide that the trustee, or an accountant engaged by the trustee, or a committee of persons who may be family members or business associates, shall have the power to determine what is income and what is principal. If the terms of a trust provide that this Act specifically or principal and income legislation in general does not apply to the trust but fail to provide a rule to deal with a matter provided for in this Act, the trustee has an implied grant of discretion to decide the question. Section 103(b) provides that the rule of impartiality applies in the exercise of such a discretionary power to the extent that the terms of the trust do not provide that one or more of the beneficiaries are to be favored. The fact that a person is named an income beneficiary or a remainder beneficiary is not by itself an indication of partiality for that beneficiary.

Section 104. Trustee's Power to Adjust.

(a) A trustee may adjust between principal and income to the extent the trustee considers necessary if the trustee invests and manages trust assets as a prudent investor, the terms of the trust describe the amount that may or must be distributed to a beneficiary by referring to the trust's income, and the trustee determines, after applying the rules in Section 103(a), that the trustee is unable to comply with Section 103(b).

(b) In deciding whether and to what extent to exercise the power conferred by subsection (a), a trustee shall consider all factors relevant to the trust and its beneficiaries, including the following factors to the extent they are relevant:

(1) the nature, purpose, and expected duration of the trust;

(2) the intent of the settlor;

(3) the identity and circumstances of the beneficiaries;

(4) the needs for liquidity, regularity of income, and preservation and appreciation of capital;

(5) the assets held in the trust; the extent to which they consist of financial assets, interests in closely held enterprises, tangible and intangible personal property, or real property; the extent to which an asset is used by a beneficiary; and whether an asset was purchased by the trustee or received from the settlor;

(6) the net amount allocated to income under the other sections of this [Act] and the increase or decrease in the value of the principal assets, which the trustee may estimate as to assets for which market values are not readily available;

(7) whether and to what extent the terms of the trust give the trustee the power to invade principal or accumulate income or prohibit the trustee from invading principal or accumulating income, and the extent to which the trustee has exercised a power from time to time to invade principal or accumulate income;

(8) the actual and anticipated effect of economic conditions on principal and income and effects of inflation and deflation; and

(9) the anticipated tax consequences of an adjustment.

(c) A trustee may not make an adjustment:

(1) that diminishes the income interest in a trust that requires all of the income to be paid at least annually to a surviving spouse and for which an estate tax or gift tax marital deduction would be allowed, in whole or in part, if the trustee did not have the power to make the adjustment;

(2) that reduces the actuarial value of the income interest in a trust to which a person transfers property with the intent to qualify for a gift tax exclusion;

(3) that changes the amount payable to a beneficiary as a fixed annuity or a fixed fraction of the value of the trust assets;

(4) from any amount that is permanently set aside for charitable purposes under a will or the terms of a trust unless both income and principal are so set aside;

(5)   if possessing or exercising the power to make an adjustment causes an individual to be treated as the owner of all or part of the trust for income tax purposes, and the individual would not be treated as the owner if the trustee did not possess the power to make an adjustment;

(6)   if possessing or exercising the power to make an adjustment causes all or part of the trust assets to be included for estate tax purposes in the estate of an individual who has the power to remove a trustee or appoint a trustee, or both, and the assets would not be included in the estate of the individual if the trustee did not possess the power to make an adjustment;

(7)   if the trustee is a beneficiary of the trust; or

(8)   if the trustee is not a beneficiary, but the adjustment would benefit the trustee directly or indirectly.

(d)   If subsection (c)(5), (6), (7), or (8) applies to a trustee and there is more than one trustee, a cotrustee to whom the provision does not apply may make the adjustment unless the exercise of the power by the remaining trustee or trustees is not permitted by the terms of the trust.

(e)   A trustee may release the entire power conferred by subsection (a) or may release only the power to adjust from income to principal or the power to adjust from principal to income if the trustee is uncertain about whether possessing or exercising the power will cause a result described in subsection (c)(1) through (6) or (c)(8) or if the trustee determines that possessing or exercising the power will or may deprive the trust of a tax benefit or impose a tax burden not described in subsection (c). The release may be permanent or for a specified period, including a period measured by the life of an individual.

(f)   Terms of a trust that limit the power of a trustee to make an adjustment between principal and income do not affect the application of this section unless it is clear from the terms of the trust that the terms are intended to deny the trustee the power of adjustment conferred by subsection (a).

Comment

Purpose and Scope of Provision. The purpose of Section 104 is to enable a trustee to select investments using the standards of a prudent investor without having to realize a particular portion of the portfolio's total return in the form of traditional trust accounting income such as interest, dividends, and rents. Section 104(a) authorizes a trustee to make adjustments between principal and income if three conditions are met: (1) the trustee must be managing the trust assets under the prudent investor rule; (2) the terms of the trust must express the income beneficiary's distribution rights in terms of the right to receive "income" in the sense of traditional trust accounting income; and (3) the trustee must determine, after applying the rules in Section 103(a), that he is unable to comply with Section 103(b). In deciding whether and to what extent to exercise the power to adjust, the trustee is required to consider the factors described in Section 104(b), but the trustee may not make an adjustment in circumstances described in Section 104(c).

Section 104 does not empower a trustee to increase or decrease the degree of beneficial enjoyment to which a beneficiary is entitled under the terms of the trust; rather, it authorizes the trustee to make adjustments between principal and income that may be necessary if the income component of a portfolio's total return is too small or too large because of investment decisions made by the trustee under the prudent investor rule. The paramount consideration in applying Section 104(a) is the requirement in Section 103(b) that "a fiduciary must administer a trust or estate impartially, based on what is fair and reasonable to all of the beneficiaries, except to the extent that the terms of the trust or the will clearly manifest an intention that the fiduciary shall or may favor one or more of the beneficiaries." The power to adjust is subject to control by the court to prevent an abuse of discretion. Restatement (Second) of Trusts § 187 (1959). See also id. §§ 183, 232, 233, Comment *p* (1959).

Section 104 will be important for trusts that are irrevocable when a State adopts the prudent investor rule by statute or judicial approval of the rule in Restatement of Trusts 3d: Prudent Investor Rule. Wills and trust instruments executed after the rule is adopted can be drafted to describe a beneficiary's distribution rights in terms that do not depend upon the amount of trust accounting income, but to the extent that drafters of trust documents continue to describe an income beneficiary's distribution rights by referring to trust accounting income, Section 104 will be an important tool in trust administration.

Three conditions to the exercise of the power to adjust. The first of the three conditions that must be met before a trustee can exercise the power to adjust—that the trustee invest and manage trust assets as a prudent investor—is expressed in this Act by language derived from the Uniform Prudent Investor Act, but the condition will be met whether the prudent investor rule applies because the Uniform Act or other prudent investor legislation has been enacted, the prudent investor rule has been approved by the courts, or the terms of the trust require it. Even if a State's legislature or courts have not formally adopted the rule, the Restatement establishes the prudent investor rule as an authoritative interpretation of the common law prudent man rule, referring to the prudent investor rule as a "modest reformulation of the Harvard College dictum and the basic rule of prior Restatements." Restatement of Trusts 3d: Prudent Investor Rule, Introduction, at 5. As a result, there is a basis for concluding that the first condition is satisfied in virtually all States except those in which a trustee is permitted to invest only in assets set forth in a statutory "legal list."

The second condition will be met when the terms of the trust require all of the "income" to be distributed at regular intervals; or when the terms of the trust require a trustee to distribute all of the income, but permit the trustee to decide how much to distribute to each member of a class of beneficiaries; or when the terms of a trust provide that the beneficiary shall receive the greater of the trust accounting income and a fixed dollar amount (an annuity), or of trust accounting income and a fractional share of the value of the trust assets (a unitrust amount). If the trust authorizes the trustee in its discretion to distribute the trust's income to the beneficiary or to accumulate some or all of the income, the condition will be met because the terms of the trust do not permit the trustee to distribute more than the trust accounting income.

To meet the third condition, the trustee must first meet the requirements of Section 103(a), i.e., she must apply the terms of the trust, decide whether to exercise the discretionary powers given to the trustee under the terms of the trust, and must apply the provisions of the Act if the terms of the trust do not contain a different provision or give the trustee discretion. Second, the trustee must determine the extent to which the terms of the trust clearly manifest an intention by the settlor that the trustee may or must favor one or more of the beneficiaries. To the extent that the terms of the trust do not require partiality, the trustee must conclude that she is unable to comply with the duty to administer the trust impartially. To the extent that the terms of the trust do require or permit the trustee to favor the income beneficiary or the remainder beneficiary, the trustee must conclude that she is unable to achieve the degree of partiality required or permitted. If the trustee comes to either conclusion—that she is unable to administer the trust impartially or that she is unable to achieve the degree of partiality required or permitted—she may exercise the power to adjust under Section 104(a).

Impartiality and productivity of income. The duty of impartiality between income and remainder beneficiaries is linked to the trustee's duty to make the portfolio productive of trust accounting income whenever the distribution requirements are expressed in terms of distributing the trust's "income." The 1962 Act implies that the duty to produce income applies on an asset by asset basis because the right of an income beneficiary to receive "delayed income" from the sale proceeds of underproductive property under Section 12 of that Act arises if "any part of principal . . . has not produced an average net income of a least 1% per year of its inventory value for more than a year. . . ." Under the prudent investor rule, "[t]o whatever extent a requirement of income productivity exists, . . . the requirement applies not investment by investment but to the portfolio as a whole." Restatement of Trusts 3d: Prudent Investor Rule § 227, Comment *i*, at 34. The power to adjust under Section 104(a) is also to be exercised by considering net income from the portfolio as a whole and not investment by investment. Section 413(b) of this Act eliminates the underproductive property rule in all cases other than trusts for which a marital deduction is allowed, and it applies to a marital deduction trust if the trust's assets "consist substantially of property that does not provide the surviving spouse with sufficient income from or use of the trust assets . . . "—in other words, the section applies by reference to the portfolio as a whole.

While the purpose of the power to adjust in Section 104(a) is to eliminate the need for a trustee who operates under the prudent investor rule to be concerned about the income component of the portfolio's total return, the trustee must still determine the extent to which a distribution must be made to an income beneficiary and the adequacy of the portfolio's liquidity as a whole to make that distribution.

For a discussion of investment considerations involving specific investments and techniques under the prudent investor rule, see Restatement of Trusts 3d: Prudent Investor Rule § 227, Comments *k-p*.

Factors to consider in exercising the power to adjust. Section 104(b) requires a trustee to consider factors relevant to the trust and its beneficiaries in deciding whether and to what extent the power to adjust should be exercised. Section 2(c) of the Uniform Prudent Investor Act sets forth circumstances that a trustee is to consider in investing and managing trust assets. The circumstances in Section 2(c) of the Uniform Prudent Investor Act are the source of the factors in paragraphs (3) through (6) and (8) of Section 104(b) (modified where necessary to adapt them to the purposes of this Act) so that, to the extent possible, comparable factors will apply to investment decisions and decisions involving the power to adjust. If a trustee who is operating under the prudent investor rule decides that the portfolio should be composed of financial assets whose total return will result primarily from capital appreciation rather than dividends, interest, and rents, the trustee can decide at the same time the extent to which an adjustment from principal to income may be necessary under Section 104. On the other hand, if a trustee decides that the risk and return objectives for the trust are best achieved by a portfolio whose total return includes interest and dividend income that is sufficient to provide the income beneficiary with the beneficial interest to which the beneficiary is entitled under the terms of the trust, the trustee can decide that it is unnecessary to exercise the power to adjust.

Assets received from the settlor. Section 3 of the Uniform Prudent Investor Act provides that "[a] trustee shall diversify the investments of the trust unless the trustee reasonably determines that, because of special circumstances, the purposes of the trust are better served without diversifying." The special circumstances may include the wish to retain a family business, the benefit derived from deferring liquidation of the asset in order to defer payment of income taxes, or the anticipated capital appreciation from retaining an asset such as undeveloped real estate for a long period. To the extent the trustee retains assets received from the settlor because of special circumstances that overcome the duty to diversify, the trustee may take these circumstances into account in determining whether and to what extent the power to adjust should be exercised to change the results produced by other provisions of this Act that apply to the retained assets. See Section 104(b)(5); Uniform Prudent Investor Act § 3, Comment, 7B U.L.A. 18, at 25–26 (Supp. 1997); Restatement of Trusts 3d: Prudent Investor Rule § 229 and Comments *a-e*.

Limitations on the power to adjust. The purpose of subsections (c)(1) through (4) is to preserve tax benefits that may have been an important purpose for creating the trust. Subsections (c)(5), (6), and (8) deny the power to adjust in the circumstances described in those subsections in order to prevent adverse tax consequences, and subsection (c)(7) denies the power to adjust to any beneficiary, whether or not possession of the power may have adverse tax consequences.

Under subsection (c)(1), a trustee cannot make an adjustment that diminishes the income interest in a trust that requires all of the income to be paid at least annually to a surviving spouse and for which an estate tax or gift tax marital deduction is allowed; but this subsection does not prevent the trustee from making an adjustment that increases the amount of income paid from a marital deduction trust to the surviving spouse. Subsection (c)(1) applies to a trust that qualifies for the marital deduction because the surviving spouse has a general power of appointment over the trust, but it applies to a qualified terminable interest property (QTIP) trust only if and to the extent that the fiduciary makes the election required to obtain the tax deduction. Subsection (c)(1) does not apply to a so-called "estate" trust. This type of trust qualifies for the marital deduction because the terms of the trust require the principal and undistributed income to be paid to the surviving spouse's estate when the spouse dies; it is not necessary for the terms of an estate trust to require the income to be distributed annually. Reg. § 20.2056(c)–2(b)(1)(iii).

Subsection (c)(3) applies to annuity trusts and unitrusts with no charitable beneficiaries as well as to trusts with charitable income or remainder beneficiaries; its purpose is to make it clear that a beneficiary's right to receive a fixed annuity or a fixed fraction of the value of a trust's assets is not subject to adjustment under Section 104(a). Subsection (c)(3) does not apply to any additional amount to which the beneficiary may be entitled that is expressed in terms of a right to receive income from the trust. For example, if a beneficiary is to receive a fixed annuity or the trust's income, whichever is greater, subsection (c)(3) does not prevent a trustee from making an adjustment under Section 104(a) in determining the amount of the trust's income.

If subsection (c)(5), (6), (7), or (8), prevents a trustee from exercising the power to adjust, subsection (d) permits a cotrustee who is not subject to the provision to exercise the power unless the terms of the trust do not permit the cotrustee to do so.

Release of the power to adjust. Section 104(e) permits a trustee to release all or part of the power to adjust in circumstances in which the possession or exercise of the power might deprive the trust of a tax benefit or impose a tax burden. For example, if possessing the power would diminish the actuarial value of the income interest in a trust for which the income beneficiary's estate may be eligible to claim a credit for property previously taxed if the beneficiary dies within ten years after the death of the person creating the trust, the trustee is permitted under subsection (e) to release just the power to adjust from income to principal.

Trust terms that limit a power to adjust. Section 104(f) applies to trust provisions that limit a trustee's power to adjust. Since the power is intended to enable trustees to employ the prudent investor rule without being constrained by traditional principal and income rules, an instrument executed before the adoption of this Act whose terms describe the amount that may or must be distributed to a beneficiary by referring to the trust's income or that prohibit the invasion of principal or that prohibit equitable adjustments in general should not be construed as forbidding the use of the power to adjust under Section 104(a) if the need for adjustment arises because the trustee is operating under the prudent investor rule. Instruments containing such provisions that are executed after the adoption of this Act should specifically refer to the power to adjust if the settlor intends to forbid its use. * * *

Examples. The following examples illustrate the application of Section 104:

Example (1)—T is the successor trustee of a trust that provides income to A for life, remainder to B. T has received from the prior trustee a portfolio of financial assets invested 20% in stocks and 80% in bonds. Following the prudent investor rule, T determines that a strategy of investing the portfolio 50% in stocks and 50% in bonds has risk and return objectives that are reasonably suited to the trust, but T also determines that adopting this approach will cause the trust to receive a smaller amount of dividend and interest income. After considering the factors in Section 104(b), T may transfer cash from principal to income to the extent T considers it necessary to increase the amount distributed to the income beneficiary.

Example (2)—T is the trustee of a trust that requires the income to be paid to the settlor's son C for life, remainder to C's daughter D. In a period of very high inflation, T purchases bonds that pay double-digit interest and determines that a portion of the interest, which is allocated to income under Section 406 of this Act, is a return of capital. In consideration of the loss of value of principal due to inflation and other factors that T considers relevant, T may transfer part of the interest to principal.

Example (3)—T is the trustee of a trust that requires the income to be paid to the settlor's sister E for life, remainder to charity F. E is a retired schoolteacher who is single and has no children. E's income from her social security, pension, and savings exceeds the amount required to provide for her accustomed standard of living. The terms of the trust permit T to invade principal to provide for E's health and to support her in her accustomed manner of living, but do not otherwise indicate that T should favor E or F. Applying the prudent investor rule, T determines that the trust assets should be invested entirely in growth stocks that produce very little dividend income. Even though it is not necessary to invade principal to maintain E's accustomed standard of living, she is entitled to receive from the trust the degree of beneficial enjoyment normally accorded a person who is the sole income beneficiary of a trust, and T may transfer cash from principal to income to provide her with that degree of enjoyment.

Example (4)—T is the trustee of a trust that is governed by the law of State X. The trust became irrevocable before State X adopted the prudent investor rule. The terms of the trust require all of the income to be paid to G for life, remainder to H, and also give T the power to invade principal for the benefit of G for "dire emergencies only." The terms of the trust limit the aggregate amount that T can distribute to G from principal during G's life to 6% of the trust's value at its inception. The trust's portfolio is invested initially 50% in stocks and 50% in bonds, but after State X adopts the prudent investor rule T determines that, to achieve suitable risk and return objectives for the trust, the assets should be invested 90% in stocks and 10% in bonds. This change increases the total return from the portfolio and decreases the dividend and interest income. Thereafter, even though G does not experience a dire emergency, T may exercise the power to adjust under Section 104(a) to the extent that T determines that the adjustment is from only the capital appreciation resulting from the change in the portfolio's asset allocation. If T is unable to determine the extent to which capital appreciation resulted from the change in asset allocation or is unable to maintain adequate records to determine the extent to which principal distributions to G for dire emergencies do not exceed the 6% limitation, T may not exercise the power to adjust. * * *

Example (5)—T is the trustee of a trust for the settlor's child. The trust owns a diversified portfolio of marketable financial assets with a value of $600,000, and is also the sole beneficiary of the settlor's IRA, which holds a diversified portfolio of marketable financial assets with a value of $900,000. The trust receives a distribution from the IRA that is the minimum amount required to be distributed under the Internal Revenue Code, and T allocates 10% of the distribution to income under Section 409(c) of this Act. The total return on the IRA's assets exceeds the amount distributed to the trust, and the value of the IRA at the end of the year is more than its value at the beginning of the year. Relevant factors that T may consider in determining whether to exercise the power to adjust and the extent to which an adjustment should be made to comply with Section 103(b) include the total return from all of the trust's assets, those owned directly as well as its interest in the IRA, the extent to which the trust will be subject to income tax on the portion of the IRA distribution that is allocated to principal, and the extent to which the income beneficiary will be subject to income tax on the amount that T distributes to the income beneficiary.

Example (6)—T is the trustee of a trust whose portfolio includes a large parcel of undeveloped real estate. T pays real property taxes on the undeveloped parcel from income each year pursuant to Section 501(3). After considering the return from the trust's portfolio as a whole and other relevant factors described in Section 104(b), T may exercise the power to adjust under Section 104(a) to transfer cash from principal to income in order to distribute to the income beneficiary an amount that T considers necessary to comply with Section 103(b).

Example (7)—T is the trustee of a trust whose portfolio includes an interest in a mutual fund that is sponsored by T. As the manager of the mutual fund, T charges the fund a management fee that reduces the amount available to distribute to the trust by $2,000. If the fee had been paid directly by the trust, one-half of the fee would have been paid from income under Section 501(1) and the other one-half would have been paid from principal under Section 502(a)(1). After considering the total return from the portfolio as a whole and other relevant factors described in Section 104(b), T may exercise its power to adjust under Section 104(a) by transferring $1,000, or half of the trust's proportionate share of the fee, from principal to income.

Section 105. Judicial Control of Discretionary Power.

(a)   The court may not order a fiduciary to change a decision to exercise or not to exercise a discretionary power conferred by this [Act] unless it determines that the decision was an abuse of the fiduciary's discretion. A fiduciary's decision is not an abuse of discretion merely because the court would have exercised the power in a different manner or would not have exercised the power.

(b)   The decisions to which subsection (a) applies include:

(1)   a decision under Section 104(a) as to whether and to what extent an amount should be transferred from principal to income or from income to principal.

(2)   a decision regarding the factors that are relevant to the trust and its beneficiaries, the extent to which the factors are relevant, and the weight, if any, to be given to those factors, in deciding whether and to what extent to exercise the discretionary power conferred by Section 104(a).

(c)   If the court determines that a fiduciary has abused the fiduciary's discretion, the court may place the income and remainder beneficiaries in the positions they would have occupied if the discretion had not been abused, according to the following rules:

(1)   To the extent that the abuse of discretion has resulted in no distribution to a beneficiary or in a distribution that is too small, the court shall order the fiduciary to distribute from the trust to the beneficiary an amount that the court determines will restore the beneficiary, in whole or in part, to the beneficiary's appropriate position.

(2)   To the extent that the abuse of discretion has resulted in a distribution to a beneficiary which is too large, the court shall place the beneficiaries, the trust, or both, in whole or in part, in their appropriate positions by ordering the fiduciary to withhold an amount from one or more

future distributions to the beneficiary who received the distribution that was too large or ordering that beneficiary to return some or all of the distribution to the trust.

(3) To the extent that the court is unable, after applying paragraphs (1) and (2), to place the beneficiaries, the trust, or both, in the positions they would have occupied if the discretion had not been abused, the court may order the fiduciary to pay an appropriate amount from its own funds to one or more of the beneficiaries or the trust or both.

(d) Upon [petition] by the fiduciary, the court having jurisdiction over a trust or estate shall determine whether a proposed exercise or nonexercise by the fiduciary of a discretionary power conferred by this [Act] will result in an abuse of the fiduciary's discretion. If the petition describes the proposed exercise or nonexercise of the power and contains sufficient information to inform the beneficiaries of the reasons for the proposal, the facts upon which the fiduciary relies, and an explanation of how the income and remainder beneficiaries will be affected by the proposed exercise or nonexercise of the power, a beneficiary who challenges the proposed exercise or nonexercise has the burden of establishing that it will result in an abuse of discretion.

Comment

* * * **Power to Adjust.** The exercise of the power to adjust is governed by a trustee's duty of impartiality, which requires the trustee to strike an appropriate balance between the interests of the income and remainder beneficiaries. Section 103(b) expresses this duty by requiring the trustee to "administer a trust or estate impartially, based on what is fair and reasonable to all of the beneficiaries, except to the extent that the terms of the trust or the will clearly manifest an intention that the fiduciary shall or may favor one or more of the beneficiaries." Because this involves the exercise of judgment in circumstances rarely capable of perfect resolution, trustees are not expected to achieve perfection; they are, however, required to make conscious decisions in good faith and with proper motives.

In seeking the proper balance between the interests of the beneficiaries in matters involving principal and income, a trustee's traditional approach has been to determine the settlor's objectives from the terms of the trust, gather the information needed to ascertain the financial circumstances of the beneficiaries, determine the extent to which the settlor's objectives can be achieved with the resources available in the trust, and then allocate the trust's assets between stocks and fixed-income securities in a way that will produce a particular level or range of income for the income beneficiary. The key element in this process has been to determine the appropriate level or range of income for the income beneficiary, and that will continue to be the key element in deciding whether and to what extent to exercise the discretionary power conferred by Section 104(a). If it becomes necessary for a court to determine whether an abuse of the discretionary power to adjust between principal and income has occurred, the criteria should be the same as those that courts have used in the past to determine whether a trustee has abused its discretion in allocating the trust's assets between stocks and fixed-income securities.

A fiduciary has broad latitude in choosing the methods and criteria to use in deciding whether and to what extent to exercise the power to adjust in order to achieve impartiality between income beneficiaries and remainder beneficiaries or the degree of partiality for one or the other that is provided for by the terms of the trust or the will. For example, in deciding what the appropriate level or range of income should be for the income beneficiary and whether to exercise the power, a trustee may use the methods employed prior to the adoption of the 1997 Act in deciding how to allocate trust assets between stocks and fixed-income securities; or may consider the amount that would be distributed each year based on a percentage of the portfolio's value at the beginning or end of an accounting period, or the average portfolio value for several accounting periods, in a manner similar to a unitrust, and may select a percentage that the trustee believes is appropriate for this purpose and use the same percentage or different percentages in subsequent years. The trustee may also use hypothetical portfolios of marketable securities to determine an appropriate level or range of income within which a distribution might fall.

An adjustment may be made prospectively at the beginning of an accounting period, based on a projected return or range of returns for a trust's portfolio, or retrospectively after the fiduciary knows the total realized or unrealized return for the period; and instead of an annual adjustment, the trustee may distribute a fixed dollar amount for several years, in a manner similar to an annuity, and may change the fixed dollar amount periodically. No inference of abuse is to be drawn if a fiduciary uses different methods or criteria for the same trust from time to time, or uses different methods or criteria for different trusts for the same accounting period.

While a trustee must consider the portfolio as a whole in deciding whether and to what extent to exercise the power to adjust, a trustee may apply different criteria in considering the portion of the portfolio that is composed of marketable securities and the portion whose market value cannot be determined readily, and may take into account a beneficiary's use or possession of a trust asset.

Under the prudent investor rule, a trustee is to incur costs that are appropriate and reasonable in relation to the assets and the purposes of the trust, and the same consideration applies in determining whether and to what extent to exercise the power to adjust. In making investment decisions under the prudent investor rule, the trustee will have considered the purposes, terms, distribution requirements, and other circumstances of the trust for the purpose of adopting an overall investment strategy having risk and return objectives reasonably suited to the trust. A trustee is not required to duplicate that work for principal and income purposes, and in many cases the decision about whether and to what extent to exercise the power to adjust may be made at the same time as the investment decisions. To help achieve the objective of reasonable investment costs, a trustee may also adopt policies that apply to all trusts or to individual trusts or classes of trusts, based on their size or other criteria, stating whether and under what circumstances the power to adjust will be exercised and the method of making adjustments; no inference of abuse is to be drawn if a trustee adopts such policies. * * *

[ARTICLE] 2

DECEDENT'S ESTATE OR TERMINATING INCOME INTEREST

Section 201. Determination and Distribution of Net Income.

After a decedent dies, in the case of an estate, or after an income interest in a trust ends, the following rules apply:

(1)   A fiduciary of an estate or of a terminating income interest shall determine the amount of net income and net principal receipts received from property specifically given to a beneficiary under the rules in [Articles] 3 through 5 which apply to trustees and the rules in paragraph (5). The fiduciary shall distribute the net income and net principal receipts to the beneficiary who is to receive the specific property.

(2)   A fiduciary shall determine the remaining net income of a decedent's estate or a terminating income interest under the rules in [Articles] 3 through 5 which apply to trustees and by:

(A)   including in net income all income from property used to discharge liabilities;

(B)   paying from income or principal, in the fiduciary's discretion, fees of attorneys, accountants, and fiduciaries; court costs and other expenses of administration; and interest on death taxes, but the fiduciary may pay those expenses from income of property passing to a trust for which the fiduciary claims an estate tax marital or charitable deduction only to the extent that the payment of those expenses from income will not cause the reduction or loss of the deduction; and

(C)   paying from principal all other disbursements made or incurred in connection with the settlement of a decedent's estate or the winding up of a terminating income interest, including debts, funeral expenses, disposition of remains, family allowances, and death taxes and related penalties that are apportioned to the estate or terminating income interest by the will, the terms of the trust, or applicable law.

(3)   A fiduciary shall distribute to a beneficiary who receives a pecuniary amount outright the interest or any other amount provided by the will, the terms of the trust, or applicable law from net income determined under paragraph (2) or from principal to the extent that net income is insufficient. If a beneficiary is to receive a pecuniary amount outright from a trust after an income interest ends and no interest or other amount is provided for by the terms of the trust or applicable law, the fiduciary shall distribute the interest or other amount to which the beneficiary would be entitled under applicable law if the pecuniary amount were required to be paid under a will.

(4)   A fiduciary shall distribute the net income remaining after distributions required by paragraph (3) in the manner described in Section 202 to all other beneficiaries, including a beneficiary who receives a pecuniary amount in trust, even if the beneficiary holds an unqualified power to withdraw assets from the trust or other presently exercisable general power of appointment over the trust.

(5)   A fiduciary may not reduce principal or income receipts from property described in paragraph (1) because of a payment described in Section 501 or 502 to the extent that the will, the terms of the trust, or applicable law requires the fiduciary to make the payment from assets other than the property or to the extent that the fiduciary recovers or expects to recover the payment from a third party. The net income and principal receipts from the property are determined by including all of the amounts the fiduciary receives or pays with respect to the property, whether those amounts accrued or became due before, on, or after the date of a decedent's death or an income interest's terminating event, and by making a reasonable provision for amounts that the fiduciary believes the estate or terminating income interest may become obligated to pay after the property is distributed.

Comment

Terminating income interests and successive income interests. A trust that provides for a single income beneficiary and an outright distribution of the remainder ends when the income interest ends. A more complex trust may have a number of income interests, either concurrent or successive, and the trust will not necessarily end when one of the income interests ends. For that reason, the Act speaks in terms of income interests ending and beginning rather than trusts ending and beginning. When an income interest in a trust ends, the trustee's powers continue during the winding up period required to complete its administration. A terminating income interest is one that has ended but whose administration is not complete.

If two or more people are given the right to receive specified percentages or fractions of the income from a trust concurrently and one of the concurrent interests ends, e.g., when a beneficiary dies, the beneficiary's income interest ends but the trust does not. Similarly, when a trust with only one income beneficiary ends upon the beneficiary's death, the trust instrument may provide that part or all of the trust assets shall continue in trust for another income beneficiary. While it is common to think and speak of this (and even to characterize it in a trust instrument) as a "new" trust, it is a continuation of the original trust for a remainder beneficiary who has an income interest in the trust assets instead of the right to receive them outright. For purposes of this Act, this is a successive income interest in the same trust. The fact that a trust may or may not end when an income interest ends is not significant for purposes of this Act.

If the assets that are subject to a terminating income interest pass to another trust because the income beneficiary exercises a general power of appointment over the trust assets, the recipient trust would be a new trust; and if they pass to another trust because the beneficiary exercises a nongeneral power of appointment over the trust assets, the recipient trust might be a new trust in some States (see 5A Austin W. Scott & William F. Fratcher, The Law of Trusts § 640, at 483 (4th ed. 1989)); but for purposes of this Act a new trust created in these circumstances is also a successive income interest.

Gift of a pecuniary amount. Section 201(3) and (4) provide different rules for an outright gift of a pecuniary amount and a gift in trust of a pecuniary amount * * * .

Interest on pecuniary amounts. Section 201(3) provides that the beneficiary of an outright pecuniary amount is to receive the interest or other amount provided by applicable law if there is no provision in the will or the terms of the trust. Many States have no applicable law that provides for interest or some other amount to be paid on an outright pecuniary gift under an inter vivos trust; this section provides that in such a case the interest or other amount to be paid shall be the same as the interest or other amount required to be paid on testamentary pecuniary gifts. This provision is intended to accord gifts under inter vivos instruments the same treatment as testamentary gifts. * * *

Administration expenses and interest on death taxes. Under Section 201(2)(B) a fiduciary may pay administration expenses and interest on death taxes from either income or principal. An advantage of permitting the fiduciary to choose the source of the payment is that, if the fiduciary's decision is consistent with the decision to deduct these expenses for income tax purposes or estate tax purposes, it eliminates the need to adjust between principal and income that may arise when, for example, an expense that is paid from principal is deducted for income tax purposes or an expense that is paid from income is deducted for estate tax purposes.

The United States Supreme Court has considered the question of whether an estate tax marital deduction or charitable deduction should be reduced when administration expenses are paid from income produced by property passing in trust for a surviving spouse or for charity and deducted for income tax purposes. The Court rejected the IRS position that administration expenses properly paid from income under the terms of the trust or state law must reduce the amount of a marital or charitable transfer, and held that the value of the transferred property is not reduced for estate tax purposes unless the administration expenses are material in light of the income the trust corpus could have been expected to generate. *Commissioner v. Estate of Otis C. Hubert*, 117 S.Ct. 1124 (1997). The provision in Section 201(2)(B) permits a fiduciary to pay and deduct administration expenses from income only to the extent that it will not cause the reduction or loss of an estate tax marital or charitable contributions deduction, which means that the limit on the amount payable from income will be established eventually by Treasury Regulations.

Interest on estate taxes. The IRS agrees that interest on estate and inheritance taxes may be deducted for income tax purposes without having to reduce the estate tax deduction for amounts passing to a charity or surviving spouse, whether the interest is paid from principal or income. Rev. Rul. 93–48, 93–2 C.B. 270. For estates of persons who died before 1998, a fiduciary may not want to deduct for income tax purposes interest on estate tax that is deferred under Section 6166 or 6163 because deducting that interest for estate tax purposes may produce more beneficial results, especially if the estate has little or no income or the income tax bracket is significantly lower than the estate tax bracket. For estates of persons who die after 1997, no estate tax or income tax deduction will be allowed for interest paid on estate tax that is deferred under Section 6166. However, interest on estate tax deferred under Section 6163 will continue to be deductible for both purposes, and interest on estate tax deficiencies will continue to be deductible for estate tax purposes if an election under Section 6166 is not in effect.

* * * Section 501(3) of this Act provides that, except to the extent provided in Section 201(2)(B) or (C), all interest must be paid from income.

Section 202. Distribution to Residuary and Remainder Beneficiaries.

(a) Each beneficiary described in Section 201(4) is entitled to receive a portion of the net income equal to the beneficiary's fractional interest in undistributed principal assets, using values as of the distribution date. If a fiduciary makes more than one distribution of assets to beneficiaries to whom this section applies, each beneficiary, including one who does not receive part of the distribution, is entitled, as of each distribution date, to the net income the fiduciary has received after the date of death or terminating event or earlier distribution date but has not distributed as of the current distribution date.

(b) In determining a beneficiary's share of net income, the following rules apply:

(1) The beneficiary is entitled to receive a portion of the net income equal to the beneficiary's fractional interest in the undistributed principal assets immediately before the distribution date, including assets that later may be sold to meet principal obligations.

(2) The beneficiary's fractional interest in the undistributed principal assets must be calculated without regard to property specifically given to a beneficiary and property required to pay pecuniary amounts not in trust.

(3) The beneficiary's fractional interest in the undistributed principal assets must be calculated on the basis of the aggregate value of those assets as of the distribution date without reducing the value by any unpaid principal obligation.

(4) The distribution date for purposes of this section may be the date as of which the fiduciary calculates the value of the assets if that date is reasonably near the date on which assets are actually distributed.

(c) If a fiduciary does not distribute all of the collected but undistributed net income to each person as of a distribution date, the fiduciary shall maintain appropriate records showing the interest of each beneficiary in that net income.

(d) A trustee may apply the rules in this section, to the extent that the trustee considers it appropriate, to net gain or loss realized after the date of death or terminating event or earlier distribution date from the disposition of a principal asset if this section applies to the income from the asset.

Comment

Relationship to prior Acts. Section 202 [provides] that the residuary legatees of estates are to receive net income earned during the period of administration on the basis of their proportionate interests in the undistributed assets when distributions are made. It changes the basis for determining their proportionate interests by using asset values as of a date reasonably near the time of distribution instead of inventory values; it extends the application of these rules to distributions from terminating trusts; and it extends these rules to gain or loss realized from the disposition of assets during administration * * * .

[ARTICLE] 3

APPORTIONMENT AT BEGINNING AND END OF INCOME INTEREST

Section 301. When Right to Income Begins and Ends.

(a)   An income beneficiary is entitled to net income from the date on which the income interest begins. An income interest begins on the date specified in the terms of the trust or, if no date is specified, on the date an asset becomes subject to a trust or successive income interest.

(b)   An asset becomes subject to a trust:

(1)   on the date it is transferred to the trust in the case of an asset that is transferred to a trust during the transferor's life;

(2)   on the date of a testator's death in the case of an asset that becomes subject to a trust by reason of a will, even if there is an intervening period of administration of the testator's estate; or

(3)   on the date of an individual's death in the case of an asset that is transferred to a fiduciary by a third party because of the individual's death.

(c)   An asset becomes subject to a successive income interest on the day after the preceding income interest ends, as determined under subsection (d), even if there is an intervening period of administration to wind up the preceding income interest.

(d)   An income interest ends on the day before an income beneficiary dies or another terminating event occurs, or on the last day of a period during which there is no beneficiary to whom a trustee may distribute income.

Comment

Period during which there is no beneficiary. The purpose of the second part of subsection (d) is to provide that, at the end of a period during which there is no beneficiary to whom a trustee may distribute income, the trustee must apply the same apportionment rules that apply when a mandatory income interest ends. This provision would apply, for example, if a settlor creates a trust for grandchildren before any grandchildren are born. When the first grandchild is born, the period preceding the date of birth is treated as having ended, followed by a successive income interest, and the apportionment rules in Sections 302 and 303 apply accordingly if the terms of the trust do not contain different provisions.

Section 302. Apportionment of Receipts and Disbursements When Decedent Dies or Income Interest Begins.

(a)   A trustee shall allocate an income receipt or disbursement other than one to which Section 201(1) applies to principal if its due date occurs before a decedent dies in the case of an estate or before an income interest begins in the case of a trust or successive income interest.

(b)   A trustee shall allocate an income receipt or disbursement to income if its due date occurs on or after the date on which a decedent dies or an income interest begins and it is a periodic due date. An income receipt or disbursement must be treated as accruing from day to day if its due date is not periodic or it has no due date. The portion of the receipt or disbursement accruing before the date on which a decedent dies or an income interest begins must be allocated to principal and the balance must be allocated to income.

(c)   An item of income or an obligation is due on the date the payer is required to make a payment. If a payment date is not stated, there is no due date for the purposes of this [Act]. Distributions to shareholders or other owners from an entity to which Section 401 applies are deemed to be due on the date fixed by the entity for determining who is entitled to receive the distribution or, if no date is fixed, on the declaration date for the distribution. A due date is periodic for receipts or disbursements that must be paid at regular intervals under a lease or an obligation to pay interest or if an entity customarily makes distributions at regular intervals.

Comment

* * * **Periodic payments.** Under Section 302, a periodic payment is principal if it is due but unpaid before a decedent dies or before an asset becomes subject to a trust, but the next payment is allocated entirely to income and is not apportioned. Thus, periodic receipts such as rents, dividends, interest, and annuities, and disbursements such as the interest portion of a mortgage payment, are not apportioned. This is the original common law rule. * * * In trusts in which a surviving spouse is dependent upon a regular flow of cash from the decedent's securities portfolio, this rule will help to maintain payments to the spouse at the same level as before the settlor's death. * * *

Nonperiodic payments. Under the second sentence of Section 302(b), interest on an obligation that does not provide a due date for the interest payment, such as interest on an income tax refund, would be apportioned to principal to the extent it accrues before a person dies or an income interest begins unless the obligation is specifically given to a devisee or remainder beneficiary, in which case all of the accrued interest passes under Section 201(1) to the person who receives the obligation. The same rule applies to interest on an obligation that has a due date but does not provide for periodic payments. If there is no stated interest on the obligation, such as a zero coupon bond, and the proceeds from the obligation are received more than one year after it is purchased or acquired by the trustee, the entire amount received is principal under Section 406.

Section 303. Apportionment When Income Interest Ends.

(a)   In this section, "undistributed income" means net income received before the date on which an income interest ends. The term does not include an item of income or expense that is due or accrued or net income that has been added or is required to be added to principal under the terms of the trust.

(b)   When a mandatory income interest ends, the trustee shall pay to a mandatory income beneficiary who survives that date, or the estate of a deceased mandatory income beneficiary whose death causes the interest to end, the beneficiary's share of the undistributed income that is not disposed of under the terms of the trust unless the beneficiary has an unqualified power to revoke more than five percent of the trust immediately before the income interest ends. In the latter case, the undistributed income from the portion of the trust that may be revoked must be added to principal.

(c)   When a trustee's obligation to pay a fixed annuity or a fixed fraction of the value of the trust's assets ends, the trustee shall prorate the final payment if and to the extent required by applicable law to accomplish a purpose of the trust or its settlor relating to income, gift, estate, or other tax requirements.

Comment

* * * *Example—accrued periodic payments.* The rules in Section 302 and Section 303 work in the following manner: Assume that a periodic payment of rent that is due on July 20 has not been paid when an income interest ends on July 30; the successive income interest begins on July 31, and the rent payment that was due on July 20 is paid on August 3. Under Section 302(a), the July 20 payment is added to the principal of the successive income interest when received. Under Section 302(b), the entire periodic payment of rent that is due on August 20 is income when received by the successive income interest. Under Section 303, neither the income beneficiary of the terminated income interest nor the beneficiary's estate is entitled to any part of either the July 20 or the August 20 payments because neither one was received before the income interest ended on July 30. The same principles apply to expenses of the trust.

Beneficiary with an unqualified power to revoke. The requirement in subsection (b) to pay undistributed income to a mandatory income beneficiary or her estate does not apply to the extent the beneficiary has an unqualified power to revoke more than five percent of the trust immediately before the income interest ends. Without this exception, subsection (b) would apply to a revocable living trust whose settlor is the mandatory income beneficiary during her lifetime, even if her will provides that all of the assets in the probate estate are to be distributed to the trust.

If a trust permits the beneficiary to withdraw all or a part of the trust principal after attaining a specified age and the beneficiary attains that age but fails to withdraw all of the principal that she is permitted to withdraw, a trustee is not required to pay her or her estate the undistributed income attributable to the portion of the principal that she left in the trust. The assumption underlying this rule is that the beneficiary has either provided for the disposition of the trust assets (including the undistributed income) by exercising a power of appointment that she has been given or has not withdrawn the assets because she is willing to have the principal and undistributed income be distributed under the terms of the trust. If the beneficiary has the power to withdraw 25% of the trust principal, the trustee must pay to her or her estate the undistributed income from the 75% that she cannot withdraw.

[ARTICLE] 4

ALLOCATION OF RECEIPTS DURING ADMINISTRATION OF TRUST

[PART 1

RECEIPTS FROM ENTITIES]

Section 401. Character of Receipts.

(a)   In this section, "entity" means a corporation, partnership, limited liability company, regulated investment company, real estate investment trust, common trust fund, or any other organization in which a trustee has an interest other than a trust or estate to which Section 402 applies, a business or activity to which Section 403 applies, or an asset-backed security to which Section 415 applies.

(b)   Except as otherwise provided in this section, a trustee shall allocate to income money received from an entity.

(c)   A trustee shall allocate the following receipts from an entity to principal:

(1)   property other than money;

(2)   money received in one distribution or a series of related distributions in exchange for part or all of a trust's interest in the entity;

(3)   money received in total or partial liquidation of the entity; and

(4)   money received from an entity that is a regulated investment company or a real estate investment trust if the money distributed is a capital gain dividend for federal income tax purposes.

(d)   Money is received in partial liquidation:

(1)   to the extent that the entity, at or near the time of a distribution, indicates that it is a distribution in partial liquidation; or

(2)   if the total amount of money and property received in a distribution or series of related distributions is greater than 20 percent of the entity's gross assets, as shown by the entity's year-end financial statements immediately preceding the initial receipt.

(e)   Money is not received in partial liquidation, nor may it be taken into account under subsection (d)(2), to the extent that it does not exceed the amount of income tax that a trustee or beneficiary must pay on taxable income of the entity that distributes the money.

(f)   A trustee may rely upon a statement made by an entity about the source or character of a distribution if the statement is made at or near the time of distribution by the entity's board of directors or other person or group of persons authorized to exercise powers to pay money or transfer property comparable to those of a corporation's board of directors.

Comment

Entities to which Section 401 applies. The reference to partnerships in Section 401(a) is intended to include all forms of partnerships, including limited partnerships, limited liability partnerships, and variants that have slightly different names and characteristics from State to State. The section does not apply, however, to receipts from an interest in property that a trust owns as a tenant in common with one or more co-owners, nor would it apply to an interest in a joint venture if, under applicable law, the trust's interest is regarded as that of a tenant in common.

Capital gain dividends. Under the Internal Revenue Code and the Income Tax Regulations, a "capital gain dividend" from a mutual fund or real estate investment trust is the excess of the fund's or trust's net long-term capital gain over its net short-term capital loss. As a result, a capital gain dividend does not include any net short-term capital gain, and cash received by a trust because of a net short-term capital gain is income under this Act.

Reinvested dividends. If a trustee elects (or continues an election made by its predecessor) to reinvest dividends in shares of stock of a distributing corporation or fund, whether evidenced by new certificates or entries on the books of the distributing entity, the new shares would be principal, but the trustee may determine, after considering the return from the portfolio as a whole, whether an adjustment under Section 104 is necessary as a result. * * *

Partial liquidations. Under subsection (d)(1), any distribution designated by the entity as a partial liquidating distribution is principal regardless of the percentage of total assets that it represents. If a distribution exceeds 20% of the entity's gross assets, the entire distribution is a partial liquidation under subsection (d)(2) whether or not the entity describes it as a partial liquidation. In determining whether a distribution is greater than 20% of the gross assets, the portion of the distribution that does not exceed the amount of income tax that the trustee or a beneficiary must pay on the entity's taxable income is ignored.

Other large distributions. A cash distribution may be quite large (for example, more than 10% but not more than 20% of the entity's gross assets) and have characteristics that suggest it should be treated as principal rather than income. For example, an entity may have received cash from a source other than the conduct of its normal business operations because it sold an investment asset; or because it sold a business asset other than one held for sale to customers in the normal course of its business and did not replace it; or it borrowed a large sum of money and secured the repayment of the loan with a substantial asset; or a principal source of its cash was from assets such as mineral interests, 90% of which would have been allocated to principal if the trust had owned the assets directly. In such a case the trustee, after considering the total return from the portfolio as a whole and the income component of that return, may decide to exercise the power under Section 104(a) to make an adjustment between income and principal, subject to the limitations in Section 104(c).

Section 402. Distribution From Trust or Estate.

A trustee shall allocate to income an amount received as a distribution of income from a trust or an estate in which the trust has an interest other than a purchased interest, and shall allocate to principal an amount received as a distribution of principal from such a trust or estate. If a trustee purchases an interest in a trust that is an investment entity, or a decedent or donor transfers an interest in such a trust to a trustee, Section 401 or 415 applies to a receipt from the trust.

Comment

Terms of the distributing trust or estate. Under Section 103(a), a trustee is to allocate receipts in accordance with the terms of the recipient trust or, if there is no provision, in accordance with this Act. However, in determining whether a distribution from another trust or an estate is income or principal, the trustee should also determine what the terms of the distributing trust or estate say about the distribution—for example, whether they direct that the distribution, even though made from the income of the distributing trust or estate, is to be added to principal of the recipient trust. Such a provision should override the terms of this Act, but if the terms of the recipient trust contain a provision requiring such a distribution to be allocated to income, the trustee may have to obtain a judicial resolution of the conflict between the terms of the two documents.

Investment trusts. An investment entity to which the second sentence of this section applies includes a mutual fund, a common trust fund, a business trust or other entity organized as a trust for the purpose of receiving capital contributed by investors, investing that capital, and managing investment assets, including asset-backed security arrangements to which Section 415 applies. * * *

Section 403. Business and Other Activities Conducted by Trustee.

(a) If a trustee who conducts a business or other activity determines that it is in the best interest of all the beneficiaries to account separately for the business or activity instead of accounting for it as part of the trust's general accounting records, the trustee may maintain separate accounting records for its transactions, whether or not its assets are segregated from other trust assets.

(b)   A trustee who accounts separately for a business or other activity may determine the extent to which its net cash receipts must be retained for working capital, the acquisition or replacement of fixed assets, and other reasonably foreseeable needs of the business or activity, and the extent to which the remaining net cash receipts are accounted for as principal or income in the trust's general accounting records. If a trustee sells assets of the business or other activity, other than in the ordinary course of the business or activity, the trustee shall account for the net amount received as principal in the trust's general accounting records to the extent the trustee determines that the amount received is no longer required in the conduct of the business.

(c)   Activities for which a trustee may maintain separate accounting records include:

(1)   retail, manufacturing, service, and other traditional business activities;

(2)   farming;

(3)   raising and selling livestock and other animals;

(4)   management of rental properties;

(5)   extraction of minerals and other natural resources;

(6)   timber operations; and

(7)   activities to which Section 414 applies.

Comment

Purpose and scope. The provisions in Section 403 are intended to give greater flexibility to a trustee who operates a business or other activity in proprietorship form rather than in a wholly-owned corporation (or, where permitted by state law, a single-member limited liability company), and to facilitate the trustee's ability to decide the extent to which the net receipts from the activity should be allocated to income, just as the board of directors of a corporation owned entirely by the trust would decide the amount of the annual dividend to be paid to the trust. It permits a trustee to account for farming or livestock operations, rental properties, oil and gas properties, timber operations, and activities in derivatives and options as though they were held by a separate entity. It is not intended, however, to permit a trustee to account separately for a traditional securities portfolio to avoid the provisions of this Act that apply to such securities.

Section 403 permits the trustee to account separately for each business or activity for which the trustee determines separate accounting is appropriate. A trustee with a computerized accounting system may account for these activities in a "subtrust"; an individual trustee may continue to use the business and record-keeping methods employed by the decedent or transferor who may have conducted the business under an assumed name. The intent of this section is to give the trustee broad authority to select business record-keeping methods that best suit the activity in which the trustee is engaged.

If a fiduciary liquidates a sole proprietorship or other activity to which Section 403 applies, the proceeds would be added to principal, even though derived from the liquidation of accounts receivable, because the proceeds would no longer be needed in the conduct of the business. If the liquidation occurs during probate or during an income interest's winding up period, none of the proceeds would be income for purposes of Section 201.

Separate accounts. A trustee may or may not maintain separate bank accounts for business activities that are accounted for under Section 403. A professional trustee may decide not to maintain separate bank accounts, but an individual trustee, especially one who has continued a decedent's business practices, may continue the same banking arrangements that were used during the decedent's lifetime. In either case, the trustee is authorized to decide to what extent cash is to be retained as part of the business assets and to what extent it is to be transferred to the trust's general accounts, either as income or principal.

[PART 2

RECEIPTS NOT NORMALLY APPORTIONED]

Section 404. Principal Receipts.

A trustee shall allocate to principal:

(1)   to the extent not allocated to income under this [Act], assets received from a transferor during the transferor's lifetime, a decedent's estate, a trust with a terminating income interest, or a payer under a contract naming the trust or its trustee as beneficiary;

(2)   money or other property received from the sale, exchange, liquidation, or change in form of a principal asset, including realized profit, subject to this [article];

(3)   amounts recovered from third parties to reimburse the trust because of disbursements described in Section 502(a)(7) or for other reasons to the extent not based on the loss of income;

(4)   proceeds of property taken by eminent domain, but a separate award made for the loss of income with respect to an accounting period during which a current income beneficiary had a mandatory income interest is income;

(5)   net income received in an accounting period during which there is no beneficiary to whom a trustee may or must distribute income; and

(6)   other receipts as provided in [Part 3].

Section 405. Rental Property.

To the extent that a trustee accounts for receipts from rental property pursuant to this section, the trustee shall allocate to income an amount received as rent of real or personal property, including an amount received for cancellation or renewal of a lease. An amount received as a refundable deposit, including a security deposit or a deposit that is to be applied as rent for future periods, must be added to principal and held subject to the terms of the lease and is not available for distribution to a beneficiary until the trustee's contractual obligations have been satisfied with respect to that amount.

Comment

Application of Section 403. This section applies to the extent that the trustee does not account separately under Section 403 for the management of rental properties owned by the trust.

Receipts that are capital in nature. A portion of the payment under a lease may be a reimbursement of principal expenditures for improvements to the leased property that is characterized as rent for purposes of invoking contractual or statutory remedies for nonpayment. If the trustee is accounting for rental income under Section 405, a transfer from income to reimburse principal may be appropriate under Section 504 to the extent that some of the "rent" is really a reimbursement for improvements. This set of facts could also be a relevant factor for a trustee to consider under Section 104(b) in deciding whether and to what extent to make an adjustment between principal and income under Section 104(a) after considering the return from the portfolio as a whole.

Section 406. Obligation to Pay Money.

(a)   An amount received as interest, whether determined at a fixed, variable, or floating rate, on an obligation to pay money to the trustee, including an amount received as consideration for prepaying principal, must be allocated to income without any provision for amortization of premium.

(b)   A trustee shall allocate to principal an amount received from the sale, redemption, or other disposition of an obligation to pay money to the trustee more than one year after it is purchased or acquired by the trustee, including an obligation whose purchase price or value when it is acquired is less than its value at maturity. If the obligation matures within one year after it is purchased or acquired by the trustee, an amount received in excess of its purchase price or its value when acquired by the trust must be allocated to income.

(c)   This section does not apply to an obligation to which Section 409, 410, 411, 412, 414, or 415 applies.

Comment

Variable or floating interest rates. The reference in subsection (a) to variable or floating interest rate obligations is intended to clarify that, even though an obligation's interest rate may change from time to time based upon changes in an index or other market indicator, an obligation to pay money containing a variable or floating rate provision is subject to this section and is not to be treated as a derivative financial instrument under Section 414.

Discount obligations. Subsection (b) applies to all obligations acquired at a discount, including short-term obligations such as U.S. Treasury Bills, long-term obligations such as U.S. Savings Bonds, zero-coupon bonds, and discount bonds that pay interest during part, but not all, of the period before maturity. Under subsection (b), the entire increase in value of these obligations is principal when the trustee receives the proceeds from the disposition unless the obligation, when acquired, has a maturity of less than one year.
* * *

Subsection (b) also applies to inflation-indexed bonds—any increase in principal due to inflation after issuance is principal upon redemption if the bond matures more than one year after the trustee acquires it; if it matures within one year, all of the increase, including any attributable to an inflation adjustment, is income.

Effect of Section 104. In deciding whether and to what extent to exercise the power to adjust between principal and income granted by Section 104(a), a relevant factor for the trustee to consider is the effect on the portfolio as a whole of having a portion of the assets invested in bonds that do not pay interest currently.

Section 407. Insurance Policies and Similar Contracts.

(a)   Except as otherwise provided in subsection (b), a trustee shall allocate to principal the proceeds of a life insurance policy or other contract in which the trust or its trustee is named as beneficiary, including a contract that insures the trust or its trustee against loss for damage to, destruction of, or loss of title to a trust asset. The trustee shall allocate dividends on an insurance policy to income if the premiums on the policy are paid from income, and to principal if the premiums are paid from principal.

(b)   A trustee shall allocate to income proceeds of a contract that insures the trustee against loss of occupancy or other use by an income beneficiary, loss of income, or, subject to Section 403, loss of profits from a business.

(c)   This section does not apply to a contract to which Section 409 applies.

[PART 3

RECEIPTS NORMALLY APPORTIONED]

Section 408. Insubstantial Allocations Not Required.

If a trustee determines that an allocation between principal and income required by Section 409, 410, 411, 412, or 415 is insubstantial, the trustee may allocate the entire amount to principal unless one of the circumstances described in Section 104(c) applies to the allocation. This power may be exercised by a cotrustee in the circumstances described in Section 104(d) and may be released for the reasons and in the manner described in Section 104(e). An allocation is presumed to be insubstantial if:

(1)   the amount of the allocation would increase or decrease net income in an accounting period, as determined before the allocation, by less than 10 percent; or

(2) the value of the asset producing the receipt for which the allocation would be made is less than 10 percent of the total value of the trust's assets at the beginning of the accounting period.

Comment

This section is intended to relieve a trustee from making relatively small allocations while preserving the trustee's right to do so if an allocation is large in terms of absolute dollars.

For example, assume that a trust's assets, which include a working interest in an oil well, have a value of $1,000,000; the net income from the assets other than the working interest is $40,000; and the net receipts from the working interest are $400. The trustee may allocate all of the net receipts from the working interest to principal instead of allocating 10%, or $40, to income under Section 411. If the net receipts from the working interest are $35,000, so that the amount allocated to income under Section 411 would be $3,500, the trustee may decide that this amount is sufficiently significant to the income beneficiary that the allocation provided for by Section 411 should be made, even though the trustee is still permitted under Section 408 to allocate all of the net receipts to principal because the $3,500 would increase the net income of $40,000, as determined before making an allocation under Section 411, by less than 10%. Section 408 will also relieve a trustee from having to allocate net receipts from the sale of trees in a small woodlot between principal and income.

While the allocation to principal of small amounts under this section should not be a cause for concern for tax purposes, allocations are not permitted under this section in circumstances described in Section 104(c) to eliminate claims that the power in this section has adverse tax consequences.

Section 409. Deferred Compensation, Annuities, and Similar Payments.

(a) In this section:

(1) "Payment" means a payment that a trustee may receive over a fixed number of years or during the life of one or more individuals because of services rendered or property transferred to the payer in exchange for future payments. The term includes a payment made in money or property from the payer's general assets or from a separate fund created by the payer. For purposes of subsections (d), (e), (f), and (g), the term also includes any payment from any separate fund, regardless of the reason for the payment.

(2) "Separate fund" includes a private or commercial annuity, an individual retirement account, and a pension, profit-sharing, stock-bonus, or stock-ownership plan.

(b) To the extent that a payment is characterized as interest, a dividend, or a payment made in lieu of interest or a dividend, a trustee shall allocate the payment to income. The trustee shall allocate to principal the balance of the payment and any other payment received in the same accounting period that is not characterized as interest, a dividend, or an equivalent payment.

(c) If no part of a payment is characterized as interest, a dividend, or an equivalent payment, and all or part of the payment is required to be made, a trustee shall allocate to income 10 percent of the part that is required to be made during the accounting period and the balance to principal. If no part of a payment is required to be made or the payment received is the entire amount to which the trustee is entitled, the trustee shall allocate the entire payment to principal. For purposes of this subsection, a payment is not required to be made to the extent that it is made because the trustee exercises a right of withdrawal.

(d) Except as otherwise provided in subsection (e), subsections (f) and (g) apply, and subsections (b) and (c) do not apply, in determining the allocation of a payment made from a separate fund to:

(1) a trust to which an election to qualify for a marital deduction under Section 2056(b)(7) of the Internal Revenue Code of 1986 [, as amended] [, 26 U.S.C. Section 2056(b)(7)] [, as amended], has been made; or

(2) a trust that qualifies for the marital deduction under Section 2056(b)(5) of the Internal Revenue Code of 1986 [, as amended] [, 26 U.S.C. Section 2056(b)(5)] [, as amended].

(e)   Subsections (d), (f), and (g) do not apply if and to the extent that the series of payments would, without the application of subsection (d), qualify for the marital deduction under Section 2056(b)(7)(C) of the Internal Revenue Code of 1986 [, as amended] [, 26 U.S.C. Section 2056(b)(7)(C)] [, as amended].

(f)   A trustee shall determine the internal income of each separate fund for the accounting period as if the separate fund were a trust subject to this [act]. Upon request of the surviving spouse, the trustee shall demand that the person administering the separate fund distribute the internal income to the trust. The trustee shall allocate a payment from the separate fund to income to the extent of the internal income of the separate fund and distribute that amount to the surviving spouse. The trustee shall allocate the balance of the payment to principal. Upon request of the surviving spouse, the trustee shall allocate principal to income to the extent the internal income of the separate fund exceeds payments made from the separate fund to the trust during the accounting period.

(g)   If a trustee cannot determine the internal income of a separate fund but can determine the value of the separate fund, the internal income of the separate fund is deemed to equal [insert number at least three percent and not more than five percent] of the fund's value, according to the most recent statement of value preceding the beginning of the accounting period. If the trustee can determine neither the internal income of the separate fund nor the fund's value, the internal income of the fund is deemed to equal the product of the interest rate and the present value of the expected future payments, as determined under Section 7520 of the Internal Revenue Code of 1986 [, as amended] [, 26 U.S.C. Section 7520] [, as amended], for the month preceding the accounting period for which the computation is made.

(h)   This section does not apply to a payment to which Section 410 applies.

Comment

Scope. Section 409 applies to amounts received under contractual arrangements that provide for payments to a third party beneficiary as a result of services rendered or property transferred to the payer. While the right to receive such payments is a liquidating asset of the kind described in Section 410 (i.e., "an asset whose value will diminish or terminate because the asset is expected to produce receipts for a period of limited duration"), these payment rights are covered separately in Section 409 because of their special characteristics.

Section 409 applies to receipts from all forms of annuities and deferred compensation arrangements, whether the payment will be received by the trust in a lump sum or in installments over a period of years. It applies to bonuses that may be received over two or three years and payments that may last for much longer periods, including payments from an individual retirement account (IRA), deferred compensation plan (whether qualified or not qualified for special federal income tax treatment), and insurance renewal commissions. It applies to a retirement plan to which the settlor has made contributions, just as it applies to an annuity policy that the settlor may have purchased individually, and it applies to variable annuities, deferred annuities, annuities issued by commercial insurance companies, and "private annuities" arising from the sale of property to another individual or entity in exchange for payments that are to be made for the life of one or more individuals. The section applies whether the payments begin when the payment right becomes subject to the trust or are deferred until a future date, and it applies whether payments are made in cash or in kind, such as employer stock (in-kind payments usually will be made in a single distribution that will be allocated to principal under the second sentence of subsection (c)). * * *

Allocations Under Section 409(b). Section 409(b) applies to plans whose terms characterize payments made under the plan as dividends, interest, or payments in lieu of dividends or interest. For example, some deferred compensation plans that hold debt obligations or stock of the plan's sponsor in an account for future delivery to the person rendering the services provide for the annual payment to that person of dividends received on the stock or interest received on the debt obligations. Other plans provide that the account of the person rendering the services shall be credited with "phantom" shares of stock and require an annual payment that is equivalent to the dividends that would be received on that number of shares if they were actually issued; or a plan may entitle the person rendering the services to receive a fixed dollar amount in the future and provide for the annual payment of interest on the deferred amount during the period prior to its payment. Under Section 409(b), payments of dividends, interest or payments in lieu of dividends or interest under plans of this type are allocated to income; all other payments received under these plans are allocated to principal.

Section 409(b) does not apply to an IRA or an arrangement with payment provisions similar to an IRA. IRAs and similar arrangements are subject to the provisions in Section 409(c).

Allocations Under Section 409(c). The focus of Section 409, for purposes of allocating payments received by a trust to or between principal and income, is on the payment right rather than on assets that may be held in a fund from which the payments are made. Thus, if an IRA holds a portfolio of marketable stocks and bonds, the amount received by the IRA as dividends and interest is not taken into account in determining the principal and income allocation except to the extent that the Internal Revenue Service may require them to be taken into account when the payment is received by a trust that qualifies for the estate tax marital deduction (a situation that is provided for in Section 409(d)). An IRA is subject to federal income tax rules that require payments to begin by a particular date and be made over a specific number of years or a period measured by the lives of one or more persons. The payment right of a trust that is named as a beneficiary of an IRA is not a right to receive particular items that are paid to the IRA, but is instead the right to receive an amount determined by dividing the value of the IRA by the remaining number of years in the payment period. This payment right is similar to the right to receive a unitrust amount, which is normally expressed as an amount equal to a percentage of the value of the unitrust assets without regard to dividends or interest that may be received by the unitrust.

An amount received from an IRA or a plan with a payment provision similar to that of an IRA is allocated under Section 409(c), which differentiates between payments that are required to be made and all other payments. To the extent that a payment is required to be made (either under federal income tax rules or, in the case of a plan that is not subject to those rules, under the terms of the plan), 10% of the amount received is allocated to income and the balance is allocated to principal. All other payments are allocated to principal because they represent a change in the form of a principal asset; Section 409 follows the rule in Section 404(2), which provides that money or property received from a change in the form of a principal asset be allocated to principal.

* * * The amount allocated to income under Section 409 is not dependent upon the interest rate that is used for valuation purposes when the decedent dies, and if the payments received by the trust increase or decrease from year to year because the fund from which the payment is made increases or decreases in value, the amount allocated to income will also increase or decrease.

Marital deduction requirements. When an IRA or other retirement arrangement (a "plan") is payable to a marital deduction trust, the IRS treats the plan as a separate property interest that itself must qualify for the marital deduction. IRS Revenue Ruling 2006–26 said that, as written, Section 409 does not cause a trust to qualify for the IRS' safe harbors. Revenue Ruling 2006–26 was limited in scope to certain situations involving IRAs and defined contribution retirement plans. Without necessarily agreeing with the IRS' position in that ruling, the revision to this section is designed to satisfy the IRS' safe harbor and to address concerns that might be raised for similar assets. No IRS pronouncements have addressed the scope of Code section 2056(b)(7)(C).

Subsection (f) requires the trustee to demand certain distributions if the surviving spouse so requests. The safe harbor of Revenue Ruling 2006–26 requires that the surviving spouse be separately entitled to demand the fund's income (without regard to the income from the trust's other assets) and the income from the other assets (without regard to the fund's income). In any event, the surviving spouse is not required to demand that the trustee distribute all of the fund's income from the fund or from other trust assets. Treas. Reg. § 20.2056(b)–5(f)(8).

Subsection (f) also recognizes that the trustee might not control the payments that the trustee receives and provides a remedy to the surviving spouse if the distributions under subsection (d)(1) are insufficient.

Subsection (g) addresses situations where, due to lack of information provided by the fund's administrator, the trustee is unable to determine the fund's actual income. The bracketed language is the range approved for unitrust payments by Treas. Reg. § 1.643(b)–1. In determining the value for purposes of applying the unitrust percentage, the trustee would seek to obtain the value of the assets as of the most recent statement of value immediately preceding the beginning of the year. For example, suppose a trust's accounting period is January 1 through December 31. If a retirement plan administrator furnishes information annually each September 30 and declines to provide information as of December 31, then the trustee may rely on the September 30 value to determine the distribution for the following year. For funds whose values are not readily available, subsection (g) relies on Code section 7520 valuation methods because many funds described in Section 409 are annuities, and one consistent set of valuation principles should apply whether or not the fund is, in fact, an annuity.

Application of Section 104. Section 104(a) of this Act gives a trustee who is acting under the prudent investor rule the power to adjust from principal to income if, considering the portfolio as a whole and not just receipts from deferred compensation, the trustee determines that an adjustment is necessary. See Example (5) in the Comment following Section 104.

Section 410. Liquidating Asset.

(a)   In this section, "liquidating asset" means an asset whose value will diminish or terminate because the asset is expected to produce receipts for a period of limited duration. The term includes a leasehold, patent, copyright, royalty right, and right to receive payments during a period of more than one year under an arrangement that does not provide for the payment of interest on the unpaid balance. The term does not include a payment subject to Section 409, resources subject to Section 411, timber subject to Section 412, an activity subject to Section 414, an asset subject to Section 415, or any asset for which the trustee establishes a reserve for depreciation under Section 503.

(b)   A trustee shall allocate to income 10 percent of the receipts from a liquidating asset and the balance to principal.

Section 411. Minerals, Water, and Other Natural Resources.

(a)   To the extent that a trustee accounts for receipts from an interest in minerals or other natural resources pursuant to this section, the trustee shall allocate them as follows:

(1)   If received as nominal delay rental or nominal annual rent on a lease, a receipt must be allocated to income.

(2)   If received from a production payment, a receipt must be allocated to income if and to the extent that the agreement creating the production payment provides a factor for interest or its equivalent. The balance must be allocated to principal.

(3)   If an amount received as a royalty, shut-in-well payment, take-or-pay payment, bonus, or delay rental is more than nominal, 90 percent must be allocated to principal and the balance to income.

(4)   If an amount is received from a working interest or any other interest not provided for in paragraph (1), (2), or (3), 90 percent of the net amount received must be allocated to principal and the balance to income.

(b)   An amount received on account of an interest in water that is renewable must be allocated to income. If the water is not renewable, 90 percent of the amount must be allocated to principal and the balance to income.

(c)   This [Act] applies whether or not a decedent or donor was extracting minerals, water, or other natural resources before the interest became subject to the trust.

(d)   If a trust owns an interest in minerals, water, or other natural resources on [the effective date of this [Act]], the trustee may allocate receipts from the interest as provided in this [Act] or in the manner used by the trustee before [the effective date of this [Act]]. If the trust acquires an interest in minerals, water, or other natural resources after [the effective date of this [Act]], the trustee shall allocate receipts from the interest as provided in this [Act].

Comment

Prior Acts. The 1962 Act allocates to principal as a depletion allowance, 27-1/2% of the gross receipts, but not more than 50% of the net receipts after paying expenses. The Internal Revenue Code no longer provides for a 27-1/2% depletion allowance, although the major oil-producing States have retained the 27-

1/2% provision in their principal and income acts (Texas amended its Act in 1993, but did not change the depletion provision). * * *

Section 411 allocates 90% of the net receipts to principal and 10% to income. A depletion provision that is tied to past or present Code provisions is undesirable because it causes a large portion of the oil and gas receipts to be paid out as income. As wells are depleted, the amount received by the income beneficiary falls drastically. Allocating a larger portion of the receipts to principal enables the trustee to acquire other income producing assets that will continue to produce income when the mineral reserves are exhausted.

Application of Sections 403 and 408. This section applies to the extent that the trustee does not account separately for receipts from minerals and other natural resources under Section 403 or allocate all of the receipts to principal under Section 408. * * *

Effective date provision. Section 9(b) of the 1962 Act provides that the natural resources provision does not apply to property interests held by the trust on the effective date of the Act, which reflects concerns about the constitutionality of applying a retroactive administrative provision to interests in real estate, based on the opinion in the Oklahoma case of *Franklin v. Margay Oil Corporation*, 153 P.2d 486, 501 (Okla. 1944). Section 411(d) permits a trustee to use either the method provided for in this Act or the method used before the Act takes effect. Lawyers in jurisdictions other than Oklahoma may conclude that retroactivity is not a problem as to property situated in their States, and this provision permits trustees to decide, based on advice from counsel in States whose law may be different from that of Oklahoma, whether they may apply this provision retroactively if they conclude that to do so is in the best interests of the beneficiaries.

If the property is in a State other than the State where the trust is administered, the trustee must be aware that the law of the property's situs may control this question. The outcome turns on a variety of questions: whether the terms of the trust specify that the law of a State other than the situs of the property shall govern the administration of the trust, and whether the courts will follow the terms of the trust; whether the trust's asset is the land itself or a leasehold interest in the land (as it frequently is with oil and gas property); whether a leasehold interest or its proceeds should be classified as real property or personal property, and if as personal property, whether applicable state law treats it as a movable or an immovable for conflict of laws purposes. See 5A Austin W. Scott & William F. Fratcher, The Law of Trusts §§ 648, at 531, 533–534; § 657, at 600 (4th ed. 1989).

Section 412. Timber.

(a)   To the extent that a trustee accounts for receipts from the sale of timber and related products pursuant to this section, the trustee shall allocate the net receipts:

(1)   to income to the extent that the amount of timber removed from the land does not exceed the rate of growth of the timber during the accounting periods in which a beneficiary has a mandatory income interest;

(2)   to principal to the extent that the amount of timber removed from the land exceeds the rate of growth of the timber or the net receipts are from the sale of standing timber;

(3)   to or between income and principal if the net receipts are from the lease of timberland or from a contract to cut timber from land owned by a trust, by determining the amount of timber removed from the land under the lease or contract and applying the rules in paragraphs (1) and (2); or

(4)   to principal to the extent that advance payments, bonuses, and other payments are not allocated pursuant to paragraph (1), (2), or (3).

(b)   In determining net receipts to be allocated pursuant to subsection (a), a trustee shall deduct and transfer to principal a reasonable amount for depletion.

(c)   This [Act] applies whether or not a decedent or transferor was harvesting timber from the property before it become subject to the trust.

(d)   If a trust owns an interest in timberland on [the effective date of this [Act]], the trustee may allocate net receipts from the sale of timber and related products as provided in this [Act] or in the manner used by the trustee before [the effective date of this [Act]]. If the trust acquires an interest in timberland after [the effective date of this [Act]], the trustee shall allocate net receipts from the sale of timber and related products as provided in this [Act].

Comment

Scope of section. The rules in Section 412 are intended to apply to net receipts from the sale of trees and by-products from harvesting and processing trees without regard to the kind of trees that are cut or whether the trees are cut before or after a particular number of years of growth. The rules apply to the sale of trees that are expected to produce lumber for building purposes, trees sold as pulpwood, and Christmas and other ornamental trees. Subsection (a) applies to net receipts from property owned by the trustee and property leased by the trustee. The Act is not intended to prevent a tenant in possession of the property from using wood that he cuts on the property for personal, noncommercial purposes, such as a Christmas tree, firewood, mending old fences or building new fences, or making repairs to structures on the property.

Under subsection (a), the amount of net receipts allocated to income depends upon whether the amount of timber removed is more or less than the rate of growth. The method of determining the amount of timber removed and the rate of growth is up to the trustee, based on methods customarily used for the kind of timber involved.

Application of Sections 403 and 408. This section applies to the extent that the trustee does not account separately for net receipts from the sale of timber and related products under Section 403 or allocate all of the receipts to principal under Section 408. The option to account for net receipts separately under Section 403 takes into consideration the possibility that timber harvesting operations may have been conducted before the timber property became subject to the trust, and that it may make sense to continue using accounting methods previously established for the property. It also permits a trustee to use customary accounting practices for timber operations even if no harvesting occurred on the property before it became subject to the trust.

Section 413. Property Not Productive of Income.

(a) If a marital deduction is allowed for all or part of a trust whose assets consist substantially of property that does not provide the surviving spouse with sufficient income from or use of the trust assets, and if the amounts that the trustee transfers from principal to income under Section 104 and distributes to the spouse from principal pursuant to the terms of the trust are insufficient to provide the spouse with the beneficial enjoyment required to obtain the marital deduction, the spouse may require the trustee to make property productive of income, convert property within a reasonable time, or exercise the power conferred by Section 104(a). The trustee may decide which action or combination of actions to take.

(b) In cases not governed by subsection (a), proceeds from the sale or other disposition of an asset are principal without regard to the amount of income the asset produces during any accounting period.

Comment

Prior Acts' Conflict with Uniform Prudent Investor Act. Section 2(b) of the Uniform Prudent Investor Act provides that "[a] trustee's investment and management decisions respecting individual assets must be evaluated not in isolation but in the context of the trust portfolio as a whole...." The underproductive property provisions in Section 12 of the 1962 Act and Section 11 of the 1931 Act give the income beneficiary a right to receive a portion of the proceeds from the sale of underproductive property as "delayed income." In each Act the provision applies on an asset by asset basis and not by taking into consideration the trust portfolio as a whole, which conflicts with the basic precept in Section 2(b) of the Prudent Investor Act. Moreover, in determining the amount of delayed income, the prior Acts do not permit a trustee to take into account the extent to which the trustee may have distributed principal to the income beneficiary, under principal invasion provisions in the terms of the trust, to compensate for insufficient income from the unproductive asset. Under Section 104(b)(7) of this Act, a trustee must consider prior distributions of principal to the income beneficiary in deciding whether and to what extent to exercise the power to adjust conferred by Section 104(a).

Duty to make property productive of income. In order to implement the Uniform Prudent Investor Act, this Act abolishes the right to receive delayed income from the sale proceeds of an asset that produces little or no income, but it does not alter existing state law regarding the income beneficiary's right to compel the trustee to make property productive of income. As the law continues to develop in this area, the duty to make property productive of current income in a particular situation should be determined by taking into consideration the performance of the portfolio as a whole and the extent to which a trustee makes principal distributions to the income beneficiary under the terms of the trust and adjustments between principal and income under Section 104 of this Act.

Trusts for which the value of the right to receive income is important for tax reasons may be affected by Reg. § 1.7520–3(b)(2)(v) *Example (1)*, § 20.7520–3(b)(2)(v) *Examples (1)* and *(2)*, and § 25.7520–3(b)(2)(v) *Examples (1)* and *(2)*, which provide that if the income beneficiary does not have the right to compel the trustee to make the property productive, the income interest is considered unproductive and may not be valued actuarially under those sections.

Marital deduction trusts. Subsection (a) draws on language in Reg. § 20.2056(b)–5(f)(4) and (5) to enable a trust for a surviving spouse to qualify for a marital deduction if applicable state law is unclear about the surviving spouse's right to compel the trustee to make property productive of income. The trustee should also consider the application of Section 104 of this Act and the provisions of Restatement of Trusts 3d: Prudent Investor Rule § 240, at 186, app. § 240, at 252 (1992). Example (6) in the Comment to Section 104 describes a situation involving the payment from income of carrying charges on unproductive real estate in which Section 104 may apply.

Once the two conditions have occurred—insufficient beneficial enjoyment from the property and the spouse's demand that the trustee take action under this section—the trustee must act; but instead of the formulaic approach of the 1962 Act, which is triggered only if the trustee sells the property, this Act permits the trustee to decide whether to make the property productive of income, convert it, transfer funds from principal to income, or to take some combination of those actions. The trustee may rely on the power conferred by Section 104(a) to adjust from principal to income if the trustee decides that it is not feasible or appropriate to make the property productive of income or to convert the property. Given the purpose of Section 413, the power under Section 104(a) would be exercised to transfer principal to income and not to transfer income to principal.

Section 413 does not apply to a so-called "estate" trust, which will qualify for the marital deduction, even though the income may be accumulated for a term of years or for the life of the surviving spouse, if the terms of the trust require the principal and undistributed income to be paid to the surviving spouse's estate when the spouse dies. Reg. § 20.2056(c)–2(b)(1)(iii).

Section 414. Derivatives and Options.

(a)   In this section, "derivative" means a contract or financial instrument or a combination of contracts and financial instruments which gives a trust the right or obligation to participate in some or all changes in the price of a tangible or intangible asset or group of assets, or changes in a rate, an index of prices or rates, or other market indicator for an asset or a group of assets.

(b)   To the extent that a trustee does not account under Section 403 for transactions in derivatives, the trustee shall allocate to principal receipts from and disbursements made in connection with those transactions.

(c)   If a trustee grants an option to buy property from the trust, whether or not the trust owns the property when the option is granted, grants an option that permits another person to sell property to the trust, or acquires an option to buy property for the trust or an option to sell an asset owned by the trust, and the trustee or other owner of the asset is required to deliver the asset if the option is exercised, an amount received for granting the option must be allocated to principal. An amount paid to acquire the option must be paid from principal. A gain or loss realized upon the exercise of an option, including an option granted to a settlor of the trust for services rendered, must be allocated to principal.

Comment

Scope and application. It is difficult to predict how frequently and to what extent trustees will invest directly in derivative financial instruments rather than participating indirectly through investment entities that may utilize these instruments in varying degrees. If the trust participates in derivatives indirectly through an entity, an amount received from the entity will be allocated under Section 401 and not Section 414. If a trustee invests directly in derivatives to a significant extent, the expectation is that receipts and disbursements related to derivatives will be accounted for under Section 403; if a trustee chooses not to account under Section 403, Section 414(b) provides the default rule. Certain types of option transactions in which trustees may engage are dealt with in subsection (c) to distinguish those transactions from ones involving options that are embedded in derivative financial instruments.

Definition of "derivative." "Derivative" is a difficult term to define because new derivatives are invented daily as dealers tailor their terms to achieve specific financial objectives for particular clients. Since derivatives are typically contract-based, a derivative can probably be devised for almost any set of objectives if another party can be found who is willing to assume the obligations required to meet those objectives.

The most comprehensive definition of derivative is in the Exposure Draft of a Proposed Statement of Financial Accounting Standards titled "Accounting for Derivative and Similar Financial Instruments and for Hedging Activities," which was released by the Financial Accounting Standards Board (FASB) on June 20, 1996 (No. 162–B). The definition in Section 414(a) is derived in part from the FASB definition. The purpose of the definition in subsection (a) is to implement the substantive rule in subsection (b) that provides for all receipts and disbursements to be allocated to principal to the extent the trustee elects not to account for transactions in derivatives under Section 403. As a result, it is much shorter than the FASB definition, which serves much more ambitious objectives.

A derivative is frequently described as including futures, forwards, swaps and options, terms that also require definition, and the definition in this Act avoids these terms. FASB used the same approach, explaining in paragraph 65 of the Exposure Draft:

> The definition of *derivative financial instrument* in this Statement includes those financial instruments generally considered to be derivatives, such as forwards, futures, swaps, options, and similar instruments. The Board considered defining a derivative financial instrument by merely referencing those commonly understood instruments, similar to paragraph 5 of Statement 119, which says that " . . . a derivative financial instrument is a futures, forward, swap, or option contract, or other financial instrument with similar characteristics." However, the continued development of financial markets and innovative financial instruments could ultimately render a definition based on examples inadequate and obsolete. The Board, therefore, decided to base the definition of a derivative financial instrument on a description of the common characteristics of those instruments in order to accommodate the accounting for newly developed derivatives. (Footnote omitted.)

Marking to market. A gain or loss that occurs because the trustee marks securities to market or to another value during an accounting period is not a transaction in a derivative financial instrument that is income or principal under the Act—only cash receipts and disbursements, and the receipt of property in exchange for a principal asset, affect a trust's principal and income accounts.

Receipt of property other than cash. If a trustee receives property other than cash upon the settlement of a derivatives transaction, that property would be principal under Section 404(2).

Options. Options to which subsection (c) applies include an option to purchase real estate owned by the trustee and a put option purchased by a trustee to guard against a drop in value of a large block of marketable stock that must be liquidated to pay estate taxes. Subsection (c) would also apply to a continuing and regular practice of selling call options on securities owned by the trust if the terms of the option require delivery of the securities. It does not apply if the consideration received or given for the option is something other than cash or property, such as cross-options granted in a buy-sell agreement between owners of an entity.

Section 415. Asset-Backed Securities.

(a) In this section, "asset-backed security" means an asset whose value is based upon the right it gives the owner to receive distributions from the proceeds of financial assets that provide collateral for the security. The term includes an asset that gives the owner the right to receive from the collateral financial assets only the interest or other current return or only the proceeds other than interest or current return. The term does not include an asset to which Section 401 or 409 applies.

(b) If a trust receives a payment from interest or other current return and from other proceeds of the collateral financial assets, the trustee shall allocate to income the portion of the payment which the payer identifies as being from interest or other current return and shall allocate the balance of the payment to principal.

(c) If a trust receives one or more payments in exchange for the trust's entire interest in an asset-backed security in one accounting period, the trustee shall allocate the payments to principal. If a payment is one of a series of payments that will result in the liquidation of the trust's interest in the security over more than one accounting period, the trustee shall allocate 10 percent of the payment to income and the balance to principal.

Comment

Scope of section. Typical asset-backed securities include arrangements in which debt obligations such as real estate mortgages, credit card receivables and auto loans are acquired by an investment trust and interests in the trust are sold to investors. The source for payments to an investor is the money received from principal and interest payments on the underlying debt. An asset-backed security includes an "interest only" or a "principal only" security that permits the investor to receive only the interest payments received from the bonds, mortgages or other assets that are the collateral for the asset-backed security, or only the principal payments made on those collateral assets. An asset-backed security also includes a security that permits the investor to participate in either the capital appreciation of an underlying security or in the interest or dividend return from such a security, such as the "Primes" and "Scores" issued by Americus Trust. An asset-backed security does not include an interest in a corporation, partnership, or an investment trust described in the Comment to Section 402, whose assets consist significantly or entirely of investment assets. Receipts from an instrument that do not come within the scope of this section or any other section of the Act would be allocated entirely to principal under the rule in Section 103(a)(4), and the trustee may then consider whether and to what extent to exercise the power to adjust in Section 104, taking into account the return from the portfolio as whole and other relevant factors.

[ARTICLE] 5

ALLOCATION OF DISBURSEMENTS DURING ADMINISTRATION OF TRUST

Section 501. Disbursements From Income.

A trustee shall make the following disbursements from income to the extent that they are not disbursements to which Section 201(2)(B) or (C) applies:

(1)   one-half of the regular compensation of the trustee and of any person providing investment advisory or custodial services to the trustee;

(2)   one-half of all expenses for accountings, judicial proceedings, or other matters that involve both the income and remainder interests;

(3)   all of the other ordinary expenses incurred in connection with the administration, management, or preservation of trust property and the distribution of income, including interest, ordinary repairs, regularly recurring taxes assessed against principal, and expenses of a proceeding or other matter that concerns primarily the income interest; and

(4)   recurring premiums on insurance covering the loss of a principal asset or the loss of income from or use of the asset.

Comment

Trustee fees. The regular compensation of a trustee or the trustee's agent includes compensation based on a percentage of either principal or income or both.

Insurance premiums. The reference in paragraph (4) to "recurring" premiums is intended to distinguish premiums paid annually for fire insurance from premiums on title insurance, each of which covers the loss of a principal asset. Title insurance premiums would be a principal disbursement under Section 502(a)(5).

Regularly recurring taxes. The reference to "regularly recurring taxes assessed against principal" includes all taxes regularly imposed on real property and tangible and intangible personal property.

Section 502. Disbursements From Principal.

(a)   A trustee shall make the following disbursements from principal:

(1)   the remaining one-half of the disbursements described in Section 501(1) and (2);

(2)   all of the trustee's compensation calculated on principal as a fee for acceptance, distribution, or termination, and disbursements made to prepare property for sale;

(3)   payments on the principal of a trust debt;

(4)   expenses of a proceeding that concerns primarily principal, including a proceeding to construe the trust or to protect the trust or its property;

(5)   premiums paid on a policy of insurance not described in Section 501(4) of which the trust is the owner and beneficiary;

(6)   estate, inheritance, and other transfer taxes, including penalties, apportioned to the trust; and

(7)   disbursements related to environmental matters, including reclamation, assessing environmental conditions, remedying and removing environmental contamination, monitoring remedial activities and the release of substances, preventing future releases of substances, collecting amounts from persons liable or potentially liable for the costs of those activities, penalties imposed under environmental laws or regulations and other payments made to comply

639

with those laws or regulations, statutory or common law claims by third parties, and defending claims based on environmental matters.

(b) If a principal asset is encumbered with an obligation that requires income from that asset to be paid directly to the creditor, the trustee shall transfer from principal to income an amount equal to the income paid to the creditor in reduction of the principal balance of the obligation.

Comment

Environmental expenses. All environmental expenses are payable from principal, subject to the power of the trustee to transfer funds to principal from income under Section 504. However, the Drafting Committee decided that it was not necessary to broaden this provision to cover other expenditures made under compulsion of governmental authority. * * *

Environmental expenses paid by a trust are to be paid from principal under Section 502(a)(7) on the assumption that they will usually be extraordinary in nature. Environmental expenses might be paid from income if the trustee is carrying on a business that uses or sells toxic substances, in which case environmental cleanup costs would be a normal cost of doing business and would be accounted for under Section 403. In accounting under that Section, environmental costs will be a factor in determining how much of the net receipts from the business is trust income. Paying all other environmental expenses from principal is consistent with this Act's approach regarding receipts—when a receipt is not clearly a current return on a principal asset, it should be added to principal because over time both the income and remainder beneficiaries benefit from this treatment. Here, allocating payments required by environmental laws to principal imposes the detriment of those payments over time on both the income and remainder beneficiaries.

Under Sections 504(a) and 504(b)(5), a trustee who makes or expects to make a principal disbursement for an environmental expense described in Section 502(a)(7) is authorized to transfer an appropriate amount from income to principal to reimburse principal for disbursements made or to provide a reserve for future principal disbursements.

The first part of Section 502(a)(7) is based upon the definition of an "environmental remediation trust" in Treas. Reg. § 301.7701–4(e) (as amended in 1996). This is not because the Act applies to an environmental remediation trust, but because the definition is a useful and thoroughly vetted description of the kinds of expenses that a trustee owning contaminated property might incur. Expenses incurred to comply with environmental laws include the cost of environmental consultants, administrative proceedings and burdens of every kind imposed as the result of an administrative or judicial proceeding, even though the burden is not formally characterized as a penalty. * * *

Insurance premiums. Insurance premiums referred to in Section 502(a)(5) include title insurance premiums. They also include premiums on life insurance policies owned by the trust, which represent the trust's periodic investment in the insurance policy. * * *

Taxes. Generation-skipping transfer taxes are payable from principal under subsection (a)(6).

Section 503. Transfers From Income to Principal for Depreciation.

(a) In this section, "depreciation" means a reduction in value due to wear, tear, decay, corrosion, or gradual obsolescence of a fixed asset having a useful life of more than one year.

(b) A trustee may transfer to principal a reasonable amount of the net cash receipts from a principal asset that is subject to depreciation, but may not transfer any amount for depreciation:

(1) of that portion of real property used or available for use by a beneficiary as a residence or of tangible personal property held or made available for the personal use or enjoyment of a beneficiary;

(2) during the administration of a decedent's estate; or

(3) under this section if the trustee is accounting under Section 403 for the business or activity in which the asset is used.

(c) An amount transferred to principal need not be held as a separate fund.

Comment

Prior Acts. The 1931 Act has no provision for depreciation. Section 13(a)(2) of the 1962 Act provides that a charge shall be made against income for " . . . a reasonable allowance for depreciation on property subject to depreciation under generally accepted accounting principles. . . ." That provision has been resisted by many trustees, who do not provide for any depreciation for a variety of reasons. One reason relied upon is that a charge for depreciation is not needed to protect the remainder beneficiaries if the value of the land is increasing; another is that generally accepted accounting principles may not require depreciation to be taken if the property is not part of a business. The Drafting Committee concluded that the decision to provide for depreciation should be discretionary with the trustee. The power to transfer funds from income to principal that is granted by this section is a discretionary power of administration referred to in Section 103(b), and in exercising the power a trustee must comply with Section 103(b).

One purpose served by transferring cash from income to principal for depreciation is to provide funds to pay the principal of an indebtedness secured by the depreciable property. Section 504(b)(4) permits the trustee to transfer additional cash from income to principal for this purpose to the extent that the amount transferred from income to principal for depreciation is less than the amount of the principal payments.

Section 504. Transfers From Income to Reimburse Principal.

(a) If a trustee makes or expects to make a principal disbursement described in this section, the trustee may transfer an appropriate amount from income to principal in one or more accounting periods to reimburse principal or to provide a reserve for future principal disbursements.

(b) Principal disbursements to which subsection (a) applies include the following, but only to the extent that the trustee has not been and does not expect to be reimbursed by a third party:

(1) an amount chargeable to income but paid from principal because it is unusually large, including extraordinary repairs;

(2) a capital improvement to a principal asset, whether in the form of changes to an existing asset or the construction of a new asset, including special assessments;

(3) disbursements made to prepare property for rental, including tenant allowances, leasehold improvements, and broker's commissions;

(4) periodic payments on an obligation secured by a principal asset to the extent that the amount transferred from income to principal for depreciation is less than the periodic payments; and

(5) disbursements described in Section 502(a)(7).

(c) If the asset whose ownership gives rise to the disbursements becomes subject to a successive income interest after an income interest ends, a trustee may continue to transfer amounts from income to principal as provided in subsection (a).

Section 505. Income Taxes.

(a) A tax required to be paid by a trustee based on receipts allocated to income must be paid from income.

(b) A tax required to be paid by a trustee based on receipts allocated to principal must be paid from principal, even if the tax is called an income tax by the taxing authority.

(c) A tax required to be paid by a trustee on the trust's share of an entity's taxable income must be paid:

(1) from income to the extent that receipts from the entity are allocated only to income;

(2) from principal to the extent that receipts from the entity are allocated only to principal;

(3) proportionately from principal and income to the extent that receipts from the entity are allocated to both income and principal; and

(4)   from principal to the extent that the tax exceeds the total receipts from the entity.

(d)   After applying subsections (a) through (c), the trustee shall adjust income or principal receipts to the extent that the trust's taxes are reduced because the trust receives a deduction for payments made to a beneficiary.

Comment

Taxes on Undistributed Entity Taxable Income. When a trust owns an interest in a pass-through entity, such as a partnership or S corporation, it must report its share of the entity's taxable income regardless of how much the entity distributes to the trust. Whether the entity distributes more or less than the trust's tax on its share of the entity's taxable income, the trust must pay the taxes and allocate them between income and principal.

Subsection (c) requires the trust to pay the taxes on its share of an entity's taxable income from income or principal receipts to the extent that receipts from the entity are allocable to each. This assures the trust a source of cash to pay some or all of the taxes on its share of the entity's taxable income. Subsection 505(d) recognizes that, except in the case of an Electing Small Business Trust (ESBT), a trust normally receives a deduction for amounts distributed to a beneficiary. Accordingly, subsection 505(d) requires the trust to increase receipts payable to a beneficiary as determined under subsection (c) to the extent the trust's taxes are reduced by distributing those receipts to the beneficiary.

Because the trust's taxes and amounts distributed to a beneficiary are interrelated, the trust may be required to apply a formula to determine the correct amount payable to a beneficiary. This formula should take into account that each time a distribution is made to a beneficiary, the trust taxes are reduced and amounts distributable to a beneficiary are increased. The formula assures that after deducting distributions to a beneficiary, the trust has enough to satisfy its taxes on its share of the entity's taxable income as reduced by distributions to beneficiaries.

Example (1)—Trust T receives a Schedule K-1 from Partnership P reflecting taxable income of $1 million. Partnership P distributes $100,000 to T, which allocates the receipts to income. Both Trust T and income Beneficiary B are in the 35 percent tax bracket. Trust T's tax on $1 million of taxable income is $350,000. Under Subsection (c) T's tax must be paid from income receipts because receipts from the entity are allocated only to income. Therefore, T must apply the entire $100,000 of income receipts to pay its tax. In this case, Beneficiary B receives nothing.

Example (2)—Trust T receives a Schedule K-1 from Partnership P reflecting taxable income of $1 million. Partnership P distributes $500,000 to T, which allocates the receipts to income. Both Trust T and income Beneficiary B are in the 35 percent tax bracket. Trust T's tax on $1 million of taxable income is $350,000. Under Subsection (c), T's tax must be paid from income receipts because receipts from P are allocated only to income. Therefore, T uses $350,000 of the $500,000 to pay its taxes and distributes the remaining $150,000 to B. The $150,000 payment to B reduces T's taxes by $52,500, which it must pay to B. But the $52,500 further reduces T's taxes by $18,375, which it also must pay to B. In fact, each time T makes a distribution to B, its taxes are further reduced, causing another payment to be due B.

Alternatively, T can apply the following algebraic formula to determine the amount payable to B:

$$D = (C - R * K)/(1 - R)$$

D = Distribution to income beneficiary

C = Cash paid by the entity to the trust

R = tax rate on income

K = entity's K-1 taxable income

Applying the formula to Example (2) above, Trust T must pay $230,769 to B so that after deducting the payment, T has exactly enough to pay its tax on the remaining taxable income from P.

Taxable Income per K-1	$1,000,000
Payment to beneficiary	230,769*
Trust Taxable Income	$769,231
35 percent tax	$269,231
Partnership Distribution	$500,000
Fiduciary's Tax Liability	(269,231)
Payable to the Beneficiary	$230,769

In addition, B will report $230,769 on his or her own personal income tax return, paying taxes of $80,769. Because Trust T withheld $269,231 to pay its taxes and B paid $80,769 taxes of its own, B bore the entire $350,000 tax burden on the $1 million of entity taxable income, including the $500,000 that the entity retained that presumably increased the value of the trust's investment entity.

If a trustee determines that it is appropriate to do so, it should consider exercising the discretion granted in UPIA section 506 to adjust between income and principal. Alternatively, the trustee may exercise the power to adjust under UPIA section 104 to the extent it is available and appropriate under the circumstances, including whether a future distribution from the entity that would be allocated to principal should be reallocated to income because the income beneficiary already bore the burden of taxes on the reinvested income. In exercising the power, the trust should consider the impact that future distributions will have on any current adjustments.

Section 506. Adjustments Between Principal and Income Because of Taxes.

(a) A fiduciary may make adjustments between principal and income to offset the shifting of economic interests or tax benefits between income beneficiaries and remainder beneficiaries which arise from:

(1) elections and decisions, other than those described in subsection (b), that the fiduciary makes from time to time regarding tax matters;

(2) an income tax or any other tax that is imposed upon the fiduciary or a beneficiary as a result of a transaction involving or a distribution from the estate or trust; or

(3) the ownership by an estate or trust of an interest in an entity whose taxable income, whether or not distributed, is includable in the taxable income of the estate, trust, or a beneficiary.

(b) If the amount of an estate tax marital deduction or charitable contribution deduction is reduced because a fiduciary deducts an amount paid from principal for income tax purposes instead of deducting it for estate tax purposes, and as a result estate taxes paid from principal are increased and income taxes paid by an estate, trust, or beneficiary are decreased, each estate, trust, or beneficiary that benefits from the decrease in income tax shall reimburse the principal from which the increase in estate tax is paid. The total reimbursement must equal the increase in the estate tax to the extent that the principal used to pay the increase would have qualified for a marital deduction or charitable contribution deduction but for the payment. The proportionate share of the reimbursement for each estate, trust, or beneficiary whose income taxes are reduced must be the same as its proportionate share of the total decrease in income tax. An estate or trust shall reimburse principal from income.

Comment

Discretionary adjustments. Section 506(a) permits the fiduciary to make adjustments between income and principal because of tax law provisions. It would permit discretionary adjustments in situations

---

* $D = (C - R * K)/(1 - R) = (500,000 - 350,000)/(1 - .35) = $230,769.$ (D is the amount payable to the income beneficiary, K is the entity's K-1 taxable income, R is the trust ordinary tax rate, and C is the cash distributed by the entity).

like these: (1) A fiduciary elects to deduct administration expenses that are paid from principal on an income tax return instead of on the estate tax return; (2) a distribution of a principal asset to a trust or other beneficiary causes the taxable income of an estate or trust to be carried out to the distributee and relieves the persons who receive the income of any obligation to pay income tax on the income; or (3) a trustee realizes a capital gain on the sale of a principal asset and pays a large state income tax on the gain, but under applicable federal income tax rules the trustee may not deduct the state income tax payment from the capital gain in calculating the trust's federal capital gain tax, and the income beneficiary receives the benefit of the deduction for state income tax paid on the capital gain. See generally Joel C. Dobris, Limits on the Doctrine of Equitable Adjustment in Sophisticated Postmortem Tax Planning, 66 Iowa L. Rev. 273 (1981).

Section 506(a)(3) applies to a qualified Subchapter S trust (QSST) whose income beneficiary is required to include a pro rata share of the S corporation's taxable income in his return. If the QSST does not receive a cash distribution from the corporation that is large enough to cover the income beneficiary's tax liability, the trustee may distribute additional cash from principal to the income beneficiary. In this case the retention of cash by the corporation benefits the trust principal. This situation could occur if the corporation's taxable income includes capital gain from the sale of a business asset and the sale proceeds are reinvested in the business instead of being distributed to shareholders.

Mandatory adjustment. Subsection (b) provides for a mandatory adjustment from income to principal to the extent needed to preserve an estate tax marital deduction or charitable contributions deduction. It is derived from New York's EPTL § 11–1.2(A), which requires principal to be reimbursed by those who benefit when a fiduciary elects to deduct administration expenses on an income tax return instead of the estate tax return. Unlike the New York provision, subsection (b) limits a mandatory reimbursement to cases in which a marital deduction or a charitable contributions deduction is reduced by the payment of additional estate taxes because of the fiduciary's income tax election. It is intended to preserve the result reached in *Estate of Britenstool v. Commissioner*, 46 T.C. 711 (1966), in which the Tax Court held that a reimbursement required by the predecessor of EPTL § 11–1.2(A) resulted in the estate receiving the same charitable contributions deduction it would have received if the administration expenses had been deducted for estate tax purposes instead of for income tax purposes. Because a fiduciary will elect to deduct administration expenses for income tax purposes only when the income tax reduction exceeds the estate tax reduction, the effect of this adjustment is that the principal is placed in the same position it would have occupied if the fiduciary had deducted the expenses for estate tax purposes, but the income beneficiaries receive an additional benefit. For example, if the income tax benefit from the deduction is $30,000 and the estate tax benefit would have been $20,000, principal will be reimbursed $20,000 and the net benefit to the income beneficiaries will be $10,000.

Irrevocable grantor trusts. Under Sections 671–679 of the Internal Revenue Code (the "grantor trust" provisions), a person who creates an irrevocable trust for the benefit of another person may be subject to tax on the trust's income or capital gains, or both, even though the settlor is not entitled to receive any income or principal from the trust. Because this is now a well-known tax result, many trusts have been created to produce this result, but there are also trusts that are unintentionally subject to this rule. The Act does not require or authorize a trustee to distribute funds from the trust to the settlor in these cases because it is difficult to establish a rule that applies only to trusts where this tax result is unintended and does not apply to trusts where the tax result is intended. Settlors who intend this tax result rarely state it as an objective in the terms of the trust, but instead rely on the operation of the tax law to produce the desired result. As a result it may not be possible to determine from the terms of the trust if the result was intentional or unintentional. If the drafter of such a trust wants the trustee to have the authority to distribute principal or income to the settlor to reimburse the settlor for taxes paid on the trust's income or capital gains, such a provision should be placed in the terms of the trust. In some situations the Internal Revenue Service may require that such a provision be placed in the terms of the trust as a condition to issuing a private letter ruling.

[ARTICLE] 6

MISCELLANEOUS PROVISIONS

UNIFORM PRUDENT INVESTOR ACT*

PREFATORY NOTE

Over the quarter century from the late 1960's the investment practices of fiduciaries experienced significant change. The Uniform Prudent Investor Act (UPIA) undertakes to update trust investment law in recognition of the alterations that have occurred in investment practice. These changes have occurred under the influence of a large and broadly accepted body of empirical and theoretical knowledge about the behavior of capital markets, often described as "modern portfolio theory."

This Act draws upon the revised standards for prudent trust investment promulgated by the American Law Institute in its Restatement (Third) of Trusts: Prudent Investor Rule (1992) [hereinafter Restatement of Trusts 3d: Prudent Investor Rule; also referred to as 1992 Restatement].

Objectives of the Act. UPIA makes five fundamental alterations in the former criteria for prudent investing. All are to be found in the Restatement of Trusts 3d: Prudent Investor Rule.

(1)   The standard of prudence is applied to any investment as part of the total portfolio, rather than to individual investments. In the trust setting the term "portfolio" embraces all the trust's assets. UPIA § 2(b).

(2)   The tradeoff in all investing between risk and return is identified as the fiduciary's central consideration. UPIA § 2(b).

(3)   All categoric restrictions on types of investments have been abrogated; the trustee can invest in anything that plays an appropriate role in achieving the risk/return objectives of the trust and that meets the other requirements of prudent investing. UPIA § 2(e).

(4)   The long familiar requirement that fiduciaries diversify their investments has been integrated into the definition of prudent investing. UPIA § 3.

(5)   The much criticized former rule of trust law forbidding the trustee to delegate investment and management functions has been reversed. Delegation is now permitted, subject to safeguards. UPIA § 9. * * *

Implications for charitable and pension trusts. This Act is centrally concerned with the investment responsibilities arising under the private gratuitous trust, which is the common vehicle for conditioned wealth transfer within the family. Nevertheless, the prudent investor rule also bears on charitable and pension trusts, among others. "In making investments of trust funds the trustee of a charitable trust is under a duty similar to that of the trustee of a private trust." Restatement of Trusts 2d § 389 (1959). The Employee Retirement Income Security Act (ERISA), the federal regulatory scheme for pension trusts enacted in 1974, absorbs trust-investment law through the prudence standard of ERISA § 404(a)(1)(B), 29 U.S.C. § 1104(a). The Supreme Court has said: "ERISA's legislative history confirms that the Act's fiduciary responsibility provisions 'codif[y] and mak[e] applicable to [ERISA] fiduciaries certain principles developed in the evolution of the law of trusts.'" *Firestone Tire & Rubber Co. v. Bruch*, 489 U.S. 101, 110–11 (1989) (footnote omitted).

Other fiduciary relationships. The Uniform Prudent Investor Act regulates the investment responsibilities of trustees. Other fiduciaries—such as executors, conservators, and guardians of the property—sometimes have responsibilities over assets that are governed by the standards of prudent investment. It will often be appropriate for states to adapt the law governing investment by trustees under this Act to these other fiduciary regimes, taking account of such changed circumstances as the relatively short duration of most executorships and the intensity of court supervision of conservators and guardians in some jurisdictions. The present Act does not undertake to adjust trust-investment law to the special circumstances of the state schemes for administering decedents' estates or conducting the affairs of protected persons.

Although the Uniform Prudent Investor Act by its terms applies to trusts and not to charitable corporations, the standards of the Act can be expected to inform the investment responsibilities of directors and officers of charitable corporations. As the 1992 Restatement observes, "the duties of the members of the governing board of a charitable corporation are generally similar to the duties of the trustee of a charitable trust." Restatement of Trusts 3d: Prudent Investor Rule § 379, Comment *b*, at 190 (1992). See also id. § 389, Comment *b*, at 190–91 (absent contrary statute or other provision, prudent investor rule applies to investment of funds held for charitable corporations).

Section 1. Prudent Investor Rule.

(a) Except as otherwise provided in subsection (b), a trustee who invests and manages trust assets owes a duty to the beneficiaries of the trust to comply with the prudent investor rule set forth in this [Act].

(b) The prudent investor rule, a default rule, may be expanded, restricted, eliminated, or otherwise altered by the provisions of a trust. A trustee is not liable to a beneficiary to the extent that the trustee acted in reasonable reliance on the provisions of the trust.

Comment

This section imposes the obligation of prudence in the conduct of investment functions and identifies further sections of the Act that specify the attributes of prudent conduct.

Origins. The prudence standard for trust investing traces back to *Harvard College v. Amory*, 26 Mass. (9 Pick.) 446 (1830). Trustees should "observe how men of prudence, discretion and intelligence manage their own affairs, not in regard to speculation, but in regard to the permanent disposition of their funds, considering the probable income, as well as the probable safety of the capital to be invested." Id. at 461.

Prior legislation. The Model Prudent Man Rule Statute (1942), sponsored by the American Bankers Association, undertook to codify the language of the *Amory* case. See Mayo A. Shattuck, The Development of the Prudent Man Rule for Fiduciary Investment in the United States in the Twentieth Century, 12 Ohio State L.J. 491, at 501 (1951); for the text of the model act, which inspired many state statutes, see id. at 508–09. Another prominent codification of the *Amory* standard is Uniform Probate Code § 7–302 (1969), which provides that "the trustee shall observe the standards in dealing with the trust assets that would be observed by a prudent man dealing with the property of another. . . ."

Congress has imposed a comparable prudence standard for the administration of pension and employee benefit trusts in the Employee Retirement Income Security Act (ERISA), enacted in 1974. ERISA § 404(a)(1)(B), 29 U.S.C. § 1104(a), provides that "a fiduciary shall discharge his duties with respect to a plan solely in the interest of the participants and beneficiaries and . . . with the care, skill, prudence, and diligence under the circumstances then prevailing that a prudent man acting in a like capacity and familiar with such matters would use in the conduct of an enterprise of like character and with like aims. . . ."

Prior Restatement. The Restatement of Trusts 2d (1959) also tracked the language of the *Amory* case: "In making investments of trust funds the trustee is under a duty to the beneficiary . . . to make such investments and only such investments as a prudent man would make of his own property having in view the preservation of the estate and the amount and regularity of the income to be derived. . . ." Restatement of Trusts 2d § 227 (1959).

Objective standard. The concept of prudence in the judicial opinions and legislation is essentially relational or comparative. It resembles in this respect the "reasonable person" rule of tort law. A prudent trustee behaves as other trustees similarly situated would behave. The standard is, therefore, objective rather than subjective. Sections 2 through 9 of this Act identify the main factors that bear on prudent investment behavior.

Variation. Almost all of the rules of trust law are default rules, that is, rules that the settlor may alter or abrogate. Subsection (b) carries forward this traditional attribute of trust law. Traditional trust law also allows the beneficiaries of the trust to excuse its performance, when they are all capable and not misinformed. Restatement of Trusts 2d § 216 (1959).

Section 2. Standard of Care; Portfolio Strategy; Risk and Return Objectives.

(a)   A trustee shall invest and manage trust assets as a prudent investor would, by considering the purposes, terms, distribution requirements, and other circumstances of the trust. In satisfying this standard, the trustee shall exercise reasonable care, skill, and caution.

(b)   A trustee's investment and management decisions respecting individual assets must be evaluated not in isolation but in the context of the trust portfolio as a whole and as a part of an overall investment strategy having risk and return objectives reasonably suited to the trust.

(c)   Among circumstances that a trustee shall consider in investing and managing trust assets are such of the following as are relevant to the trust or its beneficiaries:

(1)   general economic conditions;

(2)   the possible effect of inflation or deflation;

(3)   the expected tax consequences of investment decisions or strategies;

(4)   the role that each investment or course of action plays within the overall trust portfolio, which may include financial assets, interests in closely held enterprises, tangible and intangible personal property, and real property;

(5)   the expected total return from income and the appreciation of capital;

(6)   other resources of the beneficiaries;

(7)   needs for liquidity, regularity of income, and preservation or appreciation of capital; and

(8)   an asset's special relationship or special value, if any, to the purposes of the trust or to one or more of the beneficiaries.

(d)   A trustee shall make a reasonable effort to verify facts relevant to the investment and management of trust assets.

(e)   A trustee may invest in any kind of property or type of investment consistent with the standards of this [Act].

(f)   A trustee who has special skills or expertise, or is named trustee in reliance upon the trustee's representation that the trustee has special skills or expertise, has a duty to use those special skills or expertise.

Comment

Section 2 is the heart of the Act. * * *

Objective standard. Subsection (a) of this Act carries forward the relational and objective standard made familiar in the *Amory* case, in earlier prudent investor legislation, and in the Restatements. Early formulations of the prudent person rule were sometimes troubled by the effort to distinguish between the standard of a prudent person investing for another and investing on his or her own account. The language of subsection (a), by relating the trustee's duty to "the purposes, terms, distribution requirements, and other circumstances of the trust," should put such questions to rest. The standard is the standard of the prudent investor similarly situated.

Portfolio standard. Subsection (b) emphasizes the consolidated portfolio standard for evaluating investment decisions. An investment that might be imprudent standing alone can become prudent if undertaken in sensible relation to other trust assets, or to other nontrust assets. In the trust setting the term "portfolio" embraces the entire trust estate.

Risk and return. Subsection (b) also sounds the main theme of modern investment practice, sensitivity to the risk/return curve. * * * Returns correlate strongly with risk, but tolerance for risk varies greatly with the financial and other circumstances of the investor, or in the case of a trust, with the purposes of the trust and the relevant circumstances of the beneficiaries. A trust whose main purpose is to support an elderly widow of modest means will have a lower risk tolerance than a trust to accumulate for a young scion of great wealth. * * *

Factors affecting investment. Subsection (c) points to certain of the factors that commonly bear on risk/return preferences in fiduciary investing. This listing is nonexclusive. Tax considerations, such as preserving the stepped up basis on death under Internal Revenue Code § 1014 for low-basis assets, have traditionally been exceptionally important in estate planning for affluent persons. Under the present recognition rules of the federal income tax, taxable investors, including trust beneficiaries, are in general best served by an investment strategy that minimizes the taxation incident to portfolio turnover. * * *

Another familiar example of how tax considerations bear upon trust investing: In a regime of pass-through taxation, it may be prudent for the trust to buy lower yielding tax-exempt securities for high-bracket taxpayers, whereas it would ordinarily be imprudent for the trustees of a charitable trust, whose income is tax exempt, to accept the lowered yields associated with tax-exempt securities.

When tax considerations affect beneficiaries differently, the trustee's duty of impartiality requires attention to the competing interests of each of them. * * *

Duty to monitor. Subsections (a) through (d) apply both to investing and managing trust assets. "Managing" embraces monitoring, that is, the trustee's continuing responsibility for oversight of the suitability of investments already made as well as the trustee's decisions respecting new investments.

Duty to investigate. Subsection (d) carries forward the traditional responsibility of the fiduciary investor to examine information likely to bear importantly on the value or the security of an investment— for example, audit reports or records of title. * * *

Abrogating categoric restrictions. Subsection 2(e) clarifies that no particular kind of property or type of investment is inherently imprudent. Traditional trust law was encumbered with a variety of categoric exclusions, such as prohibitions on junior mortgages or new ventures. In some states legislation created so-called "legal lists" of approved trust investments. The universe of investment products changes incessantly. Investments that were at one time thought too risky, such as equities, or more recently, futures, are now used in fiduciary portfolios. By contrast, the investment that was at one time thought ideal for trusts, the long-term bond, has been discovered to import a level of risk and volatility—in this case, inflation risk—that had not been anticipated. Accordingly, section 2(e) of this Act follows Restatement of Trusts 3d: Prudent Investor Rule in abrogating categoric restrictions. The Restatement says: "Specific investments or techniques are not per se prudent or imprudent. The riskiness of a specific property, and thus the propriety of its inclusion in the trust estate, is not judged in the abstract but in terms of its anticipated effect on the particular trust's portfolio." Restatement of Trusts 3d: Prudent Investor Rule § 227, Comment *f*, at 24 (1992). The premise of subsection 2(e) is that trust beneficiaries are better protected by the Act's emphasis on close attention to risk/return objectives as prescribed in subsection 2(b) than in attempts to identify categories of investment that are per se prudent or imprudent.

The Act impliedly disavows the emphasis in older law on avoiding "speculative" or "risky" investments. Low levels of risk may be appropriate in some trust settings but inappropriate in others. It is the trustee's task to invest at a risk level that is suitable to the purposes of the trust.

The abolition of categoric restrictions against types of investment in no way alters the trustee's conventional duty of loyalty, which is reiterated for the purposes of this Act in Section 5. For example, were the trustee to invest in a second mortgage on a piece of real property owned by the trustee, the investment would be wrongful on account of the trustee's breach of the duty to abstain from self-dealing, even though the investment would no longer automatically offend the former categoric restriction against fiduciary investments in junior mortgages.

Professional fiduciaries. The distinction taken in subsection (f) between amateur and professional trustees is familiar law. The prudent investor standard applies to a range of fiduciaries, from the most sophisticated professional investment management firms and corporate fiduciaries, to family members of minimal experience. Because the standard of prudence is relational, it follows that the standard for professional trustees is the standard of prudent professionals; for amateurs, it is the standard of prudent amateurs. * * * Case law strongly supports the concept of the higher standard of care for the trustee representing itself to be expert or professional. * * *

The Drafting Committee declined the suggestion that the Act should create an exception to the prudent investor rule (or to the diversification requirement of Section 3) in the case of smaller trusts. The Committee believes that subsections (b) and (c) of the Act emphasize factors that are sensitive to the traits of small trusts; and that subsection (f) adjusts helpfully for the distinction between professional and amateur trusteeship. Furthermore, it is always open to the settlor of a trust under Section 1(b) of the Act to reduce the trustee's standard of care if the settlor deems such a step appropriate. * * *

Section 3. Diversification.

A trustee shall diversify the investments of the trust unless the trustee reasonably determines that, because of special circumstances, the purposes of the trust are better served without diversifying.

Comment

The language of this section derives from Restatement of Trusts 2d § 228 (1959). ERISA insists upon a comparable rule for pension trusts. ERISA § 404(a)(1)(C), 29 U.S.C. § 1104(a)(1)(C). Case law overwhelmingly supports the duty to diversify. * * *

The 1992 Restatement of Trusts takes the significant step of integrating the diversification requirement into the concept of prudent investing. Section 227(b) of the 1992 Restatement treats diversification as one of the fundamental elements of prudent investing, replacing the separate section 228 of the Restatement of Trusts 2d. The message of the 1992 Restatement, carried forward in Section 3 of this Act, is that prudent investing ordinarily requires diversification.

Circumstances can, however, overcome the duty to diversify. For example, if a tax-sensitive trust owns an underdiversified block of low-basis securities, the tax costs of recognizing the gain may outweigh the advantages of diversifying the holding. The wish to retain a family business is another situation in which the purposes of the trust sometimes override the conventional duty to diversify.

Rationale for diversification. "Diversification reduces risk . . . [because] stock price movements are not uniform. They are imperfectly correlated. This means that if one holds a well diversified portfolio, the gains in one investment will cancel out the losses in another." Jonathan R. Macey, An Introduction to Modern Financial Theory 20 (American College of Trust and Estate Counsel Foundation, 1991). For example, during the Arab oil embargo of 1973, international oil stocks suffered declines, but the shares of domestic oil producers and coal companies benefitted. Holding a broad enough portfolio allowed the investor to set off, to some extent, the losses associated with the embargo.

Modern portfolio theory divides risk into the categories of "compensated" and "uncompensated" risk. The risk of owning shares in a mature and well-managed company in a settled industry is less than the risk of owning shares in a start-up high-technology venture. The investor requires a higher expected return to induce the investor to bear the greater risk of disappointment associated with the start-up firm. This is compensated risk—the firm pays the investor for bearing the risk. By contrast, nobody pays the investor for owning too few stocks. The investor who owned only international oils in 1973 was running a risk that could have been reduced by having configured the portfolio differently—to include investments in different industries. This is uncompensated risk—nobody pays the investor for owning shares in too few industries and too few companies. Risk that can be eliminated by adding different stocks (or bonds) is uncompensated risk. The object of diversification is to minimize this uncompensated risk of having too few investments. "As long as stock prices do not move exactly together, the risk of a diversified portfolio will be less than the average risk of the separate holdings." R.A. Brealey, An Introduction to Risk and Return from Common Stocks 103 (2d ed. 1983).

There is no automatic rule for identifying how much diversification is enough. * * *

Diversifying by pooling. It is difficult for a small trust fund to diversify thoroughly by constructing its own portfolio of individually selected investments. Transaction costs such as the round-lot (100 share) trading economies make it relatively expensive for a small investor to assemble a broad enough portfolio to minimize uncompensated risk. For this reason, pooled investment vehicles have become the main mechanism for facilitating diversification for the investment needs of smaller trusts.

Most states have legislation authorizing common trust funds * * * .

Fiduciary investing in mutual funds. Trusts can also achieve diversification by investing in mutual funds. * * *

Section 4. Duties at Inception of Trusteeship.

Within a reasonable time after accepting a trusteeship or receiving trust assets, a trustee shall review the trust assets and make and implement decisions concerning the retention and disposition of assets, in order to bring the trust portfolio into compliance with the purposes, terms, distribution requirements, and other circumstances of the trust, and with the requirements of this [Act].

Comment

Section 4, requiring the trustee to dispose of unsuitable assets within a reasonable time, is old law * * * .

The question of what period of time is reasonable turns on the totality of factors affecting the asset and the trust. * * *

The criteria and circumstances identified in Section 2 of this Act as bearing upon the prudence of decisions to invest and manage trust assets also pertain to the prudence of decisions to retain or dispose of inception assets under this section.

Section 5. Loyalty.

A trustee shall invest and manage the trust assets solely in the interest of the beneficiaries.

Comment

The duty of loyalty is perhaps the most characteristic rule of trust law, requiring the trustee to act exclusively for the beneficiaries, as opposed to acting for the trustee's own interest or that of third parties. * * *

The concept that the duty of prudence in trust administration, especially in investing and managing trust assets, entails adherence to the duty of loyalty is familiar. ERISA § 404(a)(1)(B), 29 U.S.C. § 1104(a)(1)(B), extracted in the Comment to Section 1 of this Act, effectively merges the requirements of prudence and loyalty. A fiduciary cannot be prudent in the conduct of investment functions if the fiduciary is sacrificing the interests of the beneficiaries.

The duty of loyalty is not limited to settings entailing self-dealing or conflict of interest in which the trustee would benefit personally from the trust. * * *

No form of so-called "social investing" is consistent with the duty of loyalty if the investment activity entails sacrificing the interests of trust beneficiaries—for example, by accepting below-market returns—in favor of the interests of the persons supposedly benefitted by pursuing the particular social cause. * * * Commentators supporting social investing tend to concede the overriding force of the duty of loyalty. They argue instead that particular schemes of social investing may not result in below-market returns. * * * In 1994 the Department of Labor issued an Interpretive Bulletin reviewing its prior analysis of social investing questions and reiterating that pension trust fiduciaries may invest only in conformity with the prudence and loyalty standards of ERISA §§ 403–404. Interpretive Bulletin 94–1, 59 Fed. Regis. 32606 (Jun. 22, 1994), to be codified as 29 CFR § 2509.94–1. The Bulletin reminds fiduciary investors that they are prohibited from "subordinat[ing] the interests of participants and beneficiaries in their retirement income to unrelated objectives."

Section 6. Impartiality.

If a trust has two or more beneficiaries, the trustee shall act impartially in investing and managing the trust assets, taking into account any differing interests of the beneficiaries.

Comment

The duty of impartiality derives from the duty of loyalty. When the trustee owes duties to more than one beneficiary, loyalty requires the trustee to respect the interests of all the beneficiaries. Prudence in investing and administration requires the trustee to take account of the interests of all the beneficiaries for whom the trustee is acting, especially the conflicts between the interests of beneficiaries interested in income and those interested in principal.

* * * Multiple beneficiaries may be beneficiaries in succession (such as life and remainder interests) or beneficiaries with simultaneous interests (as when the income interest in a trust is being divided among several beneficiaries).

The trustee's duty of impartiality commonly affects the conduct of investment and management functions in the sphere of principal and income allocations. This Act prescribes no regime for allocating receipts and expenses. * * *

Section 7. Investment Costs.

In investing and managing trust assets, a trustee may only incur costs that are appropriate and reasonable in relation to the assets, the purposes of the trust, and the skills of the trustee.

Comment

Wasting beneficiaries' money is imprudent. In devising and implementing strategies for the investment and management of trust assets, trustees are obliged to minimize costs. * * *

Section 8. Reviewing Compliance.

Compliance with the prudent investor rule is determined in light of the facts and circumstances existing at the time of a trustee's decision or action and not by hindsight.

Comment

* * * Trustees are not insurers. Not every investment or management decision will turn out in the light of hindsight to have been successful. Hindsight is not the relevant standard. In the language of law and economics, the standard is ex ante, not ex post.

Section 9. Delegation of Investment and Management Functions.

(a) A trustee may delegate investment and management functions that a prudent trustee of comparable skills could properly delegate under the circumstances. The trustee shall exercise reasonable care, skill, and caution in:

(1) selecting an agent;

(2) establishing the scope and terms of the delegation, consistent with the purposes and terms of the trust; and

(3)   periodically reviewing the agent's actions in order to monitor the agent's performance and compliance with the terms of the delegation.

(b)   In performing a delegated function, an agent owes a duty to the trust to exercise reasonable care to comply with the terms of the delegation.

(c)   A trustee who complies with the requirements of subsection (a) is not liable to the beneficiaries or to the trust for the decisions or actions of the agent to whom the function was delegated.

(d)   By accepting the delegation of a trust function from the trustee of a trust that is subject to the law of this State, an agent submits to the jurisdiction of the courts of this State.

Comment

This section of the Act reverses the much-criticized rule that forbad trustees to delegate investment and management functions. * * *

Former law. The former nondelegation rule survived into the 1959 Restatement * * * .

The modern trend to favor delegation. The trend of subsequent legislation, culminating in the Restatement of Trusts 3d: Prudent Investor Rule, has been strongly hostile to the nondelegation rule. * * *

ERISA's delegation rule. The Employee Retirement Income Security Act of 1974, the federal statute that prescribes fiduciary standards for investing the assets of pension and employee benefit plans, allows a pension or employee benefit plan to provide that "authority to manage, acquire or dispose of assets of the plan is delegated to one or more investment managers. . . ." ERISA § 403(a)(2), 29 U.S.C. § 1103(a)(2). * * *

The delegation rule of the 1992 Restatement. The Restatement of Trusts 3d: Prudent Investor Rule (1992) repeals the nondelegation rule * * * .

Protecting the beneficiary against unreasonable delegation. There is an intrinsic tension in trust law between granting trustees broad powers that facilitate flexible and efficient trust administration, on the one hand, and protecting trust beneficiaries from the misuse of such powers on the other hand. A broad set of trustees' powers, such as those found in most lawyer-drafted instruments * * * permits the trustee to act vigorously and expeditiously to maximize the interests of the beneficiaries in a variety of transactions and administrative settings. Trust law relies upon the duties of loyalty and prudent administration, and upon procedural safeguards such as periodic accounting and the availability of judicial oversight, to prevent the misuse of these powers. Delegation, which is a species of trustee power, raises the same tension. If the trustee delegates effectively, the beneficiaries obtain the advantage of the agent's specialized investment skills or whatever other attributes induced the trustee to delegate. But if the trustee delegates to a knave or an incompetent, the delegation can work harm upon the beneficiaries.

Section 9 of the Uniform Prudent Investor Act is designed to strike the appropriate balance between the advantages and the hazards of delegation. Section 9 authorizes delegation under the limitations of subsections (a) and (b). Section 9(a) imposes duties of care, skill, and caution on the trustee in selecting the agent, in establishing the terms of the delegation, and in reviewing the agent's compliance.

The trustee's duties of care, skill, and caution in framing the terms of the delegation should protect the beneficiary against overbroad delegation. For example, a trustee could not prudently agree to an investment management agreement containing an exculpation clause that leaves the trust without recourse against reckless mismanagement. * * *

Although subsection (c) of the Act exonerates the trustee from personal responsibility for the agent's conduct when the delegation satisfies the standards of subsection 9(a), subsection 9(b) makes the agent responsible to the trust. The beneficiaries of the trust can, therefore, rely upon the trustee to enforce the terms of the delegation.

Costs. The duty to minimize costs that is articulated in Section 7 of this Act applies to delegation as well as to other aspects of fiduciary investing. In deciding whether to delegate, the trustee must balance the projected benefits against the likely costs. Similarly, in deciding how to delegate, the trustee must take costs into account. The trustee must be alert to protect the beneficiary from "double dipping." If, for example, the trustee's regular compensation schedule presupposes that the trustee will conduct the investment management function, it should ordinarily follow that the trustee will lower its fee when delegating the investment function to an outside manager.

Section 10. Language Invoking Standard of [Act].

The following terms or comparable language in the provisions of a trust, unless otherwise limited or modified, authorizes any investment or strategy permitted under this [Act]: "investments permissible by law for investment of trust funds," "legal investments," "authorized investments," "using the judgment and care under the circumstances then prevailing that persons of prudence, discretion, and intelligence exercise in the management of their own affairs, not in regard to speculation but in regard to the permanent disposition of their funds, considering the probable income as well as the probable safety of their capital," "prudent man rule," "prudent trustee rule," "prudent person rule," and "prudent investor rule."

Comment

This provision * * * is meant to facilitate incorporation of the Act by means of the formulaic language commonly used in trust instruments.

Section 11. Application to Existing Trusts. [omitted]

Section 12. Uniformity of Application and Construction. [omitted]

Section 13. Short Title.

This [Act] may be cited as the "[Name of Enacting State] Uniform Prudent Investor Act."

Section 14. Severability. [omitted]

Section 15. Effective Date. [omitted]

Section 16. Repeals. [omitted]

UNIFORM REAL PROPERTY TRANSFER ON DEATH ACT*

Section 1. Short Title.

This [act] may be cited as the Uniform Real Property Transfer on Death Act.

Section 2. Definitions.

In this [act]:

(1) "Beneficiary" means a person that receives property under a transfer on death deed.

(2) "Designated beneficiary" means a person designated to receive property in a transfer on death deed.

(3) "Joint owner" means an individual who owns property concurrently with one or more other individuals with a right of survivorship. The term includes a joint tenant[,][and] [owner of community property with a right of survivorship[,][and tenant by the entirety]. The term does not include a tenant in common [or owner of community property without a right of survivorship].

(4) "Person" means an individual, corporation, business trust, estate, trust, partnership, limited liability company, association, joint venture, public corporation, government or governmental subdivision, agency, or instrumentality, or any other legal or commercial entity.

(5) "Property" means an interest in real property located in this state which is transferable on the death of the owner.

(6) "Transfer on death deed" means a deed authorized under this [act].

---

* Copyright © 2009 by the National Conference of Commissioners on Uniform State Laws.

(7) "Transferor" means an individual who makes a transfer on death deed.

Section 3. Applicability.

This [act] applies to a transfer on death deed made before, on, or after [the effective date of this [act]] by a transferor dying on or after [the effective date of this [act]].

Section 4. Nonexclusivity.

This [act] does not affect any method of transferring property otherwise permitted under the law of this state.

Section 5. Transfer on Death Deed Authorized.

An individual may transfer property to one or more beneficiaries effective at the transferor's death by a transfer on death deed.

Section 6. Transfer on Death Deed Revocable.

A transfer on death deed is revocable even if the deed or another instrument contains a contrary provision.

Section 7. Transfer on Death Deed Nontestamentary.

A transfer on death deed is nontestamentary.

Section 8. Capacity of Transferor.

The capacity required to make or revoke a transfer on death deed is the same as the capacity required to make a will.

Section 9. Requirements.

A transfer on death deed:

(1) except as otherwise provided in paragraph (2), must contain the essential elements and formalities of a properly recordable inter vivos deed;

(2) must state that the transfer to the designated beneficiary is to occur at the transferor's death; and

(3) must be recorded before the transferor's death in the public records in [the office of the county recorder of deeds] of the [county] where the property is located.

Section 10. Notice, Delivery, Acceptance, Consideration Not Required.

A transfer on death deed is effective without:

(1) notice or delivery to or acceptance by the designated beneficiary during the transferor's life; or

(2) consideration.

Section 11. Revocation by Instrument Authorized; Revocation by Act Not Permitted.

(a) Subject to subsection (b), an instrument is effective to revoke a recorded transfer on death deed, or any part of it, only if the instrument:

(1) is one of the following:

(A) a transfer on death deed that revokes the deed or part of the deed expressly or by inconsistency;

(B) an instrument of revocation that expressly revokes the deed or part of the deed; or

(C) an inter vivos deed that expressly revokes the transfer on death deed or part of the deed; and

(2) is acknowledged by the transferor after the acknowledgment of the deed being revoked and recorded before the transferor's death in the public records in [the office of the county recorder of deeds] of the [county] where the deed is recorded.

(b) If a transfer on death deed is made by more than one transferor:

(1) revocation by a transferor does not affect the deed as to the interest of another transferor; and

(2) a deed of joint owners is revoked only if it is revoked by all of the living joint owners.

(c) After a transfer on death deed is recorded, it may not be revoked by a revocatory act on the deed.

(d) This section does not limit the effect of an inter vivos transfer of the property.

Section 12. Effect of Transfer on Death Deed During Transferor's Life.

During a transferor's life, a transfer on death deed does not:

(1) affect an interest or right of the transferor or any other owner, including the right to transfer or encumber the property;

(2) affect an interest or right of a transferee, even if the transferee has actual or constructive notice of the deed;

(3) affect an interest or right of a secured or unsecured creditor or future creditor of the transferor, even if the creditor has actual or constructive notice of the deed;

(4) affect the transferor's or designated beneficiary's eligibility for any form of public assistance;

(5) create a legal or equitable interest in favor of the designated beneficiary; or

(6) subject the property to claims or process of a creditor of the designated beneficiary.

Section 13. Effect of Transfer on Death Deed at Transferor's Death.

(a) Except as otherwise provided in the transfer on death deed[,][or] in this section[,][or in [cite state statutes on antilapse, revocation by divorce or homicide, survival and simultaneous death, and elective share, if applicable to nonprobate transfers]], on the death of the transferor, the following rules apply to property that is the subject of a transfer on death deed and owned by the transferor at death:

(1) Subject to paragraph (2), the interest in the property is transferred to the designated beneficiary in accordance with the deed.

(2) The interest of a designated beneficiary is contingent on the designated beneficiary surviving the transferor. The interest of a designated beneficiary that fails to survive the transferor lapses.

(3) Subject to paragraph (4), concurrent interests are transferred to the beneficiaries in equal and undivided shares with no right of survivorship.

(4) If the transferor has identified two or more designated beneficiaries to receive concurrent interests in the property, the share of one which lapses or fails for any reason is transferred to the other, or to the others in proportion to the interest of each in the remaining part of the property held concurrently.

(b) Subject to [cite state recording act], a beneficiary takes the property subject to all conveyances, encumbrances, assignments, contracts, mortgages, liens, and other interests to which the property is subject at the transferor's death. For purposes of this subsection and [cite state recording act], the recording of the transfer on death deed is deemed to have occurred at the transferor's death.

(c)   If a transferor is a joint owner and is:

(1)   survived by one or more other joint owners, the property that is the subject of a transfer on death deed belongs to the surviving joint owner or owners with right of survivorship; or

(2)   the last surviving joint owner, the transfer on death deed is effective.

(d)   A transfer on death deed transfers property without covenant or warranty of title even if the deed contains a contrary provision.

Section 14. Disclaimer.

A beneficiary may disclaim all or part of the beneficiary's interest as provided by [cite state statute or the Uniform Disclaimer of Property Interests Act].

Section 15. Liability for Creditor Claims and Statutory Allowances.

Alternative A

A beneficiary of a transfer on death deed is liable for an allowed claim against the transferor's probate estate and statutory allowances to a surviving spouse and children to the extent provided in [cite state statute or Section 6–102 of the Uniform Probate Code].

Alternative B

(a)   To the extent the transferor's probate estate is insufficient to satisfy an allowed claim against the estate or a statutory allowance to a surviving spouse or child, the estate may enforce the liability against property transferred at the transferor's death by a transfer on death deed.

(b)   If more than one property is transferred by one or more transfer on death deeds, the liability under subsection (a) is apportioned among the properties in proportion to their net values at the transferor's death.

(c)   A proceeding to enforce the liability under this section must be commenced not later than [18 months] after the transferor's death.

End of Alternatives

[Section 16. Optional Form of Transfer on Death Deed.

The following form may be used to create a transfer on death deed. The other sections of this [act] govern the effect of this or any other instrument used to create a transfer on death deed:

(front of form)

REVOCABLE TRANSFER ON DEATH DEED

NOTICE TO OWNER

You should carefully read all information on the other side of this form. You May Want to Consult a Lawyer Before Using This Form.

This form must be recorded before your death, or it will not be effective.

IDENTIFYING INFORMATION

Owner or Owners Making This Deed:

_____   _____
Printed name   Mailing address

_____   _____
Printed name   Mailing address
Legal description of the property:

_____   _____

PRIMARY BENEFICIARY

I designate the following beneficiary if the beneficiary survives me.

_____   _____
Printed name   Mailing address, if available

ALTERNATE BENEFICIARY—Optional

If my primary beneficiary does not survive me, I designate the following alternate beneficiary if that beneficiary survives me.

_____   _____
Printed name   Mailing address, if available

TRANSFER ON DEATH

At my death, I transfer my interest in the described property to the beneficiaries as designated above.

Before my death, I have the right to revoke this deed.

SIGNATURE OF OWNER OR OWNERS MAKING THIS DEED

_____   [(SEAL)] _____
Signature   Date

_____   [(SEAL)] _____
Signature   Date

ACKNOWLEDGMENT

(insert acknowledgment for deed here)

(back of form)

COMMON QUESTIONS ABOUT THE USE OF THIS FORM

What does the Transfer on Death (TOD) deed do? When you die, this deed transfers the described property, subject to any liens or mortgages (or other encumbrances) on the property at your death. Probate is not required. The TOD deed has no effect until you die. You can revoke it at any time. You are also free to transfer the property to someone else during your lifetime. If you do not own any interest in the property when you die, this deed will have no effect.

How do I make a TOD deed? Complete this form. Have it acknowledged before a notary public or other individual authorized by law to take acknowledgments. Record the form in each [county] where any part of the property is located. The form has no effect unless it is acknowledged and recorded before your death.

Is the "legal description" of the property necessary? Yes.

How do I find the "legal description" of the property? This information may be on the deed you received when you became an owner of the property. This information may also be available in [the office of the county recorder of deeds] for the [county] where the property is located. If you are not absolutely sure, consult a lawyer.

Can I change my mind before I record the TOD deed? Yes. If you have not yet recorded the deed and want to change your mind, simply tear up or otherwise destroy the deed.

How do I "record" the TOD deed? Take the completed and acknowledged form to [the office of the county recorder of deeds] of the [county] where the property is located. Follow the instructions given by the [county recorder] to make the form part of the official property records. If the property is in more than one [county], you should record the deed in each [county].

Can I later revoke the TOD deed if I change my mind? Yes. You can revoke the TOD deed. No one, including the beneficiaries, can prevent you from revoking the deed.

How do I revoke the TOD deed after it is recorded? There are three ways to revoke a recorded TOD deed: (1) Complete and acknowledge a revocation form, and record it in each [county] where the property is located. (2) Complete and acknowledge a new TOD deed that disposes of the same property, and record it in each [county] where the property is located. (3) Transfer the property to someone else during your lifetime by a recorded deed that expressly revokes the TOD deed. You may not revoke the TOD deed by will.

I am being pressured to complete this form. What should I do? Do not complete this form under pressure. Seek help from a trusted family member, friend, or lawyer.

Do I need to tell the beneficiaries about the TOD deed? No, but it is recommended. Secrecy can cause later complications and might make it easier for others to commit fraud.

I have other questions about this form. What should I do? This form is designed to fit some but not all situations. If you have other questions, you are encouraged to consult a lawyer.]

[Section 17. Optional Form of Revocation.

The following form may be used to create an instrument of revocation under this [act]. The other sections of this [act] govern the effect of this or any other instrument used to revoke a transfer on death deed.

(front of form)

REVOCATION OF TRANSFER ON DEATH DEED

NOTICE TO OWNER

This revocation must be recorded before you die or it will not be effective. This revocation is effective only as to the interests in the property of owners who sign this revocation.

IDENTIFYING INFORMATION

Owner or Owners of Property Making This Revocation:

_____   _____
Printed name   Mailing address

_____   _____
Printed name   Mailing address

Legal description of the property:

_____

REVOCATION

    I revoke all my previous transfers of this property by transfer on death deed.

SIGNATURE OF OWNER OR OWNERS MAKING THIS REVOCATION

_____ [(SEAL)] _____
Signature   Date
_____ [(SEAL)] _____
Signature   Date

ACKNOWLEDGMENT

(insert acknowledgment here)

(back of form)

COMMON QUESTIONS ABOUT THE USE OF THIS FORM

    <u>How do I use this form to revoke a Transfer on Death (TOD) deed?</u> Complete this form. Have it acknowledged before a notary public or other individual authorized to take acknowledgments. Record the form in the public records in [the office of the county recorder of deeds] of each [county] where the property is located. The form must be acknowledged and recorded before your death or it has no effect.

    <u>How do I find the "legal description" of the property?</u> This information may be on the TOD deed. It may also be available in [the office of the county recorder of deeds] for the [county] where the property is located. If you are not absolutely sure, consult a lawyer.

    <u>How do I "record" the form?</u> Take the completed and acknowledged form to [the office of the county recorder of deeds] of the [county] where the property is located. Follow the instructions given by the [county recorder] to make the form part of the official property records. If the property is located in more than one [county], you should record the form in each of those [counties].

    <u>I am being pressured to complete this form. What should I do?</u> Do not complete this form under pressure. Seek help from a trusted family member, friend, or lawyer.

    <u>I have other questions about this form. What should I do?</u> This form is designed to fit some but not all situations. If you have other questions, consult a lawyer.]

Section 18. Uniformity of Application and Construction. [omitted]

Section 19. Relation to Electronic Signatures in Global and National Commerce Act. [omitted]

Section 20. Repeals. [omitted]

Section 21. Effective Date. [omitted]

UNIFORM SIMULTANEOUS DEATH ACT (1940)*

PREFATORY NOTE

After more than five years study a Uniform Simultaneous Death Act has been approved by the National Conference of Commissioners on Uniform State Laws and recommended to the various legislatures for adoption. Two considerations justify the hope that the Act which is presented herewith will be received favorably by the legislative bodies of the various States. It may be a sad commentary, but the pace of modern living with its multiple forms of transportation has caused the instances of simultaneous death to occur with much greater frequency than in the past. More and more therefore courts will be called upon to administer the estates of persons who have died under circumstances that there is no evidence of survivorship, and it is desirable to have a workable and uniform rule to apply in such instances. The second consideration which should recommend this Act to the various legislative bodies is the unsatisfactory variety of methods that have been devised either as a result of jurisprudence or the result of legislation to administer this troublesome legal situation. Some States have set arbitrary presumptions which are employed by the courts to determine the devolution of property. In other States there is the "common law rule" which indulges no presumption one way or the other and leaves the matter to the respective claimants to prove survivorship. Both situations seem to be unrealistic. Prescribed presumptions frequently ignore the facts of life. For instance in some States it is presumed (conclusively) that an adult in good health survives a minor child or infant. If the minor happened to be the son or daughter of the adult it is more reasonable to suppose that the adult would have used every expedient to protect the child even at the sacrifice of his own life. In those States where there is no presumption whatever indulged courts are faced with an anachronism. The reason for the difficulty of administration is that it is impossible to know which of the persons has survived. Yet the "common law rule" in effect says that the person who claims by virtue of an alleged survivorship must prove the survivorship which is tantamount to demanding the impossible.

The theory of the present Act makes no effort whatever to resolve the unresoluble. The formula is a simple one and easily applied. The theory of the present Act is that as to the property of each person he is presumed to be the survivor and it is administered accordingly.

Perhaps a word ought to be said with respect to Section four, which deals with contracts of insurance. The Act provides that when the insured and the beneficiary in a policy of life or accident insurance have died and there is no sufficient evidence that they have died otherwise than simultaneously the proceeds of the policy shall be distributed as if the insured had survived. Obviously this section creates a conclusive presumption. The special circumstances seem to justify the creation of a presumption relative to the survivorship of the insured or beneficiary. By providing that the insured presumably survived it is thought that the result will most nearly approximate the intention of the real party in interest. If it does not, he is at liberty to provide otherwise in the contract of insurance.

Section 1. No Sufficient Evidence of Survivorship.

Where the title to property or the devolution thereof depends upon priority of death and there is no sufficient evidence that the persons have died otherwise than simultaneously, the property of each person shall be disposed of as if he had survived, except as provided otherwise in this act.

Section 2. Survival of Beneficiaries.

If property is so disposed of that the right of a beneficiary to succeed to any interest therein is conditional upon his surviving another person, and both persons die, and there is no sufficient evidence that the two have died otherwise than simultaneously, the beneficiary shall be deemed not to have survived. If there is no sufficient evidence that two or more beneficiaries have died otherwise than simultaneously and property has been disposed of in such a way that at the time of their death each of such beneficiaries would have been entitled to the property if he had survived the others, the property shall be divided into as many equal portions as there were such beneficiaries and these portions shall be distributed respectively to those who would have taken in the event that each of such beneficiaries had survived.

Section 3. Joint Tenants or Tenants by the Entirety.

Where there is no sufficient evidence that two joint tenants or tenants by the entirety have died otherwise than simultaneously the property so held shall be distributed one-half as if one had survived and one-half as if the other had survived. If there are more than two joint tenants and all of them have so died the property thus distributed shall be in the proportion that one bears to the whole number of joint tenants.

The term "joint tenants" includes owners of property held under circumstances which entitled one or more to the whole of the property on the death of the other or others.

Section 4. Community Property.

Where a husband and wife have died, leaving community property, and there is no sufficient evidence that they have died otherwise than simultaneously, one-half of all the community property shall pass as if the husband had survived [and as if said one-half were his separate property,] and the other one-half thereof shall pass as if the wife had survived [and as if said other one-half were her separate property.]

Section 5. Insurance Policies.

Where the insured and the beneficiary in a policy of life or accident insurance have died and there is no sufficient evidence that they have died otherwise than simultaneously the proceeds of the policy shall be distributed as if the insured had survived the beneficiary, [except if the policy is community property of the insured and his spouse, and there is no alternative beneficiary except the estate or personal representatives of the insured, the proceeds shall be distributed as community property under Section 4.]

Section 6. Act Does Not Apply if Decedent Provides Otherwise.

This act shall not apply in the case of wills, living trusts, deeds, or contracts of insurance, or any other situation where provision is made for distribution of property different from the provisions of this act, or where provision is made for a presumption as to survivorship which results in a distribution of property different from that here provided.

Section 7. Uniformity of Interpretation. [omitted]

Section 8. Short Title.

This Act may be cited as the Uniform Simultaneous Death Act.

Section 9. Repeal. [omitted]

Section 10. Severability. [omitted]

Section 11. Time of Taking Effect. [omitted]

UNIFORM STATUTORY RULE AGAINST PERPETUITIES*

PREFATORY NOTE

The Uniform Statutory Rule Against Perpetuities (Statutory Rule) alters the Common-law Rule Against Perpetuities by installing a workable wait-and-see element. * * *

Under the Common-law Rule Against Perpetuities (Common-law Rule), the validity or invalidity of a nonvested property interest is determined, once and for always, on the basis of the facts existing *when the interest was created*. Like most rules of property law, the Common-law Rule has two sides— a validating side and an invalidating side. Both sides are evident from, but not explicit in, John Chipman Gray's formulation of the Common-law Rule:

No [nonvested property] interest is good unless it must vest, if at all, not later than 21 years after some life in being at the creation of the interest.

J. Gray, The Rule Against Perpetuities § 201 (4th ed. 1942).

With its validating and invalidating sides explicitly separated, the Common-law Rule is as follows:

Validating Side of the Common-law Rule: A nonvested property interest is valid when it is created (initially valid) if it is then *certain* to vest or terminate (fail to vest)—one or the other—no later than 21 years after the death of an individual then alive.

Invalidating Side of the Common-law Rule: A nonvested property interest is invalid when it is created (initially invalid) if there is no such certainty.

Notice that the invalidating side focuses on a lack of *certainty*, which means that invalidity under the Common-law Rule is *not* dependent on *actual* post-creation events but only on *possible* post-creation events. Since *actual* post-creation events are irrelevant at common law, even those that are known at the time of the lawsuit, interests that are likely to, and in fact would (if given the chance), vest well within the period of a life in being plus 21 years are nevertheless invalid if at the time of the interest's creation there was a possibility, no matter how remote, that they might not have done so. This is what makes the *invalidating* side of the Common-law Rule so harsh: It can invalidate interests on the ground of post-creation events that, though possible, are extremely unlikely to happen and in actuality almost never do happen, if ever. Reasonable dispositions can be rendered invalid because of such remote possibilities as a woman, after menopause, giving birth to (or adopting) additional children (see Example (7) in the Comment to Section 1), the probate of an estate taking more than 21 years to complete (see Example (8) in the Comment to Section 1), or a married man or woman in his or her middle or late years later becoming remarried to a person born after the testator's death (see

---

Example (9) in the Comment to Section 1). None of these dispositions offends the public policy of preventing people from tying up property in long term or even perpetual family trusts. In fact, each disposition seems quite reasonable and violates the Common-law Rule on technical grounds only.

The Wait-and-See Reform Movement. The prospect of invalidating such interests led some decades ago to thoughts about reforming the Common-law Rule. Since the chains of events that make such interests invalid are so unlikely to happen, it was rather natural to propose that the criterion be shifted from *possible* post-creation events to *actual* post-creation events. Instead of invalidating an interest because of what *might* happen, waiting to see what *does* happen seemed then and still seems now to be more sensible.

The Uniform Statutory Rule Against Perpetuities follows the lead of the American Law Institute's Restatement (Second) of Property (Donative Transfers) § 1.3 (1983) in adopting the approach of waiting to see what does happen. This approach is known as the wait-and-see method of perpetuity reform.

In line with the Restatement (Second), the Uniform Act does not alter the *validating* side of the Common-law Rule. Consequently, dispositions that would have been valid under the Common-law Rule, *including those that are rendered valid because of a perpetuity saving clause*, remain valid as of their creation. *The practice of lawyers who competently draft trusts and other property arrangements for their clients is undisturbed.*

Under the Uniform Act, as well as under the Restatement (Second), the wait-and-see element is applied only to interests that fall under the *invalidating* side of the Common-law Rule. Interests that would be invalid at common law are saved from being rendered *initially invalid*. They are, as it were, given a second chance: Such interests are valid if they actually vest within the permissible vesting period, and become invalid only if they remain in existence but still nonvested at the expiration of the permissible vesting period.

In consequence, the Uniform Act recasts the validating and invalidating sides of the Rule Against Perpetuities as follows:

Validating Side of the Statutory Rule: A nonvested property interest is initially valid if, when it is created, it is then *certain* to vest or terminate (fail to vest) no later than 21 years after the death of an individual then alive. A nonvested property interest that is not *initially* valid is not necessarily invalid. Such an interest is valid if it vests within the permissible vesting period after its creation.

Invalidating Side of the Statutory Rule: A nonvested property interest that is not *initially* valid becomes invalid (and, as explained later, subject to reformation to make it valid) if it neither vests nor terminates within the permissible vesting period after its creation.

Shifting the focus from possible to actual post-creation events has great attraction. It eliminates the harsh consequences of the Common-law Rule's approach of invalidating interests because of what *might* happen, without sacrificing the basic policy goal of preventing property from being tied up for too long a time in very long term or even perpetual family trusts or other arrangements.

One of the early objections to wait-and-see should be mentioned at this point, because it has long since been put to rest. It was once argued that wait-and-see could cause harm because it puts the validity of property interests in abeyance—no one could determine whether an interest was valid or not. This argument has been shown to be false. Keep in mind that the wait-and-see element is applied only to interests that would be invalid were it not for wait-and-see. Such interests, otherwise invalid, are always nonvested future interests. It is now understood that wait-and-see does nothing more than affect that type of future interest with an *additional* contingency. To vest, the other contingencies must not only be satisfied—they must be satisfied within a certain period of time. *If* that period of time—the permissible vesting period—is easily determined, as it is under the Uniform Act, then the additional contingency causes no more uncertainty in the state of the title than would have been the case had the additional contingency been originally expressed in the governing instrument. It should also be noted that only the status of the affected future interest in the trust or other property arrangement is deferred. In the interim, the other interests, such as the interests of current income beneficiaries, are carried out in the normal course without obstruction.

The Permissible Vesting Period. Despite its attraction, wait-and-see has not been widely adopted. The greatest controversy over wait-and-see concerns how to determine the permissible vesting period, the time allotted for the contingencies attached to a nonvested property interest to be validly worked out to a final resolution.

The wait-and-see reform movement has always proceeded on the unexamined assumption that the permissible vesting period should be determined by reference to so-called measuring lives who are in being at the creation of the interest; the permissible vesting period under this assumption expires 21 years after the death of the last surviving measuring life. The controversy has raged over who the measuring lives should be and how the law should identify them. Competing methods have been advanced, rather stridently on occasion.

The Drafting Committee of the Uniform Act began its work in 1984 operating on the same basic assumption—that the permissible vesting period was to be determined by reference to measuring lives. The draft presented to the Conference for first reading in the summer of 1985 utilized that method.

The Saving-Clause Principle of Wait-and-See. The measuring lives selected in that earlier draft were patterned after the measuring lives listed in the Restatement (Second), which adopts the saving-clause principle of wait-and-see. Under the saving-clause principle, the measuring lives are those individuals who might appropriately have been selected in a well-drafted perpetuity saving clause.

A perpetuity saving clause typically contains two components, the *perpetuity-period component* and the *gift-over component*. The perpetuity-period component expressly requires interests in the trust or other arrangement to vest (or terminate) no later than 21 years after the death of the last survivor of a group of individuals designated in the governing instrument by name or class. The gift-over component expressly creates a gift over that is guaranteed to vest at the expiration of the period set forth in the perpetuity-period component, but only if the interests in the trust or other arrangement have neither vested nor terminated earlier in accordance with their other terms.

In most cases, the saving clause not only avoids a violation of the Common-law Rule; it also, in a sense, over-insures the client's disposition against the gift over from ever taking effect, because the period of time determined by the perpetuity-period component provides a margin of safety. Its length is sufficient to exceed—usually by a substantial margin—the time when the interests in the trust or other arrangement actually vest (or terminate) by their own terms. The clause, therefore, is usually a formality that validates the disposition without affecting the substance of the disposition at all.

In effect, the perpetuity-period component of the saving clause constitutes a privately established wait-and-see rule. Conversely, the principle supporting the adoption and operation of wait-and-see is that it provides, in effect, a saving clause for dispositions that violate the Common-law Rule, dispositions that had they been competently drafted would have included a saving clause to begin with. This is the principle embraced by the Uniform Act and the principle reflected in the Restatement (Second). The permissible vesting period under wait-and-see is the equivalent of the perpetuity-period component of a well-conceived saving clause.

The Uniform Act and the Restatement (Second) round out the saving clause by providing the near-equivalent of a gift-over component via a provision for judicial reformation of a disposition in case the interest is still in existence and nonvested when the permissible vesting period expires.

The Permissible Vesting Period: Why the Uniform Act Foregoes the Use of Actual Measuring Lives and Uses a Proxy Instead. The Uniform Act departs from and improves on the Restatement (Second) in a very important particular. The Uniform Act foregoes the use of *actual* measuring lives and instead marks off the permissible vesting period by reference to a reasonable approximation of—a proxy for—the period of time that would, *on average*, be produced through the use of a set of actual measuring lives identified by statute and then adding the traditional 21-year tack-on period after the death of the survivor. The proxy utilized in the Uniform Act is a flat period of 90 years. The rationale for this period is discussed below.

The use of a proxy, such as the flat 90-year period utilized in the Uniform Act, is greatly to be preferred over the conventional approach of using actual measuring lives plus 21 years. The conventional approach has serious disadvantages: Wait-and-see measuring lives are difficult to describe in statutory language, and they are difficult to identify and trace so as to determine which one is the survivor and when he or she died.

Drafting statutory language that unambiguously identifies actual measuring lives under wait-and-see is immensely more difficult than drafting an actual perpetuity saving clause. An actual perpetuity saving clause can be tailored on a case-by-case basis to the terms and beneficiaries of each trust or other property arrangement. A statutory saving clause, however, cannot be redrafted for each new disposition. It must be drafted so that one size fits all. As a result of the difficulty of drafting such a one-size-fits-all clause, any list of measuring lives is likely to contain ambiguities, at least at the margin.

Quite apart from the difficulty of drafting unambiguous and uncomplicated statutory language, another serious problem connected to the actual-measuring-lives approach is that it imposes a costly administrative burden. The Common-law Rule uses the life-in-being-plus-21-years period in a way that does not require the actual tracing of individuals' lives, deaths, marriages, adoptions, and so on. Wait-and-see imposes this burden, however, if measuring lives are used to mark off the permissible vesting period. It is one thing to write a statute specifying who the measuring lives are. It is another to apply the actual-measuring-lives approach in practice. No matter what method is used in the statute for selecting the measuring lives and no matter how unambiguous the statutory language is, actual individuals must be identified as the measuring lives and their lives must be traced to determine who the survivor is and when the survivor dies. The administrative burden is increased if the measuring lives are not a static group, determined once and for all at the beginning, but instead are a rotating group. Adding to the administrative burden is the fact that the perpetuity question will often be raised for the first time long after the interest or power was created. The task of going back in time to reconstruct not only the facts existing when the interest or power was created, but facts occurring thereafter as well may not be worth the effort. In short, not only would births and deaths have to be kept track of, but adoptions, divorces, and possibly assignments and devises, etc., also, over a long period of time. Keeping track of and reconstructing these events to determine the survivor and the time of the survivor's death imposes an administrative burden wise to avoid. The proxy approach makes it feasible to do just that.

The administrative burden of tracing actual measuring lives and the possible uncertainty of their exact make-up, especially at the margin, combine to make the expiration date of the permissible vesting period less than certain in each given case. By making perpetuity challenges more costly to mount and more problematic in result, this might have the effect of allowing dead-hand control to continue, by default, well beyond the permissible vesting period. Marking off the permissible vesting period by using a proxy eliminates this possibility. The date of expiration of the permissible vesting period under the proxy adopted by the Uniform Act—a flat 90 years—is easy to determine and unmistakable.

One final point. If the use of actual measuring lives plus 21 years generated a permissible vesting period that precisely self-adjusted to each situation, there might be objection to replacing the actual-measuring-lives approach with a flat period of 90 years, which obviously cannot replicate such a function. That is not the function performed by the actual-measuring-lives approach, however. That is to say, that approach is not scientifically designed to generate a permissible vesting period that expires at a natural or logical stopping point along the continuum of each disposition, thereby mysteriously marking off the precise time before which actual vesting ought to be allowed and beyond which it ought not to be permitted. Instead, the actual-measuring-lives approach functions in a rather different way: It generates a period of time that almost always *exceeds* the time of actual vesting in cases when actual vesting ought to be allowed to occur. The actual-measuring-lives approach, therefore, performs a margin-of-safety function, and that is a function that *can* be replicated by the use of a proxy such as the flat 90-year period under the Uniform Act.

The following examples briefly demonstrate the margin-of-safety function of the actual-measuring-lives approach:

Example (1)—Corpus to Grandchildren Contingent on Reaching an Age in Excess of 21. G died, bequeathing property in trust, income in equal shares to G's children for the life of the survivor, then in equal shares to G's grandchildren, remainder in corpus to G's grandchildren who reach age 30; if none reaches 30, to a specified charity.

Example (2)—Corpus to Descendants Contingent on Surviving Last Living Grandchild. G died, bequeathing property in trust, income in equal shares to G's children for the life of the survivor, then in equal shares to G's grandchildren for the life of the survivor, and on the death of G's last living grandchild, corpus to G's descendants then living, per stirpes; if none, to a specified charity.

In both examples, assume that G's family is typical, with two children, four grandchildren, eight great-grandchildren, and so on. Assume further that one or more of the grandchildren are living at G's death, but that one or more are conceived and born thereafter.

As is typical of cases that violate the Common-law Rule and to which wait-and-see applies, these dispositions contain two revealing features: (i) they include beneficiaries born *after* the trust or other arrangement was created, and (ii) in the normal course of events, the final vesting of the interests coincides with the death of the youngest of the after-born beneficiaries (as in Example (2)) or with some event occurring during the lifetime of that youngest after-born beneficiary (such as reaching a certain age in excess of 21, as in Example (1)).

The permissible vesting period, however, is measured by reference to the lives of individuals who must be in being at the creation of the interests. This means that the key players in these dispositions—the after-born beneficiaries—cannot be counted among the measuring lives. Since the after-born beneficiaries in both of these examples are members of the same or an older generation as that of the youngest of the measuring lives, the validity of these examples fits well within the policy of the Rule. * * * In consequence, it is clear that a permissible vesting period measured by the lifetime of individuals in being at the creation of the interests plus 21 years is not scientifically designed to and does not in practice expire at the latest point when actual vesting should be allowed—on the death of the last survivor of the after-born beneficiaries. Because of its tack-on 21-year part, the period usually expires at some arbitrary time *after* that beneficiary's death. In Example (2), the period of 21 years following the death of the last survivor of the descendants who were in being at G's death is normally more than sufficient to cover the death of the last survivor of the grandchildren born after G's death.

Thus, the actual-measuring-lives approach performs a margin-of-safety function. A proxy for this period performs this function just as well. In fact, in one sense it performs it more reliably because, unlike the actual-measuring-lives approach, the flat 90-year period cannot be cut short by irrelevant events. A key element in the supposition that the tack-on 21-year part of the period is usually ample to cover the births, lives, and deaths of the after-born beneficiaries when it is appropriate to do so is that the measuring lives will live out their statistical life expectancies. This will not necessarily happen, however. They may all die prematurely, thus cutting the permissible vesting period short—possibly too short to cover these post-creation events. Plainly, no rational connection exists between the premature deaths of the measuring lives and the time properly allowable, in Example (1), for the youngest *after-born* grandchild to reach 30 or, in Example (2), for the death of that youngest *after-born* grandchild to occur. A proxy eliminates the possibility of a permissible vesting period cut short by irrelevant events.

Consequently, on this count, too, a flat 90-year period is to be preferred: It performs the same margin-of-safety function as the actual-measuring-lives approach, performs it more reliably, and performs it with a remarkable ease in administration, certainty in result, and absence of complexity as compared with the uncertainty and clumsiness of identifying and tracing actual measuring lives.

Rationale of the 90-year Permissible Vesting Period. The myriad problems associated with the actual-measuring-lives approach are swept aside by shifting away from actual measuring lives and adopting instead a 90-year permissible vesting period as representing a reasonable approximation of—a proxy for—the period of time that would, on average, be produced by identifying and tracing an actual set of measuring lives and then tacking on a 21-year period following the death of the survivor. * * *

The adoption of a flat period of 90 years rather than the use of actual measuring lives is an evolutionary step in the development and refinement of the wait-and-see doctrine. Far from revolutionary, it is well within the tradition of that doctrine. The 90-year period makes wait-and-see simple, fair, and workable. *Aggregate dead-hand control will not be increased beyond that which is already possible by competent drafting under the Common-law Rule.*

Seen as a valid approximation of the period that would be produced under the conventional survivor-of-the-measuring-lives-plus-21-years approach, and in the interest of making the law of perpetuities uniform, *jurisdictions adopting this Act are strongly urged not to adopt a period of time different from the 90-year period.*

Acceptance of the 90-year-period Approach under the Federal Generation-skipping Transfer Tax. Federal regulations, to be promulgated by the U.S. Treasury Department under the generation-skipping transfer tax, will accept the Uniform Act's 90-year period as a valid approximation of the period that, on average, would be produced by lives in being plus 21 years. * * * For further discussion of the coordination of the federal generation-skipping transfer tax with the Uniform Act, see Comment G to Section 1, infra.

The 90-year Period Will Seldom be Used Up. Nearly all trusts (or other property arrangements) will terminate by their own terms long before the 90-year permissible vesting period expires, leaving the permissible vesting period to extend unused (and ignored) into the future long after the contingencies have been resolved and the property distributed. In the unlikely event that the contingencies have not been resolved by the expiration of the permissible vesting period, Section 3 requires the disposition to be reformed by the court so that all contingencies are resolved within the permissible period.

In effect, as noted above, wait-and-see with deferred reformation operates similarly to a traditional perpetuity saving clause, which grants a margin-of-safety period measured by the lives of the transferor's descendants in being at the creation of the trust or other property arrangement (plus 21 years).

No New Learning Required. The Uniform Act does not require the practicing bar to learn a new and unfamiliar set of perpetuity principles. The effect of the Uniform Act on the planning and drafting of documents for clients should be distinguished from the effect on the resolution of actual or potential perpetuity-violation cases. The former affects many more practicing lawyers than the latter.

With respect to the planning and drafting end of the practice, the Uniform Act requires no modification of current practice and no new learning. *Lawyers can and should continue to use the same traditional perpetuity-saving/termination clause, using specified lives in being plus 21 years, they used before enactment.* Lawyers should not shift to a "later-of" type clause that purports to operate upon the later of (A) 21 years after the death of the survivor of specified lives in being or (B) 90 years. As explained in more detail in Comment G to Section 1, such a clause is not effective. If such a "later-of" clause is used in a trust that contains a violation of the Common-law Rule, Section 1(a), by itself, would render the clause ineffective, limit the maximum permissible vesting period to 90 years, and render the trust vulnerable to a reformation suit under Section 3. Section 1(e), however, saves documents using this type of clause from this fate. By limiting the effect of such clauses to the 21-year period following the death of the survivor of the specified lives, Section 1(e) in effect transforms this type of clause into a traditional perpetuity-saving/termination clause, bringing the trust into compliance with the Common-law Rule and rendering it invulnerable to a reformation suit under Section 3.

Far fewer in number are those lawyers (and judges) who have an actual or potential perpetuity-violation case. An actual or potential perpetuity-violation case will arise very infrequently under the Uniform Act. When such a case does arise, however, lawyers (or judges) involved in the case will find considerable guidance for its resolution in the detailed analysis contained in the Comments, infra.
* * *

Section 1. Statutory Rule Against Perpetuities.

(a) [Validity of Nonvested Property Interest.] A nonvested property interest is invalid unless:

> (1)   when the interest is created, it is certain to vest or terminate no later than 21 years after the death of an individual then alive; or

> (2)   the interest either vests or terminates within 90 years after its creation.

(b) [Validity of General Power of Appointment Subject to a Condition Precedent.] A general power of appointment not presently exercisable because of a condition precedent is invalid unless:

> (1)   when the power is created, the condition precedent is certain to be satisfied or become impossible to satisfy no later than 21 years after the death of an individual then alive; or

> (2)   the condition precedent either is satisfied or becomes impossible to satisfy within 90 years after its creation.

(c) [Validity of Nongeneral or Testamentary Power of Appointment.] A nongeneral power of appointment or a general testamentary power of appointment is invalid unless:

> (1)   when the power is created, it is certain to be irrevocably exercised or otherwise to terminate no later than 21 years after the death of an individual then alive; or

> (2)   the power is irrevocably exercised or otherwise terminates within 90 years after its creation.

(d) [Possibility of Post-death Child Disregarded.] In determining whether a nonvested property interest or a power of appointment is valid under subsection (a)(1), (b)(1), or (c)(1), the possibility that a child will be born to an individual after the individual's death is disregarded.

(e) [Effect of Certain "Later-of" Type Language.] If, in measuring a period from the creation of a trust or other property arrangement, language in a governing instrument (i) seeks to disallow the vesting or termination of any interest or trust beyond, (ii) seeks to postpone the vesting or termination of any interest or trust until, or (iii) seeks to operate in effect in any similar fashion upon, the later of (A) the expiration of a period of time not exceeding 21 years after the death of the survivor of specified lives in being at the creation of the trust or other property arrangement or (B) the expiration of a period of time that exceeds or might exceed 21 years after the death of the survivor of lives in being at the creation of the trust or other property arrangement, that language is inoperative to the extent it produces a period of time that exceeds 21 years after the death of the survivor of the specified lives.

Comment

* * * **Common-Law Rule Against Perpetuities Superseded.** As provided in Section 9, this Act supersedes the common-law Rule Against Perpetuities (Common-law Rule) in jurisdictions previously adhering to it (or repeals any statutory version or variation thereof previously in effect in the jurisdiction). The Common-law Rule (or the statutory version or variation thereof) is replaced by the Statutory Rule Against Perpetuities (Statutory Rule) set forth in this section and by the other provisions in this Act.

Subsidiary Doctrines Continue in Force Except to the Extent the Provisions of Act Conflict with Them. The courts in interpreting the Common-law Rule developed several subsidiary doctrines. In accordance with the general principle of statutory construction that statutes in derogation of the common law are to be construed narrowly, a subsidiary doctrine is superseded by this Act only to the extent the provisions of the Act conflict with it. A listing and discussion of such subsidiary doctrines, such as the constructional preference for validity, the all-or-nothing rule for class gifts, and the doctrine of infectious invalidity, appears later, in Part G of this Comment.

Application. Unless excluded by Section 4, the Statutory Rule Against Perpetuities (Statutory Rule) applies to nonvested property interests and to powers of appointment over property or property interests that are nongeneral powers, general testamentary powers, or general powers not presently exercisable because of a condition precedent.

The Statutory Rule does not apply to vested property interests (e.g., X's interest in Example (23) of this Comment) or to presently exercisable general powers of appointment (e.g., G's power in Example (19) of this Comment; G's power in Example (1) in the Comment to Section 2; A's power in Example (2) in the Comment to Section 2; X's power in Example (3) in the Comment to Section 2; A's noncumulative power of withdrawal in Example (4) in the Comment to Section 2).

A. GENERAL PURPOSE

Section 1 sets forth the Statutory Rule Against Perpetuities (Statutory Rule). As explained above, the Statutory Rule supersedes the Common-law Rule Against Perpetuities (Common-law Rule) or any statutory version or variation thereof.

The Common-law Rule's Validating and Invalidating Sides. The Common-law Rule Against Perpetuities is a rule of *initial* validity or invalidity. At common law, a nonvested property interest is either valid or invalid *as of its creation*. Like most rules of property law, the Common-law Rule has both a validating and an invalidating side. Both sides are derived from John Chipman Gray's formulation of the Common-law Rule:

No [nonvested property] interest is good unless it must vest, if at all, not later than 21 years after some life in being at the creation of the interest.

J. Gray, The Rule Against Perpetuities § 201 (4th ed. 1942). From this formulation, the validating and invalidating sides of the Common-law Rule are derived as follows:

Validating Side of the Common-law Rule. A nonvested property interest is valid when it is created (initially valid) if it is then *certain* to vest or terminate (fail to vest)—one or the other—no later than 21 years after the death of an individual then alive.

Invalidating Side of the Common-law Rule. A nonvested property interest is invalid when it is created (initially invalid) if there is no such certainty.

Notice that the invalidating side focuses on a lack of *certainty*, which means that invalidity under the Common-law Rule is *not* dependent on *actual* post-creation events but only on *possible* post-creation events. *Actual* post-creation events are irrelevant, even those that are known at the time of the lawsuit. It is generally recognized that the *invalidating* side of the Common-law Rule is harsh because it can invalidate interests on the ground of possible post-creation events that are extremely unlikely to happen and that in actuality almost never do happen, if ever.

The Statutory Rule Against Perpetuities. The essential difference between the Common-law Rule and its statutory replacement is that the Statutory Rule preserves the Common-law Rule's overall policy of preventing property from being tied up in unreasonably long or even perpetual family trusts or other property arrangements, while eliminating the harsh potential of the Common-law Rule. The Statutory Rule achieves this result by codifying (in slightly revised form) the validating side of the Common-law Rule and modifying the invalidating side by adopting a wait-and-see element. Under the Statutory Rule, interests that would have been initially valid at common law continue to be initially valid, but interests that would have been initially invalid at common law are invalid only if they do not actually vest or terminate within the permissible vesting period set forth in Section 1(a)(2). Thus, the Uniform Act recasts the validating and invalidating sides of the Rule Against Perpetuities as follows:

Validating Side of the Statutory Rule: A nonvested property interest is initially valid if, when it is created, it is then *certain* to vest or terminate (fail to vest)—one or the other—no later than 21 years after the death of an individual then alive. The validity of a nonvested property interest that is not *initially* valid is in abeyance. Such an interest is valid if it vests within the permissible vesting period after its creation.

Invalidating Side of the Statutory Rule: A nonvested property interest that is not *initially* valid becomes invalid (and subject to reformation under Section 3) if it neither vests nor terminates within the permissible vesting period after its creation.

As indicated, this modification of the invalidating side of the Common-law Rule is generally known as the wait-and-see method of perpetuity reform. * * *

B. SECTION 1(a)(1): NONVESTED PROPERTY INTERESTS THAT ARE INITIALLY VALID

Nonvested Property Interest. Section 1(a) sets forth the Statutory Rule Against Perpetuities with respect to nonvested property interests. A nonvested property interest (also called a contingent property interest) is a future interest in property that is subject to an unsatisfied condition precedent. In the case of a class gift, the interests of all the unborn members of the class are nonvested because they are subject to the unsatisfied condition precedent of being born. At common law, the interests of all potential class members must be valid or the class gift is invalid. As pointed out in more detail later in this Comment, this so-called all-or-nothing rule with respect to class gifts is not superseded by this Act, and so remains in effect under the Statutory Rule. Consequently, all class gifts that are subject to open are to be regarded as nonvested property interests for the purposes of this Act.

Section 1(a)(1) Codifies the Validating Side of the Common-law Rule. The validating side of the Common-law Rule is codified in Section 1(a)(1) (and, with respect to powers of appointment, in Sections 1(b)(1) and 1(c)(1)).

A nonvested property interest that satisfies the requirement of Section 1(a)(1) is initially valid. That is, it is valid as of the time of its creation. There is no need to subject such an interest to the waiting period set forth in Section 1(a)(2), nor would it be desirable to do so.

For a nonvested property interest to be valid as of the time of its creation under Section 1(a)(1), there must then be a *certainty* that the interest will either vest or terminate—an interest terminates when vesting becomes impossible—no later than 21 years after the death of an individual then alive. To satisfy this requirement, it must be established that there is no possible chain of events that might arise after the interest was created that would allow the interest to vest or terminate after the expiration of the 21-year period following the death of an individual in being at the creation of the interest. Consequently, initial validity under Section 1(a)(1) can be established only if there is an individual for whom there is a causal connection between the individual's death and the interest's vesting or terminating no later than 21 years thereafter. *The individual described in subsection (a)(1) (and subsections (b)(1) and (c)(1) as well) is often referred to as the "validating life," the term used throughout the Comments to this Act.*

Determining Whether There is a Validating Life. The process for determining whether a validating life exists is to postulate the death of each individual connected in some way to the transaction, and ask the question: Is there with respect to this individual an invalidating chain of possible events? If one individual can be found for whom the answer is No, that individual can serve as the validating life. As to that individual there will be the requisite causal connection between his or her death and the questioned interest's vesting or terminating no later than 21 years thereafter.

In searching for a validating life, only individuals who are connected in some way to the transaction need to be considered, for they are the only ones who have a chance of supplying the requisite causal connection. Such individuals vary from situation to situation, but typically include the beneficiaries of the disposition, including the taker or takers of the nonvested property interest, and individuals related to them by blood or adoption, especially in the ascending and descending lines. There is no point in even considering the life of an individual unconnected to the transaction—an individual from the world at large who happens to be in being at the creation of the interest. No such individual can be a validating life because there will be an invalidating chain of possible events as to every unconnected individual who might be proposed: Any such individual can immediately die after the creation of the nonvested property interest without causing any acceleration of the interest's vesting or termination. (The life expectancy of any unconnected individual, or even the probability that one of a number of new-born babies will live a long life, is irrelevant.)

Example (1)—Parent of Devisees as the Validating Life. G devised property "to A for life, remainder to A's children who attain 21." G was survived by his son (A), by his daughter (B), by A's wife (W), and by A's two children (X and Y).

The nonvested property interest in favor of A's children who reach 21 satisfies Section 1(a)(1)'s requirement, and the interest is initially valid. When the interest was created (at G's death), the interest was then certain to vest or terminate no later than 21 years after A's death.

The process by which A is determined to be the validating life is one of testing various candidates to see if any of them have the requisite causal connection. As noted above, no one from the world at large can have the requisite causal connection, and so such individuals are disregarded. Once the inquiry is narrowed to the appropriate candidates, the first possible validating life that comes to mind is A, who does in fact fulfill the requirement: Since A's death cuts off the possibility of any more children being born to him, it is impossible, no matter when A dies, for any of A's children to be alive and under the age of 21 beyond 21 years after A's death. (See the discussion of subsection (d), below.)

A is therefore the validating life for the nonvested property interest in favor of A's children who attain 21. None of the other individuals who is connected to this transaction could serve as the validating life because an invalidating chain of possible post-creation events exists as to each one of them. The other individuals who might be considered include W, X, Y, and B. In the case of W, an invalidating chain of events is that she might predecease A, A might remarry and have a child by his new wife, and such child might be alive and under the age of 21 beyond the 21-year period following W's death. With respect to X and Y, an invalidating chain of events is that they might predecease A, A might later have another child, and that child might be alive and under 21 beyond the 21-year period following the death of the survivor of X and Y. As to B, she suffers from the same invalidating chain of events as exists with respect to X and Y. The fact that none of these other individuals can serve as the validating life is of no consequence, however, because only one such individual is required for the validity of a nonvested interest to be established, and that individual is A.

The Rule of Subsection (d). The rule established in subsection (d) plays a significant role in the search for a validating life. Subsection (d) declares that the possibility that a child will be born to an individual after the individual's death is to be disregarded. It is important to note that this rule applies only for the purposes of determining the validity of an interest (or power of appointment) under paragraph (1) of subsection (a), (b), or (c). The rule of subsection (d) does not apply, for example, to questions such as whether or not a child who is born to an individual after the individual's death qualifies as a taker of a beneficial interest—as a member of a class or otherwise. Neither subsection (d), nor any other provision of this Act, supersedes the widely accepted common-law principle, sometimes codified, that a child in gestation (a child sometimes described as a child *en ventre sa mere*) who is later born alive is regarded as alive at the commencement of gestation.

The limited purpose of subsection (d) is to solve a perpetuity problem caused by advances in medical science. The problem is illustrated by a case such as Example (1), above—"to A for life, remainder to A's children who reach 21." When the Common-law Rule was developing, the possibility was recognized, strictly speaking, that one or more of A's children might reach 21 more than 21 years after A's death. The possibility existed because A's wife (who might not be a life in being) might be pregnant when A died. If she was, and if the child was born viable a few months after A's death, the child could not reach his or her 21st birthday within 21 years after A's death. The device then invented to validate the interest of A's children was to "extend" the allowable perpetuity period by tacking on a period of gestation, if needed. As a result, the common-law perpetuity period was comprised of three components: (1) a life in being (2) plus 21 years (3) plus a period of gestation, when needed. Today, thanks to sperm banks, frozen embryos, and even the possibility of artificially maintaining the body functions of deceased pregnant women long enough to develop the fetus to viability * * *—advances in medical science unanticipated when the Common-law Rule was in its developmental stages—having a pregnant wife at death is no longer the only way of having children after death. These medical developments, and undoubtedly others to come, make the mere addition of a period of gestation inadequate as a device to confer initial validity under Section 1(a)(1) on the interest of A's children in the above example. The rule of subsection (d), however, *does* insure the initial validity of the children's interest. Disregarding the possibility that children of A will be born after his death allows A to be the validating life. None of his children, under this assumption, can reach 21 more than 21 years after his death.

Note that subsection (d) subsumes not only the case of children conceived after death, but also the more conventional case of children in gestation at death. With subsection (d) in place, the third component of the common-law perpetuity period is unnecessary and has been jettisoned. The perpetuity period recognized in paragraph (1) of subsections (a), (b), and (c) has only two components: (1) a life in being (2) plus 21 years.

As to the legal status of conceived-after-death children, that question has not yet been resolved. For example, if in Example (1) it in fact turns out that A does leave sperm on deposit at a sperm bank and if in fact A's wife does become pregnant as a result of artificial insemination, the child or children produced thereby might not be included at all in the class gift. * * * Without trying to predict how *that* matter will be settled in the future, the best way to handle the problem from the perpetuity perspective is subsection (d)'s rule requiring the possibility of post-death children to be disregarded.

Recipients as Their Own Validating Lives. It is well established at common law that, in appropriate cases, the recipient of an interest can be his or her own validating life. * * * Given the right circumstances, this principle can validate interests that are contingent on the recipient's reaching an age in excess of 21, or are contingent on the recipient's surviving a particular point in time that is or might turn out to be in excess of 21 years after the interest was created or after the death of a person in being at the date of creation.

Example (2)—Devisees as Their Own Validating Lives. G devised real property "to A's children who attain 25." A predeceased G. At G's death, A had three living children, all of whom were under 25.

The nonvested property interest in favor of A's children who attain 25 is validated by Section 1(a)(1). Under subsection (d), the possibility that A will have a child born to him after his death (and since A predeceased G, after G's death) must be disregarded. Consequently, even if A's wife survived G, and even if she was pregnant at G's death or even if A had deposited sperm in a sperm bank prior to his death, it must be assumed that all of A's children are in being at G's death. A's children are, therefore, their own validating lives. (Note that subsection (d) requires that in determining whether an individual is a validating life, the possibility that a child will be born to "an" individual after the individual's death must be disregarded. The validating life and the individual whose having a post-death child is disregarded need not be the same individual.) Each one of A's children, all of whom under subsection (d) are regarded as alive at G's death, will either reach the age of 25 or fail to do so within his or her own lifetime. To say this another way, it is certain to be known no later than at the time of the death of each child whether or not that child survived to the required age.

Validating Life Can Be Survivor of Group. In appropriate cases, the validating life need not be individualized at first. Rather the validating life can initially (i.e., when the interest was created) be the unidentified survivor of a group of individuals. It is common in such cases to say that the members of the group are the validating *lives*, but the true meaning of the statement is that the validating *life* is the member of the group who turns out to live the longest. As the court said in *Skatterwood v. Edge*, 1 Salk. 229, 91 Eng. Rep. 203 (K.B. 1697), "for let the lives be never so many, there must be a survivor, and so it is but the length of that life; for Twisden used to say, the candles were all lighted at once."

Example (3)—Case of Validating Life Being the Survivor of a Group. G devised real property "to such of my grandchildren as attain 21." Some of G's children are living at G's death.

The nonvested property interest in favor of G's grandchildren who attain 21 is valid under Section 1(a)(1). The validating life is that one of G's children who turns out to live the longest. Since under subsection (d), it must be assumed that none of G's children will have post-death children, it is regarded as impossible for any of G's grandchildren to be alive and under 21 beyond the 21-year period following the death of G's last surviving child.

Example (4)—Sperm Bank Case. G devised property in trust, directing the income to be paid to G's children for the life of the survivor, then to G's grandchildren for the life of the survivor, and on the death of G's last surviving grandchild, to pay the corpus to G's great-grandchildren then living. G's children all predeceased him, but several grandchildren were living at G's death. One of G's predeceased children (his son, A) had deposited sperm in a sperm bank. A's widow was living at G's death.

The nonvested property interest in favor of G's great-grandchildren is valid under Section 1(a)(1). The validating life is the last surviving grandchild among the grandchildren living at G's death. Under subsection (d), the possibility that A will have a child conceived after G's death must be disregarded. Note that subsection (d) requires that in determining whether an individual is a validating life, the possibility that a child will be born to "an" individual after the individual's death is disregarded. The validating life and the individual whose having a post-death child is disregarded need not be the same individual. Thus in this example, by disregarding the possibility that A will have a conceived-after-death child, G's *last surviving grandchild* becomes the validating life because G's last surviving grandchild is deemed to have been alive at G's death, when the great-grandchildren's interests were created.

Example (5)—Child in Gestation Case. G devised property in trust, to pay the income equally among G's living children; on the death of G's last surviving child, to accumulate the income for 21 years; on the 21st anniversary of the death of G's last surviving child, to pay the corpus and accumulated income to G's then-living descendants, per stirpes; if none, to X Charity. At G's death his child (A) was 6 years old, and G's wife (W) was pregnant. After G's death, W gave birth to their second child (B).

The nonvested property interests in favor of G's descendants and in favor of X Charity are valid under Section 1(a)(1). The validating life is A. Under subsection (d), the possibility that a child will be born to an individual after the individual's death must be disregarded *for the purposes of determining validity under Section 1(a)(1)*. Consequently, the possibility that a child will be born to G after his death must be disregarded; and the possibility that a child will be born to any of G's descendants after their deaths must also be disregarded.

Note, however, that the rule of subsection (d) does *not* apply to the question of the entitlement of an after-born child to take a beneficial interest in the trust. The common-law rule (sometimes codified) that a child in gestation is treated as alive, if the child is subsequently born viable, applies to *this* question. Thus, subsection (d) does *not* prevent B from being an income beneficiary under G's trust, nor does it prevent a descendant in gestation on the 21st anniversary of the death of G's last surviving child from being a member of the class of G's "then-living descendants," as long as such descendant has no then-living ancestor who takes instead.

Different Validating Lives Can and in Some Cases Must Be Used. Dispositions of property sometimes create more than one nonvested property interest. In such cases, the validity of each interest is treated individually. A validating life that validates one interest might or might not validate the other interests. Since it is not necessary that the same validating life be used for all interests created by a disposition, the search for a validating life for each of the other interests must be undertaken separately.

Perpetuity Saving Clauses and Similar Provisions. Knowledgeable lawyers almost routinely insert perpetuity saving clauses into instruments they draft. Saving clauses contain two components, the first of which is the *perpetuity-period component*. This component typically requires the trust or other arrangement to terminate no later than 21 years after the death of the last survivor of a group of individuals designated therein by name or class. (The lives of corporations, animals, or sequoia trees cannot be used.) The second component of saving clauses is the *gift-over component*. This component expressly creates a gift over that is guaranteed to vest at the termination of the period set forth in the perpetuity-period component, but only if the trust or other arrangement has not terminated earlier in accordance with its other terms.

It is important to note that regardless of what group of individuals is designated in the perpetuity-period component of a saving clause, the surviving member of the group is not necessarily the individual who would be the validating life for the nonvested property interest or power of appointment in the absence of the saving clause. Without the saving clause, one or more interests or powers may in fact fail to satisfy the requirement of paragraph (1) of subsections (a), (b), or (c) for initial validity. By being designated in the saving clause, however, the survivor of the group becomes the validating life for all interests and powers in the trust or other arrangement: The saving clause confers on the last surviving member of the designated group the requisite causal connection between his or her death and the impossibility of any interest or power in the trust or other arrangement remaining in existence beyond the 21-year period following such individual's death.

    Example (6)—Valid Saving Clause Case. A testamentary trust directs income to be paid to the testator's children for the life of the survivor, then to the testator's grandchildren for the life of the survivor, corpus on the death of the testator's last living grandchild to such of the testator's descendants as the last living grandchild shall by will appoint; in default of appointment, to the testator's then-living descendants, per stirpes. A saving clause in the will terminates the trust, if it has not previously terminated, 21 years after the death of the testator's last surviving descendant who was living at the testator's death. The testator was survived by children.

    In the absence of the saving clause, the nongeneral power of appointment in the last living grandchild and the nonvested property interest in the gift-in-default clause in favor of the testator's descendants fail the test of Sections 1(a)(1) and 1(c)(1) for initial validity. That is, were it not for the saving clause, there is no validating life. However, the surviving member of the designated group becomes the validating life, so that the saving clause does confer initial validity on the nongeneral power of appointment and on the nonvested property interest under Sections 1(a)(1) and 1(c)(1).

If the governing instrument designates a group of individuals that would cause it to be impracticable to determine the death of the survivor, the common-law courts have developed the doctrine that the validity of the nonvested property interest or power of appointment is determined as if the provision in the governing instrument did not exist. * * * If, for example, the designated group in Example (6) were the residents of X City (or the members of Y Country Club) living at the time of the testator's death, the saving clause would not validate the power of appointment or the nonvested property interest. Instead, the validity of the power of appointment and the nonvested property interest would be determined as if the provision in the governing instrument did not exist. Since without the saving clause the power of appointment and the nonvested property interest would fail to satisfy the requirements of Sections 1(a)(1) and 1(c)(1) for initial validity, their validity would be governed by Sections 1(a)(2) and 1(c)(2).

    The application of the above common-law doctrine, which is not superseded by this Act and so remains in full force, is not limited to saving clauses. It also applies to trusts or other arrangements where the period thereof is directly linked to the life of the survivor of a designated group of individuals. An example is a trust to pay the income to the grantor's descendants from time to time living, per stirpes, for the period of the life of the survivor of a designated group of individuals living when the nonvested property interest or power of appointment in question was created, plus the 21-year period following the survivor's death; at the end of the 21-year period, the corpus is to be divided among the grantor's then-living descendants, per stirpes, and if none, to the XYZ Charity. If the group of individuals so designated is such that it would be impracticable to determine the death of the survivor, the validity of the disposition is determined as if the provision in the governing instrument did not exist. The term of the trust is therefore governed by the 90-year permissible vesting period of paragraph (2) of subsections (a), (b), or (c) of the Statutory Rule. * * *

C. SECTION 1(a)(2): WAIT-AND-SEE-NONVESTED PROPERTY INTERESTS WHOSE VALIDITY IS INITIALLY IN ABEYANCE

    Unlike the Common-law Rule, the Statutory Rule Against Perpetuities does not automatically invalidate nonvested property interests for which there is no validating life. A nonvested property interest that does not meet the requirements for validity under Section 1(a)(1) might still be valid under the wait-and-see provisions of Section 1(a)(2). Such an interest is invalid under Section 1(a)(2) only if in actuality it does not vest (or terminate) during the permissible vesting period. Such an interest becomes invalid, in other words, only if it is still in existence and nonvested when the permissible vesting period expires.

1. *The 90-Year Permissible Vesting Period*

    Since a wait-and-see rule against perpetuities, unlike the Common-law Rule, makes validity or invalidity turn on *actual* post-creation events, it requires that an actual period of time be measured off during which the contingencies attached to an interest are allowed to work themselves out to a final resolution. The Statutory Rule Against Perpetuities establishes a permissible vesting period of 90 years. Nonvested property interests that have neither vested nor terminated at the expiration of the 90-year permissible vesting period become invalid.

As explained in the Prefatory Note, the permissible vesting period of 90 years is *not* an arbitrarily selected period of time. On the contrary, the 90-year period represents a reasonable approximation of—a proxy for—the period of time that would, *on average*, be produced through the use of an actual set of measuring lives identified by statute and then adding the traditional 21-year tack-on period after the death of the survivor.

2.   *Technical Violations of the Common-Law Rule*

One of the harsh aspects of the invalidating side of the Common-law Rule, against which the adoption of the wait-and-see element in Section 1(a)(2) is designed to relieve, is that nonvested property interests at common law are invalid even though the invalidating chain of possible events *almost* certainly will *not* happen. In such cases, the violation of the Common-law Rule could be said to be merely technical. Nevertheless, at common law, the nonvested property interest is invalid.

Cases of technical violation fall generally into discrete categories, identified and named by Professor Leach in *Perpetuities in a Nutshell*, 51 Harv.L.Rev. 638 (1938), as the fertile octogenarian, the administrative contingency, and the unborn widow. The following three examples illustrate how Section 1(a)(2) affects these categories.

Example (7)—Fertile Octogenarian Case. G devised property in trust, directing the trustee to pay the net income therefrom "to A for life, then to A's children for the life of the survivor, and upon the death of A's last surviving child to pay the corpus of the trust to A's grandchildren." G was survived by A (a female who had passed menopause) and by A's two adult children (X and Y).

The remainder interest in favor of G's grandchildren would be invalid at common law, and consequently is not validated by Section 1(a)(1). There is no validating life because, under the common law's conclusive presumption of lifetime fertility, which is not superseded by this Act (see Part H, below), A *might* have a third child (Z), conceived and born after G's death, who will have a child conceived and born more than 21 years after the death of the survivor of A, X, and Y.

Under Section 1(a)(2), however, the remote possibility of the occurrence of this chain of events does not invalidate the grandchildren's interest. The interest becomes invalid only if it remains in existence and nonvested 90 years after G's death. The chance that the grandchildren's remainder interest will become invalid under Section 1(a)(2) is negligible.

Example (8)—Administrative Contingency Case. G devised property "to such of my grandchildren, born before or after my death, as may be living upon final distribution of my estate." G was survived by children and grandchildren.

The remainder interest in favor of A's grandchildren would be invalid at common law, and consequently is not validated by Section 1(a)(1). The final distribution of G's estate *might* not occur within 21 years of G's death, and after G's death grandchildren might be conceived and born who might survive or fail to survive the final distribution of G's estate more than 21 years after the death of the survivor of G's children and grandchildren who were living at G's death.

Under Section 1(a)(2), however, the remote possibility of the occurrence of this chain of events does not invalidate the grandchildren's remainder interest. The interest becomes invalid only if it remains in existence and nonvested 90 years after G's death. Since it is almost certain that the final distribution of G's estate will occur well within this 90-year period, the chance that the grandchildren's interest will be invalid is negligible.

Example (9)—Unborn Widow Case. G devised property in trust, the income to be paid "to my son A for life, then to A's spouse for her life, and upon the death of the survivor of A and his spouse, the corpus to be delivered to A's then living descendants." G was survived by A, by A's wife (W), and by their adult children (X and Y).

Unless the interest in favor of A's "spouse" is construed to refer only to W, rather than to whoever is A's spouse when he dies, if anyone, the remainder interest in favor of A's descendants would be invalid at common law, and consequently is not validated by Section 1(a)(1). There is no validating life because A's spouse *might* not be W; A's spouse might be someone who was conceived and born after G's death; she might outlive the death of the survivor of A, W, X, and Y by more than 21 years; and descendants of A might be born or die before the death of A's spouse but after the 21-year period following the death of the survivor of A, W, X, and Y.

Under Section 1(a)(2), however, the remote possibility of the occurrence of this chain of events does not invalidate the descendants' remainder interest. The interest becomes invalid only if it remains in existence and nonvested 90 years after G's death. The chance that the descendants' remainder interest will become invalid under the Statutory Rule is small.

Age Contingencies in Excess of 21. Another category of technical violation of the Common-law Rule arises in cases of age contingencies in excess of 21 where the takers cannot be their own validating lives (unlike Example (2), above). The violation of the Common-law Rule falls into the technical category because the insertion of a saving clause would in almost all cases allow the disposition to be carried out as written. In effect, the Statutory Rule operates like the perpetuity-period component of a saving clause.

Example (10)—Age Contingency in Excess of 21 Case. G devised property in trust, directing the trustee to pay the income "to A for life, then to A's children; the corpus of the trust is to be equally divided among A's children who reach the age of 30." G was survived by A, by A's spouse (H), and by A's two children (X and Y), both of whom were under the age of 30 when G died.

The remainder interest in favor of A's children who reach 30 is a class gift. At common law, the interests of *all* potential class members must be valid or the class gift is totally invalid. *Leake v. Robinson*, 2 Mer. 363, 35 Eng. Rep. 979 (Ch. 1817). This Act does not supersede the all-or-nothing rule for class gifts (see Part G, below), and so the all-or-nothing rule continues to apply under this Act. Although X and Y will either reach 30 or die under 30 within their own lifetimes, there is at G's death the possibility that A will have an afterborn child (Z) who will reach 30 or die under 30 more than 21 years after the death of the survivor of A, H, X, and Y. The class gift would be invalid at common law and consequently is not validated by Section 1(a)(1).

Under Section 1(a)(2), however, the possibility of the occurrence of this chain of events does not invalidate the children's remainder interest. The interest becomes invalid only if an interest of a class member remains nonvested 90 years after G's death.

Although unlikely, suppose that at A's death Z's age is such that he could be alive and under the age of 30 at the expiration of the allowable waiting period. Suppose further that at A's death X or Y or both is over the age of 30. The court, upon the petition of an interested person, must under Section 3 reform G's disposition. See Example (3) in the Comment to Section 3.

D. SECTIONS 1(b)(1) AND 1(c)(1): POWERS OF APPOINTMENT THAT ARE INITIALLY VALID

Powers of Appointment. Sections 1(b) and 1(c) set forth the Statutory Rule Against Perpetuities with respect to powers of appointment. A power of appointment is the authority, other than as an incident of the beneficial ownership of property, to designate recipients of beneficial interests in or powers of appointment over property. * * * The property or property interest subject to a power of appointment is called the "appointive property."

The various persons connected to a power of appointment are identified by a special terminology. The "donor" is the person who created the power of appointment. The "donee" is the person who holds the power of appointment, i.e., the powerholder. The "objects" are the persons to whom an appointment can be made. The "appointees" are the persons to whom an appointment has been made. The "takers in default" are the persons whose property interests are subject to being defeated by the exercise of the power of appointment and who take the property to the extent the power is not effectively exercised. * * *

A power of appointment is "general" if it is exercisable in favor of the donee of the power, the donee's creditors, the donee's estate, or the creditors of the donee's estate. A power of appointment that is not general is a "nongeneral" power of appointment. * * *

A power of appointment is "presently exercisable" if, at the time in question, the donee can by an exercise of the power create an interest in or a power of appointment over the appointive property. * * * A power of appointment is "testamentary" if the donee can exercise it only in the donee's will. * * * A power of appointment is "not presently exercisable because of a condition precedent" if the only impediment to its present exercisability is a condition precedent, i.e., the occurrence of some uncertain event. Since a power of appointment terminates on the donee's death, a deferral of a power's present exercisability until a future time (even a time certain) imposes a condition precedent that the donee be alive at that future time.

A power of appointment is a "fiduciary" power if it is held by a fiduciary and is exercisable by the fiduciary in a fiduciary capacity. A power of appointment that is exercisable in an individual capacity is a "nonfiduciary" power. As used in this Act, the term "power of appointment" refers to "fiduciary" and to "nonfiduciary" powers, unless the context indicates otherwise.

Although Gray's formulation of the Common-law Rule Against Perpetuities does not speak directly of powers of appointment, the Common-law Rule *is* applicable to powers of appointment (other than presently exercisable general powers of appointment). The principle of subsections (b)(1) and (c)(1) is that a power of appointment that satisfies the Common-law Rule Against Perpetuities is valid under the Statutory Rule Against Perpetuities, and consequently it can be validly exercised, without being subjected to a waiting period during which the power's validity is in abeyance.

Two different tests for validity are employed at common law, depending on what type of power is at issue. In the case of a *nongeneral power* (whether or not presently exercisable) and in the case of a *general testamentary power*, the power is initially valid if, when the power was created, it is certain that the latest possible time that the power can be exercised is no later than 21 years after the death of an individual then in being. In the case of a *general power not presently exercisable because of a condition precedent*, the power is initially valid if it is then certain that the condition precedent to its exercise will either be satisfied or become impossible to satisfy no later than 21 years after the death of an individual then in being. Subsections (b)(1) and (c)(1) codify these rules. Under either test, initial validity depends on the existence of a validating life. The procedure for determining whether a validating life exists is essentially the same procedure explained in Part B, above, pertaining to nonvested property interests.

Example (11)—Initially Valid General Testamentary Power Case. G devised property "to A for life, remainder to such persons, including A's estate or the creditors of A's estate, as A shall by will appoint." G was survived by his daughter (A).

A's power, which is a general testamentary power, is valid as of its creation under Section 1(c)(1). The test is whether or not the power can be exercised beyond 21 years after the death of an individual in being when the power was created (G's death). Since A's power cannot be exercised after A's death, the validating life is A, who was in being at G's death.

Example (12)—Initially Valid Nongeneral Power Case. G devised property "to A for life, remainder to such of A's descendants as A shall appoint." G was survived by his daughter (A).

A's power, which is a nongeneral power, is valid as of its creation under Section 1(c)(1). The validating life is A; the analysis leading to validity is the same as applied in Example (11), above.

Example (13)—Case of Initially Valid General Power Not Presently Exercisable Because of a Condition Precedent. G devised property "to A for life, then to A's first born child for life, then to such persons, including A's first born child or such child's estate or creditors, as A's first born child shall appoint." G was survived by his daughter (A), who was then childless.

The power in A's first born child, which is a general power not presently exercisable because of a condition precedent, is valid as of its creation under Section 1(b)(1). The power is subject to a condition precedent—that A have a child—but this is a contingency that under subsection (d) is deemed certain to be resolved one way or the other within A's lifetime. A is therefore the validating life: The power cannot remain subject to the condition precedent after A's death. Note that the latest possible time that the power can be exercised is at the death of A's first born child, which might occur beyond 21 years after the death of A (and anyone else who was alive when G died). Consequently, if the power conferred on A's first born child had been a nongeneral power or a general testamentary power, the power could not be validated by Section 1(c)(1); instead, the power's validity would be governed by Section 1(c)(2).

E.   SECTIONS 1(b)(2) AND 1(c)(2): WAIT-AND-SEE-POWERS OF APPOINTMENT WHOSE VALIDITY IS INITIALLY IN ABEYANCE

Under the Common-law Rule, a *general power not presently exercisable because of a condition precedent* is invalid as of the time of its creation if the condition *might* neither be satisfied nor become impossible to satisfy within a life in being plus 21 years. A *nongeneral power* (whether or not presently exercisable) or a *general testamentary power* is invalid as of the time of its creation if it *might* not terminate (by irrevocable exercise or otherwise) within a life in being plus 21 years.

Sections 1(b)(2) and 1(c)(2), by adopting the wait-and-see method of perpetuity reform, shift the ground of invalidity from possible to actual post-creation events. Under these subsections, a power of appointment that would have violated the Common-law Rule, and therefore fails the subsection (b)(1) or (c)(1) tests for *initial* validity, is nevertheless not invalid as of the time of its creation. Instead, its validity is in abeyance. A general power not presently exercisable because of a condition precedent is invalid only if *in actuality* the condition neither is satisfied nor becomes impossible to satisfy within the 90-year permissible vesting period. A nongeneral power or a general testamentary power is invalid only if *in actuality* it does not terminate (by irrevocable exercise or otherwise) within the 90-year permissible period.

Example (14)—General Testamentary Power Case. G devised property "to A for life, then to A's first born child for life, then to such persons, including the estate or the creditors of the estate of A's first born child, as A's first born child shall by will appoint; in default of appointment, to G's grandchildren in equal shares." G was survived by his daughter (A), who was then childless, and by his son (B), who had two children (X and Y).

Since the general testamentary power conferred on A's first born child fails the test of Section 1(c)(1) for *initial* validity, its validity is governed by Section 1(c)(2). If A has a child, such child's death must occur within 90 years of G's death for any provision in the child's will purporting to exercise the power to be valid.

Example (15)—Nongeneral Power Case. G devised property "to A for life, then to A's first born child for life, then to such of G's grandchildren as A's first born child shall appoint; in default of appointment, to the children of G's late nephew, Q." G was survived by his daughter (A), who was then childless, by his son (B), who had two children (X and Y), and by Q's two children (R and S).

Since the nongeneral power conferred on A's first born child fails the test of Section 1(c)(1) for *initial* validity, its validity is governed by Section 1(c)(2). If A has a child, such child must exercise the power within 90 years after G's death or the power becomes invalid.

Example (16)—General Power Not Presently Exercisable Because of a Condition Precedent. G devised property "to A for life, then to A's first born child for life, then to such persons, including A's first born child or such child's estate or creditors, as A's first born child shall appoint after reaching the age of 25; in default of appointment, to G's grandchildren." G was survived by his daughter (A), who was then childless, and by his son (B), who had two children (X and Y).

The power conferred on A's first born child is a general power not presently exercisable because of a condition precedent. Since the power fails the test of Section 1(b)(1) for *initial* validity, its validity is governed by Section 1(b)(2). If A has a child, such child must reach the age of 25 (or die under 25) within 90 years after G's death or the power is invalid.

Fiduciary Powers. Purely administrative fiduciary powers are excluded from the Statutory Rule under Sections 4(2) and (3), but the only distributive fiduciary power that is excluded is the power described in Section 4(4). Otherwise, distributive fiduciary powers are subject to the Statutory Rule. Such powers are usually nongeneral powers.

Example (17)—Trustee's Discretionary Powers Over Income and Corpus. G devised property in trust, the terms of which were that the trustee was authorized to accumulate the income or pay it or a portion of it out to A during A's lifetime; after A's death, the trustee was authorized to accumulate the income or to distribute it in equal or unequal shares among A's children until the death of the survivor; and on the death of A's last surviving child to pay the corpus and accumulated income (if any) to B. The trustee was also granted the discretionary power to invade the corpus on behalf of the permissible recipient or recipients of the income.

The trustee's nongeneral powers to invade corpus and to accumulate or spray income among A's children are not excluded by Section 4(4), nor are they initially valid under Section 1(c)(1). Their validity is, therefore, governed by Section 1(c)(2). Both powers become invalid thereunder, and hence no longer exercisable, 90 years after G's death.

It is doubtful that the powers will become invalid, because the trust will probably terminate by its own terms earlier than the expiration of the permissible 90-year period. But if the powers do become invalid, and hence no longer exercisable, they become invalid as of the time the permissible 90-year period expires. Any exercises of either power that took place before the expiration of the permissible 90-year period are not invalidated retroactively. In addition, if the powers do become invalid, a court in an appropriate proceeding must reform the instrument in accordance with the provisions of Section 3.

F.   THE VALIDITY OF THE DONEE'S EXERCISE OF A VALID POWER

The fact that a power of appointment is valid, either because it (i) was not subject to the Statutory Rule to begin with, (ii) is initially valid under Sections 1(b)(1) or 1(c)(1), or (iii) becomes valid under Sections 1(b)(2) or 1(c)(2), means merely that the power can be validly exercised. It does not mean that any exercise that the donee decides to make is valid. The validity of the interests or powers created by the exercise of a valid power is a separate matter, governed by the provisions of this Act. A key factor in deciding the validity of such appointed interests or appointed powers is determining when they were created for purposes of this Act. Under Section 2, as explained in the Comment thereto, the time of creation is when the power was exercised if it was a presently exercisable general power; and if it was a nongeneral power or a general testamentary power, the time of creation is when the power was created. This is the rule generally accepted at common law * * * and it is the rule adopted under this Act (except for purposes of Section 5 only, as explained in the Comment to Section 5).

Example (18)—Exercise of a Nongeneral Power of Appointment. G was the life income beneficiary of a trust and the donee of a nongeneral power of appointment over the succeeding remainder interest, exercisable in favor of M's descendants (except G). The trust was created by the will of G's mother, M, who predeceased him. G exercised his power by his will, directing the income to be paid after his death to his brother B's children for the life of the survivor, and upon the death of B's last surviving child, to pay the corpus of the trust to B's grandchildren. B predeceased M; B was survived by his two children, X and Y, who also survived M and G.

G's power and his appointment are valid. The power and the appointed interests were created at M's death when the power was created, not on G's death when it was exercised. See Section 2. G's power passes Section 1(c)(1)'s test for initial validity: G himself is the validating life. G's appointment also passes Section 1(a)(1)'s test for initial validity: Since B was dead at M's death, the validating life is the survivor of B's children, X and Y.

Suppose that G's power was exercisable only in favor of G's own descendants, and that G appointed the identical interests in favor of his own children and grandchildren. Suppose further that at M's death, G had two children, X and Y, and that a third child, Z, was born later. X, Y, and Z survived G. In this case, the remainder interest in favor of G's grandchildren would not pass Section 1(a)(1)'s test for initial validity. Its validity would be governed by Section 1(a)(2), under which it would be valid if G's last surviving child died within 90 years after M's death.

If G's power were a general testamentary power of appointment, rather than a nongeneral power, the solution would be the same. The period of the Statutory Rule with respect to interests created by the exercise of a general testamentary power starts to run when the power was created (at M's death, in this example), not when the power was exercised (at G's death).

Example (19)—Exercise of a Presently Exercisable General Power of Appointment. G was the life income beneficiary of a trust and the donee of a presently exercisable general power of appointment over the succeeding remainder interest. G exercised the power by deed, directing the trustee after his death to pay the income to G's children in equal shares for the life of the survivor, and upon the death of his last surviving child to pay the corpus of the trust to his grandchildren.

The validity of G's power is not in question: A presently exercisable general power of appointment is not subject to the Statutory Rule Against Perpetuities. G's appointment, however, is subject to the Statutory Rule. If G reserved a power to revoke his appointment, the remainder interest in favor of G's grandchildren passes Section 1(a)(1)'s test for initial validity. Under Section 2, the appointed remainder interest was created at G's death. The validating life for his grandchildren's remainder interest is G's last surviving child.

If G's appointment were irrevocable, however, the grandchildren's remainder interest fails the test of Section 1(a)(1) for initial validity. Under Section 2, the appointed remainder interest was created upon delivery of the deed exercising G's power (or when the exercise otherwise became effective). Since the validity of the grandchildren's remainder interest is governed by Section 1(a)(2), the remainder interest becomes invalid, and the disposition becomes subject to reformation under Section 3, if G's last surviving child lives beyond 90 years after the effective date of G's appointment.

Example (20)—Exercises of Successively Created Nongeneral Powers of Appointment. G devised property to A for life, remainder to such of A's descendants as A shall appoint. At his death, A exercised his nongeneral power by appointing to his child B for life, remainder to such of B's descendants as B shall appoint. At his death, B exercised his nongeneral power by appointing to his child C for life, remainder to C's children. A and B were living at G's death. Thereafter, C was born. A later died, survived by B and C. B then died survived by C.

A's nongeneral power passes Section 1(c)(1)'s test for initial validity. A is the validating life. B's nongeneral power, created by A's appointment, also passes Sections 1(c)(1)'s test for initial validity. Since under Section 2 the appointed interests and powers are created at G's death, and since B was then alive, B is the validating life for his nongeneral power. (If B had been born after G's death, however, his power would have failed Section 1(c)(1)'s test for initial validity; its validity would be governed by Section 1(c)(2), and would turn on whether or not it was exercised by B within 90 years after G's death.)

Although B's power is valid, his exercise may be partly invalid. The remainder interest in favor of C's children fails the test of Section 1(a)(1) for initial validity. The period of the Statutory Rule begins to run at G's death, under Section 2. (Since B's power was a nongeneral power, B's appointment under the common-law relation back doctrine of powers of appointment is treated as having been made by A. If B's appointment related back no further than that, of course, it would have been validated by Section 1(a)(1) because C was alive at A's death. However, A's power was also a nongeneral power, so relation back goes another step. A's appointment—which now includes B's appointment—is treated as having been made by G.) Since C was not alive at G's death, he cannot be the validating life. And, since C might have more children more than 21 years after the deaths of A and B and any other individual who was alive at G's death, the remainder interest in favor of his children is not initially validated by Section 1(a)(1). Instead, its validity is governed by Section 1(a)(2), and turns on whether or not C dies within 90 years after G's death.

Note that if either A's power or B's power (or both) had been a general testamentary power rather than a nongeneral power, the above solution would not change. However, if either A's power or B's power (or both) had been a presently exercisable general power, B's appointment would have passed Sections 1(a)(1)'s test for initial validity. (If A had the presently exercisable general power, the appointed interests and power would be created at A's death, not G's; and if the presently exercisable general power were held by B, the appointed interests and power would be created at B's death.)

Common-Law "Second-look" Doctrine. As indicated above, both at common law and under this Act (except for purposes of Section 5 only, as explained in the Comment to Section 5), appointed interests and powers established by the exercise of a general testamentary power or a nongeneral power are created when the power was created, not when the power was exercised. In applying this principle, the common law recognizes a so-called doctrine of second look, under which the facts existing on the date of the exercise are taken into account in determining the validity of appointed interests and appointed powers. * * * The common-law's second-look doctrine in effect constitutes a limited wait-and-see doctrine, and is therefore subsumed under but not totally superseded by this Act. The following example, which is a variation of Example (18) above, illustrates how the second-look doctrine operates at common law and how the situation would be analyzed under this Act.

Example (21)—Second-look Case. G was the life income beneficiary of a trust and the donee of a nongeneral power of appointment over the succeeding remainder interest, exercisable in favor of G's descendants. The trust was created by the will of his mother, M, who predeceased him. G exercised his power by his will, directing the income to be paid after his death to his children for the life of the survivor, and upon the death of his last surviving child, to pay the corpus of the trust to his grandchildren. At M's death, G had two children, X and Y. No further children were born to G, and at his death X and Y were still living.

The common-law solution of this example is as follows: G's appointment is valid under the Common-law Rule. Although the period of the Rule begins to run at M's death, the facts existing at G's death can be taken into account. This second look at the facts discloses that G had no additional children. Thus the possibility of additional children, which existed at M's death when the period of the Rule began to run, is disregarded. The survivor of X and Y, therefore, becomes the validating life for the remainder interest in favor of G's grandchildren, and G's appointment is valid. The common-law's second-look doctrine would not, however, save G's appointment if he actually had one or more children after M's death and if at least one of these after-born children survived G.

Under this Act, if no additional children are born to G after M's death, the common-law second-look doctrine can be invoked as of G's death to declare G's appointment then to be valid under Section 1(a)(1); no further waiting is necessary. However, if additional children *are* born to G and one or more of them survives G, Section 1(a)(2) applies and the validity of G's appointment depends on G's last surviving child dying within 90 years after M's death. * * *

G.   SECTION 1(e): EFFECT OF CERTAIN "LATER-OF" TYPE LANGUAGE; COORDINATION OF GENERATION-SKIPPING TRANSFER TAX REGULATIONS WITH UNIFORM ACT

Effect of Certain "Later-of" Type Language. Section 1(e) was added to the Uniform Act in 1990. It primarily applies to a non-traditional type of "later-of" clause (described below). Use of that type of clause might have produced unintended consequences, which are now rectified by the addition of Section 1(e).

In general, perpetuity saving or termination clauses can be used in either of two ways. The predominant use of such clauses is as an override clause. That is, the clause is not an integral part of the dispositive terms of the trust, but operates independently of the dispositive terms; the clause provides that all interests must vest no later than at a specified time in the future, and sometimes also provides that the trust must then terminate, but only if any interest has not previously vested or if the trust has not previously terminated. The other use of such a clause is as an integral part of the dispositive terms of the trust; that is, the clause is the provision that directly regulates the duration of the trust. Traditional perpetuity saving or termination clauses do not use a "later-of" approach; they mark off the maximum time of vesting or termination only by reference to a 21-year period following the death of the survivor of specified lives in being at the creation of the trust.

Section 1(e) applies to a non-traditional clause called a "later-of" (or "longer-of") clause. Such a clause might provide that the maximum time of vesting or termination of any interest or trust must occur no later than the later of (A) 21 years after the death of the survivor of specified lives in being at the creation of the trust or (B) 90 years after the creation of the trust.

Under the Uniform Act as originally promulgated, this type of "later-of" clause would not achieve a "later-of" result. If used as an override clause in conjunction with a trust whose terms were, by themselves, valid under the Common-law Rule, the "later-of" clause did no harm. The trust would be valid under the Common-law Rule as codified in Section 1(a)(1) because the clause itself would neither postpone the vesting of any interest nor extend the duration of the trust. But, if used either (1) as an override clause in conjunction with a trust whose terms were not valid under the Common-law Rule or (2) as the provision that directly regulated the duration of the trust, the "later-of" clause would not cure the perpetuity violation in case (1) and would create a perpetuity violation in case (2). In neither case would the clause qualify the trust for validity at common law under Section 1(a)(1) because the clause would not guarantee that all interests will be certain to vest or terminate no later than 21 years after the death of an individual then alive. In any given case, 90 years can turn out to be longer than the period produced by the specified-lives-in-being-plus-21-years language.

Because the clause would fail to qualify the trust for validity under the Common-law Rule of Section 1(a)(1), the nonvested interests in the trust would be subject to the wait-and-see element of Section 1(a)(2) and vulnerable to a reformation suit under Section 3. Under Section 1(a)(2), an interest that is not valid at common law is invalid unless it actually vests or terminates within 90 years after its creation. Section 1(a)(2) does not grant such nonvested interests a permissible vesting period of either 90 years or a period of 21 years after the death of the survivor of specified lives in being. Section 1(a)(2) only grants such interests a period of 90 years in which to vest.

The operation of Section 1(a), as outlined above, is also supported by perpetuity policy. If Section 1(a) allowed a "later-of" clause to achieve a "later-of" result, it would authorize an improper use of the 90-year permissible vesting period of Section 1(a)(2). The 90-year period of Section 1(a)(2) is designed to approximate the period that, *on average*, would be produced by using actual lives in being plus 21 years. Because in any given case the period actually produced by lives in being plus 21 years can be shorter or longer than 90 years, an attempt to utilize a 90-year period in a "later-of" clause improperly seeks to turn the 90-year average into a minimum.

Set against this background, the addition of Section 1(e) is quite beneficial. Section 1(e) limits the effect of this type of "later-of" language to 21 years after the death of the survivor of the specified lives, in effect transforming the clause into a traditional perpetuity saving/termination clause. By doing so, Section 1(e) grants initial validity to the trust under the Common-law Rule as codified in Section 1(a)(1) and precludes a reformation suit under Section 3.

Note that Section 1(e) covers variations of the "later-of" clause described above, such as a clause that postpones vesting until the later of (A) 20 years after the death of the survivor of specified lives in being or (B) 89 years. Section 1(e) does not, however, apply to all dispositions that incorporate a "later-of" approach. To come under Section 1(e), the specified-lives prong must include a tack-on period of up to 21 years. Without a tack-on period, a "later-of" disposition, unless valid at common law, comes under Section 1(a)(2) and is given 90 years in which to vest. An example would be a disposition that creates an interest that is to vest upon "the later of the death of my widow or 30 years after my death."

Coordination of the Federal Generation-skipping Transfer Tax with the Uniform Statutory Rule. In 1990, the Treasury Department announced a decision to coordinate the tax regulations under the "grandfathering" provisions of the federal generation-skipping transfer tax with the Uniform Act. Letter from Michael J. Graetz, Deputy Assistant Secretary of the Treasury (Tax Policy), to Lawrence J. Bugge, President, National Conference of Commissioners on Uniform State Laws (Nov. 16, 1990) (hereinafter *Treasury Letter*).

Section 1433(b)(2) of the Tax Reform Act of 1986 generally exempts ("grandfathers") trusts from the federal generation-skipping transfer tax that were irrevocable on September 25, 1985. This section adds, however, that the exemption shall apply "only to the extent that such transfer is not made out of corpus added to the trust after September 25, 1985." The provisions of Section 1433(b)(2) were first implemented by Temp. Treas. Reg. § 26.2601–1, promulgated by T.D. 8187 on March 14, 1988. Insofar as the Uniform Act is concerned, a key feature of that temporary regulation is the concept that the statutory reference to "corpus added to the trust after September 25, 1985" not only covers actual post-9/25/85 transfers of new property or corpus to a grandfathered trust but "constructive" additions as well. Under the temporary regulation as first promulgated, a "constructive" addition occurs if, after 9/25/85, the donee of a nongeneral power of appointment exercises that power "in a manner that may postpone or suspend the vesting, absolute ownership or power of alienation of an interest in property for a period, measured from the date of creation of the trust, extending beyond any life in being at the date of creation of the trust plus a period of 21 years. If a power is exercised by creating another power it will be deemed to be exercised to whatever extent the second power may be exercised." Temp. Treas. Reg. § 26.2601–1(b)(1)(v)(B)(2) (1988).

Because the Uniform Act was promulgated in 1986 and applies only prospectively, any "grandfathered" trust would have become irrevocable prior to the enactment of the Uniform Act in any state. Nevertheless, the second sentence of Section 5(a) extends the wait-and-see approach to post-effective-date exercises of nongeneral powers even if the power itself was created prior to the effective date of the Uniform Act in any state. Consequently, a post-effective-date exercise of a nongeneral power of appointment created in a "grandfathered" trust could come under the provisions of the Uniform Act.

The literal wording, then, of Temp. Treas. Reg. § 26.2601–1(b)(1)(v)(B)(2) (1988), as first promulgated, could have jeopardized the grandfathered status of an exempt trust if (1) the trust created a nongeneral power of appointment, (2) the donee exercised that nongeneral power, and (3) the Uniform Act is the perpetuity law applicable to the donee's exercise. This possibility arose not only because the donee's exercise itself might come under the 90-year permissible vesting period of Section 1(a)(2) if it otherwise violated the Common-law Rule and hence was not validated under Section 1(a)(1). The possibility also arose in a less obvious way if the donee's exercise created another nongeneral power. The last sentence of the temporary regulation states that "if a power is exercised by creating another power it will be deemed to be exercised to whatever extent the second power may be exercised."

In late March 1990, the National Conference of Commissioners on Uniform State Laws (NCCUSL) filed a formal request with the Treasury Department asking that measures be taken to coordinate the regulation with the Uniform Act. By the Treasury Letter referred to above, the Treasury Department responded by stating that it "will amend the temporary regulations to accommodate the 90-year period under USRAP as originally promulgated [in 1986] or as amended [in 1990 by the addition of subsection (e)]." This should effectively remove the possibility of loss of grandfathered status under the Uniform Act merely because the donee of a nongeneral power created in a grandfathered trust inadvertently exercises that power in violation of the Common-law Rule or merely because the donee exercises that power by creating a second nongeneral power that might, in the future, be inadvertently exercised in violation of the Common-law Rule.

The Treasury Letter states, however, that any effort by the donee of a nongeneral power in a grandfathered trust to obtain a "later-of" specified-lives-in-being-plus-21-years or 90-years approach will be treated as a constructive addition, unless that effort is nullified by state law. As explained above, the Uniform Act, as originally promulgated in 1986 or as amended in 1990 by the addition of Section 1(e), nullifies any direct effort to obtain a "later-of" approach by the use of a "later-of" clause.

The Treasury Letter states that an indirect effort to obtain a "later-of" approach would also be treated as a constructive addition that would bring grandfathered status to an end, unless the attempt to obtain the later-of approach is nullified by state law. The Treasury Letter indicates that an indirect effort to obtain a "later-of" approach could arise if the donee of a nongeneral power successfully attempts to prolong the duration of a grandfathered trust by switching from a specified-lives-in-being-plus-21-years perpetuity period to a 90-year perpetuity period, or vice versa. Donees of nongeneral powers in grandfathered trusts would therefore be well advised to resist any temptation to wait until it becomes clear or reasonably predictable which perpetuity period will be longer and then make a switch to the longer period if the governing instrument creating the power utilized the shorter period. No such attempted switch and no constructive addition will occur if in each instance a traditional specified-lives-in-being-plus-21-years perpetuity saving clause is used.

Any such attempted switch is likely in any event to be nullified by state law and, if so, the attempted switch will not be treated as a constructive addition. For example, suppose that the original grandfathered trust contained a standard perpetuity saving clause declaring that all interests in the trust must vest no later than 21 years after the death of the survivor of specified lives in being. In exercising a nongeneral power created in that trust, any indirect effort by the donee to obtain a "later-of" approach by adopting a 90-year perpetuity saving clause will likely be nullified by Section 1(e). If that exercise occurs at a time when it has become clear or reasonably predictable that the 90-year period will prove longer, the donee's exercise would constitute language in a governing instrument that seeks to operate in effect to postpone the vesting of any interest until the later of the specified-lives-in-being-plus-21-years period or 90 years. Under Section 1(e), "that language is inoperative to the extent it produces a period of time that exceeds 21 years after the death of the survivor of the specified lives."

Quite apart from Section 1(e), the relation-back doctrine generally recognized in the exercise of nongeneral powers stands as a doctrine that could potentially be invoked to nullify an attempted switch from one perpetuity period to the other perpetuity period. Under that doctrine, interests created by the exercise of a nongeneral power are considered created by the donor of that power. * * * As such, the maximum vesting period applicable to interests created by the exercise of a nongeneral power would apparently be covered by the perpetuity saving clause in the document that created the power, notwithstanding any different period the donee purports to adopt.

H.   SUBSIDIARY COMMON-LAW DOCTRINES:
WHETHER SUPERSEDED BY THIS ACT

As noted at the beginning of this Comment, the courts in interpreting the Common-law Rule developed several subsidiary doctrines. This Act does not supersede those subsidiary doctrines except to the extent the provisions of this Act conflict with them. As explained below, most of these common-law doctrines remain in full force or in force in modified form.

Constructional Preference for Validity. Professor Gray in his treatise on the Common-law Rule Against Perpetuities declared that a will or deed is to be construed without regard to the Rule, and then the Rule is to be "remorselessly" applied to the provisions so construed. J. Gray, The Rule Against Perpetuities § 629 (4th ed. 1942). Some courts may still adhere to this proposition. * * * Most courts, it is believed, would today be inclined to adopt the proposition * * * that where an instrument is ambiguous—that is, where it is fairly susceptible to two or more constructions, one of which causes a Rule violation and the other of which does not—the construction that does not result in a Rule violation should be adopted. * * *

The constructional preference for validity is not superseded by this Act, but its role is likely to be different. The situation is likely to be that one of the constructions to which the ambiguous instrument is fairly susceptible would result in validity under Section 1(a)(1), 1(b)(1), or 1(c)(1), but the other construction does not necessarily result in invalidity; rather it results in the interest's validity being governed by Section 1(a)(2), 1(b)(2), or 1(c)(2). Nevertheless, even though the result of adopting the other construction is not as harsh as it is at common law, it is expected that the courts will incline toward the construction that validates the disposition under Section 1(a)(1), 1(b)(1), or 1(c)(1).

Conclusive Presumption of Lifetime Fertility. At common law, all individuals—regardless of age, sex, or physical condition—are *conclusively* presumed to be able to have children throughout their entire lifetimes. This principle is not superseded by this Act, and in view of new advances in medical science that allow women to become pregnant after menopause by way of test-tube fertilization * * * and the widely accepted rule of construction that adopted children are presumptively included in class gifts, the conclusive presumption of lifetime fertility is not unrealistic. Since even elderly individuals probably cannot be excluded from adopting children based on their ages alone, the possibility of having children by adoption is seldom extinct. * * * Under this Act, the main force of this principle is felt in Example (7), above, where it prevents a nonvested property interest from passing the test for initial validity under Section 1(a)(1).

Act Supersedes Doctrine of Infectious Invalidity. At common law, the invalidity of an interest can, under the doctrine of infectious invalidity, be held to invalidate one or more otherwise valid interests created by the disposition or even invalidate the entire disposition. The question turns on whether the general dispositive scheme of the transferor will be better carried out by eliminating only the invalid interest or by eliminating other interests as well. This is a question that is answered on a case-by-case basis. Several items are relevant to the question, including who takes the stricken interests in place of those the transferor designated to take.

The doctrine of infectious invalidity is superseded by this Act by Section 3, under which courts, upon the petition of an interested person, are required to *reform* the disposition to approximate as closely as possible the transferor's manifested plan of distribution when an invalidity under the Statutory Rule occurs.

Separability. The common law's separability doctrine is that when an interest is *expressly* subject to alternative contingencies, the situation is treated as if two interests were created in the same person or class. Each interest is judged separately; the invalidity of one of the interests does not necessarily cause the other one to be invalid. This common-law principle was established in *Longhead v. Phelps*, 2 Wm.Bl. 704, 96 Eng. Rep. 414 (K.B. 1770), and is followed in this country. * * * Under this doctrine, if property is devised "to B if X-event or Y-event happens," B in effect has two interests, one contingent on X-event happening and the other contingent on Y-event happening. If the interest contingent on X-event but not the one contingent on Y-event is invalid, the consequence of separating B's interest into two is that only one of them, the one contingent on X-event, is invalid. B still has a valid interest—the one contingent on the occurrence of Y-event.

The separability principle is not superseded by this Act. As illustrated in the following example, its invocation will usually result in one of the interests being initially validated by Section 1(a)(1) and the validity of the other interests being governed by Section 1(a)(2).

Example (22)—Separability Case. G devised real property "to A for life, then to A's children who survive A and reach 25, but if none of A's children survives A or if none of A's children who survives A reaches 25, then to B." G was survived by his brother (B), by his daughter (A), by A's husband (H), and by A's two minor children (X and Y).

The remainder interest in favor of A's children who reach 25 fails the test of Section 1(a)(1) for initial validity. Its validity is, therefore, governed by Section 1(a)(2) and depends on each of A's children doing any one of the following things within 90 years after G's death: predeceasing A, surviving A and failing to reach 25, or surviving A and reaching 25.

Under the separability doctrine, B has two interests. One of them is contingent on none of A's children surviving A. That interest passes Section 1(a)(1)'s test for initial validity; the validating life is A. B's other interest, which is contingent on none of A's surviving children reaching 25, fails Section 1(a)(1)'s test for initial validity. Its validity is governed by Section 1(a)(2) and depends on each of A's surviving children either reaching 25 or dying under 25 within 90 years after G's death.

Suppose that after G's death, A has a third child (Z). A subsequently dies, survived by her husband (H) and by X, Y, and Z. This, of course, causes B's interest that was contingent on none of A's children surviving A to terminate. If X, Y, and Z had all reached the age of 25 by the time of A's death, their interest would vest at A's death, and that would end the matter. If one or two, but not all three of them, had reached the age of 25 at A's death, B's other interest—the one that was contingent on none of A's surviving children reaching 25—would also terminate. As for the children's interest, if the after-born child Z's age was such at A's death that Z could not be alive and under the age of 25 at the expiration of the allowable waiting period, the class gift in favor of the children would be valid under Section 1(a)(2), because none of those then under 25 could fail either to reach 25 or die under 25 after the expiration of the allowable 90-year waiting period. If, however, Z's age at A's death was such that Z could be alive and under the age of 25 at the expiration of the 90-year permissible vesting period, the circumstances requisite to reformation under Section 3(2) would arise, and the court would be justified in reforming G's disposition by reducing the age contingency with respect to Z to the age he would reach on the date when the permissible vesting period is due to expire. See Example (3) in the Comment to Section 3. So reformed, the class gift in favor of A's children could not become invalid under Section 1(a)(2), and the children of A who had already reached 25 by the time of A's death could receive their shares immediately.

The "All-or-Nothing" Rule with Respect to Class Gifts; the Specific Sum and Sub-Class Doctrines. The common law applies an "all-or-nothing" rule with respect to class gifts, under which a class gift stands or falls as a whole. The all-or-nothing rule, usually attributed to *Leake v. Robinson*, 2 Mer. 363, 35 Eng. Rep. 979 (Ch. 1817), is commonly stated as follows: If the interest of any potential class member *might* vest too remotely, the entire class gift violates the Rule. Although this Act does not supersede the basic idea of the much-maligned "all-or-nothing" rule, the evils sometimes attributed to it are substantially if not entirely eliminated by the wait-and-see feature of the Statutory Rule and by the availability of reformation under Section 3, especially in the circumstances described in Sections 3(2) and (3). For illustrations of the application of the all-or-nothing rule under this Act, see Examples (3), (4), and (6) in the Comment to Section 3.

The common law also recognizes a doctrine called the specific-sum doctrine, which is derived from *Storrs v. Benbow*, 3 De G.M. & G. 390, 43 Eng. Rep. 153 (Ch. 1853), and states: If a specified sum of money is to be paid to each member of a class, the interest of each class member is entitled to separate treatment and is valid or invalid under the Rule on its own. The common law also recognizes a doctrine called the sub-class doctrine, which is derived from *Cattlin v. Brown*, 11 Hare 372, 68 Eng. Rep. 1318 (Ch. 1853), and states: If the ultimate takers are not described as a single class but rather as a group of subclasses, and if the share to which each separate subclass is entitled will finally be determined within the period of the Rule, the gifts to the different subclasses are separable for the purpose of the Rule. * * * The specific-sum and sub-class doctrines are not superseded by this Act. The operation of the specific-sum doctrine under this Act is illustrated in the following example.

Example (23)—Specific-Sum Case. G bequeathed "$10,000 to each child of A, born before or after my death, who attains 25." G was survived by A and by A's two children (X and Y). X but not Y had already reached 25 at G's death. After G's death a third child (Z) was born to A.

If the phrase "born before or after my death" had been omitted, the class would close as of G's death under the common-law's rule of construction known as the rule of convenience: The after-born child, Z, would not be entitled to a $10,000 bequest, and the interests of both X and Y would be valid upon their creation at G's death. X's interest would be valid because it was initially vested; neither the Common-law Rule nor the Statutory Rule applies to interests that are vested upon their creation. Although the interest of Y was not vested upon its creation, it would be initially valid under Section

1(a)(1) because Y would be his own validating life; Y will either reach 25 or die under 25 within his own lifetime.

The inclusion of the phrase "before or after my death," however, would probably be construed to mean that G intended after-born children to receive a $10,000 bequest. * * * Assuming that this construction were adopted, the specific-sum doctrine allows the interest of each child of A to be treated separately from the others for purposes of the Statutory Rule. For the reasons cited above, the interests of X and Y are initially valid under Section 1(a)(1). The nonvested interest of Z, however, fails Section 1(a)(1)'s test for initial validity; there is no validating life because Z, who was not alive when the interest was created, could reach 25 or die under 25 more than 21 years after the death of the survivor of A, X, and Y. Under Section 1(a)(2), the validity of Z's interest depends on Z's reaching (or failing to reach) 25 within 90 years after G's death.

The operation of the sub-class doctrine under this Act is illustrated in the following example.

Example (24)—Sub-Class Case. G devised property in trust, directing the trustee to pay the income "to A for life, then in equal shares to A's children for their respective lives; on the death of each child, the proportionate share of corpus of the one so dying shall go to the children of such child." G was survived by A and by A's two children (X and Y). After G's death, another child (Z) was born to A. A now has died, survived by X, Y, and Z.

Under the sub-class doctrine, each remainder interest in favor of the children of a child of A is treated separately from the others. This allows the remainder interest in favor of X's children and the remainder interest in favor of Y's children to be validated under Section 1(a)(1). X is the validating life for the one, and Y is the validating life for the other.

The remainder interest in favor of the children of Z fails Section 1(a)(1)'s test for initial validity; there is no validating life because Z, who was not alive when the interest was created, could have children more than 21 years after the death of the survivor of A, X, and Y. Under Section 1(a)(2), the validity of the remainder interest in favor of Z's children depends on Z's dying within 90 years after G's death.

Note why both of the requirements of the sub-class rule are met. The ultimate takers are described as a group of sub-classes rather than as a single class: "children of the child so dying," as opposed to "grandchildren." The share to which each separate sub-class is entitled is certain to be finally determined within a life in being plus 21 years: As of A's death, who is a life in being, it is certain to be known how many children he had surviving him; since in fact there were three, we know that each sub-class will ultimately be entitled to one-third of the corpus, neither more nor less. The possible failure of the one-third share of Z's children does not increase to one-half the share going to X's and Y's children; they still are entitled to only one-third shares. Indeed, should it turn out that X has children but Y does not, this would not increase the one-third share to which X's children are entitled.

Example (25)—General Testamentary Powers—Sub-Class Case. G devised property in trust, directing the trustee to pay income "to A for life, then in equal shares to A's children for their respective lives; on the death of each child, the proportionate share of corpus of the one so dying shall go to such persons as the one so dying shall by will appoint; in default of appointment, to G's grandchildren in equal shares." G was survived by A and by A's two children (X and Y). After G's death, another child (Z) was born to A.

The general testamentary powers conferred on each of A's children are entitled to separate treatment under the principles of the sub-class doctrine. See above. Consequently, the powers conferred on X and Y, A's children who were living at G's death, are initially valid under Section 1(c)(1). But the general testamentary power conferred on Z, A's child who was born after G's death, fails the test of Section 1(c)(1) for *initial* validity. The validity of Z's power is governed by Section 1(c)(2). Z's death must occur within 90 years after G's death if any provision in Z's will purporting to exercise his power is to be valid.

Duration of Indestructible Trusts—Termination of Trusts by Beneficiaries. The widely accepted view in American law is that the beneficiaries of a trust other than a charitable trust can compel its premature termination if all beneficiaries consent *and* if such termination is not expressly restrained or impliedly restrained by the existence of a "material purpose" of the settlor in establishing the trust. * * * A trust that cannot be terminated by its beneficiaries is called an indestructible trust.

It is generally accepted that the duration of the indestructibility of a trust, other than a charitable trust, is limited to the applicable perpetuity period. * * *

Nothing in this Act supersedes this principle. One modification, however, is necessary: As to trusts that contain a nonvested property interest or power of appointment whose validity is governed by the wait-and-see element adopted in Section 1(a)(2), 1(b)(2), or 1(c)(2), the courts can be expected to determine that the applicable perpetuity period is 90 years.

Section 2. When Nonvested Property Interest or Power of Appointment Created.

(a)   Except as provided in subsections (b) and (c) and in Section 5(a), the time of creation of a nonvested property interest or a power of appointment is determined under general principles of property law.

(b)   For purposes of this [Act], if there is a person who alone can exercise a power created by a governing instrument to become the unqualified beneficial owner of (i) a nonvested property interest or (ii) a property interest subject to a power of appointment described in Section 1(b) or 1(c), the nonvested property interest or power of appointment is created when the power to become the unqualified beneficial owner terminates. [For purposes of this [Act], a joint power with respect to community property or to marital property under the Uniform Marital Property Act held by individuals married to each other is a power exercisable by one person alone.]

(c)   For purposes of this [Act], a nonvested property interest or a power of appointment arising from a transfer of property to a previously funded trust or other existing property arrangement is created when the nonvested property interest or power of appointment in the original contribution was created.

Comment

Subsection (a): General Principles of Property Law; When Nonvested Property Interests and Powers of Appointment are Created. Under Section 1, the period of time allowed by the Statutory Rule Against Perpetuities is marked off from the time of creation of the nonvested property interest or power of appointment in question. Section 5, with certain exceptions, provides that the Act applies only to nonvested property interests and powers of appointment created on or after the effective date of the Act.

Except as provided in subsections (b) and (c), and in the second sentence of Section 5(a) for purposes of that section only, the time of creation of nonvested property interests and powers of appointment is determined under general principles of property law.

Since a will becomes effective as a dispositive instrument upon the decedent's death, not upon the execution of the will, general principles of property law determine that the time when a nonvested property interest or a power of appointment created by will is created is at the decedent's death.

With respect to a nonvested property interest or a power of appointment created by inter vivos transfer, the time when the interest or power is created is the date the transfer becomes effective for purposes of property law generally, normally the date of delivery of the deed.

With respect to a nonvested property interest or a power of appointment created by the testamentary or inter vivos exercise of a power of appointment, general principles of property law adopt the "relation back" doctrine. Under that doctrine, the appointed interests or powers are created when the power was *created* not when it was exercised, if the exercised power was a nongeneral power or a general testamentary power. If the exercised power was a general power presently exercisable, the relation back doctrine is not followed; the time of creation of the appointed property interests or appointed powers is regarded as the time when the power was irrevocably *exercised*, not when the power was created.

Subsection (b): Postponement, for Purposes of this Act, of the Time when a Nonvested Property Interest or a Power of Appointment is Created in Certain Cases. The reason that the significant date for purposes of this Act is the date of creation is that the unilateral control of the interest (or the interest subject to the power) by one person is then relinquished. In certain cases, all beneficial rights in a property interest (including an interest subject to a power of appointment) remain under the unilateral control of one person even after the delivery of the deed or even after the decedent's death. In such cases, under this subsection, the interest or power is created, for purposes of this Act, when no person, acting alone, has a power presently exercisable to become the unqualified beneficial owner of the property interest (or the property interest subject to the power of appointment).

Example (1)—Revocable Inter-Vivos Trust Case. G conveyed property to a trustee, directing the trustee to pay the net income therefrom to himself (G) for life, then to G's son A for his life, then to A's children for the life of the survivor of A's children who are living at G's death, and upon the death of such last surviving child, the corpus of the trust is to be distributed among A's then-living descendants, per stirpes. G retained the power to revoke the trust.

Because of G's reservation of the power to revoke the trust, the creation for purposes of this Act of the nonvested property interests in this case occurs at G's death, not when the trust was established. This is in accordance with common law, for purposes of the Common-law Rule Against Perpetuities. * * *

The rationale that justifies the postponement of the time of creation in such cases is as follows. A person, such as G in the above example, who alone can exercise a power to become the unqualified beneficial owner of a nonvested property interest is in effect the owner of that property interest. Thus, any nonvested property interest subject to such a power is not created for purposes of this Act until the power terminates (by release, expiration at the death of the donee, or otherwise). Similarly, as noted above, any property interest or power of appointment created in an appointee by the irrevocable exercise of such a power is created at the time of the donee's irrevocable exercise.

For the date of creation to be postponed under subsection (b), the power need not be a power to revoke, and it need not be held by the settlor or transferor. A *presently exercisable* power held by *any* person *acting alone* to make himself the unqualified beneficial owner of the nonvested property interest or the property interest subject to a power of appointment is sufficient. If such a power exists, the time when the interest or power is created, for purposes of this Act, is postponed until the termination of the power (by irrevocable exercise, release, contract to exercise or not to exercise, expiration at the death of the donee, or otherwise). An example of such a power that might not be held by the settlor or transferor is a power, held by any person who can act alone, fully to invade the corpus of a trust.

An important consequence of the idea that a power need not be held by the settlor for the time of creation to be postponed under this section is that it makes postponement possible even in cases of testamentary transfers.

Example (2)—Testamentary Trust Case. G devised property in trust, directing the trustee to pay the income "to A for life, remainder to such persons (including A, his creditors, his estate, and the creditors of his estate) as A shall appoint; in default of appointment, the property to remain in trust to pay the income to A's children for the life of the survivor, and upon the death of A's last surviving child, to pay the corpus to A's grandchildren." A survived G.

If A exercises his presently exercisable general power, any nonvested property interest or power of appointment created by A's appointment is created for purposes of this Act when the power is exercised. If A does not exercise the power, the nonvested property interests in G's gift-in-default clause are created when A's power terminates (at A's death). In either case, the postponement is justified because the transaction is the equivalent of G's having devised the full remainder interest (following A's income interest) to A and of A's having in turn transferred that interest in accordance with his exercise of the power or, in the event the power is not exercised, devised that interest at his death in accordance with G's gift-in-default clause. Note, however, that if G had conferred on A a *nongeneral* power or a general *testamentary* power, A's power of appointment, any nonvested property interest or power of appointment created by A's appointment, if any, and the nonvested property interests in G's gift-in-default clause would be created at G's death.

Unqualified Beneficial Owner of the Nonvested Property Interest or the Property Interest Subject to a Power of Appointment. For the date of creation to be postponed under subsection (b), the presently exercisable power must be one that entitles the donee of the power to become the unqualified beneficial owner of the *nonvested property interest (or the property interest subject to a nongeneral power of* *appointment, a general testamentary power of appointment, or a general power of appointment not presently exercisable because of a condition precedent).* This requirement was met in Example (2), above, because A could by appointing the remainder interest to himself become the unqualified beneficial owner of all the nonvested property interests in G's gift-in-default clause. In Example (2) it is not revealed whether A, if he exercised the power in his own favor, also had the right as sole beneficiary of the trust to compel the termination of the trust and possess himself as unqualified beneficial owner of the property that was the subject of the trust. Having the power to compel termination of the trust is not necessary. If, for example, the trust in Example (2) was a spendthrift trust or contained any other feature that under the relevant local law * * * would prevent A as sole beneficiary from compelling termination of the trust, A's presently exercisable general power over the remainder interest would still postpone the time of creation of the nonvested property interests in G's gift-in-default clause because the power enables A to become the unqualified beneficial owner of such interests.

Furthermore, it is not necessary that the donee of the power have the power to become the unqualified beneficial owner of *all beneficial* rights *in the trust*. In Example (2), the property interests in G's gift-in-default clause are not created for purposes of this Act until A's power expires (or on A's appointment, until the power's exercise) even if someone other than A was the income beneficiary of the trust.

Presently Exercisable Power. For the date of creation to be postponed under subsection (b), the power must be presently exercisable. A testamentary power does not qualify. A power not presently exercisable because of a condition precedent does not qualify. If the condition precedent later becomes satisfied, however, so that the power becomes presently exercisable, the interests or powers subject thereto are not created, for purposes of this Act, until the termination of the power. * * *

Example (3)—General Power in Unborn Child Case. G devised property "to A for life, then to A's first-born child for life, then to such persons, including A's first-born child or such child's estate or creditors, as A's first-born child shall appoint." There was a further provision that in default of appointment, the trust would continue for the benefit of G's descendants. G was survived by his daughter (A), who was then childless. After G's death, A had a child, X. A then died, survived by X.

As of G's death, the power of appointment in favor of A's first-born child and the property interests in G's gift-in-default clause would be regarded as having been created at G's death because the power in A's first-born child was then a general power not presently exercisable because of a condition precedent.

At X's birth, X's general power became presently exercisable and excluded from the Statutory Rule. X's power also qualifies as a power exercisable by one person alone to become the unqualified beneficial owner of the property interests in G's gift-in-default clause. Consequently, the nonvested property interests in G's gift-in-default clause are not created, for purposes of this Act, until the termination of X's power. If X exercises his presently exercisable general power, before or after A's death, the appointed interests or powers are created, for purposes of this Act, as of X's exercise of the power.

Partial Powers. For the date of creation to be postponed under subsection (b), the person must have a presently exercisable power to become the unqualified beneficial owner of the full nonvested property interest or the property interest subject to a power of appointment described in Section 1(b) or 1(c). If, for example, the subject of the transfer was an undivided interest such as a one-third tenancy in common, the power qualifies even though it relates only to the undivided one-third interest in the tenancy in common; it need not relate to the whole property. A power to become the unqualified beneficial owner of only part of the nonvested property interest or the property interest subject to a power of appointment, however, does not postpone the time of creation of the interests or powers subject thereto, unless the power is actually exercised.

Example (4)—"5 and 5" Power Case. G devised property in trust, directing the trustee to pay the income "to A for life, remainder to such persons (including A, his creditors, his estate, and the creditors of his estate) as A shall by will appoint;" in default of appointment, the governing instrument provided for the property to continue in trust. A was given a noncumulative power to withdraw the greater of $5,000 or 5% of the corpus of the trust annually. A survived G. A never exercised his noncumulative power of withdrawal.

G's death marks the time of creation of: A's testamentary power of appointment; any nonvested property interest or power of appointment created in G's gift-in-default clause; and any appointed interest or power created by a testamentary exercise of A's power of appointment over the remainder interest. A's general power of appointment over the remainder interest does not postpone the time of creation because it is not a presently exercisable power. A's noncumulative power to withdraw a portion of the trust each year does not postpone the time of creation as to all or the portion of the trust with respect to which A allowed his power to lapse each year because A's power is a power over only part of any nonvested property interest or property interest subject to a power of appointment in G's gift-in-default clause and over only part of any appointed interest or power created by a testamentary exercise of A's general power of appointment over the remainder interest. The same conclusion has been reached at common law. * * *

If, however, in any year A exercised his noncumulative power of withdrawal in a way that created a nonvested property interest (or power of appointment) in the withdrawn amount (for example, if A directed the trustee to transfer the amount withdrawn directly into a trust created by A), the appointed interests (or powers) would be created when the power was exercised, not when G died.

Incapacity of the Donee of the Power. The fact that the donee of a power lacks the capacity to exercise it, by reason of minority, mental incompetency, or any other reason, does not prevent the power held by such person from postponing the time of creation under subsection (b), unless the governing instrument extinguishes the power (or prevents it from coming into existence) for that reason.

Joint Powers—Community Property; Marital Property. For the date of creation to be postponed under subsection (b), the power must be exercisable by one person alone. A joint power does not qualify, except that, if the bracketed sentence of subsection (b) is enacted, a joint power over community property or over marital property under the Uniform Marital Property Act held by individuals married to each other is, for purposes of this Act, treated as a power exercisable by one person acting alone. * * *

Subsection (c): No Staggered Periods. For purposes of this Act, subsection (c) in effect treats a transfer of property to a previously funded trust or other existing property arrangement as having been made when the nonvested property interest or power of appointment in the original contribution was created. The purpose of subsection (c) is to avoid the administrative difficulties that would otherwise result where subsequent transfers are made to an existing irrevocable trust. Without subsection (c), the allowable period under the Statutory Rule would be marked off in such cases from different times with respect to different portions of the same trust.

> *Example (5)—Series of Transfers Case.* In Year One, G created an irrevocable inter vivos trust, funding it with $20,000 cash. In Year Five, when the value of the investments in which the original $20,000 contribution was placed had risen to a value of $30,000, G added $10,000 cash to the trust. G died in Year Ten. G's will poured the residuary of his estate into the trust. G's residuary estate consisted of Blackacre (worth $20,000) and securities (worth $80,000). At G's death, the value of the investments in which the original $20,000 contribution and the subsequent $10,000 contribution were placed had risen to a value of $50,000.

> Were it not for subsection (c), the permissible vesting period under the Statutory Rule would be marked off from three different times: Year One, Year Five, and Year Ten. The effect of subsection (c) is that the permissible vesting period under the Statutory Rule starts running only once—in Year One—with respect to the entire trust. This result is defensible not only to prevent the administrative difficulties inherent in recognizing staggered periods. It also is defensible because if G's inter vivos trust had contained a perpetuity saving clause, the perpetuity-period component of the clause would be geared to the time when the original contribution to the trust was made; this clause would cover the subsequent contributions as well. Since the major justification for the adoption by this Act of the wait-and-see method of perpetuity reform is that it amounts to a statutory insertion of a saving clause (see the Prefatory Note), subsection (c) is consistent with the theory of this Act. * * *

Section 3. Reformation.

Upon the petition of an interested person, a court shall reform a disposition in the manner that most closely approximates the transferor's manifested plan of distribution and is within the 90 years allowed by Section 1(a)(2), 1(b)(2), or 1(c)(2) if:

(1)   a nonvested property interest or a power of appointment becomes invalid under Section 1 (statutory rule against perpetuities);

(2)   a class gift is not but might become invalid under Section 1 (statutory rule against perpetuities) and the time has arrived when the share of any class member is to take effect in possession or enjoyment; or

(3)   a nonvested property interest that is not validated by Section 1(a)(1) can vest but not within 90 years after its creation.

Comment

Reformation. This section requires a court, upon the petition of an interested person, to reform a disposition *whose validity is governed by the wait-and-see element of Section 1(a)(2), 1(b)(2), or 1(c)(2)* so that the reformed disposition is within the limits of the 90-year period allowed by those subsections, in the manner deemed by the court most closely to approximate the transferor's manifested plan of distribution, in three circumstances: First, when (after the application of the Statutory Rule) a nonvested property interest or a power of appointment becomes invalid under the Statutory Rule; second, when a class gift has not but still might become invalid under the Statutory Rule and the time has arrived when the share of one or more class members is to take effect in possession or enjoyment; and third, when a nonvested property interest can vest, but cannot do so within the allowable 90-year period under the Statutory Rule.

It is anticipated that the circumstances requisite to reformation will seldom arise, and consequently that this section will be applied infrequently. If, however, one of the three circumstances arises, the court in reforming is authorized to alter existing interests or powers and to create new interests or powers by implication or construction based on the transferor's manifested plan of distribution as a whole. In reforming, the court is urged not to invalidate any vested interest retroactively (the doctrine of infectious invalidity having been superseded by this Act, as indicated in the Comment to Section 1). The court is also urged not to reduce an age contingency in excess of 21 unless it is absolutely necessary, and if it is deemed necessary to reduce such an age contingency, not to reduce it automatically to 21 but rather to reduce it no lower than absolutely necessary. * * *

Judicial Sale of Land Affected by Future Interests. Although this section—except for cases that fall under subsections (2) or (3)—defers the time when a court is directed to reform a disposition until the expiration of the 90-year permissible vesting period, this section is not to be understood as preventing an earlier application of other remedies. In particular, in the case of interests in land not in trust, the principle, codified in many states, is widely recognized that there is judicial authority, under specified circumstances, to order a sale of land in which there are future interests. * * * Nothing in Section 3 of this Act should be taken as precluding this type of remedy, if appropriate, before the expiration of the 90-year permissible vesting period.

Duration of the Indestructibility of Trusts—Termination of Trusts by Beneficiaries. As noted in Part G of the Comment to Section 1, it is generally accepted that a trust cannot remain indestructible beyond the period of the rule against perpetuities. Under this Act, the period of the rule against perpetuities applicable to a trust whose validity is governed by the wait-and-see element of Section 1(a)(2), 1(b)(2), or 1(c)(2) is 90 years. The result of any reformation under Section 3 is that all nonvested property interests in the trust will vest *in interest* (or terminate) no later than the 90th anniversary of their creation. In the case of trusts containing a nonvested property interest or a power of appointment whose validity is governed by Section 1(a)(2), 1(b)(2), or 1(c)(2), courts can therefore be expected to adopt the rule that no purpose of the settlor, expressed in or implied from the governing instrument, can prevent the beneficiaries of a trust other than a charitable trust from compelling its termination after 90 years after every nonvested property interest and power of appointment in the trust was created.

Subsection (1): Invalid Property Interest or Power of Appointment. Subsection (1) is illustrated by the following examples.

Example (1)—Multiple Generation Trust. G devised property in trust, directing the trustee to pay the income "to A for life, then to A's children for the life of the survivor, then to A's grandchildren for the life of the survivor, and on the death of A's last surviving grandchild, the corpus of the trust is to be divided among A's then living descendants per stirpes; if none, to" a specified charity. G was survived by his child (A) and by A's two minor children (X and Y). After G's death, another child (Z) was born to A. Subsequently, A died, survived by his children (X, Y, and Z) and by three grandchildren (M, N, and O).

There are four interests subject to the Statutory Rule in this example: (1) the income interest in favor of A's children, (2) the income interest in favor of A's grandchildren, (3) the remainder interest in the corpus in favor of A's descendants who survive the death of A's last surviving grandchild, and (4) the alternative remainder interest in the corpus in favor of the specified charity. The first interest is initially valid under Section 1(a)(1); A is the validating life for that interest. There is no validating life for the other three interests, and so their validity is governed by Section 1(a)(2).

If, as is likely, A and A's children all die before the 90th anniversary of G's death, the income interest in favor of A's grandchildren is valid under Section 1(a)(2).

If, as is also likely, some of A's grandchildren are alive on the 90th anniversary of G's death, the alternative remainder interests in the corpus of the trust then become invalid under Section 1(a)(2), giving rise to Section 3(1)'s prerequisite to reformation. A court would be justified in reforming G's disposition by closing the class in favor of A's descendants as of the 90th anniversary of G's death (precluding new entrants thereafter), by moving back the condition of survivorship on the class so that the remainder interest is in favor of G's descendants who survive the 90th anniversary of G's death (rather than in favor of those who survive the death of A's last surviving grandchild), and by redefining the class so that its makeup is formed as if A's last surviving grandchild died on the 90th anniversary of G's death.

Example (2)—Sub-Class Case. G devised property in trust, directing the trustee to pay the income "to A for life, then in equal shares to A's children for their respective lives; on the death of each child the proportionate share of corpus of the one so dying shall go to the descendants of such child surviving at such child's death, per stirpes." G was survived by A and by A's two children (X and Y). After G's death, another child (Z) was born to A. Subsequently, A died, survived by X, Y, and Z.

Under the sub-class doctrine, each remainder interest in favor of the descendants of a child of A is treated separately from the others. Consequently, the remainder interest in favor of X's descendants and the remainder interest in favor of Y's descendants are valid under Section 1(a)(1): X is the validating life for the one, and Y is the validating life for the other.

The remainder interest in favor of the descendants of Z is not validated by Section 1(a)(1) because Z, who was not alive when the interest was created, could have descendants more than 21 years after the death of the survivor of A, X, and Y. Instead, the validity of the remainder interest in favor of Z's descendants is governed by Section 1(a)(2), under which its validity depends on Z's dying within 90 years after G's death.

Although unlikely, suppose that Z is still living 90 years after G's death. The remainder interest in favor of Z's descendants will then become invalid under the Statutory Rule, giving rise to subsection (1)'s prerequisite to reformation. In such circumstances, a court would be justified in reforming the remainder interest in favor of Z's descendants by making it indefeasibly vested as of the 90th anniversary of G's death. To do this, the court would reform the disposition by eliminating the condition of survivorship of Z and closing the class to new entrants after the 90th anniversary of G's death.

Subsection (2): Class Gifts Not Yet Invalid. Subsection (2), which, upon the petition of an interested person, requires reformation in certain cases where a class gift has not but still might become invalid under the Statutory Rule, is illustrated by the following examples.

Example (3)—Age Contingency in Excess of 21. G devised property in trust, directing the trustee to pay the income "to A for life, then to A's children; the corpus of the trust is to be equally divided among A's children who reach the age of 30." G was survived by A, by A's spouse (H), and by A's two children (X and Y), both of whom were under the age of 30 when G died.

Since the remainder interest in favor of A's children who reach 30 is a class gift, at common law (*Leake v. Robinson*, 2 Mer. 363, 35 Eng. Rep. 979 (Ch. 1817)) and under this Act (see Part G of the Comment to Section 1) the interests of *all* potential class members must be valid or the class gift is totally invalid. Although X and Y will either reach 30 or die under 30 within their own lifetimes, there is at G's death the possibility that A will have an afterborn child (Z) who will reach 30 or die under 30 more than 21 years after the death of the survivor of A, H, X, and Y. There is no validating life, and the class gift is therefore not validated by Section 1(a)(1).

Under Section 1(a)(2), the children's remainder interest becomes invalid only if an interest of a class member neither vests nor terminates within 90 years after G's death. If in fact there is an afterborn child (Z), and if upon A's death, Z has at least reached an age such that he cannot be alive and under the age of 30 on the 90th anniversary of G's death, the class gift is valid. (Note that at Z's *birth* it would have been known whether or not Z could be alive and under the age of 30 on the 90th anniversary of G's death; nevertheless, even if it was *then* certain that Z could *not* be alive and under the age of 30 on the 90th anniversary of G's death, the class gift could not *then* have been declared valid because, A being alive, it was *then* possible for one or more additional children to have later been born to or adopted by A.)

Although unlikely, suppose that at A's death (prior to the expiration of the 90-year period), Z's age was such that he *could* be alive and under the age of 30 on the 90th anniversary of G's death. Suppose further that at A's death X and Y were over the age of 30. Z's interest and hence the class gift as a whole is not yet invalid under the Statutory Rule because Z might die under the age of 30 within the remaining part of the 90-year period following G's death; but the class gift might become invalid because Z might be alive and under the age of 30, 90 years after G's death. Consequently, the prerequisites to reformation set forth in subsection (2) are satisfied, and a court would be justified in reforming G's disposition to provide that Z's interest is contingent on reaching the age he can reach if he lives to the 90th anniversary of G's death. This would render Z's interest valid so far as the Statutory Rule Against Perpetuities is concerned, and allow the class gift as a whole to be declared valid. X and Y would thus be entitled immediately to their one-third shares each. If Z's interest later vested, Z would receive the remaining one-third share. If Z failed to reach the required age under the reformed disposition, the remaining one-third share would be divided equally between X and Y or their successors in interest.

Example (4)—Case Where Subsection (2) Applies, Not Involving an Age Contingency in Excess of 21. G devised property in trust, directing the trustee to pay the income "to A for life, then to A's children; the corpus of the trust is to be equally divided among A's children who graduate from an accredited medical school or law school." G was survived by A, by A's spouse (H), and by A's two minor children (X and Y).

As in Example (3), the remainder interest in favor of A's children is a class gift, and the common-law principle is not superseded by this Act by which the interests of *all* potential class members must be valid or the class gift is totally invalid. Although X and Y will either graduate from an accredited medical or law school, or fail to do so, within their own lifetimes, there is at G's death the possibility that A will have an after-born child (Z), who will graduate from an accredited medical or law school (or die without having done either) more than 21 years after the death of the survivor of A, H, X, and Y. The class gift would not be valid under the Common-law Rule and is, therefore, not validated by Section 1(a)(1).

Under Section 1(a)(2), the children's remainder interest becomes invalid only if an interest of a class member neither vests nor terminates within 90 years after G's death.

Suppose in fact that there is an afterborn child (Z), and that at A's death Z was a freshman in college. Suppose further that at A's death X had graduated from an accredited law school and that Y had graduated from an accredited medical school. Z's interest and hence the class gift as a whole is not yet invalid under Section 1(a)(2) because the 90-year period following G's death has not yet expired; but the class gift might become invalid because Z might be alive but not a graduate of an accredited medical or law school 90 years after G's death. Consequently, the prerequisites to reformation set forth in Section 3(2) are satisfied, and a court would be justified in reforming G's disposition to provide that Z's interest is contingent on graduating from an accredited medical or law school within 90 years after G's death. This would render Z's interest valid so far as the Section 1(a)(2) is concerned and allow the class gift as a whole to be declared valid. X and Y would thus be entitled immediately to their one-third shares each. If Z's interest later vested, Z would receive the remaining one-third share. If Z failed to graduate from an accredited medical or law school within the allowed time under the disposition as so reformed, the remaining one-third share would be divided equally between X and Y or their successors in interest.

Subsection (3): Interests that Can Vest But Not Within the 90-Year Permissible Vesting Period. In exceedingly rare cases, an interest might be created that can vest, but not within the 90-year permissible vesting period of the Statutory Rule. This may be the situation when the interest was created (See Example (5)), or it may become the situation at some time thereafter (see Example (6)). Whenever the situation occurs, the court, upon the petition of an interested person, is required by subsection (3) to reform the disposition within the limits of the 90-year permissible vesting period.

Example (5)—Case of an Interest, as of its Creation, being Impossible to Vest Within the 90-Year Period. G devised property in trust, directing the trustee to divide the income, per stirpes, among G's descendants from time to time living, for 100 years. At the end of the 100-year period following G's death, the trustee is to distribute the corpus and accumulated income to G's then-living descendants, per stirpes; if none, to the XYZ Charity.

The nonvested property interest in favor of G's descendants who are living 100 years after G's death can vest, but not within the 90-year period of Section 1(a)(2). The interest would violate the Common-law Rule, and hence is not validated by Section 1(a)(1), because there is no validating life. In these circumstances, a court is required by Section 3(3) to reform G's disposition within the limits of the 90-year period. An appropriate result would be for the court to lower the period following G's death from a 100-year period to a 90-year period.

Note that the circumstance that triggers the direction to reform the disposition under this subsection is that the nonvested property interest still can vest, but cannot vest within the 90-year period of Section 1(a)(2). It is not necessary that the interest be certain to become *invalid* under that subsection. For the interest to be certain to become invalid under Section 1(a)(2), it would have to be certain that it can neither vest *nor terminate* within the 90-year period. In this example, the interest of G's descendants might *terminate* within the period (by all of G's descendants dying within 90 years of G's death). If this were to happen, the interest of XYZ Charity would be valid because it would have vested within the allowable period. However, it was thought desirable to require reformation without waiting to see if this would happen: The only way that G's *descendants*, who are G's *primary* set of beneficiaries, would have a chance to take the property is to reform the disposition within the limits of the 90-year period on the ground that their interest cannot *vest* within the allowable period and subsection (3) so provides.

Example (6)—Case of an Interest after its Creation Becoming Impossible to Vest Within the 90-Year Period. G devised property in trust, with the income to be paid to A. The corpus of the trust was to be divided among A's children who reach 30, each child's share to be paid on the child's 30th birthday; if none reaches 30, to the XYZ Charity. G was survived by A and by A's two children (X and Y). Neither X nor Y had reached 30 at G's death.

The class gift in favor of A's children who reach 30 would violate the Common-law Rule Against Perpetuities and, thus, is not validated by Section 1(a)(1). Its validity is therefore governed by Section 1(a)(2).

Suppose that after G's death, and during A's lifetime, X and Y die and a third child (Z) is born to or adopted by A. At A's death, Z is living but her age is such that she cannot reach 30 within the remaining part of the 90-year period following G's death. As of A's death, it has become the situation that Z's interest cannot vest within the allowable period. The circumstances requisite to reformation under subsection (3) have arisen. An appropriate result would be for the court to lower the age contingency to the age Z can reach 90 years after G's death. * * *

Section 4. Exclusions From Statutory Rule Against Perpetuities.

Section 1 (statutory rule against perpetuities) does not apply to:

(1) a nonvested property interest or a power of appointment arising out of a nondonative transfer, except a nonvested property interest or a power of appointment arising out of (i) a premarital or postmarital agreement, (ii) a separation or divorce settlement, (iii) a spouse's election, (iv) a similar arrangement arising out of a prospective, existing, or previous marital relationship between the

parties, (v) a contract to make or not to revoke a will or trust, (vi) a contract to exercise or not to exercise a power of appointment, (vii) a transfer in satisfaction of a duty of support, or (viii) a reciprocal transfer;

(2)   a fiduciary's power relating to the administration or management of assets, including the power of a fiduciary to sell, lease, or mortgage property, and the power of a fiduciary to determine principal and income;

(3)   a power to appoint a fiduciary;

(4)   a discretionary power of a trustee to distribute principal before termination of a trust to a beneficiary having an indefeasibly vested interest in the income and principal;

(5)   a nonvested property interest held by a charity, government, or governmental agency or subdivision, if the nonvested property interest is preceded by an interest held by another charity, government, or governmental agency or subdivision;

(6)   a nonvested property interest in or a power of appointment with respect to a trust or other property arrangement forming part of a pension, profit-sharing, stock bonus, health, disability, death benefit, income deferral, or other current or deferred benefit plan for one or more employees, independent contractors, or their beneficiaries or spouses, to which contributions are made for the purpose of distributing to or for the benefit of the participants or their beneficiaries or spouses the property, income, or principal in the trust or other property arrangement, except a nonvested property interest or a power of appointment that is created by an election of a participant or a beneficiary or spouse; or

(7)   a property interest, power of appointment, or arrangement that was not subject to the common-law rule against perpetuities or is excluded by another statute of this State.

Comment

Section 4 lists seven exclusions from the Statutory Rule Against Perpetuities (Statutory Rule). Some are declaratory of existing law; others are contrary to existing law. Since the Common-law Rule Against Perpetuities is superseded by this Act (or a statutory version or variation thereof is repealed by this Act), a nonvested property interest, power of appointment, or other arrangement excluded from the Statutory Rule by this section is not subject to any rule against perpetuities, statutory or otherwise.

A.   SUBSECTION (1): NONDONATIVE TRANSFERS EXCLUDED

Rationale. In line with long-standing scholarly commentary, subsection (1) excludes (with certain enumerated exceptions) nonvested property interests and powers of appointment arising out of a nondonative transfer. The rationale for this exclusion is that the Rule Against Perpetuities is a wholly inappropriate instrument of social policy to use as a control over such arrangements. The period of the rule— a life in being plus 21 years—is not suitable for nondonative transfers, and this point applies with equal force to the 90-year allowable waiting period under the wait-and-see element of Section 1 because that period represents an approximation of the period of time that would be produced, on average, by using a statutory list identifying actual measuring lives and adding a 21-year period following the death of the survivor.

No general exclusion from the Common-law Rule Against Perpetuities is recognized for nondonative transfers, and so subsection (1) is contrary to existing common law. * * *

Subsection (1) is therefore inconsistent with decisions holding the Common-law Rule to be applicable to the following types of property interests or arrangements when created in a nondonative, commercial-type transaction, as they almost always are: options * * * ; preemptive rights in the nature of a right of first refusal * * * ; leases to commence in the future, at a time certain or on the happening of a future event such as the completion of a building * * * ; nonvested easements; top leases and top deeds with respect to interests in minerals * * * ; and so on.

Consideration Does Not Necessarily Make the Transfer Nondonative. A transfer can be supported by consideration and still be donative in character and hence not excluded from the Statutory Rule. A transaction that is essentially gratuitous in nature, accompanied by donative intent on the part of at least one party to the transaction, is not to be regarded as nondonative simply because it is for consideration. Thus, for example, the exclusion would not apply if a parent purchases a parcel of land for full and adequate consideration, and directs the seller to make out the deed in favor of the purchaser's daughter for life, remainder to such of the daughter's children as reach 25. The nonvested property interest of the daughter's children is subject to the Statutory Rule.

Some Transactions Not Excluded Even if Considered Nondonative. Some types of transactions—although in some sense supported by consideration and hence arguably nondonative—arise out of a domestic situation, and should not be excluded from the Statutory Rule. To avoid uncertainty with respect to such transactions, subsection (1) specifies that nonvested property interests or powers of appointment arising out of any of the following transactions are not excluded by subsection (1)'s nondonative-transfers exclusion: a premarital or postmarital agreement; a separation or divorce settlement; a spouse's election, such as the "widow's election" in community property states; an arrangement similar to any of the foregoing arising out of a prospective, existing, or previous marital relationship between the parties; a contract to make or not to revoke a will or trust; a contract to exercise or not to exercise a power of appointment; a transfer in full or partial satisfaction of a duty of support; or a reciprocal transfer. The term "reciprocal transfer" is to be interpreted in accordance with the reciprocal transfer doctrine in the tax law (see *United States v. Estate of Grace*, 395 U.S. 316 (1969)).

Other Means of Controlling Some Nondonative Transfers Desirable. Some commercial transactions respecting land or mineral interests, such as options in gross (including rights of first refusal), leases to commence in the future, nonvested easements, and top leases and top deeds in commercial use in the oil and gas industry, directly or indirectly restrain the alienability of property or provide a disincentive to improve the property. Although controlling the duration of such interests is desirable, they are excluded by subsection (1) from the Statutory Rule because, as noted above, the period of a life in being plus 21 years—actual or by the 90-year proxy—is inappropriate for them; that period is appropriate for family-oriented, donative transfers. * * *

B. SUBSECTIONS (2)–(7): OTHER EXCLUSIONS

Subsection (2)—Administrative Fiduciary Powers. Fiduciary powers are subject to the Statutory Rule Against Perpetuities, unless specifically excluded. Purely administrative fiduciary powers are excluded by subsections (2) and (3), but distributive fiduciary powers are generally speaking not excluded. The only distributive fiduciary power excluded is the one described in subsection (4).

The application of subsection (2) to fiduciary powers can be illustrated by the following example.

Example (1). G devised property in trust, directing the trustee (a bank) to pay the income to A for life, then to A's children for the life of the survivor, and on the death of A's last surviving child to pay the corpus to B. The trustee is granted the discretionary power to sell and to reinvest the trust assets and to invade the corpus on behalf of the income beneficiary or beneficiaries.

The trustee's fiduciary power to sell and reinvest the trust assets is a purely administrative power, and under subsection (2) of this section is not subject to the Statutory Rule.

The trustee's fiduciary power to invade corpus, however, is a nongeneral power of appointment that is not excluded from the Statutory Rule. Its validity, and hence its exercisability, is governed by Section 1. Under that section, since the power is not initially valid under Section 1(c)(1), Section 1(c)(2) applies and the power ceases to be exercisable 90 years after G's death.

Subsection (3)—Powers to Appoint a Fiduciary. Subsection (3) excludes from the Statutory Rule Against Perpetuities powers to appoint a fiduciary (a trustee, successor trustee, or co-trustee, a personal representative, successor personal representative, or co-personal representative, an executor, successor executor, or co-executor, etc.). Sometimes such a power is held by a fiduciary and sometimes not. In either case, the power is excluded from the Statutory Rule.

Subsection (4)—Certain Distributive Fiduciary Power. The only distributive fiduciary power excluded from the Statutory Rule Against Perpetuities is the one described in subsection (4); the excluded power is a discretionary power of a trustee to distribute principal before the termination of a trust to a beneficiary who has an indefeasibly vested interest in the income and principal.

Example (2). G devised property in trust, directing the trustee (a bank) to pay the income to A for life, then to A's children; each child's share of principal is to be paid to the child when he or she reaches

40; if any child dies under 40, the child's share is to be paid to the child's estate as a property interest owned by such child. The trustee is given the discretionary power to advance all or a portion of a child's share before the child reaches 40. G was survived by A, who was then childless.

The trustee's discretionary power to distribute principal to a child before the child's 40th birthday is excluded from the Statutory Rule Against Perpetuities. (The trustee's *duty* to pay the income to A and after A's death to A's children is not subject to the Statutory Rule because it is a duty, not a power.)

Subsection (5)—Charitable or Governmental Gifts. Subsection (5) codifies the common-law principle that a nonvested property interest held by a charity, a government, or a governmental agency or subdivision is excluded from the Rule Against Perpetuities if the interest was preceded by an interest that is held by another charity, government, or governmental agency or subdivision. * * *

Example (3). G devised real property "to the X School District so long as the premises are used for school purposes, and upon the cessation of such use, to Y City."

The nonvested property interest held by Y City (an executory interest) is excluded from the Statutory Rule under subsection (5) because it was preceded by a property interest (a fee simple determinable) held by a governmental subdivision, X School District.

The exclusion of charitable and governmental gifts applies only in the circumstances described. If a nonvested property interest held by a charity is preceded by a property interest that is held by a noncharity, the exclusion does not apply; rather, the validity of the nonvested property interest held by the charity is governed by the other sections of this Act.

Example (4). G devised real property "to A for life, then to such of A's children as reach 25, but if none of A's children reaches 25, to X Charity."

The nonvested property interest held by X Charity is not excluded from the Statutory Rule.

If a nonvested property interest held by a noncharity is preceded by a property interest that is held by a charity, the exclusion does not apply; rather, the validity of the nonvested property interest in favor of the noncharity is governed by the other sections of this Act.

Example (5). G devised real property "to the City of Sidney so long as the premises are used for a public park, and upon the cessation of such use, to my brother, B."

The nonvested property interest held by B is not excluded from the Statutory Rule by subsection (5).

Subsection (6)—Trusts for Employees and Others; Trusts for Self-Employed Individuals. Subsection (6) excludes from the Statutory Rule Against Perpetuities nonvested property interests and powers of appointment with respect to a trust or other property arrangement, whether part of a "qualified" or "unqualified" plan under the federal income tax law, forming part of a bona fide benefit plan for employees (including owner-employees), independent contractors, or their beneficiaries or spouses. The exclusion granted by this subsection does not, however, extend to a nonvested property interest or a power of appointment created by an election of a participant or beneficiary or spouse.

Subsection (7)—Pre-existing Exclusions from the Common-law Rule Against Perpetuities. Subsection (7) assures that all property interests, powers of appointment, or arrangements that were excluded from the Common-law Rule Against Perpetuities or are excluded by another statute of this state are also excluded from the Statutory Rule Against Perpetuities.

Possibilities of reverter and rights of entry (also known as rights of re-entry, rights of entry for condition broken, and powers of termination) are not subject to the Common-law Rule Against Perpetuities, and so are excluded from the Statutory Rule. By statute in some states, possibilities of reverter and rights of entry expire if they do not vest within a specified period of years (such as 40 years). * * *

Section 5. Prospective Application.

(a)   Except as extended by subsection (b), this [Act] applies to a nonvested property interest or a power of appointment that is created on or after the effective date of this [Act]. For purposes of this section, a nonvested property interest or a power of appointment created by the exercise of a power of appointment is created when the power is irrevocably exercised or when a revocable exercise becomes irrevocable.

(b)   If a nonvested property interest or a power of appointment was created before the effective date of this [Act] and is determined in a judicial proceeding, commenced on or after the effective date of this [Act], to violate this State's rule against perpetuities as that rule existed before the effective date of this [Act], a court upon the petition of an interested person may reform the disposition in the manner that most closely approximates the transferor's manifested plan of distribution and is within the limits of the rule against perpetuities applicable when the nonvested property interest or power of appointment was created.

Comment

Subsection (a): Act Not Retroactive. This section provides that, except as provided in subsection (b), the Statutory Rule Against Perpetuities and the other provisions of this Act apply only to nonvested property interests or powers of appointment created on or after the Act's effective date. With one exception, in determining when a nonvested property interest or a power of appointment is created, the principles of Section 2 are applicable. Thus, for example, a property interest (or a power of appointment) created in a revocable inter vivos trust is created when the power to revoke terminates. See Example (1) in the Comment to Section 2.

The second sentence of subsection (a) establishes a special rule for nonvested property interests (and powers of appointment) created by the exercise of a power of appointment. For purposes of this section only, a nonvested property interest (or a power of appointment) created by the exercise of a power of appointment is created when the power is irrevocably exercised or when a revocable exercise of the power becomes irrevocable. Consequently, all the provisions of this Act except Section 5(b) apply to a nonvested property interest (or power of appointment) created by a donee's exercise of a power of appointment where the donee's exercise, whether revocable or irrevocable, occurs on or after the effective date of this Act. All the provisions of this Act except Section 5(b) also apply where the donee's exercise occurred before the effective date of this Act if: (i) that pre-effective-date exercise was revocable *and* (ii) that revocable exercise becomes irrevocable on or after the effective date of this Act. This special rule applies to the exercise of all types of powers of appointment—presently exercisable general powers, general testamentary powers, and nongeneral powers.

If the application of this special rule determines that the provisions of this Act (except Section 5(b)) apply, then for all such purposes, the time of creation of the appointed nonvested property interest (or appointed power of appointment) is determined by reference to Section 2, without regard to the special rule contained in the second sentence of Section 5(a).

If the application of this special rule of Section 5(a) determines that the provisions of this Act (except Section 5(b)) do not apply, then Section 5(b) is the only potentially applicable provision of this Act.

Example (1)—Testamentary Power Created Before but Exercised After the Effective Date of this Act. G was the donee of a general testamentary power of appointment created by the will of his mother, M. M died in 1980. Assume that the effective date of this Act in the jurisdiction is January 1, 1987. G died in 1988, leaving a will that exercised his general testamentary power of appointment.

Under the special rule in the second sentence of Section 5(a), any nonvested property interest (or power of appointment) created by G in his will in exercising his general testamentary power was created (for purposes of Section 5) at G's death in 1988, which was *after* the effective date of this Act.

Consequently, all the provisions of this Act apply (except Section 5(b)). That point having been settled, the next step is to determine whether the nonvested property interests or powers of appointment created by G's testamentary appointment are initially valid under Section 1(a)(1), 1(b)(1), or 1(c)(1), or whether the wait-and-see element established in Section 1(a)(2), 1(b)(2), or 1(c)(2) applies. If the wait-and-see element does apply, it must also be determined when the allowable 90-year waiting period starts to run. In making these determinations, the principles of Section 2 control the time of creation of the nonvested property interests (or powers of appointment); under Section 2, since G's power was a general testamentary power of appointment, the common-law relation-back doctrine applies and the appointed nonvested property interests (and appointed powers of appointment) are created at M's death in 1980.

If G's testamentary power of appointment had been a nongeneral power rather than a general power, the same results as described above would apply.

Example (2)—Presently Exercisable Nongeneral Power Created Before but Exercised After the Effective Date of this Act. Assume the same facts as in Example (1), except that G's power of appointment was a presently exercisable nongeneral power. If G exercised the power in 1988, after the effective date of this Act (or, if a pre-effective-date revocable exercise of his power became irrevocable in 1988, after the effective date of this Act), the same results as described above in Example (1) would apply.

Example (3)—Presently Exercisable General Power Created Before but Exercised After the Effective Date of this Act. Assume the same facts as in Example (1), except that G's power of appointment was a presently exercisable general power. If G exercised the power in 1988, after the effective date of this Act (or, if a pre-effective-date revocable exercise of his power became irrevocable in 1988, after the effective date of this Act), all the provisions of this Act (except Section 5(b)) apply; for such purposes, Section 2 controls the date of creation of the appointed nonvested property interests (or appointed powers of appointment), without regard to the special rule of the second sentence of Section 5(a). With respect to the exercise of a presently exercisable general power, it is possible—indeed, probable—that the special rule of the second sentence of Section 5(a) and the rules of Section 2 agree on the same date of creation for their respective purposes, that date being the date the power was irrevocably exercised (or a revocable exercise thereof became irrevocable).

Subsection (b): Reformation of Pre-existing Instruments. Although the Statutory Rule Against Perpetuities and the other provisions of this Act do not apply retroactively, subsection (b) recognizes a court's authority to exercise its equitable power to reform instruments that contain a violation of the Common-law Rule Against Perpetuities (or of a statutory version or variation thereof) and to which the Statutory Rule does not apply because the offending nonvested property interest or power of appointment in question was created before the effective date of this Act. This equitable power to reform is recognized only where the violation of the former rule against perpetuities is determined in a judicial proceeding that is commenced on or after the effective date of this Act. See below.

Without legislative authorization or direction, the courts in [some] states * * * have held that they have the power to reform instruments that contain a violation of the Common-law Rule Against Perpetuities. * * * In * * * other states * * * the legislatures have enacted statutes conferring this power on the courts or directing the courts to reform defective instruments. * * *

Reformation Experience So Far. The existing judicial opinions and legislative provisions purport to adopt a principle of reformation that is consistent with the theme that the technique of reform should be shaped to grant every appropriate opportunity for the property to go to the intended beneficiaries. * * *

Unfortunately, all the cases that have arisen so far have been of one general type—contingencies in excess of 21 years—and all of the courts have simply ordered a reduction of the age or period in gross to 21.

Guidance as to How to Reform. The above reformation efforts are unduly narrow. Subsection (b) is to be understood as authorizing a more appropriate technique—judicial insertion of a saving clause into the instrument. * * * This method of reformation allows reformation to achieve an after-the-fact duplication of a professionally competent product. Such a technique would have been especially suitable in the cases that have already arisen, for it probably would have allowed the dispositions in all of them to have been rendered valid without disturbing the transferor's intent at all. * * * The insertion of a saving clause grants a more appropriate opportunity for the property to go to the intended beneficiaries. Furthermore, it would also be a suitable technique in fertile octogenarian, unborn widow, and administrative contingency cases. A saving clause is one of the formalistic devices that a professionally competent lawyer would have used before the fact to assure initial validity in these cases. Insofar as other violations are concerned, the saving clause technique also grants every appropriate opportunity for the property to go to the intended beneficiaries.

In selecting the lives to be used for the perpetuity-period component of the saving clause that in a given case is to be inserted after the fact, the principle to be adopted is the same one that ought to guide lawyers in drafting such a clause before the fact: The group selected should be appropriate to the facts and the disposition. While the exact make-up of the group in each case would be settled by litigation, the individuals designated in Section 1.3(2) of the Restatement (Second) of Property (Donative Transfers) (1983) as the measuring lives would be an appropriate referent for the court to consider. Care should be taken in formulating the gift-over component, so that it is appropriate to the dispositive scheme. Among possible recipients that the court might consider designating are: (i) the persons entitled to the income on the 21st anniversary of the death of the last surviving individual designated by the court for the perpetuity-period component and in the proportions thereof to which they are then so entitled; if no proportions are specified, in equal shares to the permissible recipients of income; or (ii) the grantor's descendants per stirpes who are living 21 years after the death of the last surviving individual designated by the court for the perpetuity-period component; if none, to the grantor's heirs at law determined as if the grantor died 21 years after the death of the last surviving individual designated in the perpetuity-period component.

Violation Must be Determined in a Judicial Proceeding Commenced On or After the Effective Date of this Act. The equitable power to reform is recognized by Section 5(b) only in situations where the violation of the former rule against perpetuities is determined in a judicial proceeding commenced on or after the effective date of this Act. The equitable power to reform would typically be exercised in the same judicial proceeding in which the invalidity is determined.

Section 6. Short Title.

This [Act] may be cited as the Uniform Statutory Rule Against Perpetuities.

Section 7. Uniformity of Application and Construction. [omitted]

Section 8. Time of Taking Effect. [omitted]

Section 9. [Supersession] [Repeal]. [omitted]

UNIFORM TRANSFERS TO MINORS ACT*

PREFATORY NOTE

This Act revises and restates the Uniform Gifts to Minors Act (UGMA), one of the Conference's most successful products, some version of which has been enacted in every American jurisdiction. * * *

This Act follows the expansive approach taken by several states and allows any kind of property, real or personal, tangible or intangible, to be made the subject of a transfer to a custodian for the benefit of a minor (Section 1(6)). In addition, it permits such transfers not only by lifetime outright gifts (Section 4), but also from trusts, estates and guardianships, whether or not specifically authorized in the governing instrument (Sections 5 and 6), and from other third parties indebted to a minor who does not have a conservator, such as parties against whom a minor has a tort claim or judgment, and depository institutions holding deposits or insurance companies issuing policies payable on death to a minor (Section 7). For this reason, and to distinguish the enactment of this statute from the 1956 and 1966 versions of UGMA, the title of the Act has been changed to refer to "Transfers" rather than to "Gifts," a much narrower term.

As so expanded, the Act might be considered a statutory form of trust or guardianship that continues until the minor reaches 21. Note, however, that unlike a trust, a custodianship is not a separate legal entity or taxpayer. Under Section 11(b) of this Act, the custodial property is indefeasibly vested in the minor, not the custodian, and thus any income received is attributable to and reportable by the minor, whether or not actually distributed to the minor. * * *

The Act retains (or reverts to) 21 as the age of majority or, more accurately, the age at which the custodianship terminates and the property is distributed. Since tax law permits duration of Section 2503(c) trusts to 21, even though the statutory age of majority is 18 in most states, this age should be retained since most donors and other transferors wish to preserve a custodianship as long as possible. * * *

Section 1. Definitions.

In this [Act]:

(1) "Adult" means an individual who has attained the age of 21 years.

(2) "Benefit plan" means an employer's plan for the benefit of an employee or partner.

(3) "Broker" means a person lawfully engaged in the business of effecting transactions in securities or commodities for the person's own account or for the account of others.

(4) "Conservator" means a person appointed or qualified by a court to act as general, limited, or temporary guardian of a minor's property or a person legally authorized to perform substantially the same functions.

(5) "Court" means [_____ court].

(6) "Custodial property" means (i) any interest in property transferred to a custodian under this [Act] and (ii) the income from and proceeds of that interest in property.

(7) "Custodian" means a person so designated under Section 9 or a successor or substitute custodian designated under Section 18.

(8) "Financial institution" means a bank, trust company, savings institution, or credit union, chartered and supervised under state or federal law.

(9) "Legal representative" means an individual's personal representative or conservator.

(10) "Member of the minor's family" means the minor's parent, stepparent, spouse, grandparent, brother, sister, uncle, or aunt, whether of the whole or half blood or by adoption.

(11) "Minor" means an individual who has not attained the age of 21 years.

(12) "Person" means an individual, corporation, organization, or other legal entity.

(13) "Personal representative" means an executor, administrator, successor personal representative, or special administrator of a decedent's estate or a person legally authorized to perform substantially the same functions.

(14) "State" includes any state of the United States, the District of Columbia, the Commonwealth of Puerto Rico, and any territory or possession subject to the legislative authority of the United States.

(15) "Transfer" means a transaction that creates custodial property under Section 9.

(16) "Transferor" means a person who makes a transfer under this [Act].

(17) "Trust company" means a financial institution, corporation, or other legal entity, authorized to exercise general trust powers.

Section 2. Scope and Jurisdiction.

(a) This [Act] applies to a transfer that refers to this [Act] in the designation under Section 9(a) by which the transfer is made if at the time of the transfer, the transferor, the minor, or the custodian is a resident of this State or the custodial property is located in this State. The custodianship so created remains subject to this [Act] despite a subsequent change in residence of a transferor, the minor, or the custodian, or the removal of custodial property from this State.

(b)   A person designated as custodian under this [Act] is subject to personal jurisdiction in this State with respect to any matter relating to the custodianship.

(c)   A transfer that purports to be made and which is valid under the Uniform Transfers to Minors Act, the Uniform Gifts to Minors Act, or a substantially similar act, of another state is governed by the law of the designated state and may be executed and is enforceable in this State if at the time of the transfer, the transferor, the minor, or the custodian is a resident of the designated state or the custodial property is located in the designated state.

Section 3. Nomination of Custodian.

(a)   A person having the right to designate the recipient of property transferable upon the occurrence of a future event may revocably nominate a custodian to receive the property for a minor beneficiary upon the occurrence of the event by naming the custodian followed in substance by the words: "as custodian for _____ (name of minor) under the [name of Enacting State] Uniform Transfers to Minors Act." The nomination may name one or more persons as substitute custodians to whom the property must be transferred, in the order named, if the first nominated custodian dies before the transfer or is unable, declines, or is ineligible to serve. The nomination may be made in a will, a trust, a deed, an instrument exercising a power of appointment, or in a writing designating a beneficiary of contractual rights which is registered with or delivered to the payor, issuer, or other obligor of the contractual rights.

(b)   A custodian nominated under this section must be a person to whom a transfer of property of that kind may be made under Section 9(a).

(c)   The nomination of a custodian under this section does not create custodial property until the nominating instrument becomes irrevocable or a transfer to the nominated custodian is completed under Section 9. Unless the nomination of a custodian has been revoked, upon the occurrence of the future event the custodianship becomes effective and the custodian shall enforce a transfer of the custodial property pursuant to Section 9.

Comment

This section * * * permits a future custodian for a minor to be nominated to receive a distribution under a will or trust, or as a beneficiary of a power of appointment, or of contractual rights such as a life or endowment insurance policy, annuity contract, P.O.D. Account, benefit plan, or similar future payment right. Nomination of a future custodian does not constitute a "transfer" under this Act and does not create custodial property. If it did, the nomination and beneficiary designation would have to be permanent, since a "transfer" is irrevocable and indefeasibly vests ownership of the interest in the minor under Section 11(b).

Instead, this section permits a revocable beneficiary designation that takes effect only when the donor dies, or when a lifetime transfer to the custodian for the minor beneficiary occurs, such as a distribution under an inter vivos trust. However, an unrevoked nomination under this section is binding on a personal representative or trustee (see Section 5(b)) and on insurance companies and other obligors who contract to pay in the future (see Section 7(b)). * * *

Section 4. Transfer by Gift or Exercise of Power of Appointment.

A person may make a transfer by irrevocable gift to, or the irrevocable exercise of a power of appointment in favor of, a custodian for the benefit of a minor pursuant to Section 9.

Section 5. Transfer Authorized by Will or Trust.

(a)   A personal representative or trustee may make an irrevocable transfer pursuant to Section 9 to a custodian for the benefit of a minor as authorized in the governing will or trust.

(b) If the testator or settlor has nominated a custodian under Section 3 to receive the custodial property, the transfer must be made to that person.

(c) If the testator or settlor has not nominated a custodian under Section 3, or all persons so nominated as custodian die before the transfer or are unable, decline, or are ineligible to serve, the personal representative or the trustee, as the case may be, shall designate the custodian from among those eligible to serve as custodian for property of that kind under Section 9(a).

Section 6. Other Transfer by Fiduciary.

(a) Subject to subsection (c), a personal representative or trustee may make an irrevocable transfer to another adult or trust company as custodian for the benefit of a minor pursuant to Section 9, in the absence of a will or under a will or trust that does not contain an authorization to do so.

(b) Subject to subsection (c), a conservator may make an irrevocable transfer to another adult or trust company as custodian for the benefit of the minor pursuant to Section 9.

(c) A transfer under subsection (a) or (b) may be made only if (i) the personal representative, trustee, or conservator considers the transfer to be in the best interest of the minor, (ii) the transfer is not prohibited by or inconsistent with provisions of the applicable will, trust agreement, or other governing instrument, and (iii) the transfer is authorized by the court if it exceeds [$10,000] in value.

Comment

This section [permits] custodianships to be used as guardianship or conservator substitutes, even though not specifically authorized by the person whose property is the subject of the transfer. It also permits the legal representative of the minor, such as a conservator or guardian, to transfer the minor's own property to a new or existing custodianship for the purposes of convenience or economies of administration.

A custodianship may be created under this section even though not specifically authorized by the transferor, the testator, or the settlor of the trust if three tests are satisfied. First, the fiduciary making the transfer must determine in good faith and in his fiduciary capacity that a custodianship will be in the best interests of the minor. Second, a custodianship may not be prohibited by, or inconsistent with, the terms of any governing instrument. Inconsistent terms would include, for example, a spendthrift clause in a governing trust, provisions terminating a governing trust for the minor's benefit at a time other than the time of the minor's age of majority, and provisions for mandatory distributions of income or principal at specific times or periodic intervals. Provisions for other outright distributions or bequests would not be inconsistent with the creation of a custodianship under this section. Third, the amount of property transferred (as measured by its value) must be of such relatively small amount that the lack of court supervision and the typically stricter investment standards that would apply to the conservator otherwise required will not be important. However, if the property is of significant size, transfer to a custodian may still be made if the court approves and if the other two tests are met.

The custodianship created under this section without express authority in the governing instrument will terminate upon the minor's attainment of the statutory age of majority of the enacting state apart from this Act, i.e., at the same age a conservatorship of the minor would end. * * *

Section 7. Transfer by Obligor.

(a) Subject to subsections (b) and (c), a person not subject to Section 5 or 6 who holds property of or owes a liquidated debt to a minor not having a conservator may make an irrevocable transfer to a custodian for the benefit of the minor pursuant to Section 9.

(b) If a person having the right to do so under Section 3 has nominated a custodian under that section to receive the custodial property, the transfer must be made to that person.

(c) If no custodian has been nominated under Section 3, or all persons so nominated as custodian die before the transfer or are unable, decline, or are ineligible to serve, a transfer under this section may be made to an adult member of the minor's family or to a trust company unless the property exceeds [$10,000] in value.

Section 8. Receipt for Custodial Property.

A written acknowledgment of delivery by a custodian constitutes a sufficient receipt and discharge for custodial property transferred to the custodian pursuant to this [Act].

Section 9. Manner of Creating Custodial Property and Effecting Transfer; Designation of Initial Custodian; Control.

(a) Custodial property is created and a transfer is made whenever:

(1) an uncertificated security or a certificated security in registered form is either:

(i) registered in the name of the transferor, an adult other than the transferor, or a trust company, followed in substance by the words: "as custodian for _____ (name of minor) under the [Name of Enacting State] Uniform Transfers to Minors Act"; or

(ii) delivered if in certificated form, or any document necessary for the transfer of an uncertificated security is delivered, together with any necessary endorsement to an adult other than the transferor or to a trust company as custodian, accompanied by an instrument in substantially the form set forth in subsection (b);

(2) money is paid or delivered, or a security held in the name of a broker, financial institution, or its nominee is transferred, to a broker or financial institution for credit to an account in the name of the transferor, an adult other than the transferor, or a trust company, followed in substance by the words: "as custodian for _____ (name of minor) under the [Name of Enacting State] Uniform Transfers to Minors Act";

(3) the ownership of a life or endowment insurance policy or annuity contract is either:

(i) registered with the issuer in the name of the transferor, an adult other than the transferor, or a trust company, followed in substance by the words: "as custodian for _____ (name of minor) under the [Name of Enacting State] Uniform Transfers to Minors Act"; or

(ii) assigned in a writing delivered to an adult other than the transferor or to a trust company whose name in the assignment is followed in substance by the words: "as custodian for _____ (name of minor) under the [Name of Enacting State] Uniform Transfers to Minors Act";

(4) an irrevocable exercise of a power of appointment or an irrevocable present right to future payment under a contract is the subject of a written notification delivered to the payor, issuer, or other obligor that the right is transferred to the transferor, an adult other than the transferor, or a trust company, whose name in the notification is followed in substance by the words: "as custodian for _____ (name of minor) under the [Name of Enacting State] Uniform Transfers to Minors Act";

(5) an interest in real property is recorded in the name of the transferor, an adult other than the transferor, or a trust company, followed in substance by the words: "as custodian for _____ (name of minor) under the [Name of Enacting State] Uniform Transfers to Minors Act";

(6) a certificate of title issued by a department or agency of a state or of the United States which evidences title to tangible personal property is either:

(i) issued in the name of the transferor, an adult other than the transferor, or a trust company, followed in substance by the words: "as custodian for _____ (name of minor) under the [Name of Enacting State] Uniform Transfers to Minors Act"; or

(ii) delivered to an adult other than the transferor or to a trust company, endorsed to that person followed in substance by the words: "as custodian for _____ (name of minor) under the [Name of Enacting State] Uniform Transfers to Minors Act"; or

(7) an interest in any property not described in paragraphs (1) through (6) is transferred to an adult other than the transferor or to a trust company by a written instrument in substantially the form set forth in subsection (b).

(b) An instrument in the following form satisfies the requirements of paragraphs (1)(ii) and (7) of subsection (a):

"TRANSFER UNDER THE [NAME OF ENACTING STATE]
UNIFORM TRANSFERS TO MINORS ACT

I, _____ (name of transferor or name and representative capacity if a fiduciary) hereby transfer to _____ (name of custodian), as custodian for _____ (name of minor) under the [Name of Enacting State] Uniform Transfers to Minors Act, the following: (insert a description of the custodial property sufficient to identify it).

Dated: _____

_____
     (Signature)

_____ (name of custodian) acknowledges receipt of the property described above as custodian for the minor named above under the [Name of Enacting State] Uniform Transfers to Minors Act.

Dated: _____

_____ "
(Signature of Custodian)

(c) A transferor shall place the custodian in control of the custodial property as soon as practicable.

Comment

* * * [S]ubsection (a) creates new procedures for handling the additional types of property now subject to the Act; specifically:

Paragraph (3) covers the irrevocable transfer of ownership of life and endowment insurance policies and annuity contracts.

Paragraph (4) covers the *irrevocable* exercise of a power of appointment and the *irrevocable* present assignment of future payment rights, such as royalties, interest and principal payments under a promissory note, or beneficial interests under life or endowment or annuity insurance contracts or benefit plans. The payor, issuer, or obligor may require additional formalities such as completion of a specific assignment form and an endorsement, but the transfer is effective upon delivery of the notification. See Section 3 and the Comment thereto for the procedure for revocably "nominating" a future custodian as a beneficiary of a power of appointment or such payment rights.

Paragraph (5) is the exclusive method for the transfer of real estate and includes a disposition effected by will. Under the law of those states in which a devise of real estate vests in the devisee without the need for a deed from the personal representative of the decedent, a document such as the will must still be "recorded" under this provision to make the transfer effective. For inter vivos transfers, of course, a conveyance in recordable form would be employed for dispositions of real estate to a custodian.

Paragraph (6) covers the transfer of personal property such as automobiles, aircraft, and other property subject to registration of ownership with a state or federal agency. Either registration of the transfer in the name of the custodian or delivery of the endorsed certificate in registerable form makes the transfer effective.

Paragraph (7) is a residual classification, covering all property not otherwise covered in the preceding paragraphs. Examples would include nonregistered securities, partnership interests, and tangible personal property not subject to title certificates.

The form of transfer document recommended and set forth in subsection (b) contains an acceptance that must be executed by the custodian to make the disposition effective. While such a form of written acceptance is not specifically required in the case of registered securities under subsection (a)(1), money under (a)(2), insurance contracts or interests under (a)(3) or (4), real estate under (a)(5), or titled personal property under (a)(6), it is certainly the better and recommended practice to obtain the acknowledgment, consent, and acceptance of the designated custodian on the instrument of transfer, or otherwise.

A transferor may create a custodianship by naming himself as custodian, except for transfers of securities under subsection (a)(1)(ii), insurance and annuity contracts under (a)(3)(ii), and titled personalty under (a)(6)(ii), which are made without registering them in the name of the custodian, and transfers of the residual class of property covered by (a)(7). In all of these cases a transfer of possession and control to a third party is necessary to establish donative intent and consummation of the transfer, and designation of the transferor as custodian renders the transfer invalid under Section 11(a)(2). * * *

Section 10. Single Custodianship.

A transfer may be made only for one minor, and only one person may be the custodian. All custodial property held under this [Act] by the same custodian for the benefit of the same minor constitutes a single custodianship.

Section 11. Validity and Effect of Transfer.

(a)   The validity of a transfer made in a manner prescribed in this [Act] is not affected by:

(1)   failure of the transferor to comply with Section 9(c) concerning possession and control;

(2)   designation of an ineligible custodian, except designation of the transferor in the case of property for which the transferor is ineligible to serve as custodian under Section 9(a); or

(3)   death or incapacity of a person nominated under Section 3 or designated under Section 9 as custodian or the disclaimer of the office by that person.

(b)   A transfer made pursuant to Section 9 is irrevocable, and the custodial property is indefeasibly vested in the minor, but the custodian has all the rights, powers, duties, and authority provided in this [Act], and neither the minor nor the minor's legal representative has any right, power, duty, or authority with respect to the custodial property except as provided in this [Act].

(c)   By making a transfer, the transferor incorporates in the disposition all the provisions of this [Act] and grants to the custodian, and to any third person dealing with a person designated as custodian, the respective powers, rights, and immunities provided in this [Act].

Section 12. Care of Custodial Property.

(a)   A custodian shall:

(1)   take control of custodial property;

(2)   register or record title to custodial property if appropriate; and

(3)   collect, hold, manage, invest, and reinvest custodial property.

(b)   In dealing with custodial property, a custodian shall observe the standard of care that would be observed by a prudent person dealing with property of another and is not limited by any other statute restricting investments by fiduciaries. If a custodian has a special skill or expertise or is named custodian on the basis of representations of a special skill or expertise, the custodian shall use that skill or expertise. However, a custodian, in the custodian's discretion and without liability to the minor or the minor's estate, may retain any custodial property received from a transferor.

(c)   A custodian may invest in or pay premiums on life insurance or endowment policies on (i) the life of the minor only if the minor or the minor's estate is the sole beneficiary, or (ii) the life of another person in whom the minor has an insurable interest only to the extent that the minor, the minor's estate, or the custodian in the capacity of custodian, is the irrevocable beneficiary.

(d)   A custodian at all times shall keep custodial property separate and distinct from all other property in a manner sufficient to identify it clearly as custodial property of the minor. Custodial property consisting of an undivided interest is so identified if the minor's interest is held as a tenant in common and is fixed. Custodial property subject to recordation is so identified if it is recorded, and custodial property subject to registration is so identified if it is either registered, or held in an account designated, in the name of the custodian, followed in substance by the words: "as a custodian for _____ (name of minor) under the [Name of Enacting State] Uniform Transfers to Minors Act."

(e)   A custodian shall keep records of all transactions with respect to custodial property, including information necessary for the preparation of the minor's tax returns, and shall make them available for inspection at reasonable intervals by a parent or legal representative of the minor or by the minor if the minor has attained the age of 14 years.

Section 13. Powers of Custodian.

(a)   A custodian, acting in a custodial capacity, has all the rights, powers, and authority over custodial property that unmarried adult owners have over their own property, but a custodian may exercise those rights, powers, and authority in that capacity only.

(b)   This section does not relieve a custodian from liability for breach of Section 12.

Section 14. Use of Custodial Property.

(a)   A custodian may deliver or pay to the minor or expend for the minor's benefit so much of the custodial property as the custodian considers advisable for the use and benefit of the minor, without court order and without regard to (i) the duty or ability of the custodian personally or of any other person to support the minor, or (ii) any other income or property of the minor which may be applicable or available for that purpose.

(b)   On petition of an interested person or the minor if the minor has attained the age of 14 years, the court may order the custodian to deliver or pay to the minor or expend for the minor's benefit so much of the custodial property as the court considers advisable for the use and benefit of the minor.

(c)   A delivery, payment, or expenditure under this section is in addition to, not in substitution for, and does not affect any obligation of a person to support the minor.

Comment

* * * The IRS has taken the position that the income from custodial property, to the extent it is used for the support of the minor-donee, is includable in the gross income of any person who is legally obligated to support the minor-donee, whether or not that person or parent is serving as the custodian. Rev. Rul. 56–484, C.B. 1956–2, 23; Rev. Rul. 59–357, C.B. 1959–2, 212. However, Reg. 1.662(a)–4 provides that the term "legal obligation" includes a legal obligation to support another person if, and only if, the obligation is not affected by the adequacy of the dependent's own resources. Thus, if under local law a parent may use the resources of a child for the child's support in lieu of supporting the child himself or herself, no obligation of support exists, whether or not income is actually used for support, at least if the child's resources are adequate. * * *

For this reason, new subsection (c) has been added to specify that distributions or expenditures may be made for the minor without regard to the duty or ability of any other person to support the minor and that distributions or expenditures are not in substitution for, and shall not affect, the obligation of any person to support the minor. Other possible methods of avoiding the attribution of custodial property income to the person obligated to support the minor would be to prohibit the use of custodial property or its income for that purpose, or to provide that any such use gives rise to a cause of action by the minor against his parent to the extent that custodial property or income is so used. The first alternative was rejected as too restrictive, and the second as too cumbersome.

The "use and benefit" standard in subsections (a) and (b) is intended to include payment of the minor's legally enforceable obligations such as tax or child support obligations or tort claims. Custodial property could be reached by levy of a judgment creditor in any event, so there is no reason not to permit custodian or court-ordered expenditures for enforceable claims. * * *

Section 15. Custodian's Expenses, Compensation, and Bond.

(a)   A custodian is entitled to reimbursement from custodial property for reasonable expenses incurred in the performance of the custodian's duties.

(b)   Except for one who is a transferor under Section 4, a custodian has a non-cumulative election during each calendar year to charge reasonable compensation for services performed during that year.

(c)   Except as provided in Section 18(f), a custodian need not give a bond.

Section 16. Exemption of Third Person From Liability.

A third person in good faith and without court order may act on the instructions of or otherwise deal with any person purporting to make a transfer or purporting to act in the capacity of a custodian and, in the absence of knowledge, is not responsible for determining:

(1)   the validity of the purported custodian's designation;

(2)   the propriety of, or the authority under this [Act] for, any act of the purported custodian;

(3)   the validity or propriety under this [Act] of any instrument or instructions executed or given either by the person purporting to make a transfer or by the purported custodian; or

(4)   the propriety of the application of any property of the minor delivered to the purported custodian.

Section 17. Liability to Third Persons.

(a)   A claim based on (i) a contract entered into by a custodian acting in a custodial capacity, (ii) an obligation arising from the ownership or control of custodial property, or (iii) a tort committed during the custodianship, may be asserted against the custodial property by proceeding against the custodian in the custodial capacity, whether or not the custodian or the minor is personally liable therefor.

(b)   A custodian is not personally liable:

(1)   on a contract properly entered into in the custodial capacity unless the custodian fails to reveal that capacity and to identify the custodianship in the contract; or

(2)   for an obligation arising from control of custodial property or for a tort committed during the custodianship unless the custodian is personally at fault.

(c)   A minor is not personally liable for an obligation arising from ownership of custodial property or for a tort committed during the custodianship unless the minor is personally at fault.

Section 18. Renunciation, Resignation, Death, or Removal of Custodian; Designation of Successor Custodian.

(a)   A person nominated under Section 3 or designated under Section 9 as custodian may decline to serve by delivering a valid disclaimer [under the Uniform Disclaimer of Property Interests Act of the Enacting State] to the person who made the nomination or to the transferor or the transferor's legal representative. If the event giving rise to a transfer has not occurred and no substitute custodian able, willing, and eligible to serve was nominated under Section 3, the person who made the nomination may nominate a substitute custodian under Section 3; otherwise the transferor or the transferor's legal representative shall designate a substitute custodian at the time of the transfer, in either case from among the persons eligible to serve as custodian for that kind of property under Section 9(a). The custodian so designated has the rights of a successor custodian.

(b)   A custodian at any time may designate a trust company or an adult other than a transferor under Section 4 as successor custodian by executing and dating an instrument of designation before a subscribing witness other than the successor. If the instrument of designation does not contain or is not accompanied by the resignation of the custodian, the designation of the successor does not take effect until the custodian resigns, dies, becomes incapacitated, or is removed.

(c)   A custodian may resign at any time by delivering written notice to the minor if the minor has attained the age of 14 years and to the successor custodian and by delivering the custodial property to the successor custodian.

(d)   If a custodian is ineligible, dies, or becomes incapacitated without having effectively designated a successor and the minor has attained the age of 14 years, the minor may designate as successor custodian, in the manner prescribed in subsection (b), an adult member of the minor's family, a conservator of the minor, or a trust company. If the minor has not attained the age of 14 years or fails to act within 60 days after the ineligibility, death, or incapacity, the conservator of the minor becomes successor custodian. If the minor has no conservator or the conservator declines to act, the transferor, the legal representative of the transferor or of the custodian, an adult member of the minor's family, or any other interested person may petition the court to designate a successor custodian.

(e)   A custodian who declines to serve under subsection (a) or resigns under subsection (c), or the legal representative of a deceased or incapacitated custodian, as soon as practicable, shall put the custodial property and records in the possession and control of the successor custodian. The successor custodian by action may enforce the obligation to deliver custodial property and records and becomes responsible for each item as received.

(f)   A transferor, the legal representative of a transferor, an adult member of the minor's family, a guardian of the person of the minor, the conservator of the minor, or the minor if the minor has attained the age of 14 years may petition the court to remove the custodian for cause and to designate a successor custodian other than a transferor under Section 4 or to require the custodian to give appropriate bond.

Section 19. Accounting by and Determination of Liability of Custodian.

(a)   A minor who has attained the age of 14 years, the minor's guardian of the person or legal representative, an adult member of the minor's family, a transferor, or a transferor's legal representative may petition the court (i) for an accounting by the custodian or the custodian's legal representative; or (ii) for a determination of responsibility, as between the custodial property and the custodian personally, for claims against the custodial property unless the responsibility has been adjudicated in an action under Section 17 to which the minor or the minor's legal representative was a party.

(b)   A successor custodian may petition the court for an accounting by the predecessor custodian.

(c)   The court, in a proceeding under this [Act] or in any other proceeding, may require or permit the custodian or the custodian's legal representative to account.

(d)   If a custodian is removed under Section 18(f), the court shall require an accounting and order delivery of the custodial property and records to the successor custodian and the execution of all instruments required for transfer of the custodial property.

Comment

* * * This section does not contain a separate statute of limitations precluding petitions for accounting after termination of the custodianship. Because custodianships can be created without the knowledge of the minor, a person might learn of a custodian's failure to turn over custodial property long after reaching majority, and should not be precluded from asserting his rights in the case of such fraud. * * * Other law, such as general statutes of limitation and the doctrine of laches, should serve adequately to protect former custodians from harassment.

Section 20. Termination of Custodianship.

The custodian shall transfer in an appropriate manner the custodial property to the minor or to the minor's estate upon the earlier of:

(1)　the minor's attainment of 21 years of age with respect to custodial property transferred under Section 4 or 5;

(2)　the minor's attainment of [majority under the laws of this State other than this [Act]] [age 18 or other statutory age of majority of Enacting State] with respect to custodial property transferred under Section 6 or 7; or

(3)　the minor's death.

Comment

This section * * * provides that custodianships created by fiduciaries without express authority from the donor of the property under Section 6 and by obligors of the minor under Section 7 terminate upon the minor's attaining the age of majority under the general laws of the state, since these custodianships are substitutes for conservatorships that would otherwise terminate at that time. Because property in a single custodianship may be distributable at different times, separate accounting for custodial property by source may be required. * * *

Section 21. Applicability. [omitted]

Section 22. Effect on Existing Custodianships. [omitted]

Section 23. Uniformity of Application and Construction. [omitted]

Section 24. Short Title.

This [Act] may be cited as the "[Name of Enacting State] Uniform Transfers to Minors Act."

Section 25. Severability. [omitted]

Section 26. Effective Date. [omitted]

Section 27. Repeals. [omitted]

UNIFORM TRUST DECANTING ACT*

PREFATORY NOTE

The Uniform Trust Decanting Act is promulgated in the midst of a rising tide of state decanting statutes. These statutes represent one of several recent innovations in trust law that seek to make trusts more flexible so that the settlor's material purposes can best be carried out under current circumstances. A decanting statute provides flexibility by statutorily expanding discretion already granted to the trustee to permit the trustee to modify the trust either directly or by distributing its assets to another trust. While some trusts expressly grant the trustee or another person a power to modify or decant the trust, a statutory provision can better describe the power granted, impose limits on the power to protect the beneficiaries and the settlor's intent, protect against inadvertent tax consequences, provide procedural rules for exercising the power and provide for appropriate remedies. While decanting may be permitted in some situations under common law in some states, in many

---

states it is unclear whether common law decanting is permitted, and if it is, the circumstances in which it is permitted and the parameters within which it may be exercised.

Need for Uniformity. Trusts may be governed by the laws of different states for purposes of validity, meaning and effect, and administration. The place of administration of a trust may move from state to state. It often may be difficult to determine the state in which a trust is administered if a trust has co-trustees domiciled in different states or has a corporate trustee that performs different trust functions in different states. As a result it may sometimes be unclear whether a particular state's decanting statute applies to a trust and sometimes more than one state's decanting statute may apply to a trust. A uniform statute can eliminate conflicts between different state statutes. It can also protect a trustee who decants under one state's statute when more than one state's statute might apply and protect a trustee who reasonably relies on a prior decanting. * * *

What Trusts May Be Decanted. Generally, the Uniform Trust Decanting Act permits decanting of an irrevocable, express trust in which the terms of the trust grant the trustee or another fiduciary the discretionary power to make principal distributions. See Section 3 and Section 2(3) (defining "authorized fiduciary"). The act does not apply to revocable trusts unless they are revocable by the settlor only with the consent of the trustee or an adverse party. Section 3(a). The act does not apply to wholly charitable trusts. Section 3(b). With one exception, if no fiduciary has discretion to distribute principal, the act does not apply unless the court appoints a special fiduciary and authorizes the special fiduciary to exercise the decanting power. See Section 9(1)(2). The exception is that a fiduciary who is responsible for making trust distributions may decant a trust to create a special-needs trust even if the fiduciary does not have discretion over principal if the decanting will further the purposes of the first trust.

Who May Decant. As discussed below, the decanting power is a fiduciary power, and thus must be entrusted to one of the fiduciaries of the first trust. The act entrusts the "authorized fiduciary" with the decanting power. The "authorized fiduciary" generally is the fiduciary who has discretion to distribute principal, although a more expansive definition is needed in the case of a special-needs trust. Generally, the authorized fiduciary will be the trustee. Where there is a divided trusteeship that gives the power to make or direct principal distributions to another fiduciary, such as a distribution director, such other fiduciary will be the authorized fiduciary.

Discretion Over Principal. Except in the case of special-needs trusts, the decanting power is granted only to an authorized fiduciary who by definition must have the discretion to distribute principal. The extent of the decanting authority depends upon the extent of the discretion granted to the trustee to distribute principal. When the authorized fiduciary has "limited distribution discretion" that is constrained by an ascertainable or reasonably definite standard, the interests of each beneficiary in the second trust must be substantially similar to such beneficiary's interests in the first trust. Thus when the authorized fiduciary has limited distributive discretion, an exercise of the decanting power generally can modify administrative, but not dispositive, trust provisions. When the authorized fiduciary has "expanded distributive discretion," the authorized fiduciary may exercise the decanting power to modify beneficial interests, subject to restrictions to protect interests that are current, noncontingent rights or vested remainder interests, to protect qualification for tax benefits and to protect charitable interests.

Sometimes a trust may have two or more authorized fiduciaries, some of whom have limited distributive discretion and some of whom have expanded distributive discretion. The authorized fiduciaries with limited distributive discretion may exercise the decanting power under Section 12 and the authorized fiduciaries with expanded distributive discretion may exercise the decanting power under Section 11.

Fiduciary Power. The Uniform Trust Decanting Act does not impose any duty on the authorized fiduciary to exercise the decanting power, but if the authorized fiduciary does exercise that power, the power must be exercised in accordance with the fiduciary duties of the authorized fiduciary. See Section 4. A fiduciary must administer a trust in good faith, in accordance with its terms (subject to the decanting power) and purposes, and in the interests of the beneficiaries. An exercise of decanting power must be in accordance with the purposes of the first trust. The purpose of decanting is not to disregard the settlor's intent but to modify the trust to better effectuate the settlor's broader purposes or the settlor's probable intent if the settlor had anticipated the circumstances at the time of decanting.

As a fiduciary power, the decanting power may be exercised without consent or approval of the beneficiaries or the court, except in the case of a few specific modifications that may benefit the fiduciary personally. Nonetheless, qualified beneficiaries are entitled to notice and may petition the court if they believe the authorized fiduciary has breached its fiduciary duty. Further, the authorized fiduciary, another fiduciary, a beneficiary, the settlor or, in the case of a trust with a charitable interest, the Attorney General or other official who may enforce the charitable interest, may petition the court for instructions, appointment of a special fiduciary who may exercise the decanting power, approval of an exercise of decanting power, a determination that the authorized fiduciary breached its fiduciary duties, a determination that the savings provisions in Section 22 apply or a determination that the attempted decanting is invalid.

Decanting Procedure. Initially, the power to decant was often considered a derivative of the power to make a discretionary distribution to a beneficiary. Under this construct the decanting power was exercised by making a distribution from one trust to another, and a second trust, separate and distinct from the first trust, was required.

The Uniform Trust Decanting Act views the decanting power as a power to modify the first trust, either by changing the terms of the first trust or by distributing property from the first trust to a second trust. While the act generally modulates the extent of the authorized fiduciary's power to decant according to the degree of discretion granted to the authorized fiduciary over principal, the power to decant is distinct from the power to distribute.

Thus the authorized fiduciary may exercise the decanting power by modifying the first trust, in which case the "second trust" is merely the modified first trust. The decanting instrument can, when appropriate, merely identify the specific provisions in the first trust that are to be modified and set forth the modified provisions, much like an amendment to a revocable trust. If the decanting power is exercised by modifying the terms of the first trust, the trustee could either treat the second trust as a new trust or treat the second trust as a continuation of the first trust. If the second trust is treated as a continuation of the first trust, there should be no need to transfer or retitle the trust property. Further, subject to future tax guidance, if the second trust is a continuation of the first trust, there may be no need to treat the first trust as having terminated for income tax purposes and no need to obtain a new tax identification number. * * *

Section 1. Short Title.

This [act] may be cited as the Uniform Trust Decanting Act.

Section 2. Definitions.

In this [act]:

(1) "Appointive property" means the property or property interest subject to a power of appointment.

(2) "Ascertainable standard" means a standard relating to an individual's health, education, support, or maintenance within the meaning of 26 U.S.C. Section 2041(b)(1)(A)[, as amended,] or 26 U.S.C. Section 2514(c)(1)[, as amended,] and any applicable regulations.

(3) "Authorized fiduciary" means:

(A) a trustee or other fiduciary, other than a settlor, that has discretion to distribute or direct a trustee to distribute part or all of the principal of the first trust to one or more current beneficiaries;

(B) a special fiduciary appointed under Section 9; or

(C) a special-needs fiduciary under Section 13.

(4)   "Beneficiary" means a person that:

    (A)   has a present or future, vested or contingent, beneficial interest in a trust;

    (B)   holds a power of appointment over trust property; or

    (C)   is an identified charitable organization that will or may receive distributions under the terms of the trust.

(5)   "Charitable interest" means an interest in a trust which:

    (A)   is held by an identified charitable organization and makes the organization a qualified beneficiary;

    (B)   benefits only charitable organizations and, if the interest were held by an identified charitable organization, would make the organization a qualified beneficiary; or

    (C)   is held solely for charitable purposes and, if the interest were held by an identified charitable organization, would make the organization a qualified beneficiary.

(6)   "Charitable organization" means:

    (A)   a person, other than an individual, organized and operated exclusively for charitable purposes; or

    (B)   a government or governmental subdivision, agency, or instrumentality, to the extent it holds funds exclusively for a charitable purpose.

(7)   "Charitable purpose" means the relief of poverty, the advancement of education or religion, the promotion of health, a municipal or other governmental purpose, or another purpose the achievement of which is beneficial to the community.

(8)   "Court" means the court in this state having jurisdiction in matters relating to trusts.

(9)   "Current beneficiary" means a beneficiary that on the date the beneficiary's qualification is determined is a distributee or permissible distributee of trust income or principal. The term includes the holder of a presently exercisable general power of appointment but does not include a person that is a beneficiary only because the person holds any other power of appointment.

(10) "Decanting power" or "the decanting power" means the power of an authorized fiduciary under this [act] to distribute property of a first trust to one or more second trusts or to modify the terms of the first trust.

(11) "Expanded distributive discretion" means a discretionary power of distribution that is not limited to an ascertainable standard or a reasonably definite standard.

(12) "First trust" means a trust over which an authorized fiduciary may exercise the decanting power.

(13) "First-trust instrument" means the trust instrument for a first trust.

(14) "General power of appointment" means a power of appointment exercisable in favor of a powerholder, the powerholder's estate, a creditor of the powerholder, or a creditor of the powerholder's estate.

(15) "Jurisdiction", with respect to a geographic area, includes a state or country.

(16) "Person" means an individual, estate, business or nonprofit entity, public corporation, government or governmental subdivision, agency, or instrumentality, or other legal entity.

(17) "Power of appointment" means a power that enables a powerholder acting in a nonfiduciary capacity to designate a recipient of an ownership interest in or another power of appointment over the appointive property. The term does not include a power of attorney.

(18) "Powerholder" means a person in which a donor creates a power of appointment.

(19) "Presently exercisable power of appointment" means a power of appointment exercisable by the powerholder at the relevant time. The term:

(A) includes a power of appointment exercisable only after the occurrence of a specified event, the satisfaction of an ascertainable standard, or the passage of a specified time only after:

(i) the occurrence of the specified event;

(ii) the satisfaction of the ascertainable standard; or

(iii) the passage of the specified time; and

(B) does not include a power exercisable only at the powerholder's death.

(20) "Qualified beneficiary" means a beneficiary that on the date the beneficiary's qualification is determined:

(A) is a distributee or permissible distributee of trust income or principal;

(B) would be a distributee or permissible distributee of trust income or principal if the interests of the distributees described in subparagraph (A) terminated on that date without causing the trust to terminate; or

(C) would be a distributee or permissible distributee of trust income or principal if the trust terminated on that date.

(21) "Reasonably definite standard" means a clearly measurable standard under which a holder of a power of distribution is legally accountable within the meaning of 26 U.S.C. Section 674(b)(5)(A)[, as amended,] and any applicable regulations.

(22) "Record" means information that is inscribed on a tangible medium or that is stored in an electronic or other medium and is retrievable in perceivable form.

(23) "Second trust" means:

(A) a first trust after modification under this [act]; or

(B) a trust to which a distribution of property from a first trust is or may be made under this [act].

(24) "Second-trust instrument" means the trust instrument for a second trust.

(25) "Settlor", except as otherwise provided in Section 25, means a person, including a testator, that creates or contributes property to a trust. If more than one person creates or contributes property to a trust, each person is a settlor of the portion of the trust property attributable to the person's contribution except to the extent another person has power to revoke or withdraw that portion.

(26) "Sign" means, with present intent to authenticate or adopt a record:

(A) to execute or adopt a tangible symbol; or

(B) to attach to or logically associate with the record an electronic symbol, sound, or process.

(27) "State" means a state of the United States, the District of Columbia, Puerto Rico, the United States Virgin Islands, or any territory or insular possession subject to the jurisdiction of the United States.

(28) "Terms of the trust" means:

(A) Except as otherwise provided in subparagraph (B), the manifestation of the settlor's intent regarding a trust's provisions as:

(i) expressed in the trust instrument; or

(ii) established by other evidence that would be admissible in a judicial proceeding; or

(B) the trust's provisions as established, determined, or amended by:

(i)   a trustee or other person in accordance with applicable law; [or]

(ii)   a court order[[; or]

(iii) a nonjudicial settlement agreement under [Uniform Trust Code Section 111]].

(29) "Trust instrument" means a record executed by the settlor to create a trust or by any person to create a second trust which contains some or all of the terms of the trust, including any amendments.

Comment

* * * *Ascertainable Standard.* The definition of "ascertainable standard" is similar to the definition found in Section 103(2) of the Uniform Trust Code, but also includes the regulations to the cited sections of the Internal Revenue Code.

A power that is limited to health, education, support or maintenance is limited to an ascertainable standard. * * * Other powers limited to an ascertainable standard include "support in reasonable comfort," "maintenance in health and reasonable comfort," "support in the beneficiary's accustomed manner of living," "education, including college and professional education" and "medical, dental, hospital and nursing expenses and expenses of invalidism." A power to make distributions for comfort, welfare, happiness or best interests is not limited to an ascertainable standard. In determining whether a power is limited by an ascertainable standard, it is immaterial whether the beneficiary is required to exhaust other income or resources before the power can be exercised.

The entire context of the document should be considered in determining whether the standard is ascertainable. For example, if the trust instrument provides that the determination of the trustee is conclusive with respect to the exercise of the standard, the power is not ascertainable.

A power to make distributions "as the trustee deems advisable" or in the trustee's "sole and absolute discretion" without further limitation is not subject to an ascertainable standard. * * *

Authorized Fiduciary. The definition of "authorized fiduciary" includes only a person acting in a fiduciary capacity. Only a fiduciary, subject to fiduciary duties, should have the power to decant. A distribution director who is not a fiduciary should not have the power to decant.

The definition excludes a settlor acting as a trustee. If a settlor is a trustee of an irrevocable trust, gift and estate tax problems could result if the settlor had a decanting power. The definition does not exclude a beneficiary who is acting as a trustee (an "interested trustee") because the act only permits a trustee with expanded distributive discretion to decant in a manner that would change beneficial interests. Typically trusts will not give an interested trustee unascertainable discretion over discretionary distributions because such discretion would create gift and estate tax issues. In the unusual event that a trust does give an interested trustee unascertainable discretion, the trustee will incur the tax effects of holding a general power of appointment whether or not the trustee also has a decanting power.

If the discretion to distribute or to direct the trustee to distribute is held jointly by two or more trustees or other fiduciaries, the "authorized fiduciary" is such trustees or other fiduciaries collectively. If the authorized fiduciary is comprised of two or more fiduciaries, the trust instrument or state law will generally provide whether they must act unanimously or whether they may act by majority or some other percentage vote. * * *

The term also includes a special fiduciary appointed by the court under Section 9, who may exercise the decanting power.

The term also includes a special-needs fiduciary under Section 13 even if such fiduciary does not have discretion to distribute principal of the first trust.

Beneficiary. The definition of "beneficiary" in Section 2(4)(A) and (B) is substantially similar to the definition found in Section 103(3) of the Uniform Trust Code. Section 2(4)(C) adds as a beneficiary a charitable organization identified to receive distributions from a trust. * * * Thus an identified charitable organization has the rights of a beneficiary under this act. Absent Section 2(4)(C) such charities would not be considered beneficiaries. Because a charitable interest is not created to benefit ascertainable charitable organizations but to benefit the community at large, persons receiving distributions from a charitable interest are not beneficiaries as that term is defined in the Uniform Trust Code. * * *

In addition to living and ascertained individuals, beneficiaries may be unborn or unascertained. The term "beneficiary" includes not only beneficiaries who received their interests under the terms of the trust but also beneficiaries who received their interests by other means, including by assignment, exercise of a power of appointment, resulting trust upon the failure of an interest, gap in a disposition, operation of an antilapse statute upon the predecease of a named beneficiary, or upon termination of the trust. A potential appointee of a power of appointment is not a beneficiary unless a presently exercisable power of appointment has been exercised in favor of such appointee. A person who merely incidentally benefits from the trust is not a beneficiary. * * *

While the holder of a power of appointment is not considered a trust beneficiary under the common law of trusts, powerholders are classified as beneficiaries under the Uniform Trust Code. Powerholders are included on the principle that their interests are significant enough that they should be afforded the rights of beneficiaries. * * *

Charitable Interest. The term "charitable interest" includes an interest held by a charitable organization that makes the charitable organization a qualified beneficiary. Section 2(5). See Section 2(4)(C) defining the term "beneficiary" to include an identified charitable organization that may or will receive distributions under the terms of a trust. See Section 2(20) defining a qualified beneficiary.

For example, a trust might provide for a certain amount to be distributed annually to Gentoos Need You, a charitable organization, and permit the trustee to make discretionary distributions of principal to the settlor's descendants. Upon the death of the settlor's last surviving child, $100,000 is to be paid to Gentoos Need You and the remainder to trusts for the settlor's grandchildren. The annuity interest and the remainder interest held by Gentoos Need You are both charitable interests because they are held by an identified charitable organization and make the organization a qualified beneficiary.

The term "charitable interest" also includes an interest that can benefit only charitable organizations and that, if held by an identified charitable organization, would make the charitable organization a qualified beneficiary. Section 2(5)(B). For example, if the trustee is to distribute $50,000 from the trust each year for ten years to one or more charitable organizations selected by the trustee that protect Antarctica and its wildlife, the trustee also has discretion to distribute income and principal to individual beneficiaries, and at the end of ten years the trustee is to distribute the remainder to the settlor's descendants, the $50,000 annuity is a charitable interest because it may be distributed only to charitable organizations.

As another example, if the trustee may make discretionary principal distributions to the settlor's spouse, and upon the spouse's death is to distribute one-half of the principal to charitable organizations that protect the Arctic and its wildlife, and the other one-half to the settlor's descendants, there is a charitable interest in one-half of the remainder.

The term "charitable interest" also includes an interest devoted solely to charitable purposes, even if the charitable purposes may be carried out directly by the trust rather than through distributions to charitable organizations. Section 2(5)(C). The act, however, does not apply to a wholly charitable trust. See Section 3(b).

The term does not include contingent, successor charitable interests that are not equivalent to the interests held by qualified beneficiaries. For example, if a trust permits distributions to Child A, and upon Child A's death the trust distributes to Child A's descendants, or if none, to the settlor's descendants, or if none, to the Manatee Preservation Fund, a charitable organization, and Child A or the settlor has one or more descendants living, the interest of the Manatee Preservation Fund does not make it a qualified beneficiary and therefore its interest is not a charitable interest. * * *

Current Beneficiary. The term "current beneficiary" means a beneficiary who is currently a distributee or permissible distributee of income or principal. A current beneficiary is a qualified beneficiary described in Section 2(20)(A). A mere holder of a power of appointment is not a current beneficiary unless the power is a presently exercisable general power of appointment. The term does not include the objects of an unexercised inter vivos power of appointment.

Decanting Power or The Decanting Power. The term "decanting power" or "the decanting power" means the power granted in this act to the authorized fiduciary (see Section 2(3)) to distribute all or part of the property of the first trust to a second trust or, alternatively, to modify the terms of the first trust to create the second trust. The term does not include any similar power that may be granted under the terms of the trust instrument or pursuant to common law.

If the terms of the first trust are modified, it is not necessary to treat the second trust as a newly created, separate trust, thus avoiding the need to transfer title of the property of the first trust to the second trust. If all of the property of the first trust is distributed pursuant to an exercise of the decanting power to a separate second trust, then the first trust would terminate. The termination of the first trust may impose certain duties on the trustee such as providing reports to the beneficiaries and filing final income tax returns.

Expanded Distributive Discretion. "Expanded distributive discretion" is any discretion that is not limited to an ascertainable standard (see Section 2(2)) as used in Internal Revenue Code Section 2514(c)(1) or to a reasonably definite standard (see Section 2(21)) as used in Internal Revenue Code Section 674(b)(5)(A). The tax terms are used here, one from gift tax rules and one from income tax rules, because the definitions of these tax terms are generally clearer than the definitions of nontax terms sometimes used to describe different types of trustee discretion.

First Trust. The terms "first trust" and "second trust" (Section 2(23)) are relative to the particular exercise of the decanting power. Thus when the decanting power is exercised over Trust A to make a distribution to Trust B, Trust A is the first trust and Trust B is the second trust with respect to such exercise of the decanting power. If the decanting power is later exercised over Trust B to make a distribution to Trust C, then Trust B would be the first trust and Trust C the second trust with respect to such exercise of the decanting power. * * *

Qualified Beneficiary. The definition of "qualified beneficiary" is substantially the same as the definition in Section 103(13) of the Uniform Trust Code. Note, however, that the expanded definition of "beneficiary" in Section 2(4) includes charitable organizations identified to receive distributions in charitable trusts. Such charitable organizations would be entitled to notice of an exercise of the decanting power under Section 7.

The qualified beneficiaries consist of the current beneficiaries (see Section 2(9)) and the presumptive remainder beneficiaries (see Section 11(a)(2)).

The holder of a presently exercisable general power of appointment is a qualified beneficiary. A person who would have a presently exercisable general power of appointment if the trust terminated on that date or if the interests of the current beneficiaries terminated on that date without causing the trust to terminate is also a qualified beneficiary. The term does not include the holder of a testamentary general power of appointment or the holder of a nongeneral limited power of appointment. Nor does the term include the objects of an unexercised inter vivos power of appointment.

When a trust has distributees or permissible distributees of trust income or principal who are in more than one generation of the descendants of a person and the trust continues after the deaths of the members of the most senior generation who are included among such distributees, Section 2(20)(B) should be construed to include the distributees or permissible distributees after the interests of the most senior generation of such distributees terminate and subparagraph (C) would not ordinarily be applicable if there are any current beneficiaries who are not members of the most senior generation. Assume a trust permits discretionary distributions to any of A's descendants, and only terminates if A has no living descendants, in which case it is distributed to B, and A's now living descendants are Child 1, Child 2, Grandchild 1A and Grandchild 1B. The presumptive remainder beneficiaries are Grandchild 1A and Grandchild 1B pursuant to Section 2(20)(B), and Section 2(20)(C) should not apply to cause B to be a presumptive remainder beneficiary. On the other hand, if A's then living descendants were limited to Child 1 and Child 2, then B would be the presumptive remainder beneficiary under Section 2(20)(C), because there is no presumptive remainder beneficiary under Section 2(20)(B).

Reasonably Definite Standard. "Reasonably definite standard" is defined in Treasury Regulations Section 1.674(b)–1(b)(5). "Reasonably definite standard" includes an ascertainable standard but may also include standards that would not be considered ascertainable standards. A power to distribute principal for the education, support, maintenance, or health of the beneficiary; for the beneficiary's reasonable support and comfort; or to enable the beneficiary to maintain the beneficiary's accustomed standard of living; or to meet an emergency; would be a reasonably definite standard. A power to distribute principal for the pleasure, desire, or happiness of a beneficiary is not a reasonably definite standard. A power to make distributions "as the trustee deems advisable" or in the trustee's "sole and absolute discretion" without further limitation is not a reasonably definite standard. A reasonably definite standard need not require consideration of the needs and circumstances of the beneficiary.

The entire context of a provision of a trust instrument granting a power should be considered in determining whether there is a reasonably definite standard. For example, if a trust instrument provides that the determination of the trustee shall be conclusive with respect to the exercise or nonexercise of a power, the power is not limited by a reasonably definite standard. The fact, however, that the governing instrument is phrased in discretionary terms is not in itself an indication that no reasonably definite standard exists. * * *

Second Trust. The definition of "second trust" includes (1) an irrevocable trust already in existence, whether created by the settlor of the first trust or a different settlor, (2) a "restatement" of the first trust which could be executed by the authorized fiduciary or another person as the nominal grantor, (3) the first trust as modified to create the second trust, or (4) a new trust executed by the authorized fiduciary or another person as the nominal settlor for the purpose of decanting. A decanting that is implemented by "restating" or modifying the first trust presumably would not require the issuance of a new tax identification number or the retitling of property or a final income tax return for the trust. A decanting that distributes the property of the first trust to another trust presumably would require that the property be retitled. Further, if the first trust was terminated by reason of the decanting, a final income tax return for the first trust would be required. * * *

Section 3. Scope.

(a)   Except as otherwise provided in subsections (b) and (c), this [act] applies to an express trust that is irrevocable or revocable by the settlor only with the consent of the trustee or a person holding an adverse interest.

(b)   This [act] does not apply to a trust held solely for charitable purposes.

(c)   Subject to Section 15, a trust instrument may restrict or prohibit exercise of the decanting power.

(d)   This [act] does not limit the power of a trustee, powerholder, or other person to distribute or appoint property in further trust or to modify a trust under the trust instrument, law of this state other than this [act], common law, a court order, or a nonjudicial settlement agreement.

(e)   This [act] does not affect the ability of a settlor to provide in a trust instrument for the distribution of the trust property or appointment in further trust of the trust property or for modification of the trust instrument.

Comment

The Uniform Trust Decanting Act applies to all express trusts that are irrevocable or that are revocable by the settlor only with the consent of the trustee or a person holding an adverse interest. The act does not apply to a trust revocable by the settlor without the consent of the trustee or a person holding an adverse interest, even if the settlor is incapacitated and thus unable to exercise the power to amend or revoke. * * *

The act does not permit decanting a trust held solely for charitable purposes (a "wholly charitable trust"). Section 3(b). A private foundation structured as a trust would be a wholly charitable trust that could not be decanted pursuant to the act. * * *

If an authorized fiduciary has discretion to distribute principal of a trust that is not a wholly charitable trust but that contains a charitable interest (see Section 2(5)), the charitable interest may not be diminished, the charitable purpose set forth in the first trust may not be changed and any conditions or restrictions on the charitable interest may not be changed. See subsection 14(c).

The Uniform Trust Decanting Act is not the exclusive way to decant a trust and is not the exclusive way to modify a trust. The terms of the trust instrument may grant a fiduciary or other person the power to modify the trust. This act does not supplant any authority granted under such a trust provision. Any such authority granted under the trust instrument does not affect the application of this act unless the trust instrument imposes an express restriction on the exercise of the decanting power under this act or other state statute authorizing a fiduciary to decant. See Section 15(b). * * *

Section 4. Fiduciary Duty.

(a)   In exercising the decanting power, an authorized fiduciary shall act in accordance with its fiduciary duties, including the duty to act in accordance with the purposes of the first trust.

(b)   This [act] does not create or imply a duty to exercise the decanting power or to inform beneficiaries about the applicability of this [act].

(c)   Except as otherwise provided in a first-trust instrument, for purposes of this [act] [and Sections 801 and 802(a) of the Uniform Trust Code], the terms of the first trust are deemed to include the decanting power.

Comment

Except as noted below, in exercising the decanting power, the authorized fiduciary is subject to the same fiduciary duties as in exercising any other discretionary power. * * *

An exercise of the decanting power must be in accordance with the purposes of the first trust. The purpose of decanting is not to disregard the settlor's intent but to modify the trust to better effectuate the settlor's broader purposes or the settlor's probable intent if the settlor had anticipated the circumstances in place at the time of the decanting. The settlor's purposes generally include efficient administration of the trust. The settlor's purposes may also include achieving certain tax objectives or generally minimizing overall tax liabilities. The settlor's purposes often include avoiding fruitless, needless dissipation of the trust assets should a beneficiary develop dependencies such as substance abuse or gambling, have creditor problems, or otherwise be unfit to prudently manage assets that might be distributed from the trust.

The exercise of the decanting power need not be in accord with the literal terms of the first-trust instrument because decanting by definition is a modification of the terms of the first trust. Therefore subsection 4(c) provides that the terms of the first trust shall be deemed to include the decanting power for purposes of determining the fiduciary duties of the authorized fiduciary. Nonetheless, the other terms of the first trust may provide insight into the purposes of the first trust and the settlor's probable intent under current circumstances. * * *

The Uniform Trust Decanting Act does not impose a duty on the authorized fiduciary to decant. * * *

Section 5. Application; Governing Law.

This [act] applies to a trust created before, on, or after [the effective date of this [act]] which:

(1)   has its principal place of administration in this state, including a trust whose principal place of administration has been changed to this state; or

(2)   provides by its trust instrument that it is governed by the law of this state or is governed by the law of this state for the purpose of:

(A)   administration, including administration of a trust whose governing law for purposes of administration has been changed to the law of this state;

(B)   construction of terms of the trust; or

(C)   determining the meaning or effect of terms of the trust.

Comment

* * * To provide greater certainty about whether the act applies to a trust, Section 5(2) provides that the act applies to a trust that by its terms provides that it is governed by the law of the enacting state, without further inquiry as to whether the law of the enacting state actually applies. The act also applies

where the law of the enacting state in fact governs administration of the trust, construction of the terms of the trust, or determination of the meaning or effect of terms of the trust, whether or not the trust instrument expressly so states. * * *

Alternatively, it is sufficient if the trust has its principal place of administration in the state. * * * While a change of principal place of administration will usually change the law governing the administration of the trust, that is not the result under all circumstances. To avoid the difficulties of determining whether the law governing administration has changed when the principal place of administration has changed, the act applies to any trust with a principal place of administration in the state, regardless of what state law governs its administration and meaning and effect.

Section 6. Reasonable Reliance.

A trustee or other person that reasonably relies on the validity of a distribution of part or all of the property of a trust to another trust, or a modification of a trust, under this [act], law of this state other than this [act], or the law of another jurisdiction is not liable to any person for any action or failure to act as a result of the reliance.

Comment

A trustee should be able to administer a trust with some dispatch and without concern that reliance on a prior decanting is misplaced. This section allows a trustee, other fiduciary or other person to reasonably rely on the validity of a prior decanting, whether that decanting was performed under the act or under other law of the state or another jurisdiction. Thus this section relieves a trustee or other fiduciary from any duty it might otherwise have to determine definitively the validity of a prior decanting.

The person's reliance on the validity of a prior decanting must be reasonable. Thus a fiduciary must still review the facts of the prior decanting, whether it appears to be in compliance with the statute or other law under which the decanting was performed, and whether the law under which the decanting was performed appears to be applicable to the trust. If the second trust contains provisions that clearly are prohibited by the applicable decanting law, or fails to contain provisions that are clearly required by the applicable decanting law, reliance would not be reasonable.

When trusts have changed jurisdictions, it may be difficult to determine what law governs the administration of the trust. When trusts have multiple trustees, or a trustee conducts different trust functions in different places, it may be difficult to determine where the trust is administered. Thus it may be difficult in some cases to confirm with certainty which state decanting law applied to a prior attempted decanting. In some instances more than one state's decanting law may appear to apply, creating further uncertainty if the prior attempted decanting did not comply with all of the potentially applicable statutes. Section 6 protects a trustee or other person who makes a reasonable determination about which state decanting law applied to a prior decanting.

Ordinarily, a trustee or other person relying on a prior decanting need not independently verify compliance with every procedural rule of the decanting law. For example, ordinarily, the person relying on the prior decanting need not verify that every person required by the statute to receive notice in fact received notice. If such person knew, however, that the decanting law required notice and that no notice was given, reliance would not be reasonable.

This section does not validate any or all attempted decantings. Even if a trustee or other person may reasonably rely on a prior decanting, an interested person may still have the ability to challenge the decanting as invalid.

There may be times when the trustee or other person has sufficient questions about a prior attempted decanting that additional action is required to determine whether the prior attempted decanting was valid, in whole or in part, and to clarify the operating terms of the trust. In some cases the authorized fiduciary might use a new, properly implemented decanting to clarify the terms of the trust prospectively. In other cases a nonjudicial settlement agreement between the trustee and interested parties might be used to conform the effective terms of the trust. In some cases the trustee or other person might petition the court to determine the effective terms of the trust.

Section 7. Notice; Exercise of Decanting Power.

(a)   In this section, a notice period begins on the day notice is given under subsection (c) and ends [59] days after the day notice is given.

(b)   Except as otherwise provided in this [act], an authorized fiduciary may exercise the decanting power without the consent of any person and without court approval.

(c)   Except as otherwise provided in subsection (f), an authorized fiduciary shall give notice in a record of the intended exercise of the decanting power not later than [60] days before the exercise to:

(1)   each settlor of the first trust, if living or then in existence;

(2)   each qualified beneficiary of the first trust;

(3)   each holder of a presently exercisable power of appointment over any part or all of the first trust;

(4)   each person that currently has the right to remove or replace the authorized fiduciary;

(5)   each other fiduciary of the first trust;

(6)   each fiduciary of the second trust; and

(7)   [the Attorney General], if Section 14(b) applies.

(d)   [An authorized fiduciary is not required to give notice under subsection (c) to a qualified beneficiary who is a minor and has no representative or] [An authorized fiduciary is not required to give notice under subsection (c)] to a person that is not known to the fiduciary or is known to the fiduciary but cannot be located by the fiduciary after reasonable diligence.

(e)   A notice under subsection (c) must:

(1)   specify the manner in which the authorized fiduciary intends to exercise the decanting power;

(2)   specify the proposed effective date for exercise of the power;

(3)   include a copy of the first-trust instrument; and

(4)   include a copy of all second-trust instruments.

(f)   The decanting power may be exercised before expiration of the notice period under subsection (a) if all persons entitled to receive notice waive the period in a signed record.

(g)   The receipt of notice, waiver of the notice period, or expiration of the notice period does not affect the right of a person to file an application under Section 9 asserting that:

(1)   an attempted exercise of the decanting power is ineffective because it did not comply with this [act] or was an abuse of discretion or breach of fiduciary duty; or

(2)   Section 22 applies to the exercise of the decanting power.

(h)   An exercise of the decanting power is not ineffective because of the failure to give notice to one or more persons under subsection (c) if the authorized fiduciary acted with reasonable care to comply with subsection (c).

Comment

Generally a trustee is not required to provide notice to beneficiaries prior to exercising a discretionary power. This section is not intended to change the law in this regard except with respect to exercises of the decanting power. Because qualified beneficiaries are entitled to know the terms of the trust, they should receive notice of any change in the terms of the trust. Requiring prior notice seems reasonable, in light of the significant trust modifications that can be made by decanting, and practical, in that it helps determine if any settlor, fiduciary or beneficiary has an objection to or may challenge the decanting. Any person entitled to notice under subsection 7(c) may petition the court under Section 9 for a determination of whether the proposed or attempted exercise of the decanting power is an abuse of discretion or does not otherwise comply with the act. * * *

Notice must be given to (a) each settlor of the first trust (see Section 2(25)); (b) all qualified beneficiaries (see Section 2(20)); (c) each holder of a presently exercisable power of appointment, whether or not such holder is a qualified beneficiary; (d) any person who may remove or replace the authorized fiduciary; (e) all other fiduciaries of the first trust; (f) all fiduciaries of the second trust or trusts; and (g) the Attorney General (or other official with enforcement authority over charitable interests) if there is a determinable charitable interest (see Section 14(a)(1)). If the authorized fiduciary is comprised of more than one fiduciary, notice should be given to any person who may remove or replace any of such fiduciaries. The term "replace" refers to the power to both remove and designate a successor for the authorized fiduciary, and does not refer to the power merely to designate a successor when a vacancy occurs. * * *

Although the act does not limit the amount of time that may pass between the giving of notice and the exercise of the decanting power, if the exercise of the power does not occur within a reasonable period of time from the proposed effective date set forth in the notice, a new notice should be given with a new notice period. Further, the authorized fiduciary's duties to keep beneficiaries and interested persons informed about the trust may require the authorized fiduciary to inform such persons if the decanting is not completed as proposed or when the decanting has been completed.

If after notice is given and before the decanting power is exercised, relevant facts change in a manner that entitles an additional person to receive notice, unless such additional person can be represented by another person who has already received notice, notice should be provided to such additional person. A new notice period should begin to run, unless such additional person waives the notice period. * * *

Although under Section 7(h) an exercise of the decanting power will not be ineffective because of the failure to provide the required notice to one or more persons, provided that the authorized fiduciary acted with reasonable care, the act does not override the court's ability to address breaches of fiduciary duty and to fashion appropriate remedies.

[Section 8. Representation.

(a)   Notice to a person with authority to represent and bind another person under a first-trust instrument or [this state's trust code] has the same effect as notice given directly to the person represented.

(b)   Consent of or waiver by a person with authority to represent and bind another person under a first-trust instrument or [this state's trust code] is binding on the person represented unless the person represented objects to the representation before the consent or waiver otherwise would become effective.

(c)   A person with authority to represent and bind another person under a first-trust instrument or [this state's trust code] may file an application under Section 9 on behalf of the person represented.

(d)   A settlor may not represent or bind a beneficiary under this [act].]

Section 9. Court Involvement.

(a)   On application of an authorized fiduciary, a person entitled to notice under Section 7(c), a beneficiary, or with respect to a charitable interest the [Attorney General] or other person that has standing to enforce the charitable interest, the court may:

(1)   provide instructions to the authorized fiduciary regarding whether a proposed exercise of the decanting power is permitted under this [act] and consistent with the fiduciary duties of the authorized fiduciary;

(2)   appoint a special fiduciary and authorize the special fiduciary to determine whether the decanting power should be exercised under this [act] and to exercise the decanting power;

(3)   approve an exercise of the decanting power;

(4)   determine that a proposed or attempted exercise of the decanting power is ineffective because:

(A)   after applying Section 22, the proposed or attempted exercise does not or did not comply with this [act]; or

(B)   the proposed or attempted exercise would be or was an abuse of the fiduciary's discretion or a breach of fiduciary duty;

(5)   determine the extent to which Section 22 applies to a prior exercise of the decanting power;

(6)   provide instructions to the trustee regarding the application of Section 22 to a prior exercise of the decanting power; or

(7)   order other relief to carry out the purposes of this [act].

(b)   On application of an authorized fiduciary, the court may approve:

(1)   an increase in the fiduciary's compensation under Section 16; or

(2)   a modification under Section 18 of a provision granting a person the right to remove or replace the fiduciary.

Comment

Decanting by definition is an exercise of fiduciary discretion and is not an alternative basis for a court modification of the trust.

The decanting power, however, is a very broad discretionary power. Therefore, Section 9 provides that the authorized fiduciary, any person who would be entitled to notice of the exercise of the decanting power, any beneficiary or the Attorney General or other official who has enforcement authority over a charitable interest in the first trust, may petition the court for certain purposes with respect to a prior decanting or a proposed decanting. The persons who receive notice under Section 7 and who could petition the court include the settlor, the holder of a presently exercisable power of appointment over the first trust, each person who has a right to remove or replace the authorized fiduciary and each fiduciary of the first and second trusts.

A successor beneficiary, even though such beneficiary is not entitled to notice under Section 7, could petition the court under Section 9. Even though the Attorney General is entitled to notice under Section 7 only if there is a *determinable* charitable interest, the Attorney General may petition the court under Section 9 with respect to any charitable interest.

Any such person may request instructions with respect to whether a proposed decanting complies with the act and is consistent with the fiduciary duties of the authorized fiduciary. Section 9(a)(1). The authorized fiduciary need not have provided notice of a proposed decanting or even be the person proposing the decanting in order for the court to provide instructions. Such an instruction, however, would not create in the authorized fiduciary a duty to decant.

While generally the authorized fiduciary should decide whether or not to exercise the decanting power, and may seek instructions from the court when in doubt as to whether the proposed exercise is permitted and consistent with the authorized fiduciary's fiduciary duties, there may be times when the exercise of the decanting power is appropriate but the authorized fiduciary cannot or should not be the person to exercise the power. Under such circumstances the court may appoint a special fiduciary to determine if the decanting power should be exercised and, if so, to exercise the power. Section 9(a)(2). The terms of the appointment may limit the special fiduciary's power to determine whether a proposed exercise is appropriate or may grant the special fiduciary broader power to determine the scope of a decanting. The term of appointment may also limit the period of time during which the special fiduciary may act. For example, assume a trust permits discretionary principal distributions to the settlor's descendants subject to an ascertainable standard if a beneficiary is acting as trustee and subject to expanded discretion if a disinterested person is acting as trustee. If a beneficiary is acting as trustee and believes that an exercise of the decanting power under Section 11 may be appropriate, the trustee could request that the court appoint a disinterested person as special fiduciary to determine whether the decanting power should be exercised and, if so, to exercise the power. As another example, if the authorized fiduciary is a beneficiary of the first trust and it is appropriate to create a special-needs trust for another beneficiary, but the decanting might incidentally increase the authorized fiduciary's interest in the trust, it may be advisable for the authorized fiduciary to request under subsection (a)(2) the appointment of a special fiduciary to decide whether to exercise the decanting power.

The special fiduciary essentially temporarily steps into the office of the trustee or other fiduciary who has the power to make trust distributions (the "distribution fiduciary"). If the special fiduciary, if acting as the distribution fiduciary, would have expanded distributive discretion, the court may authorize the special fiduciary to exercise the decanting power under Section 11. If the special fiduciary, if acting as the distribution fiduciary, would have limited distributive discretion, the court may authorize the special fiduciary to exercise the decanting power under Section 12. If the distribution fiduciary has no discretion to distribute principal, then the special fiduciary could not exercise the decanting power under Section 11 or 12, but could exercise the decanting power under Section 13.

For example, assume A is acting as trustee of a trust that is required to distribute income to A and upon A's death distributes to A's descendants. A special fiduciary cannot exercise the decanting power under Section 11 or Section 12 because the special fiduciary, if acting as trustee, has no distributive discretion over principal.

Now assume that the trust also provides that if a person who is not a beneficiary is acting as trustee, such trustee may make discretionary distributions of principal to A for A's health care. A special fiduciary who is not a beneficiary could be appointed and granted the authority to exercise the decanting power under Section 12.

Alternatively, assume that the trust provides that if a person who is not a beneficiary is acting as trustee, such trustee may make discretionary distributions of principal to A for A's best interests. A special fiduciary who is not a beneficiary could be appointed and granted the authority to exercise the decanting power under Section 11.

Any person described in Section 9(a) may request that the court approve an exercise of the decanting power. Such approval should be granted if the decanting complies with this act and is not an abuse of the trustee's discretion.

A petition to the court may also request that the court determine whether an attempted decanting is ineffective because it did not comply with the act. The court may also determine whether the remedial provisions of Section 22 apply to an attempted decanting and how such remedial provisions modify the second-trust instrument. If a trust has been administered after an attempted decanting under the assumed terms of the second-trust instrument, but after applying Section 22 should have been administered on different terms, the court may also instruct the fiduciary on the corr2ective action that should be taken.

For example, if an attempted decanting eliminated a noncontingent right to mandatory income distributions, and several years after the attempted decanting the income beneficiary of the first trust petitioned the court to apply Section 22 to the attempted decanting, the court might declare that the second trust must grant the income beneficiary such beneficiary's mandatory income interest and might order a makeup distribution to the income beneficiary for the period the income was not paid. * * *

Section 10. Formalities.

An exercise of the decanting power must be made in a record signed by an authorized fiduciary. The signed record must, directly or by reference to the notice required by Section 7, identify the first trust and the second trust or trusts and state the property of the first trust being distributed to each second trust and the property, if any, that remains in the first trust.

Comment

* * * The decanting power can be exercised by either an actual distribution of property to one or more second trusts or by modifying the terms of the first trust to create the second trust with or without an actual distribution of property. If the decanting power is exercised by modifying the terms of the first trust, the trustee could either treat the second trust created by such modification as a new trust, in which case the property of the first trust would need to be transferred to the second trust, or alternatively treat the second trust as a continuation of the first trust, in which case the property of the first trust would not need to be retitled.

Other actions may be required to formally complete the transfer of property from the first trust to the second trust, such as retitling accounts, executing deeds, and signing assignments.

Section 11. Decanting Power Under Expanded Distributive Discretion.

(a)   In this section:

(1)   "Noncontingent right" means a right that is not subject to the exercise of discretion or the occurrence of a specified event that is not certain to occur. The term does not include a right held by a beneficiary if any person has discretion to distribute property subject to the right to any person other than the beneficiary or the beneficiary's estate.

(2)   "Presumptive remainder beneficiary" means a qualified beneficiary other than a current beneficiary.

(3)   "Successor beneficiary" means a beneficiary that is not a qualified beneficiary on the date the beneficiary's qualification is determined. The term does not include a person that is a beneficiary only because the person holds a nongeneral power of appointment.

(4)   "Vested interest" means:

(A)   a right to a mandatory distribution that is a noncontingent right as of the date of the exercise of the decanting power;

(B)   a current and noncontingent right, annually or more frequently, to a mandatory distribution of income, a specified dollar amount, or a percentage of value of some or all of the trust property;

(C)   a current and noncontingent right, annually or more frequently, to withdraw income, a specified dollar amount, or a percentage of value of some or all of the trust property;

(D)   a presently exercisable general power of appointment; or

(E)   a right to receive an ascertainable part of the trust property on the trust's termination which is not subject to the exercise of discretion or to the occurrence of a specified event that is not certain to occur.

(b)   Subject to subsection (c) and Section 14, an authorized fiduciary that has expanded distributive discretion over the principal of a first trust for the benefit of one or more current beneficiaries may exercise the decanting power over the principal of the first trust.

(c)   Subject to Section 13, in an exercise of the decanting power under this section, a second trust may not:

(1)   include as a current beneficiary a person that is not a current beneficiary of the first trust, except as otherwise provided in subsection (d);

(2)   include as a presumptive remainder beneficiary or successor beneficiary a person that is not a current beneficiary, presumptive remainder beneficiary, or successor beneficiary of the first trust, except as otherwise provided in subsection (d); or

(3)   reduce or eliminate a vested interest.

(d)   Subject to subsection (c)(3) and Section 14, in an exercise of the decanting power under this section, a second trust may be a trust created or administered under the law of any jurisdiction and may:

(1)   retain a power of appointment granted in the first trust;

(2)   omit a power of appointment granted in the first trust, other than a presently exercisable general power of appointment;

(3)   create or modify a power of appointment if the powerholder is a current beneficiary of the first trust and the authorized fiduciary has expanded distributive discretion to distribute principal to the beneficiary; and

(4)   create or modify a power of appointment if the powerholder is a presumptive remainder beneficiary or successor beneficiary of the first trust, but the exercise of the power may take effect only after the powerholder becomes, or would have become if then living, a current beneficiary.

(e)   A power of appointment described in subsection (d)(1) through (4) may be general or nongeneral. The class of permissible appointees in favor of which the power may be exercised may be broader than or different from the beneficiaries of the first trust.

(f)   If an authorized fiduciary has expanded distributive discretion over part but not all of the principal of a first trust, the fiduciary may exercise the decanting power under this section over that part of the principal over which the authorized fiduciary has expanded distributive discretion.

Comment

Noncontingent Right. The term "noncontingent right" describes interests that are certain to occur. A right is not noncontingent if it is subject to the occurrence of a specified event that is not certain to occur. For example, if A's children who survive A are to receive trust assets upon A's death, the rights of A's children are not noncontingent, because each must survive A to take and they may not survive A. The rights of A's children are not noncontingent regardless of whether the requirement of survival is expressed as a condition precedent or a condition subsequent. Thus the result is the same if the gift upon A's death is to A's children in equal shares, but if any child predeceases A such child's share shall be distributed to such child's descendants in shares per stirpes.

A right also is not a noncontingent right if it is subject to the exercise of discretion. Thus if a trustee has discretion to make distributions to A and A's descendants for their support and health care, the interests of A and A's descendants are not noncontingent. The result is the same even if the trust directs the trustee to make distributions to A and A's descendants for their support and health care because the timing and amount of the distributions are subject to the trustee's discretion.

A right also is not noncontingent if a person has discretion to distribute the property subject to the interest to any person other than the beneficiary or the beneficiary's estate. Thus if a trust provides that all income shall be distributed annually to A, but gives the trustee discretion to distribute principal to B for B's support and medical care, A's right is not noncontingent.

A current mandatory right to receive income, an annuity or a unitrust payment where the trustee has no discretion to make distributions to others is a noncontingent right.

Presumptive Remainder Beneficiary. "Presumptive remainder beneficiary" means a qualified beneficiary (see Section 2(20)) other than a current beneficiary (see Section 2(9)). The presumptive remainder beneficiaries might be termed the first-line remainder beneficiaries. These are the beneficiaries who would become eligible to receive distributions were the event triggering the termination of a current beneficiary's interest or of the trust itself to occur on the date in question. Such a terminating event will often be the death or deaths of the current beneficiaries. A person who would have a presently exercisable general power of appointment if the trust terminated on that date or if the interests of the current beneficiaries terminated on that date without causing the trust to terminate is a presumptive remainder beneficiary.

Presumptive remainder beneficiaries can include takers in default of the exercise of a power of appointment. The term may sometimes include the persons entitled to receive the trust property pursuant to the irrevocable exercise of an inter vivos power of appointment. Because the exercise of a testamentary power of appointment is not effective until the testator's death, the qualified beneficiaries do not include appointees under the will of a living person. Nor would the term include the objects of an unexercised inter vivos power.

Successor Beneficiary. The term "successor beneficiary" means a beneficiary who has a future beneficial interest in a trust, vested or contingent, including a person who may become a beneficiary in the future by reason of inclusion in a class, other than a beneficiary who is a qualified beneficiary. Thus it includes beneficiaries who might be termed "second line" or more remote remainder beneficiaries. It also includes unborn or unascertained beneficiaries who are beneficiaries by reason of being members of a class. It does not include, however, a person who is merely a holder of a power of appointment but not otherwise a beneficiary.

Vested Interest. "Vested interest" includes a right to a mandatory distribution that is a noncontingent right as of the date of the exercise of the decanting power. Section 11(a)(4)(A). For example, if the trustee is required to distribute the trust principal to A when A attains age 30 if A is then living, and A has attained age 30 but the trustee has not yet made the distribution, A's right to receive the trust principal is a right to a mandatory distribution that is a noncontingent right. If A is age 29, however, A's right is not a noncontingent right because A must survive to age 30.

The right to a mandatory distribution does not include a right to a distribution pursuant to a standard or a right to a distribution in the discretion of a fiduciary. Thus a right to receive distributions for "support and health care," or for "best interests" would not be a mandatory distribution right for purposes of Section 11.

"Vested interest" also includes a current and noncontingent right, annually or more frequently, to a mandatory distribution of income, a specified dollar amount or a percentage of value of some or all of the trust properties. Section 11(a)(4)(B). Thus if A is currently entitled to all trust income payable annually, and the trustee has no discretion to not pay the income to A and no discretion to distribute principal to anyone other than A, A's right to income is a vested interest. A's right to income is a vested interest even if the trustee has discretion to distribute principal to A. The result is the same if instead of an income right, A has the right to receive a specified dollar amount or a percentage of value of trust assets. A's right is a vested interest even if the right will cease upon some future event, such as A's death or a particular date, so long as the future event is not an exercise of fiduciary discretion. A specified dollar amount includes a dollar amount that is dependent upon factors other than fiduciary discretion or specific events not certain to occur, such as the inflation rate. A "vested interest" includes a current right to a unitrust distribution based on the value of certain or all trust assets.

A fiduciary's power to make equitable adjustments to income or principal, whether granted under the trust instrument or state law, does not make an income interest not mandatory or not noncontingent. A fiduciary's power to exclude certain assets in determining a unitrust distribution to attain an equitable result, whether granted under the trust instrument or state law, does not make a unitrust interest not mandatory or not noncontingent. For example, a beneficiary's current right to receive an annual distribution equal to 4% of the value of the trust principal is a vested interest even if the fiduciary has a right to exclude from the value of trust principal non-income producing assets.

Even if all conditions to such right have been met, the decanting may eliminate current mandatory rights to income, annuity or unitrust distributions that have come into effect with respect to a beneficiary if the authorized fiduciary has discretion to make principal distributions to another beneficiary. For example, if the first trust provides for mandatory income distributions to A, but permits the authorized fiduciary to make discretionary principal distributions to A, B or C for their best interests, the decanting may eliminate A's mandatory income interest. In such case the first trust indirectly gave the authorized fiduciary the ability to reduce or eliminate A's income interest by making discretionary principal distributions to B or C.

A right to receive mandatory payments less frequently than annually is not a vested interest. For example, a right to receive 5% of the trust value every fifth year is not a vested interest, except with respect to any amounts currently payable. As another example, a right to receive distributions of one-third of the trust principal at ages 30, 35 and 40 is not a vested interest if the beneficiary has not attained age 30. If the beneficiary is age 30 but the trustee has not yet distributed the one-third payable at age 30, the beneficiary's right to that one-third is a vested interest, but the beneficiary's right to receive distributions at ages 35 and 40 is not a vested interest.

"Vested interest" also includes a current and noncontingent right, annually or more frequently, to *withdraw* income, a specified dollar amount, or a percentage of value of some or all of the trust property. Section 11(a)(4)(C). Thus, for example, it makes no difference whether the trustee is required to distribute income annually or whether the beneficiary may withdraw income annually. As another example, if B has a current right to withdraw annually the greater of $5,000 or 5% of the trust value each year, B's right is a vested interest. If B's right to withdraw did not begin until B attained age 25 and B has not attained age 25, B's right would not be a vested interest.

"Vested interest" also includes a presently exercisable general power of appointment. A power of appointment is presently exercisable if it is exercisable at the time in question. Typically, a presently exercisable power of appointment is exercisable at the time in question during the powerholder's life and also at the powerholder's death, e.g., by the powerholder's will. Thus, a power of appointment that is exercisable "by deed or will" is a presently exercisable power.

A power to withdraw from a trust is a power of appointment. * * * Thus if a beneficiary has already attained an age at which the beneficiary can withdraw all or a portion of the trust, the second trust may not modify or eliminate that right of withdrawal. If a Crummey withdrawal power is still in effect with respect to a prior contribution to the trust, the second trust cannot modify or eliminate the Crummey withdrawal right.

For example, if the trustee may make discretionary distributions to C and C's descendants, C has a right to withdraw one-half of trust principal after attaining age 28, and C has attained age 28, C's right is a vested interest under Section 11(a)(4)(D) even if the trustee has power to distribute trust principal to anyone other than C.

"Vested interest" also includes a right to receive an ascertainable part of the trust property on the trust's termination which is not subject to the exercise of discretion or to the occurrence of a specified event that is not certain to occur. Thus if the trustee is to distribute income to F, and upon F's death is to distribute the principal to G or G's estate, G's interest is a vested interest. G would not have a vested interest if the trustee had discretion to distribute principal to F or if G was required to survive F to take the remainder interest. Thus the right of a person to receive the trust property upon the termination of such trust if such person is then living would not be a vested interest. Any interest with a condition is not a vested interest, regardless of whether the condition is a condition precedent or condition subsequent. For example, A does not have a vested interest if upon termination the trust property passes to A or A's estate, provided that A is then married or was married at the time of A's prior death.

Expanded Distributive Discretion Decanting. Under Section 11 an authorized fiduciary who has expanded distributive discretion to distribute all or part of the principal of a trust to one or more of the current beneficiaries may exercise the decanting power over the principal subject to such expanded distributive discretion.

"Expanded distributive discretion" is defined in Section 2(11). When a trustee is granted expanded distributive discretion, that is an indication that the settlor intended to rely on the trustee's judgment and discretion in making distributions. The settlor's faith in the trustee's judgment supports the assumption that the settlor would trust the trustee's judgment in making modifications to the trust instrument in light of changed circumstances including the beneficiary's circumstances and changes in tax and other laws.

The decanting power, like most discretionary distribution powers, can be exercised over all or part of the first trust. If it is exercised over only part of the first trust, the second trust would need to be a separate trust and could not be a continuation of the first trust. If the decanting power is exercised to distribute property of the first trust to more than one second trusts, then the second trusts (or at least all but one of the second trusts) would need to be separate trusts and could not be a continuation of the first trust.

If the authorized fiduciary has expanded discretion over only part of the first trust, the authorized fiduciary may exercise the decanting power under this section only over such part. See Section 11(f). With respect to the remainder of the trust, the authorized fiduciary may have the ability to decant under Section 12 or Section 13.

The second trust may contain any terms permissible for a trust subject only to the restrictions found in the act. Thus subject to subsections (c) and (f) of Section 11 and the other restrictions in Sections 14 through 20 and subject to the fiduciary duty in Section 4(a), the second trust may (1) eliminate (but not add) one or more current beneficiaries; (2) make a current beneficiary a presumptive remainder beneficiary or a successor beneficiary; (3) eliminate (but not add) one or more presumptive remainder and successor beneficiaries; (4) make a presumptive remainder beneficiary a successor beneficiary, or vice versa; (5) alter or eliminate rights that are not vested interests; (6) change the standard for distributions; (7) add or eliminate a spendthrift provision; (8) extend the duration of a trust (subject to Section 20); (9) change the jurisdiction of the trust and the law governing the administration of the trust (subject to Section 14(e)); (10) eliminate, modify or add powers of appointment; (11) change the trustee or trustee succession provisions; (12) change the powers of the trustee; (13) change administrative provisions of the trust; (14) add investment advisors, trust protectors or other fiduciaries; (15) divide a trust into more than one trust; and (16) consolidate trusts. The foregoing list merely provides examples and is not exhaustive.

The second trust, however, cannot make a remainder beneficiary a current beneficiary. This prohibition on accelerating a remainder interest is included to avoid any argument under Internal Revenue Code Section 674 that the mere existence of a power to make a remainder beneficiary a current beneficiary causes the trust to be a grantor trust, whether or not the decanting power is ever exercised in such manner.

Section 11(c)(3) prohibits the second trust from reducing or eliminating a vested interest. A vested interest is not reduced, however, just because other changes made as a result of a decanting may have incidental effects on the interest. For example, a modification of the fiduciary's investment powers or the manner of determining the fiduciary's compensation may have incidental effects on a beneficiary's interest, but such modifications do not reduce a vested interest.

The restrictions in Section 11(c)(3) do not apply to a decanting under Section 13. Section 13(c)(2).

Subsections (d) and (e) permit the second trust to retain or omit a power of appointment included in the first trust, or to create powers of appointment in one or more current beneficiaries of the first trust. For example, if the first trust permits the authorized fiduciary to make discretionary distributions of income or principal to the settlor's child A, and upon A's death the remainder is allocated for the settlor's descendants per stirpes, to be held in further trust for each such descendant, the second trust could grant A a lifetime and/or testamentary power, general or nongeneral. The second trust could grant A a lifetime power to appoint to A's descendants, spouse and charitable organizations and a testamentary power to appoint to A's estate or to the creditors of A's estate. The second trust also could provide that each descendant of the settlor for whom a trust is established at A's death will have an inter vivos or a testamentary, general or limited, power of appointment. The second trust could even give A's now living children, D and E, powers of appointment that they may exercise in their Wills, but that will only take effect upon A's death or, if later, their deaths.

Subsection (e) makes clear that persons who are not otherwise beneficiaries of the first trust may be permissible appointees of a power of appointment granted to a current beneficiary.

Sometimes state law may provide more than one method for making the same modification to a trust. For example, a combination of trusts or a division of a trust that would be permitted under Section 417 of the Uniform Trust Code may also be accomplished under this act through decanting. When a desired modification could be accomplished by decanting or by another method, the trustee may select either method.

Section 12. Decanting Power Under Limited Distributive Discretion.

(a)   In this section, "limited distributive discretion" means a discretionary power of distribution that is limited to an ascertainable standard or a reasonably definite standard.

(b)   An authorized fiduciary that has limited distributive discretion over the principal of the first trust for benefit of one or more current beneficiaries may exercise the decanting power over the principal of the first trust.

(c)   Under this section and subject to Section 14, a second trust may be created or administered under the law of any jurisdiction. Under this section, the second trusts, in the aggregate, must grant each beneficiary of the first trust beneficial interests which are substantially similar to the beneficial interests of the beneficiary in the first trust.

(d)   A power to make a distribution under a second trust for the benefit of a beneficiary who is an individual is substantially similar to a power under the first trust to make a distribution directly to the beneficiary. A distribution is for the benefit of a beneficiary if:

   (1)   the distribution is applied for the benefit of the beneficiary;

(2) the beneficiary is under a legal disability or the trustee reasonably believes the beneficiary is incapacitated, and the distribution is made as permitted under [this state's trust code]; or

(3) the distribution is made as permitted under the terms of the first-trust instrument and the second-trust instrument for the benefit of the beneficiary.

(e) If an authorized fiduciary has limited distributive discretion over part but not all of the principal of a first trust, the fiduciary may exercise the decanting power under this section over that part of the principal over which the authorized fiduciary has limited distributive discretion.

Comment

Limited Distributive Discretion. "Limited distributive discretion" means a discretionary power of distribution that is limited to an ascertainable standard or a reasonably definite standard. Section 12(a). "Ascertainable standard" is defined in Section 2(2). "Reasonably definite standard" is defined in Section 2(21). "Limited distributive discretion" and "expanded distributive discretion" (see Section 2(11)) are mutually exclusive terms. An authorized fiduciary who has expanded distributive discretion over principal may decant under Section 11. An authorized fiduciary who has limited distributive discretion over principal may decant under Section 12. An authorized fiduciary who has no distributive discretion over principal, even if the authorized fiduciary has distributive discretion over income, may not decant under the act except as provided in Section 13.

Substantially Similar Beneficial Interests. When the authorized fiduciary has limited distributive discretion over principal, the authorized fiduciary may exercise the decanting power to effect modifications in administrative provisions, including trustee succession provisions, but may not materially change the dispositive provisions of the trust. This section requires the beneficial provisions of the second trust to be substantially the same as in the first trust, because the settlor did not choose to give the authorized fiduciary expanded discretion. Thus, for example, if a trust provides for principal distributions subject to an ascertainable standard to the settlor's child, and upon the child's death the remainder is to be distributed to Charitable Organization A, the decanting power cannot be exercised in a manner that substantially changes the interests of the child or of Charitable Organization A. Nonetheless, the settlor did entrust the authorized fiduciary with some discretion over principal distributions indicating some confidence in the trustee's judgment, justifying a limited decanting power in these situations.

"Substantially similar" means that there is no material change in a beneficiary's beneficial interests except as provided in subsection (d). A distribution standard that was more restrictive or more expansive would not be substantially similar. Thus if the first trust permitted distributions for support, health care and education, the beneficial interests would not be substantially similar if the second trust permitted distributions only for support and health care. If the first trust, however, permitted distributions for education without elaboration with respect to what was included within the term, the second trust might define education to include college, graduate school and vocational schools if otherwise consistent with applicable law.

If the first trust requires that a trust be distributed at age 35, a second trust that permits the beneficiary to withdraw any part or all of the trust at any time after age 35 would be substantially similar. A second trust that delayed the distribution to age 40 would not be substantially similar.

Changes to a fiduciary's administrative powers or investment powers, changes in a fiduciary, or changes in jurisdiction or the state law governing the administration of the trust, are not material changes in a beneficiary's beneficial interests, even though such changes may have incidental effects on the beneficial interests. For example, changing the trustee from one person to another could impact how the trustee exercises discretionary distribution authority, but is not a material change because the trustee's discretion is subject to the same standard and the trustee is subject to fiduciary duties. * * *

Section 12 is intended to permit a severance of a trust if the beneficial interests in the second trust, in the aggregate, are substantially similar to the beneficial interests in the first trust. For this purpose, an equal vertical division of a trust in which multiple beneficiaries have equal discretionary interests would usually be considered to be substantially similar. For example, if a testamentary trust created by A provides for discretionary distributions of income and principal to A's children for support, education and health care and A has three living children (B, C and D), the authorized fiduciary may exercise the decanting power under Section 12 to sever the trust into three equal trusts, one for each of B, C and D. The beneficial interest of each child in the second trusts is different because before the severance each child could conceivably receive discretionary distributions of more than one-third of the first trust and after the severance each child may only receive distributions from such child's second trust (one-third of the first trust). A child's interest would usually be considered substantially similar, however, because the loss of the possibility of receiving distributions of more than one-third of the first trust is offset by the fact that after the severance the other children may not receive discretionary distributions from such child's second trust. A child's interest after severance might not be considered substantially similar, however, if the first-trust instrument made clear that B's health care needs should be given priority and it seemed likely that B's health care needs would exceed one-third of the principal of the first trust.

Section 13. Trust for Beneficiary With Disability.

(a)   In this section:

(1)   "Beneficiary with a disability" means a beneficiary of a first trust who the special-needs fiduciary believes may qualify for governmental benefits based on disability, whether or not the beneficiary currently receives those benefits or is an individual who has been adjudicated [incompetent].

(2)   "Governmental benefits" means financial aid or services from a state, federal, or other public agency.

(3)   "Special-needs fiduciary" means, with respect to a trust that has a beneficiary with a disability:

(A)   a trustee or other fiduciary, other than a settlor, that has discretion to distribute part or all of the principal of a first trust to one or more current beneficiaries;

(B)   if no trustee or fiduciary has discretion under subparagraph (A), a trustee or other fiduciary, other than a settlor, that has discretion to distribute part or all of the income of the first trust to one or more current beneficiaries; or

(C)   if no trustee or fiduciary has discretion under subparagraphs (A) and (B), a trustee or other fiduciary, other than a settlor, that is required to distribute part or all of the income or principal of the first trust to one or more current beneficiaries.

(4)   "Special-needs trust" means a trust the trustee believes would not be considered a resource for purposes of determining whether a beneficiary with a disability is eligible for governmental benefits.

(b)   A special-needs fiduciary may exercise the decanting power under Section 11 over the principal of a first trust as if the fiduciary had authority to distribute principal to a beneficiary with a disability subject to expanded distributive discretion if:

(1)   a second trust is a special-needs trust that benefits the beneficiary with a disability; and

(2)   the special-needs fiduciary determines that exercise of the decanting power will further the purposes of the first trust.

(c)   In an exercise of the decanting power under this section, the following rules apply:

(1)   Notwithstanding Section 11(c)(2), the interest in the second trust of a beneficiary with a disability may:

(A)   be a pooled trust as defined by Medicaid law for the benefit of the beneficiary with a disability under 42 U.S.C. Section 1396p(d)(4)(C)[, as amended]; or

(B)   contain payback provisions complying with reimbursement requirements of Medicaid law under 42 U.S.C. Section 1396p(d)(4)(A)[, as amended].

(2)   Section 11(c)(3) does not apply to the interests of the beneficiary with a disability.

(3)   Except as affected by any change to the interests of the beneficiary with a disability, the second trust, or if there are two or more second trusts, the second trusts in the aggregate, must grant each other beneficiary of the first trust beneficial interests in the second trusts which are substantially similar to the beneficiary's beneficial interests in the first trust.

Comment

Section 13 permits an authorized fiduciary to exercise the decanting power over a trust that has a beneficiary with a disability to create a special-needs trust that governmental benefits programs may not consider a "resource" for purposes of the eligibility of the beneficiary with a disability for those benefits. Many governmental benefit programs restrict eligibility for those programs to only persons of limited resources. These resources may include any assets from which the beneficiary with a disability has the right to compel a distribution or a withdrawal. Special-needs trusts are drafted so as to limit the distribution rights of the beneficiary with a disability and thus better permit the beneficiary with a disability to qualify for governmental benefits. Under Section 13 the authorized fiduciary may modify the dispositive provisions for the beneficiary with a disability even if the authorized fiduciary has no discretion to make distributions or only discretion over income.

Beneficiary with a Disability. "Beneficiary with a disability" means a beneficiary who the special-needs fiduciary believes may qualify for governmental benefits based on disability. Section 13(a)(1). The beneficiary need not be adjudicated incompetent or totally incapacitated. The beneficiary need not be currently receiving governmental benefits based on disability. Nor need it be certain that the beneficiary would qualify for such benefits but for the terms of the first trust. The special-needs fiduciary need only have a reasonable belief that the decanting may permit the beneficiary to qualify for such benefits. * * *

Special-Needs Fiduciary. Because the term "authorized fiduciary" is limited to a fiduciary who has the power to make discretionary distributions of principal and Section 13 is intended to permit a fiduciary to decant even if the fiduciary does not have discretion over principal, Section 13 uses the separate term "special-needs fiduciary" to identify the fiduciary who has the power to decant. If there is no fiduciary who has discretion over principal, the special-needs fiduciary is the fiduciary with discretion over income, or if none, the fiduciary who is directed to make distributions. Section 13(a)(3). * * *

Furtherance of Purposes of Trust. The exercise of the decanting power must be in furtherance of the purposes of the first trust. Section 13(b)(2). Thus the decanting must effectuate better the settlor's broader purposes. In most cases, if the first trust did not anticipate the beneficiary's disability and the settlor's broader purpose was to provide for the beneficiary's support, a decanting that would permit the beneficiary with a disability to qualify for governmental benefits while still being eligible to receive discretionary distributions from the trust would further the purposes of the trust.

For example, assume the first trust was created and funded by A, requires all income to be distributed to the beneficiary after age 21, permits the trustee to distribute principal to the beneficiary pursuant to an ascertainable standard for the beneficiary's support, permits the beneficiary to withdraw the trust principal at age 30, grants the beneficiary a testamentary general power of appointment, and upon the beneficiary's death distributes any unappointed property per stirpes to A's descendants then living. If the beneficiary is age 25 and is disabled, the authorized fiduciary may exercise the decanting power to distribute the principal of the first trust to a trust that provides only for distributions to the beneficiary in the trustee's absolute discretion and upon the beneficiary's death distributes the remaining trust assets per stirpes to A's descendants then living. The exercise of the decanting power may eliminate the beneficiary's right to income, the beneficiary's prospective right to withdraw the trust at age 30 and the beneficiary's power of appointment. The second trust may not, however, change the remainder beneficiaries. Section 13(c)(3).

The result is the same if the beneficiary is age 31 and thus has a right to withdraw the trust assets, because Section 13(c)(2) provides that Section 11(c)(3) does not apply to the interest of the beneficiary with a disability.

If in the above example the trustee had no discretion to distribute principal, but was either required to distribute income or had discretion to distribute income for A's support, the authorized fiduciary could still decant to a special-needs trust. The trustee would be considered the special-needs fiduciary under Section 13(a)(3).

The decanting, however, must further the purposes of the first trust. Section 13(b)(2). For example, if a trust was created solely for the purpose of funding college education for the settlor's grandchildren, the authorized fiduciary may not decant to pay for the support of a grandchild who is a beneficiary with a disability. Conceivably, however, a trust for the education at all levels of the settlor's grandchildren might be decanted to a trust that permits distributions to a grandchild who is a beneficiary with a disability for such grandchild's occupational therapy and vocational training.

Pooled or Payback Trust. The second trust may be a pooled trust or a payback trust. Section 13(c)(1). For example, assume a trust was funded by the beneficiary, directly or indirectly, and provides for distributions of income to the beneficiary until age 30 and then provides for the remainder of the trust to be distributed to the beneficiary. The beneficiary is age 28. The authorized fiduciary may exercise the decanting power, and the second trust may be a "pooled trust" or a payback trust. Section 13(c)(1). The act does not require that the second trust be a "pooled trust" or a payback trust, but other state law may impose such a requirement.

Other Beneficial Interests Must Be Substantially Similar. Subsection (c)(3) generally requires that any beneficial interests of beneficiaries other than the beneficiary with a disability be substantially similar to their interests in the first trust except to the extent they are affected by changes to the interest of the beneficiary with a disability. The beneficiary's disability justifies permitting a modification of the interest of the beneficiary with a disability even when the trustee has limited or no discretion, but does not justify otherwise changing the interests of other beneficiaries. The modifications to the interest of the beneficiary with a disability, however, might affect the amount or timing of the other beneficiaries' interests.

Thus if the first trust has more than one current beneficiary, one of whom is a beneficiary with a disability, the special-needs fiduciary may decant under Section 11 as if the special-needs fiduciary had expanded discretion to distribute principal to the beneficiary with a disability, but may not alter the interests of the other beneficiaries except to the extent they are affected by the changes to the interest of the beneficiary with a disability. For example, assume the first trust was created and funded by A, continues for the rule against perpetuities period, requires that income be distributed per stirpes to A's descendants, and permits discretionary distributions of principal to A's descendants pursuant to an ascertainable standard. The exercise of the decanting power might, for example, distribute part of the principal of the first trust to a special-needs trust solely for the benefit of the beneficiary with a disability (the "Special-Needs Trust") and distribute the remaining principal to a trust solely for the benefit of the nondisabled beneficiaries (the "Non-Special-Needs Trust"), the terms of which are otherwise identical to the terms of the first trust. The Special-Needs Trust might give the trustee absolute discretion to make distributions to the beneficiary with a disability. Upon the death of the beneficiary with a disability, however, the remaining assets of the Special-Needs Trust must be distributed to the Non-Special-Needs Trust, because the decanting cannot change the interests of the non-disabled beneficiaries, except to the extent they are affected by the changes to the interest of the beneficiary with a disability. The non-disabled beneficiaries' remainder interests may be affected, for example, because the trustee of the Special-Needs Trust may make distributions to the beneficiary with a disability in the trustee's absolute discretion and is not limited by an ascertainable standard. The Non-Special-Needs Trust must have the same terms as the first trust, except that it may modify or eliminate the interest of the beneficiary with a disability. So, for example, the Non-Special-Needs Trust might provide that no distributions would be made to the beneficiary with a disability unless the Special-Needs Trust was exhausted.

Section 14. Protection of Charitable Interest.

(a)   In this section:

(1)   "Determinable charitable interest" means a charitable interest that is a right to a mandatory distribution currently, periodically, on the occurrence of a specified event, or after the passage of a specified time and which is unconditional or will be held solely for charitable purposes.

(2)   "Unconditional" means not subject to the occurrence of a specified event that is not certain to occur, other than a requirement in a trust instrument that a charitable organization be in existence or qualify under a particular provision of the United States Internal Revenue Code

of 1986[, as amended,] on the date of the distribution, if the charitable organization meets the requirement on the date of determination.

(b)   If a first trust contains a determinable charitable interest, [the Attorney General] has the rights of a qualified beneficiary and may represent and bind the charitable interest.

(c)   If a first trust contains a charitable interest, the second trust or trusts may not:

    (1)   diminish the charitable interest;

    (2)   diminish the interest of an identified charitable organization that holds the charitable interest;

    (3)   alter any charitable purpose stated in the first-trust instrument; or

    (4)   alter any condition or restriction related to the charitable interest.

(d)   If there are two or more second trusts, the second trusts shall be treated as one trust for purposes of determining whether the exercise of the decanting power diminishes the charitable interest or diminishes the interest of an identified charitable organization for purposes of subsection (c).

(e)   If a first trust contains a determinable charitable interest, the second trust or trusts that include a charitable interest pursuant to subsection (c) must be administered under the law of this state unless:

    (1)   [the Attorney General], after receiving notice under Section 7, fails to object in a signed record delivered to the authorized fiduciary within the notice period;

    (2)   [the Attorney General] consents in a signed record to the second trust or trusts being administered under the law of another jurisdiction; or

    (3)   the court approves the exercise of the decanting power.

(f)   This [act] does not limit the powers and duties of the [Attorney General] under law of this state other than this [act].

Comment

The Uniform Trust Decanting Act does not permit the decanting of a trust held solely for charitable purposes (a "wholly charitable trust"). See Section 3(b). While a split interest trust such as a charitable remainder trust or a charitable lead trust is not a wholly charitable trust, in almost all cases the trustee of such a trust would not have discretion to distribute principal to a current beneficiary and therefore there would be no authorized fiduciary (see Section 2(3)) who would have authority to exercise the decanting power under Section 11 or Section 12.

Other trusts that could be decanted under Sections 11, 12 or 13, however, may contain charitable interests. Section 14 imposes special protections for charitable interests. When a charitable interest is a "determinable charitable interest," Section 14 gives the Attorney General (or other official with enforcement authority over charitable interests) the rights of a qualified beneficiary and restricts the ability to decant to change the law governing the trust's administration. Generally, a determinable charitable interest is a charitable interest not subject to fiduciary discretion or any significant contingencies.

Determinable Charitable Interest. An interest must meet three requirements to be a determinable charitable interest. Section 14(a)(1). First, the interest must be a charitable interest. See Section 2(5). * * *

Second, a determinable interest must be a right to a mandatory distribution. A mandatory distribution is a right that is not subject to the exercise of discretion. The mandatory distribution may be a right to income, principal or both. A mandatory distribution may be a right to a current distribution, for example, where a charitable organization is entitled to a certain portion of trust principal on a date that has already occurred and the distribution has not yet been made. A mandatory distribution also includes a right to periodic distributions of income, a specific dollar amount or a percentage of value of some or all of the trust property. A mandatory distribution also includes a right to receive an ascertainable part of the trust property currently or on the occurrence of a specified event or after the passage of a specified time.

This requirement would be met, for example, if a trust required the trustee to distribute to charitable organizations or for charitable purposes one-half of the trust's net income annually or, alternatively, one percent of the value of the trust's assets annually. It would also be met if the trustee was required to distribute ten percent of the trust principal to charitable organizations or for charitable purposes ten years after the settlor's death or alternatively upon the death of the settlor's surviving spouse. This requirement would not be met if the charitable distribution was subject to the trustee's discretion.

A mandatory distribution would also include a right of withdrawal held by a charitable organization.

The third and final requirement for a determinable charitable interest is that the charitable interest either must be unconditional or must in all events be held for charitable purposes. Unconditional generally means not subject to the occurrence of a specified event that may not occur. For example, assume the trustee is to distribute $100,000 annually to the Ornithology Institute, a charitable organization, but only if it uses the funds to search for the ivory billed woodpecker, and if it does not so use the funds, to Resurrect Extinct Species, a charitable organization, but only if it uses the funds to recreate the ivory billed woodpecker from genetic material, and if it does not so use the funds, to Woods for Woodpeckers, a charitable organization. The individual interests of Ornithology Institute, Resurrect Extinct Species, and Woods for Woodpeckers are each conditional. The charitable interest to receive $100,000 annually, in the aggregate, meets the third requirement because in all events it will be held for charitable purposes for one of the three charitable organizations.

A charitable interest is conditional (i.e., not an unconditional interest) if the trustee has discretion to make or not make the distribution. For example, if the trustee has discretion to make distributions of income to Manors for Meerkats, a charitable organization, the charitable interest is not unconditional. The charitable interest would not be a determinable charitable interest unless it would in all events be held for charitable purposes. For example, if the trustee was required to distribute all income annually to Manors for Meerkats or to such other charitable organization as the trustee selected for the benefit of wildlife of the Kalahari Desert, the charitable interest is determinable even though the interest of Manors for Meerkats is not unconditional.

A charitable interest, however, would not be conditional merely because the trustee's exercise of discretion in favor of other beneficiaries could affect the charitable interest. For example, if the trustee is required to distribute $200,000 annually to Lonely George Research Fund and has discretion to distribute principal to the settlor's children, the charitable interest is unconditional because so long as there are sufficient funds in the trust the charitable distribution must be made. As another example, assume the trustee had discretion to distribute income and principal to the settlor's children, and upon the death of the surviving child the remainder was to be distributed to Gone with the Wolves, a charitable organization. The interest of Gone with the Wolves is a determinable charitable interest, even though it may be reduced, or even eliminated, by the trustee's exercise of discretion in favor of the settlor's children.

An interest held by a charitable organization is not conditional merely because it is subject to the requirement that the organization be in existence at the time the distribution is to be made. Further, an interest held by a charitable organization is not conditional merely because the organization must qualify as a charitable organization under a particular provision of the Internal Revenue Code, if the organization so qualifies on the date of determination.

For example, assume a trust provides for distributions for the education of the settlor's children and upon the youngest living child attaining age 28 distributes to Whale Whisperers, if it is then in existence and contributions to it qualify for a federal income tax charitable deduction. The interest of Whale Whisperers is unconditional if at the time of the determination Whale Whisperers is in existence and contributions to it qualify for the federal income tax deduction.

Attorney General Rights. Subsection (b) provides that if the first trust contains a determinable charitable interest, the Attorney General (or other official with enforcement authority over charitable interests) may represent the interest and has all the rights of a qualified beneficiary. The Attorney General is entitled to notice under Section 7(c)(7). The Attorney General may petition the court under Section 9, consent to a change in the compensation of an authorized fiduciary under Section 16 or consent to a change in the identity of the person who may remove or replace the authorized fiduciary under Section 18.

If the decanting changes the jurisdiction of a trust containing a determinable charitable interest, the Attorney General may block the decanting by objecting, even without petitioning the court, unless the court approves the decanting. Section 14(e).

If the determinable charitable interest is held by an identified charitable organization, the organization is a qualified beneficiary, has the rights of a qualified beneficiary and may represent and bind itself. In such a case, either the Attorney General or the organization could consent to a change in the compensation of an authorized fiduciary under Section 16 or consent to a change in the identity of the person who may remove or replace the authorized fiduciary under Section 18. If one of the Attorney General or the organization consented, but the other affirmatively objected, the other could petition the court under Section 9 for a determination.

Preservation of Charitable Interests. Although Section 14(b) gives the Attorney General the rights of a qualified beneficiary only when a charitable interest is determinable, Section 14(c) applies to all charitable interests whether or not determinable. If the first trust contains a charitable interest, whether or not determinable, the second trust may not diminish such interest. Section 14(c)(1). If the interest is held by an identified charitable organization, the second trust may not change the organization. Section 14(c)(2). If the first-trust instrument sets forth a particular charitable purpose, the second trust may not change the charitable purpose. Section 14(c)(3). If the first trust imposes certain conditions or restrictions on the charitable gift, the second trust cannot change the conditions or restrictions. Section 14(c)(4).

If a charitable trust indicates a particular charitable purpose, the exercise of the decanting power may not change the charitable purpose. Section 14(c)(3). Thus if the first trust provides that upon A's death the remainder will be paid to Companion Animals for the benefit and protection of dogs, the second trust may not change the purpose of the charitable gift to the benefit of cats. As another example, if the first trust provides that upon A's death the remainder will be distributed to such charities as the trustee selects for the purpose of preserving habitat for blue footed boobies, the second trust cannot change the charitable purpose to the protection of polar bears.

If an authorized fiduciary has limited discretion to distribute principal and exercises the decanting power under Section 12, Section 12(c) requires that the second trusts must grant each beneficiary of the first trust, including charitable organizations, beneficial interests that are substantially similar to such beneficiary's interests in the first trust. If the first trust contains a charitable interest that is not held by an identified charitable organization, Section 12(c) does not apply but Section 14(c) requires that the second trust may not diminish the charitable interest and that any stated charitable purpose must remain the same.

For example, assume a trust permits discretionary income and principal distributions to the settlor's children for their support and health care, requires that the trustee distribute $25,000 each year to one or more charitable organizations selected by the trustee for the purpose of caring for stray, neglected and abused large dogs, gives the trustee discretion to make additional distributions to charitable organizations for the same purpose, and upon the death of the settlor's last surviving child the principal is to be distributed to charitable organizations selected by the trustee for the same purpose. The trustee has limited discretion to distribute principal and therefore may decant under Section 12, but not Section 11. The exercise of the decanting power may change administrative provisions and trustee provisions, but may not alter the beneficial interests of the children. Because the charitable interests are not held by an identified charitable organization, they are not subject to Section 12(c). Section 14(c), however, requires that the second trust not diminish the charitable interests to the $25,000 annual distributions, to receive discretionary distributions and to the remainder interest. In addition, Section 14(c) requires that the charitable purpose remain the same. Thus the second trust could not change the charitable purpose to supporting dog parks for small dogs.

If the trust was as described above except that the trustee had discretion to make distributions to the children for their best interests, the trustee could exercise the decanting power under Section 11. Thus the trustee could eliminate or reduce the interest of one or more of the settlor's children. The decanting could not, however, diminish the charitable interests because Section 14(c) requires that the charitable interest not be diminished. The trustee could not, for example, grant a power of appointment to a child because such a power would diminish the charitable interests.

If a trust gave the trustee expanded discretion to make distributions to the settlor's children for best interests, and upon the death of the surviving child provided for the remaining assets to be distributed to

Howl at the Moon, a charitable organization for the peaceful co-existence of wolves and humans, the authorized fiduciary could not exercise the decanting power to provide that each child would receive an equal share of the trust assets when the youngest child attained age 25, because that would diminish the charitable interest. The authorized fiduciary also could not exercise the decanting power to change the charitable remainder beneficiary from Howl at the Moon to another charitable organization. By contrast, the authorized fiduciary could exercise the decanting power to provide that when the youngest child attained age 25 the trust would be distributed to Howl at the Moon, because that would enhance the charitable interest.

Subsection (c)(4) prohibits altering any condition or restriction related to the charitable interest. For example, if the first trust requires that the trustee consult with certain persons before making distributions or provide reports to certain persons, or gives enforcement rights to certain persons to ensure the charitable purpose is fulfilled, the second trust may not change such provisions.

Some state Attorneys General (or other officials charged with protecting charitable interests) may be concerned that trusts with charitable interests will be moved out of their jurisdiction by decanting. Section 14(e) addresses this concern by requiring that the second trust be administered under the law of the enacting state unless the court approved the decanting or the Attorney General either approved the decanting or, after receiving notice, failed to object within the notice period.

Subsection (f) makes clear that the Uniform Trust Decanting Act does not limit the powers and duties of the Attorney General under other law of the state, whether statutory or common law. For example, other law of the state may give the Attorney General the right to sue for breach of fiduciary duties with respect to charitable interests.

Section 15. Trust Limitation on Decanting.

(a)   An authorized fiduciary may not exercise the decanting power to the extent the first-trust instrument expressly prohibits exercise of:

(1)   the decanting power; or

(2)   a power granted by state law to the fiduciary to distribute part or all of the principal of the trust to another trust or to modify the trust.

(b)   Exercise of the decanting power is subject to any restriction in the first-trust instrument that expressly applies to exercise of:

(1)   the decanting power; or

(2)   a power granted by state law to a fiduciary to distribute part or all of the principal of the trust to another trust or to modify the trust.

(c)   A general prohibition of the amendment or revocation of a first trust, a spendthrift clause, or a clause restraining the voluntary or involuntary transfer of a beneficiary's interest does not preclude exercise of the decanting power.

(d)   Subject to subsections (a) and (b), an authorized fiduciary may exercise the decanting power under this [act] even if the first-trust instrument permits the authorized fiduciary or another person to modify the first-trust instrument or to distribute part or all of the principal of the first trust to another trust.

(e)   If a first-trust instrument contains an express prohibition described in subsection (a) or an express restriction described in subsection (b), the provision must be included in the second-trust instrument.

Comment

A trust instrument may expressly preclude the exercise of a decanting power under the act or any similar state statute with respect to the entire trust or with respect to one or more provisions of the trust. See Section 15(a). The exercise of a decanting power, however, is not prohibited by a statement that the trust is irrevocable or unamendable, or by a spendthrift provision. See Section 15(c). In order to preclude the exercise of the decanting power, the first-trust instrument must expressly refer to the act or to a power granted by state law to the fiduciary to distribute part or all of the principal of the trust to another trust or to modify the trust. For example, assume a first-trust instrument states: "There shall always be a trustee who is an attorney or accountant." That sentence alone would not prohibit the exercise of the decanting power to eliminate that requirement. If the first-trust instrument, however, also stated that "this provision may not be modified by the exercise of any decanting power," then the exercise of the decanting power to modify that provision would be prohibited by Section 15(a).

Any restriction in the first-trust instrument that expressly applies to decanting is honored. Thus, for example, a restriction in the first-trust instrument that requires court approval of any decanting that accelerates the distribution of trust assets would be enforced. As another example, a restriction requiring approval of any decanting by a particular third party would also be enforced.

An irrevocable trust may provide in the trust instrument a mechanism for modifying the trust, for example, by granting a trust protector the power to modify the trust. The fact that a trust instrument provides such a mechanism for modification does not preclude the application of this act. Any requirements or restrictions contained in the trust instrument for such modification mechanism do not apply to an exercise of a decanting power under this act unless such requirements or restrictions expressly apply to an exercise of a decanting power under this act or a similar state statute.

If the first-trust instrument contains a restriction on decanting, the provision must be included in the second-trust instrument. Section 15(e). This provision is intended to prevent serial decanting in which the first decanting removes the restriction on changing a particular provision in the first-trust instrument, and the second decanting then changes such provision.

Section 16. Change in Compensation.

(a) If a first-trust instrument specifies an authorized fiduciary's compensation, the fiduciary may not exercise the decanting power to increase the fiduciary's compensation above the specified compensation unless:

(1) all qualified beneficiaries of the second trust consent to the increase in a signed record; or

(2) the increase is approved by the court.

(b) If a first-trust instrument does not specify an authorized fiduciary's compensation, the fiduciary may not exercise the decanting power to increase the fiduciary's compensation above the compensation permitted by [this state's trust code] unless:

(1) all qualified beneficiaries of the second trust consent to the increase in a signed record; or

(2) the increase is approved by the court.

(c) A change in an authorized fiduciary's compensation which is incidental to other changes made by the exercise of the decanting power is not an increase in the fiduciary's compensation for purposes of subsections (a) and (b).

Comment

An exercise of the decanting power generally is an action taken by the authorized fiduciary that does not require beneficiary consent or court approval. The purpose of requiring beneficiary consent or court approval to a change in the compensation of the authorized fiduciary is to place a check on an authorized fiduciary increasing its own compensation by decanting. In this context it does not seem necessary to require the consent of all beneficiaries. Obtaining the consent of qualified beneficiaries, who would generally be immediately impacted by a change in compensation, should be sufficient.

If the first-trust instrument specifies the authorized fiduciary's compensation, the decanting may not increase the fiduciary's compensation without either the consent of all qualified beneficiaries of the second trust or court approval. Section 16(a). This subsection applies whether the increase in compensation would result from omitting the provision in the trust instrument specifying compensation, modifying such provision or replacing such provision with a different provision. If it is unclear whether a change in method of calculating compensation would result in an increase, either court approval or consent of all qualified beneficiaries should be obtained.

If the first-trust instrument does not specify the authorized fiduciary's compensation, the decanting may not increase the compensation above the compensation permitted in the trust code of the enacting state without either the consent of all qualified beneficiaries or court approval. Section 16(b).

Section 16 expressly does not prohibit an increase in compensation arising incidentally because of other changes made by the exercise of the decanting power. For example, any increase in the compensation of the authorized fiduciary because the second trust may last longer than the first trust is incidental. Also incidental are any increases in compensation that may arise because the second trust may have a greater value in the future than the first trust would have had, for example, because property is retained in the trust longer or smaller distributions are made. Other incidental increases in the compensation of the authorized fiduciary may occur because of changes in investments, changes in the law governing the administration of the trust, changes in the identity of the authorized fiduciary, or changes in the duties of the authorized fiduciary.

In many cases the consideration of a proposed decanting or the implementation of a decanting is fairly seen as an exercise of a discretionary fiduciary power that does not warrant any additional compensation for the authorized fiduciary. In some cases, however, the authorized fiduciary may be required to spend an extraordinary amount of time in evaluating a potential exercise of the decanting power, particularly when an exercise of the power is suggested by a beneficiary, or in exercising the decanting power. In such cases, and regardless of whether the authorized fiduciary ultimately exercises the decanting power, the authorized fiduciary may be entitled to additional compensation under the trust instrument or under state law. * * * In the absence of explicit authority on the appropriate amount of any such compensation, such compensation should be reasonable considering the relevant factors, including the time devoted to the decanting and the degree of difficulty. * * * The authorized fiduciary may also be entitled to have reasonable expenses related to evaluating a potential exercise of the decanting power or in exercising the decanting power paid from the first trust. * * *

Section 17. Relief From Liability and Indemnification.

(a) Except as otherwise provided in this section, a second-trust instrument may not relieve an authorized fiduciary from liability for breach of trust to a greater extent than the first-trust instrument.

(b) A second-trust instrument may provide for indemnification of an authorized fiduciary of the first trust or another person acting in a fiduciary capacity under the first trust for any liability or claim that would have been payable from the first trust if the decanting power had not been exercised.

(c) A second-trust instrument may not reduce fiduciary liability in the aggregate.

(d) Subject to subsection (c), a second-trust instrument may divide and reallocate fiduciary powers among fiduciaries, including one or more trustees, distribution advisors, investment advisors, trust protectors, or other persons, and relieve a fiduciary from liability for an act or failure to act of another fiduciary as permitted by law of this state other than this [act].

Comment

An authorized fiduciary should not be permitted to decant in order to insert in the second-trust instrument a provision directly exculpating the authorized fiduciary or indemnifying the authorized fiduciary except to the extent such provision was contained in the first-trust instrument or applicable law would have provided such exculpation or indemnification. Nonetheless, decanting may appropriately reduce the authorized fiduciary's liability indirectly. For example, if the second trust is subject to the law of a different state, the law governing the second trust may provide additional protection to the authorized fiduciary.

The terms of the second trust may reduce an authorized fiduciary's liability indirectly, for example, by modifying the rules for approving accounts or expressly permitting the retention of certain property. While such provisions may not violate Section 16, they could under certain circumstances violate the authorized fiduciary's general fiduciary duties. For example, while it may be appropriate in the second trust to expressly permit the retention of a residence used by a current beneficiary of the trust, it may not be appropriate to permit the retention of all of the current trust property without any liability.

Subsection (b) recognizes that the trustee of the first trust may be unwilling to distribute the assets of the first trust to the second trust unless the trustee is indemnified for any liability or claim that may become payable from the first trust after its assets are distributed. Subsection (b) is consistent with Section 27, which provides that decanting does not relieve the trust property from any liability that otherwise attaches to the trust property. The indemnification described in subsection (b) may be contained in the second-trust instrument or may be contained in the record exercising the decanting power.

An authorized fiduciary can decant to a trust that divides the trustee responsibilities (i.e., jobs) among various parties, but cannot eliminate the fiduciary duties that accompany those jobs. To the extent that the second trust assigns a fiduciary responsibility and the fiduciary duty that accompanies such responsibility to a particular fiduciary, the other fiduciaries may be relieved from liability for the actions of that particular fiduciary. For example, an investment advisor can be appointed and the authorized fiduciary can be relieved of fiduciary liability for the investment decisions to the extent permitted by the law of the enacting state so long as the investment advisor is acting in a fiduciary capacity and has fiduciary liability for the investment decisions. Section 17(c), (d).

Section 18. Removal or Replacement of Authorized Fiduciary.

An authorized fiduciary may not exercise the decanting power to modify a provision in a first-trust instrument granting another person power to remove or replace the fiduciary unless:

(1)   the person holding the power consents to the modification in a signed record and the modification applies only to the person;

(2)   the person holding the power and the qualified beneficiaries of the second trust consent to the modification in a signed record and the modification grants a substantially similar power to another person; or

(3)   the court approves the modification and the modification grants a substantially similar power to another person.

Comment

Section 18 authorizes a modification of a trustee removal provision only with either court approval or the consent of the person currently holding the right to remove or replace the trustee. The power to remove a fiduciary is a power to remove the fiduciary without the fiduciary's consent regardless of whether the remover has the power to designate the successor fiduciary. The power to replace a fiduciary is the power to remove the fiduciary and to designate the successor for the fiduciary without the consent of the fiduciary.

Unless the qualified beneficiaries also consent to such change, the person currently holding the right to remove the authorized fiduciary may only consent to the modification of the right with respect to himself or herself and cannot consent to the modification of such right with respect to any successor remover. Section 18(1). For example, if a trust provides that the authorized fiduciary may be removed by X (the "current remover"), so long as X is living and not incapacitated, and after X is deceased or incapacitated, by Y, X may consent to a modification that would permit the authorized fiduciary to be removed only by the joint agreement of X and Z and only with 90 days' prior notice, but such modification would not affect Y's power of removal after X is deceased or incapacitated unless Y also consents to the modification or unless the qualified beneficiaries consent to such change.

Alternatively, the removal power may be modified by the current remover and the qualified beneficiaries if the modification grants a substantially similar removal right to another person. Section 18(2). In the previous example, X (the current remover) and the qualified beneficiaries could consent to a modification that would permit the authorized fiduciary to be removed by Z, or if Z were not willing and able to act, by W. Y, the successor remover named in the first-trust instrument, would not need to consent to such modification if X and the qualified beneficiaries consent to it.

Alternatively, the power to remove or replace the authorized fiduciary may be modified if the court approves the modification and the modification grants a substantially similar power to another person. Section 18(3).

In the case of a modification with the consent of the qualified beneficiaries or with court approval, the modification must grant a substantially similar power to another person. A power to remove a fiduciary only for cause would not be substantially similar to a power to remove a fiduciary for any reason. A power to remove a fiduciary only after the fiduciary has attained age 75 or served for ten years is not substantially similar to a power to remove the fiduciary at any time. A power to replace a fiduciary is not substantially similar unless it contains substantially the same restrictions on who may serve as the replacement fiduciary. For example, a power to remove a fiduciary and replace the fiduciary with any person would not be substantially similar to a power to remove the fiduciary and replace the fiduciary with a person who is not related or subordinate to the settlor. * * *

Section 19. Tax-Related Limitations.

(a)   In this section:

(1)   "Grantor trust" means a trust as to which a settlor of a first trust is considered the owner under 26 U.S.C. Sections 671 through 677[, as amended,] or 26 U.S.C. Section 679[, as amended].

(2)   "Internal Revenue Code" means the United States Internal Revenue Code of 1986[, as amended].

(3)   "Nongrantor trust" means a trust that is not a grantor trust.

(4)   "Qualified benefits property" means property subject to the minimum distribution requirements of 26 U.S.C. Section 401(a)(9)[, as amended,], and any applicable regulations, or to any similar requirements that refer to 26 U.S.C. Section 401(a)(9) or the regulations.

(b)   An exercise of the decanting power is subject to the following limitations:

(1)   If a first trust contains property that qualified, or would have qualified but for provisions of this [act] other than this section, for a marital deduction for purposes of the gift or estate tax under the Internal Revenue Code or a state gift, estate, or inheritance tax, the second-trust instrument must not include or omit any term that, if included in or omitted from the trust instrument for the trust to which the property was transferred, would have prevented the transfer from qualifying for the deduction, or would have reduced the amount of the deduction, under the same provisions of the Internal Revenue Code or state law under which the transfer qualified.

(2)   If the first trust contains property that qualified, or would have qualified but for provisions of this [act] other than this section, for a charitable deduction for purposes of the income, gift, or estate tax under the Internal Revenue Code or a state income, gift, estate, or inheritance tax, the second-trust instrument must not include or omit any term that, if included in or omitted from the trust instrument for the trust to which the property was transferred, would have prevented the transfer from qualifying for the deduction, or would have reduced the amount of the deduction, under the same provisions of the Internal Revenue Code or state law under which the transfer qualified.

(3)   If the first trust contains property that qualified, or would have qualified but for provisions of this [act] other than this section, for the exclusion from the gift tax described in 26 U.S.C. Section 2503(b)[, as amended], the second-trust instrument must not include or omit a term that, if included in or omitted from the trust instrument for the trust to which the property was transferred, would have prevented the transfer from qualifying under 26 U.S.C. Section 2503(b)[, as amended]. If the first trust contains property that qualified, or would have qualified but for provisions of this [act] other than this section, for the exclusion from the gift tax described in 26 U.S.C. Section 2503(b)[, as amended,] by application of 26 U.S.C. Section 2503(c)[, as amended], the second-trust instrument must not include or omit a term that, if included or omitted from the trust instrument for the trust to which the property was transferred, would have prevented the transfer from qualifying under 26 U.S.C. Section 2503(c)[, as amended].

(4)   If the property of the first trust includes shares of stock in an S corporation, as defined in 26 U.S.C. Section 1361[, as amended,] and the first trust is, or but for provisions of this [act] other than this section would be, a permitted shareholder under any provision of 26 U.S.C. Section 1361[, as amended], an authorized fiduciary may exercise the power with respect to part or all of the S-corporation stock only if any second trust receiving the stock is a permitted shareholder under 26 U.S.C. Section 1361(c)(2)[, as amended]. If the property of the first trust includes shares of stock in an S corporation and the first trust is, or but for provisions of this [act] other than this section would be, a qualified subchapter-S trust within the meaning of 26 U.S.C. Section 1361(d)[, as amended], the second-trust instrument must not include or omit a term that prevents the second trust from qualifying as a qualified subchapter-S trust.

(5)   If the first trust contains property that qualified, or would have qualified but for provisions of this [act] other than this section, for a zero inclusion ratio for purposes of the generation-skipping transfer tax under 26 U.S.C. Section 2642(c)[, as amended,] the second-trust instrument must not include or omit a term that, if included in or omitted from the first-trust instrument, would have prevented the transfer to the first trust from qualifying for a zero inclusion ratio under 26 U.S.C. Section 2642(c)[, as amended].

(6)   If the first trust is directly or indirectly the beneficiary of qualified benefits property, the second-trust instrument may not include or omit any term that, if included in or omitted from the first-trust instrument, would have increased the minimum distributions required with respect to the qualified benefits property under 26 U.S.C. Section 401(a)(9)[, as amended,] and any applicable regulations, or any similar requirements that refer to 26 U.S.C. Section 401(a)(9)[, as amended] or the regulations. If an attempted exercise of the decanting power violates the preceding sentence, the trustee is deemed to have held the qualified benefits property and any reinvested distributions of the property as a separate share from the date of the exercise of the power and Section 22 applies to the separate share.

(7)   If the first trust qualifies as a grantor trust because of the application of 26 U.S.C. Section 672(f)(2)(A)[, as amended,] the second trust may not include or omit a term that, if included in or omitted from the first-trust instrument, would have prevented the first trust from qualifying under 26 U.S.C. Section 672(f)(2)(A)[, as amended].

(8)   In this paragraph, "tax benefit" means a federal or state tax deduction, exemption, exclusion, or other benefit not otherwise listed in this section, except for a benefit arising from being a grantor trust. Subject to paragraph (9), a second-trust instrument may not include or omit a term that, if included in or omitted from the first-trust instrument, would have prevented qualification for a tax benefit if:

(A)   the first-trust instrument expressly indicates an intent to qualify for the benefit or the first-trust instrument clearly is designed to enable the first trust to qualify for the benefit; and

(B)   the transfer of property held by the first trust or the first trust qualified, or but for provisions of this [act] other than this section, would have qualified for the tax benefit.

(9)   Subject to paragraph (4):

(A)   except as otherwise provided in paragraph (7), the second trust may be a nongrantor trust, even if the first trust is a grantor trust; and

(B)   except as otherwise provided in paragraph (10), the second trust may be a grantor trust, even if the first trust is a nongrantor trust.

(10) An authorized fiduciary may not exercise the decanting power if a settlor objects in a signed record delivered to the fiduciary within the notice period and:

(A)   the first trust and a second trust are both grantor trusts, in whole or in part, the first trust grants the settlor or another person the power to cause the second trust to cease to be a grantor trust, and the second trust does not grant an equivalent power to the settlor or other person; or

> (B)   the first trust is a nongrantor trust and a second trust is a grantor trust, in whole or in part, with respect to the settlor, unless:

>> (i)   the settlor has the power at all times to cause the second trust to cease to be a grantor trust; or

>> (ii)   the first-trust instrument contains a provision granting the settlor or another person a power that would cause the first trust to cease to be a grantor trust and the second-trust instrument contains the same provision.

Comment

Certain tax benefits granted under the Internal Revenue Code (the "Code") or state law are dependent upon a trust containing specific provisions. For example, a qualified terminable interest property ("QTIP") marital trust or general power of appointment marital trust requires that the surviving spouse be entitled for life to all income, and a general power of appointment marital trust also requires that the surviving spouse have a general power of appointment exercisable alone and in all events. If a trustee had the power to decant the trust in a manner that deprived the surviving spouse of the requisite income interest, or in the case of a general power of appointment marital trust, the requisite general power of appointment, then arguably the trust would not qualify for the marital deduction from the inception of the trust. Similarly, it is important to ensure that charitable lead trusts and charitable remainder trusts cannot be modified in a way that arguably would prevent them from qualifying for the charitable deduction or that would reduce the amount of that deduction at their inception.

Grantor Trust. For purposes of this section, a grantor trust means a trust as to which a settlor of the first trust is considered the owner for income tax purposes under the Internal Revenue Code. Section 19(a)(1). The term does not include a trust over which someone other than the settlor (e.g., a beneficiary) is treated as the owner under Code section 678. A "nongrantor trust" is a trust that is not a grantor trust. Section 19(a)(3).

Marital Deduction. Subsection (b)(1) protects the marital deduction. For example, for property to qualify as qualified terminable interest property, the surviving spouse must have a qualifying income interest for life and a QTIP election must be made. Code § 2056(b)(7)(B)(i). The surviving spouse has a qualifying income interest for life if the surviving spouse is entitled to all the income from the property payable annually or at more frequent intervals and no person has a power to appoint any part of the property to any person other than the surviving spouse. Code § 2056(b)(7)(B)(ii). If the first trust is a trust with respect to which a QTIP election was made, subsection (b)(1) prohibits decanting the property to a trust that does not give the surviving spouse a qualifying income interest for life. For example, if the trustee had expanded discretion to distribute principal to the surviving spouse, the trustee could not decant to give the surviving spouse a lifetime power of appointment in favor of descendants. In addition, both Section 11(c)(3) and Section 19(b)(1) would prohibit the trustee from decanting in a manner that would alter the surviving spouse's income interest.

As another example, assume the first trust qualified for the marital deduction under Code Section 2056(b)(5) because the surviving spouse is entitled for life to all the income, the surviving spouse has a testamentary power of appointment in favor of her estate, and no person has any power to appoint other than to the surviving spouse, and the trustee also has a power to make discretionary distributions to the surviving spouse subject to expanded discretion. Subsection (b)(1) prohibits decanting to a second trust that does not give the surviving spouse a right to all income or that gives any person a power to appoint to anyone other than the surviving spouse. Subsection (b)(1) also requires that the second trust qualify for the marital deduction under the same section of the Code, Section 2056(b)(5). It is not sufficient that the second trust qualify for the marital deduction under another section of the Code. Although Code Section 2056(b)(5) requires that the trust give the surviving spouse a power to appoint to either herself or her estate, the second trust could give the surviving spouse a lifetime power to appoint to herself instead of a testamentary power in favor of her estate, or could expand her testamentary power to include persons other than her estate as potential appointees, because the second trust would still qualify for the marital deduction under Code Section 2056(b)(5). If the first trust, however, gave the surviving spouse a lifetime general power of appointment, the authorized fiduciary could not decant in a manner that eliminated such power of appointment. Section 11(c)(3).

Charitable Deduction. Section 19(b)(2) protects the charitable deduction. The act does not apply to wholly charitable trusts. Section 3(b). While a split interest trust such as a charitable remainder trust or charitable lead trust would not be a wholly charitable trust, in almost all cases the trustee of such a trust would not have discretion to distribute principal to a current beneficiary and therefore there would not be an authorized fiduciary (see Section 2(3)) who would have authority to exercise the decanting power under Section 11 or Section 12. In the rare case in which a split interest charitable trust could be decanted, Section 19(b)(2) requires that the second trust qualify for the charitable deduction under the same provision of the Internal Revenue Code or state law. * * *

Gift Tax Annual Exclusion. Code Section 2503(b) grants a gift tax annual exclusion for gifts of a "present interest." Present interests are often created in trusts by granting the beneficiary a Crummey right of withdrawal over contributions to the trust. If a trustee could decant in a manner that prematurely terminated a beneficiary's existing Crummey right of withdrawal over a prior contribution to the trust, then arguably the contribution would not qualify for the gift tax annual exclusion. The restriction in Section 11(c)(3) prohibiting the modification or elimination of a presently exercisable power of appointment also protects the annual exclusion for a prior gift to a Crummey trust.

Code Section 2503(c) provides another method for qualifying gifts to a trust for the gift tax annual exclusion. Code Section 2503(c) permits a gift tax annual exclusion for a gift to a trust for an individual under age 21 provided that the property and its income may be expended for the benefit of the donee before attaining age 21, to the extent not so expended passes to the donee upon attaining age 21, and, in the event of the donee's death, is payable to the estate of the donee or pursuant to a general power of appointment.

Assume, for example that the first trust permitted distributions of income and principal subject to expanded discretion to A, provided that the trust property should be distributed to A at age 21 and directed that the trust be distributed to A's estate if A died prior to age 21. A is age 19. The authorized fiduciary could decant to a second trust that, instead of distributing the property to A at age 21, provided A a right to withdraw the trust property for 60 days and that, instead of distributing the property to A's estate, gave A a general testamentary power of appointment. Such a decanting is permitted because the second trust would still qualify under Code Section 2503(c). The authorized fiduciary could not decant to a trust that did not permit A to withdraw the assets until age 30 or that neither gave A a testamentary general power of appointment nor directed distribution of the property to A's estate.

S Corporation Stock. Under Code Section 1361, only certain types of trusts are permitted to own S corporation stock. If the first trust owns S corporation stock, the second trust must also qualify to own S corporation stock under Code Section 1361(c)(2). If the first trust qualifies because it is an electing small business trust (an "ESBT"), the second trust may either be an ESBT or qualify to hold S corporation stock because it is a grantor trust or a qualified subchapter S trust (a "QSST"). Similarly, if the first trust owns S corporation stock and is a grantor trust, the second trust may qualify to hold S corporation stock by being a grantor trust, an ESBT or a QSST.

Subsection (b)(4) imposes a more stringent rule if the first trust is a QSST. In order for a trust to qualify as a QSST, (a) the terms of the trust must require that during the life of the current income beneficiary there shall be only one income beneficiary and (b) all of the income must be distributed to such beneficiary. Code § 1361(d)(3). Thus it may be important that a trust intended to qualify as a QSST not be permitted to be decanted into a trust that would not qualify as a QSST. If the first trust owns S corporation stock and qualifies as an S corporation shareholder because it is a QSST, subsection (b)(4) requires that the second trust also be a QSST. If the first trust is a QSST, it is not sufficient that the second trust qualify to hold S corporation stock under another provision of the Code. If the authorized fiduciary had the power to modify a trust intended to qualify as a QSST to a trust that did not so qualify, the trust would not be a QSST from its inception.

GST "Annual Exclusion" Gifts. Code Section 2642(c) grants a zero inclusion ratio, essentially a "GST annual exclusion," to gifts that qualify for the gift tax annual exclusion but imposes two additional requirements for gifts to trusts. First, the trust must be only for a single individual and second, if the individual dies before the termination of the trust, the property of the trust must be included in the gross estate of such individual. Thus while gifts to trusts for multiple beneficiaries could qualify for the gift tax annual exclusion through the use of Crummey withdrawal rights, such gifts generally would not qualify for the GST annual exclusion. The Code Section 2642(c) restriction requiring a trust be for a single individual for such individual's life could be violated through decanting if the decanting permitted a remainder beneficiary to receive distributions prior to the individual's death. Section 19(b)(5) prohibits such a modification. The requirement that the trust be included in the gross estate of the individual could perhaps be violated by decanting to a trust that was not includible in the beneficiary's gross estate. Section 19(b)(5) prohibits such a decanting.

Qualified Benefits. Complicated rules determine when the life expectancy of a trust beneficiary can be considered in determining the required minimum distribution rules when a trust is the beneficiary of a qualified retirement plan or IRA. These rules are found in Code Section 401(a)(9) and the corresponding regulations, and in other Code sections that refer to Section 401(a)(9). * * *

Under the rules in Code Section 401(a)(9), only trusts with certain provisions and restrictions permit the life expectancy of the beneficiary to be used to determine required minimum distributions. If a trustee could decant to a trust that would not meet these requirements, then arguably the old trust would not qualify from the inception to use the life expectancy of the beneficiary.

Subsection (b)(6) applies not only to any trust that is currently the beneficiary of an individual retirement account ("IRA") or qualified benefit, but also to any successor trust. The need to apply subsection (b)(6) to successor trusts is demonstrated by the following example. Assume Trust A is the beneficiary of Parent's $100,000 IRA. Child is the current beneficiary of Trust A and upon Child's death the assets of Trust A will be distributed to Trusts X and Y for Child's children. Trust A is not a "conduit trust," but qualified to take IRA distributions over Child's life expectancy because Trust A, and Trusts X and Y, have only individuals as beneficiaries and all future beneficiaries must be younger than Child. If Trusts X and Y permitted the exercise of a decanting power in any way that could result in the addition of charities or individuals older than Child as beneficiaries or permissible appointees, Trust A would not have qualified to take IRA distributions over Child C's life expectancy. Therefore, the restrictions on decanting must apply to Trusts X and Y, as well as to Trust A. Trusts X and Y are indirect beneficiaries of the qualified benefit property.

If an attempted decanting violates subsection (b)(6), the qualified benefit property is deemed to be held as a separate share as of the date of the exercise of the decanting power. Holding the qualified benefit property as a separate share permits the remedial rules of Section 22 to apply only with respect to the qualified benefit property and its proceeds.

Foreign Grantor Trusts. Generally, the grantor trust rules apply only to a "grantor" who is a citizen or resident of the United States or a domestic corporation. An exception to this rule applies if (a) the foreign grantor has the power to revest title to the trust property in the grantor and such power is exercisable (1) solely by the grantor without the approval or consent of any other person or (2) with the consent of a related or subordinate party who is subservient to the grantor, or (b) distributions may be made only to the grantor and the grantor's spouse during the life of the grantor. If a foreign trust qualifies as a grantor trust because of Code Section 672(f)(2)(A), subsection (b)(7) provides that the decanting power cannot be exercised to a second trust that does not meet the requirements of Code Section 672(f)(2)(A).

Catch-all. Subsection (b)(8) is a catch-all provision intended to preserve any tax benefits not specifically listed in Section 19 for which the first trust qualified if the first-trust instrument expressly indicates an intent to qualify for the tax benefit or is clearly designed to qualify for the tax benefit. Note that subsection (b)(8) does not address any tax benefits for which the trust may qualify in the future. For example, assume that the first trust was a credit shelter trust that was not subject to federal estate tax at the death of the first to die of a married couple because of the decedent's federal exclusion. Assume that an independent person may make discretionary distributions to the surviving spouse and descendants pursuant to expanded discretion. Also assume that the credit shelter trust was designed so that it would not be included in the surviving spouse's estate. The authorized fiduciary could decant and the second trust could grant the surviving spouse a general power of appointment that would cause inclusion in the surviving spouse's estate. Although the credit shelter trust was designed to be excluded from the surviving spouse's estate, such tax benefit is one that would occur, if at all, in the future at the surviving spouse's death; it is not a tax benefit claimed in the past. Therefore subsection (b)(8) does not prohibit such a modification. If the settlor's purposes include saving taxes, and causing inclusion in the spouse's estate may save more taxes by causing a basis adjustment at the surviving spouse's death even though the trust assets would then be included in the surviving spouse's estate, then such a decanting may be appropriate and is not prohibited by subsection (b)(8).

Grantor Trusts. Subsection (b)(9) expressly permits an exercise of the decanting power to change the income tax status of the trust from a grantor trust to a nongrantor trust or vice versa. Although, absent subsection (b)(9), grantor trust status generally might be viewed as a tax benefit of the first trust, grantor trust status is treated differently under the act because the grantor does not necessarily intend that the grantor trust status be maintained until the grantor's death and because other desirable modifications of the trust may result in a loss of grantor trust status.

An exercise of the decanting power may cause a nongrantor trust to become a grantor trust either as a primary purpose of the exercise of the decanting power or as an incidental consequence of other changes made by the decanting. Subsection (b)(9)(B). It would be fundamentally unfair, however, to permit a decanting to impose on the settlor liability for the second trust's income taxes if the settlor objected to such liability. Therefore subsection (b)(10)(B) permits the settlor to block the decanting by objection during the notice period unless the settlor has the power to cause the second trust to cease to be a grantor trust. The settlor receives prior notice of the exercise of the decanting power under Section 7(c)(1).

Where the first trust is a grantor trust, often the settlor or another person has the power to cause the trust to cease to be a grantor trust. This power permits the settlor or someone acting on the settlor's behalf to relieve the settlor of the income tax liability for the trust. If the second trust is a grantor trust and does not contain the same provisions permitting the grantor trust treatment to be "turned off," the settlor may block the proposed decanting by objecting during the notice period. Subsection (b)(10)(A).

If a portion of a trust is a grantor trust and the remaining portion is a nongrantor trust, subsection (b)(10) applies to the portion that is a grantor trust.

Section 20. Duration of Second Trust.

(a) Subject to subsection (b), a second trust may have a duration that is the same as or different from the duration of the first trust.

(b) To the extent that property of a second trust is attributable to property of the first trust, the property of the second trust is subject to any rules governing maximum perpetuity, accumulation, or suspension of the power of alienation which apply to property of the first trust.

Comment

To implement the public policy of the state law applicable to the first trust, subsection (b) requires that any maximum perpetuity, accumulation, or suspension-of-the-power-of-alienation period (collectively referred to as a "perpetuities rule") applicable to the first trust apply to the second trust to the extent its assets are attributed to the first trust. This rule is also supported by pragmatic considerations. An exercise of a decanting power could inadvertently violate a perpetuities rule applicable to the first trust if the second trust does not comply with the same perpetuities rule. Even in states that have abolished the maximum perpetuity rule, the state may still impose another perpetuities rule (e.g., a suspension-of-the-power-of-alienation rule), the first trust may still be subject to a rule against perpetuities under prior law or the first trust may be subject to a rule against perpetuities under the law of a different state. Further, if a trust is grandfathered from generation-skipping transfer ("GST") tax or has an inclusion ratio less than one, decanting to a trust that does not comply with the same rule against perpetuities period (or a federal rule against perpetuities period) may have adverse GST consequences.

Thus if the first trust was created in a state with a traditional rule against perpetuities, the authorized fiduciary may not exercise the decanting power to change the governing law to a state with no rule against perpetuities and to eliminate the rule against perpetuities applicable to the first trust.

Where the maximum term of the first trust is measured by reference to lives in being on the date the first trust became irrevocable, Section 20 does not preclude the second trust from using an expanded class of measuring lives so long as the expanded class were in being on the date the first trust became irrevocable. For example, assume the first trust is subject to State A's trust duration rule, which is a traditional rule against perpetuities that requires that an interest in a trust vest within twenty-one years of the last to die of lives in being when the trust became irrevocable. The first trust contains a perpetuities savings clause that requires the trust to terminate twenty-one years after the death of the survivor of the settlor's descendants living when the first trust was created. The second trust may replace the perpetuities savings clause with a provision that requires the trust to terminate twenty-one years after the death of the survivor of the descendants of any grandparent of the settlor who were living when the first trust was created.

As another example, assume the first trust is subject to State A's trust duration rule, which is a traditional rule against perpetuities, but which permits a trust to opt out of the rule against perpetuities. The first trust does not opt out of the rule against perpetuities. The second trust may opt out of the rule against perpetuities if the first trust could have done so.

If the first trust and the state law applicable to the first trust permitted the springing of the "Delaware Tax Trap" of Code Section 2041(a)(3), the second trust may also permit the springing of the Delaware Tax Trap.

The second trust may terminate earlier than the trust duration rule applicable to the first trust would require. Assume Trust A and Trust B are both subject to State Z's trust duration rule, which is a traditional rule against perpetuities. Both trusts were created by the same settlor and contain a perpetuities savings clause that requires the termination of the trust twenty-one years after the death of the survivor of the settlor's descendants living on the date the trust was created. Trust A was created on June 6, 1966. Trust B was created May 5, 1955. Trust A may be decanted into Trust B because Trust B will terminate prior to the rule against perpetuities applicable to Trust A. Trust B may be decanted into Trust A if Trust A is modified to provide, or the decanting instrument provides, that the portion of Trust A attributable to the addition of the assets of Trust B must vest within the rule against perpetuities period applicable to Trust B. The trustee could segregate the assets Trust A receives from the decanting of Trust B. Alternatively, the trustee could determine the fractional share of the total assets attributable to Trust B, based upon values at the time of decanting, and such fractional share of Trust A will be subject to the rule against perpetuities period applicable to Trust B.

If the authorized fiduciary attempts to decant Trust B into Trust A without providing either in Trust A or the decanting instrument that the portion of the trust attributable to Trust B must vest within the rule against perpetuities period applicable to Trust B, the decanting may still be valid. First, the statutes of State Z may contain a rule against perpetuities savings clause that will cause the trust to vest or terminate within the applicable rule against perpetuities period. Second, if there is no statutory savings clause, Section 22 of this act may apply to read into Trust A an appropriate savings clause with respect to the portion of the trust attributable to Trust B.

Section 20 does not address whether, if the decanting changes the place of administration for the trust or the law governing the trust, and the new jurisdiction has a more restrictive trust duration rule, the new jurisdiction may impose its maximum perpetuity, accumulation or suspension-of-the-power-of-alienation period on the second trust. The new jurisdiction may do so if the rule of the first jurisdiction is contrary to a strong public policy of the new jurisdiction. Thus if the first jurisdiction has no rule against perpetuities, and the second jurisdiction has a traditional rule against perpetuities, the second jurisdiction may but need not determine that its rule expresses a strong public policy against perpetual trusts.

Subsection (a) provides that, except as provided by subsection (b), the second trust may have a term that is the same as or different from the term of the first trust. Thus the term of the second trust may be longer than or shorter than the term of the first trust.

Section 21. Need to Distribute Not Required.

An authorized fiduciary may exercise the decanting power whether or not under the first trust's discretionary distribution standard the fiduciary would have made or could have been compelled to make a discretionary distribution of principal at the time of the exercise.

Comment

Although the decanting power under Sections 11 and 12 is premised on the authorized fiduciary's power to distribute principal of the first trust to one or more current beneficiaries, the authorized fiduciary may exercise the decanting power even if the authorized fiduciary would not have made a distribution of principal to a current beneficiary under the distribution standard of the first trust. For example, assume a trust permits the trustee to distribute income and principal to S for S's support and health care, considering S's other resources, and that given S's other resources the trustee would not currently make a distribution to S. The trustee may still exercise the decanting power under Section 12.

Section 21, however, does not authorize an exercise of the decanting power under Sections 11 and 12 if the authorized fiduciary does not currently have a power to distribute principal. For example, if a trust permits income to be distributed to A, but does not permit principal distributions until A is age 25 or has a child, and A is age 21 and has no child, the trustee may not decant the trust under Section 11 or Section 12.

Section 22. Saving Provision.

(a) If exercise of the decanting power would be effective under this [act] except that the second-trust instrument in part does not comply with this [act], the exercise of the power is effective and the following rules apply with respect to the principal of the second trust attributable to the exercise of the power:

(1) A provision in the second-trust instrument which is not permitted under this [act] is void to the extent necessary to comply with this [act].

(2) A provision required by this [act] to be in the second-trust instrument which is not contained in the instrument is deemed to be included in the instrument to the extent necessary to comply with this [act].

(b) If a trustee or other fiduciary of a second trust determines that subsection (a) applies to a prior exercise of the decanting power, the fiduciary shall take corrective action consistent with the fiduciary's duties.

Comment

In order to provide as much certainty as possible to the trustee and the beneficiaries with respect to the operative terms of a trust, an exercise of a decanting power should not be wholly invalid because the second-trust instrument in part violates this act. Section 22(a) modifies the second-trust instrument to delete impermissible provisions in the second-trust instrument and to insert required provisions in the second-trust instrument. For example, if the second trust sets forth an impermissible rule against perpetuities period (see Section 20), the other modifications made by the decanting should be effective.

The remedial rules of Section 22 apply only to the least extent required to comply with this act. Thus if a provision in the second-trust instrument would be permissible with respect to some of the trust property but is impermissible with respect to other trust property, such provision will be void only as to the trust property with respect to which it is impermissible. Further, any modification to a provision of the second-trust instrument that is required by Section 22 should be the modification that implements the intended modifications to the greatest extent permitted under the act. Thus the authorized fiduciary's intent is relevant in determining how to apply the provisions of Section 22.

For example, assume a trust holds $500,000 of marketable assets and is the beneficiary of Grantor's $100,000 IRA. Grantor's Child is the sole current beneficiary of the trust. The trust is qualified to use Child's life expectancy in determining the distribution period for the IRA because the trust restricts all future beneficiaries, including appointees under any power of appointment and takers in default, to individuals younger than Child. The authorized fiduciary attempts to decant the trust to permit Child to appoint to her spouse. This is in violation of Section 19(b)(6) because if Child could appoint the IRA to a spouse who is older than Child, Trust would not have qualified to take IRA distributions over Child's life expectancy. Section 19(b)(6) causes the qualified benefit property and any reinvested distributions of the qualified benefit property to be treated as a separate share. Section 22 will void the power to appoint to a spouse only with respect to the qualified benefit property and any reinvested distributions of the qualified benefit property, and only if the spouse is (or could be) older than Child, because that is the least intrusive remediation required to comply with Section 19(b)(6).

As another example, assume the authorized fiduciary attempts to decant a trust to permit Child to appoint to her sibling. If Child's sibling is older than Child, this is in violation of Section 19(b)(6) because if Child could appoint the IRA to her older sibling, the trust would not have qualified to take IRA distributions over Child's life expectancy. Section 19(b)(6) causes the qualified benefit property and any reinvested distributions of the qualified benefit property to be treated as a separate share. Section 22 will void the power to appoint to a sibling only with respect to the qualified benefit property and any reinvested distributions of the qualified benefit property, which are treated as a separate share, and only if the sibling is older than Child, because that is the least intrusive remediation required to comply with Section 19(b)(6).

As yet another example, assume the authorized fiduciary attempts to decant Trust to change (1) the successor fiduciaries, (2) the manner in which the first trust instrument directed that the authorized fiduciary be compensated, which will increase the authorized fiduciary's compensation, and (3) the identity of the person who can remove the authorized fiduciary (the "Remover"). The authorized fiduciary obtains the written consent of the qualified beneficiaries of the second trust, but does not obtain consent of the Remover or approval by the court. The changes to the successor fiduciaries will be effective. The change to the authorized fiduciary's compensation will also be effective because the requirement in Section 16(a) or Section 16(b) was met. The change to the identity of the Remover will not be effective because the Remover named in the first trust instrument did not consent. See Section 18.

Section 22(b) provides that if the savings provision in Section 22(a) applies, the trustee or other fiduciary shall take corrective action consistent with the fiduciary's duties. When Section 22(a) applies, the copy of the second-trust instrument provided to qualified beneficiaries and other parties under Section 7 would not accurately state the terms of the second trust. A trustee or other fiduciary may have a duty to notify certain persons of the accurate terms of the second trust. * * *

Additional corrective action may be required, especially if distributions were made or not made in reliance on the assumed terms of the second-trust instrument and such terms are altered by Section 22(a).

Where a fiduciary is uncertain about whether corrective action should be taken, the fiduciary may apply to the court for instructions under Section 9.

Section 23. Trust for Care of Animal.

(a)   In this section:

(1)   "Animal trust" means a trust or an interest in a trust created to provide for the care of one or more animals.

(2)   "Protector" means a person appointed in an animal trust to enforce the trust on behalf of the animal or, if no such person is appointed in the trust, a person appointed by the court for that purpose.

(b)   The decanting power may be exercised over an animal trust that has a protector to the extent the trust could be decanted under this [act] if each animal that benefits from the trust were an individual, if the protector consents in a signed record to the exercise of the power.

(c)   A protector for an animal has the rights under this [act] of a qualified beneficiary.

(d)   Notwithstanding any other provision of this [act], if a first trust is an animal trust, in an exercise of the decanting power, the second trust must provide that trust property may be applied only to its intended purpose for the period the first trust benefitted the animal.

Comment

Section 408 of the Uniform Trust Code permits a trust to be created for one or more animals who are alive during the settlor's lifetime. * * *

One impediment to applying decanting to an animal trust is that animal trusts often do not technically have a beneficiary because the definition of "beneficiary" is restricted to a person who has a particular interest in the trust. The definition of the term "person" does not include a nonhuman animal. This impediment is resolved by treating the animal as if it were a person so that the animal trust does have a beneficiary for purposes of the decanting power. The extent of the decanting power would then depend upon the amount of discretion that the authorized fiduciary has to make distributions for the animal and to any other person. If the trustee has expanded discretion, then the decanting power could be exercised under Section 11. If the trustee only has limited discretion to make distributions to the animal, then the decanting power can be exercised under Section 12.

The second impediment to exercising a decanting power over an animal trust is identifying a person who can receive notice of the decanting on behalf of the animal and bring a court action with respect to the decanting if appropriate. This impediment is resolved because an animal trust will usually have a person who is designated to enforce the trust on behalf of the animal. Section 408(b) of the Uniform Trust Code provides that such a trust may be enforced by a person appointed in the terms of the trust or, if no person is so appointed, by a person appointed by the court. Thus if an animal trust did not designate a person to enforce the trust on behalf of the animal, the trustee could request that the court appoint such a person and then proceed with any exercise of the decanting power.

Section 408 of the Uniform Trust Code provides that the property of an animal trust may be applied only to its intended use, except to the extent the court determines that the value of the trust property exceeds the amount required for the intended use. Although Section 23 permits the decanting of an animal trust, it mirrors the requirement of the Uniform Trust Code that the property of the animal trust may be applied only to its intended use for the period of time the first trust was intended to benefit the animals (usually the lives of the animals). Therefore, the authorized fiduciary cannot, by decanting, reduce the value of the animal trust; such a power is reserved only to the court. Further, the authorized fiduciary cannot divert assets of the animal trust to other beneficiaries of the trust.

Assume that Trust was established for the support of Double Trouble, a husky, after the death of Double Trouble's human companion. Trust directs that the Trust shall continue to maintain Double Trouble in her Alaskan house, which is owned by the Trust, under the care of Joan, a retired musher, and permits distributions of income and principal to maintain the house and for Double Trouble's best interests so long as Double Trouble is living. Upon the death of Double Trouble, Trust is distributed to the Husky Rescue Society, a charitable organization. Double Trouble is aging and the veterinarian advises a move to a warmer climate. The assets of the Trust are diminishing, and may not be sufficient to maintain the Alaskan house and pay for Double Trouble's care. Joan is aging too, and would prefer to care for Double Trouble in Joan's house in Hawaii. The authorized trustee may, with the consent of the protector, modify Trust to permit the sale of the Alaskan house and to permit Joan to care for Double Trouble in her Hawaii home. Notice of the decanting must be provided to the protector, the Husky Rescue Society and to the Attorney General (or other official with enforcement authority over charitable interests). The second trust, however, may not add Joan as a beneficiary because such a modification would not be permitted under Section 11. Nor may the decanting provide that one year after the move to Hawaii, one-half of the principal will be distributed to the Husky Rescue Society, because Section 23(d) requires that the trust property be applied only for its intended purpose (the care of Double Trouble) for the period the first trust benefitted the animal (the life of Double Trouble). * * *

Section 24. Terms of Second Trust.

A reference in [this state's trust code] to a trust instrument or terms of the trust includes a second-trust instrument and the terms of the second trust.

Section 25. Settlor.

(a)   For purposes of law of this state other than this [act] and subject to subsection (b), a settlor of a first trust is deemed to be the settlor of the second trust with respect to the portion of the principal of the first trust subject to the exercise of the decanting power.

(b)   In determining settlor intent with respect to a second trust, the intent of a settlor of the first trust, a settlor of the second trust, and the authorized fiduciary may be considered.

Comment

* * * For most purposes, when a trust is decanted the settlor of the first trust should be considered the settlor of the second trust to the extent of the decanting. If the second trust is a pre-existing trust funded by a different settlor, then the original settlor of the second trust would continue to be considered the settlor over the portion of the trust property attributable to that person's contribution and the original settlor of the first trust would be considered the settlor of the portion of the second trust property attributable to the decanting. This general rule of Section 25(a) would apply, for example, for purposes of determining who holds the rights granted to the settlor or who must consent when the settlor's consent is required for an action and for tax purposes. * * *

For purposes of determining the settlor's intent or purpose in creating a trust, or whether the settlor did not anticipate certain circumstances, it may sometimes be appropriate to consider the intent of the original settlor of the second trust. For example, if a decanting distribution is made to a pre-existing trust with property of its own, the intent of the original settlor of the second trust may be more relevant in construing, modifying or reforming the second-trust instrument after the decanting distribution. In such a case, the decanting distribution adopts the language of the second-trust instrument, which is most appropriately construed with respect to the intent of the creator of such trust. When a decanting distribution is made to a second trust created by the authorized fiduciary for the purposes of decanting, or when the decanting is a modification of the first trust, the intent of the authorized fiduciary may be most relevant in later construing the terms of the second trust, or at least the terms modified by the decanting. The intent of the settlor of the first trust may still be relevant, however, because the decanting would have been made to better carry out the purposes of the first trust. Further, to the extent the second trust does not modify the terms of the first trust, the intent of the settlor of the first trust would be relevant in construing such terms.

Section 25(b) would apply, under the Uniform Trust Code, with respect to Section 412 (Modification or Termination Because of Unanticipated Circumstances), Section 415 (Reformation to Correct Mistakes) and Section 416 (Modification to Achieve Settlor's Tax Objectives). For example, under Section 412 of the Uniform Trust Code, a court may make certain trust modifications if because of "circumstances not anticipated by the settlor, modification or termination will further the purposes of the trust." The modification, to the extent practicable, is to be made in "accordance with the settlor's probable intention." Thus where the authorized fiduciary of the first trust, or some other person, has created the second trust, the intent of the maker of the second trust may be relevant in determining, with respect to the second trust, what circumstances were not anticipated by the settlor and what would be the settlor's probable intent.

Section 25(b) may also apply in other contexts for determining the purposes and material purposes of the trust. The material purposes of the trust may, for example, be relevant in determining whether a nonjudicial settlement agreement is valid. Settlor intent is relevant in determining a trust's purposes and material purposes.

Section 26. Later-Discovered Property.

(a) Except as otherwise provided in subsection (c), if exercise of the decanting power was intended to distribute all the principal of the first trust to one or more second trusts, later-discovered property belonging to the first trust and property paid to or acquired by the first trust after the exercise of the power is part of the trust estate of the second trust or trusts.

(b) Except as otherwise provided in subsection (c), if exercise of the decanting power was intended to distribute less than all the principal of the first trust to one or more second trusts, later-discovered property belonging to the first trust or property paid to or acquired by the first trust after exercise of the power remains part of the trust estate of the first trust.

(c) An authorized fiduciary may provide in an exercise of the decanting power or by the terms of a second trust for disposition of later-discovered property belonging to the first trust or property paid to or acquired by the first trust after exercise of the power.

Comment

If the decanting power is exercised by modifying the terms of the first trust, the trustee could either treat the second trust created by such modification as a new trust, in which case the property of the first trust would need to be transferred to the second trust, or alternatively treat the second trust as a continuation of the first trust, in which case the property of the first trust would not need to be retitled. When the second trust is a continuation of the first trust, any property owned by the first trust is still owned by the trust after the decanting, even if the authorized fiduciary is not aware of such property at the time of the decanting.

When the decanting power is exercised by distributing property of the first trust to a separate second trust, regardless of whether the terms of such second trust are set forth in an entirely separate trust instrument or a modification of the first-trust instrument, the property of the first trust needs to be transferred to the second trust(s). Inevitably, there will be cases where the trustee fails to transfer all of the property to the second trust. The trustee can protect against this possibility by, in the exercise of the decanting power, making a global assignment of all trust property to the second trust. When the property of the first trust is being divided among more than one second trusts or not all of the property of the first trust is being decanted, it is more complicated, but still possible, to specify in the exercise of the decanting power how later-discovered property should be allocated.

Section 26(c) explicitly permits an authorized fiduciary to provide, in an exercise of the decanting power or by the terms of a second trust, for disposition of later-discovered property belonging to the first trust or property paid to or acquired by the first trust after exercise of the decanting power. For example, if an authorized fiduciary exercises the decanting power over a trust to create a special-needs trust for the settlor's child J and to create a separate trust for the settlor's other children, the exercise of the decanting power might state that the trust for J will be funded with marketable securities and cash with a value of $1,000,000 and that all other property, including later-discovered property, will be distributed to and owned by the trust for the other children. Assume the trust for J is then funded with $1,000,000 of marketable securities and all other property then known to the trustee is assigned to the trust for the other children. If subsequently other trust assets are discovered, it would be clear that they belong to the trust for the other children and not the trust for J.

The trustee in transferring title to the first trust's property pursuant to a decanting may also take the precaution of executing a global assignment of all property not otherwise expressly transferred to the appropriate second trusts.

Section 26(a) and (b) specify default rules when later-discovered property and property paid to or acquired by the first trust after the exercise of the decanting power is not expressly allocated to a particular trust by the exercise, by the second-trust instrument or by an assignment.

Subsection (a) provides that if the decanting intended to distribute all of the principal of the first trust to one or more second trusts, then the property is part of the second trust or trusts. When there is more than one second trusts, the exercise of the decanting power might specify their respective interests in the property of the first trust or if it does not, the second trusts may need to reach agreement about their respective ownership interests.

Subsection (b) provides that if the decanting was not intended to distribute all of the principal of the first trust to one or more second trusts, such property remains part of the first trust.

Section 27. Obligations.

A debt, liability, or other obligation enforceable against property of a first trust is enforceable to the same extent against the property when held by the second trust after exercise of the decanting power.

Comment

It would be inequitable to permit a second trust to evade liabilities incurred by the trustee of the first trust to the extent the creditor would have been entitled to satisfaction out of the trust property. Section 27 provides that a debt, liability or other obligation of the first trust against property of a first trust is enforceable to the same extent against such property when held by the second trust. Section 27 may apply to contractual claims, obligations arising from ownership or control of trust property and to torts committed in the course of administering a trust. * * *

For example, assume Chicago Bank makes a loan to the trustee of First Trust, secured by First Trust's holdings of Fuchsia Corp. stock. The loan provides that trustee is not personally liable. The trustee decants First Trust and distributes all of its assets to Second Trust. Chicago Bank may enforce the loan against the property of Second Trust, including the Fuchsia Corp. stock, to the same extent it could have enforced the loan against the property of First Trust. If Second Trust also owns property not attributed to the decanting, Section 27 does not expose such property to Chicago Bank's claim.

Assume instead that the trustee of First Trust decanted and distributed all of the Fuchsia Corp. stock to Second Trust, and distributed all of the other assets of First Trust to Third Trust. Chicago Bank may enforce the loan against the Fuchsia Corp. stock held by Second Trust to the same extent it could have enforced the loan against the Fuchsia Corp. stock when it was held by First Trust. If prior to the decanting Chicago Bank could have enforced the loan against the property of First Trust other than the Fuchsia Corp.

stock to the extent the value of the Fuchsia Corp. stock was insufficient to satisfy the loan, after the decanting Chicago Bank may enforce the loan, to the extent the Fuchsia Corp. stock is insufficient to satisfy the loan, against the other property of Second Trust and Third Trust to the extent it was attributable to the property of First Trust.

Section 27 only applies to a debt, liability or other obligation that is in existence and enforceable against the property of the first trust at the time of the decanting.

Section 27 is not intended to impede an authorized fiduciary from exercising the decanting power in a manner that may protect the property of the second trust from debts, liabilities or obligations of the settlor or a beneficiary to a greater extent than the property of the first trust would have been protected from such debts, liabilities or obligations. For example, a decanting may add a spendthrift provision to a trust. As another example, a decanting under Section 11 could postpone or eliminate a prospective withdrawal right of a beneficiary or eliminate a general power of appointment that is not presently exercisable.

Section 28. Uniformity of Application and Construction. [omitted]

Section 29. Relation to Electronic Signatures in Global and National Commerce Act. [omitted]

[Section 30. Severability.] [omitted]

Section 31. Repeals; Conforming Amendments. [omitted]

Section 32. Effective Date. [omitted]